The Secret World

CHRISTOPHER ANDREW

The Secret World

A History of Intelligence

Yale

UNIVERSITY PRESS

New Haven and London

The Henry L. Stimson Lectures at the Whitney and Betty
MacMillan Center for International and Area Studies at Yale.
First published 2018 in the United States by Yale University Press
and in the United Kingdom by Penguin Books Ltd., London.

Yale University Press books may be purchased in quantity for
educational, business, or promotional use. For information, please
e-mail sales.press@yale.edu (U.S. office) or sales@yaleup.co.uk
(U.K. office).

Set in 10.2/13.5 pt Sabon LT Std
Typeset by Jouve (UK), Milton Keynes
Printed in the United States of America.

Library of Congress Control Number: 2018947154
ISBN 978-0-300-23844-0 (hardcover : alk. paper)

This paper meets the requirements of ANSI/NISO Z39.48-1992
(Permanence of Paper).

10 9 8 7 6 5 4 3 2 1

To Ben, Emily, Joe, Katy, Louis, Sam and Tommy

Contents

List of Illustrations   ix

Introduction: The Lost History of Global Intelligence   1

1 In the Beginning: Spies of the Bible and Ancient Egypt
   from Moses to the Last Supper   13

2 Intelligence Operations in Ancient Greece: Myth
   and Reality from Odysseus to Alexander the Great   27

3 Intelligence and Divination in the Roman Republic   40

4 *The Art of War* and the *Arthashastra*: How China
   and India Took an Early Lead over Greece and Rome   54

5 The Roman Empire and the *Untermenschen*   70

6 Muhammad and the Rise of Islamic Intelligence   86

7 Inquisitions and Counter-Subversion   100

8 Renaissance Venice and the Rise of Western Intelligence   118

9 Ivan the Terrible and the Origins of Russian State Security   141

10 Elizabeth I, Walsingham and the Rise of English Intelligence   158

11 The Decline of Early Stuart and Spanish Intelligence,
    and the Rise of the French *Cabinet Noir*   191

12 Intelligence and Regime Change in Britain: From
    the Civil War to the Popish Plot   214

13 Intelligence in the Era of the Sun King   242

14 Codebreakers and Spies in Ancien Régime Europe:
    From the Hanoverian Succession to the Seven Years War   269

15 Intelligence and American Independence   292

16 The French Revolution and the Revolutionary Wars   312

17 The Napoleonic Wars   339

18 Intelligence and Counter-Revolution. Part I:
    From the Congress of Vienna to the 1848 Revolutions   363

19 Intelligence and Counter-Revolution. Part II:
    From 1848 to the Death of Karl Marx   386

20 The Telegraph, Mid-Century Wars and the 'Great Game'   402

21 'The Golden Age of Assassination': Anarchists, Revolutionaries
    and the Black Hand, 1880–1914   425

22 The Great Powers and Foreign Intelligence, 1890–1909   449

23 Intelligence and the Coming of the First World War   472

24 The First World War. Part I: From the Outbreak
    of War to the Zimmermann Telegram   497

25 The First World War. Part 2: From American Intervention
    to Allied Victory   543

26 SIGINT and HUMINT between the Wars   573

27 The 'Big Three' and Second World War Intelligence   603

28 Intelligence and the Victory of the Grand Alliance   637

29 The Cold War and the Intelligence Superpowers   669

30 'Holy Terror': From the Cold War to 9/11   701

    Conclusion: Twenty-First-Century Intelligence
    in Long-Term Perspective   731

    Bibliography   761

    Abbreviations Used in the Notes and References   819

    Notes   821

    Acknowledgements   876

    Index   879

List of Illustrations

Integrated Illustrations

p. 168 Aldegonde's solution of Don Juan of Austria's cipher. (TNA 106/1 document 58 f.144)

p. 178 The Babington postscript and cipher, 1586. (TNA SP12/193/54)

p. 180 Forged addition to the Babington postscript and cipher, 1586. (TNA SP12/193/54)

p. 182 Letter from Pompeo Pellegrini to Jacopo Manucci, 1587. (TNA SP 94/2 part 2 f82)

p. 194 The Monteagle letter, 1605. (Paul Fearn/Alamy)

p. 197 Letter from Philip III to the 7th Duke of Medina Sidonia, 1609. (John D Rockefeller Library, Williamsburg, VA)

p. 215 *Mercurius Aulicus*, 1645. (Copyright © British Library Board/Bridgeman Images)

p. 217 Title page of 'The Kings Cabinet opened', 1645. (Copyright © British Library Board/Bridgeman Images)

p. 232 The death warrant of Charles I. (Shelfmark: HL/PO/JO/10/297A)

p. 301 Washington's letter to Colonel Elias Dayton, 1777. (Beinecke Rare Book and Manuscript Library, Yale University, CT)

pp. 350–51 The Great Paris Cipher, c. 1812. (TNA WO 37/9)

p. 451 A wanted notice for Winston Churchill, South Africa. 1899. (PA Archive)

p. 474 Frontispiece and title page of William le Queux's *Spies of the Kaiser*, Hurst & Blackett, 1909.

p. 538 Part of the Zimmermann telegram as decrypted by Room 40, 1917.

p. 540 'Germany seeks an alliance against us'. Headline from *The New York Times*, 1917.

p. 546 German conditions accepted by Lenin and others on boarding a sealed train in Zurich, 1917.

p. 554 MI5 New Year card by Eric Holt-Wilson and Byam Shaw, 1918. (Service Archives)

p. 658 The GARBO network, the largest network of bogus agents in intelligence history. (TNA WO 208/4374)

p. 686 John Walker's map of a clandestine drop point for the KGB. (Copyright © Naval Institute Heritage Group)

p. 733 Mossad logo.

Plates

1. Spies sent to scout the land of Canaan. Woodcut from the Cologne Bible, 1478–80. (Granger Collection/Alamy)
2. Clay tablet from the Amarna Letters, inscribed in Babylonian cuneiform. (Copyright © The Trustees of the British Museum)
3. A Chinese bamboo copy of *The Art of War*. (Special Collections & University Archives, University of California, Riverside)
4. A haruspex observing a liver of a sacred animal, Rome. (Falkensteinfoto/Alamy)
5. Yaqub ibn Ishaq al-Kindi. (Art Directors & TRIP/Alamy)
6. Pages from al-Kindi's *On Deciphering Crytopgraphic Messages* containing frequency analysis. (Süleymaniye Ottoman Archive MS 4832)
7. Letterbox on the wall of the Doge's Palace, Venice, Italy
8. The Doge Leonardo Loredan, by Giovanni Bellini. (Copyright © The National Gallery, London/Scala, Florence)
9. *The Return of the Prodigal Son* by Robusti Jacopo Tintoretto, Doge's Palace, Venice, Italy. (Copyright © Cameraphoto/Scala, Florence)
10. Anonymous portrait of the famous Spanish conquistador Hernán Cortés, eighteenth century. (Museum of the Royal Academy of Fine Arts of San Fernando, Madrid)
11. Cortes meets Montezuma, from 'Homenaje a Cristobal Colon' by Alfredo Chavero, 1892. (Copyright © British Library Board/Bridgeman)
12. Silver candlestick depicting Ivan the Terrible on horseback, *c.* seventeenth century. (Paul Fearn/Alamy)
13. Still from *Tsar*, directed by Pavel Lungin, 2009.
14. Sir Francis Walsingham, attributed to John De Critz the Elder, *c.* 1589. (Copyright © National Portrait Gallery, London)
15. *The Family of Henry VIII: An Allegory of the Tudor Succession*, by Lucas de Heere, *c.* 1572. (National Museum Wales/Bridgeman)
16. Queen Elizabeth I by Isaac Oliver, *c.* 1600. (Hatfield House/Bridgeman)
17. A Spy from Perugino's *Nova Iconolgia*, 1618. (Dr Cornelia Manegold)
18. The Security Services all-seeing eye. (Service Archives)
19. Wooden sculpture of a spy by Francesco Pianta, *c.* 1657–8. (Copyright © Lessing Archive)
20. Antoine Rossignol des Roches. (Copyright © Château de Versailles, Dist. RMN-Grand Palais)
21. Père Joseph. (Bibliothèque nationale de France, QB-201 (31)-FOL)
22. The visit of Louis XIV to the Château de Juvisy by Pierre-Denis Martin, *c.* 1700. (Copyright © Victoria and Albert Museum)
23. John Wallis by David Loggan. (Scottish National Portrait Gallery, bequest of William Findlay Watson)
24. Blue plaque commemorating John Thurloe, Secretary of State, 1652.
25. John Thurloe by Thomas Ross, eighteenth century. (Copyright © Image; Crown Copyright: UK Government Art Collection March 2014)
26. Aphra Behn by Peter Lely, *c.* 1670. (Yale Center for British Art, bequest of Arthur D. Schlechter/Bridgeman)
27. Tomb of Aphra Behn in Westminster Abbey.

28. *Attack on the Medway*, by Pieter Cornelisz van Soest, *c.* 1667. (Copyright © National Maritime Museum)

29. King George I, studio of Sir Godfrey Kneller, based on a work of 1714. (Copyright © National Portrait Gallery)

30. Edward Willes by John Faber Jr, after Thomas Hudson, 1750. (Copyright © National Portrait Gallery)

31. Count Wenzel Anton Kaunitz by Jean-Etienne Liotard, 1762. (Private collection. Photograph © Christie's/Bridgeman)

32. Charles Genevieve Louis Auguste André Timothée d'Éon de Beaumont, called the Chevalier d'Éon, by Thomas Stewart. (Private collection. Photograph © Philip Mould/Bridgeman)

33. George Washington as colonel of the Virginia Militia by Charles Wilson Peale, 1772. (Washington and Lee University)

34. *Surrender of Cornwallis at Yorktown* by Nathaniel Currier. (Michele and Donald D'Amour Museum of Fine Arts, Springfield, MA. Gift of Lenore B. and Sidney A. Alpert, supplemented with Museum Acquisition Funds. Photography by David Stansbury)

35. Sir George Scovell by William Salter, 1834–40. (Copyright © National Portrait Gallery)

36. Russian postage stamp depicting Barclay de Tolly. (Personal collection of Andrew Krizhanovsky)

37. *The Congress of Vienna* by Jean Godefroy, 1819. (Copyright © RMN-Grand Palais/G. Blot

38. Paul Pry at the Post Office, Punch, 1844. (Copyright © Punch Ltd)

39. Karl Marx in London, 1864. (AKG/Sputnik)

40. Bomb attack on Scotland Yard, 1884.

41. Thaddeus S. Lowe observing the battle from his balloon 'Intrepid', 1862. (Universal History Archive/UIG/Bridgeman)

42. Leadership of the Okhrana at their headquarters in St Petersburg, 1905.

43. Roman Malinovsky. (Paul Fearn/Alamy)

44. Evno Azev, 1910.

45. French President Raymond Poincaré visiting Nicholas II in Russia, 1914. (Copyright © Hulton-Deutsch/CORBIS/Getty)

46. Dragutin Dimitrijevic, *c.* 1900.

47. Dimitrijevic on trial, 1917.

48. Franz von Papen, Washington D.C., 1914. (Copyright © Hulton-Deutsch/CORBIS/Getty)

49. Franz von Rintelen, Victoria Station, 1933. (AP/Topfoto)

50. Black Tom Depot in Jersey City, NJ, shortly after the munitions explosion in 1916. (Buyenlarge/Getty)

51. Sir William Reginald Hall by Walter Stoneman, 1917. (Copyright © National Portrait Gallery)

52. 1890s advertisement for Pears soap, including the portrait of Commander William 'Bubbles' James by his grandfather Sir John Millais. (The Advertising Archives)

53. Georges Painvin, *c.* 1911–18.

54. General Allenby's entrance into Jerusalem through Jaffa Gate, 1917. (Frank & Frances Carpenter/Library of Congress)

55. Vladimir Lenin in disguise, 1917. (AKG)
56. Corpse of Sidney Reilly on private display in Lubyanka, 1925.
57. Felix Dzerzhinsky with Joseph Stalin 1924. (ITAR-TASS News Agency/Alamy)
58. Joseph Stalin and Nikolai Yezhov at the shore of the Moscow–Volga Canal, 1937. (ITAR-TASS/Getty)
59. Stalin without Yezhov. (AFP/GettyImages)
60. Lavrenti Beria with Svetlana Stalin.
61. Franklin D. Roosevelt aboard the Nourmahal, 1935. (National Archives and Records Administration, Washington D.C./Franklin D. Roosevelt Library Public Domain Photographs.)
62. Purple diplomatic cipher machine. (Courtesy of the National Cryptologic Museum, Maryland)
63. Enigma I. (Museo Nazionale della Scienza e della Tecnologia)
64. US Army Signals Security Detachment, Brickhill Manor, c. 1942.
65. Codebreaking at Bletchley Park, 1943. (SSPL/Getty)
66. National leaders gather at the Yalta Conference, 1945. (Getty. (Inset) Alger Hiss. (Everett Collection/Alamy)
67. George Abramovich Koval.
68. President Putin toasts Koval at the atom spy's posthumous 'Hero of Russia' award, 2007. (Sovfoto/UIG/Getty)
69. Marshal Tito receives Iosif Grigulevich (alias Teodoro Castro), 1953.
70. Henry Cabot Lodge Jr displays a plaque from the US Moscow embassy bugged by the KGB, 1960. (Bob Gomel/Life/Getty)
71. The headquarters of the KGB (Committee for State Security), Lubyanka Square in Moscow, 1987. (Copyright © Arnold Drapkin/Alamy)
72. St Sofia, Parish Church of the FSB in Central Moscow. (Professor Neil Kent)
73. SVR chief Mikhail Fradkov and Kim Philby's widow at the unveiling of a memorial plaque to Philby at SVR HQ, 2010. (STR/AFP/Getty Images)
74. US ambassador to the United Nations Adlai Stevenson displays imagery intelligence at a meeting of the UN Security Council, 1962. (Getty)
75. US Secretary of State Colin Powell addressing the UN Security Council, New York City, 2003. (Mario Tama/Getty)
76. Powell's UN presentation slide showing alleged mobile production facility for biological weapons, Iraq. (US Department of State)
77. Oleg Gordievsky in London, 1982. (Security Service Archives)
78. Reagan congratulates Gordievsky in the Oval office, Washington, 1987. (Able Archer Sourcebook National Security Archives)
79. Vasili Mitrokhin, 1992.
80. Moinul Abedin. (Security Service Archives)
81. Dhiren Barot. (Security Service Archives)
82. President Obama and his National Security team watch the intelligence-led operation to capture Bin Laden in 2011. (White House/Pete Souza)
83. Dangerous Love poster campaign, Beijing, 2016. (Ng Han Guan/AP/REX/Shutterstock)

Introduction: The Lost History
of Global Intelligence

Twenty-first-century intelligence suffers from long-term historical amnesia. Early in the Cold War, the historian Sherman Kent, founding father of US intelligence analysis, complained that intelligence was the only profession without a serious literature: 'From my point of view this is a matter of greatest importance. As long as this discipline lacks a literature, its methods, its vocabulary, its body of doctrine, and even its fundamental theory run the risk of never reaching full maturity.'[1] It was more difficult to learn the historical lessons of intelligence than of any other profession mainly because there was so little record of most of its past experience. Western intelligence services during and after the Second World War knew very little about intelligence before – and sometimes during – the First World War. That was true even of 'Station X' at Bletchley Park, which had greater success in breaking enemy ciphers than any codebreaking agency had ever had before. Three times over the previous 500 years, Britain had faced major invasion threats – from the Armada of Philip II of Spain in 1588, from Napoleon at the start of the nineteenth century, and from Hitler in 1940. But the Bletchley Park codebreakers who solved Hitler's ciphers, though they included some notable historians, had no idea that their predecessors had broken those of Philip II and Napoleon at other times of national crisis.* No other wartime profession was as ignorant of its own past. It is impossible, for example, to imagine an economist who had never heard of the Industrial Revolution.

For centuries before the Second World War, educated British people knew far more about intelligence operations recorded in the Bible than they did about the role of intelligence at any moment in their own history. The Christian Old Testament (the Jewish Tanakh) contains more references to

---

* The historian Sir J. H. ('Jack') Plumb, who had served at Bletchley, was, however, aware of codebreaking in the era of Robert Walpole, whose biographer he was. I had the opportunity to discuss this with him.

spies than any history of Britain or of most other countries. Most Victorian schoolchildren, as well as adults, knew, for example, how Moses had sent agents to spy out the Promised Land; how Joseph, having become the Egyptian Pharaoh's Vizier, pretended not to recognize his errant elder brothers and accused them of being spies who had come to identify weak points in Egypt's defences; and how Judas Iscariot became a paid agent of the high priests on 'Spy Wednesday' in Holy Week and betrayed Jesus. Moses (Musa) is also a Muslim prophet. There are 136 references to him in the Quran – far more than to any other human being.* In the Quran, as in the Tanakh, God instructs Moses to send twelve spies to spy out the Promised Land He has given the Israelites. Their mission ended in the first major recorded intelligence failure – due less, as was frequently the case in later centuries, to the quality of the intelligence than to the use made of it. Forty years later, after a better-organized intelligence operation, according to the biblical account, Moses' successor Joshua led the Israelites into the Promised Land.[2]

Ever since the missions of Moses' and Joshua's spies into Canaan, the first priority of intelligence operations has been to obtain secretly information unavailable from open sources. George Tenet, director of the US Central Intelligence Agency (CIA) at the beginning of the twenty-first century, summed up the Agency's main mission in three words: 'We steal secrets.'[3] During the Cold War, Allen Dulles, the longest-serving CIA director, wrote that, over the centuries, intelligence organizations had also shown themselves 'an ideal vehicle for conspiracy'.[4] From earliest times, intelligence has often involved covert operations intended to influence the course of events by methods ranging from deception to assassination – 'active measures', as the twentieth-century KGB called them. Deception involving a bogus defector played a key role in the Athenian victory at the naval Battle of Salamis in 480 BC, at a critical moment during the invasion of Greece by the Persian Empire. For the next two and a half millennia, however, the Salamis deception attracted only a tiny fraction of the interest aroused by the fictional deception of the Trojan Horse, which first featured in Homer's *Odyssey* and later, in greater detail, in the *Aeneid* by the Roman poet Virgil.[5] Even in the twenty-first century, public understanding of intelligence operations is frequently coloured – if not confused – by spy fiction. No real intelligence practitioner, alive or dead, is remotely as well known as James Bond.

No author in ancient Greece or Rome showed a grasp of strategic intelligence which compared with that of the Jewish priests who, probably during the two centuries before Athens's golden age, had written the

---

* By contrast, Muhammad is mentioned by name only four times (though there are other references which do not use his name). The Quran is about the message, not the messenger.

biblical accounts of espionage in Canaan by the spies of Moses and Joshua. Thucydides, the greatest historian of European classical antiquity, famously wrote of the origins of the Peloponnesian War in the fifth century BC, 'The growth of the power of Athens, and the alarm which this inspired in Sparta, made war inevitable.'[6] But intelligence on its rival was not a priority for either Athens or Sparta – or for Thucydides, though he was a general as well as a historian.

The first books to argue that intelligence should have a central role in war and peace were written not in Greece or Rome but in ancient China and the Indian subcontinent: *The Art of War* (*Sunzi bingfa*), traditionally ascribed to Confucius's contemporary, the Chinese general Sun Tzu (*c.* 544–*c.*496 BC); and the *Arthashastra*, a manual on statecraft attributed to a senior adviser of the founder of the Mauryan dynasty which dominated India between 322 and 187 BC. Central to the revival of interest in intelligence in twentieth-century China and India was the rediscovery, after centuries of neglect, of these two ancient works. In India today, the *Arthashastra* has a status similar to that of Aristotle's *Politics* and Machiavelli's *The Prince* in the West. Sun Tzu has been far more revered in Communist China than in any imperial dynasty since the third century AD. Even in the United States, he is more frequently quoted than any pre-twentieth-century Western writer on intelligence.[7]

During what Europeans later called the 'Dark Ages', when the influence of Sun Tzu and the *Arthashastra* was in decline in Asia, the global leaders in intelligence operations were Muhammad and the Islamic Caliphate established in the Middle East after his death in 632. While uniting the tribes of the Arabian Peninsula under the banner of Islam, Muhammad fought twenty-seven battles and instigated about fifty armed raids. Probably his most widely read Muslim biographer today, Safiur Rahman Al Mubarakpuri, claims that 'The Prophet was the greatest military leader in the entire world.'[8] The Hadiths (sacred records of Muhammad's words and deeds) give many instances of how, during his military campaigns, he paid close attention to intelligence. Al Mubarakpuri and other Muslim biographers of Muhammad, however, barely mention his intelligence operations,* which are more frequently cited by Islamist extremists.[9]

The only intelligence operations in which medieval Europe was probably

* Al Mubarakpuri refers to two cases where enemy spies were caught and executed, but to only one instance where Muhammad himself used a spy – during the conquest of the Jewish fort of Az-Zubair; *Sealed Nectar*, locs. 5729, 6432, 7293. There are no references at all to spies in Topbas, *Prophet of Mercy Muhammad*, and only one reference (to a Quraish spying on Muslim forces) in the non-Muslim biography by Karen Armstrong, *Muhammad: Prophet for Our Time*.

the world leader were devoted to what was later called counter-subversion. Catholic 'inquisitions' to root out religious heresy anticipated the very much larger campaigns by security and intelligence services in modern secular one-party states against what the KGB denounced as 'ideological subversion'. Probably no pre-twentieth-century security service was capable either of the organized mass interrogation or of the elaborate record keeping involved in, for example, mid-thirteenth-century clerical inquisitions into the Cathar heresy in Languedoc. Twentieth-century secular interrogators were often unaware that some of their methods had been devised by clerical inquisitors centuries earlier. 'Waterboarding' (simulated drowning), used by US interrogators to obtain intelligence from senior Al Qaeda personnel after 9/11, was a technique devised half a millennium before by the Spanish Inquisition.[10]

Though few historians have noticed it, the European Renaissance was a major turning point in the history of intelligence. For the first time, Europe established a global lead in intelligence which went unchallenged until the American Declaration of Independence. Like twentieth-century interrogators, few if any Renaissance advocates and practitioners of intelligence were aware of how frequently they were reinventing the wheel. It did not occur to Machiavelli that his often-quoted dictum 'Nothing is more worthy of a good general than the endeavour to penetrate the designs of the enemy'[11] merely repeated a maxim attributed to Sun Tzu almost two millennia before. The Renaissance codebreakers who believed they had invented 'frequency analysis' (a turning point in the history of cryptanalysis) had no idea that it had been discovered by the Muslim philosopher and cryptanalyst Yaqub ibn Ishaq al-Kindi in the Baghdad 'House of Wisdom' over six centuries earlier. The Ottomans, who made Constantinople the capital of their Muslim empire in 1453, seem to have been equally ignorant of al-Kindi's achievements.[12]

The Renaissance also marked a turning point in the history of diplomacy, which was closely linked to the development of Western intelligence. Hitherto ambassadors had been used only for specific diplomatic missions. The city-states in Renaissance Italy, however, established resident ambassadors in each others' capitals, a system which became the model for European diplomacy as a whole. Since most resident ambassadors were expected to collect intelligence as well as to represent their governments, the recruitment of spies increased. Early modern diplomacy and intelligence gathering thus overlapped. From 1573 until his death in 1590, Elizabeth's principal Secretary of State, Sir Francis Walsingham, successfully combined the roles of Foreign Secretary and intelligence chief, with daily access to the Queen and her Chief Minister.[13]

With one important exception, no clear separation between diplomacy and espionage emerged in Western and Central Europe until professional intelligence bureaucracies were founded in the later nineteenth century. The exception was what is now called signals intelligence (SIGINT), derived from the interception and decryption of communications. Beginning in the Renaissance, small, specialized codebreaking agencies were founded which required cryptanalytic expertise unavailable in other branches of government. Half a millennium later, the role of SIGINT remains a major gap in most histories of pre-twentieth-century politics and international relations. Even histories of Elizabethan England which recognize the importance of Walsingham's role rarely give adequate credit to the achievements of his chief cryptanalyst, who broke the ciphers of both Mary, Queen of Scots, and Philip II of Spain, and was personally rewarded with a royal pension by a grateful Elizabeth I.[14]

There was a direct, though incomplete, correlation (little noticed by historians) during the seventeenth and eighteenth centuries between the success of European statesmen in their conduct of foreign policy and their skill in the exploitation of SIGINT. The ablest French statesman of the seventeenth century, Cardinal Richelieu, was also the founder of the first French SIGINT agency, the *cabinet noir* (black chamber), a term commonly applied over the next few centuries to similar agencies in other countries. Its head, who had his own château, was better recognized and rewarded than any other pre-twentieth-century cryptanalyst. His British counterpart, a founder member of the Royal Society, was rewarded by Oliver Cromwell with a chair at Oxford University, which he kept for half a century. The ablest international statesman of the mid-eighteenth century, Count (later Prince) Wenzel Anton Kaunitz, successively leading Austrian diplomat and Chancellor, was similarly the ablest user of SIGINT.[15] The skill of both Richelieu and Kaunitz in the exploitation of intelligence was largely forgotten by later generations. Just as no French Foreign Minister before the First World War rivalled Richelieu's grasp of SIGINT, so none of Kaunitz's successors in imperial Vienna possessed his flair for diplomatic intelligence.

The first country to challenge Europe's global lead in intelligence was the United States after the Declaration of Independence in 1776. Ironically, the commander-in-chief of the rebel Continental Army, George Washington, had earlier learned the importance of military intelligence as a British army officer fighting the French, who were to become his allies against the British in the Revolutionary War. Washington's intelligence operations in both HUMINT (human intelligence) and SIGINT outclassed those of his British opponents. As first President of the United States, he was granted a fund by Congress to finance foreign intelligence which rose to about 12 per cent of the federal budget – a higher percentage than the massive US intelligence expenditure of the late twentieth and early twenty-first centuries.[16]

The history of intelligence is not linear. In both the United States and the United Kingdom foreign intelligence was a lower priority at the end of the nineteenth century than at the beginning. Save for Washington's immediate successors, no President attempted to learn from his example. Even the Civil War marked only a temporary halt in the long-term decline of US intelligence. Victorian intelligence too was in decline. As a result of the closure of the Deciphering Branch in 1844, following parliamentary protests, Britain entered the First World War, unlike any of the major wars of the late sixteenth, seventeenth, eighteenth and early nineteenth centuries, without a SIGINT agency.* At the outbreak of war in 1914, the US President, Woodrow Wilson, and the British Prime Minister, Herbert Asquith, had a weaker grasp of intelligence than their eighteenth-century predecessors, George Washington and the two Pitts. These failings passed unnoticed by both contemporaries and most subsequent historians. Also unnoticed has been the fact that, though less intelligent than Wilson and Asquith, Tsar Nicholas II regarded intelligence as a much higher priority. Because of their lack of awareness of the role of SIGINT, none of the numerous twentieth-century histories of the origins of the First World War mentions that, in both St Petersburg and Paris, the first indication in July 1914 that Austria was preparing to deliver the ultimatum to Serbia which was to trigger the outbreak of war came from diplomatic decrypts.[17]

The First World War, thanks to its unprecedented scale and intensity in an era of equally unprecedented technological change, marked an even greater turning point in intelligence history than the Renaissance. The vast increase in communications made possible by the nineteenth-century invention of the telegraph and wireless gave SIGINT a greater operational role than in any previous conflict. Particularly in the early stages of the war, however, war leaders' ignorance of past experience made them ill-equipped to put intelligence to good use. Despite the pre-war successes of Russian foreign intelligence, Russian military intelligence at the outbreak of war was far less effective than it had been a century before on the eve of Napoleon's invasion of Russia. Within weeks its incompetence had led to Russia's worst defeat of the war.

The use of intelligence by governments and high commands in the First World War thus owed much to improvisation. Though SIGINT was to

---

* The Government of India, however, had a small SIGINT agency on the North-West Frontier. See below, pp. 418–19, 467.

prove crucial to British naval operations, the Director of Naval Intelligence in August 1914 had given no thought to its wartime role until intercepted ciphered German naval messages began to pile up on his desk. These unexpected intercepts prompted the foundation in the Admiralty of the first British SIGINT agency since 1844, which, with its military counterpart, MI1b, became the wartime world leader. The creation of the Bolshevik Cheka, forerunner of the KGB, only six weeks after the October Revolution of 1917 was also the result of rapid improvisation. Though it developed between the wars into the world's largest and most powerful intelligence service, it was originally intended only as a temporary expedient to deal with an impending strike by state employees.[18]

More than any previous war, the First World War led to attempts, which varied greatly from country to country, to learn its intelligence lessons. British SIGINT successes in the Second World War owed much to lessons learned in the First – among them the need for better coordination. The failure of the United States to learn the same lesson was a major reason for the SIGINT confusion which preceded, and helped to make possible, the Japanese surprise attack on Pearl Harbor. For over a year before Pearl Harbor, the rival US military and naval cryptanalysts were bizarrely instructed to decrypt Japanese diplomatic telegrams on alternate days.[19]

All the Big Three in the Second World War – Joseph Stalin, Winston Churchill and Franklin Roosevelt – were more influenced than has usually been realized by their very different experiences of First World War intelligence. After the Bolshevik Revolution, Stalin spent years studying and annotating almost every page of the huge, multi-volume intelligence file maintained on him by the Tsarist Okhrana. Churchill had longer and more varied experience of intelligence than any previous war leader. One of the main lessons learned by both him and the less experienced Roosevelt from the First World War was the importance of Allied intelligence collaboration in the Second. Roosevelt's admiration for what he called Britain's 'wonderful intelligence service' in the First World War later led him as President to approve intelligence collaboration with Britain even before Pearl Harbor, while the United States remained officially neutral. The wartime UK/US SIGINT alliance became the cornerstone of a transatlantic Special Relationship which still continues.[20] Contrary to the belief of many of its practitioners, this is not the first SIGINT alliance in British history (which was concluded between Elizabethan England and the Dutch),[21] but it remains the most important.

Since the late twentieth century, far more has been published on intelligence operations in the Second World War than had ever been published on the role of intelligence in any previous conflict. For a generation after the war, however, historians were seriously handicapped by official concealment of the main Western (especially British) wartime intelligence successes against Nazi Germany: chief among them the ULTRA intelligence derived from breaking high-grade enemy ciphers and the Double-Cross System, the most successful strategic deception in the history of warfare. Only when these operations were declassified in the early and mid-1970s did it become possible to write accurate accounts of the war against the U-boats in the North Atlantic and the D-Day landings on the Normandy beaches.[22]

Despite the growth of intelligence history since the 1980s, study of the Cold War nowadays suffers from much the same neglect of SIGINT which diminished, and sometimes distorted, understanding of Second World War intelligence until the mid-1970s. None of President Harry S. Truman's biographers mentions that he was so impressed by his brief experience of the wartime British–American SIGINT alliance that he approved its peacetime continuation – and in so doing profoundly influenced the development of the Special Relationship. Though studies of Cold War US foreign policy invariably mention the Central Intelligence Agency (CIA), there is rarely any reference to the larger National Security [SIGINT] Agency (NSA). The virtual exclusion of SIGINT from the history of post-war international relations helps to explain why so many well-educated Americans mistakenly believed that the atom spies Julius and Ethel Rosenberg, both executed in the electric chair, and other leading Soviet agents detected in the United States were the innocent victims of official paranoia and McCarthyite hysteria. Soviet decrypts declassified by the NSA and GCHQ after the Cold War show that they were guilty as charged.[23]

The history of superpower rivalry during the Cold War has also been distorted by the KGB's ability to keep its operational secrets far more successfully than the CIA. No account of American policy in the Third World omits the role of CIA covert action. By contrast, KGB covert action ('active measures') passes almost unmentioned in most histories both of Soviet foreign policy and of developing countries. The result has been a curiously lopsided account of the secret Cold War in the Third World – the intelligence equivalent of the sound of one hand clapping. The admirable history of the Cold War by John Lewis Gaddis, for example, refers to CIA covert action in Chile, Cuba and Iran, but makes no reference to extensive KGB operations in the same countries.[24] In reality, as material exfiltrated from KGB archives after the Cold War reveals, from at least the early 1960s onwards the KGB played an even more active global role than the CIA.

In Britain, exaggerated official secrecy about the intelligence services, enforced by both Labour and Conservative governments throughout the Cold War, also inhibited the development of intelligence history. Even the existence of the Secret Intelligence Service (SIS or MI6) was not officially acknowledged until the Queen's Speech at the opening of Parliament in 1992. In the same year Stella Rimington became the first Director-General of MI5 to be publicly identified. Gender historians who had been unable to research female recruitment by MI5 even as far back as the First World War, because all its records (many since declassified)* were still secret, were surprised to discover that the Security Service had become the first of the world's major intelligence services to have a female head. The incomprehension of British tabloids at Rimington's appointment was reflected in headlines such as 'HOUSEWIFE SUPERSPY' and 'MOTHER OF TWO GETS TOUGH WITH TERRORISTS'.

For much of the Cold War, Western intelligence analysts often failed to realize the handicap imposed on them by the shortage of academic research and their own lack of historical perspective. A notable exception was the Yale historian Sherman Kent, who spent a total of seventeen years as an analyst during the Second World War and Cold War. The world's first peer-reviewed journal on intelligence, *Studies in Intelligence*, was founded in 1955, not by academics in university departments but by Sherman Kent in the CIA. Though originally classified, a majority of its articles on intelligence methodology and history are now accessible online. Like academic journals, but unlike most intelligence reports, *Studies in Intelligence* announced at the outset: 'All statements of fact, opinion, or analysis . . . are those of the Authors. They do not necessarily reflect official positions or views of the Central Intelligence Agency or any other US government entity, past or present.' The first academic journal, *Intelligence and National Security*, co-edited by Michael Handel and the author of this volume, did not begin publication until over thirty years after *Studies in Intelligence*.

Lack of long-term historical perspective was as evident in intelligence assessment at the end of the twentieth century as at the beginning of the Cold War. During the Second World War and Cold War, Western intelligence agencies had been well versed in Nazi and Communist ideology. But the increasingly secularized late-twentieth-century West found it far more difficult to grasp the appeal of Islamic fundamentalism. Its incomprehension of the political power of religious extremism was vividly displayed during the crisis in Iran which led early in 1979 to the fall of the pro-Western Shah and the rise of the 78-year-old Shia Ayatollah Ruhollah Khomeini. 'Whoever took religion seriously?' demanded one surprised State Department official after Washington had been taken aback by Khomeini's popular

---

* For many of its files, MI5 now operates an informal fifty-year declassification rule, releasing large batches to the National Archives once or twice a year.

triumph.[25] Over the next decade, many Western intelligence analysts similarly failed to grasp that understanding the appeal of Al Qaeda and the terrorist threat which it posed required serious study of its theology. Those with the best understanding of the Islamist terrorist threat before the 9/11 attacks, among them the leading academic expert on 'Holy Terror', Bruce Hoffman, were those with a long-term perspective.[26]

The dawn of cyberwarfare and the looming threat of terrorist use of weapons of mass destruction confront twenty-first-century intelligence communities with dramatic new challenges. To respond to them as effectively as possible, however, they will need a long-term perspective which has often been forgotten or ignored. Learning from past experience in intelligence, as in most other fields, is, of course, easier said than done. To quote the historian John Bew:

> History does not lend itself easily to the PowerPoints or executive summaries on which our policymakers increasingly rely . . . A genuine understanding of history requires a patience that is not easy to reconcile with the urgency of policy. A good starting point is to view the past as a source of wisdom rather than revelation.[27]

'Only long-term historical perspective', writes Quentin Skinner, former Regius Professor of History at Cambridge, can 'liberate us from the parochialism of our own forms of cultural analysis'.[28] Strategic-intelligence analysis which ignores the long term is necessarily parochial.

There are some signs of progress. The academic study of intelligence history, which barely existed little more than a generation ago, is now thriving in a growing minority of universities on both sides of the Atlantic. In the early twenty-first century, all three British intelligence agencies, as well as the Joint Intelligence Committee, commissioned official or 'authorized' histories by outside professional historians, who were given unprecedented access to their files.* All followed the pioneering principles set out by Sherman Kent in *Studies in Intelligence* half a century earlier.†

More frequently than ever before, intelligence in the twenty-first century

---

* The three UK intelligence agencies, however, differed in their views on how much of their history to make public. My authorized centenary history of MI5, *Defence of the Realm*, covers all its first hundred years, though in significantly less detail for the early twenty-first than for the twentieth century. The official history of SIS/MI6 stops in 1949. The official history of the SIGINT agency GCHQ, due for publication in 2019, is likely to omit details of diplomatic SIGINT during the Cold War.

† The Director-General of the Security Service (MI5), Jonathan Evans (now Baron Evans of Weardale), wrote in a foreword to my *Defence of the Realm*, published in 2009: 'The judgements and conclusions drawn by Professor Andrew in the History are his own, not those of the Security Service or the Government as a whole.'

has become front-page news. Official reports on 9/11 and the Iraq War, as well as unofficial whistleblowers, have published unprecedented amounts of intelligence material.[29] The significance of recent intelligence history, however, can only be adequately understood in long-term perspective. Like much else in the early twenty-first century, intelligence studies frequently suffer from what I have called Historical Attention-Span Deficit Disorder (HASDD).

The history of intelligence operations is far older than any of today's intelligence agencies. *The Secret World* sets out to recover some of the lost history of global intelligence over the last three millennia, to show how it modifies current historiography, and to demonstrate its continuing relevance to intelligence in the twenty-first century.

I

In the Beginning: Spies of the Bible and Ancient Egypt from Moses to the Last Supper

The first major figure in world literature to emphasize the importance of good intelligence was God. After the Israelites had escaped from captivity in Egypt and crossed the Red Sea, supposedly in about 1300 BC, God told Moses to send spies to reconnoitre 'the land of Canaan, which I give unto the children of Israel'. Since no trained intelligence personnel were available for the mission to the Promised Land, Moses selected, on God's instructions, one leading man from each of the twelve tribes of Israel.

> And Moses sent them to spy out the land of Canaan, and said unto them, 'Get you up this [way] southward, and go up into the mountain:
> And see the land, what it [is]; and the people that dwelleth therein, whether they [be] strong or weak, few or many;
> And what the land [is] that they dwell in, whether it [be] good or bad; and what cities [they be] that they dwell in, whether in tents, or in strongholds;
> And what the land [is], whether it [be] fat or lean, whether there be wood therein, or not.
> And be ye of good courage, and bring of the fruit of the land. Now the time [was] the time of the first ripe grapes.'[1]

Over three millennia later, the Victorian schoolboy George Aston, who went on to become a senior naval intelligence officer with a knighthood, was first attracted to secret service work by a picture in a children's book of Bible stories which showed two of Moses' agents on their way back from a forty-day mission to Canaan, staggering under the weight of a huge bunch of grapes hanging from a pole carried on their shoulders.[2] In Victorian Britain, at a time when Britain had no professional secret intelligence agencies but knowledge of Bible stories was more widespread than at any other time in British history, the use of spies by Moses and his successor Joshua was far better known than any English or British intelligence operation over the previous millennium.

The Old Testament (also known as the Tanakh, the Hebrew Bible) contains more references to spies than any published history of Britain or of most other countries. The first mention comes in the Genesis story of Joseph and his ten elder half-brothers, who were enraged by the favour-itism shown to Joseph by their father, Jacob (later renamed Israel), exemplified by his gift to him of a coat of many colours. Some of Joseph's brothers also felt, with some justification, that he was spying on them. Jacob tactlessly instructed Joseph, then aged only seventeen, to tell him how his brothers were managing the family flock; Joseph gave his father an 'evil report' of their behaviour. To rid themselves of Joseph, his brothers sold him for twenty pieces of silver to slave traders, who took him to Egypt. By ripping the coat of many colours and dipping it in goat's blood, his brothers persuaded their father that Joseph had been eaten by a wild animal.

Unknown to his family, Joseph eventually rose to become the Egyptian Pharaoh's Vizier. When his elder brothers came to Egypt to buy corn during a famine, they were received by Joseph and failed to recognize him in his now exalted position. Joseph, however, recognized them but pretended not to and accused them of being spies who had come to identify weak points in Egypt's defences. After he had subjected his brothers to several covert operations (including planting apparently stolen objects in their luggage), the story ended happily. Overcome with emotion, Joseph iden-tified himself as their brother, was reconciled with them, and invited his father and extended family to take up residence in Egypt.[3]

Whatever the historicity of the Joseph story in Genesis (which is similar to the account given in the longest chapter of the Quran),[4] it reflects one probably not uncommon reality of life in the era of the Hebrew Bible: that, in a society which was frequently in conflict, strangers and travellers who aroused suspicion were liable to be accused of being spies (which they sometimes were). Even in twentieth-century Britain, spy scares (mostly unfounded) involving supposedly suspicious foreigners were common on the eve, and at the start, of both world wars.[5]

Though the first scriptural reference to spies comes in Genesis, no organ-ized espionage operation is mentioned in the Bible until God commands Moses to 'spy out the land of Canaan'. Moses' twelve spies, sent from the desolate Wilderness of Paran (north-west of today's Aqaba), were amateurs, chosen for their social standing rather than because they had shown any talent for intelligence gathering. The intelligence they were instructed to obtain in preparation for the advance into Canaan was much in line with that sought by modern military commanders. The great nineteenth-century German military theorist, Carl von Clausewitz, defined the intelligence required by commanders on hostile territory as 'every sort of information about the enemy and his country – the basis, in short, of our own plans and operations'.⁶

All twelve of Moses' spies reported on their return that Canaan was a land flowing with milk and honey. Two of them, Caleb and Joshua, argued that, since the Israelites had God's support, they had nothing to fear from invading the Promised Land: 'Let us go up at once and possess it.' God was outraged, however, with the pessimistic intelligence assessment of the other ten – an 'evil report', according to the Bible, which concluded that the existing inhabitants would prove too strong for the Israelites: 'We be not able to go up against the people; for they [are] stronger than we.' The Canaanites, claimed the fearful ten, included giants who had made them feel no bigger than grasshoppers.⁷ The Quran contains a similar account of the spies' mission, though Joshua and Caleb are identified only as two 'God-fearing men' on whom God 'had bestowed His grace'.⁸

The Bible implies that the mission of the twelve spies was intended as a test of their faith as well as of their aptitude for intelligence gathering. All but Caleb and Joshua failed on both counts. The other ten publicly used their mission report to justify their own belief that, despite the support of the God who had delivered them from bondage in Egypt and parted the waters of the Red Sea to make possible their escape, any attempt to take possession of the Promised Land would prove impossibly dangerous. Unless, improbably, Canaan really was populated by giants, they were guilty of distorting the intelligence they had collected to dissuade the Israelites from going ahead. Both the Bible and the Quran record that the ten won the public debate. The 'whole congregation' sided with them, threatened to stone Caleb and Joshua, and ungratefully complained that the Israelites would have been better off remaining in captivity in Egypt.⁹ According to the Quran, the Israelite majority told Moses they would never enter the promised land so long as its current inhabitants remained: 'So go, you and your Lord, and fight. We are remaining right here.'¹⁰

God's furious response exceeded any other recorded instance of divine anger at the misuse of intelligence:

> And the Lord said unto Moses, How long will this people provoke me? and how long will it be ere they believe me, for all the signs which I have shewed among them? I will smite them with the pestilence, and disinherit them . . .

The ten who had produced the 'evil' report of their Canaan espionage mission all died of the plague. After intercession by Moses, God commuted the punishment of the other Israelites from pestilence and disinheritance to forty years' wandering in the wilderness. However, God decreed that no Israelite over twenty years of age, with the sole exceptions of the righteous spies Caleb and Joshua, was to live long enough to enter the Promised Land.[11]

Moses' death on Mount Nebo (at the age of 120, according to the Bible) coincided with the end of the Israelites' forty years in the wilderness. The visitor to Mount Nebo today, in present-day Jordan, can still see across the Dead Sea much the same view of the Promised Land that the Bible tells us Moses was allowed to glimpse before his death.[12] God told Joshua, Moses' successor, that the time had come for the Israelites to enter the Promised Land. The Book of Joshua tells the story of a lightning military campaign in which the Israelites, with divine assistance, defeated, one after the other, the kings of Canaan. Conquest was preceded by espionage. Joshua sent two spies (both unidentified but not, apparently, tribal leaders as forty years before) on a secret mission to the fortress city of Jericho, the first major target of the campaign.[13]

The biblical account of their mission provides the first record of a joint operation involving both of, reputedly, the world's two oldest professions (said to be prostitutes and spies). Once in Jericho, Joshua's spies found accommodation with Rahab the harlot (prostitute), whose brothel was embedded in the city wall. Though there may have been a shortage of alternatives, there were obvious disadvantages for the spies in lodging in a brothel, whose clients had no pressing reason to keep their presence secret. Indeed, within twenty-four hours the King of Jericho had received reports that Israelites with a mission to 'explore the whole country' were staying in the brothel. After hiding the two spies among bales of flax on her roof, Rahab told the King they had left Jericho: 'Pursue after them quickly; for ye shall overtake them.'[14] Despite the security problems for the spies posed by the brothel, there were some operational advantages in using it as a base. Travellers to Jericho who visited the prostitutes must have been a useful source of information about the surrounding area. Some modern intelligence agencies have made similar use of brothels' intelligence potential.*

The greatest asset of the Israelite spies staying in Rahab's Jericho brothel was Rahab herself, who told the spies, 'I know the Lord hath given you the land [of Canaan].' She said that the local inhabitants, having heard how God had rescued the Israelites from captivity in Egypt and parted the Red Sea to enable them to cross, lacked the courage to resist their

* In 1939 the Nazi Sicherheitsdienst (SD) took over the 'high-class' Berlin brothel Salon Kitty, fitted concealed microphones in the bedrooms, and connected them to a control room with monitoring desks and recording equipment. Among the clients was the Italian foreign minister, Count Galeazzo Ciano, whose recorded comments on Adolf Hitler the SD sometimes found disconcertingly frank. (Hagen (ed.), *Schellenberg Memoirs*.)

advance into Canaan. In return for a promise to ensure the safety of her family, Rahab secretly sided with the Israelites. Unlike the majority of Moses' spies, whose 'evil' intelligence report forty years earlier had aroused divine indignation, Joshua's spies told him on their return from Canaan: 'Truly the Lord hath delivered into our hands all the land; for even all the inhabitants of the country do faint because of us.'[15]

Rahab, however, had only a supporting role in the Israelites' conquest of Jericho. The success of the conquest owed far more to divine intervention than to human espionage. God enabled the Israelite army to cross the Jordan by temporarily drying up the river bed. After their arrival at Jericho, as instructed by God, they walked around the city walls for seven days in succession, blowing ram's horn trumpets. On the seventh day, after blowing the trumpets, the army 'shouted with a great shout' and the city wall fell down. Rahab and her family, who had marked the location of the brothel by hanging a scarlet cord from the window, escaped from Jericho and settled with the Israelites. All the other inhabitants of Jericho were massacred, along with their livestock.[16]

In the New Testament both St Paul and St James praise Rahab's faith and righteousness in their epistles.[17] The beginning of St Matthew's Gospel adds a new dimension to the Christian understanding of Rahab by including her in the female line of Jesus' family tree.[18] According to the very first chapter of the New Testament, Jesus was thus descended, on his mother's side, from the first female spy identified in world literature.

Attempts by twentieth-century intelligence agencies to draw lessons from the biblical account of espionage in the era of Moses and Joshua include a 1978 study in the classified in-house journal of the Central Intelligence Agency (CIA), *Studies in Intelligence*, entitled 'A Bible Lesson on Spying', which has since been declassified.[19] Its author, John M. Cardwell (possibly a pseudonym), saw analogies between the debacle which followed the Israelites' public debate of the reports of Moses' spies on Canaan and the tribulations of the CIA in the mid-1970s, when some its recent operations (including assassination plots and other 'dirty tricks') received unprecedented publicity and the Agency was subjected for the first time to Congressional oversight:

> If there is a lesson to be learned [from the Canaan espionage operation], it would appear that a strong case is made for the conduct of spying activities in secret by professionals, unencumbered by other political or military responsibilities, and that these professionals should report in secret to higher authority who would make policy decisions without debate. Spies should definitely not participate in the policy-decision-making process, nor

should they take their cases to the public. When that occurs, although stoning is passé, the people are likely to throw figurative rocks at the wrong people for the wrong reasons.

Joshua, in Cardwell's view, avoided both the main mistakes made during the first attempt to spy out the land of Canaan, which, he implied, also demonstrated the folly of the excessive publicity given to intelligence operations and Congressional interference that, he believed, undermined the CIA's effectiveness in the mid-1970s:

> Moses' operation, conducted by amateurs more or less in the public domain, resulted in a weakening of Moses' position of authority, led to a loss of the people's confidence in themselves, and precipitated an extended period of severe national punishment. Joshua's operation, conducted in private by professionals, led to an achievement of national destiny . . . Joshua certainly did not have an oversight problem, nor did he worry about defining a politically acceptable mission scenario.[20]

The modern intelligence services most concerned to draw lessons from the espionage missions sent by Moses and Joshua into the Promised Land have, predictably, been those of the state of Israel since its foundation in 1948: Mossad, the foreign intelligence agency, and Shin Bet, the domestic security service. In talks to new recruits at the start of the twenty-first century, Efraim Halevy, head of Mossad, used to cite the behaviour of ten of the spies sent by Moses to spy out the land of Canaan as a cautionary example of the importance of sticking to their assigned missions. The ten had incurred divine wrath by allowing their personal views to override their responsibilities for intelligence reporting.[21]

Both Shin Bet and Mossad take their mottoes from the Hebrew Bible. Shin Bet's comes from Psalm 121: 'He who watches over Israel shall neither slumber nor sleep.' The current Mossad motto is: 'Where no counsel is, the people fall, but in the multitude of counsellors there is safety' (Proverbs 11:14). This replaced an earlier, more contentious motto based on Proverbs 24:6: 'By way of deception, thou shalt conduct war.'[22] That motto is still sometimes cited by the current Israeli prime minister, Benjamin Netanyahu. When celebrating the Hanukkah festival with President Shimon Peres and Mossad's chief, Tamir Pardo, in December 2012, Netanyahu declared:

> On Hanukkah we traditionally say, 'Who will sing the praises of Israel's strength?', and I add to that 'Who will carry out Israel's covert operations?', as it is written: 'By way of deception, thou shalt conduct war.' This is the way the few defeat the many, and we have learned that from the days of

our forefathers. We need a body that can operate on the international level using both ancient and modern methods. The Mossad does just that in the most outstanding way.[23]

Mossad's use of deception thus claims biblical origins. According to Exodus, the Israelites' escape from captivity in Egypt began with a divinely authorized deception. Moses asked Pharaoh to permit the Israelites to go into the wilderness on a three-day religious pilgrimage, not revealing that this was intended to be the beginning of a permanent exodus.[24] Among those Jewish commentators who later concluded that Moses was acting 'by way of deception' is Rabbi Shlomo Yitzhaki (1040–1104), better known as Rashi, whose commentary on the Talmud has been included in every published edition since it was first printed in the 1520s.

Though the Israelites may have been unique in claiming divine authority for their intelligence operations in Canaan over 3,000 years ago, the ancient Egyptians were also heavily involved in intelligence collection. Despite the fact that the Bible makes no reference to an Egyptian presence in Canaan (much as surviving Egyptian sources make only a solitary reference to an Israelite presence), its city-states were ruled by vassals of the Pharaoh with a strong Egyptian military and administrative presence.[25] Canaan was the land bridge between Egypt and the four other 'Great Kingdoms' in the ancient Near East with which it had diplomatic relations: Hatti, Mittani, Assyria and Babylonia.[26] It was also a vital source of supplies for Egypt's army and navy, and therefore a priority for Egyptian intelligence collection.

The earliest reliable, though fragmentary, information on Egyptian intelligence collection in Canaan – which is also the earliest major source on intelligence operations anywhere in the world – comes from the 'Amarna letters', written on clay tablets in the mid-fourteenth century BC. These were accidentally discovered in 1887 by an Egyptian peasant woman at Tell el-Amarna on the site of the palace of Pharaoh Amenhotep IV (better known as Akhenaten). A century of research by scholars on both sides of the Atlantic culminated in the publication in 1992 of an English translation of the letters by the Harvard Egyptologist Professor W. L. Moran.[27] A total of 329 of the Amarna letters in the Moran edition were sent by vassals in Canaan to the Pharaoh about a century earlier than the Israelite conquest of Canaan recorded in the Bible. Thirty-eight of the vassals' letters contain what would nowadays be regarded as intelligence rather than open-source information, though at the time no clear distinction was made between the two.[28] Ports on the Levant coast and caravanserai along trade routes also obtained news from far-flung parts of the Mediterranean and the Fertile Crescent. Through Canaan and its harbours, there passed troops, traders and messengers, both friendly and hostile.[29] Egypt's vassals were well placed to gather information from them and knew that they were expected to do so. One vassal wrote to the Pharaoh, 'I am your loyal servant, and whatever I hear I write to my Lord.'[30] Much (almost certainly more) information was also passed on by word of mouth to local Egyptian officials.[31]

The highest-priority intelligence reported to the Pharaoh concerned threats to the Egyptian Empire from external enemies and internal traitors. On one occasion the Pharaoh threatened the ruler of Amurru (north of Canaan), Aziru, with decapitation by axe after receiving intelligence that he had been consorting with one of his enemies: 'Now the king has heard as follows: "You are at peace with the ruler of Qidša. The two of you take food and strong drink together." And it is true. Why do you act so? Why are you at peace with a ruler whom the king is fighting?' The source of this unwelcome intelligence must have been a non-Egyptian informant at the court of either Aziru or the ruler of Qidša, since an Egyptian would scarcely have been invited to witness Aziru eating and drinking with an enemy of the Pharaoh.[32] On another occasion, Abi-Milku, ruler of Tyre, reported that the ruler of Sidon, who claimed to be an exemplary vassal of the Pharaoh, had transferred his loyalty to Aziru: 'Zimredda, the king of Sidon, writes daily to the rebel Aziru . . . about every word he has heard from Egypt. I herewith write to my lord [Pharaoh], and it is good that he knows.'[33] The Amarna letters also contain the earliest, very fragmentary historical evidence of obtaining intelligence from message interception,* which, when combined with codebreaking,† later became the most important form of intelligence collection in the world wars of the twentieth century.

One intercepted Amarna letter, when compared with Hittite cuneiform records of the same period, reveals an extraordinary sequel to the death

---

* The very fragmentary evidence of message interception in the Amarna letters is sometimes difficult to interpret. One message to Aziru from his brothers may have been intercepted by the Egyptians. Or it may have been supplied by Aziru in an attempt to prove his loyalty to the Pharaoh. (Cohen, 'Intelligence in the Amarna Letters', pp. 92–3.)

† On the origins of cryptography in ancient Egypt, see Kahn, *Codebreakers*, pp. 71–3. The earliest known example is the use of unusual hieroglyphic symbols on an inscription dated *c.*1900 BC in the tomb of the nobleman Khnumhotep II. Kahn argues, however, that the aim of the symbols was not, as in modern cryptography, to make part of the inscription secret but to add to its prestige and authority. Other examples of ancient Egyptian funerary cryptography also seem to have been primarily intended to attract readers' attention and encourage them to solve the riddles that they posed.

in 1323 BC of the Pharaoh Tutankhamun. Though he died aged only about nineteen, after less than a decade on the throne, the sensational discovery in 1923 in the Valley of the Kings of his almost intact tomb and sarcophagus – the most complete of all ancient Egyptian royal tombs – has turned Tutankhamun into the best known of all the pharaohs. The most celebrated exhibit on display today in the priceless collection of the Cairo Museum of Egyptian Antiquities is Tutankhamun's death mask, made of eleven kilograms of solid gold. Other treasures from the tomb show Queen Ankhesenamen, who was probably his half-sister, at his side. A carving on a golden throne depicts her in a short Nubian wig anointing her husband. Scenes depicted on a golden shrine show her offering Tutankhamun lotus flowers and standing behind him in a skiff pointing at a duck's nest in a marsh as he hunts ducks with bow and arrow. Recent research has revealed that, immediately after Tutankhamun's death, Queen Ankhesenamun wrote to the Hittite King Suppiluliuma I, saying that she had no son and heir, and intended to remarry, but refused to marry an Egyptian without royal blood: 'They say you have many sons. So give me one of your sons. To me he will be a husband, but in Egypt he will be king.'[34]

Suppiluliuma, who seems to have been taken aback by Ankhesenamun's urgent, unexpected request to marry one of his sons, probably suspected some kind of provocation, and sent an envoy to ensure that she was in earnest. Ankhesenamun then despatched a second message reproaching the Hittite king for doubting her sincerity and again appealed to him to allow her to marry one of his sons. This time her message, which revealed her original approach to Suppiluliuma, was intercepted; part of it survives among the Amarna letters as well as in Hittite records.[35] Though Suppiluliuma seems to have been reassured that Ankhesenamun was in earnest and sent one of his sons to marry her, he was assassinated during his journey before he reached the Egyptian court. Who was responsible for the death of the Hittite prince will probably never be known with certainty. The most probable culprit, however, was Tutankhamun's elderly Vizier, Ay, who was plotting to succeed the dead Pharaoh. It was probably to avoid marriage to Ay that Ankhesenamun had tried to marry a Hittite prince. Ay, however, succeeded Tutankhamun as Pharaoh and married his widow – despite having discovered her secret plan to marry a Hittite prince instead. Though there is no proof, he may well have taken revenge on his new wife. Ankhesenamun died from unknown causes about a year after her marriage to Ay.

The Amarna letters, as well as other Egyptian records and recent archaeological discoveries in Canaan, are impossible to reconcile with the biblical account of the Israelites' conquest of the Promised Land. The only Egyptian

Jesus' awareness that he was under surveillance probably explains the secrecy with which he made arrangements to find a 'safe house' in which to have the Passover meal, now remembered as the Last Supper, with his twelve disciples. The disciples were not told the arrangements until the day of the meal, when Jesus instructed two of them:

> Go ye into the city, and there shall meet you a man bearing a pitcher of water: follow him.
>
> And wheresoever he shall go in, say ye to the goodman of the house, The Master saith, Where is the guestchamber, where I shall eat the Passover with my disciples?
>
> And he will shew you a large upper room furnished [and] prepared: there make ready for us.
>
> And his disciples went forth, and came into the city, and found as he had said unto them: and they made ready the passover.

The Passover meal, however, was penetrated by a secret agent recruited by the chief priests. As they ate, Jesus said to the disciples: 'Verily I say unto you, One of you which eateth with me shall betray me.'[42]*

The penetration agent among the Twelve was Judas Iscariot, whose motives continue to be debated two millennia later. The twentieth-century FBI acronym MICE summarizes the four main reasons why some individuals prove willing to abandon existing loyalties and work secretly for a hostile agency: Money, Ideology, Compromise and Ego. The gospel writers put Judas unequivocally into the first category. Probably on the day before Passover, a day which used to be known in, among others, the Roman Catholic and Anglican Churches as 'Spy Wednesday', in commemoration of Judas' betrayal, he had gone secretly to the chief priests and asked how much they would pay him to deliver Jesus into their hands. According to St Matthew:

> ... they covenanted with him for thirty pieces of silver.
>
> And from that time he sought opportunity to betray him.[43]

Judas would probably have been paid in silver shekels of Tyre, the only currency accepted at the Jerusalem Temple. During the reign of the Emperor Tiberius (AD 14–37) there was a rapid growth in the numbers of often mercenary *delatores* (informers) reporting on those in the Roman

---

* According to a tradition going back to the fourth century, the 'upper room' is on the first floor of a two-storey building south of Zion Gate in the walls of the Old City of Jerusalem. Though the room, known as the Cenacle, is included in many religious tours of Jerusalem, the tradition on which the identification is based is doubtful.

Empire whom they accused of disloyalty to the authorities.[44] Judas was one of the informers.

Probably because the disciples were given so little notice of the location of the Passover meal, Judas was unable to alert the chief priests beforehand. Jesus thus had time during the Last Supper, before his arrest, to teach the disciples how, by breaking bread and drinking wine from a cup, they were to commemorate him in a ceremony which most churches later used as the basis of a communion service. To enable Jesus to be arrested in the course of the night while he was at prayer in the Garden of Gethsemane, Judas left the Passover meal early in order to alert the chief priests to his whereabouts. According to St Mark, Judas told those who came to arrest Jesus:

> Whomsoever I shall kiss, the same is he ... And as soon as he was come,
> he goeth straightway to him, and saith, Master, master; and kissed him.
> And they laid their hands on him, and took him.[45]

After his arrest Jesus was tried first by the Sanhedrin, the Jewish religious court presided over by Caiaphas, high priest from AD 18 to 36, whose long period of office has been plausibly interpreted as demonstrating his capacity to work closely with the Roman authorities.* One of the keys to Caiaphas' apparently smooth working relationship with Pontius Pilate during his decade as prefect of Judaea from AD 26 to 36, appears to have been his willingness to hand over Jewish subversives for civil trials at which Pilate presided. Jesus was one of those subversives. The plaque nailed to the cross on which he was crucified, 'Jesus King of the Jews', indicates that he had been found guilty of political subversion.

In the gospel accounts Pilate shows some reluctance to sentence Jesus to death. According to St Matthew, he washes his hands to disclaim responsibility. Pilate had, however, a brutal reputation, which makes the sentence passed on Jesus unsurprising. The Jewish philosopher Philo of Alexandria (c.20 BC–AD 50) denounced 'his venality, his violence, his thefts, his assaults, his abusive behaviour, his frequent executions of untried prisoners and his endless savage ferocity'.[46] Though Philo has been accused of exaggeration, Pilate was dismissed in AD 36, a few years after the crucifixion of Jesus, by Lucius Vitellius, the Roman governor of Syria

---

* According to John 18:13, Caiaphas was the son-in-law of Annas, who is also mentioned in biblical accounts of the trial of Jesus. In 1990, archaeologists discovered what some believe are the family tombs of Annas and Caiaphas in Jerusalem's Upper City. Annas was patriarch of a family that held control of the high priesthood for most of the first century AD. (Crossan and Reed, *Excavating Jesus*.)

(of which Judaea was a province), and ordered to Rome to face charges of abuse of power.[47] Caiaphas was dismissed shortly afterwards from his position as high priest.[48]

Seen in long-term secular perspective, the treatment of Jesus of Nazareth during Holy Week up to his trial by Pilate, if not the extreme cruelty of the execution that followed, prefigured what later became a common characteristic of the use of intelligence by modern authoritarian regimes: the surveillance of those judged to be subversive of the regime combined with the attempt to penetrate the entourage of leading dissidents. Millions of alleged subversives died in the gulags, killing fields and execution cellars of twentieth-century one-party states. The crucifixion of Jesus of Nazareth, however, changed world history to an extent unequalled by any other subversive during the next 2,000 years.

2

Intelligence Operations in Ancient Greece: Myth and Reality from Odysseus to Alexander the Great

Intelligence is the only twenty-first-century profession in which a fictional character is far better known than any real practitioner, alive or dead. The fictional character, of course, is James Bond, the global brand leader in spy fiction for over half a century. A majority of the world's population have seen, and mostly enjoyed, Bond films. Their popularity shows few signs of flagging. *Skyfall*, released in 2012, almost half a century after the first Bond film, *Dr No*, was also the biggest box office success. Shortly afterwards Bond received royal recognition. The opening ceremony for the 2012 London Olympics opening ceremony began with Queen Elizabeth II, accompanied by Bond's latest incarnation, Daniel Craig, apparently parachuting into the stadium. The Queen subsequently received an honorary Bafta award.

The mass appeal of fictional secret operations goes back about three millennia to the origins of Western literature and the adventures of Odysseus, who was both a key figure in the *Iliad*, Homer's epic poem on forty days' fighting in the Trojan War, and the hero of Homer's *Odyssey*, which chronicles his long and adventurous post-war journey home. Odysseus was not primarily concerned with secret missions and intelligence operations. He was, first and foremost, a heroic warrior in search of glory and revenge who also enjoyed what might now be called recreational violence. But his remarkable talent for deception led him to be known as Odysseus the Cunning. The goddess Athena told Odysseus: 'We are both experts in trickery – you among men, I among the gods.'[1]

In both the *Iliad* and the *Odyssey*, Odysseus' trickery sometimes leads him into espionage. During the Trojan War, Odysseus volunteered to go with the young warrior-king Diomedes on a secret mission to spy on the enemy camp. Early in their mission they met a Trojan spy, Dolon, coming in the opposite direction to spy on the Greeks. By deceiving Dolon into believing that his life would be spared if he cooperated, Odysseus persuaded him to reveal important intelligence about the strength of Trojan forces. As soon as Dolon had done so, 'mighty Diomedes' said he would have to kill him.

If Dolon were set free, he would return 'either to spy or meet us in open fight'. As Dolon begged for mercy, Diomedes' sword 'caught him full on the neck ... Dolon's head met the dust while he was still speaking.' Using the intelligence Dolon had been tricked into providing, Diomedes and Odysseus secretly entered the camp of the Trojans' Thracian allies at night, slaughtered King Rhesus and some of his soldiers, and returned in triumph to the Greek camp with Thracian horses and other booty. Then, after bathing and anointing themselves with oil, they sat down to a celebration feast, pouring libations of honeyed wine to the goddess Athena.[2] Carnage, as during this spying mission, added to Odysseus' sense of a job well done. A second secret mission by Odysseus and Diomedes into Troy, this time in disguise, succeeded in capturing the 'Palladium', a sacred image of the goddess Athena, from her temple, without which, according to a Trojan seer captured by Odysseus, the Greeks could not conquer Troy. While in Troy, Helen, reputedly the most beautiful woman in the world, whose abduction by the Trojan prince Paris had begun the war, saw through the disguise of Odysseus, who was one of her former suitors. But Helen did not betray him. The two heroes were able to make their escape and enjoy the adulation which greeted their return.

The *Odyssey* ends with another famous piece of secret trickery. On his return home after a ten-year absence, Athena disguises Odysseus as a wandering beggar to enable him to discover the state of his household without being recognized and spy on the suitors who are trying to persuade his reluctant wife (and presumed widow), Penelope, to marry one of them. Failing to recognize Odysseus in his disguise, Penelope tells the suitors that she will marry whichever of them succeeds in the difficult task of stringing Odysseus' bow. After all have tried and failed, Odysseus succeeds, uses the bow to kill the suitors, orders the maids who have slept with them to bury their bodies, then kills them too. These scenes of carnage reinforce his satisfaction at reunion with the long-suffering Penelope, who finally recognizes him amid the mayhem. Odysseus thus ends his adventures by becoming first spy, then assassin, in his own home.

Odysseus' most ambitious deception, first mentioned by Homer in the *Odyssey* and later recounted in greater detail by the Roman poet Virgil in the *Aeneid*, was to order the construction of a huge, hollow, wooden 'Trojan Horse' to end the ten-year stalemate in the war. The Trojans woke up one morning to discover that the Greek army had departed in their ships, leaving only a large wooden horse behind, 'joyfully dragged the horse inside the city', and began victory celebrations. At midnight, however, when 'the clear moon was rising', Greek soldiers, led by Odysseus, emerged from their hiding place inside the horse, killed the Trojan sentries and opened the city gates to the Greek army, which had sailed back to Troy under cover of darkness.

Troy was destroyed and the war was won by the Greeks.[3] The Trojan Horse became for almost three millennia the best-known deception in the history of warfare until it was surpassed, at least in Britain, by the revelation in the 1970s of the British Double-Cross System in the Second World War. A reconstruction of the mythical Horse now stands at the entrance to the world heritage archaeological site of Troy in north-western Turkey.

The most important actual wartime deception in the golden age of Athens occurred in 480 BC at a critical moment during the invasion of Greece by the Persian Empire, the greatest power of the era, during the Battle of Salamis, the first decisive naval battle in recorded history. The deception was based on what is still sometimes termed an 'Odyssean ruse'.[4] Salamis followed the most heroic defeat in the history of ancient Greece at Thermopylae, when a small force led by King Leonidas of Sparta allegedly held at bay for seven days a Persian army many times its size in a narrow pass near the east coast of central Greece.* According to the fifth-century Greek historian Herodotus ('the father of history'), they were betrayed by Ephialtes of Trachis, the first traitor identified by name by ancient historians, who led the Persians along a goat track which outflanked the Greek lines.[5] Two and a half millennia later, Ephialtes remains the best-known traitor in Greek history, his name as much a synonym for treachery in the modern Greek language as Judas and Quisling are in English.

A monument at Thermopylae today on what is believed to be the site of the Spartans' last stand, is inscribed in Greek and English with the oft-quoted contemporary tribute to them by the poet Simonides of Ceos:

> Go tell the Spartans, passer-by.
> That here obedient to their laws we lie.

For all its heroism, defeat at Thermopylae left Athens at the mercy of the Persian army. Before the city was sacked and burned by the Persians, the Athenians and the Greek fleet, under the command of Themistocles, took refuge on the island of Salamis. While the Persians were planning a naval attack on the Greeks with their much larger fleet, they were approached by a traitor named Sicinnus, a slave who had absconded from the Greek fleet with intelligence apparently as important as that supplied by Ephialtes before Thermopylae. According to Herodotus, Sicinnus reported that the non-Athenian ships in the Greek fleet had decided to flee south and were on the point of leaving Salamis – thus presenting an ideal opportunity for a Persian attack on them. Having been deserted by his allies, Themistocles,

---

* The pass has changed beyond recognition since the time of the battle as a result of earthquakes and the receding coastline.

according to Sicinnus, was ready to change sides and lead the Athenian squadron to join the Persians as soon as their fleet approached his own.[6]

Unlike Ephialtes, however, Sicinnus was in reality a double agent – the first recorded by ancient historians. He was a loyal slave whom Themistocles had chosen to lure the Persians into the narrow strait between the island of Salamis and the Greek mainland. There he believed that the more manoeuvrable, though outnumbered, Greek triremes with their three rows of oarsmen would have an advantage in the confined space and could use the battering rams fitted well below their prows to hole the Persian vessels beneath the waterline. The enemy fleet fell into Themistocles' trap. Xerxes, the Persian monarch, sat on a golden throne on the heights above the Bay of Salamis, expecting to witness a great Persian naval victory. Instead he saw about 200 of his own fleet sunk while the Greeks lost only about forty triremes.[7] Xerxes returned home with much of his army, leaving the rest stranded in Attica without transport and with no hope of continuing the conquest of Greece by invading the Peloponnese. The remaining Persian forces were decisively defeated at Plataea the following year.

Though, thanks to Homer, Greeks were well acquainted with 'Odyssean ruses', they lacked any serious interest in organized intelligence collection. During the extraordinary flowering of Greek thought and culture in Athens's fifth-century BC golden age, no one showed a grasp of strategic military intelligence which compared with that of the Jewish priests who, probably during the previous two centuries, had written the biblical accounts of espionage in Canaan by the spies of Moses and Joshua. The Greek gods, unlike the God of the Jews, had no interest in promoting human intelligence operations at critical moments, but were thought to be willing to help those who worshipped them against their enemies. Greeks believed that, through the medium of seers (*manteis*) and oracles, the gods could provide them with far better intelligence on their enemies than any human agency. No Greek general had an intelligence officer. By contrast, most, if not all, of the leading fifth-century Athenian generals (Tolmides, Cimon, Nicias, Alcibiades and possibly Pericles) had their own personal seers; there is some evidence that the state paid for them on campaign.[8]

The two greatest historians of classical Greece, Herodotus and Thucydides, had much to say about divination but very little about intelligence operations.* Herodotus gave much of the credit for the victory at Plataea

---

* André Gerolymatos' innovative introduction to the intelligence role of the *proxenos* (*Espionage and Treason*) has yet to be followed by detailed further research. *Proxenoi* ('guest friends') were Greeks who, in an era before permanent embassies, represented foreign states in their

in 479 BC to the Spartan seer Tisamenus of Elis. On the eve of battle Tisamenus declared that the omens were 'good for the Greeks if they remained on the defensive, but not good if they cross the Asopus river and begin to attack'. While the Greeks heeded the seer's warning, the commander of the far larger Persian forces, Mardonius, riding a white horse, crossed the river and was killed in action together with the majority of his troops.[9] As in the case of Mardonius, a recurrent theme in Greek poetry from Homer to Sophocles is that those who belittle seers and ignore omens are doomed in the end to pay for their impiety and arrogance either with their own lives or with the lives of those nearest and dearest to them.[10]

Seers were so respected by military commanders in part because, contrary to modern Western assumptions, many possessed unusual insight into human behaviour – even if the insight did not, as the Greeks believed, come from the gods. Their insight sometimes provided a worthwhile substitute for intelligence assessment. As the anthropologist Philip Peek has noted: 'The European tradition tends to characterize the diviner as a charismatic charlatan coercing others through clever manipulation of esoteric knowledge granted inappropriate worth by a credulous and anxiety-ridden people.' During late-twentieth-century research in sub-Saharan Africa, Peek found that most diviners were, on the contrary, 'men and women of exceptional wisdom and high personal character'.[11] So, probably, were many seers in ancient Greece.[12] They also had a higher social status than many modern intelligence analysts who do not claim to possess either the same degree of moral virtue or power of prediction.

The methodology of ancient Greek seers, however, was more dubious than that of modern intelligence agencies. They claimed to obtain divine guidance by interpreting the entrails (especially livers) of sacrificed animals (extispicy), the behaviour of birds (augury), dreams and a great variety of portents. All these forms of divination had arrived in Greece from the Near East between the eighth and sixth centuries BC. The Greeks, however, convinced themselves that divination had been taught them not by foreign 'barbarians' but by their own mythological heroes. According to Aeschylus, it was Prometheus who 'set in order the many ways of the art of divination'. The poet Hesiod claimed that Melampus, the most celebrated seer in Greek mythology, had learned the language of birds from two snakes who licked his ears and that he had probably been taught extispicy by Apollo himself.[13]

---

own cities and supplied them with information, some of which could be classed as intelligence. They were probably least useful in time of war, when their services were needed most but connections with enemy states inevitably made *proxenoi* suspect among their fellow citizens.

The most direct access to divine guidance was believed to come from oracles – in particular, the oracle at Delphi, the leading sacred site in the ancient world,[14] where on nine days a year a virgin priestess, the Pythia, seated on a tripod, became possessed by Apollo, god of the sun, light and prophecy, and uttered incomprehensible messages from him which were 'translated' by an older priest into hexameter verse. Apollo, wrote the lyric poet Pindar, 'has the mind that knows all things'.[15] Only at Delphi did Apollo (or any other Greek god) communicate through the ecstatic trance of a priest or priestess. Though many visitors to his shrine were individuals seeking guidance on personal problems, the oracle was also consulted on affairs of state.* During the sixth and fifth centuries BC the fame of the Delphic oracle spread to the limits of the known world. The many and expensive votive offerings (some of which have survived) show that its prophecies, despite their celebrated ambiguities, must have impressed many who consulted it.† After the Greeks' victory at Plataea in 479 BC, in gratitude to the oracle which the seer Tisamenus had consulted before the battle, they erected at Delphi a nine-metre-high bronze 'Serpent column' of intertwined snakes, constructed from melted-down captured Persian weapons, supporting a golden tripod.[16]‡ The prophecies of the oracle could not, of course, have been based on inspiration from non-existent gods. What contemporaries regarded as divine revelation was probably often based on human intelligence. Nowhere attracted regular visitors from as much of the ancient world as Delphi.[17] The many questions the oracle received from a wide variety of Greek city-states and foreign potentates provided unparalleled insight into their hopes and fears which must have informed the hexameter verse that the priests claimed were messages from Apollo.

---

* It has been persuasively suggested that the Pythia produced semi-coherent prophecy and guidance which were turned into more coherent and better-composed hexameter form by better-educated religious officials at the oracle. Dr Richard Stoneman, a leading authority on ancient oracles, however, disagrees: 'All the stories we know of about the historical interventions of the Delphic oracle depict a rational functionary [the Pythia] who uttered riddling pronouncements in competent hexameter verses. It will not do to say that her ravings were composed into neat form by assistant priests at the shrine, since all sources speak as if the Pythia spoke the verses directly.' (Stoneman, *Ancient Oracles*, pp. 30–31.)

† Delphi's most celebrated sixth-century devotee was Croesus, the fabulously wealthy ruler of Lydia (western Anatolia) from 560 to 546 BC. According to Herodotus, Croesus initially sent emissaries to seven different oracles to test their powers of clairvoyance but trusted only the replies he received from Delphi and the shrine of Amphiaraos. According to Herodotus the votive offerings from Croesus were the largest Deplhi ever received. (Herodotus I.)

‡ The Serpent Column was moved by the Emperor Constantine from Delphi to Constantinople in AD 324, and remained intact until the end of the seventeenth century, when it suffered some damage. One of the serpent heads which became detached from the column is now on display in the nearby Istanbul Archaeological Museum.

By the mid-fifth century BC, though seers and oracles retained their prestige, 'Odyssean ruses' and other deceptions no longer had any place in the congratulatory self-image of Athenian democracy,[18] which, while deny-ing voting rights to women and slaves, saw itself as a role model for all other cities. At the outbreak of the Peloponnesian War with Sparta in 431, Athens declared much the same moral superiority over Sparta that Britain claimed over Nazi Germany at the outbreak of the Second World War. Pericles, the famously eloquent leading spokesman for Athenian democracy at the outbreak of war with Sparta, had no interest in either secret intel-ligence or strategic deception. He declared in his most celebrated speech, a funeral oration for the early victims of the Peloponnesian War (recorded – and probably made even more eloquent – by Thucydides), that Athens scorned all forms of surveillance, subterfuge and concealment:

> The freedom which we enjoy in our government extends also to our ordinary life. There, far from exercising a jealous surveillance over each other, we do not feel called upon to be angry with our neighbour for doing what he likes . . .
>
> We throw open our city to the world, and never by alien acts exclude foreigners from any opportunity of learning or observing, although the eyes of an enemy may occasionally profit by our liberality . . .[19]

Pericles' idyllic vision of free citizens scrupulously respecting the privacy even of annoying neighbours and foreign spies is inspirational but naïve. Athens's failure to 'spy out' Sparta in the way that the Israelites had been told to 'spy out' Canaan contributed to, even if it did not cause, the ultim-ate defeat of Athenian democracy in the Peloponnesian War.

The perils of going to war without adequate military intelligence were graphically demonstrated by the disastrous Athenian decision to send a large expeditionary force to attack the Sicilian city-state of Syracuse, a potential ally of Sparta, during a lull in the Peloponnesian War in 415 BC. Athens was lured into the expedition by an appeal for help from one of its allies, the small city-state of Egesta 600 miles away in western Sicily, which claimed to be able to finance an Athenian expedition. According to Thucydides, the greatest of ancient historians as well as a general in the Peloponnesian War, Athens was fired by the unrealistic ambition of going on from helping Egesta to conquering the whole of Sicily – despite the fact that most Athenians were ignorant even of the size of the island and its population.[20]

Before deciding to go ahead with an expedition, the Athenian Assembly sent envoys to verify the Egesteans' claim that they could finance it. Once in Egesta, both the envoys and the crews of their triremes were 'dazzled' by the profusion of gold and silver plate, drinking vessels and other treasures on display during the lavish and doubtless heavy-drinking entertainments prepared for them. Only later, according to Thucydides, was it discovered that their Egestean hosts had borrowed much of the gold and silver from neighbouring towns, some of them Phoenician settlements, and that many of the same valuables had been used in different entertainments.[21] Unaware of the deception practised on them, the envoys, accompanied by Egestean spokesmen, gave the Athenian Assembly a report on the wealth of Egesta, which Thucydides later called 'as attractive as it was untrue'. Persuaded that they had discovered El Dorado, the Assembly resolved to send to Sicily 'by far the most costly and splendid Hellenic force ever sent out by a single city'.[22] Probably the most talented and enthusiastic of the three commanders chosen to lead the expedition was the young, flamboyant and debt-ridden Alcibiades, whose enthusiasm must have been increased by his indebtedness.

Preparations for the Sicilian expedition were disturbed by a bad omen: the vandalization of the 'Herms', statues of the God Hermes with erect phallus erected all over Athens as road markers and at the entrances to both sacred sites and private property. One morning in late May or early June 415 Athenians were shocked to discover that overnight many of the Herms had been desecrated, their faces disfigured and their phalluses chopped off.[23] Since Hermes was the god of travel, the timing of this blasphemous outrage during preparations for the expedition appeared particularly ominous. A manhunt immediately began for the subversive *hermokopidai* ('Herm choppers'), who, Thucydides relates, were widely believed to be not mere vandals but part of 'a conspiracy for revolution and the overthrow of democracy'.[24]

In the absence of a police force or security service to investigate, a commission of enquiry was set up with authority to pay large rewards (eventually rising to 10,000 drachmas)* for information identifying the 'Herm choppers'. Informers were guaranteed immunity from prosecution. Though probably the main culprits were eventually uncovered (twenty-two were either executed or forced to flee from Athens), the radical demagogue Androcles and others initially claimed that the ring-leader was their flamboyant political rival Alcibiades[25] – a highly unlikely charge since Alcibiades was one of the expedition's leaders and would have done nothing to prejudice its departure. Though there was plausible evidence of his sometimes sacrilegious behaviour, it did not relate directly to the violation of the Herms.

Alcibiades and his friends countered claims that the violation was a bad omen for the expedition by paying venal diviners to predict glorious success. It seemed to Thucydides, who was probably present at the departure of the Sicilian expedition in summer 415, that almost all the citizens of Athens had come to the port of Piraeus to see the largest force ever

---

* Those building the Acropolis were being paid 1–1.5 drachmas a day.

assembled by a Greek city-state set sail. Though it was common practice for individual ships' crews to say prayers before putting to sea, on this occasion, following a trumpet fanfare, a herald led united prayers by the whole fleet, after which all on board drank wine libations.[26]

Unity did not last long. Even before the expedition reached Sicily, Alcibiades was recalled to face trial on charges of blasphemy. Instead of returning to Athens, however, he defected to Sparta. He was sentenced to death *in absentia* and his property confiscated. Instead of mounting an operation to capture or kill him (as both the Persians and Spartans were to do later in his career), the Athenian authorities had his name inscribed on a stele which was then ceremonially cursed by priests and priestesses.[27] For the Spartans, Alcibiades' defection presented an unexpected intelligence windfall. Though proof is lacking (unsurprisingly, given the shortage of sources), Alcibiades probably advised the Spartans on how to help Syracuse, the most powerful Sicilian city-state, resist Athenian forces and build a fort at Decelea in Attica to disrupt a major Athenian trade route.[28] Spartan intervention sealed the fate of the Athenian expedition.

The Athenians' belief in the illusion of a Sicilian Midas was merely the most colourful example of their recurrent failure to grasp the need for basic military intelligence before mounting a major operation. Though their defeat was hastened by the mistakes and divisions of the Athenian generals, an accurate grasp of the problems facing the expedition might well have deterred them from attempting the conquest of Sicily in the first place. According to a later history by Plutarch, even after almost two years of fighting, Athens still found it so difficult to grasp the insuperable odds it had taken on that, when news of the final defeat reached Athens in September 413 BC, the man who brought it was accused of spreading false information and tortured in an attempt to make him admit there had been no defeat, until official messengers arrived from Sicily to confirm news of the calamity.[29]

Athens's devastating defeat, which cost it 200 ships and thousands of soldiers, inevitably reduced the value of Alcibiades' intelligence to Sparta. He continued, however, as he had always done, to take risks. His career was even more colourful after his defection than it had been in Athens. The Spartan King Agis II appears to have discovered that Alcibiades had been sleeping with his wife, Timaea, thus forcing him to defect again – this time to the Persian satrap Tissaphernes.* Alcibiades so impressed Tissaphernes with the intelligence he was able to supply, based on his inside knowledge

---

* When Agis died, he was succeeded by his brother rather than by his son Leotychidas, who was declared illegitimate in the (unproven) belief that Alcibiades was his father. (Rhodes, *Alcibiades*, loc. 1261.)

of Athenian and Spartan affairs, that for a time, according to Thucydides, he became Tissaphernes' 'teacher in all things'.[30] Alcibiades, however, had an agenda of his own. Through intermediaries he tried to negotiate his return to Athens by claiming to have the power 'to make Tissaphernes a friend of the Athenians'.[31] 'Alcibiades', concluded Thucydides, 'was using Tissaphernes to frighten the Athenians and the Athenians to frighten Tissaphernes.'[32] Unsurprisingly, Tissaphernes discovered his double-dealing and threw him into jail. Alcibiades then made another of his great escapes, this time on horseback, rejoined the Athenian forces in 411 BC and became a successful admiral. He was fully reinstated as an Athenian citizen in 407, only to go into exile once again a year later. Alcibiades was probably the most versatile as well as the most colourful defector in intelligence history – driven not, like the most successful defectors and agents-in-place of the twentieth century, by ideological commitment but by self-interest. In 404, however, the consequences of his serial duplicity finally caught up with him; he was murdered in Phrygia by agents of Tissaphernes, quite possibly assisted by the Spartans.[33] In the same year, the long-drawn-out Peloponnesian War ended in the surrender of Athens to Sparta and the downfall of Athenian democracy.

The extraordinary flowering of learning and culture during the golden age of Athenian democracy in the fifth century BC did not extend to intelligence. Until the early fourth century most Greek commanders seem to have neglected even tactical intelligence gathering by reconnaissance of enemy forces and unknown or hostile terrain before battle. The historian, soldier and philosopher Xenophon of Athens (c.430–354 BC) was the first to write in any detail about reconnaissance and surveillance. He was also the first to argue that it was 'necessary to have given thought to spies before the outbreak of war'.[34] Xenophon recommended recruiting agents who were able to travel in enemy territory without arousing suspicion, such as merchants and men from neutral countries. He also advocated sending bogus deserters to mislead the enemy.[35]

But Xenophon also insisted that human intelligence collection was far less important than the use of divination to access the wisdom of the gods: 'In a war enemies plot against one another but seldom know whether these plans are well laid. It is impossible to find any other advisers in such matters except the gods. They know everything, and they give signs in advance to whomever they wish through sacrifices, birds of omen, voices and dreams.'[36] Aristotle, the leading philosopher of fourth-century BC Greece, did not dismiss divination and accepted the possibility of the transference of divine knowledge to human beings as a 'natural' phenomenon.[37] But his general attitude is sceptical: in *On Divination by Way of Dreams*, he argues that when dreams turn out to be prophetic, the main reason is 'mere coincidence'. And since some animals dream, 'it may be concluded that dreams are not sent by God'.[38]

The only references to intelligence collection in Aristotle's surviving work concern the surveillance of those who threaten to subvert the political system. In *Politics*, his classic work of political philosophy, he recommended keeping an eye on potential dissidents: 'Since people also revolt because of their private lives, it is necessary to set up some magistracy [*arkhe*] to inspect those who live in a manner deleterious to the constitution.'[39] Authoritarian regimes, Aristotle believed, required spies to infiltrate social gatherings and report on what was said: '[The tyrant must] see to it that none of the things his subjects say or do escapes his notice; rather, he must have spies [*kataskopoi*], like the women called *potagogides* at Syracuse and the spies [*otakoustai*] that Hiero used to send whenever there was any gathering or conference . . .' *Potagogides* were probably recruited from flute girls and prostitutes who provided entertainment at private drinking parties for prominent citizens.[40]

Aristotle's most celebrated pupil was the future Alexander the Great, son of King Philip II of Macedon, whom he tutored between about 343 and 340 BC, when Alexander was aged between thirteen and sixteen. 'Thus', writes the Aristotelian scholar Jonathan Barnes, 'began the association between the most powerful mind of the age and the most powerful man.'[41] Alexander owed his passion for Homer at least partly to the influence of Aristotle, who gave him an annotated copy of the *Iliad* which he later took on campaign in a golden chest. According to Plutarch, Alexander believed that Homer sometimes appeared to him in his dreams. Though Aristotle did not complete the first edition of *Politics* until almost a decade after his years as Alexander's tutor, his tutorials included politics and ethics. Aristotle composed for Alexander a treatise on monarchy which no longer survives.[42] Given the authoritarian nature of the Macedonian regime, Aristotle presumably declared the need for the ruler to 'see to it that none of the things his subjects say or do escapes his notice'. Philip II was sufficiently confident of his son's grasp of the principles of government to make Alexander regent at the age of only sixteen while he was away on campaign.

Like many modern autocrats, Alexander 'systematically exploited the tensions at his court, using conspiracies, both genuine and fictitious, to suppress opposition'.[43] Both Alexander's own plotting and the surveillance of plots by others necessarily involved the use of spies and informers, though few details of them survive. His reign began with a successful conspiracy against his father, Philip II, King of Macedon, who was assassinated at a royal wedding in 336 BC by Pausanias, a disaffected royal bodyguard, thus bringing Alexander to the throne at the age of only

twenty. Though conclusive proof is lacking, Alexander himself was probably involved in the assassination plot.[44] (He later tried to put the
blame – improbably – on the Persians.) Throughout his reign Alexander
used the suppression of alleged conspiracies as a means of reinforcing his
own authority.[45]

Only one detailed record survives of a case in which Alexander personally ordered surveillance of conspirators. Their leader was alleged to be
Philotas, commander of the Macedonian cavalry corps, which provided
bodyguards for the King. According to Plutarch, in 330 BC, after Philotas
complained to his mistress, Antigone, about the King, Alexander personally
instructed Antigone to report to him what Philotas said to her.[46] The main
warning that Philotas was preparing to go ahead with the plot, however,
came from Philotas' brother-in-law. According to the later historian Diodorus Siculus, the warning was so urgent that it was passed to Alexander
while he was in the bath. Alexander reacted immediately. On his orders,
Philotas was interrogated, tortured, tried and executed (probably by being
stoned or speared to death). Alexander then sent assassins to kill Philotas'
father, Parmenion, his most experienced general, before news of his son's
death could reach him.[47] Over the next three years, concludes Alexander's
biographer Paul Cartledge there was 'a continuous web of alleged plotting
against Alexander countered by utterly ruthless suppression by the king'.[48]

The surviving records of the extraordinary military campaigns which
led to Alexander's conquest of most of the known world from Greece to
present-day Pakistan in little more than a decade are fragmentary and of
varying reliability.[49] Like Napoleon two millennia later, Alexander
believed that an army marches on its stomach. Central to his success was
a mastery of logistics and lengthy supply chains which was probably
unequalled by any other general in the ancient world.[50] This mastery, in
turn, was based on advance information obtained more from reconnaissance than agent networks, of the resources, roads, terrain and climate of
the territory through which he planned to advance. Armed with this information, he was able to cross regions where other invading armies had been
decimated by starvation and dehydration. When possible he ordered his
troops to be supplied by boats on rivers and coastlines along his route.[51]

Though Alexander made some use of unknown numbers of spies, he
placed far more faith in seers and oracles than in espionage. His closest
adviser on campaign was a personal seer, Aristander of Telmessus, until
Aristander's death in 328 or 327 BC. Alexander attached at least as much
importance to Aristander's divinations as most modern generals attach to
briefings by their intelligence chiefs. Before battle and on numerous other

occasions Aristander examined the entrails of sacrificed animals. He did not, however, simply tailor his divinations to Alexander's wishes. According to a later historian, Arrian of Nicomedia, author of probably the most reliable account of Alexander's campaigns, in 329 BC Alexander planned to cross the River Tanais (now the Don) to attack Scythian nomads – despite a warning from Aristander that the results of two extispicies showed that crossing the Tanais would put the King's life in serious danger. 'Aristander', writes Arrian, 'refused to interpret the sacrifices in any way contrary to the signs from the divinity merely because Alexander wished to hear other things.' Against Aristander's advice, Alexander crossed the Tanais. Though he defeated the Scythians, he almost died as the result of drinking tainted water. 'In this way', argued Arrian, 'Aristander's act of divination was fulfilled.'[52]

Aristander's expertise extended to other forms of divination: among them the interpretation of bird behaviour, dreams and numerous portents. He interpreted the behaviour of a swallow which swooped over Alexander at Halicarnassus, rousing the King from his slumber, as a portent of a plot against him[53] – probably one of many occasions on which divination fed Alexander's fear of conspiracy. One example of the ingenuity of Aristander's interpretation of portents which particularly impressed ancient historians was his response to the disconcerting discovery of a perspiring statue of Orpheus. This, he claimed, foretold how much future poets and musicians would perspire while trying to compose verse and music worthy to celebrate Alexander's great deeds.[54]

After consulting the oracle of Zeus Ammon at the Siwah oasis during his occupation of Egypt, Alexander became convinced that he was the son of Zeus.[55] Belief in his own divine, or at least semi-divine, status intensified his addiction to divination in order to communicate with his fellow gods. According to Plutarch: 'Alexander became so superstitious at the end of his life, turning every unusual and strange occurrence, no matter how trivial, into a prodigy and portent, that his palace at Babylon was filled with sacrificers, purifiers and seers.'[56] Spies who kept watch on human beings were increasingly of far less interest to Alexander than seers who communicated with the divine.

3

Intelligence and Divination in the Roman Republic

The rise of Rome from small city-state to dominant regional power during the four centuries which preceded final victory over its main Mediterranean rival, Carthage, in 146 BC owed little to intelligence. As in classical Greece, most Roman generals before Julius Caesar attached more importance to divination than to intelligence collection. 'Who does not know', asked the Roman historian Livy, 'that this city was founded only after taking the auspices, that everything in war and peace, at home and abroad, was done only after taking the auspices?'[1] Those who 'took the auspices' were priests known as augurs, who specialized in studying bird behaviour to interpret the will of the gods. Coops of sacred chickens were commonly taken on campaign so that augurs could study their activity at feeding time and pronounce on the prospects for victory. As in ancient Greece, other professional seers, known as *haruspices*, practised divination by examining the entrails of sacrificed animals (extispicy).* The sceptical philosopher-statesman Cicero complained: 'There is a long-standing view which can be traced back to the age of myth and which holds its place by the unanimous assent of the people of Rome and every other nation, that there is among human beings some kind of power of divination.'[2] For believers in the Roman gods, there was a good logical argument in favour of divination rather than human intelligence collection as the most effective form of information gathering:

> If there are gods and
> (a) they love us, and
> (b) they are not ignorant of the future, and
> (c) they know that knowledge of the future would be useful to us, and

---

* The early Roman Republic sometimes summoned Etruscan augurs to interpret prodigies and portents. An engraved Etruscan mirror of about 400 BC shows the mythical diviner Calchas studying the liver of a sacrificial victim. (Hornblower and Spawforth (eds.), *Oxford Companion to Classical Civilization*, p. 595.)

(d) it is not beneath their majesty to communicate with us, and

(e) they know how to communicate with us,

then divination exists.[3]

Diviners sometimes tailored their divinations before battle to what they believed military commanders wished to hear. But not all diviners were so obsequious, and many unfavourable omens resisted optimistic interpretation. Unsuccessful generals who disregarded unfavourable omens were likely to be blamed for causing their own defeats. Before a sea battle off Sicily in 249 BC the Roman commander Claudius Pulcher ordered the sacred chickens to be let out of their coop and have corn scattered in front of them. They declined to eat, thus indicating that the omens for battle were unfavourable. When the chickens also refused to drink (another unfavourable omen), a furious Claudius Pulcher had them thrown overboard. He went on to be routed by the enemy fleet. Like Claudius' contemporaries, the historian Suetonius later condemned him for acting 'in contempt of the omen'.[4]

The low priority for Roman commanders of intelligence gathering before battle was demonstrated by their failure to make systematic use even of scouts for military reconnaissance until the third century BC.[5] During Rome's conquest of the rest of Italy, the superiority of its legions more than compensated for the deficiencies of its military intelligence. War with the Carthaginian Empire, which at the beginning of the third century was both richer and more populous than Rome, exposed these deficiencies for the first time. Carthage (near modern Tunis) derived from its Phoenician founders an awareness, which Rome lacked, of the importance of being well informed about its rivals.[6]

At their peak between about 1200 and 800 BC, the Phoenician cities on the coast of modern Lebanon controlled the greatest trading empire of the era. They also had the best Western record-keeping system, devising the ancestor of the Roman and modern alphabets chiefly to record commercial information.[7] The Phoenicians were probably the first to engage in direct long-distance trade. In the Old Testament the first book of Kings records that a Phoenician fleet brought the equivalent of about thirteen tons of gold from Ophir (probably modern India) to King Solomon's treasury.[8] Because of the destruction of Carthaginian written records, more is known about their ability to protect their own secrets than to discover those of others. Their success in concealing the location of their valuable tin mines in northern Spain was demonstrated by their ability to deceive the Greeks into believing that the tin came from islands off the north-west Spanish coast.[9]

For over three centuries, the physical and intellectual horizons of the Roman Republic were far narrower than those of Carthage. Until about

280 BC Rome's foreign relations were virtually restricted to those with other Italian states. To win the First Punic ('Phoenician') War (264–241 BC) against Carthage, however, Rome had for the first time to win command of the sea. In the Second Punic War (218–201 BC), Rome faced an even more difficult challenge from the Carthaginian general Hannibal, one of the greatest strategists in military history, who succeeded in mounting a direct threat to Rome. He also showed a greater grasp of intelligence than any previous general in the ancient world. From the age of nine Hannibal lived for most of the time with the Carthaginian army. By the time he became commander-in-chief at the age of only twenty-five, he had learned the importance of being well informed about his troops' morale. While on campaign, he often walked round the camp in disguise to judge the mood of the army and eavesdrop on what was said about him and about the enemy.[10] By contrast, as some Roman historians later noted, Hannibal was no believer in divination. When the King of Bithynia (in today's northern Turkey) queried his advice to go on the offensive after his priests had drawn ominous conclusions from the liver of a sacrificed calf, Hannibal responded scornfully: 'So you would rather believe a little chunk of calf's flesh than an experienced commander?'[11] There is no record of any Roman general during the Punic Wars ever publicly expressing similar scepticism about divination (though a minority may have done so in private).

In 218 Hannibal led an army of about 40,000 foot soldiers, 9,000 cavalry and a troop of war elephants across the Alps into Italy. Despite the lack of Carthaginian documents on Hannibal's intelligence system, it is clear from Roman records that it outclassed that of his opponents. Before crossing the Alps, Hannibal had placed spies both in Roman military camps and in Rome itself. According to Livy, the Romans discovered that one of Hannibal's spies had been active in Rome for two years and cut off his hands to deter others.[12] But other Carthaginian spies remained undetected. Rome's intelligence, by contrast, was so feeble that the arrival of Hannibal's large force in northern Italy took it by surprise. Not even the extraordinary news of elephants crossing the Alps seems to have percolated to Rome.[13]

Over the next three years, Hannibal won three major victories. Each was due not simply to his inspired leadership in battle but also to his ability, based on intelligence about the Romans and knowledge of the terrain, to surprise and deceive the enemy.[14] At Lake Trasimene in 217 BC Hannibal lured the forces of the Consul Gaius Flaminius into one of the largest and most successful ambushes in military history. In less than four hours about half of the Roman army of 30,000 were either killed in battle or drowned while attempting to escape into the lake; thousands more were taken prisoner. According to Livy, the battle was so terrible that neither army noticed that it was taking place during an earthquake.[15] Two days later, advance knowledge, from an unknown source, of the movement of a Roman cavalry force about 4,000 strong enabled Hannibal to kill or capture almost all of it.[16] According to Plutarch, the Roman commander-in-chief ('dictator'), Quintus Fabius Maximus, appointed after the disaster at Lake Trasimene, publicly blamed it not on military mistakes but on 'the neglect and scorn with which their general [Flaminius] had treated religious rites'. His aim was to persuade Roman citizens, 'instead of fearing the enemy, to propitiate and honour the gods':

> . . . The dictator, in the presence of all the people, vowed to sacrifice to the gods an entire year's increase in goats, swine, sheep, and cattle, that is, all that Italy's mountains, plains, rivers, and meadows should breed in the coming spring. He likewise vowed to celebrate a musical and dramatic festival in honour of the gods . . .[17]

The gods, however, were not propitiated. The Battle of Cannae in 216 BC was an even greater Roman disaster than Lake Trasimene – indeed one of the greatest disasters in military history. Hannibal's knowledge of the terrain and the opposing forces allowed him to make on the plains of Cannae the first known successful use in battle of a large pincer movement. Though precise statistics of the slaughter will never be known, about 50,000 Carthaginians and their allies killed most of a larger Roman force.[18] Livy relates that the rings taken from the fingers of dead Roman aristocrats were so numerous that they filled three bushels.[19] The rings were taken to Carthage and strewn on the floor at the entrance to the Senate building. Cannae is still studied in modern military colleges. The Supreme Allied Commander in the later stages of the Second World War (and later US President), Dwight D. Eisenhower, an intelligence enthusiast, once wrote: 'Every ground commander seeks the battle of annihilation; so far as conditions permit, he tries to duplicate in modern war the classic example of Cannae.'[20]

There was no investigation by Rome into why Hannibal had repeatedly been able to surprise and out-think its armies. After Cannae, Quintus Fabius Maximus appeared more concerned with interpreting omens than with improving intelligence. One of his relatives was sent to consult the Delphic oracle.[21] The Senate, at Fabius' request, turned for guidance to the Sibylline Books (*Libri Sibyllini*), a collection of oracular pronouncements in Greek hexameters supposedly purchased by Tarquinius Superbus, the last King of Rome, from the Sibyl, a mysterious Greek prophetess.[22] The Books were the Republic's greatest state secrets; the punishment for unauthorized consultation was to be sewn into a sack and thrown into the sea. Following established tradition at moments of great crisis, after Cannae specially appointed magistrates went to inspect the sacred scrolls containing the Sibylline Books in the Temple of Jupiter, where they were kept under tight security. After studying the Greek texts they concluded that, in order to propitiate the gods, two Gauls and two Greeks should be buried alive in the cattle market (Forum Boarium) – which they duly were. Livy called it a 'very un-Roman ritual' – the nearest the Romans ever came to human sacrifice.[23]

Despite his obsession with Sibylline secrets, Fabius devised a successful military strategy to contain Hannibal's advance, shadowing and intermittently harassing his forces as they moved through Italy but avoiding pitched battle. Hannibal lacked the manpower and resources to win a decisive victory by laying siege to Rome.* Tracked by Fabius, he lost the element of surprise which had been central to his early victories. Hannibal's communications became so poor that he also lost his earlier intelligence advantage. He had little idea of the whereabouts of a second Carthaginian army sent to Italy, commanded by his younger brother Hasdrubal, until Hasdrubal's head was thrown into his camp by Roman troops in 207 BC.[24]

Omens and portents continued to make Rome fearful about the threat from Carthage. After a failed harvest and several meteorite showers in 205 BC, the decision was taken to consult the Sibylline Books once again.† The conclusion of the consultation, according to Livy's later account, was that the foreign enemy would only be expelled if a sacred black meteoric stone representing the mother goddess Cybele, known to the Romans as *Mater Magna* ('Great Mother'), was imported from Rome's ally, the kingdom of Pergamum. Further advice was sought from the oracle at Delphi, which reached the same conclusion. On 4 April 204 BC, Rome ceremonially welcomed into the city the black stone representing the *Mater Magna*, along with several of her priests and priestesses, and celebrated in her honour the first Megalensia of sacrifices, feasts, dramatic productions, chariot races and games.[25] Far more thought was given to welcoming the mother goddess than to obtaining intelligence on Hannibal.

With the invasion of North Africa in 204 BC by an army led by Publius Cornelius Scipio (known after his African victories as 'Scipio Africanus'),

---

* Hannibal's own cavalry commander told him, according to Livy, that he knew how to win a victory but 'not how to use one'. (Livy, *History of Rome*, 22.51.4.)

† Though other motives have been suggested for the decision to consult the Sibylline Books, the fact that Hannibal, the most dangerous foreign enemy in the history of the Roman Republic, was still rampaging around Italy over a decade after Cannae must surely have been a central concern.

the tide of war at last turned in favour of Rome. Unlike Fabius, Scipio seems to have grasped some of the importance of Hannibal's use of espionage, making greater use of spies than any previous Roman general. While preparing for a surprise attack on King Syphax of Numidia, which supplied some of the most formidable Carthaginian cavalry, Scipio sent a series of envoys to the King's camp on the pretext of conducting negotiations. Each of the envoys had a retinue of slaves who were, in reality, centurions in disguise.[26] The disguise was far more effective than might nowadays be supposed. The modern image of disciplined Roman armies on the march usually excludes the accompanying straggling mass of slaves ministering to their needs.[27] Syphax and his court would have found the slave escorts of the Roman envoys so normal they would scarcely have noticed them. It would certainly not have occurred to the Numidians that Roman centurions would have accepted the humiliation of acting as slaves. By the time Scipio was ready to attack, most if not all of his centurions had been able to familiarize themselves in their slave disguise with the Numidian camp they were waiting to overrun. Before launching his attack, Scipio infiltrated some of his men, probably also in disguise, at night into the camps of the Numidians and their Carthaginian allies, where they set fire to wooden and thatched buildings. Believing the fires to have started by accident, the Carthaginians ran unarmed to try to put them out, only to be ambushed by Roman soldiers who were lying in wait. Both camps were destroyed.[28] Significantly, however, Scipio's use of spies and subterfuge was judged to be so alien to the Roman way of warfare that he was criticized for underhand behaviour by, among other, the leading historians Livy and Polybius.[29]

Scipio Africanus was probably second only to Gaius Julius Caesar as the ablest general in the history of the Roman Republic.* His decisive victory over Hannibal at the Battle of Zama, south-west of Carthage, in 202 BC brought to an end the Second Punic War. Before Zama, some of Hannibal's spies, who had been sent to locate Scipio's forces, were captured. Instead of killing or mutilating them, Scipio allowed them to return to Hannibal with the demoralizing news that his own forces, including cavalry, were outnumbered by the well-supplied Roman army.[30] Scipio's greater grasp of the role of intelligence than previous Roman commanders derived in part from his broader intellectual and geographical horizons. Few, if any, Roman leaders before Scipio had dreamed, like him, of an overseas empire. He spoke Greek (a sign of effeminacy in the eyes of less intellectual Roman generals), wrote his memoirs (which have not survived)

* The most recent biography, Richard Gabriel, *Scipio Africanus*, argues that he was an even greater general than Julius Caesar.

in Greek and, as a sign of admiration for Alexander the Great, became the first Roman general to be clean-shaven like Alexander – a fashion followed by subsequent Roman leaders until the era of the Emperor Hadrian.

After victory over Carthage, Rome no longer had a rival capable of collecting significant military intelligence on it. Though Rome had no foreign intelligence service, its frequent wars gave it far more understanding of its enemies and neighbours than they had of Rome. By the mid-second century BC, Romans had travelled more than any other Mediterranean people since Alexander the Great's Macedonian soldiers. Well over half the male citizens of Rome had been abroad.[31]

Julius Caesar, probably the ablest general in the history of the Roman Republic, also had the best grasp of intelligence. His interest in the mindset of his enemies was evident at the age of twenty-five when he was captured by Cilician pirates from modern-day Anatolia. When the pirates asked for a ransom of twenty talents, he asked if they realized how important he was and told them to demand fifty. Caesar warned them that, after the fifty talents were paid (which they duly were) and he was released, he would hunt them down and have them all crucified. He was as good as his word.[32]

Caesar's extraordinary political career, which led him to become consul in 59 BC and dictator in 48 BC through a combination of flair and guile, taught him both the importance of keeping track of his rivals and of concealing his tactics – lessons which he transferred to the field of battle. He paid greater attention to the security of his communications than any previous general of the ancient world. The 'substitution ciphers', which (so far as is known) he was the first general to use while on campaign, were first employed while writing to his friends and allies about Roman politics.[33] Caesar used ciphers so frequently that a later Roman writer, Valerius Probus, devoted a whole volume to them, which unfortunately has not survived.[34] Suetonius, however, gives details of one of Caesar's substitution ciphers, which replaced each letter with a letter three places further down the alphabet.[35] 'CAESAR' thus became 'FDHVDU'. No doubt Caesar also used other variations of this basic formula.*

Caesar's history of the Gallic Wars, *De Bello Gallico*, is the first to record the use of a substitution cipher for military purposes. He describes

---

* It has been claimed that the earliest military cipher was the Spartan 'skytale', a long, thin strip of parchment or leather or papyrus containing an apparently meaningless column of letters which, when wound around a baton, revealed a message which could be read horizontally (Kahn, *Codebreakers*, p. 82). Recent research has disputed this claim. It seems more likely that the skytale was simply a method of transporting, rather than enciphering, a written message (Kelly, 'Myth of the Skytale').

sending a cipher message to Cicero, who was under siege during the Gallic revolt of 54 BC and, allegedly, on the verge of surrendering. The messenger delivered the message saying that help was at hand by attaching it to a spear which he threw into Cicero's camp. According to Caesar, it had a dramatic impact on the morale of the besieged soldiers: 'For two days it was not sighted by our troops. On the third it was seen by a soldier, taken down and delivered to Cicero. He read it through and then recited it at a parade of the troops, bringing the greatest rejoicing to all.'[36] Simple though substitution ciphers seem to modern cryptographers, it was almost a millennium after Caesar's death before Arab mathematicians devised a method to decrypt them.[37]

Though Julius Caesar had no military intelligence staff, he was probably chiefly responsible for extending and differentiating the roles of reconnaissance troops: *procursatores*, who conducted reconnaissance immediately ahead of Roman forces; *exploratores*, longer-range scouts; and *speculatores*, who conducted espionage deep inside enemy territory.[38] Caesar also established a rapid-messenger system to transmit military intelligence and other information, with relay horses stationed at fixed points.

Caesar had some personal experience of espionage. Suetonius records that, on at least one occasion during the Gallic Wars, Caesar walked through enemy territory disguised as a Gaul. Though his main aim was to reach a Roman camp which had been cut off by enemy forces, his disguise also enabled him to act as a spy observing enemy activity en route.[39] Caesar's most active personal involvement in intelligence gathering during the Gallic Wars, however, was to interrogate enemy troops taken prisoner by his reconnaissance forces and enemy deserters. Before two of his most important victories – his defeat of the Germanic ruler Ariovistus in 58 BC and the Battle of the Sambre against the Belgae ('the bravest of the Gaulish peoples') in 57 BC – what Caesar learned during interrogation had a decisive influence on his battle plans. Before joining battle with Ariovistus' forces, Caesar discovered from enemy prisoners that the female seers who accompanied his army had declared that 'it was not the will of heaven that the Germans should conquer if they engaged in battle before the new moon'.[40] Caesar attacked next day, before the new moon. After fierce initial resistance, enemy morale collapsed and the Germans fled from the battlefield, pursued by vengeful Roman cavalry led personally by Caesar.[41]*

Before the battle against the Belgae at the River Sambre in the following year, Caesar once again changed his battle plan after learning from

---

* Though many Germans were massacred, including two of Ariovistus' wives, Ariovistus himself escaped and disappeared into historical obscurity.

prisoner interrogation that the enemy planned to attack the Roman legions as they crossed the river, encumbered by their baggage. Protected by an advance guard of cavalry and light troops, six legions forded the river without their baggage, which they left to be transported by two legions in the rear.[42] Even so, Caesar found himself early in the battle in what he himself acknowledged was a desperate situation. Having come without a shield, he took one from a nearby soldier, moved into the front line and ordered an advance, 'calling on the centurions by name and cheering on the rank and file'.[43] Had Caesar not changed his tactics as a result of intelligence from captured Belgae, he might well have been defeated. But Caesar survived the crisis and went on to win a decisive victory. A grateful Senate voted him a public thanksgiving of fifteen days – longer than ever awarded to any previous general.[44] During the Gallic Wars his troops killed about one million Gauls and enslaved as many more.[45]

Caesar was his own intelligence analyst as well as chief interrogator. At various points in De Bello Gallico, he mentions receiving reports from merchants, informants and envoys as well as enemy prisoners. He contrasts his own search for corroboration of reports he received with the primitive methods used by the Gauls:

> It is indeed a regular habit of the Gauls to compel travellers to halt, even against their will, and to ascertain what each of them may have heard or learnt upon every subject ... Such stories and hearsay often induce them to form plans upon vital questions ... They are the slaves of uncertain rumours, and most men reply to them in fictions made to their taste.[46]

The fact that the Gauls were illiterate makes it impossible to find written corroboration for much of Caesar's own assessment of their way of warfare in De Bello Gallico. In some cases, as in his interpretation of the religious dimension of Gallic warfare, however, archaeological excavation provides a partial substitute for the lack of a written record. According to Caesar:

> [To Mars,] when [the Gauls] have determined on a decisive battle, they dedicate as a rule whatever spoil they may take. After a victory they sacrifice such living things as they have taken, and all the other effects they gather into one place.
>
> In many tribes heaps of such objects are to be seen piled up in hallowed spots. It has often happened that a man, in defiance of religious scruple, has dared to conceal such spoils in his house or to remove them from their place, and the most grievous punishment, with torture, is ordained for such an offence.[47]

Excavation of 'war sanctuaries' of middle-Iron Age Gaul* has provided clear corroboration of Caesar's account: thousands of broken weapons piled up on what is clearly holy ground together with evidence of feasting and the remains of sacrificed animals and – sometimes – prisoners-of-war.[48]

'All the Gauls', Caesar concluded, 'are extremely devoted to superstitious rituals.' Among these rituals, especially before battle, was human sacrifice conducted by their religious leaders, the Druids. Though other Roman authors mentioned human sacrifice,† only Caesar mentions that the Druids' sacrifices sometimes used wicker men:

> ... figures of immense size, whose limbs, woven out of twigs, they fill with living men and set on fire ... They believe that the execution of those who have been caught in theft or robbery or some crime is more pleasing to the immortal gods, but when the supply of such men fails they resort to the execution even of the innocent.[49]

Caesar's description of the wicker men has caused some scepticism about his account of the Druids' human sacrifices, though they are also mentioned by the Greek author and geographer Strabo.[50] While Caesar may have embellished his account, a recent study based on archaeological as well as written evidence concludes that 'Caesar is our richest textual source for ancient Druids and he is also one of the most reliable.'[51] Caesar's own most important source was Diviciacus (or Divitiacus), joint leader of the Gallic Aedui, the only ancient Druid whose name has survived, whom he personally interrogated. 'I trusted Diviciacus', he wrote, 'more than any other Gaul.'[52]

Caesar was far less well informed about Britain than about Gaul. Part of the justification which he gave for his first invasion of Britain in 55 BC was to collect intelligence, having discovered (so he claimed) that the Britons had provided help to the Gauls during his campaigns against them:

> Even traders know nothing except the sea coast and the districts opposite Gaul. Therefore, although [Caesar] summoned to his quarters traders from all parts, he could discover neither the size of the island, nor the number or the strength of the tribes inhabiting it, nor their manner of warfare, nor the ordinances they observed, nor the harbours suitable for a number of large ships.[53]

But, as Sir Barry Cunliffe has argued, Caesar was also 'playing to the Roman gallery by crossing the ocean and setting foot in a land of

* Notably those at Gournay-sur-Aronde (Oise), Ribemont-sur-Ancre (Somme) and Mirebeau (Côte d'Or).
† Among them Cicero, Suetonius, Lucan, Tacitus and Pliny the Elder.

mystery'.[54] After landing at (or near) the site of modern Deal in 55 BC, Caesar's first cross-Channel expedition spent only a few weeks in a narrow stretch of what is now Kent countryside, added little to existing Roman knowledge of Britain and almost ended in disaster. Storms off the English coast wrecked many of his ships and prevented cavalry landing. Caesar's second landing in 54 BC, though also poorly prepared late in the campaigning season with inadequate forces, succeeded in crossing the Thames and defeated a local warlord but conquered no territory and left no garrison behind. In Rome, however, the expeditions were an enormous propaganda success. The Senate voted Caesar twenty days of public thanksgiving.[55]

Neither expedition added much to Roman understanding of the British population beyond what is now Kent. Caesar concluded that the people of Kent, whom he considered the 'most civilized', differed little from the Gauls. His information about other Britons seems to have been based mainly on the kind of hearsay of which he accused the Gauls, rather than on serious intelligence gathering. Caesar probably exaggerated their exotic appearance in order to strengthen his propaganda victory: 'All the Britons dye themselves with woad, which produces a blue colour, and gives them a more terrible appearance in battle. They wear their hair long, and have every part of their body shaved except their head and upper lip. Ten and even twelve have wives in common . . .'[56] Even after Caesar's expeditions in 55 and 54 BC, Britain remained mysterious.

The ability of Caesar and all other Roman generals to make use of any military intelligence they received was hampered by the lack of what we would now consider to be adequate maps.[57] Though Caesar, like a number of other Roman writers,* refers to maps, the only known example, a medieval copy of a fifth-century AD original, is a scroll 6.75 metres long, probably similar to earlier maps,† which consists of little more than itineraries between Roman settlements with a distorted image of the landmass between them. The role of military intelligence was partly to give Roman generals the kind of information later supplied by maps.

One of Caesar's strengths as a commander was that he paid far more attention to intelligence than to divination. There is not a single mention of divination in his history of the Gallic Wars, despite the fact that in his army, as in all Roman armies, *haruspices* regularly examined the entrails of

---

* Among them Sallust, Varro, Juvenal and Lucan.
† Because of its rarity value, in 2007 the copy of the fifth-century AD Roman map, known as the *Tabula Peutingeriana*, was placed on the UNESCO Memory of the World Register. As well as showing Constantinople, founded in AD 328, it also includes Pompeii, which had not been rebuilt after the eruption of Vesuvius in AD 79.

sacrificed animals.* Suetonius wrote later: 'No fear of unfavourable omens ever kept him from embarking on any enterprise.' When the omens were bad, Caesar either ignored them or tried to explain them away. On one occasion, even when a sacrificial animal escaped before it could be sacrificed (a particularly bad omen), he went ahead with his campaign. During the Civil War, while campaigning in North Africa against Metellus Scipio, a distant relative of the military hero Scipio Africanus, Caesar sought to discredit prophecies that the Scipio family was invincible in North Africa by including in his entourage the pathetic figure of 'Salvito' Scipio, described by Suetonius as the 'most base and abject' member of the Scipio family.[58]

Caesar's disregard for divination was curiously ironic for two reasons. First, in 63 BC, aged about thirty-seven, he had been elected High Priest (*Pontifex Maximus*) of the Roman Republic, moving into the impressive official residence, the Regia, on the Via Sacra ('Holy Way'), where he presided over numerous official sacrifices at which *haruspices* practised extispicy. Caesar's motives, however, were overwhelmingly political. The intermingling of politics and religion made his election an important political stepping stone. Caesar admitted to his mother that he spent so much on bribes to secure his election that he would have been ruined had he failed to become High Priest.[59]

Particularly ironic is the fact that before his assassination in 44 BC Caesar received probably the best-known warnings in the history of divination. In Shakespeare's *Julius Caesar* he is accosted by an unnamed soothsayer as he walks through the centre of Rome during the religious festival of Lupercalia:

> CAESAR: Who is it in the press that calls on me?
>   I hear a tongue shriller than all the music
>   Cry 'Caesar!' Speak, Caesar is turn'd to hear.
> SOOTHSAYER: Beware the ides of March.[60]

In reality, the main warning of danger on the Ides (15th) of March, so called because of the full moon on that date, came not from an anonymous soothsayer but from the *haruspex* Spurinna in Caesar's own official residence at the Regia. During one of his examinations of the entrails of sacrificed animals, Spurinna warned Caesar that he was in danger and that 'the danger threatening him would come not later than the Ides of

---

* Caesar's later revelation that he had disregarded a 'portent of death' discovered during an animal sacrifice while he was fighting Pompey during the Civil War indirectly confirmed that *haruspices* did accompany his armies. (Dando-Collins, *The Ides*, p. 78.)

March'.* At the early-morning religious ritual on 15 March, Caesar told Spurinna, 'Where are your prophecies now? The Ides of March have come. Do you not see that the day which you feared is come and that I am still alive?' 'Yes, it is come', replied Spurinna, 'but it is not yet passed.' Spurinna then proceeded to the morning sacrifice of a bird, slit its throat while it was held by his assistants and examined its entrails. Pointing to the bird's curiously shaped liver, the *haruspex* declared, 'This is a portent of death.' Caesar is said to have laughed off the warning by declaring, 'The same thing happened to me in Spain when I was fighting Pompey.'[61]

Caesar's assassination later that day, however, was made possible not by his disrespect for divination but by his failure to heed intelligence on the threat to him from within the Senate. The value of even the best intelligence is only as great as the use made of it. Caesar's assassination in 44 BC – probably the best-known political killing in history – is a prime example. In a conspiracy involving so many conspirators, chief among them about sixty senators, and in a capital city which generated as much gossip as Rome, there were bound to be rumours of a threat to Caesar's life. Though there were varied motives among the conspirators, common to all of them was probably the belief that the powers possessed by Caesar were incompatible with the survival of a free Republic. Even some of those who remained strongly loyal to him believed that his powers were excessive. Traditionally, those appointed as dictator had been limited to a six-month term. In 46, however, Caesar was given a ten-year term, and early in 44 was made dictator for life (*dictator perpetuo*). Showered with other honours, he became the first Roman whose head appeared on coins in his own lifetime. Power and glory on a scale unprecedented in the previous history of the Roman Republic, combined with success as a risk-taker (most famously in crossing the Rubicon in 49 and starting a civil war from which he emerged victorious), made Caesar overconfident. At the beginning of 44 he dismissed his large Spanish bodyguard after the Senate took an oath of loyalty to him, and he refused repeated requests from friends and supporters to form a new bodyguard and take other measures to protect his security. The conspirators were working to a tight timetable. Caesar was due to leave Rome on 18 March to embark on new military campaigns, which were expected to last for several years. His last appearance in the Senate on the 15th was thus the obvious, perhaps the only,

* Significant corroboration for Suetonius' later identification of the *haruspex* as Spurinna is provided by a letter from Cicero to a friend eight months after Caesar's assassination in which he reported that Spurinna had predicted that 'the entire Republic was threatened with grave danger unless you reverted to your old habits'. (Dando-Collins, *The Ides*, p. 77.)

opportunity to assassinate him. Killing him while he was on campaign, surrounded by loyal forces, would probably have proved impossibly difficult.[62] Though Caesar was stabbed many times by the conspirators who crowded round him in the Senate on the Ides of March, Suetonius relates that an autopsy (the first of which record survives) revealed that only one wound in the chest proved fatal.[63]

Though Caesar had made more use of military intelligence than any previous Roman general, it made only a minor contribution to Rome's emergence as a military superpower. The main role of intelligence in warfare is to act as a force multiplier, enabling a combatant who is well informed about enemy forces to make more effective use of its own. After the destruction of Carthage, however, the military superiority of the late Roman Republic was so enormous that possessing better intelligence than its adversaries added little to its power as a warrior state. Rome's armies were famed for their discipline, superior weaponry and, above all, their sheer size. By the second century BC, as well as using allied troops, Rome was enlisting about 13 per cent of its own citizens in its legions – a proportion equalled by no other European power until the era of Frederick Great and Napoleon.[64]

4

The Art of War and the *Arthashastra*: How China and India Took an Early Lead over Greece and Rome

The first books to argue that intelligence should have a central role in war and peace were written not in classical Greece or Rome but in ancient China and the Indian subcontinent: *The Art of War* (*Sunzi bingfa*), traditionally ascribed to Confucius's contemporary, the Chinese general Sun Tzu (*c.*544–*c.*496 BC); and the *Arthashastra*, a lengthy manual on statecraft attributed to Kautilya (*c.*350–*c.*283 BC), a senior adviser to the founder of the Mauryan dynasty in northern India.

The authorship of *The Art of* War remains in doubt. It was probably written not by Sun Tzu but by an unknown later author (or authors) in the early third century BC,[1] using what by then was an old-fashioned literary style in order to benefit from the prestige of the great general's reputation. Whoever the author, however, *The Art of War* is now recognized as 'the first known attempt to formulate a rational basis for the planning and conduct of military operations'.* The celebrated twentieth-century British military historian and strategist Sir Basil Liddell Hart considered Sun Tzu the greatest of all military thinkers: 'Among all the military thinkers of the past, only Clausewitz is comparable and even he is more "dated" than Sun Tzu and in part antiquated, although he was writing two thousand years later. Sun Tzu has clearer vision, more profound insight and eternal freshness.'[2]

The authors of *The Art of War* and the *Arthashastra* did what no previous work on war and statecraft had done: to insist that divination and omens (which inhibited the development of intelligence in classical Greece

---

* 'Unlike most Greek and Roman writers, Sun Tzu was not primarily interested in the elaboration of involved stratagems or in superficial and transitory techniques. His purpose was to develop a systematic treatise to guide rulers and generals in the successful prosecution of successful war.' (Griffith (ed. and trans.), *Sun Tzu: The Art of War*, p. x.)

and Rome) had no part in either.* *The Art of War* declares: 'Prohibit the taking of omens and do away with superstitious doubts':[3]†

> Now, the reason a brilliant sovereign and a wise general conquer the enemy whenever they move, and their achievements surpass those of ordinary men, is their foreknowledge of the enemy situation. This foreknowledge cannot be elicited from spirits, nor from gods, nor by analogy with past events, nor by astrological calculations. It must be obtained from men who know the enemy situation [spies].[4]

The central argument of *The Art of War* is summed up in its first and final sentences:

> War is a matter of vital importance to the state; the province of life or death; the road to survival or ruin.
>
> . . .
>
> Secret operations are essential in war; upon them the army relies to make its every move.

Spies were at the heart of secret operations. *The Art of War* distinguishes five kinds:

- 'native agents' recruited from enemy countryside
- 'inside agents' within enemy officialdom
- 'double agents', whom the enemy wrongly regards as its own loyal agents
- 'expendable agents', used to feed disinformation to the enemy
- 'living agents', who bring intelligence from within the enemy camp
  When these five types of agents are all working simultaneously and none knows their method of operation, they are called the 'Divine Skein' and are the treasure of a sovereign.

The Art of War emphasizes that both the sovereign and the military commander must pay close attention to the intelligence provided by the 'Divine Skein': 'The sovereign must have full knowledge of the activities of the five sorts of agents . . . Of all those in the army close to the commander, none

---

* Though insistent, like *The Art of War*, that the ruler pay no attention to omens and other forms of superstition, the *Arthashastra* advises him to exploit the superstitious beliefs of his enemies and rivals, and encourage the credulous populace of his own dominions to believe that he has supernatural powers.

† The Chinese philosopher Han Fei (*c.*280–233 BC) similarly listed among the ways in which states could be ruined 'dependence on the choice of a suitable season or day, service to the demons and holy spirits, trust in divination by turtle or stalks together with the accompanying devotion of prayers and sacrifice'. (Loewe, *Divination, Mythology and Monarchy*, p. 168.)

is more intimate than the secret agent . . .'[5]* Intelligence in *The Art of War* was closely linked to deception: 'All warfare is based on deception. Therefore, when capable, feign incapacity. When active, inactivity.'[6] Though there had been individual cases, as at the Battle of Salamis in 480 BC, of the use of secret agents to feed disinformation to the enemy,[7] *The Art of War* was the first to recommend their systematic use in time of war.

The Art of War, however, is sometimes guilty of hyperbole. One of its most celebrated maxims declares: 'Know the enemy and know yourself; in a hundred battles you will never be defeated.' In themselves, however, intelligence and self-knowledge cannot prevent military defeat – as Churchill discovered during his first two years as Prime Minister in the Second World War.† Good intelligence diminishes the likelihood of enemy surprise attacks, but does not guarantee victory over them. *The Art of War* damaged its credibility by promising too much. 'Know the enemy and know yourself' remains, none the less, possibly the best single-sentence advice ever given to military commanders. Any commander who reflects on that advice is also bound to draw the conclusion that knowledge about the enemy necessarily requires both the covert collection of intelligence and the ability to interpret it correctly.

The main drawback of the visionary scheme for intelligence-based warfare propounded in *The Art of War* was that within imperial China it was so far ahead of its time. Though it was closely studied over the centuries after its composition by a series of Chinese and Japanese soldiers and scholars,[8] there was no prospect that the emperors of united China would abandon the age-old Chinese belief in various forms of divination and a wide range of portents, as *The Art of War* required. Some of the very earliest examples of Chinese writing are questions inscribed on turtle shells or 'oracle bones' on matters ranging from military operations to

---

* Though poorly documented, espionage had played a role in China's civil wars for centuries before Sun Tzu. *The Art of War* identifies as the earliest major spy in Chinese history a defector from the Hsia dynasty who assisted its overthrow by the Shang in 1766 BC. Only small fragments survive of military writings earlier than *The Art of War*. (Sawyer, *Tao of Spycraft*, p. 7; Sawyer, 'Subversive Information', p. 30.)

† During the Second World War, the ULTRA intelligence obtained from breaking the German ENIGMA and other high-grade enemy ciphers, combined with detailed briefings on UK forces, made Winston Churchill, at least in the European theatre, the best-informed war leader in British history. But for his first two years as Prime Minister Britain won no significant victory. During the Battle for Crete (20 May–1 June 1941), for example, the insight provided by ULTRA into the victorious German airborne invasion, the first in military history, could not compensate for the British forces' lack of modern military equipment to resist it. Despite the British defeat, however, German losses were so heavy that Hitler forbade further large-scale airborne operations. (Antill, *Crete 1941*.)

rulers' families. Diviners heated the shells and bones until they cracked and derived answers to the questions by interpreting the patterns which emerged. Four of the ten volumes of the *Wu-pei Chih*, a massive military compendium completed in the final decades of the Ming dynasty (1368–1644), were largely devoted to divination.[9]

The first Emperor of unified China, Qin Shi Huang (221–210 BC), sought to prevent critical comparison with previous rulers by removing all historical and philosophical texts from private hands and placing them in the imperial library, where only officially approved scholars had access to them. Books judged to be of practical utility, however, were not confiscated – and these included works on divination.* Qin placed inscriptions to celebrate his achievements on mountain tops around his dominions. He claimed to rule as the agent of celestial powers, designing his new palace around the heavenly pattern of the Plough and North Star. Whether or not Qin's military operations were influenced by *The Art of War* at the close of the 'era of the Warring States' which preceded Chinese unification, as was later claimed, he was clearly more influenced as Emperor by divination and superstition. Masters of esoteric arts persuaded him to live in towers and move between them on elevated walkways in order to come into closer contact with celestial spirits and achieve immortality. The most remarkable evidence of Qin's megalomaniac ambitions in the afterlife was his mausoleum, surrounded by a model of the earth with seas and rivers made from liquid mercury and protected by an estimated 8,000 terracotta warriors, each with individual facial features (not all yet excavated), as well as terracotta horses, weapons, chariots, court officials, acrobats, strongmen and musicians.[10]

Qin's cosmic ambitions as Emperor in the afterlife blinded him to the weaknesses of his earthly empire. Within four years of his death in 210 BC, rebellion swept across the empire, its newly built capital was burned to the ground, and the last Qin emperor was killed.[11] Emperors of the Han dynasty, which succeeded its short-lived Qin predecessor and ruled China for most of the period from 206 BC to AD 220,† also showed more interest in superstition and divination than in intelligence of the kind advocated by Sun Tzu. An edict of 89 BC referred to divination by turtle shells and yarrow stalks as established imperial procedure for deciding whether to

---

* Qin did not, as was sometimes claimed, order the systematic destruction of historical and philosophical texts. (Lewis, *Early Chinese Empires*, loc. 988.)
† The Han dynasty was divided into two major periods: the Western or Former Han, which ruled from 206 BC to AD 9; and the Eastern or Later Han, which held power from AD 25 to 220. A Han dynasty official, Wang Mang, seized the throne in AD 9 and ruled until AD 23.

go ahead with projects. Divination was also sometimes used to determine the choice of generals for military campaigns.[12]*

Unlike Han emperors, Cao Cao, the most successful warlord during the final years of the dynasty, was an ardent disciple of Sun Tzu and *The Art of War*, convinced of the need for military commanders to 'prohibit talk of omens and of supernatural portents'.[13] His military victories laid the foundation for the kingdom of Cao Wei, which became the strongest state in northern China during the 'Three Kingdoms' period from AD 220 to 280 which fractured the unity of the empire.† Cao left behind him a reputation as a brutal warlord. The common Chinese saying 'Speak of Cao Cao and Cao Cao arrives' is roughly the equivalent of the English expression 'Speak of the Devil . . .' But, unlike almost any commander in Western military history, Cao was also a prolific poet. His annotations of *The Art of War* make clear that he pondered its lessons carefully. On its instruction to the 'wise general' to 'consider both favourable and unfavourable factors' for example, Cao added the comment: 'He ponders the dangers inherent in the advantages and the advantages inherent in the dangers.' On the use of spies, Cao emphasized: 'Rely upon traitors among the enemy.'[14] Eight centuries after Cao's death, his commentary on *The Art of War*, together with that of other military authorities, was collated with the text of what became in effect an official edition, further revised and annotated in the eighteenth century.[15] This was the version generally cited in China until 1977, when a complete and remarkably well-preserved text of *The Art of War*, written on thin strips of bamboo, was discovered in a tomb in Shantung province where it had been buried with its owner in 118 BC – a rare example of the rediscovery of the original version of a major text almost two millennia after it was written.‡

There is no evidence that any subsequent emperor shared Cao's devotion to *The Art of War*. None showed any interest in the world much beyond the empire's borders. As Henry Kissinger wrote later, under successive dynasties 'China was never obliged to deal with other countries or civilizations that were comparable to it in scale and civilization.'[16] It did

---

* There were, however, some dissentient voices: among them the later Han philosopher Wang Ch'ung (AD 27–c.100), who denounced the belief that 'the turtle shells or the yarrow stalks possess divine or numinous qualities such that they comprehend human fortune or misfortune and produce signs or a numerical combination by way of notification of such fortune'. (Loewe, *Divination, Mythology and Monarchy*, pp. 173–4.)
† Some historians trace the beginning of the 'Three Kingdoms' period to an earlier phase in the disintegration of Han China.
‡ The most remarkable rediscovery of manuscripts of similar antiquity was that between 1948 and 1956 of the far more voluminous Dead Sea Scrolls, probably written during the period c.200 BC–AD 68.

not feel sufficiently threatened by barbarian states to wish to be well informed about them. Covert action during internal and border conflicts was a higher priority than intelligence collection. Assassination was a much more important theme in Chinese than in Western literature. Among many heroic and semi-historical tales of the use of secret agents as assassins is the gruesome story of Yao Li, first recorded in the third-century BC, *Stratagems of the Warring States*. Before being sent by King Ho-lü of Wu to assassinate the exiled Prince Ch'ing Chi in the neighbouring state of Wei, Yao Li reputedly cut off his own right hand and killed his wife and children in order to establish his cover as a victim of Ho-lü. By posing convincingly as an enemy of Ho-Lü anxious for revenge, Yao Li gained access to Ch'ing Chi and successfully assassinated him.[17] Over 1,500 years later, in the later years of the Ming dynasty (1368–1644), the leading military thinker Jie Xuan saw the main role of secret agents as covert action: 'Agents strike fear in the enemy's General Staff, slay the enemy's beloved generals, and cause chaos in the enemy's estimates and strategies.' Apart from assassination, Jie Xuan and other military thinkers recommended bribery, seduction and disinformation.[18] The Ming emperors were notorious for ordering officials who incurred their disfavour to be viciously (and sometimes fatally) flogged on their bare buttocks in open court. Lacking an organized security service, they relied on informers to detect treachery: 'It is not difficult to conclude that the Ming emperors, through their agents among palace eunuchs and in the Imperial Bodyguard, maintained a reign of terror in the civil service.'[19]

For two millennia after the unification of the Empire in 221 BC the Middle Kingdom found it inconceivable that the barbarians beyond its borders had anything of value to offer it. After a British mission to Beijing in 1793 had tried to interest the Chinese court in trade and the products of Western civilization, the Emperor wrote to George III: 'As your ambassador can see for himself, we possess everything. I set no value on strange or ingenious objects and have no use for your country's manufactures.'[20] China owned about a third of the world's wealth and regarded all East Asia as tributary states. Not until 1861, after losing two wars against Western powers, did China establish something approximating to a Foreign Ministry to manage diplomacy with the West. Even then, as Kissinger has noted, this was regarded as only 'a temporary necessity, to be abolished once the immediate crisis subsided'. The modest building in which it was housed was intended to demonstrate, according to the leading Chinese statesman, Prince Gong, that it could not have 'a standing equal to that of other traditional government offices, thus preserving the distinction between China and foreign countries'.[21] Reluctant even to set up a Foreign

Ministry, the Qing dynasty, the last to rule China, was incapable, even after military defeats and other humiliations at the hands of the West, of grasping Sun Tzu's insistence on the importance of espionage in responding to enemy threats.

The great early Indian manual of statecraft, the *Arthashastra*, was produced at about the same time as *The Art of War*, though its dating and authorship are also controversial.[22] It has traditionally been attributed to Kautilya (also known as Chanakya), one of the chief advisers to King Chandragupta Maurya (317–293 BC), founder of the Mauryan dynasty, who halted the advance of Alexander the Great's successors and became the first ruler to unite the Indian subcontinent. Though the *Arthashastra* is less preoccupied with warfare than *The Art of War*, espionage and intelligence operations occupy centre-stage.

Spies had a long tradition in ancient Indian culture. In Vedic religion (*c.*1500–500 BC), the predecessor of modern Hinduism, the god Varuna, lord of the heavens and the earth, uses the stars as his spies to keep all human activity under constant surveillance.* The *Arthashastra* draws inspiration from references to espionage in the epic Hindu holy book, the *Mahabharata*, which probably reached its final form in the fourth century BC. Among the questions King Yudhisthira, famed for his piety, asks his equally pious adviser, the ascetic Bhishma, in the *Mahabharata* was how the ruler should use spies. For a holy man who had taken a vow of life-long celibacy, Bhishma's reply was impressively devious:

> He should employ as spies men looking like idiots or like those that are blind and deaf. Those should all be persons who have been thoroughly examined (in respect of their ability), who are possessed of wisdom, and who are able to endure hunger and thirst. With proper attention, the king should set his spies upon all his counsellors and friends and sons, in his city and the provinces, and in dominions of the chiefs under him. His spies should be so employed that they may not know one another. He should also, O bull of Bharata's race, know the spies of his foes by himself setting spies in shops and places of amusement, and concourses of people, among beggars, in his pleasure gardens and parks, in meetings and conclaves of the learned, in the country, in public places, in places where he holds his own court, and in the houses of the citizens. The king possessed of intelligence may thus ascertain the spies despatched by his foes. If these be known, the king may derive much benefit.[23]

---

* The Sanskrit word *spash*, literally 'wary watcher', is commonly translated as 'spy'.

At the end of the *Mahabharata*, Yudhisthira ascends to heaven (with his five brothers) – the first spymaster recorded as having done so.

The recommendations of the *Arthashastra* on cover professions for the ruler's numerous spies are as devious as those of the saintly Bhishma. Among the most highly recommended impersonations is that of an apparently ascetic holy man who pretends to survive on a diet of vegetables or meadow grass once or twice a month, while eating his favourite food in secret. Other spies posing as his disciples were to spread the word that he had supernatural powers as well as exceptional holiness. The holy man's prophecies, allegedly divinely inspired, were intended to buttress royal authority. He was to read the palms of those who asked him about their own future and advise them that their personal success depended on loyalty to the ruler.[24]

The *Arthashastra* was the first book anywhere in the world to call for the establishment of a professional intelligence service. It discussed in enormous detail, not since surpassed in any unclassified manual of statecraft, the recruitment, uses and twenty-nine main cover occupations (with fifty sub-types) of a huge network of spies at home and abroad. The network was such a high priority that the King was told to take personal charge of it. The royal day was to be divided into eight periods of one and a half hours each, during which intelligence was assigned a higher priority than in almost any other surviving timetable of a world leader. The one and a half hours after midday were to be devoted to writing correspondence, conferring with senior officials and receiving 'secret information from spies'; the hour and a half after sunset was allotted exclusively to 'interviews with secret agents'; and the hour and a half after midnight was devoted to consultations with advisers and sending spies on their missions.[25]

Though the King was to deal personally with leading secret agents, his senior officials were also to have their own agent networks. The *Arthashastra* thus envisaged the world's first fully organized surveillance state. The King was told to regard almost everyone within the state as a potential threat to royal authority: senior courtiers might try to usurp the throne; peasants might rebel; military commanders might challenge the Crown.[26]

Agents provocateurs were to be used both to discover potential plotters against the ruler and to identify any minister who might dare to seduce the Queen. The *Arthashastra* recommended that, from time to time, the King should go through the motions of publicly dismissing his military chief while secretly telling him to send agents to ministers offering them bribes to join him in a plot against the Crown. Potential seducers of the Queen were to be identified by sending an itinerant nun to inform any suspect minister that the Queen was in love with him and had plans to make him wealthy. Ministers who failed to respond to these provocations were presumed to be innocent.[27]

The key role assigned to *agents provocateurs* reflected the paranoid tendencies of the Mauryan and some later Indian rulers, rather than representing a serious step towards the establishment of a modern authoritarian intelligence system. An ambassador to the court of the founder of the Mauryan empire, Chandragupta Maurya, in the late fourth century BC reported that the King was so fearful of assassination that he changed bedchamber every night.[28] The *Arthashastra* declared it the duty of the sovereign to use 'secret methods' such as the following to assassinate treacherous senior officials:

- A secret agent shall tempt the brother of the traitor to kill him with the promise of being given his brother's property; when the deed is done, by weapon or by poison, he himself should be killed for the crime of fratricide.
- A mendicant woman agent, having won the confidence of the wife of a seditious minister by providing her with love potions, may with the help of the wife contrive to poison the minister.
- If the traitor is addicted to witchcraft, a spy in the guise of a holy man should inveigle him into a secret rite, during which he shall be killed by poison or with an iron bar. The death shall be attributed to some mishap during the secret rites.
- A spy in the guise of a doctor may make the traitor believe that he is suffering from a malignant or incurable disease and kill him by poisoning his medicine or diet.

Spies selected for assassination missions were to be 'recruited from the bravest in the land, particularly those who, for the sake of money, are willing to fight wild elephants and tigers, in total disregard for their own personal safety'.[29] Few, if any, early writers on statecraft and intelligence showed quite such enthusiasm for assassination as the author of the *Arthashastra*: 'A single assassin', he claimed, 'can achieve, with weapons, fire or poison, more than a fully mobilized army.'[30]

Grossly inflated though the *Arthashastra*'s estimate of the assassin's role now appears, it was shared by Stalin and his foreign intelligence service two millennia later when they were plotting the murder of the great Communist heretics of the Stalinist era, Leon Trotsky and Marshal Tito. In each case, both the priority given to the choice of assassin and the ingenuity of the method of assassination lived up to the standards demanded by the *Arthashastra*. By the outbreak of the Second World War, the assassination of Trotsky had become the main objective of Stalin's foreign policy. The assassin, Ramón Mercader, used a doctored Canadian passport in the name of Frank Jacson and gained access to Trotsky's villa near Mexico City by seducing one of Trotsky's secretaries.[31] The plot by Soviet foreign intelligence for the assassination of Marshal Tito early in the Cold War was even more ingenious. By the time the plot was called off after Stalin's sudden death in 1953, the intended Soviet assassin, Iosif Grigulevich, had succeeded in posing as a Costa Rican, become Costa Rican envoy to Belgrade, and gained an audience with Tito.[32]

Though Allen Dulles and the CIA leadership during the early Cold War were well acquainted with the *The Art of War*, they do not seem to have read the *Arthashastra*. When Richard Bissell, the CIA's Director of Plans (head of operations), began to draw up plans for the assassination of Fidel Castro in 1960, he paid no heed to the *Arthashastra*'s exhortations on the careful selection process required during the recruitment of assassins. Since the CIA, unlike the KGB, had no trained assassins, Bissell proposed to subcontract to the Mafia, which had a reputation as the United States' most professional killers. The Mafia had reasons of its own for wanting to dispose of Castro, who had wrecked its lucrative gambling and prostitution operations in Havana, but Bissell seems to have been poorly informed about its assassination skills. Contact was made with Johnny Rosselli, former lieutenant of Al Capone, and Salvatore 'Sam' Giancana, one of the FBI's ten-most-wanted criminals. Neither was attracted by Bissell's Hollywood-inspired vision of a gangland killing in which Castro would be mown down in a hail of bullets. Giancana suggested an undetectable poison instead. On Bissell's instructions, the CIA's Office of Medical Services prepared a botulinum toxin pill which 'did the job' when it was used on monkeys. Poisoning, however, was not really the Mafia's style and the pills disappeared somewhere in Cuba without ever reaching Castro. Bissell and his team persisted in devising other bizarre and impracticable schemes to use poison. A box of Castro's favourite cigars was treated with a deadly toxin. Another box was impregnated with a chemical designed to destroy Castro's credibility by making him hallucinate in public. Nothing came of these or any other of the CIA poison plots.[33] All failed to take into account the *Arthashastra*'s insistence that the use of poison required assassins with carefully planned access to the victim.

To a twenty-first-century readership the treatment of foreign intelligence in the *Arthashastra* seems less outrageous than its advocacy of a surveillance society whose leadership was committed to the secret assassination of suspected traitors. Its conclusions on handling conflict with foreign enemies broadly follow the lines of the injunction in *The Art of War* to 'know the enemy and know yourself'. The *Arthashastra* adds the advice that this self-knowledge be used to remove any weakness which might be exploited by the enemy: 'No enemy shall know [the King's] secrets. He shall, however, know all his enemy's weaknesses. Like a tortoise, he shall draw in any limb of his that is exposed.'[34] Like *The Art of War*, the *Arthashastra* emphasizes the importance of recruiting agents among the enemy population, especially senior officials.

Its proposals for agent recruitment abroad, some of which reflected the influence of the *Mahabharata*, were, however, unrealistically ambitious:

> A king shall have his own set of spies, all quick in their work, in the courts of the enemy, the ally, the middle and the neutral kings to spy on the kings as well as their eighteen types of high officials.
>
> The different types of spies are as follows:-
>
> • Inside their houses: hunchbacks, dwarfs, eunuchs, women skilled in various arts, dumb persons, *mlecchas*;
> • Inside their cities: traders, espionage establishments;
> • Near the cities: ascetics;
> • In the countryside: farmers, monks;
> • Frontiers: herdsmen;
> • Forest dwellers, such as *shramanas* and foresters.[35]

The role of the foreign agents was not limited to intelligence collection but also extended to psychological warfare and subversion. The final page of *The Art of War* claims that two Chinese rulers had been overthrown because a senior minister had defected to their enemies.[36] 'Miraculous results', claimed the *Arthashastra*, 'can be achieved by practising the methods of subversion.'[37]

It was ironic that two millennia later the KGB should have had expectations of what subversion could achieve inside India which were as exaggerated as those of the *Arthashastra*. The high-flying Oleg Kalugin, who in 1973 became the youngest general in KGB foreign intelligence, remembers India in the 1970s as 'a model of KGB infiltration of a Third World government', with 'scores of sources throughout the Indian government – in Intelligence, Counter-intelligence, the Defence and Foreign Ministries, and the police'. Helped by the streak of corruption which ran through Indian public life, by 1973, according to KGB files, it had ten Indian newspapers on its payroll as well as a press agency under its 'control'. Despite a series of tactical successes, such as persuading the Prime Minister, Indira Gandhi, that the CIA was planning to assassinate her, KGB operations had limited long-term strategic influence.[38]

Though the *Arthashastra* continued to be cited in Indian literature until the twelfth century, thereafter it disappeared from view for almost a millennium. The Sanskrit text was eventually rediscovered in 1904 by the librarian of the Mysore Oriental Library (now the Oriental Research Institute), Dr Rudrapatnam Shamashastry, who published it in 1909. The first English translation appeared in 1915, two millennia or more after it was written. The *Arthashastra* quickly became established as one of the leading Indian classics. It was praised – according to Shamashastry – even by the apostle of non-violence, Mahatma Gandhi, to whom he presented a copy in 1927.[39] The first Prime Minister of independent India, Jawaharlal Nehru, made a number of references to the *Arthashastra* in his classic popular history, *The Discovery of India*, written in jail on the eve of Independence. Its early-twenty-first-century enthusiasts include the former Indian Foreign Secretary and National Security Adviser, Shivshankar Menon, who told a conference on Kautilya and the *Arthashastra* in 2012:

> The *Arthashastra* meets one essential criterion for a great book. It bears reading again and again. Every time you read it you learn something new and find a new way of looking at events . . . This is a serious manual on statecraft, on how to run a state, informed by a higher purpose (or *dharma*), clear and precise in its prescriptions, the result of practical experience of running a state. It is not just a normative text but a realist description of the art of running a state.

Study of the *Arthashastra*, in Menon's view, is necessary to remind Indians that strategic thinking in India long predated the colonial era:

> We are afflicted with neglect of our pre-modern histories, and many of us believe [Western] orientalist caricatures of India. India's supposedly incoherent strategic approach is actually a colonial construct, as is the idea of Indians somehow forgetting their own history and needing to be taught it by Westerners who retrieved it. The version that they 'retrieved' was a construct that was useful to perpetuate colonial rule and, after independence, to induce self-doubt and a willingness to follow.
>
> . . . To be honest among ourselves, much of what passes for strategic thinking in India today is derivative, using concepts, doctrines and a vocabulary derived from other cultures, times, places and conditions. This is why, with a few honourable exceptions like the home-grown nuclear doctrine, it fails to serve our needs, impact policy, or to find a place in domestic and international discourse.[40]

To regard the *Arthashastra* as 'a realist description of the running of a state', however, requires a rather selective reading. The *Arthashastra* clearly indicates that the duties of the National Security Adviser include advising the government on, inter alia, how to conduct surveillance of the entire Indian population, how to recruit bogus holy men and women as agents, and how to liquidate, by poison if necessary, its opponents at home and abroad. It is unlikely that the passages on these topics are among those that Shivshankar Menon recommends 'reading again and again'.

Unlike the *Arthashastra*, during the twentieth century *The Art of War* acquired a major international as well as national reputation. The first largely reliable English translation was published in 1910 (five years before the first translation of the *Arthashastra*), by Dr Lionel Giles of the British Museum's Department of Oriental Books and Manuscripts.[41] The Whitehall official most likely to have paid serious attention to the publication was Vernon Kell, head of the Counter-Espionage Bureau (the future MI5) founded in the previous year. Kell was the only intelligence chief in British history with a translator's qualification in Chinese, and had been in China during the anti-Western Boxer Rebellion. The impact on him of *The Art of War*'s emphasis on intelligence-based warfare and the role of deception (which had no parallel in contemporary Western literature) must have been increased by the fact that, at the time Giles's translation was published, he was fully focused on countering German espionage in Britain which, he feared, was part of Germany's preparations for war.[42]

Within China itself *The Art of War* was probably more closely studied by Mao Zedong than it had been by any Chinese emperor. During the civil war between Communists and the Kuomintang regime he sent aides into enemy territory to find a copy of it, and Sun Tzu was later the only major figure among China's ancient thinkers to emerge unscathed from Mao's Cultural Revolution. A tract published in 1975 said that he offered useful guidance for 'criticism of the rightist opportunist military line' and the 'reactionary views of the Confucianist'.[43] Sun Tzu (or whoever wrote in his name) was equally admired by some of Mao's most committed ideological opponents in the West. Allen Dulles, Director of Central Intelligence (head of the CIA) from 1953 to 1961, gave him 'the credit not only for the first remarkable analysis of the ways of espionage, but also for the first written recommendations regarding an organized intelligence service': 'It is no wonder that Sun Tzu's book is a favorite of Mao Tse-tung and is required reading for Chinese Communist tacticians. In their conduct of military campaigns and of intelligence collection, they clearly put into practice the teachings of Sun Tzu.'[44] Henry Kissinger later criticized US commanders during the Vietnam War for their lack of attention to *The Art of War*: 'Ho Chi Minh and Vo Nguyen Giap employed Sun Tzu's principles of indirect attack and psychological combat against

France and then the United States . . . One could argue that the disregard of its precepts was importantly responsible for America's frustration in its Asian wars.'[45]

Kissinger became convinced that the sophistication of Mao, Zhou Enlai and other senior Chinese policymakers with whom he negotiated during the 1970s derived from their ability to draw on ancient strategic wisdom, first and foremost Sun Tzu. Mao's foreign policy, he believed, 'owed more to Sun Tzu than to Lenin'. Mao was 'enough of a Sun Tzu disciple to pursue seemingly contradictory strategies simultaneously'.[46]

> Even today Sun Tzu's text reads with a degree of immediacy and insight that places him among the ranks of the world's foremost strategic thinkers . . .
>
> What distinguishes Sun Tzu from Western writers on strategy is the emphasis on the psychological and political elements over the purely military.[47]

Kissinger does not mention, however, that Mao and his successors also seem to have taken to heart *The Art of War*'s insistence on the importance of using double agents within opposing powers, who were to be rewarded with 'the utmost liberality'. One such agent was the Chinese-born US citizen Larry Wu-tai Chin, who is believed to have been paid one million dollars by the Chinese while working for the CIA, which in 1980 awarded him a medal for long and, it mistakenly believed, distinguished service. At his trial for espionage, Chin admitted that among the classified documents which he passed to Beijing was a secret memorandum by Richard Nixon before his historic visit to China in 1972, the first by a US President, outlining Nixon's aim to normalize relations with the Communist regime. 'I was stunned by the about-face of President Nixon', Chin told the court. 'I wanted Zhou En-lai to see it.' Zhou, presumably, also brought Nixon's memorandum to the attention of Mao.[48]

In the early twenty-first century the CIA Center for the Study of Intelligence continued to accord Sun Tzu the central role in the history of intelligence allotted to him by Allen Dulles almost half a century earlier. One of the leading Anglophone historians writing about Sun Tzu's teachings on intelligence has been Dr Michael Warner, historian at, successively, the CIA, the Office of the US Director of National Intelligence and the National Security Agency (NSA).[49] Increasing Chinese espionage, especially in science and technology (a category of spying unknown to Sun Tzu), has left undimmed the popularity of *The Art of War* in twenty-first-century America. It became and remains a prescribed textbook at West Point and some other US armed forces academies.

During a visit to the White House in 2006 President Hu Jintao presented President George W. Bush with silk copies of *The Art of War* in

English and Mandarin. The visit itself was marred by mildly embarrassing misunderstandings. The Chinese considered the occasion a state visit; the White House did not and provided only lunch rather than the dinner reserved for major state occasions. Before the lunch began the anthem of the People's Republic of China was wrongly introduced as that of the Republic of China, the official title of Taiwan.[50] Despite these gaffes, Sun Tzu went from strength to strength, becoming a cult figure on US airport bookstalls.

By the time Hu visited the White House, the main US strategic interest in Sun Tzu was no longer in his teachings on war and espionage but on the association between *The Art of War* and the concept of 'soft power', first devised in 1990 (and further refined in 2004) by the Harvard academic and chairman of the US National Intelligence Council, Professor Joseph Nye, to describe 'the ability to get what you want through attraction rather than coercion or payments'.[51] Though *The Art of War* is chiefly concerned with the measures required to achieve military victory, ranging from use of the terrain to the role of espionage, Sun Tzu also says that the greatest achievement is 'to subdue the enemy without fighting'.[52] In his keynote speech to the 17th Congress of the Chinese Communist Party in 2007, President Hu, according to the official report, 'stressed the need to enhance Chinese culture as the country's "soft power"'. A year later Nye himself pointed to the link between soft power and *The Art of War*. Sun Tzu, he said, had concluded that 'the highest excellence is never having to fight because the commencement of battle signifies a political failure'. The 'smart' warrior had to understand 'the soft power of attraction as well as the hard power of coercion'. 'Seduction', writes Nye, 'is always more effective than coercion, and many values like democracy, human rights, and individual opportunities are deeply seductive.'[53] The problem for China is that, despite its enormous economic power, its own versions of democracy and human rights show no sign of becoming 'deeply seductive'.

Sun Tzu, however, became deeply seductive to American publishers. In 2011 Amazon had on sale 1,500 paperback titles based on the teachings of *The Art of War*: among them *Sun Tzu for Success: How to Use the Art of War to Master Challenges and Accomplish the Important Goals in Your Life* (by Gerald and Steven Michaelson), *Sun Tzu for Women* (by Becky Sheetz-Runkle) and *Golf and the Art of War: How the Timeless Strategies of Sun Tzu Can Transform Your Game* (by Don Wade). Sun Tzu also acquired a celebrity following. Paris Hilton, author of the aphorism 'Dress cute wherever you go, life is too short to blend in', was photographed studying *The Art of War*.[54]

Curiously, at a time when both Chinese espionage in the United States and the appeal to the American book market of Sun Tzu reached an all-time high, his maxims on espionage attracted much smaller US publishing and celebrity interest. The fact that he was the first to put the case for espionage as a centrally important state activity seemed largely forgotten. But it was not forgotten in Beijing. There is no reason to doubt that the Chinese regime is as committed to Sun Tzu's teachings on espionage as on soft power. China's twenty-first-century scientific and technological intelligence operations in the West, possibly the largest in history, accord well with the insistence at the end of *The Art of War* that governments and commanders 'who are able to use the most intelligent people as agents are certain to achieve great things'.

5

The Roman Empire and the
Untermenschen

The assassination of Julius Caesar in 44 BC[1] failed to save the Roman Republic. It was followed by almost two decades of civil war, which ended in the victory of Caesar's ruthlessly ambitious grand-nephew and adopted son, Octavian. Beneath an initially Republican façade, Octavian became in 27 BC the Emperor Augustus and founder of the Julio-Claudian dynasty, ruling until his death in AD 14.

The next two centuries are often remembered as the golden age of the *Pax Romana*, when Roman rule maintained the peace across much of Europe. As the result of a catastrophic defeat in AD 9 of Augustus' forces by German barbarians in the Teutoburg forest, just north of modern Osnabrück, however, the *Pax Romana* failed to extend east of the River Rhine. The defeat dramatically demonstrated the failings of Roman military intelligence, of which Augustus had a weaker grasp than Julius Caesar. At the time, the main scapegoat for the disaster was Publius Quinctilius Varus, who had been appointed governor of Germania in AD 7 with a mission to subject the province to Roman law and taxation. Nothing in Varus' previous career in North Africa and the Middle East suggests that he lacked ability as a military commander.[2] Like most Romans, however, he was seriously deficient in his understanding of the barbarians, chiefly because he regarded them as *Untermenschen* (as the Nazis two millennia later derisively described the Slavs). Varus was fortunate to possess a high-level mole among the Germanic barbarians: Segestes, a leading noble of the Cherusci tribe in the northern Rhine valley who had been granted Roman citizenship by Augustus and had transferred his main loyalty to Rome. He warned Varus in AD 9 that, though his fellow tribesmen were outwardly submissive, they were about to launch a major rebellion against Roman rule led by his main rival, Arminius (known in modern German as Hermann). While sitting (or lounging) next to Varus at a feast, Segestes suggested that he arrest Arminius and all Cheruscan leaders (himself included, presumably to avoid arousing suspicion), and then 'sort out the guilty from the innocent'. Varus, how-ever, could not bring himself to take seriously the prospect of a rebellion by the backward and apparently compliant Cherusci.[3] The Roman histor-ian Velleius Paterculus wrote later that 'Fate now blindfolded the eyes of [Varus'] mind.'[4]

In the autumn of AD 9, Varus set off from his summer camp west of the Weser river to winter quarters near the Rhine at the head of three legions and non-Roman auxiliary forces. The fact that his troops mingled with camp followers in a straggling column nine miles long strongly sug-gests that he had taken few precautions against ambush.[5] Varus' troops, however, were overwhelmed by a surprise attack from Cherusci forces led by Arminius. Recent archaeological research on the site of the Battle of Teutoburg shows that the Romans were ambushed in a mountain pass one kilometre wide, leaving them unable to manoeuvre for a counter-offensive.[6] The battle lasted three days, during which the Roman army became bogged down by heavy rain and mud. The historian Lucius Annaeus Florus gives a gruesome account of the massacre that followed:

> Never was there slaughter more cruel than took place there in the marshes and woods, never were more intolerable insults inflicted by barbarians . . . They put out the eyes of some of [the Romans] and cut off the hands of others. They sewed up the mouth of one of them after first cutting out his tongue, which one of the barbarians held in his hand, exclaiming 'At last, you viper, you have ceased to hiss.'[7]

Varus committed suicide to avoid a similarly gruesome death.[8] Augustus reacted to news of the disaster by shouting repeatedly as he banged his head against a door in his home on the Palatine hill: 'Varus, give me back my legions!'[9] Germanicus (nephew of Augustus' successor, Tiberius) later returned to Germany to take revenge on the Cherusci and was rewarded with a victory parade in Rome with a procession of captured barbarians, at which the invited guests included the still loyal Roman mole, Segestes.

The disaster at Teutoburg, which ended the Roman ambition of advan-cing to the River Elbe, was a striking example of intelligence failure. The failure, however, was more in the use, than the collection, of intelligence. The Romans could scarcely have had a better-placed agent able to keep them informed on the threat of a Cherusci uprising than Segestes. But Varus was so convinced of the inferiority of the barbarian *Untermenschen* that he paid no attention, just as two millennia later Hitler woefully underestimated the ability of the Slavs to resist his war of conquest in Eastern Europe. Half a century after Teutoburg, a similar underestimation of the threat from the barbarian Iceni was to put in doubt the survival of Roman rule in Britain.

The most visible change in intelligence collection which followed the foundation of the Roman Empire was in Rome rather than at the imperial frontiers: the increased use of informers by emperors anxious about plots (both real and imagined) against them. Augustus paid close attention to his own security. During the purge of the Senate in 18 BC, Suetonius reports, Augustus, anxious to avoid the fate of his adoptive father, Julius Caesar, carried a sword, wore a breastplate beneath his tunic, and was protected by a ten-man bodyguard. Senators were allowed to approach him only one at a time, after first being searched for hidden daggers.[10]

Much of the intelligence on alleged plots against Augustus came from informers (delatores, a word which did not carry that meaning until his reign).[11] Augustus became personally involved in the handling of the intelligence they provided. On occasion he combined intelligence collection with sexual recreation. Suetonius seems almost in awe of Augustus' sexual appetites, reporting that his friends were required to pimp for him, ordering both married and unmarried women to strip, as if they were slaves at a market, in order to ensure that their naked bodies met the Emperor's requirements. During his numerous sexual liaisons with married women, according to Suetonius, Augustus sometimes enquired whether their husbands were plotting against him. He made little attempt to hide his liaisons. According to Mark Antony, during one dinner party he led the wife of a former consul, 'before his very eyes', into a bedchamber, whence she returned 'with her hair in disorder and her ears glowing'.[12] Save for his sexual liaisons, Augustus fiercely protected his own secrets. When he discovered that his secretary, Thallus, had taken a bribe of 500 denarii to reveal the contents of one of his letters, Augustus personally broke his legs.[13] Augustus' success in protecting his own security was demonstrated by the fact that he continued to reign as emperor until the age of almost seventy-seven and then died of natural causes. (The only older emperor, Gordian I, became emperor at the age of seventy-nine in 238 – 'the year of the six emperors' – but ruled for only a month before committing suicide.)

The numbers of informers expanded considerably under the reign of Augustus' successor, Tiberius (AD 14–37), who was increasingly fearful of conspiracies.[14] The profession of delator, wrote the historian Tacitus, was often pursued for private advantage rather than in the public interest, and made some poor men rich – 'men to be feared instead of despised'. Among the victims of the informers under Tiberius were those who spread probably well-founded stories about orgies at his cliff-top palace on Capri (described in prurient detail by Suetonius and Tacitus).[15] According to the

Stoic philosopher and statesman Seneca: 'In the reign of Tiberius Caesar, there was such a common and almost universal frenzy for bringing charges of treason that it took a heavier toll of the lives of Roman citizens than any civil war.'[16]

While not literally true, Seneca's account captures the climate of fear created by the culture of denunciation during the reign of Tiberius. It was also prescient. According to Suetonius, the Emperor Gaius (better known as Caligula) declared at the start of his reign, in an attempt to win popular support, that he had 'no ears for informers'.[17] Soon after succeeding Claudius in AD 54, the Emperor Nero announced that payments to informers were to be reduced by three quarters.[18] Neither Caligula nor Nero lived up his promises. Nero ordered Seneca, his former friend and confidant, to commit suicide for complicity in a plot in which he probably played no part.[19]

The four successors to Augustus in the Julio-Claudian dynasty (Tiberius, Caligula, Claudius and Nero), like many later emperors, probably paid as much attention to omens, portents and divination as to *delatores*. According to Suetonius, Caligula was warned of his coming assassination by the astrologer Sylla and by ill omens, which included being spattered during a sacrifice by the blood of a flamingo. After being told by the oracle at Antium that Cassius was plotting against him, Caligula ordered the execution of the Asian proconsul, Cassius Longinus. He had, however, selected the wrong Cassius. The real leader of the assassination plot in AD 41 was Cassius Chaerea.[20] Though Tacitus usually writes in a no-nonsense style, his accounts of the portents which signalled regime change under the Julio-Claudian dynasty are sometimes comically credulous. The approaching death of Claudius in AD 54 was, he claims, indicated by a 'succession of prodigies': among them flames descending from the sky which set fire to soldiers' tents and standards, a swarm of bees settling on the top of the Capitol, the birth of 'a pig with hawk's talons' and 'hermaphrodite babies'.[21] Claudius' successor, Nero, believed that he was haunted by the ghost of his mother, whom he had murdered, and attempted to summon up her shade by magical rituals in order to 'soften her rage against him'. Like Caligula, he also sought help from astrologers and consulted the oracle at Delphi.[22]

The main threat to Roman imperial rule during the reign of Nero came in Britain.* The accounts by the historians Tacitus and Cassius Dio† of

---

* On the origins of the Iceni uprising, whose immediate cause was heavy-handed Roman bureaucratic incompetence, see Cunliffe, *Ancient Celts*, p. 255.
† Tacitus (AD 56–117) wrote about events which happened during his lifetime. The account by Cassius Dio (AD c.150–235) was written a century later.

the great defeat suffered by the Romans at the hands of the Celtic Iceni, who inhabited modern East Anglia, both put far more emphasis on failure to heed omens and portents of impending disaster than on the Romans' lack of elementary military intelligence about the British barbarians. As before the great defeat at Teutoburg half a century earlier, the fundamental problem remained the Roman inability to regard barbarian *Untermenschen* as worthy opponents. Taking the Iceni seriously was all the more difficult for Romans because, when the rebellion broke out in AD 60, seventeen years after the Roman conquest of southern England, they were led by a woman, Queen Boudicca. Roman soldiers had already flogged her in public and raped her two daughters: further humiliation probably appeared unnecessary. Cassius Dio did, however, later concede that Boudicca was 'possessed of greater intelligence than often belongs to women', with a commanding presence, harsh voice, stern glare, a golden torc around her neck and a long mane of tawny hair over a dark cape and coat of many colours.[23]*

To the Roman neighbours of the Iceni, however, strange portents were far more worrying than Boudicca's appearance. According to Tacitus, in AD 60 the inhabitants of Camulodunum (Colchester), then the Roman capital, become unnerved by a dramatic series of ill omens. The statue of the goddess of victory fell off her pedestal without apparent cause and lay prostrate on the ground with her gaze averted – 'as if yielding to the enemies of Rome'. Mass hysteria followed. Distraught women, claims Tacitus, 'cried that destruction was at hand', 'the theatre rang with shrieks', and 'alien cries' echoed through the council chamber. Near the mouth of the Thames the image of a Roman colony in ruins was seen beneath the water; the sea became blood-stained; and, at low tide, the imprints of human bodies were visible in the sand. Seeing the Romans 'sunk in despair, the Britons anticipated a glorious victory'.[24] Since Camulodunum had only a token garrison, its frightened inhabitants sent for reinforcements to Catus Decianus, the provincial procurator. With no intelligence on Boudicca's forces, Decianus failed to take seriously the idea that Iceni barbarians led by a woman could pose a serious military threat and sent only 200 soldiers, some of them poorly armed, to the defence of the capital.

Though Boudicca was illiterate, her spies inside the Camulodunum garrison left her better informed about Roman forces than Decianus was about the Iceni. Tacitus acknowledges that 'secret enemies' penetrated 'all the

---

* Cassius Dio writes of a large gold necklace but almost certainly means a torc, of which many examples have been discovered in former Iceni territory (200 of them in the 'Snettisham Treasure' on display in the British Museum and Norwich Castle).

deliberations' about the defence of the capital. By contrast, it did not occur to Roman commanders to recruit agents among the Iceni. Boudicca's forces overwhelmed Camulodunum, which was 'laid waste with fire and sword'.[25] A bronze head of the Emperor Claudius thought to have come from the temple dedicated to him in Camulodunum, which was destroyed by the Iceni, is now in the British Museum.[26] Boudicca moved on to burn down the Roman colonies at Londinium (London) and Verulamium (St Albans). For a time the survival of Roman rule in Britain seemed in doubt. Roman forces, however, regrouped, inflicted a crushing defeat on Boudicca at the 'Battle of Watling Street' (variously dated as AD 60 or 61)* and set up a series of garrison posts across Iceni territory which kept them better informed about the Iceni than before the rising. Boudicca disappeared from the scene and was said to have committed suicide. There were no further risings during the remaining three and a half centuries of Roman Britain.[27]

Like the Julio-Claudian dynasty, most subsequent Roman emperors paid more attention to intelligence affecting their personal security than that of the Empire. That intelligence, however, was poor. There were no adequate means of distinguishing between real threats and bogus conspiracies invented by credulous or mercenary *delatores*. Partly as a result, about three quarters of emperors were either assassinated or overthrown by pretenders to their thrones.[28]† The main responsibility for protecting the Emperor fell on the Praetorian Guard, founded by Augustus, a supposedly elite corps which enjoyed better pay and conditions than the rest of the army. In an attempt to secure their loyalty on the accession of a new emperor, the Guard was also given handsome bribes ineffectively disguised as bonuses. Claudius was particularly generous, giving praetorians a 'donative' five times their annual salary. Despite its privileges, however, the Guard was drawn into the sometimes homicidal politics of imperial Rome. Members of the Guard were involved in the assassination of Caligula as he left the Palatine games in AD 41, and in the subsequent murder of his wife and son. The Guard was also implicated in the intrigues which preceded the accessions of both Claudius and Nero.[29] So long as emperors could not rely on the loyalty of the Praetorian Guard, they could never be certain of their own security.

Praetorian plotting reached its nadir following the assassination of the Emperor Commodus in 192 as the result of a conspiracy involving the

---

* The exact location of the Battle of Watling Street is still disputed.
† No exact statistics are available on the number of assassinations. It is, for example, uncertain whether Claudius died from natural causes or was poisoned.

Praetorian Prefect. Though other members of the Guard were not involved in this assassination, they became embroiled in succession crises which produced three new emperors over the next six months. According to the historian Herodias, after killing the Emperor Pertinax, the Guard offered the throne to the highest bidder. The auction was won by Didius Julianus with an offer of 25,000 sesterces to each member of the Guard. Only two months later, however, he was decapitated by the general Septimius Severus, who then reigned as Emperor until 211. Severus also executed the praetorians who had assassinated Pertinax and dismissed the remainder. Henceforth, the Praetorian Guard differed little from the rest of the Roman army and spent more time away on campaign than stationed in Rome.* The mid-third-century crisis which brought to an end the 'golden age' of the Roman Empire dramatically demonstrated the lack of adequate security to protect the Emperor. The assassination of Alexander Severus by his own troops in 235 inaugurated a chaotic half-century in which over twenty claimants to the title of Emperor, mostly leading army generals, competed for control of all or part of the Empire.

The closest emperors came to establishing a corps of intelligence officers was their use of the *frumentarii*, who, as the name implies, had originally been responsible for the purchase and distribution of grain (*frumentum*) for the army. Because they travelled around so much of the Empire, they increasingly returned to Rome with information of interest to the imperial administration. Their intelligence role, probably chiefly prompted by emperors' desire for early warning of provincial threats to their authority, seems to date mainly from the early second century.[30]† Hadrian (117–38) was reported to have used *frumentarii* to spy even on his friends:

> He pried into all their secrets, and so skilfully that they were never aware that the Emperor was acquainted with their private lives until he revealed it himself . . . The wife of a certain man wrote to her husband, complaining that he was so preoccupied by pleasures and baths that he would not return home to her, and Hadrian found this out through his private agents. And so, when the husband asked for a furlough, Hadrian reproached him with his fondness for his baths and his pleasures. Whereupon the man exclaimed: 'What, did my wife write to you just what she wrote to me?'[31]

In addition to collecting intelligence from near and far, the *frumentarii*

---

* The Praetorian Guard was finally disbanded by the Emperor Constantine in 312 AD. (Bingham, *Praetorian Guard*, ch. 2.)
† Dating the point at which emperors began to use *frumentarii* for intelligence and police purposes is complicated by their continued connection with the grain supply.

also served as couriers, supply officers, tax collectors, police officers, even on occasion as clandestine assassins. One Roman history refers to a centurion of the *frumentarii* who was allegedly 'well known for killing senators'.[32] During the persecutions, they also hunted down Christians.[33] In the Greek-speaking part of the Roman Empire, *frumentarii* were often called 'revenue collectors' (*kollectiones*). In the Western Empire they were known as 'snoopers' (*curiosi*).[34] 'Snooping' and internal surveillance, as well as tax collection, unsurprisingly made the *frumentarii* widely unpopular. According to Aurelius Victor, 'by nefariously inventing false charges and instilling fear everywhere (especially in more remote areas), they shamefully plundered everything'.[35] An inscription in honour of a centurion *frumentarius* in the province of Asia praises him for failing to oppress his subjects – thus implying that he was an exception to the rule.[36] Complaints about the *frumentarii* led to their disbandment by the Emperor Diocletian, who replaced them by the blandly named 'general agents' (*agentes in rebus*), who performed much the same intelligence role. Unlike their predecessors, however, they were civilians, reporting to a newly established court official, the Minister of Offices. They were also more numerous, eventually numbering about 1,200[37] – about the same size as the British Security Service (MI5) in the early Cold War.[38]

Despite their desire for early warning of threats to their personal authority, successive emperors had little interest in what is now called strategic intelligence for the simple reason that they had no grand strategy. Mary Beard concludes that 'there was hardly any such thing as a general policy for running the empire or an overarching strategy of military deployment'.[39] Save for the imperial frontiers, by the late first century AD most of the Roman Empire was very lightly garrisoned because the prospect of serious rebellion was remote. Potential rebels within the Empire mostly realized they could not challenge Rome's overwhelming military might. Even during the chaos of the mid-third-century crisis, there were no serious revolts by Rome's subject peoples.[40] Intelligence on them was thus not a high priority.

The greatest policy change during the later Roman Empire was religious: the adoption of Christianity as the state religion by the Emperor Constantine in 312. Though Constantine tolerated unofficial pagan practice, he publicly denounced pagan sacrifice and divination by *haruspices* as 'foul pollution'.[41]* The period of almost a century between his conversion and the abolition of pagan rites by the Emperor Theodosius in 395 witnessed

* The oracles of Didyma and Zeus Philios (opened at Antioch under Maximin Daia, 305–13) had played a significant part in encouraging the persecution of Christians at the beginning

a protracted but ultimately unsuccessful struggle for survival by the oracles and professional diviners. Divination, traditionally a greater priority in Roman warfare than military intelligence, was made illegal in 357 and punishment prescribed for those who continued to practise it. According to pious Christian tradition, the Pythia at Delphi finally admitted defeat in verse during the reign of Julian the Apostate (360–63):

> Tell ye the king, the carven hall is fallen in decay;
> Apollo hath no chapel left, no prophesying bay,
> No talking spring. The stream is dry that had so much to say.*

The Pythia may yet have hoped to arrive at a compromise which would allow some continuing role for Apollo's sacred temple. When the proconsul of Greece complained to the Emperor Valentian (364–75) that the abolition of the ancient Mysteries 'would make life unbearable for the Greeks', the Emperor relented, but the reprieve was only temporary.[42] Though the end of centuries of official divination was not replaced by a new awareness of the importance of military intelligence, medieval generals in Christian Europe did not go on campaign with the coops of sacred chickens to provide auguries and the *haruspices* to examine the entrails of sacrificed animals which had encumbered their pagan Roman predecessors. Partly for that reason, espionage played a greater role in medieval than in ancient warfare. Spies were probably more numerous during the Hundred Years War a millennium after Constantine's conversion than they had ever been in the wars of the Greeks and Romans.†

Under Constantine the main centre of power in the Roman Empire moved from West to East: from Rome, a crumbling memorial to past glories, to a 'New Rome' on the Bosphorus named after its founder – Constantinople. For half a century after Constantine's death in 337, there were often two emperors ruling jointly, one in the East and the other in the West. In 395 the

---

of the fourth century. (Hornblower and Spawforth (eds.), *Oxford Companion to Classical Civilization*, p. 503.)

* Parke and Wormell (*The Delphic Oracle*, vol. 1, p. 290) regard the 'last utterance at Delphi' (quoted here in the twentieth-century translation of Sir William Marris) as probably authentic.

† Research on the role of espionage in medieval warfare is still a work in progress. Though Jonathan Sumption's unfinished multi-volume history of *The Hundred Years War* has discovered significant new source material on the use of spies, their organization and effectiveness remain unclear. Because of the sparsity of reliable sources, one of the most difficult areas of current research is the role of spies in the conquest of the huge Mongol Empire, which reached its peak in the thirteenth century. Because the Mongols lived off the land, as well as reconnoitring enemy defences they needed to know where to find water and pasture prior to invasion. Professor David Curtis Wright is researching the role of intelligence in the Mongol conquest of Song China.

empire was formally divided into two with separate emperors. In both West and East the Empire had become increasingly ethnically diverse. The Antonine Constitution of 212 had granted Roman citizenship to almost all inhabitants of the Empire (except, of course, for slaves). What brought down the Empire in the West was not internal collapse but external barbarian attack.*

Military intelligence on the Empire's barbarian borders improved little during the two centuries after the Battle of Teutoburg. Increasing Roman contact with the barbarians beyond the Rhine and Danube was combined with undiminished condescension to the *Untermenschen*. The deficiencies of military intelligence were starkly demonstrated by the incursions of the Goths across the Danube which took Rome by surprise during the 'mid-third-century crisis'. In AD 247, at the very moment when Rome was celebrating the thousandth anniversary of its supposed foundation by Romulus, the Goths laid waste to a great swathe of the Balkans. Barbarians had hitherto been thought incapable of organizing mayhem on this scale. Thereafter Rome sought to identify client tribal chiefs on the other side of its frontiers on the Rhine and Danube who were willing to make war against uncooperative tribes and maintain what Peter Sarris calls 'a pro-Roman balance of powerlessness' in the Germanic world. Submissive tribes could expect to be rewarded by subsidies and employment as allies (*foederati*) alongside Roman legions. Troublesome barbarians, by contrast, featured among the thousands gruesomely done to death each year in the Roman Colosseum and other places of imperial entertainment. To celebrate the pacification of the Rhine frontier in 306, Constantine ordered two captured Germanic kings to be fed to wild beasts in the arena at Trier.†

The most serious barbarian threat to the Empire to emerge during the fourth century came from the nomadic Huns from Central Asia.‡ The Romans had never heard of the Huns until reports reached their troops on the Danube early in the 370s of the arrival of savage warriors on horseback north of the Black Sea. In 372 the Huns crossed the Volga and rapidly overran the easternmost Germanic tribe, the Ostrogoths. Terrified of being similarly subjugated by the advancing Huns, their western neighbours, the Visigoths, previously settled in Dacia (in modern Romania), persuaded the

---

* The now dominant but still contested view that the barbarian invasions are the key to the understanding of the fall of the Roman Empire in the West emerged only in the nineteenth century. Its twentieth-century critics include Momigliano, 'Christianity and the Decline of the Roman Empire'.

† A total of about 200,000 people, many of them barbarian, met a violent death in the Rome Colosseum (completed in AD 80) alone. (Heather, *Fall of the Roman Empire*, ch. 2.)

‡ Where the nomadic Huns originated is still unclear; the possibilities range from Mongolia to Kazakhstan.

Romans in 376 to allow them to cross the Danube and take refuge in the Roman Empire.[43]* Despite the ability of the Huns to terrify even the warlike Goths, the Romans were curiously uncurious about them. Their lack of curiosity reflected the long-standing cultural contempt for all barbarians which over three centuries earlier had led to military disaster at Teutoburg and in Roman Britain. A later military manual of the Eastern Roman Empire was probably reflecting on the failures of the Western Empire as well as on Byzantine experience when it warned: 'Do not underestimate the barbarians, because they too have the power of wisdom, innate reason and cunning.'[44]

The Huns were illiterate and therefore left no written record of themselves. Only one, second-hand, Roman account of them in the late fourth century survives. The author, writing in about 390, was the leading Roman historian and former soldier Ammianus Marcellinus. Ammianus regarded the Huns as merely another variety of barbarian *Untermenschen* and was more concerned to pour scorn on their cultural depravity, physical ugliness and smelly clothes than to assess their military threat to the Empire:

> The Huns exceed any definition of savagery . . . They are so hideously ugly that they could be mistaken for two-legged beasts . . . They have no need of pleasant-tasting foods, but eat the roots of uncultivated plants and the half-raw flesh of all sorts of animals. This they place between their thighs and the backs of their horses and so warm it a little.
>
> . . . Once they have put on a tunic (which is drab-coloured), it is not changed or even taken off until it has been reduced to tatters by a long process of decay and falls apart bit by bit.
>
> Huns are not well adapted to battle on foot, but are almost glued to their horses, which are certainly hardy but are also ugly . . .
>
> Like unthinking animals, they are completely ignorant of the difference between right and wrong.[45]

Archaeological excavation has uncovered a number of large cooking cauldrons which Ammianus was confident the Huns did not possess. (His account, however, does contain some elements of truth. Today's *steak tartare* derives from the ancient practice by nomadic Tartars (and probably Huns) of consuming raw meat which they had kept under their saddles.[46]) Preoccupied by the Huns' contemptible barbarism, Ammianus failed, like the emperors in Rome and Constantinople, to grasp that they had emerged as the most dangerous attack force in Europe, combining 'rapid mobility with deadly firepower', 'able to shoot arrows repeatedly and accurately

* The Visigoths settled peaceably in what later became Aquitaine. (Davies, *Vanished Kingdoms*, ch. 1.)

from horseback'.[47] For over a half a century after they reached the Danube, however, the Huns' ability to mount a direct threat to Rome or Constantinople was limited by their lack of strong central leadership.

Until the accession of Attila in 434 the main direct threat to the Roman Empire came from the Goths* rather than the Huns. Ironically, the Romans themselves had increased the threat. Recent excavation of the fourth-century Visigoth village of Sobari, nearly 300 kilometres from the Roman frontier on the Danube, has uncovered 14,000 Roman terracotta roof tiles, sixteen colonnades and even some glass windows.[48] The flow of Roman money and goods across the Rhine and Danube 'led to the emergence of a warrior elite able to use their enhanced wealth and authority to draw ever larger numbers of warriors into their retinues and to cajole or coerce more and more of their inferiors and neighbours to acknowledge their overlordship'. Roman diplomacy in the frontier zone, which 'sought to identify useful clients among the tribes', contributed to the same process.[49]

The first major challenge to the cohesion of the Empire came from Visigoths who had been given refuge from the Huns in 376. Hopes that the Visigoths would become peaceful *foederati* were quickly dashed. Despite earlier trading and diplomatic contacts, the Eastern Emperor, Valens, was woefully ignorant of the strength of the forces at the command of the Visigoth leader, Fritigern. His ignorance derived both from the traditional Roman underestimation of culturally inferior barbarians and from the specific failings of his scouts (*exploratores*), who reported that Fritigern's forces numbered only 10,000, about one third the size of his own army.† Valens paid a heavy price for this intelligence failure in 378 at the Battle of Adrianople (present-day Edirne in European Turkey). Anxious to claim sole credit for the victory over Fritigern which he confidently expected, Valens decided not to await military support from Gratian, the Western Emperor. He also brushed aside Fritigern's offer of peace in return for the right of permanent settlement for the Visigoths within the Roman Empire. Valens discovered too late that Fritigern's army was as large as his own, better led and more battle-ready. According to Ammianus Marcellinus, who wrote the leading contemporary account of the battle, about two

---

* The geographic origins of the Goths remains disputed.

† Like other recent leading historians of the fall of the Roman Empire and the barbarian invasions, Christopher Kelly and Peter Heather briefly mention the inaccurate intelligence reaching Valens but do not discuss its source. Heather suggests that the inaccurate figure of 10,000 troops may have derived from 'the misconception that only Fritigern's Tervingi, and not the Tervingi and Greuthungi [another Goth tribe] combined'. (Heather, *The Fall of the Roman Empire*, loc. 2384. Kelly, *Attila the Hun*, [5].)

thirds of the Roman army were killed: 'No battle in our history except Cannae [in 216 BC] led to such a massacre.'[50]*

Adrianople was proof of how little the Romans, confident in their innate superiority over the barbarians, had improved their military intelligence since the founding of the Roman Empire four centuries before. No imperial commander equalled the grasp of intelligence shown by the two ablest generals of the Republic, Scipio Africanus during the Second Punic War and Julius Caesar during the Gallic Wars.[51] It seems not to have occurred to Ammianus, however, that lack of military intelligence was a prime cause of the disaster at Adrianople. Though tolerant of Christians, Ammianus was a pagan and blamed Valens less for his ignorance of Fritigern's forces than for failing to heed the bizarre portents observed by seers and augurs which had allegedly foretold both defeat and his death in battle:

> Dogs leaped back when wolves howled, night birds rang out a kind of doleful lament, the sun rose in gloom and dimmed the clear morning light . . . Furthermore, the ghostly form of the King of Armenia and the piteous shades of those who shortly before had been executed in connection with the fall of Theodorus [who had conspired against Valens], shrieking horrible songs at night, in the form of dirges, tormented many with dire terrors.[52]

Though fought in the East, the Battle of Adrianople had its most direct effect in the West, where it led to a huge influx of barbarians. The sack of Rome by another Visigoth leader, Alaric, in 410 marked the beginning of the end of the Western Empire. The last Western Emperor, Romulus Augustulus, was crowned in 475, not in Rome but in Ravenna, and deposed the following year. Instead of being assassinated like some of his predecessors, Romulus was simply pensioned off. The Western Emperor was by now an irrelevance. 'At the very end the western empire did not fall; it was simply declared redundant.'[53]

The most serious fifth-century threat to the Eastern Empire came from the Hunnic Empire, which at its peak stretched from the Ural river to the Rhine and from the Danube to the Baltic Sea. The threat increased after Attila became ruler of the Empire in 434 (initially as co-ruler with his elder brother, Bleda, whom he later had murdered) and for the first time provided strong central leadership. Much about Attila still remains mysterious. There is no contemporary description of his appearance and even the location of his capital has still to be discovered. By the beginning of the Attila era, however, the Huns had discovered that demanding regular tribute from prosperous communities was more profitable than mere pillaging, and were

---

* Estimates of the total size of the Roman army vary greatly.

running 'a protection racket on a grand scale'.[54] The Eastern Emperor, Theodosius II (408–50), knew little about the Huns until he became the chief victim of their protection racket. In 422 he agreed to pay them 350 pounds of gold a year, doubled by Attila in 439 to 700 pounds a year. War, however, broke out in 441 with massive Hunnic invasions of the Danubian provinces. After a series of defeats, Theodosius agreed in 447 to treble the gold payments to 2,100 pounds a year, with an additional 6,000 pounds to cover arrears. The historian Priscus of Panium denounced the cowardice towards the Huns of the Emperor and his generals which led them to accept these almost impossible demands for protection money: 'Once prosperous men were setting out their wives' jewellery and their furniture in the market place.'[55]

Theodosius and his chief advisers came to the conclusion that the best, if not the only, way to end Attila's escalating demand for huge amounts of gold as the price of peace was to assassinate him: an operation which necessitated the recruitment of a well-placed agent in his entourage. An apparent opportunity presented itself in the spring of 449 when Edekon, an envoy from Attila, arrived at the imperial court in Constantinople. He cut a strange figure in fur-lined cloak, leather jerkin and trousers (normally prohibited in the Emperor's presence) amid the silk robes of the courtiers. After prostrating himself in front of Theodosius and, in accordance with court ritual, kissing the hem of the Emperor's purple robe, he presented a letter from Attila containing various demands and complaints, and insisting that Theodosius send an envoy to respond to them. Edekon was then taken to another room for a meeting with the eunuch Chrysaphius, commander of the imperial bodyguard and *éminence grise* of Theodosius. Over a private dinner that evening, Chrysaphius, almost certainly with the approval of the Emperor, tried to persuade Edekon to lead a plot to assassinate Attila. By the end of the evening he believed that he had succeeded. According to Priscus: 'Chrysaphius said to Edekon that if he should . . . kill Attila and return to the Romans, he would live a prosperous life and would gain considerable wealth. Edekon promised to do so.' Edekon asked for fifty pounds of gold to win over Attila's bodyguard to the assassination plot. Chrysaphius promised to deliver the gold secretly to him at Attila's court when the time was right.[56]

Later in the year, as demanded by Attila, Theodosius sent a delegation (including Priscus) to his court, headed by a senior military staff officer, Maximinos, who appears to have been unaware of the assassination plot. Attila, however, had been told of the plot by Edekon, who had probably never intended to go ahead with it.[57] Shortly after Maximinos' mission, a more junior, Hunnic-speaking emissary from Constantinople named

Bigilas arrived at Attila's court to act as translator, bringing the fifty pounds of gold with which Edekon promised to bribe Attila's bodyguards. When the gold was discovered in his baggage, Bigilas confessed to the plot and was told to hand over another fifty pounds of gold – failing which his son would be executed.[58]

Attila responded to the assassination plot not by impaling the Roman delegation, as he was apt to do when seriously displeased, but by sending two Hun envoys, Orestes and Eslas, to Constantinople to humiliate Theodosius in front of his own court. According to Priscus, who was an eyewitness: '[Attila] instructed Orestes to go to the Emperor wearing around his neck the purse in which Bigilas placed the gold that was to be given to Edeco. He was to display it to the Emperor and the eunuch [Chrysaphius] and to ask if they recognized it.'[59] Eslas was instructed to tell the Emperor that, unlike Attila, he had demeaned his noble lineage. Since the following section of Priscus' history does not survive, we do not know how – or whether – Orestes and Eslas followed Attila's instructions.[60]

Attila died suddenly in 453 – not by assassination but during exuberant celebrations at the last of his many weddings, when he suffered what was probably a haemorrhage. Spies reported to the Eastern Emperor on the elaborate funeral that followed near the banks of the Danube. Attila's corpse was draped in oriental silks adorned with precious jewels which he had received as tribute from Roman emperors, then placed in three coffins. The innermost was covered in gold, the second in silver – both representing the plunder he had accumulated. The outer coffin of iron symbolized his victories in war. The tomb was filled with captured treasures and weapons. Horsemen circling the funeral intoned a dirge reported to Priscus by the spies:

> Attila the King,
> Chief of the Huns,
> Born of his father Mundiuch,
> Lord of the bravest tribes.
> He who captured cities,
> He who brought fear to the
> Romans and their empire . . .

Finally, the servants who had prepared Attila's tomb were killed to protect the secret of its location (which, at least in modern times, has never been discovered).[61]* Had the Roman spies keeping watch on the funeral been observed, they too would have been killed.

---

* Medieval grave-robbers may (or may not) have looted Attila's grave.

Though the secret operation devised by the Eastern Empire to assassinate Attila had ended in farce, the calculation behind it was rational. Attila was the first ruler to establish sufficient authority to hold the Hunnic Empire together and to harness its military resources for a direct challenge to the Roman Empire. With Attila out of the way, there was good reason to hope that Hunnic forces would fragment and end the threat to Constantinople. And so it came to pass after Attila's sudden death by natural causes in 453. His empire swiftly fell apart as his three sons fought among themselves. At a battle in 454 in what is now Slovenia, the divided Huns were routed by an alliance of some of their former subject peoples.[62]*

The attempt to use Edekon to kill Attila was the first (and last) recorded example of a Roman covert operation to assassinate a foreign head of state by recruiting an agent in the enemy camp. Though assassination had been part of the Chinese political tradition since before the unification of the Empire and was strongly recommended to the Mauryan dynasty in the Indian subcontinent by the *Arthashastra*,[63] the use of secret agents in the West to assassinate foreign rulers has been rare. None succeeded in Europe until, over a millennium after the end of the Roman Empire, King Philip II of Spain instigated the assassination of the Dutch leader, William I, Prince of Orange, in 1584.[64] During the twentieth-century Cold War, the attempts by the KGB (on Stalin's orders) to kill the Yugoslav leader, Marshal Tito,[65] and by the CIA (on the authority of Presidents Eisenhower and Kennedy) to assassinate Fidel Castro[66] were no more successful than the plot to kill Attila 1,500 years earlier.

* The exact location of the battle in Slovenia has yet to be identified.

6

Muhammad and the Rise
of Islamic Intelligence

Jesus' Kingdom, as he tried to explain to his disciples, was not of this world. Muhammad's was. Convinced, like Joshua when conquering the Promised Land, that he was doing the will of God, Muhammad established Muslim dominance in the Arabian Peninsula by force of arms as well as religious conversion. In total he fought twenty-seven battles and was responsible for about fifty armed raids. 'His achievements were of such greatness', writes a contemporary Muslim biographer, that after his death 'his followers were able to defeat the two most powerful empires of that time' – the Byzantine and the Persian.[1] As military commander, Muhammad paid close attention to intelligence collection. The Quran says of the plots of the enemies of Islam: 'Do they think that we do not hear their secrets and conspiracies? Yes indeed; our messengers are with them, recording.'[2] There are recurrent references in the Quran to the Arabic equivalent of terms such as 'intelligence', 'spy', 'agent', 'reconnaissance', 'scouting', 'deception' and 'dissembling'.[3]* Long before the birth of Islam, espionage was already a well-established tradition among the warring clans of the Arabian Peninsula.†

While the whole of Jesus' ministry was conducted in public, Muhammad's began in secret. In 610 Muhammad was a respected, though illiterate, forty-year-old merchant in the holy city of Mecca when he received his first divine revelation while sleeping in a mountain cave. Fearing that he was being attacked by a *jinn*, one of the fiery spirits who were believed to haunt the Arabian steppe, Muhammad ran down the

---

* The Quran also contains references to espionage similar to those in the Old Testament – among them the spies sent by Moses and Joshua into the land of Canaan, though Joshua, unlike Moses, is not identified by name.
† Though there are no reliable historical records of their conflicts, the celebrated anthology of Arabic poetry and prose from pre-Islamic times to the tenth century later compiled by Al-Asbahani includes tales of the attempts by tribes to uncover spies from their rivals in their midst.

mountainside in great distress to tell his first (and, at that time, only) wife, Khadijah bint Khuwaylid. Reassured by Khadijah, Muhammad began to realize that the message he had received came not from a *jinn* but from Allah, delivered by the angel Gabriel. It was followed by other messages and visions – and then by a two-year silence, which led Muhammad to fear that Allah had found him wanting and abandoned him. Then, 'by the morning hours, by the night when it is still', came God's assurance that He had chosen Muhammad as His Messenger, the last in a line of prophets which had included Abraham, Moses and Jesus, charged with teaching mankind to submit itself wholly to God's will. The words for both Islam, the religion inaugurated by Muhammad, and its Muslim adherents were derived from the Arabic verb *aslama*: total submission to another's will.

The first three years in the history of Islam were later known as the 'Secret Stage', when all Muhammad's movements and contacts with his followers were carried out clandestinely. Once the 'Open Stage' began, the Muslim campaign to convert fellow Arabs to the new faith faced vigorous opposition in Mecca from the pagan polytheists of the dominant Quraish tribe, to which Muhammad himself belonged. In 622 Muhammad narrowly escaped an assassination attempt in Mecca by the Quraish, whose leaders offered a reward of a hundred camel mares for his capture, dead or alive. While hiding from his would-be assassins in a cave near Mecca with his closest Companion, Abu Bakr, Muhammad used Abu Bakr's son Abdullah as a spy charged with mingling with the Quraish to try to discover their latest plans to assassinate him. On three successive nights Abdullah secretly visited the cave to report what he had learned. Then, after he reported that the hue and cry had died down, Muhammad fled by camel with Abu Bakr to Yathrib (now Medina), 200 miles north of Mecca, which became his home for the rest of his life.[4] For today's 1.6 billion Muslims (23 per cent of the world's population) Muhammad's flight to Medina (the *Hijrah*), whose timing was largely determined by the intelligence he received from Abdullah, was one of the major turning points in world history. The Muslim calendar dates from Muhammad's arrival in Medina.

As soon as Muhammad had established the first Islamic state in Medina, he and his military commanders began a campaign to overcome Meccan opposition by breaking the city's trading links with the outside world. Establishing an economic blockade required reliable intelligence on the movement of Meccan caravans. As well as instructing a surveillance team headed by his cousin, Abdullah ibn Jahsh, to monitor caravan routes, Muhammad also had an agent network inside Mecca which included non-Arabs who had secretly converted to Islam, non-Muslim relatives of the Muslims in Medina and non-Quraish who felt persecuted by the

Quraish majority. An Al Qaeda training manual discovered in 2011 eulogizes Muhammad's agent network as a model for militant jihadist espionage operations: 'The prophet – Allah bless and keep him – had local informants in Mecca who told him everything, big and small, that might harm the Muslims' welfare.'[5]

The head of the Mecca agent network was Muhammad's paternal uncle Abu Al-Fadl Al-Abbas, a wealthy merchant only a few years older than his nephew, who did not convert to Islam until about seven years after the *Hijrah*.[6] His wife, Umm Al-Fadl, however, claimed to be the second woman to become a Muslim, shortly after her close friend Khadijah, Muhammad's first wife. The strength of Umm Al-Fadl's personal concern for Muhammad is clear from the sacred Hadiths (sayings and deeds of the Prophet).[7] In one Hadith she recalled how, on one occasion before he left Mecca, 'some people who were with me differed about the Prophet (peace be upon him). Some said that he was fasting while others said that he was not fasting. So I sent a bowl full of milk to him while he was riding his camel, and he drank that milk.'[8] Once Muhammad moved to Medina, Umm Al-Fadl must have been anxious for him to be well informed about what the Quraish in Mecca were up to. As a wealthy merchant with a network of commercial contacts, her husband, Abu Al-Fadl Al-Abbas, was well placed to report on the movement of caravans to and from Mecca. Assisted by intelligence from the network, Muhammad's forces made several attacks on Meccan caravans in 623. These intelligence-led attacks are celebrated in the 2011 Al Qaeda training manual: 'The prophet – Allah bless and keep him – used informants in most of his attacks.'[9]

In March 624 Muhammad was informed by his intelligence sources that a caravan of 1,000 camels was making its way to Mecca from Syria, headed by the Quraish leader, Abu Sufyan, and sent a force of over 300 men to intercept it at the Badr oasis, 155 kilometres south-west of Medina. Before the battle at Badr, Muhammad's forces captured a black slave used by the Quraish as a water carrier, who was interrogated by some of the Companions about Abu Sufyan's whereabouts. The slave provided information about three other leading Quraish but said: 'I know nothing about Abu Sufyan.' He was then beaten by the Companions to persuade him to reveal what they supposed he knew about Abu Sufyan. When the beating stopped, however, the slave repeated that he knew nothing about him. The Companions then beat him again until he invented information about Abu Sufyan. Observing what was happening as he was finishing prayer before the coming Battle of Badr, Muhammad declared: 'By Allah in Whose control is my life, you beat him when he is telling the truth and you let him go when he tells you a lie.' Muhammad thus became the first religious leader to condemn brutality during interrogation not on ethical grounds (or not simply on ethical grounds), but because it was likely to produce bad intelligence.[10]

Despite the fact that the force sent from Mecca to protect the Quraish caravan at Badr outnumbered the Muslims, it broke and ran after a few hours' fighting, though the caravan itself escaped to Mecca. According to the Quran, Gabriel and thousands of angels descended from heaven to terrify the Quraish.[11] After the battle, according to a Hadith, Gabriel asked Muhammad how he rated his forces at Badr. The Prophet replied: 'As the best of the Muslims.' Gabriel added that the angels were also the best available.[12] While intelligence had played an important part in determining the planning of the battle, the Quran emphasizes that the outcome was determined by God and His Messenger's faithfulness in submitting to His will. Though the opposing human forces at Badr were small by the standards of the major battles in the history of warfare, it was a decisive victory. Defeat would have crushed what was then the only Muslim stronghold.

Muhammad's undercover agents were not simply used to collect intelligence. On a number of occasions he also instructed them to carry out assassinations.[13] Muhammad's best-known targets included two Jews who had written poetry ridiculing him and his divine message: Kab ibn Al-Ashraf and Abu Rafi, who were assassinated late in 624. The assassination squad chosen to kill Kab was led by Muhammad ibn Maslama, who asked the Prophet if, in order to carry out his mission, he could deceive Kab by telling him untruths. 'You may', replied Muhammad. After finding a pretext to visit Kab, Muhammad ibn Maslama pretended to admire his perfumed hair, declaring that he had 'never smelt a better scent than this'. Kab appeared flattered, boasting that he had 'the best Arab women who know how to use the high class of perfume'. 'Will you allow me to smell your head?', Muhammad ibn Maslama asked deferentially. Kab agreed. While Muhammad ibn Maslama was pretending to admire the perfume, he put Kab in a headlock and told the rest of the assassination team to knife him. 'So', the Hadith account concludes, 'they killed him and went to the Prophet and informed him.'[14]

Shortly afterwards, Muhammad sent a group of assassins, headed by Abdullah ibn Atik, to kill Abu Rafi. Once again the assassination plot was based on deception. Approaching Abu Rafi's castle by night, Abdullah succeeded in passing himself off as one of Abu Rafi's servants and was allowed in by the gatekeeper. In the darkness, Abdullah could not discover which room Abu Rafi was sleeping in, so shouted his name. 'Who is it?' replied Abu Rafi. Walking towards the sound of the voice, Abdullah struck Abu Rafi with his sword but, unable to see his target, failed to kill him.

Abdullah fled from the room, then returned, pretending to respond to Abu Rafi's cry for help and struck him a second time with his sword. This blow too failed to prove fatal. But, at the third attempt, Abdullah later recalled, 'I drove the point of my sword into his belly (and pressed it through) till it touched his back, and I realised I had killed him.' On his way out of the castle, however, Abdullah fell down a flight of stairs and broke his leg. Binding up the wound with his turban, he struggled home, presumably on a camel, with the help of the other members of the assassination squad. Once back in Medina, he and his Companions reported their success to Muhammad. 'Stretch out your leg', the Prophet told Abdullah. Muhammad rubbed the leg and it was miraculously healed.[15]

The most controversial killing allegedly ordered by Muhammad was of Asma bint Marwan, a woman in Medina who, like Kab and Abu Rafi, had composed poetry mocking the Prophet and his message, as well as allegedly inciting violence against him. On this occasion no undercover assassin was used, though the fact that the man who volunteered to kill her, Umayr ibn Adiy al-Khatmi, was blind made him one of history's most improbable assassins. Al-Khatmi crept into bint Marwan's house at night and plunged a knife into her chest as she lay sleeping with her children.[16]* The offence for which she, like Kab and Abu Rafi, was assassinated was not hurting Muhammad's feelings but blasphemy against the message which Allah had entrusted to him.

In 1989 the Iranian Shia leader, Ayatollah Khomeini, claimed to be following the example of Muhammad when he issued a fatwa calling for the killing of the British author Salman Rushdie and his publishers on the grounds that his novel *Satanic Verses* had insulted the Prophet and 'the sacred beliefs of Muslims'.† Khomeini's fatwa calling for the assassinations declared that 'whoever is killed in this cause will be a martyr'. This, he believed, was in accordance with the teachings of the Prophet.

---

* Ibn Ishaq was the first and most important of Muhammad's biographers, generally regarded as a reliable source by most Muslim theologians. The Quran contains only nine direct references to Muhammad, which identify him as the Messenger of Allah but provide no biographical detail. For this we are dependent on biographers (notably Ibn Ishaq) and the Hadiths.
† Though Khomeini encouraged 'all brave Muslims' to kill Rushdie if they had the opportunity to do so, the main assassination missions were entrusted to the Iranian Ministry of Intelligence and Security (MOIS). In 1992 the British Security Service (MI5) discovered that Mehdi Seyed Sadighi of the MOIS London station had been tasked with collecting operational intelligence to prepare for Rushdie's assassination. Sadighi was expelled, as was a second MOIS officer involved in the operation who operated undercover as an Iranian student in Britain. Other unsuccessful MOIS intelligence operations to target Rushdie continued intermittently for the rest of the decade. (Andrew, *Defence of the Realm*, pp. 800–801.)

Muhammad looked on those of his spies who were killed during secret missions as martyrs who, like those who died in battle, had earned a place in Paradise. Such was believed to be the fate in 628 of ten spies sent on a mission by the Prophet, led by Asim ibn Thabit, a veteran of the Battle of Badr, whose footsteps were tracked by members of the hostile Bani Lihyan tribe who discovered dates at one of their campsites which came from Medina. When the spies' hiding place was discovered, they were promised that their lives would be saved if they surrendered. Though three believed the promise and gave themselves up, they and the rest of the spies were killed. When the Quraish learned of Asim ibn Thabit's death, they sent men to mutilate his corpse. But, according to a Hadith, 'Allah sent a swarm of wasps to protect the dead body of Asim.' Thanks to divine revelation, Muhammad was able to announce the martyrdom of the spies to his followers on the day that they were killed.[17]

On a number of occasions, according to Hadiths, Muhammad's intelligence collection, like his military operations, benefited from divine assistance. The Prophet once instructed three of his followers to go on horseback 'till you reach Raudat-Khakh, where there is a pagan woman carrying a letter from Hatib ibn Abi Balta'ah [one of Muhammad's Companions] to the pagans of Mecca'. When they intercepted the woman riding a camel at Raudat-Khakh, she denied carrying a letter. 'Then', the three-man team later reported to Muhammad, 'we made her camel kneel down and we searched her, but we found no letter.' Convinced that Muhammad's intelligence about Hatib's letter must be correct, however, they had no doubt that the woman had hidden the letter in her clothes. 'Take out the letter', they told her. 'Otherwise we will strip you naked.' The woman then removed Hatib's letter from her underwear. When Muhammad was shown Hatib's letter, Umar, one of his Companions, told him: 'O Allah's Apostle! [Hatib] has betrayed Allah, His Apostle and the believers! Let me cut off his neck!' Muhammad refused and asked Hatib why he had written the letter. Hatib said he had written to the Quraish (probably about Muhammad's movements) to try to protect those of his family still living in Mecca. Muhammad spared Hatib's life because he had fought at the Battle of Badr.[18]

The struggle between Medina and Mecca continued for six years after the Battle of Badr. According to a well-known Hadith, Muhammad declared, like Sun Tzu a millennium earlier, that 'war is deception'.[19] His conquest of Mecca in 630 exemplified this maxim. Before beginning the conquest, Muhammad spread disinformation designed to persuade the Quraish that his forces were heading for Syria. During the final preparations for his assault on Mecca no one was allowed to enter or leave Medina. Even his force commanders were not told their destination until just before their departure.[20] Surprise contributed to the Muslims' success. When the Quraish leaders in Mecca finally realized the extent of the Muslim threat, they travelled by night for a meeting with Muhammad and were shocked on their arrival to see his army of 10,000 men prostrating themselves towards Mecca during morning prayer. On his return to Mecca, the main Quraish leader, Abu Sufyan, told his followers: 'Oh, Quraish, this is Muhammad who has come to you with a force you cannot resist!' Muhammad had promised to spare all who put themselves under Abu Sufyan's protection.

No religious leader, not even Jesus when he rode into Jerusalem on Passion Sunday less than a week before his crucifixion, has ever made such a dramatic entry into a holy city as Muhammad after the almost bloodless conquest of Mecca. He rode seven times round the Kaaba (Cube) in the city centre, the most sacred site in Islam, which Muslims believe was constructed by Abraham around a black stone (originally white) which had descended from Paradise. As Muhammad shouted 'Allahu Akhbar!', the words were taken up by the Muslim army and rang around the city. Then the Prophet destroyed one by one the statues of the pagan gods worshipped by the polytheists, exclaiming as he did so: 'The truth has come and falsehood has vanished away; surely falsehood is certain to vanish.'[21]

Immediately after the conquest of Mecca, some of the tribes elsewhere in the Arabian Peninsula converted to Islam and submitted to Muhammad's authority. Others resisted. The Bedouin Hawazin tribe, with its allies, assembled a force of 20,000 men to attack the Muslims. Muhammad, however, discovered their plans from his spies in the Hawazin camp. Hawazin spies found in the Muslim camp had some of their limbs amputated and were sent home to discourage their compatriots. At the Battle of Hunayn (apart from Badr, the only battle mentioned by name in the Quran), a fortnight after the conquest of Mecca, Muhammad won a great victory, capturing 24,000 enemy camels. As at Badr, according to the Quran, God sent in the angels: 'Allah did pour His calm on the Messenger and on the Believers, and sent down forces which ye saw not: He punished the Unbelievers; thus doth He reward those without Faith.'[22] When the Prophet died in 632, almost the whole of Arabia was under Muslim rule.

By the time Muhammad became God's Messenger, the authorities of the surviving Roman Empire in the East (known nowadays, though not to contemporaries, as Byzantium), with its capital in Constantinople, were better informed about the barbarians on their borders than they had ever been before the fall of the Western Empire. Byzantine writings show 'an intense curiosity' about, among others, Bulgarians, Croats, Czechs (or

Moravians), Hungarians and Serbs.[23] Since the fifth century the Byzantine emperors had had a 'Bureau of Barbarians' responsible for relations with them.* The late-sixth-century *Strategikon*, a celebrated manual on warfare attributed to the Emperor Maurice, contains a section on 'Characteristics and Tactics of Various Peoples', which contrasts the 'servile Persians', who 'obey their rulers out of fear', with 'the light-haired races [who] place great value on freedom'.[24] Byzantine military manuals also urged commanders to collect intelligence by all available means, including espionage by agents operating undercover as merchants and, where possible, 'secret friends' (agents-in-place) in the enemy camp.[25]

Byzantium had no 'secret friends' in Arabia and knew far less about the Arabs than it did about the barbarians and Persians to the north and east. Maurice's *Strategikon* contains no reference to Arabs. But even good intelligence could not have prepared Byzantium for the threat that faced it from Muhammad's successors. When Muhammad died in 632, writes Edward Luttwak, 'no reasonable person could have foreseen that the Roman empire that had possessed Syria, Egypt and all the lands between them for six centuries would lose every part of them by 646'.[26]

Under Muhammad's immediate successors, who took the title Caliph ('successor' or 'deputy'), the by now elderly Abu Bakr (632–4) and the puritanical Umar ibn al-Khattab (634–44), Arab armies overran most of the Middle East. They destroyed the thousand-year-old Persian Empire and reduced the Roman Empire to little more than a city-state around Constantinople. The Bedouin, who formed the basis of the Muslim armies, were born warriors, taught from an early age how to ride, wield a sword, use a bow and travel in difficult terrain. But it was Islam which inspired them for the first time to invade the world beyond the Arabian Peninsula. For the Arab armies who defeated the Roman and Persian Empires it was an article of faith that, whether they lived or died, God would reward them and punish their enemies. Both Arabic and non-Arabic sources agree that Muhammad preached a doctrine of Holy War (militant *jihad*) which promised Paradise to all who died for their faith.[27]

The irresistible force of the early Muslim onslaught is epitomized by the career of the greatest of the Muslim generals, Khalid ibn al-Walid, the 'Sword of Allah', one of the few generals never to lose a battle, who led the victorious armies in Iraq and Syria. Throughout the Muslim world, streets

---

* It has been argued, controversially, that the Bureau was an intelligence agency 'which gathered information from every source imaginable (even priests) and kept files on who was influential, who was susceptible to bribery, what a nation's historical roots were, what was likely to impress them, etc.' (Antonucci, 'War by Other Means'.)

are nowadays named in Khalid's honour. According to a venerable tradition, when Muhammad had his head shaved during his last pilgrimage, Khalid took some of Muhammad's hair and had it woven into a red cap which he always wore on campaign. The Prophet, he claimed, had told him: 'You will remain victorious as long as this is with you.'[28] Khalid also derived from the example of Muhammad a strong belief in military intelligence.

Though Khalid's leadership and the morale of his troops were the key to his victories, he also used intelligence as a 'force-multiplier'. The biography by the Pakistani military historian General A. I. Akram, the only historian to have studied on the spot all Khalid's known battlefields as well as researching the (sometimes contradictory) written sources, concludes that he paid 'special attention' to intelligence. Khalid took with him on campaign what would nowadays be called an intelligence staff, drawn from all the main regions in which he fought – Arabia, Iraq, Syria and Palestine. Their responsibilities covered intelligence collection, agent handling and regular briefing of Khalid.[29] According to Akram, the intelligence staff succeeded in recruiting agents within the Roman armies.[30] While no detailed evidence survives, good intelligence probably contributed to Khalid's great victory in 636 over larger Roman forces at the Battle of Yarmouk, which led to the end of Byzantine rule in Syria. The subsequent Arab victory over the Persian Empire at Qadisiyya, which opened the way to the Muslim conquest of Iraq, was assisted by the defection of large numbers of demoralized Persian troops.* Before the battle the Arabs gained a reputation for being 'adept at spying, sneaking into their opponents' camp, cutting their tent ropes and stealing their mounts to spread alarm among the enemy'.[31]

A twenty-first-century Al-Qaeda espionage training manual cites Khalid as a role model: 'Khalid Ibn Al-Walid – may Allah be pleased with him – used to take informants and spies with him in each of his wars against the Christian Orthodox. He chose them carefully and treated them well.'[32] Among the best-known of the sayings attributed to Khalid is his message to the Persian governor of Mesopotamia that Muslim forces 'love death, as you love life', a statement which currently appears on the Pakistan Defence website, among others.[33] The same claim is commonly made by twenty-first-century jihadists.[34] Osama bin Laden declared after 9/11: 'We love death. The United States loves life. That is the big difference between us.'[35]

Apart from Khalid, probably the most successful of the Muslim commanders under the first two caliphs was Amr ibn al-As, described by a

---

* The historical record of the Battle of Qadisiyya is confused. Until recently it was usually thought to have been fought in 636. Recent research indicates 640 as a more probable date.

leading British historian of Muslim expansion as 'the wily Odysseus of the early Islamic armies'.[36] Leading his forces from Arabia across the Sinai Peninsula, Amr conquered the predominantly Christian and non-Arab Egypt in under two years (639–41). Just as he was about to cross the Egyptian border in December 639, he saw a messenger galloping towards him, bringing a letter from Caliph Umar. Afraid that Umar was having second thoughts, Amr said that he would open the letter at the end of the day's march, by which time he would be inside Egypt. As he had feared, the letter contained instructions to return home. But, to his relief, the Caliph had added a postscript reading: 'If you receive this letter when you have already crossed into Egypt, then you may proceed. Allah will help you and I will send you any reinforcements you may need.'[37] Like Khalid, Amr used intelligence (which the enemy seems to have lacked) as a force-multiplier during the conquest of Egypt. As well as sending agents to spy out the enemy camp, he was reputed sometimes to do so in person.[38]

The last major target of the Arab armies in the Levant was Caesarea, the capital of Byzantine Palestine, which had the largest harbour in the eastern Mediterranean and was defended by a well-constructed city wall 2.5 kilometres long. Though the Arab armies led by Muhammad's brother-in-law Muawiyah ibn Abu Sufyan, who laid siege to the city, had good intelligence on the reinforcement of Roman forces defending Caesarea, it held out for several years.[39] According to the generally reliable later historian Al-Baladhuri, a Jewish agent named Yusef inside the city played a critical role in making possible the final conquest of Caesarea, probably in 641. In return for a promise of protection for his family, Yusef led the Arabs into Caesarea through a concealed water channel.[40] Twenty years later, the victorious Arab Muawiyah became first caliph of the Umayyad dynasty, with its capital in Damascus, conquered by Khalid, which ruled the entire Muslim world until 750.

The first Byzantine emperor to publicly identify Islam as a fundamental threat to the existence of Christianity within the Empire was Leo VI 'The Wise' (886–912).[41] The *Taktika*, a lengthy military manual attributed to Leo, recognized that what had made Muslim forces so dangerous since the seventh century was their warlike qualities: 'They are trained from childhood to live and die by the sword alone.'[42] But, because Leo dismissed Islam as blasphemous superstition, he attributed their martial ardour not to religious commitment but to temperament: 'Their temperament is hot because they dwell in such a hot climate.'[43] Byzantine generals were exhorted to 'keep an eye on [the Arabs] by means of trusted spies'.[44] 'Trusted spies', however, were in short supply – not least because Muslim agents working for non-Muslims were regarded not merely as traitors but also as apostates (as radical Islamists still insist they are in the twenty-first century). Leo's insistence on the necessity of military reconnaissance was more practical: 'Warfare is like hunting: wild animals are taken by scouting, by lying in wait, by circling around, and by other such stratagems rather than by force. And so we must accommodate ourselves to warfare by the same way, whether the enemy be few or many.'[45]

Though military intelligence was an integral part of Muhammad's way of warfare, Muslims under most circumstances were forbidden to spy on each other. The most frequently quoted reference in the Quran to 'spying' (*tajassus*) tells Muslims: 'O ye who believe! Avoid suspicion (as much as possible): for suspicion in some cases is a sin: and spy not on each other, nor speak ill of each other behind their backs.'[46] Believers were also told: 'Do not enter any houses except your own homes unless you are sure of their occupants' consent.'[47] Most Muslim rulers exempted themselves from these prohibitions in order to keep track of domestic dissidence. Key to the caliphs' system of government was the *Barid*, a messenger service which they used to communicate with the provinces. As in other pre-modern postal systems, people and horses were stationed at intervals along the various official routes to provide the messengers with food, water, shelter and fresh mounts. The Umayyad caliphs and their successors used the *Barid* to issue official orders and decrees to the provinces, which sent back confidential reports on the local state of affairs.[48] The bloodthirsty overthrow of the Umayyad dynasty in 750 was blamed by some Muslim authors writing soon afterwards on the lack of warning of growing opposition in *Barid* reports. One author writing on the *Barid* concluded: 'It used to be said: "No kingdom has ever lost its power except with the cessation of intelligence." It has reached me that the Umayyads lost power with the cessation of intelligence.'

In the opinion of another medieval Muslim commentator, the 'concealment of intelligence from [the Umayyads]', rather than their neglect of it, was the main reason for their demise.[49] The *Barid* reports, however, do not survive and it is possible that, as so often in modern history, the failure was one of intelligence analysis rather than collection. According to a number of Muslim writers, the late Umayyad caliphs neglected political intelligence, probably because they underestimated the threat from opposition to them.[50] The Umayyads paid a heavy price for this failure, whether of collection or analysis. Their last caliph, Marwan II, was killed in Egypt, fleeing from the rebel forces of the Abbasids, who claimed descent from one of Muhammad's uncles. The Umayyad dynasty met its end in one of the most grisly dinner parties of which historical record survives. Its last representatives were brought before the new Abbasid caliph, Abu'l Abbas

As-Saffah, and slaughtered in front of him. Their bodies were then laid at his feet, covered with a carpet and used as a banqueting table. 'And those who were present at the scene', it is said, 'ate while the death rattle still sounded in the throats of the expiring victims.'[51]

The early Abbasids, who moved the capital of the Muslim Empire from Damascus to Baghdad, used the *Barid* to a probably unprecedented degree as a means of internal surveillance. The second Abbasid caliph, Al-Mansur (754–75), was so obsessed with the intelligence he received from *Barid* reports that he was believed to have a magic mirror which revealed to him what was going on in the outside world.[52] Though the main priority of the *Barid* was to provide advance warning of uprisings, local postal chiefs also reported to the caliph on the peccadillos (or worse) of local governors. Al-Mansur was informed that Al-Mahdi (who later succeeded him as caliph) was spending too much money on poetry; another governor was reported to be distracted by frivolities from affairs of state.[53]

The greatest Arabic writer of the Abbasid caliphate, Al-Jahiz (776–868), had strong views on a range of topics, which included secrecy and the need to keep a close eye on civil servants. His books included *The Art of Keeping One's Mouth Shut* and *Against Civil Servants*. He died at the age of ninety-two, allegedly when a large pile of books in his library fell on top of him.[54] Al-Jahiz insisted that the caliph 'is obliged to pry into the secrets of those close to him as well as those of the general public. [The ruler] should always set his spies on them. Nothing is more important than this for the stability and steadfastness of his rule.'[55] The Abbasid caliphs seem to have agreed. A senior military commander during the reign of Al Mamun (813–33) advised the caliph's son that agent intelligence was of great importance in the government of Egypt:

> You must appoint in each hamlet a trusted agent who will keep you informed
> of how your representatives work and how they carry out their duties. Their
> letters to you will keep you abreast of developments and make you see things
> as though you were present with each of your rulers or representatives.[56]

Abu al-Faraj al-Isfahani, who compiled the celebrated tenth-century Arabic anthology and encyclopedia *Kitab al-Aghani* (Book of Songs), declared that the first priority of secret agents (*uyun*) was to safeguard the security of the caliph and his administration.[57]

Though Muhammad bequeathed to the Muslim world a tradition of warfare which attached importance to intelligence collection, none of the tradecraft used by him or the caliphs who succeeded him over the next three centuries seems to have been original. The first major Muslim intelligence innovation was a product of the golden age of Islamic science and

mathematics, which began in the ninth-century Baghdad academy of sciences known as the House of Wisdom. In present-day Baghdad nothing of
the House of Wisdom or other sumptuous Abbasid palaces remains. Unlike
the marble and stone monuments of Greece and Rome, they were built of
sun-dried mud bricks which have failed to survive the ravages of fire, flood
and invading armies. A thousand years ago, however, the now vanished
House of Wisdom was the world's leading centre of scientific and mathematical study and research. Its first great achievement was the translation
of foreign texts into Arabic. At a time when the works of Aristotle and
other great Greek writers were disappearing in Europe, they were being
preserved in Arabic, sometimes with newly composed commentaries.[58]

Thanks chiefly to the House of Wisdom, Arabic replaced Greek as the
main language of scientific research. Its leading physicist, Ibn al-Haytham,
has recently been hailed (controversially) as the greatest physicist during
the two millennia between Archimedes and Newton. The most famous
mathematician at the House of Wisdom, al-Khawarizmi, is nowadays
remembered as the father of algebra – a word derived from the title of his
book, *Kitab al-Jabr*.[59] The most prolific scholar was Yaqub ibn Ishaq
al-Kindi (*c*.800–873), a remarkable polymath known as 'the Philosopher
of the Arabs'. Few if any scholars have written on such a wide range of
subjects. Though only a fraction of al-Kindi's work survives, a tenth-
century bookseller's catalogue lists almost 300 titles by him. Al-Kindi
seems to have inspired jealousy among some less successful and prolific
scholars in the House of Wisdom. Two of his rivals succeeded in having
his library confiscated until they themselves became discredited and the
library was handed back.[60] Over forty of al-Kindi's books were devoted
to various aspects of philosophy, political philosophy, logic and ethics
(among them commentaries on Aristotle).[61] Al-Kindi's philosophical interests overlapped with theology. Mid-ninth-century Baghdad experienced
'an explosion of Islamic theological speculation'[62] in which he was actively
engaged. Probably in response to requests from the caliph's family and
other wealthy patrons, he also wrote mostly brief treatises on topics as
diverse as jewels, swords, perfume and stain removal. Apart from philosophy and theology, however, al-Kindi's main academic interests were
mathematics, science and medicine.[63]

Al-Kindi was the leading figure in the invention of what is now called
cryptanalysis, the science of decrypting ciphered messages without prior
knowledge of the cipher (popularly, if not quite accurately, known as codebreaking). The Abbasids' frequent use of ciphers to encrypt confidential
documents ranging from tax records to affairs of state made ninth-century
Baghdad the world's first centre of cryptography. Al-Kindi's seminal work,

A Manuscript on Deciphering Cryptographic Messages, which was probably allowed only limited circulation, was later lost and not rediscovered
until 1987, in Istanbul's Süleymaniye Ottoman Archive. Over half a millennium before any Western cryptanalyst, al-Kindi discovered the 'frequency'
principle, the fact that in every alphabet some letters are more frequently
used than others. In English and French, for example, the most common
letter is E, followed by T. The two commonest symbols in messages using
substitution ciphers are thus likely to represent these letters. Establishing
the frequency principle made it possible for the first time to break the kind
of ciphers used by Julius Caesar almost a millennium before.[64]

Al-Kindi's discovery was inspired by the work of Muslim theologians as
well as mathematicians. Most Muslim theologians believe that God's revelations to Muhammad were recorded in fragments by a variety of scribes
during his lifetime (though the Arabic alphabet in which the Quran was
written was simpler than today's), but it was left to the three caliphs who
succeeded him to assemble these fragments into the 114 chapters of the
Quran. To help establish the chronological order of the revelations, theologians counted the frequency of the words used in each. Revelations containing
words which had evolved relatively recently were thought to come late in the
chronological sequence. Before the publication of the three major collections
of Hadiths in the mid-ninth century, Muslim theologians also paid close
attention to etymology and sentence structure in their attempts to determine
authenticity (a topic which has given rise to some controversy among Muslim
scholars) by checking conformity to Muhammad's known vocabulary and
speech patterns. This research led for the first time to the identification of
the relative frequency with which the letters in the Arab alphabet were used –
the probable starting point for al-Kindi's invention of cryptanalysis.[65] No
other turning point in the history of intelligence owed as much to a combination of mathematical and theological research.*

---

* How far the Abbasids and other Muslim rulers used cryptanalysis remains unknown. No
evidence has yet emerged that the Abbasid dynasty set up a cryptanalytic agency similar to
the *cabinets noirs* established by some of the rulers of early modern Europe.

7

Inquisitions and Counter-Subversion

One of the defining characteristics of twentieth-century one-party states was the obsessive monitoring and repression by their security and intelligence services of what the KGB called 'ideological subversion' in order to protect their claims to a monopoly of political truth.[1] Some aspects of their counter-subversion campaigns were anticipated by the much smaller inquisitions of the Roman Catholic Church in medieval and early-modern Europe, though the subversion which the inquisitions sought to eradicate was, of course, religious rather than political. Organized counter-subversion requires both a developed bureaucracy and a capacity for record keeping which in the Middle Ages only the Church possessed. No secular medieval state could compete with the size and sophistication of the papal bureaucracy or with the network of papal legates across Christendom.

For almost 600 years after the fall of the Roman Empire, no heretics were executed in Western Europe. Not until the late twelfth century did the burning of heretics become a regular event.* From the thirteenth century onwards, inquisitions were one of the mechanisms by which the clerical hierarchy sought to enforce its monopoly of religious truth. The strengthening of the Papacy's authority over Catholic Christendom after getting the better of the 'Investiture Controversy' with the Holy Roman Empire had increased its determination to root out ideological subversion. Before the inquisitions came the 'Albigensian Crusade' against the heretical Cathars, who believed that, since the world was evil and God could not cause evil, the world must be the work of the Devil. On 14 January 1208 the Cistercian monk and papal legate Pierre de Castelnau was

---

* The first recorded medieval execution of heretics was the burning of sixteen at Orléans in 1022 on the orders of King Robert II of France. From 1028 to 1163 there were six further burnings of heretics in various parts of Western Europe. (Moore, *War on Heresy*, Prologue.)

knocked off his mule while preparing to cross the River Rhone, and fatally
wounded by an unidentified assailant who attacked him with his lance.
According to pious but plausible tradition, as Pierre de Castelnau lay
dying, he raised his arms heavenward and forgave his murderer.[2]

Pope Innocent III was much less forgiving and blamed the murder on
Raimon VI, Count of Toulouse, whom Pierre de Castelnau had excommunicated for failure to issue a public condemnation of (mostly Cathar)
heresy in his domain. Innocent proclaimed a crusade against the Count
and the heretics of Languedoc in what is now south-west France. The aim
of previous crusades had been to wrest the Holy Land from Muslim rule.
The Albigensian Crusade was the first in a Christian country waged
against other (albeit heretical) Christians. The crusade against heresy was
in part an intelligence war which required subterfuge to track down the
heretics. For the first time the Papacy explicitly sanctioned deception. In
dealing with heretics, Innocent III instructed his legates, in February
1209, 'deceit (*dolus*) should rather be called prudence.'[3] The theological
inspiration for the Pope's advocacy of deception came from St Bernard of
Clairvaux, founder of the Cistercian order to which de Castelnau had
belonged and which had become the dominant spiritual influence in Catholic Europe. St Bernard taught that Jesus had outwitted Satan with a holy
deception. By bringing about Christ's death, Satan had enabled him to
placate God the Father and so make possible the redemption of mankind.[4]
Innocent III believed that deceiving the heretics, who were necessarily
inspired by Satan, was also a holy deception. Heretics, the Pope told the
crusaders, were 'more evil' than the Muslims who had occupied the Holy
Land: 'Attack the followers of heresy even more fearlessly than the Sara-
cens.'[5] The early crusaders took him at his word.

After the citizens of Béziers refused to hand over alleged heretics in
their midst in July 1209, Arnaud Amalric, the papal legate then leading
the crusaders, informed Innocent III that 'divine vengeance raged miraculously' against the city: 'Our men spared no one, irrespective of rank, sex
and age, and put to the sword almost 20,000 people [probably an exag-
geration].' When asked by a crusader during the massacre how to
distinguish heretics from loyal Catholics, Arnaud Amalric replied, according to a later Cistercian writer: 'Kill them all! Surely the Lord will recognize
His own.'[6] There followed another twenty years of sporadic warfare.
Though there was no further war crime on the scale of the Béziers massacre, there were other episodes of horrendous cruelty. The crusaders'
capture of the town of Lavaur in 1211 was followed by the burning of 400
alleged Cathars on a gigantic funeral pyre constructed in a meadow –
probably the largest mass burning of heretics in the Middle Ages. The

Albigensian Crusade eventually ended in 1229 when Count Raimon VI's son, Raimon VII, swore submission to the Church and the French Crown, and surrendered over two thirds of his territory to King Louis IX.[7]

Henceforth the lead role in rooting out heresy was taken not by crusaders but by clerical inquisitions, initially concentrated on what remained of the Cathars in Languedoc.* Within a few years a majority of the main inquisitors were drawn from the recently founded Order of Preachers, better known as the Dominican Friars, who were thought best able both to convince heretics of the error of their ways and to dissuade the local populace from following their example. In a papal bull of 1233 Pope Gregory IX likened the Dominican inquisitors he despatched to France to Jesus' apostles.† The thirteenth-century Dominican inquisitor Humbert of Romans began each visitation by appealing to the local populace 'to help me to find and seize [the heretics], for which purpose I was sent'.[8]

The expertise of the Dominicans' inquisitorial bureaucracy grew so rapidly that during a total of 201 days in 1245–6 two Dominicans, Bernard de Caux and Jean de Saint-Pierre, with support staff, were able to question all male inhabitants aged fourteen or over and females aged twelve or over of the Lauragais region south-east of Toulouse (a total of 5,471 people) about their contacts with, or knowledge of, heretics. All were summoned to the abbey of Saint-Sernin in Toulouse, accompanied in almost all cases by their parish priests. No exceptions were allowed. Those questioned included lepers, the sick, the infirm and heavily pregnant women. Scribes translated their replies and those of witnesses into Latin. Some of those who claimed or feigned forgetfulness had their previous testimony to friar inquisitors read out. After the Latin record of their testimony had been read to them in the vernacular, all those questioned had to swear that they had told the truth.[9]‡ Probably no pre-twentieth-century security service was capable either of organized mass interrogation on this scale or of the elaborate record keeping it involved.[10]

The medieval inquisitions' hunt for heretics generated unprecedentedly large registers of suspects.§ In 1306 the Inquisitor of Carcassonne, Geoffroy d'Ablis, discovered from records kept by his predecessors that an

* The rest of Languedoc was finally annexed by France in 1271.
† Only a minority of the Dominicans became inquisitors. The majority remained chiefly concerned with preaching, teaching and pastoral care. (Ames, *Righteous Persecution*, p. 5; Ames, 'Does Inquisition Belong to Religious History?', p. 18.)
‡ This appears to have been the largest mass interrogation in the history of medieval inquisitions.
§ A number of serious riots provoked by the inquisitions had as their aim the destruction of the registers. (Sumption, *Albigensian Crusade*, loc. 3923.)

elderly inhabitant of Pézens had appeared before the Bishop of Carcassonne, accused of heresy, as far back as 1250.[11] In another instance, records showed that a female suspect in 1316 had first been arrested for heresy in 1268.[12] Inquisitors would sometimes intimidate a suspect by sitting with a pile of documents in front of them to give the impression they already knew so much that it would only make the predicament of the suspect worse if he or she tried to avoid revealing the truth. A twenty-first-century US interrogation manual recommends a similar 'file and dossier approach': 'The information is carefully arranged within a file to give the illusion that it contains more data than [is] actually there . . .'[13]

As in twentieth-century interrogations by the security services of one-party states, many of the questions put by medieval inquisitors were based on denunciations.* Though some of the hearsay in the denunciations now seems risible, at the time it could have serious consequences. The first question addressed to the suspected heretic Pierre Sabatier at his questioning in Pamiers in October 1318 was: 'Did you say that placing a consecrated candle in the anus of people during their death agonies was as much use as placing it in their mouth, as [is the practice] at present?' Sabatier insisted that this was a malicious slander spread long ago by his brother-in-law, who, before his death, had admitted the calumny and asked his forgiveness. He claimed that what he had actually said over twenty years earlier was that, in the case of someone dying in a state of mortal sin and therefore without hope of salvation, placing a consecrated candle in his mouth would do him no more good than a candle in the anus. Sabatier did, however, acknowledge that, while drunk, he had once said that priests were guilty of 'lies and buffoonery', an error of which, he insisted, he sincerely repented. Six months later Sabatier was freed from prison but required to wear on his clothing the yellow cross of the repentant heretic.[14] Harsh though this treatment now seems, a Soviet citizen who, seven centuries later, accused Communist Party officials in Stalin's Russia of 'lies and buffoonery' would not have been treated so leniently.

The growth and administrative efficiency of medieval Dominican inquisitions was not matched by their understanding of the heresy they sought to extirpate. According to pious thirteenth-century tradition, the evidence of the saintly virtues of the Friars' founder, St Dominic Guzman, included miracles which had occurred during his inquisitions. On one occasion, while St Dominic was preaching against heresy, a large, grotesque and

---

* Canon law traditionally attached considerable weight to reputation and notoriety as well as to first-hand evidence.

foul-smelling cat, presumably inspired by his sermon, was said to have leapt into the congregation and miraculously identified a Cathar.[15]

Though burnings of heretics at the stake were fewer than often supposed and carried out by the 'secular arm' rather than the Church, the Dominicans, almost from their foundation, bear much of the responsibility for them. The chronicle from 1229 to 1244 of the Dominican inquisitor in Toulouse, Guillaume Pelhisson (one of the few to survive), relates with pride the early Dominicans' instigation of a series of burnings of unrepentant heretics in the Toulouse area. He recounts, for example, that on 4 August 1234, the first feast day of their newly canonized founder, St Dominic, the Dominicans in Toulouse were about to dine with the bishop, Raymond du Falga de Miremont, a fellow Dominican who had just celebrated mass. Before the meal began, 'through the ministrations of Divine Providence and the merits of blessed Dominic', news arrived that the seriously ill mother-in-law of a prominent Cathar was being 'hereticated'* at a house nearby. The bishop and Dominican prior hastened to the house, where the bedridden old woman, mistaking them for fellow Cathars, admitted her heretical beliefs. When she refused to return to the Catholic fold, Bishop Raymond formally condemned her as a heretic in the presence of the local *viguier* (judge), representing secular justice. On the *viguier*'s orders, the woman was carried, still in her bed, to a nearby field, where she was burned on a bonfire. Bishop, prior and their fellow Dominicans then sat down to dinner, 'joyfully giving thanks to God and blessed Dominic' for this victory over heresy. Guillaume Pelhisson shared their joy: 'The Lord did this on the first feast of blessed Dominic, to the glory and praise of His name and that of His servant, blessed Dominic, and for the exaltation of the faith and the suppression of heretics and their belief.'[16]

Recent research suggests that much of the heresy that the medieval Papacy and its inquisitors denounced as Cathar was not Cathar at all,[17] just as many of the 'Trotskyists' liquidated during the Stalinist Terror seven centuries later had no connection with Leon Trotsky.[18] Because the medieval Papacy, like the twentieth-century Kremlin, refused to accept the legitimacy of any challenge to its ideological monopoly, its view of what heretics were up to in secret owed more to hostile caricature than to sober intelligence assessment. Both seized uncritically on reports which provided supposed evidence of the depravity of ideological subversives.

---

* What the Church denounced as 'heretication' was a purification ceremony usually administered to those near death by a *parfait* (Cathar minister) and known to Cathars as the *consolamentum*.

Heretics were, by definition, depraved. The inquisitors appointed by Gregory IX were charged with investigating 'heretical depravity'.

Though Gregory had a reputation as a distinguished lawyer, he was comically credulous in his response to some of the evidence of depravity presented to him. In 1233 he indignantly demanded action from the Archbishop of Mainz against a group of heretics who had been reported to him by a Dominican friar. The Pope appeared particularly shocked by the heretics' alleged initiation ceremonies at which initiates were required to kiss 'a sort of frog' or toad: 'Some bestow a kiss on his hind parts, others on his mouth, sucking the animal's tongue, and slaver. Sometimes the toad is of normal size, but at others it is as large as a goose or duck.' Next the initiate had to kiss 'a man of fearful pallor' with an emaciated body 'as cold as ice'. Then followed a banquet presided over by a black cat 'as large as a fair-sized dog', whose anus was kissed by the initiate and others present. Inevitably a sexual orgy followed.[19]* The Dominicans' second saint, the inquisitor Peter of Verona (also known as Peter the Martyr), declared that heresy was a form of diabolism. The Cathars were commonly accused, on no credible evidence, of sexual orgies, sodomy, incest and infanticide.[20]

Just as authentic Trotskyists had almost disappeared from Russia by the time of the Stalinist Terror, so few Cathars remained in southern France by the early fourteenth century. Six centuries apart, however, the Kremlin and the Papacy agreed that no trace of ideological subversion, however small, could be allowed to survive. The chairman of the KGB, Yuri Andropov (later Soviet leader), told a KGB conference in 1979: 'We simply do not have the right to permit the smallest miscalculation here, for in the political sphere any kind of ideological sabotage is directly or indirectly intended to create an opposition to our system . . .'[21] The medieval Papacy took the same attitude in the religious sphere. In 1318 the Bishop of Pamiers, Jacques Fournier, embarked on a lengthy inquisition designed to root out probably the last Languedoc remnants of the Cathar heresy in the Pyrenean mountain village of Montaillou. At intervals over the next seven years he presided over a total of 578 interrogations which, so far as is known, were the first designed not simply to identify the presence of heresy but to build up a detailed picture of the community in which it had taken root. The topics covered in villagers' responses to his questions ranged from the mundane (friends and relatives removing lice from each other's hair) to the spiritually incorrect (one of the curé's lovers arguing

---

* Though such fantasies had been common in popular culture, in Moore's view (*War on Heresy*, ch. 17) Gregory IX's letter to the Archbishop of Mainz, *Vox in Rama*, 'marks the reception into high culture of belief in the reality of such practices and phenomena'.

that her night of passion with him 'could not displease God'). Six and a half centuries later, the great French historian Emmanuel Le Roy Ladurie was able to use the records of Fournier's uniquely detailed interrogations as the basis for a history of Montaillou from 1294 to 1324, which provides the most intimate and revealing study ever written of everyday life in the Middle Ages.[22] Fournier's reputation for dealing a fatal blow to the Cathar heresy probably played a part in his election as Pope Benedict XII in 1334. He was both the first leader of an inquisition to become Pope and the last to do so for over two centuries.

Like many inquisitors and investigators of subversion in authoritarian regimes through the ages, Jacques Fournier was sometimes misled by bizarre conspiracy theories – among them rumours which swept France in 1321 that lepers were poisoning the water supply. King Philip V ('the Tall'), who believed the rumours, ordered that all lepers responsible should be burnt at the stake and their property forfeit. Among the victims of this conspiracy theory was the priest in charge of a leper colony in the diocese of Pamiers, Guillaume Agasse, who was a leper himself. In June 1321, Agasse confessed to Fournier after torture (rarely employed by Fournier) that lepers from his colony had gone to Toulouse to procure poisons to put in the wells, fountains and rivers of Pamiers so that those who drank the water would either die or become lepers. This plot, he claimed, involved leper colonies all over France. Probably to save himself from further torture, Agasse invented a grotesquely sacrilegious formula for the powder with which lepers supposedly planned to poison the water supply: the consecrated Host mixed with ground-up snakes, toads, lizards and human excrement.[23]*

The non-existent leper conspiracy of 1321 was also alleged to have been orchestrated by Jews. As R. I. Moore, one of the leading historians of medieval persecution, has noted, in the conspiracy theories of the age 'heretics, Jews and lepers were interchangeable': 'They had the same qualities, from the same source, and they presented the same threat: through them the Devil was at work to subvert the Christian order and bring the world to chaos.'[24] Jews who converted to Christianity, often through fear of persecution, and subsequently returned to their old faith were denounced in the records of Fournier's inquisition in terms such as 'dogs returning to their own vomit'.[25]

Philip V's nephew and successor, Philip VI (1328–50), was obsessed by anti-Semitic and other conspiracy theories. As Count of Anjou in 1321, he reported to Pope John XXII that a Jew named Bananias had written

---

* Following usual practice and no doubt fearing further torture, Agasse later confirmed the evidence he had given under torture.

to Muslim potentates agreeing to give them the city of Paris and the whole kingdom of France. In return the Muslims would give Jerusalem to the Jews. Absurd though the letter was, the Pope took it sufficiently seriously to include it in an encyclical.[26] Belief in homicidal plotting by Christian heretics, Jews and Muslims encouraged secular conspiracy theories about the English at the French court after the outbreak of the Hundred Years War in the 1330s. Philip VI fell prey to what the leading historian of the war, Jonathan Sumption, calls 'an extreme and irrational fear of conspirators and fifth columnists' supposedly working for the English. Among his delusions was the conviction that the princes of the Low Countries were plotting to poison his entire family. Those executed for imaginary acts of treason included the French garrison commander in Parcoul, who in 1337 was found guilty of indicating weak points in the town's defences with chalk and charcoal marks to show the English where to attack.[27]*

Save for the absence of references to the supernatural, some of the confessions forced out of the victims of Stalin's Terror by the Soviet NKVD six centuries later were no less absurd than those extracted from subjects of the French Crown during the fourteenth century. In 1937, for example, the NKVD uncovered an 'especially vicious' (and entirely fictitious) form of 'bacteriological subversion' which had killed hundreds of thousands of animals by infecting them with 'epidemic diseases'. The Politburo ordered show trials of the imaginary plotters in every republic and region of the Soviet Union.[28]

Unlike the highly centralized counter-subversion operations of Stalin's NKVD, there was never a unified medieval Inquisition. All inquisitions were ad hoc investigations carried out in specific regions, which reported to the Papacy and from time to time exchanged information with each other. Though the idea of a permanent centralized Inquisition based in Rome was first put forward in the thirteenth century, it did not come into existence until 1542.[29] The religious counter-subversion operations conducted by regional inquisitions bear some comparison with the secular operations of modern one-party states both in the priority which they accorded to rooting out heresy and in the investigative techniques which they employed. Both depended on large networks of informers, whose identity was concealed from those they incriminated. The obligation placed

---

* Though Philip VI's paranoid tendencies were exceptional, the Hundred Years War as a whole was marked by what Sumption calls 'growing fear of foreign spies and fifth columnists, an abiding characteristic of insecure societies at war' (Sumption, *Hundred Years War*, vol. 3, p. 289). Neither France nor England had any adequate means of distinguishing accurate from mistaken reports of foreign spies.

on medieval Catholics to 'persecute heretics according to their power' and report them promptly to the authorities was paralleled in Stalin's Russia by the obligation placed on Soviet citizens to denounce the ideological subversives in their midst. The Politburo declared in July 1936: 'The inalienable quality of every Bolshevik in current conditions must be to know how to discover an enemy of the Party, however well he is disguised.' Like those medieval Catholics who failed to report religious heretics, Soviet citizens who did not denounce alleged 'enemies of the people' were themselves suspected of heresy.[30] St Cyprian's maxim, 'Outside the Church there is no salvation' ('*Extra Ecclesiam nulla est salus*'), had a close parallel during the Soviet era in the doctrine that there was no political salvation outside the Party.

Like Stalinist show trials, the punishment of medieval heretics was intended as both deterrent and public education. To attract as many spectators as possible, burning heretics at the stake was usually carried out on public holidays. Ecclesiastical and secular notables from the surrounding region were invited to sit on a specially prepared catafalque while the inquisitor delivered a sermon, then read out sentences for heresy past and present in ascending order of severity. Those sentenced to execution were tied to posts above a pyre high enough for their death agonies to be visible to the crowd. The charred remains of the victims were then smashed into fragments by the executioners and thrown on a bonfire to try to ensure that as little as possible remained.[31] Surviving examples of the meticulous records kept by Languedoc inquisitions for the cost of executions show that the executioners were paid twenty sols for each of their victims, about 10 per cent less than the total cost of the stake, large logs, dry vines to start the fire and rope to bind the heretics.[32] At the burning of four heretics at Carcassonne in April 1323, the cost of wining and dining the assembled notables exceeded the wages and expenses of the executioners.[33] Though burnings were fewer in medieval England than on the Continent, the aim was the same. The English Act *De Heretico Comburendo* of 1401 laid down that relapsed heretics were to be surrendered to the secular arm and burnt 'before the people in a high place' in order that 'such punishment may strike fear into the minds of others, whereby no such wicked doctrine and heretical and erroneous opinions . . . be sustained or in any case suffered'.[34]*

Modern one-party states have sought to preserve their monopoly of the truth by control or censorship of the media as well as by repression of

---

* The number of heretics burnt at the stake in England during the fifteenth century was relatively small. Surviving records identify ten burnings for heresy between 1423 and 1503.

dissidents. The distant origins of modern media control lie in a tradition of ecclesiastical censorship which began to develop during the Middle Ages. The supposed threat posed by unorthodox or heretical writing greatly increased after the invention of movable-type printing in the 1440s, which some in the Roman Curia (the Church's central administration) regarded as the work of the Devil. By 1500 printing presses had already produced about twenty million volumes. They were crucial to the rapid spread of the Reformation after Martin Luther nailed his ninety-five theses challenging papal indulgences to the door of the Castle Church in Wittenberg on All Saints' Eve 1517. To deal with the challenges posed both by Protestant heresy and by internal Catholic dissent, in 1542 Pope Paul III founded the Roman Inquisition to establish centralized control over the investigation of heresy. Also known as the Holy Office, the Inquisition was the only Congregation (department) of the Roman Curia headed not by a prefect but by the Pope himself: Paul III attached such importance to it that for several years work on St Peter's Basilica was suspended so that its workmen could construct a new palace for the Inquisition.[35] The Roman Inquisition quickly attracted ambitious clerics. Among them was the Grand Inquisitor Antonio Ghislieri, who was elected Pope Pius V (1566–72). Later canonized, he became patron saint of the Roman Inquisition.[36]*

In 1543, a year after its foundation, the Holy Office extended its work of counter-subversion by issuing an edict forbidding the sale of 'erroneous, scandalous, seditious, suspicious and heretical works'. Initially, however, readers, customs officials and printers were left to identify which publications came into these categories. 'Intimidation', writes one historian, 'was thus combined with incompetence.'[37] Not till 1559 did the Holy Office produce its own Index of over 1,000 banned books and authors. But confusion continued. The creation in 1571 of a new Congregation for the Index of Prohibited Books did little to clear up the confusion. Good scholars such as the Jesuit theologian Robert Bellarmine (later canonized) worked alongside those whom Bellarmine's biographer calls 'the incompetents, boneheads and bunglers of the Index'. Among the books burned in Rome's Campo de' Fiori were unauthorized translations of the Bible into the vernacular.[38]†

In all authoritarian regimes, the machinery of censorship is doomed to become ridiculous. The combination of creative writing and counter-subversion leads inevitably to absurdity. The Holy Office led the way. The

---

* St Pius V's excommunications included that of Queen Elizabeth I of England in 1570.
† The most celebrated individual burned in the Campo de' Fiori was the allegedly heretical Giordano Bruno, Dominican friar, philosopher, mathematician, astrologer and astronomer.

works confiscated from the great French writer Michel de Montaigne on his arrival at Rome in 1580 included a number of books attacking heretics, on the eccentric grounds that, by naming the heretics they denounced, they made them better known. His celebrated *Essais* were also confiscated – despite the fact that they endorsed clerical censorship. Montaigne had written, probably tongue in cheek, 'The Catholic Church is right to prohibit the indiscriminate use of the Psalms of David.' To obtain approval for the publication of a revised version of the *Essais*, he thought it necessary to emphasize (though with barely disguised sarcasm) not merely his approval of censorship but his desire to 'acquiesce in the judgement of those competent to control not only my actions and writings but even my thoughts'.[39] Soviet writers, especially in the Stalin era, had to go further still and demonstrate their orthodoxy by regularly removing from new editions of their publications former role models who had been suddenly downgraded to the status of un-persons. Three successive Soviet intelligence chiefs – Genrikh Yagoda, Nikolai Yezhov and Lavrenti Beria – were executed for imaginary crimes (which included spying for Britain) and had therefore to be expunged from the historical record. After Beria's execution in 1953, subscribers to the *Great Soviet Encyclopedia* were told to use 'a small knife or razor blade' to remove the entry on him and replace it with an article on the Bering Sea.[40]

One of the main differences between counter-subversion in the Catholic Church and the later Soviet Union was the very different degree of central direction. Despite the establishment of the Holy Office in 1542, Rome never had the degree of centralized control over inquisitions in Catholic Christendom which Moscow exercised over counter-subversion in the Soviet Bloc established after the Second World War. After the beginning of the Reformation, the Roman Inquisition did not even take the initiative in the persecution of Protestants. Some Protestant states began executing Protestant 'heretics' (notably Anabaptists) at least fifteen years before the Roman Inquisition. In the decade from 1555 to 1564 the Holy Office was responsible for only about 2 per cent of Protestant executions in Catholic Christendom. Though the proportion increased during the pontificate of the former Grand Inquisitor, Pius V, the main priority of the Holy Office remained to deal with dissent within the Church rather than to persecute Protestants.*

The clearest example, before the founding of the Cheka (forerunner of

---

* Total numbers of Protestants executed for heresy declined from 882 in 1555–64 to 385 in 1566–72 to 52 in 1581–90. During these three periods the Roman Inquisition was responsible for, respectively, 15, 40 and 16 executions. A leading figure in the Counter-Reformation, Pius V was canonized in 1712. (Monter, 'The Roman Inquisition and Protestant Heresy Executions in 16th-Century Europe'. On the priorities of the Holy Office, see Godman, *Saint as Censor*.)

the KGB) six weeks after the Bolshevik Revolution, of the ability of a counter-subversion agency to enforce ideological uniformity was the role of the Inquisition in late-fifteenth- and sixteenth-century Spain. For much of the Middle Ages, Spain was the most multi-cultural part of Europe. Ferdinand III (later canonized), King of Castile from 1217 to 1252, despite his wars against Spain's Moorish (Muslim) kingdoms, called himself 'King of the Three Religions' (Christianity, Islam and Judaism). His tomb in Seville Cathedral is inscribed in the languages of all three faiths: Latin, Arabic and Hebrew, as well as an early form of Castilian.[41] Though the relationship between the three faiths was never one of equals, at a time when Jews were being expelled from England (1290), France (1306) and elsewhere, the 100,000 Jews in Spain were the world's largest Jewish community. When Ferdinand II of Aragon and Isabella I of Castile united the two crowns as joint rulers in 1474, both had Jewish doctors and financiers among their closest advisers.

However, two leading Spanish Dominicans, the royal confessor Tomás de Torquemada (later Spain's first Inquisitor General, of fearsome reputation) and the royal preacher Alonso de Hojeda, persuaded Ferdinand and Isabella that many Jewish converts to Christianity (*conversos*) were continuing to practise Judaism in secret and posed a serious threat to the integrity of the Church as well as the authority of the Crown. That belief led Ferdinand and Isabella to seek papal approval for a specifically Spanish Inquisition, established by papal bull of 1 November 1478. Pope Sixtus IV placed the Spanish Inquisition, unlike all other inquisitions elsewhere in Europe, under the control of the Crown, which for the first time had the lead role in rooting out heresy. The Spanish Inquisition became the only institution to hold authority in all the realms of the Spanish monarchy, later including the New World, thus offering the Crown the possibility of acting in provinces where its authority was limited.[42] The Spanish Inquisition was thus the first major state-controlled agency dedicated to counter-subversion – a significant milestone in the emergence of the security services of modern authoritarian regimes.

The Spanish Inquisition is nowadays best remembered for its ceremonial 'acts of faith' (*autos da fé*) at which repentant heretics were paraded in public and smaller numbers of lapsed and unrepentant heretics burnt at the stake. All six men and women executed at the first *auto da fé* at Seville in 1481 were *conversos* found guilty both of 'judaizing' (returning to the Jewish religion) and of conspiring against the Crown.[43] Though the main image bequeathed to posterity by the *autos da fé* was an almost carnival atmosphere more closely related to bullfights than to religious devotion, their principal purpose was usually to bring back as many heretics as possible into the fold through public as well as private penance. According to a contemporary account of the first *auto da fé* held at Toledo, in 1486, a procession of over 700 allegedly lapsed *conversos* were publicly 'reconciled' to the Church:

> With the bitter cold and the dishonour and disgrace they suffered from the great number of spectators (since a great many people from outlying districts had come to see them), they went along howling loudly and weeping and tearing out their hair, no doubt more for the dishonour they were suffering than for any offence they had committed against God. Thus they went in tribulation through the streets . . . until they came to the cathedral. At the door of the church were two chaplains who made the sign of the cross on each one's forehead, saying, 'Receive the sign of the cross, which you denied and lost through being deceived.'[44]*

The Spanish *autos da fé* were most brutal in their early years. About 2,000 heretics were burnt at the stake during the Inquisition's first half-century – probably three times as many as over the next century and a half. Another 15,000 were 'reconciled' to the Church.[45]

Like the security services in modern one-party states, the Spanish Inquisition greatly exaggerated the threat from ideological subversion. Its main priority, as at the first *auto da fé* in 1481, was to root out what it claimed were fraudulent or lapsed *conversos*. The population were told to watch for signs of subversive religious activity among their neighbours. A house chimney that did not smoke on Saturdays in winter, for example, might indicate that the household was observing the Jewish sabbath. In reality, it is unlikely that Spain contained a single congregation of *conversos* who practised Judaism together in secret. A mournful contemporary Jewish chronicler, whose words were echoed by others, wrote that, of the persecuted *conversos*, 'only a few of them died as Jews, and of these most were women'. The persecution created a climate of fear in which a minority of *conversos* sought to prove their own Catholic religious orthodoxy by denouncing others. A study of the Inquisition's campaign against lapsed *conversos* concludes that 'The majority seem to have been dragged before the court on the basis of neighbours' gossip, personal malice, communal prejudice and simple hearsay.'[46]

Ferdinand and Isabella, however, remained convinced that the *conversos* posed a serious threat both to the Catholic faith and to their own royal

---

* On this occasion the 'lapsed' *conversos* were spared execution, but forced to recant, fined one fifth of their property, permanently disqualified from office and forbidden to wear respectable clothes.

authority. Though anti-Semitism had some popular roots, the major influence on their decision in 1492 to expel from Spain all Jews who refused Christian baptism were alarmist reports from the Spanish Inquisition. In the words of King Ferdinand:

> The Holy Office of the Inquisition, seeing how some Christians are endangered by contact and communication with the Jews, has provided that the Jews be expelled from all our realms and territories, and has persuaded us to give our support and agreement to this, which we now do, because of our debts and obligations to the said Holy Office: and we do so despite the great harm to ourselves, seeking and preferring the salvation of souls above our own profit and that of individuals.[47]

For over forty years after the beginning of the Reformation, there was no significant Protestant challenge to the authority of the Catholic Church in Spain. Elsewhere in Europe, however, two of the main Protestant strongholds were in areas with strong dynastic links to Spain: the Holy Roman Empire and England. In 1516 the Holy Roman Emperor, Charles V, also became (the usually non-resident) King Charles I of Spain until he abdicated in favour of his son Philip II in 1556.* In the German-speaking lands of the Holy Roman Empire, Charles V lacked the authority to prevent the onward march of the Reformation in states with Protestant rulers. In the Low Countries (then the Habsburg Netherlands), which came under his direct rule, however, he, like Philip, was determined to root out heresy. Brought up to believe in the principle 'one faith, one king, one law', they and their advisers equated Protestantism with rebellion against the Habsburg monarchy. Charles V wrote after his abdication in 1556 that the pursuit of heresy 'has caused and still causes me more anxiety and pain than I can express', as well as taking a heavy toll on his health. He had been unable to establish in the Low Countries a strong centralized Inquisition on the Spanish model:

> I wanted to introduce an Inquisition to punish the heresies that some people had caught from neighbouring Germany and England, and even France. Everyone opposed this on the grounds that there were no Jews [the chief target of the Spanish Inquisition] among them. Finally an order was issued declaring that all people of whatever state and condition who came under certain specified [heretical] categories were to be *ipso facto* burnt and their goods confiscated. Necessity obliged me to act in this way.[48]

---

* Philip became ruler of Spain, its overseas empire and the Low Countries. Charles V's younger brother, Ferdinand, became Holy Roman Emperor.

Many heretics were sentenced to death in secular courts rather than after trial by inquisitors, who in the Habsburg Netherlands owed loyalty to both Pope and Emperor. Only in Flanders did the Inquisition, acting more or less independently of secular courts, become a major force in the prosecution of heresy. But, as Philip II acknowledged, despite the lack of a centralized management, the pursuit of heresy in the Netherlands 'was more pitiless than that of Spain'. At least 1,300 heretics were burned at the stake in the Low Countries between 1523 and 1566 – over two thirds of the total number of European Protestants executed for their faith during this period.[49] The burnings failed, however, to establish Catholic ortho- doxy throughout the Netherlands. In 1566 the seven, by then predominantly Protestant, United Provinces began a long, ultimately successful, struggle for independence which led to the establishment of the Dutch Republic.

The other mid-sixteenth-century state most notorious for burning Prot- estants was England during the reign of the Catholic Queen Mary (1553–8). In 1554 Mary married Philip of Spain (who continued to spend most of his time in his home country). Her zeal in pursuing heresy required no encouragement from Philip; like her absent husband, she saw Protestant- ism as a political as well as a religious threat. John Hopton, Bishop of Norwich, accused English Evangelicals of seeking to subvert the authority of the monarchy as well as of the Church. He told one of those condemned to the stake that he had sought 'to pluck the king's and the queen's majes- ties out of their royal seats through thy disobedience, in showing thyself an open enemy unto God's laws'.[50] The 280 Protestants burnt at the stake between 1555 and 1558 were greater in number than those executed any- where else in Europe during these years and greater too than the total of all previous heretics burnt at the stake in England. There was, however, no English Inquisition – further evidence, as in the Netherlands, that a zealous ruler determined to burn Protestants did not require the assistance of professional inquisitors.

As in the Low Countries, the burnings in England failed to achieve their aim. For centuries to come the reputation of Catholicism in England was stained by the memory of 'Bloody Mary', and the blood of the Prot- estant martyrs became one of the foundations of the Elizabethan Church of England. Among the best-remembered last words in English history were those of the former bishop, Hugh Latimer, who said to his fellow reformer, Thomas Ridley, as they were about to be burnt at the stake in Oxford in 1555: 'Be of good cheer, Master Ridley. We shall this day light such a candle, by God's grace, in England, as I trust shall never be put out.' Even a hostile Catholic chronicler who recorded the burning on the same spot for Protestant heresy, in 1556, of Mary's first Archbishop of

Canterbury, Thomas Cranmer, was moved by the courage with which he placed the hand which had earlier signed a recantation into the flames. If only Cranmer had died for the true religion, he lamented, 'I could worthily have commended the example, and matched it with the fame of any father of ancient time.'[51]

Until 1558, wrote a Spanish Dominican, 'Spain was untouched' by the heresies present in Marian England and the Habsburg Netherlands. In that year, however, Protestant groups, some with noble membership, were discovered by the Inquisition in Spain's two main cities, Seville and Valladolid. The first major *auto da fé* to burn Protestants (fourteen of them) was held at Valladolid on 21 May 1559 in the presence of Philip II's sister Juana (regent during his brief absence in England) and the royal court. The next was held on 8 October, also at Valladolid, in the presence of King Philip, who had returned to Spain. Twelve Protestants, including four nuns, died at the stake. The final words of the leader of the Valladolid Protestants, Carlos de Seso, who, like Cranmer, withdrew an earlier recantation, were as moving and magnificent as Latimer's: 'In Jesus Christ alone do I hope, Him alone I trust and adore, and placing my unworthy hand in His sacred side I go through the virtue of His blood to enjoy the promises that He has made to His chosen.' But de Seso's words did not echo through Spanish history as Latimer's did through English history, because no Protestant church survived the Inquisition. Four further *autos da fé* followed at Seville over the next three years. 'With these burnings', writes Henry Kamen, 'native Protestantism was almost totally extinguished in Spain.' 'Had there been no Inquisition', said Philip II, 'there would be many more heretics, and the country would be much afflicted, as are those where there is no Inquisition as in Spain.'[52] The success of the Spanish Inquisition in rooting out the practice of both Judaism and Protestant Christianity in Spain* provides depressing evidence of the ability of a strong authoritarian government with a powerful, centralized counter-subversive agency to marginalize attempts to challenge its monopoly of religious or political truth. That ability was demonstrated in even greater degree by the much more powerful one-party states of the twentieth century which possessed far more pervasive security services.[53]

The first history of inquisitions was written by the Spanish Dominican

---

* Helen Rawlings argues that the Inquisition 'successfully prevented Protestantism from establishing a native root in Spain' (Rawlings, *Spanish Inquisition*, p. 106). Kamen argues, perhaps less plausibly, given the enthusiastic Spanish following in the 1520s for Erasmian humanism before it was persecuted by the Inquisition, that, even without persecution, Protestantism would have failed to take root in Spain. Since the question of what would have happened without the Inquisition is counter-factual, there can be no definitive answer.

Luis de Páramo, doctor of theology, Canon of Leon and Inquisitor of Spanish-ruled Sicily from 1584 to 1605.[54] His three-volume *De origine et progressu officii sanctae Inquisitionis* ('On the origins and development of the office of the holy Inquisition') was published in Madrid in 1598 while he was based at the court of Philip II, who contributed an approving preface just before his death. Páramo was the first to claim to identify both the first inquisitor and the location of the first inquisition, which he asserted took place in the Garden of Eden after Adam and Eve had eaten the forbidden fruit of the tree of the knowledge of good and evil. God Himself was the first inquisitor. While God, in the words of the Authorized Version of the Book of Genesis, was 'walking in the garden in the cool of the day', Adam and Eve 'hid themselves from the presence of the Lord God amongst the trees of the garden. And the Lord God called unto Adam, and said unto him, Where art thou?' This, according to Páramo, was the first question asked by an inquisitor. In response to God's next question, Adam admitted that Eve and he had eaten the forbidden fruit. God then expelled them from Eden. Páramo compares the animal skins given by God to Adam and Eve to wear after their expulsion to the garment bearing the sign of the cross given by inquisitors to repentant heretics. His other most remarkable revelation was that Jesus Christ was 'the first Inquisitor under the Evangelical law'. Páramo demonstrates to his own satisfaction and that of the august sponsors of his history that John the Baptist and the apostles were also inquisitors. An *Approbatio* in his book written by the theologian Pedro López de Montoya certifies that it contains 'nothing adverse to the Catholic faith or good morals'.[55]

One of the long-term legacies of the Spanish Inquisition was its interrogation methods. The most controversial 'enhanced interrogation' technique used by twenty-first-century CIA interrogators to obtain intelligence from captured senior Al Qaeda personnel in the aftermath of 9/11 was 'waterboarding', a form of simulated drowning which half a millennium earlier had been used by the Spanish Inquisition in the New World as well as in Spain.[56] US forces became acquainted with waterboarding in the Philippines after the Spanish–American War of 1898 and used it to suppress a Filipino insurgency.[57] William Howard Taft, governor of the Philippines from 1901 to 1904 and later the only man ever to serve, successively, as both US President and Chief Justice, accepted its use.* So did President George W. Bush a century later, after it was declared legal by Department of Justice and CIA lawyers: 'Had I not authorized

---

* A drawing on the front cover of *Life* magazine (22 May 1902) showed US troops administering the 'water cure' (waterboarding).

waterboarding on senior al Qaeda leaders, I would have had to accept a greater risk that the country would be attacked. In the wake of 9/11, that was a risk I was unwilling to take.' Bush, who appears to have no idea that he authorized a practice made infamous by the Spanish Inquisition, is convinced that waterboarding is not torture: 'No doubt the procedure was tough, but medical experts assured the CIA that it did no lasting harm.'[58] The Spanish Inquisition knew better. It regarded waterboarding as a form of torture. Those on whom it has been practised in the twentieth and twenty-first centuries have no doubt that assessment was correct.[59]

8

Renaissance Venice and the Rise of Western Intelligence

Renaissance Venice was obsessed with secrets and secrecy. The oath taken by members of the Council of Ten, which was responsible for security and much else in the 'Most Serene Republic',* was 'Swear, forswear and do not reveal the secret' (*'jura, perjura, secretum proderi noli'*). 'Let it not be written down' (*'non scribatur'*) was a common instruction in official records. Government archives were so secret that even the Venetian Doge (duke and chief magistrate, elected for life) could not consult them except in the presence of an official. By tradition, the custodian of the archives was illiterate to prevent his reading their contents. The (probably mythical) story was told of a custodian who was caught scribbling on a piece of paper. 'So you *can* write!' said the Doge. 'No, Your Excellency', replied the custodian, 'I am doing a drawing.'[1] Doges cultivated an air of inscrutability, as in Bellini's famous portrait of the early sixteenth-century Doge Leonardo Loredan. It was said of one doge that 'one never knows whether he loves or hates anything'.[2]

In 1481 the Council of Ten forbade all members of the Senate, Colleges and secret Councils of State to have any contact with ambassadors and other foreigners not employed by the Venetian state, and ordered them to report immediately any foreign approach – failing which, they were to be exiled for two years and fined 1,000 ducats: 'Of this penalty, half shall go to the accuser whose identity shall be kept secret, and the other half to the treasury of this Council [of Ten].'[3]† Those found guilty of revealing official secrets risked the death sentence. One morning in March 1498, while crossing the Piazza San Marco, the Venetian diarist and historian Marin

---

* In reality, the Council of Ten had seventeen members. In addition to the ten who gave it its name, there were six ducal councillors and the Doge as chairman. (Iordanou, 'What News on the Rialto?', p. 320.)

† This decree reflected the Council's obsessive secrecy rather than any recent threats to state security caused by the Venetian ruling class's contacts with foreigners. As the decree acknowledged, the most recent threats to have come to the Council's attention were 'some time ago'.

Sanudo was startled to see the body of a seventy-year-old Chancery secretary, Antonio di Lando, hanging from a gallows erected on the traditional
execution site between the columns of St Mark and St Theodore:

> All the city marvelled because nobody had known anything about it, and
> he was hanged in his long-sleeved official gown, and at night. And the truth
> of the matter is that this was for having revealed secrets to one Zuan Battista
> Trevisan, who was formerly in the Chancery but had been dismissed and
> was virtually a secretary to the Marquis of Mantua.

Di Lando's downfall began when his mistress discovered his illicit dealings
with Trevisan. In order to obtain evidence against him, she asked another
lover to hide under her bed while she had sex with di Lando and then
persuaded him to talk about his disclosure of official secrets. The lover
reported what he had overheard to the authorities, presumably claimed
his 500 ducat reward (almost three times di Lando's annual salary), and
probably shared it with di Lando's mistress. Convicted by the evidence
collected beneath his mistress's bed, di Lando was subjected to a brutal
night-time execution. The hangmen had mislaid their rope and, since the
shops were shut, could not purchase a new one. The rope which they
eventually obtained from the Arsenal snapped during the hanging. Di
Lando fell to the ground, breaking an arm, but was hanged from the scaffold in the Piazza San Marco at the second attempt.[4]

The Most Serene Republic's obsession with secrets and secrecy derived
from its role as the greatest trading empire of the Middle Ages. Venice
became rich by buying high-value, low-volume goods, especially spices
and luxury articles, in the East and selling them at a large profit in European markets. Marco Polo, who probably spent over twenty years in
China, was merely the most celebrated of the thousands of medieval Venetian merchants who made their fortunes in this way. Spices have nowadays
become so cheap that it is difficult to remember that in the Middle Ages
black pepper from India and south-east Asia, used not merely for enhanc-
ing flavour but also for disguising food well past its sell-by date, was worth
its weight in silver (if not gold). Venice's mercantile success depended on
protecting its own commercial secrets and covertly obtaining those of its
rivals and trading partners. There are numerous accounts in Venice's great
Archivio Centrale, next to the Frari church, of clandestine missions sent
abroad to report on new techniques for, among others, textile, cannon,
mirror and porcelain production.[5]

Like its commercial intelligence, Venice's leading role in political-
intelligence collection derived from its medieval mercantile empire. Its
colonies along the Adriatic coast, in the Aegean and in the Mediterranean,

as well as its trading communities in Constantinople, Alexandria, Acre, Beirut, Aleppo and further afield, sent back to Venice political as well as commercial intelligence.[6] The Archivio Centrale contains the greatest medieval and Renaissance archive assembled by a single city. 'By 1450', wrote the historian and Bletchley Park veteran Sir Jack Plumb, 'Venice was the only power in Italy, save for the Papacy, that was truly cosmopolitan, one whose interests required not only a great fleet but also a complex intelligence system.'[7]* The broad horizons of Renaissance Venice at the height of its power are epitomized by the *Mappa Mundi* completed in about 1450 by Fra Mauro, a monk on the island of Murano in the Venetian Lagoon who had a previous career as a merchant and soldier, and a team of assistants. The most detailed and accurate (as well as probably the largest) world map yet produced, it incorporated over 3,000 descriptions of places together with hundreds of illustrations.[8]

Venice, followed by other states in Renaissance Europe, gained a world lead in intelligence which encountered no serious challenge until American independence. At the heart of the growing interest in intelligence by Renaissance governments and elites was a greater intellectual curiosity than ever before in European history, stimulated by the rediscovery of lost classical texts. These in turn became the basis of Renaissance humanism, whose ideas were spread with unprecedented speed by the printing revolution of the later fifteenth century. 'Merciful God', wrote the great humanist Desiderius Erasmus in 1517, 'what a world I see dawning! Why cannot I grow young again?'[9] Simultaneously, the 'Age of Discovery', which had started in the 1490s, provoked a curiosity about the outside world matched by no other culture. European mapmakers began to include empty spaces to indicate how much of the world still remained to be discovered. Unlike Fra Mauro's crowded *Mappa Mundi* and most maps produced by non-European cultures in the sixteenth century, the Salviati World Map of 1525, presented by Emperor Charles V to the Papal Legate Cardinal Giovanni Salviati, includes some of the coastline of the New World discovered since Columbus's first voyage in 1492, but is otherwise mostly empty.[10] Though the Ottomans produced operational maps of their military and naval targets (some incorporating intelligence from spies),†

---

* Plumb's years at Bletchley Park had given him a greater understanding of the significance of intelligence than most historians of Renaissance Italy, many of whom do not mention it.
† Before the invasion of Cyprus in 1570, the Ottomans had detailed plans obtained by spies of the defences of Famagusta, by far the best-fortified Cypriot city, which fell to them after an eleven-month siege. (Gürkan, 'Espionage in the 16th-Century Mediterranean', pp. 69–70.)

few had any interest in the New World.* In China the first map to show America was produced in 1602, not by a Chinese cartographer but by a Jesuit missionary.[11]†

Though firing Renaissance imaginations and changing European map-making, the Age of Discovery brought to an end Venetian mercantile supremacy. Two years after the first sea journey from Europe to India around the Cape of Good Hope, in 1498–9 by the Portuguese explorer and navigator Vasco da Gama, a Venetian agent in Lisbon reported that Portugal had begun to import spices directly from India by sea. Under pressure from the Rialto merchants, an official mission was sent from Venice to Lisbon to determine the extent of the trade. It returned with bad news. The celebrated Venetian diarist Girolamo Priuli records that, though Vasco da Gama's voyage led to 'the greatest celebrations' in Lisbon, it caused 'the greatest melancholy and distress' in Venice.[12] Within a decade the Portuguese controlled the spice trade on the Malabar coast of India and Ceylon. The 'Age of Discovery' in the Indian Ocean passed Venice by. So did transatlantic trade with the New World.‡

Within Europe, however, Venice retained its lead in diplomatic and political intelligence throughout the Renaissance. Hitherto, ambassadors had been used only for specific missions. To keep a close eye on their rivals, however, the city-states in Renaissance Italy established a new system of resident ambassadors which later became the model for European diplomacy.[13] Most ambassadors were expected to collect intelligence as well as to represent their governments. The fact that they were now based in, and not mere visitors to, foreign capitals made it easier for them to recruit spies. Andrea Spinola's sixteenth-century *Dizionario filosofico-politico-storico* asserts: 'Spying on the designs and secrets of princes is the proper business of ambassadors . . .'[14]

* A rare exception to the Ottoman lack of interest in the New World was Ahmed Muhiddin Piri (better known as Piri Reis), a privateer with an interest in cartography who became a captain in the Ottoman fleet. In 1513 he prepared a world map which included the New World and drew, he claimed, on European maps, including one by Columbus which has not survived. In 1553, then an admiral, probably in his mid-eighties, Piri was executed. (McIntosh, *Piri Reis Map of 1513*.)

† In 2006 a copy surfaced of a Chinese map of (allegedly) 1418 showing that the great Chinese admiral Zheng He sailed around the world a century before Columbus. It shows the continents of North and South America with detail which includes Alaska, the Yucatan peninsula, and the Mississippi and St Lawrence rivers, and is plainly a hoax. (https://www.theguardian.com/world/2006/jan/20/china.usa.)

‡ Venice's loss of its status as Europe's greatest trading empire, however, did not diminish its determination to protect its own commercial secrets. As late as 1745 an assassination squad was sent to poison two Venetian glass-blowers who had taken the secrets of their trade abroad. Whether the squad succeeded in its mission remains unknown. (Ackroyd, *Venice*, pp. 101–2.)

Venetian ambassadors had a probably deserved reputation for being the best diplomatic-intelligence gatherers. Many, probably most, ran agent networks as well as conducting diplomatic business. After the arrest of an agent of the Venetian ambassador in Turin in 1591, the Spanish ambassador said no real blame attached to his Venetian colleague because ambassadors 'habitually' made use of spies.[15] Venice's archives, however, reveal more about the employment of spies by its embassies than the intelligence they obtained.[16] The same is true of the agents employed directly by the Council of Ten.[17] Many were foreign merchants who passed on information during business trips to Venice.[18] Much of their information on both commercial and political developments came from open sources – among them newsletters (*avvisi*) made possible by the invention of movable type. 'The sixteenth-century Mediterranean', writes the historian Noel Malcolm, 'was a news-hungry world.'[19]

For most of the sixteenth century the greatest power in the eastern Mediterranean as well as the main threat to Venice was the Ottoman Empire, which in 1529 narrowly failed to capture Vienna. Despite the Ottomans' military might, their diplomatic and political intelligence lagged far behind that of Venice and their main Christian rivals. Constantinople suffered from two serious self-imposed long-term handicaps. The first was its continuation of the medieval practice of sending only ad hoc embassies to European capitals to conduct specific business. The Ottomans were thus deprived of the constant flow of information provided by Venetian and some other European ambassadors. After returning home at the end of their tours of duty, Venetian ambassadors presented to the Senate reports on the politics, armed forces, finances and economy of the states to which they had been accredited. Venice established a permanent diplomatic presence in Constantinople soon after it fell to the Ottomans in 1453.[20] France set up an embassy there in 1535, the Austrian Habsburgs in 1547 and England in 1578.[21] Since, in the Ottoman view, the Sultan was superior to all other rulers, it was beneath his dignity to set up permanent embassies at the courts of lesser monarchs. Instead, it was their responsibility to maintain embassies in Constantinople. Not till the end of the eighteenth century, with the Ottoman Empire in visible decline, did the Sultan deign to establish permanent embassies abroad.[22]

An even greater self-imposed limitation in the Ottomans' understanding of the outside world was their decision to prohibit printing – principally, it seems, to save the Quran from the indignity of being rendered in movable type rather than traditional calligraphy. The Ottoman Empire thus cut itself off from the explosion of open-source intelligence that printing made possible in Europe. Venice, by contrast, became the printing capital of the late fifteenth century. The first printed Quran was produced there (rather than in Constantinople) in 1537–8 by Christian publishers who probably intended it for export to the Ottoman Empire but belatedly discovered that, because of the Ottoman ban on printing, there was no market for it. All copies were believed to have been lost or destroyed until 1987, when Professor Angela Nuovo found a single copy in the library of the Franciscan Friars on the Venetian island of San Michele.[23] The first translation of the Quran (regarded by Muslims as a paraphrase since nothing can replace the Arabic original) was also published in Venice, in 1547, in Italian, and is known to have been studied by a rabbi in the Venetian Ghetto.[24] Banning printing in Ottoman Constantinople was roughly equivalent to a decision by a twenty-first-century government to ban use of the internet. The great twentieth-century Turkish leader Mustafa Kemal Atatürk identified the ban as the main cause of long-term Turkish intellectual decline:

> Think of the Turkish victory of 1453, the conquest of Constantinople, and its place in the course of world history. That same might and power which, in defiance of a whole world, made Istanbul forever the property of the Turkish people, was too weak to overcome the ill-omened resistance of the men of law and to receive in Turkey the printing press, which had been invented at about the same time.[25]

The sixteenth-century Ottomans had no shortage of spies in Europe reporting on a great variety of topics, among them Luther's challenge to the authority of the Papacy and the Holy Roman Emperor.[26] Their spies included Makarios of Chios, the Orthodox Archbishop of Thessalonica.* The lack of regular diplomatic reports and of access to printed newsletters and other publications, however, limited the ability of Ottoman policymakers to interpret the intelligence they received from espionage. When the Venetian *bailo* (who combined the role of ambassador with responsibilities for the merchant community) mentioned Rome at a meeting with the Ottoman Grand Admiral Sinan Pasha in the early 1550s, he discovered that Sinan had never heard of it. He asked whether the Venetians had learned about Rome from their merchants? Even the able Mehmed Sokollu Pasha, a former Grand Admiral who, from 1565 to 1579, was Grand Vizier to three successive Sultans, was confused about Italian geography. In 1567 he revealed to the

---

* In 1551, when Makarios came to attend the Council of Trent, which played a key role in the Catholic Counter-Reformation, he visited the court of the Emperor Charles V to offer his services in secret plots against the Ottomans. The Habsburgs eventually realized that he was an Ottoman spy. (Gürkan, 'Espionage in the 16th-Century Mediterranean', p. 107.)

bailo plans by the Ottoman navy to attack Puglia and Rome. The *bailo* reminded Sokollu, no doubt tactfully, that Rome was inland.*

The Venetian spies with the highest-level access in Constantinople tended to come from the ranks of the 'renegades': converts to Islam from Italy, Croatia, Hungary and elsewhere who had jobs, sometimes highly placed, in the Ottoman administration. Because of their linguistic skills, many were employed as dragomans (interpreters) and as secretaries for diplomatic correspondence. Some had been captured from Christian families as teenagers and retained residual loyalties to European culture. Others were successfully bribed. When a new Venetian *bailo* arrived in Constantinople, he was expected to distribute largesse to a wide range of officials. One *bailo* wrote in 1592: 'the *bailiate* is constantly visited by many Ottomans who are looking for gifts, and are like bees round a honey pot.' Some provided information in return for gifts. During Lorenzo Bernardo's years as *bailo* in 1585–7, the Sultan's chief dragoman, originally from Lucca, was on his payroll, as were secretaries of the Ottoman Chancellor, who provided him with the originals of many letters to the Sultan from European rulers (which, after translation into Turkish, were usually thrown away). Though the Venetians probably made most active use of 'renegades', some also worked for other European powers. The Jewish community in Constantinople was another important source of agents. Among the best informed was the Venetian physician Solomon Nathan Ashkenazi, whose patients included Grand Vizier Sokollu. From 1576 the Council of Ten paid Ashkenazi 300 ducats a year for his services. He also provided intelligence at various times to the Habsburg Empire, France and Spain.[27]

The dependability of Venetian agents abroad, whether employed by ambassadors or by the Council of Ten (and later by the State Inquisition), varied greatly. On the margins of the information explosion generated by printing, Renaissance humanism and the development of early-modern diplomacy, there emerged a profession of part-time or full-time agents without strong national or dynastic loyalties prepared to sell their information to the highest or most congenial bidders, whose identities might change over time.[28] Nicolò Rinaldi, who was employed as an agent by the French embassy in Constantinople, is known to have supplied intelligence to the Habsburgs and the Papacy as well. When he was imprisoned by the Ottomans, his release was paid for by the English ambassador, to whom presumably he had also supplied information. Rinaldi complained that the Venetian and French ambassadors, as well as the Habsburgs, had not also helped pay for his

---

* The Ottomans were similarly confused about the difference between Lutherans and Calvinists. (Gürkan, 'Espionage in the 16th-Century Mediterranean', pp. 53–4, 419–22.)

release, despite the services he had rendered to them.[29] On probably rare occasions even the loyalties of Venetian ambassadors were suspect. In 1591 the Council of Ten discovered that the *bailo* in Constantinople, Girolamo Lippomano, had been selling state secrets to the Habsburgs. A new *bailo* was sent to Constantinople and ordered to arrange the return of his disgraced predecessor to Venice. Shortly before Lippomano's ship arrived home, he jumped (or was pushed) overboard and drowned in the Adriatic.[30]

Despite Lippomano's treachery, Venetian ambassadors were usually the Republic's most reliable source of foreign intelligence. As well as employing spies, some had striking personal success in gaining inside information on the courts to which they were accredited. By the time the immensely experienced diplomat Sebastiano Giustiniani arrived in England early in 1515 as ambassador to the court of the 23-year-old King Henry VIII, he had already met most other European monarchs. Giustiniani quickly won the confidence of the much younger Henry. In April 1515, he reported to Venice that, one evening after dinner, the King 'embraced us, without ceremony, and conversed for a very long while very familiarly, on various topics, in good Latin and in French, which he speaks very well indeed . . . His Majesty is the handsomest potentate I ever set eyes on . . . Believe me, he is in every respect a most accomplished Prince . . .' Part of Giustiniani's success with Henry derived from his ability to play on the young king's vanity. On another occasion in 1515, he reported to Venice:

> His Majesty, . . . addressing me in French, said: 'Talk with me awhile! The King of France, is he as tall as I am?' I told him there was but little difference. He continued, 'Is he as stout [well-built]?' I said he was not; and he then inquired, 'What sort of legs has he?' I replied, 'Spare.' Whereupon he opened the front of his doublet, and placing his hand on his thigh, said, 'Look here! and I have also a good calf to my leg.'

Gratified by Giustiniani's assurance that Henry was 'the handsomest potentate' he had ever set eyes on, the King went on to reveal to him 'in detail all the events' of his recent military campaigns in France.[31]

Giustiniani also gained an insight into the King's overconfident belief that he could bend the Pope to his will. Henry told Giustiniani in 1515: 'I think I have sufficient power with the Pope to warrant hopes of my making him adhere to whichever side I choose.' By 1517 he had deluded himself into believing 'The Pope is mine' ('*Pontifex est meus*'). This delusion later powerfully informed Henry's policy in what became known as the King's 'great matter', his mistaken belief that he could persuade the Pope to annul his marriage to Catherine of Aragon, mother of the future Queen Mary.[32]

Giustiniani's frequent meetings with Cardinal Wolsey, who became

Lord Chancellor in 1515, enabled him to report on his growing ascendancy over Henry:

> [Wolsey] rules both the king and the entire kingdom. On my first arrival in England he used to say to me, 'His Majesty will do so and so.' Subsequently, by degrees, he forgot himself, and commenced saying, 'We shall do so and so.' At this present he has reached such a pitch that he says, 'I shall do so and so.' He is about forty-six years old, very handsome, learned, extremely eloquent, of vast ability, and indefatigable. He alone transacts as much business as that which occupies all the magistracies, offices, and councils of Venice, both civil and criminal; and all state affairs likewise are managed by him, let their nature be what it may.[33]

Neither Giustiniani nor, so far as is known, any other foreign observer foresaw Wolsey's overthrow a decade later.

One of Giustiniani's successors as Venetian ambassador, Carlo Capello (1531–5), who also formed a close relationship with Henry, provided an insider's account of the tortuous process leading to the King's divorce from Catherine of Aragon and his secret marriage to the ill-fated Anne Boleyn.* In May 1533, Capello reported that he had dined with, among others, Queen Anne's father and brother, 'who were most pleased to see me and told me that the King wished to speak with me':

> After I finished dining in their company, I entered the King's room where he was with many gentlemen and Queen Anne with many ladies and damsels. His Majesty immediately took me by the hand, and I congratulated him in the name of our Signoria [government] in general terms, wishing him every happiness. His Majesty showed that he was pleased to hear [the congratulations].

Henry told Capello that, though he approved of the Venetian prohibition 'upon pain of capital punishment . . . against divulging matters of the Council of Ten and the Senate', Venetian affairs were widely discussed in London.[34] As recent research has confirmed, Henry was right to claim that the level of secrecy aimed at by the rulers of Venice was not fully achievable. The famous question 'What news on the Rialto?' in Shakespeare's *Merchant of Venice* makes the same point. Gossip on the Rialto as well as in other public spaces, taverns, pharmacies and barbershops made it impossible for the Council of Ten to achieve the almost complete control of information to which it aspired.[35]

*

---

* The latest historian of the divorce, Catherine Fletcher, however, considers Capello 'excitable'. (Fletcher, *Divorce of Henry VIII*, ch. 15.)

The greatest innovation in sixteenth-century European intelligence collection was the role of SIGINT – a field in which it retained for several centuries a major lead over other continents. As well as having probably Europe's best-informed ambassadors and the leading agent network in Constantinople, the Council of Ten also established the first European codebreaking agency. Its initial head, Giovanni Soro, probably appointed in 1506, was the first great European cryptanalyst, though he probably drew on the earlier achievements of the Renaissance polymath Leon Battista Alberti: architect, painter, poet, prose-writer, priest, philosopher, composer, musician – and, for a few years in his early sixties, cryptographer. In Alberti's book *De Componendis Cifris* ('Concerning the Solution of Ciphers'), published in 1467, he recalls, with an engaging lack of discretion, a walk in the Vatican gardens with his friend Leonardo Dati, head of the Papal Secretariat, during which they discussed ciphers. The Papacy had first used ciphers during the pontificate of John XXII (1316–34),[36] though little is known about how regular their use became over the next century. Having seen other, probably more sophisticated, ciphers in diplomatic correspondence intercepted by the Papacy, Dati seems to have been anxious to improve those in current use by the Papal Secretariat. He told Alberti that he had become curious about codebreaking. 'What do you think of these decipherers?' he asked. 'Have you tried your hand at it?' Alberti had not, but agreed to try. The result was his book of 1467,[37] the first major European work on cryptanalysis, which showed how the fact that in every alphabet some letters are more frequently used than others (the 'frequency' principle) made it possible to solve ciphers which substituted a different letter or symbol for each letter of the alphabet. Alberti may have drawn on the work of other, more discreet Renaissance cryptographers whose work has not survived. But he was almost certainly unaware that, over half a millennium earlier, al-Kindi, the great Muslim mathematician of the House of Wisdom in Abbasid Baghdad, had discovered the frequency principle.[38] Alberti also devised the most sophisticated cipher so far used in Europe, based on a cipher disc with two concentric circles of letters and numbers whose positions could be altered during encipherment, thus changing their meaning in different parts of the same message (a practice since known to cryptographers as 'polyalphabetic substitution'). He proudly described his new cipher system as 'worthy of kings' and wrongly believed it to be unbreakable.[39]*

---

* In 1474, seven years after the publication of Alberti's *De Cifris*, the Milanese statesman Francesco (Cicco) Simonetta (1410–80) also produced a book on codebreaking, which was, however, significantly less advanced than Alberti's. There is no evidence that Simonetta personally decrypted ciphered correspondence.

There is no evidence, however, that Alberti personally decrypted current cipher messages. Giovanni Soro did, working on copies of intercepted despatches in a secret room at the Doge's Palace for almost forty years from his appointment in about 1506 to his death in 1544. Exactly which room Soro worked in is not known. In stark contrast to the luxurious magnificence of the public rooms, however, even the most senior of the Doge's bureaucrats worked in small, sparsely furnished rooms on the upper floors of the Palace with plain wooden walls and a cupboard for documents. In summer the rooms, as nowadays, were stiflingly hot.* As well as working as a cryptanalyst for the Venetian Republic, Soro also wrote a book on breaking ciphers. Though no copy of his book survives, there is sufficient fragmentary evidence to demonstrate the scale of his cryptanalytic achievements at a critical moment in Italian history. During the series of Italian Wars which began in 1494 and ended in 1559, only the governments of Venice and the Papacy survived intact, though both suffered serious defeats. Probably the most dangerous moment for Venice came during the early years of the War of the League of Cambrai, formed in 1508 when the Papacy, Holy Roman Emperor, France and Aragon joined in an attack on Venice in the hope of dividing its possessions between them. Mercifully for Venice, though it lost some of its territories, its enemies fell out. In April 1516, as the war was reaching its end, an intercepted despatch to the Emperor Maximilian I from the commander of his forces at Lodi in Lombardy, Marco Antonio Colonna, decrypted 'with great difficulty' by Soro, revealed – no doubt to the immense relief of the Council of Ten – that Colonna had run out of money to pay his forces. Colonna appealed to Maximilian either to send funds urgently to pay and feed his troops or else to come to Lodi in person.[40]

In both the making and breaking of codes and ciphers, the Ottomans fell far behind not merely Venice and some other European powers but also behind the Muslim Abbasid dynasty half a millennium earlier. The Sublime Porte (as the Ottoman government was known) had lost the cryptographic expertise developed in the Baghdad House of Wisdom under the Abbasid caliphs.[41] In 1567 the Venetian *bailo* was told by the Ottoman authorities not to send encrypted despatches to Venice unless he first provided details of the cipher he was using. This instruction, which seems to have been

* Most present-day visitors to the Doge's Palace are not able to visit the small upper rooms, and, like early modern ambassadors in Venice, gain a misleading impression of the interior of the Palace as uniformly spacious and magnificently decorated. The spartan upper rooms, which are mostly crammed two into a single storey, as well as the narrow staircases which lead to them, are too cramped for large groups. Those wishing to visit them have to purchase in advance an additional entry ticket giving access in small groups to the 'secret passages' of the Palace.

ignored, would not have been made if the Ottomans had been able to decrypt Venetian despatches. In 1570 Grand Vizier Sokollu asked the *bailo* to teach an Ottoman official how to cipher messages. Though Sokollu made the request with a smile on his face, it reflected the backward state of Ottoman cryptography. The *bailo* replied evasively that cipher instruction of the official would take too long for it to be practicable.[42]

The Sublime Porte had probably become at least dimly aware of some of Soro's successes half a century before. Unlike twentieth- and twenty-first-century cryptanalysts, whose identities remained officially secret during their working lives, Soro became an international celebrity. In April 1530, for example, when the Prince of Salerno visited Venice, where he was warmly welcomed and embraced by the Doge on his arrival, he asked to see three leading Venetian celebrities: the Librarian of St Mark's Basilica, Pietro Bembo, author of one of the earliest Italian grammars and later a cardinal; the leading historian Marin Sanudo; and the 'cipher master' Zuan (Giovanni) Soro (some of whose successes were known to Sanudo).[43]

Why the Venetian authorities, who protected state secrets so zealously, should have allowed probably their most important intelligence official to become an international celebrity remains mysterious. Part of the reason must have been Venice's sometimes desperate need for allies during the Italian Wars. In June 1526, for example, the Papal Legate, the Bishop of Pola, arrived in Venice with an intercepted ciphered letter sent by the ambassador in Rome of the Emperor Charles V to Naples. The Legate asked for the letter to be decrypted by Soro, whose skill as a codebreaker was, he declared, 'unique in all the world'. After discussion, the Venetian Collegio (consisting of the Doge and twenty-two high-ranking councillors) agreed to the Legate's request.[44] Two months later, a similar request was received from the French court for Soro to decrypt an intercepted ciphered letter sent by the city government of Poitiers. The Venetian diplomat Andrea Rosso reported, after Soro successfully decrypted it, that the French authorities praised his 'divine' skill as a codebreaker.[45]

Despite authorizing Soro on these, and probably other, occasions to break foreign ciphers for the Papacy and France, the Council of Ten concluded in 1539 that standards of official secrecy were too lax:

> Despite all the measures taken by this Council, it has still proved impossible to prevent the most important matters dealt with in our secret councils from being known and published, as we are reliably informed from every quarter: a disgraceful situation, and one cannot imagine anything more harmful and damaging to our state.[46]

The Council of Ten therefore appointed three state inquisitors from among their number (initially known as *Inquisitori sopra li segreti*) to 'make most diligent enquiry against offenders'.[47] The room in which the inquisitors met, though relatively modest in size, was far grander than the spartan offices of senior bureaucrats on the top floors of the Doge's Palace. A magnificent painting on the ceiling by Domenico Tintoretto showed Jesus' parable of the return of the Prodigal Son.* Tintoretto's masterpiece (probably the greatest ever produced for the offices of intelligence or security chiefs) epitomized the inquisitors' self-image of returning deviant Venetians to the path of civic virtue and respect for official secrecy. Some security services in twentieth-century repressive regimes developed a similarly pretentious self-image as upholders of civic virtue.†

The reasons for the maintenance of Venetian official secrecy went beyond the requirements of state security. Concealing disagreements in the conduct of government was also essential in preserving the illusion of near-perfect harmony which was central to Venice's self-image as 'The Most Serene Republic'.[48] To Marin Sanudo 'secrecy was a matter of collective honour.'[49] A law confirming the power of the State Inquisitors in 1583 declared that *'buon governo'* required *'segretezza'*.[50]

Like many more recent security services in authoritarian regimes, the Venetian inquisitors sometimes used torture during interrogation. The torture chamber in the Doge's Palace still contains the *strappado* ('pull' or 'tug') sometimes, though not habitually, used by the inquisitors. The victim was hoisted off the ground by his hands, usually tied behind his back, with a rope on a pulley which was then allowed to drop with a jerk, sometimes wrenching joints from sockets. The Spanish Inquisition also used the *strappado* (known in Spanish as *la garrucha*), which it called the 'Queen of tortures'.[51]

Alongside the tradition of official secrecy epitomized by the inquisitors was another, unofficial but well-established, Venetian tradition of concealing personal identity. Masks were more prevalent in Venice than anywhere else in Europe. Originating during the pre-Lenten carnival in the thirteenth century, the custom increased erratically over the next five centuries. There

* The normal entry ticket to the Doge's Palace does not give access to the inquisitors' rooms or to the torture room. Those wishing to visit them have to purchase in advance an additional entry ticket giving access in small groups to the 'secret passages' of the Palace. See footnote, p. 128.
† The KGB chairman and future Soviet leader Yuri Andropov proudly boasted at a top-secret Soviet security conference in 1979 that of 15,580 people to whom it had given warnings in the previous year after acts of 'ideological subversion', only 107 had reoffended. (Andrew and Mitrokhin, *Mitrokhin Archive*, p. 431.)

is no single explanation for the Venetian fascination with masks.[52] In a highly stratified society some enjoyed the opportunity to converse anonymously with their social superiors or inferiors. Masks also facilitated sexual assignations. The anonymity provided by masks, noted the English writer Joseph Addison in the early eighteenth century, encouraged 'an abundance of love adventures' and, he might have added, the growth of sex tourism. 'There is something more intriguing in the amours of Venice', wrote Addison, 'than in those of other countries.'[53] Giacomo Casanova, a devotee of the mask and the best-known libertine in Venetian history, agreed.

Masks also assisted espionage, making it easier for spies and informants to disguise themselves in Venice than in any other city. Among the reports in the archives of the Venetian Inquisition, for example, is one from a masked informant reporting to the Inquisition on a conversation he had overheard between the masked son of the Spanish ambassador and a masked agent reporting to him intelligence on the Council of Ten, the inquisitors and their informants.[54] Prompted by such episodes, a statute of 1608 forbade both Venetians and visitors from wearing masks when travelling through the city on foot or by boat except during carnival time. Masks were so deeply embedded in Venetian culture that such prohibitions were never fully effective. In 1626 the Great Council inveighed against those who 'mask themselves in order to pursue detestable designs, including homicide and other great offences without being known'.[55] By the eighteenth century Venetians wore masks for about half of the year, from early autumn to the beginning of Lent.*

There are still some visible traces in twenty-first-century Venice of the culture of clandestine denunciation promoted by the Council of Ten and the State Inquisition. Among the most striking are the lion's mouth (*bocca di leone*) letterboxes through which citizens were encouraged to post the names of those who subverted the authority of the state. Two survive on the walls of the Doge's Palace: one lion's mouth for unspecified denunciations, and a second (with the head of a stern bureaucrat instead of a lion) intended, more specifically, for 'secret denunciations' of officials who accepted secret bribes and favours.† The few lion's mouth letterboxes that survive in other locations also invite a mixture of general and specific denunciations. The fifteenth-century *bocca di leone* embedded in the wall of the church of Santa Maria della Visitazione, for example, calls for

---

* Masks were banned after the fall of the Venetian Republic in 1797, though they have since been reintroduced at carnival time. (Johnson, *Venice Incognito*, pp. 105–7.)
† See ill. 9. An inscription on the second letterbox reads 'secret denunciations against anyone who will conceal favours and services or will collude to hide the true revenue from them'.

'denunciations related to public health for the *Sestiere* [district] of Dorso-
duro'. This almost certainly seeks information on those responsible for
failures to isolate some suspected plague victims in the Lazzaretto Vec-
chio, an island in the Venetian Lagoon from which few returned.[56] Mark
Twain wrote of 'the terrible Lions' Mouths' after visiting Venice in the
1860s:

> These were the throats down which went the anonymous accusation, thrust
> in secretly at dead of night by an enemy, that doomed many an innocent
> man to walk the Bridge of Sighs and descend into the dungeon which none
> entered and hoped to see the sun again . . . If a man had an enemy in those
> old days, the cleverest thing he could do was to slip a note for the Council
> of Three [state inquisitors] into the Lion's mouth, saying 'This man is plot-
> ting against the Government.'[57]*

The denunciations posted in the Lions' Mouths, however, were not
anonymous. Those who made them had to give their names, though their
identities were protected. Supposedly thorough investigation preceded the
arrest of those denounced. But it is difficult not to believe that the suspicions aroused by malicious denunciations led to the imprisonment (or
worse) of some who were innocent as well as those who were guilty.

The sophistication of Venice's intelligence system failed to compensate
for its military inferiority to the Ottomans. Much of its overseas empire (*lo
Stato da Mar*) fell to greatly superior Ottoman forces after their conquest
of Constantinople in 1453. In three wars over the next century Venice lost
Negroponte, Lemnos, Morea (Peloponnese), the Cyclades (except Tinos)
and the Sporades. Though Venice was part of the Holy League, which
defeated the Ottoman fleet at the Battle of Lepanto during the Fourth
Ottoman–Venetian War (1570–73), it also lost Cyprus to the Ottomans.

By contrast, the founding of New Spain (Nueva España) following the
rapid Spanish conquest of the militarily powerful Aztec Empire† in 1521
was made possible, in part, by skilful use of intelligence (so far little
researched) by the ablest of the Spanish *conquistadores*, Hernán (Her-
nando) Cortés, as well as by his brilliance as a military commander.[58] When

---

* Contrary to Mark Twain's belief, few of those successfully denounced had their last
glimpse of Venice before imprisonment through the windows of the Bridge of Sighs, which
was not built until 1602 after the denunciations had passed their peak. It was another two
centuries before Byron gave the bridge the name by which it is now known around the world.
† The term 'Aztec Empire', though commonly used by historians, is technically incorrect.
The correct designation for the Nahuatl-speaking tribute empire of central Mexico conquered
by Cortés was *Mexica*.

the 34-year-old Cortés landed with (at most) 600 men on the coast of
Mexico on 21 April 1519, he had no intelligence on what opposition
awaited him. At a meeting with a local *cacique* (chief) on Easter Sunday,
24 April, he discovered that somewhere in the Mexican interior was a
powerful Aztec emperor, Motecuhzoma II ('Montezuma' in many Spanish
and English translations), whose dominions and vassal states extended to
the coastal plain. The Aztecs had far more experience of espionage than
Cortés. Spies had higher status in Mesoamerica than in medieval Europe;
among the Aztecs they were considered minor nobility.[59] Spies who were
caught in hostile territory faced prolonged and gruesome execution – further
evidence of the significance of their role in Mesoamerica.*

Believing that their empire covered most of the world, however, the
Aztecs had no concept of foreign espionage which went beyond their immediate neighbours. They were barely aware even of the existence of South
America and, until the arrival of Cortés, entirely unaware that, over the
previous generation, Spain had taken over most of the islands in the Caribbean. As soon as Motecuhzoma learned of Cortés's landing on the Mexican
coast, he sent emissaries bearing gifts of gold and precious feathers who
were instructed to collect intelligence on him and his men. Though the
emissaries were taken aback by Cortés's horses, armour and gunpowder,
none of which existed in Mesoamerica, the main question which concerned
the Aztec ruler and his advisers was whether the bearded, white-skinned
invaders were gods or humans. Cortés's men were not greatly impressed
by the feathers, but their response to the gold seemed to show that they
were human rather than divine: 'Like monkeys they seized upon the gold.
It was as if then they were satisfied, sated and gladdened. For in truth they
thirsted mightily for gold; they stuffed themselves with it . . . and lusted
for it like pigs.' Before allowing the emissaries to return, Cortés fired one
of his cannons, which visibly terrified them and was doubtless intended to
discourage an Aztec offensive.[60] Had Cortés's expedition come under
attack at this stage, it would have been overwhelmed by the sheer numbers
of Aztec forces. Motecuhzoma's failure to attack led within two years to
his own death and the overthrow of the Aztec Empire.

Crucial to Cortés's decisive defeat of a much stronger opponent was
intelligence on tensions between Motecuhzoma, his vassal states and
allies. He owed much of this intelligence to La Malinche, one of twenty
slave women, probably in their late teens or early twenties, given him by

---

* There are grisly images of the execution of Aztec merchants, probably suspected of being
spies, in the Codex Mendoza, part III, commissioned by Antonio de Mendoza, viceroy of
New Spain, 1535–50; Bodleian Library, Oxford.

a local *cacique* soon after his arrival in Mexico. Malinche, who spoke both Nahuatl (the language of the Aztecs) and Mayan, acted as interpreter in Cortés's dealings with the Aztecs and local tribes, and accompanied him wherever he went.* Malinche later became his mistress and bore him a son. Images and pictograms in Aztec codices always show her next to Cortés. The leading memoir of Cortés's campaign, by one of his sergeants, Bernal Díaz del Castillo, refers to her respectfully as Doña ('Lady') Marina (her baptismal name as a Catholic convert). Though she had been sold into slavery, Díaz calls her 'a truly great princess, the daughter of *caciques* and the mistress of vassals, as was very evident in her appearance . . . , being good-looking, intelligent and self-assured'. Her language skills were 'the great beginning of our successes'.[61]

Cortés had his first major intelligence success a few weeks after his landing during a visit to his camp by leaders of the local Totonac people, whose words were translated by Malinche. According to Díaz, Cortés was 'greatly delighted' by the intelligence they provided on Motecuhzoma's enemies. Soon afterwards Cortés visited some of the Totonac hill towns. The *cacique* of Cempoala complained that Motecuhzoma 'had recently brought him into subjection, had taken away all his golden jewellery, and so grievously oppressed him and his people that they could do nothing except obey him, since he was lord of many cities and counties, and ruler over countless vassals and armies of warriors'. Next day, inhabitants of Quiahuitzlan told Cortés that 'every year many of their sons and daughters were demanded of them for sacrifices . . . If their wives and daughters were handsome, Motecuhzoma's tax-gatherers took them away and raped them.' Cortés promptly arrested five tax-gatherers who arrived during his visit. The Totonacs, writes Díaz, 'could not contain their delight':

> Cortés replied with a most cheerful smile that he and his brothers who were with him would defend them and kill anyone who tried to harm them; and the *Caciques* and their villagers one and all promised to stand by us, to obey any orders we might give them, and to join their forces with ours against Montezuma and his allies.

Cortés concluded alliances with the rulers of over twenty Totonac hill towns.[62]

Cortés's next target for an alliance was Tlaxcala, a confederacy with a long history of hostility to the Aztecs. Despite a brief conflict early in

---

* A Spanish priest, Alonso Hernández Puertocarrera, who spoke Mayan but not Nahuatl, initially assisted in translation. Until she learned Spanish, Malinche (also known as Malintzin) translated from Nahuatl into Mayan, which the priest then translated into Spanish.

September caused by Tlaxalan leaders who suspected Cortés of wanting to conquer their territory, he reached agreement later in the month on an alliance against Motecuhzoma. During the negotiations, following Mesoamerican custom, Cortés made it brutally clear that he would not tolerate espionage by his allies. According to Díaz, he 'had seventeen of the [Tlaxalan] spies arrested and cut off the hands of some and the thumbs of others, which he sent to Xicotenga [their military commander] with the message that this was a punishment for their audacity in coming to our camp to spy'.[63]

Cortés's next major destination en route to the Aztec capital of Tenochtitlan (which occupied the site of today's Mexico City) was the holy city of Cholula, second only to Tenochtitlan as the largest city in central Mexico. According to Díaz, intelligence obtained by Malinche from a *cacique*'s wife revealed Cholulan plans, with the connivance of Motecuhzoma, to launch a surprise attack on the Spaniards. Cortés struck first and slaughtered hundreds, perhaps thousands, of unarmed Cholulan warriors before the attack could take place. 'If we had a reputation for bravery before', Díaz wrote later, '. . . from now on they took us for magicians and said that no plot could be so secret as to escape discovery [by us].'[64]*

Motecuhzoma's fatal inertia in confronting the threat from Cortés has been plausibly, though controversially, ascribed to his belief, at least initially, that, despite the behaviour of his troops, Cortés himself was the god Quetzalcoatl, who was believed to have once ruled the Aztecs and would one day return to his throne. According to Spanish sources written after the conquest of Mexico, the year in the Aztec calendar when Motecuhzoma's astrologers were expecting him to return was 1519. After Cortés's triumph in Quiahuitzlan in 1519, Motecuhzoma was reported to have said he was 'now certain that we were those whose coming to their country his ancestors had foretold, and must therefore be of his own race'.[65] Analysis of the intelligence on Cortés provided by Aztec spies was distorted by religious myth.

After forcing Cholula into an alliance, Cortés and his forces continued to Tenochtitlan, while he sent Motecuhzoma misleading assurances that he came in peace. The intelligence which Cortés had received on the Aztec capital left him and his men unprepared for its magnificence when they arrived in November 1519. Tenochtitlan and its setting on an island in the middle of a lake struck Díaz as an 'enchanted vision': 'Indeed, some of

---

* Malinche's discovery of the Cholulan plot was briefly reported by Cortés to Charles V (Pagden (ed), *Letters From Mexico*; 2nd letter from Cortés to Charles V). It has been suggested that Cortés used Malinche's alleged intelligence as a pretext to attack the Cholulans.

our soldiers asked whether it was not all a dream.' After a grand but probably suspicious welcome from Motecuhzoma, Cortés put him under house
arrest in the luxurious accommodation the Emperor had reserved for the
Spanish leaders. Despite her early life as a slave, Malinche gave further
proof of what Díaz called her 'manly bravery'. Though most Aztecs were
afraid even to look their Emperor in the face, Malinche told him, on
Cortés's orders, that he would not be harmed if he cooperated. Otherwise,
'you are a dead man'. Motecuhzoma duly cooperated and, while doing
Cortés's bidding, was allowed to make it appear that he was still Emperor
and Cortés merely his guest. He also continued daily human sacrifices in
the hope of obtaining divine assistance.

Unsurprisingly, after several months during which the pretence that the
Emperor remained in power wore increasingly thin and no divine assistance was forthcoming, the Aztec elite staged a coup, elected a new
emperor and drove the Spaniards from Tenochtitlan. Motecuhzoma was
killed – whether by his Aztec opponents or by the Spaniards or by some
combination of the two remains unclear. Despite his expulsion from Tenochtitlan, Cortés probably had better intelligence on the extent of opposition
to Aztec rule than the new regime which had succeeded Motecuhzoma.
The Aztecs were also overwhelmed by the sudden arrival of European
diseases, to which they had no resistance. During the last few months of
1520 at least a third of the population of Tenochtitlan died from smallpox,
a catastrophe blamed by its rulers either on the malevolence of their own
gods or on Spanish magic. In May 1521 Cortés began a siege of the demoralized capital. The great majority of his forces came from native peoples
who saw the Spanish invasion as an opportunity to rid themselves of Aztec
domination. After a brutal eighty-day siege, Tenochtitlan surrendered on
13 August 1521.[66]

In December 1530, little more than a decade after Cortés's conquest of
the Aztec Empire, another conquistador, Francisco Pizarro, invaded the
far larger Inca Empire in South America with a force of only 168 men,
less than a third the number of Cortés's troops. Pizarro's success owed
much to the Incas' complete lack of intelligence on Central America.
Though Inca rulers sometimes sent spies to neighbouring territory they
wished to add to their empire, they knew nothing about the Spanish defeat
of the Aztecs. Pizarro was thus able to imitate Cortés's winning strategy –
claiming to be a peaceful emissary from the King of Spain and arranging
a meeting with the Inca ruler, Atahualpa, at which he kidnapped him.
Like Cortés, he then embarked on a war of conquest with local allies
hostile to the Incas.[67] The illiterate Pizarro, however, lacked Cortés's flair
for intelligence. He and his men, who were obsessed with the hunt for

gold, provide extreme examples of the problems of telling truth to power. Not hesitating to use torture to force inhabitants of the Inca Empire to reveal where the gold was hidden, they failed to realize that, to try to avoid torture, those questioned were apt to exaggerate, sometimes enormously, the amount of Inca gold. Such interrogations inspired the myth of a city of gold, El Dorado, for which successive expeditions searched in vain.[68]

Spain had no foreign-intelligence successes in Europe which compared with those of Cortés during the conquest of the Aztec Empire. The Holy Roman Emperor, Charles V (King Charles I of Spain), was more concerned with rooting out heresy in his dominions than with obtaining political intelligence from foreign courts. His son Philip II, who in 1556 succeeded him as ruler of Spain, its overseas empire and the Low Countries, had similar priorities. Philip's marriage in 1554 to the Catholic Queen Mary of England, who shared his zeal for burning Protestants, offered him the prospect of extraordinary influence at her court.[69] But their marriage was childless and, on her death in 1558 at the age of only forty-two, she was succeeded by Elizabeth I, who turned down his offer of marriage and was later denounced in a papal bull of 1570 as a heretic and the 'servant of crime'. Spanish foreign intelligence under Philip II was inferior to that of both Elizabethan England and the Dutch rebels, who broke some of his ciphers. Philip himself had little if any understanding of codebreaking, which he suspected was linked to witchcraft.[70]

Within sixteenth-century Europe what most determined which country had access to the best SIGINT depended unpredictably on the nationality of the then small pool of leading cryptographic talent. Though the Venetian Giovanni Soro was widely recognized early in the century within the world of diplomacy as the leading cryptographic genius, by the later years of the century, as Venetian diplomats themselves acknowledged, Europe's leading codebreaker was the French lawyer and mathematician François Viète, nowadays remembered as the main founder of modern algebra. Viète won his reputation as a codebreaker at (for a leading mathematician) the relatively advanced age of forty-nine, during the final stages of the bitterly-fought French Wars of Religion between Catholics and Protestants (the second deadliest religious conflict in European history), which had begun in 1562. Viète became counsellor to the Protestant Henry of Navarre. Among the decrypts which he probably brought to Henry's attention was a despatch containing intelligence on Spanish support for the French Catholic League sent in 1588 by Alessandro Farnese, Duke of Parma and governor of the Spanish Netherlands.[71]

In 1589 Henry of Navarre famously decided that 'Paris is worth a Mass'

and converted to Catholicism in order to ascend the French throne as King
Henry IV. With strong support from Philip II of Spain, the Catholic League,
led by Charles de Guise, Duke of Mayenne, continued to oppose Henry's
accession. Viète succeeded in decrypting intercepted correspondence
between Philip and both his military commander in France, Comendador
Moreo, and his ambassador to the Catholic League, Bernardino de Mendoza. Remarkably, in 1590 Viète published a pamphlet containing a
decrypted despatch sent by Moreo to Phillip II on 28 October 1589. He did
so partly because of his arrogant confidence that, as he told Henry IV, there
would never be a Spanish cipher that he could not break: 'They have changed
and rechanged [their ciphers], and nevertheless have been and always will
be discovered in their tricks.' Henry probably approved publication of the
despatch because he believed it would discredit Mayenne. It revealed Mayenne's plan to surrender the cities of Picardy in northern France to Spanish
control in order to further his own ambitions to take the French throne.
Viète wrote to Henry: 'It does not seem to me at all untimely that these
cities and [their] governors, and generally all [French] people who are still
deceived by the [Catholic] League, should know this truth.'[72]

Philip II was so taken aback by the publication of Moreo's despatch
that he wrote to the ailing Pope Sixtus V to complain that Henry, like the
Dutch, must be using witchcraft to break Spanish ciphers. Sixtus was
unimpressed, not least because, as he was probably aware, papal cryptanalysts had decrypted some of Philip's correspondence thirty years earlier.
One of Henry IV's counsellors, the chronicler Jacques-Auguste de Thou,
wrote scornfully that Philip's complaint prompted only 'contempt and
indignation'.[73]* Viète had plans to publish further decrypted Spanish correspondence which he believed would demoralize Mayenne by revealing
double-dealing at his expense by both Philip II and his own followers.
Though these decrypts were never made public, Mayenne may have been
told privately of them. In 1594 he recognized Henry IV as King of France.[74]

Like Soro, Viète became an international celebrity. Remarkably, he
enjoyed boasting to foreign diplomats of his success in breaking their
ciphers. Giovanni Mocenigo, Venetian ambassador to France, reported to
the Council of Ten in 1595:

> [Viète] had just told me that a great number of letters in cipher to the King
> of Spain as well as to the [Holy Roman] Emperor and of other princes had

---

* Sixtus V died in August 1590 and was briefly succeeded by Urban VII, who died after
only a fortnight in office. The next Pope, Gregory XIV (Dec. 1590–Oct. 1591) was considerably more sympathetic to Philip II, and during his brief pontificate sent troops and money
to support the Catholic League against Henry IV.

been intercepted, which he had deciphered and had interpreted. And as I showed a great deal of astonishment, he said to me:

'I will give your government effective proofs of it.'

He immediately brought me a thick packet of letters from the said princes which he had deciphered, and added:

'I want you also to know that I know and translate your cipher.'

'I will not believe it', I said, 'unless I see it.'

And as I had three kinds of cipher – an ordinary one which I used, a different one which I did not use, and a third called *dalle Caselle* – he showed me that he knew the first. Then, to better probe so great an affair, I said to him:

'You undoubtedly know our *dalle Caselle* cipher?'

'For that you have to skip a lot', he replied, meaning that he only knew portions of it. I asked him to let me see some of his deciphered letters, and he promised to let me, but since then he has not spoken further about it to me, and, having left, I have not seen him any more.[75]

Despite his indiscretions, few codebreakers have ever been more passionately convinced than Viète of the vital importance of their work to national security. On his deathbed early in 1603 he said he wanted nothing to do with priests and doctors.* His main preoccupation was SIGINT. Viète was determined before he died to make a record for Henry IV's Chief Minister, the duc de Sully, of what he had discovered about 'solving the ciphers of Spain and Italy for the good of the service of the King and of the State of France'.[76] Spanish cryptanalytic expertise lagged far behind. Philip II's claim that French codebreaking was the result of witchcraft was as telling a confession of backwardness as Grand Vizier Sokollu's request for cipher lessons from the Venetian ambassador.

Spain's cipher security was also poor. For some years until he was caught in 1581, a Flemish-born cipher clerk in the Spanish service sent cipher material to one of the leaders of the Dutch Revolt against Spanish rule, Philips of Marnix, Lord of Saint-Aldegonde (Filips van Marnix, heer van Sint-Aldegonde).[77] Aldegonde was a polymath with a reputation as a writer and theologian, nowadays remembered as the probable author of the words of the world's oldest national anthem, the Dutch 'Wilhelmus', composed during the Revolt. The Spanish cipher material inspired him to try his hand at codebreaking. In 1577 Aldegonde published a decrypted Spanish despatch, intercepted in France, which had been sent to Philip II

---

* Viète eventually agreed to make a confession to a priest so that his daughter should not risk being disinherited as the daughter of an atheist. (Pesic, 'François Viète', p. 9, n. 22.)

by his governor-general of the Low Countries, Don Juan of Austria, emphasizing the need to crush the Dutch Revolt by force. Don Juan issued a confused and somewhat comic statement of personal outrage at the publication of his secret correspondence:

> We say that such an action . . . is a notable insult and crime of treachery, and that to intercept and open the letters of one's Sovereign is a crime of *lèse-majesté* . . . [Those responsible] cannot excuse themselves; and the more they publish what they are pleased to decipher, that is to say make up as they think fit, the more they blemish their own reputations; Even if we did write as they say, we told the King what was happening, and we are sorry that things are still in the same bad state.[78]

Aldegonde responded by publishing further decrypted despatches. He continued to attempt, sometimes successfully, to decrypt Spanish communications after the Flemish cipher clerk's arrest in 1581. The cryptographically challenged Philip II suspected Aldegonde, like Viète, of using witchcraft to break Spanish ciphers. In 1590 Aldegonde spent three months in Paris, where it is probable that he discussed cryptanalysis with Viète. Aldegonde went on to provide copies of Spanish decrypts to the courts of Henry IV and Elizabeth I, both at war with Spain.[79]

Despite Philip II's misunderstanding of codebreaking, he had an important influence on the development of European intelligence. The threat posed by his armed forces, the most powerful in Europe, stimulated codebreaking both at the court of Henry IV, which in the Viète era became the world leader, and among the Dutch rebels fighting for independence from Spanish rule. But the greatest impact of the Spanish menace on the development of intelligence systems was in England, which, in the later 1580s, was threatened simultaneously with the greatest invasion force ever sent against it and by assassination plots, supported by Philip, against Queen Elizabeth I. In response to these threats intelligence was better integrated into policymaking than ever before in English, and perhaps world, history.[80]

9
Ivan the Terrible and the Origins of Russian State Security

Ivan IV 'the Terrible', Grand Prince of Moscow in 1533 at the age of only three, who became first 'Tsar of all the Russias' in 1547, remains the most mysterious as well as the most terrifying of sixteenth-century European monarchs. Though most biographies and many histories of Russia contain portraits of him, all are imaginary. In striking contrast to the contemporary English Tudor dynasty, no authentic likeness of Ivan survives. The written sources are also more fragmentary and more frequently unreliable than in the case of any other major sixteenth-century ruler, though reports by English merchants and diplomats, which were kept secret at the time, fill some gaps in the Russian records.

The reign of Ivan the Terrible cast a long and brutal shadow over the later history of Russian intelligence and security. Stalin, his greatest twentieth-century admirer, called him a 'great and wise ruler' but blamed him for not being terrible enough. Had Ivan 'knifed through' five more noble families, Stalin claimed, the authority of the Tsar would have been maintained and Russia spared the 'Time of Troubles' which reduced it to chaos less than two decades after Ivan's death in 1584.[1] Stalin himself made no such mistake in the Great Terror of 1936–8 which killed and imprisoned millions of mostly imaginary traitors. In January 1941, Stalin sent instructions to the great film-maker Sergei Eisenstein to make a film about Ivan the Terrible. By commissioning a film showing that Ivan's Terror was necessary, Stalin sought to justify his own.*

Ivan IV lived in constant fear of conspiracies against him. In December 1564 he left the Kremlin for his fortified country estate at Alexandrovskaya Sloboda, about 100 kilometres north-east of Moscow, from which he accused boyars, other nobles and Moscow court officials of 'treasonable deeds'; even

---

* The instructions to make the film were transmitted in a letter from A. A. Zhdanov. Eisenstein, however, had no doubt that Zhdanov was acting on Stalin's orders and later referred in a letter to Stalin to 'your instructions'. (Perrie, *Cult of Ivan the Terrible*, p. 149.)

clerics, he claimed, were 'covering up' for the traitors. In January 1565 he announced his intention to divide his realm into two: the *oprichnina* (a term derived from *oprich*, 'separate') under his personal control and the *zemshchina* (from *zemlia*, 'land') ruled by the boyars in Moscow.[2] Though a complete separation between the two parts of Ivan's realm was never established and he spent much of his time in the Moscow Kremlin rather than in the country, the royal decree establishing the *oprichnina* gave the Tsar unlimited power to 'eradicate treason' and execute 'traitors'.[3]

Ivan gave responsibility for identifying and disposing of traitors to his newly established imperial guard, the *oprichniki*, who, bizarrely, he liked to think of as a monastic order with himself as 'Father Superior'.* The *oprichniki*, though their responsibilities went beyond intelligence collection and analysis, were Russia's first organized security service. Swathed in black and mounted on black horses, they must have seemed like a vision from the Apocalypse as they rode though Russia. Each had a dog's head symbolically attached to his saddle (to sniff out and attack treason) and carried a broom (to sweep away traitors). A seventeenth-century silver candlestick preserved in the museum at Alexandrovskaya Sloboda shows Ivan himself on horseback with dog's head and broom.†

The use of dogs' heads by the *oprichniki* was entirely new as well as deeply macabre.[4] Though Russians, like Western Europeans, had long been familiar with folk-tales of Hounds of Hell, dog-headed men and dog-headed monsters, no writer or artist had ever imagined dogs' heads carried on horses. Though the Russians did not practise taxidermy and so had no mounted animals' heads on the walls of their residences as in Western Europe, a dog's head, drained of blood, froze in the Russian winter and could have been carried by *oprichnik* horses when Ivan created the *oprichnina* in January 1565. But in spring the dogs' heads must have begun to decompose, thus limiting their use for six months of the year to those *oprichniki* able to obtain a regular supply.[5]

The dog's head remains the most gruesome symbol ever devised by a security or intelligence agency (far more so than the stylized skull and crossbones of the Nazi SS). It was also a fitting symbol for the chief

---

* The total numbers of *oprichniki* remain difficult, perhaps impossible, to calculate. Ivan originally spoke of 1,000. Their ranks subsequently increased, but recent estimates of 6,000 members (twice the size of today's British Security Service, MI5) may be exaggerated. (Halperin, 'Did Ivan IV's *Oprichniki* Carry Dogs' Heads?', p. 60.)

† An inscription on the base of the candlestick reads: 'the Tsar left the city with the brethren and went to the monastery'; http://www.kreml.alexandrov.ru/. When the museum opened, the restaurant gruesomely displayed the dog's head symbol to enable guests to feel they were dining 'like Ivan the Terrible'.

oprichnik, Grigory Lukyanovich Skuratov-Belski, better known as Maliuta Skuratov – against strong competition, probably the most loathsome figure in the entire history of Russian intelligence. Skuratov, a nickname inherited by Maliuta from his father, meant 'worn-out chamois', a reference to his coarse complexion. 'Maliuta' referred to his short stature. Mikhail Bulgakov, the greatest writer of the Stalin era, wrote in his forbidden masterpiece *The Master and Margarita*:

> Neither Gaius Caesar Caligula nor Messalina interested Margarita any longer, nor did any of the kings, dukes, cavaliers, suicides, poisoners, gallowsbirds, procuresses, prison guards and sharpers, executioners, informers, traitors, madmen, sleuths, seducers. All their names became jumbled in her head, the faces stuck together into one huge pancake, and only a single face lodged itself painfully in her memory – the face, framed in a truly fiery beard, of Maliuta Skuratov.*

By a curious coincidence, the most homicidal of Stalin's intelligence chiefs, Nikolai Yezhov, in whose honour the years of the Terror became known as the *Yezhovshchina*, was as diminutive and almost as unpleasant as Maliuta; he was given the nickname 'Poison Dwarf'. Though Yezhov was responsible for far more deaths than Skuratov, neither he nor any other of Stalin's intelligence chiefs rivalled Skuratov's enthusiasm for the role of executioner-in-chief or showed such sadistic pleasure in mutilating and torturing victims. Stalin's admiration for Skuratov exceeded that for any of his own intelligence chiefs. In 1940 Yezhov was secretly tried, found guilty of nonsensical charges of treason, and taken to execution, hysterically pleading for his life. He quickly became an unperson, airbrushed out of official photographs.[6] By contrast, Stalin continued to praise Skuratov's historical record. At a meeting with Eisenstein in 1941 to discuss the making of his film *Ivan the Terrible*, Stalin declared that 'Maliuta Skuratov was a great army general and died a hero's death in the war with Livonia.' When asked by the actor Nikolai Cherkasov, who played the role of Ivan, whether a scene showing Skuratov in 1569 strangling the Metropolitan of Moscow, Filipp Kolychev (who had publicly condemned Ivan's murders), could appear in the film, 'Stalin said that it was necessary to retain this scene as it was historically correct.' Filipp is now a saint in the Russian

---

* Bulgakov knew that his masterpiece, which he took twelve years to write, could not be published in his – or Stalin's – lifetime. When he died, in 1940, it was still kept in a hiding place in his house. Published a quarter of a century later, it was still regarded with deep suspicion by the KGB as 'a dangerous weapon' in Western 'ideological sabotage against the Soviet Union'. (Andrew and Mitrokhin, *Mitrokhin Archive*, p. 14.)

Orthodox Church. Skuratov was probably the only one of Ivan's closest associates whom he never suspected of plotting against him.[7]

Ultimate responsibility for Skuratov's barbarous purges lay with the Tsar himself. Ivan's way of warfare (he was at war for all but three years of his reign as Tsar)[8] was brutal even by the standards of the day. A German print made in 1561 during the Russian invasion of Livonia (present-day Estonia and Latvia) shows naked women hanging from a tree above the disembowelled bodies of their children while Russian archers use them for target practice. By the heads of the women hang their children's hearts. Though there is no corroboration for these atrocities in the sparse Russian sources, since we know that Ivan committed equally appalling acts of brutality against his Russian subjects it is unlikely that he spared the Livonians.

As during Stalin's Terror four centuries later, none of Ivan's closest associates (save, probably, for Skuratov) could be certain that they would not be suspected of plotting against him. Among the unlikely figures who figured in Ivan's conspiracy theories was Prince Ivan Petrovich Cheliadnin-Fedorov, who had been Ivan's childhood tutor and brought him up in his own household, where his wife had been Ivan's nanny. For the first two years of the *oprichnina* he had been close to Ivan. In 1568, however, Ivan's spies told him, probably wrongly, that Cheliadnin-Fedorov was leading a plot to remove him from power.[9]

According to a probably first-hand account by Albert Schlichting, a German interpreter in the Tsar's court, Ivan summoned Fedorov to the Kremlin, and ordered him to sit on his throne, dressed in royal attire, and hold the royal sceptre. Ivan bowed and knelt before him, saying: 'Now you have what you sought and strove to obtain – to be Grand Prince of Muscovy and occupy my place.' But he added: 'Since I have the power to seat you upon this throne, so I also have power to remove you from it.' He then stabbed Fedorov several times in the heart with a dagger. *Oprichniki* added other dagger blows, 'so that', according to Schlichting's gruesome account, 'his stomach and entrails poured out before the tyrant's eyes'.[10] With Ivan at their head, the *oprichniki* then terrorized Cheliadnin-Fedorov's estates. According to Baron von Standen, a German who served in the *oprichnina*: 'The villages were burned with their churches and everything that was in them, icons and church ornaments. Women and girls were stripped naked and forced in that state to catch chickens in the fields.'[11] In 1569, following rumours that Ivan's cousin Vladimir of Staritsa was planning to seize the throne (probably as baseless as those about Cheliadnin-Fedorov), he was forced by Skuratov to drink poison while his children were murdered around him.[12]

Ivan's reign of terror was no more related to real Russian security needs than Stalin's Terror in the 1930s. It reached its peak in 1570 with the *oprich-niki* massacre of the people of Novgorod, Russia's third-largest city, suspected by Ivan of collective treason.[13] Though the level of *oprichnik* violence may have run out of central control, it is clear that it was premeditated and that Ivan took a personal part in directing it. Before entering Novgorod with the *oprichniki*, he sent one of his commanders with retinue, probably in disguise, to 'spy and reconnoitre' the main targets for pillage and execution. Then, according to Standen, after plundering the bishop's palace:

> He took the largest bells and whatever he wanted from the churches . . . Every day he arose and moved to another monastery. He indulged his wantonness and had monks tortured and many of them were killed. There are 300 monasteries inside and outside the city and not one of these was spared. Then the pillage of the city began . . .
>
> The distress and misery continued in the city for six weeks without inter-ruption . . . Every day the Grand Prince [Ivan] could also be found in the torture chamber in person . . . Several thousand daughters of the inhabitants were carried off by the *oprichniki*.[14]

According to a contemporary account in a German newsletter, on their triumphal return to Moscow after the victory over imaginary treason in Novgorod, the leading *oprichnik* had on his saddle the freshly amputated head of a huge English dog (probably a bull mastiff). Ivan's horse carried a silver replica of a dog's head whose jaws opened and closed in time with the movement of the horse's hooves.[15]

During the Stalin era no suggestion was allowed that any of the killings in Ivan's reign of terror were influenced by the paranoid strain in his per-sonality.* Though the horrors of Ivan's reign of terror have long since ceased to be a taboo subject for Russian historians, they are underplayed by the official history of today's Russian foreign-intelligence service, the Sluzhba Vneshnei Razvedki (SVR), which devotes its first volume to intel-ligence under the tsars. The history makes no mention of the role (or even the name) of the leading *oprichnik*, Maliuta Skuratov. It blames Ivan's brutality in part on his disturbed upbringing in a court riven by intrigue

---

* The leading historian in the interwar Soviet Union, Sergey Platonov, who before the Revo-lution had taught history to the Tsar's children, argued that Ivan had set up the *oprichnina* to destroy the boyar and princely aristocracy and establish a new ruling class of nobles in the service of the state. But Platonov also committed the politically incorrect offence of stressing Ivan's personal responsibility for the atrocities of his reign of terror. In 1930 he was dismissed from his academic post on a trumped-up charge of involvement in a royalist con-spiracy and sent into internal exile, where he died destitute two years later. (Platonov, *Ivan the Terrible*; De Madariaga, *Ivan the Terrible*, Foreword.)

and brutal rivalries. At the age of thirteen, according to the official chronicler of Ivan's reign, he ordered the brutal murder of Prince Andrei Mikhailovich Shuisky, who he complained had treated him with disrespect, resting his dirty boots on the royal bed. Shuisky was torn to pieces by the Kremlin's pack of hunting and guard dogs.[16]

The SVR official history acknowledges the historic achievement of Ivan III 'the Great' (Ivan IV's grandfather, who reigned from 1462 to 1505) in ending Russian subjection to the Mongol 'Golden Horde', but it gives the main credit for the origins of Russian diplomacy and foreign intelligence to Ivan IV and his counsellor, Ivan Mikhailovich Viskovaty, who in 1549 became the first head of Russian diplomacy, though Russia had as yet no permanent ambassadors stationed abroad. Since there was no clear dividing line between diplomacy and intelligence work, the SVR also reasonably regards Viskovaty as Russia's first foreign-intelligence chief. His greatest achievement was probably to conclude the Treaty of Mozhaysk with King Frederick II Denmark in 1562, which gave mutual recognition to both countries' territorial claims in Livonia (modern Estonia and Latvia). The SVR official history concludes that Viskovaty overcame strong initial opposition from the Danish king by 'what is now called in professional intelligence jargon the acquisition of "agents of influence". It took money and remarkable strength of persuasion to secretly win over the Danish nobles who were then at the right moment able to influence the King . . .'[17]

Ivan the Terrible's childhood experience of internecine feuding in the Russian court gave him a natural interest in internal divisions in the foreign courts with which he dealt, such as that of Denmark, on which Viskovaty kept him informed. The SVR official history, however, exaggerates the extent to which Ivan 'appreciated intelligence that helped to orient himself correctly in foreign policy', allegedly rewarding even those who provided useless information to encourage them to remain involved in intelligence collection.[18] As the horrors of Ivan's reign of terror showed, his deeply suspicious nature made it unusually difficult for him to distinguish between real and illusory threats. His later admirer, Joseph Stalin, suffered from the same problem at the outbreak of the Second World War.[19]

Though Viskovaty's judgement was greatly superior to the Tsar's, he suffered from two major handicaps in understanding the outside world by comparison with senior officials in major Western states. First, Russia, like Turkey, had no permanent embassies. Its ambassadors were sent abroad for specific assignments and returned after they were complete or were seen to have failed. The Kremlin was thus deprived of the constant flow of information provided by English and some other European ambassadors. Also like Turkey, though in lesser degree, Russia lacked the print culture which had generated an information revolution in the West.[20] Moscow's first printing house was not founded until 1553, a century later than in Western Europe. Established by Ivan IV and Metropolitan Makarii of Moscow and All Russia, its purpose was to print religious texts. It was deeply unpopular with traditional scribes and is believed to have been burnt down by a mob in 1568. The Kremlin deacon, Ivan Federov, who was chiefly responsible for running the printing house, was forced to flee to Lithuania, though printing resumed soon afterwards.[21] The travel books which were immensely popular in Elizabethan England and help, for example, to account for Shakespeare's detailed knowledge of Italy, in which he set thirteen of his plays, did not exist in Russia. Open-source knowledge of foreign countries and cultures was extremely limited.

Ivan's and Viskovaty's first and closest diplomatic ties in Western Europe were with England. They began not as the result of a Russian policy decision but, as the SVR official history acknowledges, as the unexpected outcome of a failed attempt by the young English merchant adventurer Richard Chancellor, then in his early twenties, to reach China through the Arctic North-East Passage. Chancellor arrived on 24 August 1553 at the mouth of the Northern Dvina river on the White Sea, at the site of the future port of Archangel, which at the time was only a small fishing village. The SVR account emphasizes how effectively Ivan's 'notification system', designed to warn the authorities of the unexpected arrival of foreigners on Russian territory, operated even in this remote, sparsely populated area.[22]

The local governor came aboard Chancellor's ship, agreed to 'afford him the benefit of victuals', and sent a messenger to seek further instructions from the Tsar. When no instructions had been received after three months, Chancellor decided on 25 November to set off himself by horse-drawn sleigh on what he found a 'very long and most troublesome' journey to Moscow. Having covered the greater part of the 600-mile journey, he met coming in the opposite direction a messenger from the Kremlin, who had earlier lost his way, bearing an invitation to him from Ivan IV written 'with all courtesy'. On arrival in Moscow, Chancellor and his men were kept under surveillance for twelve days before Viskovaty informed them that they were to be received by the Tsar. In the royal court, wrote Chancellor later, 'there sat a very honourable company of courtiers to the number of one hundred, all apparelled in cloth of gold down to their ankles'. The throne room made Chancellor's men 'wonder at the Majesty of the Emperor [Tsar]':

> His seat was aloft, in a very royal throne, having on his head a diadem, or crown of gold, apparelled with a robe all of goldsmith's work and in his

hand he held a Sceptre garnished, and beset with precious stones, and
besides all . . . there was a majesty in his countenance proportionable with
the excellence of his estate . . .

Chancellor and his men were invited to an enormous dinner which gave an
unexpected insight into the nature of Ivan's personal autocracy. In the course
of the meal Ivan addressed each of the many nobles and other diners by name:
'The Russes told our men that the reason thereof . . . was to the end that the
emperor might keep the knowledge of his own household, and withal, that
such as are under his displeasure might by this means be known.'[23]

Because of difficulty in transliterating his surname into Cyrillic, official
Russian documents referred to Chancellor by his first name, 'Richard'.[24]
Following his return to England in 1554, the Muscovy Company was
founded in London to trade with Russia. At a time when Russia still had
no outlet on the Baltic coast, the new company offered an important trading link with the West and a valuable source of arms and munitions for
Ivan's many wars, as well as of luxury goods. The Muscovy Company (later
known as the Russia Company) also made a lucrative trade by importing
furs and ship-building supplies.[25] After Chancellor's second voyage to Russia in 1555, Ivan ordered the construction of an embassy for English
diplomats and merchants within the walls of the Kremlin, and gave the
Muscovy Company exemption from Russian customs duties. According to
the SVR official history, which largely agrees with Western accounts:

> Flushed with success, Chancellor returned home [in 1556] with a rich cargo
> in his ship and the first Russian ambassador [to England] on board, Osip
> Nepeya. In a stormy night at the Scottish coast, the ship crashed against
> the rocks. Whilst trying to save the Moscow ambassador, Chancellor was
> killed along with his son and most of the crew. Nepeya escaped and was
> ceremoniously received in London, where local merchants arranged a cele-
> bration in his honour.[26]

Nepeya returned to Russia in 1557 on the ship of Chancellor's successor,
the experienced sea captain Anthony Jenkinson ('Anton Iankin' in Russian
documents),[27] who acted as both English ambassador and Moscow representative of the London Muscovy Company. With them, at Nepeya's
request, travelled English craftsmen, doctors, and gold and silver prospec-
tors. Unsurprisingly, after his terrifying voyage to London, Nepeya
expressed 'great joy' on his safe return to Russia.[28]

The different roles of Nepeya and Jenkinson exemplify the gulf between
English knowledge of Ivan IV's Russia and Russian understanding of
Tudor England. Nepeya had come to London on a temporary diplomatic

mission to cement the trading relationship begun by Chancellor. He left no Russian embassy or representative behind him in London. Because of Russia's lack of any direct sources of information in Tudor England, news of the death of Edward VI, the accession of Mary, her marriage to Philip II, Mary's death and the accession of Elizabeth seem to have been brought to Moscow by Chancellor and Jenkinson. It is highly unlikely that the Tsar and his advisers understood the political and religious complexities of these regime changes. In addition to the problems of translating Tudor diplomatic communications written in Latin, they found them more generally confusing. Ivan later complained to Elizabeth: 'How many letters we have received in all this time, and all with different seals! That is not the royal custom. And such documents are not trusted in any State. Rulers of States have only one seal.' Ivan, however, claimed to have believed all these documents and to have done as Elizabeth had asked.[29]

Unlike Nepeya in London, Jenkinson established a permanent English embassy and trade mission in Moscow. He quickly became the most influential foreigner at Ivan's court.[30] Jenkinson's warm welcome in the Kremlin in December 1557, when he presented letters to Ivan from Queen Mary and her husband, Philip II, must have owed something to Nepeya's account of how Chancellor had been drowned saving his life during the voyage to England. A gargantuan dinner followed on Christmas Day, 1557. Jenkinson already knew from Chancellor's account of his first visit to the Kremlin that the dinner would enable him to judge the extent of the Tsar's favour. Ivan made clear to the whole court that Jenkinson was an exceptionally honoured guest. Seated by himself at a table of his own next to the Tsar's, 'the emperor sent me divers bowls of wine and mead, and many dishes of meat from his own hand'. Ivan showed his favour once again at the Twelfth Night dinner in Ivan's Kremlin palace, where, wrote Jenkinson, 'I sat alone as I did before directly before the emperor, and had my meat, bread and drink sent me from the emperor.' Despite the warmth of the royal welcome, Jenkinson had no illusions about Ivan's tyrannical regime: 'He keepeth his people in great subjection; all matters pass his judgment be they never so small.'[31]

Though Chancellor's and Jenkinson's accounts of their pioneering missions to the court of Ivan the Terrible are nowadays recognized as important historical sources,[32] at the time they were treated by both the Muscovy Company and the Tudor court as intelligence reports to be kept secret. None of Chancellor's reflections on his time in Russia were published until 1589, five years after Ivan's death. Ivan and Viskovaty, among others, would have been outraged by Chancellor's frank comments on Ivan's tyrannical rule, on the Tsar's court ('much surpassed and excelled by the beauty and elegancy of the houses of the kings of England')[33] and on some beliefs of the Russian Orthodox Church ('foolish and childish dotages of ... ignorant barbarians').[34] Chancellor provided military as well as political intelligence, notably a report entitled 'Of the discipline of war amongst the Russes', which would also have caused offence in the Kremlin. He made, however, the wildly exaggerated claim, probably derived from boasting in the Kremlin, that, in time of war, the Tsar 'never armeth a less number against the enemy than three hundred thousand soldiers'.[35] The Muscovy Company regarded even Chancellor's less controversial reports on the main Russian cities as commercial intelligence which was too valuable to potential rivals to be made public.

Ivan's personal favour allowed Jenkinson unlimited freedom to travel through Russia and cross its borders. After a perilous expedition to Central Asia, he returned to the Kremlin in September 1559 to a hero's welcome, bringing with him twenty-five Russians whom he had rescued from slavery, as well as six Tatar envoys. No British representative since has ever won such favour in the Kremlin. After spending a year back in London, Jenkinson returned to Russia for the third time in 1561 and, in the course of his own travels further east, became the first English envoy to be used as a secret emissary by a Russian Tsar.* In 1562 Ivan personally entrusted him with a hazardous mission to Abdullah-Khan, ruler of Shirvan in the eastern Caucasus, whence he returned a year later with a large consignment of silk and jewels as well as what Ivan regarded as favourable letters from both Abdullah-Khan and the ruler of Georgia. Jenkinson was rewarded with further concessions for the Muscovy Company.[36]†

Ivan continued to take Jenkinson into his confidence to a remarkable degree, unaware that in 1566 he wrote to William Cecil, Queen Elizabeth I's Secretary of State, denouncing the *oprichniki* campaign of terror against nobles suspected of plotting against the Tsar.[37] In the summer of 1567 Ivan began telling Jenkinson that, because of (probably largely imaginary) plots against him, he might have to seek asylum in England.[38] Having taken leave of Ivan on 22 September 1567, Jenkinson returned to England by sea with an official letter and a secret message from the Tsar, both of which he delivered personally to Elizabeth in November. Remarkably, Ivan had thus selected for what he regarded as an important secret assignment a trusted English adventurer in preference to a Russian envoy. In the messages Ivan stressed his desire for a Russian–English alliance, to be negotiated via Jenkinson, and made the extraordinary proposal (unique in the history

---

* The second was Jerome Horsey in 1580. See below, p. 155.
† His own travels also took him to the court of the Shah of Persia. (Brotton, *This Orient Isle*, pp. 52–9.)

of English foreign relations) that each monarch should have the right to take refuge in the other's country: 'The Emperor [Tsar] earnestly requireth that there may be a perpetual friendship and kindred betwixt the Queen's Majesty and him.'[39] Ivan may well have wished to conceal his request for political asylum from Viskovaty and other Kremlin officials.

Ivan had expected Jenkinson to return to Russia with Elizabeth's reply. Jenkinson, however, was replaced by a new envoy: the diplomat Sir Thomas Randolph, former Master of Broadgates Hall (now Pembroke College), Oxford. Randolph was the brother-in-law of Elizabeth's intelligence chief and Foreign Secretary, Sir Francis Walsingham, who probably had a hand in his appointment.[40] Walsingham later used his influence on three occasions to help Randolph become MP for Maidstone.* No record survives of what Randolph discovered after his arrival on the White Sea coast in July 1568 about the *oprichniki* reign of terror, but he clearly feared for his own personal safety, writing to William Cecil even before he reached Moscow that he was anxious to conclude his mission and return to England as quickly as possible.[41] George Turberville, Randolph's secretary and a former Fellow of New College, Oxford, privately denounced the Russians in poems sent to his friends as 'a people passing rude, to vices vile inclin'd'.[42] Randolph's reception on arriving at Moscow late in September added to his anxieties. There was no one to welcome him; even members of the English embassy were not 'suffered to meet us'. As he later acknowledged, the contrast between his own initial reception and that of Jenkinson 'bred suspicion in me'. Though supplied with victuals, he was disturbed by the hostile manner of the Russian appointed to ensure that he did not leave the embassy and received no visitors: 'We had no small cause to doubt that some evil had been intended unto us.'

After seventeen weeks under house arrest, Randolph was finally invited to an audience with the Tsar on 20 February 1569. Ivan failed to invite him to dinner, as he had done Chancellor and Jenkinson, but freed him from house arrest: 'I dine not this day openly, for great affairs I have; but I will send thee my dinner, and give leave to thee and thine to go at liberty, and augment our allowance to thee in token of our love and favour to our sister the Queen of England.' A few days later Ivan summoned Randolph for over three hours of secret talks in the early hours of the morning. The Tsar then left Moscow for Alexandrovskaya Sloboda, believed by

---

* Randolph was due to take part in the trial which led to the execution of Mary, Queen of Scots, at Fotheringhay Castle in 1587 but was 'forced to return home – so miserably I was tormented with the colic'. Walsingham curiously addressed his brother-in-law as 'Uncle', possibly because he was older. (*ODNB* Thomas Randolph.)

Randolph to be 'the house of his solace'. On his return to the Kremlin six weeks later, Ivan summoned Randolph for further talks, during which Randolph claimed to have secured all the 'large privileges' he had sought for the Muscovy Company.[43]

Ivan, however, was seriously dissatisfied. He had hoped to secure an alliance with England, directed mainly against Poland. Randolph stuck to his instructions to 'pass these matters with silence', leading the Tsar to complain in a letter to Elizabeth that her envoy's 'talk was of boorishness and affairs of merchants', and failed to address 'our princely affairs'.[44] To accompany Randolph on his return voyage to England in October 1569, Ivan sent his own ambassador, Alexander Grigoryevich Sovin, with a draft treaty of alliance to which he was instructed to obtain Elizabeth's signature. Sovin was told that no changes could be accepted in the draft, predictably failed in his mission, and returned to Russia in the following year.[45]

Ivan's diplomacy and intelligence collection suffered a major self-inflicted blow on 25 July 1570 with the execution of Viskovaty, who fell victim to another of the Tsar's conspiracy theories, bizarrely accused of plotting with Lithuania and urging the Ottoman Turks and the Khan of Crimea to invade Russia. In reality, as contemporary records show, so far from plotting with Viskovaty, Lithuanian envoys found him 'not well disposed' and 'intractable' in negotiations with them.[46] Having refused to beg forgiveness for treason he had not committed, Viskovaty was strung up in a market square and sliced to death. Skuratov began the execution by cutting off his nose, another *oprichnik* removed his ears and a third hacked off his genitals. Ivan complained that Viskovaty died too quickly. Over a hundred other gruesome executions followed of probably innocent victims.[47] Viskovaty's fate prefigured that of Stalin's three most powerful intelligence chiefs, all of whom were also executed for imaginary acts of treason, which, absurdly, included spying for Britain.*

The bizarre nature of Ivan's relations with England in the aftermath of Viskovaty's execution reflected the Tsar's loss of his diplomatic expertise. On 24 October 1570, outraged by Elizabeth I's refusal to sign the draft alliance delivered by Sovin, Ivan personally penned a letter to the Queen which, so far as is known, was the rudest she ever received. According to the translation prepared for Elizabeth, he said that his previous willingness to correspond with her on 'weighty affairs' of state had been based on the

---

* Genrikh Yagoda, Nikolai Yezhov and Lavrenti Beria were executed in, respectively 1938, 1940 and 1953; Beria was executed during the power struggle after Stalin's death. Though the manners of their deaths were less horrific than that of Viskovaty, both Yagoda and Yezhov were beaten before being shot.

mistaken belief that 'you had been ruler over your land, and had sought honour to yourself and profit to your Country ... But now we perceive that there be other men that do rule, and not men but boors and merchants, the which seek not the wealth and honour of our majesties, but they seek their own profit of merchandise ... And you flourish in your maidenlike estate like a maid', he added insultingly, before announcing the cancellation of the rights previously granted to the Muscovy Company: 'The privilege that we gave to your Merchants be from this day of none effect.'[48]*

Despite the rudeness of the letter, Elizabeth and her advisers clearly believed that the trading privileges of the Muscovy Company were too important to abandon. It was therefore decided to ignore Ivan's insults and send the Tsar's favourite Englishman, Anthony Jenkinson, on a new mission to Moscow as English ambassador as well as Company representative to try to restore relations.† His mission began badly. After landing on the Arctic coast in July 1571, he was stranded for over six months as the result of travel restrictions imposed after an outbreak of plague. His first report to William Cecil (newly ennobled as Baron Burghley) gave further details of atrocities committed during the *oprichniki* reign of terror. Jenkinson eventually had an audience with Ivan in the Kremlin on 23 March 1572. His instructions were to persuade Ivan to agree to reinstate the privileges of the Muscovy Company by hinting at the possibility of an Anglo-Russian political alliance but to make no binding commitments. Such was the Tsar's confidence in Jenkinson that, at their next meeting on 13 May, Ivan agreed to restore all the Company's privileges and complimented 'Anthony' on his role in restoring Russian–English relations. Jenkinson arrived back in England on 23 July after what the *Dictionary of National Biography* terms 'a brilliant culmination to a career which won him a permanent place in the history of Anglo-Russian relations'.[49]

By the time Ivan began negotiations with Jenkinson, his main anger was directed not against Elizabeth I but against his own *oprichniki*, whom he blamed for failing to defend Moscow against a devastating Tatar raid in 1571, which (as reported by Jenkinson to Cecil) laid waste much of the

* The translation slightly softened some of the insults. The sentence 'You flourish in your maidenlike estate like a maid' is more accurately translated: 'And you are in your virginal state like some old unmarried female.' (Russian text and this translation at http://eng.history.ru/content/view/131/87/.)

† Jenkinson was instructed to pass on a message from the Queen that 'No merchants govern Our State and affairs but We Ourselves take care of Our affairs'. (http://eng.history.ru/content/view/131/87/, n. 24.)

city outside the Kremlin. In 1572 Ivan formally abolished the *oprichniki*.*
Though Jenkinson did not return to Russia after 1572, Ivan continued to
make occasional secret use of other English diplomats. In 1580 he entrusted
an English diplomat in Moscow, Jerome Horsey (later knighted), with
what he regarded as a secret mission to England to obtain supplies of
'powder, saltpetre, lead and brimstone'.[50] Horsey doubtless reported his
secret mission to his patron, Sir Francis Walsingham, and later dedicated
to him a book on his travels in Russia.† Horsey's seventeen years in Moscow epitomize the frequent sixteenth-century overlap between diplomacy
and espionage.[51] What is remarkable in Horsey's case is that, because of
Russia's lack of both diplomats and spies in England, his services (like
those of Jenkinson before him) were used by the Tsar, as well as, more
frequently, by Walsingham. Horsey was so trusted by Ivan that he was
invited into his Treasury and, in 1581, given a secret letter, hidden in a
flask, to take to Queen Elizabeth.[52]

During the final years of his reign, Ivan continued to suffer from uncon-
trollable fits of rage. During one of them in 1581, he accidentally killed
his son and heir. Ilya Repin's famous painting, which shows the Tsar
grieving over the bloodstained body of his son Ivan, which was completed
in 1885, four years after the assassination of Tsar Alexander II, so disturbed his son Alexander III that he had it temporarily removed from
Moscow's Tretyakov Gallery.

The SVR official history plausibly argues that, after the death of his
son, in the final years before his own death, in 1584, Ivan began to 'repent'
that he had ordered so many executions. From 1583 all monasteries started
regular 'Remembrances of the Disgraced'. The execution Ivan most regretted was almost certainly that of Viskovaty, whose expertise had never
been replaced. Ivan personally sent to the Holy Trinity Monastery 223
rubles for the 'remembrance of the soul of Viskovaty' as well as another
twenty-three rubles to pay for candles.[53] No other intelligence chief has
ever been remembered in this way by a ruler who ordered his execution.

Ivan IV was succeeded by his devout but simple-minded younger son,
Tsar Fedor I (a 'silly prince', in the opinion of Sir Jerome Horsey).[54] Real
power, however, lay with a faction-ridden regency council in which Boris

---

* After abolishing the *oprichnina*, however, Ivan returned to the practice of dividing his
court in the mid-1570s. (Bogatyrev, 'Ivan IV', p. 260; Pavlov and Perrie, *Ivan the Terrible*,
p. 125.)
† Possibly because of Horsey's private trading missions, the Muscovy Company became
suspicious of him. Shortly before his death, Walsingham overrode objections from the Company to have him appointed ambassador to Russia in 1590. (Berry and Crummey (eds.), *Rude
and Barbarous Kingdom*, pp. 250–52.)

Godunov (best known nowadays as the anti-hero of Mussorgsky's popular nineteenth-century opera) eventually won a prolonged power struggle. Horsey, who, as under Ivan IV, was occasionally used by Godunov for secret missions, reported that at one point during the power struggle, also like Ivan, Godunov told him he might seek refuge in England.[55]* He found Godunov 'of comely person, well favoured, affable . . . not learned but of sudden apprehension, and a natural good orator'. But Godunov was also superstitious ('affected much to necromancy') and 'revengeful'.[56]† He had a sinister past both as an *oprichnik* from the age of about twenty and as the son-in-law of the most bloodthirsty of all the *oprichniki*, Maliuta Skuratov.[57] To rise in the court of Ivan the Terrible, he must have shown enthusiastic support for the brutal execution of imaginary traitors in Novgorod and Moscow. Probably largely at the expense of his victims, Godunov built up enormous wealth. The historian Catherine Merridale describes him as the nearest sixteenth-century 'equivalent of a twenty-first-century oligarch'.[58]

Unlike Ivan IV, however, Godunov tried – successfully – to avoid foreign wars. He deserves much of the credit for the twenty-year period of peace which followed Ivan's death.[59] During the regency Godunov also showed no liking for the public execution of traitors. Instead he proceeded behind the scenes, built up a large network of informers and disposed secretly of some of his main rivals.[60]‡ While ambassador in Moscow from 1588 to 1589 on a mission to settle disputes involving the Russia Company, the English writer and diplomat Giles Fletcher, a former Fellow of King's College, Cambridge, felt under almost continuous hostile surveillance. As he complained to Burghley, 'My whole entertainment from my first arrival till towards the very end was such as if they had devised means of very purpose to show their utter disliking both of the trade of the Merchants, and of the whole English nation.' Though he was eventually able to negotiate an agreement, according to the well-known writer Thomas Fuller when he returned home in the summer of 1589 'he heartily expressed his

---

* Horsey seems also to have been used by Walsingham to promote his own business ventures in Russia. Though Horsey's account is sometimes unreliable, he was sometimes used by Godunov for secret missions, which included a (successful) journey to Livonia to persuade a member of the imperial family, Mariya Vladimirovna, widow of Prince Magnus, to return to Russia. Horsey eventually fell out with Godunov; he was arrested in 1589 and sent back to England in the custody of Giles Fletcher.

† Horsey's assessment of Godunov's positive qualities is the more credible for having been written after they had fallen out and he had been expelled from Russia.

‡ Among the rivals secretly disposed of was Ivan IV's former treasurer, Petr Golovin, who was exiled from Moscow and, according to Horsey, 'dispatched of his life upon the way'. (Sir Jerome Horsey, 'Travels', in Berry and Crummey (eds.), *Rude and Barbarous Kingdom*, p. 322.)

thankfulness to God for his safe return from so great a danger; for the
Poets cannot fancy *Ulysses* more glad to be come out of the *Den* of
Polyphemus, than he was to be rid out of the power of such a *barbarious
Prince*'.[61]

In 1591 Fletcher tried to publish a book based on his experiences, entitled *Of the Russe Commonwealth, or, The manner of government by the
Russe emperor . . . with the manners, and fashions of the people of that
country*. The best and most detailed account by any Elizabethan traveller
to Russia, it made clear Fletcher's loathing for the Russian political system:
'The state and form of their government is plain tyrannical.' The worst of
the tyrants had been Ivan the Terrible:

> To show his sovereignty over the lives of his subjects, the late emperor Ivan
> [IV] Vasilevich in his walks or progresses, if he had misliked the face or
> person of any man whom he met by the way, or that looked upon him,
> would command his head to be struck off, which was promptly done, and
> the head cast before him.[62]

The governors of the Russia Company no doubt believed, as they had done
after Richard Chancellor produced an account of his mission a generation
earlier, that publication of Fletcher's book would reveal valuable commercial intelligence to their competitors. But their main fear was that, if the
Godunov regime discovered what Fletcher had written about their 'tyrannical' rule, 'the revenge thereof will light on their people and goods
remaining in Moscow, and utterly overthrow the trade forever'. Burghley
clearly agreed and the book was suppressed. Its contents were still highly
sensitive two and a half centuries later. In 1848 Tsar Nicholas I ordered
the confiscation of the first Russian translation of *Of the Russe Commonwealth* and severe punishment of the officials of the Imperial Moscow
Society of Russian History and Antiquities who had dared to publish it
in their *Proceedings*.[63] No other British intelligence report on Russia has
remained so controversial for so long.

On the death of Fedor I in 1598, Boris Godunov became Tsar. Though
most of the details of his surveillance system will probably never be
known, his network of spies and informers increased. Servants were
encouraged to inform on their masters. Even slaves were used as informants. Boris's uncle, Semen Nikitich Godunov, his chief inquisitor and an
enthusiastic torturer, reported to him regularly on the evidence of treason
he claimed to have uncovered during his brutal interrogations. But Godunov's surveillance system and secret intrigues failed to secure the succession.
On his death in April 1605 he was succeeded by his son, the well-educated
sixteen-year-old Fedor Borisovich Godunov, who was crowned Tsar Fedor

II. In May the army mutinied and many of its commanders sided with a pretender to the throne, the so-called first 'False Dmitrii'. In June Fedor II and his mother (Skuratov's daughter) were strangled in the Kremlin by Dmitrii's agents and their bodies put on public display. The hated Semen Godunov was thrown into a prison cell and left to starve to death.[64] There followed years of chaotic civil war and Russia's 'Time of Troubles'.

10

Elizabeth I, Walsingham and the Rise of English Intelligence

The long reign of Elizabeth I from 1558 to 1603 is nowadays remembered as one of the most glorious in English history. At the time it was a period of intense insecurity. Menaced by enemies at home and abroad, the Queen knew that her hold on the crown was precarious. The Catholic powers of Europe regarded her as both a bastard and a heretic. The loyalty of English Catholics, unreconciled to her Protestant Church settlement, was always in doubt. The Virgin Queen created further anxiety by persistently refusing to nominate a successor. The stability of the regime thus depended on her own survival. As one MP put it in 1567: 'If God should take her Majesty, the succession being not established, I know not what shall become of myself, my wife, my children, lands, goods, friends or country.'[1] The combined threats of foreign invasion and a Catholic fifth column at home led the Elizabethan state to create what was then the world's most sophisticated intelligence system.

From 1573 until his death in 1590, as Elizabeth's principal Secretary of State, Sir Francis Walsingham combined the roles of Foreign Secretary and intelligence chief, with daily access to the Queen and her Chief Minister, William Cecil (from 1571 Baron Burghley), who had previously borne the main responsibility for intelligence operations. In 1568 Walsingham wrote to Cecil that 'there is less danger in fearing too much than too little'. This axiom became his credo.[2] Under Walsingham's personal leadership espionage, counter-espionage, codebreaking and counter-subversion were better integrated than ever before in the history of intelligence.

Partly because of the disappearance of his private papers, much about Walsingham's early career remains mysterious. Even his date of birth (probably about 1532) is unknown. He was educated at King's College, Cambridge, which, like many others, he left, in 1550, without taking a degree. His memories of undergraduate life must have been positive, since Cambridge later became perhaps his most important intelligence recruiting ground. After leaving King's, he travelled for some years on the Continent, forming a particular affection for Protestant Basel. At difficult moments in later life, he sometimes wished himself back 'among the true hearted Swiss'. He interrupted his travels to study law at Gray's Inn, where his father had been treasurer. But there is no record of Walsingham holding any public office until 1568, when he was about thirty-six.[3]

When he became intelligence chief five years later, he seems – like the Queen and her other ministers – to have known little, if anything, about pre-Tudor intelligence operations. Elizabeth's father, Henry VIII, had made some attempt to model himself on Edward III,[4] but almost certainly had no idea of his intelligence successes and failures during the Hundred Years War:* among them his dramatic escape, guided by an English agent, across the marshes of the Somme in 1346 to avoid being trapped by French forces.[5] English government documents for the Hundred Years War (few if any of them seen by Walsingham) contain many references to the despatch of *exploratores* or *espies* across the Channel to seek intelligence on French intentions,[6]† but give little sense of an organized foreign-intelligence service. Most spies seem to have been obscure individuals, often identified only in vague terms such as 'a certain messenger', though they also included some merchants who travelled to France on business, such as the London goldsmith John Bridd in the reign of Henry IV. The usual mission given to the spies was 'to discover the intentions and plans of the enemies of the king . . . and to inform the king and council of their plans'. They were often told to proceed 'with all possible haste'.[7] The greatest successes were achieved by spies operating from English possessions in France, especially Calais and Bordeaux, in the early fifteenth century at a time during the Hundred Years War when France suffered internal collapse on a scale unmatched until the German invasion in 1940. In 1406 English spies in Paris reported to Calais on preparations for the invasion of English-ruled Gironde by Louis, duc d'Orléans, brother of King Charles VI and effective ruler of France. Bordeaux and other frontier towns organized an espionage network which provided regular, usually reliable reports of French troop movements. Their sources included a high-level informant in the camp of the duc d'Orléans whose intelligence was considered so important that it was revealed to Bordeaux *jurats* (members of the municipal council) only after they had taken an oath of secrecy.[8]

---

* Research on intelligence operations in the Hundred Years War, long neglected, remains a work in progress. Despite valuable recent work by, among others, Jonathan Sumption and Chris Given-Wilson, there are many important gaps in the very fragmentary source material.

† *Explorator* was a Latin term for spy (see above, p. 47); *espies* was Old French.

England's later loss of its French possessions, culminating in the capture of Calais by French forces in 1558, deprived Walsingham of the ability to use France as a major base for English intelligence operations. Nor was he able to learn much from the largely forgotten lessons of foreign intelligence in the Hundred Years War. Walsingham ran Elizabethan intelligence not from a set of government offices but from his own home in the Aldgate district of London, known as the 'Papey', a converted medieval hospital originally constructed to care for indigent and infirm chantry priests who had said masses for the souls of departed benefactors (a profession of which Walsingham strongly disapproved). The most secret volume in Walsingham's house was 'The book of secret intelligences', in which he recorded the names and aliases of his agents, the money they were paid and details of codes and ciphers.* No previous intelligence chief is known to have kept such a comprehensive compilation of intelligence secrets for his personal use. The size, complexity and bureaucracy of modern intelligence communities mean that no intelligence chief today possesses such a volume. But in Elizabethan England the much smaller scale of intelligence operations meant that one exceptionally hard-working and talented administrator could personally keep track of most operations. Even Walsingham, however, sometimes found his workload too much. He suffered from intermittent ill-health, probably due to a kidney stone, and was regularly forced to take sick leave, though he seems to have written almost as much when confined to bed as when sitting at his desk.[9] Unlike twentieth- and twenty-first-century intelligence chiefs in authoritarian (and some non-authoritarian) regimes, Walsingham did not fear to 'tell truth to power'. After one disagreement in 1586, an exasperated Elizabeth took off one of her slippers and threw it at his head.[10] Walsingham seems to have believed, like one of Margaret Thatcher's intelligence chiefs four centuries later, that 'My job was to tell her what she did not want to know.'[11]

Walsingham's panel portrait in the National Portrait Gallery, painted in about 1585 by John de Critz the Elder, shows a dark, brooding presence. Walsingham is dressed in black save for the obligatory white ruff around his neck, with black beard, moustache flecked with grey and receding hair beneath a scholar's cap.† Recent infrared examination of another portrait by an unknown artist has revealed a secret Walsingham never knew. This portrait was painted over a Catholic image of the Virgin and child. Walsingham would have been horrified. Dr Tarnya Cooper, chief curator at the National Portrait Gallery, suggests that the artist may have

---

* The 'Book of Secret Intelligences' has not survived. (Alford, *Watchers*, p. 18.)
† See ill. 14.

been having an irreverent private joke at the expense of the devoutly Protestant Walsingham.*

Walsingham was the most single-minded Protestant ideologue at Elizabeth's court. 'Above all things', he wrote, 'I wish God's glory and next the queen's safety.' He had been ambassador in Paris during the 1572 St Bartholomew's Day massacre, probably the century's worst religious atrocity, 'of which most horrible spectacle', he wrote later, 'I was an eye witness'. At least 2,000 Protestants were murdered in Paris and even more in the provinces amid, at times, a carnival atmosphere. Pope Gregory XIII ordered a *Te Deum* in celebration.[12] Walsingham's loathing and distrust of Catholicism were powerfully reinforced.

Better than any previous spymaster, however, Walsingham understood the importance of recruiting agents among his hated ideological opponents. Some of his best agents on the Continent were English Catholic exiles: among them Anthony Standen (alias Pompeo Pellegrini),[13] who provided vital intelligence on Philip II's preparations for the Spanish Armada. Walsingham's most important agents in the entourage of Mary, Queen of Scots, and in the French embassy in London, Gilbert Gifford and 'Henri Fagot', were both Catholic priests.[14] It would never have occurred to Philip II to recruit agents among the few remaining Spanish Protestants (whom he was determined to exterminate), though one English ambassador with serious gambling debts volunteered his services to him a few years before the Armada.[15]

For much of Elizabeth's reign as England's first Protestant queen and Supreme Governor of the Church of England, the main aim of most plots against her by English Catholics and their foreign supporters was to replace her on the English throne by Mary Stuart, Catholic daughter of James V of Scotland and his French queen, Mary of Guise. After the death of James V without a male heir in 1542, Mary Stuart had been crowned Queen of Scots at the age of only nine months, howling throughout her coronation. For the rest of her childhood, Mary's future seemed to lie in France rather than Scotland or England. At the age of four she was betrothed to the French dauphin, Francis, son and heir of King Henry II. In September 1558, two months before the 25-year-old Elizabeth succeeded Mary Tudor in England, the fifteen-year-old Mary married Francis, fourteen years old, in Paris. Less than a year later her husband became

---

* This is unlikely to have been a mere recycling of an unwanted panel painting. Infrared X-rays of 120 Tudor portraits at the National Portrait Gallery have revealed only one other case of overpainting religious iconography. (http://www.npg.org.uk/blog/under-the-skin-a-newly-discovered-piece-of-satirical-tudor-art.php, accessed 1 Sept. 2013.)

King Francis II after the sudden death of Henry II in a jousting tournament. Mary, like Elizabeth a descendant of Henry VII, publicly laid claim
to the English throne.[16]

While Mary Stuart was in France, her Catholic mother, Mary of
Guise, ruled Scotland as Queen Regent. Her rule, supported by French
troops, was challenged by Scottish Protestant nobles, the 'Lords of the
Congregation'. In 1559 the Lords appealed to William Cecil for military
support, which Cecil supplied – though he overcame opposition from
Elizabeth only by threatening to resign. By the spring of 1560 Cecil's most
valuable Scottish intelligence came from the decrypted cipher correspondence of the Queen Regent, some of it intercepted in Scotland,[17] some in
France.[18] Much, if not all, of the intercepted correspondence was decrypted
by John Somer, a mysterious figure largely ignored by historians, who
worked as secretary to the English ambassador in France, Sir Nicholas
Throckmorton.* The security of correspondence between the French
court and the Queen Regent was poorly protected in Paris. Throckmorton
reported that on one occasion the courier, a 'gentleman archer' named
Beaumont in the French royal guard, had given Somer access to one of the
letters to Mary of Guise for two hours, during which it was doubtless
transcribed before being 'made cunningly up again' to conceal the fact
that it had been opened. Throckmorton asked Cecil to ensure that, when
Beaumont arrived in England, he was 'well used' and given '100 crowns
at the least': 'Having his wife here of the French Queen [Mary Stuart]'s
privy chamber he may be able to serve some good turn and give advertisements [intelligence] from time to time.'[19]

Copies of Somer's decrypts were sent by Cecil to the Scottish 'Lords of
the Congregation', who had provided him with some of the Queen Regent's
intercepted correspondence. The Lords failed to keep the secret. One or
more of them seems to have used the intercepts in an attempt to discredit
her.† Decrypted letters of 1 May from the Queen Regent revealed that she
had 'got knowledge that her letter and [those of] the French have been
deciphered'. The inevitable consequence, Throckmorton warned Cecil,

---

* Little is known about the career of John Somer (also known as Sommer, Somers, Sommers
and Summers), who has no entry in the ODNB. He had previously worked as secretary to
Mary Tudor's ambassador in France, Nicholas Wotton. (S. Tomokiyo, 'Ciphers during the
Reign of Queen Elizabeth I', www.h4.dion.ne.jp/~room4me/america/code/elizabeth.htm.)
† It is highly unlikely, given the precautions taken by Somer to preserve the secrecy of the
decrypts, that the leak came from the English embassy in Paris. Before sending the decrypts
to Cecil in London he re-enciphered them in what he believed to be a secure cipher and took
other measures to disguise their source. (Throckmorton to Cecil, 6 April 1560, CSP Foreign
Elizabeth, vol. 3.)

would be 'an alteration of all their ciphers'. Somer, however, rose to the challenge. Throckmorton informed the Privy Council on 19 July, when forwarding further decrypts, that, though the cipher in which they were sent was 'new and difficult', following the 'dangerous intelligence' the French had received that 'their letters have been deciphered', Somer had broken it: 'Mr Somers' [sic] great travail and good service declares itself worthy [of] recompense.' Throckmorton concluded by praying that the Privy Council 'may be imbued with God's Holy Spirit'.[20]

On 17 June a French cannon shot fired from Edinburgh Castle announced the conclusion of an armistice in the civil war between the Catholic Queen Regent and the Protestant Lords of the Congregation. Peace negotiations followed, with Cecil as one of the two English negotiators. The importance Cecil attached to the intelligence provided by codebreaking was shown by his response to a ciphered letter sent by a French secretary in Edinburgh Castle which was intercepted but could not be decrypted. Cecil said he 'would have given 100 [pounds] to have had Somer here'.* The Treaty of Edinburgh, signed on 6 July, was a triumph for Cecil. French forces left Scotland and returned to France and, following the death of the Queen Regent in June, a Scottish Protestant regency was established. By the treaty Mary, Queen of Scots, and Francis II had to give up their claims to the English throne. Five months later, in December 1560, Mary also lost her place on the French throne following the death of her husband, Francis, probably from a brain tumour. In August 1561 she returned to Scotland, a devoutly Catholic queen in a country with a fiercely Protestant clique in power. After her second marriage to Lord Darnley and the birth of her son, the future James VI of Scotland and James I of England, in 1566, she was allowed no contact with him. Mary's disputes with Scotland's Protestant lords led to her abdication in July 1567 and a year later to her flight to England, where she spent the next nineteen years under house arrest in a succession of castles and stately homes.

The main threat to English security, both Cecil and Walsingham believed, came from plots backed by Philip II, with papal blessing, to depose Elizabeth and put Mary on the throne to return England to the Catholic faith. The seriousness of the assassination threat to Elizabeth was emphasized by the shooting in Linlithgow on 23 January 1570 of

---

* Cecil instructed that 'If Mr. Hampton [possibly one of his secretaries] can do nothing with it', it should be sent to Somer in Paris to be decrypted. That is probably what happened, but Somer is unlikely to have replied before the Treaty of Edinburgh was signed on 6 July. (Cecil to Petre, 21 June 1560, *CSP Foreign Elizabeth*, vol. 3.)

James Stewart, 1st Earl of Moray. After Mary's abdication, Moray had become Regent for her infant son, James, whom she never saw again. Moray's assassin was James Hamilton of Bothwellhaugh, who was motivated by both a desire to avenge Mary and personal grievance. As Moray was riding through Linlithgow, Hamilton fatally wounded him with a carbine shot fired from a window of the house of his uncle, the Archbishop of St Andrew's.[21] The murder of Moray, the first major figure to be assassinated by firearm, is commemorated in Saint Giles Kirk, Edinburgh, by one of Scotland's finest brass memorials. Cecil's papers in Hatfield House contain some of the intercepted correspondence of Hamilton while he was on the run after the assassination, among them an appeal to a servant of Mary, Queen of Scots, for financial help since he had lost 'all he had to live on for her Majesty's service'.[22]

In February 1570, by the bull *Regnans in Excelsis*, Pope Pius V excommunicated Elizabeth, 'the pretended Queen of England and the servant of crime', absolving English Catholics of their allegiance to her.* The first attempt to overthrow Elizabeth after the publication of the papal bull was the 'Ridolfi Plot', uncovered in the spring of 1571. For several years a Florentine banker resident in London, Roberto di Ridolfi, after whom the plot was named, had been secretly channelling funds from Pius V and Philip II to English Catholics. In September 1569 he had transferred almost £3,000 from the Spanish ambassador, Don Guerau de Spes, to the Scottish Catholic John Leslie, Bishop of Ross, the representative in London of Mary, Queen of Scots. In March 1571 Ridolfi travelled to Rome and Madrid to gain the support of the Pope and Philip II for a Catholic uprising in England, led by the Duke of Norfolk, supported by Spanish troops from the Netherlands. Mary was to be rescued from house arrest, marry Norfolk and replace Elizabeth as Queen of England. The plot was discovered when Charles Bailly, a servant of Mary and the Bishop of Ross, was arrested at Dover in April in possession of incriminating correspondence, including two letters from Ridolfi. Under torture on the rack in the Tower of London, Bailly revealed all he knew about the plot. He scratched on to the wall of his cell, from which he could see the executioner's scaffold on Tower Hill, two mournful messages which still survive. The first, dated 10 April 1571, reads: 'IHS [Holy Name of Jesus] Wise men ought to se[e] what they do, to examine before they speake; to prove before they

---

* The issue of the bull followed the suppression of the Catholic Rising of the North in 1569. A copy of the bull was nailed by the Catholic John Felton to the gate of the Bishop of London's home in St Paul's churchyard. Felton was executed for treason and, three centuries later, beatified as an English martyr. (*ODNB* John Felton.)

take in hand; to beware whose company they use; and, above all things, to whom they truste . . . Charles Bailly.'[23]*

Cecil and Walsingham, who was already heavily involved in intelligence operations as ambassador in Paris (1570–73), knew far more about the Ridolfi Plot than was revealed at the time or, until recently, suspected by historians. Recent research suggests, though it does not prove, that Ridolfi was a double agent. In 1569, while based in London, he was interrogated at length by Walsingham. The interrogation took place not, as usual in suspected treason cases, at the Tower but at Walsingham's house in Aldgate. The probability is that Ridolfi confessed his role as a financial conduit to English Catholics and revealed Spanish and papal plans for Mary to replace Elizabeth on the throne. Though details of what was agreed remain obscure, Ridolfi was released after a month. Walsingham, with Cecil's approval, seems to have decided that the best way to defeat the attempt to use Ridolfi as paymaster of a plot to bring Mary to the English throne was to recruit him as, in effect, a double agent who would provide intelligence on the progress of the plot, thus allowing it to be cut short at a suitable moment. The moment came when Bailly was arrested at Dover, thus allowing the plot to be exposed without revealing Ridolfi's role as a double agent.[24] The plot ended with the trial for treason and execution of the Duke of Norfolk on Tower Hill in June 1572. Before laying his head on the block, he told the watching crowd that Ridolfi was a 'stranger, a naughty man', to whom he had spoken only once: 'I found him to be a man that enjoyed the tranquillity of England and of a prompt and ready wit for any wicked design.'[25]

The Ridolfi Plot, however, failed to provide the evidence which Walsingham and Cecil needed to prove Mary's involvement in plots to assassinate Elizabeth and so bring about her own execution. Since Mary corresponded with some of her supporters by cipher, obtaining this evidence required cryptanalysis as well as agent intelligence. While Walsingham was ambassador in Paris in 1571, he acquired, with what Mary's biographer John Guy describes as 'suspicious ease', a copy of the cipher supplied by Ridolfi to the conspirators. The probability is that he obtained it from Ridolfi himself.[26] Walsingham, however, did not possess a copy of the cipher used by Mary after the Ridolfi Plot and for several years his staff struggled unsuccessfully to decrypt her letters – further circumstantial evidence that the success in decrypting her correspondence during the Ridolfi Plot may have owed more to Ridolfi than to the skill of English codebreakers.

If Ridolfi was, as seems likely, a double agent, Elizabeth was never told

---

* Bailly was spared execution and released from the Tower in 1572.

and did not suspect it. Probably shortly after the plot was unravelled and Norfolk executed, she presented Walsingham with a newly commissioned painting of Henry VIII and his three Tudor successors on the English throne, showing Elizabeth as the embodiment of the virtues of her father and half-siblings, holding the hand of Peace (pictured treading the sword of discord underfoot) with Plenty by her side. The Queen informed Walsingham that the picture was a 'mark of her people's and her own content' with him.[27] No other intelligence chief in British (and possibly world) history has ever been rewarded with such a remarkable portrait of the ruler and the dynasty for whose security he was responsible.

Early in 1573, Mary Stuart's former Secretary of State, Sir William Maitland of Lethington, and other supporters occupied Edinburgh Castle in an attempt to restore her to the Scottish throne. At the request of the Scottish Regent, Elizabeth sent troops and artillery to lay siege to the castle. In March, during the siege, the English diplomat Henry Killigrew, who accompanied Elizabeth's forces, obtained from unknown sources two intercepted letters written in cipher from Maitland to Mary's representative in France, the Catholic Bishop of Glasgow, and one letter to John Chisholm, formerly Mary's Comptroller of the Royal Artillery. Since the Regent's court at Stirling Castle was apparently unable to decrypt them, Killigrew forwarded to Somer one of the ciphered letters, addressed to the Bishop of Glasgow, and wrote to Burghley and the Earl of Leicester: 'If Mr Somers [Somer] can do anything with it, he shall have the others.'[28] There is no evidence that Somer succeeded in breaking the cipher. On 28 May, Mary's supporters in Edinburgh Castle surrendered. Their military commander was executed at the Market Cross in Edinburgh. Maitland died in Leith Prison either from disease or, by some accounts, by suicide.[29]

The revival of English codebreaking in the later 1570s owed much to Dutch assistance. In 1575 the leader of the Dutch Revolt, Prince William of Orange, commonly known as 'William the Silent', formally denounced the sovereignty of Philip II of Spain over the Netherlands. A year later, a Dutch delegation headed by William's close associate Philips of Marnix, Lord of Saint-Aldegonde, arrived in England to seek support from Elizabeth, and gained strong backing from Walsingham, whom William of Orange considered 'the chiefest friend he had in England'. The Queen, however, was unwilling to be drawn into a continental war and gave Walsingham a public dressing-down.[30] Though Aldegonde left empty-handed, he put his codebreaking expertise at Walsingham's disposal, probably revealing that he was receiving important intelligence on Spanish ciphers from a Flemish-born cipher clerk at the royal court in Madrid.[31] In March 1577 Aldegonde gave Walsingham decrypted despatches sent by the acting Spanish ambassador in London, Antonio de Guaras, which revealed that he was in frequent contact with Mary, Queen of Scots.[32] A few months later William of Orange passed to Walsingham, via the English diplomat Daniel Rogers, the contents of another Spanish decrypt, which contained plans (never implemented) by Don Juan of Austria, the governor of the Spanish Netherlands, to land a Spanish army in England under cover of taking refuge from a storm in the Channel.[33]

At about the same time[34] Walsingham received from his fellow Secretary of State, Thomas Wilson, an intercepted despatch addressed to a Spanish commander in the Netherlands, Don Bernardino de Mendoza, a supporter of Mary, Queen of Scots, and later ambassador in London, 'wherein', Wilson believed, 'may be matter of great moment, being well deciphered. If Sainte-Aldegonde cannot do it, nor Mr. Somers [Somer], I wish you would send it to your servant young Philips [Phelippes], who is with our ambassador at Paris.'[35]

Somer was near, perhaps past, the end of his career as a cryptanalyst. His precocious successor, Thomas Phelippes (pronounced 'Philips'), then aged only about twenty-one, was to become the greatest English codebreaker of his generation, though it is not known whether he succeeded in decrypting the intercepted message to Don Bernardino de Mendoza. Mary, Queen of Scots, unaware that Phelippes was decrypting much of her correspondence, later described him dismissively as 'of low stature, slender every way, dark yellow haired on the head, and clear yellow bearded, eaten in the face with smallpox [and] of short sight'. According to his father, Phelippes was 'of a staid and secret nature'. Partly because of confusion in the records over the spelling of his name, some of his early career remains uncertain. It is likely that he was a graduate of Trinity College, Cambridge. He was certainly a talented linguist with at least a good reading knowledge of Latin, Italian, French, German and Spanish. From 1578 to 1583, he was a frequent visitor to the English embassy in Paris, which succeeded in procuring a considerable amount of intercepted correspondence.[36] In a letter to Walsingham from France in 1582, Phelippes recalled that he had 'had to do, as you know, with many ciphers',* though very little indication survives of what ciphers he had so far broken.

While Phelippes was still learning his trade as a cryptanalyst, Walsingham continued to depend on Aldegonde. In March 1578 Walsingham sent

---

* At the time, Phelippes was struggling to decrypt a letter concerning the Jesuits, 'against whose practices the Lord defend us . . . I never lit upon any [cipher] wherewith I was more cumbered, nor wherein the observations which I serve myself of in these occasions did more fail me.' (Cooper, *Queen's Agent*, pp. 269–70.)

A E.P.4.

B 3

C a

D 2

E o.r.

F x1

G e

H s

I

L 3

M 7

N 8

O g.n.s

P 8

Q b

R 10

S 11

T 9

V 9

X

Y v

Z t

vocelles { A
toutes { E
aux conf- { I
namel { O
{ V

bl 3
br 3
ch
cl a
cr
dl
dr
ff
fr
gl
gr
pl
pr
tl
tr
bb
cc
dd
ff
ll
mm
nn
ll
rr

yo por lo que veo no haria estima de
que
...ra
ocupar en los lugares de tierra
firme. A lo de las islas se ha de atender
y esto tengo lo por mas dificultoso que
lo de Anglaterra y si se tomase aquello
tambien se tomara lo otro y para
hazerlo basta mediana fuerça y
no piense V. Md.

58(2)

144

◀The origins of England's first codebreaking alliance. In 1577 one of the leaders of the Dutch Revolt against Spanish rule, Philips of Marnix, Lord of Saint-Aldegonde, broke the cipher used by Don Juan of Austria, half-brother of Philip II and governor of the Netherlands, and shared Spanish decrypts with Walsingham.

a copy of an intercepted letter from the Portuguese ambassador in London to the English diplomat William Davison: 'It is very important to her Majesty's service to have this letter of the ambassador of Portugal deciphered with speed. Please therefore deal earnestly and speedily with St. Alagondye [Aldegonde] in that behalf. The cypher is so easy that it requires no great trouble.'[37] Davison replied a fortnight later that Aldegonde had had to leave before he had time to decrypt the letter, 'but he procured me another [codebreaker] to perform it. I send it herewith . . .'[38]

It is often supposed that the British–American SIGINT alliance, which began during the Second World War, and still continues, is historically unique. The codebreaking alliance between England and the Dutch rebels, however, was founded almost four centuries earlier. After the assassination of William the Silent in 1584, his son and successor as leader of the Dutch Revolt, Maurice of Nassau, was quick to reassure Walsingham that the codebreaking alliance would continue:

> Knowing your friendship to my late father, and the good correspondence you have had together in affairs touching the church and state of the kingdom of England and of these countries; and there having fallen into my hands certain letters from Don Bernardin[o] de Mendoza [Spanish ambassador in London, expelled in 1584] to the Prince of Parma [Spanish commander in the Low Countries], by which appears part of the [Spanish] negotiation in France, I send them to you but as they have been deciphered and as we must keep this cipher secret, for reasons which you know better than I do, I beg that this communication may not tend to our prejudice as regards other like letters. I pray you to keep me always in her Majesty [Queen Elizabeth]'s good graces, desiring ever to remain her very humble servant.[39]*

The assassination of William the Silent caused greater alarm in European courts than that of Henry III and Henry IV of France.[40] Unlike the French kings, who were fatally stabbed by daggers, William was the first ruler to be killed by a handgun. The bullet holes left by his assassin in the wall of his Delft home are still visible today. William's death marked a

---

* Mendoza claimed that the English 'have not been greatly pleased, according to what is understood, by the good reception and kind usage given me yesterday by the King [Henry III] and Queen Mother [Catherine de' Medici]'.

turning point in the history of royal protection. It 'preyed on the minds of European heads of state and haunted the imagination of those responsible for maintaining their security'.[41] After a similar, unsuccessful attempt, also by pistol, on the life of William the Silent two years earlier, William Herle, an English agent in the Low Countries, had claimed that Elizabeth too was in mortal danger. To prevent assassins entering England, he called for 'the passages and ports of England [to] be shut up, guarded with officers who search every man to the soles of the shoes for letters and papers of conspiracy and rebellion'.[42]

The invention of the pocket-size wheel-lock pistol, which for the first time could be loaded and primed in advance, had enabled William's French assassin, Balthasar Gérard, in 1584, to conceal the gun about his person and take William by surprise. Also deeply worrying for Walsingham and Elizabeth's court, as they meditated the security lessons of the assassination, was the fact that Gérard had managed to deceive the Dutch rebels into recruiting him as an agent to provide intelligence on the Spanish troops in the Low Countries led by the Prince of Parma. But, as Gérard admitted before his exceptionally gruesome execution, he was in reality a committed Catholic and loyal subject of Philip II, who had offered a reward of 25,000 crowns for William's assassination. Though Gérard did not live to collect the reward, Philip presented his parents with three country estates. Over a millennium after the unsuccessful plot by Emperor Theodosius II to assassinate Attila the Hun,[43] a head of state had for the first time successfully instigated the assassination of a foreign leader (albeit one whom Philip saw as a rebel subject).

The problems of protecting Elizabeth's security were exacerbated by the size and multiplicity of her courts. Whitehall, at which she spent most time, was the largest court in Europe, spanning twenty-three acres. But she also spent time at Hampton Court, Greenwich, Richmond, Westminster, St James's, Windsor Castle and, towards the end of her reign, Nonsuch, as well as making an annual royal progress around southern England. Over 1,000 people usually attended court. The fear that the Queen was being targeted for assassination rose dramatically in the summer of 1580 when a royal official, George Eliot, who had recanted his Catholic faith after serving in Catholic gentry homes in Kent and Essex, told the Queen's favourite, the Earl of Leicester, that he had discovered a huge plot, involving fifty armed men paid for by the Pope, to assassinate the Queen, Leicester, Burghley and Walsingham during a royal progress. Eliot's conspiracy theory was taken seriously by its putative victims.[44]

Though there was no plot to send Catholic assassins to England, in June 1580 a well-disguised Jesuit mission headed by Robert Persons, formerly Fellow and a popular tutor at Balliol College, Oxford, arrived in London. Persons was dressed as an army captain.[45] The other leading member of the mission, Edmond Campion, former Fellow of St John's College, Oxford, travelled separately for reasons of security, posing as a jewel salesman from Dublin.[46] The aim of the Jesuit mission, wrote Dr (later Cardinal) William Allen, the inspirational founder of the Rheims seminary which trained missionary priests to minister secretly in England, was religious, not political – 'to win our nation to God again'.[47] Persons and Campion were ordered not to discuss politics and authorized to release English Catholics from the duty of resisting Elizabeth's authority. But the terms of the authorization – 'so long as present conditions obtain' – implied that the duty to depose her might later be reimposed.[48]

For a year Persons and Campion were able to travel widely among the scattered English Catholic community. But in July 1582 Eliot strengthened the credibility of his conspiracy theory of a great Catholic plot by tracking down Campion to Lyford Grange in Berkshire, where, after a prolonged search, he was discovered hiding in a priest's hole. At his trial with seven other Catholic priests in November, Campion declared that, though he and his fellow defendants were prepared to die, their adherence to the Catholic faith was not treason and they remained loyal subjects of the Queen. All were sentenced to be hanged, drawn and quartered. Before Campion's execution at Tyburn on 1 December, according to a Catholic, Thomas Alfield, who was close to the scaffold, he 'was asked for which queen he prayed . . . [H]e answered, yea for Elizabeth your queen and my queen . . . And so he meekly and sweetly yielded his soul unto his Saviour, protesting that he died a perfect catholic.'[49]

Unlike Campion, Persons avoided arrest and escaped to the Continent. In September 1581 he wrote to the head of the Jesuit order: 'At Cambridge I have insinuated a certain priest into the very university, under the guise of a scholar or gentleman commoner, and have procured him help not far from the town. Within a few months he has sent over to Rheims [seminary] seven very fit youths.'[50] Though there is no evidence that Walsingham knew the identity of the Catholic priest 'insinuated' into Cambridge (who has still to be identified), he successfully insinuated agents of his own into the Rheims seminary. Walsingham's aim, wrote Robert Persons, was 'to put sedition among ourselves, by sending over spies & traitors to kindle and foster the same'. His first agent in Rheims was a Cambridge graduate, Richard Baines, who arrived at the seminary in 1579 and was ordained as a Catholic priest in October 1581.[51]* Baines later admitted that, though

* Baines took his BA at Christ's College and MA at Gonville & Caius College.

he had failed in an attempt to poison a well at the seminary, 'I found means to insinuate myself to the familiarity of the younger sort, that methought might easily be carried into discontentment.' His downfall came in 1582 when he tried to bribe another seminarist to work for Walsingham with a promise of 3,000 crowns for his services. The seminarist informed Dr Allen, and Baines spent the next year in jail.[52] Whether or not Walsingham had approved the plan to poison the seminarists remains unknown.

Among the agents recruited by Walsingham to replace Baines to provide intelligence from Rheims, as well as on Cambridge students planning to go to the seminary, was probably the poet and dramatist Christopher Marlowe of Corpus Christi College, who began espionage while still a student. Marlowe's recruiter was probably Nicholas Faunt, one of Walsingham's main assistants. Like Faunt, Marlowe was educated at King's School, Canterbury, and at Corpus Christi, where both held scholarships endowed by Matthew Parker, a former Master of Corpus who became Elizabeth's first Archbishop of Canterbury.* In 1578 Faunt became one of Walsingham's chief assistants and took part in numerous intelligence operations on the Continent.[53] Marlowe graduated as a BA in 1584, then began studying for his MA. The Corpus Christi Buttery Book, which recorded expenditure on food and drink, shows that from 1585 his presence at the College became irregular and his expenditure while there considerably higher.[54] The evidence of both his attendance record and his expenditure indicates that he had paid employment which took him away from Cambridge. His career in Walsingham's secret service thus probably began in 1585. The only documentary evidence was a letter of support for Marlowe sent by the Privy Council to Cambridge University on 29 June 1587, defending his reputation and designed to ensure that his absences abroad on Her Majesty's service did not delay the award of his MA:

> Whereas it was reported that Christopher Morley [Marlowe] was determined to have gone beyond the seas to Reames [Rheims] and there to remain, Their Lordships thought good to certify that he had no such intent, but that in all his actions he had behaved himself orderly and discreetly whereby he had done her Majesty good service, & deserved to be rewarded for his faithful dealing: Their Lordships request was that the rumour thereof should be allayed by all possible means, and that he should be furthered in the degree he was to take this next Commencement, because it was not her

---

* The Corpus Christi Scholars Book reveals that Faunt, who had formerly been at Gonville & Caius College, arrived at Corpus in 1573. The Buttery Book, which records expenditure on food and drink, shows that Faunt was in residence for just over four years, from late February 1573 to early March 1577. (Corpus Christi College, Cambridge, Archives.)

Majesty's pleasure that any one employed as he had been in matters touching the benefit of his Country should be defamed by those that are ignorant in th'affairs he went about.[55]

The false rumours the Privy Council was anxious to quash that Marlowe intended to take up residence in Rheims probably derived from his missions there to investigate the seminary. Marlowe's fellow Cambridge graduate, Richard Baines, who had penetrated the seminary and tried to poison its inhabitants, claimed to know Marlowe well. He was to prove an untrustworthy friend.[56]

Two major conspiracies in the mid-1580s – the Throckmorton Plot of 1583 and the Babington Plot of 1586 – dramatically demonstrated the threat to Elizabeth's life not from a supposed team of assassins paid for by the Pope but from Mary Stuart's Catholic followers in England and their foreign supporters. Francis Throckmorton, a young English Catholic after whom the first of these plots was named, was arrested early in November 1583, following 'secret intelligence given to the Queen's Majesty, that he was a privy conveyor and receiver of letters to and from the Scottish Queen'.[57] The intelligence came from inside the French embassy in London, which about two years earlier had begun to use Throckmorton to handle secret correspondence between Mary and her English supporters. The ambassador, Michel de Castelnau, also allowed Mary to use his diplomatic bag to correspond with her supporters in France. In the spring of 1583 a priest in the embassy, writing under the alias 'Henri Fagot', began sending intelligence reports written in French to Walsingham.* He reported on 29 April: 'Throckmorton dined at the ambassador's house. He has already sent the Queen of Scots 1500 ecus [crowns], which is on the ambassador's account.'[58] 'Fagot' wrote in May that Throckmorton and the Catholic nobleman Lord Henry Howard regularly delivered Mary's correspondence to the embassy under cover of darkness:

> I also advise you that, if you so wish, I have made the ambassador's secretary so much my friend that, if he is given a certain amount of money, he will let me know everything he does, including everything to do with the Queen of Scots & the cipher that is used with her. He tells me that, after

---

* The identity of 'Fagot' has yet to be established. In the original 1991 edition of *Giordano Bruno and the Embassy Affair*, Bossy identified 'Fagot' as the Italian Dominican friar, philosopher, mathematician, astrologer and astronomer Giordano Bruno, then living in England and later burnt at the stake in Rome for heresy. In the third edition, published in 2002, Bossy is much 'less confident' and concludes that 'the identification on which the book rests is not certain'. (Bossy, *Giordano Bruno and the Embassy Affair*, Preface to the 3rd edn, p. xiii.)

your Excellency has inspected any packet addressed to her, he can put something else in it without anybody knowing . . .

Your very humble and loyal servant,

Henri Fagot[59]

The 'secretary' has been identified as Laurent Feron, a London-born embassy clerk who gave Walsingham's agent Walter Williams access to the contents of the French diplomatic bag. Williams reported to Walsingham that Feron risked 'not just dishonour but death' by doing so.[60]

Lord Henry Howard was fortunate not to be tried for treason. From 1582 to 1584 he was paid by Mendoza, the Spanish ambassador, to provide regular information from Elizabeth's court. In all he was imprisoned five times on suspicion but wrote regularly to Burghley to protest his loyalty to Elizabeth.[61] The evidence against Throckmorton, who had conspired with Mendoza, was far more damning. After Walsingham put him under surveillance, he was arrested in November 1583 at his London house in possession of incriminating documents, which included details of harbours 'suitable for landing foreign forces'. When Throckmorton refused to confess, a warrant was issued 'to assay by torture to draw from him the truth of the matters'. The laconic official account of the use of the rack during his interrogation in the Tower of London on 16 November records that he was 'somewhat pinched, although not much'. Throckmorton admitted nothing and smuggled out of the Tower a cipher message to Mendoza written on the back of a playing card, promising that he would die a thousand deaths rather than betray his friends. Walsingham forecast when sending a further torture warrant to the Tower two days later: 'I suppose the grief of the last torture will suffice without any extremity of racking to make him more conformable than he hath hitherto showed himself.' And so it proved. Throckmorton admitted, without further torture, that he had carried letters to and from the Spanish ambassador in London as well as organizing secret correspondence between the French embassy and Mary Stuart. He also revealed plans for an invasion of England led by the Duke of Guise, reinforced by troops from the Spanish Netherlands and English Catholic nobles who would support the invasion. Throckmorton was convicted of treason in a trial at the Guildhall on 21 May 1584 and hanged, drawn and quartered at Tyburn on 10 July.[62]

Shortly afterwards, probably on Walsingham's initiative,[63] a propaganda pamphlet was published entitled *A discouerie of the treasons practised and attempted against the Queenes Maiestie and the realme, [by] Francis Throckemorton*, which justified torture as a necessary weapon against treason. It was also the first official publication in English history to praise the role of 'secret intelligence' in discovering and defeating treason, and to give some explanation of how it had been used. Intelligence that Throckmorton had been acting as Mary Stuart's courier was not initially acted on 'to the end there might be some proof more apparent be had to charge him therewith'. Throckmorton, the pamphlet claimed, was distraught at having let down Mary, Queen of Scots, 'who was the dearest thing to me in all the world . . . Sith I have failed of my faith towards her, I care not if I were hanged.'[64] The pamphlet, however, concealed the fact that, while awaiting execution, Throckmorton had sent a personal appeal to 'my most gracious sovereign' Elizabeth, confessing 'the great & grievous offence whereof I remain by your ma[jes]t[y's] Laws Justly Condemned' but pleading for 'some Drop of your accustomed grace & mercy'. In mitigation, he blamed his crime on 'the inconsiderate rashness of unbridled youth'.[65] It is unlikely that the letter was ever shown to the Queen.

Though official propaganda concentrated on the treason of Throckmorton, he had in reality only a supporting role in a large conspiracy which had been hatched in Spain and France. Before gaining access in 1583 to the contents of the French diplomatic bag and Throckmorton's confessions, Walsingham had thought the principal threat to Elizabeth was the possibility of a pro-Catholic invasion from Scotland. Intelligence and interrogation revealed instead that the real invasion threat was an army landing on the coasts of Sussex and Cumbria financed by Spain and led by the Duke of Guise.[66] Though the Spanish ambassador, Don Bernardino de Mendoza, was expelled from England as a result of the Throckmorton Plot, Castelnau was allowed to remain, despite the highly compromising intelligence against him obtained from examining the contents of his diplomatic bag and Mary's correspondence via the French embassy. Burghley and Walsingham prudently decided not to risk provoking a conflict with France as well as Spain, with whom war began in 1585.[67]

The Throckmorton Plot further strengthened the long-held conviction of both Walsingham and Burghley that Elizabeth could never be secure on her throne so long as Mary Stuart remained alive. The propaganda pamphlet published after Throckmorton's execution misleadingly portrayed him as a steadfast supporter of Mary willing to die for her cause while concealing his last-minute attempt to save his life by declaring renewed allegiance to Elizabeth. The plot had failed to prove Mary's complicity in attempts to overthrow or assassinate Elizabeth. The first to do so was the Babington Plot of 1586, so called after the Catholic chief conspirator, Mary's former page and devoted supporter, Anthony Babington. The plot was uncovered as the result of a remarkable intelligence coup orchestrated by Walsingham which combined agents, double agents and

codebreaking. One of the most important double agents was the English
Catholic Gilbert Gifford, who had studied at both William Allen's seminary for English missionary priests (then based at Douai) and the English
College at Rome. Gifford acted as courier between Mary's agent in Paris,
Thomas Morgan, the new French ambassador in London, the Baron de
Châteauneuf, and Mary herself. After landing at Rye in December 1585,
he was detained and taken to London to be questioned by Walsingham,
who recruited him as a double agent (if he had not already done so). Gifford agreed to collect Mary's correspondence from the French embassy
and allow Walsingham's staff to copy and decrypt it before delivering it
to Mary via a brewer (also in Walsingham's pay) who 'smuggled' letters
to and from her in the bung-hole of beer barrels delivered to Chartley,
where she was under house arrest.[68] Châteauneuf later reported to Henry
III: 'The Queen of Scots and her principal servants placed great confidence
in the said Gifford . . . and thence came the ruin of the said queen.'[69]

Another key double agent working for Walsingham was Robert
Poley, a former undergraduate at Clare College, Cambridge, a friend of
Marlowe* who penetrated Babington's entourage by posing as a Catholic
sympathizer. Poley ingratiated himself so successfully that Babington
regarded him as a close personal friend and gave him a diamond ring. On
2 June 1586 Babington and his fellow conspirators met and dined in what
they believed was 'Poley's garden' (in fact the garden of a house requisi-
tioned for him from a Queen's Messenger). On one occasion Poley was
found by Babington copying some of his papers, but somehow managed
to keep his confidence. After his arrest Babington feared that he had been
betrayed by Poley but could not quite believe him capable of such treachery. He wrote to Poley: 'Farewell sweet Robyn, if as I take thee, true to
me. If not adieu, *omnius bipedum nequissimus* [vilest of all two-footed
creatures].'† Probably by the time of the Babington Plot, Poley was well
acquainted with his fellow Cambridge graduate and Walsingham recruit
Christopher Marlowe. Like Baines, Poley was to prove an untrustworthy
friend.[70]

Mary's intercepted correspondence sealed her fate as well as Babington's. On 6 July Babington sent a long, ciphered letter seeking her approval
for the 'dispatch' (assassination) of the 'usurping Competitor' (Elizabeth
I): 'there be six noble gentlemen all my private friends, who for the zeal

---

* When Marlowe and Poley became friends is not known.
† The devious Poley was later present at the killing of Christopher Marlowe. See
below, pp. 187–8. (Honan, *Christopher Marlowe*, pp. 145–6. Riggs, *World of Christopher
Marlowe*, pp. 143–5, 150, 154, 257. Nicholl, *The Reckoning*, pp. 185–7.)

they bear to the Catholic cause and your Majesty's service will undertake that tragical execution'. An invasion from Catholic Europe would be assisted by Mary's loyal English supporters and Babington himself would rescue Mary from house arrest.[71] Mary's reply, sent on 17 July via a messenger who, unknown to her, took it straight to Phelippes, was cautious but not cautious enough. Though she did not give formal approval to the assassination, nor did she reject a straightforwardly treasonable proposal. Indeed, she expressed interest in the assassination plan, asking: 'By what means do the gentlemen deliberate to proceed?' Mary also praised Babington's 'zeal and entire affection' for the Catholic faith and her own cause, and urged him to consult with Don Bernadino de Mendoza, who, following his expulsion from England after the Throckmorton Plot, had become Spanish ambassador in Paris.[72]

When Phelippes had copied and decrypted Mary's letter to Babington he put on it the sign of the gallows, convinced that she had now provided evidence which would make it possible to convict her of treason. On the original letter, after discussion with Walsingham, he forged a ciphered postscript designed to deceive Babington into providing the names of his co-conspirators:

> I w[ould] be glad to know the names and qualities of the six gentlemen which are to accomplish the designment, for that it may be I shall be able upon knowledge of the parties to give you some further advice necessary to be followed therein; and as also from time to time particularly how you proceed and as soon as you may for the same purpose who be already and how far every one privy hereunto.[73]

So far as is known, this was the first such deception in the history of codebreaking. The doctored letter was delivered to Babington by 'a homely serving man in a blue coat'. Though Babington did not realize it, the servant was working for Phelippes, who had become an experienced agent handler as well as cryptanalyst. Babington told the servant he would send a reply the same day but did not do so. Fearful that Babington might panic and disappear, Walsingham wrote to Phelippes that, though the decision was a difficult one, 'I conclude: it were better to lack the answer than to lack the man.' By 14 August Babington and his co-conspirators were under arrest. In September they were tried, sentenced to death for treason and executed. A vengeful Elizabeth asked Burghley to ensure that their execution was particularly painful. Without giving the excruciating details of death by hanging, drawing and quartering, Burghley replied that the existing method of 'protracting' their public execution was as terrible as could be devised.[74]

Alphabet w'th the Lady Ferniherst

A B C D E F G H I K L M N O P Q R S T V X Y Z | Nulles

3. dowbleth | and . for . with . that . if . but . as . wher . off . the . from . by . so . not . when

ther . this . m . which . it . what . say . me . my . [howryth] . send . lre . receaved . bearar . I

pray . yow . inter . youre . names . myne .   the watche wordes   123
                                                     Diligently or faithfully .

Such was the alphabet w'th the Lady of Fawny hesst
                    Gilbert Curll

Alphabet w'th D. [Lew: D. Lew Am. Bab.]
Lewes.

A B C D E F G H I K L M N O P Q R S T V X Y Z | Nulles

2 dowbleth . and . for . with . that . if . but . as . wher . of . this . from

by . so . not . when . ther . this . is . with . it . what . say . me . my . Weye

send . but . receave . beare . I . pray . yow . inter . yr name . myne

Thes alphabet I such to Em w't Doct E Lewes,
                    Gilbert Curll

Cifer w'th Anthony Babington [D. Al .... An .... Bat .... Bab:]
Babington

a b c d e f g h i k l m n o p q r s t u x y z

Nuller . ff . — . — . . . — . Dowbleth . ∞

and . for . with . that . if . but . wher . as . of . the . from . by . so . not . when . ther

the . this . it . what . say . me . my . wryth . send . lre . receave . bearar . I . pray . yow

w't . youre . name . myne

This was the alphabet w't Babington
  as may be   Gilbert Curll

This is last is y'e Alphabet, by w'ch only I have writtin
unto y'e Quen'e off Scott, or receaved lettres from her :

                    Anthonie Babington

Acknowledged & subscribed by Babington
primo Sept: 1586 in y'e presence of Edwarde Barker.
                    148   [54]

During the trial of the plotters, the prosecution declared that Mary Stuart had 'willingly allowed of these treasons'.[75] She herself was tried for treason at Fotheringhay Castle in October, her protestations of innocence undermined by the evidence of her intercepted correspondence. She was, however, able to demand of Walsingham whether he was an honest man – the first, and so far the only, challenge ever made in open court to an English intelligence chief. Walsingham replied: 'I call God and all the world to witness I have not done anything as a private man unworthy of an honest man, nor as a public man unworthy of my calling. I protest before God that as a man careful of his mistress's safety I have been curious.' Walsingham's reply was carefully phrased. He declared the unblemished honesty of his private life, but implied that the defence of national security had sometimes to be conducted by different rules. The ends, he believed, might sometimes justify dishonest means. Both Mary and the commission which tried her were unaware that what Walsingham called his 'curiosity' (solicitousness) in Queen Elizabeth's service had led him to approve the insertion of a forged passage in one of the letters used to convict her. The version of the letter shown to the commission was another forgery – a facsimile of Mary's original reply to Babington without Phelippes's addition.[76] Walsingham's use of forgery to obtain the death sentence was a unique and disreputable episode in the history of English intelligence.

After months of delay, Elizabeth signed Mary's death warrant on 1 February 1587, but she did not intend it to be used. Hoping to evade personal responsibility, she would much have preferred Mary to be quietly disposed of. Burghley, however, saw to it that, without the Queen's knowledge, the royal warrant was promptly despatched to Fotheringhay. Walsingham personally chose the executioner, who travelled to the castle in the clothes of a serving man with his axe in a trunk. Mary was dead before Elizabeth was told that her warrant had been delivered. For the first time, Elizabeth angrily dismissed Burghley from her presence.[77] She was, however, full of praise for Phelippes's success in decrypting Mary's correspondence with Babington and awarded him a pension of 100 marks (worth about £10,000 today). Walsingham told Phelippes that he would 'not believe in how good part she accepteth of your service'.[78]

Mary's execution in the great hall of Fotheringhay Castle (since demolished) on 8 February 1587 did nothing to diminish the menace of Spanish

◀ Decrypted cipher letter from Anthony Babington to Mary, Queen of Scots, seeking her approval for the assassination of Elizabeth I by 'six noble gentlemen all my private friends, who ... will undertake that tragical execution'.

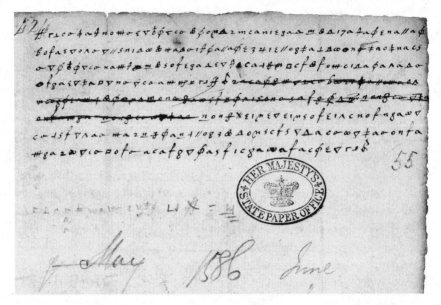

Walsingham's chief codebreaker, Thomas Phelippes, added this forged postscript in Mary's cipher to her reply to Babington, asking him to provide 'the names and qualities of the six gentlemen' who were to kill the Queen.

invasion. In January 1586 Philip II had instructed his captain-general of the ocean seas, the Marquis of Santa Cruz, to draw up an invasion plan. The plan reached Walsingham in April 1586, only days after it was first seen by Philip himself. The source of this remarkable intelligence was Walsingham's agent Antony Standen, an English Catholic émigré based in Florence who had established a new identity as 'Pompeo Pellegrini'. Though Standen's motives remain unclear, despite his Catholicism he was probably unwilling to see England overrun by Spain in the name of religion. He made friends in Florence with Giovanni Figliazzi, Tuscan ambassador to Madrid, who proved an excellent intelligence source on Spanish policy towards England.[79] Standen also recruited, at an initial cost of a hundred crowns, the brother of a trusted servant of the Marquis of Santa Cruz, who sent letters to Standen from Lisbon by the Spanish diplomatic bag. 'He is', Standen told Walsingham, 'a proper fellow and he writeth well.'[80] The brothers were Flemish and may have been motivated by secret support for the Dutch Revolt against Spanish rule as well as by money.

In April 1587 intelligence forwarded by Standen, probably from the agent in Lisbon, enabled the English privateer Francis Drake to 'singe the King of Spain's beard' and delay the departure of the Armada by attacking the Spanish fleet in Cádiz harbour – thus demonstrating, Walsingham boasted to Standen, 'how little we did fear them'. During the raid, Walsingham told him, Drake had 'fired thirty of great ships and sunk two galleys'. In congratulating Standen, whom he addressed by his initials, A B, Walsingham assured him that he had won the Queen's favour: 'Her Majesty doth accept very well of his advertisements and prayeth him that he will continue . . .'[81] The agent in Lisbon was almost certainly the source of a comprehensive list of the ships, men and supplies in the Spanish navy which reached Walsingham sometime in 1587 and showed that the Armada would not, as had been feared, be ready to sail that year.[82] This report was a prime example of the often forgotten dictum enunciated by President Dwight D. Eisenhower early in the Cold War that intelligence on what the enemy (in this case the Soviet Union) *did not* have' was often as important as information on what it did. Ignorance of a feared opponent invariably leads to an overestimation of the opponent's strength.[83] Thanks largely to Standen, Walsingham did not make this mistake in 1587. Standen travelled to Spain in person in the spring of 1588, from where he was able to report to Walsingham directly. He was rewarded with a pension of £100 – the same sum that Gilbert Gifford received for his role during the Babington Plot.[84]

Apart from Standen, the most important agent reporting on preparations for the Armada was the far less flamboyant but equally well travelled Stephen Powle, an Oxford graduate who had entered the service of Lord Burghley and was sent in 1585 to Heidelberg as his agent at the court of Duke John Casimir. There he became, in his own words, Burghley's 'feet, eyes or ears in Germany', before moving to Venice as an agent of Walsingham in March 1587. From Venice, in December 1587, Powle sent the first intelligence on Spanish preparations for the Armada.[85] He reported in February 1588:

> Letters from Spain of the last [day] of December say that the forty English vessels which were about Cape St. Vincent, on the coast of Portugal, continued to do great harm, no [Spanish] vessel being able to pass without being captured, and had already taken booty above the value of 250,000 crowns. Also that the Catholic Armada was still in the port of Lisbon, and although they were making all possible haste, it was believed that at the earliest it could not set out before the beginning of May [1588]. It is confirmed to be very powerful and exceedingly well provided with soldiers and all needful things, and that all men believe it be intended for the enterprise of England.[86]

Soon afterwards, Powle forwarded to Walsingham intelligence reporting that Madrid had decided that 'by hurrying too much', they would 'put

of yor laste letters wherby, you desire diligence in intelligence of ^{Spanish matters} ΦΩΤ–Ϙ=Φ=ΘΤ–ΟΤΨ I have borowed ii hundred crownes and dispatched ^{to Lisbone a Fleming} ΘϘ38ΤΙΟΟ4ΘΥ–ΟΟ who safe there is broker of the ^{in service to} ii–ΘΨ+ΠΨ4Η0+Ο4 ^{the Marquise Santa Croix} Ο=Ο=#ΘΤΠΨΕ+ΨΨΙ–ΟΟΙ–0ΤΨΟ4 and of his retourne I have gyven hym adresse for his letters to me att the Amb: house in Madrid who straytes will send them to me, he is a crever fellowe and wrytes well and I sent hym marye wth these laste ^{of passage} fower galleys, whose commoditie made me resolue vpon a soudaine and the safer vpon the receyte of yor letters wch so ernestlie recommended diligence and care in writinges, and this was the cause why I wisshed spedely to be sent hyther 300. crownes, for in these cases as shall avel you knowe occasions are offred vpon soudaines, and the distances do not permitt delaye. ffor my particular I am to thancke you for yor paines in procuringe me the 40. crownes of Mr Pratey, as also to see that honest man Broke railie to do some I finde my selfe much engaged me, I have written to Chr that he repayre to you about ^{Broke} the one and other, that is that Savage repayed the 100. crownes he paye hym selfe, and that the 40. he make cyfer to me. ffor the rest I am a trew Englisshman and consequentlie wisshe the good of England, the wch we all must necessarilie beloive yf it shuld come vnder the yoke of vessell devided from us by the seas and spetially of Spain, whose insolency in regiment I am to well acquainted wth neither is any intention to make a auantgardize of my zeale and affection that w^{ch}e: my want maye he supplied wth wilease w^{ch}e I will not refuse of so loued and liberall a hande all wch I maye do wth conscire and conscience and so as the Costume requbetue syget saluare la capra co cauli. God preserve you euermore the 6 of Maye 1587. newe stile

Pompeo Pellegrini:

themselves in manifest peril of losing the whole armada at sea, by sailing in the rigour of winter'.[87] As he had forecast, the Armada set sail for England in May 1588. Following the death of Santa Cruz, its commander, as Powle correctly reported in March, was the Duke of Medina Sidonia.[88]

Agent intelligence on preparations for the Armada was supplemented by SIGINT. In the few years before its despatch, Phelippes was able to break Spanish ciphers without having to seek the assistance of the Dutch. He later recalled that breaking one Spanish cipher message dealing with the Armada had 'held me twenty days in work', thus implying that code-breaking was usually more rapid. The Spanish, he believed, suspected that their ciphers were insecure and changed them quite regularly, making it necessary for Phelippes to keep detailed records of the variants they employed.[89] Walsingham probably found agent intelligence on the Armada more important than SIGINT. The closure of the Spanish embassy in London following the expulsion of the ambassador, Mendoza, because of his involvement in the Babington Plot in 1584, meant that there was no Spanish diplomatic correspondence to intercept. The most valuable Spanish intercepts probably came from the Low Countries.

As Walsingham received intelligence reports on preparations for the Armada, he was uncomfortably aware that one of England's most senior diplomats, Sir Edward Stafford, ambassador in Paris since 1583, had become a paid Spanish agent. Like the main British Soviet moles of the twentieth century, Stafford was also, like Walsingham, a Cambridge graduate educated successively at St John's and Pembroke Colleges. He was motivated by both a personal grudge towards Walsingham and heavy gambling debts in Paris. Before becoming a Spanish agent, he had given Mary Stuart's cousin, Henry, Duke of Guise, leader of the French Catholic League, access to English diplomatic despatches in return for 3,000 crowns to meet some of his debts. Stafford expressed open support for acknowledging Mary as heir to Elizabeth and was in close contact with an English Catholic conspirator in Paris, Charles Arundel. In January 1587, at a secret meeting with the Spanish ambassador in Paris, Bernadino de Mendoza, Arundel secretly offered Stafford's services as a spy. Unsurprisingly, Mendoza accepted the offer and gave Arundel an initial 2,000

◀ Walsingham's agent, Anthony Standen (alias 'Pompeo Pellegrino'), reports, partly in code, in May 1587 on his plans to obtain intelligence from the secretary of the Grand Admiral in command of the Spanish Armada.

crowns to pass on to Stafford.* As well as supplying intelligence to Mendoza, Stafford also misinformed Walsingham and Burghley by underplaying the scale of Spanish preparations for the Armada in his despatches. When sending intelligence reports to Madrid, Mendoza used three codenames to identify his English sources. It has been persuasively argued that all three were Stafford. Between April 1587 and October 1588, Mendoza's English spy or spies gave advance warning of Drake's raid on Cádiz, of instructions for the concentration of the English fleet, and details of English diplomacy on the Continent. Much other information passed to the Spaniards, however, was partly or wholly inaccurate – possibly, it has been suggested, 'because Walsingham and others were tainting its flow'.[90] This hypothesis would help to explain why Walsingham did not attempt to bring about Stafford's recall from Paris.

Unsurprisingly, Walsingham was unable to follow all the confused twists, turns and delays in Spanish invasion plans. Neither was the Duke of Parma, the Spanish governor of the Netherlands, who was supposed to provide troops for the invasion. By the time the 122 ships of the Armada arrived off Land's End in late July 1588, Parma had given up hope of its arrival and had sent the crews of his own ships to work on canals. Like Parma, the sixty-six ships of the English fleet were also taken by surprise by the timing of the Armada's arrival. After a chase in the English Channel, Sir Francis Drake, vice-admiral in command of the English fleet, was greatly helped by the unexpected and disastrous decision of the Duke of Medina Sidonia to anchor off Calais on 6 August. There Drake was able to disperse the Spanish fleet by a fireship attack. Strong winds then blew it into the North Sea, whence the only practical route back to Spain was a dangerous voyage around the Scottish and Irish coasts during which about thirty-five ships were wrecked.[91]

The defeat of the Armada was the greatest triumph and the apogee of Elizabeth's reign. Despite the surprise caused by the timing of the Armada's arrival, there is little doubt about the value of the intelligence on Spanish invasion preparations over the previous few years. Lord Henry Seymour, commander of the Narrow Seas Squadron, which joined Drake's fleet near Calais on 6 August, wrote to Walsingham twelve days later: 'I will not flatter you, but you have fought more with your pen than many have in our English navy.'[92]

The main weakness of Walsingham's intelligence system, the most

* Because of the limitations of the fragmentary sources, it is impossible to unravel the complexities of Stafford's early involvement with Spain. Before his approach to Mendoza he had supplied to Spain some intentionally inaccurate intelligence. (ODNB Edward Stafford.)

successful in sixteenth-century Europe, was the degree to which it depended on his personal management. According to his brother-in-law and close collaborator, Robert Beale, at the time of his death in 1590 he was running over forty agents and 'intelligencers' across Europe, as well as directing an apparently successful network of letter interception on continental post roads. To finance this network Walsingham was forced to spend much of his own personal fortune and became heavily indebted.[93] During 1589 Walsingham suffered increasingly from overwork and declining health. He died on 6 April 1590 and was buried the following evening in the north aisle of old St Paul's Cathedral, at his request 'without any of the ceremonies as usually appertain to a man serving in my place'. His English epitaph in the cathedral was the first ever to praise the work of an English spymaster:

> In foreign countries their intents he knew,
> Such was his zeal to do his country good,
> When dangers would by enemies ensue,
> As well as they themselves he understood.[94]

The damage to the intelligence system created by Walsingham caused by his death was compounded by budget cuts. Instead of appointing a new Secretary of State to succeed Walsingham, Elizabeth handed his responsibilities to the already overburdened, 69-year-old Burghley, who, with the royal exchequer drained by the continuing war with Spain, was forced to make serious cutbacks.[95] To try to maintain a foreign-intelligence network, the most important member of Walsingham's intelligence staff, Thomas Phelippes, appropriated some of the Crown revenues which he handled as a customs official, as well as drawing on his own income from a London property inherited from his father. This risky strategy eventually led him to debtors' prison.[96]

Some of Walsingham's agents abroad found themselves suddenly bereft of funds and support. Among them was Anthony Standen, who only a few years earlier had been congratulated by Walsingham and assured of the Queen's favour because of the importance of the intelligence he provided on the preparations of the Armada. By the time of Walsingham's death, Standen had become a double agent, deceiving the Spaniards into believing he was working for them while his real loyalty remained to England. In 1590 he was arrested in Bordeaux, accused of being a Spanish spy by the French authorities, and remained destitute in prison until he was rescued in 1591 by another of Walsingham's former agents, Anthony Bacon, elder brother of the great essayist and natural scientist, Francis Bacon. Anthony Bacon had had his own difficulties while doing intelligence work in France, being interrogated (and possibly tried) on the capital charge of sodomy with his page in 1586–7. Though, with Bacon's assistance, Standen returned safely to England, his intelligence career never fully recovered. In 1593 his Spanish employers appear to have discovered he was deceiving them.[97*]

In 1592 Nicholas Faunt, formerly one of Walsingham's chief assistants, complained about the inadequacies of some intelligence recruits: 'By experience I can say that the multitude of servants in this kind [intelligence] is hurtful and of late years hath bred much confusion with want of secrecy and dispatch.'[98] Christopher Marlowe, against strong competition probably the greatest writer ever to work for any branch of British intelligence, was, almost certainly, one of those he blamed for the confusion. Few clues survive of how Marlowe's experience of espionage influenced his writing, but when he described in *The Tragical History of the Life and Death of Doctor Faustus* how Faustus sold his soul to the Devil, he must have had in mind, among other episodes, how Richard Baines in 1581 had blasphemously taken his vows as a Catholic priest at a seminary whose members he hoped to poison.[99] In 1587 the Privy Council formally certified that 'in all his actions [Marlowe] had behaved himself orderly and discreetly whereby he had done her Majesty good service'.[100] By the early 1590s, however, his behaviour was no longer 'orderly and discreet'.

Marlowe was imprisoned in 1589 after a swordfight in Shoreditch which led to the death of an innkeeper's son, and 'bound over to keep the peace' after another fight in 1592. In the same year he was accused of attacking a tailor in Canterbury.[101] Who began each of these fights is unknown, but Marlowe's hot temper had clearly made him an intelligence liability. While in Flushing (now Vlissingen), then an English possession, early in 1592, probably on an intelligence mission with Richard Baines, he was arrested for counterfeiting. Marlowe was reported to the English governor by Baines, with whom he was sharing a room, but claimed he had made contact with a goldsmith counterfeiter only to investigate his activities.[102] Whether or not Marlowe's story was true, he had a serious falling out with Baines, which was to continue after their return to England.

Recent research provides controversial but persuasive evidence that, while quarrelling with Baines, Marlowe began collaborating with his then

---

* Bacon seems, unsurprisingly, to have suffered from stress-related illness. Walsingham had earlier implied that he was a hypochondriac, telling him he was too preoccupied with 'physic': 'you shall find in time many incommodities, if you do not break it off.' In 1604 Standen was knighted by James I.

less famous contemporary William Shakespeare.* The latest (2016) edition of the authoritative *New Oxford Shakespeare* ascribes the authorship of the three parts of *Henry VI*, probably written in 1591–2, jointly to Shakespeare and Marlowe.† During their collaboration, Marlowe must have talked to Shakespeare about his intelligence career. *Richard III*, probably written by Shakespeare in 1592, is believed to be the first play which uses 'intelligence' to mean secret information.[103]‡ The collaboration between the two greatest Elizabethan playwrights, however, was cut short by Marlowe's violent death.

On 18 May 1593, Marlowe was summoned to appear before the Privy Council, probably accused of blasphemy and atheism, and ordered to report daily until 'licensed to the contrary'. The most detailed surviving list of his alleged blasphemies, 'A note containing the opinion of one Christopher Marley [Marlowe] concerning his damnable judgment of religion and scorn of God's word', was drawn up a few days later by Richard Baines. According to Baines, Marlowe had declared 'that Christ was a bastard and his mother dishonest' and that 'Saint John the Evangelist was bedfellow to Christ [who] used him as the sinners of Sodoma'.[104] How much truth there was in Baines's 'Note' is hard to judge. As his attempt to poison the well at the Rheims seminary after being ordained as a Catholic priest had demonstrated, Baines was capable of extraordinary deception and malice. But there is corroboration for his charge of blasphemy against Marlowe in the testimony of, among others, the dramatist Thomas Kyd, with whom he had shared a room, and his fellow spy Richard Cholmeley.[105]

On 30 May 1593, twelve days after appearing before the Privy Council, Marlowe was killed after dining in Deptford, near London, with three sinister individuals: Ingram Frizer, Nicholas Skeres and Robert Poley. According to an inquest held the next day by the royal coroner with a local jury, Frizer and Marlowe fell out over the bill. 'Moved with anger', Marlowe snatched Frizer's dagger from him and struck him about the head, possibly with the blunt end. Frizer grabbed his dagger back and stabbed Marlowe above the right eye, fatally wounding him. The jury found that Frizer had acted in self-defence.[106] Much about Marlowe's death, however, remains mysterious. The evidence given to the inquest by his three dinner companions cannot be relied on. Though Nicholas Skeres was in the service of the

---

* The period from 1585 to 1592 has become known as Shakespeare's 'missing years'. No documentary evidence survives on him during this period.
† *Henry VI, Part I* was first performed on 3 March 1592.
‡ Hastings declares in *Richard III*, 'nothing can proceed that toucheth us whereof I shall not have intelligence'.

Earl of Essex, he had a track record as a swindler, having recently been accused in Star Chamber of 'entrapping young gents'. Frizer was a business associate of Marlowe's current patron, Thomas Walsingham (cousin of Sir Francis), but had also been accused of plotting with Skeres to 'undermine and deceive' a young heir.[107] Robert Poley had comprehensively deceived Sir Thomas Babington while working for Sir Francis Walsingham during the Babington Plot. Despite many complaints about his 'knavery', he was still sent on foreign missions 'in Her Majesty's service'.[108] It is quite possible that Marlowe's violent end was related to the rivalries and disruption within Elizabethan intelligence which followed Walsingham's death, but, unless further evidence is discovered, the truth is unlikely to emerge.

The most ambitious attempt to revive Elizabethan intelligence in the few years after Walsingham's death was made by the Queen's flamboyant youthful favourite, the Earl of Essex (later executed for treason), who suffered from delusions of grandeur about his ability to establish himself as a new Walsingham (and about much else). The recruitment by Essex in 1592 of Anthony Bacon to organize a spy network under his personal control was a direct challenge to Burghley.[109]* Essex's greatest self-proclaimed intelligence triumph was to discover an alleged plot to murder the Queen by Dr Roderigo Lopez, who had been appointed her physician in 1581. Lopez had also been Essex's doctor but enraged him by allegedly revealing that Essex had suffered from complaints 'which did disparage his honour' (presumably sexually transmitted disease).

Essex announced dramatically in January 1594: 'I have discovered a most dangerous and desperate treason. The point of conspiracy was Her Majesty's death. The executioner should have been Doctor Lopez. The manner by poison. This I have so followed that I will make it appear as clear as the noon day.'[110] Though a somewhat devious individual, Lopez was an unlikely assassin. He had treated Walsingham, probably for kidney stones, over twenty years earlier and had gone on to become part of his intelligence network, providing information from within the Portuguese Jewish merchant community.[111] After Walsingham's death, Burghley had also used Lopez as a double agent to penetrate Spanish attempts to spy in England.[112]† Elizabeth herself, though alive to the threat of assassination, was sceptical about Essex's charges against her physician. One of the Queen's ministers reported to her: 'In the poor man's house were found no kind of writings of intelligences whereof he is accused.' But from the moment Essex

---

* The network included the by now rather down-at-heel Standen. (*ODNB* Anthony Bacon.)
† It was probably on Walsingham's initiative, shortly before his death, that in 1590 Lopez had approached the Spanish ambassador in Paris through a double agent. (*ODNB* Roderigo Lopez.)

had staked his reputation on his claim that Lopez was guilty of 'most dangerous and desperate treason', the doctor's fate was sealed. Essex used torture to obtain an improbable admission from him. On the rack, Lopez confessed to receiving 50,000 crowns from the King of Spain to poison the Queen with exotic foreign drugs.[113] Whatever Burghley's inner doubts about Lopez's guilt, he dared not show himself less zealous than the Queen's favourite in denouncing the improbable assassination plot. Anti-Semitism played some part in the accusations made against Lopez. Burghley's son (who later succeeded him as Chief Minister), Sir Robert Cecil, denounced him as a 'vile Jew'.[114] At his trial for treason, the Attorney General, Sir Edward Coke, made much of the claim that, though nominally Christian, in secret Lopez was a practising Jew. Though Lopez retracted the confession forced out of him on the rack, he and two alleged accomplices were found guilty of treason and hanged, drawn and quartered at Tyburn on 7 June 1594. The official account of the plot, published soon afterwards, stressed the criminal conduct of Philip II in trying to murder the Queen of England, while virtuously insisting that she would never dream of becoming involved in a plot to assassinate the King of Spain.[115]

The confused management of Elizabethan intelligence in the mid-1590s was epitomized by the fate of Thomas Phelippes. By the end of 1595, unable to repay the debts incurred by trying to run an intelligence network out of his own resources, Phelippes was in debtors' prison, where he remained until mid-1597. Because of the lack of other codebreakers, however, both Essex and Sir Robert Cecil separately sent him intercepted correspondence to decrypt in his prison cell. When the Queen and Cecil unsympathetically complained at the time he was taking to complete the task, Phelippes replied that, in addition to the fact that the Spanish had developed the habit of regularly producing new ciphers of 'such kind as will ask time to tread it out', he had suffered in both 'body and mind' from his imprisonment and was denied access to his records.[116]*

Essex was preoccupied with the ambition of winning military glory as well as political power. In 1596 he became a national hero as joint commander of a naval expedition which captured, plundered and burnt the Spanish port of Cádiz. Simultaneously, however, he lost the struggle for power with the ailing Burghley, whom he had hoped to succeed as Chief Minister. On 5 July, while Essex was on the Cádiz expedition, the Queen appointed Burghley's second son, Sir Robert Cecil, as Secretary of State.

---

* Phelippes was freed from prison in, or shortly before, June 1597 after Anthony Bacon offered to pay his debts. He served another, much briefer, prison term for debt in the summer of 1598.

Among Cecil's priorities was the reform of the intelligence system. The urgency of reform was demonstrated by Philip II's despatch in October 1596 of a new Armada against England as powerful as that of 1588. One of Cecil's agents in Bayonne on the Franco-Spanish border obtained accurate intelligence on the Spanish fleet but, because of the breakdown in intelligence communications, it arrived in London far too late to be of use. Ten days before news of the Armada's departure reached Cecil, it had broken up in a storm off Finisterre and abandoned its mission.[117]*

By the time Cecil succeeded his father as, in effect (though not in title), Chief Minister on Burghley's death in August 1598, he had rebuilt a significant continental intelligence network. Its first priority was enemy Europe: Lisbon, Seville, the Spanish coast, Bayonne and the Bay of Biscay, and Rome. His highest-paid agents were in Lisbon and Seville. But, as the research of Stephen Alford has shown, Cecil also had spies in 'such states as are friends to us': Scotland, Holland and Zealand, Germany, Denmark and Sweden.[118]

Cecil's pride in his intelligence network was vividly illustrated by the last portrait of Elizabeth, 'the Rainbow portrait', which he was almost certainly responsible for commissioning. The painting was first displayed in 1602, a year before the Queen's death, during her visit to him at Theobalds, his great estate in Royston.† Attributed to the painter Isaac Oliver, the portrait gives no hint that Elizabeth was almost seventy. Her portraitists knew that she expected to be depicted as the embodiment of eternal youth. Oliver's portrait is full of the kind of symbolism which appealed to Elizabeth as well as Cecil. In one hand the Queen holds a rainbow with the motto *non sine sole iris* ('no rainbow without the sun'); with the other hand she draws attention to the eyes and ears which cover her cloak, symbolizing her supposedly all-seeing and all-hearing intelligence system. Embroidered on one arm is the serpent of wisdom. As Sir Robert Cecil knew, Elizabeth enjoyed interpreting such symbols. His father, Lord Burghley, had once written to him about the speed with which the Queen had deciphered the meaning of an 'Allegorical Letter' which he had sent her: 'I think never a lady . . . nor a decipherer in the court would have dissolved the figure as Her Majesty hath done.'[119] It was appropriate that the man who commissioned the portrait was the Queen's intelligence chief as well as Chief Minister. Nowhere in the world is there another portrait of a ruler that pays such tribute to the quality of the intelligence service.

* Another English agent in Bayonne, Henri Chasteau-Martin, about whom Burghley had had doubts for some years, was discovered to be in the pay of Spain.
† During the reign of James I, the King took over Theobalds and the Cecils moved to Hatfield House, where the portrait still hangs. See ill. 16.

11

The Decline of Early Stuart and Spanish Intelligence, and the Rise of the French *Cabinet Noir*

Britain traditionally prides itself on the continuity and stability of its institutions. The seventeenth century, however, was an era of regime change and political instability in which intelligence and secret operations played a significant role. Plans for the succession to Elizabeth I were made so secretly during the years before her death in 1603 that the Queen was told nothing about them. In May 1601 Elizabeth's Chief Minister, Robert Cecil, joined the small and secretive group who supported the claims to the English throne of James VI of Scotland and were in cipher communication with him. The informal leader of the group was Henry Howard, recommended by James to Cecil as a 'long approved and trusty' intermediary. Cecil frequently used him as a go-between with James in an attempt to keep his correspondence as secret as possible.[1] But some letters from James probably were sent to Cecil directly. According to the later recollection of the English diplomat Sir Henry Wotton, Elizabeth once noticed the arrival of a satchel of mail from Scotland and demanded to see its contents. Cecil began to open the satchel but told the Queen it was so filthy and foul-smelling that the letters would have to be aired before they could be shown to her.[2]

Walsingham and Burghley must have turned in their graves at the role played by Howard in arranging the succession to Elizabeth. A quarter of a century earlier, as a committed supporter of James's mother, Mary, Queen of Scots, Howard had played a key role in delivering her secret correspondence to the French embassy in London under cover of darkness. Howard had been imprisoned five times and come close to being accused of treason at the time of the Throckmorton Plot.[3] Unsurprisingly, given Burghley's role in Mary's execution, James's initial response to the overtures from his son was somewhat cool. Once he realized Cecil would have a crucial role in arranging an orderly succession, however, James began praising him as 'so worthy, so wise and so provident a friend'.[4] In early March 1603, with Elizabeth on her deathbed, Cecil sent to James for his approval a draft proclamation of his accession as King James I of England. Following the Queen's death, Cecil read out the proclamation on 24 March, first at the palace of Whitehall and then at the gates to the City of London. In May, during the final stages of his progress from Edinburgh, the King stayed for four nights at Theobalds, Cecil's great mansion in Hertfordshire. While there, James ennobled Cecil as Baron Cecil of Essendon. But he made Lord Henry Howard and his nephew Lord Thomas Howard earls respectively of Northampton and Suffolk, thus outranking Cecil, as well as members of the Privy Council. It was another two years before James made Cecil Earl of Salisbury.[5]

James's accession placed England's leading codebreaker, Thomas Phelippes, who had provided key evidence at his mother's treason trial, in a deeply embarrassing position. The King was later to show his continuing devotion to the memory of a mother he had never known by reburying her in Westminster Abbey and erecting a magnificent monument to her in the south aisle of the chapel of her great-grandfather Henry VII. Soon after James's arrival in London, Phelippes sent him a letter apologizing for his part in the events which had preceded his mother's execution. Phelippes claimed speciously that he had merely obeyed government instructions to decrypt letters relating to the Babington Plot.[6] Fortunately for Phelippes, James was almost certainly unaware that he had forged a ciphered postscript to a letter from Mary to Babington, asking for the names of the six gentlemen who, according to Babington, had agreed to assassinate Elizabeth.[7] Phelippes, however, remained understandably fearful about incurring 'His Majesty's further displeasure'.[8]

James lacked Robert Cecil's deep interest in intelligence. As King of Scotland he had been more interested in the supposed threat from witches, about whom he wrote a book,[9] than in espionage. As King James I of England, however, he quickly found Cecil indispensable to the conduct of his foreign policy, which was rarely referred to the Privy Council. Cecil took the lead in 1604 in bringing to an end the long war with Spain, which had begun almost twenty years earlier. Though the terms of the peace treaty were ambiguous, Spain for the first time tacitly allowed Englishmen to trade and settle in the West Indies and North America. Cecil proved even greedier than his father in using his official position to accumulate a private fortune. After 1604 he accepted both a pension and substantial presents from successive Spanish ambassadors. There was never any prospect, however, that Cecil, like Sir Edward Stafford twenty years earlier, would become a Spanish agent. The Spanish court hoped for no more than to diminish Cecil's hostility.[10]

*

Following peace with Spain, the main potential threats to national security remained attempts at regime change by irreconcilable English Catholics. With one notable exception, none came close to success. Cecil told the English ambassador in France, Sir Thomas Parry, that 'false' priests – informants who either were or pretended to be Catholic priests – were a rich intelligence source on Catholic plotting. In the autumn of 1605 Cecil's agent George Southwick, whom he described as 'very honest', returned to England in the company of priests he himself had secretly denounced to Cecil.[11]

The great exception to the inability of most Catholic plotters in early Stuart England to conspire effectively was the Gunpowder Plot of 1605, the best-remembered conspiracy in British history. According to modern calculations, the explosion of thirty-six barrels of gunpowder hidden in a cellar beneath the House of Lords during the state opening of Parliament on 5 November would have destroyed much of Westminster as well as killing the King, his ministers and many others. The fact that this terrorist attack came so close to success was the result of what several centuries later would be called 'intelligence failure'. None of the 'false priests', in whose intelligence Cecil expressed such confidence, had wind of it. A report on Catholic plotting written by George Southwick on 5 November 1605, the day the plot was discovered, contained no hint of it.[12]

With only slightly better planning, the plot to blow up Parliament would have succeeded. The charismatic Catholic leader of the plot, Robert Catesby, was described by two Jesuits who knew him well as 'more than ordinarily well proportioned, some six feet tall, of good carriage and handsome countenance'. He made, however, the fatal mistake of spreading knowledge of the plot beyond the original conspirators in order to persuade wealthy Catholics to support and finance the rising in the Midlands which he hoped would follow the assassination of the King and his ministers. One of those approached by Catesby was Francis Tresham. Though sworn to secrecy, Tresham was probably the author of an anonymous letter to his Catholic brother-in-law, Lord Monteagle, on 26 October warning him not to attend Parliament, where a 'terrible blow' was planned on 5 November.[13]

Monteagle immediately took the letter to Cecil, who showed it to the King on Friday, 1 November, the day after he returned from one of his many hunting trips. On Saturday the 2nd a group of privy councillors informed James that the Lord Chamberlain, the Earl of Suffolk, would search the Houses of Parliament 'both above and below' – but not until Monday the 4th because 'the nearer that things were to readiness', the more the search was likely to uncover.[14] If there was a plot, it was important not to scare the plotters into premature flight. Some in the Privy

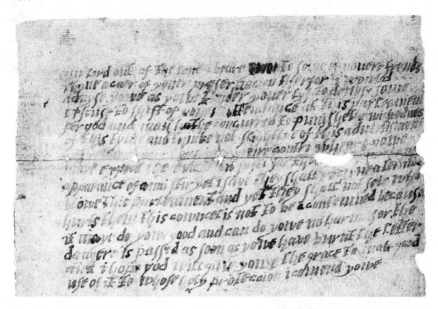

Anonymous letter to Lord Monteagle warning him of plans for 'terrible' attack on
Parliament on 5 November 1605.

Council, however, probably suspected that the curiously delivered warning
of a 'terrible blow' was a false alarm. On his first inspection during the
afternoon of the 4th, Suffolk, accompanied by Monteagle, discovered a
large pile of firewood, which a servant, who gave his name as 'John Johnson', said belonged to his master, Thomas Percy, nephew and estate
manager of the Earl of Northumberland. Though the search party seemed
to accept the explanation, Monteagle expressed surprise on returning to
Whitehall Palace that Percy had rented a cellar beneath Parliament as well
as leasing property in London, and mentioned that he was a Catholic.[15]

At a meeting of privy councillors, the King ordered a second search of
the cellars, this time led by Sir Thomas Knyvett, keeper of the Palace of
Westminster, who used the pretext of looking for wall hangings and other
'stuff' which had gone missing. Meeting 'Johnson' emerging from Percy's
cellar at about midnight, Knyvett thought his behaviour suspicious and
ordered his arrest. Beneath the firewood his men then discovered almost a
ton (thirty-six barrels) of gunpowder. Hauled before the King and his
councillors, 'Johnson' behaved with extraordinary courage: he is plausibly
alleged to have told James to his face that the purpose of the gunpowder
was to blow him and his fellow Scots back to Scotland. When the interrogation of 'Johnson' continued in the Tower, he at first refused to implicate
any of his fellow plotters, save for Percy, whose involvement was as obvious

as his own. 'You would have me discover my friends', he told his interrogators. He did not even admit that his real name was Guido ('Guy') Fawkes, until 7 November, when his interrogators, who had hitherto failed to search his pockets, found a letter in one of them addressed to 'Mr Fawkes'.[16]

Fawkes was discovered to be a Catholic ex-soldier who had fought in the Spanish army in the Low Countries. On 8 November Catesby and three other conspirators were killed in Staffordshire by a posse led by the Sheriff of Worcestershire. Next day James I addressed Parliament and took the main credit for the discovery of the plot by interpreting the Monteagle letter as a warning of a 'horrible form of blowing us up all by [Gun] Powder'.[17] Fawkes and the other surviving conspirators were tortured in the Tower, tried in Westminster Hall and sentenced to be hanged, drawn and quartered at Tyburn. Like other European rulers, James I remained vulnerable to assassination by a lone assassin prepared to die in the attempt or be horribly done to death afterwards. In 1610, after a series of unsuccessful attempts on his life, Henry IV of France was stabbed to death by the probably deranged religious fanatic François Ravaillac while his coach was stuck in Paris traffic. After prolonged and gruesome torture, Ravaillac's body was pulled apart by four horses – a method of execution reserved for regicides.[18] Though no Ravaillac emerged in Stuart England, James's favourite, the Duke of Buckingham, was later killed by a lone assassin.[19]

In early Stuart, unlike much of Elizabethan, England, Catholic plotters against the monarch could expect no help from Spain. In the decade after the Anglo-Spanish peace treaty of 1604,[20] Philip III's Council of State was more anxious to obtain intelligence on English settlement in the New World (tacitly accepted by the treaty) than on events in England.[21] Unlike his father, Philip II, 'el rey papelero', who struggled to cope with mountains of paper on his desk in the Escorial, Philip III never showed an enthusiasm for official documents (intelligence reports included) which approached his passion for hunting, riding and travel. Philip II would also have been horrified by his son's gambling debts and profligate spending on a life of luxury.[22] The initiative for intelligence collection in the New World under Philip III came chiefly from the Council of State.* A century earlier, during the rapid conquest of New Spain, it had been handled more effectively on the spot by Cortés with the assistance of the former slave Malinche, his remarkably talented interpreter and mistress.[23]

The first permanent English settlement in North America, founded in

* Philip III's *valido* (Chief Minister and favourite), the Duke of Lerma, was present at only twenty-two of the 739 meetings of the Council of State held during his term of office. (Williams, 'El reinado de Felipe III', p. 425.)

1607 by the London Virginia Company, to which James I had given a royal charter, was named Jamestown in the King's honour. Established thirteen years before the Pilgrims landed at Plymouth, the new colony barely survived its first winter. The Spanish Council of State none the less saw it as a serious potential threat, writing in the name of Philip III to the Duke of Medina Sidonia, Viceroy of New Spain, in July 1608: 'By various avenues He [the King] has been advised that the English are attempting to procure a foothold on the Island of Virginia, with the end of sallying forth from there to commit piracy.'[24] Few of the surviving colonists (all but two of them male) were as optimistic about their prospects as the Council of State. To try to save Jamestown, Captain John Smith, who became leader of the colony in September, declared a policy of 'no work, no food'. Both the Council of State and the Spanish ambassador in London remained deeply concerned, urging Philip to remove the English interlopers by force. On 11 June 1609 the King wrote to Medina Sidonia: 'You will do me great service in continuing [to gather] intelligence about the designs of the corsairs and any [intelligence] that shows the English having interest in continuing to populate the land called Virginia in the Indies.'[25]

On the same day, in anticipation of the instructions from Madrid, a Spanish ship with twenty-five soldiers on board, captained by Francisco Fernández de Écija, set sail from Florida for Virginia in order to assess the practicability of an attack on Jamestown. When Écija reached the mouth of the James river, however, he encountered a larger English ship, the *Mary and John*, which chased him back down the coast.[26] Had the Spanish intelligence-gathering mission taken place a few days earlier without encountering the *Mary and John*, Écija and his crew might well have seen for themselves the miserable condition of the English colony during the 'Starving Time' of 1609–10 and decided to launch an attack. It has been plausibly argued that mutineers among the colonists might then have sided with the small Spanish force and enlisted the support of nearby Powhatan Indian warriors. Jamestown's survival in 1609 thus owed much to Spain's lack of the intelligence which Medina Sidonia had been instructed to obtain. Over the next few years news of the hardships endured by the English colonists gradually percolated through to Spain. In 1613 the English ambassador in Madrid, John Digby, reported that the Spanish government thought that 'our Plantation in Virginia is likely to sink itself'. Philip III, however,

Anglo-Spanish rivalry in the New World: Philip III of Spain calls in 1608 for intelligence on Virginia and English designs on it. ▶

El Rey

Duque de Medina sidonia primo delmi conseso de eStado. y Capⁱᵗᵃⁿ
general del mar oceano y costa del Andalucia. Hase visto vⁿᵃ carta
de 18 del pasado. y los auisos que con ella embiastes delo que deponen
los marineros que han llegado aessa costa Vobados de Piratas. y
por agora no se ofreçe que Vosponderos mas de que se queda mirando
en todo lo que aduertis. y que me haseis mucho seruiçio encontinnar
la Anteligençia de saner los dysinios delos cosarios. y el que muestran
tener los Ingleses deproseguir en lapoblacion dela Tierra que llaman
Virginia en las Indias; de lorença a 14 — de Junio de 1609

Yo el Rey

Pormⁿ del Rey mo senõr
Antonio de Aro stepen

resisted further attempts by his Council of State to persuade him to attack Jamestown. The King's reluctance to go to war had important consequences. So long as Jamestown remained an English colony, there was no prospect of Spain extending its empire into the vast areas north of Florida.[27]*

The great Asian empires of the Ottoman Turks, the Persian Safavids, Mughal India and the Ming dynasty in China (succeeded in 1644 by the Qing), all more powerful than James I's England and Philip III's Spain, showed no interest in European conquests and rivalries in the New World. All continued to believe that the world revolved round Asia. For three centuries the main conflicts in America, Oceania, the Atlantic and the Pacific were between European powers. The Asian dynasties were to pay a heavy price for their lack of curiosity about the expansion of Europe. To quote Yuval Harari: 'The wealth and resources accumulated by the Europeans eventually enabled them to invade Asia too, defeat its empires, and divide it among themselves.'[28]

Philip III of Spain and his successor, Philip IV (1621–65), had a succession of intelligence chiefs (*espías mayores*) who were nominally in charge of all espionage and counter-espionage operations.[29] The reality, however, like much of seventeenth-century Spanish administration, was more confused.[30] Reports from both Spanish ambassadors and agents to the Council of State sometimes became stuck for long periods in the logjam of official correspondence. Late in 1617 the ambassador in Paris, the Duke of Monteleón, complained to Madrid: 'So many days have passed since I received letters from Spain that I confess to feeling the loneliest individual in the world.' He evidently received no immediate reply, since he repeated the complaint early in the following year – as did at least one of his successors.[31]

A study of 231 identified Spanish agents during the period from 1598 to 1635 shows that 101 (44 per cent) were French.[32] The great French codebreaker François Viète, who succeeded in decrypting much of the cipher correspondence of Juan Bautista de Tassis, Spanish ambassador in Paris from 1598 to 1604, concluded that he was remarkably well informed about French affairs. Viète wrote to Henry IV's Chief Minister, the duc de Sully, shortly before his death in 1603: 'These letters have made me form a judgement that he is very dangerous for France and the peace and tranquillity of the state. For he appears to me to be a very shrewd statesman and very subtle . . . His letters depict admirably to his king the moods, beliefs, weaknesses and powers of the French.'[33]

---

* In 1624, following the failure of the Virginia Company, Jamestown became a royal colony. Its fate was in striking contrast with the relative prosperity of New England.

The motives of the French agents who gave Tassis such good intelligence ranged from the mercenary to the religious. Spain's best-placed French mercenary agent in the early seventeenth century was Nicolas L'Hoste, who was employed by his godfather Nicolas de Neufville de Villeroy, probably the most accomplished French Secretary of State during the century before Cardinal Richelieu, serving successively under Charles IX, Henry III, Henry IV and Louis XIII. In 1601 Villeroy posted L'Hoste to the French embassy in Spain, where he was recruited by another French agent in the pay of Spanish intelligence, Gérard de Raffis. In 1602 L'Hoste returned to Paris to work for Villeroy, and secretly supplied the Spanish embassy with much of Villeroy's main diplomatic correspondence. The importance attached to L'Hoste's intelligence was demonstrated by the fact that he was paid 1,200 écus a year by the Spanish embassy in Paris, 20 per cent of the embassy's annual budget.[34] His three-year career as a Spanish agent came to an abrupt end in 1604 when his recruiter, Gérard de Raffis, changed sides and revealed L'Hoste's espionage to the French.[35] L'Hoste appealed for help to Tassis's successor as Spanish ambassador in Paris, Baltasar de Zúñiga, who instructed one of his servants to help L'Hoste escape. While crossing the River Marne, however, L'Hoste drowned either accidentally or, quite possibly, as the result of foul play by the ambassador's servant, who may have been instructed to avoid the embarrassment of his trial and execution for treason. After L'Hoste's death, the servant was imprisoned but later released after claiming diplomatic immunity.[36]

Probably as a result of poor security by the Spanish embassy in Paris, several other agents were caught and executed for treason.* The most dramatic embarrassment for Spanish intelligence came in December 1605 when a Provençal noble and army officer, Louis de Lagonia de Mérargues, was arrested in the act of passing plans connected with a proposed Spanish attack on Marseilles to the secretary of the Spanish embassy in Paris, Jacques Bruneau. Shortly afterwards he was executed for treason.[37] Bruneau was jailed but later released on grounds of diplomatic immunity. French suspicion about Mérargues seems to have been aroused by Zúñiga's habit of receiving him regularly at his house rather than following what became the usual tradecraft of avoiding direct contact with agents.†

Zúñiga's successor as Spanish ambassador, Diego de Irarraga, showed

---

* Among them the army officer de Bone and the Breton noble La Fontenelle, of whom little is known, executed in, respectively, 1601 and 1602. (Hugon, *Au service du roi catholique*, pp. 588, 611.)

† After Mérargues's execution, his brother also offered his services as a Spanish spy, but was turned down. (Ibid., pp. 132, 223, 620.)

equally poor judgement in handling the maverick Welshman Thomas Morgan, one of the longest-serving and, by the early seventeenth century, oldest Spanish agents, who spent much of his career in English, French and Flemish jails. Morgan had begun working for Mary, Queen of Scots, in 1568 and was involved in, among others, the Ridolfi and Babington plots. Though not a Hispanophile and later opposed to the Armada, in 1584, when working, probably unpaid, for Mary, he also became a paid Spanish agent. While spying for Spain in France, he simultaneously corresponded with the English authorities in the vain hope of obtaining a royal pardon. In 1605, after returning to England without a pardon, he was sentenced to death, but the sentence was commuted to exile. After returning to France in 1607, at the age of seventy-one, Morgan was arrested once again but escaped to seek refuge from the Spanish ambassador in Paris, whose expenses for 1608 contain the following entry: 'On 14 November 1608, on the orders of the King of France, they arrested Thomas Morgan, English gentleman, agent of this embassy, whom I had hidden in my house, looking after him for seventy-eight days.'[38]* After the embarrassments caused by L'Hoste, Mérargues, Morgan and others, the Council of State seems to have ordered greater caution in conducting espionage operations on French soil.[39] The fact that the unreliable Morgan was still being employed in his seventies is evidence of Spain's difficulty in recruiting English agents. Only six identified Spanish agents during the period from 1598 to 1635 were English or Welsh.[40]† None had direct access to English government sources.

Spain's most committed early-seventeenth-century agents came from the *parti dévot*, devout French Catholics who opposed the toleration granted to Huguenot Protestants at home by the Edict of Nantes and France's intermittent alliances abroad with German and Dutch Protestant heretics and the Muslim Ottomans. One such was the self-styled *espion divin* ('divine spy') Jean de Quercy, who in 1613 wrote Philip III a long letter declaring that in working for him he was doing God's will: 'Sacred Majesty, I am a good Frenchman and Catholic . . . I shall unceasingly seek the honour of your good graces which will be for me like the port of my salvation.'[41]

Spain's agent network in France also included some priests, including the Spaniard Antonio de Arco, who acted as intermediary for Quercy and may well have recruited him.[42] The most important of Arco's reports were probably those on the French court which he sent to the Council of State in Madrid from 1616 to 1619 during his years as confessor to the young

* Morgan was freed from prison in 1610 and, apparently, allowed to end his days in France.
† There were also four Scottish agents.

and beautiful Anne of Austria, daughter of Philip III and Queen Consort to King Louis XIII.[43] Arco's years in Paris coincided with a particularly fraught period in both the royal marriage and French politics. Married in 1615, when both were only fourteen, in a ceremony described by a hyperbolic Spanish preacher as the most beautiful since the union of Adam and Eve, Louis and Anne were put under pressure to consummate their marriage on the wedding night. So far from being a personal secret, the consummation of a royal marriage in early modern France was an affair of state because of its impact on the succession and international relations. Immediately after the wedding night, Louis's domineering mother, Marie de' Medici, Queen Regent during his minority, announced that the royal couple had successfully consummated their marriage. In reality, though Marie could not bring herself to admit it, the sexually inexperienced Louis was so traumatized by the sexual pressure put on him that he fled from the marriage bed with the marriage still unconsummated. He did not return for over three years. During these three years Louis took to visiting his wife almost every day but never dined, let alone slept, with her.[44]

As the confessor of Queen Anne, who, unlike Louis, was anxious to consummate their marriage, Arco must have discussed the issue with her. The King's confessor is known to have had such discussions with Louis and did not consider himself to have broken the secret of the confessional when he revealed that he had urged the King to return to the Queen's bed.[45*] Arco found French court politics even more fraught than the state of the royal marriage. Marie de' Medici largely ignored her daughter-in-law and continued to act as if she, not Anne, were Queen of France. Her arrogant, Italian-born favourite and Chief Minister, Concino Concini, marquis d'Ancre, made little attempt to conceal his disdain for the sexually inadequate monarch. Louis, however, developed what his leading biographer, Jean-Christian Petitfils, has called an astonishing capacity for dissimulation of which both his mother and her favourite probably thought him incapable.[46] The King was closely involved with the carefully prepared plot which assassinated Concini in Paris on 24 April 1617. Taken completely by surprise, Concini was surrounded by five assassins, who, fearing that he might have chain mail to protect him beneath his robes, each shot him in the head with a pistol. Louis appeared at a window of the Louvre Palace after the assassination and told a cheering crowd: 'Now I am King!' Marie de' Medici was ordered to leave Paris and retire to Blois. Concini's wife, Leonora Dori, was publicly beheaded in the Place de Grève (now Place de l'Hôtel de Ville).[47] Louis's teenage experience of conspiracy and

---

* Petitfils (*Louis XIII*) refers to the King's confessor but makes no mention of Arco.

deception gave him a taste for intelligence operations which lasted for the remainder of his reign.[48]

News of Concini's assassination took a fortnight to travel to Madrid. The Council of State met on 10 May 1617 to consider reports from Paris.[49] Though most of Arco's secret despatches either do not survive or have yet to be discovered in the Simancas archives, he must have reported on the response of Anne of Austria and the rest of the French court both to the rule of Marie and Concini and to its dramatic end. Arco found his presence at the French court so stressful that he several times asked the Council of State for permission to return to Spain, initially without success.* In November 1618 Louis banned the Spanish ambassador from visiting the apartments of Queen Anne.[50] Arco's continued access to her thus became even more important than before.

Following Concini's assassination, Louis came under renewed pressure to consummate his marriage from his favourite the Duke of Luynes, his confessor Father Arnoux, successive Spanish ambassadors and the papal nuncio, Guido Bentivoglio. Arco probably reported to Madrid, as Bentivoglio informed Rome, that Louis 'felt no carnal desire capable of overcoming his sense of shame' at sexual intercourse. He probably also reported that what finally roused sufficient 'carnal desire' for Louis to return to his wife's bed was the wedding on 20 January 1619 of his half-sister, Catherine-Henriette de Bourbon-Vendôme, illegitimate daughter of Henry IV, to the Duke of Elbeuf. As court custom dictated, Louis followed the newlyweds into their bedchamber. It was traditional for the king to withdraw when the newly married couple drew the curtains around their four-poster bed, but on this occasion Louis was persuaded to get into bed and watch the couple make love. What happened next appears to have been widely known within both the court and the diplomatic community. According to the Venetian ambassador, Louis became sexually aroused. The new Duchess of Elbeuf told him after her own marriage had been consummated: 'Sire, do the same thing with the Queen and it will turn out well!' It took another five days and floods of royal tears before Louis took his half-sister's advice. The news that he had done so on the night of 25 January was spread by the court and foreign ambassadors to the capitals of Europe. The newly radiant royal couple had a delayed honeymoon. Louis's doctor even became concerned that he was making love to his wife too frequently.[51] Following the beginning of regular sexual relations between the King and Queen, the Spanish Council

---

* Arco's last known secret report was in March 1619. (Hugon, *Au service du roi catholique*, pp. 421, 430, 581.)

of State finally granted Arco's repeated request to be allowed to return to Spain.[52]

Like Arco, those whom the *espias mayors* considered the most reliable of their small number of English agents were priests: the exiled Jesuits Robert Persons and Joseph Cresswell.[53] In 1580 Persons had led a secret Jesuit mission to England 'to win our nation to God again' but fled to the Continent, never to return, after the mission was discovered by Walsingham's agents.[54] Though Persons would never have considered himself a Spanish agent, he formed a close association with Philip II, whose support enabled him to found English seminaries at Valladolid (honoured by a royal visit in 1592) and at Seville. Under the pseudonym Andreas Philopater, Persons published a vigorous defence of Spanish foreign policy, which, on Philip's instructions, was published in Antwerp, Lyons, Cologne, Naples and Rome.[55] He predicted, inaccurately, in 1595 that the succession to Elizabeth I could not be settled 'without some war'.[56] Like Persons, Joseph Creswell also wrote treatises in defence of Spanish foreign policy, and in 1604 advised Philip III, to little avail, on the recruitment of English agents in Paris. On Persons's death in 1610, he succeeded him as rector of the English College in Valladolid but fell out of favour at the Spanish court.[57] By 1617 Spanish intelligence from English agents had almost dried up.[58]

The Spanish Crown's growing financial difficulties placed its intelligence system under increasing strain. During the reign of Philip III silver imports from Spanish America fell by half. Under Philip IV royal finances deteriorated further, with inevitable consequences for Spanish intelligence operations. Spain's bankruptcy in 1627 prompted a number of its unpaid agents to change sides: among them the Genoese Carlos Spina, who had previously been paid 2,000 ducats per year, and the Venetian noble and diplomat Angelo Badoer, who had begun working as a Spanish agent in 1609.[59] The capture of the Spanish treasure fleet by the Dutch in the following year prevented any rapid recovery of royal finances.

English as well as Spanish intelligence was in decline during the early seventeenth century. The death of Salisbury in 1612 deprived James of his ablest administrator and the only minister capable of organizing a coherent intelligence system. James had no one equal to the huge foreign-policy and intelligence challenge posed by the outbreak in 1618 of the Thirty Years War – a long-drawn-out struggle over the ascendancy of the Habsburg dynasty and the Catholic religion in continental Europe. By the time the war began, the dominant influence on James was his handsome, dashing favourite, George Villiers, who, despite his poor political judgement, was created successively Earl (1617), Marquess (1618) and Duke (1623) of

Buckingham. In his homoerotic correspondence with James, Buckingham commonly signed himself 'Your Majesty's humble slave and dog'.[60] James was besotted with him.

By the 1620s both the English and Spanish courts had, so far as is known, no agent intelligence on each other.* Buckingham's ignorance of intelligence was evident in the comic-opera scheme which he devised for a secret visit to Madrid in 1623 to enable the heir to the English and Scottish thrones, Prince Charles, to seek the hand in marriage of the Infanta Maria Anna, sister of Philip IV. So far from seeking intelligence before the trip on the likely reaction of the Spanish court, Buckingham did not even warn the English ambassador of his and Charles's imminent arrival. Had he done so, he would have been better briefed on the devoutly Catholic Infanta's reluctance to marry a Protestant prince. Unlike his bisexual father, Charles was not sexually attracted to the royal favourite but, after seeing the Infanta's portrait, believed himself in love with her and agreed enthusiastically to Buckingham's plan. Improbably disguised as the brothers Thomas and John Smith, Charles and Buckingham set off for Spain on horseback, wearing false beards and periwigs, accompanied by two attendants. Their disguise was compromised even before they left England when Buckingham gave such a large tip to the Gravesend ferryman that he and Charles were suspected of going to France to fight a duel and pursued all the way to Dover.[61]

Their arrival in Madrid astonished Philip IV and his Chief Minister, Don Gaspar de Guzmán, Count-Duke of Olivares, as well as the English ambassador. After two months of Spanish hospitality during which he had only two distant glimpses of the Infanta, Charles was so desperate to talk to Maria Anna that he climbed over a royal garden wall in a desperate attempt to meet her face-to-face. The Infanta and her entourage fled in terror.[62] Buckingham's temper had become seriously frayed. He became so enraged during a religious debate with a Jesuit that he took off his hat, threw it on the ground and stamped his foot on it.[63] The mission to Madrid ended, predictably, in failure. In 1624, influenced by Buckingham, James I declared war on Spain after twenty years of peace. In the following year, Charles married another Catholic princess – Henrietta Maria, younger sister of Louis XIII of France. Though Charles did not see his bride until she arrived in England, the courtship was complicated by Buckingham's undiplomatic attempts to seduce the French Queen, Anne of Austria.[64]

---

* Philip's aunt, the Archduchess Isabella, ruler of the Spanish Netherlands, had, however, an informant at Charles's court: George Lamb, secretary to the King's confidant, Sir John Coke. (Lamster, *Master of Shadows*, p. 209.)

Buckingham's disregard for intelligence extended to codebreaking as well as espionage. Though Phelippes's eyesight was failing, the Venetian ambassador in London, Girolamo Lando, described him in 1622 as still 'unequalled in deciphering'. Doubtless to Lando's relief, Phelippes was unable to break Venetian ciphers given to him in that year to test their security.[65] Lando's successor, Zuane Pesaro, sent further Venetian cipher material to Phelippes in 1624. Possibly because he was by now almost blind, Phelippes shared some of the material with a friend. Despite this apparent breach of trust, Pesaro believed that Phelippes had 'dealt sincerely' with him and had 'certainly rendered services', for which he deserved payment by the Venetians.[66] Buckingham took a different view. With his approval, if not on his initiative, Phelippes was placed in solitary confinement in King's Bench Prison. The legal justification for this decision was dubious. In April 1626 the Lord President of the Council, Sir Edward Conway, told Pesaro that 'the laws did not allow of his close confinement any longer', but Phelippes was still in prison at the end of the year. He died early in 1627; it is unclear whether or not he was released from prison before his death.[67] Unmourned by Buckingham, Phelippes's fifty-year career as the first great English codebreaker had come to a wretched end.

The demise of codebreaking in Britain with the death of Phelippes coincided with its revival in France, where it had also been in decline since the death of the great cryptographer François Viète.[68] The immediate cause of the revival of French codebreaking was the conflict between Cardinal Richelieu, now Louis XIII's Chief Minister, and the Protestant Huguenots. On 19 April 1628, Henry II of Bourbon, prince de Condé, laid siege to the Huguenot town of Réalmont. The besiegers intercepted a messenger leaving the town with a ciphered letter addressed to fellow Huguenots in Montauban. In an attempt to decrypt it, Condé summoned a 26-year-old mathematician named Antoine Rossignol, who lived twenty kilometres away in the city of Albi, and, Condé was told, had some expertise in cryptography. Appropriately, as well as meaning 'nightingale', *rossignol* was argot for a skeleton key which would unlock locked doors. Rossignol decrypted the message from the defenders of Réalmont to fellow Huguenots without difficulty. In it they pleaded for urgent supplies of gunpowder and declared that, without it, they would have to surrender. When Condé confronted them with the contents of their letter on 30 April, they capitulated.[69]

Rossignol provided equally valuable intelligence during the siege of the main Huguenot stronghold, the Atlantic port of La Rochelle, which followed that of Réalmont. From the beginning of the siege Richelieu, who commanded the besieging forces dressed in a curious combination of

ecclesiastical and military costume, took a personal interest in the interception of letters from the defenders to other Huguenots. He reported to
Louis XIII that, on one occasion, a messenger was caught carrying a note
to Montauban Huguenots in a small tin box, which he swallowed when
he was captured. Richelieu ordered him to be given a purgative to ensure
that the message passed rapidly through his system.[70] On 8 August 1628
Condé sent Richelieu a packet of intercepted letters written in cipher by
Huguenot leaders in La Rochelle, together with a covering note: 'A young
man from Albi, named Rossignol, has deciphered them very well. I am
sending you the word-by-word decipherment, from which you will see
that, since 21 June, those in La Rochelle have been complaining that they
are in a state of famine.'[71]*

Richelieu was so impressed by the decrypts that he immediately summoned Rossignol to his presence. Charles Perrault of the Académie
Française (founded by Richelieu) later included Rossignol in his book
published in 1696 on the forty most 'illustrious' Frenchmen of the seventeenth century. According to Perrault, though the usually inscrutable
Richelieu rarely displayed visible enthusiasm, at their first meeting Rossignol 'gave such astonishing proof of his ability that this great Cardinal
. . . was unable to conceal his astonishment'.[72] Richelieu made Rossignol
his cipher secretary.[73] Perrault's claim that Richelieu also handsomely
rewarded him for his services is fully corroborated by Rossignol's purchase
in 1630 of a small but elegant château at Juvisy, twelve miles south of
Paris, and by his ability to finance further building work. Louis XIII
showed his personal interest in codebreaking and his esteem for Rossignol
by paying several visits to the château.[74]† He and his son Louis XIV were
the only French monarchs to honour their chief codebreaker in this way.‡

Richelieu's victory at La Rochelle ended in humiliation for England as
well as defeat for the Huguenots. Having discovered from decrypted correspondence that the besieged garrison in La Rochelle was pinning its faith
on the arrival of a large English fleet being assembled by Buckingham,
Richelieu sought to demoralize them by sending news that Buckingham's
confidant and astrologer, Dr John Lambe, had 'been beaten to death in
London in broad daylight by the people' (a group of apprentices), thus
prompting the savage rhyme:

---

* The wording of the letter shows that Richelieu was not yet acquainted with Rossignol.
† See ills. 20 and 22.
‡ Even in the twentieth and twenty-first centuries, such public recognition by heads of state
has been very rare. No US president visited the National Security Agency (NSA), the world's
largest SIGINT agency, until Ronald Reagan in 1986 (three and a half centuries after Louis
XIII's visit to Rossignol's château). (Andrew, *For the President's Eyes Only*, p. 484.)

> Let Charles and George [Buckingham] do what they can,
> The Duke shall die like Doctor Lambe

Buckingham's first priority, Richelieu told the defenders, had become his own survival rather than help to the Huguenots.[75] The message, like the rhyme, proved prophetic. Buckingham was stabbed to death on 23 August by a soldier with a grudge against him, though confirmation of the news did not reach Richelieu for another month.[76]

The *parti dévot* had earlier been critical of Richelieu's apparent willingness to tolerate fortified heretic enclaves in France, satirically referring to him as 'Pontiff of the Calvinists' or 'Patriarch of the Atheists'.[77] His attack on Huguenot strongholds, long an ambition of the *parti dévot*, by a government led by a French cardinal made it far more difficult than earlier in the century for Spain to recruit unpaid, religiously motivated agents among its ranks. Cristobal de Benavente y Benavides, Spanish ambassador in Paris from 1632 to 1635, had only five agents, generating little intelligence, as compared with the forty-one working for his predecessor, Juan Bautista de Tassis, at the start of the century.[78]

Though Spain had no agent network in Britain, Philip IV was able to use the most celebrated painter of the era, Peter Paul Rubens, to make confidential contact with Charles I. A century earlier Venice had made similar, though more covert, use of the painter Marcello Fogolino to collect intelligence abroad.[79] The use of Rubens, a pro-Spanish Flemish Catholic, to engage in secret diplomacy with Charles I had first been suggested in 1625 by Philip's aunt, the Archduchess Isabella, ruler of the Spanish Netherlands, a year after the ailing James I, under the influence of Buckingham, had brought to an end twenty years of peace with Spain and declared war. The response to Isabella's proposal by the twenty-year-old Philip reflected his lack of grasp of secret diplomacy and intelligence operations. He wrote pompously to Isabella:

> I am displeased at your mixing up of a painter in affairs of such importance. You can easily understand how gravely it compromises the dignity of my kingdom, for our prestige must necessarily be lessened if we make so insignificant a person the representative with whom foreign envoys are to discuss affairs of such great importance.[80]

Philip failed to grasp that neither Buckingham nor Charles, probably the greatest art lover ever to come to the British throne, thought Rubens in the slightest insignificant. Buckingham so liked Rubens's grand equestrian portrait of himself, improbably attended by a large cherub, painted in

1625, that in 1627–8, though England and Spain were at war, he paid Rubens the staggering sum of 100,000 florins for thirteen of his paintings and several in his collection by other artists.[81]

Like many successful portrait painters, Rubens had a gift for chatting even with rank-conscious sitters and gaining their confidence. He won over Philip IV while painting his portrait in 1628–9 and successfully softened the inbred, jutting Habsburg jaw. The King was so pleased with Rubens's equestrian portrait of him on a charging bay horse that he put it in place of another equestrian portrait by his favourite court artist, Diego Velázquez, in the Salón Nuevo of the Alcázar Palace in Seville.[82]

In April 1629 Philip agreed to send Rubens on the mission to London that his aunt had suggested four years earlier. The mission reflected the frequent early-modern overlap between diplomacy and political-intelligence operations. Rubens's official mission was to negotiate a temporary armistice in order to make possible the exchange of official ambassadors between the two countries, who had been suspended since the outbreak of war five years earlier. But he was also given secret instructions 'to prevent as far as possible' an Anglo-French alliance which was believed to be in the final stages of negotiation.[83] He had his first meeting with Charles on 6 June, soon after his arrival in London.

When initially dismissing Isabella's proposal for Rubens's mission to London, Philip was clearly unaware that she, unlike him, had an informant in Charles's court: George Lamb, a secretary to one of the King's long-standing confidants, Sir John Coke. 'Whereas in other courts negotiations begin with the ministers and finish with the royal word and signature', Lamb wrote to Isabella, 'here they begin with the king and end with the ministers.'[84] Rubens's reports to the Spanish First Minister, Count-Duke Olivares, show that he and the King quickly established a rapport. Though there was a strong French party at court, led by the Queen, and the French ambassador was hoping for an alliance with Britain, Charles confided in Rubens that he distrusted the French and did not believe their promises. Rubens was able to reassure Olivares that Anglo-French negotiations would conclude a peace treaty but that there would be no alliance. Charles, he believed, had more sympathy for Spain than for France.[85]

By September Rubens had reached agreement with Charles on terms for the formal resumption of British–Spanish diplomatic relations. At the request of Philip IV and the Council of State, he remained in London until the arrival of the new Spanish ambassador. Rubens's rapport with Charles owed much to their shared artistic interests and Charles's admiration for his work. Rubens was greatly impressed by 'the incredible quantity of excellent pictures, statues and ancient inscriptions' in the royal collection. Charles I commissioned him to paint nine ceiling canvases for Inigo Jones's Banqueting House in Whitehall Palace. Before Rubens's departure in March 1630, Charles conferred a knighthood on him in the Banqueting House and presented him with a jewel-set sword and diamond-studded hatband.[86] By a tragic irony the ceiling canvases were to be the last seen by the King before he stepped through a first-floor window of the Banqueting House on 30 January 1649 on to the scaffold constructed for his execution.[87]

Despite the success of Rubens's secret diplomacy for Philip IV, the most successful intelligence system in Europe was the French. A common traditional image of Richelieu shows, always at his side, the shadowy figure of François Le Clerc du Tremblay, a Capuchin friar better known by his religious name, Père Joseph de Paris. Dressed in his grey habit, Père Joseph was the original *éminence grise*, a phrase which has passed into the English as well as the French language. He combined deeply mystical Catholicism with passionate loyalty to the French monarchy. Convinced that the Habsburgs in both Spain and the Holy Roman Empire were concerned only with their own dynastic glory, Père Joseph believed that Catholic Europe could be united and victorious only under the leadership of France's 'Roi Très-Chrétien'.[88] Richelieu used him as confidant, religious and political adviser, and, intermittently, for secret diplomacy – notably for bringing the Protestant King of Sweden, Gustavus Adolphus, into the Thirty Years War to help defeat the Habsburg Emperor, Ferdinand II. Père Joseph had well-placed informants within the Capuchins and other religious orders, including, at least for a time, the Jesuit confessor of the Habsburg Emperor. In the summer of 1630 Père Joseph learned from the Emperor's confessor of intrigues by Marie de' Medici which Olivares and the Spanish ambassador in Paris hoped would culminate in the downfall of Richelieu.[89]*

The intrigues culminated in the *journée des dupes*, 'day of dupes' (more properly the *journées des dupes*, 'days . . .'), on 10 and 11 November 1630. On 10 November Marie de' Medici was confident that she had recovered her old ability to dominate her son, and had persuaded Louis to dismiss Richelieu and replace him with her own candidate, Michel de Marillac. Richelieu briefly feared that his political career was at an end. The main dupe, however, turned out to be the Queen Mother. The crisis ended

---

* Richelieu and Père Joseph did not, however, always agree. In October 1630 the Cardinal unexpectedly rejected a treaty which Père Joseph and a senior French diplomat had negotiated with the Emperor at Ratisbon. (Elliott, *Richelieu and Olivares*, p. 108.)

dramatically with a public reaffirmation of the King's confidence in Richelieu and the disgrace of Marillac. Richelieu wept with relief.[90]

Like Marie de' Medici, Philip IV was no match for Richelieu. In 1633 he absurdly instructed his ambassador in Paris to use flattery to win over Richelieu to a pro-Spanish policy:

> The key stratagem . . . would be to get close to Cardinal Richelieu and make every effort to win him over by demonstrating to him that you are convinced by everything he says to you and of his sincerity . . . using this method of flattering him and praising everything which is not contrary to my service.[91]

Philip had plainly not taken Olivares's advice before devising this naïve strategy. His reign, writes Tim Blanning, 'provides a particularly compelling example of how much can go wrong when a king is not only inadequate but long-lived'. After the fall of Olivares in 1643, Philip's most influential adviser was a mystic nun, Sister María of the Ágreda convent, with whom he exchanged over 600 letters, mostly about the need for divine assistance.[92] Sister María was no Père Joseph.

Richelieu's intelligence system, however, owed even more to Antoine Rossignol, who passes curiously unmentioned in most studies of the reign of Louis XIII,[93] than to his *éminence grise*. Rossignol became the key figure, though not official head, of a new government office founded by Richelieu informally known as the *cabinet noir* (black chamber), which was fully functional by 1633 at the latest. The *cabinet noir* was responsible for the interception, opening and copying of correspondence, for decryption when required, and for resealing letters, often with imitation seals, to conceal that they had been tampered with. When it proved impossible to remedy damage caused when letters were opened, they were declared to have been lost in transit.[94]

A report to Richelieu in 1633 by Père Joseph's protégé, François Sublet de Noyers (later Secretary of State for War), reveals that cross-Channel letters and packets were secretly and routinely opened in Calais. The practice had probably begun some years earlier. The French ambassador in London, a strong supporter of the interception, emphasized the need for all correspondence to be carefully resealed: 'If it is realized in England that their packets are being opened, I fear that they will do the same and open the despatches of the [French] King.'[95]* The implication was clearly that the English were not currently suspected of intercepting French diplomatic despatches – in striking contrast with the Walsingham era. When

---

* After the death of Père Joseph in 1638, de Noyers became one of Richelieu's closest advisers (Lefauconnier, 'François Sublet de Noyers', part 3, ch. 3.)

couriers were found carrying cipher correspondence, it was routinely passed to Rossignol for decryption but not always returned to the courier if Richelieu objected to the contents. In 1634, for example, after the arrest of a courier carrying cipher correspondence from Brussels to Milan, then both Spanish possessions, he gave instructions for it to be decrypted by Rossignol 'to see if there is anything important in it, and then for it to be returned or not returned, according to the view taken of its contents'.[96]

Decrypts from the reigns of Philip III and Philip IV in the Simancas archives show that the Spanish government retained some capacity for cryptanalysis. But it is highly unlikely that Spain possessed either an organization which compared with the French *cabinet noir* or a codebreaker whose skill approached that of Rossignol. Unsurprisingly, only fragmentary evidence survives of the work of French codebreakers as of other intelligence operations. Richelieu did not keep secret intelligence files. Some of his surviving letters on secret matters to the King end with requests for them to be destroyed: 'Votre Majesté bruslera, s'il luy plaist, ceste lettre.'[97] Enough correspondence remained unburnt, however, to show that Louis XIII, as well as Richelieu, took a personal interest in Rossignol and the work of the *cabinet noir*. In 1635, for example, the King was asked to decide the fate of the intercepted correspondence from Cardinal Borgia, who was plotting (in the end unsuccessfully) to become the next Pope, to the Spanish court. Should the correspondence be seized or simply delayed long enough for it to be decrypted?[98] Louis's response, possibly burnt, does not survive.

After the outbreak of war between France and Spain in 1635, secret agents were used by both sides to destabilize the other. French agents were the more successful. Père Joseph had written in 1634: 'It is important to see if one can make use of the discontents of the Catalans and the Portuguese.' French funds were probably channelled to conspirators in Lisbon before their ultimately successful coup d'état against Spanish rule in 1640. In an attempt to diminish his own responsibility for the loss of Portugal, Olivares somewhat exaggerated the success of French secret operations. France, he told Philip IV, 'has stripped Your Majesty of entire kingdoms in Spain by resorting to hideous treachery.' The French agent most likely to have transmitted the funds to the Portuguese conspirators was Alfonso (or Alphonse) Lopez, a Jewish diamond merchant from Aragon who had settled in Paris in 1610 and had close links with the Portuguese Jewish community. Having originally been used by Richelieu for financial transactions, he was also used as an agent. But Lopez's true loyalties remain unclear. In 1638 he wrote privately to Olivares that he would like to return to Spain. Whether this was a mere ruse or whether Lopez was really willing to change sides will probably never be known.[99] If he did seriously contemplate working for

Olivares rather than Richelieu, Spain's failures in the war with France must have discouraged him.

Though royal bankruptcy was never far away in both France and Spain during the 1630s,[100] the political consequences of the war were far more serious in Spain. Olivares was forced to resign in January 1643. His biographer, John Elliott, concludes: 'The Count-Duke became a non-person, and the reforming legacy was consigned with the rest of his works to oblivion . . .' By contrast, the legacy of Richelieu, who died a month before Olivares's resignation, lived on. At meetings of the French Council of State a generation later, Louis XIV would sometimes turn to Jean-Baptiste Colbert, Minister of Finance and, in all but name, Chief Minister from 1665 to 1683, and announce: 'Here is Monsieur Colbert who is going to tell us, "Sire, the great Cardinal would have done this or that . . ."'[101]

Richelieu's least remembered legacy was the *cabinet noir*. On his deathbed in 1643, Louis XIII, aged only forty-one, commended Rossignol as 'one of the men most necessary to the good of the state' to Queen Anne, who was to become regent for their infant son Louis XIV.[102] Cardinal Jules Mazarin, who became Chief Minister on Richelieu's death in 1642, was also an admirer of Rossignol. Like much else, however, the workings of the *cabinet noir* were disrupted by the revolts of 1648 to 1653 collectively known as the *Fronde*. In 1649 some of the intercepted correspondence of the royal court at Saint-Germain-en-Laye was read out in the rebellious Paris Parlement.[103] Once royal power had been re-established, Mazarin took a detailed personal interest in the interception of the correspondence of '*mauvais Français*'. In 1660, a year before his death, for example, he sent the following instructions to Hiérosme de Nouveau, *Surintendant des Postes*, on the interception of the letters of a member of a religious order who was involved in the distribution of allegedly subversive (probably pro-Spanish) literature:

> I have received reliable information that there is in Madrid a French Dominican Friar named Jean Faure, . . . who is engaged in correspondence with bad Frenchmen. Since it is of importance to the service of the King that H[is] M[ajesty] be fully informed of their designs, I request you to order the interception all the correspondence from the said Father to the following addresses on which I have information:
>
> To Senor Huart, bookseller at Saint-Sebastien
> To Monsieur Petit, bookseller at Bayonne and St-Jean-de-Luz
> To Monsieur Philippe Bergolli at his home in the rue du Petit Judas at Bordeaux or [c/o] the postmaster
> To M. Joly bookseller, rue St-Jacques at Paris

You will also find enclosed a facsimile of the seal used by the Father [Faure] which it will be easy for you to use [in resealing his correspondence].

The letter thus far was written on Mazarin's behalf by Hugues de Lionne, his Minister of State for Foreign Affairs, but Mazarin added in his own hand thanks to de Nouveau for all the letters and information he sent him and assured him of his friendship.[104]

After Mazarin's death in 1661, Rossignol continued as royal code-breaker to Louis XIV until his own death in 1682, a total period of over half a century – the longest term of office by any important official in the history of the French monarchy. His reputation was such that in 1696 Charles Perrault of the Académie Française claimed in his book on the most illustrious Frenchmen of the seventeenth century that, in fifty years, Rossignol had almost never encountered a cipher that defeated him.[105] Perrault's assessment almost certainly reflected the views of his patron and fellow Academician, Jean-Baptiste Colbert, Louis XIV's leading minister, who died a year after Rossignol.[106]

Intelligence and Regime Change in Britain: From the Civil War to the Popish Plot

The revival of English intelligence from the torpor into which it had sunk in the early Stuart era began as a result of the Civil War (1642–9), the unexpected outcome of a conflict between Charles I and Parliament which had run of control. Though the destruction caused by the Civil War did not compare with the devastation on the Continent during the Thirty Years War, an even higher proportion of the English population may have died than during the First World War, which is usually thought of as the most homicidal conflict in British history.[1] Like the First World War, it also marked a turning point in the history of British intelligence.

In the early years of the Civil War, Charles I, who moved his court to Oxford in 1642, and his royalist ('Cavalier') supporters maintained clandestine communications with royalists in the parliamentary ('Roundhead') headquarters of London. But Charles's Secretary of State and closest adviser in 1642–3, Lucius Cary, 2nd Viscount Falkland, regarded most intelligence work as demeaningly underhand and refused either to employ spies or to authorize the opening of parliamentary correspondence.[2] The £700 which Falkland received each year for 'secret service' seems to have been spent mainly on distributing royalist propaganda.[3]

Parliament's frustration at the failure to prevent the distribution of royalist propaganda secretly infiltrated into the capital from Oxford led to the imprisonment in July 1645 of the royal bookseller and royalist agent, Richard Royston, who was accused by the parliamentary printer, John Wright, of being the 'constant factor for all scandalous books and papers against the proceedings of parliament'.[4]

If royalist supporters in London were to operate as an effective intelligence network for the King and his court in Oxford, they needed a Walsingham to coordinate their activities. Even after Falkland's death in battle in September 1643, the King paid little or no attention to the organization of intelligence. If he ever gave any thought to the appointment of an intelligence

Pag: 1519. *1535*.

MERCVRIVS AVLICVS,

Communicating the Intelligence and
affaires of the Court, to the
reft of the KINGDOME.

From Aprill 6. *to* Aprill 13. 1645.

SUNDAY. *Aprill 6.*

 He Rebels this *Eafter* have excommunicated themfelves; for lately when the *Affembly* prefented their *Directory*, the Members excepted againft that particular which debarres certaine perfons from receiving the *Communion*, alleadging it was expreffed in too generall tearmes of *Scandalous* and *Ignorant* ; therefore they voted that the Affembly fhould explaine whom they would have accounted *Ignorant* or *Scandalous* ; The *Affembly* (the *Members* Journymen) returned to their Worke-houfe , and there laying their great heads together , (as well the Preachers as thofe in Holy Orders) drew up a Character of the *Ignorant* and *Scandalous*, and brought it to the Members: In this Character they infifted much upon examination concerning the *Trinity* , fo as Mafter *Selden* ftood up and faid, *he was confident there were not Ten in the Affembly but might be pofed in That themfelves.* The Houfes being refolved into a Committee prefently paffed two votes , Firft , *That fuch perfons as are groffely ignorant fhall not come unto the Sacrament* ; Secondly, *That fuch perfons as are groffely fcandalous fhall likewife be debarred.* We will not fay
S   the

The newssheet *Mercurius Aulicus* ('Court Mercury'), distributed by royalist agents in London in 1643–5 with the aim of 'Communicating the Intelligence and affaires of the Court, to the rest of the Kingdome'.

chief in the Walsingham mould, he must have been repelled by memories of Walsingham's responsibility for the execution of his grandmother Mary, Queen of Scots. The confused conspiracy in the spring of 1643 led by the royalist poet and MP Edmund Waller, first elected to Parliament at the age of only sixteen, demonstrated the damage done to royalist covert operations by the lack of central direction. In March 1643 Charles had issued a commission to seventeen prominent London citizens authorizing them to lead an armed rising. The ensuing 'Waller Plot', which was penetrated from an early stage, ended in a major propaganda victory for Parliament. Waller was remembered by posterity as a turncoat who sullied the King's cause: the great nineteenth-century historian of the Civil War, S. R. Gardiner, denounced him as the worst of the 'rich, witty and licentious' sensualists who debased the royal court.[5] On 31 May 1643 MPs were dramatically summoned from morning worship to be told of the plot's discovery.[6] In order to save himself, Waller made an abject apology at the bar of the House of Commons and betrayed his fellow conspirators. On 5 July two of those he betrayed, Richard Chaloner and Nathaniel Tomkins, his brother-in-law, were hanged from gallows erected in front of their houses in the heart of the City. On the scaffold Chaloner acknowledged the justice of the sentence against him, while claiming that his aims had been peaceful.[7] In his own speech from the scaffold, Tomkins blamed his involvement in the plot on 'affection to a brother-in-law, and affection and gratitude to the king, whose bread I have eaten now above twenty-two years'.[8] The failed Waller Plot, as well as undermining the morale of royalist agents in London, seriously weakened the 'peace party', which sought a negotiated end to the Civil War.[9]

As the penetration of the Waller Plot demonstrated, parliamentary leaders lacked Falkland's scruples about the use of spies. Though they had no centrally organized intelligence system,* they also successfully revived English cryptanalysis for the first time since the death of Thomas Phelippes. The key to the revival was the accidental discovery early in the Civil War of a codebreaker of genius: John Wallis, a Cambridge-educated cleric and mathematician, who became chaplain to the widow of a professional army officer, Baron Vere of Tilbury.[10] One evening late in 1642 over supper at Lady Vere's London house, Wallis was shown a letter written in cipher, which he decrypted in about two hours. This was the moment, he later recalled, when he discovered his vocation as a cryptographer: 'being encouraged by this success, beyond expectation; I afterwards ventured on many others (some of more, some of less difficulty) and scarce missed of any, that I undertook, for many years, during our civil Wars, and afterwards.'[11] Wallis's most celebrated achievement came after the decisive parliamentary victory at the Battle of Naseby in June 1645, which led to the capture of the King's personal baggage. Inside the baggage were secret correspondence files, which, when decrypted by Wallis, revealed Charles's plans to seek the support of Catholic forces both in Ireland and on the

---

* Thomas Scot wrote later that, when the Commonwealth appointed him as its intelligence chief in 1649, 'I am sure I had no light, assistance, or memorial transmitted me, but whosoever had the Cognizance of the secret affairs or intrigues of State during the being of the Committee of both Kingdoms or afterwards the Committee of Safety, and were now of the Council of State, did or might keep them still to themselves, or proceed upon them as they saw cause.' (Firth (ed.), 'Thomas Scot's Account of His Actions', p. 118.)

Continent. Recognizing the propaganda value of the captured correspondence, Parliament published a substantial selection of the letters, 'written
with the King's own hand', in a volume entitled *The King[']s Cabinet
opened*, which claimed to reveal 'many mysteries of State, tending to the
justification of [the Parliamentary] cause'.[12] Among the letters decrypted by
Wallis were those from Charles to his wife, Henrietta Maria, who had taken
refuge in France, written in a cipher which, Charles assured her, was known
only to the two of them: 'none hath or shall have any copy of it but myself,
to the end thou may use it, when thou shalt find fit to write anything which
thou wilt judge worthy of thy pains to put in cypher, and to be decyphered
by none but me and so likewise from him to thee, who is eternally thine'.[13]

A commentary in *The King's Cabinet opened* claimed that the decrypted
correspondence revealed Charles as a hen-pecked husband dominated by
his wife:

It is plain here, first, that the King's Counsels are wholly managed by the
Queen, though she be of the weaker sex, born an Alien, bred up in a

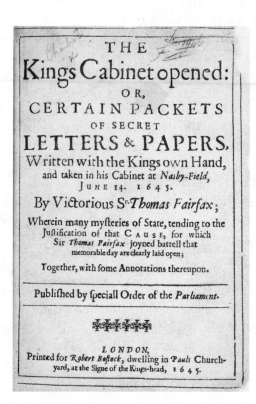

In 1645 Parliament published, for the only time in British history, the decrypted
secret correspondence of the monarch.

contrary Religion, yet nothing great or small is transacted without her
privity & consent . . .

The Queen appears to have been as harsh and imperious towards the
King as she is implacable to our Religion, Nation, and Government . . . [14]

Charles made no public comment on the correspondence with his wife
published in *The King's Cabinet opened*. Privately, he acknowledged its
authenticity, save for 'some words here and there [being] mistaken, and
some commas misplaced', probably in the course of decryption:

> . . . Though I could have wished that pains [of publication] had been spared,
> yet I will neither deny that those things are mine, which they have set out
> in my name, . . . nor as a good Protestant or honest man, blush for any of
> these papers; indeed as a discreet man I will not justify myself; and yet I
> would fain know him, who would be willing that the freedom of all his
> private letters were publicly seen, as mine have now been.[15]

No British king or queen before or since has ever had their private letters published in their lifetime. Charles admitted to only one regret about
the content of his correspondence. In one letter to Henrietta Maria he had
referred to 'our Mungrell [mongrel] Parliament', thus allowing the commentary in *The King's Cabinet opened* to claim that 'The King . . .
despiseth you [his subjects] by the name of Mungrells.'[16] Charles admitted
to a confidant that Thomas Savile, Earl of Sussex, who had sought to
ingratiate himself with parliamentary leaders while attempting to negotiate an end to the Civil War,[17]* had 'put me somewhat out of patience,
which made me freely vent my displeasure against those of his party to
my Wife'. Hence his use of the word 'Mungrell'.[18]

When Charles was put on trial for treason in Westminster Hall in January 1649, it was originally intended to quote some of his intercepted letters
to the Queen as evidence against him, much as his grandmother Mary
Stuart's decrypted correspondence had been used at her trial in Fotheringhay Castle in 1586.[19] Since, however, Charles refused to plead and so
recognize the authority of the court, the intelligence evidence was never
produced. His refusal to plead was interpreted by the court as an admission of guilt. The presiding judge, John Bradshaw (a minor circuit justice
but the most senior who could be found), wore a hat ringed with iron in
case of an assassination attempt as he catalogued the King's crimes and
pronounced sentence: 'That the said Charles Stuart, as a tyrant, traitor,
murderer and a public enemy shall be put to death, by the severing his

---

* Savile also offended Parliament by his apparent loyalty to the King.

head from his body.'[20] Charles was beheaded on a scaffold outside the Banqueting House in Whitehall on 30 January 1649. A week later the prosecutor, John Coke, published the speech he had intended to make if the King had entered a plea of 'not guilty'. He sought to refute the argument that Charles had been led astray by 'evil councillors' by citing his captured correspondence as evidence that the King was 'principal in all transactions of the state and the wisest about him but accessories'.[21]

After Charles's execution, England became a republic by default. Very few of his opponents had given any thought to drawing up a new constitution. Not until March did the Rump Parliament (so called after the purge in December 1648 of MPs opposed to Charles's treason trial) abolish the office of king, along with the House of Lords and the Privy Council. In May, an Act of Parliament replaced the monarchy by a republican regime which it named the Commonwealth of England. Committed royalists did not recognize the new republic. Britain in their view remained a monarchy. Charles, Prince of Wales, only eighteen and living in continental exile at the time of his father's execution, succeeded him, in royalist eyes, as King Charles II.* The new king is nowadays better remembered for his self-indulgence and many mistresses than for his ruthless streak. But, writing from exile in Holland, he swore vengeance on all those responsible for his father's death: 'We shall therein by all ways and means possible endeavour to pursue and bring to their due punishment those bloody traitors who were either actors or contrivers of that unparalleled and inhuman murder.'[22] The first secret operations in which he showed an active interest were missions to track down and assassinate the 'bloody traitors' rather than to collect intelligence on the policy of the republican regime. The first of the regicides to receive 'due punishment' was Isaac Dorislaus, formerly lecturer in History at Cambridge University, who had played a central part in drawing up the charges at the trial of Charles I. In late April 1649 Dorislaus sailed to The Hague to negotiate an alliance between the Commonwealth and the Dutch. On 2 May royalist assassins burst into his lodgings in the Witte Zwaan ('White Swan') inn. The lead assassin, Colonel Walter Whitford, son of the Bishop of Brechin, slashed him across the face with his sword before running him through. The others then thrust their own swords into Dorislaus's body, shouting as they made their escape: 'Thus dies one of the king's judges!' Whitford was rewarded by Charles II with two royal pensions.[23]

The hostility of foreign powers to the regicide English Republic, the

---

* After 1660, all legal documents were dated as if Charles II had succeeded his father as king in 1649.

threat of royalist invasion from Scotland and Ireland, and the danger of rebellion in England itself persuaded the Commonwealth's Council of State, which replaced the Privy Council, to give greater priority to intelligence than either James I or Charles I had done. On 1 July 1649 it appointed one of its members, the lawyer Thomas Scot (or Scott) MP, as head of 'intelligence both foreign and domestic'.[24] Though few details survive, the hot-tempered Scot had been involved in intelligence operations since late 1647,[25] and regarded Oliver Cromwell as 'my particular friend' (though he later strongly opposed his becoming Lord Protector).[26] Scot is credited with destroying in 1648 the monument at Lambeth Palace to Queen Elizabeth I's first Archbishop of Canterbury, Matthew Parker, who had supervised the drawing up of the Thirty-Nine Articles of Religion (loathed by Scot), which define the doctrine of the Church of England. Scot ordered the exhumation of Parker's remains and their reburial under a dunghill. In January 1649 he was one of the judges at the trial of Charles I and signed his death warrant.[27]

A committed republican, Scot built up a formidable network of agents and 'decoy ducks' (*agents provocateurs*) among royalist supporters and exiles.[28] He considered his most valuable agent at the royal court in exile to be the army officer Robert Werden, who had been colonel of a royalist troop of horse during the Civil War. According to Scot, Werden had 'means to know much of [Charles II's] affairs', having won the confidence of his younger brother James, Duke of York, who made him one of his grooms of the bedchamber after the Restoration. Though Werden's motives remain obscure, Scot concluded that he worked as a spy partly for sheer enjoyment: 'I believe whatever he could come to the knowledge of he communicated with as much advantage as he could, & with some impressions concerning personal things which might have been spar'd.' The 'personal things' which Werden took pleasure in revealing doubtless included prurient information on the mistresses of Charles and his brother.[29] Despite doubts about his loyalty, Werden's fraudulent protestations of innocence persuaded the royal brothers. Under James II he later became a major-general.[30]

Scot's immediate priority when he became intelligence chief was not yet the royal court in exile but the group of radical republicans derisively known as 'Levellers' to imply, inaccurately, that they wished to abolish property rights and share wealth equally. Their main demands were for an extended franchise and a written constitution to guarantee individual rights. Scot penetrated the Levellers with apprentices and other youthful agents, who were paid 'a weekly salary for their expenses in keeping them company'. He reported to the Council of State that the Levellers intended 'to raise disturbances in the Army and elsewhere, thereby to hinder the . . . recovery of Ireland' by the forces of Oliver Cromwell.[31] After the suppression of Leveller-led army mutinies in the spring of 1649, their influence rapidly declined.

As well as running the most effective agent network since the Walsingham era to penetrate royalist opposition, Scot also employed the codebreaker John Wallis, whom he praised as 'a learned gentleman incomparably able that way', and described, in strangely unrepublican language, as 'a jewel for a prince's use'.[32] In 1649 Wallis became Savilian Professor of Geometry (mathematics) at Oxford University. Though he later became a founding member of the Royal Society, his mathematical accomplishments were as yet limited.[33] His appointment to the Savilian chair was a reward for his cryptanalysis during the Civil War and, most of all, for his success in breaking Charles I's ciphers. Wallis broke Charles II's ciphers as easily as he had broken those of his father. Scot was well aware that Wallis's work was not inspired by political commitment to the Commonwealth. Wallis, he believed, broke ciphers for sheer enjoyment and 'never concerned himself in the matter [contents] but only in the art and ingenuity' of codebreaking.[34] He held his professorship for over half a century, remaining for almost all that period Britain's leading codebreaker.[35] Wallis's portrait hangs today in the office of his twenty-first-century successor, the Director of GCHQ.

The most successful intelligence-led royalist secret operation during Scot's term as England's first republican intelligence chief was to track down and assassinate another Commonwealth envoy on the Continent. On the evening of 6 June 1650 a group of seven English visitors entered a Madrid inn where the Commonwealth ambassador to Spain, Anthony Ascham, was dining. All but one were Catholics as well as royalists. After taking off their hats, one asked courteously to be introduced to the ambassador. Ascham rose from his seat and bowed to the visitors. As he did so, one of them grabbed his hair and thrust a poniard into his head. A second assassin stabbed Ascham four more times. When Ascham's interpreter tried to flee, he too was murdered. Six of the assassination squad escaped from Spain, probably with the assistance of local priests. The sole Protestant assassin was executed in Madrid.[36] There were no further royalist assassinations of regicides and Commonwealth representatives until the Restoration.

Thomas Scot's intelligence system proved far superior to the disorganized network loyal to Charles II. Charles's nearly disastrous attempt to recover his throne in 1650–51 suffered from a serious lack of reliable intelligence. Having been crowned King of Scotland at Scone on 1 January 1651, he invaded England with a Scottish army but attracted far fewer English royalists to his standard than his over-optimistic supporters had

promised him. The invasion ended in defeat at the Battle of Worcester on
3 September 1651. His close adviser, Sir Edward Hyde (later first Earl of
Clarendon), complained that 'very many' of the defeated army 'were
knocked in the head by country people' as they tried to flee. Charles,
however, escaped. The failure to catch him after the defeat was the biggest
single intelligence failure of the republican regime and of Thomas Scot in
particular. Charles's capture, followed, almost certainly, by his trial and
execution for treason, would have diminished the prospect of a Stuart
restoration and extended, perhaps greatly, the life of the English Republic.
His chances of escape after the defeat at Worcester seemed slim. An enormous reward of £1,000 was offered for his capture and there was no
shortage of people anxious to claim it. Taller at 6 feet 2 inches than the
great majority of other seventeenth-century Englishmen (taller too than
any subsequent British monarch), Charles was a conspicuous target.

Thomas Scot's leading royalist agent, Robert Werden, sent intelligence
designed to assist in Charles's capture,[37] but, since no escape plan had
been prepared in advance, it must have been of little use. Much of the
credit for Charles's improbable escape to the Continent belongs to Charles
himself. Though he showed little or no grasp of strategic intelligence, he
had some of the personal qualities of a successful secret agent. He lost no
time after the defeat both in ridding himself of his father's Garter medal,
his dearest memento of the martyred Charles I,[38] and in ordering a servant
to cut his hair in a first attempt to make himself less conspicuous. Taking
refuge in a wood, he was shown a hiding place in a large oak tree (later
famous as the 'Royal Oak', which gave its name to countless British pubs),
from where, he later told Hyde, he was able to see and hear his pursuers.
As Hyde later acknowledged, Catholics, some of whom had experience of
hiding priests in their houses, 'had a very great share in His Majesty's
preservation'.[39] With the help of his Catholic hosts, all of whom risked
execution for high treason for offering him shelter, Charles adopted a
series of disguises and aliases. He admitted to Hyde that 'he had a great
mind to have kept his own shirt, but he considered that men are not sooner
discovered by any mark in disguises than by having fine linen in ill
clothes'.[40] Among those to whom Charles expressed particular gratitude
was a Benedictine monk, Father Huddlestone, who was 'a very great
assistance and comfort to him'.[41] Over thirty years later, when Charles
was on his deathbed, Huddlestone received him into the Catholic Church.[42]

Though the republican regime showed what Huddlestone called 'great
diligence' in trying to track Charles down, it did not occur to Scot to prioritize enquiries among Catholic families and their servants, let alone look
for an undercover Benedictine monk. Charles held his nerve remarkably

on his hazardous journey from Worcester to the Channel coast. He later told Samuel Pepys (among others) of his encounter during the journey with a republican blacksmith:

> As I was holding my horse's foot, I asked the smith what news. He told me that there was no news that he knew of, since the good news of the beating the rogues of the Scots [at Worcester]. I asked him whether there was none of the English taken that joined with the Scots, He answered he did not hear if that rogue, Charles Stuart, were taken; but some of the others, he said, were taken. I told him that if that rogue were taken, he deserved to be hanged more than all the rest, for bringing in the Scots. Upon which he said I spoke like an honest man; and so we parted.[43]

After several narrow escapes, Charles eventually found a boat in Brighton, then a small fishing village, which took him to France in October 1651. Hyde, the wisest of Charles's advisers, believed that he was powerless to bring about his own restoration. He must wait patiently for 'some blessed conjuncture from the amity of Christian princes, or some such revolution of affairs in England by their own discontents and divisions amongst themselves, as might make it seasonable for his majesty again to shew himself'.[44] The court in exile 'spent more of its energy on power struggles than on efforts to regain the throne'.[45]

In 1653 regime change in the English Republic also led to a change of its intelligence chief. Thomas Scot's vehement opposition to the dissolution of the Rump Parliament by Oliver Cromwell in 1653 and to Cromwell's assumption of the office of Lord Protector led to his replacement by the loyal Cromwellian lawyer John Thurloe.* Unlike the regicide Scot, Thurloe was later able to claim, after the Restoration, that he had played no part in the execution of Charles I, 'having not had the least communication with any person whatsoever' about it.[46] Like Walsingham, Thurloe combined the role of intelligence chief with that of Secretary of State (in effect Foreign Secretary). The fact that he had greater influence on government than any other pre-twentieth-century intelligence chief save Walsingham was due, in large part, to the fact that he had the confidence of Cromwell. The Protector expected Thurloe to do his bidding, when asked, and Thurloe was usually happy to do so. Cromwell also frequently displayed a keen sense of the

---

* When a portrait of Thurloe came up at auction in 2007, it was purchased by the British Government Art Collection at the request of 'C', Sir John Scarlett, Chief of the Secret Intelligence Service (SIS or MI6), who hung it in his office in SIS's Vauxhall Cross headquarters. A slight smile plays over Thurloe's face. Scarlett's less historically minded successor as 'C' is said to have had it removed. See ill. 25.

importance of intelligence. In July 1655, for example, he wrote to ask Thurloe to arrange the admission to Charterhouse School of the son of a widow 'whose Husband was employed one day in an important secret service, which he did effectually, to our great benefit and the Commonwealth's'.[47]

The main royalist conspiracy with which Thurloe had to deal as intelligence chief was the Sealed Knot, a group of six plotters probably founded in November 1653, with the personal approval of Charles II, to prepare a royalist uprising.[48] By February 1654 Thurloe was intercepting at least some of the Sealed Knot's correspondence with Charles's court in Paris. His papers contain the copy of a letter sent on 2 February from London by one of the plotters, Edward Villiers, informing Sir Edward Hyde (alias Monsieur Barsiere) in Paris: 'The sealed knot still meet, with an intention to design somewhat for Mr Crosse [Charles II] his service, which when it comes to any maturity, a discreet chapman shall be sent over, as you appoint.'[49] The leaders of the plot, however, fell out among themselves. Villiers and his fellow plotter Sir Richard Willys were arrested in the summer of 1654, spending several months in detention; Willys suspected another member of the Sealed Knot, John Belasyse, first Baron Belasyse, of betraying him. (It seems more probable that the arrests were due to surveillance and letter interception by Thurloe's intelligence network than to betrayal.) There followed what Hyde later called 'a fatal Quarrel' within the Sealed Knot.[50]

Royalists were further demoralized by the failure of the Penruddock Uprising (so called after one of its leaders, Colonel John Penruddock), which had been planned for 8 March 1655. Charles II optimistically moved to Middelburg in the Netherlands, expecting to cross the Channel to England as the revolt gathered momentum. He sent the Earl of Rochester, one of his gentlemen of the bedchamber and senior military commander, to lead a royalist force assembled at Marston Moor near York. Royalist ranks, however, were penetrated by Thurloe's agent network. When royalists in York failed to open the city gates, as the Yorkshire rebels had expected, they fled, abandoning many of their weapons on Marston Moor. Rochester fled south in disguise but was arrested at Aylesbury and had to use bribery to escape to the Continent. Twelve leading royalist rebels in the south, including Penruddock, were captured and executed. Others were transported to Barbados.[51]

In the aftermath of the Penruddock Uprising, Charles gloomily concluded, according to Hyde, that Cromwell had 'perfect intelligence of whatsoever His Majesty resolved to do, and of all he said himself'.[52] That exaggerated belief appeared to be confirmed by the discovery in December 1655 of a double agent working for Thurloe in Charles's court in exile, then in Cologne. The agent was the mercenary royalist Henry Manning, who had written to Thurloe on 13 March 1655, offering his services in return for payment. On 16 April Manning received a cipher from Thurloe,[53] which he used to send numerous reports on royalists travelling via Dover between England and the court.[54] Manning quickly became overconfident. In November 1655 Hyde received warning from Antwerp that letters for Manning from abroad were arriving by every post and that he had letters of credit in Antwerp for 'good sums of money'. On 5 December Manning was caught red-handed at his desk writing reports in cipher intended for Thurloe. Ten days later he was executed near Cologne by members of Charles's court.[55]

Despite Manning's execution, the 'letters of intelligence' sent to Thurloe from the Continent on the prospects of further risings backed by the royal court in exile continued to be reassuring. Most also addressed Thurloe in highly, sometimes exceptionally, deferential terms – as in this report from his agent in Flushing, Thomas George, on 29 October 1656:

Noble Sir,
My devoire [duty] towards your honour is such, that though this place is (as 'twere) barren of any novelties this week, yet I must endeavour to creep to kiss your noble hands, and to acquaint your honour, how that this country rings of nothing else than the [naval] triumphs of the English against the Spaniards [during the war begun in 1654], and the sad stories of some merchants thereupon. The king of Scots [Charles II] is at a stand, yet he keeps his men together. I think he is now out of hope to attempt anything against you.[56]*

Thurloe also derived a large amount of intelligence from the interception of the post, especially after he became postmaster general in 1655. Probably his most talented assistant in dealing with the post was the mathematician and inventor Samuel Morland, MA and former Fellow of Magdalene College, Cambridge. Among Morland's inventions were devices (which do not survive) to speed up letter-opening and produce counterfeit seals. His less successful inventions included a device which attempted to copy intercepted letters by pressing damp tissue against ink writing. More importantly, while not apparently rivalling the expertise of Wallis, Morland succeeded in breaking at least some ciphers used in intercepted royalist correspondence, later publishing a book grandly entitled *A New Method of*

* The English seizure of Spanish ships and silver from the New World failed, as Cromwell and Thurloe had hoped, to meet the heavy costs of the war.

*Cryptography.** By 1657 he had also somehow contrived to become wealthy, with an income of £1,000 a year, a large house near Bow and a reputation for high living and dishonesty. Samuel Pepys, who was tutored by him, wrote later that he was generally 'looked upon . . . as a knave'. By the final years of the Interregnum Morland was playing a double game, passing intelligence to the royal court in exile. After the Restoration he gave a dramatic (if unreliable) account of his role as double agent, claiming that on one occasion he had pretended to be asleep at his desk while listening to Thurloe discuss with Cromwell a secret plan to lure Charles II to a house in Sussex with a false promise that he would find royalist forces waiting for him. According to Morland's improbable account, Cromwell suddenly noticed his presence and had to be restrained by Thurloe from attacking him with a poniard. While spreading such tall tales, Morland was simultaneously attempting to remove an effusive dedication to Cromwell from one of his books.[57]

What Thurloe learned from the post, as well as from his domestic agent network, contributed to his reputation as the 'all seeing little secretary'.[58] So did the intelligence he received from foreign capitals. His papers contain many 'letters of intelligence' from the Dutch Republic, Spain, Scandinavia and the Baltic. Like Walsingham, Thurloe was in effect Foreign Secretary as well as intelligence chief. The Protestant Dutch Republic, which had finally won its independence from Spain in 1648 and had begun a golden age of commercial success, seemed the natural ideological ally of the English Republic. Commercial rivalry, however, overrode ideological sympathy and led to the First Anglo-Dutch war in 1652.† After peace in 1654 Cromwell revived his earlier proposal for a political union between the two republics, which was rejected by the Dutch States-General. Thurloe received numerous intelligence reports in both English and French from agents in The Hague, many of them at least partly in codes which substituted numbers for names, for example:

104: the States General
105: the States of Holland, Hollanders, Holland
124: ambassador
130: the Protector, Cromwell, England
135: money
145: the Orange party

---

* Isaac Dorislaus the younger (son of the assassinated English envoy to the Dutch Republic) assisted in decrypting royalist correspondence. (*ODNB* John Thurloe.)
† The First Anglo-Dutch War secured the Commonwealth's control of the seas around England and of trade with England and its colonies.

171: peace
179: commerce, trade
198: Brussels[59]

The 'letters of intelligence' strengthened Thurloe's conviction that political union with the Dutch Republic was a lost cause. He wrote to Cromwell's son Henry that the Dutch intended 'no goodwill to this nation or indeed to the Protestant cause, however they profess the contrary'.[60] In 1657 Thurloe appointed the unscrupulous George Downing as both ambassador and head of intelligence operations in The Hague. In 1642 Downing had ranked second in Harvard's first graduating class. His intelligence career had begun in 1649 with his appointment by Cromwell as scoutmaster-general of the English army in Scotland, but he is best remembered nowadays as the property speculator who during the Restoration built the poorly constructed houses in Downing Street which are now the official home of the Prime Minister and Chancellor of the Exchequer. Downing boasted to the diarist Samuel Pepys that, while in The Hague, he 'had so good spies, that he hath had the keys taken out of [the Dutch Stadholder Johan] De Witt[']s pocket when he was a-bed, and his closet opened and the papers brought to him and left in his hands for an [hour], and carried back and laid in the place again and the keys put in his pocket again'.[61] He also informed Thurloe that a group of royalist assassins, including the 'one that killed Dr Dorislaus . . . [had] come with design and order to kill me'.[62]

Thurloe had the dominant role in running the foreign policy as well as the intelligence operations of the Protectorate. The Venetian ambassador, Francesco Giavarina, wrote of him: 'All must pass through the hands of this Secretary, who alone attends to and superintends all the most important interests of State.'[63] Thurloe's relationship with Cromwell was closer than that of any other intelligence chief with a British head of state or Prime Minister before the Second World War. Cromwell's younger surviving son, Henry, major-general of English forces in Ireland, wrote admiringly to Thurloe: 'Really it is a wonder that you can pick as many locks leading into the hearts of the wicked men as you do, and it is a mercy that God has made your labours therein so successful.'[64] According to Bulstrode Whitelocke, one of Cromwell's foreign-policy advisers, Thurloe was one of the few intimates with whom, as well as discussing policy, he would 'lay aside his greatness', relax and smoke a pipe.[65] When Cromwell lay on his deathbed in late August 1658, it was Thurloe who took the lead in persuading him to nominate his elder son, Richard, to succeed him. On 3 September, when Richard became Lord Protector on Cromwell's death, Thurloe became his chief adviser.

Mocked by his political opponents as 'Tumbledown Dick' and 'Queen Dick', Richard Cromwell was a public-spirited man who lacked the leadership skills and ruthlessness required to deal effectively with a divided, discontented army, whose pay was in arrears. In March 1659 Thurloe reported 'much underhand working' going on 'to disaffect the officers of the Army'. By April Richard Cromwell had effectively lost power to the army, which recalled the surviving members of the Rump Parliament to Westminster. On 14 May Cromwell's great seal as Lord Protector was ceremonially smashed in the House of Commons. On the 25th he sent the Rump a formal letter of abdication. Thurloe fell from power with the Lord Protector and, to the jeers of bystanders, was turned out of his Whitehall accommodation. In his place the new Council of State, which included Thomas Scot, appointed a six-man intelligence committee with Scot as its leading member. A resentful Thurloe called Scot a 'noisy windbag' and refused to pass his ciphers to him.[66]

Thurloe's downfall, followed by the increasing disarray of the republican regime now based on the authority of the Rump Parliament, led a minority of his former intelligence staff to reconsider their loyalty to the government. Probably in July 1659, Samuel Morland revealed to Charles's court-in-exile that one of its members, Sir Richard Willys (or Willis), a former member of the Sealed Knot, had been in secret contact with Thurloe.* There was still no prospect, however, that any royalist conspiracy or rebellion could succeed in overthrowing the Republic. A rising led by Sir George Booth in August 1659, with Charles's approval, ended with Booth attempting unsuccessfully to flee to the Continent, dressed in women's clothing.[67] The man who eventually ensured the peaceful restoration of Charles II to the English throne was the commander of the Republic's forces in Scotland, General George Monck.

On 1 January 1660, at the head of 5,000 foot soldiers and 2,000 cavalry, Monck began a five-week march to London, ostensibly in support of the unpopular Rump Parliament. Scot, who was formally appointed intelligence chief on 10 January,[68] was one of two emissaries from the Rump who met Monck on 22 January en route from Nottingham to Leicester, ostensibly to welcome him, in reality to try to discover his intentions and persuade him to take an oath abjuring monarchy. Monck's entourage deeply distrusted them. One of his chaplains, Dr Thomas Skinner (later his biographer), called them the 'two evil angels'.[69] Monck, however, ordered the emissaries to be treated with great deference: 'his soldiers were oblig'd, upon all occasions, to pay them greater reverence than had been

---

* Though Willys obtained a royal pardon, he was later banished from the King's presence. (ODNB Sir Richard Willys.)

us'd towards himself'.[70] At every overnight stop as Monck progressed from Leicester to St Albans, the emissaries took rooms next to his and, according to Dr Skinner, 'always found or made some hole in the door to look in or listen (which they practiced so palpably that the general found it out and took notice of it to those about him reflecting on their baseness and evil suspicions) that they might more nearly inspect his actions and observe what persons came to him'.[71] At Barnet on the final approach to London the Rump's emissaries finally moved to separate lodgings. In the middle of the night Scot received reports of noisy demonstrations in the City hostile to the Rump and in favour of Monck:

> Mr Scot was so affrighted out of his sleep with this hasty news, that he could not stay to dress him, but in the dishabit of his night-gown, cap, and slippers, hurry'd presently to the General's quarters, where he made a terrible representation of this mutiny in the City, requiring General Mon[c]k to beat his drums instantly and march forward. But the General, that did not use to be alarm'd with every little noise, or put out of his temper by an hasty tale, return'd him an answer calmly, and persuaded Mr Scot to return to his bed and put his fears under his pillow.[72]

Scot must have known that Monck had outwitted him. After a triumphal entry into the capital, Monck politely declined an invitation from the Council of State to abjure the monarchy. According to Skinner, 'the General had [secretly] design'd, before he came out of Scotland, to put an end of the excrescence of a parliament, so soon as he was well settled in London'.[73] One of Scot's sons rashly revealed in confidence to his landlord, who warned Monck's entourage, 'that the parliament had such suspicions of him, as that it was resolv'd to remove him suddenly from his command in the army, and to lay him fast in the Tower, having articles against him sufficient to endanger his life'. Such a plan, if it existed, was based on little more than wishful thinking.[74]

On 11 February, little more than a week after entering London, Monck dissolved the Rump, which, Dr Skinner wrote later, lacked the authority 'to deal with him either by tricks or force'.[75] Celebrations quickly spread across the capital. From the Strand Bridge, Pepys was able to see thirty-one bonfires in various parts of the city. By the end of February, the MPs purged over a decade earlier had been readmitted to their seats. The dissolution of the Rump ended Scot's political and intelligence career. He remained an unrepentant regicide, declaring in his final speech to Parliament that he desired no better epitaph than 'Here lies one who had a hand and a heart in the execution of Charles Stuart.'[76]

On 27 February Monck's influence secured Thurloe's reappointment as joint Secretary of State and the restoration of his Whitehall lodgings.[77] Soon afterwards a nervous George Downing, still ambassador and head of intelligence in The Hague but fearful of his prospects under the restored monarchy, wrote to Thurloe: 'I should be infinitely obliged to you, that you would a little let me know what things are like to come to.'[78] On 17 March, Monck had the first of several secret meetings late at night in St James's Palace with an agent of Charles II, Sir John Grenville. According to Grenville, Monck 'pledged his life' to the King.[79] In April, through an intermediary, Downing made his peace with the King. He blamed his father, who, he claimed, had been 'banished to New England' for the fact that, while at school and at Harvard, he 'had sucked in principles that since his reason had made him see were erroneous'. He now ardently 'wished the promoting of your Majesty's service'. To prove his indispensability at a time when Charles was planning his return to England, he passed on an intelligence report from Thurloe on the attitude of the army to the restoration of the monarchy. Downing's attempt to change sides was rapidly successful. After Charles had knighted him on 12 May, he told his secretary, Samuel Pepys, 'that I must write him *Sir G. Downing*'.[80]

On 1 May the Convention Parliament, which included a restored House of Lords, had voted to restore the King. Charles landed at Dover on 25 May, where he was received by Monck. Soon afterwards the King made Monck first Duke of Albemarle. Four days later, on his thirtieth birthday, Charles entered London amid popular rejoicings. Unlike the devious Downing, Thurloe remained a loyal supporter of Richard Cromwell and failed to make his peace with Charles II. The Convention House of Commons resolved on 14 May that 'Mr Secretary Thurloe, being accused of high treason, be secured' and questioned by a committee. Thurloe was said to have boasted that, if he was put on trial, he had 'a black book which should hang half them that went for Cavaliers'. Though there is no evidence on whether the committee was influenced by Thurloe's blackmail, he was released without charge on 27 June. Two days later the Commons authorized him to meet Charles II's secretaries of state. Thurloe seems to have prepared memoranda on foreign policy for Charles's effective Chief Minister, Sir Edward Hyde (ennobled in 1661 as Earl of Clarendon), and thereafter retired into obscurity.[81]

Despite its limitations, intelligence had been better organized and better integrated into government policy during the life of the English Republic until the end of the Commonwealth than at any other point in English or British history for the next two and a half centuries. Charles II's grasp of intelligence did not begin to compare with Cromwell's. In the early years of the Restoration, however, he took an active interest in secret operations

to track down the regicides who had fled abroad to escape trial and execution for treason in England. Thomas Scot was probably top of the
most-wanted list of the judges who had sentenced Charles I to death. 'Having been informed', he wrote later, 'that I was in danger of my life by the
rage and violence of some unreasonable men, who designed no less than a
bloody assassination upon me, I was prevailed with by my friends and
relations to withdraw out of England.'[82] After initially falling into the
hands of pirates, Scot succeeded in escaping to Brussels, where, despite
living in disguise under a false name, he was tracked down and tricked into
returning voluntarily to England by Sir Henry de Vic, the British resident.
De Vic appears to have falsely assured Scot that he was among those who
were offered a royal pardon if they surrendered within fourteen days. Those
who missed this deadline would be 'under pain of being exempted from
any pardon or indemnity for their respective lives and estates'.[83]

After returning to England in July 1660, Scot was imprisoned in the
Tower, where he was deceived again. He appears to have been promised
his life in return for a full confession and the names of agents who had
given him intelligence on Charles II's court in exile and his royalist supporters in Britain.[84] 'Initially', Scot admitted, 'I had a scruple of specifying
names, whereby others that had trusted me might be brought into trouble.'
But at the end of his interrogation, 'much discompos'd by my present condition', he swore by 'the eternal God' that he had concealed no one and
nothing which 'might endanger his Majesty's Government or Person'. Scot
was a broken man. He blamed his last speech to the Rump justifying his
role in the execution of Charles I on 'the erroneous petulancy of an intem-
perate tongue and a misguided conscience'. By the time Scot made that
admission, he must have realized that, by it, he had signed his own death
warrant.[85]

Thomas Scot was one of the first group of regicides to be tried and
found guilty of treason in October 1660. According to the diarist John
Evelyn, who had good connections with the royal court, Charles II
watched, unnoticed by the crowd, as some of them were hanged, drawn
and quartered. 'I saw not their execution', wrote Evelyn, 'but met their
quarters, mangled and cut and reeking as they were brought from the
gallows in baskets.'[86] Scot was the first, and so far the only, British intelligence chief executed for treason.

Scot's execution made it less easy to lure back to England the other
regicides who had fled abroad. Secret operations began to track down
those who had sought refuge in Calvinist communities in the Dutch
Republic, Germany, Switzerland and New England. Kidnap and assassination operations abroad were a higher priority during the early Restoration

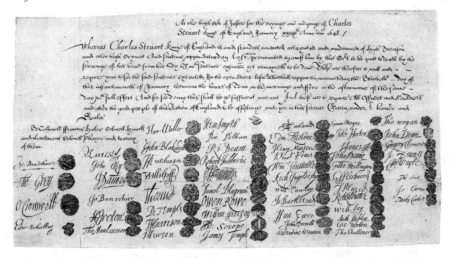

The death warrant of Charles I with Cromwell's signature third from the top of the left-hand column. Under the Restoration a series of secret operations were designed to lure back or kidnap surviving signatories and other regicides who had fled abroad. Among those hanged, drawn and quartered was Thomas Scot (sixth in the right-hand column), so far the only former British intelligence chief to be executed.

than at any other moment in the history of British intelligence. The most successful of Charles II's regicide hunters was the unscrupulous turncoat Sir George Downing, who sought to prove his loyalty to the restored monarchy by betraying his former republican associates.

Downing's first target was Edward Dendy, the sergeant-at-arms who had proclaimed the trial of Charles I and had fled to Rotterdam at the Restoration. By August 1661 Downing had assembled a kidnap team, and the royal yacht was moored in Rotterdam ready to transport Dendy back to trial in England. But at the last moment Downing's attempt to gain a warrant from the Dutch authorities for his arrest and extradition fell through, and Dendy escaped to Switzerland. Downing complained that the regicide exiles were 'perpetually changing their abode . . . never being two nights in a place'. In a despatch to the Earl of Clarendon, Downing suggested assassination rather than kidnap: 'what if the king should authorize some trusty persons to kill them . . . let me have the king's serious thoughts about this business'. Clarendon refused at first to consider assassination.[87] Later he seems to have changed his mind.[88]

After the initial rebuff from Clarendon, Downing concentrated on schemes for kidnap rather than assassination. In September 1661 he discovered that an English merchant living in Delft, Abraham Kicke, was used by three regicides living in Germany as a postbox for correspondence with their wives. Downing offered Kicke £200 for every regicide he helped to trap and threatened to ruin his business if he rejected the offer. Kicke agreed. He invited to supper at his house in Delft two regicides living near Frankfurt: Colonel John Okey, an army officer who had been one of the judges at Charles I's trial, and John Barkstead, former Keeper of the Tower of London. Downing knew Okey personally and had served in his regiment during the Civil War as chaplain (an improbable role, given Downing's lack of moral scruple). Kicke deceived both Okey and Barkstead into believing that their wives, who had remained in England, would travel to Delft to meet them after receiving news of their arrival. At Downing's suggestion, Kicke also invited to supper Miles Corbet, at eighty-three the oldest of the surviving regicides; Corbet's was the fifty-ninth and final signature on the King's death warrant. Okey and Barkstead travelled warily to Delft and arrived at Kicke's house with guns under their great-coats but left them before supper in a side-room, which their host locked without them noticing. Downing reported to Clarendon that, while Okey, Barkstead and Corbet were relaxing after dinner 'with a pipe of tobacco and a cup of beer', his snatch squad burst into the house: 'Immediately they started up to have got out at a back door but it was too late . . .'[89]

This time Downing had secured Dutch arrest warrants, but he had also to bribe local officials to allow him to put the three regicides on board a ship which took them to trial and execution in England.[90] Standing on the scaffold at Tyburn, Okey publicly forgave Downing, his former chaplain, who had 'pursued my life to the Death'.[91] Charles II, who had already knighted Downing in 1660, showed his appreciation by making him a baronet in 1662 and awarding him a series of lucrative offices. John Evelyn noted disapprovingly that 'From a pedagogue and fanatic preacher not worth a groat [Downing] has become excessive rich'; according to parliamentary gossip, 'He keeps 6 whores in pay and yet has got £40,000.'[92]*

For regicides who had taken refuge in Switzerland, kidnap was not a serious option because of the problems of smuggling them back to England. The only practical form of vengeance was assassination. Edmund Ludlow, former army officer and regicide judge, who had settled in Vevey on the northern shore of Lake Geneva, later recalled: 'Divers letters from Turin, Geneva, Lyons, and other places, which we and our friends at Vevey received, were full of advices from those parts, that so many, and such desperate persons had engaged against us, that it would be next to impossible

---

* Downing did, however, overreach himself later in 1662 and was imprisoned in the Tower for six weeks for disobeying instructions at the end of his term as envoy in The Hague. He subsequently returned to favour.

to escape their hands.'[93] The main assassination squad which pursued Ludlow and other regicides on Swiss territory was led by Germaine (or John) Riordane, an Irish soldier of fortune who had once served in the Duke of York's Regiment. Riordane was in contact with the office of Sir Henry Bennet, whom Charles II made Secretary of State in 1662 (and ennobled as Earl of Arlington a year later) with responsibilities which included dealing with (and procuring) some of the King's mistresses as well as foreign policy. Though the formal post of intelligence chief had lapsed at the end of the Interregnum, Arlington's chief assistant, Sir Joseph Williamson, a former Fellow of Queen's College, Oxford, informally took over many of the previous responsibilities of Scot and Thurloe. Riordane's contact details appear in Williamson's address book. Though, unsurprisingly, no written authorization exists for Riordane's assassination missions, there is little doubt that they had the approval of Arlington, Williamson and the King.[94]

Riordane, however, was no Downing. Instead of laying a trap for the regicides, as Downing had done, he rowed across Lake Geneva from Savoy in November 1663 at the head of a team of eight assassins with two 'lackeys' (servants) to assist them. Once they had landed in Vevey, they quickly aroused suspicion. Next day Ludlow was warned by his landlord that 'ruffian like fellows, desperadoes with long cloaks and carbines under them', were laying in wait for him and two other refugee regicides as they walked to church. Having damaged other boats moored at Vervey to hinder their pursuers, Riordane's hit squad abandoned the assassination attempt and rowed back to Savoy across Lake Geneva.[95] It is difficult to believe that, had either Scot or Thurloe ordered an assassination mission, they would have chosen Riordane to lead it.

Riordane's assassination team did, however, claim one victim. Probably early in 1664, Williamson discovered from intercepted correspondence that Sir John Lisle, a judge at Charles I's trial and later Commissioner of the Great Seal under the Commonwealth and Protectorate, who had been targeted along with Ludlow in Vevey, had moved to Lausanne. There he used the alias Mr Field but made himself conspicuous by walking round the town wearing his Commissioner's cloak. On 11 August 1664 Lisle was ambushed in a Lausanne churchyard by two of Riordane's assassins, Thomas O'Croli (aka Thomas MacDonnell) and Sémus mac Emoin Mhic Choitir (aka James Cotter), while on his way to a church service. O'Croli drew a blunderbuss from beneath his cloak and shot Lisle in the back at point-blank range. The assassins then made their escape on horseback, shouting 'Vive le Roi!', and returned safely to England, where they and Riordane were rewarded for the success of their mission.[96]

The most distant refuge of regicides fleeing from royal vengeance was New England. Thomas Goffe and his father-in-law Edward Whalley, both signatories of Charles I's death warrant, arrived in Boston in July 1660. After living initially in Cambridge, they moved in 1661 to New Haven, Connecticut, where, according to tradition, they successfully evaded agents sent by Williamson to track them down by hiding for three years in a cave outside the town. In 1664 they took up residence in Hadley, Massachusetts, where they were sheltered by sympathetic Puritan colonists. According to colonial state papers, Goffe and Whalley were held in 'exceeding great esteem for their piety and parts' and 'held meetings where they preached and prayed, and were looked upon as men dropped down from heaven'. It was also reported that, during their travels in New England, they were regularly welcomed by feasts in their honour and provided with horses and guides.[97] Goffe and Whalley were among at least a dozen refugee regicides, most of them on the Continent, who died in exile without being hunted down.*

Sir Joseph Williamson's anti-regicide intelligence operations also extended to some of their families – chief among them Thomas Scot's son William, a former Fellow of All Souls College, Oxford, who arrived in the Netherlands soon after the outbreak of the Second Anglo-Dutch War in 1665 and began working as a Dutch spy. Scot's former mistress, Aphra Behn, was sent to the Netherlands to try to turn him into a double agent operating against the Dutch. Later the first English woman to make a living as a writer, Behn was also the first female spy (codenamed ASTREA and agent 160) officially employed by any British government. Then in her mid-twenties, Behn described her intelligence mission as 'unusual with my sex, or to my years'. Behn reported that Scot (codenamed CELADON) had agreed to change sides: 'Though at first shy, he became by arguments extremely willing to undertake the service . . .' Scot did indeed provide Behn with intelligence which she forwarded to London, but he continued to be employed by the Dutch and his main loyalty as a double agent remains uncertain. Williamson's funds to Behn dried up and she narrowly avoided debtors' prison.[98]†

The Second Anglo-Dutch War ended in August 1667 in a decisive English defeat, marked by the extraordinary spectacle of the Dutch sailing up the River Medway and attacking the English fleet at its anchorages in Chatham – the most humiliating episode in the history of the Royal Navy. The English flagship, HMS *Royal Charles*, was towed back to Amsterdam,

---

* Probably the last surviving regicide, Edmund Ludlow, returned to England at the age of seventy-two after the Glorious Revolution in 1688, but was quickly denounced and took refuge again in Switzerland, where he died in 1692.
† Much about Aphra Behn's extraordinary career remains uncertain. Her leading biographer, Janet Todd, concludes: 'What is securely known about Aphra Behn outside her works could be summed up in a page.' (Todd, *Secret Life of Aphra Behn*, introduction.)

where, three and a half centuries later, its coat of arms is on display in the
Rijksmuseum. In October 1667 the Commons appointed a committee to
enquire into the war's 'miscarriages', becoming the first in British history
to consider what was later called 'warning failure'. Those chiefly responsible for the defeat complained of lack of intelligence on the Dutch plan of
attack. Sir William Morice, one of Charles II's two Secretaries of State,
claimed that his intelligence budget was only £750 a year, by comparison
with Thurloe's £70,000 during the Interregnum. The 'miscarriages' committee of enquiry reported to the House in February 1668 that there had
been 'want of intelligence from abroad'. The poet, satirist and MP Andrew
Marvell complained that 'the money allowed for intelligence [was] so small
[that] the intelligence was accordingly'.[99] Behn was, presumably, one of the
victims of the small intelligence budget. Though the report of the Commons enquiry was later largely forgotten, its 'findings about intelligence
shortcomings resemble those reached by modern enquiries three centuries
later'.[100] In 1667, however, intelligence failures probably played a smaller
role in Britain's defeat than official incompetence. The naval administrator
and celebrated diarist Samuel Pepys blamed the single greatest humiliation, the loss of the *Royal Charles*, on 'nothing but carelessness'.[101]

Foreign intelligence, during Williamson's tenure as unofficial intelligence chief, was thrown into some confusion by the private and secret
diplomacy of Charles II. In 1669, wanting British support in a war against
the Dutch, Louis XIV set out to lure Charles into an alliance, using his
sister Henriette ('Minette'), wife of the duc d'Orléans, as secret intermediary. By the secret Treaty of Dover in 1670, in return for an annual French
subsidy and a share of the spoils of war, Charles agreed to order a British
naval attack on the Dutch at a time of Louis's choosing. In two top-secret
clauses, Charles also promised to suspend anti-Catholic penal laws and
to announce his own public conversion to Catholicism at an opportune
moment. (The moment, however, did not come until Charles was on his
deathbed when he was received into the Catholic Church by the Benedictine
monk who had helped him escape after the Battle of Worcester.) Charles
revealed these clauses, which would have provoked public fury, only to his
Catholic brother, the Duke of York, and to two Catholic ministers, Arlington and the Lord Treasurer, Sir Thomas Clifford. Williamson, as a
non-Catholic, was probably not informed. To protect the secret, Charles
perfidiously instructed two leading anti-Catholic dissenters, the Duke of
Buckingham (son of the former royal favourite) and the Earl of Shaftesbury,
who were unaware of the secret treaty, to negotiate another treaty (also
secret) with Louis XIV which omitted the religious clauses.[102] No other

British monarch has gone to greater or more devious pains to mislead most of his ministers.

With the approach of the Third Anglo-Dutch War in 1672, Sir Joseph Williamson sought to insure himself against further charges of the intelligence failure reported by the Commons 'miscarriages' committee in 1668 by keeping a record of the intelligence he received from the Netherlands – the first recorded instance in British history of an intelligence chief being influenced by criticism of intelligence in a previous war. Though the war, which ended in 1674 largely as a result of parliamentary pressure, was unpopular, the role of intelligence did not, as in the previous war, become publicly controversial. While William Scott continued to work for Williamson,[103]* there is no convincing evidence that Aphra Behn had any further involvement in espionage. She used the Third Anglo-Dutch War as an opportunity to exploit anti-Dutch feeling in her tragicomedy *The Dutch Lover*, which combined cruelty with sexual intrigue. Among those to whom Behn dedicated later plays was Charles II's best-known mistress, Nell Gwyn.† After her death in 1689 she became the first former spy to be buried in Westminster Abbey.‡

The main continuity in intelligence operations between the Interregnum and the Restoration was the continued employment of John Wallis as chief cryptanalyst. Despite his role in breaking the ciphers used by Charles I during the Civil War, as well as by Charles II and leading royalists during the Republic, his skills as cryptanalyst were regarded as irreplaceable. He was given early assurance of royal favour by being made a royal chaplain in 1660 and a member of the commission appointed a year later to revise the Prayer Book.[104] Ironically, Charles's first Chief Minister, the Earl of Clarendon, became one of Wallis's chief targets after he went into exile in France in 1668 to escape the threat of impeachment. Though almost none of Wallis's decrypts survive, Williamson's assistant, John Ellis, wrote to him in 1669 that his success in decrypting Clarendon's correspondence 'gives me very great satisfaction'.[105] Wallis also had considerable success in decrypting Dutch despatches during the Third Anglo-Dutch War. In the middle of the war, clearly impressed by Wallis's achievements, Charles's Secretary of State, the Earl of Arlington, summoned Wallis 'and did (without me asking) give me 50 Guineas in hand; and promised me 50 guineas

---

* Williamson's most productive spy seems to have been Jerome Nephro, an agent in Antwerp.
† Behn dedicated to Nell Gwyn her 1679 comedy *The Feign'd Curtizans*. (Todd, *Secret Life of Aphra Behn*, ch. 18.)
‡ Behn's grave is in the East Cloisters of Westminster Abbey. See ill. 27.

a quarter (which were duly payd me) to attempt the deciphering of such letters as should be sent me from time to time'.[106]*

Like his abler predecessors, Walsingham and Thurloe, Sir Joseph Williamson also kept watch on domestic subversion. Early in the Restoration there were attempts to make an example of seditious speakers. In 1661 a Fifth Monarchist preacher who denounced Charles II as a ' bloody tyrant', whose 'death and destruction . . . drew very near', was found guilty of high treason and sentenced to be hanged, drawn and quartered. Most of what Williamson's spies and *agents provocateurs* reported, however, was alehouse chatter. Instructions to one spy tell him to enquire 'very slyly at the next alehouses'. It was not difficult to note subversive utterances such as that of the probably intoxicated Mary Greene of St Paul's, Covent Garden, who declared: 'A pox on all the kings!' She 'did not care a turd for never a king in England for she never did lie with any'. Though Greene's fate is unknown, most magistrates were likely to treat such utterances as evidence of disorderly conduct rather than of treason.[107] By 1666 the Earl of Clarendon was less concerned by alehouses than by the growing number of coffee houses, which he denounced as centres of sedition where 'the foulest imputations [were] laid upon the government'; their customers 'generally believed that those houses had a charter of privilege to speak what they would without being in danger to be called into question'. To judge by the numbers of seditious conversations reported to Williamson, there was a significant increase in coffee house informers over the next few years.[108] As in alehouses, however, seditious talk in coffee houses never threatened the regime.

The greatest challenge to Williamson's domestic security system came from the 'Popish Plot' in the late 1670s, the most sensational bogus conspiracy in British history. At the heart of the Popish Plot was Titus Oates, who developed a remarkable gift for providing sensational, though fraudulent, intelligence on Catholic conspiracies. Nothing in Oates's early career gave any hint of how influential he was to become. While studying at Gonville & Caius College, Cambridge, he gained a reputation for 'canting, fanatical' behaviour, as well as sodomy; he transferred to St John's College, where he was no more popular, and left Cambridge without a degree in 1669. Falsely claiming to have a BA, Oates embarked on a remarkable career as fantasist and fraudster. He took holy orders as an Anglican priest but was dismissed from his first living in Kent for bad behaviour in 1673. He then became curate to his father in Hastings but had to flee to London to

* Wallis claimed that he was ten times more successful in decrypting despatches for William and Mary's first Secretary of State, the Earl of Nottingham.

escape prosecution for perjury after falsely accusing the local schoolmaster of sodomy with a pupil. In London Oates began a new career as naval chaplain but was dismissed from the Royal Navy after a voyage to Tangier on a charge of sodomy (a recurring theme in accusations against him).

In 1677, with his career as an Anglican cleric at an end, Oates persuaded an apparently deranged Catholic priest to receive him into the Roman Catholic Church. Claiming to have given up a rich benefice in the Church of England for the sake of his Catholic convictions, he gained entrance to the English Jesuit College at Valladolid, but was expelled after a month. He returned to England, falsely claiming to have received a doctorate from the University of Salamanca. At the end of 1677 Oates was admitted to the Jesuit seminary at Saint-Omer, where he quickly became so unpopular that another student 'broke a pan about his head for recreation'. Oates was then despatched to another Jesuit seminary, where he caused so much trouble that he was sent back to Saint-Omer, from which he was finally expelled in the summer of 1678 and forced to return to London. The moves between seminaries, as well as giving him authentic insights into plans for Jesuit missions to England, which he was later to transmute into conspiracy theories, also enabled him to claim that the Jesuits had used him as a courier of secret correspondence.

Once back in London, Oates succeeded in persuading an eccentric retired cleric, Dr Israel Tonge, author of a series of tracts denouncing the Jesuit menace, that the Jesuits had singled him out for vengeance. Tonge asked him to write down all he had discovered about Jesuit and other Catholic conspiracies. Oates did so in a series of forty-three 'depositions' which claimed to reveal a 'Popish Plot' whose main aim was to murder Charles II. He claimed to have been present at a secret Jesuit conclave at the White Horse tavern in London on 24 April 1678, when details of the plot were discussed. Teams of assassins hired by French Jesuits were, he reported, already in London completing their preparations. In September Tonge took Oates to meet a long-serving justice of the peace, Sir Edmund Berry Godfrey, who made copious notes of his conspiracy theories and passed them to the Lord Chief Justice. Godfrey was reluctant to become involved and is said to have told one acquaintance, 'I shall have little thanks for my pains . . . I did it very unwillingly and would fain have [had] it done by others.' When Godfrey's body was found, run through by a sword, in a ditch in Primrose Hill on 17 October, many believed he had been assassinated by the supposed Popish plotters denounced by Oates.[109]

In October, Oates was summoned to give evidence to the Commons, which resolved, after being taken in by his conspiracy theories, that 'There hath been, and still is, a damnable and hellish plot contrived and carried out by Popish Recusants, for the assassination and murdering of the King, and for subverting and rooting out and destroying the Protestant religion.' Williamson's fellow Secretary of State, Sir Henry Coventry MP, wrote that 'If [Oates] be a liar, he is the greatest and adroitest I ever saw.'[110] The Commons resolution reflected not merely Oates's remarkable talent for deception and self-deception but also long-standing fears of Catholic conspiracy, exemplified by the annual celebrations of Guy Fawkes Day and exacerbated by the fact that the heir to the throne, the Duke of York, was a Catholic convert. The 'Popish Plot' gained further credibility after the discovery of allegedly treasonable correspondence between the Catholic Edward Coleman (or Colman), secretary to the Duchess (and formerly to the Duke) of York, and the confessor of Louis XIV. Oates was chief witness at Coleman's trial for treason in King's Bench on 27 November 1678. Despite flimsy evidence, the jury took less than fifteen minutes to find him guilty. He was hanged, drawn and quartered at Tyburn a week later.[111] Coleman's was the first of more than twenty gruesome executions of imaginary Catholic conspirators.

Though Williamson almost certainly regarded Oates's revelations as deeply suspect, his nerve cracked under the strain of the public and parliamentary rage which they provoked. Amid the hysteria of the Popish Plot, the discovery that Williamson had approved warrants excusing some Irish Catholic army officers from swearing allegiance to the Church of England led the Commons on 18 November 1678 to consign him to the Tower. Though he was speedily released on the orders of a furious Charles II, Williamson was a broken man, unable to summon up the nerve to return to the Commons. In February 1679 he was replaced as Secretary of State by the arrogant, cynical Robert Spencer, second Earl of Sunderland. Though able, Sunderland disliked detail and showed no aptitude for intelligence. A disaffected member of his staff complained, probably with some exaggeration, that he preferred state papers to be taken to him not in his office but in his house, 'where he was usually at cards, and he would sign them without reading, and seldom asked what they were about'.[112]

By the time Williamson was succeeded by Sunderland, the organized agent network of the Interregnum and the early Restoration had been adulterated by volunteer, sometimes self-serving, anti-Catholic informers. Among their victims was William Stayley, a Catholic London goldsmith, who in November 1678 was overheard speaking in French to a foreigner in a London victualling house over 'a quart of ale and a slice of roast beef'. According to an informer, who claimed to understand French, Stayley declared that the King 'was the greatest heretic in all the world, that he was a great rogue'. Clapping his hand on his heart, he added: 'I will with this hand kill him.' Though Stayley denied that he had said these words, the jury at his treason trial preferred the word of the informer. He was hanged, drawn and quartered.[113]

By 1681 Oates's credibility had begun to disintegrate under the cumulative weight of his own inventions. He brought and lost several libel suits against those who challenged his conspiracy theories. In May 1684 he was arrested in a coffee house on a charge of *scandalum magnatum* after he had called the Duke of York a traitor. In May 1685, three months after the Duke succeeded his brother on the throne as King James II, Oates was sentenced to life imprisonment, brought to Westminster Hall wearing a paper hat inscribed 'Titus Oates convicted upon full evidence of two horrid perjuries', placed in the pillory in Palace Yard, Westminster, and repeatedly whipped through the streets of London, emitting, according to an unsympathetic observer, 'hideous bellowings' along the way.[114]* What had seemed to both Houses of Parliament only six years earlier the most important intelligence on a Catholic conspiracy against the monarchy since the Gunpowder Plot was now utterly discredited.

* Oates was released from prison after the 'Glorious Revolution' and the flight of James II in 1688.

13

Intelligence in the Era of the Sun King

Louis XIV is far better remembered for self-glorification than for secret intelligence. When moving his court to the Palace of Versailles in 1682, he confined God to the chapel. The rest of the largest and grandest palace in European history was devoted to the cult of the Sun King, Louis's favourite image of himself. By the end of his reign the resident devotees numbered about 10,000 nobles, soldiers, priests, officials, tradesmen and servants. Versailles was second only to the army as France's largest employer.[1] But Louis also regarded secrecy as essential to his royal authority. A medal struck to commemorate the beginning of his personal rule after the death of Cardinal Mazarin in 1661 had a portrait of the King on the front and, on the reverse, Harpocrates, the Greek god of silence and secrecy, raising a finger to his lips. A painting on the ceiling of the Versailles Hall of Mirrors, the most magnificent room in the palace, shows Louis ordering a simultaneous attack on four Dutch strongholds. By his side is an allegorical figure also holding a finger to his lips. Another figure puts his hand over his mouth as the King prepares to take the city of Ghent.[2]

Louis XIV paid some interest to intelligence collection as well as official secrecy. He took a personal interest in the work of the *cabinet noir*. Like his father, Louis XIII, he honoured Antoine Rossignol, France's leading codebreaker until his death in 1682, by visiting his château at Juvisy.[3] Neither of the two great seventeenth-century English codebreakers, Thomas Phelippes and John Wallis, received any sign of royal appreciation from the Stuart kings. Lord Hollis, the English ambassador in Paris, complained in 1665 that his despatches were always opened and read before he received them. His successor, Ralph Montagu, made the same complaint in 1669.[4] Their awareness, like that of some French courtiers, that their correspondence was intercepted must have diminished the value of the intelligence obtained from it by the *cabinet noir*. The celebrated letter-writer Madame de Sévigné sometimes made personal appeals in her correspondence to those who opened it during the second half of the seventeenth century:

'Alas! I beseech those who take this trouble to consider the little pleasure which they gain from reading it and the sorrow they cause to us. Messieurs, at least take the trouble to put [the letters] back in their envelopes so that, sooner or later, they reach their destination.'[5]

Louis's first direct involvement in an intelligence operation, crucial to the establishment of his personal rule in 1661, was the plot to overthrow Mazarin's superintendent of finance, Nicolas Fouquet, marquis de Belle-Île and vicomte de Melun et Vaux, who hoped to step into Mazarin's shoes. Fouquet was a classic example of an overmighty subject whose power and prestige threatened royal authority. At his magnificent château at Vaux-le-Vicomte, he lived in greater opulence than the King. On the island of Belle-Île off the coast of Brittany, with the assistance of Sébastien Le Prestre de Vauban, the foremost military engineer of his age, he sought to construct an impregnable private fortress with its own garrison.

Fouquet's nemesis was the shrewder and less ostentatious Jean-Baptiste Colbert, whose chilly exterior led Madame de Sévigné to give him the sobriquet *le nord* ('the north').[6] Colbert came from a family of Rheims merchant bankers, trained as an accountant, and helped Mazarin amass the greatest private fortune in the history of the Ancien Régime.[7] On his deathbed Mazarin recommended Colbert to Louis XIV.[8] It was not long before Colbert succeeded in involving Louis in a plot against Fouquet, which, because of Fouquet's numerous informants in the court and administration, had to be conducted in great secrecy. One of the first steps was to send a spy, disguised as a fisherman, to reconnoitre Fouquet's Belle-Île fortress. The spy returned with a map of the fortress and details of its 200-man garrison, 400 cannon and the fortifications being built by 1,500 labourers to Vauban's design. Colbert's agents also reported that Fouquet had plans to take over the Caribbean island of Martinique and export its produce to Belle-Île. 'In short, Fouquet was building a miniature kingdom and a small empire.'[9]

Colbert devised a secret plan, approved by the King, for Fouquet to be arrested without warning after a meeting of the provincial Estates in Nantes, well away from his strongholds of Vaux-le-Vicomte and Belle-Île. Louis went out of his way to allay Fouquet's suspicions by giving him repeated signs of royal favour before his sudden arrest in Nantes immediately after a meeting with the King on 5 September 1661. Since the commander of the royal bodyguard, the *Garde du Corps*, was an informant of Fouquet, he was arrested instead by Charles d'Artagnan, leader of the musketeers who accompanied the King on his travels. The fictional d'Artagnan in Alexandre Dumas's celebrated mid-nineteenth-century novel *The Three Musketeers*, famous for the cry 'All for one, one for all!', has become far better known than the elusive and less romantic figure of the real musketeer. There is some evidence that the real d'Artagnan had carried out espionage missions for Mazarin and thus had the experience required for the secret operation which culminated in his arrest of Fouquet.[10]*

Colbert arranged for the simultaneous seizure of Fouquet's files, chief among them the *Cassette*, a massive folio volume hidden behind a large armoire in his office containing financial secrets, evidence of corruption, and details of his agents, informers and mistresses. After a controversial three-year trial, Fouquet was sentenced to life imprisonment. Louis was proud of his own role in the sophisticated intelligence operation orchestrated by Colbert. The King later claimed that 'the whole of France', as well as approving the overthrow of Fouquet, 'particularly praised' his success in keeping secret the plan to arrest him for three or four months, despite the fact that Fouquet's informers were all around him. Colbert's critics said privately that his family crest of a climbing snake had proved highly appropriate.[11]

From 1665 until his death in 1683 Colbert was Controller-General of Finance and First Minister in all but name. He regarded the royal account books, financial reports and all other state financial information as classified intelligence for official use only, believing that all ministers and government officials should take oaths of secrecy and lose their jobs if they broke them.† Colbert's ultimate aim was to assemble a classified audit of all the local resources and administrative systems of the French kingdom, sending officials to obtain information on population numbers, land holdings, economic activity, local regulations, laws and important individuals. He expanded the audit to include neighbouring states, drawing much of his inspiration from the sixteenth-century trading and banking empire of the Augsburg Fugger family, whose sophisticated filing system included regular reports from a far-flung network of correspondents. Colbert told his son (whom he hoped would succeed him) before sending him on a mission to Italy in 1671:

> In each state, look at ... its situation, its military forces, the size of its population, the greatness of the state, the number and size of cities, towns,

---

* In Dumas's novel, d'Artagnan is not himself one of the three musketeers (the inseparable friends Athos, Porthos and Aramis) but devises for them the motto 'All for one, one for all!'
† The influence of Colbert on Louis XIV was so remarkable that, as recent research has shown, he even persuaded the Sun King to take a serious interest in accounting. Louis was the first major European monarch to do so. Almost from the start of his personal rule in 1661 he carried in his coat pockets miniature account books prepared by Colbert which recorded his expenditure, revenue and assets and were changed at the end of each fiscal year. (Soll, *Reckoning*, ch. 6.)

and villages . . . ; the form of State government, and if it is aristocratic . . . the names and status of noble families that have taken or will take part in governing the Republic; their different functions; their general and particular councils; who represents the State, in whom the sovereign power lies and who resolves peace and war, who makes laws; etc . . . the results of elections; the particular councils for the militia, the admiralty, justice, for the city and for the rest of the State; the laws and the customs . . . Visit the public works, maritime and on land, all the palaces, public buildings, and generally all that is remarkable.

Faced with this demanding agenda, Colbert's son had more than once to apologize to his father for failing to live up to his high expectations.[12]

Colbert, concludes a recent study of him, aimed to construct a 'secret state intelligence system'.[13] Though only fragmentary evidence of Colbert's use of the *cabinet noir* survives, his intelligence system involved the interception (and, where necessary, decryption) of correspondence. Colbert wrote to the Intendant of Toulouse in 1682 that letters from Flanders to Toulouse had revealed the existence of an important plot (possibly involving the spread of Jansenist heresy) which it was 'very important to clarify'. Other intercepted correspondence to and from Toulouse revealed (unspecified) commercial ventures in Rome, which Colbert declared 'prejudicial to the service of the King'.[14]*

Apart from its ambitiousness, a major obstacle to the development of Colbert's state intelligence system was his rivalry with the marquis de Louvois, Secretary of State for War from 1662 until his death in 1691.† From 1668, Louvois was also superintendent of the posts, a position which brought him an income of about a million livres a year, as well as giving him greater authority than Colbert over the operations of the *cabinet noir*, which he used for military as well as political intelligence.‡ In 1668, at the request of the French military commander, the prince de Condé ('le grand Condé'), who was in Dijon, preparing for the invasion of Franche-Comté, Louvois postponed the delivery of the post to Dijon until the invasion had begun, to prevent correspondents in Paris giving advance warning of it.[15]

---

* Like Louis XIV, Colbert was an admirer of the great French codebreaker Antoine Rossignol, though no evidence survives of his access to decrypts; see above, p. 213.
† Louvois's father, Michel Le Tellier, had been Secretary of State for War under Mazarin and arranged for his son to be appointed to the same post in 1662, at the age of only twenty-one. Though the two men administered the War Department together, Louvois had the lead role by the end of the decade. (Corvisier, *Louvois*, 2ème partie.)
‡ The celebrated memoirs of Louis XIV's godson, the duc de Saint-Simon, written two decades after his death, mistakenly attribute the creation of the *cabinet noir* to Louvois. In fact, it had been founded by Richelieu; see above, p. 210.

Louvois attached more importance to intelligence than any other European War Minister of his time. The growth in the size of armies in the age of Louis XIV, as well as of the munitions and rations they required, combined with the immense improvements in fortifications pioneered by Vauban to increase the importance of military intelligence.* In the forty years after 1667, Vauban directed the construction of thirty-seven new fortresses and fortified harbours, as well as upgrading the fortifications of about 300 cities in France and the Low Countries.[16] Before beginning his victorious advance along the River Meuse at the start of the Franco-Dutch War in 1672, Condé sent a fortifications expert to reconnoitre enemy fortresses.[17] This reconnaissance probably contributed to the rapid conquest of four fortresses on the Rhine, for which Louis XIV claimed personal credit: 'I hope no one complains that I disappointed public expectations.' In 1673 the King's army, after a siege conducted by Vauban, also took the Dutch fortress of Maastricht.[18] French victories and Vauban's fortifications increased the priority of military intelligence among France's opponents. French military archives in the château de Vincennes contain an intelligence questionnaire given by his superiors to a military engineer in the Rhine army of the Habsburg Emperor Leopold I who was also working as a French agent. He was asked to collect intelligence on French fortifications from both their designers and builders. In addition to identifying French military units and their commanders (later known as battle-order intelligence), the engineer was also asked for details of their stocks of munitions and rations, as well as information on their finances and how recently their troops had been paid.[19] Even at the beginning of the seventeenth century such an attempt to collect this kind of military intelligence would have been very unusual.

Improved military intelligence contributed to the superiority of French armies over their foreign opponents in the 1660s and 1670s, though the fact that, thanks largely to Louvois, Louis XIV had both the largest European army of the era (possibly the largest since the fall of the Roman Empire) and the greatest generals – Condé, the vicomte de Turenne and the duc de Luxembourg – contributed far more. Louvois acted as his own intelligence chief. In dealing with Louis XIV, however, he had to face the classic problem of 'telling truth to power'. This problem presented itself in an acute form in the autumn of 1673, when, following a Dutch and Habsburg offensive, combined with declarations of war on France by Spain and Brandenburg–Prussia, Louvois favoured a strategic withdrawal

---

* Historical controversy continues over whether, as Geoffrey Parker was the first to argue, these military changes amounted to a 'Military Revolution'.

by French forces from some conquered territory. Louis, however, regarded retreat as incompatible with *gloire*. 'In the King's present mood', wrote Louvois gloomily, 'he would rather give up Paris or Versailles than Maastricht.' French forces were thus pinned down defending conquests of the previous year while Dutch and Habsburg forces advanced to the Rhine.[20]

Over the next decade Louis XIV lost both his greatest generals and his leading intelligence experts. Turenne died in battle in 1675. Soon afterwards the 64-year-old Condé, worn out by the exertions of his long military career and tortured by gout, retired. In 1682 the death of Rossignol, regarded by Colbert as one of the 'most illustrious Frenchmen' of the century, deprived France of the greatest codebreaker of the French Ancien Régime.[21] With Colbert's sudden death (probably from a kidney stone) in 1683, his still unfinished project to create a classified database was abandoned. Louis XIV gave up the attempt to centralize official information and dispersed responsibility for its collection and management to ministries and officials who lacked the accountancy skills required to conduct serious audits. Claude Le Peletier, who became Controller-General of Finance on Colbert's death, complained to Louis XIV that he was unable to understand the state's financial workings, for Colbert had kept them secret – 'enclosed in his very self'.[22]*

After Colbert's death, Louis XIV also lost interest in state finance and gave up the attempt to balance the books.† He retained an active interest, however, in the operations of the *cabinet noir*. Louvois wrote to the French military commander in Alsace, Baron Joseph de Montclar, during the formation in 1685 of the anti-French League of Augsburg: 'The King has been informed that in a few days' time a courier of the Emperor [Leopold I] is due to return from Spain [through Alsace]. H[is] M[ajesty] judges it important in present circumstances to seize the courier's valise and take possession of the despatches.' On royal instructions, the attack on the imperial courier was to be disguised as a robbery: 'Make sure that those whom you instruct to seize the courier's valise do not fail to take all his money in order to strengthen the belief that they are robbers . . .'[23] Louis XIV also took a personal interest in what the *cabinet noir* revealed about gossip at court. The main topic for gossip in the mid-1680s and beyond was the King's morganatic marriage to his mistress, Madame de Maintenon. The marriage remained so secret that its exact date (possibly in

---

* Some vestiges of Colbert's attempt to create a large royal database remain, chief among them the 36,000 books and 10,500 manuscripts in the Royal Library, which became the core of today's Bibliothèque Nationale in Paris.
† Louis no longer received account books after Colbert's death. (Soll, *Reckoning.*, ch. 6.)

October 1683) will probably never be known.[24] Three young members of leading noble families were banished from Versailles in 1685 after their intercepted letters were found to contain satirical references comparing the royal couple to a decrepit provincial noble and his ageing mistress. Maintenon, who was fifty in 1685 (slightly older than Louis) and sensitive about her age, was outraged by 'the very great irreverence' of such gossip, which she denounced as an 'abominable vice'.*

The expulsions from Versailles in 1685 and other sanctions against 'irreverent' gossip must have inspired greater prudence in courtiers' correspondence. Among those at court who were indignant about the invasion of their personal privacy by the *cabinet noir* was Louis XIV's sister-in-law the Princess Palatine, who regularly corresponded with her German relatives. In one letter to a female relative, intended to shame those who opened it, she described how, while answering an urgent call of nature, the earthenware chamber pot on which she was sitting had broken. But for the fact that she clung on to a nearby table, she believed that the jagged fragments of the broken pot would have lacerated her *derrière*. This 'fine story', the princess added for the benefit of the letter-openers, would no doubt be considered 'worthy of the attention of the Secretary of State [for foreign affairs] and I am sure that M. de Torcy will make a report on it to the King'.[25]†

Thanks chiefly to Charles II and his successor, James II, Louis XIV's best foreign intelligence came from Britain. Charles II concealed the Treaty of Dover, secretly negotiated with Louis in 1670, from all but two of his ministers.[26] The French ambassador in London from 1677 to 1688, Paul Barillon, marquis de Branges, reported that Charles was 'so secret and impenetrable that even the most skillful observers are misled'.[27] Barillon found James II, who succeeded his elder brother in 1685, much easier to deal with. James had received military training in the French army, was converted to Catholicism by a French Jesuit, and was strongly influenced by Louis XIV in his choice of the Catholic Mary of Modena as his second wife. Sir William Trumbull, James's ambassador in Paris, later recalled that 'all matters of moment were to be transacted by Barillon', who was in close contact with Louvois as well as communicating directly with Louis XIV. James, Trumbull believed, 'no doubt communicated to Barillon all that he knew'. Louis XIV's special envoy, Usson de Bonrepaus, was also taken

* Their intercepted letters were to Louis Armand de Bourbon and his brother François Louis de Bourbon, who succeeded him as prince de Conti in 1685. (Vaillé, *Cabinet noir*, pp. 78–83.)
† Torcy became Secretary of State in 1699.

into James's confidence. But James's often expressed hopes to Barillon and Usson de Bonrepaus of returning England to the Catholic faith proved hopelessly optimistic.[28] Given the difficulty of telling truth to power at the court of the Sun King, it is highly unlikely that any of Louis's advisers dared tell him, even if they realized it, that James's impossible project of a Catholic England risked putting his throne in jeopardy.

The English 'Glorious Revolution' of 1688 was, in part, an anti-Catholic revolution. James II was overthrown by an invasion led by the Dutch Stadholder and Protestant hero William of Orange. Until 1688 William's wife, Princess Mary, the Protestant daughter of James II by his Protestant first wife, Anne Hyde, had been James's heir. On 10 June, however, Mary of Modena gave birth to a son and heir, James Francis Edward, thus threatening the Protestant succession. William sent his close friend William Nassau van Zuylestein (later 1st Earl of Rochford) to London, ostensibly to convey his congratulations to James and Mary of Modena on the birth of their son. Zuylestein's real mission, however, was to continue secret talks with James's leading opponents which he and others had begun in the previous year. He also reported to William a widespread belief that James's alleged son was a baby who had been secretly smuggled into the Queen's bedchamber in a warming pan.[29] On 30 June, at William's private request, seven of James's opponents, later known as the 'Immortal Seven', sent a letter assuring him that, if he landed in England to protect English liberties, his forces would receive widespread support.

The timing of William's landing was influenced by top-secret intelligence ('*secretum secretorum*') which he received from the court of the Holy Roman Emperor in Vienna, Leopold I. William kept the identity of his informant in Vienna so secret that he refused to reveal it even to the leading Dutch supporters of his invasion of England. Recent research shows that the informant was the Emperor himself. Leopold warned William that Louis XIV was planning an attack on the Dutch United Provinces and other Protestant states, and was trying to persuade him to join an alliance against them. Though Catholic, Leopold had hitherto been an ally of the Protestant Dutch, but he now informed William that, if Louis XIV defeated the United Provinces and James II crushed English opposition to his rule, he would be obliged to change sides. The Protestant nightmare, shared by William, of a Roman Catholic grand alliance of Bourbon France, Habsburg Austria and Stuart England would become a reality. We now know that Leopold's claims that the French were offering him the cession of Alsace and other inducements to form an alliance were fraudulent – part of his successful campaign to win Dutch support against

Louis XIV.* William, however, was completely taken in by the false intelligence he received from Vienna, and used it repeatedly from July 1688 to
demonstrate the urgency of intervention in England.[30]

Though William had good intelligence from England while planning
his invasion, James II had virtually none from the Dutch Republic. Deceived
by disinformation from Dutch envoys, he was so confident that William's
military preparations were for war with France rather than the invasion of
England that, when Louis XIV offered to place the French Atlantic fleet
at his disposal, James assured him it would not be needed. By the time he
discovered his mistake in September, it was too late; the fleet had been
deployed elsewhere. It also took some weeks for James to discover that
William had printed 60,000 copies of a declaration intended to justify his
invasion for distribution in England. William declared that his purpose
was 'to preserve and maintain the liberties, laws and customs of England'.
Despite the fact that he had earlier congratulated James on the birth of his
son and heir, he also declared the need to investigate the circumstances of
the birth, thus appearing to give credence to the conspiracy theory that the
baby had arrived in the Queen's bedchamber in a warming pan.[31]

Obtaining intelligence on where William's forces intended to land was
impossibly difficult. When the invasion fleet first set off in mid-October,
storms drove it back to port. Driven west by a 'Protestant wind' at the second
attempt, William decided at the last minute to land at Torbay in Devon on 5
November.[32] Most support for James II quickly melted away. 'The reason we
have so little intelligence' from the West Country, complained his Secretary
of State, Charles Middleton, was that 'none of the gentry of this or adjacent
counties come near the court and the common [folk] are spies to the enemy'.
Government spies continued to take Stuart money only to transfer their allegiance to William's forces at the first opportunity.[33] Among those who
changed sides was James's ablest general, John Churchill (later Duke of Marlborough). Even his younger daughter, the future Queen Anne, deserted him.

William could not have predicted that, with a larger army than his own,
James would give up without a fight. On 11 December James threw the
Great Seal of England into the Thames (hoping thus to prevent the passing
of legislation in his absence) and travelled in heavy disguise to the Kent
coast, where a small ship was waiting to take him to France. Before he
could escape, however, he was caught by fishermen looking for fleeing
Catholic priests, and suffered the humiliation of becoming the only British
monarch ever to be strip-searched. Not until James had been frog-marched

* By a treaty of May 1689 Leopold succeeded in winning Dutch support for the Austrian
succession to the imperial throne and against Bourbon ambitions in Spain.

to the nearest town (another unique experience for an English monarch) was he recognized as the King. A crucifix stolen from him by the fishermen was given back. After briefly returning to London, James made a second attempt to flee, which William allowed to succeed. James's flight to France, where he arrived on Christmas Day 1688, enabled his opponents to claim that he had abdicated and left the throne vacant. In February 1689 William and Mary were declared joint rulers.[34]

William became simultaneously King William III of England and Ireland, William II of Scotland and Stadholder of the Dutch Republic. He immediately embroiled England as well as the Dutch Republic in the Nine Years War (1688–97) between Louis XIV (who continued to recognize James II as King of England and Ireland, and as James VII of Scotland) and a Grand Alliance dominated by William which also included the Austrian Habsburgs, princes of the Holy Roman Empire, Spain and Savoy. Among William's main wartime intelligence assets, little noticed by historians, was John Wallis, by now in his early seventies and in fragile health but still active as an Oxford mathematician and theologian as well as Britain's chief cryptanalyst.[35] Though Wallis had been distrusted by James II, probably in part because he was an Anglican priest, William was quick to recognize his talents.[36] His correspondence with the leading Dutch statesman Anthonie Heinsius shows his admiration for Wallis as the greatest codebreaker of the era.[37] The King's personal interest in Wallis was in striking contrast with the distance he kept from most other British officials. He spent much of his time with foreign advisers in Hampton Court and Kensington, away from the great palace of Whitehall, the main seat of Stuart government. Unlike his sociable wife, Queen Mary, William was one of the most reserved and reclusive monarchs in British history. Mary's death from smallpox in 1694 made the monarchy even more remote from most of its subjects.[38]

Some of the first important decrypts produced by Wallis during William and Mary's reign followed James II's landing in Ireland in March 1689 with Jacobite and French forces, who began a siege of the Protestant stronghold of Londonderry (Derry) a month later. The relief of the 105-day siege, which, despite heavy loss of life, failed to starve the defenders into submission, is still celebrated by Unionists every August with the firing of a cannon to commemorate the apprentice boys who shut the city gates against James's advancing armies. Wallis wrote to the Earl of Nottingham, one of the King's two Secretaries of State, when sending him a decrypted despatch from an unidentified French commander soon after the relief of Londonderry: 'I have met with better success than at first I could promise your lordship or myself and with more expedition than I could hope for.'[39] The decrypt gave William III welcome intelligence on dissension between Jacobite and French forces. The French commander complained that arms suppliers chosen by James II's staff to provide munitions for his forces during the siege had defrauded him:

> Orders were given for a supply of cannon and ammunition for our use, but they took care that, of the two cannon sent, only one would take the cannon balls supplied and the fuses were nearly worn out. Nothing I could do could then remedy these defects. I have made the [Jacobite] general officers understand the state of affairs so that they may inform the King, their master, of it, who I am sure will deal with those who are guilty in a fitting manner. The mistake cannot have been committed in ignorance, because, in my despatch, on which they acted, I particularly directed that the shot was to be tried, to see if it fitted the cannon and the fuses that they fitted the touch holes. If like faults are committed with impunity one cannot feel the same ardour for King [James's] service. Shame will be acquired and reputation lost, if the public simply hear that supplies have been sent to the [French] camp without being also told that those supplies were useless. It will be thought that nothing was done, because the [French] officers were incapable. I am on my mettle, not being willing to be overcome by their malice.

As well as revealing dissension between French and Jacobite officers, increased by the failure of the Londonderry siege, the decrypted despatches of the French commander also reported disputes within James's own high command. The Earl of Tyrconnell, commander-in-chief of his Irish army, was said to have faced 'almost insurmountable resistance' by James and, it was believed, his Secretary of State, Lord Melfort, to authorizing essential expenditure: 'I am assured that Lord Tyrconnell's discontent, as much as his indisposition, has contributed to his retirement to a country house.'[40] Wallis noted that one of the intercepted French despatches sent to him was in very poor condition: 'Nor know I how it becomes so rotten and discoloured in so short a time: Unless possibly it may have been thrown overboard into salt water & recovered from thence.'[41] This was a distinct possibility, since some French despatches were intercepted at sea.

When sending Nottingham the decrypt from a French commander in Ireland, Wallis reported that another intercepted despatch, addressed to Louis XIV, 'was in a hard cipher . . . I cannot yet see my way to break it.'[42] Within a fortnight, however, he had begun to decrypt highly sensitive correspondence between Louis XIV and his ambassador in Warsaw:

> I am almost ashamed to tell yo[u]r Lordship how much time & pains on that very perplexed cypher in the Letter from Poland, & have not yet

dispatched it. But by what I have done all ready, I find two things (which seem to me) of moment. One is a Treaty (or entreaty rather) of the French King with the King of Poland presently to make a war on Prussia. The other, about a marriage of the Princess of Hanover with the Prince of Poland, promoted by the French King. How far it may be of concernment to us to know it, I am no competent Judge. But I thought it did become me to give this timely notice of it (lest there might be a prejudice by delay) while I am preparing to give a fuller account of that letter . . . [43]

William immediately saw the opportunity to provoke a political crisis between France and Poland by revealing the contents of the decrypted French despatches. Wallis was quick to claim much of the credit: 'The deciphering some of those letters . . . quite broke off all the French King's measures in Poland . . . & caused his Ambassadors to be thence thrust out with disgrace. Which one thing was of much greater advantage to his Ma[jes]ty & his Allies than I am like to receive on that account.'[44] Contrary to his initial expectation, Wallis was given by Nottingham 'a Present (from the King, I suppose) of Fifty pound. Which I looked upon as a handsome gratuity for the service then done and as a testimon[y] of his Ma[jes]ty's acceptance (which I valued) and returned my acknowledgements.' Wallis was anxious, however, that future French decrypts be kept secret in order not to lead France to change its ciphers.[45]

Wallis's success in revealing Louis XIV's plans to provoke war between Poland and Prussia so impressed Frederick I, Duke (later King) of Prussia and Elector of Brandenburg, that he asked Wallis to decrypt further (probably French) despatches for him. Having done so, Wallis was told that Frederick was sending him 'a rich medal with an honourable inscription, & a gold chain of a great value'. Two years later, Wallis had still received neither and complained to the English ambassador in Berlin of being 'treated like a child, as if I were to be wheedled on to difficult services by a few fair words, & a promise of a few sugar-plums, which should in the issue signify nothing'.[46] The 'rich medal' and gold chain did, however, eventually arrive. Both appear on a small table by Wallis's side in a portrait of him by the leading court painter, Sir Godfrey Kneller, presented to Oxford University by Wallis's friend and admirer Samuel Pepys.[47] Wallis was the first, and so far the only, British codebreaker to receive an award from a foreign ruler.

By the end of 1689, Wallis had succeeded in breaking a series of French diplomatic and military ciphers used by, among others, Louis XIV's Foreign Minister, Colbert de Croissy, as well as by Louis himself.[48] When sending the Earl of Nottingham the decrypt of a despatch to Croissy in December, Wallis added:

I am very ready to serve his Majesty the best I can, gratis, and to lay [aside] all my own affairs, as I have done this half year, to attend this service. I have been indisposed as to my health all this winter, my eyesight fails me so that I must be forced to quit this service. I have had assistance from my son who with some directions from me could pretty well perform it. I have lost the sight of one eye in the service already this winter.[49]

Nottingham replied:

I . . . am very sorry this service has so much prejudiced your health. I have acquainted the King with it, who is very sensible of your zeal and good affection, and will, I believe, in a short time give you some mark of his favour, wherein my endeavours shall not be wanting to serve you. If I have occasion, hereafter, to send you any more of these letters, I will not press you to despatch them in so much haste as formerly, but leave it to you to do them more at leisure.[50]

In fact, despite his fragile health, Wallis continued breaking ciphers for the remainder of the reign of William III, and outlived him by nearly two years.[51] Wallis, however, continued to resent the fact that he received no regular salary as royal codebreaker and depended on irregular payments. Anxious to provide for his family, he told Nottingham he would be grateful for 'any kindness' in finding employment for his son and son-in-law, both struggling lawyers. Despite his age and infirmity, Wallis also declared himself 'capable of any promotion Ecclesiastical'.[52] Despite complimenting Wallis on his work, Nottingham failed to respond to his requests. As Wallis complained:

. . . Having (for my Lord Nottingham) condescended to do clarks[clerk's]-work: I might at least expect clarks-wages (without being thought mercenary or ungentle). And I presume there is never a clark his Lo[rdshi]p keeps, but is (one way or other) better payd, for the work he doth, than I am.

He may say perhaps, This is (not his, but) the King's service. Very true. And so is all the service his Lo[rdshi]p doth as Secretary. Yet he is well payd for it. And, so well, that he may (out of his allowance) afford to gratify those that work under him.[53]

William III's main military priority in 1690 was to drive James II and his forces from Ireland. Convinced that 'nothing worthwhile would be done' to end James's rule in Ireland unless he took personal charge of the campaign, William crossed the Irish Sea in June 1690. The intelligence provided by Wallis's decrypts was of great importance. Had Louis XIV sent further forces to add to the French regiments already in Ireland, James's prospect of victory would have been much greater. Though the French fleet was stronger than those of the British and Dutch combined, William knew from intelligence reports (probably including decrypts) that the French fleet had no soldiers on board, and therefore that no French reinforcements were on the way to Ireland. At the Battle of the Boyne, north of Dublin, on 1 July 1690, William won a crushing victory over James II, who left Ireland never to return, angrily blaming his poorly led Irish troops for having 'basely fled the field'. His Irish forces conferred on James the nickname Seamus an Chaca ('James the Shithead').[54] The victory of the French fleet over the British and Dutch at the Battle of Beachy Head on 10 July did nothing to restore his fortunes.*

William III's understanding of foreign intelligence, and in particular of black chambers (so called after the French *cabinet noir*), exceeded that of any other ruler of his time – or any other monarch in British history, with the possible exception of George I. As well as receiving decrypts from Wallis, from 1693 William III was also able to make use of a black chamber established at Celle in Lower Saxony, the official residence until 1705 of one of the two branches of the house of Brunswick-Lüneburg. William III was a personal friend of the last member of the dynasty, Duke George William of Celle, who had probably been inspired to found a black chamber by William's diplomatic coup after Wallis's decryption of Louis XIV's correspondence with his ambassador in Poland. The two rulers had a common interest in monitoring French diplomacy in Germany and Northern Europe. Copies of intercepted French despatches obtained in Celle were forwarded to London. Inspired by the Celle example, the other branch of the house of Brunswick-Lüneburg in Hanover also set up a black chamber, at Nienburg. After Duke George Louis I, the future King of England, became Elector of Hanover in 1698, the two black chambers cooperated closely.† By 1701 they even had a joint bonus scheme. When George William died in 1705, George I inherited the duchy of Celle and the two black chambers as well as the two duchies combined. As well as

---

* An intercepted French account of the naval victory, dated 10 July 1690, reached William. (*CSP Domestic 1690.*) Unionists celebrate victory at the Boyne on 12 July, not on the anniversary eleven days earlier.

† The black chambers in Celle and Hanover also had a common interest in intercepting the despatches of the Danish representatives in the rival nearby duchy of Wolffenbüttel, as well as the correspondence of the envoys of Wolffenbüttel and Denmark in Paris, Berlin and Dresden. George William and George Louis did not routinely pass these intercepts to William III. Occasionally they passed some of the intercepts to the Habsburg emperor in Vienna as well. (Leeuw, 'Black Chamber in the Dutch Republic', pp. 138–41.)

taking over Celle's codebreakers, George removed the contents of the
ducal palace and took them to Hanover. The development of codebreaking
in both Celle and Hanover probably owed much to the inspiration of the
great mathematician Gottfried Wilhelm von Leibniz, who, though not a
codebreaker himself, had a keen theoretical interest in the principles of
cryptanalysis.[55]

Despite the achievements of the black chambers in Celle and Hanover,
Leibniz deferred to Wallis, even when Wallis was in his early eighties, as
the greatest codebreaker of the age. Wallis wrote in 1701:

> I have been solicited by . . . Leibnitz, more than once, in behalf of the Elector
> of Hanover: who is willing to send hither some young men, whom he desires
> I would instruct therein; leaving it to me to make my own proposals on what
> terms I would undertake it. To which I have returned answer, That I shal be
> ready, my selfe to serve his Electoral Highness if there be occasion: but the
> skill of doing it, being a curiosity which may be of use to my own Prince, I
> do not think it proper to send it abroad, without his Ma[jes]ty's leave.[56]

In 1701, two years before his death, Wallis at last secured the regular
salary he had sought for the past decade. While training his precocious
grandson William Blencowe, who had just graduated from Magdalen
College, Oxford, at the age of only eighteen, to succeed him, Wallis was
granted £100 a year, backdated to 1699. At Wallis's request, the salary
was paid to him during his lifetime, 'which is not like to be long (being
now in my 85th year), and thenceforth to the young man during his Majesty's pleasure'.[57]

William III's most important foreign agent network was at James II's court
in exile at Saint-Germain-en-Laye, near Paris.[58] The agent penetration of
Saint-Germain became so notorious that the Abbé Renaudot, its French
liaison with Versailles, mistakenly concluded that James's Secretary of
State, Lord Melfort, was in the pay of William III. At Louis XIV's insistence, James dismissed Melfort in 1694 and banished him to the provinces.[59]
William's agents at Saint-Germain enabled him to feel some confidence
that, as was to happen early in 1696, he would receive advance warning
of any attempt by James to launch a cross-Channel invasion with French
support. But William could not hope to keep the whole Jacobite exile community in France under surveillance. Numbering about 50,000,[60] it was
much larger, in proportion to the size of the British population, than the
membership of the British Communist Party at any time in the twentieth
century, as well as a far more diffuse and elusive target. Until the last minute, there was no intelligence warning of a serious plot to assassinate

William which had been devised by a group of Jacobite exiles in 1695 and timed to precede the planned invasion of 1696.

Assessing the threat posed by Jacobite conspiracy in England was also difficult. Much public denunciation of William and Mary was simply alehouse talk which posed no significant threat to national security. The usual penalty imposed at the Middlesex assizes for such seditious talk was a fine combined with a sentence to spend an hour at the busiest time of the day in the pillory at Charing Cross, Covent Garden, St James's Street, St John Street, Bow Street, the Strand or New Palace Yard.[61] Most informers' reports of Jacobite sympathizers contained nothing of real importance. An informant named James Ormiston wrote, for example, in 1695 to one of the secretaries of state, Sir William Trumbull, to report that a Captain Clifford had mistaken him for a Catholic and told him in an alehouse, under the influence of drink, that preparations for a Jacobite rising were going very well (though he declined to give details) and 'in a short time we should have home our sovereign King James again'. A more experienced agent told Trumbull that such claims were 'trumpeted in all [Jacobite] coffee houses'.[62] There were similarly exaggerated reports that many French and other foreign travellers were Jacobite spies. Even John Wallis, not usually an alarmist, feared that many of the 'great concourse' of foreign students he saw in Oxford were really Jacobite agents sent 'to take measure of the inclinations of the Kingdom'.[63]

William III was more concerned with Jacobite sympathies among leading members of his own government and armed forces, some of whom had only recently changed sides in his favour and were quite capable of changing back again. Among them was the man who later emerged as the greatest British general of his generation: John Churchill, Earl (later Duke) of Marlborough. Though Marlborough had defected from James II's forces a few weeks after William landed in England, in 1691 he began a secret correspondence with both James and the Duke of Berwick, James's illegitimate son by Marlborough's sister Arabella, and maintained contact with more than one Jacobite agent. Early in 1692 William dismissed Marlborough without warning. Those close to the King let it be known that Marlborough's recent correspondence with James II had been intercepted and that he was suspected of revealing a secret plan by William to attack Dunkirk. Marlborough was sent to the Tower of London for six weeks and it took him several years to regain the King's confidence.[64] His later belief in the importance of 'getting intelligence of the enemy's motions and designs'[65] must have owed something his experience of William's discovery of his own 'designs'.

The majority of those with Jacobite connections in the government and

armed forces were of what was called the 'fire insurance' variety – men who
had no personal loyalty to James II but thought it prudent to keep some
contact with his supporters in case he unexpectedly regained the throne.
Keeping track of more serious Jacobite conspiracies was made more difficult
by the diffuse nature of William III's domestic intelligence system. William
himself was partly responsible. He appointed no Scot or Thurloe to coordinate intelligence operations at home and abroad, as had happened during
the Interregnum. William's ministers were guilty of a classic failure to learn
from past intelligence experience. In the mid-1650s the exiled Charles II
had come to the pessimistic (and exaggerated) conclusion that Cromwell's
spymasters supplied him with 'perfect intelligence of whatsoever His Majesty resolved to do'.[66] The disorganized surveillance of Jacobites after the
Glorious Revolution never approached in efficiency the penetration of royalist opposition by Scot and Thurloe a generation earlier. William's two
(sometimes three) secretaries of state independently ran their own agents,
as well as receiving spasmodic reports on suspected Jacobites from local
justices and mayors. Two Whig MPs, John Arnold and Henry Colt, ran
their own spy networks to track down Jacobites, as did the Earl of Monmouth. Some county lords lieutenant, who led the local militias, took it on
themselves to investigate subversive activity and arrest suspects.[67]

The confused domestic intelligence system (far less effective than foreign intelligence), combined with widespread fear of Jacobite conspiracy,
created new opportunities for confidence tricksters, much as earlier fears
of 'popish plots' had enabled Titus Oates (undeservedly rehabilitated after
the Glorious Revolution) to embark on a career as a celebrity fraudster.
The confidence trickster who made the most sensational use of fraudulent
intelligence on Jacobite plots after the Glorious Revolution was William
Fuller, who claimed to have been brought up as a Catholic and employed
both as a servant to James II's adviser Lord Melfort and as a page to the
Queen, Mary of Modena. By his own unreliable account, Fuller then
secretly changed sides and worked as a Williamite agent at James's court
in exile at Saint-Germain. After assisting in the arrest of a Jacobite courier,
Matthew Crone, in 1690 and giving evidence at his trial, Fuller extracted
large sums of money to finance his supposed intelligence operations from
William and his government.[68]* Among those deceived by Fuller was
Queen Mary, who ordered him to be paid £100.[69] Other sums paid to
Fuller of which record survives are £180 'by his Majesty's commands' and
£110 from the Earl (later Duke) of Shrewsbury. Fuller's conspiracy

---

* Given the difficulty of separating fact from invention in Fuller's career, it is unsurprising
that there are discrepancies between these two accounts.

theories, like those of Titus Oates just over a decade earlier,[70] alarmed a nervous House of Commons. During two appearances at the bar of the House in 1691, he claimed that Louis XIV had spies in both the Privy Council and the offices of the secretaries of state. The truth of these and his other allegations of Franco-Jacobite conspiracy, he declared, could be proved by two witnesses who were currently abroad but willing to return if given safe passage and protection. The witnesses, however, failed to turn up as promised by Fuller. Early in 1692, Fuller claimed to be 'very ill, with great vomiting and looseness' of the bowels after being poisoned by Jacobites and unable to return to the Commons to give further evidence. Pretending to be on his deathbed, he gave a group of MPs who visited him a sworn statement directing them to the house of an apothecary where the elusive witnesses were allegedly lodging. But the witnesses were, once again, nowhere to be found and Fuller did not die. Embarrassed by their previous gullibility in taking seriously Fuller's fraudulent inventions, the Commons angrily resolved that he was an impostor and cheat who had 'scandalized Their Majesties and the government and abused this House and falsely accused several persons of honour and quality'. After prosecution by the Attorney General, he was sentenced to stand in the pillory, like Oates in 1685, and to pay a fine of 200 marks.[71]

The most serious authentic Jacobite conspiracies uncovered by intelligence operations were linked plans to invade England and to assassinate William III in 1696. According to William's informants at the court of Saint-Germain, James was confident, despite his humiliating flight from England and defeat in Ireland, that, with French assistance, he could recover his throne. In January 1696 he sent his illegitimate son, the Duke of Berwick, secretly to England to prepare an insurrection. Berwick rashly assured Louis XIV, who ordered troops to assemble on the Channel coast to support the insurrection, that 'King James has a great party both in England and Scotland who will take up arms as soon as they hear he is landed.' William's closest adviser, the Dutch-born William Bentinck, first Duke of Portland, received intelligence reports from Flanders 'that the enemy had collected a great body of troops at Dunkirk and Calais as well as a large number of transport vessels and ships of war, that the troops were either on board or being embarked and that it was well known there that they were assembled for the invasion of England'. Portland later confided to the English diplomat Baron Lexington: 'We were on the brink of a precipice and ready to fall. When, by a manifest interposition of providence, we were made aware of the danger which threatened us and all Europe.'[72]

What Portland called the 'interposition of providence' was intelligence received on the evening of 14 February 1696 that, in addition to the planned French invasion in support of a Jacobite rebellion, a well-prepared attempt would be made next day to assassinate the King as he returned by coach from a hunting expedition down a narrow street. Portland's informant, Thomas Prendergast, had been chosen as one of a group of eight assassins led by Sir George Barclay, a Jacobite army officer at James's court in exile who had travelled to London in disguise. Prendergast's allotted role was to fire a musketoon repeatedly into the royal coach but, he told Portland, his conscience would not allow him to go ahead. With some difficulty, Portland persuaded William to postpone his hunt until 22 February. On the evening of the 21st, Prendergast went to Kensington Palace to report that the assassins had reassembled and intended to kill the King after the hunt next day. His report was confirmed by a double agent, Francis Delarue. Prendergast was shown into the presence of the King and for the first time revealed the names of his Jacobite associates. When the royal hunt was again cancelled, rumours spread that a plot had been discovered and the would-be assassins fled. Though most, including Barclay, eventually escaped to France, eleven of those involved in the plot – some peripherally – were executed or imprisoned. Plans for a French invasion, which would probably have gone ahead if the assassination had succeeded, were cancelled. The exposure of the plot did great damage to the Jacobite cause and strengthened William's popularity at a time of economic crisis.[73] The Duke of Berwick, who also escaped to France, despite the offer of a £1,000 reward for his capture, later claimed that 'he came over to stir up rebellion, but knew nothing of the assassination'. He admits in his *Memoirs*, however, that he was informed of a plot to 'kidnap' the King, which he did not countermand. Since no such plot existed, 'kidnap' may have been a euphemism for assassination. After his escape, Berwick never returned to Britain.[74]

    The death in exile of James II in 1701 was hastened by an English intelligence coup involving his former Secretary of State Lord Melfort, whom James had allowed back to Saint-Germain from provincial exile in 1697 and restored to favour as gentleman of the bedchamber. In 1701 a French messenger mistakenly delivered a letter written by Melfort to his brother Lord Perth to the English court at Whitehall instead. The letter contained secret details about Jacobite supporters in Scotland and discussed the possibility of a French invasion. Seizing this unexpected opportunity to embarrass both James and Louis, William ordered the publication of the letter. Versailles was so furious that it accused Melfort of having deliberately sent the letter to Whitehall in the hope of provoking another war between France and England. James was so shocked when told of the letter's publication that he suffered a stroke from which he never fully recovered. At Louis XIV's insistence, the unfortunate Melfort was once again banished to provincial exile.[75]

Within a year, for reasons unconnected with Melfort's letter, England and France were once again in conflict with the outbreak of the War of the Spanish Succession (1702–14), a further episode in the long-drawn-out struggle to contain the power of Louis XIV's France that had dominated European politics for almost half a century. For much of the war the armies of England and its allies, under the leadership until 1711 of the Duke of Marlborough, the British commander-in-chief ('captain-general'), triumphed over those of Louis XIV. The Battle of Blenheim in Bavaria in 1704 was both the first great English land victory on the Continent since the Hundred Years War and Louis XIV's first decisive defeat. Marlborough was given the royal estate at Woodstock and a blank cheque to construct on it the great palace named after his victory. 'For a time', writes the historian Mark Kishlansky, 'Marlborough was the most famous man in the world.' He won further decisive victories at Ramillies in 1706, which enabled him to take possession of the Spanish Netherlands in a lightning campaign, and at Oudenarde in 1708, a battle which ended all prospect of a French invasion of the Dutch Republic.[76]

Good intelligence, as well as Marlborough's inspired generalship, contributed to Allied victories. Unlike British intelligence successes in the Nine Years War, however, those in the War of the Spanish Succession owed nothing to the monarch. Intelligence was beyond the mental horizons of William's successor, Queen Anne. As her confidante, the Duchess of Marlborough, complained, Anne's mind was so taken up with 'ceremonies and customs of courts and such like insignificant trifles' that her chief topics of conversation were 'fashions and rules of precedence'. Though only thirty-seven when she became queen, Anne had to be carried to her coronation in a sedan chair, prematurely aged by seventeen pregnancies, all of which had ended tragically in miscarriages, still births or the birth of babies who died in infancy. Her pleasures were limited to dining and gambling.[77]

The moving force in English intelligence during Anne's reign (1702–14) was the Duke of Marlborough. The latest and best biography of Marlborough, by the military historian Richard Holmes, concludes that 'The acquisition and analysis of intelligence underlay everything he did.'[78] When Marlborough assumed command of the Allied army in the Low Countries in April 1702, he appointed William (later General Earl) Cadogan his quartermaster-general; unofficially, he was also Marlborough's intelligence chief – the first appointed by any English general. Cadogan was an excellent linguist, fluent in French, Dutch and German.

While leading a reconnaissance expedition near Tournai in July 1706, he
was taken prisoner by a French cavalry patrol. Aware of Marlborough's
high regard for him, the French chivalrously released him in a prisoner
exchange.[79] Lord Strafford claimed that the Dutch Grand Pensionary,
Heinsius, had told him: 'If you want to have a Duke of Marlborough, you
need a Cadogan.'[80]

As well as collating tactical intelligence from enemy prisoners and desert-
ers, Cadogan also ran an agent network in France, much of it at the main
French ports. The inducements given to his agents were not simply financial.
Cadogan told Marlborough's private secretary, Adam de Cardonnel, in
1705: 'You will give me leave to remember my good friend the *Conseiller
Intime*. I hope the Tokay and the lady are provided for him as promised.'[81]
Cardonnel also ran an intelligence network through a former private secretary of William III, the Huguenot refugee Jean de Robethon, who had
become private secretary and influential adviser to the Elector of Hanover,
the future King George I.[82] A few months before Blenheim, Robethon gave
him a captured memorandum by Louis XIV's Secretary of State for War,
Michel de Chamillart, which summarized Louis's instructions to his
commanders. 'We find . . . the utmost designs of the enemy in this memorial',
wrote Cardonnel, 'and I hope we shall be able to traverse them.' Marlborough thus knew the French campaign plan – that French commanders were
to engage in battle only disunited Allied forces.[83] Before Blenheim, by contrast, the French commander, Marshal Camille de Tallard, professed 'total
ignorance of the strength of the enemy'; he had no idea that the combined
forces of Marlborough and his chief ally, the imperial commander-in-chief,
Prince Eugène of Savoy (French-born but rejected by Louis XIV for service
in the French army), were so close to him. Whereas Marlborough had devised
his own campaign plan with the help of good intelligence, Tallard complained to Chamillart that a bad campaign plan had been imposed on him
and that his Bavarian allies were impossible to deal with. He also blamed
his own forces for his humiliating defeat: 'The bulk of the cavalry did badly,
I say very badly, for they did not break a single enemy squadron.'[84] Tallard
spent the next eight years as prisoner-of-war in relative comfort in Nottingham, teaching his English captors how to make lace, bake *proper* bread, and
grow celery, all skills hitherto unknown to them.[85]

Following Marlborough's victory at Ramillies and his unopposed entry
into Brussels, previously under French control, in May 1706, he and the
Dutch acquired a major new intelligence source. In December François
Jaupain, who had taken charge of the Brussels post office, offered his ser-
vices to Marlborough and the Earl of Sunderland, newly appointed
Secretary of State. Jaupain gained control of all mail delivery between

those parts of the Spanish Netherlands still under French or Bavarian control and Northern Europe. In the summer of 1707 and again in the spring of 1708, he joined Marlborough on his military campaigns, running an intelligence unit which collected information on enemy troop movements and provisioning. Jaupain's main contribution to the Allied war effort, however, was to provide a regular flow of French intercepted messages to the youthful royal decipherer in England, William Blencowe, who had succeeded his grandfather John Wallis on Wallis's death in 1703. Blencowe, then a twenty-year-old Fellow of All Souls College, Oxford, was paid the salary of £100 a year negotiated by Wallis two years earlier. He initially made slow progress in breaking French ciphers, partly because of the limited number of intercepts sent to him. On one occasion Marlborough sent him a captured despatch from Chamillart, the French Secretary of State for War, but Blencowe failed to decrypt it in time for Marlborough to make use of it.[86] Blencowe's 'French Ministers Letterbook' contains only three decrypts for the period up to 1706. Thereafter, thanks to the intercepts from Jaupain, their numbers greatly increased.[87] There were also a smaller number of letters from the court of James III, 'the Old Pretender', son of James II, to Jacobites in Scotland. Ironically, some of the correspondence intercepted in Brussels contained warnings of the dangers of letter interception in London.

Blencowe was rewarded for his success in decrypting French despatches by the doubling of his salary to £200 a year. Queen Anne, no doubt at the prompting of her secretaries of state, also took his side in a dispute with his Oxford college. In 1709 Blencowe sought a dispensation to permit him to retain his fellowship at All Souls without, as was customary, taking holy orders. The Warden, Bernard Gardiner, refused and tried to force Blencowe either to take orders or to resign his Fellowship. Queen Anne's intervention on Blencowe's behalf led to the abolition of the Warden's veto on dispensations. Blencowe's precocious career as royal decipherer came to a tragically early end in 1712 at the age of only twenty-nine. During a bout of insanity following serious illness, Blencowe shot himself. His memorial in All Saints' Church, Northampton, records his expertise in 'the art of deciphering letters wherein he excelled, and served the public for ten years'.[88]

Marlborough was so anxious to keep secret Blencowe's decrypts of the French correspondence intercepted by Jaupain during the War of the Spanish Succession that he did not share them with his Dutch allies. He had good reason to doubt whether the Dutch could keep the secret. Following the death of the 'Stadholder-King', William III, day-to-day management of Dutch foreign policy had passed to Heinsius. Heinsius, in turn, had to answer to a supposedly secret committee of the States-General consisting of representatives of all the provinces, who on important matters had to consult their provincial States. 'This meant, in effect', writes the Dutch historian Karl de Leeuw, 'that in the Dutch Republic more people were involved in the making of foreign policy than anywhere in the world and that it was extremely difficult to conduct any form of secret diplomacy.'[89]

Marlborough was unaware that Jaupain was sending copies of French intercepts to Heinsius, as well as to himself, and that Heinsius was sending them on to the Elector George I's black chamber in Hanover. From 1707 to 1711 he paid Hanover's leading codebreaker, Ludwig Neubourg, 1,000 guilders a year. 'This', Neubourg told Heinsius in 1707, 'will greatly enhance my enthusiasm.'[90] Like Heinsius, George I's mother, Sophia of Hanover, heiress presumptive to Queen Anne under the 1701 English Act of Settlement, was an enthusiastic admirer of Neubourg's codebreaking expertise, calling him 'one of the wonders of the century'.[91] George, however, changed his mind about Neubourg's cooperation with the Dutch after the leak in The Hague in 1711 of a French diplomatic decrypt which personally embarrassed him. The decrypt revealed a scheme by the French court to cause dissension among the Allies by promoting the election of the Elector of Hanover as Holy Roman Emperor after the death of the Emperor Joseph I in April. During a visit to The Hague two months later, George's influential personal secretary, Jean de Robethon, reported to him that rumours were circulating about the contents of the French decrypt: 'It is out of the question that these rumours originate from the Grand Pensionary, but one cannot be sure of the deputies of the secret committee of the States-General, who get the intercepts to read as well, after our people [in Hanover] have decoded them.' The Hanover black chamber ceased work for Heinsius soon afterwards. However, Heinsius's private secretary, Abel Tasien d'Alonne, believed to be an illegitimate son of the Stadholder William II, had begun to set up a Dutch black chamber, which grew in importance over subsequent decades.[92]

Blencowe's decrypts provided Marlborough, on occasion, with valuable intelligence about his Dutch allies as well as his French enemies. Correspondence intercepted by Marlborough's agents in 1709 revealed secret peace negotiations between Heinsius and Torcy, Louis XIV's Secretary of State. Cadogan provided confirmation in May that Torcy had passed through Brussels, and sent Sunderland as well as Marlborough details of the peace terms which Torcy had secretly offered the Dutch. British pressure on Heinsius helped to ensure the failure of the Franco-Dutch negotiations.[93] Faced with attempts by Louis XIV to break up the Grand Alliance by offering generous concessions to the Dutch and Germans, Britain publicly pledged to make no separate peace.[94]

Cadogan ended 1709 with a strikingly confident intelligence assessment: 'Great numbers of deserters come in daily, they are half starved and quite naked, and give such an account of the misery the French troops are in as could not be believed were it not confirmed by the reports and letters from all their garrison towns on the frontier.'[95] Cadogan was too optimistic. Unlike Marlborough's previous triumphs at Blenheim, Ramillies and Oudenarde, the Battle of Malplaquet in September 1709 was a Pyrrhic victory which left him with double the casualties of the French. For the first time he received no congratulations from Queen Anne. Marshal Claude Louis Hector de Villars, the last great French general of the Louis XIV era, wrote to the King: 'If God will have the goodness to lose us another battle like this one, Your Majesty can count on the destruction of all our enemies.'[96] In the aftermath of Malplaquet, a war-weary British government was ready for peace negotiations.

The transformation of the English government in London into a *British* government by the Act of Union in 1707 had owed much to a domestic intelligence operation run by Queen Anne's future First Minister Robert Harley, then Northern Secretary of State, who a few years earlier had claimed that he 'knew no more of Scotch business than of Japan'.[97] During the negotiations which preceded the passage of the Act, Harley had sent secret agents to Scotland to report on, and seek to influence, Scottish opinion. Chief among them was the great writer, polemicist and unscrupulous businessman Daniel Defoe, whom Harley had already used as an agent in England.[98] Defoe, who arrived in Edinburgh in September 1706, was later described by a contemporary as 'a Spy amongst us, but not known to be such, otherways the Mob of Edinburgh had pulled him to pieces'. When the draft Act of Union was published in October, a 'villainous and outragious mobb' threatened members of the Scottish Parliament and judiciary. Despite the street protests, Defoe acquired sources in the Scottish Parliament, the Church of Scotland, and major business and civic groups, as well as gaining control of all the newspapers. Though Defoe publicly denied being a spy, writes the Cambridge literary scholar John Kerrigan, 'he so liked to cut a dash in coffee houses that he couldn't resist hinting at his role. This mixture of concealment and showing off is typical of the man . . .'[99] Economic 'inducements' certainly played a major part in winning a majority for the Union in the Scottish Parliament. Harley said cynically of the negotiations which won Scottish support for the Act of Union: 'We bought them.'[100]

Harley's most dangerous encounter with intelligence work came in 1711, when, to quote the usually authoritative *Oxford Dictionary of National Biography*, he narrowly 'survived an assassination attempt by a French spy,

the marquis de Guiscard'. Antoine de Guiscard, Abbé de la Bourlie, marquis de Guiscard, was, in reality, a talented fantasist who spent more of
his fraudulent career as an English than as a French agent. While living in
Lausanne in 1704 Guiscard met and greatly impressed the English diplomat
Richard Hill, who reported to the Earl of Nottingham, Secretary of State,
that he 'would engage to raise a revolt in Dauphine and Languedoc among
the Catholics, if I would promise him such a protection and assurance as
was absolutely necessary to begin the work. I liked the character of the
man, and his temper so much, a man of figure, and family, very well
known, that I promised him every thing.' Guiscard claimed to have access
to many French secrets and to carry with him a vial of poison in case he
was caught by the agents of Louis XIV who were allegedly pursuing him.

   Guiscard's bizarre career is evidence of the vulnerability of Queen
Anne's governments (and, to a lesser extent, William's) to intelligence
fraud and the high-level access which a plausible impostor such as Guiscard could achieve. At the height of his influence, in 1706, he enjoyed the
strong support of the Secretary for War, Henry St John, received 600
guineas from Queen Anne and a pension from the Dutch, and was given
command of a regiment to land on the French coast and foment the uprising he had promised Hill two years earlier. The landing never took place
and Guiscard's credibility and income steadily declined over the next few
years. In 1711 he sought to transform himself into a double agent working
for Louis XIV, promising Torcy that, in so doing, he would 'expiate his
crimes towards [His Majesty] and towards his fatherland'. Though aware
of Guiscard's villainous reputation, Torcy was so impressed by his past
high-level access to the British government that he sent an agent to England to make contact with him.[101]

   Guiscard's correspondence, however, had been intercepted, and by the
time Torcy's agent arrived he was under arrest in London. On 8 March
he was questioned by the members of the Cabinet (meeting without the
presence of the Queen). Charged with treasonable correspondence with
France, Guiscard at first denied it but was then confronted with his intercepted letters, which until that point had been hidden under a hat on the
Cabinet table. He then lunged at Harley, head of the government elected
in the previous year, and stabbed him with a penknife from his
pocket. According to dramatic contemporary accounts, since many times
repeated, though Harley was badly wounded, his life was saved by the
heavy gold-thread embroidery lovingly sewn on his coat by his devoted
sister Abigail, which broke the blade of the knife. Though the gold embroidery may have been a myth, the knife did break during the attack. A
second attempt by Guiscard to stab Harley with the broken blade also

failed to kill him, though Harley was confined to bed for the next six weeks. Harley's attempted assassination by a French spy greatly increased his popularity among a public unaware of Guiscard's earlier career as a fraudulent British agent. Guiscard died in Newgate Prison on 17 March from wounds sustained after his attack on Harley. Public interest in the assassination attempt was so great that the jailer pickled Guiscard's corpse in a barrel, put it on display and charged a penny for admission. His remains were eventually interred at Newgate by royal command and the jailer, somewhat undeservedly, given £5 'to repair the damages done to the floor and ceilings of 2 rooms by the salt water that ran out of [Guiscard's] cofin'.[102] No double agent in British history has met a stranger end.

In June 1711 Harley, now Earl of Oxford, decided to begin secret negotiations with Louis XIV. On 12 July the poet and diplomat Matthew Prior was sent to France, travelling on a false passport in company with the French secret negotiator, Abbé François Gaultier, also travelling incognito. After ten days of negotiations with Torcy and an audience with Louis XIV, Prior returned to England with another French negotiator, Nicolas Mesnager. On landing in England he was briefly jailed by a customs official, whose suspicions may have been aroused by his false passport. The secret negotiations suddenly ceased to be secret. The Whig opposition to Harley's Tory government derisively called the preliminary peace treaties signed on 8 October 'Matt's peace'.[103]

Marlborough told Harley that 'there is nothing on earth I wish more than an end to the war', but disagreed with him on what constituted reasonable terms. His position was weakened by investigation of his military accounts, which uncovered a large shortfall. Marlborough maintained in his defence, not very persuasively, that he had personally received 'no more than what has been allowed as a perquisite to the general, or commander-in-chief of the army' and, rather more persuasively, that he had spent much of the money on 'getting intelligence of the enemy's motions and design'.[104] On 30 December 1711 he was dismissed as commander-in-chief. His successor, the Duke of Ormond, was instructed to avoid engaging the enemy. On 11 April 1713 France, England, Holland, Portugal, Prussia and Savoy finally signed the Treaty of Utrecht, ending their involvement in the War of the Spanish Succession. The Emperor and his German allies continued for another year but achieved nothing of significance.

Obsessed by his increasingly unsuccessful quest for glory, Louis XIV ruled France less successfully at the end of his reign than at the beginning. In the 1660s, guided by Colbert, he showed a serious interest in understanding his account books and maintaining national solvency. After Colbert's death he gave up. On his death in 1715 Louis left a bankrupt

France with no effective accounting system and little more territory than at the beginning of his personal rule, despite the ruinous cost of his almost continuous wars in human lives as well as money. Half a century earlier, Colbert had had a broader vision of intelligence than any other European statesman of his time. In the Nine Years War, by contrast, William III made far better use of foreign intelligence than Louis or any of his ministers. During the War of the Spanish Succession, no French general matched Marlborough's intelligence flair. Louis XIV's grasp of intelligence, as of much else, did not compare with that of Cardinal Richelieu, who had died when he was only four. Under Richelieu, France had been the world leader in intelligence. It has never been so since.

14

Codebreakers and Spies in Ancien Régime Europe: From the Hanoverian Succession to the Seven Years War

After the accession of George Louis, Elector of Hanover, as King George I in 1714, the main British intelligence priority was to monitor and disrupt the threat of a Jacobite rising to restore the Stuart dynasty to the British throne. Under the terms of the peace treaty signed by Britain and France at Utrecht in 1713, James II's son, James Stuart, later called the 'Old Pretender', was forced to leave his palace at Saint-Germain, departing first for Avignon, then for Bologna and finally for Rome. Jacobite plotting was complicated by his disorganized and sometimes chaotic intelligence network. In addition to using a motley collection of unofficial informants, James employed a small number of 'official' salaried agents, who wrote him regular reports from Britain (few of which survive) and helped maintain contact between James's British supporters and his peripatetic court. The security of the Jacobite agent network has been fairly described as 'haphazard and primitive even for the time'. Its confused communications system included what were later called 'dead-letter boxes' maintained by merchants in Dunkirk and Rotterdam. Though aware their letters might be intercepted, some agents used such transparent codewords as 'Joseph' (James), 'Stirling' (Scotland) and 'Estmor' (England).[1]

Lacking any coherent method of assessing the reliability of the intelligence they received, James and his entourage vainly hoped that he might peacefully recover his throne on the death of Queen Anne. Buoyed by unreliable agent reports of the Jacobite sympathies of Robert Harley, Earl of Oxford, Anne's Chief Minister from 1711 to 1714, the Duke of Berwick, James's half-brother and best general (also, from 1706, a Marshal of France), wrote to him in 1712:

> I do really believe that they [the British government] mean well for your interest, and that they intend to act with all speed imaginable, but they are so afraid of its being known before the conclusion of the peace [in the War of the Spanish Succession], that they are unwilling of trusting anybody with the secret.

In reality, despite Harley's contacts with the Jacobite minority in the Tory Party and other Jacobite sympathizers, he and the Tory majority (as well as the Whig party) remained committed to the Hanoverian succession which he had helped to negotiate.[2]

Preparations for the 1715 Jacobite Rebellion were as chaotic as Jacobite intelligence – plans for a rising in southern England were never coordinated with those for risings in the north and Scotland. In July 1715 it became obvious to the plotters in the south that their intentions had been discovered by government spies. The rebellion in Scotland, however, posed the most serious Jacobite threat since the Glorious Revolution. By October the leader of the rising, John Erskine, Earl of Mar, had won control of all of Scotland north of the Firth of Forth except for Stirling Castle. Mar's delay and military inexperience then allowed government forces to recover the initiative.[3] His leadership has been fairly described as 'a disastrous combination of chronic indecision and strategic incompetence'.[4] Mar and a despondent James Stuart, who had landed at Peterhead on 22 December, secretly took ship to France on 4 February 1716, leaving the remnants of the Jacobite forces with orders to negotiate surrender terms.

The common element in Jacobite plots which followed the 1715 Rebellion were the attempts to secure backing from a European power. George I's governments had good intelligence on most of the attempts from codebreakers as well as from their agent network. The King himself was personally responsible for establishing a secret alliance between his Hanoverian codebreakers at Nienburg and those in Britain, who exchanged both intelligence and personal visits. Decrypts from Nienburg were forwarded by the Hanoverian minister in London to the King and distributed to leading ministers.[5] After the suicide of Queen Anne's royal decipherer, William Blencowe, in 1712,[6] he had been succeeded by a 39-year-old Fellow of the Royal Society, John Keill, who, like Blencowe, was an Oxford don. Keill had been about to accept a post as mathematician in the Venetian Republic when Robert Harley offered him the post of decipherer. The fact that the offer came directly from Queen Anne's Chief Minister (not yet called 'Prime Minister') is evidence of the importance of the post, though Keill was paid only £100 a year – half the salary of Blencowe. From 1712, however, Keill earned an additional salary as Savilian Professor of Astronomy. He established himself as one of Britain's most influential natural philosophers, helping to disseminate Newtonian principles.* But

---

* Though Leibniz had been an admirer of Wallis, he had a serious falling out with Keill. (*ODNB* John Keill.)

Keill's skill, and perhaps commitment, as a codebreaker did not compare with that of Wallis and Blencowe.*

In 1716 Keill was replaced as royal decipherer by the far abler 22-year-old Edward Willes, who had been taught codebreaking by Blencowe while a teenage undergraduate at Oriel College, Oxford, from which he graduated in 1712. Despite his youth, Willes was paid an initial salary of £200 a year, the same as Blencowe's and twice as much as Keill's. Unlike his predecessors, he was also given a secret government office (in effect a British black chamber) as well as working from his London home.† By 1717 Willes had succeeded in breaking some French,[7] Prussian[8] and Swedish, as well as Jacobite, ciphers.

In the aftermath of the failed rising of 1715, Jacobite hopes of mounting another rebellion centred on obtaining military assistance from Charles XII of Sweden, who was at war with Hanover. In 1716 Willes succeeded in decrypting correspondence on Swedish negotiations with the Jacobites exchanged between the Swedish Chief Minister, Georg Heinrich von Görtz,‡ and his ambassador in London, Count Karl Gyllenborg, who was married to a wealthy Jacobite heiress. Their correspondence, which included reports from Swedish diplomats in Paris and The Hague, discussed raising Jacobite loans to finance Charles XII's war against Hanover and his other campaigns in Northern Europe in return for Swedish support for another Jacobite rebellion in Britain. George I was so outraged by the intercepted correspondence that he probably ordered, and certainly approved, the arrest of Gyllenborg in January 1717 – an open violation of an embassy's diplomatic immunity which Britain has never repeated since. Gyllenborg was released in August and promptly returned to Sweden. His correspondence with Görtz was given greater publicity than any intercepts since the publication by Parliament of Charles I's secret letters during the Civil War. Much of the correspondence appeared in a government White Paper, with folio and quarto editions in English, French, German and Dutch, designed to score a propaganda victory over James Stuart and the Swedes.[9] The House of Commons voted a fulsomely sycophantic address to the King praising the divine as well as official surveillance

---

* Kahn's judgement that Keill was 'totally incompetent' (*Codebreakers*, p. 170) may be too harsh. Though he was not in the same class as Wallis, Blencowe and Willes (see below), at least one example of a successful decryption by him survives. (Leeuw, 'Cryptology in the Dutch Republic', p. 19, n. 40.)

† Willes was fluent in Latin, French, Spanish and Swedish. (*ODNB* John Willes.)

‡ Görtz's position was highly unusual. Officially, he was the Holstein-Gottorp envoy at the court of Charles XII. In practice, despite not being a Swedish subject, he was Swedish Chief Minister.

which had defeated the plots of the Jacobites and their Swedish collaborators: 'We adore the watchful eye of Heaven that has so wonderfully guarded and protected your sacred person and cannot too much extol the wisdom and vigilance that have been used in so early and seasonably discovering this desperate attempt.'[10] The Jacobites' last hope of Swedish armed support for a rebellion in Britain ended with Charles XII's death in battle on 11 December 1718.

The publication of the correspondence between Görtz and Gyllenborg seems, unsurprisingly, to have persuaded the Swedish Foreign Ministry to adopt more secure ciphers, which Willes was usually unable to break. Willes, however, had other major successes. As well as continuing to break the diplomatic ciphers of France and Prussia, he broke those of Spain in 1720, Sardinia in 1721 and Austria in 1722.[11]* Willes succeeded, where Wallis had failed,[12] in using his codebreaking successes to obtain ecclesiastical preferment. In 1718 he was given the valuable living of Barton-in-the-Clay, Bedfordshire.[13] A year later he was also given an assistant: the 32-year-old Anthony Corbiere, educated at St Paul's School and Trinity College, Cambridge, who had previously served in the embassies in Lisbon and Madrid, before becoming private secretary and translator to the secretaries of state.[14]

Over the next three years Corbiere assisted Willes in decrypting correspondence which revealed contacts between the Bishop of Rochester, Francis Atterbury, undeclared leader of Jacobites in England, and Jacobites in exile abroad.[15] Public outrage at the 'South Sea Bubble' in 1720 seems to have persuaded Atterbury that the time was ripe for another rising. In three months, the share price of the South Sea Company, of which George I was nominally governor, fell from £1,050 to £175, devastating the fortunes of both individuals and institutions. Investigations during 1721 revealed a web of official and company corruption. In November 1721 Atterbury agreed to proposals for an armed rebellion brought to him from James Stuart by the Jacobite courier, George Kelly.[16]† The rebellion was to begin with an invasion led by the Duke of Ormond timed to coincide with the British general election due in 1722.[17]

Alerted by the publication of the Swedish intercepts to the possibility that his correspondence too might be intercepted, Atterbury wrote nothing about the plot in his own hand and talked about it only in his bishop's residence in Bromley, where he trusted his chaplains and servants not to

---

* Research has yet to take place on the great majority of Willes's decrypts, which have been surprisingly neglected by historians of eighteenth-century Britain.
† Kelly was an Irish Protestant from a Catholic family and may have been an Anglican priest.

inform on him. Instead of corresponding directly with James Stuart and his court-in-exile, Atterbury left it to Kelly to do so.[18] Within a few months, however, the plot itself had collapsed in confusion. Atterbury quarrelled with the other leading Jacobite conspirators, 'whose collective caution', it has been said, 'amounted to inertia'.[19] James Stuart showed his usual lack of judgement in approving a separate plot devised by Christopher Layer, an eccentric Norfolk lawyer. At a meeting in Rome, Layer presented James with the names of 114 'persons of fortune' in Norfolk 'now desirous to show their loyalty and affection by joining in any attempt that shall be thought advisable to bring about a speedy and happy restoration'. Instead of recognizing Layer as a fantasist, James gave him his enthusiastic blessing; he and his wife, 'Queen' Clementina, became godparents to Layer's baby daughter.[20] Layer planned to begin his rebellion by seizing the Tower, the Bank of England and the Royal Mint, and then to take George I into protective custody if he did not promptly depart for Hanover. The lead which led to Layer's discovery seems to have come from the French Regent, Philippe, duc d'Orléans, then seeking a rapprochement with the British government.[21] When arrested in September 1722, Layer tried, improbably, to explain his hoard of swords and firearms by telling the arresting officer: 'You must know my clerk and I are great shooters when we are in the country.'[22] He was convicted of high treason in November.[23]*

The prime mover in the attempt to prove Atterbury guilty of treason was Sir Robert Walpole, who in 1721 had become Britain's first Prime Minister (though the title itself was not commonly used for another decade). Atterbury was betrayed by a man he believed to be a fellow Jacobite. Though he had broken contact with the other Jacobite plotters and withdrawn from the conspiracy by the spring of 1722, his involvement in its origins was revealed by the Scottish leader of the failed Jacobite rebellion of 1715, the Earl of Mar. After a period in exile as James Stuart's Secretary of State, the disillusioned Mar became a British double agent.[24] In the spring of 1722, writing under the pseudonym 'Mr Musgrave', Mar acted as an *agent provocateur* by engaging in incriminating ciphered correspondence with Atterbury, whom he addressed as 'Mr Illington'. Unaware that Mar had become a double agent, Atterbury dictated replies to George Kelly, which were delivered to Mar, who then handed them to one of Walpole's agents for decryption by Willes.[25]

Atterbury was arrested on 24 August 1722 and sent to the Tower. The

---

* Layer's execution was repeatedly delayed in the hope that he could be persuaded to incriminate his co-conspirators. He refused to do so and was hanged, drawn and quartered at Tyburn in May 1723.

warrant for his arrest claimed that he was 'carrying on a treasonable cor-respondence against His Majesty's government and hath endeavoured to engage several of His Majesty's liege subjects to execute and stir up a rebellion, towards the support of which he had promised them foreign assistance'.[26] A declaration issued by James Stuart (styling himself James III) from Italy in September showed him to be comically out of touch with his prospects of recovering the throne but at the same time deeply con-cerned at agent penetration of his supporters. He offered to make peace with George I, provided that George would 'deliver quietly to us the pos-session of our own Kingdoms', but complained 'that divers of our Subjects continue dayly to be question'd and imprison'd upon pretence of intelli-gence with us', and that 'informers, Spy's and false witnesses are become so numerous . . . that no innocence is safe'.[27]

By the beginning of 1723 Walpole and his advisers had concluded that the evidence against Atterbury, which included nothing written in his own hand, was too uncertain to risk a treason trial. They decided instead to opt for a 'bill of pains and penalties', which simply required Parliament to agree that Atterbury was a danger to the state, who should be deprived of all his ecclesiastical preferments and exiled for life. Atterbury turned the proceed-ings in the House of Lords before the third reading of the bill in May into a form of state trial during which at one point he cross-examined his chief accuser, Walpole.[28] Among a number of eccentric moments during the proceedings in the Lords was the questioning of a widowed landlady, Mrs Jane Barnes, by the Archbishop of Canterbury and others about the owner-ship of 'a very fine spotted Dog' named Harlequin, which George Kelly was alleged to have brought earlier from France as a gift for Atterbury's wife from the Earl of Mar.[29] Atterbury's friend Jonathan Swift wrote a satirical poem on the episode, entitled 'Upon the Horrid Plot discovered by Harlequin, the Bishop of Rochester's French dog'.

Among the most reluctant witnesses to give evidence in the Lords against Atterbury was Edward Willes, the only codebreaker ever to appear before Parliament. On 6 May counsel for the bill produced 'copies of let-ters intercepted at the Post Office, part of them written in cypher and afterwards decyphered'. The bishop and his counsel demanded that Willes 'give an account of his decyphering several letters, by what rule it was he judged that these cyphers meant what he pretended'. Willes refused to answer questions on codebreaking as 'disserviceable to the Government' and helpful to its enemies. Atterbury at the Bar of the House then exclaimed: 'In the name of God, what are these decypherers? They are a sort of officers unknown to the English nation. Are they the necessary implements and instruments of ministers of state?' He demanded that 'this

blind art' should be explained to the House 'that he might have an opportunity perhaps of unravelling it'. He desired to have 'the key itself which
they had discovered as belonging to these letters and from which they
made out these several words that are pretended' to be laid before the
Lords, but this was rejected by a great majority. His demand that Willes
should produce the key of the cipher was defeated by 80 votes to 43.[30]

Next day, 7 May 1723, before counsel for the bill read out several letters intercepted by the Post Office, Atterbury tried to insist that the Post
Office clerks be examined as to

1. Whether they had sufficient warrant and authority to stop and open the
    said letters, and from whom they had such authority?
2. Whether the clerks of the post-office who copied the letters, whose
    originals had been forwarded, had intercepted the said letters themselves,
    or received them from somebody else?

Despite protests by Atterbury and his counsel, the Lords voted to disallow
the questions on the grounds that they were 'inconsistent with public
safety'.[31] Atterbury's protests had more effect next day, 8 May. After three
decrypted letters of April 1722 had been read out to the Lords, Atterbury
'desired that he might have copies of them with the cyphers as they were
in the original, that he might have an opportunity of examining into the
justness of the decyphering that was pretended on the side of the King. He
thought this could not be denied him since so much depended upon it.'
Despite opposition by the counsel for the bill, Viscount Townshend, Walpole's chief political ally, who presided over the judicial proceedings in
the Lords, allowed Atterbury to have 'a copy of the letters and cyphers
together with the words as decyphered'. Townshend also permitted a
demonstration of the basic method of producing counterfeit seals to seal
the envelopes of intercepted letters to conceal that they had been opened,
but rejected Atterbury's demand for further details as 'going too far into
the secrets of state'.[32]

The 'bill of pains and penalties' duly passed its third reading, and
Atterbury was exiled to the Continent, where he spent the next five years
as James Stuart's increasingly despondent Secretary of State. With Atterbury's departure, Jacobitism ceased to be a significant force in southern
(though not northern) England. His was the first major trial (or near
equivalent) since that of Mary, Queen of Scots, 137 years earlier, in which
codebreaking was of central importance to the verdict.[33] Jonathan Swift,
like many of Atterbury's supporters, believed the evidence of the codebreakers was fraudulent. His *Gulliver's Travels* contains the first (and so
far the only) satire of codebreaking by a major British writer. Gulliver

explains that he has spent many years 'in the kingdom of Tribunia by the natives called Langden' (anagrams for 'Britain' and 'England'), where ministers and their minions have in their pay and under their control huge numbers of informers, accusers and false witnesses, who manufacture plots against the government:

> It is first agreed and settled among them what suspected persons shall be accused of a plot: then effectual care is taken to secure all their letters and other papers, and put the owners in chains. Their papers are delivered to a set of artists [decipherers], very dexterous in finding out the mysterious meaning of words, and syllables, and letters. For instance, they can decipher a close-stool [traditional toilet] to signify a privy council ...
>
> By their mastery of acrostics and anagrams, the most skilled decipherers can discover 'the deepest designs of a discontented party':
>
> So, for example, if I should say in a letter to a friend, [']Our brother Tom has just got the piles['], a man of skill in this art would discover how the same letters which compose that sentence may be analysed into the following words: [']Resist – a plot is brought home – [signed] The Tour.['][34]

'The Tour' probably refers to the Jacobite Viscount Bolingbroke, who after the 1715 rebellion fled for several years to France, where he was known as *La Tour*.

After the Atterbury Plot, Willes was rewarded by being made Canon of Westminster, his salary rising to at least £500 a year. Even more lucrative ecclesiastical preferments followed further codebreaking successes. Willes became Dean of Lincoln in 1739, Rector of Bonsall, Derbyshire, in 1734 and of St John Millbank, Westminster, in 1736. His next step was to 'put in for a bishopric' as soon as his son Edward junior, born in 1721, had completed his education at Westminster School and Queens' College, Cambridge, and was ready for appointment as a decipherer. Edward junior was duly appointed in 1742, sharing £1,000 a year with his father. In the same year Willes senior became Bishop of St David's, moving to the wealthier bishopric of Bath and Wells in the following year. Willes turned the Deciphering Branch into a fully fledged family business. Two of his younger sons also became decipherers: the Revd William Willes, born in 1732 and educated at Westminster and Wadham College, Oxford, in 1752, and Francis, born in 1735 and educated at Westminster, in 1758. Willes's reputation for nepotism was reinforced by the appointment of William and two of his sons-in-law as archdeacons of Wells. For some years, despite cryptanalytic assistance from his sons, Willes continued to take the lead role: coded messages for decryption arrived regularly at the magnificent Bishop's Palace in Wells, next to the cathedral.[35]

*

From 1722 to 1744 the Deciphering Branch was regularly able to decrypt Austrian despatches. For the next half-century, however, it had only occasional success in doing so.[36] By the mid-eighteenth century, the Deciphering Branch, despite continuing success in decrypting (among others) French, Spanish and Prussian diplomatic despatches,[37] had been overtaken by the Austrian 'black chamber', the *Geheime Kabinets-Kanzlei*, in Vienna. The French *cabinet noir*, a world leader only a century earlier, was in relative decline,[38] unaware that its ciphers were so vulnerable to the Austrian black chamber and the British Deciphering Branch. Until 1743 the French Foreign Ministry was also unaware that Russia, which until recently had possessed no black chamber, had acquired one of the leading codebreakers of his generation. This was the Prussian mathematician Christian Goldbach, now chiefly remembered as the originator of 'Goldbach's conjecture' that every even integer greater than 2 is the sum of two prime numbers. Goldbach was a founding member of the Russian Academy of Sciences in 1725 and tutor to Peter II, who became Tsar in 1727 but died three years later at the age of only fourteen. When Peter the Great's daughter Elizabeth (Elizaveta) became Empress in 1741, she sacked most German officials but kept Goldbach, who joined her Foreign Ministry a year later to work as a codebreaker.[39]

In 1744 Goldbach's decrypts led to the public humiliation of the French ambassador, the marquis de La Chétardie, then on his second tour of duty in St Petersburg. During his first tour, La Chétardie had won the favour of the then Princess Elizabeth and became well informed about her affairs with handsome commoners: among them a sergeant in a Guards regiment, a coachman, a waiter and a Ukrainian peasant in a church choir. After Elizabeth became Empress, La Chétardie reported to Paris that she remained 'so frivolous and so dissipated' that she was 'given entirely to her pleasures'. The Empress was shown a decrypt of the ambassador's despatch by her Grand Chancellor, Count Aleksey Bestuzhev-Ryumin, on 16 June 1744. Next day, La Chétardie was informed that he was to be expelled from Russia. When he protested, some of his decrypted despatches to Paris were read out to him. 'That's enough', he replied and began preparations for his departure. The British ambassador reported to London, 'I never saw a pickpocket drummed out of a garrison with more infamy than La Chétardie was *culbuté* out of this Empire.'[40]*

---

* La Chétardie's judgements on Elizabeth, though imprudent, were not greatly exaggerated. According to the great Russian historian Vasily Klyuchevsky, at the end of her twenty-year reign she left behind 15,000 dresses, two chests of silk stockings, a half-built Winter Palace and a mountain of debt. Christian Goldbach, however, had prospered under her rule, being richly rewarded with both land and money. He died in 1764 at the age of seventy-four.

It was probably the Austrian black chamber, the *Geheime Kabinets-Kanzlei* in Vienna, which in the mid-eighteenth century had the greatest success in decrypting French diplomatic despatches. Viennese codebreakers, often on duty around the clock, worked, except in emergencies, one week on and one week off. Translators too were always on hand. Each morning at 7 a.m. the bags of mail for delivery to embassies in Vienna were brought to the black chamber, where their seals were melted with a candle. Senior officials identified the despatches, or parts of despatches, to be copied. Lengthy documents were sometimes dictated to save time. Up to four people might be involved in copying different sections of a single important despatch in order not to delay its delivery. By 9.30 a.m. the despatches were supposed to be back in their envelopes, fastened with facsimile seals and ready to be delivered to embassies.[41]

French decrypts were a particularly important source of intelligence during the reorientation of Austrian foreign policy after the War of the Austrian Succession. Austria's leading diplomat, Count (later Prince) Wenzel Anton Kaunitz, sought an alliance with the traditional enemy, France, against the new enemy, Prussia. As ambassador to France from 1750 to 1752, he was sent a stream of intelligence from decrypted French diplomatic despatches (including some in the most secret French cipher) by Baron Ignaz von Koch, head of the *Geheime Kabinets-Kanzlei*. By the beginning of 1751, French decrypts revealed that the French appeared to regard the outbreak of a European war as inevitable and were simultaneously suspicious of the intentions of Britain, Russia and the Habsburg Empire.[42] During the first nine months of 1751, the *Geheime Kabinets-Kanzlei* broke eighteen different French ciphers.[43] Decrypted French diplomatic despatches, Koch wrote to Kaunitz on 4 September 1751, 'reveal more and more clearly the guiding principles of the French cabinet'.[44] While in Paris, Kaunitz was also supplied with decrypted British despatches from, among others, the Duke of Newcastle, then one of the secretaries of state.[45]

On his return to Vienna and appointment as Chancellor (with the formal title 'House, Court and State Chancellor') in 1753, Kaunitz became the dominating figure in Habsburg foreign policy. Assisted by intelligence from French and other diplomatic decrypts, Kaunitz achieved his ambition of concluding an alliance with France by the two treaties of Versailles in 1756 and 1757. These were the centrepieces of the 'Diplomatic Revolution' which led to the Seven Years War (1756–63) between the rival alliances of Austria, France and Russia on the one hand and of Britain and Prussia on the other. Kaunitz's manner gave no hint of his fascination with intelligence and the high priority he attached to it. The Habsburg Empress Maria Theresa and her court chamberlain, both admirers of Kaunitz's administrative and diplomatic skills, wondered 'how one man can combine the qualities of a superior genius with ridiculousness bordering on extravagance'. Kaunitz was both an incurable hypochondriac, fearful of contact with the slightest infection, and absurdly vain, spending hours at his elaborate toilette, attended by a bevy of handsome male servants.[46]

The work of the Austrian black chamber never received official publicity comparable to that endured by its British counterpart during the first decade of the reign of George I as a result of government publication of decrypted Swedish diplomatic despatches and evidence on codebreaking given in the House of Lords during proceedings against Atterbury. The existence of the *Geheime Kabinets-Kanzlei* none the less became an open secret to foreign diplomats in Vienna. Its head, Baron von Koch, complained: 'Unfortunately we have the reputation of being too skilful in this art and as a result, the courts which fear that we could be in possession of their correspondence change their [cipher] keys and each time adopt ones which are more difficult and troublesome to decipher.' Though such errors by the black chamber seem to have been rare, the British ambassador in Vienna reported on one occasion that official correspondence in an envelope addressed to him from London had consisted of Austrian copies rather than the English originals. Kaunitz, to whom he complained, replied, 'How clumsy these people are!'[47]

Spies received far more publicity than codebreakers, much of it hostile. 'Spy' (*espion*) was a pejorative term in Ancien Régime France, used predominantly to denote enemy agents. The French usually called their own spies by the less pejorative term 'agents'. The French word *espionnage*, which has entered the English language, was first used only in 1796. French dictionaries and the celebrated *Encyclopédie* (published in instalments between 1751 and 1772) defined the use of spies primarily in the context of military intelligence: 'C'est un vilain métier que d'espionner.' The leading mid-eighteenth-century French general Maurice de Saxe, whose great victory at Fontenoy in 1745 was personally witnessed by Louis XV and the future Louis XVI, was far more enthusiastic: 'It is impossible to pay too much attention to spies and guides.'[48] Eighteenth-century military commanders tended to make greater use than in previous centuries of spies for strategic intelligence on the enemy's resources and intentions, as well as for the traditional tactical battlefield reconnaissance.

Frederick II ('the Great') of Prussia claimed to make far more use of spies than Louis XV: 'My brother of France has twenty cooks and one spy. I have twenty spies and one cook.'[49] Probably unknown to Frederick, however, in 1745 Louis XV set up a secret department, the *Secret du Roi*

('King's Secret'), to conduct espionage and secret diplomacy independently of the Foreign Ministry. Its initial priority was to attempt to place Louis's cousin, the prince de Conti, on the throne of Poland. Despite years of subterranean intrigue, the attempt failed. The *Secret du Roi* seems to have achieved little until after the Seven Years War.[50]* Louis XV was, in any case, more concerned with intelligence on Frenchmen who dared to mock his royal authority than on the policies of foreign courts.

In 1749, with the backing of Louis XV, the comte d'Argenson, Minister of War and an ally of Madame de Pompadour, the King's *maîtresse en titre*, embarked on a major campaign to ban scurrilous popular songs and verse about the royal couple. No expense was spared and the campaign became obsessional. During the search for those spreading a verse about the King which began 'Monstre dont la noire furie' ('Monster, whose black fury'), one informer sent a crumpled note which read: 'I know someone who had a copy of the abominable verse against the king in his study a few days ago and spoke approvingly of them. I can tell you who he is, if you want.' The informer was richly rewarded for identifying the malefactor, a medical student named François Bonis, receiving twelve louis d'or, almost a labourer's year's wage. Bonis's arrest prompted 'an extraordinary poetry hunt and manhunt' which, writes the Princeton historian Robert Darnton, generated 'the richest dossiers of literary detective work that I have ever encountered'. Bonis confessed to getting the verse from a priest, who turned out to be one link in a chain of fourteen students, priests, notaries and clerks who had passed the verse from hand to hand. All were imprisoned in the Bastille.[51]† No known foreign-intelligence case in the reign of Louis XV was as intensively pursued as the 'Affair of the Fourteen'.

Antoine Louis Rouillé, successively French Secretary of State for the Navy (1749–54) and Foreign Secretary (1754–57), had a low opinion of the achievements of French foreign intelligence. Most of his own agents, he complained, failed to give value for money. In 1756 he denounced 'the danger of spies who, provided that they can make money out of it, sell indiscriminately and with equal facility truth and lies to one and all'.[52] As a long-serving British Foreign Secretary and later Prime Minister, the Duke of Newcastle‡ was far more positive about the benefits of espionage. About 100 of the over 300

---

* The *Secret du Roi* became more active after the Seven Years War; see below, pp. 292–3.
† In Britain, by contrast, the authorities were usually relaxed about spoken disrespect for the Crown. 'If commoners spoke ill of government, that was among the crosses that authority had to bear'. (Cressy, *Dangerous Talk*, p. 243.)
‡ Newcastle was Secretary of State for the Southern Department from 1724 to 1748, for the Northern Department from 1748 to 1754, and Prime Minister, save for a brief interval, from 1754 to 1762.

boxes of his (incompletely researched) papers contain intelligence material.[53] British ambassadors were among his main agent recruiters. Some eighteenth-century diplomats loathed being involved in espionage. 'I abhor this dirty work', wrote Sir James Harris (later Earl of Malmesbury) while minister at The Hague in 1785, 'but when one is employed to sweep chimneys one must black one's fingers.'[54] Other British diplomats enjoyed collecting secret intelligence – none more so than the immensely suave first Earl Waldegrave, ambassador to France from 1730 to 1741.

Waldegrave's courtly manners and engaging personality so impressed Louis XV that the King invited him to a day's hunting and presented him with a large amount of game – an unheard-of royal gift to a foreign ambassador. Louis would have been outraged to discover that, at the very moment he bestowed on Waldegrave such a mark of his favour, the ambassador was running a French diplomat as a British agent. In October 1734 Waldegrave had sought Newcastle's approval for an attempt to recruit an official at the French foreign affairs secretariat, François de Bussy, whose extravagance and debts had attracted his attention. Newcastle replied that George II personally authorized Waldegrave to undertake this 'Affair of the greatest Consequence'. By the following summer, Waldegrave had recruited Bussy as a paid agent, codenamed 101, financed by Walpole's Secret Fund. Bussy continued to supply the British with French diplomatic documents and other intelligence (including copies of the correspondence of the Foreign Minister, Germain Chauvelin)[55]* until the outbreak of war between the two countries ten years later.[56]

Waldegrave's intelligence operations were facilitated by poor French security. In October 1736 Chauvelin handed him, in error, a secret letter from the 'Old Pretender', James Edward Stuart, urging France to take the lead in forming an alliance with the Habsburgs to restore the Stuart dynasty. Without revealing the source of his intelligence, Waldegrave used the contents of the letter to complain to Louis XV's 83-year-old Chief Minister, Cardinal Fleury, about French support for the Jacobites. Queen Caroline, British Regent during the absence in Hanover of her husband, George II, sent her personal congratulations to Waldegrave on the 'great Prudence and Discretion' he had shown in using this intelligence windfall to confront Fleury.[57] In striking contrast to Walpole and Newcastle, as well as to the two great seventeenth-century *cardinaux ministres*, Richelieu and Mazarin, Cardinal Fleury showed little visible interest in foreign

---

* From 1727 to 1737 Chauvelin was the only minister in the history of the Ancien Régime to be simultaneously *Secrétaire d'État des Affaires étrangères* and *garde des sceaux*.

intelligence.* Largely because of Louis XV's deep affection for him, he remained Chief Minister until his death in 1743 at the age of almost ninety. Louis wept at the news.[58]

Bussy's career as a British agent was facilitated by his posting to the French embassy in London in 1737.[59] With the approach of the oddly named War of Jenkins' Ear two years later, Bussy was used to obtain intelligence on France's relations with Spain as well as with the Jacobites. The war arose out of a trading dispute which had earlier led a Spanish coastguard to sever an ear of the British Captain Robert Jenkins, who reputedly displayed it during testimony to an outraged House of Commons. Waldegrave's intelligence operations in France were not limited to recruiting Bussy. In June 1739, Newcastle instructed him to establish an agent network at French ports and report on French military recruitment in Ireland. On 8 August 1739 Waldegrave reported, probably partly on the basis of information from Bussy, that 'there seems to be a perfect arrangement made between this court and the court of Spain'.[60] In October Walpole reluctantly gave in to parliamentary pressure and declared war on Spain.

By the time Bussy was promoted to chargé d'affaires in London in 1740, he had a reputation for greed and corruption. The fact that he remained *en poste* is further evidence of the lack of priority given to French diplomatic security.[61] 'Surely', Waldegrave wrote to Newcastle in January 1739, 'there is not a more brazen-faced wretch.' Newcastle appears to have hinted to Waldegrave at some point that Bussy was in British pay.[62] Some of Bussy's intelligence was of the first importance. On 14 February 1744 he provided the entire plan for a French invasion of England in support of the 'Young Pretender', Charles Edward Stuart, better known to posterity as 'Bonnie Prince Charlie', and gave the names of the leading English Jacobites involved. He was paid the then enormous sum of £2,000. The government of Henry Pelham (Prime Minister from 1743 to 1754 and younger brother of the Duke of Newcastle) summoned troop reinforcements from Ireland and Netherlands, and rounded up some leading Jacobites. At almost the moment that Bussy betrayed the French invasion plan, the Young Pretender arrived at Gravelines, using the pseudonym 'Chevalier Douglas' and impatient for the invasion to begin. But the arrest of his leading English supporters, doubts over whether the majority would give effective support, and storm damage to French landing craft assembled at Dunkirk, led Louis XV to cancel the invasion plan.[63]

---

* There is no mention of Fleury in the 510 pages of Genêt, *Espions des lumières*. There is also 'no trace' of Fleury's direct involvement in the affairs of the *cabinet noir*, known during the reign of Louis XV as the *bureau du secret*. (Vaillé, *Cabinet noir*, p. 139.)

In the summer of 1745 Charles sailed to Scotland, confident that, even without the support of French forces, his faithful Highlanders would rally to him. So far as Scotland was concerned, his optimism was largely justified. The Jacobite victory at Prestonpans in September, only two months after he landed, gave him control of most of Scotland. By early December, Charles had reached Derby. Among his forces was a government spy named Dudley Bradstreet who posed as Captain Oliver Williams, an ardent Jacobite. Bradstreet later claimed that he had been personally instructed by Newcastle to delay Charles's advance to London 'by some Stratagem' and that he successfully persuaded Charles's council to retreat to Scotland. Though Bradstreet did indeed penetrate the Jacobite army, it is far more likely that most of the council decided to retreat, against Charles's wishes, not because of any 'Stratagem' by Bradstreet but because they feared to take on the three English armies they believed were preparing to do battle with them. They were unaware that, encouraged by Charles's success thus far, the French were hurriedly assembling an invasion force. After the retreat of Jacobite forces, Bradstreet received a reward of £120 from George II, though not the army commission he claimed he had been promised. He later made a living as confidence trickster and conjurer.[64]

The Jacobite Rising ended disastrously on 16 April 1746 at Culloden near Inverness in the last pitched battle fought on British soil. Charles's forces, largely composed of Highlanders, supported by Irish and Scots units from the French army, were decisively defeated by a mostly English army, commanded by the Duke of Cumberland, a younger son of George II. Bonnie Prince Charlie's escape after Culloden 'over the sea to Skye' has passed into British folklore much as Charles II's flight after the Battle of Worcester almost a century earlier is commemorated by 'Royal Oak' public houses.[65] Both Stuarts owed their improbable escapes partly to the fact that they possessed some of the qualities of resourceful secret agents, adept at concealment and disguise. But the Young Pretender's escape would have been impossible without the success of the informal Jacobite intelligence network in tracking his pursuers and helping Charles evade them. His most famous helper was Flora Macdonald, who had grown up in the Jacobite household of the chief of the Macdonalds of Clanranald and agreed, after some hesitation, that Charles should escape with her from Benbecula in the Outer Hebrides, where he had taken refuge, disguised as her Irish maid, Betty Burk. She later recalled that she had forbidden Charles to carry pistols under his petticoat in case they were searched. Charles objected, in vain, that 'If we shall happen to meet with any that will go so narrowly to work in searching as what you mean, they will certainly discover me . . .'

On the night of 28/29 June he set sail with Flora Macdonald in a small boat from Benbecula to Skye. Though Flora was arrested soon afterwards, Charles, still with a price on his head of £30,000 (a seven-figure sum by today's values), escaped first to the neighbouring island of Raasay and then to the mainland. At one point, while soldiers were searching for him in the hills round Glenfinnan, he passed close enough to the sentry posts to hear the sentries talking. Charles remained in hiding until he was rescued on 19 September by a French ship, which took him to safety in France.[66]

Over the next few years, British agents pursued Charles around Europe as he made plans for a Jacobite coup in London. With the help of what his biographer Frank McLynn claims was 'a cell structure of agents',[67] Charles, often disguised as a priest, regularly evaded his pursuers. Even more remarkably, in 1750 he succeeded in visiting London undetected. Charles prepared for his visit by sending misleading correspondence to an English female supporter which he believed, probably correctly, would be intercepted and confuse the government. On 13 September he landed at Dover in disguise and reached London three days later, staying with Anne Drelincourt, Lady Primrose, at her house off the Strand. He later held a meeting at a house in Pall Mall, once again without being detected, with fifty leading English Jacobites. They held out no hope of a successful coup and Charles returned despondently to France from Dover on 23 September.[68] He never returned to Britain.

Over the next decade, the British government had a penetration agent of major importance in Jacobite ranks who chose the codename 'Pickle', presumably in honour of Tobias Smollett's fictional hero Peregrine Pickle.[69]* Pickle's identity was so closely guarded that it was not discovered until the end of the nineteenth century, when the historian Andrew Lang discovered, while examining the papers of Alasdair Ruadh, chief of clan Macdonnell of Glengarry (c.1725–61), that he had Pickle's habit of writing 'how' when he meant 'who'.[70] Pickle usually addressed the Prime Minister, Henry Pelham, as his 'Great friend' and the Duke of Newcastle as 'Mr Kenady'. Other leading figures were designated by numerals. The Old Pretender was no. 8, Charles Stuart was no. 80. In the aftermath of Charles's return to the Continent in 1750, Pickle provided detailed intelligence on continued Jacobite plotting. He had the complete confidence of Charles, who discussed details of the plots with him. Pickle wrote in one report on a meeting with the Young Pretender: 'The discourse turn'd chiefly upon

---

* He also sometimes used the pseudonyms 'Alex Pickle', 'Jeanson' (his father's name was John), 'Alex Johnson' and 'Roderick Random' (another of Smollett's fictional heroes).

the Scheme in England . . .' Warned by Pickle, Pelham's agents monitored the secret correspondence and movements of the Jacobites he identified.[71]

The most important intelligence provided by Pickle concerned what became known as the 'Elibank Plot', a conspiracy led by the forty-year-old Jacobite peer Alexander Murray of Elibank.* As in the Layer Plot thirty years earlier, the conspirators planned to seize St James's Palace and the Tower of London, on 10 November 1752, and – even more unrealistically – to kidnap George II and members of the royal family. Charles Stuart would then sail to England and reclaim the throne. When Murray arrived secretly in England in October to prepare for the attack, he found English Jacobites close to panic, fearing – correctly – that the plot had been betrayed. Though the culprit was believed to be Charles's current mistress, Clementine Walkinshaw, the real source of government information about the Elibank Plot was MacDonnell, alias Pickle. One of the plotters, Dr Archibald Cameron, was hanged, drawn and quartered – not, however, for his part in the plot but for his role in the '45 rebellion. Pelham's government seems to have decided not to put the other Elibank plotters on trial, for fear of giving any clues to the identity of its main informant.† With the failure of the plot and Cameron's execution, any realistic Jacobite threat to the Hanoverian dynasty disappeared. Only Charles and the most diehard of his demoralized supporters believed any longer in the possibility of a Stuart restoration. Even Charles, increasingly prone to alcoholic despair, spent less of his time making plans to return to Britain than in trying to evade the Hanoverian spies and assassins he believed were pursuing him around the Continent. His followers often found him 'so disguised as to make it extremely difficult to know him', with rouge on his cheeks, eyebrows blackened and wearing one of a variety of false noses.[72]

The eighteenth-century ruler who was the most enthusiastic advocate of spies was Frederick the Great of Prussia. Experience in the War of the Austrian Succession, during which he conquered Silesia from the much

---

* In February 1751 Murray had been summoned before the Commons, accused of stirring up pro-Jacobite mob violence during an election, and was sent to Newgate Prison. When brought before the House again, he was found guilty of contempt for refusing to kneel before the House to receive sentence, and was sent back to Newgate. He was freed in June when Parliament was prorogued. In November a motion was carried in the Commons sending Murray back to prison. By then, however, he had fled to France. (ODNB Alexander Murray of Elibank.)

† ODNB Alexander Murray of Elibank, ODNB Archibald Cameron. Other leading Jacobites discovered to be involved in the Elibank Plot were Sir John Graeme, Henry Goring, Lady Primrose, Jeremy Dawkins, MacDonald of Lochgarry, and George Keith, Earl Marischal, then Frederick of Prussia's envoy in Paris.

larger Habsburg Empire, had persuaded Frederick of the importance of intelligence. Only 'with accurate intelligence', he insisted, 'can we, even with inferior numbers, always be more than a match for the enemy'.[73] His 'Military Instructions' to his commanders, written between the War of the Austrian Succession and the Seven Years War, emphasized the importance of espionage: 'I must further add that in the payment of spies we ought to be generous, even to a degree of extravagance. That man certainly deserves to be well rewarded, who risks his neck to do your service.'[74]

Frederick distinguished four categories of spies. The first were 'common people', local inhabitants who could reveal the location of enemy forces (but, in Frederick's view, little else of value).[75] During the Seven Years War, French generals regularly complained that, when fighting in German states, they found the population resolutely pro-Prussian. After the occupation of Hesse by France in 1759, reported the baron de Bonneval, not a single French soldier could be moved without 'the peasants leaving to tell the enemy'. The Duke of Württemberg complained in 1760 that, though he personally was an ally of France, his pro-Prussian populace were willing 'to spy for the enemy with the greatest pleasure'.[76] Deserters, in Frederick's view, were of very limited value, in his experience usually able to reveal reliably only the movements of their own regiments, rather than the enemy army as a whole.

Frederick seems to have been the first eighteenth-century ruler to advocate the use of double agents (his second category of spies) to feed disinformation to the enemy. He was a rare, perhaps unique, example of an eighteenth-century monarch who sought to learn from the past history of intelligence operations. In commending the use of double agents to his generals, he cited William III's successful use of a double agent in 1692 at the Battle of Steenkerque in present-day Belgium. Shortly before William launched an attack, the double agent inaccurately informed the French commander, Marshal Luxembourg, that there would be no attack until the day after a large foraging party had been sent out. 'The consequence', claimed Frederick, 'was that the French very narrowly escaped being surprised at Steenkerque, and would have been cut to pieces if they had not defended themselves with extraordinary valour.'

If 'milder methods' of recruiting spies failed, Frederick was prepared to use blackmail. On one occasion in the War of the Austrian Succession he put pressure on a wealthy landowner to enter the enemy camp with one of Frederick's spies disguised as his servant, on the pretext of seeking medical treatment for injuries he had sustained. Frederick later told his generals that he had warned the landowner that if he failed to return with the spy, 'his houses shall be burned, and his wife and children hacked in pieces'. He admitted this was a 'harsh and cruel' way of collecting intelligence, but claimed that cruelty was sometimes a wartime necessity. On this occasion, according to Frederick, blackmail enabled him to obtain important intelligence.[77]

Frederick placed 'spies of consequence' in a category by themselves.[78] The spy of most consequence to Frederick on the eve of the Seven Years War was an agent in the Foreign Ministry of Saxony, a state which he dramatically likened to a 'dagger pointed at the heart' of Brandenburg/Prussia. The agent warned him that the Elector of Saxony was planning to attack Prussia in alliance with Maria Theresa, Louis XV and Catherine the Great. Frederick struck first, and invaded Saxony in late August 1756, quickly overrunning the whole electorate. One of his first acts was to search the government archives in Dresden for incriminating documents to prove his agent's warning that the Elector was planning to attack Prussia. Once discovered, Frederick triumphantly published the documents, claiming in self-justification that 'whoever anticipates a secretly planned attack . . . is not the aggressor'.[79]

Frederick's decision to make what he considered a preemptive strike against Saxony was also influenced by good intelligence from a Prussian agent in the Austrian embassy in Berlin, supplemented by despatches from the Dutch envoy in St Petersburg, intercepted and decrypted in Berlin en route to The Hague (a rare example of diplomatic decrypts apparently having some influence on Frederick's policy). According to intelligence received by Frederick on 17 June, the Russians were assembling 170,000 regular troops and 70,000 irregulars on their western borders. Ten days later, he was told that Russian mobilization had been halted and on 21 July that they had decided to postpone an attack until the following year. Frederick was thus reassured that he had time to launch an attack on Saxony in late August before the Russians entered the war.[80]

The most important spy working for Prussia's ally, Britain, at the outbreak of the Seven Years War probably remained François de Bussy. How much intelligence he was able to provide after the breach in Anglo-French diplomatic relations remains unclear: the closure of the French embassy in London also greatly diminished opportunities for the interception of ciphered French diplomatic despatches.[81] Lack of French intelligence, however, mattered little in the early successful years of the Seven Years War, with British triumphs over France in the New World (discussed in Chapter 15) and Frederick's victories on the Continent, assisted by the British. Though the Duke of Newcastle had become Prime Minister in 1754 after the death of his brother, in 1757 the popular War Minister, William Pitt (later dubbed 'the Elder'), became effective head of an apparently victorious government. Horace Walpole wrote in 1759: 'Our bells are worn out threadbare with ringing for victories.'[82]*

The most celebrated of Frederick's victories was won against the Austrians at Leuthen in December 1757. Napoleon later called it a 'masterpiece of movements, of manoeuvres and of resolution; enough to immortalize Frederick and rank him among the greatest of generals'. But it was achieved despite, not because of, the quality of Prussian intelligence and Frederick's assessment of it. Before the battle, Frederick believed the size of enemy forces was about the same as his own. In reality the Austrians outnumbered the Prussians almost two to one.[83]

Until 1761 Pitt had better intelligence on his Prussian allies than on his French opponents. Frederick the Great, who had less interest in codebreaking than in espionage, seems to have been unaware that Prussian diplomatic despatches were regularly decrypted by the British Deciphering Branch.† He wrote to his envoy in Paris in 1755:

> I have received letters from London that, to my great surprise, contain all the details of what has happened between France and me since the time of the Anglo-French rupture in America. They are so well informed that they have my very phrases. Clearly there is either no secrecy in the French Council or a leak. You are to press Rouillé on the need for France to take better arrangements in order to ensure that secrecy is maintained. Tell him that unless this happens I will be unable to confide in France, as secrecy is crucial to me.[84]

Clearly, it did not even occur to Frederick that the British knew the 'very phrases' of his communications with France not because of a French failure to 'maintain secrecy' but because the British had broken his ciphers.

British intelligence on France during the Seven Years War improved, probably dramatically, in May 1761 when, despite the breach in diplomatic relations, Bussy was sent by the French Foreign Ministry on a mission to London to explore the possibility of peace negotiations to end the Seven Years War.[85]‡ Bussy almost certainly continued (or resumed) his role as mercenary British Agent 101, thus making unusually ironic his remarkably flattering assessment of Pitt's abilities which he sent the French Foreign Minister, the duc de Choiseul:

---

* Walpole added: 'PS. You shall hear from me again if we take Mexico or China before Christmas.'

† With the exception of the period 1741–7, the Deciphering Branch was able to break Prussian diplomatic ciphers from 1717 until the end of the eighteenth century. (Ellis, *Post Office in the Eighteenth Century*, p. 73.)

‡ Some recent studies of Bussy's involvement in the peace talks of 1761 surprisingly fail to mention his role as a British agent. (Black, *George III*, p. 308.)

The minister is, as you know, the idol of the people, who regard him as the sole author of their success, and they do not have the same confidence in the other members of the council [Cabinet] . . . Pitt joins to a reputation of superior spirit and talent, that of most exact honesty . . . with simple manners and dignity, he seeks neither display nor ostentation . . . Pitt seems to have no other ambition but to elevate Britain to the highest point of glory and to abase France to the lowest degree of humiliation.[86]

Such opinions were not welcome at Versailles. The unusually censorious entry on Bussy in the *Dictionnaire de biographie française* accuses him of *'extrême maladresse'*, 'alienating the partisans of both peace and war by his thoughtlessness, capriciousness and insolence'. Bussy had become a loose cannon and was recalled to France in September 1761.[87*]

Probably for the first time in the British Cabinet's foreign-policy debates, intercepted diplomatic despatches played a prominent part during discussions of peace negotiations with France. On 14 August 1761 the Earl of Bute, joint Secretary of State, read out to ministers a despatch from Choiseul to the French envoy in Stockholm, possibly provided by Bussy, revealing that France had decided to continue the war but was continuing to negotiate with Britain to conceal its intentions.[88†] Bute was the favourite, former tutor and for many years close adviser of George III, who succeeded his father, George II, in 1760. It was at the new monarch's wishes that, on his accession, Bute joined the Cabinet as Secretary of State.[89] Bute undoubtedly drew the intercepted diplomatic correspondence to the attention of George III, who read his state papers conscientiously.

Pitt also read diplomatic intercepts avidly. As well as providing an important insight into the failure of peace negotiations with France, they yielded valuable intelligence on Franco-Spanish negotiations for an alliance directed against Britain. At Cabinet on 18 September Pitt argued in favour of a preemptive attack by Britain on Spain: 'Loss of time [is] loss of opportunity . . . Prevarication will increase the danger.'[90] Having failed to convince most of his colleagues, Pitt tried again on 2 October and read out to the Cabinet an intercepted despatch between the Spanish ambassadors in London and Paris, decrypted by the Deciphering Branch, which clearly pointed to the conclusion of a Franco-Spanish alliance.[91] Three

---

* Bussy retired in 1767, dying about twenty years later.

† Black (*Pitt the Elder*) believes that the despatch was 'provided by the excellent postal interception system that served Britain so well in the mid-eighteenth century'. It is unclear, however, how the British Post Office could have intercepted a wartime despatch en route from Paris to Stockholm. The fact that the incomplete surviving records of the Deciphering Branch contain no French decrypt for 1761 makes it more likely that the source was Bussy.

days later, with the Cabinet still opposed to war, Pitt resigned. Bute took charge of foreign policy, declared war on Spain in January 1762, resumed peace negotiations with the French, and loosened connections with Britain's ally Prussia.

Bute succeeded Newcastle as Prime Minister in May 1762. Though his unpopular ministry lasted only eleven months, he concluded peace with France and Spain by the Treaty of Paris, which confirmed British dominance overseas and did serious damage to France's international prestige.* Bute is believed to have set aside £80,000 from the Secret Service Fund to ensure the ratification of the Treaty of Paris by the Commons on 10 February 1763. His secretary to the Treasury, John Ross Mackye, claimed to have paid forty MPs £1,000 each and eighty others £500.[92]

For Prussia the Seven Years War almost ended in disaster. By 1762 Frederick's only reliable major ally was the unpopular German-born heir to the Russian throne, Grand Duke Peter, who was also Duke of Holstein-Gottorp in north Germany, spoke little Russian and made no effort to conceal his preference for all things Prussian. To keep Frederick informed of the Empress Elizabeth's secret war councils, Grand Duke Peter passed him what he learned of the plans of the Russian high command via Robert Keith, the British ambassador in St Petersburg. Keith included this intelligence in his despatches to London, which he sent via Prussia, so that the British ambassador in Berlin could make copies for Frederick. Peter's admiration for Frederick and contempt for the Russian army were so blatant that Keith reported to London: 'He must be mad to behave in this way.'[93] Like the rest of the Tsarist administration, Peter was doubtless unaware that from 1758 the British Deciphering Branch had considerable success in decrypting Russian diplomatic despatches, most of them written in French.[94]

Just when Frederick was facing defeat in the Seven Years War at the beginning of 1762 and praying for a 'miracle', he was saved by the death of the Empress Elizabeth and the accession of Grand Duke Peter as Tsar Peter III. Only three days after the accession, Keith reported to London that 'at a dinner, His Imperial Majesty, with whose good graces I have always been honoured, came up to me and smilingly told me in my ear that he hoped I would be pleased with him as the night before he had sent couriers to the different corps of his army with orders not to advance further into Prussian territory and to cease all hostilities'. Had the new Tsar remained on the throne, he might have proved an extraordinary source for Britain of intelligence on Russian policy. 'Not a day passes', complained

---

* Prussia and Austria signed the separate Treaty of Hubertusburg five days later.

the Austrian ambassador, 'that the Emperor does not see Mr Keith, or send him fruit, or pay him other attentions.'

After the arrival in March 1762 of a new Prussian envoy in St Petersburg, Baron Bernhard von der Goltz, Peter paid even closer attention to him than to Keith. Peter gave him a mansion and visited him twice a day. Goltz was taken aback by the Tsar's ardent admiration for both Frederick and the Prussian army. In April Peter signed an 'eternal' alliance with Prussia and returned all the territory conquered by Russian forces during the Seven Years War. Had Peter sought intelligence on the threat of a coup against him, it would not have been difficult to obtain. Frederick warned him as he was about to leave St Petersburg to start a private war against Denmark to win back Schleswig for his German Duchy of Holstein-Gottorp, 'Frankly, I distrust these Russians of yours. What if, during your absence, a cabal were formed to dethrone Your Majesty?' Peter's contempt for the Russian army persuaded him that it was incapable of launching a coup. He told Frederick that he would have no difficulty in coping with Russian opposition: 'I assure Your Majesty that when one knows how to deal with the Russians, one can be quite sure of them.'[95]

The Tsar, however, had grossly underestimated his wife, Catherine, whom he was planning to divorce so that he could marry his mistress. Though German-born like Peter, Catherine had learned fluent Russian and immersed herself in Russian culture. Late on 28 June 1762, during one of St Petersburg's midsummer 'white nights', Catherine walked from the unfinished Winter Palace, holding a sabre and wearing the green uniform of a captain of the Preobrazhensky Guard, then mounted 'Brilliant', her thoroughbred grey stallion. Accompanied by 12,000 Guards who had rallied to her cause, she set off to the palace at Peterhof, where Peter had taken refuge. By the time she arrived, Peter had already capitulated. Catherine's lover, Grigory Orlov, forced him to sign an unconditional abdication. Frederick II later said scornfully: 'He allowed himself to be dethroned like a child being sent to bed.' A few days later, Peter was throttled by a group headed by Orlov. Catherine, who had probably not been consulted before his murder, announced that he had died of 'a haemorrhoidal colic', a phrase which in other European courts quickly became a satirical euphemism for political assassination. The French philosopher Jean d'Alembert, when invited by Catherine to visit Russia, joked to Voltaire that, because he was prone to haemorrhoids, a potentially fatal condition in Russia, he dared not accept the invitation.[96]

15

Intelligence and American Independence

The duc de Choiseul, Louis XV's Anglophobe Chief Minister from 1758 to 1770, as well as Foreign Minister for much of this period, told him in 1765 that 'only a revolution in America . . . will return England to the state of weakness in which Europe will no longer have to fear her'.[1] Though Choiseul used spies to report on the growth of American opposition to British rule,[2] they are unlikely to have discovered anything of significance not available from public sources. Choiseul's most successful intelligence operations seem to have been in the royal bedchamber rather than North America. After the death in 1764 of the King's mistress, Madame de Pompadour, who had been one of Choiseul's chief supporters at court, he tried to influence the choice of her successor to ensure his continued influence. Dissatisfied with the new incumbent, he secured her downfall by obtaining information on the King's sexual inadequacies, then maliciously telling Louis that his new mistress was gossiping about them. Choiseul met his match when Louis chose as his mistress one of the great beauties of her generation, Madame du Barry, a prostitute previously known as Mademoiselle Ange ('Miss Angel'), who appears to have stimulated some improvement in the King's sexual performance. She also became a sworn enemy of Choiseul.[3]

French intelligence operations in England were less successful than those run by Choiseul in the royal bedchamber. Louis XV took a personal interest in the spies sent to England by his own personal intelligence agency, the *Secret du Roi*,* which had incurred the wrath of Madame de Pompadour a year before her death when she discovered its papers hidden by Louis in his private quarters. The chief spy sent to England was the flamboyant and unpredictable Chevalier d'Éon de Beaumont, who was appointed temporary Minister Plenipotentiary to the Court of St James

---

* The *Secret du Roi* was often at odds with the Foreign Ministry. French envoys sometimes received two sets of instructions, both signed by the King, which contradicted each other. (Scott, *Birth of a Great Power System*, p. 82.)

in the spring of 1763, pending the arrival of the new French ambassador, the comte de Guerchy. D'Éon was outraged by the prospect of being relegated to a mere embassy secretary when the new ambassador arrived in London. He refused to hand over his official papers to Guerchy, ignored letters of recall, and threatened to reveal his secret assignment as agent of the *Secret du Roi*. In March 1764 d'Éon caused a sensation in both London and Paris by publishing some of the official diplomatic correspondence he had refused to hand over to Guerchy. Though his book stopped short of revealing d'Éon's role as secret agent, Horace Walpole pronounced it 'full of wit' with 'a thousand curious circumstances'.[4]

Guerchy began, and lost, a pamphlet war with d'Éon. The ambassador was accused of attempting to assassinate d'Éon and jeered by mobs as he travelled round London. The philosopher David Hume, then working as secretary to the British ambassador in Paris, warned the French Foreign Ministry that, if they tried to kidnap d'Éon, the French embassy in London would be stormed and 'nobody would be able to stop the British people having their revenge on the French ambassador and his retinue'. The standoff continued for a decade, complicated by widespread rumours from 1770 onwards that d'Éon was really a woman. Despite secret attempts by agents of the *Secret du Roi* to purchase d'Éon's compromising documents from him, they were still in his possession on the death of Louis XV in 1774. On becoming king, Louis XVI was initially inclined to wind up the *Secret du Roi*. One of its agents, the prominent playwright Pierre-Augustin Caron de Beaumarchais, fresh from his success with *The Barber of Seville*, claimed, however, to be able to reach a settlement with d'Éon. He was as good as his word, though the agreement was both eccentric and unprecedented.

The agreement (or 'Transaction'), signed by d'Éon on 4 November 1775, required him to 'readopt' women's clothing, thus implying that his real gender was female. Though there is no reliable evidence that d'Éon had ever dressed as a woman during his earlier career as soldier and diplomat, he had since become an enthusiastic transvestite. Beaumarchais claimed in a letter to Louis XVI's Foreign Minister, the comte de Vergennes, that 'this crazy woman is insanely in love with me' and that they were to be married – another of the flights of fancy which made Beaumarchais a successful dramatist but, like d'Éon, an unreliable spy. For Vergennes, the 'Transaction' had the advantage that, if the unpredictable d'Éon did reveal the correspondence linking him with the *Secret du Roi* or cause other embarrassments, it would be possible to dismiss him as a hysterical female fantasist.[5]

Though d'Éon never mastered the art of walking in high heels, he so enjoyed life in London as 'Britain's first openly transvestite male'[6] that he did not return to France until twenty-one months after signing the 'Trans-action' with Beaumarchais. On 21 November 1777, following a four-hour toilette supervised by Marie-Antoinette's dressmaker, Rose Bertin, the 49-year-old d'Éon was at last presented in female dress at court to Louis XVI and his queen. 'She had nothing of our sex except the petticoats and the curls', complained the vicomtesse de Fars (among others). After a fortnight at Versailles, the court ended the embarrassment by banishing d'Éon to the provinces.[7]* Today's British support group for transgender people, the Beaumont Society, is named in honour of the Chevalier d'Éon de Beaumont.[8]

While d'Éon languished in the provinces, Beaumarchais continued to combine a flamboyant career in both drama and intelligence. In May 1776, two months before the American Declaration of Independence, Vergennes authorized him to found a company, 'at your own risk', to supply arms to the American rebels: 'It is important that the operation should have in the eyes of the British government and even the Americans the character of a private speculation of which we know nothing.' With secret financial support from both the French and Spanish crowns, Beaumarchais founded the front company Roderigue Hortalez et Compagnie, which by April 1777 had sent the rebels nine vital shiploads of military supplies, only one of which was intercepted by the British.[9]

The Continental Congress had been quick to grasp the need for foreign intelligence at the outbreak of the Revolutionary War. On 29 November 1775 it created the Committee of Secret Correspondence, the distant ancestor of today's CIA, for the sole purpose of 'Corresponding with our friends in Great Britain, Ireland and other parts of the world'.† Two weeks after its foundation the Committee wrote to one of the first of its secret correspondents, Arthur Lee, an American-born Old Etonian lawyer resident in London:

> It would be agreeable to Congress to know *the disposition of foreign powers toward us*, and we hope this object will engage your attention. We need not hint that *great circumspection and impenetrable secrecy* are necessary. The Congress rely on your zeal and ability to serve them, and will readily compensate you for whatever trouble and expense a compliance with their desire may occasion. We remit you for the present £200.

---

* D'Éon's career has, unsurprisingly, generated a considerable mythology, such as the claim that he penetrated the court of the Russian Empress Elizabeth, dressed as a woman.
† The Committee of Secret Correspondence became the Committee of Foreign Affairs in April 1777 but retained its intelligence functions.

Arthur Lee was a disastrous choice as secret correspondent in London. Though he later became notorious for his paranoid tendencies, he failed for some time to realize that his secretary, John Thornton, was a British agent.[10]

Like Berlin in the Cold War two centuries later, Paris during the American War of Independence attracted more spies than anywhere else in Europe. Britain's chief intelligence target at the outbreak of war was the seventy-year-old Benjamin Franklin, who arrived in France in December 1776 as principal commissioner of the Continental Congress (chief American envoy), after a difficult Atlantic crossing which, he complained, 'almost finished me'. Franklin's welcome in France made up for the voyage. He was already famous as scientist, man of letters and champion of the liberties of the New World against British oppression. In 1752 Louis XV had publicly thanked him for his electrical experiments and discovery of the lightning rod, which saved the spires of many churches. Not till the visit to Paris almost two centuries later by President John F. Kennedy and his wife, Jackie, did any American visitor receive similar acclaim. Parisians lined the streets to witness Franklin's entry into the capital. According to John Adams:

> His name was familiar to government and people, to kings, courtiers, nobility, clergy, and philosophers, as well as plebeians, to such a degree that there was scarcely a peasant or citizen, a *valet de chambre*, coachman or footman, a lady's chambermaid or a scullion in a kitchen, who was not familiar with it, and who did not consider him as a friend to human kind.

Appearing without a wig among 'the Powder'd Heads of Paris', Franklin succeeded in creating an image of homespun New World virtue, which he successfully maintained throughout his decade as American envoy in France. 'Figure me', he wrote to a friend, '. . . very plainly dress'd, wearing my thin grey strait Hair, that peeps out under my only Coiffure, a fine Fur Cap, which comes down my Forehead almost to my Spectacles.'[11]

In 1997 the Central Intelligence Agency declared Franklin a 'Founding Father of American Intelligence': 'His efforts in what is known today as covert action were wide-ranging and usually successful.'* The secret side of Franklin's role as chief American commissioner has often been overlooked or underestimated. From the moment he arrived in France, he began a covert propaganda campaign against Britain by planting anonymous articles in the press. One of his targets was Britain's use of mercenaries from the German state of Hesse. Shortly after his first meeting with

---

* In 1997 one of the three meeting rooms in the CIA's newly founded Liaison Conference Center was named in his honour. (Rose, 'Founding Fathers of American Intelligence'.)

Vergennes, Franklin arranged the publication of a fabricated letter to the commander of the Hessian mercenaries from a German aristocrat, who was supposedly paid a bounty by the British government for every American soldier they killed. The fictional count advised the Hessian commander that, because the British paid no bounty for wounded soldiers, as many as possible should be allowed to die: 'I do not mean by this that you should assassinate them; we should be humane, my dear Baron, but you may insinuate to the surgeons with entire propriety that a crippled man is a reproach to their profession, and that there is no wiser course than to let every one of them die when he ceases to be fit to fight . . .' Franklin was a clear winner in his propaganda battle with the British ambassador in Paris, Lord Stormont, who also made use of disinformation, thus introducing into fashionable French conversation the verb 'stormonter' as a synonym for telling untruths – a pun of sorts on *mentir* ('to lie').[12] Franklin was both more talented and more unscrupulous than Stormont.

While conducting psychological warfare against the British, however, Franklin was himself successfully deceived by British intelligence. His chief assistant at Passy, near Paris, where he established the American mission, was his protégé, Edward Bancroft. Born in Massachusetts, Bancroft had moved to London in 1767, studied at St Bartholomew's Hospital and begun a successful career as scientist and writer. With Franklin's backing, he was elected Fellow of the Royal Society (FRS) in 1773 at the age of only twenty-nine. Bancroft was the first FRS to become a major spy. Franklin instructed Silas Deane, who arrived in Paris five months before him as the first American commissioner in July 1776, to make secret contact with Bancroft, whom Deane had once taught at school: 'Procure a meeting with Mr. Bancroft by writing a letter to him, under cover to Mr. Griffiths at Turnham Green near London, and desiring him to come over to you.'[13] Having received the letter, Bancroft arrived in Paris at the same time as Deane and was given a key role in the American delegation. He was regularly sent by Deane and, later, Franklin on intelligence-gathering missions to London. In March 1777, while on one of his missions, Bancroft was arrested in London and imprisoned as an American agent. A distraught Deane wrote to the Congress: 'Dr Bancroft is arrested in London for corresponding with and assisting us . . . I feel more for Dr Bancroft than I can express.'

Unknown to Franklin and Deane, Bancroft was a double agent in the pay of the British; his arrest in London had been arranged simply to strengthen his cover. After a few weeks he was released from prison and allowed to return to France. Bancroft had been recruited as a British agent in December 1776 by Paul Wentworth, who had moved from New Hampshire to London a decade earlier and made a successful living by speculating in stocks and land, as well as running an agent network in France for William Eden (later 1st Baron Auckland), who combined the roles of spymaster and Undersecretary in the Northern Department in the government of Lord North. The Eden papers contain an undated, draft memorandum[14] in which Edward Bancroft, using the rather transparent pseudonym 'Dr Edward Edwards', agreed to 'correspond with P. Wentworth whatever may come to his knowledge' on matters which included:

> The progress of the [American] treaty with France and of the assistance expected . . . The same with Spain and of every other court in Europe . . . The means of obtaining credit, effect and money and the channels and agents used . . . Franklin's and Deane's correspondence with Congress in secret . . . Descriptions of the ships and cargoes, the times of sailing and the ports bound to . . . The intelligence that may arrive from America.[15]*

Among Bancroft's intelligence reports on French ship movements across the Atlantic were full details of the departure of the twenty-year-old marquis de La Fayette for America in April 1777 from the Spanish port of San Sebastian, headed 'directly to Port Royal South Carolina', aboard a ship paid for by himself, as well as the names of the French officers accompanying him. 'To harm England', declared La Fayette, 'is to serve (dare I say avenge) my country.' Bancroft reported that, though the French court pretended to disapprove of La Fayette's private expedition to support the American rebels, Marie-Antoinette and all the ladies at court were passionate supporters of the dashing marquis. La Fayette felt such confidence in Bancroft that he later invited him to join an attack on the English coast (which, however, failed to materialize).[16] The marquis went on to become both a French national hero and one of the heroes of the American Revolution, commemorated by a series of cities (Fayettevilles in Arkansas, Georgia, North Carolina and Tennessee) and monuments erected in his honour. But if the Royal Navy had been able to use Bancroft's intelligence to intercept La Fayette's initial expedition, he would have become a mere footnote in the history of the American Revolution. In April 1778 another intelligence report from Bancroft revealed that Admiral d'Estaing was

---

* Opinions differ on the date of the memorandum. Walter Isaacson, who cites this passage, gives the date as December 1776; more recently, Thomas Schaeper has argued persuasively for a later date. Whatever the date of the document, however, it probably accurately summarizes the intelligence Bancroft was expected to collect from the time of his recruitment by Wentworth.

about to leave Toulon with a fleet of seventeen ships of the line and frigates 'to destroy or secure the English fleet'.[17] D'Estaing, like La Fayette, was not intercepted during his crossing of the Atlantic. Despite the superiority of the Royal Navy, there is no evidence that intelligence from Bancroft or any other informant led to the capture of a single French vessel.[18] Intelligence was at the time poorly integrated into British naval operations.

Once a week Bancroft walked through the Tuileries gardens in Paris next to the Louvre and left messages for Wentworth written in secret ink between the lines of bogus love letters hidden in the hollow of a box tree. Initially paid £500 a year for his work as a British agent, Bancroft did so well that his salary was doubled.* Even though Bancroft was not fully trusted, partly because of his speculation on the Stock Exchange, the British government was often better informed than Congress about the work of the American commissioners in Paris.[19] The reports from Bancroft most valued by Eden and British ministers were probably those on the negotiations, begun by Franklin, which led early in 1778 to the conclusion of two Franco-American treaties by which France recognized the independence of the United States and signed an alliance promising support in the war with Britain.

As well as giving Wentworth copies of American documents during the negotiations, Bancroft also took part in drafting some of them. In September 1777 he informed Wentworth that 'we' (Franklin, himself and probably Deane) were drawing up an important document to be submitted to both Vergennes and the Spanish ambassador in Paris.[20] Thanks largely to Bancroft, the negotiations with Vergennes got off to a bad start. He gave Wentworth advance details of a request by the American commissioners for seven times as much French aid as they were already covertly receiving. The British ambassador, Lord Stormont, was thus able to protest to Vergennes about the request even before Franklin had delivered it. Vergennes, in turn, complained to the Americans at their failure to keep secret their negotiations with him.[21] Bancroft suspected that Vergennes and the French negotiators were engaged in a devious strategy designed to avoid making a public commitment to support the Americans. He reported to Wentworth: 'It seems to me impossible to conjecture the real intentions of 60 [France] & 136 [Spain]. The former is so addicted to deception that it would appear to me very doubtful whether its assurances to America ought to be more candid than those to 57 [England].'[22] The French mood changed early in December 1777, when news reached Paris of the first major American victory of the Revolutionary War, at Saratoga

---

* Bancroft also made money by using his inside information to speculate on the stock markets. (Isaacson, *Benjamin Franklin*, ch. 13.)

in October, and the surrender of almost 7,000 British troops commanded by General John Burgoyne. Madame de Brillon, a talented musician, composed a triumphal march (still sometimes performed today) in honour of the victory, which she played for Franklin at a private concert.[23]

The Franco-American treaties concluded in February 1778 were a diplomatic triumph for Franklin: indeed, one of the greatest triumphs in the history of American diplomacy. But the CIA is also justified in claiming that France's agreement to provide open, rather than covert, support for the Americans was facilitated by Franklin's 'influence operations'. After Saratoga, Wentworth was instructed to offer secret peace terms to Franklin which offered the Americans almost everything they wanted – except independence. Franklin had no intention of accepting the offer but fuelled French fears that he might do so if France failed to sign an open military alliance. During the first week of 1778, Franklin secretly encouraged press articles reporting that British envoys were in Paris and that he might reach agreement with them unless the French promptly agreed to an alliance. He also privately passed on to the French Foreign Ministry a distorted account of his meeting with Wentworth. Franklin succeeded in what the CIA now calls 'perception management'. Two days later Vergennes sent his secretary to ask the American commissioners: 'What is necessary to be done to give such satisfaction to the American commissioners as to engage them not to listen to any proposition from England for a new connection with that country?' Franklin responded by proposing the outline of the treaties signed on 6 February.[24] Among those present at the signing was Edward Bancroft, who promptly hired a special courier to take copies of the treaties to London. He later boasted that Lord North's government knew within forty-two hours. It seems likely that this was only a minor exaggeration. On 9 February Lord North, who had probably received Bancroft's intelligence report on the 8th, informed George III of its contents.[25]

Bancroft was very much more than unpaid secretary to the American commissioners. John Adams, who arrived in Paris in 1779, praised his 'clear head' and 'good Pen'.[26] Impatient to obtain the latest intelligence from Bancroft as quickly as possible, Wentworth travelled to France at least eight times between May 1777 and February 1778, as well as meeting Bancroft twice in the Netherlands and once in London.[27] Bancroft boasted, probably accurately, of providing more intelligence than all other British agents in France combined.[28] Not until the Soviet agents Larry Duggan and Alger Hiss penetrated the State Department during the presidency of Franklin Roosevelt a century and a half later did American diplomacy suffer such a serious penetration.[29]

Unlike Franklin and Deane, Arthur Lee, who had become the third

Congressional commissioner in Paris, was deeply suspicions of Bancroft: 'I have evidence in my possession that makes me consider Dr Bancroft as a criminal with regard to the United States.' But Lee was equally suspicious about Franklin, and his paranoid tendencies had become so notorious that his warnings about Bancroft were disregarded. His credibility was further undermined when his own private secretary was exposed as a British agent.[30] Franklin, meanwhile, followed the conclusion of the Franco-American treaties by plotting with the celebrated American naval commander Captain John Paul Jones an attack on the port of Whitehaven, where Jones had begun his naval career. The original plan was to burn the hundreds of ships crowded in the port's anchorage. But, having lost the element of surprise, Jones had to make a hasty retreat after burning only a single ship and spiking a number of cannon. A recent historical assessment by the CIA Center for the Study of Intelligence concludes, however, that the raid was 'an important achievement for America in terms of propaganda and morale'. A hostile landing had taken place at a British town for the first time in almost a century, causing an increase in the price of shipping insurance rates and considerable anxiety in the British shipping industry.[31]

The breach in British–French diplomatic relations in March 1778 caused by the conclusion of the Franco-American alliance made the task of Edward Bancroft and of British intelligence in general more difficult. With the closure of the French embassy in London, the Deciphering Branch no longer had intermittent access to intercepted diplomatic despatches from Paris, which it had successfully decrypted since the Seven Years War.[32] From March 1778 Bancroft ceased to leave intelligence reports in the dead-letter box in the Tuileries gardens, because there was no longer any British agent to collect them. Until the Dutch entered the war against Britain at the end of 1780, it was possible for Bancroft to communicate secretly with Wentworth via the United Provinces. Thereafter most of his messages were probably taken by small boats across the Channel under cover of darkness.[33]

Though only fragmentary evidence survives of the contents of Bancroft's intelligence reports during the years following the breach of British–French diplomatic relations, it is clear that he provided a wide range of reports on Franco-American relations and some of the key figures involved in them – notably his friend Benjamin Franklin, who became US Minister Plenipotentiary in 1778. Bancroft was able to spend hours alone reading (and sometimes helping to draft) confidential American documents in the newly recognized US embassy at Passy.[34] In the years before the British defeat at Yorktown in October 1781, he was often the bearer of unwelcome intelligence and had to face the classic problem of 'telling truth to power'. While generally well informed on international relations,

George III was a poor judge of intelligence. Though taken in by the inventions of a mercenary spy, who reported directly to him,[35] he took a personal dislike to Bancroft, complaining that some of his reports were 'exaggerated' or 'without foundation', and 'calculated to intimidate'.[36]

In 1780 George III was also shown a packet of intercepted despatches which La Fayette had sent to Vergennes on a French ship captured by the Royal Navy in the Atlantic. Though thrown overboard, it was recovered by British sailors who jumped into the sea. Its contents were successfully decrypted by Francis Willes, who had become head of the Deciphering Branch after the death of his father, Bishop Willes, in 1773. George III cannot have been encouraged by what he read – though, as in the case of Bancroft's reports and with more justification, he may have doubted its reliability. In a despatch dated 20 May, La Fayette eulogized the ability, honesty and constancy of 'mes amis Américains'. He reported over-optimistically that, if French troops arrived in time, New York could be captured from Sir Henry Clinton, and that George Washington was thinking of conquering Canada.[37]

Though Britain, unsurprisingly, had the advantage over the American rebels in intelligence operations in Europe, the reverse was true in America. 'First in war, first in peace, first in the hearts of his countrymen', as Henry Lee famously described him, George Washington also ranks first in the early history of US intelligence. He wrote in July 1777:

> The necessity of procuring good intelligence is apparent & need not be further urged. – All that remains for me to add is, that you keep the whole matter as secret as possible. For upon Secrecy, success depends in most Enterprises of this kind, & for want of it, they are generally defeated, however well planned . . .[38]

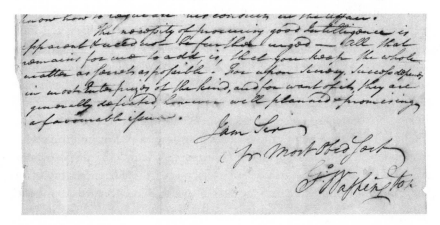

George Washington on the 'necessity of procuring good intelligence' and keeping it 'as secret as possible'.

Ironically, Washington's understanding of the importance of military intelligence, and his success in using it, owed much to his ability to learn from his earlier experience as a British army officer operating against the French, who were to become his allies against the British in the Revolutionary War.[39] In 1753, at the age of only twenty-one, Washington, then a major in the Virginia militia, was sent with an Indian scout on a mission from Virginia to the Ohio wilderness to discover whether French forces were on English soil and, if so, to instruct them politely to withdraw. Part of his assignment was secret: to collect intelligence on French forts, garrisons and communications. At dinner one night in the fort of Venanges (since renamed Fort Franklin), Washington drank little while French officers 'dos'd themselves pretty plentifully': 'The Wine . . . soon banished the restraint which at first appeared in their Conversation, & gave license to their Tongues to reveal their sentiments more freely. They told me it was their absolute Design to take possession of the Ohio, & by G – they would do it.'[40] Two years later Washington fought under General Edward Braddock during his crushing defeat by the French at Fort Duquesne (now Pittsburgh), a disaster due largely to British ignorance of the strength of enemy forces.* Lack of intelligence proved fatal to Braddock and nearly fatal to Washington; two horses were shot from under him and he emerged from battle with four bullet holes in his coat. Had the enemy pursued him instead of stopping to plunder English supplies of rum, Washington would probably have perished.[41] His experience of the 'French and Indian Wars', as they became known, convinced him that 'There is nothing more necessary than good intelligence to frustrate a designing enemy, & nothing that requires greater pains to obtain.'[42]

When he took command of the US Continental Army at Cambridge, Massachusetts, on 3 July 1775, Washington was determined to be better informed than Braddock twenty years before. 'Gaining intelligence' about the British forces, he wrote, was 'one of his most immediate and pressing Duties'.[43] On 15 July he recorded in his accounts a payment for the curious sum of $333.33 (presumably one instalment of a 1,000-dollar payment) to an unidentified agent, whom he instructed to enter British-occupied Boston 'to establish a secret correspondence for the purpose of conveying intelligence of the Enemys movements and designs'.[44] Washington's correspondence with officers of the Continental Army contains frequent requests for 'the earliest Advises of every piece of intelligence which you shall judge of importance'.[45] He was also deeply concerned about the

---

* Washington had, however, received an accurate plan of Fort Duquesne by Major Robert Stobo. (Stobo, *Memoirs of Major Robert Stobo*, pp. x, 20–23.)

threat posed by British espionage. 'There is one evil that I dread', he wrote to Joseph Quincy, '& that is their Spies . . . I think it is a matter of some importance to prevent them from obtaining Intelligence of our Situation.'[46]*

The most famous, though far from the most talented, of Washington's spies was one of the first: a 21-year-old Yale graduate, Nathan Hale, who was sent to collect intelligence on British forces in Long Island in September 1776. Though Hale was selected for the mission by Lieutenant-Colonel Thomas Knowlton, commander of his newly organized Ranger Regiment, Knowlton's choice was personally approved by Washington. Hale, however, who operated under his own name, was badly prepared for his first experience of espionage. His cover as a schoolteacher looking for work after the start of the academic year was unconvincing and he had never previously been to Long Island. All that is known with certainty about Hale's mission to Long Island from his landing on the morning of 16 September to the night of the 21st is an entry in the daybook of the commander of British forces, General Sir William Howe, for 22 September: 'A spy from the Enemy (by his own full confession) apprehended last night, was this day Executed at 11 o'Clock in front of the Artillery Park.'[47] According to a patriotic but plausible tradition, Nathan Hale declared just before he was hanged: 'I only regret that I have but one life to lose for my country.' His British executioners, impressed by his bravery, may have recognized his now famous last words (possibly the most famous in the history of espionage) as the paraphrase of a line from the well-known tragedy *Cato* by Joseph Addison. Statues of Hale, hands trussed behind his back as he awaits execution, stand today both on Yale's Old Campus and in front of CIA headquarters at Langley, Virginia – the only statues ever erected in honour of an American spy.[48] To most Americans, as they looked back on espionage during the Revolutionary War, Nathan Hale's bravery and patriotism mattered more than the failure of his mission. His hanging by the British in September 1776 must surely have been in Washington's mind when he refused a personal appeal four years later from the captured British spy Major John André to be executed by firing squad rather than 'die on the gibbet'. On the orders of George III, André became the second British spy to be buried in Westminster Abbey.†

* Washington's main counter-espionage organizer was the future Chief Justice John Jay, who organized a network of at least ten counter-intelligence agents. In 1997 the CIA named him as 'America's first counterintelligence chief'. (Rose, 'Founding Fathers of American Intelligence'.)
† The first spy to be buried in Westminster Abbey was Aphra Behn in 1689 (see above, p. 237.) – not a precedent which George III is likely to have had in mind. In 1782, two years after André's execution, a monument to him designed by Robert Adam was erected in the nave at the King's expense. André's remains were brought from the United States and buried close to the monument in 1821. www.westminster-abbey.org/our-history/people/john-andre.

Washington was personally involved in so many intelligence operations that, in the absence of an intelligence staff, he sometimes found it difficult to keep track of them all.* He wrote absentmindedly to one of his agents: 'It runs in my head that I was to corrispond [*sic*] with you by a fictitious name, if so I have forgotten the name and must be reminded of it again.'[49] His reluctance to delegate much of the running of intelligence operations reflected the lack of professional staff officers among the citizen soldiers of the Continental Army. Had Washington possessed an adequate intelligence staff, he would surely not have lacked the basic intelligence on battlefield terrain that led to his nearly disastrous defeat at Brandywine Creek in September 1777. The failure of local militia to send scouts to reconnoitre the British advance, combined with Washington's ignorance that there was a ford across the creek immediately to his north, led to the loss of at least 1,200 of his 11,000 troops. Deception was central to Washington's survival strategy during the terrible winter that followed in Valley Forge, Pennsylvania. He prepared fake documents in his own hand, full of references to non-existent infantry and cavalry regiments under his command, which were then passed to the enemy by double agents. The British credited Washington with over 8,000 troops he did not have and mistakenly concluded he was too strong to attack when he was, in reality, at his most vulnerable. But for his successful deception operation, the Continental Army might not have survived the winter. Overall, Washington avoided more battles than he fought – which goes far to explain why he won the Revolutionary War. His strategy was less to engage the enemy than to outlast him.[50]

During 1778 Washington gave the commander of his light infantry, Brigadier-General Charles Scott, additional responsibilities as his 'intelligence chief'. Scott gave up this role after only a few months for unspecified personal reasons, of which the most important may well have been his lack of aptitude for intelligence. Soon after his appointment, Scott sent five men on simultaneous, independent scouting missions to Long Island, intending to compare their reports. Probably as the result of inadequate preparations and poor cover, three were quickly caught.[51] Scott was succeeded as intelligence chief by the much more junior but far more talented Major Benjamin Tallmadge, who had been a contemporary at Yale of Nathan Hale. At the

---

* Unsurprisingly, Washington's involvement in espionage has given rise to a number of myths. Among them, it appears, is the supposed contribution of an alleged double agent, John Honeyman, to his victory at Trenton in December 1776. (https://www.cia.gov/library/center-for-the-study-of-intelligence/csi-publications/csi-studies/studies/vol52no2/the-spy-who-never-was.html.)

age of only thirteen, the precociously intelligent Tallmadge had been offered a place at Yale by the college president but, at his father's insistence, delayed enrolment until he was fifteen. He was well ahead of many of his older college contemporaries. 'Being so well versed in the Latin and Greek languages', Tallmadge wrote later, 'I had not much occasion to study during the first two years of my collegiate life.'[52]

Tallmadge quickly grasped the importance of intelligence in the Revolutionary War. His most important agent network was the Culper spy ring set up in August 1778 to gather intelligence on the British troops commanded by General Sir Henry Clinton, who had recently occupied New York City.* Two centuries later, a study published by the CIA Center for the Study of Intelligence concluded that the most important intelligence obtained by the Culper ring was a report in July 1780 from Agent 355 (also known as 'Lady'), whose identity has never been discovered, that Clinton intended to send British troops by sea from New York City to Newport, Rhode Island, to attack newly arrived French forces under General Rochambeau before they could recover from their two-month crossing of the Atlantic. As soon as he received Agent 355's report on the afternoon of 21 July, Washington began drawing up a deception plan to persuade Clinton to change his mind. Bogus orders signed by Washington ordering preparations for an attack on New York City were handed to a British military outpost by a local farmer who claimed to have found them by the roadside. Believing that an attack was imminent, Clinton recalled troops then on their way to attack Rochambeau in order, needlessly, to strengthen the city's defences. The Culper ring and Washington's talent for deception thus saved the vulnerable French forces from probable defeat and enabled them to join with the understrength American army.[53]†

So far from suspecting that he was the victim of a deception operation by Washington, Clinton had reason to believe that he had achieved a major penetration of the Continental Army. In May 1779 General Benedict Arnold sent a secret message to Clinton in New York, using the codename 'MONK', offering to change sides at an agreed moment, as well as to provide intelligence in the meantime. His choice of codename is significant. Arnold saw himself as the successor of the British republican General George Monck (or Monk), who had changed sides at the end of the

---

* The leading members of the Culper ring were Abraham Woodhull, a farmer from Setauket, New York (codenamed Samuel Culper Sr), and Robert Townsend, a Manhattan merchant (codenamed Samuel Culper, Jr.).

† Given his previous use of deception, it is scarcely conceivable that Washington would have failed to try to deceive Clinton on this occasion. Unsurprisingly, however, no document survives ordering the bogus documents signed by him to be passed to the British.

Interregnum and taken the leading role in restoring the monarchy in 1660[54] – just as Arnold planned to do in America. Though nowadays remembered (even by the Simpsons) as the ultimate American traitor, Arnold had begun the Revolutionary War as a patriot role model. Had he been killed during the American victory at Saratoga in 1777, Arnold might stand next to Washington in the American pantheon of revolutionary military heroes.

In August 1780, at Arnold's request, Washington put him in command of the forts at West Point fifty miles north of Manhattan on the Hudson River, later home of the US Military Academy. Washington thought of West Point as the 'key to America', from which it would be possible to neutralize Clinton's base in New York. Arnold planned to hand over West Point to the British and agreed a price with Clinton of £20,000 if he succeeded – half that if his plan failed. Major John André, a young officer on Clinton's staff disguised as a merchant, travelled to meet Arnold in late September to arrange the final details of his defection and the surrender of West Point. Had Arnold's plan succeeded, Washington might have lost the war. On André's way back to New York, however, he was captured by American militia, who found incriminating papers hidden in his boots. Their commanders failed to grasp the significance of the papers and informed Arnold, giving him just time to flee down the Hudson on a British warship. André, captured in his civilian disguise, was hanged as a spy. Arnold, rewarded for his defection with a lump sum of £6,315 and an annual pension of £360, became a British brigadier-general.[55]

Unaware that he had been deceived by Washington about the threat to New York, Clinton must have been reassured by the regular, detailed intelligence he received on his movements in the summer of 1780. Agents reported on 27 June that Washington was moving towards Peekskill, on 6 July that he was staying at the house of Joseph Appleby, on 8 July at Thomas Tompkins's and on 14 July at Edward Brown's. Clinton also received accurate and detailed battle-order intelligence on the forces of both Washington and Rochambeau.[56] What no agent could tell him, however, was Washington's plan of campaign. When Washington decided in mid-August 1781 to move south against the forces of Lord Cornwallis, he arranged for more fake despatches, indicating that his objective remained New York, to fall into British hands. Washington strengthened the deception by setting up camp at Chatham, New Jersey, and assembling boats along the Jersey shore in preparation for a crossing to Staten Island.[57]

George III, meanwhile, was seriously confused by bogus intelligence sent personally to him by a fraudulent mercenary agent in his sixties, codenamed 'Aristarchus', whose real identity remains unknown. 'My last

Dispatches from Paris', he warned the King in 1780, 'happily discover a secret Plot against your Majesty's Life.' The French had chosen as the 'most favourable spot' for their 'horrid and bloodthirsty machination' the Queen's Garden in Buckingham Palace, where George sometimes went for an evening walk. Characteristically, 'Aristarchus' gave no indication of why Louis XV's notoriously diffident successor, Louis XVI, who had taken seven years to consummate his marriage to Marie-Antoinette, should have become the only French ruler of the Ancien Régime to approve the assassination of a foreign monarch. Nor did he explain how he had 'happily discovered' this improbable plot. Early in 1781 'Aristarchus' reported that Benjamin Franklin (whom he misspelt 'Franklyn') had discovered that a secret meeting was to take place in Antwerp between the Emperor Joseph II and the French 'Duke of G.' Franklin had recruited 'a Frenchman some time residing at Brussels on account of a Duel' to spy on the meeting: 'The method projected by Franklyn is for this Spy to get himself concealed in the Chimney or behind the Arras of the Room, in which the Emperor and his royal Highness ['the Duke of G.'] shall from time to time hold their secret conference. Money is not to be spared on this account.' How the exiled French duellist was to evade the numerous royal guards and gain access to either the chimney or the arras during the secret meeting was not explained.[58]* Washington, unlike George III, would never have taken such nonsense seriously.

The crucial gap in British intelligence during the final stages of the Revolutionary War was naval rather than military or political. Without good naval intelligence, Clinton and other British commanders could not keep track of the assistance from France, which was to prove crucial to Washington's victory. Though the Royal Navy lacked the means to track French fleets as they crossed the Atlantic, it missed repeated opportunities to monitor their movements in the West Indies and off Rhode Island. Admirals de Grasse and de Barras were able to evade British surveillance and reinforce French forces in the Chesapeake Bay area, thus effectively isolating Cornwallis's 7,000-strong army on the Yorktown peninsula in Virginia in the autumn of 1781, and making his position untenable. While the French fleet prevented Cornwallis from escaping by sea, La Fayette, who had at least one agent among Cornwallis's servants, cut off his escape route by land.[59] The 11,000 American forces under Washington's command were reinforced by 9,000 French troops and French artillery from Rhode Island.[60]

* When the reports from 'Aristarchus' to George III were first released early in 2017, commentators surprisingly took them seriously.

Once Washington had begun the siege of Yorktown, his most valuable intelligence came from intercepted British despatches decrypted by the Boston schoolteacher and founder member of the Committee of Secret Correspondence, James Lovell, today remembered as the father of American codebreaking. On 21 September 1781 Lovell sent the current British cipher, which he had solved, to Washington, to enable intercepted British despatches to be decrypted as quickly as possible. Two weeks before Cornwallis's surrender on 19 October, Washington wrote to Lovell:

> I am much obliged by the Communication you have been pleased to make me in your Favr. of 21st ulta.
>
> My Secretary has taken a copy of the Cyphers, and by help of one of the Alphabets has been able to decipher one paragraph of a letter lately intercepted going from L[or]d Cornwallis from Sir H[enr]y Clinton.[61]

Lord North famously remarked on hearing the news from Yorktown: 'Oh God, it is all over.' George III disagreed. Though Cornwallis's surrender had settled the outcome of the war, skirmishing thus continued for almost a year. A peace treaty with Britain recognizing US independence was not concluded until 1783. The Yorktown campaign and the scattered fighting which followed left Washington with a fascination for codebreaking often overlooked by his biographers.

The lead role in psychological warfare during the peace negotiations was taken by Benjamin Franklin. A printer by trade, Franklin had set up a printing press at Passy soon after his arrival in France and specialized in disseminating 'hoaxes' (disinformation), which he used as black propaganda. One of his most successful productions was a forged copy in 1782 of a Boston newspaper, complete with local news and bogus advertisements. The main article in the paper claimed that the British governor of Canada was paying his Indian allies for American scalps, many of them from women and children. It quoted a bogus letter from a Captain Samuel Gerrish, of the New England militia, claiming that a British officer, James Craufurd, intended to send to England 'eight Packs of [colonists'] Scalps, cured, dried, hooped and painted, with all the Indian triumphal Marks'. Packet 'No. 1' allegedly contained:

> 43 Scalps of Congress Soldiers killed in different Skirmishes; these are stretched on black Hoops, 4 Inches diameter; the inside of the Skin painted red, with a small black Spot to note their being killed with Bullets. Also 62 of Farmers, killed in their Houses; the Hoops red; the Skin painted brown, and marked with a Hoe; a black Circle all round, to denote their being

surprised in the Night; and a black Hatchet in the Middle, signifying their
being killed with that Weapon.

The story was used by opposition Whig politicians in Britain to attack the
conduct of the war. It was frequently reprinted in the United States until
finally exposed as fraudulent in 1854.[62]*

Throughout the skirmishing which followed Yorktown and the prolonged peace negotiations, Washington continued to pore over intercepted
despatches and agent reports, personally sifting and collating the intelligence, recognizing that the whole picture was usually more important
than any single item of intelligence, however sensational. After Lovell had
sent him a number of decrypted British despatches in March 1782, Washington wrote to him:

> I thank you for the trouble you have taken in forwarding the intelligence
> which was inclosed in your letter . . . It is by comparing a variety of infor-
> mation, we are frequently enabled to investigate facts, which were so intricate
> or hidden, that no single clue could have led to a knowledge of them[. I]n
> this point of view, intelligence becomes interesting which but from its
> connection and collateral circumstances, would not be important.[63]

As this letter shows, Washington was his own chief intelligence analyst
as well as his own spymaster. His sophisticated grasp of intelligence,
unequalled by any British commander in North America, was at the heart
of his strategic vision.

Though Washington, in the view of most military historians, was no
more than a competent field commander, he was, in very difficult circumstances, an exceptional commander-in-chief who, as well as defeating the
enemy, had to deal with internecine warfare both in a faction-ridden
Congress and among the officers of the Continental Army (who, according
to John Adams, 'quarreled like cats and dogs'). Washington dealt with the
immense stresses and strains of his role as commander-in-chief in part by
what a recent study of his accounts calls an 'almost compulsive spending
on luxury goods in midst of war'. He regularly spent, entirely from his
and his wife's resources, five times the salary of one of his generals on
casks of Madeira. As Washington pored over intelligence reports, trying
to assess their significance, and drafted instructions to agents, it is easy

* A study by the CIA Center for the Study of Intelligence cites the article as an example of
Franklin's skill in the use of disinformation (Rose, 'Founding Fathers of American Intelligence'). There is, however, no mention of disinformation in a number of Franklin's recent
biographies, which appear to find difficulty in coming to terms with the unscrupulous side
of the great man's personality.

to imagine him with a glass of Madeira at hand. Other wartime luxuries included expensive clothes, fine tablecloths, the best English carriages and grand dinners, some prepared by a French chef.[64]

As President of the United States from 1789 to 1797, Washington continued to take personal responsibility for foreign intelligence. In his first State of the Union message to Congress on 8 January 1790, he requested a 'competent fund' to finance intelligence operations. Congress responded six months later with an Act setting up the Contingent Fund of Foreign Intercourse, better known as the Secret Service Fund ('for spies, if the gentleman so pleases', as was later acknowledged in the Senate). For the first year the fund was $40,000. By the third year it had risen to over $1 million, about 12 per cent of the federal budget – a far higher proportion than the massive intelligence expenditure of the late twentieth century. The fund was used for a great variety of purposes, not all strictly related to intelligence, ranging from bribing foreign officials to ransoming American hostages in Algiers. Washington correctly foresaw that all his actions as first President would set precedents for his successors. Thus it was with the Secret Service Fund. Congress required him to certify what sums he had spent but allowed him to conceal both the purposes and recipients of payments from the fund. A century and a half later the Central Intelligence Act of 1949 authorized the Director of Central Intelligence to adopt similar accounting procedures.[65]

During his lifetime Washington's role as spymaster was little mentioned. But in 1821 it provided the plot for the first major American spy novel, James Fenimore Cooper's *The Spy*. The central character is Harvey Birch, an English spy 'possessed of a coolness and presence of mind that nothing seemed to disturb', who, after being killed in action, is finally unmasked as a patriotic American double agent working in the enemy camp for Washington. Clasped to Birch's dying breast is 'a tin box, through which the fatal lead had gone'. Inside the box is a secret document whose contents, though not revealed until the last page of the novel, will have been guessed by attentive readers about 200 pages earlier:

> Circumstances of a political nature, which involve the lives and fortunes of many, have hitherto kept secret what this paper now reveals. Harvey Birch has for years been a faithful and unrequited servant of his country. Though man does not, may God reward him for his conduct!
>   Geo. Washington

Though James Fenimore Cooper is now best remembered as the author of *The Last of the Mohicans* and *The Leatherstocking Tales*, it was *The Spy* which made his reputation, going through fifteen US and many foreign editions before his death in 1851. No other American spy novel achieved such popularity until the Cold War.⁶⁶*

For one and a half centuries after Washington, none of his successors as President came close to rivalling his grasp of intelligence. Even the great wartime presidents, Abraham Lincoln, Woodrow Wilson and Franklin Roosevelt, made no significant attempt to learn from his example. Though the United States had led the world in military intelligence during the Revolutionary War, by the outbreak of the First World War it lagged behind all the major combatants.⁶⁷

* Like the fictional Birch, James Rivington, who had posed as a wartime British propagandist, was afterwards hounded by American patriots unaware of his true role.

16

The French Revolution and
the Revolutionary Wars

On 14 July 1789 even a well-organized security service, which the Ancien Régime did not possess, could not have foreseen the subsequent course of the French Revolution. Those who began the Revolution that day by storming the Paris fortress prison of the Bastille, in the belief that they were striking a blow against tyranny, were surprised to discover, instead of the many prisoners of despotism they had expected to find, only four convicted forgers, two 'lunatics' and a dissipated noble imprisoned at the request of his family. (The more seriously dissipated marquis de Sade had been transferred from the Bastille to an asylum ten days earlier.) The symbolism of the fall of the Bastille, however, proved so powerful that its anniversary has since become France's National Day. The initial values of the Revolution were enshrined in the 'Declaration of the Rights of Man and of the Citizen', passed by France's National Constituent Assembly on 26 August. It began by declaring, 'Men are born and remain free and equal in rights.' British reactions were mostly favourable. The government of William Pitt the Younger, who had been Prime Minister for the past six years and was still only thirty years of age, believed that the Revolution would make France weaker and war less likely. The Foreign Secretary, Lord Carmarthen, expressed personal delight at the news from Paris: 'I defy the ablest Heads in England to have planned, or its whole Wealth to have purchased, a Situation so fatal to its Rival as that to which France is now reduced by her own intestine Commotions.'[1]

The British embassy in Paris and its small group of informants* were ill equipped to interpret the 'intestine Commotions' which followed. John

---

* The only British embassy informant in 1789 whose name has survived is one Hippisley (of whom no further details are available), who informed the ambassador of the hostility of the Paris population after the fall of the Bastille. Unlike the Spanish ambassador, the Duke of Dorset appears to have had no informants in the French Foreign Ministry. (Marquis, *Agents de l'ennemi*, p. 33.)

Frederick Sackville, 3rd Duke of Dorset, ambassador at the outbreak of the Revolution, is far better remembered for his enthusiasm for cricket and aristocratic mistresses (among them such celebrities as Georgiana, Duchess of Devonshire) than for his unremarkable diplomacy. The outbreak of the Revolution forced him to cancel what would have been the first English cricket tour of France.[2] The circumstances which led to his recall from Paris in August 1789 were later described by the deferential Cambridge historian Oscar Browning: 'the Duke of Dorset, a fine gentleman in mind and manners, an ornament to the inner circle at Versailles, was recalled because his liveried servant had been seized by the mob and a letter from the Duke to the Comte d'Artois [a younger brother of Louis XVI] found in his pocket.'[3]

Earl Gower, who was appointed ambassador in Paris in June 1790 at the age of thirty-two,* did not, like Dorset, have the opportunity to become 'an ornament at Versailles'. In October 1789 a revolutionary mob had forced Louis XVI to abandon the palace of the Sun King and move to the Tuileries Palace in the centre of Paris. Gower was scarcely better equipped than his predecessor to understand the complexities of revolutionary politics. He had no previous experience of diplomacy and, after two difficult years in Paris, gave up his diplomatic career.[4]

At the same time as Gower's arrival in Paris, the Foreign Office, with Pitt's approval, sent two agents, William Miles and Hugh Elliot, on a secret mission to negotiate directly with leading members of the National Assembly without informing the court and the King's ministers.[5] Miles, a political writer whose pen, he assured Pitt, had been 'indefatigable in your service', posed as an English supporter of the Revolution and succeeded in gaining admission to the Jacobin Club of radical revolutionaries.[6] Elliot was an extrovert Scottish adventurer who had held various second- and third-rank diplomatic posts, and had known since childhood the leader of the moderate revolutionaries, the comte de Mirabeau, who was chairman of the Assembly's foreign affairs committee (*comité diplomatique*) and favoured a French constitutional monarchy on the British model. His brother-in-law, William Eden, then ambassador to The Hague, informed Elliot of the widespread view that there was 'a predominancy of the Hotspur vivacity in your character'.[7] The main purpose of the mission by Miles and Elliot was to persuade Mirabeau and other leaders of the National Assembly not to support the Spanish in the crisis with Britain caused by their occupation of Nootka Sound, at the centre of a rich

* The chargé d'affaires between Dorset's departure and Gower's arrival was the former embassy secretary, Lord Robert Fitzgerald.

whaling region off Vancouver Island. Though Gower believed that, since Mirabeau was not a minister, he could have 'no communication' with him or other members of the National Assembly, he reported to the Foreign Office on 22 October 1790 that, despite Louis XVI's personal support for Spain, the 'popular party' in the Assembly 'has signified to me, through Mr Elliot, their earnest desire to use their influence with the Court of Madrid in order to bring it to accede to the just demands of His Majesty [King George III] . . .'[8] How far Miles's and Elliot's confidential discussions with Mirabeau and other Assembly leaders contributed to this success is uncertain, but Pitt had no doubt that he had achieved a major diplomatic triumph. 'In short', Eden wrote to him, 'there never was a business better conducted or better concluded . . .'[9]

Gower's priority was to provide news from the French court, however trivial. 'I am sorry to inform Your Grace', he wrote to the Foreign Secretary on 2 August 1790, 'that His Majesty has been confined, for some days past, with a tooth-ache and swelled face, accompanied by a slight fever.'[10] Though Gower also reported some popular 'disturbances',* he had little comprehension of the broader political climate. He arrived in Paris at a remarkably idealistic moment in French political history that would have confused any intelligence analyst past or present. The positive achievements of the Revolution continued to be celebrated over much of France. The historian Alfred Cobban picks out as an example of the unprecedented political euphoria in the Paris region a fête on 20 June 1790 which culminated with a banquet for 300 in the bois de Boulogne 'served by young patriotic nymphs on tables decorated with busts of the friends of humanity, Rousseau, Mably, Benjamin Franklin'. Grace consisted of the first two articles of the Declaration of the Rights of Man and of the Citizen, after which the great revolutionary orator Georges Danton proposed a toast to the liberty and happiness of the whole world. Maximilien Robespierre, later the chief organizer of the greatest Terror in French history, and other prominent revolutionaries followed with similarly idealistic toasts. Women dressed as shepherdesses then placed crowns of oak leaves on the heads of deputies present from the Constituent Assembly. The climax came when four of those who had stormed the Bastille a year earlier placed a model of it on a table, destroyed it with their swords and

---

* Gower had some paid informants. He wrote to Grenville on 10 February 1792: 'I have today received His Majesty's additional instructions on the subject of foreign secret-service money, to which I shall punctually conform myself upon all occasions which may occur during my employment abroad' (Browning (ed.), *Despatches of Earl Gower*, p. 154). Almost no information survives, however, about Gower's use of secret-service money.

revealed in its midst a baby dressed in white, symbol of innocence and new-born liberty. Amid applause, the red Phrygian cap of the freed slave was placed on the baby's head. Cobban concludes:

> It seems all very fresh and innocent and even naïve, but unless we can recapture some of the spirit in which such fêtes were held and trees of liberty were planted, and judge them without undue cynicism or wisdom after the event, we shall fail to understand an essential element in the revolutionary victory.[11]

The romantic poet William Wordsworth, who witnessed such innocent euphoria while staying with young revolutionaries in Blois, understood this 'essential element' far better than most:

> Bliss was it in that dawn to be alive,
> But to be young was very Heaven!

By the summer of 1791, by contrast, France was a divided country. A year to the day after the joyful fête in the bois de Boulogne, Louis XVI attempted to escape from Paris with his immediate family to Montmédy, close to the Belgian border, where he planned to put himself at the head of a counter-revolutionary army led by royalist officers. To mark what would have been Louis's first military operation, he took with him a magnificent red uniform. Since the royal family was effectively under house arrest in the Tuileries, the escape required a full-scale intelligence operation. Within the Tuileries, the operation was known only to Louis, Marie-Antoinette and the Queen's favourite (and possibly lover), the Swedish diplomat Count Hans Axel von Fersen. The escape plan was devised by the marquis de Breteuil, who had become Louis's Chief Minister only four days before the fall of the Bastille and later took on the secret role of his Chief Minister in exile. Breteuil's despatches, many of them sent to Paris in the Swiss ambassador's diplomatic bag to avoid interception, have not survived. But it is clear that, partly because of his emphasis on secrecy, they were not easy to read. Fersen wrote to Breteuil, probably quoting Marie-Antoinette, after receiving one of his despatches: 'The ink which you used was so faint that it could only be deciphered by holding it up against the window, and to enable the king to read it I had to copy it out in full; as I dare not trust anyone to do it for me, this took a very long time.' To avoid arousing suspicion from his guards, Louis XVI hid some of his replies to Breteuil in the bindings of pro-revolutionary books which he gave to senior clerics to take out of the Tuileries.[12]

The details of the plan were worked out in secret correspondence between the marquis de Bouillé, commander of forces loyal to Louis at

Montmédy, and Fersen, acting for the King and Queen, in the Tuileries. The royal couple carried out the most difficult part of the plan, the escape from the heavily guarded palace, with courage. During dinner on 20 June 1791, Marie-Antoinette left the table and went to her children's bedrooms, where their governess, the marquise de Tourzel, was waiting. She then accompanied the governess, her daughter Marie-Thérèse, and the dauphin, Louis-Charles, who was disguised as a girl, across the courtyard of the Tuileries in full view of members of the National Guard to a hackney coach driven by Fersen. The Queen returned to the dinner table and, after the departure of the guests, she and the King retired as usual to their separate apartments. Each put on less regal attire and made their way individually to the waiting hackney. At the Barrière Saint-Martin, one of the northern gates of Paris, they changed into a larger *berline* coach, amply supplied with food, drink and chamber pots. The marquise de Tourzel posed as a Russian noblewoman, Baroness Korff, and Louis as her steward, Monsieur Durand.[13] Unsurprisingly, in view of the tight security preserved about the escape plan, the Pitt government received no intelligence warning. Gower was taken completely by surprise. 'The way in which the Royal Family contrived to leave the Thuileries is not yet known', he informed the Foreign Secretary on 23 June, 'the thing is wonderful . . .'[14]

The King's attempted flight to Montmédy was only the second time in his life that he had travelled beyond the confines of Paris and Versailles. Once the *berline* had left Paris in the early hours of 21 June, Louis was rashly confident the Royal Family would not be caught and no longer thought it important to maintain his false identity. At Châlons, Marie-Thérèse later recalled, 'many people praised God for the sight of the king, and offered up prayers for his safe passage'. It failed to occur to Louis that reports of his presence at Châlons would alert hostile forces further along his escape route. Fersen had written to Bouillé on 26 May: 'Everything should depend on speed and secrecy, and if you are not sure of your detachments, it would be better to have none at all, or only to place them after Varennes [130 miles from Paris], so as not to excite attention in the countryside.' Instead of relying on speed and secrecy, however, the escape plan involved stationing detachments of troops along the route. The detachment sent by Bouillé to Varennes arrived too late to prevent Louis being captured there and returned to Paris. By contrast, Louis's younger brother, the comte de Provence (the future Louis XVIII), travelling in a fast carriage disguised as an English merchant, arrived safely in Belgium on 23 June.[15] Had the King also relied on speed and secrecy he too might have escaped, thus making it likely that he, rather than his brother, would later reclaim the throne after the overthrow of Napoleon.

In the aftermath of Louis XVI's return to Paris on 25 June, republicanism emerged for the first time as a serious political force. The main issue
radicalizing the Revolution, however, was the attempt to nationalize the
Church and turn priests into civil servants by the Civil Constitution of
the Clergy. A decree of 27 November 1790 by the National Assembly
(successor of the Constituent Assembly), requiring clergy to sign an oath
of loyalty to the Civil Constitution or lose their benefices, led to a decade
of civil strife. In the west, Brittany, the Vendée, Flanders, Lyons and
Alsace, most priests refused to take the oath and were supported by their
parishioners. A third of the population of the Vendée died in a long-
drawn-out conflict which many saw as a holy war to defend the Catholic
Church. Pitt's government had no contact with the rebels until secret
agents were sent from Jersey in the spring of 1793.[16]

Despite the dark suspicions about Pitt's supposed anti-French plotting
held by many revolutionaries, his main aim for the first three years of the
Revolution was to avoid war. He told the Commons optimistically in February 1792: 'Unquestionably there never was a time in the history of this
country, when, from the situation of Europe, we might reasonably expect
fifteen years of peace, than we might at the present moment.'[17] Even when
France went to war with Austria and Prussia only two months later, British policy remained, in the words of the newly appointed Foreign Secretary,
Lord Grenville, to maintain 'the most scrupulous neutrality in the French
business'.[18]

The Legislative Assembly's decision in April 1792 to declare war on
Austria did even more than religious conflict to radicalize the Revolution.
The combination of foreign war and internal conflict turned France into
the world's first police state, committed to the surveillance and repression
of all opposition. Pressure for its creation came less from revolutionary
leaders than from popular hysteria in Paris, whipped up by conspiracy
theories of a secret alliance between enemies abroad and counter-
revolutionary traitors at home. Many believed that Louis XVI and the
Austrian-born Marie-Antoinette were part of an aristocratic plot to join
forces with the invading Austrian army and its Prussian allies. On 10
August an insurrection by the newly established Paris Revolutionary Commune drove the royal family from the Tuileries. Three days later Louis
was arrested and imprisoned in the Temple, a former medieval fortress.
Britain broke off diplomatic relations in protest.

The closure of the British embassy meant that intelligence operations
could no longer be run from it. In place of the ambassador, the Foreign
Office sent an army officer, Captain George Monro, who had previous
experience of intelligence work, to send secret reports from Paris.[19] With

him went a French-speaking courier to convey his reports to London.[20]*
Monro arrived in Paris at a dangerous time. The dominating figure in the
new government set up after the arrest of the King was the mercurial mob
orator Georges Danton, who sent armed patrols, usually late at night or
in the early hours of the morning, to search houses for weapons and take
suspected traitors into custody. With 3,000 arrests in the final weeks of
August, the prisons were soon full to bursting point. The round-up of
counter-revolutionary traitors in Paris prefigured, on a less enormous
scale, the arrest of 'enemies of the people', also at night, by the NKVD,
Stalin's security and intelligence service, during the Great Terror of 1936–
8. In both cases, most of the victims were probably innocent of the charges
against them, which were motivated more by paranoia than by credible
evidence. But, whereas the Great Terror was state terror, the main impetus
for the Parisian Terror came from the street.

Popular hysteria in revolutionary Paris reached its peak early in September 1792 after the fall of Verdun to the Prussians appeared to open
the way for the invading armies to advance on the capital. In the 'September massacres', paranoid mobs descended on the prisons to butcher
prisoners who they claimed, on no credible evidence, were part of a monstrous fifth column preparing to deliver Paris into the hands of the invaders.
More than two thirds of the approximately 1,400 victims of the mobs
were, in reality, common criminals. Monro's eyewitness reports on some
of the massacres were among the most gruesome ever sent to London by
an intelligence official. Unable at first to credit reports of the savagery, he
visited the Abbaye prison 'to be convinced of what I could not believe',
and found 'some of the mob distributing their justice':

> Those they found guilty were seemingly released, but only to be precipitated
> by the door on a number of piques [pikes], and then amid the savage cries
> of *vive la nation*, to be hacked by those that had swords and were ready to
> receive them. After this their dead bodies were dragged by the arms or legs
> to the Abbaye, which is distant from the prison about two hundred yards.
> Here they were laid up in heaps till carts could carry them away.

The whole area, Monro reported, was 'swimming with blood'.

Among the aristocratic victims was the princesse de Lamballe, mistress
of the Queen's household (and, according to popular fantasy, her lesbian
lover), who was stripped and hacked to death after a mock trial. Though

---

* Monro was recommended to the Foreign Secretary by his Undersecretary, George Burges,
who saw Monro as a man of 'great talent' and integrity (Marquis, *Agents de l'ennemi*,
pp. 36–7).

Monro was not an eyewitness, he reported that 'Lamballe, after having been butchered in the most shocking manner, had her head severed from her body, which these monsters carried about, while others dragged her body through many of the streets. It is even said they attempted to carry it to the Queen, but the guards would not permit that.'[21] Other sources confirm Monro's account. The princess's head, impaled on a pike, was paraded through the streets of Paris to the royal residence in the Temple, where one of the crowd burst inside to demand that the Queen show herself at a window to see the princess's head, 'so you may know how the people avenge themselves on tyrants'. Marie-Antoinette fainted on the spot. She and Louis must by now have had premonitions of the fate that awaited them.[22] Monro concluded his first report to Grenville on the September massacres:

> I ask pardon for giving such a detailed account of such uncommon barbarity, which I am sure must be as disagreeable for you to read as it is for me to commit such acts to paper, but they ought to be particularized to the eternal disgrace of a people who pretend to be the most civilized among the nations of Europe.[23]

One of Monro's main intelligence assignments in Paris, posing as a republican, was to monitor the activities of British republican expatriates, who met regularly at White's Hotel near the place des Victoires. The tone of his reports on them was more mocking than alarmist. In December 1792 he informed Grenville that 'The party of conspirators have now formed themselves into a society . . . ; they have however as yet met with but few subscribers . . .' The great hero of British expatriate republicans was Thomas Paine, author of the international best-seller *Rights of Man*, fêted in France, made honorary citizen and elected deputy to the Convention for the Pas-de-Calais, despite speaking little or no French. Paine, however, seemed shocked by the September massacres and made an unsuccessful appeal in the Convention for clemency for Louis XVI, who, he proposed, might be exiled to the United States. While Monro was drafting a report on the expatriate republicans in Paris, Paine was convicted *in absentia* in England of seditious libel against the Crown. Monro informed Grenville that Paine had left Paris and was 'in the country unwell or pretending to be so'. (In fact he was probably genuinely unwell.) In Paine's absence, the president of the expatriate republican society was the Old Harrovian poet Robert Merry, whom Monro described as 'the author of some pretty poetical pieces', including an ode on the fall of the Bastille. But, Monro added, Merry 'seems ashamed of his associates' and never socialized with them. He returned to England in the following year. Monro picked out seven other 'leading men' in the society. Three of them – two Irish brothers named Sheare and a Mr York (or Yorke) from Derby – were given to violence but lacked the 'weight or abilities to do much mischief'.[24] Monro reported on 31 December:

> Our countrymen here, who have been attempting to ruin their country, are now really much beneath the notice of anyone; struggling for consequence among themselves, jealous of one another, differing in opinions, and even insignificant in a body, they are, excepting a few, heartily tired of politics and addresses. Tom Payne[Paine]'s fate and the unanimity of the English [against the trial of Louis XVI] has staggered the boldest of them, and they are now dwindling into nothing.[25]

The dominating political issue in France at the end of 1792 was the fate of Louis XVI. A new National Convention (replacing the Legislative Assembly) had met on 20 September and voted unanimously next day to abolish the monarchy and establish a republic. The ex-king, henceforth officially known as Citoyen Louis Capet, was placed in even greater jeopardy in November after the discovery in his former bedroom at the Tuileries Palace of the *armoire de fer*, a concealed cupboard containing his secret archive. Though the most incriminating documents had been burnt, no doubt on the King's orders, what remained, including correspondence with the Austrian court, was sufficiently damaging to ensure that he was put on trial on 3 December. Monro was confident that the lengthy trial would not end in a death sentence, reporting to Grenville on 7 January 1793: 'The people of Paris are at present quiet and I flatter myself there is a party strong enough to protect the lives of Their Majesties in case Robespierre's party should arm his banditti against them . . .'[26] Despite the dubious legal basis for the case against him, however, Louis was found guilty on 15 January 1793 of conspiring against liberty and the safety of the state. Though there was a majority of only one in the Convention for an unconditional death sentence, Louis was sentenced to the guillotine two days later. An emotional Monro reported to Grenville on 21 January:

> I am sorry it has fallen to my lot to be the messenger of the most disagreeable intelligence, that I, or perhaps any one else, was ever obliged to communicate. The National Convention after sitting near thirty-four hours on Thursday night [17 January], voted that the punishment of death should be inflicted upon His Most Christian Majesty.[27]

Louis went to the guillotine on 21 January. 'Son of St Louis', said his Irish confessor as he mounted the scaffold, 'ascend to heaven!'[28]

*

By the time Louis was executed, Monro's role as head of the British intelligence station in Paris had been fatally compromised. His earlier work penetrating groups in England sympathetic to the French Revolution had always threatened to blow his cover in Paris. On 10 January he reported to Grenville that a republican English bookseller named Thomson, who had recently arrived in Paris, 'recollected my face and reported that I was a spy in London and that I was here for the same purpose'. Though Monro denied Thomson's charge, he informed Grenville that 'in all the coffee-houses it still gains ground'.[29] Even if Monro had not left Paris at the end of January, the French declaration of war on Britain on 1 February would probably have forced him to do so. Save for the fourteen months after the Peace of Amiens in 1802, France and Britain would now be continuously at war for over twenty years.

After the outbreak of war, probably Monro's most important French contact, the Abbé Michael Somers, a cleric of Irish extraction also known as Charles Somers, became Grenville's main informant in Paris. Somers was a classic example of an ideological agent, inspired by what he called 'the most ardent and disinterested love for the sacred person of my king and for the constitution of my country, which I have seen indignantly outraged'.[30] He had already been asked by his friend Edmund Burke to keep him informed on 'the troubles in France'. Somers wrote to Grenville shortly before Monro's departure:

> If Monro leaves, I shall need to inform you about everything, and perhaps [do so] better than him. The time that I have spent in this country, the obscure environment in which I have been living since the Revolution, the prudence and circumspection which guide my words and actions, all make me hope that I could stay here for some time to come.

According to Monro, Somers had contacts in the *Comité de défense générale* founded on 1 January 1793, a predecessor of the far better known *Comité de salut public* (Committee of Public Safety). What information Somers obtained from the *Comité de défense générale* remains unclear, though some of it came from his friend Admiral Louis-Antoine de Bougainville, who knew members of its naval subcommittee. Somers's regular reports to Grenville ceased after his arrest in August. Though a police search found eleven letters written in English in his apartment, he had destroyed all correspondence with Grenville and claimed to have stopped practising as a priest.[31]

In the aftermath of Louis XVI's execution, the power of the republican police state continued to expand. On 11 March a Revolutionary Tribunal was established in Paris to try suspected counter-revolutionaries. Ten days

later every commune in the country was instructed to set up its own committee of surveillance (*comité de surveillance*). All citizens were told they
had a duty to denounce counter-revolutionaries. As during the Stalinist
Terror almost a century and a half later, many feared that, if they did not
denounce others first, they would be denounced themselves. Apparent
proof of the continuing power of counter-revolutionary conspiracy was
provided by the defection in April of General Charles-François Dumouriez, who tried unsuccessfully to persuade his troops to march on Paris and
overthrow the revolutionary government. The Convention responded by
creating the nine-man (later twelve-man) Committee of Public Safety. In
theory only a supervisory committee of the Convention, in practice it
became the first effective executive government in the history of revolutionary France. Central to its authority and to the Terror over which it
presided were its powers of surveillance, investigation and repression. The
Convention gave the Committee of Public Safety 100,000 livres to pay for
secret agents and another 100,000 livres for secret expenses. Its agent
network was used to monitor public opinion and spread revolutionary
propaganda, as well as to track down traitors.[32]

By July 1793 conscription had given the Committee of Public Safety by
far the biggest army in Europe, which from the autumn onwards won a
series of victories against foreign foes. The Revolutionary Wars were to
transform the nature of European warfare from conflicts between relatively modest professional armies to warfare between large armies of
civilians. France's ability to combine the largest army in world history
with the most inspired generalship since ancient times led it to victory in
the Revolutionary Wars. France's unprecedented military power, in turn,
helped to bring about the military dictatorship which the political theorist
Edmund Burke, the most far-seeing British opponent of the Revolution,
had famously forecast in 1790.[33]

Like twentieth-century police states, the Committee of Public Safety
refused to tolerate the slightest dissent. Jokes at its expense, by the few who
dared to make them, were regarded as evidence of potential treason. Little
more than four years after the Declaration of the Rights of Man and of the
Citizen had guaranteed freedom of expression, the Committee of Public
Safety abolished it. By the Law (in reality a decree) of Suspects of 17 September 1793, the Committee made insults and defamatory remarks against the
authorities, as well as written or spoken disparagement of patriotism, the
Revolution and the Republic, criminal offences. Over the next ten months,
thousands throughout France were arrested for politically incorrect comments. More than one third of the indictments brought before the Revolutionary
Tribunal in Paris were for criminal use of the spoken or written word.[34]

In September, authorized by the Convention and promoted by the Committee of Public Safety, Terror became official government policy for the first time in an allegedly democratic state. In October the Convention issued the Decree on Emergency Government, suspending peacetime rights and legal safeguards, and authorizing coercion and violence. Louis-Antoine de Saint-Just, the youthful chief ideologue of Terror, decreed that, so long as the war continued, the government would be 'revolutionary', in effect a police state without a constitution. The expansion of the police state was reflected in the rapid but still little-studied growth of its personnel. Between the summers of 1793 and 1794, the staff of the Committee of Public Safety increased twenty-fold from 26 to 523.[35]

As well as spying on French citizens, the Committee of Public Safety was obsessed with the threat from foreign spies. A common element in charges during the Terror against many of the revolutionaries unfairly denounced as covert counter-revolutionaries was that they were enemy agents. Robespierre declared, and probably believed, that the revolutionary administration was riddled with foreign spies: 'It would be somewhat strange for us to have the generosity to pay spies from London or from Vienna to help us police the Republic. Yet I have no doubt that we have frequently done so . . .'[36] The mastermind most frequently blamed for the plots was William Pitt.

Pitt's government was indeed trying to set up paid agent networks in Paris during the Terror by using royalist émigrés who claimed to have contacts in Paris. During 1793, however, the émigrés, whose motivation appears to have been more mercenary than that of the Abbé Somers, probably produced more bogus than accurate intelligence. Potentially the most important French network working for British intelligence was run by Antoine-Claude Rey, an ultra-royalist émigré based in Coblenz, which had become a refuge for many counter-revolutionary French exiles. In February 1793 one of Rey's agents, named Ponthou, who was paid £300 per month, claimed to have set up in only three days an espionage network in Paris with four chief agents (each paid two guineas a day) and eight assistants. By June he was also claiming to have working for him 'someone in the Committee of Public Safety' who 'could not be providing me with better service'. William Huskisson, first superintendent of the London Alien Office (of which more below) and later a leading British politician, was rightly sceptical. In July Huskisson wrote to Rey that the intelligence provided by his network, some of it based on well-known rumours, was often ridiculous as well as inaccurate. Rey replied indignantly that he had sent the same intelligence to King Frederick-William II of Prussia and Prince Louis V of Bourbon-Condé, who, he claimed, had warmly thanked him for it.* Beginning early in 1793, another British-financed network run by a royalist émigré, using the name Martin Blanchardie (whose real identity remains unknown), seems to have provided some reliable intelligence on the naval defences of French colonies from official sources in Paris. His financial demands, however, became exorbitant and his claims of access to influential members of the Convention almost certainly exaggerated. British contact with Blanchardie was broken off after he asked for £30,000 to pay members of Convention committees to provide intelligence and for formal appointment as His Britannic Majesty's head of secret affairs in France.[37]

The obsessional hunt for counter-revolutionary traitors and foreign spies during the Terror made Paris too hard an operating environment for British intelligence. The record numbers imprisoned during the Year II of the Republic (September 1793 to September 1794) led to the use of a record number of stool pigeons (*moutons des prisons*) in the cells to report on alleged plots by the prisoners. 'There is no rigged trial of the Year II', wrote Richard Cobb, 'without its *complots des prisons*.' About a third of the surviving papers of the sinister public prosecutor, Antoine Fouquier-Tinville, and of the Revolutionary Tribunal consist of reports of plots, many of extraordinary complexity, from the stool-pigeon informers. Most of the reports were fabricated. The *moutons*, who were prisoners themselves, had to invent or exaggerate prison plots if they were to ingratiate themselves sufficiently with the authorities to win their freedom. If they failed to discover plots, they risked drawing suspicion on themselves.[38]

The most celebrated victim of the *moutons* was Georges Danton. On the first day of his trial, 3 April 1794, Danton put up a vigorous defence. Overnight in the Luxembourg Prison where he was held, however, a fellow prisoner, the former diplomat Alexandre de Laflotte, who had turned informer, sent a letter reporting that Danton and his supporters were planning a prison break-out and had joined a plot to restore the monarchy.

* Marquis (*Agents de l'ennemi*, pp. 43–7) takes a more positive view of the intelligence provided by Ponthou and the rest of Rey's agent network. Huskisson, however, was well informed about French affairs and his judgement was probably correct. Partly educated in France, he had been present at the fall of the Bastille and in August 1790 became a member of the newly established Société de 1789, whose leading light was the liberal aristocrat the marquis de Condorcet, who favoured a French constitutional monarchy on the British model. In December 1790, aged only twenty, Huskisson became private secretary to the British ambassador, Earl Gower, returning with Gower to London after the breach of diplomatic relations in August 1792. He was appointed superintendent of the Alien Office in January 1793, overseeing arrangements for the influx of French émigrés and helping to set up Pitt's main intelligence agency. In July 1794 Huskisson became chief clerk at the War Office. (*ODNB* William Huskisson.)

Saint-Just used the letter to persuade the Convention to bring the trial to an end before Danton could complete his defence. The jury obediently brought in a guilty verdict. Danton went to the guillotine on 5 April with characteristic bravado. As he passed Robespierre's lodging in the tumbril, he pointed a finger and roared: 'You're next!' At the scaffold, he told the executioner: 'Don't forget to show my head to the people. It's well worth a look.'[39] Laflotte was not, however, Fouquier-Tinville's most active *mouton*. The most productive of them, Charles Joubert, was moved from prison to prison, uncovering imaginary plots in, successively, Sainte-Pélagie, the Luxembourg, Saint-Lazare and the Abbaye. Though Fouquier-Tinville must sometimes have doubted the detail in the *moutons'* reports, like Robespierre he had no doubt that all those arrested during the Terror were guilty of counter-revolutionary conspiracy and must therefore be plotting with other traitors.[40] Paranoia was an essential constituent of the collection and assessment of what passed for intelligence during the Terror.

The French revolutionary police state was confused as well as paranoid. The administration of the Terror had increasing difficulty in coping with the sheer volume of mostly bogus intelligence on alleged counter-revolutionary plots. By the summer of 1794 there were at least six different police organizations variously reporting to the Committee of Public Safety, to the Committee of General Security, to the Minister of the Interior, to the Minister of War, to the *mairie*, to the Paris Commune, to Fouquier-Tinville, to the Administration of Police (a body which itself controlled the fifteen sections of *la police criminelle*), and to the *Commission des subsistances*.[41]

Despite, or perhaps because of, the growing administrative confusion, executions during the Reign of Terror rose steadily during the spring and summer of 1794 from 155 in the republican month of Germinal (20 March to 19 April) to 796 in Messidor (19 June to 18 July), There were 342 in the first nine days of Thermidor (19 to 28 July).[42] Almost all the victims of the Terror were accused of involvement in counter-revolutionary conspiracy. Though the rhetoric of conspiracy was common currency during the Revolution,[43] its supreme exponent was Robespierre, who saw behind all individual plots a gigantic overarching conspiracy.[44] Robespierre's extraordinary final speech to the Convention on 8 Thermidor (26 July) was that of a man consumed by incurable conspiracy theory. Counter-revolutionary 'monsters', he warned, were organizing a huge plot which threatened to destroy the Republic. With secret foreign assistance, they had already taken over the Republic's financial administration. Robespierre denounced the head of the National Treasury as 'a counter-revolutionary hypocrite'. France's foreign relations had also, he claimed, been taken over by counter-revolutionaries: 'Almost all [French] officials working abroad . . . have openly betrayed the Republic with an audacity which has gone unpunished right up to this day.' Behind their treason, Robespierre detected, once again, England's 'infernal genius' at organizing counter-revolution.[45] In authoritarian regimes, particularly at times of crisis, conspiracy theory commonly degrades intelligence assessment. In Robespierre's case it almost entirely replaced reliable intelligence on national security. 'Telling truth to power' was impossible. Anyone who had dared to tell Robespierre that there were no significant prison plots would have feared for his life. With a greater volume of intelligence on domestic opposition than any previous regime, the Committee of Public Safety had a far more distorted view than Pitt's government in Britain

Because of his obsession with conspiracy, Robespierre failed to realize that his speech on 8 Thermidor would convince some members of the Convention that the only way they themselves could escape the guillotine in the next stage of the Terror was to guillotine Robespierre himself. The day after, when Robespierre and Saint-Just tried to speak to the Convention, they were shouted down with cries of 'Down with the tyrant!' The Convention voted for the arrest of Robespierre and his closest supporters before they could seek help from the streets. After Robespierre had failed in a suicide attempt, he and twenty-one others went to the guillotine on 10 Thermidor (28 July). France's leading conspiracy theorist had failed to identify the conspiracy which cost him his life. As Cardinal de Retz had written during the Ancien Régime: 'The most distrustful persons are the biggest dupes.'*

Pitt's main anxiety as the French Republic became increasingly violent and extreme was how far it would gain support in Britain. In historical hindsight, the prospect of a British republic never had any chance of generating mass enthusiasm. There were eventually about 2,000 Loyalist societies in England, many times as numerous as those who wanted to follow the French example.[46] During the early years of the French Republic, however, given the speed with which republicanism had taken hold in France despite insignificant support for it at the time of the storming of the Bastille, Pitt could not afford to disregard the threat from English republicans. The tiny existing 'secret service', headed by one of the Home Office

---

* Almost a century and a half later, despite numerous intelligence warnings of a German invasion, Stalin, whose paranoid tendencies during his own Terror equalled those of Robespierre during the French Terror, was completely taken by surprise when the attack came in the early hours of 22 June 1941. (Andrew and Gordievsky, *KGB*, ch. 7.)

undersecretaries, Evan Nepean, expanded into the Alien Office, which was made responsible for monitoring immigration after the passage of the Aliens Act in January 1793.[47]

Though William Huskisson was the first superintendent of the Alien Office, its leading figure by 1794 was William Wickham, a well-connected graduate of Christ Church, Oxford, where he was a younger contemporary of a future Foreign Secretary, William Grenville, and a future Undersecretary at the Home Office, John King, both influential in his later career. As a stipendiary magistrate with the Whitechapel police office from 1792, Wickham was expected to maintain a register of aliens in the Whitechapel area and, almost certainly with the help of informers, to report suspicious foreigners to the Home Office. Though Wickham was not taken in by obviously alarmist reports, at least two other London magistrates were. A Queen Street magistrate reported to the Home Office that '25 Marseillois were sent over to this country armed with daggers for the purpose of assassinating and cutting off any obnoxious characters';[48] a magistrate in Great Marlborough Street passed on a report that eight French soldiers in full uniform had been seen in Parliament Street.

Through his patrician Swiss wife, Eleonore, Wickham had connections with leading families in Geneva, which after the outbreak of war became an important point of departure for British intelligence operations in France. Though no detailed records survive, in the summer of 1793 he was secretly employed by Grenville for an intelligence mission to Switzerland. On his return he wrote to John King, asking to be considered for further Swiss assignments but emphasizing that all communications on the subject 'must *be* and *remain* in strict and perfect confidence between you and me'.[49]

The main intelligence priority of the Pitt government, in which Wickham was closely involved, remained to monitor British sympathizers with the French Republic. The most active were believed to be the members of the London Corresponding Society (LCS), founded in January 1792 in a tavern off the Strand by nine 'well meaning, sober and industrious men'. Six months later, it claimed to have 1,000 members committed to the principle of universal male suffrage, introduced by the French Revolution. Even before the foundation of the Alien Office, the Home Office had a spy in the LCS. An ironmonger named George Lynam seems to have volunteered his services in October 1792, probably in the correct expectation of being paid by the Home Office, and remained its only informant inside the Society until the end of 1793. In November 1792 Lynam sent an alarmist report that the LCS and similar societies were intent on 'corrupting the minds of the lower order of the people by inflaming their imaginations with imaginary grievances and working them up to commit some great excess which may alarm and throw the Country with the greatest confusion'.[50]* In the same month another informer reported that an LCS member, John Frost, a radical lawyer who had just returned from the French Republic, had said in a Marylebone coffee house that there should be 'no kings in this country'. Six months later Frost was put on trial for 'maliciously, turbulently and seditiously' seeking to 'bring our most serene sovereign lord George III . . . into great hatred and contempt'. The defence barrister, Thomas Erskine, denounced the prosecution as an attack on freedom of speech. What Englishman, he demanded, would consent to 'have his loosest and lightest words recorded and set in array against him in a court of justice? . . . If malignant spies were properly posted, scarcely a dinner would end without a duel and an indictment.' Frost, however, was found guilty, sentenced to be struck off the roll of attorneys, to stand for an hour in the pillory at Charing Cross, and be imprisoned for six months in Newgate.[51]

In February 1794 an Alien Office agent reported a conversation with an LCS member who claimed, improbably, that thousands of nine-inch daggers had been ordered and that 'it was determined to put an end to Mr. Pitt and all the leading Men on that side'.[52] Though Wickham may have doubted the detail of this and other agent reports, he took the threat of violence seriously. He also feared that the English Convention which the LCS intended to call later in the year would take its inspiration from the French Convention which had abolished the monarchy and set up a republic. Wickham reported on 8 May: 'The language formerly holden in these Societies was confined to Parliamentary Reform and the correction of abuses; if ever it went further it was only in hints. *Now* the intention to overturn the Government of the Country is openly avowed.' A few days later, the shoemaker Thomas Hardy, secretary of the LCS, and other leading members were arrested and charged with treason.[53] On becoming Home Secretary in July 1794, the Duke of Portland made Wickham superintendent of the Alien Office.[54]† Pitt showed how seriously he took intelligence reports of LCS subversion from Wickham and the Alien Office by personally taking part in the Privy Council interrogation of the Society's leaders. Though no record survives of most of the interrogations,

* Records of payments made to Lynam in 1792 and much of 1793 do not survive. However, on 2 December 1793 he was paid £50 by Nepean and on 25 March 1795 £100 (probably his severance pay) by John King. (Durey, *William Wickham, Master Spy*, loc. 971.)
† Wickham's appointment as superintendent of the Alien Office was not formally gazetted until September 1794.

one of Hardy's co-accused, the radical writer John Thelwall, left this satirical account of his appearance before the Privy Council:

ATTORNEY-GENERAL   [*piano*]. Mr Thelwall, what is your Christian name?

T[HELWALL]   [*somewhat sullenly*]. John.

ATT. GEN.   [*piano still*] . . . With two I's at the end or with one?

T.   With two – but it does not signify [*Carelessly, but rather sullen, or so*] You need not give yourself any trouble. I do not intend to answer any questions.

PITT.   What does he say? [*Darting round, very fiercely, from the other side of the room, and seating himself by the side of the* CHANCELLOR]

LORD CHANCELLOR   [with silver softness, almost melting to a whisper]. He does not mean to answer any questions.

PITT.   What is it? . . . What is it? . . . What? [*fiercely*]

When Thelwall turned his back on his questioners and 'began to contemplate a drawing in water-colours', the Prime Minister ended the interrogation. In November 1794, after spending seven months in the Tower and Newgate, Hardy, Thelwall and their fellow accused from the LCS were tried on a charge of treason. All were acquitted.[55] As a result of evidence at their trial, Lynam's role as a government spy in the LCS became public knowledge. He complained to the Alien Office official who had acted as his controller: 'My name is wrote as a Spye every night in Wallbrook, I have been personaly threatened by a person of one of the Societys at Aldgate, and yesterday received a threatening letter from another quarter . . .'[56] Pitt's administration remained sufficiently alarmed to push through Parliament the Treason Act and the Seditious Meetings Act, both of 1795, which gave the government temporary powers to hold suspects without trial and ban meetings. The Acts were little used. 'There was something restrained, even amateurish', writes the historian Robert Tombs, 'about England's "Terror".'[57]

As well as working for the Home Secretary as head of the Alien Office, Wickham was also given the main responsibility for Foreign Office intelligence. In October 1794 he was sent on a secret mission to Geneva to follow up what appeared to be peace overtures from moderates in the post-Robespierre French government. Conscious of the failure to set up reliable agent networks in Paris during 1793, Grenville wrote to Wickham in December:

We receive little intelligence from France, on which much reliance can be placed, respecting the general disposition of the Country, or the events in the inland and southern Provinces, except what comes thro' Swisserland. It would therefore be extremely material that you should exert yourself to the utmost to procure constant and detailed information from thence: and it will generally be as early as any other that we shall receive . . . respecting the general situation of the Country. It is hardly necessary to add that expense for that purpose will be considered as very well employed.[58]

Though the peace overtures came to nothing, Wickham stayed in Geneva for three years, conducting a great variety of intelligence operations.[59]

The complexities of French revolutionary politics continued to complicate British intelligence gathering. The five-man Directory which seized power in 1795 was an unstable and unpredictable regime throughout the four years of its existence. Much of Wickham's intelligence on it came from the royalist intelligence service, the Agence Royale, which operated secretly in Paris. After the death in prison of the terribly maltreated ten-year-old Louis XVII (the former dauphin, Louis-Charles) in June 1795, the elder of Louis XVI's two younger brothers, the exiled comte de Provence, took the title Louis XVIII. Anxious to gain access to 'Pitt's gold' (also known as the 'cavalry of St George'), Louis XVIII instructed the Agence Royale to cooperate with British intelligence 'and even, if they consider it useful, to establish communication with British ministers'. On the British side, Wickham was put in charge of providing funding for the Agence.[60] Like the rest of Louis XVIII's administration, the Agence Royale was a rather rambling organization. The author of a forty-six-page Agence report passed to the Foreign Office on the 'present state of France', based on four months' investigations, acknowledged that readers might find some details in the report 'futile', but insisted that they were necessary to explain the complex 'evils' caused by the republican regime.[61]

It has been calculated that the Foreign Office spent £665,222 on secret-service operations during 1795–9, as compared with £76,759 in the previous five years. Wickham and James Talbot, his successor in Switzerland, were responsible for 80 per cent of all secret-service money spent by the British on the Continent during the period 1790–1811.[62] Though never short of ideas, Wickham does not seem to have delivered value for money. In 1795 he attempted unsuccessfully to suborn republican generals and to provoke a royalist rising in Lyons, which had a reputation as the most counter-revolutionary city in France.[63] 'Whenever one of his grand designs collapsed', writes the historian Boyd Hilton, 'he simply erected another.'[64] Probably the most successful grand design was to influence, largely by bribery and funding moderate ('constitutional') royalist candidates, the outcome of the spring 1797 'partial elections' to the Council of 500, the lower house of the bicameral parliament which had replaced the Convention two years earlier. Most of those elected in the one third of seats which came up for election were constitutional royalists rather than republicans.[65] 'If the royalists had been united and competently led, and the *émigrés* capable of offering a modicum of concessions', writes Alfred Cobban, 'France was theirs.'[66] But the royalists were neither.

Louis XVIII was incapable of effective leadership. 'It is a great publick calamity at the present time', wrote Wickham to Grenville in April 1797, 'that there should be no one person about the French King at all acquainted with the real state of the interior and of publick opinion in France . . .'[67] Even the members of the Agence Royale intelligence network in Paris were riven by internal feuds. A member of the Agence who arrived in Paris in April 1797 reported that the network had disintegrated into 'a mass of agents, divided into three factions who were tearing themselves apart'.[68] Despite the divisions of the royalists, Wickham still tried to persuade himself that the result of the elections would prove fatal for the Directory. He told Grenville on 25 August: 'I own I have the most confident hope that all is going for the best, and that before the year be over this monstrous edifice will be pulled down.'[69] Less than a fortnight later, three of the French directors, backed by the young general Napoleon Bonaparte and the army, carried out what became known as in the 'Coup of 18 Fructidor', annulled the elections and arrested royalist leaders. The fourth director fled. The fifth, two generals and forty deputies were deported to a penal colony in French Guiana.[70] There were also numerous arrests of royalist agents.[71] Wickham's plotting against the Directory was publicly exposed and he was forced to return to London, believing that he had been betrayed. He wrote to Talbot, who replaced him in Switzerland: 'You must find the spy in our midst: the man who is said to be a spy of the Directory, for there is no spy so good as a double one.'[72]

Wickham's intelligence networks had failed to provide warning earlier in 1797 of what proved to be the last foreign invasion in English history. In February 1,400 Frenchmen, some freed from prison to take part in the invasion, set off under the command of the American pirate William Tate to burn Bristol, then the second-largest city in England, but were forced by gales to land further north, at Fishguard in Pembrokeshire, where they spent their time hunting for food. According to local tradition, the French invaders surrendered after mistaking a group of Welsh women in red cloaks for British soldiers, 'and the Lord took from our Enemies the Spirit of War and to him be the Prais'. Farcical though the episode was, news of the invasion caused financial panic in London and a run on the Bank of England which forced Pitt's government for the first time to end the convertibility of paper money into gold.[73]

The invasion of February 1797 produced periodic scares over the following months, strengthened by spring mutinies in the Royal Navy, that French spies in England were preparing a further invasion. During the summer a doctor who lived near the Somerset coast reported to the Home Secretary 'a very suspicious business concerning an emigrant family who have contrived to get possession of a mansion house at Alfoxden' and were going round the countryside on 'nocturnal or diurnal excursions which they have been heard to say were almost finished'. The doctor suspected they were 'under-agents' working for a French spy in Bristol. James Walsh of the Alien Office, who was sent to investigate, discovered that what the doctor suspected was a French spy ring were in reality William Wordsworth, Samuel Taylor Coleridge and Wordsworth's sister, Dorothy. Walsh lodged at a local inn and began spying on the poets and their guests from behind sand dunes as they sat talking on a beach. He also took a statement from a man who, while waiting at table during a large dinner party at the poets' rented house in Alfoxden, had been alarmed by one of the guests: 'a little stout man with dark cropt hair and wore a white hat and glasses who after dinner got up and talked in such passion that I was frightened and did not like to go near them since'.[74] The passionate dinner guest was probably the radical writer John Thelwall, who had been tried and acquitted of treason three years earlier.[75]

Walsh's surveillance mission illustrates the difficulties of eavesdropping in an era before recording devices. Coleridge was often a difficult man to listen to in normal conversation and even more difficult to eavesdrop on during the long, rambling monologues for which he was notorious. At dinner with Coleridge one evening, his friends and fellow poets, Samuel Rogers and Wordsworth, had the impression they were listening to a single, unpunctuated sentence which lasted for much of the evening. Rogers later recalled that he said to Wordsworth after dinner: 'For my own part, I could not make head nor tail of Coleridge's oration. Pray, did you understand it?' 'Not one syllable', replied Wordsworth.[76] Coleridge mischievously claimed twenty years later in *Biographia Literaria* that the ignorant Alien Office eavesdropper, Walsh, had misunderstood his comments about the great Dutch philosopher Spinoza. Since Walsh had never heard of Spinoza, he allegedly reported back to Whitehall that Coleridge and Wordsworth had been talking about a sinister figure called 'Spy Nozy'. In reality, Walsh said no such thing. 'I think', he informed the Alien Office, 'this will turn out no French affair but a mischievous gang of disaffected Englishmen.' Wordsworth, he added, was already known to the Alien Office, as was Thelwall.[77]

The main threat of French invasion in 1798 was in Egypt rather than in England. General Bonaparte had told the Directory in August 1797: 'To destroy England thoroughly, the time is coming when we must seize Egypt.'[78] On 5 March 1798 the Directory gave him command of the army of Egypt. Had Napoleon been less obsessed by following in the glorious footsteps of his heroes, Alexander the Great and Julius Caesar, he would have realized that he was taking a huge strategic risk that might well end in disaster. Though plans for the Egyptian expedition were kept secret, it was impossible to conceal the assembly of the 40,000 soldiers and 15,000 sailors who set sail from Toulon on 18 May in 300 transport vessels and warships.* Word also inevitably leaked out on some of the 165 *savants* chosen to accompany Napoleon. A distinguishing feature of European imperialism was its interest in obtaining new knowledge from the territories it conquered. Previous imperial conquerors as various as the Romans, Arabs, Mongols and Aztecs had no such interest. By contrast, all major European military expeditions to other continents in the eighteenth and nineteenth centuries, like Napoleon's, took with them scientists and other scholars to study their conquests.[79]

Napoleon's expeditionary force was able to reach Egypt in the summer of 1798 only because of the most serious British intelligence failure of the Revolutionary and Napoleonic Wars. The underlying reason for the blunder was lack of imagination by the Admiralty combined with reluctance by Whitehall departments to share intelligence in time for it to be of operational use.[80] The First Lord of the Admiralty, Earl Spencer, had intelligence reports showing that many of the troop transports being assembled by Napoleon at Toulon were too unseaworthy to venture into the Atlantic and support rebellion in Ireland. The destination of the French fleet was thus almost certainly in the Mediterranean. Spencer wrote on 1 May that it was 'most probable that they are destined either for the coast of Spain or Naples, or (though I can scarce believe it) for the Levant'. He made no mention of Egypt even as a possible destination.[81] Within Whitehall only the Secretary of State for War, Henry Dundas, who was urged by Grenville to 'think with a map in your head', concluded that Napoleon was heading for Egypt.[82] Grenville received some confirmation in May from copies obtained by a British agent of two letters written by a geologist at the Paris École des Mines who was

---

* These are the figures arrived at by research at the Paris Musée de l'Armée. Some other estimates of the size of the expedition vary.

part of the expedition. The geologist reported that other *savants* accompanying Napoleon included professors of Arabic, Turkish and Persian – one
indication that the likely initial destination, though secret, was Egypt.*

The success of Napoleon's reckless gamble in embarking for Egypt also
depended on remarkable good fortune. Admiral Horatio Nelson, who was
sent to the Mediterranean with seriously inadequate intelligence from the
Admiralty to discover what the French fleet was up to, suffered an early
setback when his flagship, the *Vanguard*, lost its masts in a gale on 21
May. The previous day Napoleon's expedition had set sail from Toulon
to Malta, which it was to capture on its way to Egypt. Napoleon travelled
to Egypt in opulent quarters on his magnificent flagship, *L'Orient*, with
his bed on castors to try to prevent sea-sickness, fantasizing about travelling from Egypt 'on the road to Asia, riding on an elephant, a turban on
my head'.[83] While the damage to the *Vanguard* was being repaired in
Sardinia, the slower French fleet passed Nelson's unseen in fog.[84] Nelson
received his best intelligence on Napoleon's destination not from the
Admiralty but in a private letter from John Udney, the British consul in
Livorno. Udney had witnessed Napoleon's victorious Italian campaigns,
which raised him from obscurity to international renown, and, unlike the
Admiralty, grasped the 'unbounded' scale of the 28-year-old's ambitions,
correctly forecasting that he was set on 'getting possession of Egypt . . .
seizing and fortifying Alexandria, Cairo and Suez'.†

Persuaded by Udney that Napoleon was heading for Egypt, Nelson
arrived in Alexandria on 28 June, only to find no sign of the French expedition. On 30 June he left Alexandria to search for Napoleon in Sicily.[85]
Had Nelson received earlier intelligence on the destination of the slow-
moving French fleet, he could probably have caught and crippled Napoleon's
overcrowded warships and transport vessels carrying 40,000 soldiers
before they reached Egypt.[86] If Nelson had caught the French at sea, he
would not have allowed Napoleon to escape; his chances of becoming
dictator as First Consul in the following year would have been slim. The
British intelligence failure which allowed Napoleon to reach Egypt before
Nelson could catch him thus had major consequences for French political
and military history.

---

* The letters, written by the geologist Déodat Gratet de Dolomieu, were secretly sent to
Grenville by Jean-André de Luc, a Genevan philosopher who had been employed by George
III for a confidential mission in the previous year. Though dated 28 March and 11 April
1798, the letters did not reach Grenville until sometime in May. (Marquis, *Agents de
l'ennemi*, pp. 254–5.)
† Grenville failed to circulate a similar warning from Udney outside the Foreign Office.
(Knight, *Britain Against Napoleon*, pp. 145, 147.)

On 1 July 1798, only twenty-four hours after Nelson had left Alexandria, Napoleon landed nearby with his expeditionary force in the greatest amphibious operation since Xerxes' invasion of Greece over two millennia earlier. The *savants* who travelled with him were to become the first Egyptologists. A month later, at Aboukir Bay on the mouth of the Nile, Nelson at last caught up with the French warships he had failed to intercept en route to Egypt and destroyed all but two of them (both of which he was to capture later). His victory brought the Mediterranean under British control and left Napoleon marooned on the Nile with his flagship, *L'Orient*, blown up.[87] British national rejoicing at Nelson's triumph cut short recriminations about the failure to prevent Napoleon's forces reaching Egypt in the first place. Dundas, however, began the first known detailed enquiry into an intelligence failure. After finishing his review in September, he told Grenville that he was full of 'depressed melancholy' at the missed opportunity to prevent Napoleon's Egyptian campaign.[88]

Early in 1799 there was another major British intelligence blunder, though of a different kind. The impetuous James Talbot, who succeeded Wickham in running intelligence operations from Switzerland, became involved in a failed French royalist plot to assassinate the heads of the Directory in Paris. Possibly owing to confusion in the Foreign Office, Talbot mistakenly believed he had the support of Grenville. As soon as Grenville learned of the plot, he told Talbot 'to lose no time in entirely and distinctly putting an end' to his involvement, though recognizing that Talbot had been motivated by nothing more than excess of zeal 'for the advantage of your country'. It was an expensive error of judgement. By the time Talbot had disentangled himself from the assassination plot, he had spent the enormous sum of £377,807 on it.[89] Ten months later the Directory was to be overthrown not by royalist or British plotters but by Napoleon Bonaparte.

'If I am lucky enough to get back to France', Napoleon told a friend while stranded in Egypt, 'the reign of the chattering classes is over.'[90] Boarding a corvette on 23 August 1799, he evaded a series of Royal Navy patrols off the Egyptian coast and in the Mediterranean, reaching Provence after a forty-one-day voyage. Like the British failure to intercept Napoleon before he reached Egypt in the previous summer, failure to prevent his escape just over a year later was to change French political and military history. Though Napoleon had lost most of his expeditionary force during the Egyptian campaign, he claimed on his return to France that he had won a glorious victory. Privately, he knew the campaign had been a strategic blunder and regretted it for the rest of his life. 'If, instead of the expedition to Egypt', he said after Waterloo, 'I had undertaken one against

Ireland, what could England have done now?'[91] At the beginning of 1798 Pitt had indeed been convinced Napoleon was planning a large-scale invasion of Ireland. British agents sent detailed and accurate reports of preparations in French embarkation ports on the Channel. They also reported that Napoleon had visited the ports but were unaware that on 23 February, with the Egyptian expedition secretly in mind, he had decided not to go ahead.[92] The British difficulty in coping with even the small French force under General Humbert which landed in County Mayo in support of Irish rebels in August 1798 shows how much a major invasion of Ireland led by Napoleon might have achieved.[93]

On his return to London at the beginning of 1798, William Wickham had been promoted to the position of Undersecretary at the Home Office, with responsibility for the 'Inner Office', a security and intelligence department within the Alien Office of whose existence few people in Whitehall were aware.[94] The closeness with which Pitt followed intelligence matters in 1798–9 was demonstrated by his many meetings with Wickham, who became his unofficial intelligence chief. As well as having regular access to Grenville and Portland, the Foreign and Home Secretaries, he frequently called on Pitt late at night in his London home, Burlington House, to deliver the latest intelligence. 'On those occasions', Wickham wrote later: 'I was often received in his dressing room, more than once in his Bedroom . . .' Pitt either made a written note on what Wickham told him or 'desired me to report verbally his observations to the D[uke] of P[ortland]': '[Pitt] always conversed with me on every subject contained in the despatches with apparent openness and confidence. I had constant, at one time almost daily opportunities of knowing his private opinion on all great questions then under consideration.'[95] No subsequent intelligence chief had such close contact with the Prime Minister until the Second World War, when the Chief of the Secret Intelligence Service, (Sir) Stewart Menzies, called frequently on Winston Churchill.

By the time Napoleon became First Consul in the coup d'état of November 1799, Whitehall had learned some lessons from Dundas's post-mortem on its failure to foresee the Egyptian campaign. Intelligence henceforth was somewhat better shared between the main departments of Pitt's government.[96] It continued to be so during the three-year ministry of Pitt's friend Henry Addington (later Viscount Sidmouth) which followed his resignation in February 1801. Nelson was far better briefed before his expedition to Copenhagen in March 1801, which led to a hard-fought naval victory and the bombardment of the Danish capital, than he had been when pursuing Napoleon in the Mediterranean in 1798.[97]

War weariness on both sides of the Channel led in March 1802 to the peace treaty of Amiens, which lasted only fourteen months. From February 1802 until January 1804, Wickham was Chief Secretary in Ireland with the rank of privy councillor and, outside Ireland, no longer had any intelligence role.[98] Had he still been unofficial intelligence chief, he might well have saved the Addington administration from at least one intelligence blunder. The new government refused a pension to the Frenchman Le Clerc de Noisy, who had worked for Wickham in both Switzerland and the Inner Office. Le Clerc took his revenge after the Peace of Amiens by returning to France, where he revealed the secrets of the Inner Office and at least some British intelligence sources in France. His former colleague in the Inner Office, Charles Flint, described Le Clerc's defection as a disaster 'of which we shall often have to repent'.[99]*

Neither the Pitt nor the Addington government addressed, or perhaps understood, the most serious gap in British foreign-intelligence collection. British codebreaking was less effective at the beginning of the nineteenth century than for more than a century. The decline of the Deciphering Branch was due partly to the fact that, before his death in 1773, Edward Willes, Bishop of Bath and Wells, royal decipherer for fifty-seven years, had turned the Branch into a family business in order to provide employment for his less talented sons and grandsons. From 1762 until its abolition in 1844, the entire staff were members of the Willes family.[100] The problems created by the Branch's declining cryptanalytic ability were compounded by wartime difficulty in intercepting diplomatic communications. The nine-and-a-half-year breach of diplomatic relations with France from 1792 to the Peace of Amiens meant that there was no French embassy in London whose correspondence could be intercepted. Codebreaking thus had a smaller influence on British policy during the French Revolutionary Wars than during the Seven Years War, when on at least two occasions important diplomatic decrypts had been discussed in Cabinet.[101]

The most ambitious intelligence operation undertaken by the Addington government was its secret support for a French royalist plot to assassinate Napoleon, which began within weeks of the resumption of war with France in May 1803. Addington, who had never previously held ministerial office, may have been unaware of Talbot's expensive involvement in a failed royalist plot to assassinate the heads of the Directory four years earlier. The few ministers and officials who knew of the plot in 1803 were probably motivated, at least in part, by intelligence on Napoleon's

---

* It is possible, but by no means certain, that Le Clerc de Noisy already had a track record as a double agent and had been the unidentified 'spy in our midst' whom Wickham believed had betrayed him in Switzerland (see above, p. 331). Wickham, however, did not suspect Le Clerc.

preparations for an invasion of England which eventually led him to mass 167,000 men in the French Channel ports.[102]*

Unsurprisingly, details of the British part in the plot to assassinate Napoleon were not committed to paper. Some traces of it, however, survive in official correspondence. One of the British agents working with the French royalist plotters wrote on 22 June to Lord Castlereagh, a senior Cabinet minister, asking for £150 for himself and £1,000 for one of the royalist plotters engaged in 'a political intrigue planned by Lord Castlereagh to abduct Bonaparte in 1803'. 'Abduct' was probably a euphemism for 'assassinate'. Castlereagh's closest friend in Parliament, George Holford MP, replied to the agent that if he would 'take the trouble of calling in Downing Street his Lordship will see him upon it'. Though no record survives of what was said at the meeting, in the early hours of 23 August a Royal Navy ship secretly landed the chief plotter, Georges Cadoudal, and some of his associates, on the coast of Brittany. Further plotters landed on 16 January 1804. Following the arrest of a British agent on 29 January, however, the plot began to unravel. Cadoudal was arrested on 9 March after a dramatic chase through the streets of Paris in which he shot one policeman dead and seriously wounded another before being captured. He went to the guillotine on 25 June, shouting 'Vive le Roi!'[103] After the restoration of the monarchy ten years later he was posthumously made Marshal of France. So far as is known, following the failure of the Cadoudal conspiracy, no British government or government agency approved another plot to assassinate a foreign leader until the Second World War.†

* Napoleon did not finally abandon the invasion plan until Nelson's great victory at Trafalgar destroyed much of the French fleet in October 1805.
† In 1944 the Special Operations Executive (SOE) prepared, but never implemented, a plan to assassinate Hitler, codenamed Operation FOXLEY. Wellington, among others, regarded British involvement in attempts on the life of Napoleon as ungentlemanly behaviour. At the Battle of Waterloo in 1815, when told that Napoleon was in British gunsights, he replied that it was 'not the business of commanders to be firing upon one another'. (Roberts, *Napoleon and Wellington*, loc. 4739.)

17

The Napoleonic Wars

By the time Napoleon crowned himself Emperor of the French at Notre-Dame Cathedral in 1804, he had a larger and better-organized military intelligence headquarters than any previous French general. As well as assembling data, the Statistical Bureau in his *cabinet* was responsible for strategic intelligence: questions such as whether the Austrian Habsburg Emperor intended to go to war and, if so, how the King of Prussia would react. The Bureau's sources included agents in most foreign capitals.[1]* Napoleon, however, was not much interested in intelligence reports:

> Nothing is so contradictory and nonsensical as this mass of reports brought in by spies and officers sent on scouting missions. The former see corps in place of mere detachments, the latter report weak detachments in places where corps are present. Often they do not even report their own eyesight, but only repeat that which they have heard from panic-stricken or surprised people. To draw the truth from this mass of chaotic reports is something vouchsafed only to a superior understanding . . .[2]†

This 'superior understanding', Napoleon believed, was his alone.‡ Like many autocrats, he was usually impressed only by intelligence which confirmed his preconceived views.

---

* The imperial *cabinet* took its final form in 1808. (Arboit, 'Napoléon et le renseignement'.)

† Napoleon had high, though conventional, expectations as regards tactical military intelligence: 'Carrying out a rapid reconnaissance of passes and fords, making sure to obtain reliable guides, questioning the priest and the postmaster, making rapid contact with local inhabitants, sending out spies, seizing, translating and analysing postal correspondence, and, finally, responding to all the questions of the commander-in-chief when he arrives at the head of the army – these are the qualities required of a general in a forward position'. (Arboit, 'Napoléon et le renseignement'.)

‡ Professor Van Creveld concludes, after detailed analysis of the Battle of Jena in October 1806, that, despite Napoleon's great victory, his letter before the battle to his brother, King Louis of Holland, 'shows how little he really knew of the Prussians and the extent to which his understanding of their intentions was based simply on map study'. (Van Creveld, *Command in War*, pp. 82, 96.)

The reports of his Statistical Bureau to which the Emperor paid most attention were translations of the foreign press. Napoleon seems to have read British newspaper reports with greater attention than most secret intelligence, believing that they frequently gave more reliable accounts of operations than his own generals. Wellington envied Napoleon his control over the French press. He complained to the Secretary for War and Colonies, Lord Liverpool, in November 1809 that the detailed information published by the uncensored British press on 'the position, the numbers, the objects and means of attacking possessed by the armies in Spain and Portugal' would 'increase materially the difficulty of all operations'. Napoleon agreed. A year earlier, he had written to his Foreign Minister, Jean-Baptiste de Champagny: 'I am angry that you have not sent me the English newspapers, because they give us information about their positions.'[3]

Napoleon was far more imaginative in his use of open sources than of secret intelligence. He was a rapid reader and before each of his campaigns he read as much published literature as possible on the theatre of war and on the history, geography, armed forces, religion and legal systems of his opponents. Eyewitness reports agree that he rarely read any book from cover to cover; he moved on to another book as soon as he had extracted what he regarded as relevant information.[4] He studied in detail the campaigns of Frederick the Great, who had fought in some of the same areas of Central Europe as himself, and later paid tribute to his generalship in a number of lengthy monologues in exile on St Helena.[5] As a student at the École Militaire Napoleon had taken extensive notes on English history. In exile on St Helena he compared Waterloo with French defeats during the Hundred Years War at Agincourt and Crécy: 'Poor France! To be beaten by these rascals!'[6] Napoleon also found time to read plays, poetry and novels, though he was a demanding reader. When reading while travelling in his *berline*, as he frequently did, he would throw any book which displeased him out of the window.[7] Probably no previous commander-in-chief had ever been such a voracious reader. He took with him on campaign his librarian and a personal library of several hundred volumes.[8]

Though the *cabinet noir* (and sometimes the Foreign Ministry)[9] continued to attempt to intercept and decrypt diplomatic communications, Napoleon showed greater enthusiasm for reading books about his foreign enemies and allies than for breaking their ciphers. Unlike Tsar Alexander I and the Duke of Wellington, who were to prove his most dangerous enemies in the final years of his reign and were both keenly interested in decrypted French despatches, Napoleon showed little discernible interest in codebreaking. When shown evidence in 1806 that the Prussians had broken French diplomatic ciphers, he seems to have brushed it aside.[10] The foreign leader whose correspondence he monitored most attentively was Pope Pius VII, whom Napoleon had stripped of the papal states and kept under house arrest first in Savona on the Italian Riviera (1809–12), then in Fontainebleau (1812–14). From time to time members of the Pope's entourage were searched to prevent their conducting secret correspondence on his behalf. The Pope, said Napoleon, could communicate 'as many blessings as he wishes'. Everything else he wrote had to be kept carefully under control.[11]

In general, Napoleon took a more active personal interest in domestic than in foreign intelligence. On St Helena, he revealed to a confidant that he had refused to allow his ministers direct access to domestic correspondence intercepted by the *cabinet noir*. Indeed, the correspondence he was most anxious to monitor was that of his own ministers, senior officials and high command. He retained a jaundiced recollection of the frequent expressions of 'ill humour' he found in their letters during his military campaigns 'because I was taking them away from the pleasures of Paris to be in my service and serve the interest of the state'.[12]*

The man on whom Napoleon depended most for internal surveillance during his first six years as Emperor was his Minister of Police, Joseph Fouché, a former Oratorian teacher who had turned regicide during the Revolution. Napoleon's aide-de-camp, comte Philippe Segur, said (with evident distaste) that Fouché's 'long mobile face' reminded him of 'an excited ferret; one remembers his piercing keen gaze, shifty nevertheless, his little bloodshot eyes, his brief and jerky manner of speech which was in platitudes'. Napoleon, however, believed that Fouché's talent for surveillance was unrivalled. 'Fouché, and Fouché alone', he declared, 'is able to run the ministry of police. We cannot create such men; we must take as we find.'[13]† Surveillance reports to senior government officials on public opinion in many parts of France had become commonplace during the French Republic.[14] Fouché, however, was the first to produce a daily intelligence digest which he presented to Napoleon each morning.[15]‡ From time to time Napoleon sent Fouché correspondence intercepted by the *cabinet noir* for further investigation.§

---

* Charles-Tristan de Montholon was one of the most loyal followers of Napoleon and stayed with him throughout his exile on St Helena. Though his account of the exile was written twenty years later, he is unlikely to have misrepresented what Napoleon told him on the *cabinet noir*.
† Fouché's unreliable 'memoirs' were the work of the ghost-writer Alphonse de Beauchamp.
‡ The reports were drawn up by a former royalist barrister named François, who had been sentenced to death under the Directory but reprieved after informing on other royalists. Fouché added his own comments to François's drafts.
§ In November 1807, for example, he sent Fouché intercepted correspondence from the comte de Lille (Louis XVIII) and asked for a report on its contents. (Vaillé, *Cabinet noir*, p. 313.)

Fouché's agent network was partly financed by levies on brothels and gaming houses, which were also a plentiful source of informers. Fear of his ubiquitous agents helps to account for the lack of conspiracies during the Empire to overthrow Napoleon.[16] Fouché also had some success in intimidating British spies. Having discovered in 1804 that Sir George Rumbold, the British minister in the free city of Hamburg, was running an agent network in France, Fouché sent a detachment of troops by boat to force their way into Rumbold's country residence and seize his files, in breach of international law. Rumbold himself suffered the indignity of being taken to Paris. Following protests by Prussia, which had placed Hamburg under its protection, Rumbold was released after a few days. By that time, as Fouché had intended, British spies operating against French targets had no doubt been intimidated.[17]

Though an admirer of Fouché's black arts, Napoleon never fully trusted him and ensured that he also received domestic-intelligence reports from other sources: among them his loyal aide-de camp, Géraud Duroc. Napoleon later called Duroc 'the only man who had possessed his intimacy and entire confidence'. (Unlike Fouché, Duroc was one of the few outside the Bonaparte family to call the Emperor by the familiar '*tu*'.[18] Even Duroc's correspondence, however, was opened by the *cabinet noir* on Napoleon's orders.[19]) Other confidential sources who reported to Napoleon included Fouché's enemy, Joseph Fiévée, editor of the *Journal des Débats*, which became the *Journal de l'Empire*.[20] Napoleon also directly employed twelve informers, each paid 12,000 francs a year, to send him reports, which he burnt after reading them. He later claimed in exile on St Helena that his personal intelligence network 'worked very well': 'I should have extended this system.' Napoleon admitted, however, that he did not always have time to read the informers' reports before burning them.[21] The Emperor's insatiable appetite for mostly domestic news was not matched by a coherent method for digesting it.

Napoleon also ensured that Fouché did not obtain a monopoly of police or security investigations, some of which he entrusted to the Paris prefect of police, Louis Dubois, and to one of his senior adjutant generals, René Savary. Fouché's intrigues, Napoleon complained, made it necessary to keep him under 'constant supervision, which fatigues me'. In 1810 Fouché began secret, unauthorized peace negotiations with the British Foreign Secretary, Lord Wellesley, Wellington's elder brother. Napoleon told him on 5 June:

> I am aware of all the services you have rendered me, and I believe in your attachment and your zeal; however, it is impossible for me to allow you to keep your portfolio. The post of minister of police requires an absolute and

entire confidence, and that can no longer exist because you have compromised my tranquillity and that of the State.

Napoleon sent Fouché to Rome as governor and replaced him with his
rival, Savary.[22] Both Fouché and Savary played a key role in the suppression of political rights. Though the Empire never came close to creating a
reign of terror, it had about 2,500 political prisoners.[23]

Intelligence played a far more effective part in the British than the French
war effort. Following Pitt's return to power in May 1804, the Secret Service
Vote reached a record £172,830 in 1805, a sum not exceeded for the rest
of the nineteenth century. During the governments which followed Pitt's
premature death in January 1806 at the age of only forty-six, the annual
Vote remained above £100,000 until after the Battle of Waterloo.[24] Senior
ministers during the Napoleonic Wars took a more active interest in intelligence from across Whitehall departments than in any previous conflict.
Before the naval expedition to Copenhagen in 1807, the future Prime
Minister Spencer Perceval, then Chancellor of the Exchequer in the government of the Duke of Portland, noted that: 'Intelligence from so many
and such various sources of B[onaparte]'s intention to force or seduce
D[enmark] into an active confederacy against this country leaves no doubt
of his design.' Napoleon, by contrast, had no intelligence on British preparations for the naval expedition. The British capture of the Danish fleet
at Copenhagen took him completely by surprise.[25]

During parliamentary debates early in 1808 the Portland government
used intelligence to justify the Copenhagen expedition against opposition
criticism, but refused to identify the source.* Government supporters
accepted that the origin of the secret information should not be divulged
'to the curiosity of [Parliament], or to the vengeance of Bonaparte'.[26] For
the first time, the Portland administration publicly declared the principle,
since accepted by all subsequent British governments, that its secret agents
were guaranteed indefinite anonymity. The Foreign Secretary, George

* The main intelligence source was a letter to Canning of 21 July 1807 from the comte
d'Antraigues, a French royalist émigré then resident in London who had been intermittently
involved in intelligence work for over a decade. D'Antraigues's informant was Prince Vasili
Troubetzkoi, an aide-de-camp to Tsar Alexander I during his meeting with Napoleon at Tilsit.
Though there is no proof that, as d'Antraigues claimed to have been informed by Troubetzkoi,
Napoleon and Alexander had secretly discussed at Tilsit the formation of an anti-British
maritime league, on 7 November 1807 the Tsar broke off diplomatic relations with Britain,
annulling all existing British–Russian conventions. Alexander publicly declared that he 'pro-
claims anew the principles of the armed neutrality' previously directed against Britain, 'and
engages never to recede from them'. (Munch-Petersen, 'Secret Intelligence from Tilsit'.)

Canning, put to the Commons the rhetorical question: 'Was this country to say to the agents, who served it from fidelity, or from less worthy motives, "You shall never serve us but once, and your life shall be then forfeit"?'[27] Senior ministers retained unfettered control of intelligence expenditure. Secret Service, said Canning in 1808, remained 'the only fund which has not been pried into by Parliament'.[28]

Napoleon later traced the origins of his downfall to the debilitating effect of the 'Spanish ulcer' on the *Grande Armée*. In 1807 French forces invaded Portugal. A year later Napoleon made his brother Joseph King of Spain, provoking a nationwide revolt which French forces were never able to crush. When Wellington, his eventual nemesis, took charge of British and Portuguese forces in the peninsula in 1809, Napoleon used British press reports sent to him by the Statistical Bureau to justify his overconfidence about the outcome of the Peninsular War. After reading the English press in May 1810, he wrote to the chief of staff of the French army in Spain, Marshal Berthier: 'According to the news that we have from England, General Wellington is no stronger than 24,000 men, English and German, and the Portuguese are not quite 25,000.'[29] Napoleon failed to mention that about three quarters of the far larger French army were tied down by Spanish forces and guerrilla groups.[30] His distorted assessment of the military balance in the Iberian peninsula reflected both the reluctance of the Statistical Bureau to confront him with unpalatable truths (a characteristic example of the problems of 'telling truth to power' in authoritarian regimes) and Napoleon's own tendency to disregard evidence which challenged his own views. Napoleon's military genius did not extend to intelligence.

As well as being the two greatest generals of the age, Wellington (born Arthur Wellesley) and Napoleon had much else in common (including two mistresses). They were the same age, born in 1769. For both French was their second language. The official language of Napoleon's native Corsica (acquired by France a year before he was born) was Italian and remained so until 1859. He learned to speak French fluently only after entering the Brienne Military Academy. Wellington also learned French in France, and became a life-long Francophile after leaving Eton College for the more congenial Royal Academy of Equitation at Angers in 1786.[31] Probably no British general in the Second World War was as fluent in German as Wellington had been in French during the Napoleonic Wars. Though the scale, range and brilliance of Napoleon's many victories exceeded those of Wellington, Wellington not only received better intelligence than Napoleon: he had a better understanding of it too. He also understood France far better than Napoleon understood Britain.

Napoleon's lack of understanding of Wellington was demonstrated by his dismissal of him as a 'sepoy general' – a reference to the Indian private soldiers (*sepoys*) who had served under him in India, most of them excellent fighting men (something the Statistical Bureau may have known from French officers in India but would have shrunk from telling the Emperor). During the wars against the Marathas, the last major obstacle to the establishment of the British Raj, and other campaigns, Arthur Wellesley and his brother Richard conquered an even larger empire in India than Napoleon did in Europe.[32] It was also in India that Wellesley learned the importance of military intelligence. Intelligence played an important part in what he later said was his greatest (though far from his best-known) victory: the Battle of Assaye in 1803 against the larger armies of the Maratha Empire. Wellesley's most valuable strategic intelligence came from senior mercenaries in the service of the Marathas who worked as paid agents in place before they defected with the promise of a British pension. Among them was Colonel J. F. Mieselbach, a battalion commander in the central Indian region of Bundlekund (now Bundelkhand) who, for two years before he left Maratha service in 1803, provided a regular supply of high-quality intelligence. The ruler of Bundlekund, Himmat Bahadur Gosavi, had made Mieselbach both his closest political adviser and head of his personal honour guard.[33]

The most important tactical intelligence before Assaye probably came from two Maratha horsemen captured by Wellesley's forces who revealed on 21 September 1803 that the main Maratha army was much closer than he had thought. Wellesley saw an opportunity for a preemptive attack that would be lost if he delayed – despite the fact that not all his forces were ready for battle.* The attack ended in a famous victory two days later against a much larger army, led by French officers. Like Waterloo, the Battle of Assaye almost ended in defeat. Over a third of Wellesley's 4,500 troops were killed or wounded. One horse was killed under him, a second badly wounded, and he was fortunate to survive. His dragoon orderly was decapitated by a Maratha cannon shot; 'the body being left kept in its seat by the valise, holsters, and other appendages of a cavalry saddle, it was some time before the terrified horse could rid himself of the ghastly burden'.[34]

Wellesley gave more thought than Napoleon to improving the quality of intelligence collection. He quickly became suspicious of the *harkarrah*s, traditional Indian messengers who moved ahead of armies, relaying back information and intelligence but who were apt to tell their employers what

* Wellesley also apparently feared that failure to go on the offensive would jeopardize the safety of his troops. (Cooper, *Anglo-Maratha Campaigns*, pp. 99–100.)

they thought they wished to hear. On 7 November 1803 he wrote in evident annoyance to an East India Company administrator, Sir William Clarke, whom he believed had been misled by his *harkarrah*s:

> Allow me to assure you, my dear Sir, that these hircarrahs [sic] are not to be believed: they never bring any intelligence that is worth hearing, and when they circulate their false reports they do infinite mischief to our cause. I shall be obliged to you if you will be so kind as to desire your hircarrahs to confine their reports to yourself.[35]

A fortnight later Wellesley wrote contemptuously to another correspondent: 'There is no foundation for any of Sir William Clarke's reports.'[36] Wellesley wrote in 1804, the year he won promotion to major-general, that 'one of the great difficulties of war in this country is to obtain intelligence of the enemy's movements and intentions sufficiently early to take advantage of them'. He devised a plan for a new, if rather unwieldy, intelligence department which would be divided into three sections, each separate from the others and reporting separately to him as a way of guarding against the supply of bogus or misleading intelligence brought by individual *harkarrah*s:

> Great care was taken that the persons employed in one department should not be known to those employed in the others, and that they should not communicate. The *hiccarah*s [sic] were highly rewarded, besides receiving monthly pay, particularly when they brought any intelligence on which an operation could be founded; and were punished and turned out of the service when they brought any which was known to be false . . .

To broaden the range of his intelligence sources, Wellesley encouraged local traders (*vakeel*s) to make evening visits to him to pass on 'all that they had heard in the course of the day', and kept in contact with local *amildar*s (governors) and other officials whom he hoped might 'throw light on the enemy's designs'.[37] Despite his improvements to military intelligence, the East India Company remained less well informed about its great empire than either its Mughal predecessors or, probably, the Mauryas two millennia before.[38]

During the Peninsular War in Spain and Portugal, which turned Wellesley (from 1809 Viscount Wellington) into a British military hero and won him a dukedom even before his apotheosis at Waterloo, he remained committed to using agent networks (necessarily rather different to those in India) as one method of gaining 'intelligence of the enemy's movements and intentions sufficiently early to take advantage of them'. In the Iberian peninsula he took advantage of popular hostility to the French invaders. 'Everywhere', he wrote later, 'I received intelligence from the peasants and priests. The French learned nothing.' By 1810 Wellington was receiving plentiful intelligence from networks of correspondents and agents which had been established by his friend Charles Stuart and younger brother, Henry Wellesley, British ministers to Portugal and Spain respectively. Stuart's network included agents based in Bayonne in south-west France, through which most French troops passed on their way to the peninsula.[39]

The key to the success of British intelligence in the Peninsular War was Wellington's management of it. Though the surviving records are incomplete, cryptanalysis (a much greater priority for Wellington than for Napoleon) probably contributed at least as much as agent intelligence. Attacks by Spanish guerrillas against French lines of communications produced a regular supply of intercepted military despatches. Until 1811 Napoleon's generals used simple substitution ciphers which could be broken by using the frequency principle discovered by al-Kindi 1,000 years before.* Over the next few years French ciphers became more challenging. Wellington, however, was fortunate that one of the quartermasters in his army, George Scovell, turned out, probably to his as well as Wellington's surprise, to be a codebreaker of genius. In the spring of 1811 the French army introduced a new cipher known as the 'Army of Portugal Cipher', based on combinations of 150 numbers. George Scovell cracked it within two days. Far more complex was the 'Great Paris Cipher', introduced early in 1812, with 1,400 numbers that could be applied to both words and parts of words in a wide variety of permutations, together with meaningless 'blanks' which could be randomly inserted to confuse codebreakers. The frequency principle enabled Scovell to make a start. Certain numbers – 2, 13, 210, 413 – appeared more frequently than the rest. Scovell was quickly able to establish that 210 stood for 'et', the most commonly used two-letter word in the French language. He was also assisted by despatches which combined unciphered and ciphered phrases. One simple example was '918 ne negligerai'. Since 'negligerai' ('shall neglect') was in the first person, it followed that '918' must mean 'je' ('I'). Though most clues were far more

---

* In April 1811, for example, General William Beresford, commander of an Anglo-Portuguese force operating on the Spanish border east of Lisbon, received an intercepted message sent by the French General Latour Maubourg, written in a cipher which merely replaced each letter of the alphabet by a single symbol. Beresford's quartermaster-general and his deputy were able to decrypt and translate the message on the day it was received. It revealed details of the build-up of a large French force preparing to challenge Beresford on the plains of Estremadura and was probably largely responsible for Wellington's decision to send reinforcements to the area. (Urban, *Man Who Broke Napoleon's Codes*, pp. 89–90.)

difficult, Scovell had largely solved the cipher by the summer of 1812.[40]
The information on enemy troop movements gathered by Scovell's Army
Guides helped him make informed guesses about the identities of persons
and places mentioned in ciphered despatches.[41]

The first decrypted message in the 'Great Paris Cipher' of major operational importance to Wellington was a letter from King Joseph to
Napoleon of 9 July 1812, captured by Spanish guerrillas. Written in small
writing on a sliver of paper, probably to enable it to be hidden in a riding
crop, it revealed that Joseph was bringing reinforcements to join forces
with Marshal Auguste Marmont near Salamanca between the Portuguese
border and Madrid. On 22 July, about two days before the decrypt indicated that Joseph's forces would arrive, Wellington attacked Marmont at
Salamanca and won a major victory. Wellington was able to plan his
campaign for 1813 with a knowledge of French operational plans obtained
from intercepted despatches. He was so enthused by Scovell's decrypts
that he could not resist boasting about them. He wrote to a prominent
Spanish politician, Don Andres de la Vega, in January 1813: 'I enclose an
extract of a letter from King Joseph to Napoleon which was in cipher and
which we have de-ciphered, which is well deserving of your attention and
that of your friends in the Cortes.' The decrypt poured scorn on the Cortes, absurdly claiming that the Spanish people preferred the Bonaparte
dynasty to their own parliament.[42] In circulating the letter, Wellington's
aim was clearly to expose Joseph's regime to parliamentary ridicule. He
showed no awareness, however, of the huge intelligence risk he was taking
by circulating the decrypt. If Napoleon or his senior generals had realized
that the *grand chiffre* had been broken, they would probably have ceased
to use it, thus depriving Wellington of his best intelligence source. Wellington was almost certainly unaware of the historical precedents for his
monumental indiscretion, which went back to Parliament's decision to
publish the decrypted correspondence of Charles I during the English Civil
War.[43] In 1717, after a government White Paper had published decrypted
Swedish diplomatic correspondence, the Swedes adopted new diplomatic
ciphers which for some years the Deciphering Branch was unable to
break.[44] Wellington and Scovell were more fortunate in 1813. Napoleon
and his senior commanders did not realize that the *grand chiffre* had been
broken by the British and continued to use it.

Scovell was far ahead of the few cryptanalysts in what remained of the
Deciphering Branch in London. Though the Branch survived, the official
post of decipherer, occupied successively by a series of members of the
family of Bishop Edward Willes, was abolished in 1812 after the death of
Edward Willes junior[45] – a sign of its declining status. Before the Battle

of Salamanca in July 1812, Wellington sent the new Secretary of State for War, Earl Bathurst, copies of the latest intercepted ciphered French despatches. It was another nine months before Bathurst forwarded a reply from the Deciphering Branch. During that period the London cryptanalysts had found meanings for only 164 of the 1,400 numbers in the Great Paris Cipher. On 24 May 1813 Wellington replied sardonically to Bathurst: 'I am very much obliged to your Lordship for the key of the cipher as far as it had been discovered, which you transmitted to me on the 5th April last; I now enclose for your information such parts of it as have been made out by Lieut Colonel Scovell without reference to the key received through your Lordship.'[46]

Cryptanalysis made a major contribution to Wellington's great victory in June 1813 at Vitoria in north-east Spain which virtually ended French rule. An intercepted despatch of 13 March from King Joseph to the commander of the Army of Portugal, General Charles Reille, revealed that the French were reducing the forces facing Wellington in order to launch an offensive against the guerrillas. Among other important despatches decrypted by Scovell was a message of 14 March sent to Joseph Bonaparte by one of his staff officers, Colonel Lucotte, who was returning from Paris, where he had been given the Emperor's directives on the future conduct of the Peninsular War. Since use of the *grand chiffre* was reserved to senior commanders and the imperial court, Lucotte used a less complex cipher. Though Scovell had not previously encountered it, he wrote dismissively on the decrypted message: 'de-cyphered at Frenada [Wellington's Portuguese HQ] with ease in 6 hours'. Probably having belatedly realized the risk he had taken by passing an earlier intercept to a Spanish politician, Wellington informed Earl Bathurst that 'this letter was in cypher and it is desirable that its contents should not be published'.[47]

Though Vitoria was Wellington's most decisive victory of the Peninsular War, it led to a cryptanalytic setback. Seeing the rout of his forces on 21 June, King Joseph abandoned his royal carriage and fled from the battlefield on horseback. Inside the carriage, in addition to four rolled-up paintings which Joseph had removed from Madrid, Scovell found the King's leather document case and extracted from it a large document inscribed '*Sa Majesté Catholique*', which he immediately identified as Joseph's personal copy of the Great Paris Cipher. Unaware that an important part of his ciphered correspondence had been decrypted by the British for several years, Joseph warned the French War Minister after the battle that his document case with the *grand chiffre* had been lost: 'It may be that it has fallen into the hands of the enemy. You will doubtless think it prudent, Monsieur le duc, to order the creation and dispatch of a new

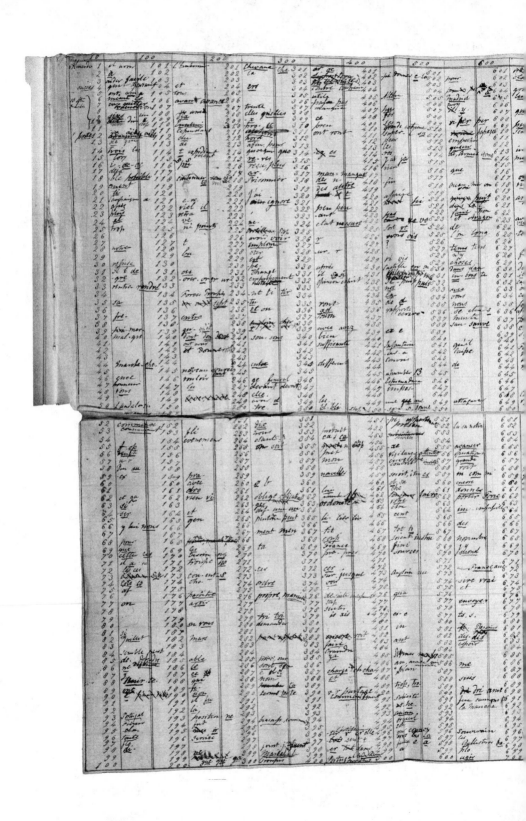

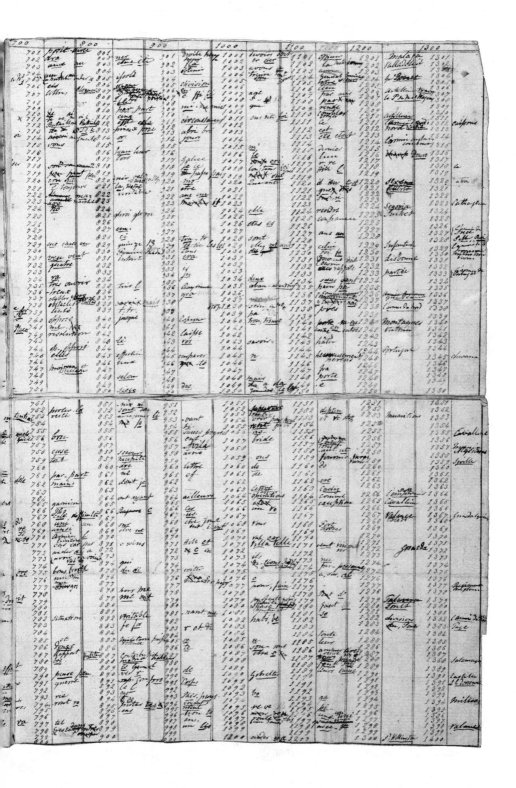

◀ The greatest British codebreaking coup of the nineteenth century: part of George Scovell's solution in 1812 of Napoleon's 'Great Paris Cipher'.

cipher.' The War Minister took Joseph's advice. An intercepted despatch which he sent in July to the commander of the French Army of Catalonia, Marshal Louis-Gabriel Suchet, used a new cipher. Though Scovell began work on the cipher, he (and probably Wellington) seems to have regarded breaking it as a low priority because of the rapid decline in the number of messages they were able to intercept. As the Army of Catalonia fell back towards the frontier, despatches from Paris passed mainly through French territory where Spanish guerrillas did not operate.[48]

After four years fighting an unwinnable war with poor intelligence in the Iberian peninsula, Napoleon invaded Russia with the largest invasion force yet assembled anywhere in the world. During the Russian campaign, as in the Peninsular War, Napoleon's intelligence system was outclassed by that of his opponents. Six months before the campaign began, he had hopelessly unrealistic expectations about the intelligence likely to be available to him. On 20 December 1811 Napoleon told his Foreign Minister, Hugues-Bernard Maret, that, if the invasion went ahead, he was to become head of a new 'secret police' with responsibilities which 'would include being in charge of intelligence on the Russian army and enemy countries, the translation of intercepted letters and documents, and information from POWs, etc.' Little came of this grand design. The head of the Foreign Ministry archives informed Maret on 1 January 1812 that the ministry's Russian files were 'out of date, incomplete and uncertain': 'We have no really certain information on Russia.' On 19 June the French minister in the Grand Duchy of Warsaw, Louis de Bignon, reported to Paris: 'We no longer receive good reports from Russian territory, and at present are only able to form a very vague judgement on the position of their armies.' Four days later, Napoleon's *Grande Armée* crossed the River Nieman to begin the invasion of Russia.[49]

Mikhail Barclay de Tolly, whom Tsar Alexander I appointed Defence Minister in January 1810, had much greater success in acquiring intelligence from France than the Napoleonic Empire did from Russia. Barclay is still remembered as the founding father of Russian military intelligence. A postage stamp was issued in his honour as recently as 2011.

Barclay, whose Scottish ancestors had settled in the Baltic in the mid-seventeenth century, was an experienced commander who, like Wellington, had learned the importance of intelligence at first hand on campaign.

Among his first proposals as Defence Minister, accepted by the Tsar, was the establishment of the Special Chancellery, an intelligence service based on the appointment of military attachés (then called military agents) for the first time in major Russian embassies. (Military attachés were not posted to French embassies until the 1820s.) The existence of the Chancellery, whose establishment took two years to complete, was, to use later intelligence jargon, top secret. Its operations were never mentioned in the annual Defence Ministry reports.[50] Napoleon may never have known of its existence.

Nor is there any evidence that Napoleon, any more than many more recent historians, suspected that Russia had an active *cabinet noir*. At the start of the nineteenth century the Foreign Ministry in St Petersburg set up an Encryption Committee of Russia's leading cryptographers to report to both the ministry and the Tsar on the introduction of new cipher systems, the phasing out of outdated ciphers, and the operation of encipherment and decryption.[51] In March 1800 the Foreign Minister, Nikita Petrovich Panin, wrote to the Russian ambassador in Berlin:

> We possess the ciphers of the correspondence of the [Prussian] King with his chargé d'affaires: if you should suspect [Prussian Foreign Minister Count Christian von] Haugwitz of bad faith, it is only necessary to get him to write [to his chargé d'affaires] here on the subject in question under some pretext, and as soon as his or his King's despatch is deciphered, I will not fail to apprise you of its contents.[52]

By, and probably well before, Napoleon's invasion of Russia, the Tsar's *cabinet noir* was also able to break the ciphers used by the British embassy in St Petersburg.[53] The Prussians too were able, at least intermittently, to break French diplomatic ciphers. In August 1806 King Frederick William III discovered from a decrypted French despatch that Napoleon was engaged in negotiations with Britain, and, in defiance of his treaty obligations to Prussia, had secretly offered to return Hanover to Britain as part of a broader peace settlement. In September, under pressure from his advisers, the King wrote a letter full of recrimination to Napoleon, who sent a mocking reply:

> I am extraordinarily sorry that You have been made to sign such a pamphlet. I write only to assure You that I will never attribute the insults contained within it to Yourself personally . . . I despise and pity at the same time the authors of such a work . . . Believe me, I have such powerful forces that all of Yours will not suffice to deny me victory for long! But why shed so much blood? For what purpose? . . . Sire, Your Majesty will be vanquished! You

will throw away the peace of Your old age, the life of Your subjects without being able to produce the slightest excuse in mitigation![54]*

Napoleon was so contemptuous of the Prussian army and government that he paid little, if any, attention to the source of the intelligence which had alerted Frederick William to his secret negotiations with the British. But, at the time, his inattention scarcely mattered. Once again, sheer military might overwhelmed the advantage drawn by Prussia from its superior intelligence. At Jena in October 1806 the Emperor won one of the greatest victories of his career, later commemorated by the Pont de Iéna over the Seine in Paris.

Though Napoleon had much greater respect for Tsar Alexander than for the King of Prussia, it never occurred to him that the intelligence available to Alexander on France was greatly superior to his own on Russia. Alexander's intelligence on France during the five years of Franco-Russian alliance inaugurated at the meeting between Tsar and Emperor aboard an elaborately decorated raft on the River Niemen at Tilsit in 1807 came from agents and informants in Paris. The most successful military attaché working for the Special Chancellery set up by Barclay de Tolly was the Tsar's aide-de-camp and former page, Alexander Chernyshev, who was already stationed in Paris as the Tsar's personal representative to Napoleon's court. The young and handsome Chernyshev, who was only twenty-two when the Tsar first used him to deliver a message to Napoleon in 1808, was welcomed into the Emperor's household and, quite possibly, also into the bed of his sister Pauline Borghese, a celebrated beauty who posed nude for the Italian sculptor Antonio Canova. Chernyshev became a romantic hero in Paris after rescuing the wives of two French marshals from the palace of the Austrian ambassador when it caught fire during a ball. Prussian diplomats complained to Berlin that they could not match Chernyshev's range of contacts in the imperial court and administration. His paid-agent network included at least three imperial officials, of whom probably the most important, codenamed 'Michel', worked at the heart of the War Ministry. Though 'Michel' had first supplied information to the Russian embassy in 1804, Chernyshev ran him more successfully than ever before.[55] Each month the War Ministry produced a classified printed report with details of the size, movements and deployment of every regiment in the French army, which 'Michel' promptly passed to Chernyshev, who copied it overnight and sent it to St Petersburg. Barclay de Tolly was thus able to

---

* Clark's outstanding history (*Iron Kingdom*, pp. 303–4) gives only this single example of Prussian codebreaking.

follow in detail, month by month, the eastward deployment of Napoleon's forces. Everything, he informed the Tsar, pointed to preparations for a French invasion of Russia. Chernyshev reported to Barclay before leaving Paris at the end of 1811 that all his sources, among them 'officers of great merit and knowledge' with no affection for Napoleon, agreed that his campaign strategy in Russia would be based on big battles and quick victories. The Russian army, he argued, should avoid giving battle and instead use light mobile forces to harass the *Grande Armée* – which, for the most part, was exactly what it did after the French invasion.[56]

The French Minister of Police, Savary, was far more suspicious than Napoleon of Chernyshev's activities but seems never to have identified any of his main sources while he was stationed in Paris. Chernyshev was not deceived by the informers sent him by Savary bearing bogus intelligence. When burning his intelligence files before returning to St Petersburg in December 1811, however, he overlooked a report from 'Michel', which a police search after his departure discovered under a carpet. The identity of 'Michel' was discovered from the handwriting and he became probably the only Russian spy ever to be sent to the guillotine.[57]

Chernyshev's friend, Count Carl von Nesselrode, who had become deputy head of the Paris embassy in 1808 at the age of only twenty-eight, ran a parallel Russian intelligence network before the French invasion concentrating on diplomatic sources. Bypassing the Russian ambassador, from 1809 he sent his intelligence reports to the Tsar via his favourite and chief adviser, Mikhail Speransky,* whom he asked to ensure that none of the confidential details he had obtained on Napoleon's personal habits and eccentricities were mentioned at the Russian court, for fear of compromising his sources. Probably the single most important document obtained by Nesselrode from a paid agent was a secret memorandum on future foreign policy submitted to Napoleon, at his request, by the French Foreign Minister, Jean-Baptiste de Nompère de Champagny, on 16 March 1810. Russia and Britain, concluded Champagny, were natural allies and likely to draw together. France must therefore support Russia's natural rivals: Poland, Sweden and Turkey. Champagny reported that French agents were already encouraging the Ottomans to ally with France in the event of war with Russia. He also forecast that victory over Russia would make possible a 'more grandiose and decisive' policy, 'perhaps more worthy of Your Majesty's genius', which would push the Russian border back beyond the River Dnieper and make possible a full-scale restoration of

---

* Because of opposition to Speransky's plans for liberal reforms, the Tsar gave way in 1812 to noble demands for him to be sent into internal exile.

the kingdom of Poland. Within weeks of Champagny's memorandum being submitted to Napoleon, it was also on the desk of the Tsar.[58]

Nesselrode's highest-level informant in Paris was Charles Maurice de Talleyrand-Périgord, the most sophisticated diplomat of his era as well as an expert in transferring allegiance from one regime to another. Born an aristocrat under the Ancien Régime, he had become an atheist and begun a career as a bishop before becoming, successively, a prominent revolutionary, Napoleon's Foreign Minister, restorer of the Bourbon dynasty after his defeat, and, finally, French ambassador in London. Napoleon knew that Talleyrand was untrustworthy and dismissed him as Foreign Minister in 1807, after complaints from the kings of Bavaria and Württemberg about the large bribes he was demanding from them. On another celebrated occasion, Napoleon, in a fit of rage, accused Talleyrand of betraying everyone, called him 'a turd in a silk stocking', threatened to hang him from the iron railings outside the Tuileries Palace, then stormed out. Talleyrand said regretfully after his departure: 'What a pity, such a great man and so ill-mannered!' Despite Talleyrand's incurable disloyalty, Napoleon remained so captivated by his intelligence, wit and diplomatic expertise that he kept him in his inner circle.*

The Emperor took Talleyrand to his meeting with the Tsar at the Congress of Erfurt in 1808, at which he sought a promise of Russian support in the event of war between France and Austria. Each evening during the Congress, unknown to Napoleon, Talleyrand had a secret meeting with Alexander and urged him not to give the assurance Napoleon was seeking. Talleyrand's best-known twentieth-century biographer, Duff Cooper, calls his action at Erfurt 'treachery, but treachery on a magnificent scale', motivated by concern for the French national interest. But Talleyrand also made a personal profit out of treachery which helped to finance his fabulously opulent lifestyle. He maintained both a magnificent château in the provinces and several *grandes mansions* in Paris, chief among them a luxurious residence on the corner of the Tuileries Palace gardens and the place de la Concorde with, reputedly, the best table in France – and therefore in the world – as well as an excellent library. The large sums which Talleyrand sought and frequently obtained from foreign powers went to subsidize his domestic extravagance. He once secretly asked for (but on this occasion did not obtain) 1.5 million francs from the Tsar to meet some of his debts. 'My heart, in writing to you', he declared, 'is full of gratitude, affection,

---

* Napoleon told his aide-de-camp Jean Rapp after Talleyrand's dismissal: 'You are aware of the esteem and attachment I entertain for that minister.' (Roberts, *Napoleon the Great*, loc. 9423.)

devotion and respect.' Alexander did not, as Talleyrand requested, burn his letter, though it did not surface for many years after Talleyrand's death.[59] Some recipients of such requests doubtless did burn letters of that kind, though there is no means of knowing how numerous they were.

Talleyrand also betrayed Napoleon to Prince Klemens von Metternich, Austrian ambassador in Paris from 1807 to 1809 and future Chancellor. Austria, he told him, should prepare for war with France. Metternich was aware that, no doubt on Napoleon's orders, his diplomatic correspondence was opened by the *cabinet noir*. On one occasion he sent a facetious letter to the *directeur de la Poste*, pointing out an error in the facsimile seal used to reseal his despatches and asking him to improve the facsimile 'so that I continue not to notice anything [amiss]'.[60] In his despatches to Vienna, Metternich started referring to Talleyrand as 'X'. 'X', he told Emperor Francis, advised him not to allow Napoleon to take the initiative in declaring war on him, but to strike first. Talleyrand made clear in January 1809 that he expected financial recompense for his services – 'a few hundred thousand francs, say'. Metternich urged Francis to make a payment of 400,000 francs: 'However large this sum may seem, it is far smaller than the sacrifices to which we are accustomed and the results can be immense. Moreover I cannot tell you how useful X has been to me since our relations assumed this new character. I beg Your Excellency to make your calculations on the high side.'

Before Metternich received a reply he reported new intelligence from Talleyrand in February 1809, revealing that Marshal Nicolas Oudinot had been ordered to lead his army corps to Bavaria: 'X believes that we should use Oudinot's movements as a *casus belli*. We should waste no time. It would be criminal to nurse illusions about Napoleon. He definitely wants war.' Though recognizing the importance of the intelligence, the Austrian Foreign Minister, Johann von Stadion, sent a first instalment of only 100,000 francs. Metternich replied: 'I beg Your Excellency to go as high as the sum I mentioned.' X had supplied two documents of 'immense interest' from Napoleon's office which were so important that he was reluctant to send them to Vienna even by diplomatic bag. They demonstrated that Napoleon was planning war with Russia as well as Austria.[61]

On the eve of Napoleon's Russian campaign, Russian foreign intelligence was the best in Europe. Britain's lack of a Paris embassy meant that its French agent network could not compare with those of Chernyshev and Nesselrode. The *cabinet noir* in St Petersburg was also more successful than the Deciphering Branch in London, which achieved much less than it had done during the Seven Years War. Napoleon underestimated the ability of the Russians to break his ciphers even more than he underestimated

Wellington's codebreakers. For most of the Russian campaign he used the relatively straightforward *petit chiffre* instead of the *grand chiffre*, which he employed for despatches to the Iberian peninsula.[62]

Since the summer of 1810 it had been clear to the Tsar and most of his key advisers that Napoleon was planning a massive invasion of Russia. In January 1812 the French War Minister boasted that the *Grande Armée* had never before been so well equipped for war: 'We have been making preparations for more than fifteen months.' It never occurred to him that he made his boast within earshot of a Russian informant. Most French forces preparing to invade Russia were either deployed in Prussia or travelled across it. From the Russian mission in Berlin, Christoph Lieven (later a long-serving ambassador in London) provided detailed intelligence on their movements.[63] Napoleon, by contrast, suffered not merely from lack of intelligence but also from a reluctance by his generals and other subordinates to give him unwelcome news. Throughout the invasion Napoleon's commanders frequently lied to him about both the health and the food supply of his army. On some occasions he was told that units whose rations were exhausted still had ten days' food supply.[64]

The Tsar, Barclay de Tolly and Prince Mikhail Kutuzov, who became commander-in-chief in August 1812, out-thought and ultimately outfought Napoleon. Save for the Battle of Borodino on 7 September, a week before Napoleon entered the, by then, mostly deserted city of Moscow, Kutuzov avoided set-piece battles and, like the Roman general Quintus Fabius Maximus two millennia earlier,[65] wore down the *Grande Armée* through a strategy of attrition and harassment by Cossack cavalry. Napoleon later admitted that, when he reached Moscow, even though he had lost half the *Grande Armée* with which he had begun the campaign, he 'considered the business as done' – in other words, that he had defeated the Russian army.[66] He also acknowledged that he 'ought not to have stayed in Moscow more than two weeks', in order to give himself time to reach Smolensk before the first winter snows and the arrival of Kutuzov's Cossack regiments from the Don. Instead he made the fatal mistake of delaying his departure for six weeks.[67] Unwilling to accept responsibility for this disastrous error of judgement, he later claimed that he was 'deceived from day to day' by hints that the Tsar was ready to offer peace terms. In reality Alexander had no intention of doing so.[68] Only about 6,000 of the *Grande Armée* made it back to France. Napoleon himself had a narrow escape. Sixty miles after leaving Moscow, he was almost taken prisoner by Tatar *uhlans* (light cavalry). Thereafter he wore a phial of poison around his neck, which he intended to swallow if he were captured.[69]

It became increasingly clear during the invasion of Russia that the Tsar's understanding of whatever intelligence he received was also much better than the French Emperor's. As well as seeking intelligence on the *Grande Armée*, Alexander valued the objectivity of foreign opinions on Russian forces. Alexander attached particular importance to the views of the British military observer Sir Robert Wilson, who published in 1810 *Brief remarks on the character and composition of the Russian army, and a sketch of the campaigns in Poland in the years 1806 and 1807*. In the summer of 1812 Wilson reached the headquarters of the Russian army under Barclay de Tolly in time to take part in the Battle of Smolensk on 16 August. Three weeks later he was invited to an audience with the Tsar in St Petersburg. He then joined the Russian army as British liaison officer ('commissioner') as it harassed Napoleon's forces during their retreat, reporting to the British ambassadors in St Petersburg and Constantinople as well as to London.[70] The Tsar valued Wilson's independent assessment of the performance of Russian forces and their generals, and encouraged him to send him his views on the campaign. The decryption of Wilson's cipher despatches to London, like those of the British embassy, enabled Alexander to judge whether Wilson and British diplomats were equally frank in what they said to him.[71] Wilson may well have been reluctant to repeat to the Tsar his (probably decrypted) report to London that Kutuzov feared a heavy French defeat in the Napoleonic Wars would make Britain too powerful. Kutuzov declared himself 'by no means sure that the total destruction of the Emperor Napoleon and his army would be such a benefit to the world; his succession would not fall to Russia or to any other continental power, but to that which already commands the sea whose domination would then be intolerable'.[72] Wilson became an important intelligence source for London on Prussian and Austrian, as well as Russian, forces. The British ambassador in Vienna, Lord Aberdeen, wrote to the Foreign Secretary, Lord Castlereagh, in 1813: 'From his intimate knowledge of the Russian and Prussian armies, and the great respect invariably shown him by the emperor of Russia and the king of Prussia, he is able to do a thousand things which no one else could do.'[73]

Remarkably, by the spring of 1813 Napoleon had assembled a new army of 200,000 men. But he now had ranged against him his former allies, Prussia and Austria, as well as Russia and Britain. Defeat in October 1813 in the 'Battle of the Nations' at Leipzig, the biggest battle so far in the history of warfare, forced him to retreat across the Rhine to France. Allied strategy during the final offensive in 1814 which led to the fall of Paris and the overthrow of Napoleon was strongly influenced by the Russian light cavalry's interception of secret French despatches. On 22 March Russian

Cossacks captured a courier carrying a letter from Napoleon revealing that he was heading for the Marne 'in order to push the enemy as far as possible from Paris'.[74] The document was discussed next day at an Allied council of war.[75] Further enemy despatches captured by the Russian cavalry on 23 March disclosed the low morale of French forces, their generals included, and the fact that Paris's arms depots and arsenals were almost empty. The Police Minister, Savary, reported to Napoleon in an intercepted despatch that he could no longer count on the loyalty of the capital if Allied armies approached.[76] On 24 March Alexander summoned his senior commanders for a meeting to discuss the latest intelligence from intercepted French despatches before deciding on a plan of campaign.[77]

Most of the French intercepts were in cipher. Alexander, the best-educated monarch of his time and the only one who may have been able to understand some of the principles of cryptography, was proud of the success of his codebreakers, which Napoleon and his generals had never suspected. Some years after Waterloo, at a state dinner in Moscow given by the Tsar for French marshals, he revealed publicly for the first time that Russia had decrypted French despatches during the Napoleonic Wars. One of the guests, Marshal Jacques Macdonald, who had commanded a corps in the *Grande Armée* during Napoleon's invasion, assumed that the Russians must have been given French ciphers by a French general who had defected. 'It is not surprising that Your Majesty was able to decipher them', Macdonald told the Tsar. 'Someone gave you the key.' Hand on heart, Alexander denied it and gave his word of honour that the credit belonged to Russia's codebreakers.[78]

Though in early 1814 Napoleon fought a brilliant rearguard action, on 30 March Allied troops entered Paris with Tsar Alexander and Frederick William of Prussia at their head – the first time any foreign army had captured Paris since 1415. On the same day in Paris Talleyrand set up a provisional government, including Fouché, which promptly began peace negotiations with the Allies. On 2 April the Senate invited Louis XVI's younger brother, who had styled himself Louis XVIII since the death of the child Louis XVII, to assume the throne. Napoleon abdicated on 6 April. By the Treaty of Fontainebleau between France and the Allies on 11 April he was exiled to Elba but allowed to keep the courtesy title of Emperor. In the early hours of the 13th, before he had left for Elba, Napoleon took the poison he had carried round his neck since his narrow escape from capture during the retreat from Moscow. But the poison had lost its potency and he survived. On 4 May he arrived on Elba.

Nine months later, on 26 February 1815, Napoleon escaped from Elba and landed on 1 March with about 600 supporters in the south of France in a bid to regain his throne. The escape was made possible by an agent network in France. Napoleon was so grateful to one of its leading members, Joseph Emmery, a surgeon from Grenoble, that he left him 100,000 francs in his will.[79] But his success in assembling an army owed almost nothing to agents or advance planning. All along Napoleon's route to Paris, the troops sent to arrest him rallied to his cause. On 19 March Louis XVIII fled across the Belgian border. Next day Napoleon entered Paris to a hero's welcome.[80] The Hundred Days of the restored Napoleonic Empire came to an abrupt end at Waterloo, south of Brussels, on 18 June. Though the battle, in Wellington's famous (often misquoted) phrase, was 'a damned nice thing', the numerical superiority of the Allied forces would have ensured their victory if the war had continued. The armies of Wellington and the Prussian commander, Gebhard Leberecht von Blücher, though dispersed, outnumbered Napoleon's by 209,000 to 120,000.[81]*

Three days before the battle, the head of the intelligence department in Wellington's army, Colquhoun Grant, who had the rank of assistant adjutant-general, received information from one of his French agents that Napoleon was planning to attack his defensive position at Waterloo on 18 June. Grant had established himself as a highly successful intelligence officer during the Peninsular War. When he was taken prisoner in 1811, Wellington said that his capture was as serious a blow as the loss of a brigade. Grant, however, escaped, persuading an unsuspecting French general that he was an officer in the US army. But the intelligence he obtained on 15 June 1815 of Napoleon's battle plans for the 18th was accidentally delayed in transit, and did not reach Wellington until Grant delivered it personally to him on the field of Waterloo.[82]

Immediately before the battle, Napoleon brushed aside important last-minute intelligence. Over breakfast he was told by his brother Jérôme that a (presumably English-speaking) waiter in an inn at Genappes, where Wellington had dined two days earlier, had overheard a British aide-de-camp say that Prussian forces were due to join them in the forest of Soignes. Though the intelligence was correct, Napoleon insisted that it would be another two days before the two armies could link up.[83] Had Napoleon taken seriously the possibility that Prussian forces would begin to arrive to support Wellington in the early afternoon, he might well have begun his attack at sunrise rather than after 11 a.m.[84]† Until evening, Napoleon seemed to be winning. The main cause of his defeat was the

---

* The Austrian and Russian forces, who invaded France in 1814, had departed.

† In a dawn attack, however, he would have contended with rain and more-muddy conditions.

arrival at 7 p.m. of General von Zieten's Prussian 1st Army Corps, 'which', as Wellington said later, 'I was expecting with the utmost impatience'.[85] 'Incomprehensible day', Napoleon said later of Waterloo. He did not, he admitted, 'thoroughly understand the battle'.[86] He would have understood it better if he had taken seriously information that Wellington was counting on Prussian support. But, as Napoleon acknowledged after his exile to St Helena, 'I do not allow myself to be governed by advice' – including intelligence which contradicted his own opinions.

18

Intelligence and Counter-Revolution.
Part I: From the Congress of Vienna to the 1848 Revolutions

The Congress of Vienna, held in 1814–15 to redraw the map of post-Napoleonic Europe, was the largest gathering of sovereigns and diplomats ever assembled in European history. On Sunday, 25 September 1814, Tsar Alexander I of Russia and King Frederick William III of Prussia made a ceremonial entry on horseback into Vienna, where they were welcomed, with further ceremony, by Emperor Francis (Franz) I of Austria. Others at the Congress included three lesser monarchs (the kings of Bavaria, Denmark and Württemberg), two crown princes (of Prussia and Württemberg), a series of other royal princes (including, for a time, the British Prince Ernest, Duke of Cumberland), thirty-two minor German royals and three grand duchesses.[1]

Behind the scenes more informers and spies were also at work than at any previous diplomatic conference. The largest contingent were Austrian. Prince Metternich, the German-born Austrian Foreign Minister (later Chancellor), had calculated, correctly, that holding the congress in Vienna would increase both his influence on the negotiations and the opportunities to spy on other delegations. Metternich's intelligence chief, who had the official title of Head of Police and Censorship (*Oberste Polizei und Cenzur Hofstelle*), was Baron Franz von Hager, whose promising military career had been cut short by a riding accident.[2] Hager and Metternich had access to three forms of intelligence: intercepted correspondence* and stolen documents; agent reports; and intelligence obtained directly from foreign officials and policymakers.[3] As in the Kaunitz era,[4] the most valuable intelligence source was diplomatic correspondence decrypted by the *cabinet noir*, which Metternich increased in size. He boasted privately that one of his codebreakers, named Eichenfeld, had personally broken eighty-three ciphers. One French ambassador who had served in Vienna told a colleague

---

* The Vienna Haus-, Hof- und Staats-Archiv contains very large numbers of intercepts which still await historical research.

he believed that none of his ciphers had taken Austrian codebreakers more than a month to decrypt.[5] The work of the *cabinet noir* was assisted by low-level agents who scoured embassy and other wastepaper baskets for scraps of torn-up official documents (*chiffons*).[6] Its operations fascinated the Emperor, who read – apparently avidly – a selection of the latest intercepts each day after early morning mass.[7] Francis, however, was unaware that Metternich had ordered the interception of some of his own private correspondence and that of the Imperial family.[8]

On 1 July 1814 Hager instructed the Vienna police chief, Silber:

> The imminent arrival of the foreign sovereigns imposes on us the obligation to take special measures to reinforce surveillance and ensure that we are informed on a daily basis and in complete detail of everything about their august personages, their immediate entourage, all individuals who seek to approach them, as well as the plans, projects, enterprises that arise from the presence of these illustrious guests.[9]

The 1,500 servants required by foreign delegations for everything from serving at table to emptying chamber pots offered numerous opportunities for 'reinforced surveillance'. Police agents employed as servants were instructed to eavesdrop on conversations, if necessary pressing their ears against closed doors, to 'borrow' letters and documents for secret copying, to take keys to the police or make wax impressions on the spot, and to go through pockets and wastepaper baskets – even to look for burnt remains of documents in fireplaces.[10] The royal guests and their entourages who stayed at the imperial palace, the Hofburg, were subject to similar surveillance.[11] The *chiffons* collected by police agents were often of sufficient interest to be sent by Hager to the Emperor and Metternich.[12]

Keeping track of the expenditure of delegates to the Congress offered another means of 'reinforced surveillance'. Hager ordered the head of the police bureau responsible for the surveillance of Jews to identify potential informers 'either among the heads of the [Jewish] banks or the most intelligent of their sons' in order to monitor the financial transactions of foreign delegations. The limited civil rights of the growing Jewish community made it dependent on the goodwill of the police, and Hager had no doubt that the 'influence' the police was able to exert over Jewish bankers would make informers 'easy' to find.[13] The financial problems of Congress delegates revealed by the bankers assisted Hager's agent recruitment. A senior Viennese police official reported in October 1814: 'Most delegations from small states . . . are distressed by the high cost of living and have already emptied their pockets.' It was important, he argued, to try to keep them in Vienna until their financial needs had become desperate. At that point, offering them monetary 'gratifications' could not fail to 'loosen their tongues'.[14] Thanks to the personal intervention of the Emperor, Hager did not lack the means to do so. 'The present moment', he wrote, 'is of the greatest importance for the State's political police. His Majesty has therefore deigned to put at my disposal all necessary resources.'[15]

Metternich's obsession with surveillance was so well known that some of his main targets took precautions against it. Though an Austrian agent quickly gained employment as a valet in the Russian embassy,[16] a senior police official complained to Hager in October 1814 that the French plenipotentiary, Prince Talleyrand, had tried to turn his residence at the Kaunitz Palace into a 'fortress' containing only trusted staff. He had not, however, completely succeeded. The police had persuaded an elderly servant and a *garçon de chancellerie* to purloin some documents from Talleyrand's office.[17] The French embassy was less secure than the Kaunitz Palace and its correspondence was frequently intercepted. In November 1814, however, one of its correspondents noticed that the embassy's seal on the envelope had been tampered with. Hager assured the Emperor that in future the *cabinet noir* would take even greater precautions to avoid detection.[18]

Initial Viennese police attempts to penetrate the British embassy and the lodgings of the Foreign Secretary, Lord Castlereagh, both failed. Silber complained to Hager that the British had recruited two chambermaids without Austrian official assistance, absurdly condemning this prudent procedure as 'excessively cautious'. What outraged Silber was that the British failure to accept pre-selected police spies as chambermaids involved him in unnecessary work at a busy time: 'It is therefore necessary for me, before attempting to procure papers torn up in the [British] offices and thrown into wastepaper baskets, to check on these two women and see if they can be depended on.'[19] An agent report on 4 October informed Hager that it appeared 'almost impossible' to intercept Castlereagh's correspondence: 'The Lord sends everything by his own couriers, and his secretaries collect and burn all his papers' after use.[20] The report proved too pessimistic. Only ten days later Hager succeeded in intercepting British diplomatic correspondence. On 15 October he proudly informed the Emperor that he was enclosing decrypts of correspondence which Castlereagh had received by courier from London two days earlier.[21] The British, however, had intelligence successes of their own. Metternich was shocked to discover in December 1814 that a secret agent of the British ambassador, Sir Charles Stewart (later 3rd Marquess of Londonderry), had 'plundered' secret papers from his chancellery. Having been shown the papers, Stewart's predecessor as ambassador, Lord Aberdeen, jumped to the conclusion, probably wrongly on this occasion, that Metternich had tried to deceive him and accused him of dishonesty. Stewart's embassy secretary, George Jackson, commented: 'More chicane and manoeuvring have been, and still are, going on concerning this business than on any that has hitherto come within my experience.'[22]

Hager's intelligence reports to the Emperor and Metternich were unusually frank and show few signs of a reluctance to 'tell truth to power'. He did not hesitate to include serious criticism of Metternich himself. An intercepted despatch to Copenhagen from the Danish plenipotentiary before the Congress opened reported that Metternich found himself in 'the greatest embarrassment' because of his failure to secure the diplomatic support of Lord Castlereagh, 'on which he had been counting'.[23] According to agent reports, 'a great storm' of criticism from his coalition partners against Napoleon was also about to descend on him.[24] The papal nuncio 'could not contain his bile against Metternich'.[25] The Tsar's 'dearest wish' was said to be Metternich's dismissal as Austrian Foreign Minister.[26] Hager's reports also contained embarrassing intelligence on Metternich's sexual liaisons. Some of the most embarrassing concerned his former mistress and the mother in 1810 of his illegitimate daughter, Princess Catherine Bagration, the young and merry widow of a Russian war hero, who had since become the mistress of Tsar Alexander I. Bagration's diaphanous gowns earned her the Viennese nickname 'naked angel'. Alexander visited her as soon as he arrived in Vienna.[27] According to a confidante of the princess, the Tsar had asked her for the 'full history' of her affair with Metternich and how he had subsequently begun a liaison with Wilhelmine, Duchess of Sagan. Alexander told her: 'Metternich never loved either you or Sagan . . . He is a cold-blooded creature.'[28] Most embarrassing was an agent report that Bagration had shown the Tsar all Metternich's many letters to her. As a result, according to the agent, 'Metternich's enemies are over the moon (*aux anges*).'[29] Like his letters to Sagan (many of which have been published), Metternich's private correspondence with Bagration was doubtless full of detailed comments on both politics and international relations.[30]

According to another agent report, Bagration was so anxious to revenge herself on Metternich that she also revealed embarrassing confidences about him to Nesselrode, the leader of the Russian delegation, and several other Russian statesmen.[31] The Tsar was not the princess's only lover during the Congress. A police agent reported that on one occasion, when arriving at her palace, Alexander found her on a staircase dressed in a negligée. In her chamber he noticed a man's hat. Bagration claimed it belonged to a decorator who had been preparing her palace for a ball on the following day. Why he had been in her private chamber was not explained. The agent report concludes: 'The Tsar spent two and a half hours with the princess. *Honi soit qui mal y pense!*'[32]*

As in the case of Bagration, much of the intelligence collected during the Congress of Vienna came from pillow-talk. The police reports sent to Emperor Francis and Metternich reveal the Congress as the most promiscuous in diplomatic history. The handsome, dissolute young British diplomat Frederick Lamb (later ambassador in Vienna) began an affair with Metternich's main current mistress, the Duchess of Sagan, from whom he sought information about the Austrian Chancellor to pass on to London.[33] Metternich's frank and voluminous correspondence with the Duchess shows that she had much to tell Lamb.[34] It is easy to imagine the affront to Metternich's pride when he learned from, at times almost daily, police reports in the spring of 1815 that the Duchess was also having an affair with Charles Stewart, the British ambassador, whose posturing and extravagant wardrobe in Vienna earned him the nickname 'golden peacock'.[35] Though he and Sagan usually spent the night together in the Duchess's Vienna mansion, an intercepted letter from a Swiss doctor revealed that they also had 'a certain inn near Laxenburg which they use for f***[ing]'.[36] Hager reported (accurately) that Stewart frequented brothels as well as Sagan. After Castlereagh's return to London, the British embassy in the Starhemberg Palace and the British plenipotentiary's residence were transformed, according to police reports, into combinations of 'brothel and pothouse', where actresses and chambermaids worked as prostitutes.[37] Police reports on behaviour at the Russian embassy, where one of the valets was a Russian agent,[38] were even more censorious. According to a report by 'Agent D' forwarded to Hager on 9 November, 'the Russians lodged at the [Hof]Burg, not content with keeping it in a filthy condition, are behaving very badly and constantly bringing in girls'.[39] One officer in the Tsar's entourage tried to blame Russian bad behaviour on 'the unbelievable depravity of the female sex of the [Austrian] lower orders'.[40]

Intelligence reports to the Emperor and Metternich revealed that a number of leading Congress delegates had brought remarkably youthful mistresses to Vienna. The Russian Prince Volkonsky had a nineteen-year-old mistress from Cologne who had been disowned by her family. According to surveillance reports, she came to visit him at the Hofburg almost every day, often disguised in male clothing.[41] The chief Prussian

---

* Bagratian's other lovers in Vienna included a Bavarian prince, the Prince Royal of Württemberg and, probably, the Tsar's brother Grand Duke Constantine. (Zamoyski, *Rites of Peace*, loc. 4180.)

representative at the Congress, Prince Karl August von Hardenberg, was reported to have with him a young Parisian actress named Jubille.[42] Talleyrand installed as hostess at the Kaunitz Palace his current mistress, the beautiful 21-year-old Dorothée de Périgord, thirty-nine years younger than himself and daughter of one of his former mistresses, the Duchess of Courland. One of Dorothée's roles was to charm those whom Talleyrand wished to influence. According to the French writer Sainte-Beuve, she had 'eyes of an infernal brilliance that shone in the night'. While in Vienna, however, she began an affair with a dashing young cavalry officer, Count Karl Clam-Martinic, a confidant of Metternich and later Austrian War Minister.[43] Clam-Martinic had earlier sent intelligence reports to Vienna on the situation at Russian military headquarters. The Tsar, he reported, had become 'easy prey to all those who praised his ideas with most eloquence'.[44] His pillow talk with Dorothée doubtless turned to Talleyrand's diplomatic manoeuvres in Vienna.

Intelligence operations during the Congress collected a record quantity of high-level scandalous gossip, much of which probably did more to divert than to inform the recipients. Intelligence also increased, at least modestly, the level of distrust among the victorious allies – as when Lord Aberdeen accused Metternich of bad faith after reading papers purloined from his chancellery. But the sometimes exotic mix of gossip and intelligence in Vienna did little to affect the outcome of the Congress. While negotiating the future of post-Napoleonic Europe and following the intrigues and private lives of their allies, the victors largely lost sight of Napoleon himself and made no serious attempt to obtain intelligence on his behaviour in exile. The news which reached Vienna early in March 1815 of Napoleon's escape from Elba took all the negotiators by surprise. Talleyrand was reported to have heard the news from Dorothée de Périgord, who read out his morning correspondence to him while he was still in bed.[45] The news was of some personal interest to Dorothée since her current lover, Karl Clam-Martinic, had escorted Napoleon into exile on Elba less than a year before.[46]

The fact that Allied representatives were gathered together in Vienna enabled them to respond quickly to the news of Napoleon's return to France. On 13 March, they issued a proclamation, written by Talleyrand, branding him an outlaw, 'beyond the pale of civil society'.[47] The Vienna Final Act, concluded at the only formal meeting of the Congress, on 9 June 1815, nine days before Napoleon's defeat at Waterloo, redrew the map of Europe to the advantage of the ruling dynasties in Russia, Prussia and Austria. The Act also created the German Confederation (*Deutscher Bund*), a loose association of Austria and thirty-nine German states, to replace the defunct Holy Roman Empire (which Napoleon had abolished in 1806). Metternich ended the Congress with a much enhanced reputation. According to a police report, the representatives of the German states 'continue to sing the praises of Prince Metternich'.[48]* After Waterloo, Talleyrand was less content. The second Treaty of Paris concluded on 20 November 1815 was less generous than the first treaty of May 1814, forcing France to surrender territory to her smaller neighbours, pay an indemnity of 700 million francs, and submit to a five-year occupation of its northern departments.

The aim of the victorious rulers of Russia, Prussia and Austria (all former allies of Napoleon) was to use the peace settlement not merely to increase their own territories but also to reinforce their own security against any revived revolutionary or Bonapartist threat to the established order. On 20 November, the same date as the second Treaty of Paris, the three powers and Britain signed the Quadruple Alliance committing them to defend the new status quo established by the Congress of Vienna and hold regular congresses of their foreign ministers to review current threats and consider how to respond to them. The congresses, which continued in various European cities until 1822, have been likened to 'a kind of security council dedicated to the preservation of the status quo'. The four victorious great powers regarded themselves as 'the policemen of Europe'.[49]

Emperor Francis I and Metternich, whom he was to make Austrian Chancellor in 1821, shared an almost obsessive fear of conspiracy and revolution. In the aftermath of the Congress of Vienna they believed that the main revolutionary threat came from France, as it had done ever since 1789. Metternich 'equated change and reform with subversion and revolution'. All threats to the existing political order, he believed, were plots organized by a (non-existent) Central Revolutionary Committee in Paris.[50] Metternich sought to monitor these imaginary plots by both agent reports and the operations of the *cabinet noir*. His capacity to monitor even real plots, however, was severely limited. The origins of the Galician uprising of 1846, the last peasant jacquerie in European history, which had been several months in preparation and killed about 1,000 nobles before being brutally suppressed,[51] went entirely unobserved by Metternich's famed intelligence network.[52]

The Vienna *cabinet noir* was at its most effective in intercepting and

---

* Since police reports early in the Congress had not hesitated to report serious criticism of Metternich, the report of the praise accorded to him at the end of the Congress is probably reliable.

decrypting foreign diplomatic despatches.[53]* Metternich was unaware, however, that some of his own correspondence was itself intercepted by the French during his affair from 1818 to 1825 with Countess (later Princess) Dorothea Lieven, wife of the Russian ambassador in London. Writing to Lieven during the Congress of Aix-la-Chapelle at midnight on 15 November 1818, Metternich appealed to her to 'love me with all your heart from this moment, tomorrow and for ever, and do not fear regrets'.[54] Since their correspondence was personal, Metternich did not use a diplomatic cipher but instead went to elaborate lengths to try to ensure that it was not intercepted. He arranged for Lieven's letters to him from London to be sent by British diplomatic bag to the secretary of the Austrian embassy in Paris, Baron Franz von Binder. Inside each sealed package from the Countess, Binder found another package, also addressed to him, which contained a further sealed envelope with no address but which he had instructions to send via the Austrian diplomatic bag to one of Metternich's secretaries in Vienna. Inside this sealed envelope was yet another, also unaddressed, which the secretary handed personally to Metternich, who was entirely unaware that the letter it contained from Countess Lieven had been secretly intercepted, copied and resealed during transit by the Paris *cabinet noir*.[55]

The French Foreign Ministry thus enjoyed for some years a regular secret commentary not merely on Metternich's latest affair but also on British policy. Countess Lieven was particularly contemptuous of George IV. The King, she told Metternich (and, unintentionally, the French), was 'a dangerous madman', much more interested in his current mistress than in affairs of state. Well aware that Lieven was Metternich's mistress, Castlereagh used her as a secret intermediary to communicate with him. There were some matters, he explained to Metternich, on which he could not communicate directly, 'on account of his colleagues, who would think it too official a step', but which would be privately 'made clear to you' on his behalf by Lieven. The Countess vividly reported Castlereagh's changing moods as well as his policies. Following dinner with him after the failed Cato Street Conspiracy to murder the British Cabinet in 1820, Lieven wrote to Metternich that he kept 'two loaded pistols in the pockets of his breeches'. By the early summer of 1822 Castlereagh, for reasons which will never be fully clear, was under enormous stress. Lieven wrote to Metternich on 10 June: '[Castlereagh] looks ghastly. He has aged five years in the last week; one can see that he is a broken man.' He had come to

---

* Metternich established special *Postlogen* to intercept and decrypt diplomatic traffic during the Congresses at Troppau and Laibach. A *Postloge* was already in existence at Verona during the Congress in 1822.

distrust all his colleagues, even his old friend Wellington.[56] In August Castlereagh committed suicide by cutting the carotid artery in his throat with a penknife. Lieven, 'in great grief', wrote to Metternich that she was 'shaking like a leaf'. Metternich, more charitable than usual, described Castlereagh as 'irreplaceable . . . the only person in his country who had experience in foreign affairs'.[57]

In the years after the Vienna Congress a new element appeared in Metternich's conspiracy theories about the supposed international revolutionary threat. Students had played no significant part in the French Revolution. Metternich, however, became convinced that they posed a revolutionary threat in Germany, which had more university students than any other country in Europe. His conspiracy theories were fuelled by police reports on the *Burschenschaften*, nationalist German student associations. Hager's successor as Austrian police chief, Count Sedlnitsky, was convinced that the *Burschenschaften* had 'a deep and carefully laid plan to kindle and encourage, not only among students but also among most teachers, a political and religious fanaticism which evidently has as its end the revolutionary overthrow of all monarchical institutions in favour of a demagogic, representative freedom and unity of the German people'.[58]

Such alarmist intelligence assessments derived from a grotesque exaggeration of the threat of student revolution. Among conservative opinion in the German Confederation, however, they were given credibility on 18 October 1817 by a conference of a few hundred students, mainly from Jena, Kiel, Vienna and Berlin, at the castle of Wartburg in the Grand Duchy of Weimar. Though the conference had been summoned to mark the 300th anniversary of the Reformation and the fourth anniversary of the victory over Napoleon at Leipzig, some students also used it to denounce the undemocratic government of the German states and Austrian interference in German affairs. According to some accounts, Metternich was burned in effigy. Student political activism was such a new phenomenon that the British ambassador in Berlin, George Rose, like most German rulers, was deeply shocked. He wrote to Castlereagh:

> A scandalous scene of revolutionary effervescence, and concerted in revolutionary views, took place on the 18th Instant, . . . on the Wartburg . . . It is of particular evil omen, as indicating the spirit, which reigns to a considerable extent in the German universities . . .
>
> Inflammatory speeches were made by Professors at the repast, which followed [the conference], the health of no Sovereign was drunk, but that of the Grand Duke of Saxe Weimar; and various books written in opposition to revolutionary doctrine were with much solemnity consigned to the

flames of a large bonfire . . . It is said, I know not if correctly, that the act of the congress of Vienna underwent the same fate. In order to insult the governments, and regular armies of Prussia, Austria, and Hesse Cassel, they burnt a Prussian pair of stays (such, as they assume, the officers of this Army wear), an Austrian Corporal's cane, and a Hessian Queue [soldier's wig]: and it is said they did the same by a Hanoverian Cat o'-nine tails, an implement of punishment which, I believe, is not used in that army.[59]

On 23 March 1819 Karl Sand, a 24-year-old former theology student and *Burschenschaft* member, called at the house in Mannheim of the famous playwright August von Kotzebue. Though Kotzebue's work was then performed in Germany even more frequently than that of Goethe and Schiller, his conservative anti-nationalist views had made him deeply unpopular with the *Burschenschaften*; his history of Germany had been thrown on the bonfire at the Wartburg festival. After receiving a friendly welcome from Kotzebue, Sand drew a dagger from his sleeve, denounced him as a 'traitor to the fatherland' and stabbed him to death, then tried unsuccessfully to commit suicide. Though Sand was probably mentally ill, Metternich declared himself 'absolutely certain' that the murder had been ordered by a secret student tribunal at Jena University. He put most blame on the evil influence of the students' professors: 'They can produce a whole generation of revolutionaries if one does not manage to check the evil.'[60]

Metternich's fear of 'a whole generation' of revolutionary students derived from conspiracy theories which distorted intelligence collection. The purpose of intelligence, he believed, was to provide evidence of the great revolutionary conspiracy of whose reality he had no doubt. It is highly unlikely that any intelligence reports sent to Metternich dared to downplay the extent of the conspiracy. Metternich used alarmist intelligence on subversion in German universities to convince a meeting of ministers of the German Confederation of the urgent need for action. Rose wrote to Castlereagh after a conversation with the Prussian Foreign Minister, Count Bernstorff:

> He speaks in high terms of the energy, and ability displayed by Prince Metternich, who seems to have been so wholly engrossed by the sense of the danger menacing the German States, and by the necessity of averting it . . . The Prince laid before the assembled Ministers authentic information proving that danger, – the effect of the machinations of the revolutionists, – to be far more imminent, than had been supposed.[61]

The Carlsbad Decrees, drafted by Metternich with Prussian support, introducing heightened surveillance and censorship in German universities, were ratified by the entire German Confederation on 20 September. The decrees laid down that:

1. A special representative of the ruler of each state shall be appointed for each university . . . to see to the strictest enforcement of existing laws and disciplinary regulations [and] to observe carefully the spirit which is shown by the instructors in the university in their public lectures and regular courses . . .

2. The confederated governments mutually pledge themselves to remove from the universities or other public educational institutions all teachers who, by obvious deviation from their duty, or by exceeding the limits of their functions, or by the abuse of their legitimate influence over the youthful minds, or by propagating harmful doctrines hostile to public order or subversive of existing governmental institutions, shall have unmistakably proved their unfitness for the important office intrusted to them . . .

3. Those laws which have for a long period been directed against secret and unauthorized societies in the universities shall be strictly enforced. These laws apply especially to that association established some years ago under the name Universal Students' Union (*Allgemeine Burschenschaft*) . . .[62]

So far as Austria was concerned, Metternich regarded even these draconian decrees as inadequate. In 1825 all foreign students, including those from other members of the German Confederation, were banned from Austrian universities in an attempt to keep out revolutionary contagion. In 1829 Austrian students were banned from attending any foreign university.[63]

Like Metternich, Tsar Nicholas I, who succeeded his childless elder brother Alexander I in December 1825, was obsessed with the necessity for surveillance of the revolutionary menace. In Nicholas's case, the menace was real. The origins of the failed Decembrist Revolt on 26 December to put the unwilling (but supposedly less autocratic) Grand Duke Constantine on the throne instead of Nicholas went back to the foundation in 1816 of Russia's first secret political society, the Union of Salvation (succeeded two years later by the Union of Welfare). The 1825 revolt was quickly and brutally crushed. Five of the leaders were hanged and over 120 exiled to Siberia. Nicholas, who was horrified to discover that the revolt had been led by nobles and army officers, personally took part in the interrogations and studied carefully the reports on them. He was so shaken by the investigation that he wrongly concluded that the Decembrists were part of a much larger Europe-wide conspiracy to destroy all hereditary monarchies,[64] and commissioned the Prussian Police Minister, Karl Albert von Kamptz, to write an article blaming the rebellion on an international network of secret societies. In April 1826 Nicholas ordered all those who had been members of subversive societies to make full confessions.[65]

On 3 July the Tsar issued an imperial *ukaz* establishing a new Third Section of his chancellery to take charge of political policing, under the 44-year-old General Aleksandr Kristoforovich von Benckendorff. Nicholas began with a hopelessly unrealistic view of Third Section as a force for good which would heal the troubles of Mother Russia. When he appointed Benckendorff, he was reputed to have told him, holding a handkerchief: 'Here is your directive. The more tears you wipe away with this handkerchief, the more faithfully you will serve my aims.' Benckendorff in turn told a new recruit: 'In you, everyone will see an official who can, through my agency, bring the voice of suffering humanity to the Imperial Throne and immediately place the defenceless and voiceless Citizen under the protection of the Tsar.'[66] The reality, inevitably, was very different. The Third Section became best known for its pervasive surveillance. Benckendorff's executive director, Maksim Yakovlevich von Vock, rapidly built up a network of 5,000 informers. Vock privately acknowledged that there was a widespread belief that it was becoming 'impossible to sneeze in one's home . . . without the Sovereign finding out about it within the hour'.* The Third Section was also seen as a threat by other police forces, who tried to demonstrate their own commitment to countering political subversion. Only two months after the founding of the Section, Vock complained to Benckendorff that he himself was under surveillance by the St Petersburg city police, who followed him wherever he went: 'Surveillance itself is being made the object of surveillance, in defiance of all sense and propriety.'[67]

The Third Section was also responsible for letter-opening on an industrial scale, which was carried out throughout the Russian Empire, according to Benckendorff, by postmasters 'known for their meticulousness and zeal'.[68] Probably the primary purpose of letter-opening was to conduct Russia's first (classified) opinion polls. Benckendorff's first overview of Russian opinion in 1827 concluded, much like Metternich's assessment of subversion in German universities, that the main subversive threat came from an educational system which was spreading 'gangrene' through noble youth: 'Our youth, that is to say the young gentry between the ages of 17 and 25, constitute as a group the most gangrened element in the empire.

---

* On Vock's death from cholera in 1831, he was succeeded by another civilian, A. A. Mordvinov, until 1839. (Ruud and Stepanov, *Fontanka 16*, p. 23.)

Among these madcaps we can see the germs of Jacobinism, a revolutionary reformist spirit.' 'Our infected youth', insisted Vock, 'needs vigilant and persistent surveillance.'[69] As in Metternich's Austria, fear of 'the germs of Jacobinism' distorted intelligence collection. Vock had no interest in reports of uninfected youth.

France, under the restored Bourbon monarchy, proved a less dangerous hotbed of revolutionary conspiracy than Metternich and other leading counter-revolutionaries had anticipated. At the accession of Charles X in 1824, following the death of his childless elder brother Louis XVIII, the Paris police reported that in recent years there had been a decline in the number of secret societies.[70] Metternich concluded two years later that France itself was no longer in danger of revolution. He complained, however, that it was spreading 'moral poison' across the rest of Europe by permitting the publication of subversive literature.[71] Among the titles which must have offended him was the greatest European best-seller of its time, Las Cases's *Mémorial de Sainte-Hélène*, published in 1823, in which Napoleon portrayed himself as the continuer of the French Revolution, committed to the doctrine of popular sovereignty.

Other 'moral poison' appeared in the published French parliamentary debates, where prominent liberals were able to challenge government policy. Each year from 1818 onwards, the French parliament, alone in Europe, had to approve the budget for (though not the use of) the *fonds secret*, which paid for surveillance and espionage. Though the liberal minority was never able to prevent approval of the budget, its attacks on government intelligence gathering were frequently ferocious and sometimes produced parliamentary uproar. Among the government's leading critics was the great liberal political philosopher Benjamin Constant, later praised by Isaiah Berlin as 'the most eloquent of all defenders of freedom and privacy', who sat in the Chamber of Deputies for most of the period from 1819 to 1830. In 1822 Constant denounced the repeated attempts by government agents 'to corrupt all those in contact with every [liberal deputy] not simply to get reports on their dealings with [deputies] but also to persuade them to steal their papers and give them to [the agents] who solicited the crime'. As evidence of the vileness of the agents, another liberal deputy, Alexandre-Edme Méchin, described the case of a 'depraved son' who had been persuaded to inform on his father, as well as the routine corruption of those 'who deliver our letters and a keep a register of our visitors'. Méchin also derided both the fascination of all new Ministers of the Interior with police intelligence reports and their exaggerated fears of revolutionary plots: 'New men in power love the police. They are alarmed by everything, and fear is a passion which, like other passions, likes to be tended.'[72] No such public scepticism of alarmist intelligence would have been tolerated in Vienna or St Petersburg.

For most of the reign of Charles X there was no sign of a threat to his regime. Departmental and police prefects reported a national mood of 'complete tranquillity' and widespread 'devotion to the monarchy', with little interest in politics between elections. Charles's government was undermined not by the plots of professional revolutionaries but by his own policies. The mood began to change with Charles's appointment of the extreme 'ultra-royalist', the prince Jules de Polignac, as his Prime Minister in April 1829. On 25 July 1830 Charles signed the Four Ordinances: an attempted royal coup d'état dissolving the Chamber, reducing the already small electorate by 75 per cent, limiting the powers of deputies, and requiring publications to have a government licence. 'The King has thrown down the gauntlet to the liberals', wrote Metternich to the Emperor. Neither Charles nor his ministers had made contingency plans to deal with resistance to the royal coup. The next day, 26 July, Charles went hunting, oblivious of the anger he had aroused among the people of Paris.[73] There followed what were later eulogized as the 'Three Glorious Days' of 27, 28 and 29 July, when rioters erected barricades (unknown during the revolution which had begun in 1789) and more than 1,000 died in clashes with the army. On 30 July Charles abdicated and fled to England.

The July Days brought about a change of regime rather than a revolution; the Bourbon dynasty was replaced by that of Orléans, whose head, Louis Philippe, agreed to a more liberal constitution. Charles X and Polignac fell back on conspiracy theory to explain their overthrow, repeatedly claiming that a revolutionary *comité directeur* had been planning an insurrection and distributing money to workers, manufacturing daggers and acquiring firearms.[74] Tsar Nicholas I became obsessed by similar conspiracy theories, particularly after an uprising in Russian Poland in November took him by surprise. The unofficial Russian Viceroy, his elder brother Constantine, who had been the target of an unsuccessful assassination attempt, wrote to him on 13 December: 'All my measures of surveillance proved useless.' There had been a major intelligence failure.[75]

Early in 1831 Nicholas was reduced to a temporary state of panic by reports that the Illuminati, a secret society of small real significance which became the subject of grandiose conspiracy theories, had infiltrated the highest circles of the Russian administration, including the Third Section, and was planning to assassinate him.[76] The extent to which Russian intelligence assessment continued to be degraded by conspiracy theory was demonstrated by the Lukovsky case four years later. In 1835 an informant named Lukovsky, probably Polish, arrived in St Petersburg from England and informed the Third Section that a secret Russo-Polish society in England was preparing to overthrow the Russian monarchy by an invasion of Russia which would begin in British India and advance through Persia, Georgia and Astrakhan. Though Lukovsky was unable to identify any of those involved or to provide other details of this preposterous invasion plan, Nicholas I, despite describing the intelligence as 'unclear', ordered it to be followed up. 'In our times', he insisted, 'nothing should be ignored.'[77]

Western travellers to Russia thus found themselves treated with deep suspicion as potential, if not actual, spies and subversives. The French marquis de Custine was asked on his arrival at St Petersburg in 1839:

What are you going to do in Russia?
See the country.
That is not a motive for travelling.
I have no other . . .
Do you have a public diplomatic mission?
No.
Secret?
No.
Some scientific purpose?
No.
Have you been sent by your government to observe social and political conditions in this country?
No.
By a commercial company?
No.[78]

Nicholas I's Russia had become a surveillance society. 'The Tsar', wrote Custine, 'is the only man in the Empire with whom one can talk without fear of informers.'[79] He ended one letter home by saying he was:

busy hiding my papers because any of my letters, even one which would appear most innocent to you, would suffice to send me to Siberia. I take care to shut myself up when I write; and when my courier or someone of the post knocks at my door, I lock my papers before opening the door and pretend to be reading. I am going to slip this letter between the crown and the lining of my hat.[80]

For many Western diplomats and intelligence officers in the Soviet Union during the early Cold War, Custine's journal seemed to be prophetic. Walter Bedell Smith, the US ambassador in Moscow from 1946 to 1949 and head of the Central Intelligence Agency (Director of Central Intelligence) from 1950 to 1953, found Custine's journals 'the greatest single contribution in helping us to unravel, in part, mysteries that seem to envelop Russia and the Russians'. While in Moscow, 'My own position and that of my staff as foreign diplomats in the Soviet Union showed little variation from that of our predecessors accredited to the Tsarist court a century before. In both eras one finds the same restrictions, the same surveillance, the same suspicion.'[81] Bedell Smith overstated the continuities: nothing in the era of the Third Section truly compared with the Gulag of the Stalinist era. But Aleksandr Herzen, the first Russian socialist, found Custine's evocation of the surveillance and climate of suspicion in Nicholas I's Russia compelling: 'unquestioningly the most diverting and intelligent book written about Russia by a foreigner'.[82]

After the accession of the July Monarchy of Louis-Philippe, French parliamentary debates during the 1830s to approve the *fonds secret* used to fund spies and informers (held twice yearly from 1831) were no less boisterous than during the Bourbon Restoration. During one particularly uproarious debate on 13 March 1838, the Minister of the Interior, the comte de Montalivet, fainted at the tribune when seeking additional funds. In the wake of a republican rising in Paris in 1839, however, there seemed to be a general acceptance in the Chamber that some sort of police surveillance was necessary. The Interior Minister, Charles Marie Tanneguy Duchâtel, one of the leading politicians of the July Monarchy, told the Chamber in February 1841: 'We believe it is no longer necessary to defend the *fonds secrets* against charges that they are either unnecessary or immoral.'[83]*

The 1839 rising had been organized by the secret *Société des Saisons*, founded two years earlier by the veteran revolutionary Auguste Blanqui, who based it on a theoretically secure cell structure. Though the reality was sometimes more confused, every cell was supposed to consist of seven republican revolutionaries, each named after a day of the week. Four weeks combined to form a month, whose leader was given the name of the month; three months made one of the four seasons. The fact that the *Société des Saisons* succeeded in launching a Paris rising on 12 May 1839, which for a few hours was able to occupy the National Assembly, the Hôtel de Ville and the Palace of Justice, strongly suggests that attempts at high-level penetration of the society by police agents had failed.

---

* Karila-Cohen's important study ('Fonds secrets ou la méfiance légitime') does not make the connection between the Paris rising of 1839 and increased parliamentary acceptance of the *fonds secrets*.

However, the belief by Blanqui and his followers that his secret organization, which never had a membership greater than about 1,500 (considerably
more than took part in the rising), could launch a successful insurrection
was a revolutionary fantasy – epitomized by their manifesto, 'Aux armes,
citoyens!', which proclaimed on 12 May 1839: 'People, rise up! And your
enemies will disappear like dust before a hurricane.' The manifesto named
Blanqui as 'commander-in-chief' of the rising, assisted by the 29-year-old
Armand Barbès and four other alleged 'divisional commanders of the
republican army'.[84] Though the rising was a fiasco, the revolutionaries
fought bravely; seventy-seven were killed as compared with twenty-eight
of the troops who defeated them.[85]

By far the largest and best-organized popular protest against any European political system before the 1848 revolutions was that of the Chartists
in unrevolutionary Britain. The Chartists united widely differing groups in
support of a People's Charter demanding the vote for all adult males, secret
ballots, annual general elections, equal constituencies, salaries and no property qualifications for MPs. In June 1839, a few weeks after the failure of
the Blanquist rising in Paris, a National Petition for the Charter with 1.28
million signatures was presented to the House of Commons. A second petition in 1842 gathered 3.32 million signatures, more than all the registered
voters in the United Kingdom. Both petitions, however, won the support of
fewer than fifty MPs. Because of the immense publicity which the Chartists
obtained, they were far easier to track than secretive revolutionary groups
such as the Société des Saisons and the Italian Carbonari on the Continent.
Thanks to the unprecedented expansion of the British press, more information was publicly available on the Chartists than on any previous popular
movement. Sales of newspapers which paid stamp duty rose from less than
33 million in 1833 to over 53 million in 1838, the year in which the People's
Charter was drawn up. Weekly sales of the Leeds-based Chartist newspaper,
Northern Star, reached an extraordinary 50,000 during 1839, giving it
probably the second-largest circulation in Britain; perhaps twenty times as
many heard it read aloud in pubs and meeting places.[86]*

In 1842 there was a wave of strikes and riots across much of the north
and Midlands. During the 'Plug Plot' 50,000 strikers forced factories to
close by removing the plugs from boilers to immobilize their steam engines.
Official concern at Chartism's growing support and fears that it would
end in serious violence led to the widespread official use of informers. The
Northern Star regularly warned its readers of the presence of government

* In 1833 the fourpenny tax on newspapers was reduced to one penny. Originally Leeds-
based, the Northern Star moved to London in 1844.

spies at Chartist meetings. Abram Duncan, one of the organizers of the
1842 National Petition, told a Chartist demonstration of 100,000 people
at Newcastle upon Tyne that 'hired moral assassins, the scoundrel minions
of a tyrant government' had been sent to inform on them.[87] The Home
Office, however, was no longer at the centre of domestic intelligence collection as it had been during the Revolutionary and Napoleonic Wars.[88]
Though there were numerous British informers, there was no centralized
political police intelligence system as in the main continental powers. 'We
have no political police, no police over opinion', boasted Charles Dickens's
Household Words in the 1850s. 'The most rabid demagogue can say in
this free country what he chooses ... He speaks not under the terror of
an organised spy system.' The Metropolitan Police Force ('Met'), founded
by Sir Robert Peel in 1829, originally contained no plain-clothes officers
at all. The detective department, established in 1842, still had only fifteen
men a quarter of a century later.[89]

Most of those who informed on the Chartists were freelance. In London
their main employers were the Met Commissioners. Over the rest of the
country, informers were used in varying numbers by magistrates, lords
lieutenant, military commanders, chief constables and local notables. Disraeli's friend W. B. Ferrand, the Tory factory reformer, personally persuaded
Michael Flynn, secretary of the Bradford Chartist Executive, to turn
informer. Ferrand, however, was exceptional. Like many mid-nineteenth-
century criminal investigations, most surveillance of the Chartists depended
on volunteer informers of varying reliability. 'Pardons, rewards, and a host
of other incentives', writes the historian J. C. Belchem, 'provided a lucrative
trade for the enterprising common informer as well as encouraging robbers,
thieves, embezzlers and murderers, let alone radicals, to betray their accomplices and spy upon their companions.' Most juries were untroubled by the
frequent unreliability of the informers' evidence.[90]

Metternich was less worried by the prospect of a Chartist revolution
than by England's role as a safe haven for continental revolutionaries. The
revolutionary exile who concerned him most was the Italian nationalist
Giuseppe Mazzini, whom he called the most dangerous man in Europe.
Metternich set up an eighty-strong police department to monitor plots by
Italian nationalists. In reality, though Mazzini was a romantic hero, he
was an incompetent revolutionary. During the decade after he fled to
London in 1837, he planned or inspired eight attempted revolts in Italian
states. All ended in fiasco.[91]

Through the Austrian ambassador in London, however, Metternich
successfully put pressure on the Conservative government of Sir Robert
Peel, which came to power in 1841, to intercept Mazzini's correspondence.

By the spring of 1844 Mazzini suspected his letters were being opened. To test his suspicion he placed grains of sand and poppy seeds in the envelopes which had disappeared by the time his letters reached their destination. Thomas Carlyle thundered in the letter columns of *The Times*:

> Whether the extraneous Austrian Emperor and the miserable old chimera of a Pope shall maintain themselves in Italy, or be obliged to decamp from Italy, is not a question in the least vital to Englishmen. But it is a question vital to us that sealed letters in an English post-office be, as we all fancied they were, respected as things sacred; that opening of men's letters, a practice near of kin to picking men's pockets, and to others still viler and far fataler forms of scoundrelism, be not resorted to in England, except in cases of the very last extremity.

The *Times* leader-writer agreed: 'the proceeding cannot be English, any more than masks, poisons, sword-sticks, secret signs and associations, and other such dark inventions'.[92]

The *Northern Star* denounced the Home Secretary, Sir James Graham, the main target of complaints at letter-opening, as 'the English Fouché':

> It has always been the boast of England that the friends of freedom, when driven from the other countries by the bloodhounds of despotism have ever found a refuge in England. Hence the exiles of all other countries flock in crowds to our shores. If the espionage system introduced by Sir James Graham were to be sanctioned or winked at by Parliament, this would be so no more.[93]

Punch portrayed Graham as 'Paul Pry at the Post Office'.*

On 14 June 1844 the radical MP for Finsbury, Thomas Duncombe, who had brought the 1842 Chartist petition to the Commons, presented to the House a petition from Mazzini and others complaining that the opening of their letters had introduced to Britain 'the odious spy system of foreign countries', a system 'repugnant to every principle of the British constitution'. 'It was', he said, 'disgraceful to a free country that such a system should be tolerated – it might do in Russia, aye, or even in France, or it might do in the Austrian dominions, it might do in Sardinia; but it did not suit the free air of this free country.' Robert Wallace MP, a leading advocate of reform of the postal service, told the Commons that 'he believed [mistakenly] that persons had been sent abroad to study in the school of Fouché, how to open, fold, and reseal letters in the Post Office in London'.[94]

In a debate prompted by the Mazzini case on 24 June, the most remarkable speech was that of the great historian Thomas Babington Macaulay,

* See ill. 38.

a Whig MP for over a quarter of a century.* Macaulay accepted that useful intelligence could be obtained by the interception of correspondence, by police spies and (more controversially) by torture, but denounced all three as un-British:

> There could be no doubt there might be an advantage in breaking open letters. No one denied it; but then was it fitting that it should be done? In the same way, did any one doubt that there was an advantage in having police spies? But then the country did not approve of them. The French had an advantage in having police spies. No one doubted that the spy system enabled them to bring to justice many who must otherwise have escaped. It was the same thing as to torture. There could be no doubt that as long as the English law sanctioned the use of the torture a great many crimes were detected by it. It had, too, its advantages. [*Cries of "Oh, oh."*] Yes; for the instant that Guy Fawkes was shown the rack, out came at once the entire story of the gunpowder plot. Even this torture, as well as the spy system, had these advantages, but then this country had determined long ago that such were pernicious, debasing, and dangerous modes of maintaining its institutions.[95]

The leading Whig politician Lord John Russell MP, who was to succeed Peel as Prime Minister two years later, claimed that Austria was not the only authoritarian regime which had been secretly supplied by the Home Secretary with the intercepted correspondence of political exiles in Britain: 'to the complaisance of the right hon. Baronet [Sir James Graham] Russia has an equal claim. Letters addressed to unfortunate Poles, who have found a refuge in this country, have been broken open. Poland has been abandoned: she is bound hand and foot, and the boot of the Tartar is on her neck . . .'[96] Thomas Wakley, Duncombe's fellow MP for Finsbury, told the Commons that the interception of correspondence was being 'denounced in every quarter and in every house':

> A gentleman – a politician – had said to him, only last Saturday, that he had always considered a Government that employed spies was the most odious that could exist, but he had at length discovered a worse – that was a Government that became spies themselves, and the present Government was clearly becoming a spy Government.[97]

In response to the public uproar over the Mazzini case, the Commons appointed a Committee of Secrecy 'to inquire into the State of the Law in respect of the Detaining and Opening of Letters at the General Post-office,

* Though a Whig MP for over a quarter of a century, Macaulay several times changed seats.

and into the Mode under which the Authority given for such Detaining and Opening has been exercised'. In August the committee produced a 116-page report. Lord John Russell expressed surprise, given the extent of the committee's 'antiquarian research' into postal history, that they had not considered Shakespeare's account of how Hamlet, having opened secret letters asking the King of England to order his execution, was able to arrange for Rosencrantz and Guildenstern to be executed instead.[98]

The Mazzini affair marked a turning point in British intelligence history. After the report of the Committee of Secrecy, the Peel government decided to close down both the Deciphering Branch and the Secret Office of the Post Office.[99] Francis Willes, the last of the Willes dynasty of cryptanalysts founded by Bishop Edward Willes, was given a pension of £700 a year; he died a year later. His assistant, 'Mr Lovell' (almost certainly his nephew, the Reverend William Willes Lovell), received £200 a year.[100] As a result of the closure of the Deciphering Branch in 1844, Britain entered the First World War, unlike any of the major wars of the seventeenth and eighteenth centuries, with no codebreakers.[101]

During the 1840s, as before the 1830 revolutions, the ruling regimes in the four main continental powers continued to believe that the main threat to their survival came from revolutionaries. Surveillance of French republican revolutionaries was far more effective after the failed Paris rising of 1839 than previously. The leaders of the rising – chief among them Auguste Blanqui, Armand Barbès and Martin Bernard – were imprisoned until the 1848 Revolution, closely watched by *moutons de prison*. Republican groups outside prison were also penetrated by agents working for the Paris *préfet de police*, Gabriel Delessert.[102] One of Delessert's leading agents, Lucien Delahodde, later published a highly critical history of French secret societies which appears to draw on police files of varying reliability. The New York publisher of the English translation of Delahodde's history identified him on the title page as a 'member of the detective police' as well as 'a sparkling and witty French writer': 'The object of translating this work ... is to show the dangerous consequences, to society and government, arising from the practices of secret associations.'[103] Both before and after the 1848 Revolution there were rumours in republican ranks that some of them had been recruited as police informers. The most prominent of those accused was France's leading professional revolutionary, Auguste Blanqui. In April 1848 Blanqui published a pamphlet protesting his innocence in an attempt to clear his name.[104] Though the charges against him by his chief accuser, Jules Taschereau, a former senior official of the July Monarchy, were almost certainly unfounded, they were believed by, among others, Armand Barbès, his ally in the failed revolt of 1839, who publicly denounced Blanqui.[105]* Controversy still continues over whether Aloysius Huber, another leading republican imprisoned under Louis Philippe, became a police spy and *agent provocateur*.[106]

Writing in 1864, Delahodde – a genuine police spy – poured scorn on the ineffectiveness of republican revolutionaries: 'not one of our revolutions, during the last sixty years, has been the work of conspirators. However blasphemous this assertion may appear to the grumblers of the mob, we hold it to be irrefragably true.'[107] The February Revolution which overthrew the July Monarchy in 1848 was caused not by republican conspirators but by Louis Philippe's incompetent response to a political reform movement, exacerbated by economic crisis. With the Hôtel de Ville in the hands of the mob, and an angry crowd advancing on the Tuileries Palace, Louis-Philippe abdicated on 24 February. After hurriedly shaving off his luxuriant side whiskers, he slipped out of a side door of the palace and fled ignominiously to England, wearing dark glasses, a cap and scarf, and with a false passport identifying him as Bill Smith, uncle of the British vice-consul in Le Havre.[108]

In no European capital did intelligence reports provide advance warning of the 1848 Revolution. Surveillance was focused on revolutionary groups – or those thought to be so. As in 1789, however, the Revolution produced revolutionaries, rather than the other way around. In Paris political demonstrations and clubs proliferated, and universal male suffrage was declared. The head of the provisional government, Alphonse de Lamartine, a conservative turned republican and the first major lyric poet to become French leader, was quick to reassure the rest of Europe that the Second Republic wanted peace and would not imitate the wars of the First Republic.[109]

Though Metternich and Frederick William IV read intelligence reports from their spies and *cabinets noirs* attentively, the news of the February Revolution in Paris and the enthusiasm it aroused in Vienna and Berlin took them by surprise. In March 1848 rioters forced Frederick William and his army to flee from Berlin. For several months 'unrespectable' and 'unruly' crowds dominated the capital.[110] Seeing revolutionary demonstrators in front of Schönbrunn Palace in Vienna, the intellectually challenged Austrian Emperor Ferdinand I is said to have asked Metternich: 'Well, are they allowed to do this?' ('Ja, dürfen's denn des?'). When they continued demonstrating, Ferdinand abdicated in favour of his nephew Franz Joseph, who was to rule Austria for the next sixty-eight years. 'Afterwards', he

---

* In April 1848 Taschereau was elected to the Constituent Assembly.

wrote in his diary with evident relief, 'I and my dear wife heard Holy Mass . . . After that I and my dear wife packed our bags.' Metternich fled from Vienna on 13 March and, after a difficult journey, found refuge from revolution in London on 20 April.[111] Despite a revival of Chartism in 1848, most British people believed that revolutions were only for foreigners.

19

Intelligence and Counter-Revolution. Part II: From 1848 to the Death of Karl Marx

Ultimately, by far the most influential revolutionaries who came to the fore in 1848 were the Prussians Karl Marx and Friedrich Engels, both in exile in Brussels at the time of the February Revolution in Paris. Two years earlier Marx, his wife, Jenny, and Engels had been among the eighteen founder members in Brussels of the Communist Correspondence Committee, from which all modern Communist parties are descended.[1] On receiving news of the February Revolution, Engels wrote exultantly but over-optimistically in the *Deutsche-Brüsseler Zeitung*: 'The flames of the Tuileries and the Palais Royal are the dawn of the proletariat. Everywhere the rule of the bourgeoisie will now come crashing down, or be dashed to pieces.'* In the nervy atmosphere in Berlin created by the February Revolution in Paris and its resonance in Central Europe, some Prussian officials took Engels's forecast more seriously than it deserved. A Prussian police spy in Brussels wrote of the *Deutsche-Brüsseler Zeitung*:

> This noxious paper must indisputably exert the most corrupting influence upon the uneducated public at whom it is directed. The alluring theory of the dividing-up of wealth is held out to factory workers and day labourers as an innate right, and a profound hatred of the rulers and the rest of the community is inculcated into them.[2]

Expelled from Brussels in early March, Marx moved to Paris, where he stayed for the next month. Like Alexis de Tocqueville, he saw the February Revolution and the Second Republic, which succeeded the July Monarchy, as 'a revolution made up of memories', inspired by romanticized folk memories of the events which followed 1789. Marx wrote later: 'Hegel remarks somewhere that all great world-historic facts and personages appear, so to speak, twice. He forgot to add: the first time as tragedy, the second time as farce.' The Second Republic, he believed,

---

* Marx and Engels had begun writing in the *Deutsche-Brüsseler Zeitung* in April 1847.

became a farce. Like the First, it fell into the hands of a Bonaparte. In December 1848 Napoleon's nephew, Louis Napoleon, was elected President by an electorate most of which knew nothing about him but his name. On 2 December 1851 he staged a coup which Marx considered a 'caricature' of the coup in 1799 which had made his uncle First Consul and effectively dictator.[3] A year later, like Napoleon in 1804, Louis Napoleon became Emperor and founded the Second Empire.

After a month in Paris during the spring of 1848, Marx left for Cologne to become editor of the *Neue Rheinische Zeitung*, which began publication on 1 June. As Engels privately admitted, the management of the newspaper was 'a simple dictatorship' by Marx. It quickly built up a daily circulation of 5,000, very large by the standards of the day, and inevitably attracted close police attention. During July Marx was twice summoned to appear before examining magistrates for offences which included 'insulting or libelling the Chief Public Prosecutor'.[4] In August, at the height of the German revolutionary upheavals, Marx called a congress in Cologne to coordinate agitation against the Prussian government. The Prussian police must have been delighted by reports they received from the informers in attendance. Convinced as always of his own ideological infallibility, Marx disastrously mishandled the congress. Among the revolutionary students present was Carl Schurz from the University of Bonn, who had arrived 'eager to gather words of wisdom from the lips of the famous man'. He was bitterly disappointed:

> Marx's utterances were indeed full of meaning, logical and clear, but I have never seen a man whose bearing was so provoking and intolerable. To no opinion which differed from his own did he accord the honour of even condescending consideration. Everyone who contradicted him he treated with abject contempt; every argument that he did not like he answered either with biting scorn at the unfathomable ignorance that had prompted it, or with opprobrious aspersions on the motives of him who had advanced it. I remember most distinctly the cutting disdain with which he pronounced the word 'bourgeois'; and as a 'bourgeois' – that is, as a detestable example of the deepest mental and moral degeneracy – he denounced everyone who dared to oppose his opinion. Of course, the propositions advanced or advocated by Marx in that meeting were voted down, because everyone whose feelings had been hurt by his conduct was inclined to support everything that Marx did not favour. It was very evident that not only had he not won any adherents, but had repelled many who might otherwise have become his followers.[5]*

---

* In 1852, Carl Schurz emigrated to the United States, where he later became the first German-American senator and Secretary of the Interior.

Marx even succeeded in alienating the workers in the print room of the *Neue Rheinische Zeitung*, who took a day off to celebrate a royal visit to the Rhineland by Frederick William IV, forcing him to cancel an issue.[6]

By now the old order in both Vienna and Berlin was recovering its nerve and rediscovering the underlying strength of traditional authority and the armed forces. At the end of October 1848 Vienna was retaken by government troops with the loss of 2,000 lives.[7] Behind the scenes Frederick William IV gathered round him a cabal of conservatives determined to end the revolution in Prussia. In November the Prussian army expelled the Prussian National Assembly, elected the previous May, from its Berlin premises.[8] From April to July 1849 there was a new wave of insurrections in the German states. 45,000 revolutionaries, including men such as Carl Schurz whom Marx had alienated at the Cologne congress, fought and lost pitched battles against the Prussian army.[9] In May 1849 the *Neue Rheinische Zeitung*, founded by Marx a year earlier, was closed down, defiantly printing its last issue in red ink with a declaration that the editors' 'last word is and always will be: *emancipation of the working class!*'[10]

The increasing number of revolutionary refugees from the Continent in Britain after the suppression of the 1848 revolutions led the Metropolitan Police to show greater interest in émigré activities. It had four main sources of intelligence: investigations by its small group of detectives, diverted from their usual duties; unsolicited and often alarmist information from the public; reports from foreign police spies forwarded by the Foreign Office; and a modest number of paid informers. Probably the Met's most reliable informer was John Hitchens Sanders, a French-speaker able to pass himself off as a refugee. In 1849 and 1850 Sanders attended meetings of political exiles and sent detailed reports to the Met and the Foreign Office. In January 1851 he joined Scotland Yard's 'A' (Whitehall) Division and for the next eight years reported directly on émigré activities to the Commissioner, Sir Richard Mayne.[11] A dramatic report, possibly by Sanders, of a London meeting of 600 mainly French republican exiles in March noted vociferous disagreements, with 'the words Canaille, Voleur, Brigand, Coquin, Jean-foutre continually used in speaking of each other' by rival speakers.[12]

Ultimately the most influential of the political refugees in London was Karl Marx, who arrived in August 1849 and established the new headquarters of the Communist League at the offices of the German Workers' Education Society. London became his home for the remainder of his life. Earlier in 1849 Marx had joked to his wife: 'Your brother [Ferdinand von Westphalen] is so stupid that he will become a Prussian Minister yet!' The fellow revolutionary who recorded the conversation noted that 'Mrs Marx blushed at this over-frank remark and turned the conversation to another subject.'* A year later the right-wing Westphalen fulfilled Marx's prophecy by becoming Prussian Interior Minister. The Prussian hunt for subversives intensified after an unsuccessful assassination attempt against Frederick William IV on 22 May 1850 at a Berlin railway station by a former soldier, Maximilian Joseph Sefeloge.† Thanks in large part to Westphalen, the Prussian government was more active than any other in sending police spies and *agents provocateurs* to track down émigré revolutionaries in foreign capitals, especially London. High on the list of targets was his brother-in-law, Karl Marx.

On 15 June 1850 the London *Spectator* published a protest signed by Marx, Engels and another Prussian revolutionary, August Willich, written by Marx in his Soho flat, protesting at the intensiveness of their surveillance by 'Prussian spies and English informers' in the aftermath of an attempt to assassinate Frederick William IV:

> Really, Sir, we should have never thought that there existed in this country so many police-spies as we have had the good fortune of making the acquaintance of in the short space of a week. Not only that the doors of the houses where we live are closely watched by individuals of a more than doubtful look, who take down their notes very coolly every time any one enters the house or leaves it; we cannot make a single step without being followed by them wherever we go. We cannot get into an omnibus or enter a coffee-house without being favoured with the company of at least one of these unknown friends. We do not know whether the gentlemen engaged in this grateful occupation are so 'on her Majesty's service'; but we know this, that the majority of them look anything but clean and respectable.
>
> Now, of what use can be, to any one, the scanty information thus scratched together at our doors by a lot of miserable spies, male prostitutes of the lowest order, who mostly seem to be drawn from the class of common informers, and paid by the job? Will this, no doubt exceedingly trustworthy information, be of such value as to entitle any one to sacrifice, for its sake, the old-established boast of Englishmen, that in their country there is no chance of introducing that spy system from which not one country of the Continent is free?
>
> . . . We believe, Sir, that under these circumstances, we cannot do better than bring the whole case before the public. We believe that Englishmen

---

* Marx's comment and his wife's reaction were recorded by Simon Buttermilch (also known as Stephan Born). (McLellan (ed.), *Karl Marx, Interviews and Reflections*, p. 16.)

† Marx later claimed that Sefeloge was 'not a Revolutionist, but an ultra-Royalist' as well as 'a notorious madman'. (Letter from Marx, Engels and Willich, *The Spectator*, 14 June 1850. *MECW*, vol. 10, p. 381.)

are interested in anything by which the old-established reputation of England, as the safest asylum for refugees of all parties and of all countries, may be more or less affected.[13]

Marx's complaint that Britain was giving aid and comfort to the continental 'spy system' aroused only a small fraction of the public interest provoked by Mazzini's somewhat similar complaint six years earlier. On 1 September 1850, just over a fortnight after the publication of the letter in *The Spectator*, Marx's irascible co-signatory, August Willich, who grandly described himself as 'Colonel in the Insurrectionary Army in Baden'[14] and had a reputation as a crack-shot, challenged Marx to a duel. Marx refused.[15]

Chief among the Prussian police spies sent to London in 1850 to report on Marx and other émigré revolutionaries was Wilhelm Stieber, later Bismarck's intelligence chief, who posed as a journalist named Schmidt. Stieber sent an alarmist and fraudulent report to Westphalen, claiming that Marx and his fellow revolutionaries were plotting the assassination of the crowned heads of Europe:

> At a meeting the day before yesterday at which I assisted and over which [the German Communist, Wilhelm] Wolff and Marx presided, I heard one of the orators call out: 'The Moon Calf [Queen Victoria] will likewise not escape its destiny. The English steel wares are the best, the axes cut particularly sharply here, and the guillotine awaits every Crowned Head.' Thus the murder of the Queen of England is proclaimed by Germans a few hundred yards only from Buckingham Palace ... Before the close of the meeting Marx told his audience they might be perfectly tranquil, their men were everywhere at their posts. The eventful moment was approaching and infallible measures are taken so that not one of the European crowned executioners can escape.[16]

'Stieber', writes a leading British historian of Germany, Sir Richard Evans, 'developed many of the techniques which were to give the Prussian police so much notoriety in subsequent decades: deliberate provocations, bribery, deception, theft of documents, forgery and perjury were all his stock in trade.'* Westphalen was taken in by Stieber's report that Marx and other revolutionaries were planning the assassination of Queen Victoria and

---

* Among other preposterous claims, Stieber's memoirs say that, while Bismarck's intelligence chief in the late 1860s, he had a network of 30,000 agents in France. Though the authenticity of the memoirs has been challenged, as Sir Richard Evans observes: 'Since Stieber was an accomplished, indeed professional liar, the obvious falsehoods in his book do nothing in themselves to suggest that he did not write it himself.' (Stieber, *The Chancellor's Spy*. Evans, *Rereading German History*, pp. 70, 84, n. 25.)

other royals, and forwarded it to the British government. Palmerston, the Foreign Secretary, wisely ignored it.[17]

Continental governments were horrified by the revolutionary potential of the huge crowds likely to attend the Great Exhibition which was due to open on 1 May 1851 in the astounding glass and iron Crystal Palace constructed in Hyde Park, four times the length of St Paul's Cathedral. According to one, exceptionally alarmist foreign police report (ignored by the Met) some revolutionaries planned to disguise themselves as trees.[18*] The British minister in Dresden reported in April: 'there is universal terror respecting the Great Exhibition & the Plots probably concerting there'. Similar expressions of alarm came from other European capitals.[19] Shortly before the Exhibition opened, Lord Palmerston suggested that if the French government was alarmed by émigré plots, it should send 'Some sharp Directors' to keep an eye on them in London, as 'our police are good for ~~nothing~~ [sic] little for such purposes, and besides they are not *linguists*'.[20] During April and May, however, in collaboration with continental police spies, the Metropolitan Police recruited informers to report on émigré meetings. In September the Chartist *Northern Star* reported rumours of a 'recently established foreign branch of the English police force'. The rumours probably referred to the increase in intelligence liaison with continental police prompted by the Great Exhibition.[21]

During 1851, twenty years ahead of German political unification, the main German states and Austria set up a police union to exchange intelligence and coordinate operations against political subversion. For the next fifteen years the union organized annual meetings, exchanged confiscated subversive documents, and shared intelligence on wanted revolutionaries, political parties with democratic tendencies, religious groups and the press.[22] According to Wilhelm Hirsch, a Hamburg-born Prussian police spy in London, surveillance of German and Austrian émigrés during the 1851 Exhibition was coordinated on the spot by 'a police triumvirate': Stieber from Prussia, Herr Kubesch from Austria and Police Commissioner Huntel from Bremen.[23] Instead of discovering signs of revolutionary disorder in the Crystal Palace, they witnessed instead a triumphant display of British capitalism and national pride. Queen Victoria, who opened the exhibition on 1 May amid massed choirs singing the Hallelujah Chorus, declared it 'the *greatest* day in our history' and 'the *happiest, grandest* day of my life'. Over the six months of the Exhibition, it was visited by six million people, one third of the British

---

* The intention may have been to warn that revolutionaries would be hiding behind trees in Hyde Park.

population – the largest, and among the most orderly, indoor crowds ever
assembled. 'There is about as much chance of a revolution in England',
wrote Macaulay, 'as of the falling of the moon.'[24]

There was, however, no slackening of Prussian police surveillance in
London. Wilhelm Hirsch later described how agents to spy on Prussian
refugees were recruited at Ye Olde Cock Tavern, which then, as now
(though the tavern has since crossed the street), had the narrowest frontage
of any London pub:

> The Cock, in Fleet St., Temple Bar, is so unobtrusive that but for a golden
> cock pointing to the entrance the casual passer-by would hardly notice it.
> I went through a narrow passage leading to the interior of this old English
> tavern and asked for Mr. Charles, whereupon a corpulent personage intro-
> duced himself to me with such an amiable smile that anyone seeing us would
> have taken us for old friends. The Embassy agent (for this is what he was)
> seemed to be in very high spirits and his mood was still further improved
> by brandy and water.

'Mr Charles' revealed that his real name was Alberts and that he was the
Prussian embassy secretary. At a second meeting, at his home in Brewer
Square, he introduced Hirsch to Police Lieutenant Greif, who, like Alberts,
initially identified himself as 'Mr Charles':

> Greif looked the true policeman: medium height, dark hair and a beard of
> the same colour cut in the regulation style, with the moustache meeting the
> side-whiskers and the chin left shaven. His eyes looked anything but intel-
> ligent and they protruded fiercely in a permanent glare, apparently the result
> of frequent association with thieves and rogues.

At a later meeting, after expressing satisfaction with Hirsch's early surveillance work, Greif announced that the priority was reports on 'the
secret meetings of the Marx party': 'Do it any way you wish as long as
you don't overstep the limits of credibility.'[25]*

During 1852 the Prussian police agent who had most success in winning
Marx's confidence was the Hungarian journalist János Bangya, who assured
Marx that he was 'the only capable German man' and entertained both him
and his wife to dinner. Marx's correspondence to Engels and others showed
that by the spring of 1852 he trusted Bangya completely and invited him to
join the Communist League. Bangya praised a series of satirical sketches
which Marx had written about other leading revolutionary exiles in

---

* In producing reports on 'Marx's party', Hirsch took instructions from Greif's subordinate,
Fleury-Krause.

London, and told him a Berlin publisher would pay £25 for a short selection and publish them anonymously.[26]* Instead, almost certainly, Bangya forwarded them to Berlin police headquarters. The two most important twentieth-century Communist leaders, Lenin and Stalin, were similarly deceived before the February Revolution by police spies posing as loyal comrades. Like Lenin, Marx at first refused to believe that he had been taken in.[27] Bangya later also worked as an agent for Napoleon III.[28]

In the autumn of 1852 the Prussian political police in London sent Berlin an agent report on Marx, possibly by Bangya, which was highly complimentary about his wife, Jenny, 'the sister of the Prussian Minister von Westphalen, a cultured and charming woman, who out of love for her husband has accustomed herself to his bohemian existence, and now feels perfectly at home in this poverty'. The agent, however, was plainly anxious not to offend the Prussian authorities by giving too positive a report on Marx himself: 'In private life he is an extremely disorderly, cynical human being, and a bad host. He leads the existence of a real bohemian intellectual. Washing, grooming and changing his linen are things he does rarely, and he likes to get drunk.' Later in the report, however, the agent contradicted himself and acknowledged that, so far from being 'a bad host', both Marx and his wife had given him a hospitable welcome:

> You are received in the most friendly way and cordially offered pipes and tobacco and whatever else there may happen to be; and eventually a spirited and agreeable conversation arises to make amends for the domestic deficiencies, thus making the discomfort tolerable. Finally you grow accustomed to the company, and find it interesting and original.[29]

Though still supremely confident of his own ideological infallibility, Marx had plainly learned some social skills since he had alienated revolutionary sympathizers at the Cologne congress four years earlier.

During 1852 Marx became heavily embroiled from London in the show trial which opened in Cologne in October of eleven members of the Communist League charged with conspiring to overthrow the government. Marx sent evidence to the defence attorneys through secret intermediaries, unaware, however, that one of the intermediaries, Hermann Ebner, was an Austrian spy. The star witness at the trial was Wilhelm Stieber, who gave hair-raising details of the planned Communist insurrection and presented in evidence a mixture of forgeries and genuine documents stolen by his spies from Prussian refugees in London. He claimed that, while he

---

* Bangya paid Marx £18 for the satirical sketches, partly because he had already loaned him £7.

was assisting the French police to arrest some of the conspirators, the émigré revolutionary Joseph Cheval had attacked him in his Paris flat and that Frau Stieber had been wounded in the ensuing fracas. In reality, Cheval was an *agent provocateur* employed by Stieber. In November 1852 seven of the defendants were sentenced to imprisonment. Marx and his London followers agreed that all prospect of effective political action had disappeared for the foreseeable future and dissolved the Communist League.[30] There was no longer a 'Marx party' for the Prussian political police in London to keep under surveillance. Marx wrote in 1858: 'since 1852 I had not been associated with *any* association and was firmly convinced that my theoretical studies were of greater use to the working class than my meddling with associations which had now had their day on the Continent.'[31] His priority was the writing of *Das Kapital* and his main workplace was the Reading Room of the British Museum.

By the mid-1850s informers had established themselves as part of the Prussian political system at the highest level. Rival factions in the Prussian court employed agents to spy on each other. Otto von Manteuffel, Minister-President (Chief Minister) from 1850 to 1858, who was deeply suspicious about the plotting of ultra-conservatives in the entourage of Frederick William IV, paid a former army lieutenant, Carl Techen, to steal copies of confidential documents from the homes of leading ultras, among them the King's adjutant-general, Leopold von Gerlach, and Frederick William's secretary, Marcus Niebuhr. On 2 November 1855 the police arrested servants of Gerlach and Niebuhr, on charges of making and selling copies of their masters' correspondence and diaries. Following further investigation, Techen, for whom these copies had been made, was arrested on 29 January 1856. Wilhelm Stieber and the veteran police inspector Friedrich Goldheim extracted a signed confession from him. 'For a long time', Techen admitted, 'I have been employed as a secret agent of the Minister-President, Baron von Manteuffel.' Gerlach and Niebuhr, Manteuffel believed, were among those who 'were constantly intriguing against him'. Techen, it emerged, believed himself poorly paid for his espionage by the Minister-President and had also sold copies of the stolen documents to the French embassy in Berlin. (Bismarck observed that Manteuffel had indeed paid Techen with 'Prussian frugality'.) Further investigation of what one recent historian has called the 'Prussian Watergate' revealed that Gerlach himself, as well as being spied on, had been employing a spy of his own to report to him on the King's brother, Prince William.*

---

* Techen had first been arrested in October 1855 but had been released for lack of evidence. (Barclay, *Frederick William IV*, pp. 152–4.)

Like Manteuffel and others at the Prussian court, Louis Napoleon in France took a close personal interest in intercepted correspondence. Among the letters he read regularly as Emperor were those of his Spanish wife, the Empress Eugénie, to the Spanish court. He formed the habit of destroying those letters of which he disapproved. Napoleon's most eloquent critic, the writer Victor Hugo, an even greater global celebrity than Charles Dickens, was well aware that his correspondence to France was regularly intercepted during his years in exile on Guernsey, and used envelopes on which were printed the article of the penal code forbidding the opening of letters. When this had no effect, he took to writing on the envelope: 'Family matters – no point in reading' – also without result. Agents of the *cabinet noir* at the Interior Ministry bribed the concierges, valets and maids of important people to give them access to their correspondence. The leading politician Adolphe Thiers, one of Louis Napoleon's ablest political opponents (later first President of the Third Republic), dismissed his valet after hearing the Interior Minister quote from one of his purloined letters.[32]

Louis Napoleon had greater personal interest in intelligence than any other ruler of his time outside Russia – an interest derived in part from his own experience of being under surveillance during the July Monarchy. In 1836 and 1840 he had attempted two woefully inept coups d'état. In 1846 he made a rather better-planned escape from the fortress of Ham in the department of the Somme, where he was imprisoned, shaving off his beard and moustache, donning a wig, dressing as a labourer and walking out of the fortress with a plank of wood balanced on his shoulder.[33] As French ruler, Louis Napoleon shared his uncle's fascination with intelligence reports on French public opinion but, unlike most autocrats, was preoccupied by the problems of 'telling truth to power'. On 22 January 1852 he established a new Ministry of Police under Charlemagne de Maupas, who had played a leading role in his coup d'état on 2 December 1851. Maupas's role, Louis Napoleon told him, was to ensure he was told 'the truth which is too often kept from those in power'.[34]

Assessments of the prefects of the eighty-six French departments in the summer and autumn of 1852 by the Ministry of Police seem to have been as uninhibited as Louis Napoleon had intended. Very few prefects received the accolade *très dévoué, très intelligent*. Five were assessed as so 'incapable' that they deserved to be dismissed. Another eighteen were recommended for transfers to other jobs because of failings ranging from laziness to tactlessness.[35] The ministry, unsurprisingly, survived for only seventeen months. Having aroused the ire of the rival Interior and War Ministries as well as probably numerous prefects, it was closed down in

June 1853.[36] Louis Napoleon, who had declared himself the Emperor Napoleon III in December 1852, probably concluded that its usefulness had been undermined by the disputes which it provoked. During the Second Empire the internal-intelligence reports to which he paid most attention were those of the *procureurs généraux*, the attorney-generals in the French departments, who monitored not merely public opinion but also the performance of the prefects. The most recent detailed study of their role concludes that they functioned as a 'political police'.[37]

The greatest intelligence bungle of the Second Empire was the failure to provide warning of a nearly successful attempt by four Italian republican nationalists, led by Felice Orsini (son of a survivor of Napoleon's Russian campaign), to assassinate the Emperor and Empress as they arrived at the Paris Opéra in January 1858. Though Napoleon III and Eugénie survived the bombs thrown at their carriage, eight bystanders were killed and almost 150 injured. The British embassy in Paris believed that the French police had failed to act on intelligence pointing to an assassination plot. The French government and its supporters, however, placed all the blame on Britain's failure to keep under surveillance the dangerous foreign revolutionaries to whom it had given refuge. The bomb attack had been planned in England, where Orsini and his accomplices were political exiles. Detective-Constable John Sanders, Scotland Yard's chief investigator of political exiles in London, had warned the Commissioner in 1856 and 1857 that plotting by Italian and a smaller number of French émigrés was becoming 'really dangerous', and that they were actively preparing an attempt on the life of Napoleon III. But Sanders's warning seems not to have been followed up. It was later discovered that a prototype of the bombs used by Orsini's group had been tested in a Sheffield quarry by George Holyoake, a former Chartist parliamentary candidate.[38]

The Foreign Secretary, the 4th Earl of Clarendon, felt privately 'ashamed of the protection wh[ich] assassins enjoy here'. Lord Palmerston, the Prime Minister, agreed that the reaction of the French was 'perfectly natural and would have been ours in as great a Degree if attempts and outrages of the same kind had been repeatedly committed in London by criminals issuing from Paris'.[39] To try to persuade the French that some action was being taken, Palmerston made an ill-judged attempt to gain parliamentary support for a Conspiracy to Murder bill. When the Commons voted it down, the government resigned. Though most of Orsini's helpers in Britain escaped arrest, the French bomb-maker Simon Bernard was put on trial. Bernard's barrister, the flamboyant former actor Edwin James (later disbarred for fraud and corruption), denounced what he claimed was 'foreign police spy' involvement in the case, telling the jury that the prosecution

had been 'directed by foreign dictation, to bring about a state of subservi-
ency to foreign governments which the Executive of this country has not
the courage to submit to the sanction of the English House of Commons . . . to gratify a foreign potentate'. Against the clear direction of the
judge, Bernard was acquitted and hailed as a hero outside the court in
what Clarendon called 'a rascally demonstration, disgraceful to our country'.[40] John Sanders died from 'apoplexy' in August 1859 at the age of only
thirty-five.[41] Scotland Yard does not seem to have replaced him as its
specialist on the activities of political refugees.

Marx followed the trial of Orsini and his accomplices in Paris in February 1858 with deep, though misplaced, suspicion: 'For the first time, a
prisoner was decently treated in an Imperial court of justice. There was,
as an eye-witness says, "little or no bullying, brow-beating or attempt at
declamation." It thus becomes evident that an infernal double game was
here played.' Though Orsini and one of his accomplices were sentenced
to death and went to the guillotine in March, Marx wrongly concluded
that Orsini had been comparatively well treated because he 'had revelations to make', particularly about Louis Napoleon's earlier involvement
in the *Carbonari*, secret Italian revolutionary societies, but had agreed
not to make them.[42] A year later Marx became involved in bitter mutual
recriminations with a left-wing German scientist, Karl Vogt, who had
taken refuge in Switzerland. After Marx repeated allegations that Vogt
was in the pay of Napoleon III, Vogt replied, amid a flurry of writs, with
a book denouncing Marx as 'a revolutionary charlatan who sponged off
the workers while consorting with the aristocracy', which became an
instant best-seller in German.[43] Marx spent most of 1860 writing a detailed
reply entitled *Herr Vogt*, denouncing him as 'one of the countless mouth-
pieces through whom the grotesque ventriloquist in the Tuileries spoke in
foreign tongues'.[44] Since no German publisher would touch it, Marx had
to beg and borrow the money for an English edition. Jenny Marx wrote
to an old friend: 'You cannot imagine how many worries and sleepless
nights the affair brought us.'[45] Documents discovered after the overthrow
of Napoleon III in 1870 revealed that in 1859 alone Vogt had been paid
50,000 francs by the French authorities.[46]

Marx never deviated from his insistence in *The Communist Manifesto*
that 'The history of all hitherto existing society is the history of class
struggle.' Class struggle did not depend on secret conspiracy. Marx, however, had been targeted by so many secret agents that he came to see spies
in improbable places. Among the most improbable was 10 Downing Street.
During the Crimean War he convinced himself that, despite being at
war with Russia, the Prime Minister, Lord Palmerston, formerly Foreign

Secretary for fifteen years, was a long-standing, paid Russian agent. Further research in the Reading Room at the British Museum bizarrely convinced Marx that continuous secret collaboration between the Cabinets of London and St. Petersburg went back to the era of Peter the Great.[47]

With the foundation in London in 1864 of the International Working Men's Association (IWMA), later called the First International, Marx became of some renewed interest to continental police intelligence. By 1865 he was effectively leader of the International, though his formal title was simply 'corresponding secretary for Germany'.[48] The early years of the International, however, faded into apparent insignificance by comparison with the momentous changes taking place in Germany. Prussia's victory in the war with Austria in the summer of 1866 led to the dissolution of the German Confederation, the creation of a new Prussian-dominated North German Confederation and Prussian annexation of a number of its neighbours. Among the casualties of the Austro-Prussian War was the Police Union of German States founded in 1851 to coordinate police counter-subversion operations in Austria and the main German states, and which ceased to function in 1866.[49] Marx attracted less attention in London from the Prussian police as leader of the International than he had done at the time of the Great Exhibition. It is highly unlikely that spies of any nationality ever followed him to the British Museum and watched as he put the final touches to the first volume of *Das Kapital* ('Capital'), which was published in German in 1867. It is equally improbable that Palmerston paid attention to, or was even aware of, Marx's repeated published claims that he was a long-standing Russian spy.

Marx returned to notoriety and the serious interest of continental intelligence services after the fall of the Second Empire and France's defeat in the Franco-Prussian War. The most serious civil war of the century broke out in March 1871 between patriotic radicals of the Paris Commune, who were unwilling to accept defeat, and the forces of the newly elected French government led by Adolphe Thiers, referred to by Marx as 'that monstrous gnome'. Though seventeen of the ninety-two elected leaders of the Commune, named in honour of the Paris Commune of the 1790s, were members of the International, the majority looked back to an older revolutionary tradition. It suited the Thiers government, however, to blame the Commune on Marx and the International; forged documents were used in an attempt to prove the connection.[50] Marx seems to have concluded, probably correctly, that the forgeries were the work of police agents:

> The police-tinged bourgeois mind naturally figures to itself the International Working Men's Association as acting in the manner of a secret

conspiracy, its central body ordering, from time to time, explosions in different countries. Our Association is, in fact, nothing but the international bond between the most advanced working men in the various countries of the civilized world.[51]

After the *Pall Mall Gazette* denounced him as 'head of a vast conspiracy' responsible for atrocities by the Commune, Marx threatened the editor with a duel. Privately, however, after years in which the British press had largely ignored him, he was pleased to be 'the best calumniated man in London': 'It really does one good after a boring twenty-year-long swamp idyll.'[52]

Marx was well aware that the Paris Commune did as much to defend middle-class as workers' interests and later complained that it had failed to seize the assets of the Bank of France. But after the Commune was crushed by French government forces with horrendous violence during *la Semaine Sanglante* in May,[53] Marx sprang to its defence in one of the most eloquent political pamphlets ever written, *The Civil War in France,* originally composed as an address by the General Council of the International to its members:

> Working men's Paris, with its Commune, will be forever celebrated as the glorious harbinger of a new society. Its martyrs are enshrined in the great heart of the working class. Its exterminators history has already nailed to that eternal pillory from which all the prayers of their priest will not avail to redeem them.

Claims that Marx was behind the Commune made him once again a target for police spies, this time from the newly united Germany. At the next Congress of the International at The Hague in 1872, he seems to have outmanoeuvred most, if not all, the spies by limiting attendance to those with credentials from their local associations, all of them carefully checked. A German police agent, who tried to eavesdrop after being excluded from the meeting, reported to Berlin that it was impossible even to 'make an attempt to hear through the open window a single word of what is taking place within'. The *Times* correspondent achieved marginally more by listening through a keyhole but could hear only 'the tinkling of the President's bell, rising now and again above a storm of angry voices'.[54] Out of earshot of the spies, Marx pushed through a motion (doubtless responsible for some of the 'angry voices') moving the headquarters of the Council of the International to New York. His motives, though unclear, probably included fear of police surveillance and harassment if it remained in Europe, concern that his own failing health would prevent him remaining the effective leader of the International, and his desire to return to writing the rest of *Das Kapital*. As Marx had probably foreseen, once in New York the International went into rapid decline and dissolved itself in 1876.[55]

After the suppression of the Paris Commune, the Home Office was faced with a series of urgent requests from foreign governments for information on alleged 'Communists' who had taken refuge in London. Initially, it had little idea how to respond. The Home Secretary, Lord Aberdare, however, had the bright idea of asking his secretary to write to Marx, who obligingly replied with literature on the activities of the International and a copy of his *Civil War in France*.[56] Scotland Yard had less success with its own direct enquiries. In May 1872 a police sergeant was sent to investigate a meeting of French 'Communist refugees' at the Canonbury Arms in Islington. On his way into the meeting, the sergeant was asked if he was a Communist, replied that he was not but insisted on his right to attend the meeting: 'Upon that a person (whom I can identify) caught hold of me and assisted by others carried me out of the room and intimated that if I returned they would break my head. I did not return in order that no breach of the peace should take place.' A month later the sergeant tried again. This time he was able to stay but all the Communists departed.[57]

The lack of police harassment left Marx sufficiently confident to apply for British citizenship in 1874, with the support of four British-born referees. The Home Office, however, rejected the application after Scotland Yard reported that, though the referees were 'respectable householders', Marx was 'the notorious German agitator, the head of the International Society, and the advocate of Communistic principles. He has not been loyal to his own King and Country.'[58] Thereafter Scotland Yard seems to have lost interest in Marx and his few followers in London. In a graveside oration at Highgate cemetery after Marx's death on 14 March 1883, Engels described him as a revolutionary genius, whose 'name and work will endure throughout the ages'. Only eleven mourners, however, were present at the funeral.[59] No English edition of *Das Kapital* appeared until 1887. Scotland Yard, almost certainly, did not acquire a copy. The English version became possibly the least-read masterpiece written in Victorian England. Britain's best-educated twentieth-century Labour leader, Harold Wilson, a former Oxford don, boasted while Prime Minister that he had never got beyond page two.[60]

Some foreign governments, however, retained an interest in subversive émigrés in London throughout the 1870s and beyond, and sought intelligence, usually with little success, from the British authorities. In October 1878 the Russian ambassador asked for the help of the Met in obtaining information on the activities of Russian political exiles in London. The

Met Commissioner, Sir Edmund Henderson, who may have been unaware of the intelligence passed to continental police in the 1850s, claimed wrongly that such assistance had never been provided before 'except when some overt act had been committed and materials were required in a prosecution in this country': 'The Police action even in the Orsini case visited [*sic*] great animosity against the Government of the day among a large class of the people.' Henderson added that investigation by the Met of Russian political exiles would, in any case, be 'worse than useless'.[61] Despite the creation of the Criminal Investigation Department (CID) in 1877, Superintendent Adolphus 'Dolly' Williamson complained in 1880 that detective work remained unpopular within the Met:

> The uncertainty and irregularity of the duties . . . are . . . no doubt in many cases very distasteful and repugnant to the better class of men in the service, as their duties constantly bring them into contact with the worst classes, frequently cause unnecessary drinking, and compel them at times to resort to trickey [*sic*] practices which they dislike.[62]

20

The Telegraph, Mid-Century Wars and the 'Great Game'

The invention of the telegraph, first successfully demonstrated at the beginning of the reign of Queen Victoria, began 'the greatest revolution in communications since the development of the printing press'.[1] The Crimean War (1853–6), the first war between great powers since Waterloo, was also the first in which the telegraph played a major role. At the start of the Anglo-French campaign on the Crimean peninsula in September 1854, news took at least five days to reach London: two by steamship from Balaklava to Varna on what is now the Bulgarian Black Sea coast, then three by horseback to the nearest telegraph link at Bucharest. When the French extended the telegraph to the coast of the Black Sea during the winter of 1854, it took only two days. After the British laid an underwater cable from Varna to the Crimean peninsula in April 1855, news could reach London in a few hours.[2]

For the first time ministers were likely to see reports of wars and major events in freshly ironed copies of *The Times* brought to them by their butlers at home before they read official despatches from British commanders and diplomats in their Whitehall offices. Never before had newspaper readers in foreign capitals as well as London been able to follow British military campaigns in such immediate detail. The British commander-in-chief, Lord Raglan (promoted to Field Marshal in November 1854), complained that, thanks to *The Times*, the Russians had little need for spies and 'need spend nothing under the head of "Secret Service" '.[3] Writing to the Secretary of War, the Duke of Newcastle, in January 1855, Raglan effectively accused the *Times* war correspondent, William Howard Russell, of treason:

> I pass over the fault the writer finds with every thing and every body, however calculated his strictures may be to excite discontent and encourage indiscipline, but I ask you to consider whether the paid agent of the Emperor of Russia could better serve his Master than does the correspondent of the paper that has the largest circulation in Europe . . . I am very doubtful, now

that Communications are so rapid, whether a British Army can long be maintained in the presence of a powerful Enemy, that Enemy having at his command thro' the English press, and from London to his Head Quarters by telegraph, every detail that can be required of the numbers, condition, and equipment of his opponent's force.[4]

The Times, however, caused British forces, after their arrival in the Crimea, far fewer problems than lack of intelligence. Raglan, whose last experience of combat was almost forty years earlier at Waterloo, where he had lost his right arm, had learned the importance of military intelligence while serving under Wellington. He had contributed to the success of Wellington's siege of Pamplona in 1813 by personally decrypting an intercepted message from the commander of the French garrison to Marshal Nicolas Soult.[5] In contrast with his experience in the Peninsular War, Raglan arrived in the Crimea in 1854 not merely without secret intelligence on the enemy but also without even much basic information. He complained when setting off for Sevastopol that it was as much a mystery to him as it had been to Jason and the Argonauts during their mythical hunt for the Golden Fleece three millennia earlier.[6]

The lack of much basic information on the Crimea, though chiefly the responsibility of the War Office, was also partly Raglan's fault. Early in 1854 Major Thomas Best Jervis, a retired Bombay sapper who had spent much of his career as a surveyor in India, discovered in Brussels a copy of the latest secret Russian staff map of the Crimea, which he excitedly described as 'a document which no money could purchase', as well as an Austrian staff map of European Turkey. Hurrying back to London to take the maps to the War Office, he found both Newcastle and Raglan surprisingly unenthusiastic. Raglan, it transpired, already had a copy of the secret Russian map but, unable to read its Cyrillic 'hieroglyphics', had put it to one side. His and Newcastle's interest in it was somewhat revived by Jervis, who was offered what he later described as 'a parsimonious proposition'. Jervis was told that, if, at his own expense, he translated the maps into French and produced ten-sheet chromolithograph versions of them, the War Office would buy two copies. To raise the £850 needed to finance the project, he was forced to sell much of his own treasured library. Once in the Crimea, Jervis's translated Russian map quickly proved invaluable to both British and French commanders, and he was asked to produce more copies. These were probably the first maps printed in Britain to delineate marine contours in blue, high ground in brown and the rest in black.[7]

The Anglo-French campaign got off to a good start with victory over the Russians at the Battle of Alma on 20 September (later commemorated by a bridge over the Seine in Paris). Lack of local intelligence in the Crimea, however, led Raglan to take the fatal decision not to follow the victory with an immediate attack on Sevastopol from the south.[8] Russian commanders, who also suffered from a lack of basic intelligence, had not expected the Allies to invade the Crimea until the following spring. As a result, 'Russian forces were in disarray' and Sevastopol virtually defenceless. In all probability, an Allied attack on 21 September would have taken the Russians by surprise and succeeded at the cost of relatively few casualties. Raglan's delay resulted in a siege which lasted almost a year and cost tens of thousands of lives.[9]

The advance of Russian forces on 25 October towards the British lines between their base at Balaklava and Sevastopol led to the Battle of Balaklava, now best remembered for the Charge of the Light Brigade. The disastrous but heroic charge of the Brigade into the 'Valley of Death' (as Tennyson later called it) was due to confused communications between Raglan and his senior commanders. Raglan wanted the Light Brigade to prevent British guns on Causeway Heights lent to his Turkish allies being captured by the Russians. The Duke of Wellington had never lost a single gun to the enemy, and to lose British guns to the Russians in the Crimea would have been a major humiliation. Raglan's order to 'try to prevent the enemy carrying away the guns', became hopelessly garbled as it passed down the chain of command. The message to the commander of the cavalry division, George Bingham, 3rd Earl of Lucan, was delivered by Captain Louis Nolan. The two men loathed each other. Having read the message, Lucan asked Nolan: 'Attack, sir? Attack what? What guns, sir?' Possibly waving his arm indistinctly, Nolan replied: 'There, my Lord, is your enemy. There are your guns.' Lucan then sent an order to the commander of the Light Brigade, James Brudenell, 7th Earl of Cardigan, with whom he was barely on speaking terms, to attack the wrong target. Of the 661 members of the Light Brigade who charged in the wrong direction, 113 were killed and 134 were wounded. Only a French cavalry charge saved the Brigade from complete destruction. On hearing that Nolan had been killed during the charge, Lucan declared with characteristic lack of compassion: 'He met his deserts, a dog's death –and like a dog let him be buried in a ditch.'[10]

The confused communications between Raglan and his commanders, worsened by personal animosities, inevitably affected the circulation of intelligence. Some lessons, however, were learned. The man mainly responsible for the improvement of British military intelligence in the Crimea was Charles Cattley (alias Calvert), formerly British vice-consul at the eastern Crimean trading port of Kerch, who became a civilian member of Raglan's staff late in August 1854. Cattley, who spoke Russian, French and Italian, was initially taken on as an interpreter, but he also improvised and ran a military intelligence department. In addition to his consular salary of £200 a year, he was paid one guinea a day plus expenses for food and travel. Some of Cattley's intelligence came from Polish deserters from the Russian forces. He also recruited agents from the Muslim Crimean Tatars, who regarded the Allied invasion as a liberation. Probably just as important was basic information about the Crimea of which Raglan was ignorant. On 21 October 1854 Cattley sent a memorandum warning Raglan that over the next month 'bleak winds, heavy rains, sleet [and] snow' would replace the autumn sunshine. There was also the danger that, as happened every few years, 'Russian cold' would settle over the peninsula: during it 'if a man touches metal with an uncovered hand the skin adheres'. Enclosing Cattley's memorandum, Raglan wrote to Newcastle two days later: 'We must be prepared either for wet or extreme cold, and in neither case could our troops remain under canvas . . . the country hardly produces wood enough to cook the men's food.' Newcastle replied that Raglan must be 'greatly misinformed'; the Crimean climate was 'one of the mildest and finest in the world'.[11] Due to the War Office's refusal to acknowledge its own ignorance, British troops thus lacked both warm clothing and winter accommodation.[12]

Cattley's intelligence played an increasing role in operational planning. It probably contributed to the Allies' decision to reinforce their forces in the west Crimean port of Eupatoria before their defeat of a major Russian attack, ordered by Tsar Nicholas I, in February 1855. Grief at the defeat may have contributed to Nicholas's death a fortnight later. Intelligence from Cattley also had a major influence on the amphibious operations in the Sea of Azov which from May onwards destroyed large quantities of Russian supplies and tied down many Russian troops. Only two weeks after Raglan's death on 28 June 1855, Cattley died of cholera in the British camp at Balaklava. 'His loss', wrote Raglan's successor, Lieutenant-General Sir James Simpson, 'is irreparable!'[13]

Like Raglan, Simpson complained bitterly about the intelligence the Russians were supposedly obtaining from telegraphed war reports in *The Times*: 'Our spies give us all manner of reports [for money], while the enemy never spends a farthing for information. He gets it all for five pence from a London paper.'[14] The main victim of the *Times* reports, however, was not the British Army but the British government. The combination of the telegraph and the new profession of war correspondent brought the reality of war and the suffering of British soldiers home to the public as never before. On 30 January 1855 the Prime Minister, Lord Aberdeen, resigned after losing a Commons vote of confidence. 'It was you', the Duke of Newcastle accused the *Times* correspondent William

Howard Russell, 'who turned out the government.'[15] The seventy-year-old Palmerston succeeded him as the man to win the war.

Russia never recovered from the fall of Sevastopol in September 1855, after almost a year's siege. Isolated in Europe, Alexander II, who had succeeded Nicholas I in March, sued for peace at the end of the year. The Treaty of Paris, which ended the war in March 1856, as well as undermining Russian plans to partition the Ottoman Empire, also prohibited it from maintaining a Black Sea fleet. Alexander believed that Russian recovery from humiliating defeat in the Crimea required major reforms. The best-known and most far-reaching of these was the abolition of serfdom, which he first announced in March 1856 but did not implement until five years later. The Tsar was far quicker to reform military intelligence, which had performed less well in the Crimea than during the Napoleonic Wars, deriving little, if any, benefit from the uncensored articles in *The Times* which outraged both Raglan and Simpson.

On 10 June 1856 Alexander II personally appointed military attachés in London, Paris, Vienna and Constantinople, with instructions on fifteen categories of intelligence collection: among them the strength, organization, weaponry, transport, communications, mindset and morale of foreign armed forces. Today's Russian foreign intelligence service, the SVR, like the military GRU, regards this as 'a momentous day in the history of Russian intelligence' – the foundation of modern military intelligence.[16] The Tsar was probably inspired by the example of the intelligence operations using military attachés run by the secret Special Chancellery in St Petersburg during the final years of the Napoleonic Wars.[17] The most influential of the new military attachés was Nikolai Ignatiev, who was posted to London at the age of only twenty-four, determined to seek revenge for Russia's defeat in the Crimean War. Quickly identified by the Foreign Office as a 'clever, wily fellow', he became a major player in the 'Great Game' with Russia on the North-West Frontier – and later the model for the sinister villain of the same name in two of the Flashman novels who tortures and attempts to assassinate the British hero. The outbreak of the Indian Mutiny in 1857 persuaded Ignatiev that Russia should take advantage of India's 'will to free itself from the hateful yoke of foreigners'.[18]

The foreign yoke in India was still officially that not of the British government but of the East India Company (EIC), whose headquarters were in the City of London, though it was subject to growing interference from Whitehall and Downing Street. Despite their ethnocentrism, India's British rulers were far more curious about the lands they conquered than their Mughal predecessors had been, and discovered much more about Indian geography and history. Over a period of seventy years, the Great Trigono-metrical Survey of India, begun in 1802 under the auspices of the EIC, which employed tens of thousands of Indian labourers, guides and scholars, succeeded in mapping the whole subcontinent with a scientific precision which enabled it to calculate for the first time the height of Mount Everest and other Himalayan peaks.[19]

Despite the success of the Survey, Britain lacked a cultural understanding of Indian life, which contributed to a serious intelligence failure before the Mutiny of 1857–8 (later called by Indian writers the 'First War for Independence'). This lack of understanding was epitomized by the confusion among British administrators during the few months before the outbreak of the Mutiny caused by the so-called 'chupatty (or *chapatti*) movement'. Chapattis, unleavened flatbread, were, and remain, a staple part of Indian diet. Early in February 1857, Mark Thornhill, a British magistrate in a small town near Agra, entered his office one morning to find four chapattis, which he disdainfully described as 'dirty little cakes of the coarsest flour, about the size and thickness of a biscuit', lying on his desk. He was informed that they had been put there by an Indian police officer, who had been handed the chapattis by a puzzled village *chowkidar* (watchman): 'A man had come out of the jungle with them, and given them to the watchman with instructions to make four like them and to take these to the watchman in the next village, who was to be told to do the same.' Numerous similar reports followed. Thornhill's boss, George Harvey, in Agra, calculated that chapattis were advancing across his province at a speed of between 100 and 200 miles a night, more rapidly than the fastest British mail service. 'The British', writes the historian Kim Wagner, 'regarded with deep suspicion, bordering on paranoia, any type of communication in India which they could not understand.' Even the unexplained circulation of the harmless chapatti appeared sinister. It seemed even more sinister after the outbreak of the Mutiny. The 'chupatty movement', it was believed, had been the work of a cunning group of conspirators who had begun planning the Mutiny months, if not years, in advance. In reality, the marauding chapattis had no connection with the Mutiny. As Kim Wagner has shown, their circulation probably began as a well-intended, though ill-conceived, attempt to prevent the spread of cholera and developed into a novel form of chain letter which those involved were superstitiously afraid to break.[20]

British failure to understand Indian sensitivities was also at the root of the unintended provocation caused by the introduction of a new model of Enfield rifle in the East India Company's armies, which was the immediate cause of the Mutiny. The cartridge case for the rifle, which sepoys (Indian soldiers) had to bite open, was believed to contain grease from lard (unclean to Muslims) and tallow from cows (which were sacred to Hindus). Though not a single greased cartridge was actually issued to the Indian Army, the belief among some sepoys that there had been a British plot to defile them was the immediate cause of the Mutiny. Sepoys of the Bengal Army in Meerut shot their British officers and marched on Delhi. A number of the mutineers, who had been trained to operate the telegraph, were well aware of its use in military operations and broke the telegraph cables in the areas they held – but not before the Delhi station had telegraphed a warning to other stations. The warning enabled the Punjabi authorities to disarm Indian regiments before they received news of the rebellion in Meerut.[21] Robert Montgomery, then judicial commissioner in the Punjab at Lahore, made the dramatic claim that 'The electric telegraph has saved India.' His words are inscribed on the Telegraph Memorial, a twenty-foot granite obelisk in old Delhi, which was later erected 'to commemorate the loyal and devoted services of Delhi telegraph office staff, on the eventful 11th May 1857'. Montgomery (the grandfather of Field Marshal Earl Montgomery of Alamein) was awarded a knighthood for disarming the sepoy garrison in Lahore after receiving the warning from the Delhi telegraph station.[22]

A sepoy rebellion had previously seemed unthinkable. Most British officers were convinced that, as one of them put it, the native soldier was 'perfectly happy with his lot, a cheerful, good-natured fellow, simple and trustworthy'.[23] Sir John Kaye, secretary of the foreign department of the India Office established in Whitehall after the Mutiny, wrote later: 'There was not a gentlewoman in the country who did not feel measureless security in the thought that a guard of Sepoys watched her house, or who would not have travelled, under such an escort, across the whole length and breadth of the land.'[24] During the Mutiny, some gentlewomen became victims of attacks by sepoys which *The Times* claimed were:

> so abominable that they will not even bear narration . . . We cannot print these narratives – they are too foul for publication. We should have to speak of families murdered in cold blood – and murder was mercy! – of the violation of English ladies in the presence of their husbands, of their parents, of their children – and then, but not till then, of their assassination.[25]*

Having previously taken the loyalty of the sepoys for granted, British administrators mistakenly concluded after the Mutiny began that the

---

* Marx wrote in the *New York Daily Tribune*: 'It should not be forgotten that, while the cruelties of the English are related as acts of martial vigour, told simply, rapidly, without dwelling on disgusting details, the outrages of the natives, shocking as they are, are still deliberately exaggerated.'

native soldiers were in reality the most cunning of conspirators – a conclusion which exemplified the capacity of racist stereotypes to distort intelligence assessment. The leading British missionary in India, the Reverend Alexander Duff, blamed the sepoys' 'Asiatic' mentality:

> Throughout the ages the Asiatic has been noted for his duplicity, cunning, hypocrisy, treachery; and coupled with this, – and indeed, as necessary for excelling in his accomplishment of Jesuitism, – his capacity of secrecy and concealment . . . In almost every instance, the sepoys succeeded in concealing their long-concocted and deep-laid murderous designs from the most vigilant officers to the very last . . .[26]

Thomas Babington Macaulay, once an influential figure in Calcutta, where he had been immersed twenty years earlier in educational and penal reform, condemned the inhabitants of Bengal, where British power was at its mightiest, in even more purple prose:

> What horns are to the buffalo, what the paw is to the tiger, what the sting is to the bee, what beauty, according to the old Greek song, is to woman, deceit is to the Bengalee. Large promises, smooth excuses, elaborate tissues of circumstantial falsehood, chicanery, perjury, forgery, are the weapons, offensive and defensive, of the people of the Lower Ganges.[27]

The problems of suppressing the Mutiny turned intelligence into a major priority. Robert Montgomery and the newly appointed 36-year-old head of the army's Intelligence Department, Major W. S. R. Hodson, coordinated intelligence operations against the rebel sepoys and their supporters who were in control of Delhi during the summer of 1857.[28] Their agent networks gave steadily more detailed and more optimistic reports of the rebels' increasingly difficult position – somewhat biased, however, by a tendency to tell Montgomery and Hodson what it was believed they wanted to hear. The sycophantic claim that 'the citizens pray anxiously for the return of British power' became a regular refrain.[29]

Hodson was one of the most unscrupulous senior British intelligence officers since Sir George Downing two centuries before.[30] Before the Mutiny he had been accused, probably correctly, of embezzling regimental money, the pay of a fellow officer and the funds of an asylum. In 1855 he had been temporarily stripped of his command. During the Mutiny he killed an Indian officer, Bisharat Ali, allegedly because he owed Ali money.[31] Immediately after the reconquest of Delhi, Hodson tracked down and arrested the last Mughal ruler, Bahadur Shah, on whom the British had bestowed the title of King of Delhi, and who was later found guilty of complicity in murder and sent into exile with his wives. Hodson borrowed a carbine from one of his soldiers and summarily executed Bahadur's three sons, stripping their bodies of rings and swords. It would, he boasted, be 'quite something' for him 'to wear a sword taken from the last of the House of Timur [Tamerlane]'.[32]

The Mutiny changed the nature of British rule in India. A Royal Proclamation of 1 November 1858, followed by the Government of India Acts, replaced the rule of the East India Company with that of the British Crown, represented by a Viceroy with his capital (until 1911) in Calcutta (moving to Simla in the summer heat). A new Indian Army was created, one third of whom were British troops (as compared with 10 per cent before the Mutiny), with a strengthened intelligence department. Intelligence was a higher priority in Calcutta than in London. Despite the closure of the Deciphering Branch in London in 1844, the Government of India maintained its own independent system of message interception and decryption. Since 1836 magistrates had also been head postmasters for their districts with orders to arrange for the opening and scrutiny by British officials of all Indian letters.[33] During the Mutiny the authorities intercepted very few clearly 'treasonable' letters, but found evidence of hostility to white rule in statements such as 'White wheat has become very scarce and country produce very abundant' and 'Hats were hardly to be seen and white turbans plentiful.'[34]

The Mutiny made at least some senior British officials aware for the first time just how little they knew about local conditions in much of the subcontinent. The Chief Justice of Bombay complained in 1863 that 'the chief administrators of our vast Indian Empire . . . are often, if not habitually, in complete ignorance of the most patent facts . . . around them'.[35] Attempts to track down former rebels in the countryside continued for almost a decade after the Mutiny. In Punjab, Robert Montgomery paid large rewards to informers who revealed the whereabouts of 'proclaimed offenders'. Once caught, the offenders were publicly flogged. An 1860 'Report on Village Police' concluded that in North-Western Province the police were mostly ignorant of what was happening in the countryside. Attempts were made over the next two decades to establish a better-informed system of rural police distinct from local officials.[36] The delusion remained, however, that the Mutiny had been the result of a long-prepared sepoy plot. Ironically, the British conspiracy theory became so well established that it was taken over by early-twentieth-century Indian nationalists, who saw the Mutiny as a carefully planned war of independence designed to rid India of British oppression. On its fiftieth anniversary, V. D. Savarkar described how an immense (though in reality non-existent) 'Revolutionary Organization' had sent secret agents to sepoys across the subcontinent to prepare the rebellion with such success that 'not much inkling of what was going on could reach even such cunning people as the English, until the explosion took place'.[37]

As during the Indian Mutiny, the telegraph played a major role in the American Civil War of 1861–5. When not in the White House, President Abraham Lincoln was usually to be found next door in the War Department's telegraph office and cipher section, studying the stream of telegraphed orders and reports that gave him more detailed and up-to-date information on the war than any other source.* The young telegrapher and cipher clerk David Homer Bates wrote later: 'Outside the members of his cabinet and his private secretaries, none were brought into closer or more confidential relations with Lincoln than the cipher-operators . . .' Bates and his two colleagues, Arthur B. Chandler and Charles A. Tinkler, also introduced Lincoln to the mysteries of codebreaking. Aged only seventeen, twenty and twenty-three respectively at the outbreak of war, the 'Sacred Three', as they grandly called themselves, were probably the youngest group of cryptanalysts in American history. Among the codebreaking coups which particularly impressed the President was their success in decrypting private correspondence in 1863 which revealed that plates for printing Rebel currency were being manufactured in New York. The Confederate Secretary of the Treasury enthused in one of the intercepted letters, 'The engraving of the plates is superb.' After the engraver had been tracked down in Lower Manhattan, the plates and several million newly printed Confederate dollars were seized by a US marshal.[38] Though both sides tapped telegraph lines, most message interception resulted from the capture of telegraph stations, which also enabled the captors to send false messages to the enemy. The Confederate General Robert E. Lee ordered his officers to 'send no dispatches by telegraph relative to . . . movements, or they will become known'.[39]

Lincoln was the first President to show interest in overhead reconnaissance, which was to lead, a century later, to the use of spy planes and satellites to collect imagery intelligence (IMINT). He was greatly impressed by a remarkable demonstration on 18 June 1861 by a 28-year-old balloonist and self-styled professor, Thaddeus S. C. Lowe. From 500 feet above Washington, Lowe telegraphed a message 'to the President of the United States' down a cable linking his balloon to the ground: 'This point of observation commands an area nearly fifty miles in diameter. The City, with its girdle of encampments, presents a superb scene.' The balloon experiment achieved three firsts: the 'first electrical communication from

---

* In 1862 Lincoln authorized his Secretary of War, Edwin M. Stanton, to reroute telegraph lines through his office. (Mindich, 'Lincoln's Surveillance State'.)

an aircraft to the ground, first such communication to a president of the United States, and first "real-time" reconnaissance data from an airborne platform'. With Lincoln's enthusiastic support, a balloon corps was founded two months later with Lowe as 'chief aeronaut' in charge of seven balloons and nine balloonists. Before the Battle of Fair Oaks, the culmination of a Unionist offensive up the Virginia peninsula in early summer 1862, 'Professor' Lowe succeeded in detecting a large concentration of Confederate forces preparing to attack. The early IMINT experiments, however, were a false dawn. Though Lowe made some military converts, his unwieldy balloon trains and cumbersome gas generators were heavily criticized because of their inability to move at more than a snail's pace. The balloon corps was disbanded in June 1863.[40]*

Despite his interest in SIGINT and IMINT, Lincoln failed to establish adequate centralized direction or analysis of Union intelligence during the Civil War. Intelligence reports were liable to be directed unpredictably to any one or more of a great variety of recipients: the President, the Secretary of War, the General-in-Chief, governors of threatened states, army and divisional commanders. During the Gettysburg campaign of 1863, the major Union commands, as well as the Military Railway Department, all ran their own independent intelligence operations.[41]

The best-run intelligence agency of the Civil War was the Bureau of Military Information (forerunner of the later Military Intelligence Division of the US Army), founded early in 1863 by the new commander of the Unionist Army of the Potomac, General 'Fightin' Joe' Hooker. Under Hooker's intelligence chief, Colonel George G. Sharpe, a New York lawyer, the Bureau collated open and secret information from sources ranging from newspapers to spies, and prepared regular and usually reliable intelligence assessments. Hooker, however, proved incapable of making effective use of the Bureau's intelligence. Before and during the Battle of Chancellorsville in May 1863, Sharpe provided detailed, accurate intelligence on the Confederate forces of Robert E. Lee. 'Instead of using this information', writes Jay Luvaas in his study of Chancellorsville, 'Hooker seemed overwhelmed by it . . .' In Lee's greatest victory, his 60,000 troops defeated a Union army of 130,000 men.[42] Hooker refused to accept that he had been beaten by inferior forces. The Provost Marshal General, Marsena Rudolph Patrick, wrote in his diary:

> We get accurate information [from the Bureau], but Hooker will not use it and insults all those who differ from him in opinion. He has declared that

* See ill. 41.

the enemy are over 100,000 strong – it is his only salvation to make it appear that the enemy's forces are larger than his which is all false and he knows it. He knows that Lee is his master and is afraid to meet him in fair battle.

The fortunes of the Bureau of Military Information improved dramatically after Lincoln sacked Hooker on 27 June and replaced him as commander of the Army of the Potomac with General George G. Meade (after whom the headquarters of today's US SIGINT agency, NSA, is named). Before and during the victorious Battle of Gettysburg (1 to 3 July) Meade made far better use of the Bureau's accurate intelligence on Confederate forces than Hooker had done at Chancellorsville. Lee, by contrast, had less information on Union forces than in any of his previous battles. 'He was forced', writes Jay Luvaas, 'to fight a battle without intelligence.' That was one of the reasons for his defeat.[43]*

The growing reputation of the Bureau of Military Information as a result of the Gettysburg campaign led to Sharpe's appointment as intelligence officer to the new General-in-Chief of the Union armies, Ulysses S. Grant. Henceforth the Bureau served both Grant and Meade. The success of Grant's war of attrition over the next year, though due chiefly to his larger forces and the superior resources of the North, was assisted by good intelligence. Sharpe himself gave most of the credit for the Bureau's successes in the months before Lee's surrender at Appomattox in April 1865 to an agent network in the Confederate capital of Richmond, Virginia, run by Elizabeth Van Lew, an ardent abolitionist who had persuaded her mother to free the family slaves. For most of the previous year Van Lew had maintained five intelligence 'depots' around Richmond, where her agents delivered reports for collection by Union couriers slipping through Confederate lines. The agents included her African-American servants, who concealed messages in eggshells hidden among real eggs and in seamstresses' paper patterns. To protect her agents from post-war retribution in Richmond, Van Lew destroyed the intelligence reports which she had asked the War Department to return to her. Though, as a result, little detailed evidence survives, she was probably the most successful female spy of the mid-nineteenth century. Financing the agent network out of her own pocket cost 'Miss Lizzie' most of her fortune. After the War, Grant tried and failed to persuade Congress to refund $15,000 which she had secretly spent in the Union cause. When he became President four years later, in order to provide her with an income Grant made her

---

* Gettysburg and General Ulysses S. Grant's simultaneous success at the siege of Vicksburg turned the tide of the Civil War.

Richmond postmaster, then one of the highest federal posts available to a woman. The *Richmond Enquirer and Examiner* declared the appointment of 'a Federal spy' a 'deliberate insult to our people'. Grant's successor, President Rutherford B. Hayes, failed to reappoint her. Though Van Lew later worked for a few years in Washington, she died in Richmond as a recluse, 'shunned like the plague'.[44]

After the Civil War the Bureau of Military Information, the first professional US intelligence agency, which had analysed as well as collected intelligence, was disbanded. Since the Crimean War, British military intelligence had been similarly run down. In February 1855 the War Office had founded a Topographical and Statistical Department (T&S) under the cartographer Major (later Lieutenant-Colonel) Thomas Jervis, who had obtained a secret Russian map of the Crimea on the eve of war.[45] Jervis hoped to turn T&S into the War Office's first intelligence department, but progress was painfully slow; after his death in 1857, even its cartography declined. By the mid-1860s T&S was being given such trivial tasks as preparing illustrations for army dress regulations. When Captain (later Major-General Sir) Charles Wilson became director of T&S on 1 April 1870, he reported that its foreign-map collection was 'very incomplete', its intelligence on foreign armies shamefully deficient, and the 'means for keeping the office supplied with information from abroad' non-existent. On the last point Wilson overstated his case. Since the Crimean War, military attachés had been posted for the first time in Berlin, Paris, St Petersburg, Turin and Vienna (together with a solitary naval attaché in Paris). But the outbreak of the Franco-Prussian War in July provided further evidence of the inadequacies of British military intelligence. 'Had any complications arisen with France . . . and had we been asked for information', Wilson said later, 'we should have had to translate a German work on the French army as giving a better account of it than we could have produced ourselves.'[46]

The French Minister of War, Marshal Leboeuf, boasted to the *Corps Législatif* on the declaration of war with Prussia: 'So well prepared are we that, if the war were to last two years, not a gaiter button would be found wanting.'[47] In reality Prussia proved far better prepared for war than the French Second Empire in both the organization of its forces and the use of intelligence. Unlike the Prussian cavalry, the French cavalry remained stuck behind the lines and made little attempt to scout for the enemy. A war correspondent noted scornfully on 30 July 1870: 'At the moment, nothing could be less aggressive than the French army. Inhabitants of the border region, though accustomed to regular Prussian visits, have not seen a single French dragoon in more than ten days.' Leboeuf, who became Chief of

Staff of the Army of the Rhine, complained from Metz next day: 'Twenty-four hours have passed without a scrap of intelligence on troop movements in north or south . . .' Leboeuf and the Emperor Napoleon III received most of their intelligence from newspapers, from Swiss, Belgian and British war correspondents, whose annotated press cuttings were placed in thick files optimistically entitled 'Renseignements'.[48]

Prussia's first victory at Wissembourg on the French frontier on 4 August was facilitated by French intelligence failure. When General Douay inspected the town on the previous day, he had no idea that 80,000 Prussian and Bavarian troops were rapidly closing in from the north-east. For weeks the Prussian forces had been concealed in the Niederwald, a pine forest on both banks of the River Lauter which hid the Prussian advance. French infantry officers later complained that, to their knowledge, not a single French cavalry patrol had entered the forest to look for the enemy.[49] The capture of Wissembourg enabled the Prussians and their allies to cross into France. Though the war continued into the following year, its outcome was decided by the French defeat at Sedan and the capture of Napoleon III on 2 September.

In 1873 the reforming British Secretary of State for War, Edward Cardwell, announced the transformation of T&S, whose limitations had been exposed once more by the Franco-Prussian War, into 'a real Intelligence Department' to be known as the Intelligence Branch (IB) and directed by Major-General Sir Patrick MacDougall, formerly first commandant of the Staff College at Camberley, with 'that most excellent officer Captain Wilson' as his deputy. Its duties were defined not merely as the collection and collation of military intelligence but also as planning for war in the light of that intelligence. But though the IB quickly gained support among civilian administrators in the War Office, it was viewed with suspicion by the high command at Horse Guards and in particular by Field Marshal the Duke of Cambridge, cousin to Queen Victoria, a vigorous opponent of Cardwell's reforms and commander-in-chief from 1856 to 1895. One IB officer later recalled how at Staff College dinners the Duke, 'a great favourite with the Army . . . always spoke most scornfully of "Pwogress"' and was always 'cheered to the echo'.[50]

The priorities of Victorian soldiers and statesmen during the years of 'splendid isolation' from the Continent were imperial rather than European: above all the threat from the expanding Russian Empire to India's North-West Frontier. By the mid-1860s Russia had crushed the Muslim tribes of the Caucasus and begun to annex or to turn into protectorates the independent states of Central Asia: Tashkent in 1865, Samarkand in 1868, Khiva in 1873 and the remaining territory east of the Caspian Sea in 1881–5. Its advance was accelerated by a series of alarmist intelligence reports that the British were set on establishing control over Central Asia and driving out Russian trade. This belief, writes a later British ambassador in Russia, Sir Rodric Braithwaite, 'affected and distorted policymaking in St Petersburg and Orenburg, just as policy-making in London and Delhi was affected and distorted by the belief that the Russians intended to come through Afghanistan into India. Paranoia affected judgement in all four cities.'[51] The long-drawn-out intelligence duel between the British and Russian empires became romanticized as the 'Great Game'. In Rudyard Kipling's novel *Kim*, 'the Great Game that never ceases day and night, throughout India', is played in the service of the British Raj by many itinerant traders, horse dealers and preachers recruited from the local population:

> But Kim did not suspect that Mahbub Ali, known as one of the best horse dealers in the Punjab, a wealthy and enterprising trader, whose caravans penetrated far and far into the Back of Beyond, was registered in one of the locked books of the Indian Survey Department as C.25.1B. Twice or thrice yearly C.25 would send in a little story, baldly told but most interesting, and generally – it was checked by the statements of R.17 and M.4 – quite true. It concerned all manner of out-of-the-way mountain principalities, explorers of nationalities other than English, and the gun trade [and] was, in brief, a small portion of that vast mass of 'information received' on which the Indian Government acts.

After being recruited to the 'Secret Service' by Mahbub Ali, the orphan Kim O'Hara helped capture important documents from Russian spies.

Though the Great Game was actually played on nothing like the scale portrayed by Kipling, the Indian Army and the Government of India's Political Department did send hillmen, often disguised as Buddhist pilgrims or Muslim holy men, on secret missions. The idea of using the hillmen came from the Survey of India during the mapping of the subcontinent[52] but it was forbidden by the governor-general to send its officers to northern Afghanistan, Turkestan and Tibet, which he considered too dangerous. The Survey officer chiefly responsible for beginning the recruitment of the hillmen was Captain Thomas Montgomerie of the Royal Engineers. 'When I was in Ladakh', Montgomerie later told the Royal Geographical Society, who presented him with its Founders' Medal, 'I noticed that natives of India passed freely backwards and forwards between Ladakh and Yarkand, in Chinese Turkestan, and it consequently occurred to me that it might be possible to make the exploration by that means.'[53]

Each native explorer recruited by Montgomerie and his colleagues was known as a *pandit* (Sanskrit for 'knowledge owner'), the origin of the English word 'pundit'. Because of the dangers they were running, the pandits' identities and missions were kept secret. Even within the Survey of India they were known merely by a number or a codename (as in *Kim*). They were trained personally by Montgomerie at Dehradun, the Survey's headquarters in the Himalayan foothills, which now houses the Indian Military Academy. Montgomerie taught the pandits always to take a pace of the same length whether walking uphill, downhill, or on the level. Next he taught them ways of keeping a precise but discreet count of the number of such paces taken during a day's march. This enabled them to measure immense distances with remarkable accuracy and without arousing suspicion.

Montgomerie supplied the pandits with secret equipment manufactured by the Survey of India's workshops at Dehradun to measure the distances they covered, calculate direction and altitude, and record observations en route. Many travelled as Buddhist pilgrims, crossing mountain passes to visit the holy sites of the ancient Silk Road. Montgomerie adapted both the Buddhist rosary of 108 beads, used to count prayers, and the spinning Buddhist prayer-wheel. He removed eight beads from the rosaries, not enough to be noticed, but leaving a mathematically convenient 100. At every hundredth pace the pandit would slip one bead. Each complete circuit of the rosary thus represented 10,000 paces. Concealed in the copper cylinder of the prayer-wheels (some of which are preserved in Indian State Archives), instead of the usual scroll of prayers, was a roll of blank paper on which the total distance covered each day was recorded along with observations en route. Hidden in the lid of the prayer-wheel was a compass to enable the pandit to take regular bearings as he travelled. Thermometers, which helped to calculate altitude, were hidden in the tops of pilgrims' staves. Mercury, used in taking sextant readings, was concealed in cowrie shells and poured out into a pilgrim's begging bowl when required. False bottoms, in which sextants could be hidden, were built into the chests which most native travellers carried with them. To preserve their cover on their travels, the pandits chanted the traditional Sanskrit mantra '*Om mani padme hum*' ('Oh Jewel in the Lotus') as they turned their bogus prayer-wheels.[54]

The most famous of Montgomerie's pandits was the headmaster of a Himalayan village school, Nain Singh, who became known as Pandit Number One, or the Chief Pandit. One year after beginning his journey disguised as a Buddhist holy man, Nain reached the Tibetan capital of Lhasa, a city forbidden to Europeans. He spent three months there, gained an audience with the Dalai Lama, gathered intelligence about the city, and calculated its altitude and geographical position. After witnessing the public beheading of a Chinese who had entered Lhasa without permission, and having revealed his true identity to two Muslim traders, Nain Singh felt in personal danger. He left Lhasa in April 1866 as part of the same caravan with which he had arrived and reached India eighteen months later, having surveyed some 1,200 miles. His data led to a complete revision of the Indian Survey's map of Tibet. Other pandits were less fortunate. At least two never returned from their missions and a third was sold into slavery (though he eventually escaped). Between 1868 and 1877 Montgomerie and his superior officer, Colonel James Walker, publicly reported the geographical data collected by the pandits during their secret missions in the *Journal* and *Proceedings* of the Royal Geographical Society. The intelligence they obtained, however, was usually omitted. There was no public mention, for example, of a pandit report that the Mir of Badakhshan was 'given to drinking' and allowed 'his petty officials to do very much as they like: he is consequently very unpopular'. In 1877 Nain Singh became the first Asian to be awarded the Royal Geographical Society's gold medal, for contributing 'a greater amount of positive knowledge to the map of Asia than any other individual of our time'.[55]

The thirty years of pandit missions at the height of the Great Game from 1863 to 1893 explored a million square miles of unmapped territory.[56] Despite their sometimes extraordinary achievements, however, there were large gaps in the Government of India's knowledge of what was happening across the North-West Frontier. Lord Salisbury, one of the few late Victorian statesmen to attach high priority to intelligence collection, was highly critical when he became Secretary of State for India in 1874 of the state of Indian intelligence under the current Viceroy, the Earl of Northbrook: 'Northbrook's intelligence department is very bad. He disdains the use of secret service money: and without a liberal use of that kind of investigation it is impossible to know what is going on in Affghanistan [sic].'[57] Salisbury was deeply suspicious, as well as ignorant, of dealings between the Russians and the Afghan Amir, Sher Ali. Though he would never have attempted the interception of diplomatic correspondence in Europe, Salisbury insisted on it in the case of Afghanistan. 'You ought', he told Northbrook, 'to be in possession of any correspondence that is passing between the Ameer and the Russian agents.'[58] Northbrook, however, was sceptical of the use of 'native' agents, whether Indian or Afghan, because of their racial inferiority. Natives would, he claimed, only 'collect a mass of lies' and – he added cryptically – 'perhaps, some truths we are better ignorant of'.[59]

On succeeding Northbrook as Viceroy in 1876, Edward Bulwer-Lytton, 1st Earl Lytton, found the Government of India in 'an extraordinary state of ignorance' about the states on its borders. During the expedition against the Jowakis tribal area on the Punjab border in 1877–8, he complained that 'we were more completely ignorant of its interior than we now are of the centre of Africa'.[60] Lytton was equally critical about the intelligence obtained from Afghanistan. Russia, he believed, had superb intelligence from the court of Sher Ali: while 'the Government of India is dependent on the merest guesswork for what is happening in the mind of Sher Ali, the Russian Cabinet know every rupee that we give him and almost every word that we write or talk about him'.[61] When Sher Ali received a Russian mission at Kabul while turning back a mission sent by Lytton at the Khyber Pass in September 1878, Great Britain's prestige as a great power, as well as the security of India, was thought to be at stake, and a show of force necessary to demonstrate to the Russians Great Britain's will and ability to protect her sphere of influence, and to the Amir that he could have no allies but the Government of India. Lytton was confident that Sher Ali would be 'brought to heel', quickly and cheaply.[62]

As with the expedition against the Jowakis, Lytton was confident that the strength of the Indian Army would more than compensate for the lack of intelligence. In what was to become the *cause célèbre* of his viceroyalty, in November 1878 he launched an invasion (originally intended to be a mere show of force) across the Khyber and Bolan passes which began the Second Anglo-Afghan War. Initially, Indian forces swept all before them, becoming the first to reach Kabul since the First Anglo-Afghan War of 1839–42.[63] Sher Ali was forced to flee and died in exile in February 1879. In the course of the invasion, correspondence between Sher Ali and the Maharajah of Kashmir fell into British hands by means unknown. Lytton noted that 'part of it is in a cipher of which the key is yet to find' – which implies that attempts continued to be made in Calcutta (unlike London) to decrypt, as well as to intercept, cipher correspondence.[64] Major Sir Louis Cavagnari, 'self-confident to the point of arrogance, bold to the point of rashness',[65] established himself as British political resident, never doubting that he could turn the new Amir, Yakub Khan, son of Sher Ali, into an obedient client of the Raj.*

Cavagnari did not allow his over-confidence to be disturbed by ominous reports concerning the arrival in Kabul of six regiments of near-mutinous Afghan soldiers, who had not been paid for months. Though Cavagnari

---

* Cavagnari dismissed intelligence reports that Yakub Khan could not be trusted. He cabled Lytton on 30 August 1879: 'I personally believe Yakub Khan will turn out to be a very good ally, and that we shall be able to keep him to his engagements.' (Meyer and Brysac, *Tournament of Shadows*, p. 192.)

had the authority to pay them, he did not do so, dismissing reports from a Pathan guide of violent threats to him made by the soldiers with the flippant claim that 'Dogs that bark do not bite.' 'Sahib', replied the guide, 'these dogs *do* bite.' Cavagnari paid no attention, cabling regularly to Lytton about Afghan 'support' for his forces and the 'calm' which they had restored to Kabul. The simplest explanation for what proved to be his disastrous failure to heed intelligence that the unpaid regiments were ready to 'bite' is most simply explained as a belief that he was dealing with inferior peoples. In this case the simplest explanation is probably correct. Had Cavagnari been willing to address the grievances of the unpaid regiments and secure a strong defensive position in Kabul, he might well have survived. But he did not believe he needed to do so. He did not even bother to close the gates of his residency compound. On 2 September 1879 he cabled Peshawar: 'All well in the Cabul embassy.' The next day Cavagnari and his entire staff were massacred inside the residency by the unpaid Afghan regiments, who began a large-scale revolt.[66]

Lytton responded to the disaster by despatching a new invasion force. Among its acts of vengeance was the hanging of forty-nine Afghans on a gallows set up in the ruins of Cavagnari's residence for their alleged part in his murder. Outside Kabul, however, Afghan resistance continued. British forces were hampered by inadequate intelligence; reconnaissance expeditions were discouraged by Indian political officers afraid of arousing the hostility of local tribes.[67] At Marwand in July 1880 Afghan irregulars overwhelmed much of a British field force, 1,000 of whom were killed. Intelligence from Kabul remained poor, a weakness exacerbated by alarmist reports about Russian designs on Afghanistan.*

---

* Sir Arthur Conan Doyle later included Dr Watson, who had supposedly served as assistant surgeon on the North-West Frontier, among those wounded at Marwand. On meeting Dr Watson for the first time, Sherlock Holmes astonished him by saying: 'You have been in Afghanistan, I perceive.' Holmes later explained to Watson how he reached this conclusion:

'The train of reasoning ran, "Here is a gentleman of a medical type, but with the air of a military man. Clearly an army doctor then. He has just come from the tropics, for his face is dark, and that is not the natural tint of his skin, for his wrists are fair. He has undergone hardships and sickness, as his haggard face says clearly. His left arm has been injured. He holds it in a stiff and unnatural manner. Where in the tropics could an English army doctor have seen much hardship and got his arm wounded? Clearly in Afghanistan." The whole train of thought did not occupy a second. I then remarked that you came from Afghanistan, and you were astonished.' (Conan Doyle, *A Study in Scarlet*, ch. 2.)

For once, there was a flaw in Holmes's reasoning. Afghanistan is not in the tropics. Holmes's error reflected the widespread ignorance about Afghanistan even among those generally well informed about the Empire and its frontiers. (Meyer and Brysac, *Tournament of Shadows*, pp. 202–3.)

The Second Afghan War ended in a British victory and the emergence of a new imperial hero, General (later Field Marshal Lord) 'Bobs' Roberts, who avenged the defeat at Marwand by reconquering Kabul. But it was a pyrrhic victory. There was no successor to Cavagnari. Britain had to accept as Amir Abdur Rahman, who they knew had spent eleven years in exile under Russian protection in Tashkent but about whom they otherwise had little intelligence. Though Abdur Rahman ceded the Khyber Pass to the Raj, he refused to accept a British resident at Kabul. Despite recurrent fears to the contrary, however, a mixture of bribes, threats and promises of support against its neighbours kept Afghanistan out of the orbit of Russia and within that of India. By far the most successful intelligence service inside Afghanistan was that of Abdur Rahman, whose hold on power was reinforced by what Sir Rodric Braithwaite calls 'a ruthless and omnipresent secret police'.[68] 'The Iron Amir', as he became unaffectionately known, crushed two major rebellions and killed approximately 100,000 of his own subjects.[69]

By the 1880s the practice of diplomacy had been profoundly changed by increasing use of the telegraph. The cipher telegram became the most frequent form of diplomatic communication. In 1878 the Foreign Office, which had long numbered its despatches, also began numbering its telegrams.[70] By greatly simplifying the interception of diplomatic correspondence, use of the telegraph marked a turning point in intelligence history. One of the great problems of Ancien Régime *cabinets noirs*, how to lay hands on foreign diplomatic traffic, was largely resolved. Governments, if they chose to do so, could gain ready access to telegrams which passed through telegraph offices in their capitals. Henceforth, the main problem was to decrypt the ciphers in which the telegrams were written.

Because of the closure of the Deciphering Branch in 1844,[71] however, Britain, unlike (notably) France and Russia,[72] was unable to decrypt any diplomatic telegrams until the First World War. Having abandoned the interception of foreign communications, some British statesmen were naïve about foreign interception of their own correspondence. Perhaps the most naïve was William Ewart Gladstone, whose four terms as Prime Minister (1868–74, 1880–85, 1886 and 1892–4) are still a record. On one occasion while on holiday in Cannes during his second term as Prime Minister, Gladstone asked a friend to write the address on the envelope of a letter which he sent to the Foreign Secretary, Earl Granville – confident, he told Granville, that, if the French authorities failed to recognize his writing on the envelope, they would not bother to open it. Granville replied in some exasperation that the mere fact that a letter from Cannes was addressed to the Foreign Office was enough to attract the attention of the *cabinet noir*. 'You would', he told Gladstone, 'have been a good clergyman, a first-rate lawyer and the greatest of generals, but you would have been an indifferent Fouché in dealing with the Post Office.'[73] Twenty years later, the Foreign Secretary, Lord Lansdowne, showed himself almost as naïve as Gladstone, sending letters to his ambassador in Paris, Sir Edmund Monson, by post rather than the diplomatic bag. 'I think it right to tell you', wrote Monson in 1902, 'that your recent letters by post have been palpably opened by the bureau noir . . .'[74]

Most US secretaries of state were at least as naïve as Gladstone. After the opening of the transatlantic cable connecting America and Europe in 1866, the US minister in Paris, John Bigelow, warned the Secretary of State, William Seward, of the need for improved US ciphers:

> While joining in the chorus of congratulation with which this triumph of modern science is received by the civilized world I deem it my duty to suggest . . . that the State Department provide itself at once with a new cypher . . . It is not likely that it would suit the purpose of the Government to have its telegrams for this Legation read first by the French authorities, and yet you are well aware that nothing goes over a French telegraph wire, that is not transmitted to the Ministry of the Interior.

Seward ignored the warning. The sixty-year-old State Department code was, he foolishly assured Bigelow, 'believed to be the most inscrutable ever invented'. Seward had little notion of cipher security. When he sent his first ciphered transatlantic diplomatic cable, he also gave a copy of the plain text to the press, thus making it possible for French cryptanalysts to compare the two.[75]

The great powers of Europe, however, did not require *cabinets noirs* to gain access to much of the most important US diplomatic correspondence. To satisfy Congressional requests for information on foreign relations during the Civil War, the Lincoln administration had begun publishing its main diplomatic correspondence in annual volumes entitled *Foreign Relations of the United States (FRUS)*. Subsequent peacetime administrations continued to do so, even at the cost of embarrassing their envoys abroad.[76] In 1870, for example, when the Italian government was about to take over the Papal State of Rome, the US minister, George P. Marsh, sent a confidential ciphered despatch to Washington accusing the Italians of 'vacillation, tergiverzation and duplicity'. The State Department published it in *FRUS 1870*. For over a year, its publication went unnoticed by the Italian media. One evening in January 1872, however, as Marsh was dressing for dinner with the Italian Foreign Minister, one of his servants brought him a copy of a newspaper prominently featuring extracts from his despatch. Marsh is said to have almost fainted with shock. Only his friendship with the Italian Prime Minister and Foreign Minister and the fact that his denunciation applied chiefly to a previous government made it possible for him to remain in Rome. Marsh and his first secretary believed that the despatch had been 'treacherously printed by the Department of State in the volume of *Foreign Relations* with the malicious object of making the legation in Italy untenable any longer by its minister'. They may well have been right. The Republican Congressman John Bingham, a friend and strong supporter of President Ulysses S. Grant and Secretary of State Hamilton Fish, wanted his job in Rome. As a recent study by a State Department historian concludes, 'What better way to clear the way for Bingham than to let slip a dispatch from Marsh that would enrage the Italians?'[77]

Similar embarrassments continued. A decade later, Isaac P. Christiancy, former US minister in Lima, was outraged by the publication in *FRUS* of a 'private and personal' letter he had sent Secretary of State James G. Blaine in 1881 denouncing the 'debauched' state of the Peruvian people. 'The laboring class', he declared, was 'sunk beyond redemption' and the ruling class so dishonest that it had 'no idea even of that self-sacrificing patriotism which is essential to a proper and honest administration of government'. 'This letter', he told Blaine, 'must be treated as perfectly confidential, for your own eye and that of the president alone. My own life would not be safe here for one day if it were made public.' Fortunately for Christiancy, by the time his letter made newspaper headlines he had left Lima. Whereas nowadays US administrations criticize the media for publishing WikiLeaks and other classified official documents, in the late nineteenth century the roles were reversed. There was widespread support for the attack on the State Department by the New York *Herald-Tribune*: 'If it is possible for confidential dispatches to be divulged by so important an office as the State Department, the result will be that ministers will not send such dispatches, but prefer to communicate their substance orally.' In 1886 the former US minister to Greece Eugene Schuyler claimed that 'our ministers do not feel free to express to the Secretary their real opinions, for they have always in view the possibility that their dispatches may be published . . .' Aaron A. Sargent, minister to Germany, one of whose published despatches led to uproar in the German press, told the State Department formally that he would no longer send it frank reports on controversial issues.[78]

Even war with Spain in 1898 failed to persuade the State Department to take seriously either cipher security or the confidentiality of its correspondence. At the height of the pre-war diplomatic crisis, the Department received a credible report that Madrid was in possession of the main US diplomatic code, the 'Red Code', introduced in 1876. American diplomacy appears to have been unaffected by this discovery. The US minister in Spain carried on with his negotiations as before. A recent study by a State Department historian 'detects no meaningful change in the minister's communications with Washington even after he learned that the Spanish were reading them'.[79] Successive secretaries of state from the Civil War to the First World War were naïvely unaware of, or little interested in, the extent to which they were conducting what President Woodrow Wilson later famously called 'open diplomacy'.

21

'The Golden Age of Assassination': Anarchists, Revolutionaries and the Black Hand, 1880–1914

In the generation before the First World War, Europe endured what was later called 'the golden age of assassination'.* The 'golden age' began in 1878 with the founding of a secret Russian terrorist group, the People's Will (*Narodnaya Volya*), the first to use systematic terror for political ends.[1] A year later its executive committee condemned Tsar Alexander II to death for 'crimes against the people'. In 1880 the People's Will succeeded in blowing up the main dining room in the Winter Palace, killing eleven and injuring fifty-five – not, however, including the Tsar, who was late for dinner. In March 1881 a bomb was thrown under the Tsar's sleigh in St Petersburg. Alexander was unhurt but, as he left his sleigh to inspect the injuries to his Cossack escort, he was fatally injured by a second bomb thrown by another People's Will terrorist. His assassination, like the earlier attack on the Winter Palace, was made possible by the invention of dynamite by the Swedish chemist Alfred Nobel, particularly in its more malleable and powerful gelatinous form, better known as gelignite, invented in 1875 and adopted a few years later by the People's Will. Its chief bomb-maker, Nikolai Kibalchich, was also a pioneering rocket scientist. In the Soviet era a crater on the dark side of the moon was named after him.[2]

Discredited by its failure to prevent the assassination of the Tsar in 1881, the Third (Intelligence) Section of the Imperial Chancellery founded by Nicholas I in 1825,[3] was replaced by the Okhranka (better known as the Okhrana), a larger intelligence and security agency within the police department. From its St Petersburg headquarters the Okhrana ran a network of agents and informers which by the end of the century was about 20,000 strong, as well as opening tens of thousands of letters in post

---

* It was not the first golden age. The founder of the Indian Mauryan Empire in the early fourth century BC was said to be so fearful of assassination that he changed bedchamber every night. About three quarters of Roman emperors were either assassinated or toppled from their thrones. See above, pp. 62, 75.

offices across the Russian Empire in its search for subversive correspondence. Within two years of the assassination the Okhrana had succeeded
in disrupting operations of the People's Will. For the remainder of the
century there were no further political assassinations or successful bomb
attacks in Russia.[4]

To monitor and disrupt the activities of political dissidents abroad, the
Okhrana set up a Foreign Agency (*Zagranichnaya Agentura*), whose headquarters were located in the Russian embassy in Paris, the main émigré
centre. According to French Sûreté records, the Foreign Agency began
work in Paris, probably on a modest scale, in 1882.[5] By 1884 it was fully
operational under the direction of the formidable Pyotr Rachkovsky, who
seems to have had revolutionary sympathies during his early career before
becoming an informer for the Third Section. He went on to become probably the most influential of all Okhrana foreign intelligence officers.[6] Far
from objecting to Okhrana covert operations on French soil, the Sûreté
welcomed them. It concluded after thirty years' experience of secret collaboration with the Foreign Agency: 'It is impossible, on any objective
assessment, to deny the usefulness of having a Russian police operating
in Paris, whether officially or not, whose object is to keep under surveillance the activities of Russian revolutionaries.'[7] Unlike KGB residents
(heads of station) in Paris during the Soviet era, Rachkovsky, despite
conducting secret operations, became a prominent figure in Parisian high
society, making a fortune by speculating on the Bourse, entertaining lav-
ishly at his villa in Saint-Cloud, and numbering directors of the Sûreté,
presidents, ministers and leading diplomats among this guests. A writer
in the *Écho de Paris* said of him in 1901:

> If you ever meet him in society, I very much doubt whether you will feel the
> slightest misgivings about him, for nothing in his appearance reveals his
> sinister function. Fat, restless, always with a smile on his lips . . . he looks
> more like some jolly fellow on a spree . . . He has one rather noticeable
> weakness – that he is passionately fond of our little Parisiennes – but he is
> the most skilful operator in the ten capitals of Europe.[8]

Save for Russia, where the Okhrana became virtually a law unto itself,
most European states responded to increasing security threats not, as in
the twentieth century, by establishing specialized security services (such
as the British MI5) but by extending the responsibilities of the growing
nineteenth-century police forces. At the beginning of the century, Fouché,
Napoleon's Police Minister, had distinguished between 'low' policing of
such matters as 'prostitutes, thieves and lampposts', which he was content
to delegate, and 'high' policing on matters of national security, in which

he took a personal interest.[9] In the late nineteenth century 'the golden age of assassination' increased the priority given to 'high' policing.

During the years following Alexander II's assassination, the European capital which suffered the largest number of bomb attacks was London. In the 'Dynamite War' of 1881–5, Irish-American Fenians tried to end British rule in Ireland by a terrorist bombing campaign. More bombs exploded in London in 1883–5 than during any of the IRA campaigns a century later. They were also the first terrorist bombs fitted with timing devices. The Fenians successfully bombed the Local Government Board in Whitehall, the Houses of Parliament, the Tower of London, the offices of *The Times*, several main railway stations, the London Underground and Scotland Yard. 'The Houses of Parliament', reported *The Times* in March 1883, 'are searched as if continually on the eve of a GUY FAWKES plot . . .' The Home Secretary, Sir William Vernon Harcourt, wrote to the Prime Minister, William Gladstone, in May: 'This is not a temporary emergency requiring a momentary remedy. Fenianism is a permanent conspiracy against English rule [in Ireland] which will last far beyond the term of my life and must be met by a permanent organization to detect and control it.' At the heart of the 'permanent organization' created by Harcourt was a new intelligence department within the Metropolitan Police, the Special Irish Branch, established in March 1883. Its offices were imprudently situated on the first floor of a building in the centre of Great Scotland Yard, immediately above a public urinal. Though a police constable on duty in front of the building 'observed nothing suspicious in any person who entered the urinal', the Fenians succeeded in planting a large time-delay bomb which demolished the Special Irish Branch offices (which were fortunately empty at the time) on the evening of 30 May 1884.*

After a search for other strategically placed urinals, a public lavatory near Windsor Castle was closed down, and there was a flurry of alarm when it was discovered that the entire sanitation of the Houses of Parliament was being overhauled by Irish workmen. Queen Victoria was 'in a great state of fuss about the situation in general', fearful that her royal train might be bombed on the way to Balmoral.[10]

After the arrest of twenty Fenians, however, the 'Dynamite War' came to an abrupt end early in 1885 without further damage either to Scotland Yard or to public urinals. A subsequent attempt to arrange a Fenian 'firework display' to disrupt Queen Victoria's golden jubilee in 1887 with explosions in Westminster Abbey and Parliament ended in fiasco. Scotland Yard was forewarned of the bomb plot by informers and had the

---

* See ill. 40, the first photograph of the aftermath of a terrorist attack.

Irish-American bombers under surveillance from the moment they left the United States. Two of the bombers were arrested as soon as they reached England. A third died before the police could arrest him. The remnants of the Special Irish Branch and other anti-Fenian forces were combined in a new body, the Special Branch of the Metropolitan Police, which was given responsibility for all political crime.[11]

The best-publicized terrorist attack in the later 1880s was the blowing up in November 1886 of a printing house in Geneva used by émigré Russian Populists, some of them former members of the People's Will. The Populists, as Rachkovsky had intended, blamed the explosion on their revolutionary rivals, the Marxists. But the man actually responsible for the explosion was Rachkovsky himself, who reported to Okhrana headquarters by coded telegram: 'On Saturday night I was happy to destroy in Geneva the typography of the People's Will, along with . . . all revolutionary publications.' When the Populists established a new printworks in Paris, that too was destroyed in February 1887. The Foreign Agency, perhaps Rachkovsky personally, paid the leading Populist propagandist, Lev Tikhomirov, to write pamphlets denouncing the Marxists for the destruction of the printing presses.[12] Rachkovsky's greatest triumph of black propaganda was to draw a group of Populist émigrés into a bogus plot to assassinate Tsar Alexander III. One of his agents, Abram Landezen, who had penetrated Populist ranks, provided funds secretly supplied by Rachkovsky to set up a bomb factory in woods near Paris. When work on bomb construction was well advanced, Rachkovsky reported the plot to the Russian ambassador, Baron Morenheim, who had no idea that it had been orchestrated from his embassy by the Okhrana Foreign Agency. Morenheim demanded that the French police arrest the plotters. In 1890 two were sentenced to three years in prison. The ringleader, Landezen, who escaped, was sentenced to three years *in absentia*. Rachkovsky's propaganda coup convinced the French media and public of the reality of the threat posed by Russian 'nihilist' émigrés. Under the name Arkady Harting, Landezen re-emerged some years later as head of the Foreign Agency in Paris.[13]

The total numbers of victims during 'the golden age of assassination' were relatively modest by the standards of twenty-first-century terrorism. Between 1880 and 1914 about 150 people were killed and fewer than 500 injured. Those killed, however, included an unprecedented – and still unsurpassed – number of heads of state and government: among them Tsar Alexander II of Russia (1881), the Empress Elisabeth of Austria (1898), King Umberto I of Italy (1900), King Carlos I of Portugal and his heir apparent (1908), King George I of Greece (1913), President Sadi

Carnot of France (1894), President William McKinley of the United States (1901), and the prime ministers Antonio Cánovas del Castillo of Spain (1897) and Pyotr Stolypin of Russia (1911). Even more had narrow escapes. In 1906, for example, King Alfonso XIII and Queen Victoria of Spain survived a bomb attack on their wedding day which killed thirty-one soldiers and bystanders.

Anarchists were responsible for a majority of the attacks. Though most anarchists were non-violent, a violent fringe of the movement across Europe and the United States believed in the assassination of rulers as 'propaganda of the deed' designed to demonstrate the limitations of state power and encourage popular revolt against it. Anarchist assassination attempts tended to be low-tech. No French anarchist terrorist in the 1890s, for example, possessed expertise in the construction or use of gelignite bombs comparable with that of the People's Will in Russia or the Fenians in England a decade earlier. The first terrorist to use dynamite in France was a dyer's assistant, François-Claudius Ravachol, who with other anarchists stole a considerable amount of dynamite from a quarry south-east of Paris in February 1892. But two attempts by Ravachol a month later to use some of the sticks of dynamite to blow up a French magistrate both failed. On each occasion the magistrate was unhurt, though eight others were injured.[14] Despite the amateurishness of the first French terrorist use of dynamite, the alarmist prefect of the Seine concluded in 1893 that terrorist attacks on the Continent were ordered and coordinated by a (mythical) international anarchist committee (the so-called 'Dynamite Club') based in London, whose members included the Russian Pyotr Kropotkin as well as the French anarchists Charles Malato and Louis Matha.[15]

The two most celebrated French anarchist terrorist attacks of the 1890s – against the Chamber of Deputies and the President of the Republic – were no more sophisticated than Ravachol's. On 9 December 1893 Auguste Vaillant, an unemployed worker who had been imprisoned four times for theft and begging, obtained a pass permitting him to observe a session of the French Chamber of Deputies from a seat in the second row of the public gallery. Hidden in his trousers was a poorly constructed homemade bomb which he had filled with gunpowder, sulphuric acid, small nails and tacks. In the middle of a debate he threw the bomb into the Chamber, where it caused only minor injuries and the Speaker (president of the Chamber) famously announced that the debate would continue as normal: '*Messieurs, la séance continue.*' Security in the Chamber was so poor that Vaillant, despite being injured by his own bomb, was able to escape and seek hospital treatment. He was arrested when hospital staff discovered traces of gunpowder on his hands, tried and sentenced to the guillotine, shouting before his execution, 'Death to the Bourgeoisie! Long live Anarchy!'[16]

In France, as in most other continental countries, there was an extraordinary contrast between increasing police surveillance and investigation of anarchists on the one hand and the failure to give serious attention to the protection of political leaders from anarchist attacks. Before dawn on New Year's Day 1894, three weeks after Vaillant's arrest, French police began searching 552 supposedly subversive addresses. Over the next two months they arrested 248 suspected anarchists.[17] The arrests in France and other European countries, though undoubtedly including many non-violent political dissidents, removed some potential assassins from circulation. Those arrested in Italy in 1894, for example, included the homicidal anarchist Gaetano Bresci, who after a year in detention on the island of Lampedusa emigrated to New Jersey, whence he returned in 1900 to assassinate King Umberto with an American revolver.[18]

In February 1894 the Paris prefecture of police centralized its intelligence gathering under a former senior bureaucrat at the Interior Ministry, Louis Puibaraud (or Puybaraud), who was given the title *directeur-général des recherches*. His intelligence empire included a *brigade* of over 100 detectives (several times the size of Scotland Yard's Special Branch) which monitored anarchists' activities and compiled a detailed directory listing their names and addresses.[19]* Puibaraud, however, had no responsibility for overseeing what was later called 'protective security' against anarchist attacks.

The assassination on 24 June 1894 of President Sadi Carnot was the result of an even less sophisticated, though more successful, anarchist attack than Vaillant's. The Italian anarchist assassin, Sante Caserio, who set out to avenge Vaillant by killing Carnot, was armed only with a dagger, spoke very little French, and relied on the assistance of local anarchists as he made his way through France. As he acknowledged at his trial: 'Every forty or fifty kilometres on the way to Lyons I found small groups of *compagnons* [fellow anarchists], all French but very good and supportive in the welcome they gave to other *compagnons*.' Once in Lyons, Caserio must also have depended on local anarchists to discover the route to be taken by Carnot and where he would be most vulnerable.[20] The protective security around the President, despite the bomb attack on the Chamber of Deputies only six months earlier, was so feeble that Caserio needed to do no more than position himself along Carnot's route. The President's magnificently attired cavalry escort was almost purely ceremonial and

* Puibaraud served as *directeur-général des recherches* from 1894 to 1903.

proved powerless to prevent Caserio clambering onto Carnot's open carriage:

> I heard the 'Marseillaise' and the cries of 'Vive Carnot!' I saw the cavalry come up. I understood that the moment had come and I held myself ready. On seeing the President's carriage I drew my dagger and threw away the sheath. Then, when the carriage was passing close by me, I sprang forward to the step, supported myself by resting my left hand on the carriage, and with my right hand buried the dagger in the President's breast.[21]

Similar basic failures of protective security enabled other anarchists in the space of only three years to assassinate the Prime Minister of Spain, the Empress of Austria and the King of Italy. When the Italian anarchist Michele Angiolillo arrived in the spa resort of Santa Águeda to assassinate the Spanish Prime Minister, Antonio Cánovas del Castillo, in August 1897, he found Cánovas sitting alone on a bench in the spa. Angiolillo drew a revolver from an inside pocket of his coat and shot him dead. A year later another Italian anarchist, Luigi Lucheni, found the Empress Elisabeth of Austria (thinly disguised as an Austrian noblewoman) walking along the Geneva promenade with her lady-in-waiting but without a bodyguard. Lucheni had come to Geneva intending to assassinate the duc d'Orléans, the pretender to the French throne. On discovering that Orléans had left, he seized the unexpected opportunity to kill the Empress instead with a homemade dagger constructed from a sharpened four-inch needle. Lucheni said later: 'I came to Geneva to kill a sovereign, with the object of giving an example to those who suffer and those who do nothing to improve their social position; it did not matter to me who the sovereign was whom I should kill.'[22]

The threat from anarchist terrorism in Britain was probably lower than in any other major power. A few inexpert bomb-makers were arrested in Walsall in 1892; the local police are still in possession of one of their bombs. The French anarchist Martial Bourdin, who unintentionally blew himself up while attempting to demolish Greenwich Royal Observatory in 1894, is remembered chiefly for providing Joseph Conrad with the inspiration for his novel *The Secret Agent*. With little terrorism to investigate, the Special Branch turned its attention to the alleged threat posed by vaguer forms of subversion. It began, for example, to suspect a sinister purpose behind the activities of the Legitimation League, which campaigned to end discrimination against illegitimate children. Inspector John Sweeney of the Special Branch became convinced that the League was being used by anarchists to promote free love and subvert the social order. Sweeney purchased a copy of Havelock Ellis's *Psychology of Sex* from the League's secretary, George Bedborough, then promptly arrested him for selling it. Following Bedborough's conviction for obscene libel in 1898 and a police raid on its offices, the League was wound up.[23]

Though anarchists such as Caserio, Angiolillo and Lucheni moved across borders, most anarchist assassinations and attempted assassinations were the work of individuals or small groups. The successive killing of the French President, Spanish Prime Minister and Austrian Empress by Italian anarchists, however, encouraged the belief by some governments and their police forces in a great international anarchist conspiracy. After the assassination of the Empress Elisabeth, the Italian Prime Minister, General Luigi Pelloux, informed his Minister of Justice that both foreign governments and 'our confidants abroad' had sent warning of 'a vast conspiracy against the life of every head of state, and especially against the King of Italy'.[24]

The Italian government took the initiative in convening a secret 'International Conference for the Defence of Society against the Anarchists', which met in Rome from 24 November to 21 December 1898 – the first international gathering ever called to combat terrorism. It was also the only Europe-wide anti-anarchist conference ever held, attended by diplomats and police chiefs from all but one of the twenty-one European countries. (Montenegro, the only state to send no delegate, was represented by Russia.)[25] Despite a series of anarchist attacks in France during the mid-1890s, Léopold Viguié, director of the French Sûreté Générale, proudly informed the conference that all anarchist suspects in France were under constant surveillance and that the Sûreté had files on all potentially dangerous individuals which included both full-face and profile photographs.[26] In reality, Viguié was often privately sceptical of the reliability of reports even from some of the Sûreté's best-placed informants. The less experienced, and usually transient, interior ministers in the short-lived governments of the French Third Republic tended to take alarmist agent reports more seriously.[27]

All delegates to the Rome conference except the British (who abstained) agreed to a German proposal that agencies in every country keep resident anarchists under close surveillance, and exchange intelligence on them with other agencies.[28] In the aftermath of the conference there were a number of anarchist complaints of increased surveillance and cross-border cooperation between police forces. The London anarchist newspaper *Freedom* reported in March 1899:

> The so-called secrets of the anti-anarchist conference begin to slowly leak out. An Italian comrade, a working mason, who had the audacity to speak at a meeting in Hungary, three weeks ago, has been arrested and handed over to the Italian police. In England the Italian comrades are being systematically coerced and terrorized by Scotland Yard.[29]

But the Rome conference led to little improvement in police protection of royalty and ministers against assassination attempts. On 4 February 1900 the Prince of Wales, the future King Edward VII, came close to assassination at Brussels Nord railway station, where he had just boarded a royal train which was to take him and his Danish wife, Princess Alexandra, to Copenhagen. Security at the station was so poor that a fifteen-year-old Belgian anarchist, Jean-Baptiste Sipido, was able to mount the step to the royal carriage, put his hand through the open window and fire two shots at Edward from a distance of only two yards. 'If he had not been so bad a shot', Edward wrote later, 'I don't see how he could possibly have missed me.' In the absence of adequate police protection, it was left to the station manager to wrestle Sipido to the ground. Edward retained his sang-froid throughout. According to Charlotte Knollys, who was in his carriage, 'Bertie never even changed colour and the Princess behaved equally well.' As their train steamed out of the station, Edward and Alexandra leant through the open window to acknowledge the cheers of the crowd on the platform – a brave gesture which was also an elementary security lapse, since it was quite possible another would-be assassin was at large.[30] When he arrived at Copenhagen, unknown to his wife, Edward sent a telegram to his mistress, Alice Keppel, to assure her that he was unharmed.[31]

He was, however, furious with his cousin, King Leopold II, and the Belgian courts for failing to make an example of Sipido. The jury at Sipido's trial acquitted him on the grounds that 'by reason of his age he had not acted with discernment' and was thus not legally responsible. Sipido immediately fled to France.[32]

Neither the Prince of Wales's narrow escape in Brussels nor the Rome conference did anything to improve protective security in Italy. The assassination in July 1900 at Monza of King Umberto, who had survived two previous attempts on his life, was made possible, as in the case of President Carnot, by basic failure to protect a head of state travelling in an open carriage. His anarchist assassin, Gaetano Bresci, was less than twelve feet from the royal carriage when he fired three shots at Umberto with a revolver he had practised firing many times. An autopsy revealed that two of the shots had been lethal. Since capital punishment had been abolished in Italy in 1889, Bresci was the first European regicide not to be executed. He died in prison a year later, allegedly as the result of suicide – more probably at the hands of the prison guards.[33]

After the attempt to assassinate the Prince of Wales in Brussels, he was accompanied on his foreign travels by Superintendent William Melville, head of Scotland Yard's Special Branch. Melville was probably aware that during Edward's many, usually incognito, trips to Paris since the 1870s without a British bodyguard, he had been kept under discreet surveillance by the Paris police – partly because of the possibility of Fenian or anarchist attacks, partly to monitor his political and social contacts. Some of Edward's aristocratic friends were hostile to France's republican regime. The police also sought to discover whether any of the mistresses he entertained in his suite at the Hôtel Bristol in the place Vendôme were royalist agents of influence. They went to great pains to identify his mistresses both by surveillance and by questioning their neighbours, servants and concierges, and noted that he had a taste for tall, well-dressed blondes.[34] Scotland Yard was less well informed than the Paris police about Edward's private life.

As well as being put in charge of Edward's personal protection in 1900, Melville was also responsible for security arrangements (modest in scale by contemporary standards) at Queen Victoria's funeral in February 1901, which was attended by almost fifty members of foreign royal families. Kaiser Wilhelm II, who as Victoria's grandson was one of the three chief mourners, brought with him as his personal bodyguard a former *Kriminalkommissar* of the Berlin police, Gustav Steinhauer, who had trained as a private detective at the Pinkerton Agency in Chicago and spoke English fluently with an American accent. Melville worked closely with Steinhauer on security arrangements for the Kaiser, entertaining him to dinner with cigars and 'one or two bottles of wine' at Simpson's Grand Cigar Divan in the Strand. Steinhauer later gave a melodramatic, and probably unreliable, account of how he had accompanied Melville in a hunt for three homicidal Russian nihilists, who made their escape after allegedly killing a female informant of the Special Branch. Melville told the Kaiser he had been impressed by Steinhauer's intelligence expertise. 'Yes, Steinhauer is a splendid fellow!' replied the Kaiser. Melville also had frequent meetings, some of them at Scotland Yard, with Pyotr Rachkovsky and other Okhrana Foreign Agency officers during their regular visits to London. While investigating the activities of Russian revolutionary émigrés such as Lenin, who first stayed in London in 1902–3, Rachkovsky stayed in considerable opulence in a suite of rooms at the Savoy Hotel.[35]

In March 1901, only a month after Queen Victoria's funeral, an attack on the Kaiser in Bremen by a worker said to be 'of unsound mind' left him with a permanent scar beneath his right eye.[36] Thereafter Wilhelm II was probably the best protected European monarch; his bodyguard was increased to more than sixty for his travels outside Berlin.[37] Melville continued to assist in his personal protection during visits to Britain. The Kaiser presented him at various times with a gold watch and chain, a ring and a cigarette case. On his official retirement from the Special Branch in

1903, Melville was made a Member of the Royal Victorian Order (MVO) in recognition of his services to royal security at home and abroad. *The Times* reported that Scotland Yard had lost the services of 'the most celebrated detective of the day'. Melville, however, remained secretly involved in intelligence work for the War Office, later becoming 'chief detective' of MI5.[38]

Among the major powers, heads of state were probably at greatest risk in the United States. Three presidents – Abraham Lincoln, James A. Garfield and William McKinley – were assassinated in the half-century before the First World War. The Warren Commission on the assassination of President John F. Kennedy later concluded that security failures were largely responsible.[39] On the evening of 14 April 1865, the actor John Wilkes Booth was able to enter the President's box at Ford's Theatre in Washington and shoot Lincoln at point-blank range. Booth then jumped from the box to the stage and, despite fracturing his leg, escaped amid the pandemonium (though he was captured and shot a fortnight later). The President's bodyguard for the evening, Patrolman John F. Parker, who had been instructed to stand guard outside Lincoln's box, first wandered off to watch the play, then left the theatre to drink in a nearby saloon. Presidents after the Civil War had no bodyguard at all. In 1881 James A. Garfield was fatally wounded by a gunman with delusional grievances at a Washington railway station.

Today's presidents are protected by the US Secret Service, which is now part of the Department of Homeland Security. Founded in 1865, the Secret Service originally had a quite different role. As part of the Treasury Department, its main responsibility was to deal with the spate of forgeries which had followed the introduction of paper money three years earlier. Since, however, it was the only federal law enforcement agency until the founding in 1908 of the Justice Department's Bureau of Investigation (which later became the FBI), it was intermittently employed for other purposes as well. After the Secret Service discovered a plot against President Grover Cleveland in 1894, it was used for presidential protection, initially on an ad hoc basis. The protection became permanent after the assassination of President William McKinley in September 1901 during a public reception at the Pan-American Exposition in Buffalo at which three Secret Service agents, together with four Buffalo detectives and four soldiers, shared responsibility for the President's security. The assassin, a self-styled anarchist named Leon Frank Czolgosz, was among a long line of people waiting to shake McKinley's hand. When his turn came, Czolgosz shot the President twice with a gun concealed beneath a handkerchief. The poorly trained Secret Service agents, along with several others, immediately jumped on Czolgosz – despite the fact that, by doing so, they were leaving McKinley unguarded and vulnerable to the possibility of attack by a second assassin. After Czolgosz had been disarmed, and despite the fact that he was not resisting arrest, the senior Secret Service agent, George Foster, 'hit him between the eyes when he stood up' and knocked him down.[40]

Despite the lack of professionalism shown by the Secret Service in dealing with the attack on McKinley, the White House gave it full-time responsibility for presidential protection in 1902 – largely because there was no other federal investigative agency capable of doing so. It was another four years, however, before it received formal approval and funding from Congress. The earliest files on suspected anarchists in the Service's records, dating apparently from 1901–2, are primitive by the standards of leading European police forces, recording names of suspected anarchists, their places of residence (usually without exact addresses) and some comments such as 'very dangerous', but without biographical detail or physical descriptions.[41]

By far the most active European intelligence service both at home and abroad before the First World War was the Okhrana, which was unique in both the extent of its powers and the scope of its activities. Other European police forces operated under the law. The Okhrana was a law unto itself. In matters of political crime it had the right to search, to imprison and to exile on its own authority. Tsarist Russia, however, never became a fully fledged police state. By subsequent Soviet standards, the enormous powers of the Okhrana were used on only a modest scale. Even during the repression of the 1880s, only seventeen people were executed for political crimes – all actual or attempted assassinations. Among the terrorists who went to the scaffold was Alexander Ulyanov, condemned to death for his part in an unsuccessful plot to kill Alexander III on 1 March 1887, the sixth anniversary of Alexander II's assassination. Ulyanov's seventeen-year-old brother Vladimir (better known by his later alias Lenin) is said to have sworn vengeance against the Tsarist regime. By 1901, 4,113 Russians were in internal exile for political crimes, 180 of them on hard labour.[42]

The most persecuted group in the Russian Empire were the Jews. Popular anti-Semitism, state-encouraged pogroms, disabling laws and multiple forms of discrimination during the reigns of Alexander III (1881–94) and Nicholas II (1894–1917) led to the exodus of several million Jews, mainly to the United States. The regime, from the Tsar downwards, found the Jews a convenient scapegoat on which to focus popular discontents. Though the Okhrana did not originate state-sponsored anti-Semitism, it helped to implement it. One of its officers, M. S. Komissarov, received an official reward of 10,000 roubles for inciting anti-Jewish riots with pamphlets printed on Police Department presses. While head of the Foreign Agency, Pyotr Rachkovsky was probably responsible for fabricating the infamous anti-Semitic forgery, *The Protocols of the Elders of Zion*, which purported to reveal a secret Jewish plot for world domination. Though the *Protocols* had limited influence before the First World War, it was later a key text of Nazi and fascist anti-Semitism, becoming probably the most influential forgery of the twentieth century.[43]

Twenty years after the killing of Alexander II by the People's Will, Russia became once again the main arena for political assassination. The immediate cause was student protests against restrictions on political meetings and demonstrations. On 14 February 1901 an expelled university student, Peter Karpovich, shot and fatally wounded N. P. Bogolepov, the reactionary Minister of Education. Many students saw Karpovich as a hero. They were further radicalized by the brutal dispersal by Cossacks on 4 March of a large student demonstration in front of St Petersburg's Kazan Cathedral. Karpovich's strongest support came from student members of the newly formed Socialist-Revolutionary (SR) Party, dedicated to the establishment of a socialist state based on the communal traditions of rural Russia. In 1902 one of the SR founders, the charismatic Grigory Gershuni, founded a 'Combat Organization' to carry out terrorist attacks. Police reports described him as 'an artist in terror'. According to an Okhrana official, he had 'an incredible gift . . . for taking hold of inexperienced, easily carried-away youth'. A fellow SR said he had 'eyes that penetrated one's soul'. The first major target of the Combat Organization was the Interior Minister, S. N. Sipiagin. On 2 April 1902 a student member of the Organization, Stepan Balmashov, entered the Marinsky Palace, dressed in the uniform of an aide-de-camp, handed Sipiagin an envelope which was later discovered to contain a document sentencing him to death, then shot him twice at point-blank range. After the assassination, the SR leadership for the first time formally declared the Combat Organization part of the party, and that the use of terror was compatible with peaceful agitation. Political assassination would 'awaken even the sleepiest philistines . . . and force them, even against their will, to think politically'. Though officially under the control of the party Central Committee, however, the Combat Organization chose its own targets.[44]

The Okhrana's main source of intelligence on the SRs was agent penetration. Its prize agent was Evno Azev, who first appears in Okhrana files in the early 1890s as 'a Jewish revolutionary'. In 1893 he volunteered his services as a paid agent.[45] In 1902, no doubt to the delight of the Okhrana, he became a member of both the SR Central Committee and the Combat Organization, of which he later became leader.*

Among the Combat Organization's targets was the brutal, anti-Semitic Interior Minister, V. K. Plehve, whose responsibilities included the Okhrana. Though Azev informed the Okhrana of a plot to assassinate Plehve, fear of blowing Azev's cover prevented its taking adequate precautions, and on 28 July 1904 he was killed by a bomb thrown beneath his carriage as he was being driven to a St Petersburg railway station. Even more sensational was the assassination on 17 January 1905, also by a bomb thrown at his carriage, of the Tsar's uncle, Grand Duke Sergei, governor-general of Moscow. Sergei was so reactionary that he forbade his wife to read *Anna Karenina* for fear that it might arouse in her 'unhealthy curiosity and violent emotions'.[46] The Combat Organization's next major target was the Prime Minister, Pyotr Stolypin. On 12 August 1906 it infiltrated his villa and detonated several bombs. Though more than a dozen people were injured, including one of Stolypin's children, on this occasion Stolypin himself survived unscathed.

Throughout the period of these assassinations, Azev had regular meetings with the head of the St Petersburg Okhrana, A. V. Gerasimov, who seems to have taken the view that, despite the difficulty of acting on much of Azev's intelligence, the wave of assassinations would have been even worse without his penetration of the Combat Organization. Counter-terrorism was further complicated by the widespread upheavals of the 1905 Revolution, when the Combat Organization terrorist Boris Savinkov declared that 'anyone in uniform' was a target.[47] The Romanov dynasty survived the 1905 Revolution not because of the Okhrana but because the army remained loyal.

Azev's parallel careers as leading Socialist Revolutionary and top Okhrana agent came to a dramatic end in 1908. The man mainly responsible for revealing his double life was Vladimir Burtsev, an SR who had made it his mission to track down police spies in revolutionary ranks. When seeing Azev walking openly around St Petersburg in 1906, Burtsev asked himself: 'If I have recognized Azev so easily from a distance, why cannot police detectives, who most certainly know him by sight, recognize him when he appears so conspicuously in St Petersburg?' Azev, he concluded, must be working for the Okhrana. Though Azev protested his innocence with some success for the next two years, an investigation late in 1908 conducted by leading SRs in Paris (a safer location for the investigation

---

* When the SR Central Committee was reduced in size to five in December 1905, Azev remained a member of it. (Ruud and Stepanov, *Fontanka 16*, ch. 7.)

than St Petersburg) established his guilt. He was given twenty-four hours to confess, and preparations were made for his execution. Azev fled from Paris at dawn the next day. The Russian Duma ordered an enquiry into the Azev case. Stolypin, as Prime Minister, responded to the scandal in February 1909 with a rare official public justification for agent penetration of subversive organizations: 'While revolutionary terror exists, there will always be a need for police action.' The Socialist Revolutionaries, humiliated by the revelation that the head of the Combat Organization had been an Okhrana agent, gave up assassination. Controversy has continued ever since on where Azev's real loyalty lay. While there will probably never be a definitive answer, the probability is that he worked for money and excitement rather than from commitment either to the SRs or to the Tsarist regime. Though well paid by the Okhrana, he also embezzled money from Combat Organization funds (much of them obtained from bank robberies) and lived in some style, gambling on both the stock exchange and in casinos, where he was often accompanied by a former *chansonnière*.[48]

Just over two years after Stolypin publicly justified agent penetration of revolutionary organizations, he himself fell victim to an Okhrana agent of uncertain loyalties. On 1 September 1911 both the Tsar and Stolypin attended a gala evening at the Kiev opera house to mark the fiftieth anniversary of the emancipation of Russian serfs. Also present was a 24-year-old Okhrana agent, Dmitri Bogrov, who had earlier won the confidence of the head of the Kiev Okhrana by providing intelligence on terrorist manufacture and distribution of explosives. During an interval in the gala evening, while Stolypin was standing talking by the orchestra pit, Bogrov shot him twice with a pistol. According to an eyewitness, the Prime Minister 'unbuttoned his white frock coat and, looking at his blood-soaked vest, he waved his hand as though signalling, "Everything is over." Then he dropped heavily into a chair and said clearly and distinctly, in a voice which was heard by all those standing near him, "I am happy to die for the Tsar."' Stolypin survived another five days before dying of his wounds. Bogrov told one of his jailers as he was being led to execution on 12 September: 'The only happy moment in my life was the moment when I learned that Stolypin had died.' In the course of his lengthy interrogation, however, he had given a confused account of his motives. A central element in his motivation seems to have been remorse for the anarchists he had betrayed to the Okhrana. He claimed that his betrayal had been discovered by revolutionaries who had told him he could only 'rehabilitate' himself by killing a state official.[49]

The Okhrana found the Marxist Russian Social Democratic Labour Party (RSDLP), which in 1903 divided into Bolshevik and Menshevik wings, more straightforward to penetrate than the populist SRs, partly because it did not pose a terrorist threat. Despite Lenin's deep suspicions about non-Bolshevik revolutionaries, he was curiously naïve about the danger of Okhrana penetration. Even after the sensational unmasking of Azev, it did not occur to him that Dr Yacov Zhitomirsky, the Bolshevik representative in Berlin, had been an Okhrana agent since 1902, regularly reporting on Lenin's travels while in foreign exile. After being expelled from Berlin in 1907, Zhitomirsky attended the fifth RSDLP congress, held that year in London, and moved his permanent base to Paris, where he continued to report to the Foreign Agency.[50] S. P. Beletsky, the director of the Police Department, later said that 'the whole purpose' of his pre-war policy had been to prevent, at all costs, the unification of Russian socialism. 'I worked', he said, 'on the principle of divide and rule.' The man he believed most likely to keep Russian socialists divided was Lenin.[51] Though many Bolsheviks hoped for reunion with the Mensheviks, Lenin stood out resolutely against it.* Whereas the Ohkrana believed that a disunited RSDLP would mean a weaker socialist movement, Lenin was convinced that, on the contrary, the existence of a separate Bolshevik Party was the key to victory. Only a disciplined, doctrinally pure, 'monolithic' elite of hardened revolutionaries could lead the Russian people to the promised land.

The Okhrana's most successful Bolshevik penetration agent was Roman Malinovsky, a Moscow worker with a criminal record recruited in 1910, who, two years later, was one of six Bolsheviks elected as deputies in the Duma. 'For the *first* time', wrote Lenin excitedly, 'we have an *outstanding leader* from among the workers representing us in the Duma.' In a party dedicated to proletarian revolution but as yet without proletarian leaders, Lenin saw Malinovsky, whom he brought on to the Bolshevik Central Committee, as a figure of great importance: 'It is really possible to build a workers' party with such people, though the difficulties will be incredibly great!' After the 1912 election the Bolshevik and Menshevik deputies in the Duma sat as members of a single RSDLP group. But when the group split in 1913, Malinovsky became chairman of the Bolshevik 'fraction'.

By 1912 Lenin had belatedly grasped the potential seriousness of Okhrana penetration. On his initiative, the Bolshevik Central Committee appointed a three-man 'provocation commission' to consider the problem. One of the members was Malinovsky. In July 1913 Lenin discussed the

---

* Beletsky was probably responsible for the exile to Siberia in 1912 of the leading Bolshevik champion of reunification with the Mensheviks, Alexei Rykov. (Billington, *Fire in the Minds of Men*, p. 476.)

problem of penetration at a meeting with him and two other leading Bolsheviks, Lev Kamenev and Grigory Zinoviev. Only Malinovsky saw the irony of their conclusion that there must be an Okhrana agent 'close' to the six Bolshevik deputies whose chairman he was. He was instructed to be 'as conspiratorial as possible' to minimize the threat of police penetration. Almost simultaneously, Malinovsky persuaded Lenin to appoint his fellow Okhrana agent, Miron Chernomazov, as editor of *Pravda*.[52] The work of the 'provocation commission', like the Azev revelations, increased Lenin's awareness of the effectiveness of Okhrana operations, even if they did not alert him to the role of Malinovsky. There was much to be said, he wrote, for revolutionary parties being run by 'a few professionals, as highly trained and experienced as our security police'.[53]

Though Beletsky described Malinovsky as 'the pride of the Okhrana', the strain of his double life eventually proved too much. Even Lenin, Malinovsky's strongest Bolshevik supporter, became concerned by his heavy drinking. In May 1914, at a time when Malinovsky was reported to be drinking vodka from teapots, the Ministry of the Interior probably fearing public scandal if Malinovsky's increasingly erratic behaviour led to the revelation that the Okhrana employed him as an agent in the Duma, decided to get rid of him. Malinovsky resigned from the Duma and fled from St Petersburg with a 6,000-rouble pay-off which the Okhrana urged him to use to start a new life abroad. Rumours quickly spread that he had been an Okhrana agent. Yuli Martov, the Menshevik leader, wrote in June: 'We are all certain, without the slightest doubt, that he is a provocateur ... but whether we will be able to prove it is another matter.' Lenin, by contrast, dismissed the charges against Malinovsky, though acknowledging that he had committed 'political suicide'.[54]

Because Lenin spent so much time in foreign exile, Okhrana surveillance of him was less close than of Stalin (born Iosip Dzhugashvili), who was usually in Russia. Lenin was in London during the 1905 Revolution (as on five other occasions before the First World War) and in Zurich during the February 1917 Revolution, which took him completely by surprise. The Okhrana file on Stalin was probably the most detailed yet produced on any political subversive by any intelligence agency. It fills over 100 volumes, which are currently being researched by the historian Svetlana Lokhova. After the Bolshevik Revolution, Stalin placed all the volumes in his own personal archive and brooded over them for many years, making numerous annotations and occasional doodles. So far as is known, no other world leader has ever spent so much time brooding over the intelligence record of his past life.

As Lokhova's research shows, there was much to brood over, ranging from his private life to his career as a revolutionary. Though Stalin knew he had been under surveillance, he must have been taken aback by the immensely intrusive detail in his voluminous file – such as the erotic post-card which, at the age of thirty-four, he had sent from abroad in 1912 to a friend's sixteen-year-old fiancée, promising her a 'hotttttt' kiss, because that was the only way worth kissing. Between 1902 and 1916 Stalin spent more time in prison and internal exile than at liberty, but escaped from exile six times. In 1906 he was able to evade Okhrana surveillance and attend the fourth congress of the RSDLP in Stockholm, at which Lenin led Bolshevik attacks on the rival Mensheviks. In 1907, again unnoticed by the Okhrana, he succeeded in leaving for London to attend the even stormier fifth congress of the RSDLP, at which Lenin was the leading Bolshevik delegate.[55]

Over most of Europe during the years immediately before the First World War, the 'golden age' of political assassination seemed to have gone out of fashion. The major exception was the Balkans, where there was a long and homicidal rivalry between Serbia's two dominant families, the Obrenović and Karadjordjević dynasties, and some Serbian intelligence officers looked on assassination as an instrument of policy. The most gruesome killing of any head of state during the 'golden age' was that of King Alexander Obrenović and Queen Draga of Serbia in the royal palace at Belgrade. Plotting the violent overthrow of the Obrenović dynasty began in 1901, led by a powerfully built lieutenant on the Serbian General Staff, Dragutin Dimitrijević, known to his admirers as 'Apis', because of his supposed resemblance to the broad-shouldered bull-god of ancient Egypt. By the spring of 1903 the conspirators numbered over 120, among them officers of the palace guard and the King's aide-de-camp.

In the early hours of 11 June 1903 twenty-eight mutinous Serbian army officers, determined to replace Obrenović rule by the rival and more com-pliant Karadjordjevićs, burst into the royal palace. Apis had chosen himself as one of the assassination squad but was shot and injured by loyal guards near the palace entrance. The rest of the squad found Alexander and Draga behind the royal bedroom, cowering in a tiny room used by the Queen's maid to iron her clothes. They shot and bayoneted both the royal couple, disfigured their faces beyond recognition, partly disembowelled their bodies with sabres, then threw the mutilated corpses out of a palace window into the courtyard below. Members of the assassination team also broke into the apartments of the Prime Minister, Dimitrije Cincar-Marković, and the War Minister, Milovan Pavlović. Both were killed. The Interior Minister,

Belimir Theodorović, was also shot and left for dead but recovered from his wounds. The British minister in Belgrade, Sir George Bonham, was shocked by the 'entire absence of decent regret' at the brutal assassinations. The following day was celebrated as a public holiday and Belgrade streets were festooned with flags. The wounded Apis became a national hero. King Peter I, head of the Karadjordjević dynasty, then in exile in Geneva, returned to rule Serbia (and later the future Yugoslavia) as a constitutional monarch, with army support, for the next eighteen years.[56*]

Henceforth the main target of plotting by Apis and the Serbian regicides was increasingly Austrian rule in the Balkans, especially after the neighbouring, formerly Ottoman provinces of Bosnia and Herzegovina, which had a large ethnic Serb population, were incorporated into the Austro-Hungarian Empire in 1908. Apis, who had been appointed to a professorship at the Serbian Military Academy, was one of the seven founders in 1911 of a supposedly secret military society, 'Unification or Death!' (*Ujedinjenje ili smrt!*), better known as the Black Hand (*Crna Ruka*), dedicated to the creation of a greater Serbia populated by all the Serbs of the Balkan peninsula. The violence of the Black Hand's methods was epitomized by its insignia of skull and crossbones, knife, poison and bomb. When challenged later about the choice of such macabre symbols, Apis replied that it was the duty of all Serb nationalists 'to save Serbdom with bombs, knives and rifles'. He also defended the use of poison by the Black Hand 'both as a means of attack and to save someone if he fell into enemy hands' – in other words, to commit suicide. Within Belgrade coffee houses the existence of the Black Hand became an open secret. Its members penetrated both the officer corps and the Foreign Ministry. Apis was sent to conduct covert operations by the army in Macedonia, then part of the Ottoman Empire, before the Serbian invasion in the First Balkan War of 1912. During the Serbian occupation of much of Ottoman Albania in 1913, the Black Hand was used by the Belgrade Foreign Ministry to negotiate with local Albanian chieftains.

In August 1913, a year before the outbreak of the First World War, Apis was promoted to the position of chief of General Staff Intelligence. No other intelligence chief in pre-war Europe had as much freedom from political control. Nikola Pašić, leader of the Serbian People's Radical Party and Prime Minister for most of the period from 1904 to 1918, like many of his colleagues, regarded Apis as a threat to national security. The Interior Minister, Milan Protić, called him 'a menace to democracy'. Like many Serbian army

---

* From 1918 to his death in 1921 Peter I was first King of the Serbs, Croats and Slovenes (later Yugoslavia).

officers, Apis despised the Radical Party. In the spring of 1914 Pašić is reported to have called the Black Hand 'a state within a state'.[57]

Within Austrian-ruled Bosnia and Herzegovina, the Black Hand and an older Serb nationalist organization, the Narodna Odbrana, worked closely with pro-Serb activists, of which the most important were the members of 'Young Bosnia' (*Mlada Bosna*). At the opening of the Bosnian parliament in June 1910, one 'Young Bosnian', Bogdan Žerajić, fired five bullets at the Austrian governor. When all missed their target he shot the sixth into his own head (which the Austrian police kept as a gruesome exhibit in their black museum). Žerajić became a hero of the nationalist press in Belgrade and the grave of his headless corpse a shrine for 'Young Bosnians'. His attack on the Austrian governor marked the beginning of the systematic use of political terrorism against Austrian rule. There were seven similar attacks as well as a dozen other abortive plots in the South Slav provinces of the Austrian Empire during the four years between Žerajić's death and the assassination of the Archduke Franz Ferdinand in Sarajevo in 28 June 1914.[58]

The key figures in carrying out the Sarajevo assassinations were three 'Young Bosnian' students, who were further radicalized while living in Belgrade from 1912 to 1914: Gavrilo Princip, Nedeljko Čabrinović and Trifko Grabež.* The Black Hand supplied them with Browning semi-automatic pistols and bombs, provided weapons training in a forest near Belgrade, and later helped to smuggle them across the Serbian border. Their original assassination target, decided in 1913, was General Oskar Potiorek, the authoritarian Austro-Hungarian governor of Bosnia. In the spring of 1914, the main target in Sarajevo was changed from Potiorek to the heir to the Austro-Hungarian throne, Archduke Franz Ferdinand, after his decision to pay an official visit to the Bosnian capital with his wife, Sophie. Apis was probably first informed that the Archduke and Sophie were to visit Sarajevo on 28 June 1914 by Rade Malobabić, a Serb born in Austria–Hungary who provided Austrian military intelligence to Black Hand members among Serbian frontier officers. They in turn forwarded it to Apis and Serbian military intelligence.[59]

Though Apis was probably the first to decide on the assassination of Franz Ferdinand in Sarajevo, the change of target was welcomed by Princip, Čabrinović and Grabež, who did not discover plans for the Archduke's

---

* Tim Butcher's mostly impressive interpretation of Gavrilo Princip in *The Trigger* argues unpersuasively that his radicalization owed little to his years in Belgrade and the influence of the Black Hand, but was a straightforward response to the poverty and oppression suffered by all Bosnian South Slavs.

visit until they read them in a newspaper. Before leaving Belgrade for Sarajevo about a month ahead of the Archduke's visit, Princip wrote to his confidant and former Young Bosnia room-mate in Belgrade, Danilo Ilić, to inform him of the plan to kill the Archduke and seek more recruits to the assassination team. Ilić found three further would-be assassins: the eighteen-year-old Cvetko Popović and seventeen-year-old Vaso anČubrilović, both Bosnian Serb students, and Muhamed Mehmedbašić, a Bosnian Muslim carpenter in his mid-twenties.[60]

How much the Prime Minister, Nikola Pašić, knew about Apis's assassination plans will probably never be known. The Bosnian peasant who guided Princip and Grabež across the Bosnian frontier was a Serbian government informer who told the Belgrade Interior Ministry about their movements and the weapons they were carrying, though his report made no mention of the assassination plan. Pašić ordered weapons smuggling from Serbia to Bosnia to be stopped. The Belgrade government, however, was no longer in control of the Serbian border. One minister later claimed that the Prime Minister told the Cabinet approximately a month before the Archduke's visit that assassins were on their way to Sarajevo to kill him. The Serbian envoy in Vienna, apparently on Pašić's instructions, passed on only a vague warning about an assassination plot, which was not taken very seriously by the Austrian authorities.[61]

Despite the unprecedented number of assassinations of crowned heads and their chief ministers over the previous generation, in most of Europe as it approached the First World War protective security remained a remarkably undeveloped branch of intelligence work – nowhere more so than in Sarajevo. Though the Archduke was the most conspicuous of targets, travelling in an open car, wearing a helmet adorned with green peacock feathers and a sky-blue tunic with gold collar, security during his visit to Sarajevo was perfunctory. Franz Ferdinand dismissed the idea of protection by bodyguards or of soldiers standing between himself and the crowds along his route as personally demeaning. The governor of Bosnia, General Potiorek, who was in charge of security for the visit, mocked those on his staff who believed the 'children' of Young Bosnia were capable of mounting a serious assassination threat. Such security as there was in Sarajevo was in the hands of its 120-strong police force woefully lacking in counter-terrorist intelligence. The seven youthful assassins lying in wait with bombs and guns along the Archduke's route were willing to give their lives in order to strike a dramatic blow for the freedom of Balkan Slavs who remained under Austrian rule. The first assassin waiting in line as the royal motorcade drove along the banks of the River Miljacka in central Sarajevo was Muhamed Mehmedbašić, who, however, lost his nerve at the critical moment and later escaped to Serbia. Next in line was the more determined Nedeljko Čabrinović, who drew a bomb from his coat pocket, struck its percussion cap against a lamp post, and threw it at the Archduke as his car passed by. Seeing the bomb being thrown, Franz Ferdinand raised his arm to ward it off, and succeeded in deflecting it into the street behind. Though the bomb explosion caused injuries among spectators and the occupants of the following car, the royal couple survived unscathed. On arrival at the City Hall, a furious Franz Ferdinand told the Mayor: 'Mr Mayor, one comes here for a visit and is received by bombs! It is outrageous!' But, despite the obvious risk of another assassination attempt, the royal visit continued.

Security in Sarajevo continued to be so incompetent that, after the reception at the City Hall, the drivers of the two cars containing the royal couple and the mayor were not told that changes had been made to the route in order to allow Franz Ferdinand to visit in hospital those who had been wounded in the bomb attack. In the confusion, the royal car took the wrong road and was forced to reverse. While moving slowly backwards, it passed one of the team of assassins, Gavrilo Princip. Though taken by surprise to be presented with such an easy target, Princip drew a pistol from his pocket and fired two shots at close range, fatally wounding both Franz Ferdinand and Sophie.*

Apis covered his tracks in the planning of the Sarajevo assassination so successfully that his exact role is no longer discoverable. The Austro-Hungarian police, however, discovered more about the team of assassins than he had expected. After the assassinations, as Apis was aware, all had planned to commit suicide so that they could not be interrogated. But, for unknown reasons, the poison given them by the Black Hand failed to do its job. As soon as Čabrinović had thrown his bomb, he swallowed cyanide, as did Princip after shooting the royal couple. Though both foamed at the mouth and became violently ill, they did not die. Less than an hour after Princip's arrest, in a state of shock and surprised to be alive, he admitted to the police that, on returning to Sarajevo from Belgrade, he had registered his address in Oprkanj Street. There the police found Ilić, whom they arrested, and discovered the bags he had used to store the assassins' weapons beneath his bed. Hundreds of Bosnian Serbs who had

---

* The most famous photograph of the aftermath of the Sarajevo assassination is commonly believed to show the manhandling of Gavrilo Princip. In fact it shows the arrest of an innocent bystander, Ferdinand Behr, during the confusion which followed the killing of the royal couple. (Sarajevo History Museum.)

nothing to do with the assassination were rounded up and maltreated. To try to protect the innocent, Princip told Ilić and Grabež, as soon as he was allowed to see them: 'Confess everything, how we got the bombs, how we travelled and in what society we were, so that just people do not come to harm.'[62] Under Austrian law, no one under twenty could be executed. Princip died in prison from tuberculosis in 1918. The youngest of the assassination team, Čubrilović, survived to become a minister in Marshal Tito's post-Second World War Communist government in Yugoslavia. Ilić and two older individuals, who were also involved in the Sarajevo assassination plot, were tried and executed.

Without the support and guidance of the Black Hand, the young and inexperienced assassins in Sarajevo on 28 June 1914 would have been unable to attempt the assassination of Franz Ferdinand. Even with Black Hand assistance to the assassins, only elementary failures of Austro-Hungarian security, which seems to have learned nothing from the homicidal attacks on other European royals and political leaders over the previous generation, enabled the assassination to succeed. The lack of protection given to the Archduke and his wife in their open-topped Gräf & Stift motorcar replicated the errors which had made possible the earlier killing of, among others, President Carnot of France and King Umberto of Italy in their open horse-drawn carriages.

The Black Hand was able to play a crucial role in planning the assassination and assisting the assassins because Apis headed the only significant intelligence agency in pre-war Europe which was largely out of the control of its government. Had Pašić been able to reassert political control of Serbian intelligence, the Young Bosnian assassins in Sarajevo would have been deprived of the support they needed. Apis's part in the assassinations gave him a more important role in the origins of the First World War than any other intelligence chief. Not until eight months after the outbreak of the war was his authority seriously challenged. In March 1915 Prince Regent Alexander, heir to the Serbian throne, sacked him as chief of intelligence and moved him to military operations. Thereafter Apis maintained a low political profile until his arrest late in 1916.[63] In 1917 the Serbian government-in-exile put Apis on trial on a number of dubious charges unconnected with the Sarajevo assassinations which included the attempted killing of the Prince Regent. Though Apis denied the charges, he was found guilty of treason. During the trial, probably to embarrass the Pašić government, he claimed – with some exaggeration – that the Black Hand had been in complete charge of every stage of the operation which led to the Sarajevo assassinations. Pašić wrote to his envoy in London:

'Dimitrijević [Apis], besides everything else, admitted he had ordered Franz Ferdinand to be killed. And now who could reprieve [him and his associates]?' Apis and three fellow officers were shot by firing squad.[64]* He thus became the first intelligence chief of the twentieth century to be executed.†

* The case was retried in 1953 by the Serbian Supreme Court, which posthumously exonerated all the defendants.
† Others to be executed later in the twentieth century included three successive heads of Soviet intelligence: Genrikh Yagoda, Nikolai Yezhov and Lavrenti Beria. Like Apis, all were found guilty on at least partly trumped-up charges.

22

The Great Powers and Foreign Intelligence, 1890–1909

Between the Franco-Prussian and the First World Wars, the great powers of Europe were at peace between themselves (though not with colonial peoples and minor powers) for longer than ever before in modern history. Partly for that reason, foreign intelligence was usually a low priority for their governments. British intelligence at the outbreak of the Boer War in 1899 was less productive than during the Napoleonic Wars a century earlier. Britain had not possessed a codebreaking agency since the closure of the Deciphering Branch in 1844, and the Intelligence Department (ID) in the late-Victorian War Office had only an amateurish, underfunded espionage network. The total ID budget for all 'Secret Service' work before the Boer War was a mere £600 a year, occasionally supplemented by funds from the Foreign Office. The ID's far-flung informants included a riverboat captain in the Belgian Congo, the head of telegraphs in Persia, and British railway officials at various points of the globe, all of whom gave their occasional services either free of charge or for token payment. Most of the War Office's £600 Secret Service budget went to finance foreign travel by ID officers to the parts of the world which they were responsible for monitoring. Nevertheless, they usually ended up out of pocket. Lord Edward Gleichen complained that his reconnaissance of Montenegro in 1899 cost him nearly £90 of his own money. Other ID officers were grateful simply to receive part of their travel costs. 'In those days', Major-General Charles Callwell later recalled, 'one was expected by the financial authorities to be out of pocket when away on public service.' Secret Service funds, he claimed, allowed ID officers to 'have interesting and often very pleasant trips abroad at trifling cost to their own pockets'.[1]

The intelligence-gathering missions of ID staff were supplemented by those of other army officers and 'patriotic folk'. The most enthusiastic of the officers was the future founder of the Boy Scout Movement, Robert (later General Lord) Baden-Powell, who developed a taste for intelligence work during a series of 'jolly larks' on the North-West Frontier in the early

1880s. Baden-Powell was a firm believer in the superiority of the gentle-man amateur over the career professional. 'The best spies', he declared, 'are unpaid men who are doing it for the love of the thing.' Espionage also had great 'sporting value':

> For anyone who is tired of life, the thrilling life of a spy should be the very finest recuperation. When one recognises also that it may have valuable results for one's country in time of war, one feels that even though it is time spent largely in enjoyment, it is not by any means time thrown idly away; and though the 'agent' if caught, may 'go under', unhonoured and unsung, he knows in his heart of hearts that he has done his 'bit' for his country as fully as his comrade who falls in battle.[2]

Before the First World War, there was not much danger that British 'agents' would 'go under'. Until less than a decade before the outbreak of war, all the great powers took a remarkably tolerant attitude towards amateur espi-onage by foreign army officers. R. B. Haldane, the Secretary of State for War, told the Commons in 1908: 'That officers of all nations, when abroad, look about for useful information I have no doubt.' 'But that', he believed (though Baden-Powell disagreed), 'is a different thing from coming as spies.'[3]

The outbreak and early months of the Boer War had brutally exposed the limitations in the War Office's ability to use, as well as to collect, intel-ligence. The Royal Commission on the War in South Africa later concluded that, though the ID had been 'undermanned for the work of preparation for a great war', its eighteen officers had achieved 'a considerable meas-ure of success'. The ID had argued as early as June 1896 that, contrary to prevailing military opinion, 'the two Boer states may make a dash at Natal' – which in October 1899 is precisely what they did. Subsequent ID reports also correctly identified the Boer threat to Cape Colony, and pro-vided accurate estimates of Boer forces and ammunition. Some of the most important ID strategic intelligence was simply not believed – largely because of the arrogant belief that unkempt, long-haired Boer farmers would be no match for disciplined British troops. The Colonial Secretary, Joseph Chamberlain, convinced that the ID must be exaggerating the numbers and capacity of Boer guerrilla forces, opposed sending large troop reinforcements to South Africa in the summer of 1899. Much other ID intelligence was simply ignored. When a copy of the ID manual on South Africa was sent to General Sir Redvers Buller (nicknamed 'Blunder' by the ID and others) on his appointment as commander-in-chief of the exped-itionary force, he sent it back with, according to Britain's best-paid war correspondent, the 25-year-old Winston Churchill, who travelled with Buller to Cape Town, the message that he 'knew everything about South

Africa'. Buller's defeat at Colenso, the climax of the military disasters of 'Black Week' in December 1899 which cost him his command, was due at least in part to his neglect of intelligence on Boer movements.

Churchill's enthusiasm for intelligence, which was in striking contrast to Buller's indifference, lasted for the rest of his life. It began during his early adventures, first as army officer, then as war correspondent, at the outposts of the late-Victorian Empire on the North-West Frontier and with Kitchener in Sudan. 'The great mass of those who took part in the little wars of Britain in those light-hearted days', Churchill later claimed (speaking chiefly for himself), found them 'full of fascinating thrills'. During the Boer War, Churchill's 'thrills' included escaping from a Boer prisoner-of-war camp with a price on his head. Later in the war, he cycled through Johannesburg in disguise, on reconnaissance work. He admitted that, had he been caught, 'No court martial that ever sat in Europe would have had much difficulty in disposing of such a case.' Churchill would have been shot as a spy.[4]

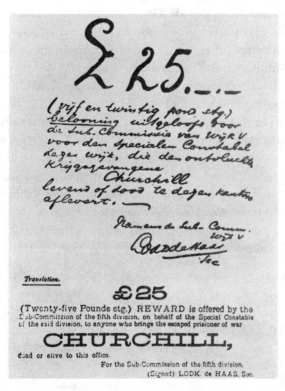

£25 reward offered by Boers for Churchill's recapture after his escape from POW camp in December 1899. He left behind this note: 'I have the honour to inform you that as I do not consider that your Government has any right to detain me as a military prisoner, I have decided to escape from your custody.'

The diminutive, white-haired Field Marshal Lord 'Bobs' Roberts VC, who landed at Cape Town to succeed Buller in January 1900, had a less blinkered view of intelligence than his predecessor. The Field Intelligence Department in South Africa, belatedly set up at the outbreak of war, was rapidly expanded, new and better maps distributed, and reconnaissance improved. By war's end in May 1902, the Field Intelligence Department numbered 132 officers, 2,321 white civilians and several thousand 'natives'. The very pace of expansion, however, meant that most intelligence officers were inexperienced. Since most of the guerrilla war was fought on Boer territory, the expanded Field Intelligence Department could also not hope to match the Boers' tactical intelligence. But without the intelligence the Department provided, the long-drawn-out British victory against much smaller Boer forces would have been even longer delayed.[5]

Like its predecessors in earlier conflicts, the Field Intelligence Department failed to survive the war for which it had been created. The 1904 report of a committee chaired by the army reformer Lord Esher led, however, to radical reform of the War Office and the long overdue introduction of a British General Staff in 1906 (almost a century after Prussia). However, there was little place for secret-service operations in the reorganized Directorate of Military Operations and Intelligence (DMO&I), often referred to simply as the Directorate of Military Operations (DMO). When Major (later Major-General Sir) James Edmonds became head of the DMO Special Section (renamed MO5) in 1907, he found that 'its activities had been allowed to die down'.[6] Intelligence officers at the War Office made forays on to the Continent with much the same enthusiastic amateurism as in the heyday of the late-Victorian ID. In Lord Edward Gleichen's account of his early months as Director of Military Operations and Intelligence in 1907, espionage sometimes appears simply as part of his hectic social round. In the autumn of that year he went with his old friend and military-intelligence officer, Sir George Aston, on a 'little spying journey' to Holland:

> We wanted to see what sort of resistance the Dutch would be able to put up against the Germans if attacked by them ... We were not very favourably impressed. And then I went via Copenhagen and the delightful old castle of Aaleholm [Alholm], belonging to my excellent friends Count and Countess Raben, to Sweden, where to my delight I was invited by the King to attend some manoeuvres ... After a pleasant two days at the end of the manoeuvres at the castle of Tjolöholm [Trolleholm], near Göteborg, belonging to Count Bonde, the Rodds very kindly put me up at the Legation.[7]

Not everyone in the War Office was impressed with Gleichen's mix of a 'little spying' and a lot of high society. 'The only consolation', noted a memorandum in 1907, 'is that every foreign government believes that we already have a thoroughly organised and efficient European Secret Service.'[8]

Like Britain, the Germany of Kaiser Wilhelm II had no codebreaking agency. Secret intelligence was a relatively low priority within its General Staff. Most German military intelligence came from published sources, contacts with foreign officers and attendance at military manoeuvres. Military attachés in foreign capitals, however, also had modest numbers of paid informers and secret agents. A small department in the German General Staff, Sektion IIIb, had overall responsibility for agent-running by military attachés, as well as counter-intelligence operations.[9] The French hunt in 1894 for an agent of the German military attaché in Paris, wrongly identified as the only Jewish officer on the French General Staff, Captain Alfred Dreyfus, led to the greatest *cause célèbre* in modern French history.[10] Bitter, prolonged public controversy over the identity of the agent in Paris must have strengthened the existing dislike of many German ambassadors for the covert operations run by military attachés from their embassies.[11]

To supervise German cross-border intelligence collection, *Nachrichtenoffiziere* were stationed at six posts near the French frontier* and five on the Russian border.† Open sources were generally more important than covert operations in obtaining intelligence on the French army. It was from reports in the French newspaper *Le Matin*, for example, that the German General Staff learned in October 1905 of the first Anglo-French army staff talks and in 1911 that French and Russian army and navy chiefs had attended each other's autumn manoeuvres. In time of war, German military intelligence expected the French high command to deploy five armies (each of four to five army corps) from Mézières–Sedan in the north to Belfort in the south – crucially omitting the Belgian border region through which the Germans planned to invade France – with the heaviest French concentration near Neufchâteau–Saint-Menehould. In contrast to this assessment, which proved to be broadly accurate,[12] the German General Staff was far less well informed about Russia's mobilization plans.

German military intelligence failed in its most important pre-war objective on the Eastern Front: to forecast how rapidly Russia would mobilize and the speed of its initial attack. When the Russian First and Second Armies invaded East Prussia barely two weeks after the declaration of war, 'German military intelligence was as startled as the German army was unprepared.' It was later claimed by Russian military intelligence that both Berlin and Vienna had built up pre-war networks of paid 'distance

---

* Münster, Coblenz, Metz, Saarbrücken, Karlsruhe and Strassburg.
† Königsberg, Allenstein, Danzig, Posen and Breslau.

agents' in major Russian cities who communicated with espionage bureaux based in Stockholm, Christiana (Oslo), Copenhagen and Berne. Given the surprise caused by the invasion of East Prussia in August 1914, they were clearly of very limited use.[13]

Pre-war German military intelligence ran no British agent operations. Growing British–German naval rivalry, however, led the naval Nachrichten-Abteilung ('N') to begin setting up its own agent network in Britain in 1901. The network was run by the Kaiser's English-speaking former body-guard, Gustav Steinhauer, who had accompanied him to Queen Victoria's funeral.[14] The Kaiser's confidence in him largely explains why Steinhauer was put in charge of naval-intelligence operations in Britain. The 'N' network included both 'reporters' (*Berichterstatter*), who provided in-formation on the Royal Navy in peacetime, and 'confidential agents' (*Vertrauensmänner*), who were to be mobilized after the outbreak of war. Though Steinhauer's recruitment methods, which usually involved sending letters to German citizens living in Britain, written under an alias from a cover address in Potsdam and asking for their services, were somewhat hit-and-miss, the 'Kaiser's spy' also developed a more sophisticated system of 'intermediaries' (*Mittelsmänner*) to act as cut-outs between him and his agents in Britain. Steinhauer was left largely to his own devices with little active tasking by the German Admiralty.[15] It seems probable, how-ever, that Wilhelm II took a personal interest.

The Kaiser, who thought of himself as both Supreme Warlord and 'Admiral of the Atlantic', was frequently disdainful of diplomats' opinions – as of civil-ians' views in general. By contrast, he was one of the most avid readers of service attaché reports and other military and naval intelligence. Among the reports he read with greatest attention were those from Paul von Hintze, who in 1903 was appointed German 'Naval Attaché for the Northern Empires residing in St Petersburg'. The Kaiser forwarded Hintze's reports, together with his own enthusiastic comments on them, to the General Staff and Admir-alty Staff – but not to the Chancellor, Bernhard von Bülow, or to the Foreign Ministry. Wilhelm later made Hintze a baron. In the final months of the Kaiser's reign, Hintze was to become his Foreign Minister.[16]

At a meeting with the Tsar in Hesse in 1903, Wilhelm persuaded the Tsar to allow him to telegraph to him military information in a 'private' cipher which would allow the two monarchs to correspond secretly without inform-ing their ministers. Without informing the Kaiser, Nicholas immediately passed the 'private' cipher to Count Lamsdorf, the Foreign Minister, who arranged for all Wilhelm's supposedly secret telegrams to be deciphered in the Foreign Ministry.[17] By contrast, Bülow and the German Foreign Office were entirely unaware of the correspondence between Kaiser and Tsar.

Despite Nicholas II's lack of interest in private correspondence with the Kaiser, some of the intelligence forwarded by Wilhelm during the Russo-Japanese War was of real significance. After the outbreak of war the Kaiser began receiving well-informed reports direct from a German corvette captain, Albert Hopman, inside the beleaguered Russian naval base of Port Arthur.[18]

But the Kaiser's reaction to the military intelligence he received was impulsive and his judgement poor – as it frequently was on other matters. His recurrent nightmares about the Asiatic 'Yellow Peril' he believed was threatening Western civilization led him to send the Tsar and others a series of bizarre warnings. On one occasion during the Russo-Japanese War, the Kaiser solemnly assured the Tsar that a German agent had personally 'counted 10,000 Japanese men in the plantations in South Mexico, all in Military Jackets with brass buttons', who were preparing to seize the Panama Canal. He was, he told Nicholas II, willing to send a German army to defend the Californian coast if Japan attacked the United States.[19]

It never occurred to the Kaiser that, save on Japan, the less impulsive and more discreet Tsar Nicholas II, whom Wilhelm foolishly believed he could influence, had access to better intelligence than he did. For most of his reign, Nicholas II's first priorities were military and diplomatic affairs.[20] In addition to diplomatic despatches, which he read with greater attention than the Kaiser, the Tsar received almost daily intelligence summaries, intercepted communications (some of them decrypted by the *cabinet noir*), attaché reports and captured documents from the War and Foreign Ministries, and read them with, at times, almost obsessional interest. He marked everything he read with a blue crayon, sometimes adding comments.[21] (A generation later Stalin too marked with blue crayon those official documents he selected for his personal archive.)[22]

Unknown to the Kaiser, throughout Nicholas II's reign the St Petersburg *cabinet noir* was frequently able to decrypt German diplomatic telegrams. The Russian diplomat Count Lamsdorf, who became Foreign Minister in 1900, copied some of the decrypts into his diary together with comments (if any) on them written by the Tsar. Among them was the telegram sent to the Kaiser from St Petersburg on 30 September 1895 by his aide-de-camp, Helmuth von Moltke 'the Younger' (later Chief of the General Staff), reporting on his meeting with the Tsar. The fact that Nicholas II made no comment on the decrypt led Lamsdorf to note in his diary: 'Moltke's report regarding the audience with His Majesty must be accurate.' Within the privacy of his diary Lamsdorf was sometimes critical of the Tsar's comments on the decrypts. Soon after the arrival in St Petersburg of Prince Hugo von Radolin as the new German ambassador in 1895, the Tsar noted on a decrypted telegram to him from Berlin, 'Childishly foolish advice!' Lamsdorf wrote in his diary: 'I do not particularly see why this is stupid. I confess that, on the contrary, I am delighted with the thorough care and great prudence with which Berlin directs the first steps of its new ambassador to the region, which is not yet familiar enough to him. It would not be a bad thing for us to follow this example.'[23]*

Nicholas II seems to have paid particular attention to comments in decrypts about Russian statesmen and diplomats. In 1898 the Tsar warned his Finance Minister, Sergei Witte, 'Sergei Iulevich, I advise you to be more careful in your conversations with foreign ambassadors.' Lamsdorf told him afterwards that Nicholas had read a report in a German decrypt that Witte had sent a personal message to the Kaiser, via the German ambassador.[24] Lamsdorf also noted in his diary satirical ('naughty') comments by the Tsar about the long-serving ambassador to Vienna, Pyotr Kapnist, which reminded him of comments he had heard from Alexander III about the elderly general and statesman Prince Mikhail Gorchakov, who at his coronation had the misfortune to drop the orb on to the floor.[25]

By the beginning of the twentieth century, if not before, German decrypts were having a significant influence on Russian foreign policy.[26] For three years, beginning late in 1898, Russia tried secretly, without informing her French ally, to negotiate with Germany an agreement on spheres of influence in the Middle East which would have opened the Turkish Straits to Russian warships. By the end of 1901, however, German decrypts had convinced Lamsdorf that the German government had no intention of concluding such an agreement, and negotiations were broken off.[27]

British ciphers usually posed little difficulty to Tsarist codebreakers. 'I had a disagreeable shock last night which will also have its impact on you', wrote the British ambassador to Russia, Sir Charles Hardinge, to the Permanent Undersecretary (PUS) at the Foreign Office, Sir Thomas Sanderson, on 3 June 1904. At a banquet the previous evening a prominent Russian politician had told Hardinge he 'did not mind how much I reported in writing what he told me in conversation, but he begged me on no account to telegraph as all our telegrams are known!' Hardinge and the embassy secretary, Cecil Spring Rice, already had well-founded doubts about embassy security, which improved little over the next two years. Spring Rice reported in a secret despatch in February 1906: 'For some time past papers have been abstracted from this Embassy . . . The porter and other

* It is possible that some of the 'Childishly foolish advice' to which the Tsar took exception belittled his own role in Russian policymaking. Nicholas II also probably disliked the fact that Radolin was a Catholic. St Petersburg preferred Protestant diplomats and Radolin was the only pre-war German Catholic ambassador. (Cecil, *German Diplomatic Service*, p. 96.)

persons in connection with the Embassy are in the pay of the Police department and are also paid on delivery of papers.' He wrote two months later:
'Emissaries of the police are constantly waiting in the evening outside the
Embassy in order to take charge of the papers procured.' The US, Swedish, Belgian and probably other St Petersburg embassies reported similar
experiences. What the Okhrana was most anxious to obtain from foreign
embassies were copies of their ciphers to assist the *cabinet noir*. After
returning to London in 1906 to succeed Sanderson as PUS, Hardinge
wrote a furious minute describing his experience in St Petersburg:

> The proceedings of the secret police in the British Embassy during the past
> 10 months have really been a scandal . . . During my occupancy of the
> Embassy a sum of £1000 was offered to the Head Chancery servant for one
> cypher and he made an attempt to break open one safe in which he was
> detected. A letter was also extracted at night from one of my desp[atch]
> boxes by means of a false key and photographed by the secret police.

For a time, to try to prevent night-time intrusion by Okhrana agents,
Spring Rice slept in a room next to the Chancery with a connecting door
open and all other doors bolted. However, he reported after Hardinge's
return to London that classified documents continued to be abstracted
from the embassy and photographed by the Okhrana.[28] The enormous
sums the Okhrana was willing to pay for foreign diplomatic ciphers were
evidence of the importance it attached to them. A British cipher clerk paid
£1,000 by the Okhrana would have been able to purchase four three-
bedroom London terrace houses on his return home. The Foreign Office
was no match for the Okhrana. Until the outbreak of the Second World
War, it did not possess a single security officer, let alone a Security
Department.[29]

The official in the St Petersburg *cabinet noir* chiefly responsible for
breaking British ciphers was the cryptanalyst Ernst Fetterlein (born Vater-
lein), son of a German language teacher and the only Russian Jew to hold
the rank of Admiral.[30] Like Kaiser Wilhelm II, Edward VII was splendidly
unaware that, with Fetterlein's assistance, Nicholas II prepared for meetings with him by studying decrypted diplomatic despatches.[31] One such
meeting was at the Cowes Regatta in August 1909. Arriving on board the
imperial yacht *Standart*, escorted by Russian cruisers and destroyers, the
Tsar and his family were given a spectacular welcome. As bands played,
seamen cheered and cannons roared, Nicholas II, dressed in the uniform
of a British admiral, boarded the royal yacht *Victoria and Albert* to review
with Edward VII the Royal Navy, the mightiest battle fleet in world history. There followed extravagant dinners hosted by the two monarchs on

their yachts and meetings by the Tsar with the Prime Minister, Herbert Asquith, and Foreign Secretary, Sir Edward Grey.[32]

Fetterlein was among the officials in the Tsar's entourage. According to one of his Russian colleagues, he was initially disconcerted by a word he could not understand in a British diplomatic telegram:

> he sat morosely through breakfast until suddenly a great change took place. He beamed, began to laugh and jest, and when one of the embassy officials asked him what the matter was, confessed that he had been worried by an indecipherable word which occurred in one of the English telegrams he had deciphered. Someone in conversation mentioned the name of a small English castle to which the King [Edward VII] had gone to shoot, and this was the word in the telegrams which had bothered him.[33]*

Though neither the British decrypts nor any record of the Tsar's response to them survive, they must have provided further reassurance that both Edward VII and his government were committed to the 'Triple Entente' with Russia and France. As the Tsar was well aware, Edward and Wilhelm II loathed each other. A year earlier the Kaiser had boasted to his Chancellor, Prince von Bülow, that, in a conversation with Sir Charles Hardinge, witnessed by Edward, 'I showed my teeth in no uncertain terms . . . That is how one always has to behave with the English.'[34]

Few (if any) St Petersburg embassies took adequate precautions to protect their cipher rooms from Okhrana intrusion. In 1905 the American ambassador in St Petersburg reported to the State Department: 'I have discovered beyond a doubt that the Russian Government has in their possession our entire cable code.' An Okhrana agent in the US embassy had photographed the whole codebook. For the next five years, however, the same 'Blue' code, though in the possession of the Russian *cabinet noir*, remained in regular use by the State Department.[35] A generation later American embassy security in Russia had not improved. Throughout the Stalinist era, the US embassy, which had moved to Moscow, remained one of the most productive sources for Soviet intelligence.[36]

Like the St Petersburg *cabinet noir*, the Russian foreign-intelligence service, the Okhrana's Foreign Agency, was the most active in Europe. Though its first priority was to monitor and neutralize the threat from émigré revolutionaries,[37] it also played a major role in secret diplomacy, especially with France. The Foreign Agency head, Pyotr Rachkovsky,[38] was regularly used as a secret intermediary in negotiations for the Franco-Russian 'Dual

---

* Presumably, the telegrams decrypted by Fetterlein were the latest to have been intercepted before the Tsar left Russia for England.

Alliance', concluded by stages in 1891–4, and for the modification of the terms of the Alliance in 1899. Among Rachkovsky's closest contacts in Paris was Théophile Delcassé, the longest-serving Foreign Minister (1898–1905) in the seventy-year history of the Third Republic. In arranging both his own visit to St Petersburg in 1899 to modify the alliance, Tsar Nicholas II's state visit to France in 1901 and President Émile Loubet's return visit to Russia in 1902, Delcassé bypassed the French ambassador, the marquis de Montebello, and worked instead through Rachkovsky. The Russian Foreign Minister, Count Mikhail Muravyov, informed the unfortunate Montebello: 'We have the fullest confidence in Monsieur Rachkovsky and he seems to have gained that of the French government also.' Rachkovsky eventually overreached himself and was recalled from Paris in 1902. What led to his downfall, however, was not his intrusion into Franco-Russian diplomacy but the outrage of the Tsarina at his revelation that a French doctor who had gained her confidence was an unqualified charlatan.[39]

Apart from Russia, until almost the eve of the First World War the only other great power to possess an active *cabinet noir* was France. During the late nineteenth century the *cabinet noir* at the Quai d'Orsay decrypted intermittently the diplomatic telegrams of Italy (from 1887), Britain (probably for the first time in 1891), Turkey (from 1898) and Germany (from 1899 at the latest). Though the earliest Spanish decrypts so far discovered in French archives date only from 1906, Spanish ciphers were probably broken some years earlier. Russian diplomatic ciphers, the most sophisticated used by any great power, were never broken before the fall of the Tsarist regime.[40] French codebreakers, like their Russian counterparts, were assisted by documents purloined from embassies and consulates. Within French military intelligence, the Deuxième Bureau, Major Hubert-Joseph Henry of the 'Statistical' (espionage) Section ran an agent from the Parisian underworld, Martin-Joseph Brücker, whose job was to suborn clerks, chambermaids and valets working in Paris embassies.[41] In 1891 the valet of the British ambassador, Lord Lytton, provided the Statistical Section with copies of deciphered British diplomatic telegrams[42] which the codebreakers were able to compare with intercepted cipher versions. A French cleaner in the German embassy, Madame Marie-Caudron Bastian, codenamed 'Auguste', was paid by Henry to pass to him the contents of the embassy wastepaper baskets, which she was supposed to burn. Madame Bastian successfully avoided suspicion in the embassy by her dutiful demeanour and pretending to be illiterate. A report from a German agent in the French General Staff which she found in a wastepaper basket in 1894 was to give rise to the Dreyfus Affair.[43] Other torn-up classified documents removed by her from the embassy may well have included cipher material. Between August and December 1896 an agent of the Sûreté in the Italian consulate-general in Marseilles succeeded in copying five lengthy extracts from the Italian diplomatic codebook which the Sûreté forwarded to the Quai d'Orsay.[44] There were no doubt other examples of cipher material purloined from embassies and consulates which no longer survives in French archives.

The successes of the codebreakers of the Quai d'Orsay also reflected advances in French cryptography. During the last twenty years of the nineteenth century twenty-nine books on cryptography were published in France – more than in any other country. (During the same period only six were published in Germany.)[45] The successes of the Foreign Ministry's *cabinet noir* during the 1890s were due chiefly to Étienne Bazeries, an army officer seconded to the Quai d'Orsay,[46] who became well known in 1893 for decrypting secret correspondence between Louis XIV and Louvois, his Minister of War, which he believed, probably wrongly, revealed the identity of the celebrated 'man in the iron mask'.[47] Bazeries was one of the greatest cryptographers of his age. But he was also, as one of his superiors later recalled, 'a man of unusual Bohemian habits, an inveterate gambler, always short of money and an alcoholic into the bargain. He was like a hound with a marvellous scent who had to be kept on a lead.' Unhappily, during the 1890s he was allowed free rein by colleagues and superiors who regarded the brilliance of his cryptanalysis as an almost magical gift beyond their comprehension. As a result, from time to time, he was liable to mix correct solutions with guesses which proved to be mistaken.[48] One of his guesses was to add a further layer of complexity to the Dreyfus Affair.

The affair exposed both the incompetence and the politicization of French military intelligence. Its origins lay in the contents of the wastepaper basket of the German military attaché in Paris, Colonel Maximilian von Schwartzkoppen. On 27 August 1894 Madame Bastian was paid 100 francs for the latest wastepaper from the attaché's room, probably at an evening rendezvous in the church of Sainte-Clotilde, conveniently situated opposite the War Ministry. Two days earlier, however, Major Henry, who was in charge of the infiltration of the embassy, had gone on a month's hunting holiday in his native Péronne and did not examine Schwartzkoppen's documents until a few days after his return on 25 September. The key document from the wastepaper basket, Henry quickly concluded, was a torn-up unsigned *bordereau* (memorandum) promising to provide technical details of new French cannon and other classified military information. The anonymous traitor was clearly a French army officer, who reported that he was 'off on manoeuvres'. Henry took the document to the anti-Semitic head of the Statistical Section, Colonel Jean Sandherr.

Unknown to Henry, Sandherr and their colleagues, the author of the *bordereau* was Ferdinand Esterhazy, a heavily indebted French major who had first offered to sell military secrets to Schwartzkoppen on 20 July. From 13 October onwards Esterhazy visited the German embassy once a fortnight, bringing classified military documents, sometimes with his own comments on them. On one document he wrote dismissively about the French army he was betraying: 'A fine bit of stage machinery, charming and deceptive; one imagines there is something behind; one pricks it; there is nothing!'[49]

The most convenient scapegoat was the only Jewish officer on the General Staff, Captain Alfred Dreyfus. On 1 November news of Dreyfus's arrest a fortnight earlier was published in the French press. The threadbare case against him was briefly reinforced by a codebreaking error. On 2 November the Italian military attaché in Paris, Alessandro Panizzardi, despatched a telegram to Rome which concluded: 'If Captain Dreyfus has not had relations with you, it would be a good idea to instruct the [Italian] ambassador to publish an official denial in order to avoid press comment.' Though the *cabinet noir* at the Quai d'Orsay had already decrypted a number of Panizzardi's previous telegrams, he used a new cipher on 2 November which took the codebreakers over a week to break completely.[50] Bazeries was almost certainly involved in the decryption. His *dossier personnel* records that he was seconded to the Foreign Ministry from 29 September 1894 to 26 February 1895[51] and, given the difficulty of breaking the new Italian cipher, his assistance must surely have been required. On 6 November the *cabinet noir* sent Sandherr a provisional decryption with an erroneous conclusion. Instead of 'in order to avoid press comment', it concluded 'Our emissary has been warned', thus implying that Dreyfus had been in contact with an emissary of Italian intelligence. On 10 November the codebreakers finally produced a completely accurate version of the decrypted telegram. But, because it tended to exonerate rather than incriminate Dreyfus, Sandherr refused to accept it. The correct version of the decrypt was not included in the secret dossier of evidence shown to the judges at Dreyfus's incompetently conducted trial in December, which found him guilty of high treason and sentenced him to deportation for life. Over the next few years a series of outrageous forgeries were produced by or for French military-intelligence officers designed to cover up the errors and frauds which had led to Dreyfus's conviction and demonstrate his guilt. Among them was a bogus version of the Panizzardi telegram which read: 'Captain Dreyfus arrested. The Minister has proofs of his relations with Germany. Parties informed in the greatest secrecy. My emissary is warned.'[52]

Few changes of intelligence chief in parliamentary democracies have made as much difference to a human rights case as the appointment of

Colonel Georges Picquart to succeed Sandherr as head of the Statistical
Section in July 1895. Within a year Picquart found proof that Esterhazy,
not Dreyfus, was the German spy in the General Staff. When he informed
the Chief of the General Staff, General Raoul de Boisdeffre, and the head
of the Deuxième Bureau, General Charles-Arthur Gonse, they ordered
him not to try to reopen the Dreyfus case. 'What does it matter to you',
asked Gonse, 'if one Jew stays on Devil's Island?' More documents were
forged in an attempt to prove Dreyfus's guilt and discredit Picquart. Left
with no other way to ensure justice was done, Picquart became the first
major French intelligence officer to turn whistle-blower. As well as briefing
the Vice-President of the Senate, Auguste Scheurer-Kestner, late in 1897,
he gave Émile Zola the information for 'J'Accuse . . . !', his celebrated open
letter to the French President, denouncing the official framing of Dreyfus,
in January 1898. Picquart was dismissed from the army, falsely accused
of forgery, and kept in solitary confinement in a military prison for more
than a year. Though Dreyfus was pardoned in 1899, his conviction was
not quashed until 1906. In the same year, the new Prime Minister, Georges
Clemenceau, who had published 'J'Accuse . . . !' in his newspaper, made
Picquart Minister of War, a post he retained for the three years of the
Clemenceau government. 'Dreyfus was the victim', said Clemenceau, 'but
Picquart was the hero.'[53]

In 1896, in the midst of the Dreyfus Affair, at about the time Picquart
began his campaign to overturn Dreyfus's conviction, the Foreign Minister, Gabriel Hanotaux, approved the recruitment of a Hungarian nobleman,
Jules de Balasy-Belvata, as a French agent. Over the next decade Balasy
sent several hundred reports to Hanotaux and his successor, Théophile
Delcassé. For much of that time he was also working for the German
embassy in Paris. At the turn of the century Balasy was receiving 6,000
francs a year from the German embassy and more than twice as much
from the Quai d'Orsay. By 1903 Prince Hugo von Radolin, German
ambassador in Paris, had concluded that Balasy's ' "sensational information" – which usually turns out to be wrong – is of no value to the
Embassy'.[54] It seems to have been of slender use also to the Quai d'Orsay.
Balasy, however, impressed Hanotaux and Delcassé by claiming an
impressive range of high-level contacts, whom he quoted in his reports:
among them Bernhard von Bülow, successively German Foreign Minister
and Chancellor; Friedrich von Holstein, the influential head of the German
Foreign Ministry's political department; Count Agenor Maria Gołuchowski,
the Austro-Hungarian Foreign Minister; and Joseph Chamberlain,
Britain's long-serving Colonial Secretary.[55] Most of Balasy's alleged conversations with these and other policymakers (none recorded by any other

source) were doubtless based either on second-hand information or on his own imagination.

Codebreakers had a much greater influence than spies on French foreign policy before the First World War. The Quai d'Orsay's *cabinet noir* had a major impact on both the last of the late-nineteenth-century British–French imperial crises in 1898, the most serious since Waterloo, and the first of the Franco-German crises which preceded the First World War in 1905. As in the early stages of the Dreyfus Affair, a partially inaccurate decrypt, for which Bazeries was probably responsible, added notably to the complications of the British–French crisis caused by the arrival at the ruined Sudanese fort of Fashoda on the Upper Nile on 10 July 1898 of eight French officers and 120 Senegalese soldiers led by Major Jean-Baptiste Marchand after an epic two-year journey from French West Africa.[56] They were confronted on 18 September by a large force led by General Sir Herbert Kitchener, who was in the process of bringing the Sudan under Anglo-Egyptian control. 'Our poor Froggies are virtually our prisoners', wrote one British officer condescendingly of Marchand's men, 'they cannot budge a step.'[57]

The diplomatic crisis began in earnest when news of Kitchener's confrontation with Marchand at Fashoda reached Europe on 26 September. Four days later, at a critical point in the crisis, an intercepted telegram from the Italian ambassador in Paris to Rome was incorrectly decrypted by the Quai d'Orsay's *cabinet noir*. The decrypt shown to the new French Foreign Minister, Delcassé, incorrectly reported that the British ambassador, Sir Edward Monson, had instructions to deliver a formal ultimatum demanding Marchand's withdrawal and threatening war if France refused. Though Delcassé was well aware that the French government would have to instruct Marchand to leave Fashoda, he was desperate to avoid the humiliation of doing so in response to a British ultimatum. When Monson called at the Foreign Ministry later the same day, 30 September, he found Delcassé in an emotional mood. Before Monson could utter a word, Delcassé began an impassioned plea, appealing to him not to ask for the sacrifice of French national honour. When Monson then failed to deliver an ultimatum he did not possess, Delcassé believed he had achieved one of the great triumphs of French diplomacy. 'Posterity', he wrote to his wife, might well consider 30 September 1898 'an historic day'. And, he added melodramatically, 'It is at times like this that a man realises the full meaning of patriotism.' Delcassé could not resist leaking news of his supposed triumph to his friends in the press.[58]

Such errors by the *cabinet noir* seem to have ceased after Octave Homberg became its head in 1903. Though probably unaware of the decryption error during the Fashoda crisis, Homberg knew of the damage done by the first, incorrect decrypt of the Panizzardi telegram during the Dreyfus Affair and made it an inflexible rule not to pass on to the Foreign Minister decrypts whose accuracy could not be guaranteed.* Researching the influence of SIGINT on French foreign policy before the First World War has been made very difficult by official censorship. No reference to codebreaking was permitted in the many official volumes of *Documents diplomatiques français* on the period 1871 to 1914 published by the Foreign Ministry between 1929 and 1962. To take only one example, a secret report on 30 September 1913 by the *directeur des affaires politiques* now accessible in the Quai d'Orsay archives concludes: 'According to a telegram decrypted yesterday, the Italian government wishes the negotiation relative to the Mediterranean balance of power to be reopened as soon as possible before the elections.'[59] The editors of the *Documents diplomatiques français* removed this sentence from the published version of the report and substituted an editorial note which made no reference to codebreaking: 'The *directeur des affaires politiques* has reason to believe that the Italian government wishes to reopen the negotiation as soon as possible.'[60] The pre-1914 records of the *cabinet noir* appear to have disappeared. Its role and influence can, however, be partly reconstructed from private papers (such as those of Delcassé and President Raymond Poincaré), Sûreté and military files, from which important SIGINT records have not been 'weeded'.

Agent reports were also excluded from the *Documents diplomatiques français*. At least one of Balasy's reports seems, however, to have made a considerable impression on Delcassé. He reported that on 20 November 1903, during a private conversation (which almost certainly never took place), Joseph Chamberlain told him that he believed that a Triple Entente of Britain, France and Russia would one day shape the destinies of the world. This was exactly the intelligence that Delcassé wanted to hear at a time when his main policy objective was an Anglo-French *Entente Cordiale*, which he eventually concluded in April 1904. (A Triple Entente followed three years later.) The credibility of Balasy's invented conversation of 20 November 1903 was greatly increased a few weeks later when Delcassé received a report from the French chargé d'affaires in Cairo that Chamberlain, while in Egypt en route to South Africa, had revealed that he had recommended to the British Cabinet an entente with France and a rapprochement with France's ally, Russia. Though Chamberlain had stepped down from the Cabinet, he remained one of Britain's most

---

* Other errors in the decryption of Italian telegrams, which deceived Delcassé, occurred in 1901. (Andrew, 'Déchiffrement et diplomatie', pp. 44–50.)

influential politicians.[61] Unlike the German embassy in Paris, Delcassé failed to realize that Balasy, though sometimes plausible, was a fraud.

The most remarkable pre-war agent of French military intelligence was believed by the Deuxième Bureau to be a senior officer on the German General Staff, who used the pseudonym 'Le Vengeur' ('The Avenger'). A French officer who had three meetings with him at different luxury hotels reported that Le Vengeur tried to conceal his identity by swathing most of his head in bandages. The only parts of his face visible beneath the bandages were piercing eyes and a (possibly artificial) 'Prussian moustache'. On 25 April 1904 the Chief of the French General Staff, General Jean-Marie Pendézec, visited the Quai d'Orsay to warn Maurice Paléologue, the *sous-directeur* responsible for top-secret matters, that Le Vengeur had provided Germany's plan of attack in the event of war with France, which revealed that they intended to launch their main invasion through Belgium. 'Do I need to tell you that we could not resist such an attack?' Pendézec asked him. 'We should be immediately overwhelmed.' Le Vengeur claimed that his motive for betraying his country was, as his pseudonym implied, a desire for revenge. But he also asked for, and received, 60,000 francs. The source of the intelligence he provided has never been satisfactorily identified. The 'Schlieffen Plan' for an invasion through Belgium, the basis for the German attack in August 1914, was not completed until 1906, two years after the attack plan provided by Le Vengeur.[62] His bizarre behaviour and attempt to conceal his probably mercenary motives cast further doubt on the authenticity of his intelligence. There had long been speculation in France about the possibility of a German attack through Belgium,[63] and it is quite possible that he invented a plan of attack inspired by this speculation which turned out to be quite close to the genuine Schlieffen Plan. (Between the wars there were to be similar cases of forged communications from the Communist International (Comintern) sold to Western intelligence services which were quite similar to authentic Comintern documents.)[64] During 1905 Le Vengeur's credibility appeared to be strengthened by accurate reports that, in January 1904, three months before his revelations to the Deuxième Bureau, the Kaiser, at his most bombastic, had personally demanded of King Leopold II of the Belgians:

> A written declaration now in time of peace to the effect that in case of conflict Belgium would take her stand on our side, and that to this end the King should amongst other things guarantee to us the use of Belgian railways and fortified places. If the King of the Belgians did not do so, he – His Majesty the Kaiser – would not be able to give a guarantee for either his territory or the dynasty. We would then, if the case arose, immediately invade Belgium.

King Leopold was so taken aback by the Kaiser's tirade that, when he stood up to depart, he put on his helmet back to front, with the eagle facing backwards.[65] The irony at the outbreak of the First World War was that, despite Pendézec's alarm at Le Vengeur's revelations a decade earlier, the French high command was to be taken by surprise by the German invasion of France through Belgium.[66]

The greatest military and intelligence disaster experienced by any great power in the decade before the First World War was Russia's defeat in the Russo-Japanese War of 1904–5, fought mainly in Manchuria. Russia's superiority in intelligence in Europe did not extend to the Far East, where the inability of most Russian attachés to speak oriental languages handicapped intelligence collection by forcing them to work through interpreters and other intermediaries. Western attachés and other observers at Japanese manoeuvres were permitted to view only what the Japanese military wanted them to see.[67] By contrast, Japan had numerous agents in Russia's Far Eastern naval base at Port Arthur, who contributed to the success of the surprise attack on Port Arthur on the night of 8–9 February 1904 which began the Russo-Japanese War.[68] During the attack two Russian battleships and a heavy cruiser were torpedoed and Russia's Pacific Fleet was trapped in Port Arthur's harbour. Japanese troops were then able to land in Korea unopposed, cross the Jalu river into Manchuria, and lay siege to Port Arthur by land as well as by sea.

The main weakness of Russian strategic intelligence assessment of Japan was an underestimation of Japanese troops so severe that it can be fairly described as racist. An assessment of the 'primary causes of Japanese success' on the centenary of the great Japanese naval victory at Tsushima in May 1905 by Vice-Admiral Yoji Koda, Director-General of the Japanese Defence Agency's Joint Staff Office, identified racism as a major reason for Russia's defeat:

> The Russians overestimated their own power, ignored that of Japan, and provoked the Japanese people – whom many Russians, particularly Tsar Nicholas II, called 'Asian small yellow monkeys.' They did not study Japan or the Japanese people carefully. Because of the significant difference of power between the two nations, the Russians even thought that Japan would never opt for war, whatever the Japanese security concern was. Without sufficient knowledge of Japan, they first optimistically thought that war was not possible for Japan; even in case of war, they felt, they could knock down the weak and barbarous Japanese forces at the first blow.[69]

Nicholas II had personal reasons for despising the Japanese. During his visit to Japan as Crown Prince in 1891, a probably deranged Japanese police escort, Tsuda Sanzo, attempted to assassinate him with a sabre. The Tsarevich's life was probably saved only by the quick thinking of his cousin, Prince George of Greece and Denmark, who parried a second sabre blow with his cane. Nicholas was left with a nine-centimetre scar on his forehead. Unlike Franz Ferdinand at Sarajevo in 1914, he cancelled the remainder of the royal visit.*

The Russian War Minister, General Alexei Kuropatkin, reported on his return from a Far Eastern inspection tour in the summer of 1903 that 'everything is going well' and that 'the Japanese Army does not constitute a serious threat for us'. Port Arthur, he claimed, could withstand a ten-year siege. Russian naval attachés were much less dismissive about the Japanese fleet than the military high command about the Japanese army. In part this was as a result of information from French naval intelligence about Japanese vessels under construction in French shipyards who passed to the Russians their observations and conclusions about the Japanese navy.[70] The Japanese leadership never underestimated the Russian armed forces as Kuropatkin and the Tsar underestimated the Japanese, and went to great lengths to be well informed about them – for example, by establishing an agent network in Port Arthur before the outbreak of war. Vice-Admiral Yoji Koda concludes that both Japanese intelligence collection and the use made of it in the Russo-Japanese War were far superior to those in the Second World War.[71]

The British Raj in India showed greater interest than the government in London in expanding intelligence collection during the Russo-Japanese War, probably because of fear of Russian contacts with Indian opponents of British rule. In 1904 two Indian Army officers, Major G. R. M. Church and Captain G. S. Palmer, neither of whom is known to have had any experience of codebreaking, were sent to Simla to organize the interception and attempt the decryption of Russian messages sent on Indian telegraph lines.† The acting Viceroy, Lord Ampthill, worried that 'the regular interception of correspondence telegraphic and otherwise is contrary to all English practice', but was persuaded to agree to their posting. Among the probably low-grade cipher communications they succeeded in decrypting were those of the Russian commander-in-chief in Manchuria and a Russian consul in Iran.[72]

Codebreaking by the Raj did not, however, compare with that by the Russian and French *cabinets noirs*, which began to collaborate during the

* Though the Emperor apologized in person and the Interior and Foreign Ministers resigned, Tsuda was sentenced to only life imprisonment. (Keene, *Emperor of Japan*, pp. 448–58.)
† Church had earlier been a telegraph censor in Aden; Palmer was a Russian linguist.

Russo-Japanese War, following a joint operation between Ivan Manasevich-Manuilov of the Okhrana Foreign Agency in Paris and the Sûreté. Hitherto Manasevich-Manuilov's main role seems to have been to bribe leading French newspapers (among them *Le Figaro*, *L'Écho de Paris* and *Le Gaulois*) to support Russian policy and encourage French investors to continue making large investments in Russian government loans (all of which were lost after the Bolshevik Revolution).[73] Early in 1904, in collaboration with the Sûreté, he succeeded in abstracting from the Japanese embassy fragments of its diplomatic code (then in the English language). Bazeries, who worked for the *cabinet noir* of the Sûreté as well as the Quai d'Orsay, was unable to make sense of the fragments. For the first time, one of his deputies at the Sûreté, Commissaire Jacques-Paul-Marie Haverna, succeeded where Bazeries had failed.* With the help of what he described as an 'assistant', Haverna pulled off the extraordinary feat of reconstructing almost the entire Japanese codebook of 1,600 pages with 100 lines to the page. On the recommendation of Delcassé, he was awarded the *Légion d'honneur* as well as a monetary reward from the Quai d'Orsay's *fonds secret*.[74] Haverna's 'assistant', not identified in his report, was a polyglot Russian codebreaker from the St Petersburg *cabinet noir*, Vladimir Krivosh-Nemanich, who had studied at both the University of St Petersburg and the Sorbonne. The main credit for breaking the Japanese code may well belong to Krivosh-Nemanich, who later went on to work for Soviet intelligence, rather than to the less experienced Haverna.[75] This was the first example of collaboration between Russian and French crypt-analysts. Throughout the Russo-Japanese War, thanks to the collaboration between Haverna and Krivosh-Nemanich, both Delcassé and the Russian Foreign Ministry were thus supplied with decrypts of most diplomatic telegrams between Tokyo and its Paris embassy, as well as some telegrams exchanged with other Japanese embassies. Delcassé was able to follow in detail the Japanese response to his attempts to mediate in the war, which he began at the secret request of Russia in the spring of 1905.[76]

The *cabinet noir* of the Quai d'Orsay achieved a major success of its own in 1905 by decrypting German diplomatic telegrams during the Franco-German First Moroccan Crisis, precipitated by German opposition to French attempts to turn Morocco into a French protectorate. The

---

* Andrew ('Déchiffrement et diplomatie', p. 50) was the first to discuss the breaking of the Japanese codes but used only French archives, which make no reference to collaboration with the Okhrana Foreign Agency. Russian sources have since revealed the role of Manasevich-Manuilov in penetrating the Japanese embassy in Paris (Chiharu, 'Franco-Russian Intelligence Collaboration against Japan').

1. The best-known operation in intelligence history until the twentieth century: two of Moses' spies return from the Promised Land with a bunch of grapes so large it takes both of them to carry it.

2. The world's earliest surviving intelligence reports: ancient Egyptian 'Amarna letters' written in cuneiform on clay tablets. Some report threats to the Pharaoh from external enemies and internal traitors.

3. The oldest surviving book on warfare and intelligence, still studied in military academies: *The Art of War*, traditionally ascribed to Confucius' contemporary, Sun Tzu. This bamboo edition belonged to the eighteenth-century Qianlong emperor.

4. Relief sculpture in Trajan's Forum, Rome, of a *haruspex* (diviner) studying the liver of a sacrificed animal. Most Roman generals paid more attention to divination than to military intelligence.

5. Al-Kindi, Muslim polymath in the ninth-century-Baghdad 'House of Wisdom' and the first known codebreaker, commemorated here in an Iraqi postage stamp of 1962 (a rare honour for a codebreaker).

6. Al-Kindi's *On Deciphering Cryptographic Messages* discovered the frequency principle, central to cryptanalysis, over 500 years before European codebreakers. This key text was lost by the Ottomans and not rediscovered until 1987.

7. A letterbox in the Doge's Palace for 'secret denunciations against those hiding favours and commissions or conspiring to hide the true value of them'.

8. Giovanni Bellini's 1501 portrait of the inscrutable Doge Leonardo Loredan epitomizes the Venetian official obsession with secrecy.

9. The Hall of the (secular) Inquisitors in the Doge's Palace includes in its decoration this fresco by Tintoretto (the finest ever commissioned for any intelligence HQ) of the return of the Prodigal Son, symbolizing the inquisitors' mission to return deviant Venetians to the path of civic virtue.

10. The Spanish *conquistador* Hernán Cortés, whose rapid conquest of the Aztec Empire (1519–21) with only 600 men owed much to intelligence on tensions between Emperor Motecuhzoma II, his vassal states and allies.

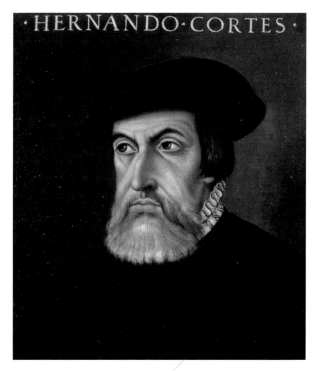

·HERNANDO·CORTES·

Tenochtitlan.

11. This intelligence was interpreted by the female former slave Malinche, shown here with Cortés at a meeting with Motecuhzoma II. She became Cortés's mistress and mother of his son.

12. The earliest, rather crude, surviving portrait of Ivan the Terrible, on this seventeenth-century silver candlestick, shows him on horseback with a severed dog's head to sniff out treason and a broom to sweep it away – symbols of the authority of his brutal *oprichniki*, Russia's first organized security service.

13. Portrayal of an *oprichnik* from *Tzar*, 2009.

14. Sir Francis Walsingham combined the roles of Elizabeth I's Foreign Secretary and intelligence chief from 1573 to 1590. He had a daily audience with the Queen.

15. Elizabeth gave Walsingham this painting of Henry VIII and his Tudor successors on the English throne, showing her holding the hand of Peace with Plenty by her side. The message around the frame says the picture was a 'mark of her people's and her own content' with him – a unique gift by an English (or British) monarch to an intelligence chief.

NON SINE SOLE
IRIS.

16. In the 'Rainbow portrait' (*c.*1600–1602), the last of Elizabeth I's reign, the eyes and ears covering the cloak symbolize her supposedly all-seeing, all-hearing intelligence service.

17. The spy in Cesare Ripa Perugino's *Nova iconologia* of 1618 also has a cloak covered in eyes and ears. Winged feet show that he is fleet of foot, the lantern that he spies by night.

18. After the First World War the British Security Service (MI5) used the same symbol of the all-seeing eye.

19. The first three-dimensional image of a spy, with stereotypical cloak, hat pulled well down, winged feet and lantern: a wood carving by Francesco Pianta in the Scuola Grande di San Rocco, Venice (*c.*1657–8).

Antoine Rossignol
M^e. des Comptes.

Vraye effigie du P. P. Ioseph de Paris predicateur Capucin Prouincial
de Touraine superieur des missions estrangeres et de Poitou fon-
dateur des Religieuses de Caluaire. A rendu lesprit entre les
mains de ses Superieurs le 18 Decembre 1638.

20. Antoine Rossignol, first head of the *cabinet noir* (SIGINT agency), later identified by Charles Perrault of the Académie Française as one of the most 'illustrious' Frenchmen of the seventeenth century.

21. The original éminence grise: Père Joseph (François Le Clerc du Tremblay), a Capuchin friar in grey habit who ran Richelieu's most important network of informants.

22. Rossignol was so well rewarded that he was able to buy the château de Juvisy, where he was honoured by visits from Richelieu, Louis XIII and Louis XIV.

23. After breaking Charles I's ciphers during the Civil War, John Wallis was rewarded with a chair at Oxford University, which he held for half a century while remaining chief codebreaker to successive regimes.

24. John Thurloe, close adviser to Oliver Cromwell, was the first intelligence chief (1653–9) to be commemorated by a blue plaque – though it makes no reference to intelligence.

25. An eighteenth-century portrait of Thurloe (probably commissioned by some of Cromwell's descendants), purchased in 2007 for the office of the chief of today's SIS (MI6).

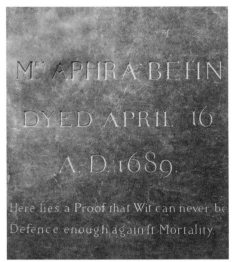

26. A portrait (*c*.1670) by Sir Peter Lely of Aphra Behn, the first woman to make a living as an English playwright and, while still in her twenties, also the first official female spy.

27. Behn later became the first spy, male or female, to be buried in Westminster Abbey.

28. Dutch attack on the English fleet in 1667 at its anchorages in Chatham: the greatest humiliation in the history of the Royal Navy. The Commons committee of enquiry was the first in parliamentary history to blame 'want of intelligence from abroad'.

29. George Louis, Elector of Hanover, 1698–1727, King George I of Britain and Ireland, 1714–27. Though his role in intelligence has often passed unnoticed, he had more influence on the development of SIGINT than any other ruler in German or British history.

30. Edward Willes, Royal Decipherer 1716–73. Rewarded for his codebreaking successes with the bishopric of Bath and Wells, he turned the Deciphering Branch into a family business.

31. Austria's leading eighteenth-century statesman, Count (later Prince) Wenzel Anton Kaunitz. SIGINT played a major role in his best-known diplomatic coup: alliance with the traditional enemy France and the 1756 'diplomatic revolution'.

32. The first known transvestite spy, the flamboyant French Chevalier d'Éon de Beaumont (with five o'clock shadow), who enjoyed his life in London so much that for some time he refused instructions to return to France.

33. The earliest authenticated portrait of George Washington (1772) as Colonel of the Virginia Militia. Fighting for the British during the French and Indian War taught him the importance of intelligence, which he put to good use against the British in the Revolutionary War.

34. The British commander, Lord Cornwallis, surrenders to Washington at Yorktown in October 1781. His defeat was hastened by Washington's greatly superior use of intelligence.

35. The first codebreaker to be knighted (and the last until after the Second World War): Sir George Scovell, who broke Napoleon's supposedly unbreakable *grand chiffre* during the Peninsular War.

36. Barclay de Tolly, founder of Russian military intelligence, which outclassed that of Napoleon during the invasion of Russia; a postage stamp marking the 250th anniversary of his birth.

37. The Congress of Vienna, 1815. Wellington is on the extreme left; Metternich is standing in front of a chair; and Castlereagh is cross-legged in the centre. More spies, as well as rulers and statesmen, were present than at any previous congress.

38. The Home Secretary, Sir James Graham, satirized by *Punch* during the scandal in 1844 caused by intercepting correspondence of the Italian revolutionary Giuseppe Mazzini. The Foreign Office closed its Deciphering Branch and SIGINT operations ceased until the First World War.

39. While in London exile, Karl Marx (photographed in 1864) saw spies in improbable places. Lord Palmerston, he believed, was a long-standing paid Russian agent.

40. The first photograph of a bomb attack on an intelligence agency, the Special Irish Branch (later Special Branch) of the Metropolitan Police, during the Fenian 'Dynamite War', as well as the first of the aftermath of a terrorist attack.

41. The beginnings of imagery intelligence during the American Civil War: 'Professor' Thaddeus Lowe prepares to ascend in his balloon 'Intrepid' to begin surveillance of Confederate forces before the Battle of Fair Oaks in 1862.

42. The well-dressed leadership of the Okhrana, the Tsarist political police, in their St Petersburg HQ at the time of the 1905 Revolution.

43. Roman Malinovsky, the Okhrana's most successful penetration agent in the Bolshevik Party, comprehensively deceived both Lenin and Stalin.

44. Evno Azev, the main Okhrana agent in the Socialist Revolutionaries, from whom he embezzled funds to spend on gambling and mistresses.

45. The French President, Raymond Poincaré, with the Tsar on a state visit to St Petersburg during the 1914 July crisis; they were both avid consumers of SIGINT from the world's two most proficient *cabinets noirs*.

47. 'Apis' (left end of front row) on trial for treason in 1917. After conviction he became the first twentieth-century intelligence chief to be executed.

46. Dragutin Dimitrijević ('Apis'), leader of the Serbian terrorist 'Black Hand' group and, from 1913, chief of the Serbian General Staff Intelligence, who helped to plan the assassination in Sarajevo on 28 June 1914 of Archduke Franz Ferdinand of Austria.

48. Franz von Papen: German military attaché in Washington in 1914, in charge of sabotage operations in the United States. He later became German Chancellor (1932) and Vice-Chancellor to Adolf Hitler (1933–4).

49. Papen faced competition in 1915 from the flamboyant fantasist and naval reserve officer Franz Rintelen von Kleist (interwar photo). Rintelen's boastful bungling compromised Papen's sabotage operations as well as his own. Both were expelled from the United States.

50. The first major terrorist attack on US soil by a foreign power: aftermath of the sabotage of ammunition supplies by German agents at Black Tom pier, New Jersey, on 30 July 1916.

51. Captain (later Admiral Sir) William Reginald 'Blinker' Hall, British Director of Naval Intelligence 1914–19, used SIGINT to become probably the most influential intelligence chief of the First World War.

52. Portrait of William 'Bubbles' James by his grandfather, the painter Sir John Millais, which became a famous advert for Pears Soap. In 1917 James was appointed head of ID25 in the Naval Intelligence Division, which ran SIGINT operations.

53. Georges Painvin, the greatest military codebreaker of the First World War, at work in elegant French surroundings.

54. General Sir Edmund Allenby enters the Holy City of Jerusalem on foot on 11 December 1917 after a victory greatly assisted by SIGINT.

55. Lenin in disguise, clean-shaven with wig, in August 1917, after being wrongly denounced as a German agent.

56. After his execution in a forest near Moscow in 1925, the corpse of the so-called British 'masterspy', Sidney Reilly, was put on private display at Soviet intelligence HQ.

57. The first head of Soviet intelligence, Felix Dzerzhinsky, with his friend Joseph Stalin in 1924.

58. Stalin with the NKVD chief and 'poison dwarf', Nikolai Yezhov, chief perpetrator of the Great Terror in 1936–8.

59. After Yezhov's dismissal and execution in 1940, he was airbrushed out of Soviet history.

60. Stalin's daughter, Svetlana, on the lap of Yezhov's sinister successor as intelligence chief, Lavrenti Beria, later exposed as a serial rapist.

61. Franklin D. Roosevelt's amateurish approach to espionage before and after becoming President was epitomized by holidays on Vincent Astor's *Nourmahal* with intelligence enthusiasts whom he encouraged to go on spy cruises.

62. The PURPLE diplomatic cipher machine (from Japan's Berlin embassy). After the US broke the Japanese PURPLE cipher in 1940, Roosevelt signed bizarre instructions for military and naval codebreakers to decrypt PURPLE messages on alternate days.

63. The origins of ULTRA, the most important intelligence of the Second World War. In May 1940, less than a fortnight after Churchill became Prime Minister, Bletchley Park began to decrypt traffic from this Luftwaffe version of the Enigma cipher machine.

64. A US Army Signals Security detachment posted to Bletchley Park in 1942 (photographed at its Brickhill Manor billet): the first foreign codebreakers to work at a British SIGINT agency since the reign of George I.

65. Wrens (Women's Royal Naval Service) in Hut 3 at Bletchley Park operating 'Colossus', the world's first programmable, electronic computer.

66. The Yalta conference of the Big Three in session at the Livadia Palace in February 1945. Just to the left of Roosevelt, sitting behind him, is a Soviet spy in the State Department: Alger Hiss (inset).

67. Zhorzh ('George') Koval: a Soviet Second World War atom spy whose identity was revealed only in 2007.

68. In 2007, President Putin posthumously declared Koval 'Hero of Russia' and proposed a champagne toast.

69. The Yugoslav head of state, Marshal Tito (left), receives the Costa Rican envoy, 'Teodoro B. Castro', in 1953, unaware that 'Castro' is a Soviet illegal (real name Iosif Grigulevich) planning his assassination – a mission aborted after Stalin's death.

70. The American representative at the UN, Henry Cabot Lodge, Jr, displays a bugging device in a wooden replica of the Great Seal, presented by Russian schoolchildren, which had hung in the office of the US ambassador in Moscow from 1946 to 1952.

71. The Lubyanka, KGB HQ, during the 1987 May Day celebrations. Dzerzhinsky's statue outside was the tallest in Moscow. It was pulled down after the failure of the hardline coup in August 1991 – an act which symbolized the end of the Soviet era.

72. The biggest change in the public image of Russian intelligence in the post-Soviet era: the consecration in 2002 of St Sofia in central Moscow as the parish church of the FSB, successor to the militantly atheistic KGB.

73. The unveiling in 2010 of a memorial plaque to Kim Philby (looking to both east and west) at SVR (Russian foreign intelligence) HQ in the presence of Philby's widow, Rufina, and the SVR's director, Mikhail Fradkov.

74. The first public peacetime use of imagery intelligence at the UN General Assembly, 25 October 1962: the US representative, Adlai Stevenson (seated, right), displays U-2 photographs of the construction of Soviet missile bases in Cuba.

75. On 5 February 2003, the US Secretary of State, Colin Powell, tries to repeat Stevenson's success by displaying to the UN Security Council intelligence on Saddam Hussein's alleged (but non-existent) WMD programme – such as this supposed replica of an Iraqi vial of anthrax.

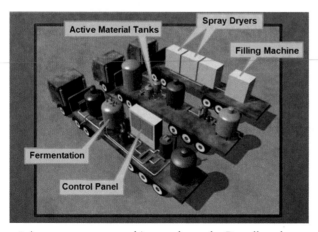

76. A computer-generated image shown by Powell to the UN of Saddam's mobile production facilities for biological weapons (also non-existent).

77. Oleg Gordievsky, stationed at the KGB London residency 1982–5. The MI5 surveillance team which took this photograph in 1982 had no idea he had been a leading British agent since 1974.

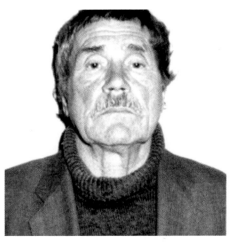

78. In 1987, President Reagan and his Chief of Staff, Howard Baker, congratulate Gordievsky in the Oval Office beneath a portrait of Washington, two years after the Russian's escape from the Soviet Union – the first successful attempt by an agent under KGB surveillance.

79. The most successful whistleblower in Soviet intelligence history: Vasili Mitrokhin, who in 1992 (the year of this photo) escaped to London, with the assistance of the British SIS, bringing with him a huge archive of top-secret KGB material.

81. An MI5 surveillance photograph of Dhiren Barot, the first Islamist terrorist whose ultimate (unrealized) ambition was to explode a radioactive 'dirty bomb', probably in the heart of London.

80. An MI5 surveillance photograph of Moinul Abedin, convicted in 2000, over a year before 9/11, of setting up the first Islamist bomb factory in Britain.

| Admiral Mike Mullen Chairman of the Joint Chiefs of Staff | Tom Donilon Assistant to the President for National Security Affairs | William M. Daley White House Chief of Staff | Tony Blinken National Security Advisor to the Vice President | Audrey Tomason Director for Counterterrorism for the National Security Council | John O. Brennan Assistant to the President for Homeland Security, later CIA Director | James R. Clapper Director of National Intelligence |

| Joe Biden Vice President | Barack Obama President | Brigadier General Marshall B. "Brad" Webb Assistant Commanding General of the Joint Special Operations Command | Denis McDonough Deputy National Security Advisor | Hillary Rodham Clinton Secretary of State | Robert Gates Secretary of Defense |

82. 1 May 2011: the first photo of a policymaker and advisers watching an intelligence-led operation – President Obama and his national security team in the White House situation room during Operation NEPTUNE SPEAR to capture Osama bin Laden. In a TV address that evening, Obama announced that Bin Laden had been killed.

83. Counter-espionage in Beijing: 'Dangerous Love' poster campaign in 2016 warns Chinese women of foreign spies out to seduce them.

most dramatic of these decrypts was a telegram from the German embassy in Paris to Berlin on 26 April which reported that the French Prime Minister, Maurice Rouvier, had offered to dismiss Delcassé in order to resolve the crisis. Instead of confronting Rouvier with the decrypt – which would have risked making the Germans aware that their cipher had been broken – Delcassé tried instead to convince Rouvier that it was important for him to remain Foreign Minister because of his planned mediation in the Russo-Japanese War. The Japanese naval victory at Tsushima at the end of May, the first Asian defeat of a Western power since the days of the Mongol Empire, made it clear that Russia had no option but to sue for peace. Its preferred mediator, unsurprisingly, remained Delcassé. For Berlin, however, the prospect of Delcassé's mediation was an added reason to press for his dismissal. On 6 June, faced with a German ultimatum, Rouvier demanded and obtained Delcassé's resignation. The only revenge Delcassé allowed himself was to show the Prime Minister the German decrypt in which Rouvier had offered to dismiss him.[77] Delcassé's successor at the Quai d'Orsay during the next major Moroccan crisis six years later was to be less discreet.[78]

Shortly before his resignation, Delcassé had requested intelligence from Russia on 'German intentions in Morocco'. Lamsdorf, as he told his ambassador in Paris, considered it his duty to his French ally to supply 'in absolute confidence and complete secrecy the copy of a secret telegram from Chancellor Bülow to Count Alvensleben [German ambassador in St Petersburg] on the subject of Moroccan affairs'.[79] Because of Delcassé's resignation, the decrypt was delivered to Rouvier, who took over the foreign-affairs portfolio on 6 June as well as remaining Prime Minister. In return Rouvier instructed the Sûreté to give the Russians all Japanese telegrams decrypted by its *cabinet noir*.[80] Given the closure of the Japanese embassy in St Petersburg during the Russo-Japanese War, Russian access to decrypted wartime diplomatic traffic between Tokyo and its Paris embassy was an important intelligence source. During Russo-Japanese peace negotiations in Portsmouth, New Hampshire, mediated, after Delcassé's resignation, by President Theodore Roosevelt during August and September 1905, the St Petersburg *cabinet noir* was also able to keep abreast of US mediation policy by decrypting correspondence between the State Department and the US Russian embassy.*

---

* See above, p. 458. The official State Department account of American mediation in the Russo-Japanese peace negotiations, which culminated in the Portsmouth Treaty of September 1905, makes no reference to the Russian breaking of US ciphers (https://history.state.gov/milestones/1899-1913/portsmouth-treaty).

Franco-Russian intelligence collaboration, however, was temporarily disrupted by a scandal involving Ivan Manasevich-Manuilov, the Okhrana Foreign Agency officer in Paris who had been instrumental in obtaining cipher material from the Japanese embassy. On 11 July 1905 he was recalled to St Petersburg by the Okhrana, apparently on charges of corruption which later led to his dismissal.[81] The Quai d'Orsay appears to have taken the decision to suspend cooperation with the Okhrana. Having discovered that the Sûreté was continuing to forward Japanese decrypts to St Petersburg via the Okhrana Foreign Agency, Bazeries demanded an explanation from its director, René Cavard. Regarding Rouvier's instructions to do so as secret, Cavard refused to reveal them. The Quai d'Orsay concluded that there had been a major breach of security at the Sûreté and instructed Bazeries to break off all contact with its *cabinet noir*. Henceforth he was ordered to work exclusively for the Foreign Ministry.[82]

For the next eight years, until the outbreak of war, the two rival French *cabinets noirs* independently decrypted a substantial amount of diplomatic traffic – sometimes the *same* diplomatic traffic – without showing each other their results. Since the Prime Minister during this period was usually also Minister of the Interior (and thus responsible for the Sûreté), he and the Foreign Minister were thus sometimes in the extraordinary position of receiving decrypts of the same diplomatic telegrams (among them those of Spain and Italy) from different sources. Haverna wrote later: 'Foreign Affairs noted with regret that at the Interior [Sûreté] Spanish and Italian diplomatic despatches were being decrypted. Its bitterness is easily understandable, because the Interior was thus informed of issues which were the responsibility of Foreign Affairs.'[83]

Despite the distant relationship between the Russian Foreign and War Ministries, no such interdepartmental disputes damaged the work of the St Petersburg *cabinet noir*, the world's leading SIGINT agency. The diplomatic decrypts which made the greatest impression on the Tsar seem to have been those of Germany.* Within what the German Chancellor, Bernhard von Bülow, mistakenly believed was the secrecy of his cipher telegrams to the German ambassador in St Petersburg, Friedrich von Pourtalès, he made much plainer than in public his belief that the success of Britain, France and Russia in resolving their differences by the *Entente Cordiale* of 1904 and the Triple Entente of 1907 had weakened Germany's international position. Pourtalès's personal courtesy in his dealings with the

---

* Detailed research is still required on many of the numerous decrypts in the Russian Foreign Ministry Archives. Until recently these archives had been closed for several years as a result of building work.

Russian Foreign Ministry contrasted with the sometimes peremptory tone of Bülow's decrypted telegrams. In 1909, for example, the Chancellor instructed his ambassador to obtain Russia's 'unreserved' assent to Austria–Hungary's annexation of the former Turkish province of Bosnia–Herzegovina: 'a precise answer – yes or no'. 'Any evasive, unclear or qualified answer', wrote Bülow, 'would be regarded as a rejection.' No doubt with the Chancellor's disrespectful telegrams in mind, Nicholas II wrote to his mother, the Dowager Empress Marie: 'It is true that the form and method adopted by the Germans in their treatment of us was rude, and that we won't forget. I think that once again they were seeking to split us from France and England but once again did not succeed. Such methods generally lead to the opposite result.'[84]

23

Intelligence and the Coming of the First World War

The revival of British intelligence five years before the First World War was prompted by naval rivalry with Germany. Following the 1907 Triple Entente with Britain's former imperial rivals, France and Russia, both later wartime allies, the main threat to British security came from the expanding German High Seas Fleet. The security of Victorian Britain had depended on Britannia's ability to rule the waves with by far the largest navy in the world. But, paradoxically, after the launching of the new British battleship *Dreadnought* in 1906, the Royal Navy could no longer take its global supremacy for granted. By its size and firepower, the *Dreadnought* threatened to make all other battleships obsolete. With ten 12-inch guns, each with a range of over eight miles, it was more than a match for any two of its predecessors. Overnight, the existing Grand Fleet of the Royal Navy, like every other navy in the world, seemed out of date. It was feared that the German High Seas Fleet, which also began building the Dreadnought class of battleship, might soon catch up with the Grand Fleet and threaten the naval supremacy on which British security depended. Fear of the naval threat from the growing High Seas Fleet encouraged the myth that it was to be used for a surprise invasion of England and that German spies were actively preparing the invasion route.[1]

The supposed German threat began a fashion for spy fiction, one of the few creative arts in which Britain became the world leader for the next century. The most successful of the Edwardian spy novelists was William Le Queux, who assumed the highly paid role of alarmist-in-chief. Despite his slender literary talent, Le Queux's work was so popular that publishers paid him the same rate per thousand words as Thomas Hardy. Le Queux's best-seller *The Invasion of 1910*, published in 1906, described how German spies were hard at work in England, preparing the way for future invasion. It sold a million copies and was published in twenty-seven languages, including German. *The Invasion of 1910* was serialized ahead of publication in 1906 in Britain's first mass-circulation newspaper, the *Daily*

Mail, which published daily maps to show which part of Britain the Germans would be invading in the next morning's edition. The proprietor, Lord Northcliffe, had objected to the original invasion route, which included too many villages, where the market for the *Daily Mail* was small. In the interest of circulation, the route was changed to include as many major towns as possible from Sheffield to Chelmsford. The serial added 80,000 to the *Mail*'s daily readership. Le Queux later complained of 'many imitators who obtained much kudos and made much money' by jumping on the German-invasion bandwagon.*

Success on so heady a scale launched Le Queux on a Walter Mitty career as secret agent and spycatcher extraordinary. He became a member of a 'new voluntary Secret Service Department': 'Half-a-dozen patriotic men in secret banded themselves together. Each, paying his own expenses, set to work gathering information in Germany and elsewhere that might be useful to our country in case of need.' Le Queux published the results of his own farcical investigations, assisted by an unidentified (and possibly non-existent) 'well-known detective officer', in another best-seller, *Spies of the Kaiser*, published in 1909. For 'obvious', though unexplained, reasons, he 'refrained from giving actual names and dates'. But he assured his readers: 'I am an Englishman and, I hope, a patriot. What I have written in this present volume in the form of fiction is based upon serious facts within my own personal knowledge.' Though the spineless British authorities refused to take action, he complained, over 5,000 German spies were hard at work in England: 'Every six months an "inspection" is held, and monetary awards made to those whose success has been most exemplary.'[2]

Excitable readers of Le Queux and other best-selling alarmists sent the press so many reports of German spies, or people looking suspiciously like German spies, that some in the War Office began to take them seriously. By 1907 Major (later Major-General Sir) William Thwaites, head of the German Section at the War Office, was convinced that there was 'much truth' in newspaper reports that German intelligence officers were at work in every county of England. The Director of Military Operations, Major-General (later Lieutenant-General Sir) John Spencer Ewart, also believed that Germany was pouring 'hosts of agents and spies' into Britain. A press campaign backed by the ageing military hero Field Marshal Lord Roberts VC (who had collaborated with Le Queux in working out the German invasion

---

* Le Queux's most successful rival, E. Phillips Oppenheim, however, embarked independently on his own 'crusade against German militarism', making enough money from it to give up the family leather business and begin a full-time career as one of Britain's most prolific popular novelists. (Andrew, *Secret Service*, pp. 38–44.)

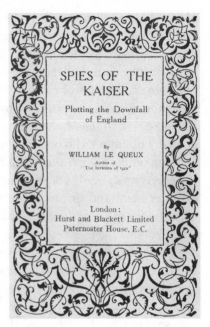

Left German female spy with radio concealed in her bottom drawer, allegedly discovered by the alarmist spy writer William Le Queux.

Right Le Queux's alarmist books on mostly non-existent German spies were the most influential yet published on intelligence in Britain, helping to generate public support for a major reform of counter-espionage.

route) and some of the Conservative front bench had persuaded the Liberal government to appoint a subcommittee of the Committee of Imperial Defence to consider the invasion threat. The membership of the subcommittee bears witness to the importance of its task. The chair was taken by Herbert Asquith, then Chancellor of the Exchequer but soon to become Prime Minister. With him sat four senior ministers (the Lord President, the Foreign Secretary, the Secretary for War and the First Lord of the Admiralty) and an impressive array of service chiefs. They met sixteen times between November 1907 and July 1908, completing a report on 22 October 1908 which demolished most of the arguments of the invasion theorists and showed surprise attack to be impossible. The subcommittee's conclusions, however, failed to carry conviction with most of those whose arguments it had demolished.[3]

Since becoming head of the diminutive counter-espionage department of the War Office, MO5, late in 1907, Major (later Brigadier-General Sir) James Edmonds had been compiling reports of alleged German espionage. During the 1890s, initially through exchanging intelligence on Russia, Edmonds became friendly with several German military intelligence officers. In 1901 his informants told him – correctly – that German intelligence had set up a new department to target Britain. Neither Edmonds nor anyone else in the War Office, however, realized that the department was purely naval and had no involvement with Sektion IIIb, military intelligence. It was therefore wrongly assumed that Germany had begun to develop a military espionage network in Britain similar to its successful network in France before the Franco-Prussian War, which had been studied by Edmonds. MO5 mistook some of the operations of the naval Nachrichten-Abteilung ('N'), founded in 1901, directed by Melville's old acquaintance Gustav Steinhauer, for those of the military Sektion IIIb.[4] Though Steinhauer's recruitment methods were somewhat hit-and-miss (usually involving letters by him to German citizens living in Britain written under an alias from a cover address in Potsdam and asking for their services), he also developed a more sophisticated system of 'intermediaries' (Mittelsmänner) to act as cut-outs between him and his agents in Britain. After the outbreak of war, he intended to introduce a 'war intelligence system' (Kriegsnachrichtenwesen), using agents travelling to Britain under false identities to conduct specific missions. Steinhauer was left largely to his own devices with little active tasking by the German Admiralty.[5] It seems probable, however, that, because of their previous connection,[6] Wilhelm II took a personal interest in his agent-running.

In March 1909 Asquith's Liberal government instructed the Committee of Imperial Defence (CID), the chief defence-planning council of the realm, to consider 'the nature and extent of foreign espionage that is at present taking place within this country and the danger to which it may expose us'. A CID subcommittee, chaired by Viscount Haldane, the Secretary of State for War, reported on 24 July: 'The evidence which was produced left no doubt in the minds of the subcommittee that an extensive system of German espionage exists in this country and that we have no organisation for keeping in touch with that espionage and for accurately determining its extent or objectives.' In reality, the evidence was extremely flimsy. When presenting the reports he had compiled of German espionage to the subcommittee, Edmonds acknowledged: 'We have . . . no regular system or organisation to detect and report suspicious cases, and are entirely dependent on casual information.' According to the minutes, Edmonds 'laid great stress on the fact that none of these cases were reported by the police authorities, and that he was indebted for information regarding them to private individuals'. He seems, at the very least, to have been insufficiently surprised by the failure of the police to detect a single suspicious German, as well as insufficiently sceptical of the information supplied by 'private individuals', many of them influenced by Le Queux and other alarmist press coverage. As Edmonds acknowledged, 'it is only since certain newspapers have directed attention to the subject that many cases have come to notice'.[7]

Edmonds's first twelve cases concerned 'alleged reconnaissance work by Germans'. In half these cases the suspicious persons were not even clearly identified as Germans. The most eccentric 'reconnaissance' report seems to have come, appropriately, from Le Queux (though, like other informants, he is not identified by name and is referred to only as a 'well-known author'):

> Informant, while motoring last summer in an unfrequented lane between Portsmouth and Chichester, nearly ran over a cyclist who was looking at a map and making notes. The man swore in German, and on informant getting out of his car to apologize, explained in fair English, in the course of conversation, that he was studying at Oxford for the Church, and swore in German to ease his conscience. He was obviously a foreigner.[8]

Since, in reality, Germany had no military-intelligence network in Britain at the time, the evidence of its operations considered by the subcommittee was necessarily mistaken (with the possible exception of a few private intelligence-gathering initiatives by German citizens and occasional reports to the German military attaché in London by informants not employed by military intelligence). Lacking any long-term perspective on the history of counter-espionage, Haldane's subcommittee failed to realize that, for centuries, war and the approach of war had commonly produced spy scares. Though they were, for example, undoubtedly aware of the great English (if not French) victories of the Hundred Years War from Crécy to Agincourt, they probably had no knowledge of what the leading historian of the war, Jonathan Sumption, calls the 'growing fear of foreign spies and fifth columnists' which it generated on both sides of the Channel.[9]

After a somewhat uncritical consideration, hampered by historical ignorance, of the evidence presented to it, Haldane's subcommittee recommended the founding of a Secret Service Bureau 'to deal both with espionage in this country and with our own foreign agents abroad, and to serve as a screen between the Admiralty and the War Office on the one hand and those employed on secret service, or who have information they wish to sell to the British Government, on the other'. Their report was considered 'of so secret a nature' that only a single copy was made and handed over for safekeeping to the Director of Military Operations. Despite the absence of German military-intelligence operations in Britain and the absurdity of the best-selling spy scares whipped up by Le Queux and others, the case for establishing the Bureau was none the less a strong one.

A German naval espionage network concentrating on the Royal Navy *was* operating in Britain and, until the establishment of the Bureau, there was, to quote the subcommittee report, 'no organisation for keeping in touch with that espionage and for accurately determining its extent or objectives'. The continuing naval arms race between Britain and Germany, a persistent cause of tension between the two countries until the First World War, made such an organization an obvious priority. The successes achieved by the Nachrichten-Abteilung before the outbreak of war, even after the founding of the Secret Service Bureau, were sufficient to indicate that if naval espionage in Britain had been allowed a free rein, it might well have provided the German Admiralty with a major flow of classified information on its leading rival.

The Secret Service Bureau, whose foundation was approved by the Asquith government, was staffed initially by only two officers: Commander Mansfield Cumming RN, fifty years old, and an army captain fourteen years his junior, Vernon Kell, who met for the first time on 4 October 1909. According to Cumming's diary, they 'had a yarn over the future and agreed to work together for the success of the cause'. Kell and Cumming later parted company to become the first heads of, respectively, what later became the Security Service (MI5), which operated on British territory, and the Secret Intelligence Service (SIS or MI6), which collected foreign intelligence. For several months, however, they were based in the same room, struggling, with minimal resources, 'to deal both with espionage in this country and with our foreign agents abroad'.[10] The Bureau remained so secret that its existence was known only to a small group of senior Whitehall officials and ministers, who never mentioned it to the uninitiated. More than half a century later, the main biographers of Asquith and his ministers were still apparently unaware of its existence and made no mention of it in their books. Even the eight-volume official biography of Winston Churchill, who was the main supporter of the Secret Service Bureau in the Asquith Cabinet, contains no reference to it.

The extraordinary secrecy which surrounded the Secret Service Bureau in Britain was in striking contrast to the governmental indiscretion in France which undermined the work of its codebreakers during the Agadir crisis of 1911, the most serious of the Franco-German crises which preceded the First World War. By the summer of 1911 it was clear that France was on the verge of making Morocco a French protectorate. Alfred von Kiderlen-Wächter, the German Foreign Minister, concluded that a dramatic gesture was necessary to secure compensation for Germany for the expansion of the French Empire. 'It is', he claimed, 'necessary to thump the table, but the only object is to make the French negotiate.' Kiderlen's method of thumping the table was a classic example of gunboat diplomacy. On 1 July the German gunboat SMS *Panther* appeared at the Moroccan port of Agadir, allegedly to protect German civilians whose lives were supposedly threatened by a rebellion in Morocco. However, as A. J. P. Taylor noted, the nearest German was at the more northerly port of Mogador. He was therefore ordered to proceed at once to Agadir, in order that his life might appear to be in danger, but it was three days after his arrival at Agadir before the crew of the *Panther* noticed him standing on the beach and rescued him.[11] Despite its farcical beginnings, however, the Agadir crisis 'was allowed to escalate to the point where it seemed that a western-European war was imminent'.[12]

The French government's handling of the crisis provides a curious parallel with the First Moroccan Crisis of 1905. Once again the Prime Minister, this time Joseph Caillaux, made secret contact with the German embassy – though on this occasion only to offer better terms to end the crisis and not, like Rouvier in 1905, to offer to sack the Foreign Minister. Once again, the Foreign Minister, this time Justin de Selves, learned of the Prime Minister's actions through decrypted German diplomatic telegrams. This time, however, the denouement was very different. Both de Selves and Caillaux were far less discreet than Delcassé and Rouvier six years before. On 28 July de Selves angrily confronted Caillaux with an intercepted German telegram sent the previous day and decrypted by the *cabinet noir* of the Quai d'Orsay. Immediately after this stormy encounter, Caillaux told Hyacinthe Fondère, a businessman he had used as intermediary with the Germans, what had happened. Fondère lost no time in telling the embassy counsellor, Oskar von der Lancken, that German telegrams were being decrypted by the French. The Germans, predictably, changed their ciphers. Save on a few isolated occasions, the *cabinet noir* at the Quai d'Orsay was able to decrypt no further German diplomatic telegrams from August 1911 until the outbreak of war three years later. France had lost its most valuable intelligence source.[13] The St Petersburg *cabinet noir* continued, however, to decrypt German diplomatic traffic sent in the new ciphers.*

In the aftermath of the Agadir crisis, the Kaiser showed greater awareness of the importance of secret diplomacy than during the Russo-Japanese War, when his impulsive indiscretions had seriously worried the

---

* In the year before the outbreak of war, the St Petersburg *cabinet noir* decrypted 171 telegrams exchanged between Berlin and its embassy in St Petersburg. (Soboleva, *Istoriia Shifrovalnogo Dela v Rossii*, pp. 283–4.)

Chancellor, Bernhard von Bülow, and other ministers.* During negotiations for the secret naval agreement between the members of the Triple Alliance (Germany, Austria–Hungary and Italy) concluded in June 1913, according to a memorandum by the Chief of the German Admiralty Staff, Hugo von Pohl:

> His Majesty pointed to the need to keep the agreement and these goings-on absolutely secret. Special precautions must be taken when informing the Foreign Ministry, the General Staff and the Secretary of State at the Reich Navy Office of the conclusion of the agreement as far as it concerns them. Likewise the Chief of the Mediterranean Division. And the Head of the Kaiser's Naval Cabinet, in so far as the commanding of officers is concerned.

Before Caillaux's revelation that German diplomatic ciphers had been broken during the Agadir crisis, there is no sign of any interest in cipher security on the Kaiser's part. Thereafter, he took a personal interest in the adoption, as part of the naval agreement between Germany, Austria–Hungary and Italy, of a secret code devised in Berlin, the 'Triplecodex', by all three navies. In May 1914 the Kaiser formally congratulated the German Admiralty on the creation and implementation of the 'Triplecodex'.[14] Neither the Kaiser nor the Admiralty, however, had more than a very basic grasp of cipher security. It did not occur to them that sharing a cipher with the Italians, whose cipher security was poor, automatically increased its vulnerability. Unknown to anyone in Berlin, in October 1913 the *cabinet noir* of the Quai d'Orsay had discovered the terms of the secret Triple Alliance naval agreement by decrypting Italian diplomatic telegrams.† So, almost certainly, had the even more expert Russian codebreakers.[15]

It also did not occur to either Kaiser or his Admiralty that the communications of the German naval intelligence ('N') agent network in Britain were being regularly intercepted. Instead of reporting by cipher telegrams, which Britain, without a codebreaking agency, would have been unable to decrypt, the network communicated through the post by letters which were frequently opened. Kell's section of the pre-war Secret

---

* The Kaiser's biographer, Professor John Röhl, notes, for example, that on the eve of the Russo-Japanese War Bülow was 'pleading desperately for German support for Russia's East Asia policy to be kept secret. He quite rightly feared that the covert goals of German policy would be exposed by Wilhelm II's excessive enthusiasm and would filter out of St Petersburg to Paris, London and Washington.' (Röhl, *Wilhelm II: Into the Abyss*, ch. 11.)

† The Quai d'Orsay wrongly assumed, however, that the secret naval agreement of June 1913 dated back to the renewal of the Triple Alliance in the previous year. Italian diplomatic telegrams were regularly decrypted by the French. (Andrew, 'Déchiffrement et diplomatie', pp. 50, 55–6.)

Service Bureau, the future MI5, was run on a shoestring. Even at the out-break of war, his permanent staff numbered only sixteen (including the caretaker). With such minimal resources, the key to Kell's initial counter-espionage strategy was to gain the assistance of police chief constables around the country. That, in turn, required the support of the Home Secretary. It was Kell's good fortune that the Home Secretary for most of 1910 and 1911 was Winston Churchill, who in the course of his long car-eer showed greater enthusiasm for, and understanding of, intelligence than any other British (or foreign) politician of his generation. In April 1910 Churchill minuted: 'Let all facilities be accorded to Captain Kell.' Next day his private secretary provided Kell with a letter of introduction to the chief constables of England and Wales which concluded: 'Mr Churchill desires me to say that he will be obliged if you will give Captain Kell the necessary facilities for his work.' In June the Scottish Office gave Kell a similar introduction to chief constables in Scotland. Churchill also added a major weapon to Kell's armoury by greatly simplifying the interception of suspects' correspondence. Hitherto, individual warrants signed by the Home Secretary had been required for every letter opened. Despite Post Office opposition, Churchill introduced a system of Home Office War-rants (HOWs), which is still in operation over a century later, authorizing the interception of 'all the correspondence of particular people', for whom Kell and his successors submitted secret evidence that they represented actual or potential threats to national security. HOWs for each of the targeted individuals, then as now, were personally signed by the Home Secretary.[16] Churchill failed, however, to grasp that the espionage detected through the operations of the HOWs which he signed was conducted solely by German *naval* intelligence. On leaving the Home Office for the Admiralty in November 1911, he informed the Foreign Secretary, Sir Edward Grey, that the intercepted letters 'show that we are the subject of a minute and scientific study by the German military and naval authori-ties, and that no other nation in the world pays us such attention'.[17]

From September 1911 Kell kept a cross-referenced index of the inter-cepted letters. An in-house MI5 history written in 1921 noted that, though the pre-war letters between Steinhauer and his agents in Britain had been destroyed, the surviving index to them contained 1,189 entries for the period from 1911 to 1914. During the three years before the outbreak of war, Kell's Bureau thus received, on average, more than one intercepted letter a day from Steinhauer and his British network. In December 1911 intercepted correspondence revealed that an unidentified German intelli-gence officer was travelling through Britain. By the time sufficient evidence had been assembled to justify his arrest, however, he had left the country.

Another intercepted letter in February 1912 revealed that the German officer had been Steinhauer himself.[18]

Among the most successful of Steinhauer's British agents was the chief gunner on HMS *Agamemnon*, George Parrott. Kell's Bureau later established that in 1910–11 Parrott had supplied 'N' with four volumes of a classified Royal Navy report on developments in gunnery and a total of twenty-three classified naval manuals. The lengthy report on gunnery must have been highly valued by Steinhauer at a time of steady increase in firing range. In 1906 it was expected that fire would be opened at 9,000 yards. By 1912 the War Orders of Admiral Sir John (later Earl) Jellicoe, then in command of the Second Division of the Home Fleet, specified that firing by guns of 9.2 inch calibre and above would begin at 14,000 yards.[19] Kell's Bureau obtained the first evidence that Parrott was part of Steinhauer's agent network from intercepted correspondence late in 1911. In July 1912 Kell's 'chief detective', William Melville, shadowed Parrott on a ferry to Ostend, where he met a man who, Melville reported, was 'evidently a German . . . Age about 35 to 40. Height 5ft 9 inches – hair and moustache medium dark. Dress light tweed jacket suit and straw hat. Typical German walk and style.' Parrott was arrested on his return to England and dismissed from the Royal Navy, but, like the majority of pre-war naval spies identified by Kell's Bureau, was not put on trial, in order to avoid revealing intercept evidence in court. Parrott's correspondence revealed that he remained in touch with German intelligence after his dismissal. On 18 October 1912 he travelled to Hamburg to meet his case officer, 'Richard', who handed him the then considerable sum of £500, enough to buy two London terrace houses and a certain sign of the importance attached to his intelligence. While in Hamburg, Parrott was extensively debriefed by gunnery, torpedo, naval engineering and intelligence experts, and agreed to continue work as a German agent. By the time he returned home, enough evidence had been assembled for a prosecution without making use of intercepted correspondence. Parrott was found guilty in January 1913 of breaking the Official Secrets Act and sentenced to four years' hard labour.[20]

The naval-intelligence targets in Germany of Mansfield Cumming, Chief of the Foreign Department of the Secret Service Bureau (the future SIS or MI6), were quite similar to those of Steinhauer in Britain. According to a post-war report on Cumming's pre-war operations: 'With the funds then available attempt could only be made to unravel a few technical problems, and for this purpose use had to be made of casual agents whose employment as a class has by war experience been clearly demonstrated to be undesirable.'[21] Fragments of the technical intelligence obtained by Cumming and his 'casual agents' survive in the logbooks of the head of the German section of the Naval Intelligence Division, Fleet Paymaster Charles Rotter, who collated information from open and secret sources on U-boat and battleship construction.[22]* Cumming noted in his diary in March 1914: 'Rotter asked me to get him information about secret building of submarines . . . He says they have about 50 built & projected.' Some of Cumming's intelligence reports, however, were greeted sceptically by Admiralty experts who underestimated German advances in the construction of submarines, torpedoes, mines and aircraft.[23] The military and naval attachés in Berlin had greater influence than Cumming in pre-war Whitehall. From 1906 onwards they were unanimous in reporting that German armed forces were being built up for offensive, not defensive, purposes. Sir Eyre Crowe, Assistant Undersecretary (later PUS) at the Foreign Office, minuted on a series of reports from the naval attaché in Berlin, Captain (later Admiral Sir) Herbert Heath, in 1912: 'They expose in a crushing manner the dishonest manoeuvres by which the German Admiralty deliberately misinform the Reichstag and public.'[24]†

The Director of Military Operations (DMO), General Ewart, had told Cumming in January 1910 that he 'did not wish any espionage work done in France just now, as our present excellent relations might be damaged thereby'.‡ These instructions were reaffirmed by General (later Field Marshal Sir) Henry Wilson, who succeeded Ewart as DMO in August 1910. Though British–French staff talks on wartime military cooperation against Germany had begun in 1905, it was only under Wilson that they acquired real substance. By 1913, with Wilson's support, Cumming was exchanging intelligence with the French. He noted on 6 March that 'a large packet of valuable stuff came in from our friends', and that Wilson thought it 'extremely valuable'.[25]

Cumming enjoyed going on operations himself, carrying a swordstick and sometimes in disguise.§ At a rendezvous in Paris in July 1910, he was, in his own words, 'slightly disguised (toupee and moustache) and had on a rather peculiar costume'. For a meeting in January 1911 with a potential agent who had offered to report on Austrian ship-building in Trieste, Cumming had himself made up at a theatrical costumier in Soho.[26] He kept in his office a photograph of a stereotypical German and was delighted

---

* Only 2 per cent of the pre-war Admiralty dockets registered in the pre-1914 era now survive in the National Archives. (Seligmann, 'Naval History by Conspiracy Theory', p. 969.)
† Only a minority of the reports of the military and naval attachés in Berlin survive.
‡ Ewart used the French spelling 'espionnage'. (Jeffery, *MI6*, pp. 31–2.)
§ Christopher Andrew was able to demonstrate the swordstick, the property of Cumming's niece, Miss Diana Pares, when presenting a BBC2 *Timewatch* documentary on Cumming in 1985.

when visitors failed to recognize it as himself. During the First World War, he once asked his young niece what she would do if she met the German in London. The little girl suggested shooting him. 'Well, my dear', replied Cumming, 'in that case you'd have killed your uncle!'[27] During the war he looked back nostalgically to the fun he had had on pre-war intelligence expeditions. 'That is when this business was really amusing', he told the writer and wartime intelligence officer Compton Mackenzie. 'After the War is over, we'll do some amusing secret service work together. It's capital sport!'[28] In honour of Cumming, the present Chief of the Secret Intelligence Service (SIS or MI6), Alex Younger, is still known as 'C' (not 'M', as in the James Bond novels) and, like Cumming, is the only Whitehall official to sign his name in green ink.

The pre-war offices of the Secret Service Bureau's Foreign Department and Cumming's London flat were both at the top of 2 Whitehall Court in 'a regular maze of passages and steps, and oddly shaped rooms', reached by a private lift.* Bernard Shaw and the other celebrities who lived on the lower floors seem never to have realized that the headquarters of British foreign intelligence were directly above them. Cumming called those who were privy to the secret work of his top-floor offices his 'top-mates'. Cumming told his secretary that, in retirement, he planned to publish his memoirs: 'I shall call them "The Indiscretions of a Secret Service Chief". It will be a splendid-looking publication bound in red with the title and my name embossed in gold, and consisting of 400 pages – every one of which will be blank!'[29] British ministers and officials were equally discreet about both Cumming's and Kell's operations. Even the existence of the British foreign-intelligence agency was not officially acknowledged until 1992.

In France, by contrast, during the few years before the First World War, SIGINT, potentially the most valuable foreign-intelligence source, was handled with less discretion than ever before in French history. The internecine warfare which characterized many of the short-lived Cabinets of the Third Republic hampered the work of the *cabinet noirs* at both the Sûreté and the Quai d'Orsay. In the spring of 1913 Commissaire Haverna

---

* A British Heritage blue plaque in honour of Sir Mansfield Cumming was unveiled outside 2 Whitehall Court (now the Royal Horseguards Hotel) on 30 March 2015. The current 'C', Alex Younger, said at a reception afterwards, attended by the author: 'I sense [Cumming] would share the delight I experience today, when I watch a small group of people, embodying the best of modern Britain, penetrate our enemies and disrupt their plans. And doing this, not by force of arms, but by guile, creativity and that thing that he would most certainly recognise: the sheer satisfaction of putting one over on those who mean us harm.' ('Sir Mansfield Cumming, first MI6 chief, commemorated with blue plaque', *Guardian*, 31 March 2015.)

and his assistants decrypted three telegrams from the Italian ambassador in Paris, Tommaso Tittoni, which suggested that both Stephen Pichon, the Foreign Minister, and Raymond Poincaré, the President of the Republic, were secretly plotting to restore diplomatic relations with the Vatican – a highly charged subject in the anticlerical atmosphere of the pre-war Third Republic, where it was virtually impossible for practising Catholics to become ministers. On 6 May 1913 Louis-Lucien Klotz, who as Interior Minister was responsible for the Sûreté, brought the Italian intercepts to the attention of the Cabinet. There was immediate uproar. The Foreign Minister's indignation at the references to himself further fuelled the Quai d'Orsay's growing resentment at the Sûreté's meddling with diplomatic intelligence. Pichon threatened to resign unless the Sûreté was immediately denied access to diplomatic telegrams. Though Klotz protested, Pichon won the argument within the Cabinet. From May 1913 until the eve of the First World War, the Sûreté was no longer supplied by the post office with copies of telegrams sent and received by Paris embassies.[30]

Because of political mishandling, SIGINT did as much to confuse as to inform French policymakers during the few years before the outbreak of war. Though the French government received almost no current German intercepts after 1911, the German decrypts of the Agadir crisis[31] returned to plague it in 1914. In the winter of 1913–14 *Le Figaro* began daily attacks against the former Prime Minister, Joseph Caillaux, then leader of the Radical Party. During January 1914 its editor, Gaston Calmette, took up the theme of 'secret negotiations' during the Agadir crisis, suggesting that Caillaux had been working in the German interest. Among the documents in Calmette's possession were copies of three top-secret decrypts of German diplomatic telegrams dealing with the 'secret negotiations'. Caillaux believed, probably correctly, that Calmette had procured them from another journalist, named Albin, who in turn had obtained copies from de Selves's *chef de cabinet*, Maurice Herbette. Caillaux's own copies of the decrypts had been stolen from Albin's desk drawer.

On 14 January 1914 Caillaux called on President Poincaré to warn him that the *Figaro* was about to publish the German decrypts. The inevitable result, as the German ambassador was soon to warn the Quai d'Orsay, would be German protests at the violation of the secrecy of its diplomatic communications and an international scandal. At Poincaré's request, Louis Barthou, a former Prime Minister, went to see Calmette and persuaded him, in the national interest, not to go ahead with publication. Caillaux, however, had already taken devious precautions of his own in case the decrypts were published. During a week as caretaker Interior Minister in December 1913 he had raided the Sûreté archives (a raid condemned by its director, Pujalet, as 'burglary') and removed copies of the Italian intercepts which had embarrassed Poincaré the previous spring – no doubt as a potential means of putting pressure on the President. In the course of the 'burglary' Caillaux also removed copies of Spanish decrypts which showed that Calmette had been bribed by the Spanish government to support some of its territorial claims in North Africa. He also succeeded in acquiring by means unknown German telegrams of 1905–6 decrypted by the *cabinet noir* at the Quai d'Orsay which revealed potentially embarrassing contacts between some French ministers and the German embassy – probably including Rouvier's offer to dismiss Delcassé during the First Moroccan Crisis.[32]

The whole extraordinary affair took a new and even more sensational turn on the afternoon of 16 March 1914, when Madame Henriette Caillaux walked into the office of Gaston Calmette, drew a revolver from her muff and shot him dead. Her immediate motive for murder was to prevent *Le Figaro* publishing love letters between herself and Caillaux, written while he was still married to his first wife. It was quickly rumoured, however, that Madame Caillaux's main motive had been to prevent publication not of the love letters but of the German telegrams intercepted during the Agadir crisis. The German ambassador called at the Quai d'Orsay to deliver a warning that, if the telegrams were published, his government would regard their publication as a public insult. If that happened, said the ambassador menacingly, 'a bomb would explode'. Caillaux called on Poincaré and threatened that if there were any reference to the German decrypts during his wife's forthcoming murder trial, he would retaliate by 'divulging plenty of others' from the *cabinets noirs* of both the Quai d'Orsay and the Sûreté. He demanded an official statement during the trial that the government possessed no documents casting doubt on his honour or patriotism. Though Poincaré privately denounced Caillaux's demand as blackmail, René Viviani, who became Prime Minister in June, agreed to it. Even in the final days of the July Crisis, however, the French government continued to fear that the German decrypts would be revealed and cause an international scandal.[33]

The great power with the best foreign intelligence during the few years before the First World War continued to be Tsarist Russia. In 1913–14 the codebreakers of the St Petersburg *cabinet noir* (who were not, like their French counterparts, distracted by the use of SIGINT for political infighting and the threat of international scandal) decrypted almost 3,000 diplomatic telegrams, among them 569 exchanged between the Austro-Hungarian embassy in St Petersburg and Vienna and 171 between the German embassy and Berlin.[34] Nicholas II probably read intercepted

German diplomatic telegrams more attentively than Wilhelm II read the originals.[35]

Russia's most productive foreign agent during the pre-war decade was Colonel Alfred Redl, who served as an Austro-Hungarian counter-intelligence officer (1901–5) before becoming Deputy Chief of Military Intelligence in the General Staff (1907–12). As a promiscuous homosexual, Redl may initially have been blackmailed into working for Russian military intelligence; his main motive thereafter was his need for money to fund an extravagant lifestyle and numerous male lovers. For the period between 1908 and early 1913, the Russian military archives contain copies of *Fall R*, the Austro-Hungarian strategic deployment plan for war against Russia, *Fall B* (against Serbia, and possibly Montenegro) and *Fall I* (against Italy). The source was probably Redl, who provided detail on deployments down to division level. Early in 1912 Redl's intelligence strongly influenced General Mikhail Alekseev to make the substantial alterations to Russian deployment plans against Austria–Hungary which, with some further modifications in 1913 and 1914, laid the basis for Russian mobilization at the beginning of the First World War.[36] Redl was also able to provide classified documents on links between Austrian military intelligence and the Polish Socialist Party (PPS) led by Józef Piłsudski, future President of the interwar Polish Republic. The PPS, which had a 'terrorist' training school in Cracow, provided military intelligence from Russian Poland and received substantial Austrian arms supplies in return. Piłsudski's key negotiator with the Austrian General Staff was also an Okhrana agent. Thanks to its Austrian agents, St Petersburg was better informed about Galicia, the northernmost province of the Austro-Hungarian Empire, than the civilian authorities in Vienna.[37]

Redl's career as a Russian spy came to a dramatic end in March 1913 when letters to him containing large numbers of banknotes were intercepted in Vienna. He was handed a revolver and left to commit suicide. Redl left behind a note which said: 'Levity and passion have destroyed me. Pray for me. I pay with my life for my sins. Alfred.'[38] Though the evidence is incomplete, the probability is that, even after Redl's suicide, the Russians retained at least three other highly placed agents in Vienna.[39] According to Colonel Mikhail Svechin, pre-war Chief of Military Intelligence for the St Petersburg military district, one of these agents was Kurt Conrad von Hötzendorf, the eldest son of Franz Conrad von Hötzendorf, Chief of the Austro-Hungarian General Staff. Svechin alleged that the young Conrad entered his father's study to photograph documents on war planning, then passed them to Russian intelligence.[40]

Despite the successes of its cryptanalysts and foreign agents, Russia suffered from poor coordination between diplomatic and military intelligence.

'From the most insignificant consulate in Persia to the Council of State, civilian diplomats were blindly ignorant of Russian military reality, while soldiers were confused about the goals of foreign policy.'[41] One of Russia's leading military attachés, A. A. Ignatiev (who was stationed in Paris at the outbreak of war), later recalled that in almost all Russian embassies the military attachés preserved their independence from the diplomats and thus 'faced Petersburg with an insoluble dilemma: whom to believe – the ambassador or the military attaché?'[42] The Russian government made no serious attempt to resolve the dilemma. The Foreign Ministry predictably sided with its diplomats, the War Ministry with the military attachés. Sergei Sazonov, the Foreign Minister and Nicholas's most important political adviser, scarcely spoke to the Minister of War, the bon vivant Vladimir Sukhomlinov, who was also popular with the Tsar but knew little about international relations.[43]

By February 1914 the great powers had been at peace with each other for the record period of forty-three years since the 1871 Treaty of Versailles had ended the Franco-Prussian War. Tensions between them seemed to be declining rather than rising. The Permanent Undersecretary at the Foreign Office, Arthur Nicholson, said in May 1914 that it was some years since international relations had been so calm.[44] No foreign government or intelligence agency could have predicted either that the heir to the Austro-Hungarian throne would put his life at risk by visiting Sarajevo on 28 June 1914, or that his security would be so appallingly mishandled after the failure of the first assassination attempt that day.[45] No other major European leader in 1914 would have taken similar risks. On security grounds, the Kaiser did not even attend his friend Franz Ferdinand's funeral in the far safer city of Vienna.[46]

But for the Sarajevo assassinations there would have been no European war in 1914, though an Austro-Serb crisis in later years might well have provoked one. The killing of Franz Ferdinand, however, quickly persuaded both military and civilian leaders in Vienna that the survival of their multi-national empire depended on the military defeat of Serbia. The key figure was General Franz Conrad von Hötzendorf, Chief of the Austro-Hungarian General Staff since 1906 (except for an interval in 1912). During previous Balkan crises he had called for war against Serbia on more than fifty occasions. After the Sarajevo assassinations he argued vehemently and repeatedly that the time for a final reckoning had come. His demands for an attack on Serbia during the Balkan Wars in 1912–13 had been rejected by both the Archduke Franz Ferdinand and the Foreign Minister, Leopold Berchtold. The assassination of Franz Ferdinand changed Berchtold's mind. War with Serbia, he believed, could now 'hardly be avoided' and Austria could not afford to 'show weakness to Serbia once more'.[47] All the main Austro-Hungarian policymakers except, temporarily, the Hungarian leader, István Tisza, were in favour of war.[48] On 30 June 1914, only two days after the Sarajevo assassinations, the German minister in Vienna, Heinrich von Tschirsky, reported to Berlin that his official contacts in the Foreign Ministry and elsewhere were united in their desire for a 'thorough settling of accounts with Serbia'.[49] The Germans too believed that only this 'settling of accounts' could ensure the survival of the Habsburg Empire, their only dependable ally. On 5–6 July Berlin secretly gave Vienna the famous 'blank cheque' – an unconditional guarantee of support even if the consequence of conflict with Serbia was a European war, which the Austrians would have preferred to avoid but were willing to risk.

A century later large (but little-noticed) gaps still remain in the source material on the role of intelligence in the 'July Crisis' of 1914. Both as Prime Minister in 1912 and President from February 1913, the dominating figure in the making of French foreign policy was Raymond Poincaré, who followed with passionate interest the work of the Quai d'Orsay's *cabinet noir*. In 1912 one of France's leading diplomats, Camille Barrère, the long-serving ambassador in Rome, claimed, no doubt with some exaggeration, that French foreign policy was 'wholly based' on intercepted foreign diplomatic telegrams. By comparison, he complained, 'the reports of our own ambassadors count for nothing'.[50] Yet neither the *Documents diplomatiques français* nor Poincaré's published journal contains a single one of the decrypts which had such an influence on French foreign policy. Poincaré's unpublished diary, however, contains enough extracts from, and comments on, diplomatic decrypts to demonstrate their importance.[51] Both the Tsar and Sazonov similarly paid close attention to the larger volume of decrypts produced by the St Petersburg *cabinet noir*, which, unlike the Quai d'Orsay, was able at least intermittently to decrypt German and Austro-Hungarian telegrams.[52] The recent closure for several years of the Russian Foreign Ministry Archives delayed the detailed research in the surviving files of decrypts which is still required.

The biggest gaps in the available archives are probably in Germany. German army records, including many military-intelligence files, were destroyed in a massive Allied bombing raid on Potsdam in April 1945, a few days before Hitler committed suicide. The papers of the German Chancellor, Bethmann Hollweg, disappeared at about the same time, either during the Red Army advance or as the result of a Nazi rearguard action to prevent their capture. Though the files of Moltke the Younger, Chief of the General Staff, have survived, they are inaccessible – kept from public view by a cult bizarrely convinced that Moltke was the reincarnation of a ninth-century pope and will one day be reborn in another important role.*

In one important respect, Austro-Hungarian intelligence collection during the few years before the First World War became more sophisticated than Germany's. From late in 1911, Vienna, unlike Berlin, possessed a SIGINT agency. The immediate stimulus for the belated re-establishment of the once famous Viennese *cabinet noir*[53] was the outbreak of the Balkan Wars. In November 1911, Andreas Figl, a former Austrian infantry officer who had been accidentally blinded in one eye a year earlier, was appointed head of a new military codebreaking unit. Before long, his unit was approached by a Serb who claimed that his nephew worked in the cipher room at the Serbian embassy in Vienna and had succeeded in copying its diplomatic codebook. With the help of the codebook, the Viennese codebreakers were able to decrypt the next two telegrams sent to the Serbian embassy and paid the informant 10,000 kroner. No further Serbian telegrams, however, were sent using the code Figl had purchased. Only then did he discover that he had been the victim of an ingenious sting operation. The two telegrams successfully decrypted had been sent to the Serbian embassy by the mysterious informant himself in a code quite unlike that used by Serb diplomats. The greatest pre-war success of Figl's unit, assisted by poor Italian cipher and embassy security, was to break the main Italian diplomatic code. To assist their attack on the code, Viennese codebreakers resorted to a technique first used in the Kaunitz era when the Austrian *Geheime Kanzlei* contained Europe's most successful cryptanalysts. Figl's unit planted in the press a series of articles calculated to be of particular interest to the Italian embassy which were duly quoted in its telegrams to Rome.[54] Further research is required to establish what decrypts were available to Austrian policymakers during the July Crisis. It is unlikely, however, that Figl's unit was in the same league as the *cabinets noirs* of St Petersburg and the Quai d'Orsay.

Some leading policymakers were more confused than enlightened by the intelligence that reached them during the July Crisis. Among them was the German Chancellor, Bethmann Hollweg, who was seriously misled by political intelligence from a German agent in London, Benno von Siebert, a second secretary at the Russian embassy. Born in St Petersburg into an aristocratic Baltic German family in 1876, Siebert went to Heidelberg University and joined the Russian diplomatic corps in 1898, serving

---

* The sect has, however, published letters 'dictated' by Moltke from beyond the grave to Rudolf Steiner. (Röhl, 'Goodbye to All That (Again)?' pp. 160–61.)

initially in Brussels and Washington. His loyalties, however, remained German rather than Russian and he began supplying Russian diplomatic documents to German contacts after being posted to London in 1908.* How many documents he supplied remains unknown.[55] Early in July 1914 Bethmann received from the German embassy in London a Russian document on Anglo-Russian naval talks in June secretly provided by Siebert. Bethmann was alarmed by its contents. Kurt Riezler, his closest adviser and confidant, noted this conversation with Bethmann on the evening of 6 July as both sat on a verandah under the night sky at Bethmann's country estate forty miles north-east of Berlin:

> The secret information [from Siebert] he divulges to me conveys a shattering picture. He sees the Russian–English negotiations on a naval convention, a landing in Pomerania, as very serious, the last link in the chain.
>   . . . Russia's military power growing swiftly
>   . . . Austria steadily weaker and less mobile[56]

Hitherto Bethmann Hollweg had always been convinced that, despite its involvement in the Triple Entente, Britain would never support a war of aggression against Germany by either Russia or France.[57] Now he began to doubt the honesty of the British Foreign Secretary, Sir Edward Grey. Neither Siebert nor Bethmann, however, realized that the British view of the negotiations was very different from the Russian. Grey informed the British ambassador in St Petersburg in a telegram probably decrypted by the Russians (who must have been dismayed by its contents) that the talks 'could not amount to very much' and that there was no question of the Royal Navy operating in the Baltic 'at the sufferance of, let alone in combination with, the imperial Russian fleet'.[58] Bethmann's alarmism reflected both his inexperience at dealing with intelligence and his misunderstanding of British–Russian relations. He had failed to grasp that Russia was far keener than Britain on naval cooperation and made the classic mistake of relying on one-sided intelligence.

For both St Petersburg and Paris the first indication that Austria was preparing to deliver an ultimatum to Serbia as a preliminary to war came from SIGINT. On 11 July 1914 the German Foreign Minister, Gottlieb von Jagow, a former ambassador in Rome, informed the current German ambassador, Hans von Flotow, that the ultimatum was in preparation.[59]

---

* Siebert seems to have been recruited in 1908 as the result of a personal initiative by Baron Hilmar von dem Bussche-Haddenhausen, then department head for British affairs in the German Foreign Ministry (later ambassador in Buenos Aires and Bucharest). (West, *Historical Dictionary of World War I Intelligence*, p. 285.)

Because Germany, uniquely of the great continental powers, had no SIGINT agency and Jagow had as little grasp of intelligence as Bethmann, he was wholly unaware of the risks he was taking. Flotow passed this information to the Italian Foreign Minister, Antonio di San Giuliano, at a spa where he was taking a cure for his recurrent attacks of gout. On 16 July 1914 San Giuliano informed the Italian ambassadors in Vienna, Paris and St Petersburg in telegrams which are known to have been decrypted by Figl's SIGINT unit in Vienna and, almost certainly, by the far more experienced *cabinets noirs* in the other two capitals.[60] The St Petersburg *cabinet noir* also decrypted the telegram from Vienna to the Austro-Hungarian ambassador, Frigyes (Friedrich) Szapáry, containing the full text of the forthcoming ultimatum to Serbia.[61]

By about 20 July, when President Poincaré, with the Prime Minister, René Viviani, arrived in St Petersburg for a long-arranged state visit, both the Russian and French governments, thanks chiefly to their codebreakers, thus knew the terms of the forthcoming ultimatum to Serbia. Sazonov's later claim that the ultimatum came as a terrible shock to both him and the French when it was delivered to Serbia on 23 July was thus false.[62] Poincaré and Viviani, however, also had domestic matters on their minds. Their arrival in Russia coincided with the opening in Paris of the trial of Madame Caillaux, charged with murdering Gaston Calmette, editor of *Le Figaro*, on 16 March.[63] Poincaré privately complained that Viviani was woefully ignorant of foreign affairs[64] – by which he probably meant that the Prime Minister's support for Russia and the Dual Alliance was less unconditional than his own. Viviani's socialist background, including his role as co-founder of the socialist (later Communist) *L'Humanité*, a fierce critic of the Tsarist regime during and after the 1905 Revolution, did not commend him to his Russian hosts.[65] Throughout the state visit, however, Viviani was too preoccupied by the progress of the trial in Paris, and the major political scandal he feared would erupt from it, to focus on the mounting diplomatic crisis and urge moderation on the Russian government.[66]

On the second day of the trial, which was also the second of the state visit, came the reference in open court to German decrypts which the government had dreaded. Louis Latzarus, a *Figaro* journalist, blurted out in evidence that, at the time of his murder, Calmette had in his possession 'horrifying documents' which 'every good Frenchman who read them would have thought established the infamy and treason of a certain person', but had declined to publish them 'because their publication might be dangerous to the country'. The identity of the 'certain person' was clear to all in the courtroom. Caillaux immediately demanded that, as Viviani had previously agreed, the *procureur-général* officially exonerate him.

Jean-Baptiste Bienvenu-Martin, Minister of Justice and acting Prime Minister in Viviani's absence, consulted a few colleagues and drafted a statement asserting that the documents referred to in court were forgeries and that the Quai d'Orsay possessed no documents adversely reflecting on Caillaux's honour and patriotism. The draft was telegraphed to Poincaré and Viviani in Russia. Though Poincaré insisted that Caillaux was still engaged in 'blackmail', Viviani feared that Caillaux would go ahead with his earlier threat to reveal decrypts from the *cabinets noirs* of both the Quai d'Orsay and the Sûreté, and telegraphed his consent.[67] Poincaré noted in his diary that, since receiving the news from Paris of Caillaux's latest demands, Viviani had been 'overcome with gloom. He is becoming more and more nervous and sullen, and his bad temper is noticed by everyone who approaches him.'[68] The *procureur-général* made the courtroom statement in Paris demanded by Caillaux even before Viviani's formal approval had been received from St Petersburg. Abel Ferry, Undersecretary for Foreign Affairs, noted in his diary that the 'fantastic declaration' in open court deceived no one: 'We declared non-existent documents which were only too real.' The primary purpose of preventing political crisis and international scandal had, however, been achieved.[69]

While Viviani remained too preoccupied by events in Paris to focus on anything else, Poincaré constantly reaffirmed France's commitment to the Dual Alliance and made no attempt to urge moderation on his hosts. Soon after the President and Prime Minister began their return journey to Paris on 24 July, Szapáry arrived at the Russian Foreign Ministry to deliver a copy of the Austrian ultimatum to Serbia which, though the ambassador did not say so, was intended to be too harsh for Serbia to accept. The minister, Sazonov, was used to reading decrypts which gave him advance warning of the messages which ambassadors had been instructed to deliver to him. Thus it was on 24 July. It never occurred to Szapáry that, thanks to the St Petersburg *cabinet noir*, Sazonov already knew the terms of the ultimatum. Though Sazonov kept up the pretence of surprise at the news brought by Szapáry, he had had plenty of time to prepare his apparently spontaneous response. 'I know what it is', he told Szapáry, 'You want to make war on Serbia! The German newspapers have been egging you on. You are setting fire to Europe.'[70] The ultimatum had indeed been intended to justify war with Serbia, though Vienna would have preferred to avoid a wider conflict. The beginning of Russian military mobilization on 25 July increased the likelihood of a general European war.[71]

German policy for most of the July Crisis, though not after the outbreak of war, was ultimately dependent on decisions taken by the Kaiser. Even a well-informed intelligence service would have found it difficult to predict his mood swings. A century later historians still disagree on what these mood swings were.* On 6 July, at the request of Bethmann Hollweg, to make it appear that Germany had no inkling of any Austrian plan to attack Serbia, Wilhelm left for his usual summer cruise along the Norwegian coast and into the fjords. To diminish his personal responsibility for the outbreak of war, he later claimed that he was sent 'only meagre news' of the crisis from Berlin and 'was obliged to rely principally on the Norwegian newspapers'.[72] In reality, the Kaiser received many despatches from Berlin and intervened a number of times in the crisis, seeking, for example, to persuade Italy, which was believed (correctly) to be detaching itself from the Triple Alliance, to join with Germany and Austria–Hungary if there was war with France and Russia.[73] On 25 July, following the announcement of the Austrian ultimatum to Serbia, which he later claimed improbably to have 'learned from the Norwegian newspapers – not from Berlin', Wilhelm decided to return to Germany. His decision was also partly prompted by risible intelligence 'from a Norwegian source that it was said that a part of the English fleet had left secretly for Norway in order to capture me'. Wilhelm took the intelligence seriously enough to quote it in his post-war memoirs, complaining that England had apparently been prepared to contemplate kidnapping his royal person at a time when 'peace still reigned!'[74]

On his return to Germany, Wilhelm brushed aside proposals for mediation between Austria and Serbia. When Sazonov warned that an Austrian attack on Serbia would lead to wider European war, Wilhelm responded: 'Well then, go ahead!' The Kaiser was taken aback, however, by Serbia's acceptance of most of the terms of the Austrian ultimatum. It was, he declared, 'a capitulation in the humblest style, and with it there disappeared all reason for war'. But, when Austria rejected his proposal that its forces 'halt in Belgrade' and wait for the Serbian government to accept its demands, the Kaiser seemed at a loss on what to do next. The Prussian War Minister, Erich von Falkenhayn (later Moltke's successor as Chief of the German General Staff), noted after calling on the Kaiser on the evening of 28 July: 'He makes confused speeches, from which the only clear thing that emerges is that he does not want war any more and to this end is even determined to leave Austria in the lurch.' Earlier in the July Crisis, Wilhelm would have been outraged to be told by Falkenhayn that he was 'no longer in control of the matter'. But now he accepted it. Having

---

* Christopher Clark, among other historians, for example, quotes the Kaiser as saying early in the July Crisis that he wanted to return to Berlin 'to take the situation in hand and preserve the peace of Europe'. John Röhl persuasively challenges the authenticity of this statement. (Röhl, *Kaiser Wilhelm II*, pp. 151–2.)

concluded that 'the ball which has started to roll cannot be stopped', the confused Kaiser was back in warlike mood.[75]

For continental governments and intelligence services, divining British intentions was almost as difficult as judging the Kaiser's mood swings. The Asquith government was deeply divided over the extent of its moral obligation to support France against German attack. The Prime Minister and his Foreign Secretary, Sir Edward Grey, were resolved to resign unless the Cabinet agreed to send an expeditionary force. Had Germany not violated Belgian neutrality, the Cabinet would probably have refused to do so, and the government would have fallen.[76] On 30 July Field Marshal Sir John French had been officially informed that in the event of war he would command a British Expeditionary Force, but he was not fully convinced.[77] On 2 August, only two days before Britain declared war, French telephoned Lord Riddell of the Newspaper Proprietors' Association to ask: 'Can you tell me, old chap, whether we are going to be in this war? If so, are we going to put an army on the Continent and, if we are, who is going to command it?'[78] Continental governments asked themselves the same questions.

The final element of confusion in the outbreak of war was the telegram from Berlin to the German ambassador in Paris, Wilhelm von Schoen, on 3 August (two days after Germany declared war on Russia), containing the declaration of war he was to deliver to the French government. 'Unfortunately', wrote Schoen later, 'the telegram was so mutilated that, in spite of every effort, only fragments of it could be deciphered.' Errors by the cipher clerk in Berlin had produced such meaningless phrases as *Schon gestern herab mp* ('already yesterday downward mp'). Schoen had to construct his own declaration of war on France from the fragments he could understand. As he later acknowledged, he made a number of errors which gave the French 'abundant ground for asserting that we had trumped up excuses to justify our attack'.[79]

The early success of the German invasion of France through Belgium, which began on the same day, 3 August 1914, owed much to the deficiencies of French military intelligence and, especially, the use made of it by the French high command. When Marshal Joseph Joffre became Chief of Staff and commander-in-chief-designate in July 1911, he took seriously the threat of an invasion through Belgium. In October 1911 he identified as a major strategic concern 'the need to defend against a German violation of Belgium', which he then judged more likely than not. By 1914 Joffre had changed his mind. He had become fixated by the doctrine of *attaque à l'outrance* embodied in the final pre-war military Plan XVII based on all-out attack by French forces through Lorraine, which paid little attention to German invasion plans.[80] 'The French Army', declared its Field

Regulations, 'knows no law but the offensive.' Some of Joffre's leading generals, however, were seriously concerned by the German threat to Belgium. When General Charles Laurent assumed command of the Fifth Army in the spring of 1914, he questioned Joffre's commitment to a full-scale offensive in Lorraine while leaving much of the Belgian border open to German invasion. The commander of the Third Army, General Pierre Ruffey, was convinced that a large-scale German attack through Belgium was a certainty.[81] It is difficult to resist the conclusion that some pre-war military intelligence reports to Joffre were designed to tell him what he wanted to hear. As late as May 1914 the Deuxième Bureau insisted that the main German attack would come against Nancy, Verdun and Saint-Dié, that any German operation in Belgium would stay well south of the Sambre and the Meuse, and that Germany would not deploy reserve units with regular forces.[82] It was wrong on all three counts. Joffre later claimed that he had believed German discussion of an attack through Belgium was disinformation intended to disguise Germany's real intentions.[83] By the beginning of September the German attack through Belgium, for which Joffre had failed to prepare, had reached the River Marne, Paris was in a panic, and the French government had left for Bordeaux.

German military and naval intelligence also had serious deficiencies. The speed of Russia's mobilization, followed by the Russian invasion of East Prussia barely a fortnight after the declaration of war, took Sektion IIIb (military intelligence) by surprise.[84] Because of the superiority of German forces, the surprise did little damage to German operations on the Eastern Front.[85] Far more serious was the destruction of the Nachrichten-Abteilung naval espionage network in Britain, run by Gustav Steinhauer, which had been under surveillance for several years by Kell's counter-espionage Bureau (the future MI5).[86] On 29 July, six days before Britain entered the war, Kell began sending chief constables 'warning letters' with the names and details of twenty-two German spies working for Steinhauer. During the final days of peace, he remained in his London office at Watergate House twenty-four hours a day, sleeping surrounded by telephones, ready to order the spies' arrest as soon as war was declared. Never before in British history had plans been prepared for such a large number of arrests of enemy agents at diverse locations. The final arrests were made on 15 and 16 August. Though the identification of the agents arrested on Kell's instructions owed much to police investigations, the key role in their detection usually belonged to his Bureau. The correspondence of at least seventeen (probably more) of the twenty-two spies, which provided the most reliable method of monitoring their contacts with the Nachrichten-Abteilung, had been intercepted under Home Office Warrants obtained by Kell.[87]

When Steinhauer reported that there had been 'a wholesale round-up of our secret service agents in England', the Kaiser instantly abandoned his earlier belief that Steinhauer was a 'splendid fellow'. Wilhelm, Steinhauer later recalled, was beside himself with fury when told the news of the arrests: 'Apparently unable to believe his ears, the Kaiser raved and stormed for the better part of two hours about the incompetence of his so-called intelligence officers, bellowing: "Am I surrounded by dolts? Why was I not told? Who is responsible?" and more in the same vein.'[88]* The Kaiser's fury was due largely to the fact that Germany no longer had any agent in Britain capable of reporting on the departure and destination of the British Expeditionary Force (BEF). This ignorance significantly reduced the prospects of a quick victory on the Western Front. Crown Prince Wilhelm ('Little Willy') wrote later:

> on September 5, on the eve of the fateful battle of the Marne, the fear of English troops landing in Antwerp and Ostend and threatening the German rear led General von Moltke to take two army corps and one division of cavalry from the Sixth and Seventh German armies in Lorraine and send them to Belgium. If these troops had been sent to support the First Army of General von Kluck, or had been used to reinforce the German thrust south of Verdun – the two vital points – the 1914 campaign on the Western Front might have had a wholly different ending. The whole course of the war would have been changed.[89]

---

* Steinhauer is scarcely likely to have fabricated such a devastating denunciation of his own incompetence.

24

The First World War. Part I: From the Outbreak of War to the Zimmermann Telegram

During the opening weeks of the First World War, Russia paid a heavy price for its pre-war failure to coordinate foreign and military intelligence.[1] Its diplomatic ciphers were the best in the world, unbroken (so far as is known) by the codebreakers of any other state. In striking contrast, before and during the Battle of Tannenberg in East Prussia (the first great battle of the war) at the end of August 1914, Russian military ciphers were in such confusion that radio operators did not use them. The architect of the German victory, Colonel Max Hoffmann, Deputy Chief of Operations of the German Eighth Army, wrote after the war: 'We had an ally that I can only talk about [now] it is all over – we knew all the enemy's plans. The Russians sent out their wireless in clear.' Having discovered the positions of the two Russian armies in East Prussia from eavesdropping on their radio communications, the Germans surrounded and overwhelmed each in turn. The commander of the Russian Second Army, which was almost completely destroyed, committed suicide.

Tannenberg was the greatest German victory of the war. It was also a turning point in the history of German intelligence. For the first time since unification Germany acquired a SIGINT agency. After Tannenberg German forces on the Eastern Front, commanded by General Erich Ludendorff, continued to intercept Russian radio communications.[2] Though these communications were usually enciphered, many were successfully decrypted by a group of linguists headed by Ludwig Deubner, Professor of Philology at the University of Königsberg. Max Hoffmann called the linguists 'quite geniuses in deciphering'.[3] The Russian military ciphers cracked by Deubner's team of apprentice cryptanalysts were, however, very basic. In the spring of 1915 Russian forces were using the 'Caesar cipher', first used by Julius Caesar two millennia earlier, successfully broken by the great Muslim cryptographer al-Kindi in the ninth century, which had been well known to most European cryptographers since the sixteenth century. Ludendorff, who had shown no pre-war interest in SIGINT, paid great

attention to the wartime Russian decrypts he received.[4] Another major
German SIGINT source was in Switzerland. The Russian General Staff
routed all telegrams to its military attachés in Western Europe through the
Berne telegraph office. With the help of pro-German sympathizers in the
Swiss federal government, the German military attaché in Berne, Major
Busso von Bismarck, succeeded in obtaining copies of all the telegrams. It
was probably this source that alerted the Germans to Russia's planned
offensive in January 1915 and led to the German counter-offensive which
culminated in February in the destruction of the Russian XX Corps.[5]
German agents on the Eastern Front, by contrast, provided little significant
intelligence. According to the head of German military intelligence, Colonel Walter Nicolai, 'espionage in the Russian theatre of war . . . could
only provide material for very limited local tactical successes.'[6] SIGINT,
however, remained of strategic importance throughout the war on the
Eastern Front. Max Hoffmann later claimed that, largely as a result of
SIGINT, the Russian advance in Latvia between the Tirul marsh and the
River Aa in January 1917 was the only occasion when German forces were
taken by surprise.[7]*

Russian military intelligence at the outbreak of the First World War
was far less effective than it had been a century before on the eve of Napoleon's invasion of Russia. Mikhail Barclay de Tolly, whom Tsar Alexander
I made Minister of War in 1810, is still remembered in the Putin era as
the founding father of Russian military intelligence. No European War
Minister of the time had a more sophisticated grasp of both SIGINT and
espionage. Barclay's most successful military attaché, Alexander Chernyshev, who ran a remarkable agent network in Paris before Napoleon's
invasion, later became a long-serving Minister of War (1827–52), as well
as chairman of the Council of State and Cabinet of Ministers (1848–56).[8]
By contrast, General Vladimir Sukhomlinov, an impeccably dressed cavalry commander with little grasp of intelligence, who served as Nicholas
II's Minister of War from 1909 to 1915, was not in the same class as
Barclay or Chernyshev. His main claim to fame is for what has become
known as 'the Sukhomlinov effect': the principle that there is an inverse
correlation between the attention a general pays to his uniforms and his
military skill.[9] Anxious to ensure that he was not overshadowed by the
Chief of the General Staff, he appointed three in succession who were not
up to the job – with disastrous consequences for Russian military planning
at the outbreak of war.[10] Though Sukhomlinov was a personal favourite

---

* The Austrians were taken by surprise on a much larger scale during the offensive of General Alexei Brusilov (the most successful Russian offensive of the war) in June 1916.

of the Tsar, who must have mentioned during their private meetings some of the diplomatic decrypts which he read attentively,[11] the Minister of War showed no observable interest in SIGINT. A century earlier, Tsar Alexander I would never have tolerated the divorce between diplomatic and military intelligence which characterized the reign of Nicholas II.[12]

The weakness of First World War Russian military ciphers, though successfully exploited by German intelligence, was only a subsidiary reason for Russia's defeats on the Eastern Front. Far more serious was the acute shortage of munitions and the superiority of German generals. In May 1915, 150,000 Russian soldiers on the South-West Front had no rifles. As late as January 1916, 286,000 soldiers of the West Front were still without them. The British military attaché reported during the German offensive in May 1915 that Russian forces were so short of shells that they had no alternative but to retreat when faced with German artillery fire. Russia's military disasters in the spring and summer of 1915 eclipsed even those of the previous autumn. From May to September Russian armies lost an average of 300,000 men per month killed or wounded; another 200,000 men were captured or surrendered. Russia's 'Great Retreat' before German and Austrian forces also produced at least three million refugees.[13] The British government found it difficult to grasp some of the basic facts about the Russian war effort, let alone the latest intelligence. On 29 August 1914, Asquith wrote to his daughter Violet about the idea that the Russians might send three or four army corps to the Western Front via the port of Archangel in the White Sea: 'Don't you think this is rather a good idea?' The Prime Minister had clearly had no recent contact with a Russian atlas. Two days later, having presumably been shown one, he had second thoughts: 'the Russians can't come – it w[oul]d take them about 6 weeks to get to Archangel'. Asquith wrote SECRET at the top of this geographical revelation.[14]

Though Russian military ciphers in the First World War were frequently substandard, the St Petersburg *cabinet noir* remained the best in the world. Much of its energies were devoted to decrypting the diplomatic telegrams of its British and French allies, as well as its enemies. This is reflected in a list of the large secret awards made to codebreakers in 1916, mostly for breaking new ciphers:

Ernst Fetterlein: 2,400 rubles (for successes with Persian and French codes)
Ziegler: 2,300 rubles (English and Greek ciphers)
Ramming: 1,150 rubles (Japanese ciphers)
Von Berg: 1,100 rubles (Austrian and German ciphers)
Nan'ersky: 1,000 rubles (Italian ciphers)
Struve: 900 rubles (English ciphers)

In addition to these monetary awards, Court Counsellor Yuri Pavlovich, who worked for the wartime *cabinet noir*, was given the Order of St Stanislaus, class 2, for unspecified services.[15]* Once Russia and Britain became wartime allies, the pre-war Okhrana attempt to recruit British cipher clerks from the British embassy,[16] if it did not cease entirely, was far less aggressive than before. The St Petersburg *cabinet noir* seems to have been able to break British ciphers without the need for agent penetration. Indeed, it was fearful that the ciphers were so straightforward that German codebreakers might also be able to decrypt British diplomatic telegrams. When the Russian-speaking Sir Samuel Hoare MP became MI1c (later MI6) representative in St Petersburg in 1916, one Russian intelligence officer 'implored me as a friend and ally to ask the British Foreign Office to change a cypher that he could read almost as easily as his daily paper'.[17] Ironically, Hoare was awarded the Tsarist Orders of St Anna and St Stanislaus, both of which were also bestowed on members of the *cabinet noir* who broke Allied ciphers.[18]

No longer faced with the Okhrana penetration of the British embassy which had outraged some of their peacetime predecessors,[19] neither the British ambassador, Sir George Buchanan, nor the chief military attaché, General Sir John Hanbury Williams, seems to have given any thought to the likelihood that their telegrams to London were being decrypted.† The Foreign Ministry doubtless found most of what it read in British decrypts reassuring. Both Buchanan and Hanbury Williams were committed supporters of the Russian alliance and the Tsar enjoyed their company. Nicholas would have been distressed, however, by their reports on the unpopularity of the German-born Tsarina Alexandra and rumours about her (in reality innocent) relationship with the dissolute holy man, Grigory Rasputin, who she believed could cure the haemophilia of the Tsarevich Alexei. In August 1915 Buchanan reported to the Foreign Secretary, Lord Grey: 'The unpopularity of the Empress is assuming serious proportions [since] it is known that she still sees the monk Rasputin whose private life is a scandal.' He wrote two months later: 'hatred is the only word to describe the feeling against the Empress'. She and Rasputin were regarded as the Tsar's 'malignant counsellors'.[20] How far such decrypts were kept from the Tsar may never be known. The flow of diplomatic intercepts to

---

* The noble Boris Orlov, who also worked for the *cabinet noir*, was awarded the Order of St Stanislaus, class 3. This, however, was a routine award given to many military and civilian recipients for blameless careers rather than particular distinction.
† Neither their official despatches to London nor their surviving private correspondence appear to show any awareness of the likelihood of Russian interception.

Nicholas probably decreased after he appointed himself commander-in-chief in August 1915 and spent much of his time at the Stavka (GHQ) at Mogilev, almost 800 kilometres from St Petersburg.

The most difficult wartime problem faced by the St Petersburg *cabinet noir* was its greatly diminished access to Germany's diplomatic traffic after the closure of the German embassy. Unlike British wartime code-breakers, their Russian counterparts had no regular access to German diplomatic despatches sent by either radio or cable. In the twenty months between the outbreak of war and April 1916, the *cabinet noir* decrypted only sixty German diplomatic communications, 10 per cent of the number of Austrian and Bulgarian decrypts.* During 1915 some of the expertise of the St Petersburg *cabinet noir* was reassigned to decrypting German and Austrian military communications. In January 1915 the Stavka forwarded to the *cabinet noir* photographs of German cipher material which had probably been captured during fighting. Only very fragmentary information survives on Russian success in breaking the military codes and ciphers of the Central Powers over the next two years. A note in Russian Foreign Ministry files records that eight telegrams sent by German and Austrian army officers to Berlin, Vienna and Romania in April 1915 were successfully decrypted. Another document reveals that an unspecified number of Austrian military telegrams, which may have provided intelligence on German as well as Austrian operational plans, were decrypted in August.[21] It is probable, though not certain, that these and other decrypts provided evidence of the German decision to make its main priority the Western rather than the Eastern Front. The Chief of the German General Staff, Erich von Falkenhayn, concluded by August 1915 that, despite German successes on the Eastern Front, a decisive victory over Russia was for the moment unobtainable: 'it is impossible to annihilate an enemy who is far superior in numbers, must be attacked frontally, and has excellent lines of communications [and] any amount of time and space at his disposal . . .' The centrepiece of his strategy for 1916 was to be a massive offensive against the French fortress of Verdun.[22] Following Falkenhayn's decision, from the autumn of 1915 to the spring of 1916 the Eastern Front was relatively quiescent. In February 1916 Ernst Fetterlein, probably the ablest of the Russian codebreakers, was awarded the Order of St Anna (2nd class), which conferred noble status, 'for the implementation of special orders of great military significance'.[23] Though the 'special

---

* Between the outbreak of war and April 1916, the *cabinet noir* decrypted 588 Austrian, 606 Bulgarian, 457 Italian and 225 Turkish diplomatic communications. (Soboleva, *Istoriia Shifrovalnogo Dela v Rossii*, ch. 13.)

orders' do not seem to have survived, they were plainly related to SIGINT on enemy operations on the Eastern Front.

The first Russian general to learn the main intelligence lesson of Tannenberg was Alexei Brusilov, who in April 1916 was appointed commander-in-chief on the South-West Front. He found his predecessor, General Nikolai Ivanov, 'in a state of utter dejection'. 'Amid sobs', Ivanov declared the Russian army 'quite unfit to undertake any sort of offensive'.[24] The Brusilov offensive, however, which began on 4 June and demolished the Austrian Fourth and Seventh Armies, proved to be the most successful Russian offensive of the war. Its success was due to both the brilliance of Brusilov's generalship and to meticulous preparation which for the first time gave priority to intelligence and deception. False Russian military orders were broadcast *en clair* to deceive the Austrians, who probably assumed that Russian radio operators were guilty of the same security breach as before Tannenberg. Brusilov's real orders were delivered personally to Russian commanders. He was also the first Russian general to use other forms of deception, such as setting bogus artillery batteries to deceive enemy aerial reconnaissance. Brusilov was a pioneer of the deception (*maskirovka*) which in the Soviet era became part of Russian military doctrine. He was also a rare example of a Tsarist general who went on to serve in the Red Army.[25]

The massive Russian defeats on the Eastern Front before the Brusilov offensive, combined with evidence of German foreknowledge of Russian troop movements, were widely blamed on huge (but non-existent) networks of German spies. It never occurred to the many Russians addicted to spy mania that German intelligence success on the Eastern Front was based on SIGINT rather than on espionage. In two days of rioting in Moscow at the end of May 1915, 475 shops, offices and factories whose owners had German (or German-sounding) names were attacked, 700 supposed Germans were beaten up, sometimes fatally, and 207 apartments looted. Sir George Buchanan was so convinced of the threat from German spies that he reported to the Foreign Office that he believed the Germans had instigated the riots themselves in order to disrupt already inadequate munitions production and undermine the Russian war effort.[26]

Widespread conspiracy theories claimed that Russia's military disasters could only be explained by the actions of 'traitor generals' in league with the enemy – chief among them the Minister of War, General Vladimir Sukhomlinov. In March 1915 a former associate of Sukhomlinov, Lieutenant-Colonel Sergei Miasoiedov, was sentenced to death by a field court-martial on charges of treason, of which he was almost certainly entirely innocent. In June the Tsar reluctantly gave in to pressure to sack Sukhomlinov as War Minister. 'A sinister cabal', Nicholas wrote to his wife from Stavka, 'wants to implicate [Sukhomlinov] in the Miasoiedov case but will not succeed.' The cabal, however, won much more support than the Tsar had expected. In secret session in July 1915 the Duma voted by 245 to 30 votes for the prosecution of Sukhomlinov and others they held responsible for the munitions crisis. Many believed that Germany had paid him to sabotage shell production. One deputy demanded: 'Miasoiedov has been executed, but where is the head of his protector [Sukhomlinov]? Still resting on his star-studded shoulders.' For some months Sukhomlinov and his wife lived in a small flat out of public view. In April 1916, however, he was arrested and, amid widespread jubilation, imprisoned in the Fortress of Peter and Paul.[27]

Sukhomlinov's young and attractive wife, Ekaterina, realized that the best hope of freeing her husband from prison was to persuade Rasputin to intercede with the Tsarina. The police agents who, almost certainly unknown to the royal couple, kept Rasputin under surveillance reported that in the summer and autumn of 1916 Ekaterina paid two visits to Rasputin's home and received him at her own home on no fewer than sixty-nine occasions. Despite a strong personal dislike for Sukhomlinov, Rasputin agreed to intercede on his behalf. The price he probably demanded was sex. Despite his many other aristocratic lovers, he was exceptionally attracted to Ekaterina, confiding to a crony that she was 'one of only two women in the world to have stolen my heart'. In September 1916 Alexandra wrote to Nicholas at the Stavka: 'Our Friend [Rasputin] has said that it is necessary to release General Sukhomlinov, lest he die in prison . . . He has already been in prison for six months – which is long enough (since he is no spy).' Soon afterwards the Tsar took the deeply unpopular decision to transfer Sukhomlinov from prison to the relative comfort of house arrest.[28]

In November 1916 Sukhomlinov was told to prepare his defence. The trial, however, did not begin until some months after the overthrow of the Russian monarchy in the February Revolution of 1917. The 116-page indictment in small print, a sometimes surreal product of spy mania, accused him of espionage and high treason, as well as personal corruption and malfeasance in the munitions supply to the Russian army. Over a hundred, sometimes delusional, witnesses gave evidence during a trial which lasted just over a month in August and September 1917. 'It is a psychological feature of this war', Sukhomlinov told the court, 'that all failures are ascribed first and foremost to treason.' As Minister of War, he had demonstrated incompetence on such a scale, combined with corruption in awarding contracts which had made him a personal fortune, that the prosecution used both as evidence that he must be in the pay of the Germans. Sukhomlinov's incompetence extended to his handling of military intelligence. The best study of his treason trial, by Professor William C. Fuller, which shows conclusively that Sukhomlinov was innocent of all charges of treason, also concludes that he had shown 'a mindboggling nonchalance about the handling of classified material'.[29]

Sukhomlinov's evidence was notable for what he did not say as well as for what he did. He could have countered preposterous claims that he had a leading role in a great German spy ring at the outbreak of war by revealing that at Tannenberg enemy commanders owed their intelligence not to spies but to the fact that Russian forces had sent radio messages *en clair*. Sukhomlinov's failure to mention SIGINT did not derive from a patriotic determination to keep Russian intelligence secrets. After the overthrow of the monarchy he owed no allegiance to the republican Provisional Government which subjected him to a show trial for treason. Soon after the February Revolution, the new Minister of Justice, Alexander Kerensky, later head of the Provisional Government, had humiliated him by publicly removing the general's epaulettes from Sukhomlinov's greatcoat with his penknife.[30] It is far more likely that Sukhomlinov feared that, if he mentioned the real source of German military intelligence at Tannenberg, it would be claimed that the fact that Russian forces lacked a usable cipher system had been a deliberate act of betrayal rather than further evidence of incompetence. His judges found him guilty of most of the charges against him, including treason. Because the death sentence could be imposed only for crimes committed at the front, Sukhomlinov was sentenced instead to hard labour for life.*

In varying ways and differing degrees, spy mania afflicted all the combatants in the First World War – though nowhere more than Russia. On his arrival as head of the MI1c (later MI6) station in St Petersburg in 1916, Sir Samuel Hoare compared the current wave of Russian spy scares with 'the spy mania that swept England in the first year of the war'.[31] War with Germany raised British, as well as Russian, spy mania to unprecedented heights. On 4 August 1914, the day that Britain went to war, Basil Thomson, Assistant Commissioner at Scotland Yard and head of the Metropolitan Police Special Branch, was informed that secret saboteurs had blown up a culvert near Aldershot and a railway bridge in Kent. An inspection next day found both to be intact. Spy mania, wrote Thomson later, 'assumed a virulent epidemic form accompanied by delusions which defied treatment': 'It attacked all classes indiscriminately and seemed even to find its most fruitful soil in sober, stolid, and otherwise truthful people.'

* Amnestied some months after the Bolshevik Revolution, Sukhomlinov fled abroad and died in Berlin in 1926.

MI5 files still contain a small sample of the letters forwarded to it after the outbreak of war by the War and Home Offices from correspondents even more deluded than those who had contributed to the spy scares of Edwardian England. An army officer reported that 'the first and foremost spy' was Viscount Haldane, the Secretary for War: 'His houses should be raided, as he has got a wireless set behind the cupboard in one of his bedrooms.' Other correspondents claimed that German coalminers in the Kent coalfields had secretly dug a series of tunnels which were to be used for wartime sabotage. One of the tunnels was said to pass under Canterbury Cathedral.[32]

The spy manias of the First World War showed how little the public in all combatant countries, in many cases misled by spy novels, understood about the role of intelligence. Governments, themselves sometimes subject to spy scares, understood public hysteria about espionage so little largely because, as in intelligence matters generally, they lacked historical perspective. Spy mania in the First World War never approached, for example, the intensity it had achieved over a century earlier in the French Revolutionary Wars, notably during the 'September massacres' of 1792 when paranoid mobs descended on Paris prisons to butcher prisoners alleged, on no credible evidence, to be part of a monstrous fifth column preparing to deliver the capital into the hands of an enemy invasion.[33]

On the Western Front the main intelligence innovation at the outbreak of war was aerial reconnaissance, first attempted half a century earlier, with little success, by the Balloon Corps during the American Civil War.[34] The most valuable operational intelligence during the early war of movement on the Western Front came for the first time in the history of warfare from aircraft. On 16 August 1914 the newly founded Royal Flying Corps (RFC) assembled four squadrons with sixty-three aeroplanes, 105 officers and 755 other ranks at Maubeuge. Airpower, however, remained in its infancy. At the outbreak of war Britain lacked even an aero-engine industry and remained for six months totally dependent on France for its engine supply. During these six months, none the less, the magnificent men in their flying machines had the freedom of the skies. Aircraft armed with Lewis or Vickers guns were a rarity until the Germans introduced the Fokker *Eindecker* (monoplane) in May 1915. In the early phases of the war, air battles consisted of little more than airborne observers discharging rifles and carbines at each other.

The RFC flew its first reconnaissance sorties on 19 August but saw no large influx of enemy troops. Next day, however, it observed a column of troops passing through Louvain, 'stretching as far as the eye could see'. The morning of the 21st was too foggy for planes to take off, but the weather cleared in time for RFC reconnaissance in the afternoon to report a large body of cavalry with infantry and guns south-east of Nivelles. The report was confirmed by an Intelligence Corps officer actually in Nivelles when the German cavalry arrived, who managed to escape by car. Largely on the basis of these reports the head of intelligence (GSO1) at BEF GHQ, Colonel (later General Sir) George Macdonogh, correctly deduced that a column of all German arms was rapidly advancing on Mons from Brussels. Operations loftily declared his intelligence appreciation 'somewhat exaggerated'.[35] Aerial reconnaissance played an even more important role during the Battle of the Marne in September, where it revealed German forces wheeling to the south-east of Paris, exposing themselves to a brilliantly successful counter-attack on the Marne by the Paris garrison. Marshal Joffre paid an emotional, even extravagant, tribute to the quality of the intelligence produced by the BEF as well as by the French Aéronautique Militaire:

> Please express most particularly to Field Marshal French [the British c-in-c] my thanks for the services rendered to us every day by the English Flying Corps. The precision, exactitude and regularity of the news brought in by them are evidence of their organisation and also of the perfect training of pilots and observers.[36]

Airborne artillery observers guided shells to their target by wireless messages such as the following:

> 4.2 pm Very little short. Fire. Fire.
> 4.4 pm Fire again. Fire again.
> 4.12 pm A little short; line O.K.
> 4.15 pm Short. Over, over and a little left
> 4.20 pm You were just between two batteries. Search 200 yards each side of your last shot. Range O.K.
> 4.22 pm You have them.
> 4.26 pm Hit. Hit. Hit.
> 4.3 pm About 50 yards short and to the right.
> 4.37 pm Your last shot in the middle of three batteries in action; search all round within 300 yards of your last shot and you have them.
> 4.42 pm I am coming home now.[37]

Aerial reconnaissance during trench warfare on the Western Front, though less critical than during the early war of movement, grew in importance as photography improved. In January 1915 Lieutenant (later Wing Commander) W. S. Douglas was appointed air photographer in RFC number 2 Squadron simply because he had possessed a box camera as a child. He cut a hole in the bottom of his cockpit and thrust a folding bellows camera

through it to photograph enemy positions below. Each photographic plate
had to be changed by hand and he 'spoilt many plates by clumsy handling
with frozen fingers'. In March a slight advance was made with the introduction of a Thornton-Pickard camera which the photographer held over
the side of the plane. Lieutenant (later General Sir) James Marshall later
recalled 'leaning out of the cockpit with a hand-held camera at a height of
800 feet being peppered by German machine guns'. By the summer a method
had been devised of fixing the camera to the plane together with a semi-
automatic plate-changing mechanism. But aerial reconnaissance became
even more dangerous in the autumn of 1915 when the Fokker monoplane,
fitted with a light machine-gun capable of firing through the orbit of the
propeller, established its supremacy in the skies over the Western Front.
After a series of losses by the RFC, General Sir Douglas (later Field Marshal
Earl) Haig, who became British Commander-in-Chief in December 1915,
gave instructions in January 1916 that, because the RFC had to 'fight in
the air for information', armies should 'avoid the despatch of daily reconnaissance as a matter of routine'.[38] RFC HQ ordered soon afterwards:

> Until the Royal Flying Corps are in possession of a machine as good or
> better than the German Fokker, it seems that a change in the tactics
> employed becomes necessary ... It must be laid down as a hard and fast
> rule that a machine proceeding on reconnaissance must be escorted by at
> least three other fighting machines. These machines must fly in close forma-
> tion and a reconnaissance should not be continued if any of the machines
> become detached.[39]

When the Germans began their great offensive at Verdun on 21 February
1916, they achieved total surprise.[40] The combination of bad weather,
German deception and the superiority of the Fokker *Eindecker* fighters
deprived the French of effective aerial reconnaissance before the battle. For
the first time at the beginning of a major battle on the Western Front, the
Germans achieved air superiority.[41] During the spring of 1916, however,
Fokker air supremacy began to be disputed by both Farman Experimental
2Bs and De Havilland Scouts. In the course of the year the RFC completed
a photographic map of 'Hun-land', the territory immediately opposite British lines in the British sector of the Western Front.[42] But it provided little
operational intelligence before the Battle of the Somme in July 1916. Haig's
intelligence chief at GHQ, Brigadier-General John Charteris, wrote to
Macdonogh after the first few weeks of the battle: 'Air reconnaissance as
a battle means of information has failed us. Aeroplanes have to go too high
now to do much good, and in any case the number of machines is very
limited and the information they give meagre and amateurish.'[43] Aerial

reconnaissance as well as air warfare was increasingly dangerous. During the Battle of the Somme, which began on 1 July 1916 and ended on 19 November, the RFC lost 782 aircraft and 576 pilots.[44]

During the final two years of the war aerial reconnaissance became a greater asset for the Allies on the Western Front.[45] In the middle of the war, however, it was at its most effective in the Middle East, playing an important role in operations against Turkish forces and in support for the Arab Rising against Turkish rule which began at Mecca in June 1916. Photographic reconnaissance in the Middle East was usually able to benefit from both clear skies and the absence of enemy aircraft. Far more than on the Western Front, it was thus able to undertake strategic reconnaissance behind enemy lines.[46] In late July and early August 1916, Sir Archibald Murray, GOC-in-C of Egyptforce, ordered a photographic survey of the strategically important Red Sea port of Aqaba and the surrounding mountains. Nine months later, intelligence from this reconnaissance played a key role in the ambitious plans drawn up by T. E. Lawrence, 'Lawrence of Arabia', to take Aqaba from the Turks by a surprise overland attack with his Arab allies. Nowadays, Lawrence is best remembered as a superb practitioner of guerrilla warfare. But he was also a leading pioneer of what later became known as imagery intelligence (IMINT), clearing aircraft landing grounds on his own initiative, promoting photographic reconnaissance, and coordinating flight plans to meet the Arabs' operational needs.[47] By 1917 the three aircraft stationed in Egypt at the outbreak of war had increased to three squadrons, whose primary purpose was intelligence gathering.[48]

Despite the new contribution made by aerial reconnaissance to military intelligence in both Europe and the Middle East, the First World War did even more to transform intelligence at sea than on land. Thanks chiefly to SIGINT, Britain had access to far more naval intelligence than any power had ever possessed in any previous war. Since ancient times naval intelligence had been a very scarce commodity. Until the radio era, the horizon was an impenetrable barrier to intelligence collection at sea. Though the Royal Navy was the most powerful in the world by the end of the seventeenth century, for the next two centuries it spent much less time in battle than in scouring the seas, often without success, for enemy fleets. Before Admiral Lord Howe's great victory on 'the Glorious First of June' 1794, for example, he had to spend eight days searching for the nearby French convoy of 139 merchantmen he planned to attack.[49] During the Napoleonic Wars, Wellington had access to vastly better intelligence on land than Nelson possessed at sea. In the First World War, by contrast, Britain, for the first time in its history, had better naval than military intelligence.

Soon after midnight on 4 August 1914, the day Britain declared war, the British cable ship *Telconia* began cutting Germany's overseas telegraph cables, forcing it either to send radio messages, which could be intercepted, or to use foreign cables which might be tapped by her enemies. Radio was also the only practicable way for the German Admiralty to communicate with both its surface fleet and U-boats. As a result German intercepts arrived daily in the Admiralty. Attempting to decrypt the German naval cipher messages sent by radio was the main stimulus to the rebirth of British codebreaking after a gap of seventy years. For the first fortnight of the war, Rear-Admiral (later Admiral of the Fleet Sir) Henry 'Dummy' Oliver, the taciturn Director of Naval Intelligence (DNI or DID), had little idea what to do with the German intercepts which piled up on his desk. Then, while walking one day in mid-August to lunch with the Director of Naval Education, Sir Alfred Ewing, it suddenly struck Oliver that Ewing was 'the very man I wanted'. Ewing was a short, softly spoken Scot with, in Oliver's view, 'very great brainpower, in fact a man who stood out among clever men'. In the course of a career as Professor of Engineering at Tokyo, Dundee and Cambridge Universities, he had acquired 'an expert knowledge of radio-telegraphy' and had briefly dabbled in codes and ciphers. Oliver, as usual, did not mince words. He told Ewing that, since 'education would probably be considered of little importance over the next few months', he would do better to apply himself to the intercepted enemy signals. Ewing agreed.

Since British official codebreaking (save on India's North-West Frontier) had ceased seventy years before,[50] Ewing was forced to improvise. The fact that, from a standing start, British wartime codebreaking became the best in the world, was a triumph of improvisation. As Director of Naval Education, Ewing began his search for potential codebreakers in the naval colleges at Dartmouth and Osborne, which sent him four of their language teachers. The ablest of them, A. G. 'Alastair' Denniston, a short-statured Scottish hockey international known to colleagues as 'the little man', was later to become operational head of interwar SIGINT and first head of Bletchley Park in the Second World War. Denniston and Ewing's other First World War recruits, however, had no qualification for codebreaking save a knowledge of German and 'a reputation for discretion'. None knew anything about cryptography. As Denniston wrote later, 'Cryptographers did not exist, so far as we knew.'[51]* It had been so long since Britain

---

* Denniston's statement that he was unaware of any British cryptographic expertise at the outbreak of war was not an attempt at public self-justification. It was made in a classified document which he did not expect to be published in his lifetime, if ever.

possessed any cryptanalytic expertise that, save for a handful of SIGINT specialists in India, all memory of it had disappeared.

The apprentice codebreakers had several major strokes of luck. The first was the news brought to Churchill by the Russian naval attaché that the German light cruiser *Magdeburg* had been wrecked in the Baltic: 'The body of a drowned German under-officer was picked up by the Russians a few hours later, and clasped to his bosom by arms rigid in death were the cypher and signal books of the German Navy . . .' On 13 October Churchill and the First Sea Lord, Prince Louis of Battenberg, 'received from our loyal allies these sea-stained priceless documents'. Churchill's account is heavily romanticized. The copy of the *Signalbuch der Kaiserlichen Marine* (*SKM*) in the British National Archives shows no sign of being 'sea-stained' and was probably recovered from the *Magdeburg* more prosaically than Churchill was led to believe.[52] At the end of October the Admiralty also received, belatedly, from the Royal Australian Navy a copy captured on 11 August of the *Handelsverkehrsbuch* (*HVB*) used by the German Admiralty and warships to communicate with merchantmen (and also sometimes used by the High Seas Fleet). On 30 November a British trawler fishing off the Texel found in its nets a lead-lined chest from a German destroyer sunk by the Royal Navy. Among the papers recovered from the chest was a copy of the *Verkehrsbuch* (*VB*), the last of the three main German naval codes.[53]

These windfalls and the early successes of the Admiralty codebreakers together fired Churchill with an enthusiasm for SIGINT which was to last for the rest of his life. On 8 November he composed a memorandum for which he devised the unique, though ephemeral, formula 'Exclusively Secret' (briefly Britain's highest security classification), initialled by himself and by Battenberg's successor as First Sea Lord, Admiral Sir John Fisher:

> An officer of the War Staff, preferably from the I[ntelligence] D[ivision], should be selected to study all the decoded [decrypted] intercepts, not only current but past, and to compare them continually with what actually took place in order to penetrate the German mind and movements and make reports. All these intercepts are to be written in a locked book with their decodes [decrypts] and all other copies are to be collected and burnt. All new messages are to be entered in the book and the book is only to be handled under instructions from the COS [Chief of Staff].
>
> The officer selected is for the present to do no other work. I shall be obliged if Sir Alfred Ewing will associate himself continuously with this work.[54]

Churchill was the first minister in Asquith's wartime Cabinet to grasp the potential importance of SIGINT. Asquith, by contrast, despite his high intelligence and political skill, seems to have paid no attention to it. Had he known of the role played by SIGINT in previous conflicts from the attempted Spanish invasion of 1588 to the Napoleonic Wars, he would surely have shown greater interest in 1914.

The Prime Minister disposed of the regular carbon copies ('flimsies') he was sent of major diplomatic despatches with little regard for security. On 15 August, after showing a selection to his mistress Venetia Stanley (forty years his junior) as their carriage passed along Roehampton Lane in south-west London, Asquith tore up the flimsies, made them into a paper ball, and, despite Venetia's protests, threw it through the window of the carriage. Asquith was not the only minister to tear up flimsies after reading them and throw them away. He wrote to Venetia:

> It appears that the police have discovered fragments of them, in St James' Park, in Oxfordshire near Goring, & one or two other places in the country. These they have laboriously collected and the pieces came round in a box this morning with a severe admonition from E. Grey as to the dangers to wh[ich] the Foreign Office cypher was exposed from such loose handling of secret matters! My conscience was quite clear as to St Jas's Park & Goring: so I simply wrote 'not guilty' . . . but what damning evidence you might have given![55]*

Asquith was equally lax with military secrets. He wrote to Venetia Stanley after a Cabinet meeting on 18 August: 'Everyone is very pleased with the smoothness & secrecy of the Exped[itionar]y Force.'[56] On 24 August Sir John French sent Lord Kitchener a secret telegram with details of the retreat by the BEF to the River Marne and precise details of the defensive lines, unknown to the Germans, which the BEF and the French Fifth Army planned to take up. Asquith immediately sent a copy to Venetia Stanley, telling her: 'I wish we had something like a code that we cd. use by the telegraph. This morning for instance I longed to let you know before anyone else what had happened & was happening.'[57]

Churchill's enthusiasm for SIGINT was in stark contrast to Asquith's indifference. His belief in November 1914 that a single officer in Room 40 was capable of studying all decrypts, not only current but past, and comparing them 'continually with what actually took place' shows, however, that even he failed to foresee the future volume of wartime SIGINT.

---

* In August 1914 the other ministers apart from Grey, the Foreign Secretary, who were given the diplomatic flimsies were Kitchener, the Secretary of State for War; Churchill, First Lord of the Admiralty; and Lewis Harcourt, Secretary of State for the Colonies. The most likely culprit in the careless disposal of the torn-up flimsies found by the police was the badly behaved Harcourt.

The single 'locked book' of intercepts which he had ordered quickly proved impracticable and Churchill authorized additional copies of decrypts to be sent in sealed envelopes to the COS and DNI/DID.[58]

Following 'Dummy' Oliver's promotion to COS early in November 1914, he was succeeded as Director of the Intelligence Division by the 44-year-old Captain (later Admiral Sir) William Reginald 'Blinker' Hall, whose uncertain health had forced him to give up command of the battle cruiser *Queen Mary* in favour of a desk job. Hall was a Punch-like figure, prematurely bald with a hook-nose. The writer and wartime member of MI1c (the future SIS or MI6) Compton Mackenzie found him rather like his own chief, Mansfield Cumming: 'His nose was beakier; his chin had a more pronounced cutwater. Nevertheless, when I looked at the two men I could have fancied that each was a caricature of the other.'[59]

Hall quickly performed two important services for the naval code-breakers. First, he found them less-cramped accommodation in Room 40 in the Admiralty Old Building. As their numbers grew, the codebreakers spilled over into a series of adjoining rooms but continued to be known collectively as Room 40 OB, a name sufficiently innocuous to give no hint of their activities. Secondly, he appointed Commander (later Admiral) W. W. Hope to analyse the German intercepts and provide the professional naval expertise that the codebreakers lacked – or, as Hall put it, 'to sift the messages and extract the juice'. The very success of Room 40 led to a dispute for control of it between Ewing and Hall. Ewing wished to retain personal control of the codebreakers; Hall wanted to incorporate them into the Intelligence Division. Hall eventually won.[60]

By the end of the year, thanks to German dependence on radio communications, British naval cryptanalysts were providing operational intelligence on a scale unprecedented in the previous history of SIGINT. Room 40's greatest achievement was to make German surprise attack impossible. Until its cryptanalysts got into their stride, the Grand Fleet, based inconveniently far north at Scapa Flow in the Orkneys, was forced to spend much of its time scouring the North Sea for an enemy it failed to find, continually fearful of being caught off its guard. But from December 1914 onwards no major movement by the German High Seas Fleet – save, briefly, in 1918 – escaped the notice of the cryptanalysts. The first warning by Room 40 of a major German sortie came on 14 December 1914 when the commander-in-chief of the High Seas Fleet, Admiral Friedrich von Ingenohl, ordered a raid by battle cruisers commanded by Admiral Franz von Hipper on British east-coast towns, combined with a minelaying expedition off Yorkshire. On the evening of the same day, Admiral Sir John (later Earl) Jellicoe, commander-in-chief of the Grand Fleet, was warned that German battle cruisers would be setting out for the east coast next day. Oliver, however, wrongly deduced from incomplete intelligence – without consulting Room 40 – that German battleships were 'very unlikely to come out'. Unaware that the German High Seas Fleet had been ordered to support Hipper's raid from a position in the middle of the North Sea, the Admiralty therefore ordered only part of the Grand Fleet to come south from Scapa Flow to lay a trap for the German battle cruisers.[61]

At 8.30 a.m. on 16 December while Churchill lay soaking in his bath, the door burst open and an officer hurried in, holding a naval signal which the First Lord 'grasped with dripping hand'. The signal reported: 'German battle-cruisers bombarding Hartlepool.' Jumping out of the bath 'with exclamations', Churchill pulled on his clothes over a still damp body, raced downstairs to the War Room, conferred excitedly with Fisher and Oliver, and ordered the trap to be sprung.[62] What happened in the remainder of that day later appeared to both sides as a tragically wasted opportunity to win a major victory. The first contact between the opposing fleets took place between Vice-Admiral Sir George Warrender's Second Battle Squadron and the light forces screening the High Seas Fleet. Wrongly believing he was facing the whole, rather than only a part, of Jellicoe's forces, Ingenohl broke away and thus missed an opportunity which would never recur to engage a detachment of the Grand Fleet with superior German forces. 'On 16 December', wrote Tirpitz later, 'Ingenohl had the fate of Germany in the palm of his hand. I boil with inward emotion whenever I think of it.'[63]

By 11 a.m., his mission completed but denied the protection of the High Seas Fleet, Hipper was heading, without realizing it, for a trap laid by the battle cruisers of Admiral Sir David (later Earl) Beatty and the six battleships of Warrender. At 11.25 the two sides' light cruisers made contact. Beatty wrote later with the same sense of exasperation as Tirpitz: 'We were within an ace of bringing about the complete destruction of the Enemy Cruiser Force – and failed.' Scarcely had the British light cruisers made contact with the enemy than a signalling error by Beatty's flag-lieutenant, led them to break it off. Thereafter Hipper was saved by poor visibility and the Admiralty's misinterpretation of a Room 40 decrypt referring to the presence of the High Seas Fleet in the North Sea. Unaware that the enemy battleships had been there all the time, the Admiralty wrongly assumed that Ingenohl was advancing rather than retreating and warned Beatty not to pursue Hipper too far.[64]

'All concerned', wrote Fisher furiously, 'made a hash of it.' The enemy had escaped from 'the very jaws of death!' Jellicoe too was 'intensely unhappy'. 'We had', he said, 'the opportunity of our lives.'[65] And yet, for all the intense frustration which followed Hipper's escape, the outcome of the German raid was ultimately reassuring. So long as Room 40 could decrypt German naval signals, the Admiralty would always be forewarned of any major German move into the North Sea. As the naval staff concluded at the end of 1914:

> The result was that it was no longer necessary for the Grand Fleet either to carry on the continual sweeps of the North Sea, as prescribed in the War Plans, or to be constantly in a state of complete readiness. It was now possible for rest and training to be looked upon as matters of essential routine. On the whole, the Grand Fleet was less harassed, more secure, and stronger than when war broke out.[66]

On 23 January 1915 Admiral Sir Arthur Wilson, whom Churchill had recalled from retirement to advise him, walked unannounced into Churchill's room in the Admiralty, a 'glow' still in his eye from reading the latest Room 40 decrypts. 'First Lord', he declared, 'these fellows are coming out again!' 'When?' demanded Churchill. 'Tonight. We have just got time to get Beatty there.' At 5.45 p.m. Admiral Hipper set out with four battle cruisers from the Jade estuary unaware that his plans were known and his movements followed by an enemy who was intercepting his signals and planning to ambush him with a larger naval force in the North Sea. For Churchill, 'Only one thought could reign – battle at dawn! Battle for the first time in history between mighty super-Dreadnought ships! And there was added a thrilling sense of a Beast of Prey moving steadily hour by hour towards the trap.'

Churchill was up before dawn on the 24th, waiting impatiently with Fisher, Wilson and Oliver in the Admiralty War Room. Just after 8 a.m. came the news that the enemy had been sighted off the Dogger Bank. In a long life crowded with dramatic incident, Churchill underwent 'few purely mental experiences more charged with cold excitement' than the silent hours which he spent in the War Room following the course of the battle.[67] At 10.47 Beatty signalled to his ships: 'Close the enemy as rapidly as possible consistent with keeping all guns bearing.' One of Hipper's outnumbered battle cruisers, the *Blücher*, was hit and began sinking. Beatty was confident he could sink the other three. But at 10.54 submarines were reported on the starboard bow. Beatty thought he saw a periscope and immediately ordered a ninety-degree turn to port, placing his ships astern of the enemy. Room 40 decrypts had shown that, in reality, the nearest U-boats were hours away, but the Admiralty had failed to pass this crucial intelligence to Beatty. Though Beatty and his flag-lieutenant made subsequent errors of judgement, the Admiralty's continuing failure, as in December, to make full use of SIGINT in naval operations was probably the main reason why three of Hipper's four battle cruisers escaped. 'The disappointment of that day', wrote Beatty to a friend, 'is more than I can bear to think of.'[68]

Despite the 'disappointments' of December 1914 and January 1915 in the North Sea, SIGINT had a bigger influence on British policymaking during the First World War than in any previous war in British history. It was of great strategic importance during the war at sea, especially the Battle of the Atlantic against the U-boats; in discovering German intentions on issues ranging from the introduction of unrestricted U-boat warfare to the attempt to find new wartime allies; and in monitoring the policy of the United States, whose entry into the war was a vitally important aim of British policy. In no other combatant country did SIGINT play a role of comparable importance. Had Winston Churchill not been forced to resign as First Lord of the Admiralty in May 1915, he might have taken the leading role in overseeing the use of SIGINT, as he did during the Second World War. Instead, after Churchill's resignation, the leading role was taken not by another minister (or even by Churchill himself in his uninfluential role of Chancellor of the Duchy of Lancaster until November 1915 or as Minister of Munitions outside the Cabinet from July 1917) but by 'Blinker' Hall, the most influential intelligence chief of the First World War and the most powerful intelligence chief in British history since Sir Francis Walsingham. Hall did not always trouble to consult ministers before he made policy decisions. During the 1915 Dardanelles campaign, before Churchill's resignation from the Admiralty, he sent secret emissaries to Constantinople with authority to offer up to four million pounds to secure the passage of the Royal Navy. Hall left the following account of the interview which ensued with Churchill and the First Sea Lord, Lord Fisher:

> [Churchill] was frowning. 'Who authorised this?' he demanded.
> 'I did, First Lord.'
> 'But – the Cabinet surely knows nothing about it?'
> 'No, it does not . . .'
> It was one of those moments when dropped pins are supposed to be heard. Then Mr Churchill turned to Lord Fisher . . . 'D'you hear what this man has done? He's sent out people with four millions to buy a peaceful passage! On his own!'[69]

Part of Hall's willingness to act without ministerial approval derived from his generally well-founded belief that he understood intelligence (SIGINT in particular) far better than the Cabinet. With much less justification, Hall had no doubt also that he understood the national interest, particularly in wartime, in a way that most politicians could not. The national interest, as Hall interpreted it, overrode all other considerations. Central to Hall's extraordinary ability to get his own way was one of the most magnetic personalities in the history of twentieth-century intelligence. The US wartime ambassador in London, Dr Walter Hines Page, was, quite literally, spellbound in his presence; he wrote to President Wilson:

> Neither in fiction nor in fact can you find any such man to match him . . . The man is a genius – a clear case of genius. All other secret service men are amateurs by comparison . . . I shall never meet another man like him; that were too much to expect.
>
> For Hall can look through you and see the very muscular movements of your immortal soul while he is talking to you. Such eyes as the man has! – which is well, because he hasn't a hair on his head nor a tooth in his mouth . . . – My Lord! I do study these men here most diligently who have this vast and appalling War Job. There are most uncommon creatures among them – men about whom our great-grandchildren will read in their school histories; but of them all, the most extraordinary is this naval officer – of whom, probably, they'll never hear.[70]

Hall had the knack of winning over people he wished to influence by taking them into his confidence – or pretending to do so. Page told Wilson that Hall was in the habit of revealing both to him and to Eddie Bell, the US diplomat in London responsible for military and intelligence liaison, 'certain things . . . which he doesn't tell his own Government'. 'That's my claim to distinction', Page told the President.[71] It did not occur to Page that, while telling him secrets allegedly not known to the British government, Hall was simultaneously reading his decrypted telegrams to and from the State Department.[72] Though Hall was one of the founders of the intelligence 'special relationship' with the United States, in which he was a true believer, he could not resist – in what he believed was the national interest – mixing deception with collaboration. Like Sun Tzu over two millennia earlier, Hall believed that 'All warfare is based on deception.'[73] The backwardness of American intelligence at the outbreak of the First World War made British deception easier than it would have been in the Second World War – or the Revolutionary War. Hall would have found George Washington far more difficult to deceive than Woodrow Wilson.

In addition to decrypting German naval signals, Room 40 also broke the German diplomatic code. In the autumn of 1915 a diplomatic codebreaking department, dealing chiefly with German intercepts, was created in Room 45, reporting directly to Hall. Ewing continued to focus on naval codebreaking until he left to become Vice-Chancellor of Glasgow

University in October 1916. Though his own skills as a cryptographer turned out to be limited, he had an enduring influence on British code-breaking in the Second as well as the First World War. Ewing recruited to Room 40 what Denniston was to call in the early days of Bletchley Park 'men of the professor type': civilian intellectuals whom most admirals would never have dreamed of involving in naval matters. The single most valuable source of 'professor types' in both world wars was Ewing's former Cambridge college, King's, with which he retained strong links, notably through his son-in-law, who was a Fellow. Despite Ewing's background in engineering, none of Room 40's academic recruits were professional mathematicians – though some had considerable mathematical talent. Room 40 seems to have shared the arts graduate's traditional suspicion that, whatever their dexterity with numbers, the best mathematicians tend to have withdrawn, uncommunicative personalities which make them unsuitable for the collaborative solution of practical problems.[74] When the first American codebreaking unit, founded after US entry into the war, later sought advice from its British allies on the right kind of recruit, it was told to beware mathematicians. What was needed was 'an active, well trained and scholarly mind, not mathematical but classical'.[75]

The King's College classicist Alfred Dillwyn Knox, recruited by Ewing early in 1915, was just such an individual. Reputed to be Room 40's 'most brilliant member', 'Dilly' Knox was the second of four remarkable sons of the Bishop of Manchester. Edmund, the eldest, became editor of *Punch*; Wilfred was an Anglo-Catholic theologian, later elected Fellow of Pembroke College, Cambridge; Ronald, the youngest, who also worked for a time in Room 40, was the most influential Catholic convert of his generation and, according to the *Daily Mail*, 'the wittiest young man in England'. 'Dilly' had established himself as a leading King's eccentric and prominent supporter of his friend, the great economist Maynard Keynes's campaign against the Bursar. In successive issues of the King's journal, *Basileon*, Dilly called on the Bursar to inspect the rats in Fellows' rooms, then to protect the rats from water rats attracted by the rising damp, and finally to have a care for the water rats whose 'nasty cough' was disturbing the repose of younger Fellows. Knox did some of his best work for Room 40 lying in a bath in Room 53, claiming that codes were most easily cracked in an atmosphere of soap and steam.[76] His belief in the creative powers of bathtime lasted into the Second World War. One of his colleagues at Bletchley Park was to write of him:

> At his billet [Dilly] once stayed so long in the bathroom that his fellow
> lodgers at last forced the door. They found him standing by the bath, a faint

smile on his face, his gaze fixed on abstractions, both taps full on and the plug out. What was then passing in his mind could possibly have solved a problem that was to win a battle.[77]

Ewing also recruited a series of other academics, mostly classicists and German linguists, from Cambridge and other universities. They included, in addition to Knox, two other Fellows of King's College, Cambridge. Frank Adcock (later knighted and Professor of Ancient History at Cambridge University) arrived at about the same time as Dilly. The Old Etonian King's historian Frank Birch arrived in 1916.[78] Birch was a brilliant conversationalist and comic actor who later appeared in pantomime at the London Palladium and wrote a comic history of Room 40, *Alice in ID25*, which included a celebration by Knox of his bathtime brainwaves:

> The sailor in Room 53
> Has never, it's true, been to sea
> But though not in a boat
> He has yet served afloat –
> In a bath at the Admiralty[79]

In the Second World War Birch and Adcock were to take the lead in recruiting one third of the King's Fellowship to Bletchley Park (including its greatest cryptanalyst, Alan Turing).[80] But for the experience of the contribution made by King's eccentrics to codebreaking in the First World War, it is unlikely that Turing would have been recruited in 1939.

Like Ewing, Hall was actively involved in recruiting for Room 40 from the moment he became DID. Hall seems to have had a weakness for Old Etonians. In December 1914 he made one of Room 40's earliest recruits, the Old Etonian Lord Herschell, Lord in Waiting to George V, his personal assistant. Convinced that he required 'men of wider experience of the world' than the Admiralty or Whitehall could provide, he took on as a second personal assistant the Old Etonian stockbroker Claude Serocold, who struck Frank Birch as a 'slim, well groomed creature with a black moustache' (later removed). Through Herschell and Serocold, Hall recruited mostly well-connected German-speakers from a variety of professions. The Old Etonian publisher Nigel de Grey, depicted by Birch in *Alice in ID25* as 'the Dormouse' ('very quiet and apparently asleep'), rivalled his fellow Old Etonian Dilly Knox as the ablest codebreaker in Room 40.[81]

After the Germans' transatlantic cable was cut by the British at the outbreak of war, the officially neutral but pro-German Swedes allowed them to use the Swedish cable to communicate with German diplomatic missions in the New World. When Britain protested in the summer of 1915, Sweden agreed to stop allowing Germany to use its cables, but in fact continued cabling German messages, disguised by re-encipherment in Swedish ciphers, by a roundabout route from Stockholm via Buenos Aires to Washington. This circuitous itinerary also included Britain, and by the spring of 1916 Room 40 had detected the Swedish ruse. This time, however, Britain made no protest, because of the opportunity offered by the 'Swedish roundabout' to intercept German diplomatic traffic undetected. At the end of 1916 the Germans acquired a second and more direct communication link with North America. Bernstorff successfully argued that President Wilson's peace initiatives would make speedier progress if the German embassy in Washington could use the American transatlantic cable to communicate with Berlin. This cable too went via Britain, and Room 40 was 'highly entertained' to discover German ciphers among the American diplomatic traffic that, unknown to Wilson and Page, was routinely intercepted.[82]

German diplomatic telegrams were also regularly decrypted by the *Section du Chiffre* at the French War Ministry, which replaced the pre-war *cabinets noirs* of the Quai d'Orsay and the Sûreté as France's main SIGINT agency. In the course of the war the *Section du Chiffre* decrypted over 28,000 enemy and neutral diplomatic intercepts, in addition to German military and naval traffic. The most regularly intercepted diplomatic traffic was that of Germany and neutral Spain with their embassies in, respectively, Madrid and Berlin.[83] The French War Ministry was able to discover from the decrypts details of the bribery of the Spanish press by the German ambassador in Madrid, Prince Max von Ratibor, who assured Berlin in February 1915 that a number of leading Madrid newspapers 'will now work for our side with redoubled enthusiasm. And they will also persuade others to become Germanophiles.' Ratibor reported that the French were also bribing Spanish newspapers but implied that they were less successful.[84] For the first time British and French codebreakers decrypted more German diplomatic traffic than their Russian counterparts.[85]

Germany, by contrast, failed entirely to decrypt any British, French or Russian diplomatic communications. The German Foreign Ministry was visibly taken aback when the worldwide publicity given to the 'Zimmermann telegram' in March 1917 revealed that its own diplomatic code had been broken.[86] The German Admiralty similarly failed entirely to grasp the vulnerability of its naval ciphers. Room 40's ability to break U-boat ciphers was to be central to Germany's defeat in 1917 in the Battle of the Atlantic.[87] The records of the Abhorchdienst, the German military codebreaking unit established at Neumünster in 1916, have not survived. But there is no evidence that it achieved significant success during the era of trench warfare on the Western Front.[88] German military intelligence was, however, able to benefit from poor British telephone security in the trenches. In 1915 a 32-year-old German telegraph inspector devised the 'Moritz' apparatus which allowed the interception of messages from British field telephones by amplifying the current in the single-wire transmission system which used the ground of No Man's Land as the return path for the signal. British GHQ first discovered German use of the Moritz apparatus in March 1916 but, as the Battle of the Somme was to show a few months later, greatly underestimated its effectiveness.[89]

The distinguishing feature of Germany's wartime intelligence operations was the priority given to sabotage. In November 1914 the German Admiralty Staff issued a circular to naval attachés and their agents ordering the recruitment of 'agents for arranging explosions on ships bound for enemy countries'. Almost simultaneously, German military intelligence established a sabotage department, Sektion P, under Captain Rudolf Nadolny.[90] Falkenhayn awarded Nadolny the Iron Cross for his success in blowing up a Russian gunpowder factory at Ochta on the outskirts of Petrograd (as St Petersburg was renamed in wartime).[91] In the spring of 1916 naval intelligence set up a dedicated sabotage department, NIV, headed by Lieutenant-Commander Alfred Lassen.[92] Neither Nadolny nor Lassen succeeded in carrying out sabotage in Britain and France.[93]* German sabotage operations achieved their greatest success in the neutral United States. Germany, writes President Wilson's biographer, Arthur S. Link, 'mounted a massive campaign on American soil of intrigue, espionage and sabotage unprecedented in modern times by one allegedly friendly power against another'.[94] The campaign must have drawn some inspiration from Bismarck's notorious Prussian intelligence chief, Wilhelm Stieber, whose operations at home and abroad had included 'provocations, bribery, deception, theft of documents, forgery and perjury'. Karl Marx, among others, had complained about Stieber's operations in London during the 1850s.[95]

The main objective of German covert operations in the wartime United States was to prevent American industry from supplying Britain and its allies with the sinews of war. Because of Britain's dominance of the seas and financial reserves (increased by American loans), it was able to import hugely more from the United States than the Central Powers. American exports to Britain and France rose to $2.75bn in 1916, while those to Germany dwindled to a mere two million dollars.[96] The invention of dynamite and TNT made possible German sabotage operations of a kind that

---

* A number of industrial accidents, however, were wrongly blamed on German sabotage.

would not have been possible in any previous war between great powers. On 21 May 1915 the British merchant ship *Bayropea* caught fire on its way to Le Havre after the explosion of what the British called a German 'infernal machine'. Despite a series of similar sabotage operations over the next year,[97] the German secret war in the New World ended in strategic defeat. Like the German sinking of the British liner *Lusitania* in May 1915 with the loss of 128 American lives, the gradual revelation of Germany's covert operations in the United States proved a public-relations disaster for the German cause. The disaster was skilfully exploited by British intelligence. Profiting from German bungling and American innocence, it gradually succeeded in winning the confidence not merely of the fragmented US intelligence community but also of President Wilson.[98]

At the outbreak of the war in Europe, neither the US Justice Department's Bureau of Investigation (forerunner of the FBI) nor the Treasury Department's Secret Service[99] yet had significant experience of counter-espionage. Each made matters worse by its reluctance to cooperate with the other. Both the German and British intelligence services thus found it easier to operate in the neutral United States than in war-torn Europe. The first substantial evidence of German intelligence operations to reach the White House was in December 1914. Reports from the Bureau of Investigation revealed the involvement of the German ambassador, Count Johann Heinrich von Bernstorff, in the wholesale forgery of American passports to enable German reservists in the United States to return to Germany via neutral ports. In May 1915, on Wilson's instructions, the Secret Service began investigating other suspected violations of American neutrality, some involving the German commercial attaché, Dr Heinrich Albert. On 23 July Albert boarded a Sixth Avenue elevated train in New York, shadowed by a Secret Service operative, Frank Burke, who had his eyes on the attaché's bulging briefcase. Burke could scarcely believe his luck when Albert got off at Fiftieth Street and absent-mindedly left his bag behind. Seeing Burke make off with his briefcase, Albert gave chase. Burke hurriedly boarded another train and told the conductor he was being pursued by a madman. According to Burke's report, 'The wild-eyed appearance of the Doctor corroborated my statement and the conductor called to the motorman to pass the next corner without stopping so the nut could not get on.'

The stolen briefcase contained documents detailing the planting of pro-German news stories in the American press, subsidies paid to German-American and Irish-American organizations and media, the purchase with German money of a large munitions plant to prevent its production going to the Allies, and various secret schemes to influence US opinion. Wilson's

confidant and chief adviser, 'Colonel' Edward M. House, Secretary of
State Robert Lansing and Secretary of the Treasury William G. McAdoo
(Wilson's son-in-law) jointly agreed to publish selected items from Albert's
briefcase in the New York *World* on condition that the source was not
revealed. The publication produced the expected press uproar. 'Woe to
the newspaper or lecturer who takes the German side', declared the New
York *Nation*. ' "How much are you being paid by the Germans?" will be
an inevitable question.' Wilson wrote to House in August 1915: 'I am sure
that the country is honeycombed with German intrigue and infested with
German spies. The evidences of these things are multiplying every day.'[100]

Wilson's main concern was German sabotage operations. The main
initial organizers of sabotage were the military and naval attachés at the
Germany embassy, Major Franz von Papen (later German Chancellor and
Hitler's Vice-Chancellor) and Captain Karl Boy-Ed. Apparently dissatisfied
with the initial results achieved by the attachés, in April 1915 the German
War Ministry despatched the flamboyant international banker and naval
reserve officer Franz Rintelen von Kleist to step up the tempo of the secret
war. Rintelen promised rapid results. 'I'll buy up what I can and blow up
what I can't', he told the Admiralty. Within a few months he had set up a
successful sabotage network, which used east-coast dockworkers and long-
shoremen to conceal time bombs on munitions ships before they set off
across the Atlantic. In the process Rintelen aroused the indignation of
Papen and Boy-Ed, who pressed successfully for his recall to Berlin on the
grounds that his covert operations were interfering with theirs. Rintelen's
memoirs, in which he grandly entitles himself 'The Dark Invader', recap-
tures some of the absurdity of his wartime braggadocio: 'Singlehandedly,
I . . . ventured an attack against the forty-eight United States! . . . The word
"fear" did not and does not exist in my vocabulary . . .'[101]

Hall was quick to see the propaganda opportunities offered for British
influence operations by the revelation of German covert operations in the
United States. The extrovert Australian-born British naval attaché, Captain (later Admiral Sir) Guy Gaunt, who operated out of the British
consulate in New York, worked closely with Hall on what he called the
'Intelligence-cum-Propaganda line'. Soon after the outbreak of war, Gaunt
breezily informed the British ambassador, Sir Cecil Spring Rice, that he
intended to concentrate on covert operations and that 'It might be advisable . . . that he should be able to say: "I didn't know what the fool was
doing" – the fool being me.'[102] Gaunt's social circle included former President Theodore Roosevelt, Assistant Secretary of the Navy (and future
President) Franklin D. Roosevelt, J. P. Morgan partner (and future Secretary of State) Edward Stettinius, and Wilson's closest adviser, 'Colonel'

Edward M. House. Gaunt boasted to House, and probably to his other influential friends, that 'the British Intelligence Service is marvellously good. They have reports of everything going on in Berlin.' House had no idea that Gaunt was engaged in secret influence operations in the United States. He wrote to Arthur J. Balfour, who succeeded Churchill as First Lord of the Admiralty in May 1915:

> I want to express my high regard and appreciation of Captain Gaunt. I doubt whether you can realize the great service he has rendered our two countries. His outlook is so broad and he is so self-contained and fair-minded that I have been able to go to him at all times to discuss, very much as I would with you, the problems that have arisen.

The American journalist with whom Gaunt worked most closely on the 'Intelligence-cum-Propaganda line' was the editor of the *Providence Journal*, John R. Rathom, also Australian-born and staunchly pro-British. At their almost daily meetings Gaunt handed over intelligence on German covert operations which Rathom published in his newspaper and occasionally in *The New York Times*, for which he had worked previously.[103]

On 3 August 1915, after being ordered back to Berlin, Franz Rintelen boarded a ship bound for Holland, travelling under the alias 'Émile Victor Gaché'. Hall was alerted by a Room 40 decrypt to Rintelen's return and arranged for his arrest and the seizure of compromising papers in his luggage on German covert operations in the United States during a search of his ship off Ramsgate on 13 August. The papers which Hall passed to the US embassy to forward to Washington contained proof of Papen's and Boy-Ed's, as well as Rintelen's, involvement in illegal covert operations. With Hall's approval Gaunt ran a spy ring of Czech-Americans headed by Emanuel Voska. Some were Austrian citizens with jobs at the Austrian embassy, where they discovered that both German and Austrian officials sometimes used the US journalist James F. J. Archibald as a confidential courier to Europe. Soon after Rintelen's arrest, Gaunt informed Hall that Archibald was to be sent on a mission to Europe aboard a Dutch ship, carrying with him top-secret Austrian documents. When the ship stopped at Falmouth, Archibald was arrested and the documents seized. The documents, which Hall forwarded to the US embassy without authorization from Balfour, implicated the Austrian embassy in Washington in attempts to instigate strikes by workers of Hungarian descent in American arms factories. As a result, the Austrian ambassador, Constantin Dumba, was declared *persona non grata* in September 1915. The evidence of German covert operations in both the Rintelen and Archibald papers led to the recall of Papen and Boy-Ed three months later. When Papen's ship stopped at Falmouth, his papers too, with further embarrassing revelations of German covert operations, were confiscated on Hall's orders and handed to the US embassy for transmission to Washington.[104]

The Admiralty as a whole lacked Hall's flair for intelligence. Some of its failings in dealing with the new phenomenon of naval SIGINT were due to Admiral Oliver's overwork and reluctance to delegate as COS. He slept in the War Room, rarely left it by day, and frequently insisted on drafting signals based on SIGINT himself. Beatty complained that Room 40 gave Oliver 'priceless information . . . which he sits on until it is too late for the Sea Forces to take action'. The underlying problem for Room 40 was the weight – often the dead weight – of naval tradition. An Admiralty which had long resisted the creation of the Naval Staff (forced on it by Churchill only in 1912) was unlikely to adjust itself overnight to the even greater novelty of Room 40. Traditionally minded naval officers were bound to look askance at civilian meddling in naval matters. Initially at least, the prejudices of the Admiralty Operations Division were reinforced by the inexperience of the new cryptographers. An enlightened Director of Operations would have regarded Room 40, despite its lack of naval experience, as a new organization of enormous potential. But Rear-Admiral Thomas Jackson was not an enlightened man. One of the Room 40 recruits, the banker Lionel Fraser, later recalled 'many odd incidents' when professor types, 'plonked into the uniform of an officer of the RNVR', forgot to salute senior officers or mislaid parts of their uniform. As stories leaked out of Dilly Knox's bathtime brainwaves and the practical jokes played on and by Frank Birch, Admiral Jackson's suspicions must surely have deepened and darkened.[105] According to a memoir by one of the lawyer recruits to Room 40, William F. Clarke:

> Admiral Thomas Jackson . . . displayed supreme contempt for the work of Room 40. He never came into the room except on two or three occasions, on one of which he came to complain that one of the locked boxes in which the information was sent him had cut his hand, and on another to say, at a time when the Germans had introduced a new code book, 'Thank God, I shan't have any more of that damned stuff!'[106]

Not merely was Room 40 not allowed to send intelligence direct to commanders at sea: it was also denied the information it needed to interpret fully the signals it decrypted. Not until Room 40 was fully incorporated into the Naval Intelligence Division (NID) as ID25 in 1917 was it allowed the flagged charts where enemy naval movements were plotted.

The Admiralty's failure to make adequate use of Room 40 arguably denied the Royal Navy victory at the Battle of Jutland on 31 May and 1 June 1916, the greatest naval battle of the war, when, writes Professor Keith Jeffery, 'the most powerful and technologically advanced fighting machines of the age engaged in a distinctly old-fashioned way which would have been broadly familiar to Nelson a century before'.[107] The plan of the new German commander-in-chief, Admiral Reinhard Scheer, was to lure part of the Grand Fleet into battle, then suddenly confront it with the whole of the High Sea Fleet. On 30 May, Room 40 decrypted signals revealing Scheer's intention to put to sea early next day. The Admiralty's handling of SIGINT, however, served to undermine the confidence in Room 40 of both Jellicoe, the commander-in-chief of the Grand Fleet, and Beatty, commander of the battle cruiser squadron at Rosyth. On the morning of 31 May Admiral Jackson made one of his rare visits to Room 40 to ask the meaning of the German call-sign 'DK'. He gave no explanation for his question and was told that it was the call-sign of Admiral Scheer. Had he enquired further or explained his question, he would have been told that when Scheer went to sea he used a different call-sign and transferred DK to the Wilhelmshaven wireless station in an attempt to conceal his movements. But Jackson left Room 40 without this information and so misread an intercepted signal from Wilhelmshaven bearing the call-sign DK to mean that Scheer had yet to put to sea. Soon after midday the Admiralty sent Jellicoe and Beatty the disastrously erroneous signal: 'At 12 noon our directional stations place the German fleet flagship [at its Baltic base] in the Jade.' The news deprived Jellicoe of any sense of urgency as he steamed south from Scapa Flow to rendezvous with Beatty; he stopped en route to inspect neutral ships to make sure they were not enemy scouts. When Beatty made contact with the German fleet at 2.20 p.m., Jellicoe was still seventy miles away. Beatty, however, was confident of victory. He believed himself faced only with Hipper's battle cruisers and that Scheer had yet to put to sea. The battle began badly. In little more than half an hour two of his battle cruisers, their magazines unprotected against flash, had been sunk and his flagship badly damaged. Then, unexpectedly, the battleships of the High Seas Fleet appeared on the horizon and the nature of the battle changed. Turning north, apparently in flight, Beatty succeeded in luring Scheer towards the whole of the Grand Fleet. Suddenly, Scheer found himself outnumbered and the Royal Navy in sight of victory.[108]

Jellicoe, however, was acutely aware that he was, in Churchill's words, 'the only man on either side who could lose the war in an afternoon', and deeply conscious of the threat to the Grand Fleet from enemy torpedoes. Twice during the Battle of Jutland the hail of fire from the Grand Fleet forced Scheer to break off the engagement and turn his fleet away. On both occasions a determined pursuit *might* have led to a decisive British victory. Each time Jellicoe refused a pursuit because of the danger of torpedo attack. When night fell on 31 May, Jellicoe still lay between the High Seas Fleet and its Baltic base, and hoped for victory on the following day. Scheer, however, had two alternative routes back to base. Tragically, Jellicoe chose to cover the wrong one. Part of the blame lies with Jellicoe himself. Even with the information he possessed, he might have deduced that Scheer was heading for home, under cover of darkness, by the Horn Reef passage off the coast of Denmark.[109] A much greater share of the blame, however, belongs to the Admiralty. Room 40 produced a series of decrypts identifying Scheer's escape route, but most of this crucial intelligence was not passed on to Jellicoe. The one intercept pointing to the Horn Reef passage which was passed on to Jellicoe (at 10.41 p.m.) failed to impress him, partly because a slightly earlier signal from the Admiralty (at 9.58 p.m.) had given a position which he knew to be inaccurate, but mainly because his confidence in Admiralty intelligence had been badly undermined by the disastrously mistaken signal earlier in the day that Scheer was still in port. 'What am I to think', Beatty later demanded, '. . . when I get that telegram and in three hours time meet the whole German fleet well out at sea?' Jellicoe insisted that the failure to send him all the SIGINT identifying Scheer's escape route was 'absolutely fatal': 'It is impossible to understand this extraordinary omission on the part of the Admiralty Staff, but there can be no doubt whatever that the escape of the High Seas Fleet from being engaged at daylight off the Horn Reef was due to this neglect.'[110]

In the aftermath of Jutland, the Admiralty's main intelligence priority was to discover how much damage had been done to the High Seas Fleet during the battle. SIGINT could not supply the answer; there were no German damage assessments to intercept. For probably the first time in the war at sea, espionage was able to provide naval intelligence of major importance which was beyond the reach of Room 40. MI1c's most successful wartime agent, Karl Krüger, a naval engineer codenamed TR/16, was able to provide the answer. Krüger had offered his services to the British legation in The Hague in November and was recruited as an agent by Cumming's representative in Rotterdam, Richard Tinsley. His motives were a mixture of avarice and desire for revenge. According to a post-war SIS report, he worked for 'very large sums of money, for which he is still always greedy'. It also emerged that, while serving in the German navy, Krüger had 'insulted a relative of the Kaiser', after which he was 'courtmartialled and degraded, thereby becoming very embittered against his country'. His sixty surviving wartime reports show that he toured, and reported on, German shipyards about once a month from May 1915 to January 1919. Between 3 and 20

June, in the aftermath of Jutland, he visited ten shipyards, including Kiel, Bremen, Rostock and Danzig. Hall praised Krüger's comprehensive damage assessment as '100%'. Krüger reported that eight capital ships would be out of action for at least three months.[111]* A second MI1c agent, D.15, who operated out of Denmark, produced further detail, including remarkably accurate estimates of German casualties.†

The success of Krüger and D.15 highlights the weakness of wartime security in German shipyards by comparison with those in Britain. Port security in the neutral United States was even weaker. In the early hours of 30 July 1916 German saboteurs achieved their greatest success of the war in the Black Tom railroad yard opposite the Statue of Liberty in New York harbour. A barge packed with fifty tons of TNT and sixty-nine railroad freight cars containing more than 1,000 tons of ammunition, all awaiting shipment to the Allies, were destroyed in an explosion which was the equivalent of an earthquake measuring up to 5.5 on the Richter scale – the biggest before 9/11. Thousands of plate-glass windows from skyscrapers in Brooklyn and Manhattan cascaded into the streets. The blast also blew out most windows in Jersey City. The torch of the Statue of Liberty was badly damaged; the interior staircase, which visitors had hitherto been able to climb to enjoy a spectacular view, was later closed.[112]

The success of German sabotage operations made glaringly obvious the weakness of American counter-espionage. Both Lansing and Frank L. Polk, the State Department counsellor responsible for intelligence, had a far better grasp than the President of the problems caused both by the inadequate resources of the Bureau of Investigation and the Secret Service and by the sometimes bitter rivalry between the two. In the summer of 1916 Lansing made Polk head of a new unit, later known as U-1, to coordinate intelligence gathering by acting as 'the "Clearing House" or at least the repository of information gathered from various sources'. As Lansing later told Wilson, the Bureau and the Secret Service were 'willing to report to the State Department but not each other'. Wilson could not bring himself either to tackle the problem of intelligence coordination personally or to delegate it to Lansing. The Secretary of State's stuffy, bureaucratic manner increasingly grated on the President. As one of Lansing's critics complained, it seemed that he 'worked at being dull'. Wilson acted largely as his own Secretary of State and showed greater confidence in the

* The most successful British spy of the First World War, Krüger was not detected by the Germans until 1939.
† D.15 estimated German casualties as 2,477 killed and 490 wounded; the final official figures were 2,551 and 507 respectively. (Jeffery, *1916*, loc. 2299.)

inexperienced diplomacy of Colonel House than in the State Department and US missions abroad. Lansing's understanding of the problems of intelligence collection and assessment, however, while it did not approach that of George Washington, greatly exceeded that of Wilson and House.[113]

The climax of German sabotage operations in the United States with the Black Tom attack in July 1916 coincided with the bloodiest British offensive of the war on the Somme. British military intelligence, whose organization was itself confused with divided responsibilities between the War Office and GHQ in France, was still poorly integrated with Cumming's MI1c, which was to play a major role on the Western Front during the final year of the war.[114] Sir Douglas (later Earl) Haig, who succeeded Sir John French as Commander-in-Chief on the Western Front at the end of 1915, had little grasp of how to integrate intelligence into his military planning. His own wishful thinking became a substitute for serious intelligence assessment both before and during the Battle of the Somme. In a staff lecture at GHQ in February 1916, Haig's intelligence chief, Brigadier John Charteris, placed 'the desire to please' as first among the 'great pitfalls that every Intelligence Officer must avoid'. He failed to heed his own advice. James Marshall-Cornwall, who served under Charteris, was alarmed by his 'breezy optimism'. His intelligence summaries 'seemed intended to bolster up our own morale rather than to paint a true picture of the enemy's strength and fighting qualities'.[115] Though Charteris did not consciously fabricate intelligence, he tended to tell Haig what he wanted to hear.[116] At the beginning of the Battle of the Somme on 1 July, there were six divisions in the German reserve, all with satisfactory morale, facing the British sector on the Western Front. Charteris reported that there were only three divisions, all with poor morale.[117] Serious underestimation of German reserves continued to distort GHQ intelligence assessment until the end of September.[118]

When the Battle of the Somme began, by far the ablest group of British intelligence officers in theatre were stationed not at GHQ in France but at the Arab Bureau in Cairo. The Bureau's success shows what could have been achieved in France with better leadership and personnel. The head of the Arab Bureau, Brigadier-General Gilbert F. Clayton, a veteran of the Egyptian Army, had, in high degree, the qualities of imagination and openness to new ideas which Charteris lacked. The Bureau's most famous member, T. E. Lawrence, who had begun his career as an Oxford archaeologist, wrote of Clayton in his classic memoir, *Seven Pillars of Wisdom*:

> Clayton made the perfect leader for such a band of wild men as we were.
> He was calm, detached, clear-sighted, of unconscious courage in assuming

responsibility. He gave an open run to his subordinates. His own views were general, like his knowledge: and he worked by influence rather than by loud direction. It was not easy to descry his influence. He was like water, or permeating oil, creeping silently and insistently through everything. It was not possible to say where Clayton was and was not, and how much really belonged to him.[119]

The Bureau's intelligence officers tended to be unorthodox rather than 'wild': a creatively eclectic mix from both civilian and military backgrounds with a remarkable range of regional and professional expertise, including archaeology, politics, journalism, Turkish forces, the Sudan Service and the Royal Engineers.[120] As well as being supplied with better imagery than GHQ in France, thanks to the clear skies of the Middle East, from 1916 the Bureau also had better SIGINT, due partly to the weakness of Turkish ciphers. Late in 1916 Admiral Sir Rosslyn Wemyss, Commander-in-Chief of the Royal Navy East Indies and Egypt station, assured the Admiralty that SIGINT would provide ample warning of any Turkish advance, 'as a large number of enemy W/T [wireless] messages transmitted by Stations in Sinai and Arabia are intercepted by us and the Military stations and deciphered by the [Cairo Military] Intelligence Department. The news thus obtained is of great value.'[121]

In collaboration with Military Intelligence in Cairo, the Arab Bureau collated and analysed imagery, SIGINT, and human and open-source intelligence, produced daily intelligence bulletins, and wrote intelligence assessments for interdepartmental and government distribution.[122] These gave greater emphasis to political intelligence, as well as including a longer-term perspective, than the reports sent to Haig. The Bureau's most celebrated secret intelligence report was *The Arab Bulletin*, which it issued several times a month to twenty-five senior recipients, including the Foreign Office, Admiralty, Director of Military Intelligence (War Office), the Secretary of the Foreign Department (India), the Sirdar of the Egyptian Army (Khartoum), the High Commissioner of Egypt and other senior officials in the Middle East. Its unofficial audience was probably far wider.[123] The issues of *The Arab Bulletin* were both the most readable and most scholarly intelligence reports produced in either the First World War or any previous war. The archaeologist D. G. Hogarth, who, like Lawrence, was one of the early editors, wrote in 1917:

Since it was as easy to write it in decent English as in bad, and much more agreeable, the Arab Bulletin had from the first a literary tinge not always present in Intelligence Summaries. Firstly, it aims at giving reasoned, and as far as possible definitive summaries of intelligence, primarily about the

Hejaz and the area of the Arab Revolt. Secondly, the Arab Bulletin aims at giving authoritative appreciations of political situations and questions in the area with which it deals at first hand. Thirdly, it aims at recording and so preserving all fresh historical data concerning Arabs and Arabic-speaking lands, and incidentally rescuing from oblivion any older facts which might help to explain the actual situation: likewise, any data of geographical or other scientific interest, which may be brought to light by our penetration of the Arab Countries during the present war. It is part of the Editor's purpose that a complete file on the Bulletin since its beginning should be indispensable to anyone who hereafter may have to compile for official use a history of the Arabs during the last three years, an Intelligence Handbook of any Arab district or even a map of Arabia.[124]

Hogarth, wrote Lawrence, was 'our untiring historian', who 'brought us the parallels and lessons of history'.[125] Lawrence reported in November 1916: 'Again and again I have heard from [the Bedouin] about acts of the early Arabs or things that the Sherif and his sons have said which contain all that the exalted Arab patriot would wish. They intend to restore the Sh[a]ria . . .'[126]

The Arab Bureau was sometimes remarkably frank in criticizing other Allied intelligence agencies with whom it disagreed. Lawrence, for example, described the head of the British Intelligence Department in Basra as 'very excellent but he has never been to Turkey, or read about it, and he knows no Arabic. This would not necessarily matter, but unfortunately his staff do not supply the necessary knowledge.'[127] Unsurprisingly, the frankness of the Arab Bureau in 'telling truth to power' and its commitment to the Arab Revolt made it enemies in the Indian government, the Mesopotamian military administration, the Egyptian high command and the India Office in London.[128] Though *The Arab Bulletin* went to the DMI at the War Office, there is no evidence that either Haig or Charteris ever saw a copy.* They would have been unlikely to approve of it.

The ability of German military intelligence to intercept British field telephone messages – probably its most important operational intelligence on the Western Front – helped to deny Haig the element of surprise on which he had been counting before the start of the Somme offensive. A good-luck message from General Henry Rawlinson was intercepted on the eve of the attack.[129] On 1 July 1916 British troops, weighed down by sixty-six-pound packs, advanced at walking pace in even lines towards the enemy trenches,

---

* There is, for example, no reference to the Arab Bureau or any of its members in Beach, *Haig's Intelligence.*

presenting German machine-gunners with their best target of the war. As one line of troops was cut down, so others came on, regularly spaced at intervals of a hundred yards. At the end of the first day's fighting, the British had lost almost 60,000 killed or wounded, more than on any other day in the history of the British army, more too than the losses suffered by any other army on any day of the First World War. Haig seemed unable to grasp the extent of the catastrophe. He wrote in his diary on the following day, 'The enemy has undoubtedly been severely shaken. Our correct course, therefore, is to press him hard with the least possible delay.' A fortnight later, despite continuing heavy losses, Haig's optimism was undimmed. He described the fighting on 14 July as 'the best day we have had in this war'.[130] When the battle ended four and a half months later amid a wilderness of mud, although the front line had here and there advanced about five miles, some of the objectives set by Haig for the first day's fighting had still to be achieved. Comforting himself with inflated intelligence estimates of enemy casualties, however, he persuaded himself that he had fought a successful battle of attrition. 'The results of the Somme', he wrote, 'fully justify confidence in our ability to master the enemy's power of resistance.'

Both Charteris and Haig were, however, horrified by the failures of their communications security revealed during the offensive by captured German intelligence documents which included transcripts of intercepted messages sent by British field telephones. Charteris claimed, possibly with some exaggeration, that the Germans had obtained an 'extraordinary amount of information from this source' which had helped them resist the British offensive.[131] A summary of POW interrogations in September 1916 reported that 'special personnel who are good linguists', identified by the letter T on their epaulettes, listened in to British telephone calls: 'These men are kept well behind the lines to reduce the possibility of capture. A prisoner also said that the use of telephones, except for urgent messages, is forbidden during alternate hours so as to facilitate the hearing of [British] messages.'[132]

Field Marshal Sir William Robertson, Chief of the Imperial General Staff (CIGS), had warned Haig on 29 July 1916 that some ministers were 'beginning to get a little uneasy' about the numbers of British casualties, and 'persist[ed] in asking me whether I think a loss of say, 300,000 men will lead to really good results because if not we ought to be content with something less'.[133] In an attempt to limit ministerial criticism, Robertson restricted the flow to the Cabinet of bad news and pessimistic intelligence about the Battle of the Somme. Lloyd George, who became Secretary of State for War in July, complained to Haig in October that the 'Gen. Staff at the War Office don't let him know *everything* but only feed him with what *they think* is suitable for him to know'.[134]

Robertson's ability to decide what should or should not reach the Prime Minister and the Cabinet owed much to Asquith's personal lack of interest in intelligence. Though his pre-war government had founded the Secret Service Bureau, whose home and foreign departments, headed by Kell and Cumming, became MI5 and MI1c (later SIS or MI6), as wartime Prime Minister Asquith showed no interest in meeting either. Like all his ministers except Churchill, who had to resign in May 1915 after the blunders of the Gallipoli expedition, Asquith was almost totally ignorant of British intelligence history. He had no idea, for example, that Walsingham had seen Elizabeth I and Burghley almost every day during the wars with Spain,[135] or that, during a critical phase in the French Revolutionary Wars, Pitt the Younger's intelligence chief, William Wickham, had frequently called on Pitt late at night in his London home to deliver the latest intelligence, 'often . . . in his dressing room, more than once in his Bedroom'.[136] Asquith's only known meeting with an intelligence chief was with Hall late in 1914 after an MP discovered that Hall, without ministerial authority, had organized the opening of foreign mail, including his own, on security grounds. Hall said later that, while meeting the Prime Minister at Number 10, 'I could not rid myself of the idea that I was witnessing some strange kind of stage play. Things had suddenly become unreal.'[137] Though Asquith accepted the case for wartime postal censorship, neither then nor later did he show any interest in discussing intelligence with Hall. Had he grasped the importance of the rebirth of British codebreaking in Room 40 to the war effort after a gap of seventy years, he would surely have done so. But perhaps he was not even informed of it. There is no record of Asquith ever being shown a decrypt. On only one recorded occasion was he even informed of the contents of one of them. On 20 November 1916, less than three weeks before Asquith was succeeded at Number 10 by Lloyd George, Maurice (later Baron) Hankey, secretary of the War Committee (and soon to become Britain's first and longest-serving Cabinet Secretary), considered a German intercept containing what he believed was 'absolutely reliable but very secret information that the German Chancellor is trying to get American mediation' so important that he informed the Prime Minister of its contents.[138]

Had Churchill, then on the back benches after a period as lieutenant-colonel on the Western Front, still been a minister, there is no doubt that he would have challenged the accuracy of the military intelligence supplied by Robertson to Asquith's Cabinet during the Battle of the Somme. On 1 August, his friend the Attorney General, F. E. Smith, circulated to ministers a fierce attack (which he did not personally endorse) by Churchill on the futility of Haig's offensive, demanding that it be brought to an end:

'In *personnel* the results of the operation have been disastrous; in *terrain* they have been absolutely barren . . . From every point of view, therefore, the British offensive *per se* has been a great failure.' Robertson replied with possibly the most inaccurate intelligence supplied to the British government at any stage of the First World War. In the past month, he claimed, Germany had suffered 1.25 million casualties. In reality, during the entire four and a half months of the battle on the Somme, German casualties amounted to less than half a million.[139]

The fumbling use of intelligence by the Admiralty Operations Division during the Battle of Jutland and by GHQ in France during the Battle of the Somme was in stark contrast to 'Blinker' Hall's sophisticated, if sometimes unscrupulous, handling of it. In addition to overseeing naval codebreaking in Room 40 after the departure of Ewing, Hall secured the leading role in the exploitation of both American and German diplomatic SIGINT. The decrypted US diplomatic telegrams came to him from the military SIGINT agency, MI1b, the War Office counterpart of Room 40. Originally known as MO5e, the unit had been tasked during the early war of movement with intercepting German army radio messages in collaboration with the French *Section du Chiffre*. When these radio messages dried up with the beginning of trench warfare, MI1b concentrated instead on attempting to decrypt American diplomatic traffic between Washington and Europe, to which it had virtually complete access. Though US codes and ciphers were relatively weak, its codebreakers made slow progress. As MI1b's official history acknowledges: 'The work was entirely fresh to all members of the staff, there were no past records as guidance, and the problem of how to solve large code books had to be thought out ab initio.'[140] The official history does not mention, however, that MI1b's slow progress was also due to the fact that it felt unable to seek the help of the more experienced *Section du Chiffre* in attacking the codes and ciphers of the neutral United States as it had done when intercepting enemy messages.

By the end of 1915 the attack on US codes and ciphers had finally succeeded.* Though the codebreakers of MI1b and Room 40 refused to collaborate until the spring of 1917 as a result of what Denniston later condemned as 'mere official jealousy',[141] Hall was supplied with copies of MI1b's US decrypts. The most important of the early decrypts were

---

* The earliest surviving decrypt of a US diplomatic telegram, dated 25 September 1915, is incomplete. The next decrypts to survive, from January 1916, are both complete and accurate – evidence that the codebreakers had fully resolved the problems they had encountered a few months earlier. (Larsen, 'British Intelligence and American Neutrality', ch. 3.)

reports by President Wilson's main foreign-policy adviser, Colonel Edward M. House, on his attempts to persuade the British, French and German governments to agree to a peace conference. House spent almost two months early in 1916 in shuttle diplomacy between London (his main port of call), Paris and Berlin. Hall, who strongly opposed the peace conference proposal, made selective and unscrupulous use of the decrypts to undermine House's efforts. Hankey wrote after Hall had shown him some of the decrypts, 'This information is of course priceless.'[142]

Late in 1916, with Hall's knowledge (and, no doubt, approval), the MI1c head of station in the United States, Sir William Wiseman, a former Cambridge boxing blue, had succeeded in establishing himself as a confidant of Colonel House. At his first meeting with House, on 17 December, Wiseman impressed him as 'the most imp[ortan]t caller I have had for some time'. Knowing that the Republican sympathies and indiscreet wit of the ambassador, Sir Cecil Spring Rice, had made him unpopular with Wilson, Wiseman set out to supplant him as the most influential British representative in the United States by boldly misrepresenting his true role. Seduced by Wiseman's charm and ancient baronetcy, House naïvely concluded that Wiseman was well qualified to become a direct channel of communication with the government of David Lloyd George which had taken power ten days before their first meeting. House wrote to Wilson on 26 January 1917:

> [Wiseman] told me, in the *gravest confidence*, a thing which I had already suspected and that is that he is in direct communication with the Foreign Office, and that the Ambassador and other members of the Embassy are not aware of it.
>
> I am happy beyond measure at this latest conference with him, for I judge that he reflects the views of his government.

In reality, so far from Wiseman being a spokesman for the British government, Lloyd George and most (perhaps all) of his ministers were as yet unaware of his existence. Wiseman was not, as he claimed, 'in direct communication with the Foreign Office'. Instead he reported to Mansfield Cumming, chief of MI1c, who passed on to the Foreign Office and other Whitehall ministries whatever intelligence he judged appropriate. Having won over House by a mixture of charm and deception, Wiseman then used House's confidence in him to persuade Whitehall that he could provide a direct link with the White House. A later SIS head of station in the United States during the early 1950s, John Bruce Lockhart, believed that Wiseman was arguably Britain's 'most successful agent of influence' in, and perhaps beyond, the first half of the twentieth century.[143]

As well as deceiving House and Wilson about his role in the United

States, Wiseman also directed an imaginative array of covert operations of which both would have strongly disapproved. Among the most imaginative was the success of Wiseman's deputy in New York, Norman Thwaites, during a Long Island house party in stealing a photograph showing the German ambassador, Count Johann Heinrich von Bernstorff, with his arms round two young women in bathing costumes. Though the photograph was innocent, Thwaites quickly grasped its propaganda value. It was taken to New York, copied and returned to the owner's photograph album before she had noticed its absence. Thwaites then arranged for an enlarged copy of the apparently compromising photo to be prominently displayed in the office of the Russian ambassador, thus exposing Bernstorff to ridicule in the Washington diplomatic corps. According to Thwaites: 'poor Bernstorff heard of it promptly and cursed the Muscovite, quite definitely of the opinion that some rascally secret servant in Russian pay had purloined the picture.' When the photo appeared in the press, House and Wilson probably assumed the source was the Russian embassy.[144]

The greatest obstacle faced by Wiseman in attempting to win the confidence of House and Wilson during the early months of the Lloyd George government was the new Prime Minister's angry reaction to American decrypts. Since becoming Secretary of State for War in June 1916, Lloyd George had developed an active, though initially poorly informed, interest in SIGINT. He jumped to the erroneous conclusion, after reading a decrypt in late September, that the Americans and Germans were working together against the British interest to make a peace proposal. Without mentioning the President by name, Lloyd George promptly gave an interview to an American journalist warning Wilson not to interfere: 'There can be no outside interference at this stage.' 'The fight', Lloyd George announced, 'must be to a finish – to a knockout.' To make sure that Wilson, then in the middle of a presidential election campaign, got the message, he arranged for the text of the interview to be delivered directly to the White House. Lord Grey, the Foreign Secretary, was one of a number of ministers who responded furiously to the interview. Lloyd George replied by producing a copy of the US decrypt he had misinterpreted. 'I wonder whether you are still of the same opinion after reading M.I.1[b]'s secret information?' he wrote to Grey.[145]

Though Lloyd George did not reveal the decrypt to the Commons, he hinted to MPs that his warning to the United States had been prompted by secret intelligence. 'Members pricked their ears and waited for revelations from secret history', reported the *Daily Mail*, 'but Mr. Lloyd George had only whetted their appetite without satisfying it.' Lloyd George gave the editor of the *Manchester Guardian* a clearer hint of the nature of the intelligence on which he had acted. He had, he said, 'documentary evidence' that the Germans had made 'a proposal to Wilson that he should propose mediation'. Within days of his becoming Prime Minister, two more American decrypts, misinterpreted by Lloyd George, who did not understand their context, convinced him that Germany and the U.S. were still conspiring together. Privately, Lloyd George denounced Wilson's peace proposal of 20 December as a 'German move'. 'They knew, absolutely knew', Lloyd George told the editor of the *Manchester* Guardian, 'that it was put forward at the inspiration' of Germany. Though Lloyd George was persuaded not to give an angry response in public, he remained deeply mistrustful of Wilson.[146]

Hall had hitherto concealed Room 40's success in breaking German codes and ciphers from the Americans for fear of alerting them to the vulnerability of their own communications. He must have feared that Lloyd George's indiscretions were already in danger of doing so. On the morning of 17 January 1917, however, Hall found himself faced with a difficult dilemma. One of his leading cryptanalysts, the Old Etonian publisher Nigel de Grey, who had been working the night shift, dramatically enquired of Hall: 'Do you want to bring the Americans into the war?' 'Yes, my boy', replied Hall. 'Why?' 'I think I've got something here for you', said de Grey, and handed Hall an incomplete decrypt of an intercepted telegram from the German Foreign Minister, Arthur Zimmermann, to the Washington embassy for onward transmission to Mexico City.

The Zimmermann telegram, as it became known, contained a German offer of alliance with Mexico if war broke out between Germany and the United States, which would include a German 'undertaking that Mexico is to recover the lost territory in Texas, New Mexico and Arizona'. Because of its importance the telegram was transmitted from Berlin by both the 'Swedish roundabout' and the American transatlantic cable. By an unprecedented diplomatic impertinence, the United States had been hoodwinked into providing one of the channels through which Germany hoped to persuade Mexico to enter the war against it. Hall quickly recognized the potential risks as well as the advantages of publicizing the decrypt. If Washington realized that Britain had been tapping the US transatlantic cable and intercepting American as well as German diplomatic traffic, the Zimmermann telegram might lead not to a triumph for Room 40 but to a spectacular intelligence disaster. Before the intercept could be used to enrage the Wilson administration and American opinion, therefore, Hall had to devise a method of disguising its origins.[147]

For almost three weeks Hall kept the secret of the Zimmermann telegram to himself and Room 40 – in the hope that the United States might enter the war without the telegram being publicized. On 1 February 1917

Germany began unrestricted U-boat warfare. In response Wilson broke off diplomatic relations with Germany two days later but declared his hope that peace could still be preserved. On the 5th Hall cabled Gaunt in New York 'to try and get copies of all telegrams from German Embassy Washington to German Minister Mexico since Jan. 18th'. Hall's main aim was to get the version of the Zimmermann telegram which had arrived in Mexico City in order to conceal the fact that British intelligence had intercepted it en route.[148]* He was successful in doing so. Gaunt passed on his request to the British consul-general in Mexico City, Edward Thurstan, who obtained copies of German diplomatic telegrams from a source in the telegraph office.† Also on 5 February, probably soon after telegraphing Gaunt, Hall at last presented himself at the Foreign Office with a not quite complete decrypt of the Zimmermann telegram. On 19 February, assisted by the copy of the Zimmermann telegram obtained from Mexico City, Room 40 produced a complete version of what was to become the best-publicized decrypt in intelligence history:

19.1.17

We intend to begin on the first of February unrestricted submarine warfare.

We shall endeavour in spite of this to keep the U.S.A. neutral. In the event of this not succeeding we make Mexico a proposal of alliance on the following terms:-

Make war together.

Make peace together.

Generous financial support and an undertaking on our part that Mexico is to reconquer the lost territory in Texas, New Mexico and Arizona. The settlement in detail is left to you.

You will inform the [Mexican] President of the above most secretly as soon as the outbreak of war with U.S.A. is certain, and add the suggestion that he should on his own initiative invite Japan to immediate adherence and at the same time mediate between Japan and ourselves.

Please call the President's attention to the fact that the ruthless employment of our submarines now offers the prospect of compelling England in a few months to make peace.

ZIMMERMANN

* The German legation in Mexico City, Hall correctly believed, did not possess the more difficult variant of the diplomatic code employed by Berlin in messages to the Washington embassy. The version of the telegram forwarded to the Mexico City legation, he believed, also correctly, would thus prove easier for Room 40 to decrypt in its entirety.
† Thurstan is often referred to as the British envoy in Mexico City. *The London Gazette* for 23 November 1915 identifies him as consul-general. He probably also worked for MI1c.

A few hours after receiving the decrypt, Hall rang Eddie Bell at the US embassy. Bell arrived at the Admiralty half an hour later to read the Zimmermann telegram. Hall said later that he had rarely seen anyone 'blow off steam in so forthright a manner': 'Mexico to "reconquer the lost territory"! Texas and Arizona? Why not Illinois and New York while they were at it?' After briefly raising and abandoning the possibility that the telegram might be a hoax, Bell asked if it was to be given officially to the United States government. That, said Hall, had still to be decided by the Foreign Office. He failed to tell Bell that Lord Hardinge, the PUS, disliked the idea of admitting that the British government engaged in codebreaking, even in wartime.[149]

Recent research by Dr Dan Larsen shows that Lloyd George almost sabotaged Hall's plan to exploit the Zimmermann telegram by warning Page that his diplomatic correspondence with Washington was known to the British. In February 1917, Page went to 10 Downing Street to deliver

Part of the Zimmermann telegram as decrypted by Room 40. Because 'Arizona' did not appear in the German naval codebook, it had to be split into phonetic syllables.

a lengthy message from Washington, containing a number of questions. Before Page had time to put the questions, Lloyd George interrupted him with a long speech that 'answered every question [Page] had prepared to ask him' – leaving the ambassador somewhat bewildered. When Page later returned to Downing Street with another message from Wilson, Lloyd George could not resist the temptation to show off again, and said he had already seen Wilson's message. The Prime Minister claimed that the message had leaked in Washington. Page wrote in a draft report to Wilson: '[Lloyd George] knows that news of your instructions to me got out at Washington somehow and was telegraphed here by someone in the British Embassy or in the British spy service. Although this implies a compliment to their [spy] service, he is afraid that other persons also may hear of it.' Since Page now knew that the British had broken German codes, the obvious implication was that they had broken US codes as well.[150] Page, however, was a passionate Anglophile and believed Hall was 'a clear case of genius'. Aware of the damage Lloyd George's revelation that Britain had intercepted his communications with the President would do to British–American relations, perhaps even to the prospect of the United States entering the war, Page suppressed it. He never sent his report to the President, crossed out the text, and placed the document in his personal files, where it remained undiscovered for almost a century.[151] The most likely explanation for Lloyd George's extraordinary indiscretion is unfamiliarity with intelligence. Until he became Prime Minister, he had probably never seen intercepts and may well have been uncertain how they were obtained. He understood less about SIGINT on taking office than, among other British political leaders, Lord Burghley, Oliver Cromwell, Walpole, Pitt the Elder and Pitt the Younger.

Lloyd George seems never to have been consulted about the use to be made of the Zimmermann telegram. His Foreign Secretary, Arthur Balfour, who had got to know Hall and Room 40 as First Lord of the Admiralty in the previous Cabinet, overrode Lord Hardinge's objections to passing the telegram to the US government. 'I think Captain Hall may be left to clinch this problem', he told the PUS. 'He knows the ropes better than anyone.' Lengthy discussions followed at the US embassy between Hall, Bell and Page. The ambassador insisted that if the Foreign Secretary would personally present him with a copy of the telegram, the impact on the President would be greatly heightened. Balfour's patrician calm was rarely ruffled. But, when he received Page at the Foreign Office on 23 February, he found it difficult to suppress his excitement, later recalling that handing the telegram to Page was 'as dramatic a moment as I remember in all my life'.[152]

On reading the telegram on Sunday, 25 February, Wilson was as shocked and angry as Hall and Page had hoped he would be. At the very moment when he had been negotiating in good faith with Germany on ways to bring the war to an end, Germany had simultaneously been trying to entice Mexico into attacking the United States. But his handling of the decrypt over the next few days shows how strange, and even bewildering, he found his first experience of SIGINT. As an experienced user of SIGINT, George Washington would have found it easier to cope. Wilson's first instinct on 25 February was to publish the Zimmermann telegram at once. By the time his Secretary of State, Lansing, returned to Washington, after a short holiday, on Tuesday the 27th, the President had had second thoughts. He told Lansing he had been wondering how the telegram could actually have reached Bernstorff in Washington, and was now 'a little uncertain as to its authenticity'. Lansing reminded Wilson that Berlin had been allowed to communicate with its Washington embassy via the US transatlantic cable and explained how the telegram had been sent first to Bernstorff, then forwarded by him to Mexico City. Wilson several times exclaimed 'Good Lord!' during Lansing's explanation but was convinced by it. On 28 February he decided that the telegram should be published in the following day's papers.

The publication of the Zimmermann telegram on 1 March created an even greater sensation than the German invasion of Belgium or the sinking of the *Lusitania*. 'No other event of the war', writes Arthur S. Link, 'so

The publication of the Zimmermann telegram turned SIGINT for the first time into front-page news on both sides of the Atlantic.

stunned the American people.' Partly because of previous revelations of German sabotage and other covert action, most newspaper readers assumed the telegram was authentic. All doubt was removed on 3 March by Zimmermann himself. 'I cannot deny it', he admitted. 'It is true.' Lansing heard the news 'with profound amazement and relief . . . By admitting the truth he blundered in a most astonishing manner for a man engaged in international intrigues. Of course the message itself was a stupid piece of business, but admitting it was far worse.' Zimmermann, like Wilson, was bewildered by his first experience of SIGINT and found it difficult to know how to respond to it. Had he claimed that the telegram was a British forgery and that Britain was illegally intercepting US communications, Britain would have found it difficult to refute his claim. Many German-Americans and other opponents of US entry into the war would have believed him. Zimmermann's admission, however, cut the ground from beneath their feet.[153]

In both London and Cairo, cryptanalysts were anxious that the worldwide publicity given to the Zimmermann telegram should not undermine the secrecy of British codebreaking. The publication of the telegram coincided with SIGINT of major importance in the Middle East, where GHQ Egyptforce intercepted a Turkish radio message from Constantinople ordering the Hejaz Expeditionary Force (HEF) to evacuate Medina. The GOC Egyptforce, Sir Archibald Murray, telegraphed the CIGS, Sir William Robertson, at the War Office: 'It is now quite obvious that the Turkish campaign in Arabia has failed, and that the Hejaz Expeditionary Force is about to be withdrawn to Palestine.' Probably with the Zimmermann telegram in mind, Murray insisted on the need to keep the interception of Turkish military radio communications absolutely secret and ensure that no premature announcement of the HEF's withdrawal appear in Parliament or the press. Murray even asked the Egyptian High Commissioner, Sir Reginald Wingate, not to reveal the Turkish decrypts to the Foreign Office – probably fearing that it might treat them as indiscreetly as the Zimmermann telegram. If it was absolutely necessary for the Foreign Office to be informed, Robertson should do so under conditions of the greatest possible secrecy. 'For obvious reasons', Murray added, 'I have not told the French.'[154]*

To Hall's delight (and possibly Murray's relief), much of the American press gave the credit for obtaining the Zimmermann telegram to US secret agents rather than to British codebreakers. Hall had 'no little fun' covering the tracks of Room 40 by deceiving American journalists in London. Much of the 'fun' centred on a trunk of Swedish diplomatic documents on board the ship that had brought Bernstorff across the Atlantic after

---

* The HEF commander proved reluctant to withdraw as rapidly as he had been instructed.

the breach of German–American diplomatic relations in February. Hall spread rumours that the trunk contained some of Bernstorff's secret papers. He wrote gleefully to Guy Gaunt in New York:

> [The journalists] are quite convinced that the American Secret Service abstracted the Zimmermann telegram from the trunk ... They tackled me yesterday about it, and I had to admit that all the evidence pointed to the seals having been broken before we opened the chest. It is a very safe line and I think we will stick to it.

Wilson's address to a joint session of Congress on 2 April 1917, calling for a declaration of war on Germany, was one of the great speeches of American political history. It is best remembered for Wilson's vision of a post-war world 'made safe for democracy' with peace 'planted upon the tested foundations of political liberty'. The responsibility for American entry into the war lay with 'Germany's irresponsible government which has thrown aside all considerations of humanity and is running amok'. Proof that Germany was 'running amok' included its intelligence operations in the United States:

> One of the things that has served to convince us that the Prussian autocracy was not and could never be our friend is that from the very outset of the present war it has filled our unsuspecting communities and even our offices of government with spies and set criminal intrigues everywhere afoot against our national unity of counsel, our peace within and without, our industries and our commerce. Indeed it is now evident that its spies were here before the war began ... That it means to stir up enemies at our very doors the intercepted note to the German Minister in Mexico is eloquent evidence.

Even without the Zimmermann telegram, the United States would doubtless have declared war on Germany. But Hall and Room 40 had accelerated the decision to do so and helped Americans to go to war as a united nation, without significant protests from German-Americans and the neutralist lobby. On 6 April the United States declared war on Germany. That night Hall and de Grey celebrated with champagne.[155]

25

The First World War. Part 2:
From American Intervention
to Allied Victory

The spectacular public impact of the decrypted Zimmermann telegram won the DNI, 'Blinker' Hall, a knighthood. More important from the viewpoint of wartime intelligence, it also gained him for the first time direct control of the naval as well as the diplomatic section of Room 40.* In May 1917 Room 40 was formally incorporated into the Naval Intelligence Division (NID) as section 25 (ID25) under Commander William 'Bubbles' James, whose portrait was more widely and eccentrically displayed than that of any other intelligence chief in British history. The new head of ID25 owed his nickname to a portrait by his grandfather, the celebrated painter, Sir John Millais, which showed him as a child with golden curls, dressed in a green velvet suit watching seraphically as soap bubbles he had blown floated into the air. For many years an advertising campaign by Pears Soap, who had purchased the portrait, plastered this cherubic image of the new head of ID25 on billboards up and down the country.

Room 40's transformation into ID25 came at a critical moment in the naval war. In the spring of 1917 Britain seemed to have no answer to the unrestricted U-boat warfare which had begun in February. In April alone German U-boats sank 835,000 tons of Allied shipping. Jellicoe, now First Sea Lord, told Admiral Sims of the US navy: 'The Germans will win this war unless we can stop these losses – and stop them quickly.' Sims asked if there was any solution. 'Absolutely none that we can see now', Jellicoe replied. The solution Jellicoe failed to see was the convoy. When Germany began its all-out submarine offensive, opinion in both the Royal and Merchant Navies was still overwhelmingly against the convoy system. Beaverbrook's famous description

---

* There is no direct documentary evidence on the reasons for placing Room 40 under Hall's direct control in May 1917. But the date at which it happened surely indicates official recognition by Balfour, Hankey and others of Hall's brilliant handling of the Zimmermann telegram, in contrast to Oliver's and Jackson's confused use of German intercepts during the Battle of Jutland. See above, pp. 524ff.

of Lloyd George descending on the Admiralty on 30 April, seating himself in the First Lord's chair and ordering the introduction of the convoy system is doubtless overwritten. But the War Cabinet, urged on by Hankey, whom Lloyd George made the first Cabinet Secretary, saw sense before the admirals.[1]

Convoys did not defeat the U-boat menace overnight but they reduced it to manageable proportions. In the remaining eighteen months of the war, less than 1 per cent of ships in convoy were lost from any cause. Before May 1917 Room 40 had worked in almost total isolation both from NID's German Section (ID14), which collated intelligence on the German navy, and from the Enemy Submarines Section (E1), which kept track of the U-boats. As a post-war 'Naval Staff Appreciation' concluded, Room 40 could have supplied both ID14 and E1 with 'priceless information' but was not allowed to do so. All that changed with the foundation of ID25, whose intelligence was of particular importance to the Admiralty Convoy Section, founded in June 1917 to provide escorts and organize 'evasive routing' to steer convoys away from the U-boats: 'For the first time one could see the latest information as to enemy submarines side by side with the track of a convoy, and as the Commodore's ship was always equipped with wireless, it was possible to at once divert a convoy from a dangerous area.' As convoy losses fell, U-boat losses rose. In each of the first two quarters of 1917 ten U-boats were sunk; in the third and fourth quarters sinkings jumped to twenty-two and twenty-one, thanks in large part to the use of mines, depth charges and hydrophones (acoustic underwater listening devices).[2]

At the very moment when Germany was losing the Battle of the Atlantic, it was winning the war on the Eastern Front, conquering more territory than in any previous war in European history. Though the main reasons for the conquests were German military superiority and the disintegration of the Russian war effort, Hindenburg, Ludendorff and the German high command also implemented a covert strategy designed to destabilize the Russian Provisional Government and reduce Russia to revolutionary chaos. In March 1915 the German Treasury had approved an initial grant of two million marks 'for the support of Russian revolutionary propaganda', followed by another five million marks in July. The main channel for passing German money to the Bolsheviks was Alexander Helphand, a corrupt but ideologically driven revolutionary tycoon who seems to have laundered some of the secret German subsidies through an import–export company in neutral Copenhagen, the Handels og-Eksport Kompagniet. Probably the most obese Russian revolutionary, Helphand adopted in exile the new name Alexander Parvus ('Small').[3]

The most successful German subversion operation of the war was to transport Lenin back from exile in Switzerland though Germany in a 'sealed' train ('like a plague bacillus', said Churchill) to the Baltic ferry port of Sassnitz, whence he continued via Sweden and Finland to Petrograd in the spring of 1917.[4] The operation had the strong personal support of the Kaiser, who joked that Lenin and his Bolshevik comrades should be given copies of his speeches to take with them on their train journey.[5] In the view of both the high command and the German government, Lenin's 'revolutionary defeatism' was tantamount to acceptance of German victory. Cumming passed on to MI5 a report from an agent in Berne that the Germans had required Lenin to give a guarantee that he and all his fellow revolutionaries on the train, which left Zurich on 9 April, were 'partisans of an immediate peace'.[6] The detailed regulations for the train journey which Lenin imposed upon his fellow travellers, covering such issues as smoking and the use of lavatories, gave an early indication of the authoritarian one-party state which he was later to create in Russia.[7]

On 16 April (3 April by the Russian calendar) Lenin arrived to a tumultuous reception at the Finland Station in Petrograd, where he issued a call for 'worldwide socialist revolution'. Next day a German representative in Stockholm cabled Berlin: 'Lenin's entry into Russia successful. He is working exactly as we wish.' His 'April Theses', promulgated after his return to Petrograd, denounced the Provisional Government, which had replaced the Tsarist regime, demanded the dissolution of the regular army, and called for an immediate end to the war. Lenin dismissed any suggestion that he should have turned down the offer of German help to return to Petrograd as 'silly bourgeois prejudices': 'If the German capitalists are so stupid as to take us over to Russia, that's their funeral.'[8] The German covert operation to return Lenin to Petrograd changed the course of the Russian revolution. When Lenin returned, he found the Bolsheviks agreed on a policy of 'vigilant control' over, rather than outright opposition to, the Provisional Government, and contemplating cooperation with the rival Mensheviks. The first condition of the strategy which Lenin succeeded in imposing on his followers after his return was that, on the contrary, they should adopt a policy of total opposition to the government and refuse all cooperation with other parties. The revolutionary wisdom of this policy became clear in May when the Mensheviks and Socialist Revolutionaries joined the Provisional Government. While their rivals became increasingly compromised by the government's growing unpopularity, the Bolsheviks were able to claim that they alone had a revolutionary programme totally independent of the government.[9] Lenin had been in exile in London during the most important phase of the 1905 Revolution. But for German help

Ich bestätige.

1) dass die eingegangenen Bedingungen, die von Platten mit der deutschen Gesandtschaft getroffen wurden, mir bekannt gemacht worden sind;

2) dass ich mich den Anordnungen des Reiseführers Platten unterwerfe;

3) dass mir eine Mitteilung des "Petit Parisien" bekanntgegeben worden ist, wonach die russische provisorische Regierung die durch Deutschland Reisenden als Hochverräter zu behandeln drohe.

4) dass ich die ganze politische Verantwortlichkeit für diese Reise ausschliesslich auf mich nehme;

5) dass mir von Platten die Reise nur bis Stockholm garantiert worden ist.

Bern - Zürich, 9. April 1917.

1 Lenin.
2 Frau Lenin
3 Georg Safaroff
4 Valentina Safaroff — Mortotchkine
5 Gregor Ussijevitch
6 Helene Kon
7 Inès Armand
8 Nikolai Boskov.
   F. Grebelsky
8 A. Konstantinowitsch
   G. Mirinhoff
   M. Mirinhoff
9 A. Skowno
10 G. Zinoview
11 G. Radomyslski (und Sohn)
   G. Slussareff
12 D. Slletaninoff.

13 M. Kaumanuch
   G. Brillant
   D. Rosenblum
14 A. Abramovitch
   S. Scheinesohn
   Mi. Khar.
   H. Gobermann
15 M. Linde
   M. Aisenbud
   Prigorvskolo
   Souliachvili
16 Ravitsch
   Chantouff

he would have remained in exile in Zurich for most of 1917, probably unable to impose his will on his Russian followers.

While Lenin was demanding an end to the war, German military intelligence simultaneously set out to break the morale of Russian forces on the Eastern Front with a pioneering campaign of psychological warfare. Though both sides had earlier dropped leaflets over enemy lines, neither had attempted anything as ambitious as the Germans' propaganda offensive in 1917. The Foreign Ministry chose the propaganda themes: Germany wished for, but did not need, peace; the Russian Provisional Government, by contrast, was a British puppet, prolonging the war for the benefit of Western imperialists. The German army and its Habsburg ally developed innovative methods to disseminate this subversive message. Russian-speaking intelligence officers were posted in the front line to make contact with Russian units. At Easter, German commanders permitted unofficial ceasefires and fraternization along the front to give the impression of goodwill.[10] Russian soldiers were lured from their trenches with vodka (officially banned during the war), music, even 'makeshift brothels'.[11] German commanders were enthusiastic about the combined impact of revolutionary propaganda and psychological warfare on the Eastern Front. The 12th Infantry Division, for example, reported that 'the disintegration of the Russian Army through revolution is becoming widespread'.[12]

To counter German propaganda and Bolshevik influence, British intelligence embarked on less successful influence operations of its own in an attempt to keep Russia in the war. The chief organizer was Cumming's head of station in the United States, Sir William Wiseman, who used his close contacts with Colonel House to seek US support for a two-part operation: first, black propaganda 'to expose present German intrigues and their undoubted [in reality, non-existent] connection with the late reactionary [Tsarist] government'; second, a more straightforward attempt 'to persuade the Russians to attack the Germans with all their might and thus accomplish the overthrow of the Hohenzollern dynasty and autocracy in Berlin'. Wiseman gained funding for the operation by an ingenious deception in both Washington and London. He won American support

◀ List of conditions, including acceptance of full personal responsibility for the risks of returning to Russia, signed by Lenin and other travellers on the German 'sealed train', which left Zurich in April 1917. All agreed to take instructions from their German escort, Reichsführer Fritz Platten. The first to sign was Lenin; the second his wife, Nadezhda Krupskaya, who signed herself 'Frau Lenin'. Grigory Zinoviev (no. 10) became head of the Communist International but was executed on trumped-up charges in 1936 after a Stalinist show trial.

by implying that his scheme had Foreign Office backing, then used American backing to gain Foreign Office support. On 26 May Wiseman triumphantly reported to Cumming that the Americans were willing to leave the running of the operation to the British – in effect, to MI1c:

> The U.S. authorities are willing to facilitate this propaganda in every possible way, and join with the British Government in putting up the necessary funds; but, as they have no organization through which to conduct such an operation, they would like the matter left entirely in my hands, on behalf of both the Governments.

Wiseman asked Cumming to see Balfour's private secretary, Sir Eric Drummond, 'immediately and obtain his authorization'. The proposed covert action would, he believed, 'work in very well' with the operations of the MI1c station in Petrograd, headed by the future Foreign Secretary, Sir Samuel Hoare MP.

Wiseman did not mention his project to Spring Rice, the British ambassador in Washington. He did, however, discuss it with House, Polk and Lansing – all of whom gave their enthusiastic support.[13] They would have been far less likely to give their support had they known that until the United States entered the war, Britain's most valuable agents in Germany included two Americans who had agreed to work for German military intelligence but were in reality double agents reporting to MI5.*

On 15 June Wilson authorized $75,000 to fund what he naïvely believed was an Allied propaganda exercise rather than a covert operation run by British intelligence. The next day Wiseman cabled Drummond to ask for the same amount from London. The Foreign Office, unlike Cumming, was not keen on the idea of a joint operation with the Americans, even if it was effectively run by MI1c. Wiseman won Balfour over by stressing Wilson's alleged interest in the operation and the intelligence on American policy that he expected to obtain if it went ahead:

> It is possible that by acting practically as a confidential agent for Remus [the Wilson administration] I might strengthen the understanding with Caesar [Colonel House] that in future he will keep us informed of steps taken by Remus in their foreign affairs which would ordinarily not be a matter of common knowledge to the Governments of the two countries.

* One of the double agents, Roslyn Whytock, became a captain in American military intelligence after the US entry into the war. The identity of MI5's second double agent, codenamed COMO, in accordance with assurances given to him, has never been revealed. (Andrew, *Defence of the Realm*, pp. 72–7.)

The Foreign Office agreed to contribute $75,000 to the Russian operation on the grounds that 'the scheme seems to afford sound measures for checking German pacifist propaganda to Russia and that [the] President is interested in it'.[14]

To head the covert influence operation in Petrograd, Wiseman chose the celebrated playwright and novelist W. Somerset Maugham, a Russian-speaker who used his writing career to provide cover for his work as a wartime MI1c agent. Maugham was 'staggered' by his Petrograd mission. 'The long and short of it', he wrote later, 'was that I should go to Russia and keep the Russians in the war.' With Maugham, in a supporting role, went Gaunt's former agent, Emanuel Voska, with instructions to 'organise the Czechs and Slovaks of the Empire to keep Russia in the war'.[15] As well as organizing pro-Allied propaganda in Petrograd, Maugham succeeded, through his former mistress, Sasha Kropotkin, in gaining an introduction to Alexander Kerensky, the head of the Provisional Government. With Sasha acting as hostess and, when necessary, interpreter, Maugham entertained Kerensky or members of his government once a week at the Medved, reputedly the best restaurant in Russia, paying for the finest caviar and vodka from the ample funds provided by the British and American governments. The famously austere Woodrow Wilson, who had cancelled the inaugural ball on taking office, can scarcely have imagined that some of the $75,000 'propaganda' budget he had authorized in 1917 was being used to fund such lavish entertainment. 'I think Kerensky must have supposed that I was more important than I really was', wrote Maugham later, 'for he came to Sasha's apartment on several occasions and, walking up and down the room, harangued me as though I were at a public meeting for two hours at a time.'[16]

Despite his remarkable success in gaining access to the head of the Provisional Government, there was nothing Maugham or any other Allied agent could do to keep Russia in the war. On the eve of the Russian summer offensive, which began on 16 June, General Alexei Brusilov warned Kerensky that there were mass mutinies among Russian troops. 'He paid not the slightest attention to my words', Brusilov later complained, 'and from that moment on, I realized that my own authority as the Commander-in-Chief was quite irrelevant.' The offensive, which Kerensky and his ministers had persuaded themselves would rally the country in defence of democracy, collapsed in only three days, with Russian forces fleeing in panic from a German counter-attack. Hundreds of thousands of soldiers were killed and millions of square miles of territory lost.[17]

Rumours that Lenin was a German spy were unreliably confirmed in Petrograd by a Russian officer who claimed to have been told so by his

German captors when a prisoner of war. On 6 July the Justice Ministry of the Russian Provisional Government ordered Lenin's arrest on a charge of high treason. Lenin was forced to shave off his beard, disguise himself as a worker and take temporary refuge in Finland. 'We understand', wrote Claude Dansey of MI5 (later Assistant Chief of SIS) in August, 'that the Russian General Staff have proof now of Lenin's guilt.'[18] Like MI5, most Western intelligence agencies mistakenly believed, or at least strongly suspected, that Lenin was in the pay of the Germans.

Under the Provisional Government, much of the Tsarist military intelligence system disintegrated. In April 1917 all intelligence officers who had previously served in the Okhrana or police were expelled. General N. S. Batiushin and several other leading officers in military counter-intelligence were arrested on charges of corruption and abuse of authority. Amid the confusion caused by the collapse of Brusilov's June offensive and subsequent disintegration of the Russian war effort, German and Austrian spies were routinely blamed for what were in reality accidental mishaps ranging from stockyard fires to failures in army boot production. In August military counter-intelligence circulated a warning that Russia's enemies

> persistently work not only in the area of military espionage in its purest form, but are also seeking by all means possible to destroy Russia's military power, for example by spying on trade and commerce, by smuggling in contraband as well as pacifist, nationalist, political and all other forms of propaganda, by arson, and by bombing factories and other structures.

During the somewhat paranoid final months of the Provisional Government, military counter-intelligence sought powers to investigate enemy subversion throughout Russian society which were almost as extensive as those later obtained by Stalin's NKVD to uncover even more extensive, though almost wholly imaginary, imperialist subversion.[19]

Though on a smaller scale, there were mutinies within the French as well as the Russian army during the spring and summer of 1917. The catastrophic failure of the offensive led by the French commander-in-chief, General Robert Nivelle, in April 1917, with 130,000 troops killed or wounded in only five days, led to mutinies of varying severity involving 40,000 men in half the divisions of the French army. Some historians have suggested that, had the Germans been aware of the mutinies, 'they might have won the war'. Ludendorff, however, did not learn of the mutinies until 30 June, when the crisis in the French Army was nearly at an end.[20] There are few better indications of how much better informed German military intelligence was on the Eastern than on the Western Front in 1917.

Unaware that the Germans knew nothing about the French mutinies until two and a half months after they began, French ministers and military intelligence wrongly suspected Germany of promoting them – as it had done in Russia. On 15 May Émile-Joseph Duval, a director of the allegedly defeatist, left-wing newspaper *Bonnet Rouge*, was caught returning from Switzerland with a large cheque from a German banker. He was later found guilty of treason and sent to the guillotine. In August the editor of the *Bonnet Rouge*, Miguel Almereyda, committed suicide in prison. Georges Clemenceau, soon to become Prime Minister, claimed that the refusal of the Interior Minister, Louis Malvy, to prosecute Almereyda and other 'defeatists' was responsible for the French army mutinies. Malvy was later found guilty of 'culpable negligence in the discharge of his duties' and sentenced to five years' exile. The radical former Prime Minister Joseph Caillaux, who had given financial support to the *Bonnet Rouge* before the war, was also arrested. The British ambassador reported that Clemenceau hoped he would be shot. (In a post-war trial Caillaux was found guilty of treason with, somewhat bizarrely, 'extenuating circumstances'.)[21]

Though it later emerged that Clemenceau and his supporters had greatly exaggerated the threat to the French war effort of German-financed subversion, many British observers at the time took it at face value and believed that similar dark forces were at work in Britain. Given the priority which Germany had given to assisting the Bolsheviks to undermine the Russian war effort, it was reasonable – though, as it later turned out, mistaken – for MI5 to conclude that it was also assisting the Bolsheviks' British sympathizers. Russian 'proof' that Lenin was in the pay of the Germans encouraged the belief that German money was also subsidizing British Bolshevism. On 3 October 1917 Sir Edward Carson, Minister Without Portfolio in Lloyd George's War Cabinet, declared it a 'fact' that German money had been 'promoting industrial trouble' in Russia, France, Italy, Spain, the United States, Argentina, Chile – 'in fact wherever conditions were suitable for their interference'. Carson's claims were taken seriously by his colleagues. At the War Cabinet on 4 October: 'It was pointed out . . . that the only really efficient system of propaganda at present existing in this country was that organised by the pacifists, who had large sums of money at their disposal and who were conducting their campaign with great vigour.' The Cabinet minutes record no challenge to this preposterous allegation.[22]

During 1917 counter-subversion became for the first time a higher priority for MI5 than counter-espionage. With the help of the police it had tracked down all the German spies of any significance infiltrated into wartime Britain. It was far less successful in detecting significant German finance for the British anti-war movement – for the simple reason that there was none to find. The War Cabinet discussed the question of German finance for pacifism again at its meeting on 19 October. The minutes reveal, as on 4 October, extravagant conspiracy theories, this time that 'anti-war propaganda was being financed by wealthy men, who were looking forward to making money by opening up trade with Germany after the war'. This claim too appears to have gone unchallenged. The War Cabinet decided that the head of the Special Branch, Sir Basil Thomson, rather than the director of MI5, Vernon Kell, should 'undertake the co-ordination and control of the investigation of all pacifist propaganda and of the wider subjects connected therewith', and report back. Thomson groaned inwardly at the news. While he considered ministers naïvely alarmist, he was conscious that failure to give their alarms due – or rather undue – weight might be interpreted as complacency in the face of subversion. He complained to his diary on 22 October:

> The War Cabinet . . . are not disposed to take soothing syrup in these matters. Being persuaded that German money is supporting [pacifist and revolutionary] societies they want to be assured that the police are doing something. I feel certain that there is no German money, their expenditure being covered by the subscriptions they receive from cranks.

Thomson's report contrived to show a prudent awareness of the dangers of German-financed subversion, while none the less arriving at a reassuring conclusion. German money, he informed ministers, had been neither widely nor effectively deployed.[23] Ministers' alarmism derived, at least in part, from their historical ignorance of all matters relating to intelligence. Had they possessed a long-term perspective, they would have realized that alleged subversive threats were frequently exaggerated – particularly in time of war.*

The news of the Bolshevik Revolution in Russia on 7 November (25 October by the traditional Russian calendar) raised ministers' fears of Bolshevik subversion in Britain to new heights. On 30 October Kerensky had asked Somerset Maugham to warn Lloyd George that his government was unlikely to survive.[24] Maugham, however, was unable to telegraph this important message to London from the British embassy in Petrograd. His relations with the non-Russian-speaking ambassador, Sir George Buchanan, were frosty. In Maugham's fictionalized account of his experiences as a

---

* During the 1820s, 1830s and 1840s, the ruling regimes in the four main continental powers wrongly believed that the main threat to their survival came from professional revolutionaries. See above, pp. 375, 376, 383.

secret agent, *The Ashenden Papers*, Buchanan appears as Sir Henry With-
erspoon, who receives Ashenden (Maugham) 'with a frigidity that would
have sent a little shiver down the spine of a polar bear'.[25] Maugham's
account of his meeting with Kerensky did not reach the Foreign Office until
18 November, eleven days after the Provisional Government had been toppled by the Bolsheviks.*

Alarmism in the Foreign Office fuelled the anxieties of Lloyd George's
War Cabinet caused by the news from Petrograd. It reported on 12 November that Bolshevism had been 'fastened on and poisoned by the Germans
for their own purposes' to undermine the Russian war effort: 'It is not yet
possible to say which of the Bolshevik leaders have taken German money;
some undoubtedly have, while others are honest fanatics.' Some ministers
inevitably feared that British subversives had taken German money too. The
Home Secretary, Sir George Cave, suspected that German-financed subversion had been more widespread than Thomson had earlier reported, and
ordered 'further investigations' by a joint committee of MI5 and Special
Branch officers, including an examination of the records of pacifist and
revolutionary societies seized in police raids to trace the source of their
income. No evidence of German funding for British pacifists and revolutionaries emerged from investigations by either MI5 or the Special Branch.
Thomson's dismissive comments on the No-Conscription Fellowship, circulated to the War Cabinet on 13 December, were typical of his contemptuous
attitude to pacifists in general: 'The documents disclose no evidence of
Enemy influence or financial support. The Fellowship is conducted in an
unbusinesslike way by cranks, and its influence outside the circle of Con-
scientious Objectors seems to be small.'[26]

The MI5 New Year card for 1918, sent to the privileged circle in Whitehall and beyond with whom it had contact, was designed to demonstrate
that Vernon Kell took the threat of Soviet subversion seriously. The card,
personally designed by Kell's long-serving deputy, Eric Holt-Wilson (initials in bottom left-hand corner) and drawn in the Pre-Raphaelite manner
by the leading illustrator Byam Shaw (identified bottom right), shows the
loathsome, remarkably hirsute figure of Subversion, smoke billowing from
its jaws, crawling on all fours towards a British fighting man, improbably attired as a Roman soldier, who is oblivious of the danger to his rear,
his eyes fixed firmly on the vision on the horizon of 'Dieu et Mon Droit'
and Victory in 1918. Just in time MI5, depicted as a masked Britannia,

---

* Jeffery, *MI6*, p. 119. The chronology in Maugham's account of this episode and his own
recall from Petrograd, written from memory almost half a century later, is confused.
(Maugham, 'Looking Back', part 2.)

impales Subversion with a trident marked with her secret monogram before it can stab the British warrior in the back.

In January 1918 Kell began an investigation into possible Soviet subversion in munitions factories, urging chief constables to:

> report to us any change of attitude on the part of Russians on Munitions, which would be denoted by: pacifist or anti-war propaganda, a disinclination to continue to help in the production of Munitions, or any active tendency towards holding up supplies, either by restriction of out-put, or destruction of out-put of factories.[27]

There was, in reality, nothing of importance for chief constables to discover. Despite the alarmism of British and French ministers, Communist-inspired subversion posed no significant threat to the war effort of any of the Western Allies.

The Bolshevik seizure of power none the less marked a major turning point in intelligence history. The first Communist security and intelligence agency, the All-Russian Extraordinary Commission for Combating Counter-Revolution and Sabotage (*Vserossiiskaya Chrezvychainaya Kommisiya po Borbe s Kontr Revolyutsiyei i Sabotazhem*), better known by the abbreviation 'Cheka', was founded on 20 December 1917, only six weeks after the Bolshevik Revolution, and became central during 1918 to the structure of the world's first one-party state. Like British income tax on its introduction in 1799, however, the Cheka was originally intended only as a temporary expedient to deal with opposition on a scale Lenin had never expected. The immediate cause for its creation was an impending strike by state employees. Lenin wrote to the Polish head of the Cheka, Felix Edmundovich Dzerzhinsky: 'The bourgeoisie is intent on committing the most heinous of crimes ...'[28] Though Russian intelligence agencies changed their names a number of times during the three quarters of a century of the Soviet era, their members continued to call themselves 'Chekists' (*Chekisti*) and were paid their salaries on the 20th, not the 1st, of each month ('Chekist's Day') in honour of the Cheka's birthday. The Cheka's emblems of the shield and the sword – the shield to defend the Revolution and the sword to smite its foes – were retained by all future Soviet security and intelligence agencies. In the Stalin era the Cheka's successors became the largest, most powerful and most brutal secret agencies in the peacetime history of Europe.

Before their seizure of power, it had never occurred to Lenin or other

◀ MI5's 1918 New Year card, sent to its contacts in and beyond Whitehall, looks forward to 'Mankind's Immortal Victory'.

leading Bolsheviks that they would need any intelligence agency at all. They confidently expected their own revolution to spark off an international revolution which would overthrow world capitalism. In the new post-revolutionary world order there would be no need for conventional diplomats, let alone for spies. Trotsky declared on his appointment as People's Commissar for Foreign Affairs after the Bolshevik Revolution: 'I will issue a few revolutionary proclamations to the peoples of the world and then shut up shop.' He ordered the publication of Tsarist Russia's secret treaties with its allies, then announced: 'The abolition of secret diplomacy is the primary condition of an honourable, popular, really democratic foreign policy.'[29] Without realizing it, Trotsky himself largely abolished secret diplomacy when negotiating the Treaty of Brest-Litovsk with Germany, concluded in March 1918. The British military attaché in Moscow during the talks leading up to the treaty had access to intercepts of telegraph messages sent back and forth between Russian negotiators in Brest-Litovsk (where German military headquarters were located) and the Bolshevik government in Petrograd. The telegrams were copied by political opponents of the Bolsheviks at the Moscow telegraph office and passed to British diplomats. The US Russian expert George Kennan, who became ambassador in Moscow two decades later, concluded that the main source of the telegrams, intentionally or not, was Ivan Zalkind, Trotsky's deputy commissar.[30] The Treaty of Brest-Litovsk, signed on 3 March, was 'the most humiliating end to a war for Russians since the Mongol invasion in the thirteenth century'.[31] A quarter of the Russian Empire passed under German control. Lenin insisted that Russia had no option but to give way to German demands. 'If you do not know how to adapt yourself', he said, 'if you are not inclined to crawl on your belly through the mud, then you are not a revolutionary but a chatterbox.' In the aftermath of Brest-Litovsk, the Bolshevik Party changed its name to Communist. The Council of People's Commissars (*Sovnarkom*) moved its seat of government and the Russian capital from Petrograd to Moscow.

The original measures approved by Sovnarkom to combat counter-revolution were non-violent: 'seizure of property, resettlement, deprivation of [ration] cards, publication of lists of enemies of the people, etc'. The Cheka's main weapon, however, rapidly became terror. One of Dzerzhinsky's lieutenants, Martyn Yanovich Latsis, wrote in the Cheka journal, *Krasny Terror* ('Red Terror'):

> We are not waging war against individuals. We are exterminating the bourgeoisie as a class. During investigation, do not look for evidence that the accused acted in word or deed against Soviet power. The first questions

that you ought to put are: 'To what class does he belong? What is his origin? What is his education or profession?' And it is these questions that ought to determine the fate of the accused. In this lies the significance and essence of the Red Terror.

Like Lenin, Dzerzhinsky and his chief lieutenants were not personally brutal individuals. They supported Red Terror because of what they saw as the objective needs of class conflict, especially after the beginning in May 1918 of the Civil War against counter-revolutionary 'White' armies, which threatened the survival of the Soviet regime. Some Cheka recruits, however, enjoyed the opportunity both to brutalize both 'former people' from the Tsarist ruling class and to carry out acts of personal vengeance. Yakov Khristoforovich Peters, one of Dzerzhinsky's early deputies, later acknowledged that 'filthy elements' had tried to attach themselves to the Cheka. Some of them succeeded.[32]

Until the summer of 1918 the Cheka's propensity to terror was partly held in check by the Left Socialist Revolutionaries (LSRs), on whose support the Bolsheviks initially depended. One of the four LSRs appointed to the Cheka Collegium, Vyacheslav Alekseevich Alexandrovich, became for a time probably Dzerzhinsky's most influential deputy. In March 1918 the LSRs left Sovnarkom in protest against the peace of Brest-Litovsk, but, remarkably, remained in the Cheka. Indeed, according to the LSR version of events, Dzerzhinsky pleaded with them to stay, telling their leader, Maria Spiridonova, that, without their support, he would 'no longer be able to tame the bloodthirsty impulses in [Cheka] ranks'. So long as the LSRs remained in the Cheka Collegium, there were no authorized executions for political crimes. Dzerzhinsky had such confidence in his LSR deputy, Alexandrovich, that, after the move to Moscow, he handed over to him the main responsibility for day-to-day administration so that he could concentrate on operational work.[33]

The only power with which the Bolshevik regime had formal diplomatic relations after Brest-Litovsk was Germany. On 23 April 1918 a German embassy under Count Wilhelm Mirbach installed itself in Moscow. Six days later a member of Mirbach's mission wrote in his diary: 'Here we must be ever on the alert for approaches by agents and provocateurs. The Soviet authorities have rapidly revived the former Tsarist Okhrana . . . in at least equal size and in more merciless temper, if in somewhat different form.' Penetration of the German embassy was made the responsibility of a counter-espionage section of the Cheka, set up in May under the twenty-year-old LSR, Yakov Blyumkin, probably the youngest section chief in Soviet intelligence history. Blyumkin successfully penetrated the German embassy by recruiting as an agent Count Robert Mirbach, an Austrian relative of the German ambassador who had become a Russian prisoner of war. In June he extracted from Mirbach a signed undertaking to supply the Cheka with intelligence from the embassy.[34]

Dzerzhinsky had been unwise to entrust the penetration of the German embassy to Blyumkin, for the LSRs remained bitterly opposed to the Treaty of Brest-Litovsk. On 4 July the LSR Central Committee approved a plot to assassinate the German ambassador, in the naïve belief that they would thus dramatically bring to an end Bolshevik 'appeasement' of the Germans, renew the war on the Eastern Front and advance the cause of world revolution. The assassination was entrusted to Blyumkin and an LSR photographer working for him in the Cheka, Nikolai Andreev. On the morning of 6 July, Blyumkin prepared a document on Cheka notepaper, authorizing himself and Andreev to hold talks with the German ambassador. Dzerzhinsky's LSR deputy, Alexandrovich, was then brought into the plot by Blyumkin and affixed the official Cheka seal to the document. The same afternoon, Blyumkin and Andreev drove to the German embassy and secured a meeting with the ambassador on the pretext of discussing the case of his relative, Count Robert Mirbach. Blyumkin later claimed that he himself fired the shots which killed the ambassador, Count Wilhelm Mirbach. According to the evidence of embassy staff, however, after three shots from Blyumkin's revolver all missed their target, the ambassador was gunned down by Andreev.[35]

The Cheka's role as 'the sword and shield of the Revolution' thus almost ended in disaster. Instead of ensuring the survival of the world's first Communist state, the Cheka nearly became the instrument of its destruction. Lenin telegraphed Stalin that Mirbach's assassination had brought Russia within 'a hair's breadth' of renewed war with Germany. The assassination was followed by an LSR rising in which the Cheka's headquarters, the Lubyanka in central Moscow, was seized and Dzerzhinsky taken prisoner. But the LSRs had no coherent plan of campaign and their rising was crushed within twenty-four hours by Latvian troops loyal to the Communists. On 8 July, a chastened Dzerzhinsky stepped down from the Cheka leadership at his own request, while a commission of enquiry investigated the rising and the Cheka was purged of LSRs. By the time Dzerzhinsky was reinstated as Chairman on 22 August, the Cheka had become an exclusively Communist agency whose use of terror against its political opponents was no longer restrained by the moderating influence of the LSRs. 'We represent in ourselves organised terror', said Dzerzhinsky. 'This must be said very clearly.'[36]

There were, however, still idealists within the Cheka prepared to challenge the brutality of its onslaught on 'counter-revolution'. Among them was the chairman of the Petrograd Cheka, Moisei Solomonovich Uritsky, who complained to Dzerzhinsky on 30 August at the methods used by a group of Chekists to extort a confession from a fourteen-year-old suspect, Vsevolod Anosov. At his first interrogation, Anasov was threatened with being shot; at the second, a gun was fired at him but used a blank; on the third occasion, the gun shot a real bullet through a cloak lying on a chair next to him. Anasov was told that a warrant had been signed for his execution at dawn next day, which, however, was never carried out. Uritsky told Dzerzhinsky in an unpublished letter: 'I think that such interrogation methods are absolutely unacceptable, and especially for children who are 14 years of age. I therefore ask you to investigate this case and hold the guilty responsible. I am hoping that you will not refuse to let me know the results of the investigation and about the decision you took.'[37] Uritsky did not live to hear the outcome of the investigation – if it ever took place. Later the same day, 30 August, in an unconnected attack, he was assassinated by a Tsarist military cadet.

Soon afterwards Lenin himself was shot and seriously wounded by a possibly deranged Socialist Revolutionary, Fanya (Dora) Kaplan. These two attacks on Bolshevik leaders unleashed a reign of terror. In Petrograd alone over 500 political prisoners were executed in two days. While still recovering from his wounds, Lenin instructed: 'It is necessary secretly – and *urgently* – to prepare the terror.' On 5 September 1918 the decree 'On Red Terror' ordered a pitiless campaign by the Cheka against counter-revolution.[38] Lenin took an active, if naïve, interest in the application of technology, as well as terror, to the hunt for counter-revolutionaries. Though his many biographers do not mention it, he favoured the construction of a large electro-magnet to detect concealed weapons in house-to-house searches, and pressed the idea on the Cheka. Dzerzhinsky was politely unimpressed. 'Magnets', he informed Lenin, 'are not much use in searches. We have tested them.' But he agreed, as an experiment, to take large magnets on house searches in the hope that counter-revolutionaries would be frightened into handing over their weapons themselves. The experiment was soon abandoned.[39]

In the course of the Civil War the Cheka claimed to have uncovered and defeated a series of major conspiracies by Western governments and their intelligence agencies to overthrow the Bolshevik regime. The best known of the Western conspirators in Moscow was the junior British diplomat Robert Bruce Lockhart, the leading figure in the inept 'envoys' plot' (sometimes called the 'Lockhart Plot'), which was easily penetrated and disrupted by the Cheka. The KGB later claimed, with characteristic hyperbole, that this 'shattering blow dealt by the Chekists to the conspirators was equivalent to victory in a major military battle'.[40] In reality, the 'envoys' plot' was the brainchild not of an organized coalition of capitalist governments but of a group of politically naïve Western diplomats and secret agents left largely to their own devices during the first chaotic year of Bolshevik rule.

Though arrested after the 'envoys' plot' was publicly revealed, Lockhart and other British officials were allowed to return to London in October 1918 in return for the release of Soviet officials imprisoned in Britain, among them the future Commissar for Foreign Affairs, Maxim Litvinov. Lockhart's memoirs contain an extraordinary (but probably authentic) account of his final meeting before his return home with Yakov Peters, deputy head of the Cheka. 'I have a favour to ask of you', Peters said. 'Will you give this letter to my English wife?' To help Lockhart identify his wife, Peters gave him several photos of her, but then had second thoughts. 'No', he said, 'I shan't trouble you. As soon as you're out of here you'll blaspheme and curse me as your worst enemy.' Lockhart told Peters not to be a fool, took the letter and delivered it to Mrs Peters on his return to England. Lockhart is unlikely to have known just how violent Peters' career as an underground revolutionary in pre-war London had been. Though details remain obscure, Peters was involved in the murder of several policemen in 1910 prior to the celebrated 'Siege of Sidney Street', during which the Home Secretary, Winston Churchill, famously appeared in the front line.[41]

The most colourful of the secret agents who set out to topple the early Bolshevik regime was the so-called British 'ace of spies', Sidney Reilly, whose exploits oscillated between high adventure and low farce. Reilly announced his arrival in Moscow on 7 May with characteristic bravado by marching up to the Kremlin gates, telling the sentries he was an emissary from Lloyd George, and demanding to see Lenin personally. Remarkably, he managed to get as far as one of Lenin's aides, Vladimir Bonch-Bruevich, who was understandably bemused. The Commissariat for Foreign Affairs rang Lockhart to enquire whether Bonch-Bruevich's visitor was an impostor. Lockhart later admitted that he 'nearly blurted out that [Reilly] must be a Russian masquerading as an Englishman or else a madman'. On discovering from the MI1c head of station, Ernest Boyce, that Reilly was a British agent, Lockhart lost his temper, summoned Reilly to his office, 'dressed him down like a schoolmaster and threatened to have him sent home'. But, recalled Lockhart, Reilly was 'so ingenious in his excuses that in the end he made me laugh'. Probably the most laughable of Reilly's many non-implemented schemes was a plan to capture Lenin and Trotsky, remove their trousers and 'nether garments', and expose them to public ridicule by parading them through the streets dressed only in their shirts.[42]

The Cheka's success in penetrating the 'envoys' plot' and 'counter-revolutionary' Russian groups derived in large part from its imitation of the techniques employed by Roman Malinovsky and other Tsarist penetration agents.[43] Dmitri Gavrilovich Yevseev, the author of two of the Cheka's earliest operational manuals, 'Basic Tenets of Intelligence' and 'Brief Instructions for the Cheka on How to Conduct Intelligence', based his writings on detailed study of Okhrana tradecraft. Though the Cheka was 'an organ for building the dictatorship of the proletariat', Yevseev insisted – like Dzerzhinsky – that it must not hesitate to learn from the experience of 'bourgeois' intelligence agencies.[44]

The Cheka's early priorities were overwhelmingly domestic. It was, said Dzerzhinsky, 'an organ for the revolutionary settlement of accounts with counter-revolutionaries', a label increasingly applied to all the Bolsheviks' opponents and 'class enemies'.[45] The memorial erected next to the Lubyanka in the closing years of the Soviet era to commemorate 'the victims of totalitarian oppression' consists of a large block of granite taken not from Stalin's Gulag but from a concentration camp established by Lenin on Solovetsky Island in the White Sea in the autumn of 1918.* Many Chekists regarded brutality against class enemies as a revolutionary virtue. According to a report from the Cheka in Morshansk: 'He who fights for a better future will be merciless towards his enemies. He who seeks to protect poor people will harden his heart against pity and will become cruel.'[46]

When agreeing to the humiliating Treaty of Brest-Litovsk with Germany, Lenin had insisted that it was only a temporary reverse which would be swept aside by the tide of revolution advancing irresistibly across Europe. In the event, however, Brest-Litovsk was swept away not by the tide of revolution but by the Allied victory on the Western Front only eight months later. Because Germany's forces were no longer needed in the East, it had, by March 1918, twenty divisions more on the Western Front than the combined total of the Allies. Ludendorff was well aware that this advantage could not last. In March 1918 there was still only one American division fighting in the Allied line with three others in training areas. As soon as US forces began to arrive in France in large numbers, the tables would be turned and the Allies could expect to win the war by sheer weight of numbers. Ludendorff drew the conclusion, therefore, that Germany must gamble on a last, all-out offensive before its numerical advantage was lost.

---

* Though 'Gulag' was officially the acronym for the organization which ran the prison camp system, the Main Administration of Corrective Labour Camps, it is commonly used to indicate the prison camps themselves.

The intelligence on the Western Front available in 1918 to Haig and Brigadier Edgar Cox, who, after a brief interregnum, succeeded Brigadier John Charteris as head of intelligence at GHQ in January, was better than ever before. At thirty-five, Cox is believed to have been the youngest brigadier in the British army – a sign of the priority given to intelligence assessment – and was among the ablest British military-intelligence officers of the war. His arrival at GHQ did much to restore the standing and morale of the intelligence staff. In the spring of 1915 he had been the first to compile a comprehensive battle order of the German army, which had since become a basic handbook for all British intelligence officers on the Western Front. In January 1918 he introduced the first weekly GHQ intelligence summaries, including forecasts of German operational plans.[47]

For much of the final year of the war, the most valuable British intelligence source was the train-watching agent network in occupied Belgium, known as *La Dame Blanche* after the legendary White Lady of the Hohenzollerns whose appearance was supposed to herald the downfall of the dynasty. The agents, mostly Belgian patriots, who provided important intelligence on German troop movements, grew in numbers from 129 in July 1917 to 408 by January 1918 and to 919 by the Armistice. Captain Henry Landau of MI1c, who ran the network from Holland, wrote to its leaders in January 1918: 'There is no doubt that at this critical moment you represent by far the most abundant Allied intelligence source and that the results you are achieving are of inestimable value.' Some of the intelligence passed to Cox from *La Dame Blanche* concerned preparations for the last great German offensive of the war which opened in March 1918.[48] At the turn of the year *La Dame Blanche* and other train-watchers had revealed the transfer of forty German divisions from Russia and Romania to the Western Front. During February aerial reconnaissance disclosed almost daily extensions to the German light-railway network. On 16 February Brigadier Cox told a conference of British army commanders chaired by Haig that they must 'be prepared to meet a very severe attack at any moment now'. According to Haig: 'All felt confident on being able to hold their front'. Then in early March came intelligence that German artillery units from Antwerp and Liège, along with 'Force D', a new body of shock troops, were on the move. Cox was now convinced that the offensive would begin within a month. Though Haig accepted Cox's forecast, he remained, as usual, over-optimistic about the outcome, 'only afraid that the enemy would find our front so strong that he will hesitate to commit his Army to the attack with the almost certainty of losing very heavily'.[49]

The German attack began on 21 March at almost precisely the point Cox had predicted. Cox was also right about the strength of the attack. The commander of the Fifth Army, General Sir Hubert Gough, told Cox's deputy: 'You were right, right to the tick, and thanks.' Haig too phoned his congratulations to Cox, but woefully overestimated the ability of his forces to withstand the attack. No previous advance since the beginning of trench warfare over three years earlier had much exceeded ten miles. The German offensive on 21 March, however, advanced forty miles in a few days. A second wave of the offensive opening in Artois on 9 April carried the Germans ten miles in three days. On this occasion Haig made a different error of judgement. Convinced that the Germans would attack the Vimy ridge, the target he would have chosen in their place, he discounted aerial reconnaissance reports which correctly pointed to an attack further south. On 11 April Haig issued his famous Order of the Day: 'With our backs to the wall and believing in the justice of our cause each one of us must fight on to the end.' Before the third and final wave of the German offensive on 27 May, GHQ intelligence at first misread the enemy's intentions. As late as 24 May Cox still expected the attack to come in the Albert–Arras sector. But on the 26th he reported to Haig the movement south from Belgium of four enemy divisions and heavy artillery towards Laon, on the German side of the Chemin des Dames sector of the front – intelligence which chimed with a captured letter from a German soldier reporting a coming attack on the Chemin des Dames. Haig thought such an attack quite likely. However, Marshal Ferdinand Foch, who had been appointed first 'Commander in Chief of the Allied Armies in France' on 14 April, did not believe the intelligence, and on 27 May was taken by surprise.[50]

Cox was tragically drowned off Le Touquet at the end of August. A few days earlier Marshall-Cornwall had found him 'disheartened by the fact that Douglas Haig appeared to ignore his advice on intelligence and still placed his confidence in the wishful thinking of Charteris'.[51] Whether or not Cox's suspicions about the influence of Charteris were correct, Haig was right to believe that Germany had lost all chance of victory. His invincible optimism, which had hitherto sometimes been a liability, became a valuable asset in the Allied cause. With the gift of hindsight, it is possible to see the three waves of the German attack not as a strategy which stood a serious chance of success but as a desperate gamble on short-term victory as the only means to stave off long-term defeat: a defeat made inevitable by the prospect of five million Americans fighting on the Western Front if the war continued into 1919 and by the growing success of the Allied naval blockade. The Germans lacked the resources to extend, or even to sustain, their early successes.

The most telling evidence of the turning of the tide came from French rather than British intelligence. The greater German use of radio to communicate with forward positions during their offensive made it much easier to intercept their communications than during the era of trench warfare. On the eve of the offensive, however, the Germans introduced the new ADFGX (later modified as ADFGVX) cipher, which the head of the French Bureau du Chiffre, Colonel François Cartier, initially feared might prove unbreakable. The cipher was broken by probably the ablest cryptanalyst of the war, the 32-year-old Georges Painvin, a polymath who had graduated in second place in his class at the École Polytechnique, taught paleontology at the École Nationale Supérieure des Mines, and won first prize as a cellist at the Conservatoire de Nantes.[52] Painvin was the greatest French codebreaker since Antoine Rossignol (of whose achievements he was probably unaware) in the seventeenth century. On 2 June 1918 he decrypted a radio message from German HQ to its 18 Corps, which revealed that its forces were desperately overstretched. The message, which came to be known as the 'Radiogramme de la Victoire' by the Bureau du Chiffre, instructed: 'Rush munitions Stop even by day if not seen.' Forewarned of plans for a German assault on the French lines between Montdidier and Compiègne which began on 9 June, the French resisted the German onslaught. For the first time since the opening of his offensive on 21 March, Ludendorff was forced to suspend an operation before it had reached its target.[53] The secret of the 'Radiogramme de la Victoire' was remarkably well kept. Colonel Fritz Nebel, the German inventor of the ADFGX cipher, did not discover that it had been broken until 1967.[54]

Though the French had to resist further German attacks during June, the tide of battle swung thereafter decisively in favour of the Allies. Yet it was Haig rather than the French who drew the correct conclusions from intelligence on the crumbling of the German offensive. Even after the great British victory at Amiens on 8 August 1918, which Ludendorff later called 'the black day for the German army in the history of the war', Foch did not foresee a decisive breakthrough until April 1919. Haig was convinced that, on the contrary, the war could be won in the autumn of 1918 before the demoralized enemy had a chance to recover. Cox's intelligence assessments were much more cautious. Partly because Charteris had exaggerated morale problems among German forces based on selective use of evidence from POWs, Cox made no attempt before his untimely death to analyse morale among the thousands of captured German soldiers (13,000 on 8 August alone). Haig understood the military importance of declining German morale rather better than Cox.[55]

During the final year of the war, intelligence played an even more important role in the Middle East than on the Western Front. SIGINT was central in the campaign which led to the conquest of Jerusalem from the Turks by

General Sir Edmund (later Field Marshal Viscount) Allenby, the first Christian conqueror for many centuries, who famously showed his respect for the holy city by dismounting and entering on foot through the Jaffa Gate on 11 December 1917. Yigal Sheffy's pioneering study of intelligence during the Jerusalem campaign concludes that Allenby found SIGINT 'practically the sole source for up-to-date information' at a time when 'air reconnaissance was restricted by the winter weather and information from [Turkish] prisoners became rapidly outdated'.

Aerial reconnaissance had a much greater role in Allenby's next great Palestine offensive – at Megiddo (best known as the site of the battle of Armageddon prophesied in the Book of Revelation) in September 1918. Allenby's forces had a hundred serviceable aircraft, heavily outnumbering the fifteen German planes sent to support their Turkish allies. Before the battle the RFC took 42,000 photographs of enemy territory, while preventing significant enemy surveillance of Allenby's movements. SIGINT, however, was once again Allenby's main intelligence source, convincing him that the Turks had no inkling of his plan of attack at Megiddo. After the initial artillery bombardment and infantry attack, Allenby's Australian, British, Indian and New Zealand cavalry swept through Turkish lines, captured Damascus and advanced to Aleppo in northern Syria. Megiddo is remembered as the last great cavalry victory in modern warfare. Three Turkish armies and supporting German units were routed, and the entire Levant came under British control.[56]

The outcome of the war, however, was determined on the Western Front. Part of the reason for Haig's optimism that the war could be won in 1918 was that US forces were now arriving in large numbers. Beginning on 12 September, over half a million of them, commanded by General John J. 'Black Jack' Pershing, fought in the Battle of Saint-Mihiel, the largest offensive operation in American history. During the Meuse–Argonne offensive, which began on 26 September and continued until the Armistice, Pershing commanded more than one million American and French troops.[57]

During 1918 the Western Allies shared more intelligence than ever before, much of it through an Inter-Allied Commission which, from August, included the Americans.[58] The British–American intelligence 'Special Relationship', often believed to be a product of the Second World War, was already well established in the later stages of the First. Before leaving Haig's staff, Charteris had cultivated the young (later celebrated) US codebreaker William F. Friedman, who became personal cryptographer to General Pershing. It was due largely to the influence of Charteris that Friedman maintained closer contact with British than with French wartime SIGINT operations.[59] Almost certainly unaware of British success in decrypting communications between President Wilson and Colonel House,[60] he was later a leading supporter of US SIGINT collaboration in the Second World War.[61]

The lead role in developing the wartime intelligence special relationship with the United States was taken by MI1c. While Sir William Wiseman continued to spend much of his time cultivating Colonel House,[62] the MI1c station in New York, run by his deputy, Norman Thwaites, had established itself as the dominant partner in an informal alliance with most of the fragmented American intelligence community. It boasted in March 1918:

> As this office has been in existance [sic] longer than any of the other organi-
> zations of investigation and intelligence, it is naturally regarded as the best
> source of experienced information. There is complete cooperation between
> this office and
>
> 1. United States Military Intelligence
> 2. Naval Intelligence
> 3. U.S. Secret Service
> 4. New York Police Department
> 5. Police Intelligence
> 6. U.S. Customs House
> 7. The American Protective League and similar civic organizations
> 8. U.S. Department of Justice, Bureau of Investigation.
>
> . . . Everyone of them is in the habit of calling us up or visiting the office
> daily. They have access to our files under our supervision and we stand
> ready to give them all the information in our possession. They, on the other
> hand, are equally ready to reciprocate, and the spirit of friendly cooperation
> makes the week extremely pleasant and, I venture to think, useful.
> . . . With regard to 'agents and enquiries', it might be possible to curtail
> our activities and leave such matters to the U.S. Intelligence Bureaux but
> the [MI1c] London office frequently send us questionnaires which in no
> way concern America. Also we have facilities of gaining information which
> the U.S. has not. For months Major Thwaites has been the only intelligence
> officer in New York who was able to speak and read German. He has spent
> many nights at Police headquarters, etc. examining captured enemy docu-
> ments. None of the U.S. Bureaux employ Germans whereas this office has
> several most dependable German agents who are trusted acquaintances in
> enemy circles. This office supplied the addresses of all the persons appre-
> hended this last week when the U.S. authorities were at a loss.[63]

Had President Wilson known that MI1c conducted operations on American soil 'which in no way concern America' and employed its own

'dependable agents' in the United States, his trust in Wiseman would surely have been destroyed. But Wilson did not know. Wiseman reported to Cumming two months before the Armistice that, though 'Our cooperation with the many intelligence branches of the U.S. Government has always been most cordial, and I believe of value . . . The details of our organization they have never known and do not know to this day.'[64]

In the summer of 1918 Wiseman saw his main intelligence role as maintaining 'close touch' with the Inquiry, a group of experts assembled by House on Wilson's instructions to study political and territorial problems likely to arise at the peace conference. In July he wrote to Lord Reading, who had replaced the unpopular Spring Rice as ambassador early in 1918: 'It must be quite clear to you that when in New York I occupy practically the position of political secretary to House. I think he shows me everything he gets, and together we discuss every question that arises.' Wiseman reported that he had gained access to 'much of the data which will be used by the American delegates at the Peace Conference'.[65]

Simultaneously 'Blinker' Hall went to extraordinary lengths to influence the impressionable young Assistant Secretary of the Navy and future US President, Franklin D. Roosevelt, who was responsible for US naval intelligence. Roosevelt's meeting with Hall during a visit to London in the summer of 1918 made a profound impression on him that still influenced his attitude to British intelligence at the beginning of the Second World War. 'Their intelligence unit is much more developed than ours', he wrote after the visit, 'and this is because it is a much more integral part of their Office of Operations.' What struck Roosevelt most was the apparently phenomenal success of the Admiralty's secret agents. Still anxious to conceal from his American allies how much of his intelligence was obtained from SIGINT rather than from HUMINT, Hall arranged an elaborate charade. As he and Roosevelt discussed German troop movements, Hall, probably blinking furiously as he did at moments of excitement, said suddenly to Roosevelt: 'I am going to ask that youngster at the other end of the room to come over here. I will not introduce him by name. I want you to ask him where he was twenty-four hours ago.' When Roosevelt put the question, the young man replied: 'I was in Kiel, sir.' The Assistant Secretary was as astonished as the DNI had intended. Hall then explained that British spies crossed the German–Danish border each night, went by boat to the island of Sylt, and thence by flying boat to Harwich. Roosevelt was deeply impressed. He went to his grave never realizing that he had been taken in by one of Hall's deceptions.[66]

While Roosevelt was meeting Hall in London, Woodrow Wilson's enthusiasm for Wiseman's company even extended to his summer holidays. While spending a week's vacation at Magnolia in August, the President lunched on most days at House's summer house with Wiseman and House. Each evening Wiseman and House dined with the Wilsons. Though Wiseman, with his customary tact, waited to discuss the problems of war and peace until these subjects were raised by the President, he was able to report to London in some detail Wilson's views on most 'questions of the moment'. The most important topic of the week's discussions was Wilson's plans for a new world order based on the League of Nations. It is difficult to imagine Wilson choosing to spend so much of his vacation talking with any American intelligence officer or, indeed, with Lansing or most members of his administration. No British intelligence officer since Wiseman has spent so much time in policy discussions (or discussions of any kind) with the President of the United States. Arthur C. Murray of the Foreign Office Political Intelligence Department wrote to Wiseman after his return from Magnolia: 'The importance of the hours that you spent with House and the President cannot, I feel sure, be exaggerated.' Wiseman agreed. He boasted in September: 'House and the President have come to regard me as perhaps their chief source of information.'[67]

Despite Wilson's interest in some of the intelligence provided by Wiseman and Hall, he paid little attention to the organization and functioning of his own intelligence agencies. Immediately after the declaration of war on Germany, Lansing had tried to impress on the President 'the very great importance' of 'the coordination of the secret service work of this government'. Despite Polk's attempt to organize an intelligence 'clearing house' in the State Department, Lansing reported that two serious obstacles remained: the divorce between foreign and domestic intelligence, and the 'extreme jealousy' of the two domestic agencies, the Secret Service and the Bureau of Investigation (later the FBI). Lansing proposed solving these problems by putting all intelligence agencies 'under the general control of one efficient man' (possibly himself) in the State Department.[68] Wilson, however, remained unwilling either to delegate the problem of intelligence coordination to his Secretary of State or to tackle it himself. While he accepted the need to monitor German policy and domestic subversion of the US war effort, the idea of a strengthened and coordinated American intelligence community seemed so at odds with his post-war vision of a brave new world of open diplomacy that he could not bring himself to face up to the wartime problems of intelligence gathering. The consequence of entry into the First World War, combined with lack of presidential direction, was thus the rapid but uncoordinated growth of the fragmented American intelligence agencies.[69]

Although the United States, unlike the other major combatants, continued to lack a specialized foreign-espionage agency, the war produced a rapid expansion of the small pre-war naval- and military-intelligence personnel. By the Armistice, the permanent staff of the Office of Naval Intelligence had been augmented by almost 3,000 reservists and volunteers. In August 1918 military intelligence was raised in status to become one of four divisions of the War Department General Staff; the Military Intelligence Division personnel increased from only three in 1916 to 1,441 in 1918. The most significant innovation in wartime military intelligence was the founding of the first specialized US SIGINT agency. In June 1917 Herbert Yardley, a 28-year-old State Department code clerk who later claimed to have disconcerted his superiors by breaking a presidential code,* was commissioned as first lieutenant (later promoted to major) and placed in charge of a new military-intelligence cipher unit, MI-8. Over the next year MI-8 compiled new code and cipher systems for army use, translated foreign-language messages in various forms of shorthand passed on by the censors, produced chemical preparations to reveal messages written in secret ink, and deciphered messages sent in known codes and ciphers. But, reported Yardley at the end of the war, 'it was not until the beginning of August, 1918, that the staff was enlarged sufficiently to permit of serious attack upon the large number of code messages in various [unknown] codes which had been accumulating in the files'. By the November Armistice, MI-8 employed eighteen army officers, twenty-four civilian cryptographers, and 100 typists and stenographers. Wilson gave no sign of interest in this turning point in the history of American intelligence. Possibly he was not informed. Perhaps he preferred not to know.[70]

On 5 October 1918 a new German government, headed by Prince Max of Baden, appealed directly to Wilson for an armistice over the heads of his European allies. Unsurprisingly, Britain and France resented the President's independent negotiations with the enemy. Fearing that Wilson might be seduced by the newly conciliatory Huns, Hall sent him a series of intercepts designed to demonstrate Germany's continuing duplicity. One decrypt, forwarded to the White House on 14 October, which contained evidence of German double-dealing over the evacuation of conquered territory in Eastern Europe, clearly enraged the President. 'Every word', he told Wiseman, 'breathed the old Prussian trickery and deceit. It was difficult to see how we could trust such people.' But he made it clear that even 'Prussian trickery' would not deter him from armistice

---

* Though Yardley probably did break one of Wilson's ciphers, the details in his memoirs are unreliable. He also claimed, inaccurately, to have made contact with Room 40 in early 1915. In reality he had no access to its diplomatic work until 1919. (Kahn, *Reader of Gentlemen's Mail*, pp. 46–7. Larsen, 'British Intelligence and American Neutrality', pp. 40–42.)

negotiations: 'Of course, ... we must never trust them ... But we must not appear to be slamming the door on peace.'[71]

At the end of October, Wilson despatched House to Europe to inform his allies of the armistice terms he had negotiated with Germany. With him, as earlier in the year, went Wiseman. Hall redoubled his efforts to convince Wilson of the error of his ways, apparently manufacturing intelligence calculated to demonstrate that the Kaiser would not honour the armistice terms. Hall reported that on 30 October he had 'learned from an absolutely sure source that at a recent council in Berlin the German Emperor said: "During peace negotiations or even after peace, my U-boats will find an opportunity to destroy the English fleet."' Though asking 'to be excused from divulging the source of this astonishing piece of information', Hall insisted that it was just as reliable as German radio and cable intercepts. Lansing was 'inclined to give full credence to this information' on the grounds that Hall's intelligence had been 'most reliable in the past'.[72]

In reality, Hall's claim that he had 'an absolutely sure source' at the highest level in Berlin was as fraudulent as his claim to Roosevelt that his spies crossed the German border each night before being brought by flying boat to Harwich.[73] MI1c's best-informed source of political intelligence from Germany, a retired Bavarian general named Monteglas, whose brother was a senior German diplomat, gave a quite different perspective. Monteglas reported on 17 October:

> The military situation is desperate, if not hopeless, but it is nothing compared to the interior condition due to the rapid spread of Bolshevism. Owing to this development, news of which has just reached me, nothing can save Germany but an immediate acceptance of an armistice and peace, no matter what the terms.

This and similar intelligence reports on the decline of German morale probably reinforced Haig's belief in imminent German defeat.[74] The success of the Allied blockade in reducing much of the German population to a near-starvation diet encouraged a revolutionary mood which spread with astonishing speed on both the home and war fronts. A hysterical Kaiser responded to calls for his abdication, which he was eventually forced to accept, by demanding that revolutionaries be met 'with machine guns in the streets'.[75]

On the evening of 29 October Admiral Scheer, the commander of the High Seas Fleet, began preparations for a final, desperate sortie on the following day. The duty officer in ID25 that night was the musician and journalist Francis Toye, who had served there for less than a year. As evidence from intercepts pointing to a sortie began to multiply, Toye became increasingly agitated. At about 2 a.m. on the 30th he visited Operations Division to report 'various signs and portents'. Operations, however, was not satisfied with signs and portents, and demanded to know definitely whether the High Seas Fleet was leaving harbour. Toye later recalled:

> It was just before four, I think, that I made up my mind. Over I went again to Operations to tell them that it was my opinion that the German fleet was moving and that they must act as they thought fit. So in the space of an hour or two England spent some half a million pounds; the DNI and, in all probability, the First Lord of the Admiralty, not to mention the sea lords and a whole bevy of admirals and captains, were roused from their beds by the insistent ringing of the telephone. How I sweated! The cold, clammy sweat of sheer funk!

A signal intercepted at about 8 a.m. ('All officers on board the flagship') gave the first hint of a major mutiny in the German navy.[76] The High Seas Fleet was not moving after all. Though Scheer believed it 'a question of honour' for his fleet to go down fighting, most of his sailors disagreed. By 4 November the red flag of revolution flew at all Germany's naval bases.[77] During the first week of November, Room 40's cryptanalysts read with mounting excitement the flow of intercepts which revealed the High Seas Fleet, unbeaten in battle, collapsing as a fighting force in its home ports.[78]

MI1b also decrypted all the cables exchanged between House and Wilson during the talks which led up to the Armistice of 11 November.[79] Hall, whose doctored intelligence had failed to disrupt the talks, cannot have been pleased to read a cable of 5 November in which House told Wilson: 'I doubt whether any other heads of government with whom we are dealing realize how far they are now committed to the American peace program.' He must have been further disturbed by House's comment that Wiseman had been 'splendidly helpful' in resolving differences with Lloyd George over Wilson's proposals.[80] Just as Wiseman influenced House, so House influenced Wiseman, who became increasingly sympathetic to American mediation as a way of ending the war.[81]

By the Armistice, the *La Dame Blanche* train-watching organization, which reported on German troop movements, had become the largest agent network in the history of British intelligence, with 919 committed agents (more than twice as many as at the beginning of 1918) reporting from ninety observation posts. Cumming had written to the leaders of the network, possibly with some exaggeration, in July:

> The work of your organisation accounts for 70 per cent obtained by all the Allied armies not merely through the Netherlands [MI1c station] but

through other neutral states as well ... It is on you alone that the Allies
depend to obtain intelligence on enemy movements in areas near the
Front ... The intelligence obtained by you is worth thousands of lives in
the Allied armies.[82]

During the final months of the war, the most valuable source of intelligence on the growing demoralization of the German army came from the unprecedented number of POWs. In the three months between the Battle of Amiens and the Armistice, British forces captured 188,700 prisoners of war, far more than ever before in its history. 'Never at any time in its history', said Foch, 'has the British army achieved greater results in attack than in this unbroken offensive.'[83] A GHQ Intelligence summary concluded on 27 September: 'While no-one could say that the discipline of the German army has gone, or that the German soldier may not still be expected to put up a good fight, there is no doubt that ... the moral[e] of the German army has depreciated very considerably during the past five months.' During October, GHQ Intelligence summaries, based on POW interrogation and captured documents, reported further deterioration of morale and cases of breakdown of discipline among German forces. Haig wrote to his wife in the middle of the month: 'I think we have their army beaten now.'[84] Intelligence about the deployment of enemy forces was better than it had ever been in British military history. On Armistice Day, 11 November, GHQ Intelligence produced the last in the series of weekly 'Order of Battle' summaries, introduced by Cox in January. Of the 186 German divisions whose location was given, only two were shown in the wrong position.[85]

Despite its poor morale and decline in discipline, the German army mostly remained loyal to its officers and marched back from the front in good order after the Armistice.[86] Germany's military collapse was only partly due to the defeats inflicted on it and its allies in the closing months of the war. It was due still more to the conviction that the success of the British blockade and the prospect of large-scale American intervention made Germany's future prospects even bleaker than at present. The longer the war continued, the more the odds would turn against Germany. No intelligence agency six months before the Armistice could have foreseen that, for the first time in the history of warfare, a major power would give up the fight, as Germany did, without being invaded and with its front line still on enemy territory. Germany capitulated, not because it had been beaten in the field, but because its leaders and its people had lost hope in the future.[87]

26

SIGINT and HUMINT between the Wars

In the aftermath of the First World War intelligence services were drastically cut back in all but one of the major combatants. Headquarters personnel in the US Military Intelligence Division (MID) fell from 1,441 at the time of the Armistice to ninety in 1922.[1] Unlike its wartime allies, the United States still had no foreign-espionage agency. Neither, officially, did the newly established German Weimar Republic. As well as limiting the German army to 100,000 men, the 1919 Treaty of Versailles forbade Germany to engage in espionage. The main interwar German intelligence agency, the Abwehr ('defence'), was founded in 1920 as a *counter*-espionage service. Since other countries continued to spy on Germany, the Abwehr reasonably regarded the prohibition on German espionage, which it later disregarded during the Nazi era, as hypocritical.[2] Most of the thirty-three overseas stations of the British Secret Intelligence Service (SIS) in the early 1920s were one-man operations.[3] All interwar governments in Britain upheld the convention that there should be no mention whatever even of the existence of SIS. In 1927 Arthur Ponsonby, former junior Foreign Office minister during the first MacDonald Labour government of 1924, attacked 'the hypocrisy which pretends that we are so pure': 'The Secret Service [SIS] is supposed to be something we do not talk about in this House ... I do not see why I should not talk about it. It is about time we did say something about the Secret Service.'[4] Such parliamentary outbursts were very rare.

The great exception to post-war intelligence cutbacks was in Russia. During the Russian Civil War of 1918–20, the Cheka played a significant supporting role in the Red Army's victory over its White enemies. Like its later successor, the KGB, the Cheka liked to quantify its successes. In the autumn of 1919, probably the turning point in the Civil War, it proudly claimed that during the first nineteen months of its existence it had discovered and neutralized '412 underground anti-Soviet organisations'. The Cheka's most effective method of dealing with opposition was Terror.[5]

Though its liking for quantification did not extend to calculating the number of its victims, it is clear that the Cheka enormously outstripped the Tsarist Okhrana in both the scale and the ferocity of its onslaught on political opposition. Executions for political crimes in the reign of Nicholas II were limited to those involved in actual or attempted assassinations. During the Civil War, by contrast, Cheka executions probably numbered as many as 250,000, and may well have exceeded the number of deaths in battle.[6] 'The terror and the Cheka are absolutely indispensable', declared Lenin in December 1919.[7]

The brutality of the Cheka has distracted historical attention from its domestic bungles, in particular elementary failures to safeguard Lenin's security, documented in the archive of its chief, Felix Dzerzhinsky. In January 1919, unprotected by the Cheka, Lenin was held up by a gang of robbers while being driven in his official limousine to visit his long-suffering wife, Krupskaya. Thanks to the failure of the Cheka to provide security, Lenin became the first, and so far the only, head of government to be the victim of a carjack. The gang also robbed Lenin of all his possessions, including his Browning pistol, and ignored his protests as they drove off in his car. The gang leader, Iakov Kuznetsov, alias 'Koshelek' ('Wallet'), was not caught for another six months.[8]

In September 1922, after the Cheka had failed once again to provide basic security for Lenin, he returned home one day to find that his furniture had been vandalized during the renovation of his flat. A deeply embarrassed Dzerzhinsky personally led the investigation and produced a report entitled 'Inquiry into the damage to Lenin's furniture'. Among his initial instructions was an order 'To identify from an inspection of the damages whether they were caused with: chisel, hammer etc., and to find those guilty using these indications.' The ten pages of inspection and enquiry reports suggest that the damage had been done by bungling (or malevolent) builders rather than counter-revolutionary vandals. Unable to find the keys to Lenin's drawers, the builders had forced them open and damaged the locks, as well as leaving scratches with their tools on some of the furniture. It was clear, however, that GPU personnel had paid no attention to what the builders were up to in Lenin's apartment.[9]

In the West, unlike the Soviet Union, security services were peripheral to post-war systems of government. By 1925 the staff of MI5, which had numbered 844 at the end of the First World War, had shrunk to only thirty-five. Its operations were so reduced that in that year it sought and obtained only twenty-five Home Office Warrants allowing it to intercept the correspondence of individuals under investigation.[10] In Soviet Russia, by contrast, the Cheka and its interwar successors (the GPU, OGPU and

NKVD) were central to the functioning of the world's first one-party
state. By the mid-1920s their foreign operations were outclassing those of
their Western opponents. The most successful were the deception operations SINDIKAT ('Syndicate') and TREST ('Trust'), both of which
made sophisticated use of *agents provocateurs*. SINDIKAT was targeted
against Boris Savinkov, the man judged by the OGPU to be the most
dangerous of the White Guards, the successors in Western exile of the
White Armies defeated during the Civil War. Churchill, among others,
was captivated by his anti-Bolshevik fervour and included him in his book
Great Contemporaries. In 1924 Savinkov was lured across the Soviet
frontier for secret talks with a supposedly anti-Bolshevik resistance movement fabricated by the OGPU. Savinkov quickly capitulated, publicly
confessed his counter-revolutionary sins at a show trial, and died (or was
murdered) in prison a year later.

TREST was the cover name given to a fictitious monarchist underground, the MOR, cleverly fabricated by the GPU in 1921 and used as
the basis for a six-year deception operation against the White Guards and
their Western supporters. By 1923 the OGPU officer Aleksandr Yakushev,
posing as a secret MOR member able to travel abroad in his official capacity as a Soviet foreign trade representative, had won the confidence
during visits to Paris of both the Grand Duke Nikolai Nikolyaevich, cousin
of the murdered Tsar, and General Aleksandr Kutepov, leader of the White
Guards.[11] The leading victim of the TREST deception, however, was the
former SIS agent Sidney Reilly, a fantasist whose operational flair gave
him an undeserved posthumous reputation as a British 'masterspy'. In September 1925, like Savinkov a year earlier, Reilly was lured by the OGPU
across the Russian frontier for a meeting with bogus MOR conspirators.
Reilly's resistance after his arrest lasted little longer than Savinkov's. His
KGB file contains a letter written soon after his arrest to Dzerzhinsky, the
OGPU chief, in which, doubtless hoping to escape execution, he promised
to reveal all he knew about Western intelligence as well as Russian émigrés.
Reilly's letter failed to save him. Six days after writing it, he was taken for
a walk in woods near Moscow and, without warning, shot from behind.
Reilly's corpse was put on display in the Lubyanka sickbay to allow OGPU
officers to celebrate their triumph.[12]*

The TREST deception was finally exposed in 1927, to the embarrassment of intelligence agencies in Britain, France, Poland, Finland and the
Baltic states, who, in varying degree, had been taken in by it.[13] Not till

---

* The SIS head of station in Helsinki, Ernest Boyce, was 'carpeted' by the Chief, Admiral
Sir Hugh 'Quex' Sinclair, for having assisted Reilly.

the British 'Double-Cross System' deceived the Germans during the Second World War did a Western intelligence agency engage in an intelligence operation as sophisticated as TREST.

Though well ahead of Western HUMINT operations during the post-war decade, Soviet intelligence lagged seriously behind in SIGINT. After the Bolshevik Revolution, the codebreakers of the Tsarist *cabinet noir* had dispersed. Probably the ablest of them, Ernst Fetterlein, had escaped to Britain, where he became head of the Russian section at the interwar British SIGINT agency, the Government Code and Cypher School (GC&CS), formed from combining the wartime naval and military SIGINT units, Room 40 and MI1b.[14] His colleagues in GC&CS found that 'on book ciphers and anything where insight was vital he was quite the best'.[15] The great American cryptographer William Friedman, who met 'Fetty' (as he became known in GC&CS) soon after the First World War, noticed a large ruby ring on the index finger of his right hand: 'When I showed interest in this unusual gem, he told me that the ring had been presented to him as a token of recognition and thanks for his cryptanalytic successes while in the service of Czar Nicholas, the last of the line.'[16] Fetterlein, however, blamed Nicholas II's weakness for contributing to the Bolsheviks' success. Though he said little about his life in Tsarist Russia while working for GC&CS, one of his British colleagues would occasionally draw him out by making a disingenuous comment with which he was expected to disagree. 'And the Tsar, Mr Fetterlein', he was once asked, 'I believe he was a very strong man, with good physique?' 'Fetty' rose to the bait and replied indignantly: 'The Tsar was a weakling with no mind of his own, sickly and generally the subject of scorn.'[17]

Lord Curzon, who succeeded Balfour as Foreign Secretary in October 1919, initially expected GC&CS to produce little of diplomatic interest. He quickly changed his mind. By the summer of 1920 he was studying the Soviet decrypts produced by Fetterlein and his colleagues with almost obsessional interest. The Foreign Office was eventually embarrassed into taking over direct responsibility for GC&CS from the Admiralty after its codebreakers had decrypted a telegram from the French ambassador in London reporting that Curzon had secretly criticized British Cabinet policy. Curzon, a former Viceroy of India, had long been convinced that the French were not the kind of people 'to go tiger-shooting with', but decrypted French telegrams during the Turkish War of Independence (1919–23) raised his suspicions to new heights.* Both Curzon and the War

---

* No attempt had been made to decrypt French diplomatic traffic during the First World War. (Denniston, 'Government Code and Cypher School', pp. 54–5.)

Office were outraged by the evidence of secret dealings between the French and Turkish nationalists. French intercepts, wrote the DMI, Major-General Sir William Thwaites, sarcastically, were 'a nice savoury disclosure'. The British Commander-in-Chief in Constantinople, Sir 'Tim' Harington, complained a year later that there was still 'plenty of dirty work going on, as our intercepts show'. The intercepts persuaded Curzon that the former French President, Raymond Poincaré (Prime Minister and Foreign Minister, 1922–4), 'lied shamelessly'.[18] Curzon's mounting indignation at what he believed were Poincaré's attempts to deceive him, combined with the knowledge that he could not confront him with the secret evidence of his deceit obtained by intercepting French diplomatic correspondence, reduced the Foreign Secretary to a state of nervous collapse during the Chanak crisis in 1922. Looking across the conference table at Poincaré during a meeting in London in September, Curzon felt physically sick. One of the diplomats present wrote later: 'Curzon's wide white hands upon the green baize cloth trembled violently. He could stand it no longer.' His Permanent Undersecretary, Lord Hardinge, helped him to another room, 'where he collapsed upon a scarlet settee. He grasped Lord Hardinge by the arm. "Charley", he panted, "I can't bear that horrid little man, I can't bear him." He wept.'[19]

Curzon was also deeply unsettled by Russian intercepts during trade negotiations in 1920–21 which ended in the first *de facto* recognition of the Soviet regime by a major Western power. Leonid Krasin, head of the Russian trade delegation, paid his first visit to 10 Downing Street at the beginning of the negotiations on 31 May 1920. Churchill, Secretary of State for War and Air in Lloyd George's coalition government, stayed away to avoid having to 'shake hands with the hairy baboon'. Curzon turned up at Number 10 but initially refused to shake Krasin's hand. 'Curzon!' exclaimed Lloyd George. 'Be a gentleman!' Curzon took Krasin's still outstretched hand.[20]

During the six months of trade negotiations which followed, by far the most important intelligence available to Lloyd George, who took personal charge of the negotiations, and other ministers was the Soviet diplomatic traffic decrypted by Ernst Fetterlein and his British colleagues at GC&CS. Georgi Chicherin, the Soviet Commissar for Foreign Affairs, instructed Krasin not to 'yield to British blackmailing'. Lenin was blunter still: 'That swine Lloyd George has no scruples or shame in the way he deceives. Don't believe a word he says and gull him three times as much.' Unlike Curzon, Lloyd George took such insults in his stride. He tried to persuade ministers that 'the trickery of the Russians was not worse than that of the French'.[21]

Since his early indiscretions as Prime Minister in the use of SIGINT,[22] Lloyd George had learned the importance of preserving its secrecy. But

for Lloyd George, the evidence in the intercepts of the Russian trade delegation's secret dealings with British sympathizers with the Soviet regime would
almost certainly have led the Cabinet to expel the delegation and bring the
trade negotiations to an end. One cause of particular outrage among ministers and some service chiefs were the secret payments by the trade
delegation to the socialist *Daily Herald* and to the Communist Party of
Great Britain (CPGB) on its foundation in August. The payments were made
possible by the sale of Tsarist jewels which the delegation had smuggled into
Britain. 'Rumour of these large disposals has brought Jew dealers from all
parts of Europe', reported Sir Basil Thomson, head of the Special Branch
and of the short-lived Directorate of Intelligence. He obtained a photograph
of 'two of the largest gems' and noted the banknote numbers of much of
the proceeds from the sales of jewels. Krasin was dismayed to discover that,
as he informed Litvinov in a telegram decrypted by GC&CS, 'All our payments in banknotes are controlled [monitored] by Scotland Yard.'

As the price for continuing trade negotiations, Lloyd George had to
agree to demands from within the Cabinet for public disclosure of the secret
Soviet subsidies. On 18 August copies of eight intercepts revealing payments to the *Daily Herald* were given to all national newspapers (except
the *Daily Herald*) for publication on the following day. In an attempt to
protect the SIGINT source, the press was asked to say that the messages
had been obtained from 'a neutral country' – in the hope that Moscow
would conclude that there had been a leak from the entourage of Maxim
Litvinov in Copenhagen. To Lloyd George's fury, however, *The Times*
began its story with the words, 'The following wireless messages have been
intercepted by the British Government.' Moscow, surprisingly, paid little
attention. Either it did not read *The Times* attentively or it wrongly concluded that only the cipher in which the eight messages were sent had been
compromised.[23]

Pressure rapidly built up within Whitehall for further public revelations
of Soviet subversion. On 1 September, Sir Basil Thomson, Sir Henry Wilson, Chief of the Imperial General Staff, and Admiral Sir Hugh Sinclair,
Director of Naval Intelligence (and later Chief of SIS), sent Churchill a
joint memorandum which concluded:

> The presence of the Russian Trade Delegation has become in our opinion
> the gravest danger which this country has had to face since the Armistice.
>   This being so, we think that the publication of the de-cyphered cables
> has become so imperative that we must face the risks that will be entailed.

As Prime Minister in the Second World War, Churchill would have been
horrified by any action that might compromise the work of GC&CS. But

in 1920 he was 'convinced that the danger to the state which has been wrought by the intrigues of these revolutionaries and the disastrous effect which will be produced on these plans by the exposure of their methods outweighs all other considerations'.[24] On this occasion, the Cabinet did not approve the publication of further intercepts, though two were leaked from an unknown Whitehall source to the right-wing *Daily Mail* and *Morning Post*, which published them on 15 September. The Cabinet 'deplored' the publication but showed little interest in discovering the source of the leak.[25]

Lloyd George's restraining influence on the publication of Soviet intercepts disappeared with his resignation and the fall of his coalition government in October 1922. His Conservative successor, Andrew Bonar Law, the shortest-lived Prime Minister in British history, made no visible attempt to curb the calls for publication by Lord Curzon, who regarded Soviet subversion in India and on India's borders as a more serious menace than in Britain itself. On 23 April 1923, Curzon obtained Cabinet authority to prepare a protest note to Moscow, appropriately known to posterity as 'the Curzon ultimatum', threatening to cancel the trade agreement unless the Soviet Union promised to mend its ways. Curzon decided to base his ultimatum on SIGINT evidence. On 3 May, less than three weeks before the resignation of the terminally ill Bonar Law, the Cabinet considered a draft by Curzon. After prolonged discussion, which was considered too secret to include in the Cabinet minutes, it was agreed:

> That the advantages of basing the published British case on actual [telegraphic] despatches which had passed between the Soviet Government and its agents outweighed the disadvantages of the possible disclosure of the secret [SIGINT] source from which these despatches had been obtained, more especially as this was actually known to the Russian Soviet Government.[26]

The claim that Moscow already knew the intelligence source of Curzon's ultimatum was disingenuous. Though it was aware that GC&CS had decrypted telegrams exchanged earlier with the trade delegation, it is unlikely that it was fully aware of the extent to which its current ciphers were compromised. The Curzon ultimatum remains unique in the history of British diplomacy. Not content with quoting from Russian intercepts, the Foreign Secretary repeatedly taunted the Soviet government with Britain's success in decrypting their communications:

> The Russian Commissariat for Foreign Affairs will no doubt recognise the following communication dated 21st February, 1923, which they received from M. Raskolnikov . . . The Commissariat for Foreign Affairs will also

doubtless recognise a communication received by them from Kabul, dated the 8th November, 1922 . . . Nor will they have forgotten a communication dated the 16th March, 1923, from M. Karakhan, the Assistant Commissary for Foreign Affairs, to M. Raskolnikov . . . [27]

The Soviet reply virtuously declared its own refusal 'to base its protests upon reports of informers and intercepted documents'. The ultimatum none the less had the effect that Curzon had intended. Moscow was determined to preserve the trade agreement and therefore accepted the humiliation of promising 'not to support with funds or in any other form persons or bodies or agencies or institutions whose aim is to spread discontent or to foment rebellion in any part of the British Empire'. Even more humiliatingly, the Soviet government also recalled its envoy in Kabul, Fedor Raskolnikov, to whose 'subversive' activities Curzon's ultimatum had taken particular exception.[28]

No British Foreign Secretary has ever reacted so emotionally, at times even hysterically, as Lord Curzon to the contents of decrypted diplomatic telegrams. During his final months in office before the Conservative election defeat in January 1924, he became obsessed by the belief that the French were plotting against him.[29] In October 1923 he discovered from French diplomatic decrypts what he believed was an 'intrigue between M. Poincaré [French premier and Foreign Minister], Comte de Saint-Aulaire [French ambassador], H. A. Gwynne [editor of the *Morning Post*] to supplant me at [the] F.O.'[30] According to intercepted telegrams exchanged between Poincaré and Saint-Aulaire, the French hoped through the intermediary of Gwynne to persuade Bonar Law's successor, Stanley Baldwin, to replace Curzon by a more Francophile Foreign Secretary. Curzon could no longer bring himself even to meet the French ambassador, whom he henceforth 'declined to see . . . on one excuse or another': 'This is the worst thing that I have come across in my public life . . . I had not realised that diplomacy was such a dirty game.' Baldwin, though secretly anxious to replace Curzon, declared himself 'unaware that such dirty things were done in diplomacy'.[31]

At the opposite extreme to Curzon's frequent obsession with intelligence was the distaste for it of Britain's first Labour Prime Minister, J. Ramsay MacDonald, who took office on 22 January 1924 at the head of a Labour minority government, dependent on Liberal support. When Churchill returned to office in November 1924, anxious to catch up on the backlog of decrypts, he discovered that 'In MacDonald's time, he was himself long kept in ignorance of them by the Foreign Office.'[32] Arthur Ponsonby, MacDonald's Undersecretary at the Foreign Office who had the main responsibility for day-to-day diplomacy, was refused all access to intercepts and SIS reports on the dubious grounds of his 'subordinate position'. Ponsonby regarded all intelligence work as a 'dirty' business, though probably 'you have to do it'. By his own admission he was not sorry to be kept in ignorance of it:

> It is part of the etiquette of the Secret Service [SIS] that Under-Secretaries are not told about it . . . When I mentioned the Secret Service, the officials, the most genial of them, used to become rigid. I was not allowed to know, and even when we got to the verge of that awful mud-bath which surrounded the Zinoviev letter, I was never allowed to come in, and I am glad it was so.[33]

Allegedly despatched by Grigory Zinoviev and two other members of the Communist International (Comintern) Executive Committee to the CPGB on 15 September 1924, the letter instructed them to put pressure on their sympathizers in the Labour Party, to 'strain every nerve' for the ratification of a recent treaty concluded by MacDonald's government with the Soviet Union, to intensify 'agitation-propaganda work in the armed forces', and generally to prepare for the coming of the British revolution. On 9 October SIS forwarded copies to the Foreign Office, MI5, Scotland Yard and the service ministries, together with an ill-founded assurance that 'the authenticity is undoubted'. Though the letter resembled some genuine Comintern correspondence, it was a forgery obtained by the SIS station in Reval (now Tallinn), which had been deceived by other forgeries three years earlier.

The unauthorized publication of the letter in the Conservative *Daily Mail* on 25 October turned it into what MacDonald called a 'political bomb' during the final week of a general election campaign. Those responsible intended the 'Red Letter' to sabotage Labour's prospects of victory by suggesting that it was susceptible to Communist pressure: though they were partly successful in covering their tracks, they probably included a senior MI5 officer, Joseph Ball (later director of the Conservative Research Department and a confidant of Neville Chamberlain), acting without the knowledge of the director, Sir Vernon Kell. Conservative Central Office, with which Ball already had close contacts, probably had a copy of the Zinoviev letter by 22 October, three days before publication. Ball's subsequent lack of scruples in using intelligence for party-political advantage while at Central Office in the later 1920s strongly suggests, but does not prove, that he was willing to do so during the election campaign of October 1924. But Ball was not alone. Other senior figures involved in the publication of the Zinoviev letter probably included the former DNI, Admiral 'Blinker' Hall, and Lieutenant-Colonel Freddie Browning, Cumming's former deputy and a friend of both Hall and the editor of the *Mail*.[34] All belonged to a deeply conservative, strongly patriotic establishment network who were accustomed to sharing state secrets between themselves: 'Feeling themselves part of a special and closed community, they exchanged confidences secure in the knowledge, as they thought, that they were protected by that community from indiscretion.'[35] Those who conspired together in October 1924 convinced themselves that they were acting in the national interest – to remove from power a government whose susceptibility to Soviet and pro-Soviet pressure made it a threat to national security. Though the Zinoviev letter was not the main cause of the Tory election landslide on 29 October (which owed more to Conservative success in overcoming internal divisions and withdrawal of Liberal support for Labour), many politicians on both left and right believed that it was. Labour leaders felt they had been tricked out of office. And their suspicions seemed to be confirmed when they discovered the part played by Conservative Central Office in the publication of the letter.

As Prime Minister, Ramsay MacDonald preferred to keep the intelligence agencies quite literally at arm's length. It is unlikely that he ever knowingly met any officer from SIS, MI5 or GC&CS. When he finally decided to question the head of the SIS political section, Major Malcolm 'Woolly' Woollcombe, about the Zinoviev letter in the aftermath of his election defeat and before the formation of the second Baldwin Conservative government, MacDonald could not bring himself to conduct a face-to-face interview. Instead, Woollcombe was placed in a room adjoining MacDonald's at the Foreign Office while the PUS, Sir Eyre Crowe, positioned himself in the doorway between the two. The Prime Minister then addressed his questions to Woollcombe via Crowe, who reported the answers to MacDonald. At no point during these bizarre proceedings did Woollcombe catch sight of the Prime Minister.[36]*

One of the consequences of the Zinoviev letter furore was a drastic tightening of SIGINT security procedures by the incoming Conservative administration led by Stanley Baldwin after it took office in November 1924. Winston Churchill, now Chancellor of the Exchequer, returned to power eager to catch up on the backlog of Soviet intercepts and was outraged to be denied access to them. He protested to Austen Chamberlain, the new Foreign Secretary, against 'such serious changes in the system which was in vogue when we were last colleagues':

> I have studied this information over a longer period and more attentively than probably any other minister has done. All the years I have been in

* By permission of the then Foreign Secretary, Sir Geoffrey Howe, Christopher Andrew presented a re-enactment of this remarkable episode in the Foreign Secretary's room at the FCO for BBC2's *Timewatch* in November 1987.

office since it began [in Room 40] in the autumn of 1914[37] I have read every one of these flimsies and I attach more importance to them as a means of forming a true judgement of public policy in these spheres than to any other source of knowledge at the disposal of the State.

Churchill's protests were to no avail. Henceforth, to reinforce their secrecy, a complete set of intercepts from GC&CS was sent only to the Foreign Office. The service ministries, and India, Colonial and Home Offices, saw only intercepts which directly concerned them.[38]

In 1927, however, the Baldwin government breached its own SIGINT security procedures in a way which caused more long-term damage than the Curzon ultimatum. In the spring of that year, under pressure from a vociferous backbench Conservative campaign against Soviet subversion, strongly supported within the government by Churchill and some other ministers, the Baldwin government decided to break off diplomatic relations with Moscow. To justify its decision it originally intended to use documents seized in a police raid on the Moorgate offices of the All-Russian Co-operative Society (ARCOS), which acted as a front for Soviet intelligence operations as well as to promote trade with Britain. Contrary to expectation, however, the documents did not provide significant evidence of espionage. The Cabinet therefore concluded that the only available proof of serious misbehaviour by the Soviet legation came from diplomatic telegrams exchanged with Moscow which had been decrypted by GC&CS. The first public reference to the decrypts was made by the Prime Minister on 24 May in a Commons statement on the ARCOS raid. Baldwin read out four Russian telegrams which had, he drily observed, 'come into the possession of His Majesty's Government'. An Opposition MP challenged Baldwin to say how the government had obtained the telegrams, but there was uproar (or, as Hansard put it, 'interruption') before he could finish his question. The Speaker intervened and deferred further discussion until the debate two days later on the decision to end diplomatic relations with the Soviet Union.

The debate, on 26 May, developed into an orgy of governmental indiscretion about secret intelligence for which there is no parallel in modern parliamentary history. Both the Foreign Secretary, Austen Chamberlain, and the Home Secretary, William Joynson-Hicks ('Jix'), followed Baldwin's bad example by quoting intercepted Russian telegrams. Jix became quite carried away while accusing the Soviet Trade Delegation of running 'one of the most complete and one of the most nefarious spy systems that it has ever been my lot to meet'. 'I happen to have in my possession', he boasted, 'not merely the names but the addresses of most of those spies.'

On the day of the debate Chamberlain informed the Russian chargé d'affaires of the decision to break off diplomatic relations (which were not renewed until 1929) because of 'anti-British espionage and propaganda'. Chamberlain gave his message an unusually personal point by quoting a decrypted telegram from the chargé to Moscow on 1 April 'in which you request material to enable you to support a political campaign against His Majesty's Government'. Baldwin's government was able to prove the charge of covert Soviet dabbling in British politics. But the documents seized in the ARCOS raid and the decrypts published in a White Paper contained only a few oblique allusions to the more serious sin of espionage. The government contrived in the end to have the worst of both worlds. It compromised the work of its most secret and productive intelligence agency, GC&CS, and yet, at the same time, it failed to produce evidence to support Jix's dramatic charge that Britain was threatened by an extraordinarily nefarious Soviet 'spy system'.

The effect of the government's publication of the Soviet intercepts on the intelligence services was traumatic. The Soviet Union responded by adopting the theoretically unbreakable 'one-time pad' for its diplomatic traffic. As Fetterlein informed his colleagues, the system had been first used by the Tsarist Foreign Ministry in 1916–17.[39] Between 1927 and the Second World War, GC&CS was able to decrypt almost no high-grade Soviet communications (though it continued to have some success with the communications of the Communist International). Alastair Denniston, the operational head of GC&CS, wrote bitterly that Baldwin's government had 'found it necessary to compromise our work beyond question'. New entrants to GC&CS over the next decade were told the story of the loss of the Soviet ciphers as a warning of the depths of indiscretion to which politicians were capable of sinking.[40]

The post-war French politician most indiscreet about SIGINT was probably Georges Clemenceau. According to Sir Maurice Hankey, British Secretary of the Paris Peace Conference in 1919 (as well as Cabinet Secretary) and usually a reliable witness, Clemenceau boasted to the other members of the Council of Four (Lloyd George, Woodrow Wilson and Vittorio Orlando of Italy) about the success of French SIGINT, claiming with considerable exaggeration that 'the Quai d'Orsay decoded every message that reached Paris'.[41] His boast was all the more remarkable because some American, British and Italian telegrams were among the decrypts.[42] The repeated revelations between 1920 and 1927 that GC&CS had broken Soviet ciphers failed to alert the Quai d'Orsay to the danger that its own ciphers might also be at serious risk. Not until 1935 did any French diplomatic cipher defeat GC&CS. As Denniston wrote later, until then the codebreakers' only problem was that the proximity of Paris and London meant that much French diplomatic traffic between them went via diplomatic bag and was therefore beyond their reach.[43]

As before the war, some of the intercepts decrypted by French codebreakers led to disputes within the French government.[44] Among them was a conflict in January 1921 between Alexandre Millerand, Poincaré's successor as President of the Republic, and Aristide Briand, then at the start of the seventh of his eleven terms as Prime Minister. Millerand took a hard line over negotiations for the payment of the war reparations imposed on Germany by the Treaty of Versailles. Germany, he believed, was 'an adversary of whose bad faith there is no doubt'.[45] He was shocked to read in a decrypted despatch from the German ambassador in Paris to Berlin that Briand had told him in private: 'I shall do everything possible to improve relations with Germany. It is essential to reach an agreement . . . My policy will not be one of intransigence; I shall always take account of reality and shall never ask for the impossible.'[46]* Though detailed research is still required on French SIGINT during the 1920s, it was a period of sharp decline. After 1919 the École Supérieure de la Guerre no longer offered courses in cryptography, and the *Section du Chiffre* of the Deuxième Bureau was drastically cut back. The personnel of the *Section du Chiffre* at the Quai d'Orsay during the 1920s numbered no more than a dozen, with few cryptanalysts among them.[47] The cutbacks in the *Section du Chiffre* doubtless help to explain the relative ease with which GC&CS broke French diplomatic ciphers.

Apart from French diplomatic ciphers, GC&CS had its greatest success during the 1920s with those of Japan. To translate the Japanese decrypts, Denniston recruited a retired diplomat, Ernest Hobart-Hampden, who had spent thirty years in the Far East:

> With his knowledge of the habits of the Japanese he soon acquired an uncanny skill in never missing the important . . . Throughout the period down to [the Japanese invasion of Manchuria in] 1931, no big conference was held in Washington, London or Geneva in which he did not contribute all the views of the Japanese government and of their too verbose representatives.†

---

* Agreement on reparations was not reached until 1932.
† In 1926 Hobart-Hampden was joined by another retired Japanese-speaking diplomat, Sir Harold Parlett, who, in Denniston's view, had 'an equal sense of the essential'. The two men combined their work at GC&CS with compiling an *English–Japanese Dictionary of the Spoken Word*. (Denniston, 'Government Code and Cypher School', pp. 55–6.)

Probably the main success of US codebreakers during the 1920s was also in decrypting Japanese diplomatic traffic. In August 1918, Herbert Yardley, wartime head of the military intelligence cipher unit, MI-8,[48] established a peacetime Cipher Bureau, better known as the Black Chamber, at a secret address in Manhattan, funded jointly by the Departments of War and State. Unlike GC&CS, Russian diplomatic traffic was a low priority and not easy to intercept until the United States belatedly established diplomatic relations with the Soviet Union in 1933. The Black Chamber's main priority was Japan. Its greatest success came at the Washington Conference on the Limitation of Armaments, the first major international conference to meet in the nation's capital, which began four months of deliberations in November 1921.[49]

Yardley's later account of his codebreakers' achievements is characteristically untainted by modesty:

> The Black Chamber, bolted, hidden, guarded, sees all, hears all. Though the blinds are drawn and the windows heavily curtained, its far-seeing eyes penetrate the secret conference chambers at Washington, Tokio [sic], London, Paris, Geneva, Rome. Its sensitive ears catch the faintest whisperings in the foreign capitals of the world.[50]

Though never approaching the omniscience suggested by Yardley's hyperbole, the Black Chamber was strikingly successful in decrypting Japanese traffic. Secretary of State Charles Evans Hughes was initially alarmed by the aggressive rhetoric contained in Japanese intercepts. Before the conference opened, he told the British ambassador, Sir Auckland Geddes, that the intercepts indicated 'that Japan intends to seize Eastern Siberia', and asked Britain to 'take action to persuade [the Japanese Government] to desist from attempting to carry out their projects'. Geddes did not reveal that Britain was also decrypting Japanese diplomatic traffic.[51] The US Secretary of State almost certainly did not suspect that GC&CS was also able to decrypt some American communications.*

Japanese decrypts from the Black Chamber during the Washington conference gave the US delegation a remarkable negotiating advantage. The American negotiators called for a 10:6 naval ratio between the United States and Japan. The Japanese insisted they would not go below 10:7. Then, in early December 1921, the Black Chamber decrypted a message from Tokyo of 28 November that Yardley later claimed was 'the most important and

---

* Denniston later modestly recalled that the American section of GC&CS was able to be 'of some assistance' to British policymakers during the Washington conference. (Denniston, 'Government Code and Cypher School' p. 54.)

far reaching telegram that ever passed through its doors'. Tokyo instructed its delegates to 'redouble your efforts' to obtain the 10:7 ratio. 'In case of unavoidable necessity', it was authorized to accept 10:6.5. Since, however, it was necessary to avoid any clash with Great Britain and America, particularly America', even a 10:6 ratio would in the last resort have to be accepted. The US delegation knew henceforth that it had only to stand firm to achieve the ratio it wanted. Yardley, a poker aficionado, later commented: 'Stud poker is not a very difficult game after you see your opponent's hole card.' Finally, on 10 December, Tokyo cabled its delegation: 'There is nothing to do but accept the ratio proposed by the United States . . .'*

'Christmas in the Black Chamber', wrote Yardley, 'was brightened by handsome presents to all of us from officials in the War and State Departments, which were accompanied by personal regards and assurances that our long hours of drudgery during the conference were appreciated by those in authority.'[52] On this occasion, Yardley probably did not exaggerate. Other records reveal that he received a curiously calculated Christmas bonus of $998 to distribute among his staff. The award to Yardley of the Distinguished Service Medal in 1923 was, almost certainly, primarily in recognition of the Black Chamber's achievements during the Washington conference.

'It was all downhill from there', concludes the veteran US cryptographer, Thomas R. Johnson, author of a four-volume classified history of American cryptologic operations during the Cold War. 'Yardley's organization was starved for money – by 1929, the budget stood at one-third of what it had been eight years earlier.'[53] The decline in the fortunes of the Black Chamber (much like French diplomatic SIGINT in the 1920s but unlike GC&CS) was due partly to the lack of interest in the outside world of Calvin Coolidge, President from 1923 to 1929. The former Secretary of War and State Elihu Root said of 'Silent Cal', the least active and most taciturn of twentieth-century presidents: 'He did not have an international hair in his head.' Coolidge's *Autobiography* contains no mention of foreign policy, still less of foreign intelligence.[54]

But Herbert Yardley's leadership was also partly to blame for the decline of the Black Chamber. He failed to provide the dependable leadership and sound judgement which characterized Denniston's years at GC&CS. After the strain of the Washington conference, Yardley suffered a temporary breakdown. When he returned to work, he was plagued by fantasies of

---

* Yardley (*American Black Chamber*, ch. 16) published the text of a number of Japanese telegrams decrypted during the conference, including a photograph of the decrypted telegram of 28 November 1921.

beautiful female agents attempting to seduce him. Unable to tolerate Prohibition, he stopped off after work each day at a speakeasy in the Manhattan
West Forties. There he encountered a 'gorgeous creature' with 'golden hair
which curved in an intriguing manner about her ears' but who 'showed a
bit too much of her legs as she nestled in the deep cushions'. 'Very beautiful
legs too', Yardley reflected 'at the end of the third cocktail.' On further
reflection, he became convinced that she had been sent to spy on him and
thus discover the closely guarded cryptanalytic secrets of the Black Chamber. According to his own improbable account, Yardley decided, in the
national interest, to get the 'lovely creature' drunk, then took her back to
her apartment in the East Eighties. While she slept on a couch, he searched
her dressing table and found a note that appeared to provide proof that she
was on a secret mission: 'See mutual friend at first opportunity. Important
you get us information at once.' Yardley hurriedly let himself out of the
apartment.[55] Since he was left to run the Black Chamber more or less as
he pleased, his mostly harmless fantasies of sex and espionage seem to have
attracted little or no attention from the administrations he served.

The end of the Black Chamber owed more to a change in the presidency
than to Yardley's failings. Following Herbert Hoover's inauguration as
President in succession to Coolidge in March 1929, Henry L. Stimson
became Secretary of State. In view of Stimson's well-advertised insistence
on high moral standards in public affairs, his officials decided not to bring
the existence of the Black Chamber to his attention until he had had some
weeks to acclimatize himself to the lower moral tone of everyday diplomacy.
In May the State Department finally decided, with some trepidation, to
place a few Japanese decrypts on Stimson's desk. According to a confidential
account of the sequel later compiled by the leading codebreaker, William
F. Friedman:

> His reaction was violent and his action drastic. Upon learning how the
> material was obtained, he characterized the activity as highly unethical and
> declared that it would cease *immediately*, so far as the State Department
> was concerned. To put teeth into his decision he gave instructions that the
> necessary funds of the State Department would be withdrawn *at once*.[56]

Stimson's own account in his diary, though less dramatic, agreed with
Friedman's. On seeing the decrypts on his desk, he immediately summoned his friend Joseph P. Cotton, a New York lawyer whom he had made
his Undersecretary:

> We both agreed it was a highly unethical thing for the Government to do
> to be reading the messages coming to our ambassadorial guests from other

countries. So then and there . . . I discontinued these payments [to the Black Chamber] and that put an end to the continuing of this group of experts who subsequently disbanded.[57]

It was only with difficulty that Stimson was persuaded to allow the Black Chamber two months to close down and hand its files to the Army Signal Corps, which carried on some work on Japanese ciphers.[58]*

Yardley, the sacked head of the Black Chamber, who was given no government pension, took a terrible revenge. Hitherto, he had been strongly opposed to 'disclosing anything about codes and ciphers'. 'My reason', he wrote, 'is obvious: it warns other governments of our skill and makes our work more difficult.' Large posters in the Manhattan offices of the Black Chamber warned its staff: 'SECRET! If enemies learn that we can decipher their present codes, they will try to devise more difficult forms.'[59] Between April and June 1931, Yardley broke his own rules by publishing sensational memoirs, first as a magazine serialization, then as a book entitled *The American Black Chamber*. As well as revealing classified information on cryptanalysis, Yardley's memoirs listed a series of countries (some of them American allies), some of whose ciphers had been broken by the Black Chamber: Argentina, Brazil, Britain, Chile, China, Costa Rica, Cuba, France, Germany, Japan, Liberia, Mexico, Nicaragua, Panama, Peru, San Salvador, Santo Domingo, the Soviet Union and Spain. The most explosive chapters dealt with the breaking of Japanese Foreign Ministry ciphers, and the intelligence about Tokyo's negotiating stance during the Washington Naval Conference.[60] The State Department flatly denied that Japanese ciphers had been broken during the conference but deceived no one. The Japanese Foreign Ministry sent 138 copies of *The American Black Chamber* to its embassies and legations around the world to warn them that their ciphers might be compromised.[61]

Nine months after Yardley published Japanese decrypts, the Soviet Union also did so. Though the Soviet publication attracted far less attention in the Western media than Yardley's memoirs, it was even more remarkable, because it was done on Stalin's instructions. Stalin had become so concerned by the threat of Japanese attack on the Soviet Far East and Eastern Siberia that in March 1932 he took the unprecedented step of ordering the OGPU to publish in *Izvestia* extracts from top-secret Japanese documents obtained both from breaking Japanese ciphers and from an (unidentified)

---

* Stimson had fewer moral qualms about military intelligence operations. By 1936 the Signal Intelligence Service had succeeded in breaking the main Japanese diplomatic cipher, to which it gave the code name RED.

OGPU agent in the office of the Japanese military attaché in Moscow,
Lieutenant-Colonel Yukio Kasahara. Though not identifying him by name,
Izvestia quoted Kasahara as reporting to Tokyo:

> It will be [Japan's] unavoidable destiny to clash with the USSR sooner or
> later ... The sooner the Soviet–Japanese war comes, the better for us. We
> must realize that with every day the situation develops more favourably for
> the USSR. In short, I hope the authorities will make up their minds for a
> speedy war with the Soviet Union and initiate policies accordingly.

In the spring of 1932 Kasahara was appointed chief of the Russian section
in the second department of the Japanese General Staff. His equally bel-
ligerent successor as military attaché in Moscow, Torashiro Kawabe,
reported to Tokyo that a Russo-Japanese war was 'unavoidable'. Kasahara
replied that military preparations were complete: 'War against Russia is
necessary for Japan to consolidate Manchuria.' For the next few years the
top priority of Soviet codebreakers was probably to monitor the danger
of a Japanese attack which was never to materialize.[62]

Despite the discovery that both the United States and the Soviet Union
had broken its ciphers, the Japanese Foreign Ministry did little to improve
them for some years. GC&CS decrypted more Japanese telegrams in
1932–3 than in 1930–31.[63] The OGPU also continued to produce a steady
stream of Japanese decrypts. Some of the decrypts which worried Stalin
most concerned Japanese intelligence penetration of the Soviet Union. On
10 June the OGPU sent Kliment Voroshilov, Commissar for the Army
and Navy, decrypted Japanese intelligence reports which gave largely
accurate details of the transfer of Soviet land and air forces to the Far East
from European Russia, as well as on the strengthening of Soviet naval
forces. It seemed clear that the intelligence came from Japanese agents in
Transbaikalia and Primorye, as well as from Moscow and Japanese contacts in the General Staffs of Poland and Latvia.[64]

A few weeks later Stalin angrily denounced the 'criminal' conduct of
'subversive operations' by both the OGPU and the military Fourth
Department in Manchuria which, he claimed, risked 'provoking a new
conflict with Japan'. Those responsible, he believed, might well be Japanese agents who had penetrated Soviet intelligence. He wrote to Kaganovich, who chaired the Politburo in his absence: 'We cannot put up with
this outrage any longer! Have a chat with Molotov and take Draconian
measures against the criminals at the OGPU and [military] Intelligence
Bureau (it is quite possible that these gentlemen are agents of our enemies
in our midst).'[65]

In the autumn of 1933, Hirota, the former Japanese ambassador to

Moscow, was appointed Foreign Minister in Tokyo. In late November, the OGPU sent Stalin a decrypted despatch from the US ambassador in Japan to the State Department, predicting a more aggressive Japanese foreign policy under Hirota and war with the Soviet Union in the spring of 1934.[66] Stalin continued to use SIGINT as a means of monitoring the threat of a Japanese attack. Though the attack never came, there were over a hundred minor military incidents between Soviet and Japanese troops, culminating in an undeclared border war in 1939.[67]

By the early 1930s Russian codebreakers were once again the best in the world, as they had been in the reign of Tsar Nicholas II.[68] Stalin's largely unresearched files of diplomatic intercepts had a major influence on his foreign policy. These were not merely additional pieces of information which he added to the other sources available to him. Often, as in the case of Japan, they were the sources to which he paid most attention.*

As in the reign of Nicholas II, Russian SIGINT operations were greatly assisted by agent penetration of foreign embassies.[69] The most successfully penetrated British embassy was in Rome. According to the diplomat Sir Andrew Noble, who was stationed in Rome in the mid-1930s, security was 'virtually non-existent'. Embassy servants had the keys to red boxes and filing cabinets containing classified documents, as well as – probably – the number of the combination lock on the embassy safe. Among the servants was Francesco Constantini, who was recruited as a Soviet agent in 1924 and for more than a decade sold his case officers a remarkable quantity of British diplomatic despatches.[70] An NKVD report of 15 November 1935 notes, for example, that no fewer than 101 of the British documents obtained from Francesco Constantini (or his brother Secondo) since the start of the year had been judged sufficiently important to be 'sent to Comrade Stalin': among them the Foreign Office records of talks between Sir John Simon, Anthony Eden and Hitler in Berlin; between Eden and Maksim Litvinov, the Soviet Commissar for Foreign Affairs, in Moscow; between Eden and Josef Beck, the Polish Foreign Minister, in Warsaw; between Eden and Eduard Beneš, the Czechoslovak Foreign Minister, in Prague; and between Eden and Mussolini in Rome.[71] Successive British ambassadors in Rome noticed nothing amiss until January 1936, when

---

* No one would nowadays dream of writing a book or even an article on Churchill in the Second World War without acknowledging his passion for ULTRA. By contrast, no existing biography of Stalin or study of his foreign policy mentions that his enthusiasm for SIGINT was as great as Churchill's. Stalin's SIGINT files are currently being researched by Svetlana Lokhova.

Secondo Constantini stole a diamond necklace belonging to the ambassador's wife from one of the locked red boxes normally used for classified documents. An investigation by Valentine Vivian, head of SIS counterintelligence, quickly identified Secondo Constantini (codenamed DUDLEY by the NKVD) as the probable thief. The ambassador, Sir Eric Drummond (later Lord Perth), refused to believe the results of Vivian's investigation. Instead of being dismissed, agent DUDLEY and his wife were invited to London as guests of His Majesty's government in May 1937 to attend the coronation of King George VI, as a reward for his long and supposedly faithful service.[72]

The US embassy in Moscow was even more comprehensively penetrated than the British embassy in Rome.* When the embassy opened in 1933, it had virtually no security and initially no ciphers either. The future US ambassador in Moscow, George Kennan, one of the original members of the embassy staff, later recalled: 'Communications with our government went through the regular telegraphic office and lay on the table for the Soviet government to see.' Stalin must have found it difficult to believe his luck. The US Marines supposed to guard the embassy were quickly provided with attentive girlfriends (some of them ballerinas) by the NKVD. 'Chip' Bohlen, like Kennan both a founder member of the embassy and a future ambassador, was sitting in the lobby of the Savoy Hotel one day, when a heavily made-up Russian woman walked up to the reception desk and said she wished to go up to Marine Sergeant O'Dean's room. 'I', she announced, 'am his Russian teacher.'[73] With the assistance of other 'Russian teachers', at least one of the first group of cipher clerks posted to the embassy, Tyler Kent, was recruited as a Soviet agent. Despite the restrictions imposed on most foreign diplomats, Kent was able to acquire a car, a gun and a studio, where he took nude photographs of his Russian teacher. He also collected US diplomatic correspondence, allegedly for 'historical purposes', more probably for the NKVD.†

Without realizing it, the US embassy, so far as Soviet intelligence was concerned, practised something akin to open diplomacy. The first ambassador, William C. Bullitt Jr, bequeathed both to his successors and to the NKVD a deeply penetrated US embassy and ambassador's residence. In 1937 the embassy electrician discovered an NKVD microphone hidden

* No existing history of US/Soviet relations grasps the importance of (or usually even mentions) the extraordinary haemorrhage of classified documents from the US embassy in Moscow over a period of thirty years from its foundation after the establishment of diplomatic relations in 1933.
† In 1939, Kent was transferred to London as code clerk in the US embassy. (Rand, *Conspiracy of One.* Andrew and Gordievsky, *KGB*, p. 238.)

in an attic above the desk of Bullitt's naïve successor, Joseph E. Davies, US ambassador from 1936 to 1938. Davies was entirely unconcerned and refused to take seriously the protests of his staff. He wrote condescendingly in his diary: 'The youngsters were all "het up" . . . I cooled them off and "kidded" them about their "international sleuthing" . . . My position was if the Soviets had a Dictaphone installed so much the better – the sooner they would find that we were friends, not enemies.'[74]

By the mid-1930s, as well as having the world's best SIGINT, the Soviet Union had more foreign agents in more countries (most, but by no means all, of them ideological) than any intelligence agency had ever had before. The high-flying Ivy League recruits in the United States – Larry Duggan, Alger Hiss, Harry Dexter White and Duncan Lee chief among them – were very like their equally high-flying Cambridge UK counterparts.

In the mid-1930s, more recent Cambridge graduates were recruited by Soviet intelligence than by MI5 and SIS. Probably the ablest of them, Kim Philby, later began his memoirs with a preface by his friend Graham Greene comparing him and his fellow Soviet recruits to the committed 'Catholics who, in the reign of Queen Elizabeth I, worked for the victory of Spain' over Protestant England.[75] The main recruiter in Elizabethan Cambridge was a deep-cover Catholic priest operating 'under the guise of a scholar'.[76] The main Soviet recruiter in the 1930s was Arnold Deutsch, a Viennese PhD with an academic record more brilliant than any of the Cambridge 'Magnificent Five', living in Hampstead and operating undercover as a graduate student at University College London. As well as being seduced by the myth-image of the Soviet Union as a worker-peasant state where, for the first time, ordinary citizens were able to make the most and the best of themselves in the service of the common good, the ideological recruits saw themselves as secret warriors in the struggle against international fascism. Julian Wadleigh, a Soviet agent who entered the State Department in 1936, wrote later: 'When the Communist International represented the only world force effectively resisting Nazi Germany, I had offered my services to the Soviet underground in Washington as one small contribution to help stem the fascist tide.'[77]

Potentially the most valuable NKVD ideological agent networks were those in Nazi Germany, headed by Arvid Harnack, an official in the Economics Ministry, and Harro Schulze-Boysen, a lieutenant in Luftwaffe intelligence, who were both capable of providing advance warning of a German attack on the Soviet Union. So was the Fourth Department (later GRU) illegal Richard Sorge, operating undercover in Tokyo as a German journalist. Sorge had close contact in the German embassy with both

Colonel Eugen Ott, military attaché from 1934, and Frau Ott, with whom he had one of his numerous affairs. Sorge saw much of the intelligence on the Japanese armed forces and military planning which Ott forwarded to Berlin, as well as many of the classified documents received by the embassy on German policy in the Far East. When Ott was promoted to ambassador in April 1938, Sorge had breakfast with him each day, briefing him on Japanese affairs and drafting some of his reports to Berlin.

There was a growing gulf, however, between the extraordinary successes of Soviet HUMINT and SIGINT collection during the 1930s and the Stalinist regime's ability to interpret it. The warnings of Harnack, Schulze-Boysen and Sorge in June 1941 of impending German invasion were ignored.[78] In all one-party states, intelligence analysis is distorted by the insistent demands of political correctness. Analysts are rarely willing to challenge the views of the political leadership (which in June 1941 were that there would be no German invasion). Foreign intelligence in authoritarian regimes commonly acts as a mechanism for reinforcing rather than correcting the regimes' misconceptions of the outside world. In Stalinist Russia the distortions produced by political correctness were made worse by a recurrent tendency to conspiracy theory (another common characteristic of authoritarian regimes), of which Stalin himself was the chief exponent. The tendency to substitute conspiracy theory for evidence-based analysis was made worse by Stalin's increasing determination to act as his own intelligence analyst. Stalin, indeed, actively discouraged intelligence analysis by others, which he condemned as 'dangerous guesswork'. 'Don't tell me what you think', he is reported to have said, 'give me the facts and the source!' As a result, INO (the foreign-intelligence department of the Cheka and its interwar successors) had no analytical department. Soviet intelligence reports throughout, and even beyond, the Stalin era characteristically consisted of no more than compilations of information on particular topics.[79]

During the Great Terror of 1936–8, the main priority of Soviet intelligence was the pursuit of imaginary 'enemies of the people'. Stalin's obsession with liquidating opposition was more recent than most studies of him have realized. As the neglected photographic record of Stalin mingling with passers-by as he walked though Moscow during the early 1930s shows, he had then been unconcerned with his personal security. The lack of reaction on the faces of Muscovites shows that he was a familiar sight on the streets of the capital.

Stalin's attitude to his own security changed dramatically after the assassination of his closest friend, Sergei Kirov, the Leningrad party boss, on 1 December 1934 by a lone gunman, Leonid Nikolaev, inside Party headquarters.* Though it has often been wrongly assumed that Stalin was behind the killing, in reality he was deeply shocked by it. The investigation of the Kirov assassination by the NKVD led early in 1935 to the discovery of what was called the 'Kremlin Plot' to kill Stalin. The investigations of both the Kirov assassination and the Kremlin Plot disprove the common contention that both Stalin and the NKVD were already obsessed with security. In both cases security, as in the earlier failure to prevent Lenin's carjacking and the vandalization of his flat,[80] was remarkably feeble. Genrikh Yagoda, head of the NKVD, acknowledged that Kirov's murder would not have been possible but for 'the complete disintegration and collapse of the NKVD apparatus in Leningrad':

> The shame which has shrouded the organs of the NKVD . . . is only worsened by the fact that the assassination could without a doubt have been prevented, if those officers of the Leningrad NKVD Directorate responsible for the guard of Comrade Kirov had worked to take even the most elementary measures to protect and guard Comrade Kirov.[81]

The investigation of the Kremlin Plot, whose voluminous files have recently been discovered by Svetlana Lokhova, revealed a security shambles on an even larger scale. The Kremlin was a miniature city which provided a privileged lifestyle for the Communist elite, with superior food, heating, electrical supply, telephones – even its own private hospital, cinema and library. But it emerged during the NKVD investigation that its many employees had been taken on without any vetting system or background checks. The official responsible for issuing security passes, Pavel Federovich, told NKVD interrogators that if job applicants had 'a mother or a sister already working in the Kremlin', that was an adequate guarantee of their reliability. It was discovered, however, that the staff included relatives of jailed political prisoners and former members of the Tsarist nobility. The investigation also revealed that the chief administrator of the Kremlin site, Abel Enukidze, a Georgian 'Old Bolshevik' and friend of Stalin, led a life of extraordinary and sometimes ostentatious dissipation, including involvement in organized prostitution. A Kremlin secretary described Enukidze's habit of travelling by train from Moscow to Leningrad with four of his lovers, who were rewarded with places in the government box at the Bolshoy Theatre and other privileges.[82]

Stalin was sent copies of all 110 (often multi-volume) interrogation protocols during the investigation of the 'Kremlin Plot' and made many

---

* The most recent study of the Kirov assassination shows that Nikolaev 'very probably' acted alone. (Lenoe, *The Kirov Murder and Soviet History*, p. 689.)

annotations on them. They show that, contrary to the conclusions of most historians, Stalin was not yet obsessed with personal criticisms of himself. By the time the Great Terror began in the autumn of 1936, the NKVD would never have shown him uninhibited criticism of him by his own personnel. But in 1935 it still dared to tell him what the staff in the Kremlin were secretly saying about him. They included these scathing comments by four cleaners:

> Comrade Stalin eats well and works little. People work for him, that's why he is fat. He has all kinds of servants, and all sorts of pleasures. (A.M. Konstantinova)
>
> Stalin gets a lot of money, and lies to us about it. (B. Y. Katynskaya)
>
> He divorced his first wife and shot the second. He is not a Russian. (M. S. Zhalybina)
>
> Stalin has killed his wife. He's not Russian but Armenian. He is very mean and gives everyone the evil eye. (A. E. Avdeeva)

What is striking about this and similar testimony during the investigation of the Kremlin Plot is that those who gave it were unafraid to criticize Stalin. The interrogations bore little resemblance to those during the Terror less than two years later, when the accused were expected to make abject confessions of their responsibility for mostly imaginary crimes and scrupulously avoid any criticism of the regime. Only six of the 110 interrogated by the NKVD during the investigation of the Kremlin Plot made significant confessions of involvement in it. Some others admitted minor offences such as spreading slander.[83]

The leading conspirator in the plot was a disillusioned Fourth Department (military intelligence) officer, Mikhail Cherniavsky, a chemical warfare expert who studied chemistry at the Massachusetts Institute of Technology (MIT) under an assumed name while actively engaged in scientific and technological espionage (S&T). While at MIT he lost his Communist faith and became secretly convinced that the Stalinist command economy could never compete with American capitalism. Cherniavsky revealed to his interrogators that, since his return to Russia from MIT, he had repeatedly asked himself: 'Is this really my motherland?' For most of the first three weeks of his interrogation, he claimed that he had plotted only to replace Stalin as Soviet leader – not to kill him. On 26 March, however, Cherniavsky admitted that he too had been part of a 'terrorist' assassination plot. Following the killing of Kirov by a lone gunman inside the insecure Leningrad Party headquarters, the plotters believed that, thanks to equally poor security in the Kremlin, they could smuggle in pistols and shoot Stalin. Though there is no evidence that Cherniavsky was subjected to the torture which was later commonly used against recalcitrant suspects during the Terror, he was also persuaded to admit that he had been recruited while working in the United States by an alleged American Trotskyist named Ryaskin 'for carrying out terrorist activity and creation of Trotskyist groups in the [Soviet] Union'. But, when asked two days later for details of 'precise assignments' from Ryaskin, Cherniavsky was unable to provide any – probably because there were none.[84]

Pressure for executing the Kremlin plotters came not from Stalin, its main target, but from the NKVD and, in particular, from its chief, Genrikh Yagoda. Stalin's response to the list of twenty-six people to be executed which was submitted to him by Yagoda was astonishingly unlike his reaction to similar lists sent him by Yagoda's successor, Nikolai Yezhov (or Ezhov), during the Great Terror. After receiving one list of names from Yezhov in August 1938, Stalin replied curtly: 'All 138 to be shot.' Shortly afterwards, Yezhov sent him four further lists totaling 736 'enemies of the people', with the covering note: 'I request your approval to shoot them all.' Stalin gave his approval with the single word 'For'.* When given Yagoda's list of 'enemies of the people' responsible for the Kremlin Plot in 1935, however, Stalin deleted all but two of the names marked for execution: those of Mikhail Cherniavsky and a deputy commandant of the Kremlin, Alexei Sinelobov. Only Cherniavsky was executed. Sinelobov's sentence was later commuted by Stalin to ten years' imprisonment. In the light of the NKVD files on the investigation of the Kremlin Plot discovered by Svetlana Lokhova, it is no longer possible to believe either that Yagoda was simply acting on Stalin's orders or that in 1934–5 Stalin was in unchallenged control of state security.[85]

Stalin did not gain unchallenged control until September 1936 when, at his insistence, the Politburo sacked Yagoda and replaced him by Nikolai Yezhov as head of the NKVD. The US ambassador, Joseph E. Davies, reported to Washington in 1937 in a despatch probably decrypted by the NKVD: 'The secret police is the personal agency of Stalin and the party. It is in the saddle and riding hard! The new head of this organization, Yezhov, is comparatively a young man. He is constantly seen with Stalin and is regarded as one of the strongest men in the government.' Though Yezhov was so short that he was 'almost a dwarf', Davies admired his 'very fine head and face'.[86] During the Terror, sometimes called the 'Yezhovshchina' in his honour, Yezhov spent more time with Stalin than probably any other intelligence chief has ever spent with any political

---

* The lists were co-signed by the obedient Molotov as Chairman of Sovnarkom. (Watson, *Molotov*, pp. 141–2.)

leader before or since. In 1937–8, Yezhov called on Stalin 278 times in the Kremlin for lengthy meetings lasting an average of three hours each (a total of 834 hours).[87] In 1935 a total of 1,229 Soviet citizens were sentenced to death by shooting, euphemistically termed 'the Highest Level of Punishment'. Two years later, at the height of the Terror, the total was 353,074.

The transition from the relatively moderate NKVD investigation of the Kremlin Plot in early 1935 to the surreal paranoia of the Great Terror in 1936–8, whose victims were forced to confess to mostly imaginary, and sometimes preposterously improbable, crimes has still to be adequately explained. Part of the explanation is that it was ideologically unacceptable to blame the many Soviet economic problems caused by collectivization and the Five Year Plans on administrative and policy failures by Stalin and the Soviet leadership. They had to be attributed instead to vast and non-existent conspiracies. In 1937, for example, the NKVD uncovered an entirely fictitious but 'especially vicious form of sabotage' by 'veterinarians, zoological technicians and laboratory assistants', whose 'bacteriological subversion by infecting cattle, horses, herds of sheep and swine with plague, foot-and-mouth disease, anthrax, brucellosis, anaemia and other epidemic diseases', it reported, had killed hundreds of thousands of animals. The Politburo ordered each republic and region of the Soviet Union to organize three to six show trials of the imaginary plotters in order to alert the 'broad masses of peasants' to their non-existent campaigns of sabotage.[88]

The increasingly paranoid strain in Stalin's world view also owed much to his growing obsession with his great opponent Leon Trotsky, who had been expelled from the Soviet Union in 1929 (to Stalin's subsequent regret) and was thus unavailable for what would have been the most sensational of the show trials. As Trotsky's biographer Isaac Deutscher wrote later:

> The frenzy with which [Stalin] pursued the feud [with Trotsky], making it the paramount preoccupation of international communism as well as of the Soviet Union . . . beggars description; there is in the whole of history hardly another case in which such immense resources of power and propaganda were employed against a single individual.

In 1937, having despaired of finding a secure European base, Trotsky left for Mexico, where he remained until his assassination three years later.[89] The chief Trotskyist organizer in Europe for most of the 1930s was not Trotsky but his elder son, Lev Sedov, who was based in Paris from 1933 until his death in 1938. For both Stalin and Soviet intelligence no foreign HUMINT operations in the mid-1930s equalled in importance the penetration of Trotsky's and Sedov's entourages. From 1934 onwards Sedov's closest confidant and collaborator in Paris was the Russian-born Polish

NKVD agent Mark Zborowski, known to Sedov as Étienne. Similarly no SIGINT operation had greater priority than the interception of Trotsky's and Sedov's correspondence. Most of the interception proved remarkably straightforward. Sedov trusted 'Étienne' so completely that he gave him the key to his letterbox, allowed him to collect his mail (including that with his father), and entrusted him with Trotsky's most confidential files and archives for safekeeping.* An emergency, however, arose in 1936 when Zborowski reported to the Centre (NKVD headquarters) that, because of financial problems, Trotsky was selling part of his personal archive (previously entrusted to his keeping) to the Paris branch of the International Institute of Social History. The Centre immediately instructed Yakov 'Yasha' Serebryansky, head of its Administration for Special Tasks, which specialized in abduction and assassination, to recover the archive. A task force assembled by Serebryansky, codenamed the HENRY group, burgled the Institute offices at night and recovered the archive. The Centre attached such importance to this minor burglary that it awarded the Order of the Red Banner to the whole of the HENRY group – further evidence of its lack of any sense of proportion in operations against Trotsky.†

The Centre also regarded as a major success its penetration of the main Trotskyist organization in the United States, the Socialist Workers Party (SWP). In 1937 Dr Grigory Rabinovich, an officer of the NKVD New York residency operating undercover as head of the US office of the Soviet Red Cross, recruited a young Communist social worker, Sylvia Callen (codenamed SATYR), who agreed to join the Trotskyist SWP under the alias Sylvia Caldwell. Callen succeeded in becoming private secretary to the SWP leader, James Cannon, and for almost a decade handed over large amounts of SWP correspondence and files to Soviet intelligence.‡

Within the Soviet Union most of those expelled from the Communist Party were publicly branded either Trotskyists or Zinovievists. To Trotsky

---

* Sedov died from a mysterious illness in Paris on 16 February 1938. It is possible but by no means certain that he was murdered by Serebryansky's Administration for Special Tasks.
† The operation was as pointless as it was professional. The Trotsky papers stolen from the Institute were of no operational significance and of less historical importance than the part of the Trotsky archive which remained in the hands of Zborowski and later ended up at Harvard University. (Andrew and Mitrokhin, *Mitrokhin Archive*, pp. 90–93.)
‡ Rabinovich used as an intermediary in Callen's recruitment Louis Budenz, a senior Communist Party of the USA member who became managing editor of the *Daily Worker*. Other agents to penetrate the SWP included Thomas Black, previously an S&T agent, who became secretary of its Newark branch. (Haynes, Klehr and Vassiliev, *Spies*, pp. 165–6, 474–9. 'Security and the Fourth International, the Gelfand Case and the deposition of Mark Zborowski: An open letter from David North to Susan Weissman', 10 Nov. 2015; https://www.wsws.org/en/articles/2015/11/10/weis-n10.html.)

in exile this was vastly encouraging news – proof, he claimed in January 1936, that the 'strongest, most numerous and most hardened branch' of what became the Trotskyist Fourth International was in the Soviet Union. Both Stalin and Trotsky now inhabited, at least intermittently, a world of make-believe in which each fed the other's fantasies. Stalin's belief in mostly non-existent Russian Trotskyists infected Trotsky, whose pleasure at discovering these imaginary followers in turn persuaded Stalin that the Trotskyist menace was even worse than he had supposed.

The real reason why Trotskyists had disappeared from view within the Soviet Union was simply that, with very few exceptions, they had in fact disappeared. No Soviet citizens who valued their life expectancy dared say as much. Stalin and the many conspiracy theorists in the NKVD believed that the apparent disappearance of Russian Trotskyists merely meant that they had gone underground, often posing deceitfully as loyal party members. In the summer of 1936 a secret Central Committee resolution, passed on Stalin's initiative, gave the NKVD extraordinary powers to destroy all 'enemies of the people'.[90] A press campaign over the next few weeks reported that, 'thanks to corrupt liberalism and a blunting of vigilance on the part of some Communists', 'Trotskyist–Zinovievist degenerates' were still concealed in party ranks.

The trial of some of the leading 'degenerates' opened in August 1936. Grigory Zinoviev and Lev Kamenev, who, with Trotsky, had competed unsuccessfully with Stalin for the succession to Lenin, confessed, together with their associates, that since 1932 they had acted on instructions from Trotsky himself, conveyed to them by secret agents. The NKVD was left to manufacture the evidence for this preposterous tale, but made some blunders. One of the accused, no doubt sticking to a script prepared by his NKVD interrogators, confessed in court to meeting Sedov in a Copenhagen hotel which turned out to have been pulled down twenty years earlier. On instructions from the NKVD, the defendants made the equally fraudulent confession that they were the 'direct organizers' of Kirov's murder and had also been plotting Stalin's assassination in order to overthrow the Soviet regime.[91]

A Central Committee review in 1937 of NKVD operations against 'Japanese–German–Trotskyist agents' complained that over the previous two years they had been 'directed not against organized counter-revolutionary organizations but chiefly against isolated incidents of anti-Soviet agitation'. It would have been politically incorrect in the highest degree to point out that there were no 'organized counter-revolutionary organizations' to investigate. At a time when the Terror was at its height, the Central Committee complained, equally absurdly, that the NKVD were sending 'enemies of the people' to locations that 'resembled forced vacation homes more than prisons'.[92]

The final revelation of the extent of the imaginary counter-revolutionary conspiracy against Stalinist Russia came in February 1938 with the show trial of twenty-one members of the 'Bloc of Rightists and Trotskyites', chief among them Bukharin, Rykov and Yagoda, who were accused of an expanded version of what had become the usual catalogue of Trotskyist crimes: espionage, 'wrecking', terrorism and making preparations for foreign invasion, the dismemberment of the USSR, the overthrow of the Soviet system and the restoration of capitalism. Previously the Trotskyists had been allegedly conspiring only with the German and Japanese secret services; now they were accused of working for British and Polish intelligence as well. Trotsky himself was declared to have been a German agent since 1921 and a British spy since 1926. For years German, Japanese and Polish spies had surrounded Yagoda 'like flies'.[93]

The most important novelty in the conspiracy theory unveiled at the trial of the 'Bloc of Rightists and Trotskyists' was the heightened emphasis given to the alleged secret role of Western governments and their intelligence agencies. The Trotskyists were no longer the mere auxiliaries of foreign secret services but their 'slaves', 'bondmen of their masters'. The state procurator, Andrei Vyshinsky, declared during his paranoid peroration: 'The "Bloc of Rightists and Trotskyists" is no political grouping; it is a gang of spies, of agents of foreign intelligence services. This has been proved fully and incontestably. Herein lies the enormous social, political and historical significance of the present trial.'[94] Among those who attended the trial was Sir Fitzroy Maclean, then a young diplomat at the British Moscow embassy. At one point during the trial a clumsily manoeuvred arc light illuminated a private box at the back of the courtroom, and Maclean saw, to his astonishment, the drooping moustache and sallow complexion of Stalin himself.[95]

The Soviet spy mania of the 1930s, which reached its apogee in the Great Terror and made Western intelligence operations in Moscow almost impossibly difficult, derived not simply from the general sense of insecurity within the Soviet system generated by its encircling capitalist neighbours, but also from what Khrushchev later famously described as Stalin's 'pathologically suspicious personality': 'Everywhere and in everything he saw "enemies", "two-facers" and "spies".' Most of the Soviet population accepted the official doctrine that they were threatened by a major conspiracy of spies and saboteurs in the pay of foreign secret services. In every factory NKVD officers lectured workers on the dangers from non-existent imperialist agents in their midst. Films at Soviet cinemas, comedies included, invariably

contained their obligatory quota of spies. On 10 October, probably at Stalin's initiative, the Politburo approved NKVD operational order No. 00693,
classing all embassies and consulates as bases of foreign intelligence agencies, and ordering the immediate arrest of 'all Soviet citizens linked with
the personnel of diplomatic representations and visiting their offices and
homes'. 'Ceaseless surveillance' was to be maintained over all staff of major
embassies. Unsurprisingly, a series of foreign consulates closed down.[96]

By a macabre irony, allegedly the most dangerous 'enemies of the
people' were discovered in the three institutions which shared responsibility for defending the Soviet state against them: the Communist Party,
the Red Army and the NKVD. Of the 139 members of the Central Committee elected at the 1934 Party Congress, 110 were shot or sent to the
Gulag. Only fifty-nine of the 1,966 delegates reappeared at the next Congress in 1939. Seventy-five of the eighty members of the Supreme Military
Council were shot. More than half the Red Army officer corps, probably
well over 35,000 men, were executed or imprisoned. The NKVD hierarchy was purged twice. All eighteen of Yagoda's Commissars of State
Security, grades one and two, were shot (save for the foreign-intelligence
chief, Abram Slutsky, who was probably poisoned) under Yezhov. Of
Yezhov's top 122 officers in 1937–8, only twenty-one still held office under
his successor in 1940.[97]

Though Stalin did not, of course, supervise every detail of the Terror
or even know the names of the great majority of its victims, his was none
the less the guiding hand. The chief author of the gigantic conspiracy theory, which became undisputed orthodoxy within the NKVD and provided
the ideological underpinning of the Great Terror, was Stalin himself. Stalin
personally proofread the transcripts of the show trials before their publication, amending the defendants' speeches to ensure that they did not
deviate from their well-rehearsed confessions to imaginary conspiracies.
NKVD records of the period proclaim with characteristic obsequiousness
that 'The practical organization of the work exposing the right-wing Trotskyist underground was supervised personally by Comrade Stalin, and in
1936–8 crippling blows were delivered to the rabble.'[98]

27

The 'Big Three' and Second World War Intelligence

The Second World War, even more than the First, was an intelligence war. Unlike Adolf Hitler and Imperial Japan, the victorious Big Three – Churchill, Stalin and Roosevelt – recognized from the outset that intelligence would have a key role to play. More than any war leaders since George Washington, all, in different ways, were deeply influenced by their own previous intelligence experience.

Churchill had longer and more varied involvement in intelligence than any previous political leader. After first-hand experience of espionage at the frontiers of the late-Victorian and Edwardian empire, Churchill had been a member of the Asquith Cabinet which in 1909 founded the Secret Service Bureau, whose home and foreign departments (for which he had an enthusiasm which Asquith lacked) later became MI5 and SIS. As First Lord of the Admiralty at the outbreak of war in 1914, he presided over the rebirth of British SIGINT after a break of seventy years. Ten years later Churchill rightly claimed that he had studied decrypts 'over a longer period and more attentively than probably any other minister has done'.[1] Stalin's experience of intelligence work, though quite different from Churchill's, went back almost as long. He spent much of the two decades before the February Revolution trying to evade Okhrana surveillance. After the Bolshevik Revolution Felix Dzerzhinsky, first head of the Cheka, was one of his closest political allies. He also brooded for many years over the many volumes of his Tsarist intelligence file. During the 1930s, however, his understanding of intelligence became distorted by his obsession with hunting down 'enemies of the people' at home and abroad.[2]

Though Roosevelt lacked Churchill's and Stalin's passion for intelligence, during the First World War he developed a rather naïve fascination with espionage which continued between the wars. As Assistant Secretary of the Navy from 1913 to 1920, Roosevelt was fond of contrasting his own proactive approach with the allegedly deskbound inertia of the Secretary, Josephus Daniels. In 1920 he made the preposterous boast that, to prepare the US navy for war without the knowledge of Daniels and President Wilson, 'I committed enough illegal acts to put me in jail for 999 years.' The main area for which Roosevelt had direct responsibility as Assistant Secretary was the Office of Naval Intelligence (ONI). Initially ONI found his enthusiasm for its work somewhat disconcerting. In January 1916 the Director of Naval Intelligence (DNI), Captain James Harrison Oliver, complained that FDR was recruiting his own espionage network and interfering in intelligence operations. Roosevelt got on far better with Captain Roger Welles, who succeeded Oliver as DNI shortly after the US entry into the war. Welles seems to have been happy to appoint as naval-intelligence officers a number of the Assistant Secretary's socialite friends: among them his golf partner, Alexander Brown Legare, founder of the Chevy Chase Hunt Club; the leading polo player Lawrence Waterbury, husband of FDR's sister-in-law; and Roosevelt's Harvard classmate Steuart Davis, commander of Roosevelt's Volunteer Patrol Squadron, which became the nucleus of the Naval Reserve.[3]

The discovery of German secret agents and sabotage operations in the United States, culminating in the massive Black Tom explosion in New York harbour in July 1916,[4] increased Roosevelt's fascination with covert operations. His grasp of the potential threat from German agents, however, owed at least as much to spy novels as to intelligence files. In April 1917, as the United States entered the war, he instructed ONI to investigate the possibility that German-Americans in New Hampshire might be planning to purchase an aircraft to bomb Portsmouth Navy Yard. Roosevelt began to speculate, and later to fantasize, that he had been personally marked down for assassination by German secret agents. He subsequently told a deeply improbable tale of how, in the spring of 1917:

> the Secret Service found in the safe of the German Consul in New York a document headed: 'To be eliminated'. The first name on the list was that of Frank Polk [intelligence coordinator at the State Department]; mine was the second followed by eight or ten others. As a result the Secret Service asked us both to carry revolvers as we both habitually walked to and from our offices. I was given the revolver and the shoulder holster.

Roosevelt claimed that, after a few days, he stopped carrying the revolver and kept it in a desk drawer instead.[5]

During a visit by Roosevelt to London in 1918, the able and unscrupulous British DNI, Admiral 'Blinker' Hall, conscious of the US Assistant Secretary's naïve fascination with espionage, successfully persuaded him that British spies crossed the German–Danish border every night with important intelligence and were then taken by flying boat to Harwich.[6] Roosevelt was also taken in (as was Woodrow Wilson) by forged documents designed to discredit the Bolshevik regime. Among the most ridiculous of the forgeries which deceived Roosevelt was a 'Decree on the Socialization of Women' which declared them 'the property of the whole nation': 'Men citizens have the right to use one woman not oftener than three times a week for three hours.' Roosevelt told a ladies' luncheon club that the League of Nations offered the best defence against this evil doctrine.[7]

In 1919 Roosevelt and his wife almost became the unintended victims of an anarchist bomb attack on the Washington home of the Attorney General, Alexander Mitchell Palmer. They walked past Palmer's house only minutes before the bomb exploded. One of the bomber's body parts landed on their nearby doorstep.[8] Ten years later Roosevelt used this experience as the inspiration for a fictitious claim that a bomb had been sent to him during the war at the Assistant Secretary's office, but had been discovered before it detonated.[9]

Intelligence was a low priority after Roosevelt's inauguration in 1933 during the frenetic Hundred Days that launched the New Deal and created an alphabet soup of new federal agencies. The new President found time, however, to renew contact with ONI and to begin cultivating his own private sources of information. The Washington journalist John Franklin Carter ('Jay Franklin'), later head of a wartime intelligence unit in the White House, began providing him with confidential reports on his own administration.[10] Roosevelt's attitude to espionage when he became President was reminiscent of those of the gentlemen amateur spies of late-Victorian and Edwardian Britain. Chief among FDR's gentlemen spies was the multimillionaire publisher and property developer Vincent Astor. In 1927 Astor had set up an amateur intelligence group known as 'The Room' that met monthly in New York City in an apartment at 34 East 62nd Street with a mail drop and unlisted telephone number. Prominent members of The Room included FDR's cousin, the soldier, explorer and businessman Kermit Roosevelt, son of President Theodore Roosevelt; the banker Winthrop W. Aldrich; Judge Frederic Kernochan; the philanthropist William Rhinelander Stewart; the Assistant Secretary of Air, F. Trubee Davison; and David Bruce, who later served in London both as wartime chief of the Office of Strategic Services (OSS) and as post-war ambassador.[11]

By the time Roosevelt became President, Astor was one of his closest friends. Roosevelt spent his last holiday before his inauguration aboard Astor's luxurious 263-foot motor yacht, the *Nourmahal*; he wrote to his mother while on the cruise, 'Vincent is a dear and perfect host.'[12] During his first presidential term, FDR took annual holidays of up to two weeks on board the *Nourmahal*, accompanied by several members of The Room.

The eccentric male bonding and well-lubricated hilarity aboard the *Nourmahal* were itemized in bogus bills that Astor sent his guests after every voyage. In September 1934 each was charged $187.50 for 'Expenses incurred for Alcoholic Stimulants and repeated Correctives (NOTE: The Chief Steward reports that consumption of the above Stores was so vast as to overwhelm his accounting system)'.[13] Roosevelt loved every moment of both the voyages and the somewhat adolescent shipboard humour. In his private collection of 'Amusing Things' he kept a card sent him by Astor showing a naked woman concealed in a picture of 'A Dirty Dog'.[14]

FDR encouraged Astor to go on unofficial intelligence-gathering voyages on the *Nourmahal*, initially in the Caribbean and along the Pacific and Atlantic coasts of Latin America, mainly to investigate Japanese activities. In 1938 Astor went on a more ambitious cruise to gather intelligence from some of the Japanese Pacific islands, telling Roosevelt that his instructions for the trip 'could not be more clear'. Though the instructions themselves do not survive, his letter of acknowledgement makes clear that they concerned a voyage to the Marshall Islands and 'possible trouble'. Astor was pleased with the rather basic intelligence he collected. Eniwetok, he reported to Roosevelt, was Japan's 'principal naval base in the Marshall Islands' with Bikini 'probably their second string base'. Wotje contained a new Japanese airfield and a submarine base.[15]

Sir Mansfield Cumming, first Chief of the British SIS, had described pre-First World War espionage operations as 'capital sport'.[16] Roosevelt and Astor agreed. 'I don't want to make you jealous', Astor wrote to the President before the *Nourmahal* left on its 1938 intelligence-gathering mission, 'but aren't you a bit envious of my trip?' Despite creating a record number of new federal agencies at record speed during his first term, it did not yet occur to Roosevelt that the United States might require a *professional* foreign-intelligence agency.[17]

Several senior figures, however, sent Roosevelt private foreign-intelligence reports which bypassed the State Department. Probably FDR's most valued source was one of his friends from Columbia Law School, the war hero and wealthy New York lawyer Colonel (later General) William J. 'Wild Bill' Donovan, who had links with The Room, even if he was not a regular member of it. In 1935 Donovan began a series of transatlantic intelligence missions with the President's blessing, and perhaps at his request. In December of that year he paid a private visit to the Italian dictator, Benito Mussolini. At a meeting in Mussolini's absurdly grandiose study at the Palazzo Venezia in Rome, Il Duce authorized Donovan to tour the East African battlefront, where the Italian army was engaged in the brutal conquest of Ethiopia. A guided tour for Donovan, arranged by the Italian commander, Marshal Pietro Badoglio, was, however, a well-organized Italian deception, which persuaded Donovan that Fascist forces were not merely greatly superior to the Italian troops he had encountered in the First World War but, improbably, on excellent terms with the Ethiopians they had conquered. The use of mustard gas and other horrors were successfully concealed from him. At a private meeting with Roosevelt on his return, Donovan emphasized the determination of the Italian people, under Mussolini's allegedly inspirational leadership, not to yield to international pressure to stop the war. His briefing may have contributed to Roosevelt's decision not to seek to impose an embargo on oil exports to Italy.[18]

Among Roosevelt's other private, ill-informed sources of foreign intelligence was his friend William C. Bullitt Jr, successively first US ambassador to Moscow (1933–6) and ambassador to Paris (1936–40). On 28 September 1938, during the Munich Crisis, Bullitt sent an urgent personal message to the President, allegedly containing 'secrets of the highest importance' for his '*most private eye*' only: 'To the certain knowledge of the French Military Intelligence, the Germans have ready for battle at this moment six thousand five hundred planes of the very latest types . . .' In the event of war, 'The [French] Minister for Air felt that the destruction in Paris would pass all imagination. He said that he had sent his wife and children to Brittany already . . .' Roosevelt juggled Bullitt's and other woefully inaccurate statistics around in his head and arrived at a figure for annual German aircraft production of 12,000 planes (almost fifty per cent higher, he calculated, than the combined capacity of Britain and France), which he produced at a White House conference on 14 November, called to consider US air power requirements. In reality, at the time of the Munich Crisis, Germany possessed 2,928 aircraft of all kinds, of which only 1,669 were serviceable – markedly fewer than the combined total of British, French and Czechoslovak aircraft.[19]

Roosevelt's greater interest in foreign intelligence than any previous President since Washington reflected a growing preoccupation during his second term (1937–41) with 'national security', a term he used more frequently than all previous presidents combined. Most Americans before the Second World War were 'isolationist' in the sense that they wanted to avoid involvement in the conflicts brewing in Europe and East Asia. Roosevelt, however, without saying so openly, did what he could to bring the United States into the Second World War in the interest, as he saw it, of American national security.[20]

With the outbreak of war in Europe, Vincent Astor and 'The Room' (henceforth renamed 'The Club') acquired an increased sense of self-importance. 'Things are going really well up our alley', Astor assured the

President. Mindful of the importance of gathering intelligence on Japan, The Club was consuming 'a considerable amount of Saki'.[21] Astor's most important role, however, was to begin intelligence liaison within Britain in defiance of the United States' official policy of neutrality. Soon after Britain declared war on Germany, Astor reported to Roosevelt that he had made contact with Sir James Paget, the head of the Secret Intelligence Service station in New York: 'I asked [Paget] for unofficial British [intelligence] cooperation, but made it clear that we, for obvious reasons, could not return the compliment in the sense of turning over to them any of our confidential information. This somewhat one-sided arrangement was gladly accepted.' Astor's now almost forgotten meeting with Paget was to mark the first step in the creation of the Anglo-American intelligence alliance, which still endures. In February 1940, however, the Assistant Secretary of State, George S. Messersmith, was outraged to discover that Paget had been supplying intelligence direct to Astor and the FBI's director, J. Edgar Hoover. At his insistence, the SIS station was ordered henceforth to communicate exclusively with the State Department. Following Messersmith's replacement as Assistant Secretary shortly afterwards by Adolf A. Berle Jr, the State Department agreed, in principle, to allow SIS to resume its previous contacts with Astor and Hoover.[22] In the spring of 1940 Paget was succeeded as head of station by William Stephenson, a wealthy Canadian businessman who had worked part-time for SIS in the 1930s. A year later Astor told Roosevelt that relations between the SIS station and the FBI were 'working perfectly'. 'Little Bill' Stephenson was a close friend of Astor and probably had long-standing links with The Room. His engaging personality, business contacts and dry martinis won him many friends in the United States.[23]

Among them was William Donovan. On 3 July 1940 Roosevelt summoned Donovan to the Oval Office and sent him on a mission to Britain to investigate the alleged threat to its security, in the wake of the rapid German conquest of France and the Low Countries, from the alleged (but, in reality, almost non-existent) German Fifth Column. Rightly convinced that Donovan had the ear of the President, Stephenson insisted that he be shown the red carpet, indeed a whole series of red carpets. Donovan was received by Churchill, granted an audience with King George VI, and taken to secret meetings with Stewart Menzies, Chief of SIS, and most of Britain's other intelligence chiefs. After his return to Washington in August, Stephenson cabled SIS headquarters: 'Donovan believes you will have within days very favourable news, and thinks he has restored confidence as to Britain's determination and ability to resist.' The 'very favourable news' was an agreement on 2 September 1940 by which it received, as Churchill had requested, fifty mothballed American destroyers to help defend British sea lanes and repel a German invasion, in return for leasing to the United States naval and air bases in the Caribbean and Western Atlantic: the forerunner of the Lend-Lease Act of March 1941 which made the United States 'the arsenal of democracy' eight months before it entered the war.[24]

Donovan also urged on Roosevelt 'full intelligence collaboration' with the British. The President's willingness to move in that direction reflected both the influence of Donovan and other advisers, and his own admiration for the achievements of Britain's 'wonderful intelligence service' in the First World War.[25] He had concluded after his visit to British naval intelligence in the summer of 1918: 'Their intelligence unit is much more developed than ours and this is because it is a much more integral part of their Office of Operations.'[26] At a meeting in London on 31 August 1940 between the British chiefs of staff and the American Observer Mission, the US Army representative, Brigadier-General George V. Strong (later G-2), announced that 'the time had come for a free exchange of intelligence'. To conduct the exchange, Stephenson set up the British Security Coordination (BSC) on the thirty-fifth and thirty-sixth floors of the International Building in Rockefeller Center on New York's Fifth Avenue. For much of the war BSC included officers from MI5 and the Special Operations Executive (SOE) as well as SIS.[27]

At a meeting of his Cabinet on 4 April 1941 Roosevelt returned to the problem of US intelligence coordination which he had so far failed to solve. He praised the way the British solved the problem but was muddled about how they did so, mistakenly informing his Cabinet that all interdepartmental disputes were resolved by a mysterious ' "Mr. X", whose identity was kept a complete secret'.[28] On 10 June, strongly supported by the British (chiefly in the person of Stephenson), Donovan submitted to the President a proposal for the establishment of a 'Coordinator of Strategic Information who would be responsible directly to the President' and oversee a new 'central intelligence organization that would itself collect either directly or through existing departments of government, at home and abroad, pertinent information concerning potential enemies'. At a meeting in the Oval Office on 18 June, Roosevelt accepted the main features of Donovan's proposal and offered him the newly created post of Coordinator of Information (COI). Donovan accepted on three conditions:

1. That I would report only to him [FDR]
2. That his secret funds would be available
3. That all the departments of the government would be instructed to give me what I wanted.[29]

The third condition woefully overestimated the likely level of cooperation from the Washington bureaucracy, but accurately reflected the optimism with which Donovan embarked on his new career as COI. During a visit to the United States shortly before Donovan's appointment, the British DNI, Admiral John Godfrey, accompanied by his assistant, Commander Ian Fleming (later famous as the creator of James Bond), found that collaboration between the ONI, MID and FBI 'hardly existed': 'These three departments showed the utmost good will towards me and Ian Fleming but very little towards each other.'[30]

The biggest weakness in Donovan's new role as COI was that he was given no responsibility for SIGINT, whose importance Roosevelt, despite his interest in espionage, failed to grasp. A secret post-war report on SIGINT concluded that the two main pre-war problems had been 'lack of unified control' and 'extremely limited funding'. For much of the 1930s the military Signal Intelligence Service (SIS) and the navy's Code and Signal Section, which shared responsibility for SIGINT after the closure of the Black Chamber in 1929, were not on speaking terms. Each sought independently to break the same diplomatic codes and ciphers 'to gain credit for itself as the agency to which the information obtained was made available to the Government'. By 1936 SIS had succeeded in cracking the main Japanese diplomatic cipher, to which it gave the codename RED.[31]

RED decrypts were probably the first SIGINT to be seen by FDR as President. Early in 1937, for the first time in American history, SIGINT began to be regularly delivered to the White House, initially at the rate of about one decrypt a day. The first major revelation of the RED intercepts was probably the disclosure in March 1937 that Italy was considering joining the German–Japanese Anti-Comintern Pact. It was another six months before similar information reached the State Department from US diplomats abroad. RED decrypts also revealed part of the text of the treaty. Roosevelt, however, was far more interested in the less reliable but superficially more exciting intelligence supplied by Astor's Room, Bullitt and other informants. The cryptanalysts, unlike the amateur agents, received no sign of the President's interest in their work.

During 1938 RED decrypts revealed that a new Japanese cipher machine was under construction. On 20 March 1939, the first diplomatic messages were intercepted in a new machine cipher, codenamed PURPLE by SIS. Over the next three months RED was gradually replaced by the new cipher. The head of SIS, the redoubtable William F. Friedman, later established a reputation as 'the man who broke PURPLE'. But, though he supervised the team, headed by the former schoolteacher Frank B. Rowlett, which led the eighteen-month attack on PURPLE, Friedman played no direct part in its solution. Following the appointment of Major-General Joseph Mauborgne as the army's Chief Signal Officer in October 1937, relations with the naval Code and Signal Section, now renamed OP-20-G, had somewhat improved. Though chiefly occupied with work on Japanese naval ciphers, OP-20-G cooperated with SIS in the attack on PURPLE before abandoning the attempt. PURPLE was finally broken by SIS on the afternoon of 20 September 1940. Unable to contain his excitement, the usually soft-spoken Rowlett jumped up and down, exclaiming: 'That's it!' His principal assistant, Robert O. Ferner, also abandoned his customary reserve and shouted: 'Hooray!' Junior cryptanalyst Albert W. Small was less outspoken, but ran around the room with his hands clasped in triumph above his head. The victorious codebreakers then jointly celebrated the greatest success in the history of US intelligence thus far by sending out for a case of Coca-Cola. Mauborgne began referring to Rowlett and his fellow cryptanalysts as 'magicians'. The name stuck and MAGIC became a code word for the Japanese decrypts (or, sometimes, for high-grade SIGINT in general).[32]

PURPLE was broken at a critical time. Only a week later Japan began stationing troops in northern French Indochina and signed the Tripartite Pact establishing the Berlin–Rome–Tokyo Axis. Ironically, one of the chief consumers of MAGIC was the Secretary of War, Henry Stimson, who as Secretary of State in 1929 had closed down the Black Chamber. Stimson no longer felt bound to treat Japanese diplomats as 'gentlemen' whose correspondence it was ungentlemanly to intercept. He noted excitedly in his diary the 'wonderful progress' made by SIS, but added: 'I cannot even in my diary go into some of the things that they have done.' There is no evidence of similar excitement in the Oval Office.[33]

Once PURPLE had been broken, OP-20-G began to cooperate with SIS in the laborious work of cracking the daily changes in the machine cipher settings. Inter-service rivalry, however, led to an absurdly bureaucratic formula intended to prevent either of the SIGINT agencies gaining an advantage over the other. According to a post-war report:

> It was agreed after lengthy negotiations that the Army and the Navy would exchange all diplomatic traffic from their intercept facilities, and that both services would work on this traffic. But in order to avoid as much duplication of effort as possible it was agreed that the Army would receive all traffic of days with an even date and the Navy all traffic of days with an odd date. This arrangement was ... to give both services equal opportunities for training, 'credit' and so on.[34]

Roosevelt either did not care or did not know about this bizarre arrangement – so far as is known, the only odd-/even-date collaboration agreement in the history of intelligence. It continued to cause confusion in the production of MAGIC until after Pearl Harbor.

Churchill would never have tolerated such SIGINT confusion. After the First World War he had been a member of the Secret Service Committee which had brought cryptanalysis for both the Foreign Office and the armed services under one roof at the Government Code and Cypher School (GC&CS). Despite his continuing passion for SIGINT,[35] however, he had no access to it during his 'wilderness years' on the backbenches during the 1930s. Churchill had a number of informants who passed him classified intelligence from other sources, chief among them Desmond Morton of SIS,[36]* head of the Industrial Intelligence Centre, and Ralph Wigram of the Foreign Office until his premature death at the end of 1936.[37] But Churchill had no access to the intelligence obtained by MI5 from inside the German embassy, which he would have seized on as evidence that 'Appeasement' of Hitler did not work. Neville Chamberlain, the most influential advocate of Appeasement, who became Prime Minister in May 1937, ignored it.

MI5's main source in the German embassy was the aristocratic anti-Nazi diplomat Wolfgang zu Putlitz, whose family had owned the castle at Putlitz in Brandenburg since the twelfth century. Putlitz (codenamed PADGHAM by the Security Service) later recalled that, at his fortnightly meetings with the MI5 agent Jona 'Klop' Ustinov, 'I would unburden myself of all the dirty schemes and secrets which I encountered as part of my daily routine at the Embassy. By this means I was able to lighten my conscience by the feeling that I was really helping to damage the Nazi cause . . .'[38] Putlitz insisted, and MI5's leadership believed, that the only way to deal with Hitler was to stand firm. Appeasement would make him even more aggressive. For several years, MI5, headed by Sir Vernon Kell, sent regular reports on the intelligence supplied by Putlitz and other sources in the German embassy to Sir Robert Vansittart ('Van'), Permanent Undersecretary at the Foreign Office from 1930 to early 1938. More than any other Whitehall mandarin, Van stood for rearmament and opposition to Appeasement. In September 1936 Putlitz reported that the German ambassador, Joachim von Ribbentrop (the 'von' was fraudulent), and his staff regarded a German war with Russia as being 'as certain as

---

* Morton later claimed, unreliably, that in the early 1930s Ramsay MacDonald had verbally authorized him to pass intelligence to Churchill: 'Tell him whatever he wants to know. Keep him informed.' MacDonald then allegedly put that permission in writing, and it was endorsed by his successors, Stanley Baldwin and Neville Chamberlain. This is highly unlikely. (Morton to Liddell Hart, 9 July 1961, 9 May 1963, 20 March 1967; KCL Liddell Hart Centre for Military Archives, Liddell Hart MSS 1/153.)

the Amen in church', and were confident that Britain would not lift a finger when Hitler began his invasion.[39]

The only way to deal with the English, Ribbentrop maintained, was to give them 'a kick in the behind' (*ein Tritt in den Hintern*). In February 1938 Hitler made Ribbentrop his Foreign Minister, a post he retained for the remainder of the Third Reich. Ustinov summed up Putlitz's assessment as follows:

> The Army will in future be the obedient instrument of Nazi foreign policy. Under Ribbentrop this foreign policy will be an aggressive, forward policy. Its first aim –Austria – has been partly achieved . . . Austria falls to [Hitler] like a ripe fruit. After consolidating the position in Austria the next step will be against Czechoslovakia.

Putlitz's constant refrain during 1938 was that 'Britain was letting the trump cards fall out of her hands. If she had adopted, or even now adopted, a firm attitude and threatened war, Hitler would not succeed in this kind of bluff. The German army was not yet ready for a major war.' When the Wehrmacht crossed into Austria on 12 March, it left in its wake a trail of broken-down vehicles ill prepared even for an unopposed invasion. The probability is that it would also have proved ill prepared for a war over Czechoslovakia that autumn. In May 1938 Putlitz left London and was posted to the German embassy in The Hague. During the summer of 1938 Whitehall received a series of intelligence reports, some of them from Putlitz, warning that Hitler had decided to seize the German-speaking Czech Sudetenland by force. There were contradictory reports, however, on when Hitler planned to attack. Putlitz apart, Ustinov's most important source from mid-August onwards was the German military attaché in London, General Baron Geyr von Schweppenburg, who told Ustinov: 'We simply must convince the British to stand firm . . . If they give in to Hitler now, there will be no holding him.'[40]

Among the material handed over to Ustinov by Schweppenburg which MI5 forwarded to the Foreign Office was a memorandum by Ribbentrop of 3 August, reporting that a decision to settle the Czechoslovak question '*in unserem Sinne*' ('in accordance with our wishes') would be taken before the autumn, and expressing confidence that Britain and France would not intervene. Even if war followed, Germany would be victorious. At the beginning of September Sir Alexander Cadogan, who had succeeded Vansittart as Permanent Undersecretary in January, arrived back in the Foreign Office after a disturbed French holiday to find 'enough in the Secret Reports to make one's hair stand on end'. 'It's obviously touch and go', he believed, 'but not gone yet.' On 6 September Whitehall received the most direct warning so far. The German chargé d'affaires, Theodor Kordt, in Cadogan's view a brave man who 'put conscience before loyalty', paid a secret visit to 10 Downing Street, where he was admitted through the garden gate, and warned Chamberlain's close adviser, Sir Horace Wilson, that Hitler had decided to invade Czechoslovakia. Next day he returned to Number 10 and repeated the same message to the Foreign Secretary, Lord Halifax.

On 15 September the Prime Minister made a dramatic flight to Munich to parley with the Führer in his grandiose mountain retreat at Berchtesgaden. Schweppenburg quickly contacted Ustinov with a warning, which MI5 forwarded to the Foreign Office, that 'It is Hitler's intention to bring about the dissolution of the Czechoslovak state by all or any means.' Chamberlain continued the policy of Appeasement. After he had made three round-trips by air and attended a disorganized four-power conference at Munich, the Prime Minister returned to a hero's welcome in London on 30 September, brandishing an agreement which surrendered the Czech Sudetenland to Germany and meant, he claimed, not only 'peace with honour' but 'peace for our time'. Ustinov's case officer, Jack Curry, later recalled the 'growing sense of dismay' in the Security Service as the negotiations with Hitler continued: 'When Chamberlain returned from Munich waving his piece of paper we all had an acute sense of shame.'[41]

SIS saw things differently. Before and during the Munich Crisis, its chief, 'Quex' Sinclair, probably to a greater degree than ever before, set out to influence government policy in the opposite direction to Kell. Unlike Kell, Sinclair was an appeaser. There is no evidence he paid attention to MI5 intelligence from the German embassy. Because of the lack of coordination between MI5 and SIS, he may not even have seen it.* SIS's own policy was set out in a memorandum of 18 September entitled 'What Should We Do?', drafted by its head of political intelligence, Malcolm Woollcombe, and personally approved by Sinclair. SIS argued strongly that the Czechs should be pressed to accept 'the inevitable' and surrender the largely German-speaking Sudetenland to Germany. They should 'realise unequivocally that they stand alone if they refuse such a solution'. Britain, for its part, should continue with a policy of calculated appeasement. It should not wait until German grievances boiled over and threatened the peace of Europe. Instead the international community should take the initiative and decide 'what *really legitimate* grievances

---

* There is no mention of MI5 intelligence from the German embassy in the official history of SIS by the late Keith Jeffery, who had unrestricted access to surviving interwar SIS files, which remain classified.

Germany has and what surgical operations are necessary to rectify them'. Some of Germany's colonies, confiscated after the last war, should be restored. If genuine cases for self-determination by German minorities remained in Europe they should be remedied. Britain should try to ensure *'that Germany's "style is cramped", but with the minimum of provocation'*. Sir Warren Fisher, head of the Civil Service, told Sinclair that 'What Should We Do?' was 'a most excellent document'.[42]

MI5 disagreed. But there was no mechanism for discussing the differences between its own assessment of Hitler's policy and that of SIS. MI5 therefore followed the Munich Crisis by preparing a controversial report on the intelligence from Putlitz and other German sources (none of them identified by name) which it had forwarded to the Foreign Office over the previous few years, and was entirely at odds with the SIS memorandum 'What Should We Do?' Probably on 7 November Kell personally delivered the MI5 report to Vansittart. Van, who earlier in the year had been kicked upstairs to the post of (not very influential) chief diplomatic adviser to the Chamberlain government, forwarded the note to Cadogan, who made a few comments on it, then passed it to Lord Halifax, the Foreign Secretary. This report represented probably the first, barely concealed, indictment of government foreign policy ever prepared by a British intelligence agency. Page 1 of the MI5 report included the provocative statement that, in view of the intelligence the Service had provided from 'reliable sources' over the past few years:

> There is nothing surprising and nothing which could not have been foreseen in the events of this summer in connection with Czechoslovakia. These events are a logical consequence of Hitler's Nazi Weltanschauung and of his foreign policy and his views in regard to racial questions and the position of Germany in Europe.

The report went on, with unusual frankness, to record the frustration and 'feelings of dismay' of Putlitz (identified only as 'Herr Q') at the failure of the British government to stand up to Hitler. Schweppenburg ('Herr von S') too had been 'risking his life' to pass on a similar message. British policy during the Munich Crisis, MI5 reported, had convinced Hitler of 'the weakness of England': 'There now seems to be no doubt he is convinced that Great Britain is "decadent" and lacks the will and power to defend the British Empire.' MI5's aim was to stiffen Chamberlain's resolve by demonstrating that Appeasement had encouraged, rather than removed, Hitler's aggressive designs. In order to try to ensure that the Prime Minister paid attention to the report, it was decided, at Curry's suggestion, to include samples of Hitler's insulting references to him – the first known occasion of a British intelligence agency using this simple but effective tactic to attract a policymaker's attention. Halifax was so struck by Hitler's reported description of Chamberlain as an 'arsehole' (*Arschloch*) that he underlined it three times in red before, reportedly, showing it to the Prime Minister. According to Curry, the insult made, as intended, 'a considerable impression on the Prime Minister', who was known to be infuriated by mockery and disrespect. But it had little impact on his policy. 'All the information I get', wrote Chamberlain cheerfully on 19 February 1939, 'seems to point in the direction of peace.' On 15 March Hitler's forces occupied Prague and announced the annexation of the Czech provinces of Bohemia and Moravia. Slovakia became a German vassal state.[43]

When Churchill entered 10 Downing Street on 10 May 1940, he became the first twentieth-century Prime Minister to insist not merely on frequent intelligence reports but on seeing much raw intelligence as well – particularly SIGINT. At first he demanded to see all the intercepts decrypted by GC&CS at their main wartime base at Bletchley Park. When persuaded that there were now too many decrypts for him to inspect personally, he agreed to a daily delivery of the most important of them. Sir Stewart Menzies, who had succeeded 'Quex' Sinclair as Chief of SIS, as well as Non-Operational Director of GC&CS, arranged for their delivery in a red box marked 'Only to be opened by the Prime Minister in person', to which only he and Churchill had keys. Churchill kept the key on his personal keyring. He called the intercepts 'my golden eggs' and the cryptanalysts 'the geese who laid the golden eggs and never cackled'.[44]

By an extraordinary coincidence, the most valuable intelligence source in British history began to come on stream less than a fortnight after Churchill became Prime Minister. On 22 May GC&CS succeeded in breaking the Luftwaffe version of the Enigma machine cipher. From this date onwards it was able to read current German traffic using the air force Enigma without a break for the remainder of the war. In the spring of 1941 Bletchley mastered the naval Enigma, and in the spring of 1942 the army Enigma. At first the Enigma decrypts were referred to by the codeword 'Boniface' in order to suggest, if the enemy caught wind of them, that they derived from a secret agent rather than cryptanalysis. By 1941 they were known as ULTRA to Churchill and the small circle of initiates. ULTRA was an Allied rather than a purely British triumph: the culmination of a decade of intelligence work involving the Poles and French as well as GC&CS.

ULTRA was probably the best-kept secret in modern British history. Churchill had learned from his mistakes in the 1920s when he had repeatedly been willing to compromise GC&CS's ability to decrypt Soviet traffic by revealing the contents of decrypts, culminating in the cryptanalytic disaster of 1927.[45] As wartime Prime Minister, he kept even his private secretaries in ignorance of the contents of the mysterious red boxes he received each day from Menzies. At Churchill's personal insistence, the Whitehall circle who shared the secret of the 'golden eggs' was limited to about thirty of those most closely concerned with the direction of the war, and included only half a dozen of his thirty-five ministers. Within the Foreign Office, which was responsible for GC&CS, only Cadogan and Victor Cavendish-Bentinck, chairman of the Joint Intelligence Committee (JIC), knew the ULTRA secret.*

Churchill was the first British Prime Minister to visit GC&CS. No other Prime Minister did so until Margaret Thatcher forty years later.[46] Churchill left the cryptanalysts in no doubt about his personal support for them. When the four leading codebreakers of Bletchley Park found themselves critically short of resources in October 1941, they deputed the youngest of them, Stuart Milner-Barry, to deliver an appeal for help to 10 Downing Street. Milner-Barry went on to become a Treasury knight and ceremonial officer in the Civil Service Department. 'The thought of going straight from the bottom to the top', he wrote after his retirement, 'would have filled my later self with horror and incredulity.' Churchill, however, responded immediately to the codebreakers' appeal with the now celebrated minute: 'ACTION THIS DAY. Make sure they have all they want on extreme priority and report to me that this has been done.' Milner-Barry was in no doubt about the importance of Churchill's personal support to Bletchley Park:

> ... the cryptographers were hanging on to a number of crucial keys by their coat-tails and if we had lost any or all of them there was no guarantee (given the importance of continuity in breaking) that we should ever have found ourselves in business again ... Almost from that day the rough ways began miraculously to be made smooth ...[47]

At least as important as Churchill's grasp of the importance of SIGINT was the priority which he gave to coordinating the wartime intelligence effort. The intelligence agencies and intelligence assessment had been poorly coordinated throughout the interwar years. The Joint Intelligence Committee (JIC), founded in 1936, was virtually boycotted by the Foreign Office until July 1939 and achieved little until after the outbreak of war. During the Munich Crisis MI5 and SIS, neither represented on the JIC,

---

* Even Desmond Morton, formerly of SIS, who had advised Churchill on intelligence in the 1930s and continued to do so as his personal assistant at Number 10, almost certainly had no access to ULTRA. (Bennett, *Churchill's Man of Mystery*, p. 251.)

had produced contradictory assessments. In the final years of peace and the early months of war Whitehall received a remarkable mixture of good and dreadful intelligence, and was frequently incapable of distinguishing between the two. As a result, it was deceived by a series of German intelligence plants, culminating in humiliation at Venlo in November 1939 when two leading SIS officers were lured to the Dutch border and captured by German intelligence officers posing as members of an anti-Hitler resistance movement.[48]

On 17 May 1940, only a week after Churchill became Prime Minister, he gave the JIC enhanced status as the central body responsible for producing operational intelligence 'appreciations'. It was instructed to take the initiative, whenever it saw fit, 'at any time of day or night' (a phrase repeated twice in its new terms of reference) to submit appreciations to the Prime Minister, the War Cabinet and the chiefs of staff. Its membership was expanded to include SIS, MI5 and the Ministry of Economic Warfare. The Foreign Office, service departments and intelligence agencies were no longer allowed to bypass the JIC and submit independent assessments. The JIC, however, lacked the staff to enable it to fulfil its much enhanced role. This weakness was remedied early in 1941 with the foundation of the Joint Intelligence Staff (JIS) as a JIC subcommittee, charged with coordinating, assessing and disseminating the administration and policy of the intelligence community as a whole. Without such assessment machinery, Whitehall would have found it difficult, if not impossible, in June 1941 to overcome its long-held conviction that Hitler saw the 'overwhelming' advantage of remaining at peace with Russia.[49]

Churchill's conviction during the year when Britain stood alone after the Fall of France and the withdrawal of British forces from Dunkirk that Germany could be defeated, however, sprang not from a cool assessment of the intelligence but from a patriotic conviction that Britain could somehow defy the odds. His Foreign Secretary, Anthony Eden, privately dismissed Churchill's belief that the German economy could be brought to its knees by British bombing and guerrilla warfare as 'the most frightful rot'.[50] Churchill entered Number 10 with an exaggerated faith in secret operations behind enemy lines. He was, however, far from alone in Whitehall in believing that Germany's six-week victory over France and the Low Countries demonstrated the enormous power of subversion and sabotage. The sheer rapidity of the German Blitzkriegs was mistakenly ascribed to the assistance of large 'fifth columns' working behind the lines. Sir Nevile Bland, the British minister in the Netherlands, reported that the rapid collapse of the Dutch, who surrendered after only five days' fighting, on 15 May, had been made possible by the cooperation between the fifth column and German parachutists. He gave the (probably fictitious) example of a German maid who had led the parachutists to one of their targets – a story reminiscent of the spy scares of the First World War.[51]

When Bland's report was presented to the War Cabinet on 15 May, Churchill demanded 'urgent action'. On 16 July he gave control of 'a new instrument of war', the Special Operations Executive (SOE), to conduct 'subversion and sabotage' behind enemy lines in collaboration with local resistance movements, to the brash, dynamic Labour politician Hugh Dalton, Minister of Economic Warfare in Churchill's coalition government. 'And now', Churchill famously told Dalton, 'set Europe ablaze!' During Dalton's two years in charge of SOE, however, occupied Europe did no more than 'smoulder'.[52]

Churchill's exaggerated expectations of SOE derived, in part, from a romantic belief in the power of patriotic terrorism. Despite his hostility to Indian nationalism, Churchill said of Madan Lal Dhingra, who in 1909 assassinated Sir William Curzon Wyllie, political aide-de-camp to the Secretary of State for India: 'He will be remembered two thousand years hence, as we remember Regulus and Caractacus and Plutarch's heroes.' Churchill called Dhingra's last words before his execution 'the finest ever made in the name of patriotism'.[53] After the First World War, Churchill's awed admiration for the Russian terrorist Boris Savinkov came close to farce. Savinkov had, he acknowledged, 'described with brutal candour the part he played in the murders of M. de Plehve and the Grand Duke Serge' in Tsarist Russia. Yet, 'Amid these miseries, perils and crimes he displayed the wisdom of a statesman, the qualities of a commander, the courage of a hero, and the endurance of a martyr.' Churchill's support for Savinkov's impracticable plans to overthrow Lenin and the Bolsheviks during the early 1920s shows how far his judgement could be impaired by his love of daring. Shortly before Christmas 1921 Churchill drove down to Chequers with Savinkov in an effort to win over Lloyd George to his visionary schemes. 'He is', he told Lloyd George, 'the only man who counts.' The Prime Minister was rightly unimpressed. Yet even after Savinkov's fantasies had been exposed and he had been lured back to a show trial in Russia,[54] Churchill still retained an enduring admiration for him. As recently as 1937 he had included Savinkov in his volume of *Great Contemporaries*: 'With all the stains and tarnishes there be, few men tried more, gave more and suffered more for the Russian people.'

For all Churchill's sometimes excessive enthusiasm for intelligence, his grasp of it outclassed that of Roosevelt and Stalin. While Churchill enhanced the role of intelligence in Britain, Stalin degraded it in the Soviet

Union. In the five years from the onset of the Terror in 1936 to the German invasion in 1941, thanks chiefly to Stalin's paranoid tendencies, Soviet intelligence spent less time dealing with real than imaginary threats. Intelligence personnel who failed to subscribe with sufficient enthusiasm to Stalin's conspiracy theories put at risk not merely their career prospects but also their life expectancy. The Terror at home ushered in an era of competitive denunciation in embassies and residencies abroad. Diplomats and intelligence officers hastened to denounce colleagues before their colleagues could denounce them. After the show trial of Zinoviev, Kamenev and other 'degenerates' in August 1936, the NKVD Paris residency denounced its Fourth Department colleague Abram Mironovich Albam (codenamed BELOV):

> BELOV does not appear to feel a deep hatred or a sharply critical attitude towards these political bandits. During discussions of the trial of the Trotskyite–Zinovievite bandits, he retreats into silence. BELOV was hoping that the seven convicted men would be shown mercy, and, when he read about their execution in the newspaper today, he actually sighed.

Albam's subversive sigh helped to convict not merely himself but also a number of his colleagues of imaginary crimes. His file lists thirteen of his acquaintances who were subsequently arrested; some, probably most, were shot. Albam's wife, Frida Lvovna, tried to save herself by disowning her arrested husband. 'The most horrible realization for an honest Party member', she wrote indignantly to the NKVD, 'is the fact that he was an enemy of the people surrounded by other enemies of the people.'[55]

In 1937–8, following the recall and liquidation of all or most of their officers, some NKVD residencies ceased to function. Though the residencies in London, Berlin, Vienna and Tokyo did not close, they were reduced to one or, at the most, two officers each. Over 60 per cent of Soviet diplomats and Narkomindel (Foreign Ministry) officials were also purged.[56] During 1938 three successive heads of INO (NKVD foreign intelligence) were liquidated. Abram Slutsky was probably poisoned. Zelman Pasov and Sergei Shpigelglass were both shot.[57] INO collapsed into such confusion that, as the SVR official history acknowledges, for 127 consecutive days during 1938, it sent not a single intelligence report to Stalin.[58] In December Yezhov was replaced as head of the NKVD by Lavrenti Pavlovich Beria, later remembered by Stalin's daughter, Svetlana, as 'a magnificent modern specimen of the artful courtier, the embodiment of oriental perfidy, flattery and hypocrisy'. He became closer to Stalin than any other member of his entourage, acting as his unofficial toastmaster at his heavy-drinking late-night dinner parties.[59] Yezhov was found guilty of the charge (preposterous even by his own paranoid standards) of simultaneous conspiracy with Britain, Germany, Japan and Poland. Until, and even after, the Terror wound down during 1938, all NKVD officers worked under tremendous strain. As they went home each evening, they must have wondered whether this was the night when a knock at the door in the early hours would signal that they too were about to be unmasked as enemies of the people.

So many mostly imaginary traitors were purged from Soviet foreign intelligence that by 1939 the NKVD London residency was manned only by a single officer, Anatoly Veniaminovich Gorsky, who knew little about even its most important agents. In the summer of 1939, when Kim Philby, now honoured by a memorial at SVR headquarters, was about to return to London from Spain, where he had been working for the NKVD under cover as a *Times* journalist, Gorsky telegraphed the Centre: 'When you give us orders on what to do with SÖHNCHEN [Philby], we would appreciate some orientation on him, for he is known to us only in the most general terms.' By this time, the Centre had developed serious doubts about all five of the main young Cambridge graduates it had recruited in the mid-1930s: Philby, Donald Maclean, Guy Burgess, Anthony Blunt and John Cairncross, later sometimes known as the 'Magnificent Five'. Several case officers and residents in Britain who had dealt with them had since been (wrongly) identified as 'enemies of the people' in contact with Western intelligence services. One, Alexander Orlov, fearful that he was about to be arrested, had defected to the United States (though he revealed nothing about the Five). An assessment by the Centre in the summer of 1939 concluded that intelligence work in Britain 'was based on doubtful sources, on an agent network acquired at the time when it was controlled by enemies of the people and was therefore extremely dangerous'. It concluded with a recommendation to break contact with all British agents. Though contact with the Five was not actually broken, all seem to have been held at arm's length for most of 1939. Intelligence from them was accepted, often without any visible interest in it, while the Centre continued to debate the possibility that some or all of them were *agents provocateurs*. All the Five, however, remained ideologically committed Soviet agents, successfully suppressing most of their inner doubts about the Nazi–Soviet Pact of August 1939.[60]

During the later 1930s the hunt for 'enemies of the people' replaced intelligence collection as the main priority of NKVD foreign-intelligence operations. Residencies abroad were regularly berated for their lack of energy in pursuing Trotskyists. One angry telegram to Stockholm and Oslo, at a time when Trotsky was living in Norway, was typical of many: 'The campaign against Trotskyist terrorist bandits is being pursued in your countries with intolerable passivity.'[61] In Stalin's conspiratorial mental universe, Trotsky remained a more dangerous opponent than Hitler. With Hitler, perhaps as early as the mid-1930s, Stalin envisaged the possibility of a Nazi–Soviet Pact. With Trotsky it was a struggle to the death.

The NKVD struggle against Trotskyism in Spain produced a civil war within the Civil War. By 1937 Stalin was less interested in helping Spain's left-wing Republican government defeat the nationalist rebellion led by General Franco than in pursuing his obsessional vendetta against Trotskyism in all its forms. His chief target in Spain was Andreu Nin, the pro-Trotsky leader of the Partido Obrero de Unificación Marxista (POUM).* Nin's assassination was such a high priority that, despite a generally poor record in Spain, the NKVD resident, Alexander Orlov, who helped to organize Nin's abduction in the summer of 1937, was awarded (necessarily with Stalin's personal approval) the Order of Lenin. Though Orlov helped to organize Nin's abduction, the subsequent murder of the POUM leader was almost certainly carried out by the NKVD's most intellectual assassin, Iosif Romualdovich Grigulevich, a much more talented intelligence officer than Orlov. It was a measure of Grigulevich's skill in assuming false identities that, though born a Lithuanian Jew, he was to succeed, a decade later, in passing himself off as a Costa Rican diplomat. After initially training saboteurs and arsonists to operate behind Franco's lines, he took the leading role in liquidating Trotskyists. Success against Troskyists in the Spanish Civil War led Grigulevich to be chosen to lead the first operation to assassinate Trotsky himself in Mexico.[62]

The NKVD's most active foreign operations department was Yakov 'Yasha' Serebryansky's Administration for Special Tasks, which specialized in abduction and assassination rather than intelligence collection. By 1938, at a time when NKVD foreign residencies were in rapid decline, the Administration for Special Tasks claimed to have 212 illegals operating in sixteen countries.[63] Its leading Trotskyist victims in that year included the German Rudolf Klement, who was in charge of the founding conference of Trotsky's Fourth International, which was due to be held in the autumn. On 13 July Klement mysteriously vanished from his Paris home. About a fortnight later Trotsky received a letter ostensibly written by Klement and posted in New York, denouncing him for forming an alliance with Hitler and other imaginary crimes. Trotsky dismissed the letter, no doubt correctly, as either an

---

* On ideological grounds, Nin's categorization as Trotskyist may be debatable. His public denunciation in August 1936 of Kamenev, Zinoviev and other 'old Bolsheviks', combined with his invitation to Trotsky, then in exile in Norway, to come to Barcelona, sealed his fate in Moscow. (Volodarsky, Stalin's Agent, p. 281.)

NKVD forgery or a document written by Klement with an NKVD revolver held to his head. The NKVD probably intended Klement simply to disappear after his fictitious denunciation of Trotsky. Soon after the denunciation was delivered, however, a headless corpse was washed ashore on the banks of the Seine. Two French Trotskyists were able to recognize it as the body of Klement by identifying distinctive scars on his hands. The Fourth International was stillborn. Its founding 'conference' opened at the house near Paris of the French Trotskyist Alfred Rosmer, on 3 September, attended by only twenty-one delegates claiming to represent mostly minuscule Trotskyist groups in eleven countries. The 'Russian section', whose authentic members had by now probably been entirely exterminated, was represented by the NKVD agent Mark Zborowski ('Étienne').[64]

The majority of operations by the Administration for Special Tasks were spent in hunting down imaginary, rather than real, Trotskyists among Soviet intelligence and diplomatic personnel stationed abroad. Serebryansky's persecution of INO officers steadily diminished the flow of foreign intelligence and degraded the Centre's understanding of it. Even the executioners abroad, however, were not immune from the Terror at home. Serebryansky himself became one of the victims of his own witch-hunt. Though awarded the Order of Lenin for hunting down alleged enemies of the people, in November 1938 he was recalled to Moscow and absurdly exposed as 'a spy of the British and French intelligence services'. A surreal enquiry later concluded that his network contained 'a large number of traitors and plain gangster elements'.[65]

Serebryansky's successor was Pavel Anatolievich Sudoplatov, who a few months earlier had assassinated the émigré Ukrainian nationalist leader Yevhen Konovalets with an ingeniously booby-trapped box of chocolates. In March 1939 Sudoplatov became deputy head of INO (foreign intelligence), thus bringing 'special tasks' and INO into closer association than ever before. Stalin personally instructed him to despatch a task force to Mexico to assassinate Leon Trotsky. The killing of Trotsky, codenamed operation UTKA ('Duck'), had become the main objective of Stalin's foreign policy. Even after the outbreak of the Second World War in September 1939, discovering the intentions of Adolf Hitler was a lower priority than liquidating the great heretic. Stalin naïvely expected Hitler to stick to the Nazi–Soviet Pact.

The first, nearly successful attack on Trotsky's villa near Mexico City in the early hours of 24 May 1940, organized by Iosif Grigulevich with the aid of an assault group led by the Stalinist Mexican artist David Alfaro Siqueiros, left Trotsky's bedroom walls pockmarked with machine-gun bullets. Trotsky and his wife survived by throwing themselves, just in time, beneath their bed. The second, successful assassination attempt was led by Sudoplatov's deputy, Leonid Eitingon, whose experience of 'special actions' included the liquidation of enemies of the people in Spain. The assassin was the Spanish Soviet agent Ramón Mercader (alias Jacques Monard, alias Frank Jacson), lover of the American Trotskyist Sylvia Ageloff, who had access to Trotsky's villa. Posing as a supporter, Mercader persuaded Trotsky to give him advice on an article he had written. On 20 August, as Trotsky sat reading it at his study desk, Mercader took an icepick from his pocket and brought it down with all the force he could muster on the back of Trotsky's skull. Mercader had expected Trotsky to die instantly and silently, thus allowing him to make his escape to a car nearby where his mother and her lover, Eitingon, were waiting. But Trotsky let out 'a terrible piercing cry' which alerted his guards. He died in hospital the next day. Mercader spent the next twenty years in a Mexican prison. His mother escaped with Eitingon to Moscow, where she was received by Stalin in the Kremlin and awarded the Order of Lenin – the first female Soviet agent to be so honoured.[66]*

Even Trotsky's murder did not come close to ending Stalin's Trotskyist obsession. In January 1941 the Centre instructed the head of the New York legal residency, Gayk Ovakimian, 'to intensify the struggle against the Trotskyists by making use of the disarray among the Trotskyists since the death of the "Old Man" [Trotsky], the departure of many of them, and the uncertainty and disillusionment among them'. It was 'essential that we acquire agents who are capable of vigorous actions to demoralise their ranks'. No doubt mirroring Stalin's own fears, the Centre convinced itself, on no credible evidence, that Trotsky's supporters had a 'secret spy "kitchen"' in the United States, which continued to infiltrate agents into the Soviet Union. It also persuaded itself that American Trotskyists were lying in wait for the crews of Soviet ships which called at US ports:

> To facilitate our activities in uncovering Trotskyite contacts on the part of Sov[iet] ship commanders, we must know possible sites of meetings between Sov. sailors and Trotskyite agitators – public places, bars, stores and others that are most often visited by our sailors who come to US ports and that are used by the Trotskyites. Immediately wire any new information about these 'activities' of the Trotskyites.[67]

The Centre also pored over the many documents from Agent SATYR (Sylvia Callen), private secretary to James Cannon, leader of the Trotskyist

---

* The icepick which killed Trotsky is now in the Keith Melton intelligence collection in the United States; DNA tests have established its authenticity.

Socialist Workers Party.[68] It attached particular priority to an inventory provided by SATYR of some of Trotsky's files which had been stored in a vault of the National City Bank in New York, and instructed Ovakimian to follow up references in 1939 documents to Intourist, 'a provocateur among the Trotskyites in San Francisco' and 'connections among Ukrainians': 'If the opportunity presents itself, we need to obtain these archives.' The New York residency was also instructed to attempt to recruit an agent to photograph other Trotsky archives at Harvard University.[69]

During the first half of 1941, at the very moment when the New York residency was instructed to give high priority to pointless anti-Trotskyist operations in the United States, NKVD networks in Germany headed by Arvid Harnack, an official in the Economics Ministry, and Harro Schulze-Boysen, a lieutenant in Luftwaffe intelligence,[70] were providing vitally important intelligence on Hitler's preparations for Operation BARBA-ROSSA, the invasion of Russia. On 16 June, the deputy NKVD resident in Berlin, Aleksandr Korotkov, cabled Moscow that intelligence from the two networks indicated that 'All of the military training by Germany in preparation for its attack on the Soviet Union is complete, and the strike may be expected at any time.' Similar intelligence arrived from as far afield as China and Japan. The head of foreign intelligence, Pavel Fitin, had been appointed in 1939 at the age of only thirty-one, owing his unprecedentedly rapid promotion largely to the liquidation of so many INO officers. Though doubtless prompted chiefly by grave concern for the threat to Mother Russia, he showed great moral courage in forwarding to a deeply sceptical Stalin reports of impending German attack. KGB historians later counted 'over a hundred' such intelligence warnings sent by Fitin to Stalin between 1 January and 21 June 1941. Other reports came from military intelligence, the Fourth Department. All were wasted.[71]

The British diplomat R. A. Sykes later summed up Stalin's world view as 'a curious mixture of shrewdness and nonsense'. The shrewdness which had helped him win the power struggle after Lenin's death was to show itself again in his wartime dealings with Churchill and Roosevelt. But before BARBAROSSA his understanding of both German and British policy was undermined by paranoid nonsense. Stalin convinced himself that the Soviet Union's best German and British agents were part of an elaborate conspiracy to deceive him. Though many NKVD officers shared, if often to a less grotesque degree, his addiction to conspiracy theory, the main blame for the catastrophic failure to foresee the German surprise attack on 22 June belongs to Stalin himself. Stalin not merely ignored a series of accurate warnings. He denounced many of those who provided them. His response to an NKVD report from Schulze-Boysen on 16 June was the obscene minute: 'You can tell your "source" in German airforce headquarters to go fuck himself. He's not a "source", he's a disinformer. J. Stalin.' Stalin also heaped abuse on the Fourth Department illegal Richard Sorge, posthumously recognized as one of the heroes of Soviet intelligence, who sent similar warnings from Tokyo, where he had penetrated the German embassy and seduced the ambassador's wife. Sorge's warnings of impending German invasion were denounced by Stalin as disinformation from a lying 'shit who has set himself up with some small factories and brothels in Japan'.[72] Even in marginal comments, Stalin almost never used obscenity. His comments on Schulze-Boysen in June 1941 show the stress he was under.

Stalin was less suspicious of Hitler than of Churchill, who had preached an anti-Bolshevik crusade in the Civil War twenty years before and, Stalin believed, had been plotting against the Soviet Union ever since. Behind many of the reports of impending German attack, Stalin claimed to detect a disinformation campaign by Churchill designed to continue the long-standing British plot to embroil him with Hitler. Churchill's personal warnings to Stalin of preparations for BARBAROSSA only heightened his suspicions. From the intelligence reports sent by the London residency, Stalin almost certainly knew that until June 1941 the British Joint Intelligence Committee (JIC) did not believe that Hitler was preparing an invasion. It reported to Churchill as late as 23 May that 'the advantages . . . to Germany of concluding an agreement with the USSR are overwhelming'. The JIC assessments were probably regarded by Stalin as further proof that Churchill's warnings were intended to deceive him. Stalin's deep suspicions of Churchill and of British policy in general were cleverly exploited by the Germans. As part of the deception operation which preceded BARBAROSSA, the Abwehr spread reports that rumours of an impending German attack were part of a British disinformation campaign.[73]

Lavrenti Beria sought to protect his position as head of the NKVD in succession to Yezhov by expressing mounting indignation at those inside and outside the NKVD who dared to send reports of preparations for German invasion. On 21 June 1941 he ordered four NKVD officers who had patriotically persisted in sending such reports to be 'ground into concentration camp dust'. He wrote to Stalin the same day:

> I again insist on recalling and punishing our ambassador to Berlin, Dekanozov, who keeps bombarding me with 'reports' on Hitler's alleged preparations to attack the USSR. He has reported that this attack will start tomorrow . . .
> But I and my people, Iosif Vissarionovich, have firmly embedded in our memory your wise conclusion: Hitler is not going to attack us in 1941.

Beria probably also intended to liquidate Fitin for daring to 'bombard' Stalin with false reports of impending German attack. According to an SVR official biography: 'Only the outbreak of war [next day] saved P. M. Fitin from the firing squad.'[74]

BARBAROSSA was the mightiest invasion in military history. Hitler's unshakeable belief in the Slavs' racial inferiority left him in no doubt that the Wehrmacht would be victorious before winter set in: 'We have only to kick in the door and the whole rotten edifice will come crashing down.' His forces advanced at fifty miles a day, sweeping all before them even more rapidly than in the Blitzkriegs in Western Europe. The Soviet Union also faced the terrifying prospect of a simultaneous Japanese attack in the east. Sorge reported from Tokyo that Ribbentrop was urging the German embassy to persuade the Japanese to break their treaty with the Soviet Union concluded only three months before BARBAROSSA began. 'Do everything', Ribbentrop instructed, 'to rouse the Japanese to begin war against Russia . . . the quicker this happens the better. Our goal remains to shake hands with the Japanese on the Trans-Siberian railway before the beginning of the winter.' Initially opinions were divided within the Japanese government and high command between the 'northern solution' (war with the Soviet Union) and the 'southern solution' (war with Britain and the United States).[75]

Before his arrest on 18 October with most of his spy ring, Sorge was able to keep Moscow informed, chiefly from intelligence supplied by Hotsumi Ozaki, a member of the entourage of the leading Japanese statesman Prince Konoye, as supporters of the 'southern solution' gained ground.[76] The intelligence which did most to persuade Stalin that the Russians would not, however, attack came from SIGINT. Like GC&CS and the US SIS, NKVD codebreakers broke what the Americans called the Japanese PURPLE cipher. The NKVD's chief Japanese specialist, Sergei Tolstoy of the Fifth (Cipher) Directorate, became the most decorated Soviet cryptanalyst of the war. The successes of his group allowed the Fifth Directorate to take over responsibility for decrypting military communications from the Fourth Department (renamed in 1942 the GRU). One of the responsibilities of the First Section of the Fifth Directorate was to monitor the traffic of the Japanese Kwantung Army to detect any preparations for an attack on the Soviet Far East.[77]

Tolstoy's initial successes, as in many other Russian codebreaking coups since Tsarist times,[78] probably owed much to assistance from espionage. In the autumn of 1938, a Japanese diplomat in Prague, Kozo Izumi (code-named NERO), mainly through the intermediary of his Russian wife, Elena, sold the NKVD resident seven Japanese codebooks and a substantial number of diplomatic telegrams exchanged between Tokyo and its embassies in Berlin, Prague, London, Rome and Moscow. He handed over further important code and cipher material during postings in Helsinki in 1939 and in Sofia from 1940 to 1944.[79] At a crucial early stage in the Great Patriotic War, the reassurance provided by Fifth Directorate cryptanalysts and Richard Sorge that Japan did not intend to attack the Soviet Union enabled Stalin to shift to the West half the divisional strength of the Far Eastern Command. During October and November 1941 between eight and ten rifle divisions, together with approximately 1,000 tanks and 1,000 aircraft were transferred to the fight against Germany. SIGINT continued to provide reassurance about Japan's intentions. A decrypted telegram of 27 November 1941, from Tokyo to the Berlin embassy, probably copied to the Moscow embassy, instructed the Japanese ambassador: 'See Hitler and Ribbentrop, and explain to them in secret our relations with the United States . . . Explain to Hitler that the main Japanese efforts will be concentrated in the south and that we propose to refrain from deliberate operations in the north [against the Soviet Union].'[80]

Despite his interest in espionage, Roosevelt attached far less importance to Japanese SIGINT than either Stalin or Churchill. In the autumn of 1940 he had approved a bizarre arrangement by which the military and naval SIGINT units, SIS and OP-20-G, produced MAGIC decrypts on alternate days.[81] By the beginning of 1941, the Secretary for War, Henry Stimson, who, since ordering the closure of the Black Chamber in 1929, had become an ardent supporter of SIGINT, was increasingly concerned by Roosevelt's apparent lack of interest in MAGIC. On 2 January he called at the White House, where he found FDR working in bed: 'I told him he should read the important [MAGIC] reports which had come in from Berlin giving the summary which the Japanese ambassador there had made of the situation and others like it. He hadn't read them. They were extremely interesting.'[82] To ensure that important decrypts were brought to the President's attention, it was agreed, after further inter-service wrangling, that MAGIC should be supplied to the President by his naval aide in even-numbered months and by his military aide in odd months.[83] But there was no arrangement for providing FDR with SIGINT on either Sundays or weekday evenings.[84] It is impossible to imagine Churchill or Stalin tolerating these arrangements for a single day.

By the summer of 1941, this extension of the bizarre odd/even-date arrangement for MAGIC production by SIS and OP-20-G had begun to break down. The immediate cause of the breakdown was the carelessness of Roosevelt's genial, long-serving military aide, General Edwin 'Pa'

Watson, who had the responsibility for supplying MAGIC during the army months. 'Pa' was the court jester of the Roosevelt White House. When FDR commented on his aftershave ('Do all generals smell this nice?') or made other jokes at his expense, Watson never failed to laugh appreciatively. G-2 (military intelligence) was less happy about his understanding of security. Probably in May, a MAGIC summary went missing. A prolonged search of the White House eventually discovered it in Watson's wastepaper basket.[85] During June, a navy month, the President received MAGIC decrypts from his new naval aide, Captain John R. Beardall. But in July, an army month, the Military Intelligence Division (MID) refused (with possibly a few exceptions) to supply SIGINT to the White House because, it later admitted, of 'lack of confidence in General Watson's idea of security'. Though dissatisfied by the interruption in the supply of decrypts, Roosevelt curiously did not insist that it be resumed. Instead, even though July was an army month, he asked his naval aide about the latest MAGIC revelations. Having read the decrypts in OP-20-G, Beardall was able to inform the President of their contents. But, to comply with the odd-/even-months arrangement with SIS, he did not take the decrypts themselves into the White House.[86]

During 1941, apart from the press, MAGIC was almost the only significant source of information on Japanese policy reaching the President. The ambassador to Tokyo, Joseph C. Grew, told the State Department:

> Please remember that in Japan we are generally groping in the dark and that now, more than ever, it is exceedingly difficult to ascertain what is going on behind the scenes, especially since few of our former Japanese contacts dare come to the Embassy or meet us elsewhere. Many have been warned by the police to avoid us.[87]

Despite its increasing importance, however, MAGIC continued to reach the President erratically. During August (a navy month) the supply was normal. In September (an army month), because of the distrust of 'Pa' Watson by SIS, it dried up once again. As in July, Beardall was allowed to brief Roosevelt on the contents of the September decrypts but not to show them to him for fear of offending G-2. By the latter part of the month, FDR's patience was wearing thin. He told Beardall he wished to see the decrypts themselves. Beardall asked the chief naval-intelligence translator, Lieutenant-Commander Alwin D. Kramer, who approached Colonel Rufus S. Bratton, head of the G-2 Far Eastern section. Faced with a direct request from the commander-in-chief, G-2 grudgingly allowed the navy to trespass on an army month.[88] At the beginning of the next army month in November, the flow of MAGIC to the White House dried up once again. This time the President had had enough. Henceforth army months were abolished and all decrypts were channelled to him through his naval aide. Inter-service rivalry ensured, however, that the nonsense of odd (navy) and even (army) days for the production of MAGIC continued.[89]

Despite the worsening of US–Japanese relations, it did not occur to the Office of Naval Intelligence or to the President's naval aide that Japan was preparing a plan for a surprise attack on the US Pacific Fleet at Pearl Harbor in Hawaii. Though Imperial Japan had little grasp of strategic intelligence, the tactical-intelligence operations which prepared the way for Pearl Harbor were efficiently conducted. In March 1941 a junior Japanese naval-intelligence officer, Takeo Yoshikawa, was posted to Hawaii under diplomatic cover under the alias 'Tadashi Morimura'. He reported on the size, strength and location of the US Pacific Fleet at Pearl Harbor both by telegraph to Tokyo and in person to his superior, Minato Nakajima, who visited Hawaii on a Japanese liner en route to San Francisco. Other Japanese naval officers reconnoitred the seaway from Japan to Hawaii, as well as gathering intelligence from agents in Hawaii. Japanese naval direction-finding monitored the movements of US warships based in Hawaii.[90]

On 5 November a Japanese imperial conference made the final decision to go ahead with the attack at Pearl Harbor on 8 December, Tokyo time (7 December in the United States). The decision was not mentioned in Japanese diplomatic telegrams and therefore did not figure in MAGIC decrypts. But MAGIC did make clear that Japan was moving towards a rupture of relations with the United States and that the risk of war was growing. The first major indication of the tougher line being adopted by the government of General Hideki Tojo had come in a telegram to its Washington embassy on 5 November (the day of the imperial conference), decrypted the same day, declaring it 'absolutely necessary' to settle the dispute with the United States not later than 25 November. It was probably news of this decrypt that finally persuaded Roosevelt to insist on uninterrupted access to MAGIC. In a further decrypt of 15 November, the new Foreign Minister, Shigenori Togo, reaffirmed that the 25 November deadline was 'absolutely immoveable'. In fact another telegram extended the 'immoveable' deadline by four days to 29 November, but it did so in language that was more ominous than ever: 'This time we mean it, that deadline absolutely cannot be changed. After that things are automatically going to happen.'[91]

Roosevelt had little doubt that Togo was referring to plans for a surprise attack. He told a meeting in the White House on 25 November that 'we were likely to be attacked next Monday [1 December] for the Japs are notorious for making an attack without warning . . .' But the idea of a surprise attack on the Pacific Fleet did not occur to either him or his advisers. Though

US intelligence failed to detect the threat to Pearl Harbor, it provided clear evidence that war was on the way. On 26 and 28 November US cryptanalysts decrypted in two parts the now celebrated 'Winds Messages' sent by Tokyo to its foreign embassies on 19 November, containing the coded signals that would indicate the intention to break off diplomatic relations with the United States, Britain and the Soviet Union. For the US, it would be 'East Wind Rain'; for Britain 'West Wind Clear'; for the Soviet Union 'North Wind Cloudy'. As soon as the embassies received these messages, they were to destroy all codebooks and secret papers.[92]

Further evidence of impending conflict was contained in instructions from Tokyo to a number of foreign missions on 1 and 2 December to destroy codes and cipher machines. The message to the Washington embassy (which instructed it to retain one PURPLE machine for the time being) was decrypted on 3 December and probably shown to Roosevelt by Beardall on the 4th.* Hitherto FDR's naval aide had usually handed him his daily MAGIC without comment. On this occasion, as Beardall quaintly put it, 'I took the liberty of inviting [his] special attention.' 'Mr President', he declared, 'this is a very significant despatch.' Roosevelt read it attentively, then asked, 'Well, when do you think it will happen?' Beardall understood him to be asking 'when war is going to break out, when we are going to be attacked, or something.' 'Most anytime', he replied. This brief dialogue is the first recorded discussion of the contents of a MAGIC decrypt between the President and his naval aide.[93]

At a meeting of the War Cabinet on Friday, 5 December, the Secretary for War, Frank Knox, announced: 'We have very secret information that mustn't go out of this room that the Japanese fleet is out. They're out of the harbour. They're out at sea.' But he was referring to fleet movements off Japan, not to the undetected carrier force which was now less than two days from Pearl Harbor. Attention was still focused on discovering the likely targets of Japanese aggression in south-east Asia.[94]

The production of intelligence during the critical day and a half before the attack on Pearl Harbor was confused by the continuing absurdity of the odd/even navy/army day cryptanalytic compromise. A decrypted telegram from Tokyo to the Washington embassy, which became known as the 'pilot' message, announced that the situation was now 'extremely delicate' and that a fourteen-part reply to the final US terms to end the dispute

* Beardall later remembered the date as 'about the 4th or 5th' (*PHA*, part 11, p. 5284). Given the importance of the Japanese telegram, it is unlikely that it was not shown to FDR until the 5th, two days after it was decrypted. Churchill too was shown the decrypt on 4 December (TNA HW1/297).

with Japan would follow shortly. The message was intercepted by the navy's West Coast listening station near Seattle at 7.20 a.m. EST on Saturday, 6 December, and forwarded by teleprinter to the Navy Department in Washington. Since 6 December was an even date and therefore an army day, the navy sent the message to be decrypted by the military SIS, which received it at 12.05 p.m. The first thirteen parts of the fourteen-part message were intercepted by the West Coast listening station between 8.05 and 11.52 a.m., and sent by teleprinter to Washington at intervals from 11.45 a.m. to 2.51 p.m. (The fourteenth part did not arrive until the following day.)[95]

Having received from the navy the most important intercepts in its history, SIS now found itself in a deeply embarrassing position. Its civilian translators and other staff went off duty for the weekend at midday on Saturday, and there was no provision for overtime. SIS was thus forced to return the intercepts to the navy and ask OP-20-G to deal with them.[96] Ironically, when the Japanese reply rejecting the American terms was decrypted, it was discovered to be in the English language and thus not to require translation. While OP-20-G spent the afternoon decrypting most of the intercepts, SIS succeeded in arranging its first-ever evening shift to help deal with overnight messages. Military cryptanalysts also decrypted two of the thirteen parts of the fourteen-part message so far intercepted, though all the typing was done by the navy.[97]

While naval and military cryptanalysts continued work on the thirteen parts of the Japanese message, the President finished drafting a final appeal to Emperor Hirohito 'to restore traditional amity and prevent further death and destruction in the world'. At 3.30 a.m. on Sunday, 7 December, the senior naval-intelligence translator, Lieutenant-Commander Alwin D. Kramer, arrived at the White House with the decrypted thirteen parts in a locked pouch. Beardall's assistant, Lieutenant Lester R. Schulz, who had begun work at the White House only the previous day, was waiting to take it to the President. Remarkably, this was the first MAGIC decrypt judged sufficiently important to be given to Roosevelt outside normal office hours. He had been warned, probably by Beardall, to expect its arrival. Schulz found him in his study, seated at his desk, talking to his confidant and adviser, Harry Hopkins. Schulz later testified that the President 'turned toward Mr Hopkins and said in substance – I am not sure of the exact words but in substance – "This means war".'[98]

Kramer delivered the final part of the decrypted fourteen-part message to the White House at 9.45 a.m. Beardall, who had come to work on a Sunday for the first time since becoming the President's naval aide, took the message to his bedroom. Roosevelt said: 'Good morning', read the decrypt, told Beardall: 'It looks like the Japanese are going to break off negotiations', then returned the document to him. There was nothing in Roosevelt's manner, Beardall later testified, to indicate that he expected war in a matter of hours. This brief exchange was, according to Beardall, only the second conversation he had had with the President on Far Eastern affairs.[99] Roosevelt spent the next two hours with his personal physician, Rear Admiral Ross T. McIntire. According to McIntyre, the President thought the Japanese might 'take advantage of Great Britain's extremity and strike at Singapore or some other point in the Far East, but an attack on any American possession did not enter his thought'.[100] At about 11 a.m. Kramer left two further Japanese decrypts at the White House. But, not expecting another morning delivery, Beardall had taken the final part of the fourteen-part message to the Navy Department and did not return to the White House until after lunch. So it appears that the President did not receive the two final pre-war MAGIC decrypts until after news of the Japanese attack.[101]

First news of the attack on Pearl Harbor reached Roosevelt in a phone call from Knox at about 1.40 p.m. while he was lunching in his study with Hopkins, 'chatting about things far removed from war'. Hopkins's immediate reaction was that 'there must be some misunderstanding . . . that surely Japan would not attack in Honolulu'. Roosevelt shook his head. This was 'just the kind of unexpected thing the Japanese would do'.[102] By 3 p.m. the President's advisers had begun to gather in the White House. Details of the attack came in a series of telephone messages from the Chief of Naval Operations, Admiral Harold R. 'Betty' Stark, his voice registering stunned disbelief. When the Cabinet met that evening, Roosevelt could hardly bring himself to describe what had happened. According to his Labor Secretary, Frances Perkins: 'His pride in the Navy was so terrific that he was having actual physical difficulty in getting the words out that put him on record as knowing that the Navy was caught unawares, that bombs dropped on ships that were not in fighting shape and not prepared to move, but were just tied up.'[103] Eighteen ships (ten of them battleships) were sunk or seriously damaged, almost 200 aircraft destroyed on the ground, and 2,400 people killed.

Over a week before Pearl Harbor, a MAGIC decrypt had revealed that on 29 November the German Foreign Minister, Count Joachim von Ribbentrop, had promised the Japanese ambassador in Berlin that if Japan went to war with the United States: 'Germany, of course, would join the war immediately . . . The Fuehrer is determined on that point.'[104] But, in the absence of any centralized system of intelligence assessment, in the aftermath of Pearl Harbor Roosevelt's advisers gave him bewilderingly different interpretations of the intentions of the Axis powers. Stimson insisted, quite wrongly: 'We know from the intercepts and other evidence that Germany had pushed Japan into this.'[105] Assistant Secretary of State Adolf A. Berle Jr, perhaps confused by a misreading of Italian intercepts, argued, also wrongly, that SIGINT made 'plain' that the Japanese had the enthusiastic backing of the Italians but not yet of the Germans.[106] There was further confusion in Washington over who had access to MAGIC and who did not. Stark laboured under the delusion that Admiral Husband Kimmel, Commander-in-Chief of the Pacific Fleet at Pearl Harbor, was regularly supplied with MAGIC. In fact, Kimmel had received only a few fragments since July. Military intelligence similarly believed, also mistakenly, that the army commander at Pearl Harbor, General Walter Short, was on the MAGIC circulation list. Kimmel and Short later became the chief scapegoats for the disaster.[107]

The confusion of MAGIC assessment and circulation before Pearl Harbor was ultimately the responsibility of the President himself. When giving General William J. Donovan responsibility for the coordination of intelligence assessment in June 1941, he had failed to include SIGINT in his responsibilities – despite the fact that it provided by far the most important intelligence. Until November, Roosevelt had tolerated an extraordinary level of confusion in the distribution of MAGIC, even to himself. In Britain, by contrast, Churchill took an active personal interest in both the coordination of intelligence assessment (SIGINT included) through the JIC system and in its orderly and secure application to the war effort.[108]

Even if MAGIC production and delivery to the White House had been competently handled, however, it would not have identified the main Japanese target as Pearl Harbor. Since no Japanese mission abroad was given advance notice of the attack, MAGIC made no mention of it. But if diplomatic cables failed to point to an attack on Pearl Harbor, Japanese naval traffic did. Though thousands of naval signals were intercepted during the last six months of 1941, however, the great majority could not be decrypted. While the cryptanalysts had made progress in solving the basic Japanese naval code, known to OP-20-G as JN25, the attack on the variant, JN25b, introduced in December 1940, had so far failed.[109] A detailed study by the post-war SIGINT service, the National Security Agency (NSA), concluded that the failure to break JN25b was due solely to a shortage of resources. For most of the three years before Pearl Harbor, usually only two cryptanalysts (and never more than five) were assigned to work on all Japanese naval code and cipher systems. Faced with a similar lack of resources, the leading codebreakers of GC&CS would have appealed directly to Churchill. It did not occur to OP-20-G to appeal to Roosevelt, who had given little sign of interest in its work. Only after Pearl Harbor was the number of cryptanalysts working on JN25 and JN25b increased to eight. 'If the Japanese navy messages had enjoyed a higher priority and [had been] assigned more analytic resources', wrote the NSA historian, Frederick D. Parker, 'could the U.S. Navy have predicted the Japanese attack on Pearl Harbor? Most emphatically yes!' When the unsolved intercepted messages of late 1941 were decrypted as part of a secret post-war study, they were found to reveal many of the preparations for Pearl Harbor. There were numerous indications in the intercepts of planning for a surprise attack by a naval task force including six aircraft carriers on an enemy fleet at anchor somewhere in the North Pacific. There were references also to the modification of large numbers of torpedoes for an attack in shallow waters. (Pearl Harbor was believed in Washington to be too shallow for a conventional torpedo attack.) The telegraphed order from Tokyo on 2 December, 'Climb Mount Nikita 8 December, Repeat 8 December', would have revealed, if decrypted, that the attack was planned for 8 December Japanese time (7 December in Hawaii).[110]

American successes in breaking Japanese naval ciphers after Pearl Harbor[111] confirm the conclusion of the NSA study that, had their importance been recognized and an adequate number of cryptanalysts set to work on them, JN25b could have been broken in time to reveal preparations for the surprise attack on 7 December 1941. The low priority given to the attack on JN25b was due, in part, to the myopia of the Navy Department, which had failed to grasp the importance of SIGINT in naval warfare. But it also reflected the shortsightedness of a President who, despite his passion for the navy, his long-standing enthusiasm for intelligence, and his first-hand experience of the value of Japanese diplomatic intercepts, showed little interest in Japanese naval signals. Given the brevity of his comments to his naval aide about MAGIC, it seems unlikely that he ever asked Beardall what progress was being made in the attack on naval ciphers.

It is inconceivable that Churchill would have shown a similar indifference. During the weeks before Pearl Harbor, Churchill frequently telephoned Bletchley Park himself to ask for the latest intelligence. One of GC&CS's leading Japanese cryptanalysts, Captain Malcolm Kennedy, wrote in his diary on 6 December: 'The All-Highest [Churchill] . . . is all over himself at the moment for latest information and indications re Japan's intentions and rings up at all hours of day and night, except for the 4 hours in each 24 (2 to 6 A.M.) when he sleeps.' Captain Kennedy, like Churchill, first learned of the attack on Pearl Harbor next day not from SIGINT but from the BBC:

A message received just before leaving the office this evening had indicated that the outbreak of war was probably only a matter of hours, but the news

on the 9 P.M. wireless, that Japan had opened hostilities with an air raid
on Pearl Harbour, more than 3000 miles out in the Pacific, came as a
complete surprise.[112]

By chance, Churchill was dining at Chequers with John Winant, the US
ambassador, and Averell Harriman, Roosevelt's special representative,
when the BBC broadcast the news of the Japanese attack. Churchill and
his guests were uncertain exactly what the newsreader had said. 'What
did he say?' asked Churchill. 'Pearl Harbor attacked?' Churchill's butler,
Sawyers, entered the room. 'It's quite true', he told Churchill and his
guests, 'We heard it ourselves [on the BBC]. The Japanese have attacked
Pearl Harbor.'[113] Only in a British country house could the news of world
war have been announced by the butler.

The 'complete surprise' of both Roosevelt and Churchill at the news
from Pearl Harbor reflected a failure of imagination as well as of intelligence. It did not occur to either the President or the Prime Minister that
the 'little yellow men', as Churchill sometimes spoke of them and Roosevelt
thought of them, were capable of such an astonishing feat of arms. When
General Douglas MacArthur first heard the news of the attack by carrier-
borne aircraft on Pearl Harbor, he insisted that the pilots must have been
white mercenaries. Had the Japanese been taken more seriously as political
opponents, had they been considered the racial equals of Americans, intelligence on their navy would have been given a higher priority in the White
House as well as in the Navy Department.

28

Intelligence and the Victory
of the Grand Alliance

The Pearl Harbor disaster led to a long overdue reorganization of United States SIGINT. The initiative came from the Secretary of War, Henry Stimson, who on 18 January 1942 recruited the New York lawyer (later Colonel) Alfred McCormack 'to make order in MAGIC'. At almost the same moment the absurd arrangement that had given military and naval cryptanalysts responsibility for producing MAGIC decrypts on alternate days was abandoned. The naval OP-20-G agreed, no doubt reluctantly, that the military SIS should henceforth have sole responsibility for diplomatic cryptanalysis. To soften the blow to naval pride, diplomatic SIGINT, though produced by the army, continued illogically to be supplied to the President by his naval rather than his military aide. Captain John McCrea, who succeeded Beardall as naval aide in January, usually took MAGIC decrypts, as well as important naval documents, to Roosevelt twice a day. When he arrived at the White House each morning, he found Roosevelt either working in bed or shaving in the bathroom. If the President was still in bed, McCrea would give him the papers to read. If he was in the bathroom, McCrea would close the toilet lid, sit on it and read top-secret intelligence aloud to the President. When McCrea came on his afternoon visit, Roosevelt was most frequently to be found in the map room (which became the White House war room), where he would read the documents selected for his attention by his naval aide. If not in the map room, the President would usually be nearby in his doctor's office, having his withered legs massaged or his sinuses packed, and McCrea would read the afternoon MAGIC to him.[1]

The SIGINT read to or by Roosevelt in bed, in his bathroom, in the map room and in his doctor's office was the most remarkable intelligence yet received by a President of the United States. Within six months of Pearl Harbor, it had helped to turn the tide of the Pacific War. By the spring of 1942 cryptanalysts in the Pearl Harbor SIGINT unit codenamed HYPO (later known as FRUPac), had made enough progress in decrypting the latest variant of the JN25 naval cipher to reveal the plan by Admiral

Isoroku Yamamoto to attack Port Moresby in New Guinea.* Though the Battle of the Coral Sea (4–8 May 1942) ended without a clear victory for either side, it effectively stopped the Japanese advance towards Australia. A few weeks later HYPO achieved one of the great cryptanalytic coups of the war by revealing Yamamoto's plan to capture Midway Island, in the middle of the North Pacific, as a base from which to repel any future US advance towards Japan. Yamamoto calculated that the capture of Midway would lure out the US Pacific Fleet to be destroyed by his own superior forces, thus opening the way to a Japanese attack on Hawaii. Forewarned of the enemy battle plan, the Commander-in-Chief of the US Pacific Fleet, Admiral Chester W. Nimitz, positioned his three aircraft carriers 350 miles north of Midway, from where, on the morning of 4 June, he was able to launch a surprise attack on the larger Japanese fleet. Midway, Nimitz said later, 'was essentially a victory of intelligence. In attempting surprise, the Japanese were themselves surprised.'[2] Following the sinking of four of the six aircraft carriers that had carried out the attack on Pearl Harbor, Yamamoto was forced back on the defensive. Two months later the US Army landed at Guadalcanal in the Solomon Islands, thus taking the first step in its long 'island-hopping' advance towards the Philippines and Japan. In April 1943 US fighters based at Guadalcanal shot down Yamamoto's plane, whose flight plan had been discovered from Japanese decrypts. In authorizing Yamamoto's mid-air assassination, Roosevelt, probably without realizing it, risked compromising US SIGINT security. According to Captain Jasper Holmes of HYPO: 'It became an item of widespread interservice gossip that the dramatic interception of Yamamoto's plane had been contrived through broken Japanese codes. It was a miracle that the story did not break in American newspapers.'[3]†

The weakest link in the communications security of the Grand Alliance was the American 'Black Code' (so called after the colour of its binder), used for US diplomatic and military attaché communications, which had been broken by German, Italian and British codebreakers.[4] On 25 February 1942 Churchill made a remarkable, though incomplete, confession to Roosevelt about British success in breaking the Black Code:

---

* HYPO was helped not merely by increased resources but by the capture of codebooks from the Japanese *I-go 124* submarine sunk off northern Australia in January 1943. (Kotani, *Japanese Intelligence in World War II*, p. 87.)

† The threat was all the greater in view of the fact that the *Chicago Tribune* and other US media had come close to revealing that victory at Midway had been made possible by breaking Japanese ciphers.

Some time ago . . . our experts claimed to have discovered the system and constructed some tables used by your diplomatic corps. From the moment when we became allies, I gave instructions that this work should cease. However, danger of our enemies having achieved a measure of success cannot, I am advised, be dismissed.[5]

Roosevelt's lack of interest in SIGINT may partially explain why US diplomats and military attachés continued to use the Black Code after Churchill's warning. But unless, improbably, the White House failed to pass on the warning, the State Department and War Department were guilty of basic security lapses.

Among those who continued to make regular use of the compromised Black Code was Colonel Bonner Fellers, the US military attaché in Cairo, who sent regular, highly classified reports on the British Eighth Army to Washington and, thanks to German codebreakers, inadvertently to Rommel also. Fellers was given the German codename *Gute Quelle* ('good source'). One of Rommel's staff officers later claimed that the intelligence from the *Gute Quelle* was 'stupefying in its openness' and even, possibly with some exaggeration, that it 'contributed decisively to our victories in North Africa' during the first six months of 1942, which brought the Afrika Korps close to the conquest of Alexandria and Cairo.[6] According to the Chiffrierabteilung (code department) of the Armed Forces High Command (OKW) in Berlin, through the first six months of 1942, until the Black Code was replaced on 29 June, Colonel Fellers unwittingly provided 'all we needed to know, immediately, about virtually every enemy action'. Dr Herbert Schaedel, director of the Chiffrierabteilung's main intercept station, later claimed that, thanks to the *Gute Quelle*, 'Rommel, each day at lunch, knew exactly where the Allied troops were standing the evening before.'[7]

On 20 June 1942 Fellers transmitted a devastating critique of British military operations in Libya which must have given Rommel particular pleasure:

With numerically superior forces, with tanks, planes, artillery, means of transport, and reserves of every kind, the British army has twice failed to defeat the Axis forces in Libya. Under the present command and with the measures taken in a hit or miss fashion the granting of 'lend-lease' alone cannot ensure a victory. The Eighth Army has failed to maintain the morale of its troops; its tactical conceptions were always wrong; it neglected completely cooperation between the various arms; its reactions to the lightning changes of the battlefield were always slow.[8]

Next day the British and Commonwealth garrison at Tobruk surrendered. Rommel took more than 30,000 prisoners, 2,000 vehicles, 2,000 tons of fuel, and 5,000 tons of rations, and declared: 'I am going on to Suez.' Adolf Hitler promoted Rommel to field marshal. Had Rommel forced the British out of Egypt, control of the Middle East, its strategic oil reserves, and the Suez Canal would have been in Axis hands. Unable to contain his excitement, Mussolini flew to Libya, ready to make a triumphal entry into Cairo.[9] In one of his after-dinner monologues on 28 June 1942, Hitler expressed the hope that Fellers would continue 'to inform us so well over the English military planning through his badly enciphered cables'.[10] Fearful that Rommel was about to break through British lines, GHQ Middle East and the British embassy in Cairo frantically incinerated huge piles of classified documents to prevent their falling into his hands. 1 July 1942 became known as 'Ash Wednesday' because of the cloud of partially burnt documents which descended on the city. Some street vendors sold peanuts in paper cones made from the charred remains of secret documents.[11]

Rommel, however, never reached Cairo. His 'good source' was lost on 29 June when Fellers returned to Washington and his successor as US military attaché in Cairo ceased to send reports in the compromised Black Code. Bletchley Park discovered Rommel's previous access to Fellers' reports from German decrypts. Somewhat unfairly, Eisenhower put much of the blame for the security breach on Fellers personally. 'Any friend of Bonner Fellers', he declared, 'is no friend of mine.'[12] Rommel's loss of the 'good source' left Britain with a decisive SIGINT advantage in the North African campaign. At a time when Rommel no longer had significant SIGINT on the Eighth Army, ULTRA made a major contribution to the failure of his attempt to break through the British line defending Egypt at the Battle of Alam Halfa from 30 August to 7 September 1942. Rommel reported his battle plan on 15 August in an Enigma message to Hitler decrypted by Bletchley Park. Within forty-eight hours the decrypt was in the hands of the recently appointed commander of the Eighth Army, Lieutenant-General (later Field Marshal Sir) Bernard Montgomery. Never naturally inclined to give credit to others, Montgomery failed to acknowledge the debt he owed to Bletchley. ULTRA, however, was a major, perhaps crucial, element in Rommel's defeat at Alam Halfa.[13]

Monty's far better-known victory at El Alamein (23 October–4 November) was due more to the fact that he outgunned and outmanned Rommel, who was critically short of fuel, than to superior intelligence. Churchill was unable to resist interfering in the use of SIGINT during the battle. Having found in his daily box of intercepts from Bletchley Park an ULTRA decrypt from Berlin reassuring Rommel that an Italian convoy was bringing him more fuel and ammunition, Churchill ordered an attack on the convoy. To prevent Rommel realizing that the message from Berlin had been intercepted, a bogus British message was sent in an insecure cipher congratulating a group of non-existent Italian agents on providing the intelligence which had led to the sinking of the convoy. ULTRA revealed that the Germans duly intercepted the message and were taken in by it.[14] The promised fuel failed to reach Rommel.

On the morning of 3 November Montgomery must have been elated to read a despairing decrypted message from Rommel to Hitler, warning him that his army had run out of fuel and faced annihilation.[15] Next day Rommel began a long retreat, during which Montgomery made too little use of ULTRA intelligence. The Cambridge historian Ralph Bennett, then a cryptanalyst in Hut 3 at Bletchley Park, later recalled after the victory at El Alamein:

> the fierce indignation in the Hut at Montgomery's painfully slow advance from Alamein to Tripoli, incomprehensible in the light of the mass of Ultra intelligence showing that throughout his retreat Rommel was too weak to withstand serious pressure . . . [Montgomery's] delay seemed to cast doubt on the whole point of our work.

By the beginning of 1943 Montgomery and his staff had developed complete confidence in ULTRA and, to the relief of Hut 3 at Bletchley, made more rapid operational use of it.[16]

Despite defeat in North Africa, until the spring of 1943 Germany still had the advantage in what Churchill called the 'Battle of the Atlantic'. 'The only thing that ever really frightened me during the war', he later recalled, 'was the U-boat peril.'[17] As in 1917, U-boats threatened to halt the flow of vital war supplies across the Atlantic.[18] Between June 1941 and February 1943, 885 ships were lost but only thirteen U-boats sunk. The introduction in February 1942 of a more complex variant of the U-boat version of Enigma, codenamed SHARK (involving the addition of a fourth rotor to the cipher machine), defeated Bletchley Park until the end of the year. In March 1943 there was another ten-day period when SHARK messages could not be decrypted. Thereafter much U-boat traffic was read within hours of transmission. Though sophisticated direction-finding techniques also helped locate U-boats, SIGINT probably made the critical difference. Between April 1943 and May 1945, 286 U-boats were sunk, as compared with 178 ships.[19] An enquiry ordered by Admiral Karl Dönitz mistakenly concluded that U-boat communications remained secure but that the Allies were probably receiving intelligence from agents inside submarine bases on the French Atlantic coast.[20]

ULTRA was used so effectively during the Battle of the Atlantic because of the British–American intelligence alliance, the most special part of the 'special relationship' created during the war.[21] From early 1943 British and American cryptanalysis of naval Enigma was carried out according to a single programme coordinated by Bletchley Park.[22] Communication via direct signal links between the U-boat tracking rooms in London, Washington and (from May 1943) Ottawa became so close that, according to the British official history, for the remainder of the war 'they operated virtually as a single organisation'.[23]

Though there was no formal agreement until 1943 between Bletchley Park and the US military SIGINT service (renamed the Signal Security Agency, SSA, in 1943), unofficial collaboration was crucial to Bletchley's success in breaking the German FLORADORA diplomatic cipher in 1942.[24] American pressure also contributed to better use of the tactical SIGINT produced by Bletchley's Air Section. Unlike the Admiralty, the Air Ministry (founded only in 1918) had failed to learn from First World War experience the importance of passing intelligence to local commanders. Until 1942 the ministry stubbornly refused to allow the Air Section to report directly to RAF commands. It eventually yielded to pressure from the US Army Air Force which wanted the most up-to-date tactical intelligence to attempt to reduce heavy losses in its strategic bombing missions over Germany. The Air Section's head of Luftwaffe analysis, Arthur 'Bill' Bonsall, a future Director of the post-war GCHQ, wrote later that the USAAF became 'our best customers'.*

On 17 May 1943 a top-secret agreement signed in Washington by Commander Edward Travis, who had succeeded A. G. Denniston as head of Bletchley Park, and Major-General George Strong, head of US military intelligence (G-2), formalized and greatly extended collaboration between British and American military cryptanalysts.[25] The Travis–Strong agreement became better known as 'BRUSA', an acronym devised by the 25-year-old Harry Hinsley, who had been recruited by Bletchley Park at the outbreak of war while still a Cambridge history undergraduate. Hinsley believed that Americans 'loved acronyms' but initially worried – needlessly, as it turned out – that putting Britain ahead of the United States in BRUSA might cause offence.[26]†

When the agreement was signed in Washington, a three-man delegation of senior US military cryptanalysts was in the middle of a six-week

---

* Until 1943 most of the Air Section, unlike the Naval Section, was also denied access to ULTRA. (Bonsall, 'Bletchley Park and the RAF Y Service'; Bonsall, *Uphill Struggle*.)
† In January 1944 Bletchley and OP-20–G concluded a 'naval BRUSA' on collaboration in the decryption of Japanese traffic.

fact-finding mission at Bletchley Park and other British SIGINT instal-lations.* The most experienced member of the delegation, the celebrated cryptographer William F. Friedman, whose first dealings with British SIGINT went back to the First World War,[27] wrote in his diary while at Bletchley: 'The no. & varieties of their sources are striking & very much better than our own.' Friedman was also passionately Anglophile. He wrote after being taken by a senior Bletchley cryptanalyst, Professor E. R. Vincent, to visit his Cambridge College, Corpus Christi: 'The atmosphere of Cambridge, which I drank in in great gulps, gives one a feeling of "solidity" – the solidity that is England. Here stand in quiet dignity and great strength buildings devoted to learning and democratic institutions and the dignity of man – for nine centuries – still going strong.'[28]†

Though not all US cryptanalysts, of course, were as Anglophile as Friedman, SSA and the naval OP-20-G were far more suspicious of each other than of Bletchley. As Hinsley later recalled: 'The Navy didn't like me talking to the Army. But I wasn't allowed to tell the Navy any details [of BRUSA] because the Army would have been furious.' Hinsley privately tried to reassure OP-20-G that the BRUSA agreement was not 'anything like as intimate' as its own, less formal collaboration with Bletchley Park. Whereas naval cryptanalysts on both sides of the Atlantic attempted to decrypt the same German naval messages and exchanged keys as soon as they succeeded, the military cryptanalysts agreed instead on a division of labour in decrypting German signals and an exchange of missions between Bletchley Park and the SSA HQ in Arlington Hall, Virginia.[29]‡

Members of the SSA mission at Bletchley preferred their personal contact with British colleagues to the more impersonal, though effective, trans-atlantic collaboration in naval SIGINT. Many enduring friendships were formed. Among the US cryptanalysts at Bletchley was William F. Bundy, later special adviser to President John F. Kennedy and Assistant Secretary of State under President Lyndon B. Johnson. Bundy said in retirement: 'Although I have done many interesting things and known many interesting people, my work at Bletchley Park was the most satisfying of my career.'[30]

Unlike the largely forgotten mission to London by early-eighteenth-century Hanoverian codebreakers at the invitation of George I,[31] the exchange of cryptanalysts by Bletchley and Arlington Hall during the

* Ralph Erskine argues persuasively that this was a fact-finding mission without substantive negotiating powers. (Erskine, 'William Friedman's Bletchley Park Diary'.)
† Cambridge University was a century younger than Friedman believed.
‡ Though Hinsley never completed the final year of his history degree, a generation later he went on to become official historian of British wartime intelligence, Vice-Chancellor of Cambridge University and Master of St John's College.

Second World War set an important precedent which has continued ever since. Today's allied British and American SIGINT agencies, GCHQ and NSA, continue to have active liaison offices in each other's headquarters.

During the Second World War, Western intelligence entered the era of mass production.[32] By 1943 the British–American SIGINT alliance was decrypting between 3,000 and 4,000 German signals a month as well as a large, but somewhat smaller, volume of Italian and Japanese traffic. By contrast, though Germany had as many SIGINT personnel as Britain (about 30,000), it was no longer able to break any significant Allied ciphers. Neither were its Italian and Japanese allies.[33] After the loss of the SIGINT 'good source' in North Africa, Hitler occasionally enquired about current progress in breaking Allied ciphers. In May 1944, for example, he asked the naval SIGINT agency, B-Dienst, what progress it was making in breaking British naval ciphers, some of which it had been able to decrypt early in the war. B-Dienst replied, no doubt with embarrassment: 'The two main English systems cannot be read.'[34]

German SIGINT was far less effective than British SIGINT for two main reasons. First, its organization was more confused. Though British SIGINT had been centralized under the control of GC&CS since shortly after the First World War, in Germany during the Second World War the Chiffrierabteilung of the OKW, Pers Z at the Foreign Ministry and Göring's Forschungsamt competed with each other. In addition, for a time the Sicherheitsdienst (SD), the intelligence arm of the SS, had its own SIGINT department. The army, navy and air force also had their own agencies.[35] Hitler was unaware of the damage done by a lesser degree of interdepartmental rivalries to the development of SIGINT in France before the First World War, in Britain during the First World War, and in the United States during the 1930s.[36] Even had he been aware of the previous history of SIGINT, however, he would have paid little attention to it. Central to Hitler's style of government was his habit of assigning similar responsibilities to different departments so that ultimate control remained in his hands.

At least as important as the administrative confusion of the rival German SIGINT agencies was their failure to attract the extraordinary talent recruited by Bletchley Park and its US allies. Hundreds of Bletchley recruits went on to become leading academics after the Second World War. The fellowships at most post-war Oxbridge colleges, for example, contained one or more Bletchley veterans.* Recruits to the US armed

* Bletchley alumni also included leading members of other professions such as the senior politicians Roy Jenkins and Edward Boyle.

forces were given IQ tests; many of the wartime SIGINT personnel were chosen from those with the highest marks. Dr Solomon Kullback, one of the leading wartime and post-war American cryptanalysts, said later that the military SIS could have staffed all the departments of a first-class university.[37] As well as taking no sustained interest in the development of German SIGINT, Hitler rather despised the profession of intelligence. He declared in February 1942 over lunch with Heinrich Himmler, Reichsführer of the Schutzstaffel (SS) and the most powerful of his intelligence chiefs: 'It's difficult to conceive that a genuine officer can be a sneaking spy.'[38]* His views about spies seem to have been influenced by vague memories of spy novels rather than serious attention to intelligence reports. Hitler declared during another opinionated lunchtime monologue in May 1942: 'Spies nowadays are recruited from two classes of society: the so-called upper classes and the proletariat. The middle classes are too serious to indulge in such activity.'[39] Though most German spies sent to Britain, like most Soviet spies caught in Germany, were middle class, no one, as usual, dared to contradict the Führer.

Despite Hitler, unlike Churchill and Stalin, having had only a spasmodic interest in intelligence, he was personally responsible for the most monstrous secret operation in European history. During the six months after the beginning of BARBAROSSA, Himmler was Hitler's most frequent visitor at his Eastern Front headquarters in East Prussia, the 'Wolf's Lair'. Though no record was kept of their discussions, the chief topic was undoubtedly the 'Final Solution of the European Jewry problem', a phrase first used in official German documents in late October 1941. In January 1942 one of Himmler's chief deputies, SS General Reinhard Heydrich, head of the Reich Security Main Office (Reichssicherheitshauptamt, RSHA), invited senior representatives of various Reich ministries to a secret conference at an elegant lakeside villa on the Wannsee, south-west of Berlin, where he announced that Hitler had instructed the SS to coordinate the Final Solution. From the outset, the Final Solution was based on elaborate deception and as much secrecy as possible. No Jews were killed near their places of residence. Instead, throughout German-occupied Europe, they were interned (whenever possible, as in Paris, by the local police) in holding camps, then deported long distances by train for 'resettlement' – in reality to death camps. The destination of the 'Special Resettlement Trains' was identified only as 'somewhere in the East'. Even the drivers who drove the 'resettlement' trains to within a few miles of

* The transcript of Hitler's lunchtime monologue records that Himmler was present as a 'special guest'.

their destinations were kept in ignorance of the death camps (four in German-occupied Poland, one in the occupied Soviet Union), where a majority of the Jews were gassed. Himmler told a meeting of SS major-generals in 1943: 'We will never speak of it publicly . . . The Jewish race is being exterminated . . . This is a page of glory in our history which has never been written and is never to be written . . .' Hitler agreed. He gave no written order for the Final Solution, and avoided speaking about it even to his entourage.[40]

Hitler had no time for intelligence which challenged his views on the conduct of the war. In 1944 the head of the German section of SOE, R. H. Thornley, opposed plans to assassinate Hitler in Operation FOXLEY on the grounds of the continuing advantages to the Allies of his strategic incompetence: 'As a strategist, Hitler has been of the greatest possible assistance to the British war effort.'[41] General Alfred Jodl, Chief of Operations at OKW, wrote shortly before his execution for war crimes in 1946:

> Hitler was willing to have a working staff that translated his decisions into orders which he would then issue as Supreme Commander of the Wehrmacht, but nothing more . . . He did not care to hear any other points of view; if they were even hinted at he would break into short-tempered fits of enraged agitation. Remarkable – and, for soldiers, incomprehensible – conflicts developed out of Hitler's almost mystical conviction of his own infallibility as leader of the nation and of the war.[42]

In the winter of 1942–3 Hitler's refusal to heed contrary advice from his generals contributed to disaster at Stalingrad, the main turning point in the war. Hitler insisted that German troops remain encircled in Stalingrad even when an orderly retreat might have been possible. German racial superiority and willpower would defeat the subhuman Slavs.

The Slavs, however, made more intelligent use of deception than the so-called master race. The first major Soviet deception of the war, Operation MONASTYR, drew its inspiration from the SINDIKAT and TREST deceptions twenty years earlier which had deceived a number of Western intelligence services by creating a bogus anti-Bolshevik monarchist underground.[43] Late in 1941 the NKVD and GRU jointly fabricated an anti-Soviet, pro-German underground, codenamed THRONE, supposedly operating at the heart of the Russian high command. The key figure in the THRONE deception was Alexander Demyanov (codenamed HEINE by the Centre), whose aristocratic father had been killed fighting for the Tsar in 1915. Having originally volunteered his services to the Abwehr, posing as a Red Army deserter, Demyanov reported to his case officer in the autumn of 1942 that he had been posted as communications officer at the Soviet high command HQ in Moscow, from which he would be able to supply intelligence of major importance. The head of German intelligence on the Russian front, Colonel (later Major-General) Reinhard Gehlen, remained convinced for the rest of his life of the importance of Demyanov's intelligence on the Red Army order of battle and strategic intentions.

Demyanov's most important role came during the Battle of Stalingrad. On 12 September 1942, General Friedrich Paulus's Sixth Army entered Stalingrad, though it never won control of more than two thirds of the city. The Soviet counter-offensive at Stalingrad, Operation URANUS, began on 19 November. Only four days later, the German Sixth Army was encircled in what Stalin called 'the decisive moment of the war'.[44] On 25 November the Red Army launched a deception operation, codenamed MARS, to dissuade forces of the German Army Group Centre moving from their positions west of Moscow to support the Sixth Army at Stalingrad. Surviving reports in German archives from Demyanov's bogus agent network show that he gave Gehlen accurate operational intelligence designed to demonstrate the opportunity for the German Army Group Centre to defeat Russian forces west of Moscow and thus deter it from moving east to support Paulus's Sixth Army. Operation MARS succeeded in its aim of limiting the concentration of German forces at Stalingrad – but at a terrible price. 70,000 Russian lives were lost during an offensive by the German Army Group Centre. Demyanov sent the Abwehr a bogus report of a Moscow conference on 3 December at which Stalin expressed personal outrage at what appeared to be a major German intelligence coup which had made possible the success of the offensive: 'Stalin is sure that there have to be treacherous informants at the top, since the Germans are so well informed about Soviet movements, plans and troop strengths'. The military historian Antony Beevor calls Operation MARS a 'massive sacrificial tragedy that was kept secret for nearly sixty years'. 'Only in Stalin's dreadful world', writes Sir Max Hastings, 'could 70,000 lives have been sacrificed, without sentiment or scruple, to serve the higher purposes of the state.' Whether Demyanov's deception made a critical contribution to victory at Stalingrad is very doubtful. He later became, however, the only wartime intelligence operative to be awarded both the Soviet Order of the Red Banner from the People's Commissariat for State Security (NKGB) and the German Iron Cross.[45]*

---

* Demyanov was not, as has been claimed, codenamed MAX; this was the codeword given by the Germans to intelligence from his network. The NKGB succeeded the NKVD from February to July 1941 and after April 1943.

On 2 February 1943 German resistance at Stalingrad ceased. 171,000 German troops had been killed; 91,000 were taken captive. Though Russian losses were even heavier, the myth of the Wehrmacht's invincibility had been destroyed. To celebrate victory, Stalin promoted both General Georgi Zhukov and himself to the rank of marshal, with uniforms adorned for the first time since the Tsarist era with gold braid and epaulettes. For the rest of the war, Stalin rarely appeared in public out of marshal's uniform.[46] In Germany the news from Stalingrad had a devastating impact on morale and damaged the personal prestige of the Führer. A secret opinion survey by the Sicherheitsdienst (SD) concluded: 'People ask, above all, why Stalingrad was not evacuated or relieved, and how it was possible, only a few months ago, to describe the military situation as secure? Fearing that an unfavourable end to the war is now possible, many compatriots are seriously thinking about the consequences of defeat.'[47] In the summer of 1943 Himmler and Goebbels agreed that Hitler should no longer be shown the increasingly depressing monthly SD reports on German public opinion and declining morale.[48]

Victory at Stalingrad produced an intelligence windfall which Soviet SIGINT was unable to exploit. German forces in Stalingrad had at least twenty-six Enigma machines which must have been difficult to destroy before their surrender. On at least one occasion, a German unit carried on transmitting until Soviet troops were at the door. A number of Enigma key settings almost certainly fell into the hands of the Red Army. The 91,000 German prisoners taken at Stalingrad also included signals and cipher personnel, not all of whom can have resisted the pressing demands of their captors to assist Soviet SIGINT operations. On 17 January 1943, even before the Stalingrad surrender, the Signals Division of the Wehrmacht High Command concluded that it was a 'certainty' that the Russians had decrypted a number of Enigma messages, and introduced improvements in cipher security. Soviet cryptanalysts, however, were unable to read Enigma traffic on a regular basis. Captured machines, keys and cipher personnel made possible the retrospective solution of some German intercepts. But the NKVD and GRU lacked the state-of-the-art technology which was crucial to the ULTRA intelligence produced at Bletchley Park. There was no Soviet equivalent either of the powerful electronic 'bombes' first built at Bletchley in 1940 to break Enigma, or of 'Colossus', the world's first electronic computer, constructed in 1943 to decrypt *Geheimschreiber* messages (radio signals based on teleprinter impulses enciphered and deciphered automatically), which for the last two years of the war yielded more important operational intelligence than the Enigma traffic.[49]

The most important SIGINT received by the NKVD during and after Stalingrad came not from Soviet cryptanalysts but from a British agent, John Cairncross (the 'Fifth Man' of the Cambridge Five), who, beginning in the summer of 1942, spent a year at Bletchley Park. Cairncross later claimed misleadingly that 'Except for the work and the routine, I remember very little of what happened there during my twelve months' service. My territory was limited to my hut and to the functional and austere cafeteria, which could hardly be described as having a relaxed and inviting atmosphere.'[50] Though Cairncross did indeed make few friends at Bletchley, he provided intelligence of major importance to his Soviet case officer. Most important of all were ULTRA decrypts on German preparations for the Battle of Kursk in June 1943 when the Red Army defeated Hitler's last offensive on the Eastern Front. ULTRA intelligence enabled the Red Air Force to launch massive pre-emptive strikes against German airfields which destroyed over 500 enemy aircraft. Two years later the NKGB awarded Cairncross the Order of the Red Banner.[51]*

Other important intelligence on German plans for the Kursk offensive had come from the 'Lucy Ring' in Switzerland headed by a mercenary, anti-Nazi German émigré, Rudolf Roessler, who reported to a GRU network headed by the Swiss agent Alexander Radó. Surviving fragments of Roessler's reports include a warning in March of a forthcoming offensive at Kursk offensive, Hitler's operational plan in April, followed by details of delays in beginning the attack. Roessler claimed that his intelligence came from a series of sub-agents. It seems more likely, however, that his source was stolen teleprinter tapes of messages from the OKW operations centre to Hitler's HQ, sent on a secure landline and therefore not encrypted. The problem for the professionally suspicious minds in the Centre was that Roessler's access to top-secret German operational planning seemed too good to be true.[52]

Some of the Centre's most successful deception operations were those it unconsciously practised against itself. The Cambridge Five (Kim Philby, Donald Maclean, Guy Burgess, Anthony Blunt and John Cairncross), later acknowledged as probably the ablest group of foreign agents in KGB history, aroused deep suspicion by failing to provide any evidence of the non-existent British intelligence operations against the Soviet Union which Stalin and the Centre had convinced themselves must be taking place.[53] Neither Kim Philby in SIS nor Anthony Blunt in MI5 identified 'a single

---

* At a meeting with Christopher Andrew in August 1990, Cairncross admitted that he had supplied intelligence from Bletchley Park to his Soviet case officer before the Battle of Kursk but declined to give details.

valuable British agent either in the USSR or in the Soviet embassy in Britain'. The Centre did not consider for one moment the possibility that there were no British agents operating against the Soviet Union for Philby and Blunt to identify. In October 1942 Stalin wrote to Ivan Maisky, the Soviet ambassador in London: 'All of us in Moscow have gained the impression that Churchill is aiming at the defeat of the USSR, in order then to come to terms with the Germany of Hitler or [his predecessor] Brüning at our expense.' A year later the Centre informed the London residency that it was now clear the Five were double agents. Their failure to reveal details of the British anti-Soviet conspiracy and agents working against Soviet targets proved that, while pretending to work for the NKGB, they were operating under orders from SIS and MI5.[54]

The Centre's belief that the Five were double agents was reinforced by what Blunt told his case officer about the extraordinary success of MI5's double agents against Germany. As in the First World War, all German spies of any significance sent to Britain were caught. By March 1943, twenty-eight of the captured Second World War spies had been turned into double agents feeding disinformation to Germany. 'In addition', according to a top-secret MI5 report, 'twelve real and seven imaginary persons have been foisted upon the enemy as double-cross spies.'[55] Stalin and Soviet intelligence were convinced that some of its British agents were also 'double-cross spies'. 'Our task', the Centre instructed its London resident, Anatoli Gorsky, 'is to understand what disinformation our rivals are planting on us.'[56]*

The Centre tied itself in knots as it tried to explain why, despite the British Double-Cross, some intelligence from its British agents appeared to be genuine. It told the London residency that the sheer quantity of Foreign Office documents supplied by Maclean *might* indicate that, unlike the other four, he was not consciously engaged in deception. The Centre also thought that the Five might be passing on important genuine intelligence which did not harm British interests, such as some ULTRA decrypts on German military operations, in order to make more credible the disinformation they were supplying about British policy to the Soviet Union. While attempting to decide how much intelligence from the Five to believe, the Centre instructed Gorsky to maintain contact with them 'in such a manner as to reinforce their conviction that we trust them completely'. A special eight-man surveillance team was sent from Moscow to the London residency to trail the Five and other supposedly bogus Soviet

---

* It is unfair to blame suspicions of the Five on personal failings of the head of the Centre's British desk, Zoya Rybkina. Her paranoid tendencies were widely shared.

agents in the hope of discovering contacts with their (non-existent) British case officers.[57]

Unlike the deception operations of the Soviet Union, those of British intelligence were not confused by conspiracy theory. No agency in British history, probably none in the history of intelligence, had ever devised such a wide range of ingenious deceptions with such a high success rate as MI5's B1a, the double-agent section of its counter-espionage division during the Second World War. Most new recruits to the section were so enthused by the ethos created by its head, Thomas 'Tar' Robertson, that they took to the art of deception with unusual speed and ingenuity.[58] The success of British wartime deception was also made possible by a degree of interdepartmental cooperation which was unimaginable in any of the other major combatants. The day-to-day selection of information and disinformation to feed to the enemy was entrusted to the imaginatively named Twenty Committee, so called because the Roman numeral for twenty (XX) is a double cross. The Committee, which had representatives from MI5, SIS, the War Office, the three service intelligence departments, GHQ Home Forces and, when necessary, other interested departments, began meeting in January 1941 and thereafter met weekly for the remainder of the war under the inspired leadership of its MI5 chairman, the Oxford history don J. C. Masterman (later knighted). Masterman preceded the first meeting of the Twenty Committee with what he later called 'a small but important decision, to wit that tea and a bun should always be provided for members':

> In days of acute shortage and of rationing the provision of buns was no easy task, yet by hook or crook (and mostly by crook) we never failed to provide them throughout the war years. Was this simple expedient one of the reasons why attendance at the Committee was nearly always a hundred per cent?

Masterman also had a gift for creating consensus. At only one of the 226 meetings was a disagreement pressed to a vote.[59] Initially the Twenty Committee found it difficult to credit the extent of its success. But, even at its first meeting, it began to suspect what it soon realized was the astonishing truth that, in Masterman's words, thanks to the Double-Cross System, *we actively ran and controlled the German espionage system in this country*. In close cooperation with B1a and the Twenty Committee, the London Controlling Section (LCS) coordinated global strategic deception 'with the object of causing the enemy to waste his military resources'.[60]

For almost two years after Churchill became Prime Minister, the Double-Cross System was the only major intelligence secret kept from him. Unlike Menzies, Chief of SIS, who was a regular visitor to Number 10, Sir David Petrie, Director-General of MI5 from 1941 to 1946, kept Churchill at arm's length. Well aware how much the Double-Cross would fascinate the Prime Minister if he knew about it, the DG preferred to keep him in ignorance for fear that he might interfere in the running of it. Though Churchill's enthusiasm for intelligence exceeded that of any previous British Prime Minister, Petrie was right to be nervous about where that enthusiasm might lead him.[61]

Before Operation MINCEMEAT in the spring of 1943, however, the head of the LCS, Colonel J. H. Bevan, considered it necessary for the first time to obtain the Prime Minister's approval for a deception operation. The basis of MINCEMEAT, devised by B1a and supervised by the LCS, was to obtain a corpse from a London hospital, dress it in the uniform of a staff officer of the Chief of Combined Operations, Vice-Admiral Lord Louis Mountbatten, attach to it a briefcase containing bogus top-secret documents, and arrange for a submarine to drop the disguised corpse off the Spanish coast. When Bevan called at 10 Downing Street on 15 April, he found Churchill sitting up in bed, smoking a cigar, 'surrounded by papers and black and red Cabinet boxes'. Churchill gave his enthusiastic approval. If the operation did not succeed at the first attempt, he told Bevan, 'we shall have to get the body back and give it another swim'.

On 30 April the body of the fictitious staff officer, whose forged documents identified him as Major William 'Bill' Martin of the Royal Marines, was picked off the coast of south-west Spain by a local fisherman. Though the body of 'Major Martin' was handed over to the British, pro-German Spanish officials, as expected, allowed the Abwehr to photograph the documents in his briefcase. They included handwritten letters by Mountbatten and the Vice-Chief of the Imperial General Staff, Lieutenant-General Sir Archibald Nye, as well as proofs of a manual on Combined Operations to which Eisenhower (who had given his approval to the deception) had, supposedly, agreed to write a foreword. The letters falsely indicated that the Allies were planning a landing in Greece, codenamed Operation HUSKY. Soon afterwards ULTRA decrypts revealed that the Germans had been comprehensively deceived. A message sent to Churchill during a visit to Washington said simply: 'MINCEMEAT swallowed whole.' Even when the Allied attack in July took place in Sicily rather than Greece, the Germans did not doubt the authenticity of the MINCEMEAT documents but concluded that Allied plans had changed.[62]

The need to inform Churchill of the preparations for Operation MINCEMEAT persuaded MI5's leadership and the head of the Security Executive, Duff Cooper, that the time had come to send Churchill a monthly report on MI5 operations against the enemy – in particular the deceptions devised by B1a and practised by its double agents. The first monthly 'Report on Activities of Security Service', submitted on 26 March 1943, was an instant success with the Prime Minister. Churchill wrote on it in red ink: 'deeply interesting'. Henceforth, Petrie wrote later, Churchill 'took a sustained personal interest in our work'. MI5 was careful to include particularly colourful cases which it knew would appeal to the Prime Minister. These included Eddie Chapman (codenamed ZIGZAG), a flamboyant London career criminal, who, after being recruited by the Abwehr, offered his services to MI5 late in 1942. A year later Chapman became the first British subject to be awarded the Iron Cross in recognition of his 'outstanding zeal and success'. His main success was a major sabotage operation against the de Havilland aircraft factory at Hatfield which built the Mosquito bombers then pounding German cities. Chapman provided the Abwehr with dramatic photographs of wrecked factory buildings covered in tarpaulins with debris strewn around. The 'sabotage', however, was a hoax, orchestrated by B1a.

The first monthly 'Report on Activities of Security Service' to Churchill set the pattern for its successors. Various sections of MI5 produced drafts totalling about sixteen single-spaced typed pages. Anthony Blunt prepared a précis, and the final draft of about two and a half pages was produced in collaboration between him and the future DG, Dick White. Since Blunt continued to draft the monthly reports to Churchill for the remainder of the war, it is highly probable they went to Soviet intelligence as well – and quite possibly to Stalin personally. Indeed, Moscow may well also have received the longer version before it was condensed by Blunt and thus have seen more detailed reports than Churchill.[63]

Though the British Double-Cross System was the most successful strategic deception in the history of warfare, the outcome of the war was decided on the Eastern Front. The Soviet victory at Kursk in June 1943 opened the way to a virtually continuous advance by the Red Army which ended almost two years later with Marshal Georgi Zhukov accepting the surrender of Berlin. Partisans for the first time made a significant contribution to the victory of the Red Army at Kursk, notably through sabotaging the Wehrmacht's transport network.[64] A Soviet official history later claimed that partisans were responsible for killing 137,000 Germans, including eighty-seven senior Nazi officials specifically targeted for assassination.[65]

Though the claim was probably exaggerated, the Abwehr felt swamped by the sheer number of partisans operating secretly behind German lines. By the summer of 1944 it believed there were 20,000 of them and estimated that their numbers were growing at the rate of 10,000 every three months.[66] Among the most difficult to detect were the *Besprisorniki*, teenage children who had been trained in reconnaissance and sabotage. Even the Wehrmacht admired their bravery. A report from one German unit described the case of 'a half-grown boy' who had been caught making notes on troop movements. Under interrogation he steadfastly refused to say who had given him his orders and 'kept telling clumsy lies'. Finally, it was decided to frighten him into submission. First, he was forced to witness the shooting of seven adult prisoners. Then he was told to prepare himself for execution. At the last moment, just as the firing squad was taking aim, the child was told that his life would be spared if he told the truth:

> The youth smiled cheekily and said he knew he would be killed even if he did speak up. When the interrogator assured him again that he could only save his life by naming his employer, the boy replied: 'I know very well that I shall be shot even if I do tell you the truth. I'll tell you the truth now: I have lied to you six times and I'll do it a seventh!'

The report does not mention the child's fate. He was probably shot.[67]

Soviet accounts of the undeniably heroic deeds of the partisans did not mention that they were used at least as frequently against Russian 'collaborators' as against the enemy; indeed, they probably killed more collaborators than Germans. Beria reported in 1943 that the NKVD had arrested and interrogated 931,549 suspects in territory liberated by the Red Army, of whom 80,296 had been 'unmasked as spies, traitors, deserters, bandits and criminal elements'.[68] The future KGB officer (and defector to SIS) Vasili Mitrokhin, later told Christopher Andrew that, even a generation later, his wartime memories of the brutal punishment of many thousands of 'anti-Soviet' Ukrainians sometimes gave him nightmares. He could not bring himself to tell Andrew what he witnessed. 'I was deep in horrors', was all he would say.[69]

One of the chief wartime roles of Soviet intelligence was ethnic cleansing. Whole peoples were branded as collaborators by Stalin and the NKVD. The first to be deported were the Karachai, Turkic shepherds in the north-west Caucasus. Though most Karachai did not collaborate with the German invaders, some even putting themselves in danger by giving refuge to Jewish children, a minority hoped that Hitler would give them their independence. The NKVD claimed that they had guided German forces through mountain passes into Georgia. Beria and his deputy, Ivan Serov, denounced the Karachai as a 'traitor-nation'. In October 1943 the Karachai autonomous district was abolished. 53,000 NKVD troops deported over 69,000 Karachai, mostly women and children, to Kazakhstan. Refused permission to take warm clothing, about 40 per cent perished on the journey. Karachai soldiers in the Red Army were also deported as soon as they were demobilized.*

Next the NKVD took its revenge on the Kalmyks, Buddhist Mongol herdsmen who lived between Stalingrad and the Caspian Sea and were accused of providing cattle to feed the German forces. In December 1943 the autonomous Kalmyk republic was abolished and over 90,000 Kalmyks (later followed by 20,000 Kalmyks in the Red Army) were deported in freezing weather to the Arctic and eastern Siberia to work as slave labourers. In April 1944 Beria reported to Stalin that the deportation had been carried out without untoward events or 'excesses'. In reality well over half the Kalmyks died from starvation.†

The NKVD's most ambitious ethnic-cleansing operations were in the north Caucasus against the Chechens and Ingush, who had fought an intermittent guerrilla war against Russian rule for the past two centuries. On 17 February 1944 Beria announced plans to deport almost 460,000 Chechens and Ingush (as well as some of their neighbours) in eight days. As with the Kalmyks' deportation, Beria reported to Stalin that the whole operation went smoothly. He failed to mention that, where heavy snow hampered deportation, the NKVD burnt villagers alive in barns, stables and mosques. Chechnya and Ingushetia were wiped from the map. The Supreme Soviet awarded Beria, Serov and two NKVD generals the Order of Suvorov (First Class).‡

In May 1944 about 240,000 Crimean Tatars, some of whose Red Army soldiers were accused by the NKVD of deserting to the Germans, were rounded up by 32,000 NKVD troops and deported in cattle trucks, mainly to Uzbekistan. Some were used as forced labour, 6,000 were arrested for 'anti-Soviet' activity, and 700 executed as spies. Within six months about half the deportees were dead. When Stalin, Churchill and Roosevelt met at Yalta in February 1945, probably not a single Tatar remained in the Crimea.[70]

The horrors of Soviet ethnic cleansing do not, of course, compare with those of the Nazi Holocaust, which killed about six million Jews, one third

---

* In March 1944, 37,000 Balkars, Turkic shepherds like the Karachai, were deported from the Caucasus. (Rayfield, *Stalin and His Hangmen*, pp. 391–4.)

† The Kalmyk population in 1939 totalled 134,000; in the 1953 census there were 53,000. (Rayfield, *Stalin and His Hangmen*, pp. 390–91.)

‡ The Chechens and Ingush, hardened by highland life, withstood deportation better than the Karachai and Kalmyks. By October 1945, however, about a fifth of the deportees were dead. (Rayfield, *Stalin and His Hangmen*, pp. 392–3. Burds, 'Soviet War against "Fifth Columnists"')

of the world's Jewish population at the outbreak of war. How much intelligence the Allies received on the 'Final Solution' remains controversial. It seems, however, that details of the mass killing of Jews at Auschwitz II (Birkenau) did not reach London and Washington until the summer of 1944, over two years after they began.[71]

The Holocaust was more efficiently conducted, as well as being a much higher priority for Hitler, than German foreign-intelligence collection. Following the defeats at Stalingrad and Kursk, the inevitability of Germany's defeat made it impossible for the Abwehr to attract worthwhile foreign informants.[72] After lengthy study of Abwehr decrypts, Hugh Trevor-Roper concluded that it was 'unable to evaluate its own reports . . . Berlin has no knowledge or solid opinion about the strategic future and therefore has to let the local generals and admirals make up their own mind by giving them prompt access to all the reports that come in.'[73] Ironically, some of the intelligence about which the Abwehr was most confident was a product of the British Double-Cross System. It had, for example, no doubt whatever about the reliability and importance of the disinformation fed to it in the MINCEMEAT deception.[74]

In February 1944, following the defection to the British of an Abwehr officer in Istanbul,* Hitler abolished the Abwehr as an independent organization, placing it under the control of Himmler and the SD. The SD believed it had gained control of a major network of Abwehr agents in Britain. In reality, all were double agents, controlled by MI5, feeding disinformation to their German case officers. The SD, however, had one major genuine agent of its own: Elyesa Bazna (codenamed CICERO), the valet of the British ambassador in Ankara, Sir Hughe Knatchbull-Hugessen. From October 1943 to February 1944 Bazna photographed the ambassador's classified diplomatic correspondence. Among the documents was a record of negotiations between Churchill, Roosevelt and Stalin at their Tehran conference in November 1943, from which, wrote Trevor-Roper later, the Allies' most closely guarded secret, plans for the invasion of occupied northern France in Operation OVERLORD, 'might have been inferred'. But analysis was poor and the secret was not discovered. Until the spring of 1944, by which time Bazna had ceased to supply documents, he was suspected in Berlin of operating a British deception – ironically,

---

* The Abwehr representative in Zurich, Hans-Bernd Gisevius, passed intelligence to SIS via Halina Szymańska, an informant for both British and Polish intelligence. Despite much speculation to the contrary, SIS records indicate that the head of the Abwehr, Admiral Canaris, did not do so. (Jeffery, MI6, pp. 380–82.)

at a time when the disinformation of the Double-Cross System was accepted as genuine. Bazna was handsomely rewarded for his services with money which he later discovered was forged. Unaware that the Germans had made such poor use of CICERO's intelligence, Stewart Menzies, the Chief of SIS, called the case 'an appalling national disaster'.[75]

What Churchill learned about the Double Cross during 1943 left him with the conviction that, 'In wartime, truth is so precious that she should always be attended by a bodyguard of lies.'[76] No military operation in British history has ever been so successfully protected by deception as OVERLORD, the Allied invasion of occupied northern France in 1944. Late in 1943 conferences of the British and American Combined Chiefs of Staff in Cairo and Tehran took the decision to launch the invasion in May 1944 (a date later deferred until the D-Day landings on 6 June). Colonel Bevan of the LCS was instructed to prepare the deception plans for OVERLORD. Their key aims were:

a. To induce the German Command to believe that the main assault and followup will be in or east of the Pas de Calais area, thereby encouraging the enemy to maintain or increase the strength of his air and ground forces and his fortifications there at the expense of other areas, particularly of the Caen area [in Normandy].

b. To keep the enemy in doubt as to the date and time of the actual assault.

c. During and after the main assault, to contain the largest possible German land and air forces in or east of the Pas de Calais for at least fourteen days.

All three aims were achieved.[77] By a mixture of double-agent disinformation and bogus Allied signals sent in low-grade ciphers which were intended to be intercepted by the Germans, the OKW was persuaded that the huge (and entirely fictitious) First United States Army Group (FUSAG), commanded by the formidable General George S. Patton, with its headquarters in Dover, was waiting to invade the Pas-de-Calais.[78] FUSAG was the biggest phantom force in military history. In the weeks leading up to OVERLORD, SIGINT revealed a number of plans for German aerial reconnaissance which might have discovered the deception. All were foiled by Fighter and Coastal Commands.[79]

The double agent who contributed most to the success of the FORTITUDE deceptions which preceded the D-Day landings was the anti-fascist Spaniard Juan Pujol, codenamed GARBO as a tribute to his star quality. During the first six months of 1944, working with his MI5 case officer,

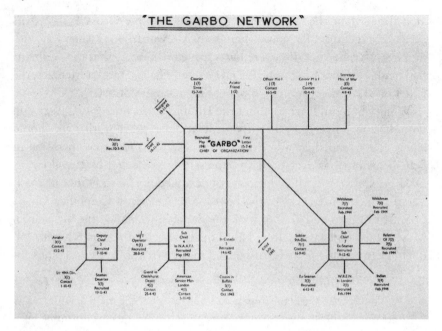

The largest network of bogus agents in intelligence history, who made possible during the Second World War the biggest strategic deception in the history of warfare.

Tomás Harris, he sent more than 500 messages to the Abwehr station in Madrid, which, as ULTRA revealed, forwarded them to Berlin, many marked 'Urgent'.*

Despite friction in OSS relations with SOE and SIS, the counter-intelligence section of OSS, X-2, founded in 1943, was fully briefed on GARBO and the rest of the Double-Cross System. An X-2 officer was given a desk in the office of the head of MI5's double-agent section. X-2 privately expressed astonishment at the closeness of its cooperation with MI5:

> For even an Ally to be admitted to a full access to all secret files and to a
> knowledge of their sources; to information on most secret methods and
> procedures; and to a knowledge of personnel and the system of organization

---

* After being initially turned down by British intelligence, Pujol offered his services to the Germans, who recruited him as Agent ARABEL. Decrypted Abwehr traffic revealed that, instead of sending reports to the Abwehr from Britain, as he claimed, Pujol was sending disinformation invented by himself from Lisbon. Pujol was recruited by SIS in March 1942 and, after moving to England, transferred to MI5 control a month later. (Andrew, *Defence of the Realm*, pp. 253–4.)

and of operations – in short to the innermost arcana, in this case, of perhaps the world's most experienced and efficient, and therefore most carefully safeguarded, security systems – was beyond precedent or expectation. Yet the British did it. The implications of this fact are staggering – and completely inexplicable in terms of merely cheap exchange of mutual advantages.[80]

The final act in the pre-D-Day deception was entrusted, appropriately, to its greatest practitioners, GARBO and Tomás Harris. After several weeks of pressure, Harris finally gained permission for GARBO to be allowed to radio a warning that Allied forces were heading towards the Normandy beaches just too late for the Germans to benefit from it. GARBO added a warning that the landings were a diversion and the main attack was still planned for the Pas-de-Calais. Though the Abwehr radio station in Madrid normally shut down from 11.30 p.m. to 7.30 a.m., GARBO warned it to be ready to receive a message at 3 a.m. on 6 June (D-Day). For unknown reasons, Madrid did not go on air until after 6 a.m., and received the warning several hours later than intended. But GARBO's credibility was powerfully reinforced.[81]

At noon on 6 June, Churchill, watched by his wife and eldest daughter from the Speaker's Gallery, announced to a packed and expectant House of Commons: 'During the night and early hours of the morning, the first of the series of landings in force upon the European continent has taken place.' The Prime Minister must have thought his reference to other land-ings which were to follow D-Day would help to reinforce the German belief that an even bigger Allied assault was being planned in the Calais region. Tar Robertson and others in B1a, however, were shocked by Churchill's statement, which – though he did not realize it – contradicted an earlier message sent by GARBO to the Abwehr reporting a bogus Political Warfare Executive (PWE) directive on the need to avoid any public reference to 'further attacks and diversions'. The Prime Minister's faux pas seemed to justify MI5's earlier fear that, if Churchill was informed of deception operations (as he was in this case), he might take some rash initiative of his own. At 8 p.m. on D-Day GARBO radioed Madrid, say-ing that he had spoken to the PWE's director, who was dismayed that Churchill had ignored his directive. The Prime Minister, claimed GARBO rather lamely (without, however, arousing the suspicions of the Abwehr), had felt obliged not to distort the facts when announcing the invasion to the Commons and to the country.

GARBO rounded off his radio message with a withering denunciation of the failure of Madrid to come on air at 3 a.m. that day to receive vital intelligence on the imminent Allied landings on the Normandy beaches:

'This makes me question your seriousness and sense of responsibility. I therefore demand a clarification immediately as to what has occurred.' By the following morning, after a supposedly sleepless night, GARBO radioed a further message of recrimination, this time combined with self-pity:

> I am very disgusted as in this struggle for life and death I cannot accept excuses or negligence . . . Were it not for my ideals and faith I would abandon this work as having proved myself a failure. I write these messages to send this very night though my tiredness and exhaustion due to the excessive work I have had has completely broken me.

The errant Abwehr case officer in Madrid, who had failed to ensure that the radio station came on air at 3 a.m., replied apologetically with a glowing tribute to the quality of GARBO's intelligence: 'I wish to stress in the clearest terms that your work over the last few weeks has made it possible for our command to be completely forewarned and prepared.' That tribute, which probably caused GARBO and Harris to laugh out loud, was quoted in the Security Service's June report to the Prime Minister.[82]

Before D-Day it had been expected that the fiction of a planned attack on the Pas-de-Calais could not be maintained for more than ten days after the Normandy landings. ULTRA, however, revealed that the deception remained firmly embedded for far longer in the minds of both Hitler and his high command. For the rest of June GARBO and BRUTUS, another double agent, continued to send alarming intelligence reports on the waves of fresh American forces supposedly flooding into Britain and the growing troop concentrations in the south-east of England, apparently poised for an assault on the Pas-de-Calais. Four weeks after D-Day the German high command still had twenty-two divisions waiting to repel an attack by the non-existent FUSAG. The Security Service's monthly report for June, despatched to Churchill on 3 July, concluded:

> It is known for a fact that the Germans intended at one time to move certain Divisions from the Pas de Calais area to Normandy but, in view of the possibility of a threat to the Pas de Calais area, these troops were either stopped on their way to Normandy and recalled or it was decided that they should not be moved at all.

Churchill was also informed that Berlin had awarded GARBO the Iron Cross (Second Class); the following German radio message from his case officer was cited as an example of the praise lavished on him and his imaginary sub-agents: 'I reiterate to you, as responsible chief of the service, and to all your collaborators, our total recognition of your perfect and cherished work and I beg of you to continue with us in the supreme and decisive hours of the struggle for the future of Europe. Saludos.' The Security Service's June report to the Prime Minister also cited 'an effusive message of encouragement' from his German case officer: 'Your messages about concentrations and movements (more especially signs of troops preparing for action) can be not only fabulously important, but can even decide the outcome of the war.'[83]

A month after D-Day Eisenhower declared: 'I cannot overemphasize the importance of maintaining as long as humanly possible the Allied threat to the Pas-de-Calais area, which has already paid enormous dividends and, with care, will continue to do so.' Not till the last week of July did the HQ of Field Marshal Gerd von Rundstedt, Commander-in-Chief West, conclude that 'The more ground Montgomery gains southward from the [Normandy] bridgehead, and the quicker he does this, the less probable it will be that the forces still in England will carry out a seaborne landing at a new point.'[84]

In Moscow the preparations for D-Day re-established the Centre's trust in the Cambridge Five. On 26 May 1944 Blunt passed on a complete copy of the entire deception plan devised as part of OVERLORD. On 7 July he provided a comprehensive account of B Division's role in the deception and, in particular, its use of double agents. (The stress of his own double life took a greater toll on Blunt than on the rest of the Five. He was under such visible strain that the Centre did not object to his decision at the end of the war to return to his career as an art historian and accept an appointment as Surveyor of the King's Pictures.[85]) On 29 June the Centre informed the London residency that important recent SIS documents provided by Kim Philby (codenamed SÖHNCHEN) had been largely corroborated by material from 'other sources' (probably the American OSS, which also contained Soviet agents): 'This is a serious confirmation of S[ÖHNCHEN]'s honesty in his work for us, which obliges us to review our attitude to him and the entire group.' It was now clear, the Centre acknowledged, that intelligence from the Five was 'of great value' and must be maintained at all costs: 'On our behalf express much gratitude to S[ÖHNCHEN] for his work . . . If you find it convenient and possible, offer S[ÖHNCHEN] in the most tactful way a bonus of 100 pounds or give him a gift of equal value.' After years in which Philby's phenomenal work as a penetration agent had been frequently undervalued, ignored or suspected by the Centre, he was almost pathetically grateful for this long overdue recognition of his achievements. 'During this decade of work', he told Moscow, 'I have never been so deeply touched as now with your gift and no less deeply excited by your communication [of thanks].' High among the intelligence which restored the Centre's faith in Philby were his reports, beginning early in 1944, on the founding by SIS of a new Section IX 'to study past records of Soviet and Communist activity'. Urged on by his new controller, Boris Krötenschield, Philby succeeded at the end of the year in becoming head of an expanded Section IX, charged with 'the collection and interpretation of information concerning Soviet and Communist espionage and subversion in all parts of the world outside British territory'. As one of his SIS colleagues, Robert Cecil, wrote later: 'Philby at one stroke had ... ensured that the whole post-war effort to counter Communist espionage would become known in the Kremlin. The history of espionage records few, if any, comparable masterstrokes.'[86]

Soviet intelligence penetration of the United States was equally remarkable. Throughout the war there was a breathtaking gulf between the intelligence supplied to Stalin on the United States and that available to Roosevelt on the Soviet Union. While the Centre penetrated every branch of Roosevelt's administration, OSS – like the British SIS – had not a single agent in Moscow. The Roosevelt administration seemed indifferent to the problem of Soviet espionage in the United States. On 2 September 1939, the day after the outbreak of war in Europe, the former Fourth Department courier Whittaker Chambers revealed much of what he knew about the military intelligence agent network in the United States (a large part of it recently taken over by the NKVD) to Adolf Berle, Assistant Secretary of State and Roosevelt's adviser on internal security. Immediately afterwards, Berle drew up a memorandum for the President which identified such high-level agents as Alger Hiss, Harry Dexter White and one of Roosevelt's own leading aides, Lauchlin Currie (misspelt Lockwood Curry). Roosevelt was not interested. He seems to have dismissed the idea of Soviet penetration of his administration as absurd. Equally remarkably, Berle simply pigeonholed his own report. He did not even send a copy to the FBI until the Bureau requested it in 1943.[87]

Molotov, the Soviet Foreign Minister, regarded intelligence reports from the US as clearly more important than Soviet diplomatic despatches from the Washington embassy, which, he told Stalin in September 1942, were rarely of much interest.[88] During 1944 there was a temporary interruption in the flow of intelligence on US foreign policy from what had hitherto been the Centre's most productive source: the American embassy in Moscow. A long-overdue electronic sweep of the embassy by an FBI expert found 120 hidden microphones in the first twenty-four hours. Thereafter, according to an eyewitness, 'they kept turning up, in the legs of any new tables or chairs which were delivered, in the plaster of walls, any and everywhere'.[89] The loss of intelligence from the US embassy was to prove only temporary.[90]

As the Great Patriotic War approached its end, the most valuable Soviet political intelligence agent in the United States was the high-flying young US diplomat Alger Hiss, agent ALES of the GRU. Soviet agents within the Roosevelt administration never attracted the same level of suspicion in Moscow as the Cambridge Five, partly because Roosevelt was thought less likely than Churchill to conspire against his Russian allies. At the Yalta conference of the Big Three in February 1945, Stalin had an extraordinary encounter with Hiss, which remains unique in intelligence history. As he looked across the conference table in the Livadia Palace, he could see agent ALES just behind Roosevelt's right shoulder. Stalin had, no doubt, already read Hiss's briefing on the US negotiating position at Yalta.

The NKGB 'legal' resident in Washington, Anatoli Gorsky, reported to the Centre a month later:

> Recently ALES and his whole group were awarded Soviet decorations. After the Yalta conference, when he had gone to Moscow, a Soviet person-age in a very responsible position (ALES gave to understand that it was Comrade Vyshinsky [deputy Foreign Minister]) allegedly got in touch with ALES and at the behest of the military NEIGHBOURS [GRU] passed on to him their gratitude and so on.[91]

Stalin undoubtedly approved, and may well have been responsible for, the decision to make the award to Hiss.

Though the Soviet Union had better wartime intelligence on its allies (some of which it wasted) than any power had ever had before, the Western allies had better intelligence on their enemies. From Midway onwards,[92] US intelligence outclassed Japanese intelligence in the Pacific War. In the Japanese armed forces intelligence was looked on as an inferior posting; the ablest officers were sent to operations.[93] In practice, it was the Operations (First) Departments of the Army and Navy General Staffs, not their better-informed intelligence departments, who were responsible for strategic intelligence assessment.[94]* Attempts to create a Cabinet Intelligence Bureau in 1940 to coordinate and share intelligence assessment, somewhat on the model of the British JIC, failed.† The Chief of Army Intelligence played no significant role in war planning during the Pacific War.[95] Operations

---

* The Japanese military and naval intelligence departments, only a fraction of the size of their US equivalents, were the Second Department of the Army General Staff and the Third Department of the Navy General Staff.

† After interdepartmental disputes on intelligence, the Cabinet Intelligence Bureau was limited to propaganda work. (Kotani, *Japanese Intelligence in World War II*, p. 161.)

Departments commonly preferred reports from operational units in the field to intelligence assessments.[96] The Foreign Minister, Yosuke Matsuoka, usually disregarded intelligence which failed to conform to his views.[97] In February 1943, after the Japanese defeat by the United States at the Battle of Guadalcanal and the German defeat by the Red Army at Stalingrad, Tokyo sent a delegation to Berlin headed by a former head of army intelligence, Major-General Kiyotomi Okamoto. The delegation reported that German military strength was 'lower than we had expected' when Japan began the Pacific War. If Germany was to emerge victorious, it would have to 'overcome many challenges'. Save for the army intelligence department, most Japanese officers were surprised and shocked by the clear implication that Germany would probably be unable to do so.[98]

Major-General Seizo Arisue, chief of the Army Intelligence Department during the Pacific War, later condemned the 'self-righteous' mindset of the Operations Department, which 'disliked even listening to opinions of others'. Arisue was summoned only once to the operations room of the Imperial HQ, shortly before the attack on British and Indian forces at Imphal on the Burmese front in March 1944. Arisue advised against the operation, his advice was rejected, and Japanese forces were defeated.[99] The award for the worst intelligence assessment of the Pacific War may well belong to the official announcement by Japanese Imperial HQ, just over six months later, that Japanese aircraft had won an even more devastating victory than Pearl Harbor. It reported that, in the air battle which preceded the great naval Battle of Leyte Gulf, nineteen US aircraft carriers had been sunk. The announcement caused widespread popular rejoicing in Japan. In reality, only seventeen US aircraft carriers were present and none was sunk. Imperial HQ had relied on hopelessly optimistic operational reports and ignored entirely intelligence reports based on SIGINT traffic analysis which showed that the US navy had suffered no losses.[100]

The greatest Soviet intelligence triumph during the final months of the war was to obtain the plans of the atomic bomb with which the United States planned to defeat Japan. As late as November 1944, only eight months before the explosion of the first atomic bomb at Alamogordo, the Centre sent a stern rebuke to the New York residency on its lack of success in penetrating the top-secret MANHATTAN Project to build the bomb. Most significant atomic intelligence, it complained, was coming to the Centre from England rather than the United States.[101] The Centre was no doubt annoyed that the rival GRU was doing considerably better. Only two Soviet intelligence officers, Arthur Alexandrovich Adams and Zhorzh ('George') Abramovich Koval, were later made Heroes of Russia for their wartime operations in the United States to penetrate the MANHATTAN

Project. Adams and Koval, both GRU illegals of Jewish origin, are barely mentioned in existing histories of atomic espionage.

Arthur Adams remains one of the most mysterious of all Second World War intelligence officers. Many details of his complex career have still to be adequately researched. Probably born in Sweden in 1885, as a child he moved with his mother to her native Russia, where he became an anti-Tsarist revolutionary in his teens and escaped police persecution by fleeing to the United States. Remarkably, he served in the US Army during the First World War, rising to the rank of major before becoming in 1919 a founder member of the Central Committee of the Communist Party of America. Adams spent most of the interwar years in the Soviet Union, joining military intelligence in 1935 and becoming head of an illegal GRU residency in the United States in 1939. Probably Adams's most productive wartime agent was Clarence Hiskey, who worked for the MANHATTAN Project at the Chicago University Metallurgical Laboratory. Before he came under FBI surveillance in November 1944, Adams obtained over 5,000 pages of classified documents as well as samples of radioactive materials.*

Unlike Adams, 'George' Koval (codenamed DELMAR by the GRU) was born a US citizen in 1913 and grew up in Sioux City, Iowa. His father, Abram, was secretary of the Association for Jewish Colonization in the Soviet Union (ICOR), a Communist rival to the Zionist movement which sought a Jewish homeland in Palestine. In 1932, before George had completed a degree majoring in electrical engineering at the University of Iowa, the family moved to the Jewish autonomous region near the Soviet border with Manchuria. A few years later, they claimed in an interview with a New York Yiddish-language newspaper to have 'exchanged the uncertainty of life as small storekeepers in Sioux City' during the Depression for a 'worry-free existence' in the Soviet Union. In 1939 Koval graduated from the Mendeleev Institute of Chemical Technology in Moscow, joining the GRU soon afterwards. He was an ideal candidate for scientific and technological espionage (S&T) operations in the United States, a well-educated scientist who gave no hint of his Soviet nationality. 'I always thought he was straight out of Iowa', said one of his American friends. Koval later revealed how, in October 1940, he had entered the United States at San Francisco without a passport: 'I came over on a small tanker and just walked out through the control point together with the captain,

---

* Adams's MI5 file, based largely on intelligence received from the United States, was declassified in 2014; TNA KV 2/3787-8. Ironically, the file contains a note on him written by Kim Philby in 1946, while Philby was still a rising star in SIS. Adams returned to Moscow in 1946 to escape FBI surveillance, possibly after a warning from Philby.

his wife and little daughter, who sailed with him.' In February 1943 he
enlisted in the US Army, was admitted six months later to the newly
established Army Specialized Training Program and sent to study electrical engineering at the City College of New York, where he was quickly
identified as a high flier. Early in 1944 Koval was drafted to the Oak Ridge
facility in Tennessee to work for the MANHATTAN Project, thus
becoming the only Soviet intelligence officer (as opposed to agent) to penetrate the Project.[102]

Until November 1944 the New York NKGB 'legal' residency had only
one atomic spy, Russell 'Russ' McNutt (codenamed PERSIAN).[103]
McNutt was one of a series of S&T agents recruited by Julius Rosenberg
(codenamed successively ANTENNA and LIBERAL), a 26-year-old
New York Communist with a degree in electrical engineering. The members of the Rosenberg S&T network included, besides McNutt, the
scientist William Perl (codenamed GNOME), who provided intelligence
on jet engines, and the military electronics engineers Joel Barr (METRE)
and Alfred Sarant (HUGHES), both of whom were radar experts. The
members of the Rosenberg network, who included his wife Ethel, were
rewarded by the Centre with cash bonuses in the summer of 1944. The
network produced so many classified S&T documents that the New York
residency complained that it was running out of film to photograph them.
The residency reported to Moscow that Rosenberg was receiving so much
intelligence from his agents that he was finding it difficult to cope: 'We
are afraid of putting LIBERAL out of action with overwork.'[104]

After a promising start, however, Russ McNutt, like Rosenberg a New
York Communist, proved a serious disappointment to the NKGB. While
working at a Kellex design office in New York, he was for a time a useful
source of intelligence on the massive uranium separation plant being
constructed by Kellex at Oak Ridge, Tennessee. But, to the dismay of
Rosenberg and the New York residency, McNutt refused an offer of a job
at Oak Ridge, unwilling to move from his comfortable New York apartment to a facility where there was no housing for his wife and child.[105]
The New York residency was unaware that the GRU already had an illegal
officer, George Koval, working at Oak Ridge since early 1944. Koval
reported that Oak Ridge scientists had discovered that reactor-produced
plutonium was too unstable for the plutonium version of the atomic bomb
they were designing. To enable the plutonium core of the atomic bomb to
achieve the necessary chain reaction, Oak Ridge was manufacturing
another rare element, polonium 210, to act as 'initiator'. He transmitted
intelligence on polonium production to Moscow via couriers, coded cables
and diplomatic bag from the Soviet embassy in Washington. Koval also

revealed that polonium was being sent from Oak Ridge to the Los Alamos laboratories in New Mexico, where both plutonium and uranium versions of the atomic bomb were being constructed.[106]

The first NKGB agent to penetrate Los Alamos was the German-born British physicist Klaus Fuchs, who had been recruited by the GRU in 1941. Fuchs was a committed, doctrinaire Communist, who during the Terror had been an enthusiastic participant in dramatized readings of the transcripts of the show trials organized by the British Society for Cultural Relations with the Soviet Union. He impressed his research supervisor, the future Nobel Laureate Sir Nevill Mott, with the passion with which he played the part of the prosecutor, Andrei Vyshinsky, 'accusing the defendants with a cold venom that I would never have suspected from so quiet and retiring a young man'. When Fuchs left Britain late in 1943 as a member of the British team to take part in the MANHATTAN Project, he was unaware that, at Beria's insistence, he had been transferred from GRU to NKGB control and given the codename REST (later changed to CHARLES). Fuchs arrived at Los Alamos in August 1944. The NKGB, however, did not succeed in renewing contact with him after his arrival at Los Alamos until he visited New York in February 1945.[107]

In November 1944 the NKGB New York residency reported to the Centre that the precociously brilliant Harvard physicist Theodore 'Ted' Hall, also working at Los Alamos, had also agreed to become a Soviet agent. Because Fuchs later confessed to working as a Soviet agent, he remains a better-known figure than Hall, whose atomic espionage did not become public knowledge for half a century after Hiroshima. Hall, however, was an even abler scientist. Entering Harvard at the age of fifteen as a physics major, he graduated with highest honours (*summa cum laude*) in 1944, a few months before his nineteenth birthday. As the youngest of the atom spies, Hall was given the rather obvious codename MLAD ('Young'). He was a convinced believer in the myth-image of the Soviet worker-peasant state, which he believed had solved the problems of mass unemployment which plagued the United States and, for the first time in history, given all its citizens the opportunity to make the most and the best of themselves. As a thirteen-year-old Hall had been deeply impressed by the Soviet pavilion at the 1939 New York World Fair. Among the exhibits was a full-size copy of the celebrated Mayakovskaya Station on the Moscow Metro, designed by Alexei Dushkin, which won the World Fair's Grand Prize. 'The Soviet pavilion was so damn good', Hall later told Christopher Andrew, 'that the others would have liked to close it down.' Hall also told Andrew that he had believed an American nuclear monopoly would threaten the peace of the post-war world. Passing the secrets of the MANHATTAN Project to Moscow was thus, in his view, a way to 'help the world' as well as the Soviet Union. At Los Alamos, Hall established himself as the youngest major spy in modern history.[108]

In February 1945 lower-level atomic intelligence from Ethel Rosenberg's Communist brother-in-law, David Greenglass (codenamed BUMBLE-BEE and CALIBRE), a technical sergeant at Los Alamos, also began reaching the NKGB. Stalin and the Soviet leadership, Greenglass believed, were 'really geniuses, every one of them'. 'My darling', he wrote to his wife, 'I most certainly will be glad to be part of the community project [espionage] that Julius and his friends [the NKGB] have in mind.'[109]

Hall and Fuchs each independently gave the NKGB the plans of the first plutonium atomic bomb, successfully tested at Alamogordo on 16 July 1945. The Centre was thus able to crosscheck each set of plans against the other. The plans, however, did not provide everything Soviet scientists needed to replicate the US bomb. They also needed to understand the manufacturing process, particularly the use of the polonium 'initiator'. That crucial intelligence was provided by George Koval. On 27 June 1945 he was transferred from Oak Ridge to another top-secret facility in Dayton, Ohio, where the polonium-based initiator went into production. Koval's key role in atomic espionage was not revealed by the GRU until after his death in 2006 at the age of ninety-three. In 2007 the Russian Defence Ministry newspaper *Krasnaya Zvezda* disclosed for the first time that the initiator for the first Soviet atomic bomb exploded in 1949 had been 'prepared to the "recipe" provided [in 1945] by military intelligence officer DELMAR – Zhorzh Abramovich Koval'. At a public ceremony President Putin posthumously declared Koval 'Hero of Russia' and proposed a champagne toast in his honour.[110]

29

The Cold War and the
Intelligence Superpowers

No new world leader ever had more extraordinary top-secret briefings than Vice-President Harry S. Truman when he became President after Roosevelt's sudden death on 12 April 1945. 'Boys', he told reporters the next day, 'if you ever pray, pray for me now. I don't know whether you fellows ever had a load of hay fall on you, but when they told me yesterday what happened, I felt like the moon, the stars and all the planets had fallen on me.' Over the next few days, Truman was told the two greatest secrets in the history of warfare, both of which had been kept from him as Roosevelt's Vice-President: the making of the atomic bomb and ULTRA intelligence. SIGINT gave Truman a dramatic insight into the last days of the Third Reich and, more importantly, into the final four months of the Pacific War.

Truman had no idea, however, that Soviet intelligence penetration of the United States and of the West in general had achieved a level of success during the Second World War unprecedented in any previous conflict. Never before had any state learned so many of its allies' secrets as the Soviet Union. There is an unusual irony about Truman's decision at the conference of the Big Three at Potsdam in July 1945 to reveal to Stalin that 'we had a new weapon of unusual destructive power'. Stalin seemed unimpressed by the news – as well he might, since, thanks to Soviet espionage, he had known about plans to build the atomic bomb for fifteen times as long as Truman. Truman was returning to the United States from Europe aboard the USS *Augusta* when he heard the news that the first atomic bomb had been dropped on Hiroshima on 6 August. His first reaction was a sense of relief that the bomb had exploded successfully rather than of foreboding that the nuclear age had dawned. 'This is the greatest thing in history', he told the crew of the *Augusta*.

Over the next week MAGIC enabled the President to follow what some of the SIGINT summaries shown to him called 'Japan's surrender maneuvers', as its warlords struggled to avoid the humiliation of unconditional surrender. MAGIC did not, however, disclose that at a meeting of Japan's six-man Supreme War Council on 9 August, the day on which a second atomic bomb obliterated Nagasaki, three of its members supported the proposal by the Foreign Minister, Shigenori Togo, to surrender, provided that Emperor Hirohito's position was safeguarded, while the other three members wanted to continue the war. Nor did MAGIC disclose the Emperor's decision in the early hours of 10 August that 'We must bear the unbearable', followed by the War Council's acceptance of Togo's proposal. SIGINT did, however, reveal the sequel. At 8.47 a.m. (Japanese time) on 10 August, Tokyo sent cables to the Japanese legations in the neutral capitals of Berne and Stockholm for onward transmission to the Allied governments, agreeing to surrender, provided the 'prerogatives' of the Emperor were preserved. Truman learned of the Japanese decision from MAGIC even before he received official notification.

At 6 p.m. on 14 August, Japan's formal acceptance of the surrender terms was delivered by the Swiss chargé d'affaires in Washington to Truman's Secretary of State, James F. Byrne, who immediately took it to the White House. At 7 p.m. Truman read the Japanese message to newspaper correspondents gathered in the Oval Office, then went outside to acknowledge the cheers of the crowd, making what he described as 'a V sign in the manner of Churchill'. As the crowds continued to grow, the President returned to the north portico of the White House and made a short speech through a loudspeaker. 'This is the day', he declared, 'when Fascism and police government cease in the world.' His denunciation of 'police government', which he lumped together with fascism, reflected Truman's confused suspicion of peacetime HUMINT agencies which he was apt to liken to 'Gestapos'.[1]

SIGINT bothered Truman far less than HUMINT. On 12 September Henry Stimson (shortly to retire as Secretary for War), James Forrestal (Knox's successor as Secretary of the Navy) and Dean Acheson (acting Secretary of State in the absence of Byrne) jointly submitted to Truman a top-secret memorandum reminding him of 'the outstanding contributions to the success of the Allied forces in defeating Germany and Japan' made by Allied cryptanalysts, and recommending 'that you authorize continuation of collaboration between the United States and the United Kingdom in the field of communications intelligence'.[2] Truman responded remarkably promptly, signing on the same day a top-secret one-sentence memorandum authorizing continued collaboration 'as determined to be in the best interests of the United States'.[3] There followed the British–American SIGINT accords of March 1946 and June 1948 (the latter known as the UKUSA agreement), also involving Australia, Canada and New Zealand.[4] The five intelligence allies have become known as the 'Five

Eyes'.[5] No member of the post-war GCHQ had a long enough historical perspective to compare the UKUSA agreement with Britain's SIGINT alliance with Hanover in the reign of George I.[6] Michael Herman, who joined in 1952, recalls that 'We were all *very* unhistorical, me included.'[7]*

Since the post-war SIGINT agreements, the United States and Britain have shared more secrets than any two independent powers had ever shared before. During the Cold War, SIGINT secrecy on both sides of the Atlantic was far more successfully maintained than it had been between the wars.[8] The terms of the SIGINT accords of 1946 and 1948 were not declassified until 2010.[9] At the end of the Second World War, GCHQ (the British SIGINT agency) wanted to keep secret indefinitely the wartime ULTRA intelligence derived from breaking Enigma and other high-grade enemy ciphers, but expected it to be uncovered within a few years. Despite the classification of SIGINT records, it believed that the clues to ULTRA were too obvious for historians to miss.[10] It was also common knowledge that British cryptanalysts had broken German ciphers during the First World War; indeed one well-publicized German decrypt – the Zimmermann telegram – may even have hastened American entry into the war. Historians, however, proved much less curious than GCHQ had expected. Until the revelation of ULTRA in 1973, almost no historian considered the possibility that German ciphers had been extensively broken during the Second World War as well as the First.[11]†

Even after the revelation of the wartime ULTRA secret, historians and international relations specialists remained remarkably uncurious about the role of SIGINT in the Cold War. Truman's role in authorizing SIGINT collaboration with Britain passed unmentioned by his biographers. Sir Martin Gilbert's epic eight-volume biography of Sir Winston Churchill makes much of his passion for ULTRA as war leader but neglects entirely his continued interest in SIGINT as peacetime Prime Minister from 1951 to 1955. General Dwight D. Eisenhower regarded ULTRA as 'of priceless value' to his conduct of the war, and in 1945 sent to 'each and every one'

---

* Some years later, Herman, who had graduated with first-class honours in Modern History at Queen's College, Oxford, became probably the first intelligence officer to compare the experience of SIGINT collaboration with early-eighteenth-century Hanover and with the Cold War United States: 'For . . . Sigint practitioners international contacts are their only chance of honing techniques and interpretations with other professionals – rather as the British and Hanoverian Black Chambers had a dialogue about their recondite art in the eighteenth century.' (Herman, *Intelligence Power*, p. 209.)

† Post-war historians' lack of curiosity about the role of SIGINT during the war against Germany was all the more remarkable in view of the public disclosure of the breaking of the Japanese PURPLE diplomatic cipher during the meetings of the Congressional Pearl Harbor Committee in 1945–6.

of the cryptanalysts at Bletchley Park 'my heartfelt admiration and sincere thanks for their very decisive contribution to the Allied war effort'. Though Eisenhower's enthusiasm for SIGINT, like Churchill's, continued into the Cold War,[12] there is no mention of it in Stephen Ambrose's otherwise excellent biography of Eisenhower as President.

The National Security Agency (NSA), founded in 1952 to unite for the first time the previously fragmented American SIGINT community, quickly became the biggest and best-funded Western intelligence agency. Studies of US foreign policy in the Cold War, however, rarely mention it – despite the acknowledgement by the last Cold War President, George H. W. Bush, that SIGINT was a 'prime factor' in his foreign policy.[13] The small circle of those in the know in Washington used to joke that NSA stood for 'No Such Agency'.* No Republican President visited NSA headquarters at Fort Meade, Maryland, until Ronald Reagan in 1986.[14]† Over thirty years later no Democratic President has yet made a public visit.‡ By contrast, almost four centuries earlier, the great French codebreaker Rossignol was publicly visited at his château by both Louis XIII and Louis XIV.[15]

The virtual exclusion of SIGINT from the history of international relations after the Second World War has distorted understanding of the Cold War in significant ways. That point is illustrated by the very first Cold War SIGINT to be declassified in 1995–6: the approximately 3,000 intercepted Soviet intelligence and other telegrams (codenamed VENONA) for the period 1939–48, partially decrypted by American and British codebreakers in the late 1940s and early 1950s, thanks to Soviet errors in the use of the 'one-time pad'.[16] A majority of the most important decrypts were messages exchanged between Moscow and its intelligence residencies in the United States; they have large implications for American political history as well as for Soviet–American relations.§ The outrageous exaggerations and inventions of Senator Joseph McCarthy's self-serving anti-Communist

* The Cold War Canadian and Norwegian SIGINT agencies, also rarely mentioned by historians, were among a number which were probably larger than any interwar agency. (Ferris, 'Signals Intelligence in War and Power Politics', p. 167.)

† Reagan's visit seems to have been prompted by the need to apologize for revealing in a broadcast SIGINT (at least some of it from GCHQ) on the instructions given by Gaddafi's regime for a terrorist attack on US forces in West Berlin. Reagan stayed to pay the first public tribute by a US President to the work of NSA.

‡ President Obama, however, is believed to have made an unpublicized visit to Fort Meade in 2015.

§ Though declassification of the VENONA decrypts began only in 1995, their existence had been unofficially revealed in the early 1980s and some of their contents leaked out over the next decade. VENONA was, however, ignored by most US historians until the late 1990s.

witch-hunt in the early 1950s made liberal opinion sceptical for the remainder of the Cold War of the reality of the Soviet intelligence offensive. McCarthy arguably performed the role, albeit unconsciously, of the KGB's most successful Cold War agent of influence. The mostly reliable public evidence of Elizabeth Bentley and Whittaker Chambers, who had worked as couriers for Soviet intelligence, was widely ridiculed. The VENONA decrypts provide compelling corroboration for both. It is now clear that the wartime Roosevelt administration, from Los Alamos to OSS, was successfully penetrated by Soviet intelligence.[17] The discovery of this penetration through the VENONA decrypts helped to prevent most of it continuing into the Cold War.

The VENONA secret was shared with Clement Attlee, the British Prime Minister, and with all three British intelligence agencies but, due chiefly to the insistence of J. Edgar Hoover, Director of the FBI, not with President Truman, or, until late 1952, with the Central Intelligence Agency. When Kim Philby was posted to Washington as SIS representative in 1949, he was thus told that he could discuss VENONA with the FBI but not with the CIA; he obeyed instructions not to mention the decrypts to the CIA but revealed them to his KGB case officer. Thanks to Philby and a Soviet agent in US SIGINT, William Weisband, Stalin was thus better informed than Truman about the early Cold War successes of American codebreakers.[18] In 1949 Philby was able to report to Moscow that the leading atom spy at Los Alamos, successively codenamed REST and CHARLES in a number of the decrypts, had been identified as the German-born British physicist Klaus Fuchs – thus giving Moscow time to warn those of its American agents who had dealt with Fuchs that they might have to flee through Mexico. Among those who made their escape were Morris and Lona Cohen, who later reappeared in Britain as KGB illegals using the aliases Peter and Helen Kroger and were convicted of espionage in 1961. After his death in 1995, Morris Cohen was posthumously declared Hero of the Russian Federation by President Boris Yeltsin.[19] In the spring of 1951 Philby had been able to pass a warning, via Guy Burgess, to Donald Maclean in the Foreign Office that he too had been identified as a Soviet agent by a VENONA decrypt. In May 1951 Burgess and Maclean fled to Moscow.[20]*

Once Moscow discovered and corrected the errors in its use of the one-time pad which had made possible the VENONA decrypts, the UKUSA

---

* The fact that Burgess, while posted to the Washington embassy, had stayed in Philby's house led to Philby's recall to London at US insistence and the end of his career as an SIS officer. Unlike MI5, most of Philby's SIS colleagues continued to believe in his innocence. SIS remained in contact with Philby until his defection to Moscow in January 1963.

alliance had very little high-grade Soviet SIGINT for the remainder of the Cold War. Among the less publicized achievements of Bletchley Park, however, overshadowed by ULTRA and the invention of the first electronic computer, had been its success, notably in the Air Section, in extracting valuable intelligence from low-level cipher communications and electronic signals (ELINT). Early in the Cold War, the wartime head of Luftwaffe intelligence analysis in the Air Section, Arthur ('Bill') Bonsall, took the lead in initiating similar low-level SIGINT operations which identified the order of battle of the Soviet forces in East Germany and provided broader insights into Soviet military readiness and defence spending. In 1955 GCHQ founded a new J Division responsible for SIGINT on the Soviet Union and the Warsaw Pact, with Bonsall as its first head.[21] Better than any previous SIGINT agency, GCHQ had learned the lessons of the last war. Until 1978 all its Cold War directors were veterans of Bletchley Park.*

Though the highest-grade cipher systems of the Cold War were harder to break than those of the Second World War, the total volume of SIGINT generated by both Soviet intelligence and the UKUSA alliance greatly increased. Much of the diplomatic traffic of Third World states, many of whom lacked state-of-the-art cipher systems, was vulnerable to cryptanalysts in both East and West. On the eve of the 1956 Suez Crisis the British Foreign Secretary, Selwyn Lloyd, formally congratulated the director of GCHQ on both the 'volume' and the 'excellence' of the decrypts he had supplied to the Foreign Office 'relating to all the countries of the Middle East. I am writing to let you know how valuable we have found this material . . .'[22] Though Selwyn Lloyd did not mention it, the decrypts were the product of joint GCHQ/NSA operations under the terms of the UKUSA agreement. It is likely that Soviet cryptanalysts enjoyed a similar level of success against Middle Eastern diplomatic traffic. There was probably never a year during the Cold War, at least from the 1950s onwards, when the KGB sent less than 100,000 diplomatic decrypts to the Communist Party Central Committee (chiefly, no doubt, to its International Department). By 1967 the KGB was able to decrypt 152 cipher systems employed by a total of seventy-two states.[23]

The KGB owed much of its SIGINT success to the recruitment of cipher clerks and other personnel in foreign embassies in Moscow. Few, if any, embassies escaped some degree of KGB penetration. The US embassy was

---

* The last was Bonsall, GCHQ director from 1973 to 1978. 'In the opinion of his staff', writes Sir David Omand, 'Bonsall was the cleverest Cold War director even if his reserved and austere working style was not ideally suited to Whitehall jostling for prestige and budget.' (ODNB Sir Arthur Bonsall.)

penetrated virtually continuously from the beginning of Soviet–American diplomatic relations in 1933 until at least the mid-1960s.[24] Remarkably, most studies of US–Soviet relations continue to take no account of the haemorrhage of diplomatic secrets from the Moscow embassy for more than thirty years. The KGB and GRU were also able to profit from poor security at NSA. In 1960 two NSA staff members, Bernon F. Mitchell and William H. Martin, who had made contact with the KGB a year earlier, defected to Moscow, where they continued being debriefed for several years. On 6 September 1960, in Moscow's House of Journalists, Mitchell and Martin gave perhaps the most embarrassing press conference in the history of the US intelligence community. The greatest embarrassment was the public revelation that NSA had been decrypting the communications of some US friends and allies. Among them, said Martin, were 'Italy, Turkey, France, Yugoslavia, the United Arab Republic [Egypt and Syria], Indonesia, Uruguay – that's enough to give a general picture, I guess.'[25]*

Though security at the US embassy in Moscow improved after the mid-1960s, that at many other embassies did not. According to Admiral Fulvio Martini, head of SISMI (Italian foreign intelligence) from 1984 to 1991, the attitude to security in Italian embassies in the Soviet Bloc frequently continued to be characterized by *'leggerezza e superficialità'*.[26] Soviet SIGINT throughout the Cold War was also assisted by the penetration of foreign ministries in the West as well as the Third World. In 1945 the Paris residency of the MGB (predecessor of the KGB) recruited a 23-year-old cipher officer, codenamed JOUR, in the Quai d'Orsay who was still active in the early 1980s. DARIO in the Italian Foreign Ministry had an almost equally long career as both KGB agent and talent-spotter.[27] The incomplete evidence currently available suggests that, at a number of periods during the Cold War, France and Italy were unconsciously conducting towards the Soviet Union something akin to open diplomacy. In 1983, for example, the French embassy in Moscow discovered that bugs in its teleprinters had been relaying all incoming and outgoing telegrams to the KGB for the past six years.[28] François Mitterrand, the French President at the time of the discovery, was one of a number of Cold War political leaders with a deep interest in the SIGINT obtained from domestic eavesdropping. While in opposition in the 1970s, he had publicly denounced those intelligence officials who, he claimed, were bugging him as 'idiots': 'What do they actually do with these thousands of stolen words?' As President, however, Mitterrand set up a secret office in the Elysée Palace which organized the bugging

---

* In 1963 Staff Sergeant Jack E. Dunlap committed suicide after several years spent smuggling top-secret documents from Fort Meade, the NSA HQ, for the GRU.

of a wide variety of people in public life ranging from some of his political opponents to the wife of one of his prime ministers.[29]

The role of HUMINT in the Cold War is better understood than that of SIGINT. Though quickly convinced of the need for peacetime SIGINT, Truman took much longer to be persuaded of the need for a post-war espionage agency. On 20 September 1945, just over a week after authorizing continued SIGINT collaboration with Britain, he closed down the wartime foreign-intelligence agency, OSS.* The eventual outcome of bureaucratic wrangling over the future of peacetime US intelligence was a plan, embodied in a presidential directive of 22 January 1946, establishing a National Intelligence Authority (NIA) composed of the Secretaries of State, War and the Navy with Truman's Chief of Staff, Admiral Leahy, representing the President. Truman's directive also established the post of Director of Central Intelligence (DCI), who was to attend the NIA as a non-voting member and direct the work of a new Central Intelligence Group (CIG), a small analytical agency set up to collate and process intelligence collected by the rest of the intelligence community. The chief architect of this reorganization, Admiral Sidney W. Souers, agreed to Truman's request that he become the first DCI on condition that he serve no longer than six months. The President celebrated the occasion with probably the most eccentric lunch in White House history, personally presenting each guest with a black cloak, black hat and wooden dagger. He then called Leahy forward and stuck a large black moustache on his upper lip. Souers, Truman announced, had been appointed 'Director of Centralized Snooping'. As this comic ritual indicates, Truman still found it difficult to take seriously the idea of peacetime American espionage. Conscious of his lack of experience in international relations, what he wanted from the CIG was 'a digest every day, a summary of the dispatches flowing from the various departments, either from State to our ambassadors or from the Navy and War departments to their forces abroad, wherever such messages might have some influence on our foreign policy'.[30]

The beginning of the Cold War transformed Truman's attitude to espionage and covert operations. On 12 March 1947 he appeared before a joint session of Congress, asked for $400m to help save Greece and Turkey from the Communist threat, and pronounced what became known as the

---

* Executive Order 9621 gave the R&A section of OSS to the State Department and transferred the espionage and counter-espionage elements to the army as a new Strategic Services Unit (SSU). Neither received much of a welcome. (Andrew, *For the President's Eyes Only*, pp. 160–61.)

Truman Doctrine: 'I believe that it must be the policy of the United States to support free peoples who are resisting subjugation by armed minorities or by outside pressures.' For the next forty years 'Containment' of the Soviet threat became the basis of US foreign policy. All Cold War presidents accepted that 'Containment' must have a covert dimension. The National Security Act of 26 July 1947 created the National Security Council (NSC), which Truman intended as 'the place where military, diplomatic and resources problems could be studied and continually appraised'. The Act also created the Central Intelligence Agency (CIA) 'for the purpose of coordinating the intelligence activities of the several Government departments and agencies in the interest of national security'. The director of the CIA held the additional title of Director of Central Intelligence (DCI) with, in principle but never fully in practice, authority over the rest of the foreign-intelligence community.[31]

The CIA was the first foreign-intelligence agency in any major power to be publicly created by Act of parliament. Congress gave its unqualified approval not because of the onset of the Cold War but because of memories of Pearl Harbor less than six years earlier. Representative Ralph Edwin Church (R, Illinois) declared during the House hearings on the National Security bill: 'There is no better proof that we have been extremely backward in our intelligence work than the fact that we were so completely surprised at Pearl Harbor. It is somewhat reassuring to have this emphasis placed on intelligence as part of our national security.' During the remarkably non-partisan hearings, Church was supported by, among others, Carter Manasco (D, Alabama): 'If we had had a strong central intelligence organization, in all probability we would never had had the attack on Pearl Harbor; there might not have been a World War II.'[32] No parliamentary debate on the case for a British foreign-intelligence service took place at any point during the Cold War. Even the existence of SIS was not officially admitted until the Queen's Speech at the opening of Parliament in 1992.

By the 1950s intelligence as well as international relations was dominated by two superpowers, the United States and the Soviet Union, which operated on a global scale. Truman in retirement found it difficult to come to terms with his own role in the early stages of the intelligence Cold War. 'I never had any thought when I set up the CIA', he claimed, 'that it would be injected into peacetime cloak and dagger operations.' It is indeed difficult to imagine Truman authorizing the landing at the Bay of Pigs in 1961 or other operations intended to overthrow Fidel Castro in Cuba. But it is equally difficult to take at face value his later attempts to disclaim all responsibility for covert action (operations primarily designed not to collect intelligence but to influence the course of events). The original role allocated to the CIA by the National Security Council included, in addition to intelligence collection and analysis, 'such other functions and duties related to intelligence affecting the national security as the National Security Council may from time to time direct'. Truman's special counsel, Clark Clifford, later testified that this studiously vague formula was intended to include covert operations, albeit 'of limited scope and purpose': 'We did not mention them by name because we felt it would be injurious to our national interest to advertise the fact that we might engage in such activities.' When Truman later tried to deny any responsibility for 'peacetime cloak and dagger operations', Allen Dulles (DCI from 1953 to 1961) privately reminded him of his own 'very important part' in its origins.[33]

The earliest covert action authorized by Truman, for which he later tried to evade personal responsibility, was prompted by fear of a Communist victory in the Italian elections of April 1948. The first numbered document secretly issued by the National Security Council, NSC 1/1 of 14 November 1947, warned: 'The Italian Government, ideologically inclined toward Western democracy, is being subjected to continuous attack by a strong Communist Party.' The NSC recommended, in addition to American public support for the beleaguered Italian government, a programme to 'Actively combat Communist propaganda in Italy by an effective U.S. information program and by all other practicable means, including the use of unvouched funds'. Over ten million dollars of captured Axis funds were laundered for use in the Italian election campaign in the spring of 1948. Some were secretly handed over to the Christian Democrat Prime Minister, Alcide de Gasperi, whose party won 307 of the 574 seats.[34]

SIS also became more actively involved in covert action than ever before, partly as a result of taking over the remains of the wartime Special Operations Executive (SOE), founded in 1940 in the optimistic hope of 'setting Europe ablaze'.[35] A 1944 Foreign Office report on the future of SIS, while not expecting a major role for post-war covert action, concluded that it would be 'a mistake to abandon the principle that in almost any foreign country occasions may arise when it may be useful for His Majesty's Government to resort to bribery, &c., for the furtherance of their foreign policy (this in contrast to the strict S.I.S. practice of only paying money for the collection of intelligence)'.[36] Attlee, Britain's first Cold War Prime Minister, agreed. A supporter of SIS Operation VALUABLE, begun in 1948 in a failed attempt to incite rebellion in Communist Albania, Attlee proposed bribery as one of the methods to be used. Asking for 'an appreciation of Albanian personalities', he enquired: 'Are they not possibly for sale?'

Though SIS was unable to identify whom to bribe, the Permanent Under-secretary at the Foreign Office, Sir William Strang, assured Attlee that bribery was 'certainly one of the covert methods we would bear in mind for possible use in due course'.[37] Attlee's successor, the ailing Winston Churchill, was a covert action enthusiast. After the CIA/SIS combined operation in 1953 which overthrew the anti-Western Prime Minister of Iran, Mohammed Mossadeq, and restored the Shah to his throne, Church-ill summoned the CIA leader of the operation, Kermit Roosevelt (cousin of FDR), to his bedroom in Number 10, where he was recovering from a stroke. According to Roosevelt, Churchill told him: 'Young man, if I had been but a few years younger, I would have loved nothing better than to have served under your command in this great venture.'[38]

Throughout the Cold War, the main Western practitioner of covert action remained the CIA. The apparent success of CIA covert action in the 1948 Italian elections led to its rapid expansion. Over the next six years, the Korean War and the election of the intelligence enthusiast Dwight D. Eisenhower as President from 1953 to 1961 turned covert action into a major arm of US foreign policy. Eisenhower's enthusiasm for covert action represented, in part, a misreading of the HUMINT lessons of the Second World War. The experience of wartime support for resistance movements behind German lines provided little guidance for covert action in support of opponents of Communist rule in Cold War Europe, all of which failed.

Between 1951 and 1975 there were, according to the 1976 Church Committee report, about 900 major US covert actions, as well as many minor ones. The Doolittle report, commissioned by Eisenhower in 1954, gave a chilling endorsement of the case for them:

> It is now clear that we are facing an implacable enemy whose avowed object-ive is world domination by whatever means and at whatever cost. There are no rules in such a game. Hitherto acceptable norms of human conduct do not apply. If the United States is to survive, long-standing American concepts of 'fair play' must be reconsidered.

Eisenhower agreed. He exaggerated both the danger of Soviet 'world domination' and the efficacy of US covert action. The apparent rapid suc-cess of covert action in overthrowing supposedly pro-Soviet regimes in Iran and Guatemala during the first eighteen months of the Eisenhower administration in 1953–4 led it to ignore the warning signs later left by other, less successful operations. After a failed attempt to overthrow Presi-dent Achmed Sukarno of Indonesia in 1958, the CIA's future Deputy Director for Intelligence (DDI), Ray Cline, wrote prophetically: 'The weak point in covert paramilitary action is that a single misfortune that reveals CIA's connection makes it necessary for the United States either to abandon the cause completely or convert to a policy of overt military intervention.'[39] Failure to learn that lesson led to public humiliation. After the farcically inept invasion by a CIA-backed 'Cuban brigade' of anti-Castro exiles at the Bay of Pigs in April 1961, President John F. Kennedy despairingly asked his special counsel, Theodore Sorensen: 'How could I have been so stupid, to let them go ahead?' The American people, however, rallied round the flag and the President. It did not occur to Congress to investigate the débâcle.[40]

Because of the global publicity given to such episodes, amplified by best-selling conspiracy theories, it was little realized during the Cold War that the KGB used covert action on a larger scale than the CIA. Covert action played a central role in the post-war establishment of the Soviet Bloc in Eastern and Central Europe. The East German Communist leader, Walter Ulbricht, announced to his inner circle after returning to Berlin from exile in Moscow on 30 April 1945: 'It's got to look democratic, but we must have everything under our control.' Because a democratic façade had to be preserved in all the states of the new Soviet Bloc, the open use of force to exclude non-Communist parties from power had, so far as possible, to be avoided. Instead, Communist-controlled security services, newly created in the image of the MGB (which later became the KGB) and overseen by Soviet 'advisers', helped to implement the post-war transition to so-called 'people's democracies' by intimidation largely behind the scenes. Finally, the one-party Stalinist regimes, purged of all visible dissent, were legitimized as 'people's democracies' by huge and fraudulent Communist majorities in elections rigged by their security services.[41]

One of the distinguishing characteristics of Stalinist intelligence operations during the early Cold War, as for much of the 1930s, was the degree to which they targeted imaginary enemies as well as real opponents. The pre-war hunt for real or, more commonly, imaginary Trotskyists[42] was paralleled by post-war search-and-destroy operations against mostly imaginary Titoist and Zionist conspirators. Stalin and the MGB interpreted the break with Moscow by Marshal Tito's Yugoslavia in 1948 as part of a wide-ranging imperialist conspiracy to undermine the Soviet Bloc. Some of the allegations of Tito's involvement with Western secret services were part of a deliberate attempt to discredit him. Others were the product of the paranoid tendencies of Stalin and the Centre. In the end, the two strands became inextricably intertwined.

During the early Cold War, Soviet advisers kept the security services of the Soviet Bloc on a tight rein. The witch-hunts and show trials which purged the ruling Communist parties of alleged Titoists and Zionists were orchestrated from Moscow.⁴³ One of the alleged accomplices of the Hungarian Minister of the Interior, László Rajk, in the non-existent Titoist plot for which Rajk was executed in 1949, noted how, during his interrogation, officers of the Hungarian security service, the AVO (later AVH), 'smiled a flattering, servile smile when the Russians spoke to them' and 'reacted to the most witless jokes of the [MGB] officers with obsequious trumpeting of immoderate laughter'. The show trial of Rajk and seven accomplices in Budapest in 1949 was devoted to the elaboration of a vast conspiracy theory linking Tito with the subversive schemes of Western intelligence services. The prosecutor declared in his closing address:

> This trial is of international importance . . . Not only Rajk and his associates are here in the dock but with them sit their foreign masters, the imperialist instigators from Belgrade and Washington . . . The plot in Hungary, planned by Tito and his clique to be put into action by Rajk's spyring, cannot be understood out of context of the international plans of the American imperialists.

The most vivid memory of one of the MGB advisers in Budapest, Valeri Krotov, was of Rajk's last words before his execution: 'Long live Communism!'⁴⁴

On Stalin's instructions, plans for Tito's assassination were prepared with the same care as Trotsky's a decade earlier. The chosen MGB assassin, the illegal Iosif Romualdovich Grigulevich, had played a leading role in the first, narrowly unsuccessful assassination attempt on Trotsky in Mexico City in May 1940,⁴⁵ had run a Latin American sabotage group during the Second World War, and in 1951, posing as the Costa Rican 'Teodoro Castro', had become Costa Rica's chargé d'affaires (later Minister Plenipotentiary) in Rome. Since Costa Rica had no diplomatic mission in Belgrade, Grigulevich (then codenamed MAKS) was also able to obtain the post of non-resident envoy to Yugoslavia. The MGB reported to Stalin in February 1953: 'While fulfilling his diplomatic duties in the second half of the year 1952, [MAKS] twice visited Yugoslavia, where he was well received. He had access to the social group close to Tito's staff and was given the promise of a personal audience with Tito.' At a secret meeting with MGB officers in Vienna early in February 1953, Grigulevich discussed a number of assassination methods either at the audience or at a diplomatic reception involving the use of a silenced pistol, poison or poison gas. The use of an accredited Central American diplomat as Tito's assassin was intended to conceal as effectively as possible the hand of the MGB. Using his alias 'Teodoro Castro', Grigulevich composed a farewell letter to his Mexican wife to be made public and reinforce his Costa Rican cover in case he was captured or killed during the assassination. At about midnight on 1 March Stalin read a progress report on the operation to 'rub out' Tito. It may well have been the last document he saw before he suffered a fatal stroke in the early hours of 2 March.[46]

After Stalin's death on 5 March, plans for Tito's assassination were suspended. In May, when the pre-war Soviet defector Aleksandr Orlov began publishing reminiscences of Stalin and the NKVD in *Life* magazine, Grigulevich was hurriedly withdrawn to Moscow. The Centre feared that Orlov, who knew of Grigulevich's sabotage missions before and during the Spanish Civil War, might blow his cover – though, in the event, he did not do so. So far as the puzzled Costa Rican Foreign Ministry and Rome diplomatic corps were concerned, 'Teodoro Castro' and his wife simply vanished into thin air. A note on his KGB file in 1980 records that Western intelligence services had, apparently, never identified the missing diplomat Castro as the illegal Grigulevich. Back in Moscow, Grigulevich, under his real name, completed a doctorate and made a successful new career for himself as an academic expert and writer on Latin America at the Academy of Sciences.[47] A number of his books were translated into English and purchased by British and US university libraries.

Intelligence operations served, in different ways, both to stabilize and to destabilize the Cold War. Assessing the role of intelligence in helping to prevent the Cold War turning into the hot war which some predicted and many feared is impossible without a modest degree of the counterfactual analysis that most scholars are reluctant to engage in. Only by imagining, at least in outline, what the policy of East and West would have been *without* reliable intelligence on their opponents' military (especially nuclear) capabilities is it possible to estimate the importance of the stabilizing role which intelligence actually played. Imagining what US Cold War policy would have been like from the late 1950s onwards with little reliable intelligence on the Soviet nuclear strike force is relatively straightforward because in the early and mid-1950s the United States was in precisely that position. The destabilizing effect of that ignorance provides a valuable insight into the importance of the much better intelligence which subsequently came on stream.[48]

Studies of the Cold War frequently forget the truth of Eisenhower's dictum that intelligence on 'what the Soviets *did not* have' was often as important as information on what they did. Ignorance of a feared opponent invariably leads to an overestimation of the opponent's strength. Shortage of reliable intelligence in the early 1950s generated the dangerous American myth of the 'bomber gap', soon followed by that of the 'missile gap' – the delusion that the Soviet Union was increasingly out-producing the United States in both long-range bombers and ICBMs. In 1955 US Air Force intelligence estimates calculated that by the end of the decade the Soviet Long-Range Air Force would be more powerful than US Strategic Air Command, whose head, General Curtis LeMay, became dangerously attracted by the idea of a pre-emptive strike to prevent the Soviet Union achieving nuclear superiority. That each superpower was able by the middle years of the Cold War to monitor the other's nuclear strike force was crucially dependent on a revolution in imagery intelligence (IMINT) which began with the top-secret contract concluded by the CIA with Lockheed in December 1954 for the construction of the U-2, the world's first high-altitude spy-plane, fitted with the world's highest-resolution cameras.[49] The introduction of the U-2 in 1956, followed four years later by the launch of the first spy satellites, produced IMINT which convinced the Eisenhower administration that the Soviet nuclear strike force was not in fact overtaking that of the United States. The U-2 missions, wrote Eisenhower, 'provided proof that the horrors of the alleged "bomber gap" and "missile gap" were nothing more than the imaginative creations of irresponsibility'.[50] Without the IMINT revolution, US policy towards the Soviet Union would doubtless have continued to be confused by other destabilizing myths about the extent of Soviet nuclear capability. The course of the 1962 Cuban Missile Crisis would also have been quite different. But for IMINT from U-2s (whose interpretation owed much to top-secret documents supplied by a British–American agent in the GRU, Oleg Penkovsky),* Khrushchev would almost certainly have achieved his ambition of concealing the construction of the missile bases until they were fully operational. The option of declaring a US naval 'quarantine' (blockade) around Cuba in the hope of preventing the delivery of the material necessary to complete the bases would thus not have existed. The world would have come even closer to thermonuclear warfare.[51]

But the world did come closer than was realized at the time. Unknown to Washington, the submarine escorts accompanying Soviet surface vessels approaching the US naval blockade around Cuba were armed with nuclear torpedoes. Because of problems in communicating with the submarines, their commanders had authority to fire the torpedoes without authorization

* All the evaluations of the 'Soviet Missile Threat in Cuba' circulated daily (or more frequently) to EXCOMM during the Missile Crisis carry the codeword IRONBARK – a reference to the documents on missile site construction supplied by Penkovsky which had been used in interpreting the U-2 imagery. Facsimiles of some of the evaluations are published in McAuliffe (ed.), *CIA Documents on the Cuban Missile Crisis 1962*.

from Moscow. When the US fleet began dropping practice depth charges in an attempt to force the Soviet Foxtrot-class submarine *B-59* to come to the surface for identification, the submarine captain wanted to launch a nuclear torpedo. He would have done so but for the presence on board of the flotilla commander, who refused to permit the launch.[52]

After the Cuban Missile Crisis, the intelligence available to both East and West on the extent and deployment of their opponents' nuclear strike force became an essential element in stabilizing the Cold War. According to Robert Gates, whose quarter-century career in the CIA and the White House staff culminated in his appointment as DCI from 1991 to 1993:

> The great continuing strength and success of the analysts of CIA and the intelligence community was in describing with amazing accuracy from the late 1960s until the Soviet collapse the actual military strength and capabilities of the Soviet Union . . . And these numbers and capabilities would be relied upon, with confidence, by the Executive Branch (including the Defense Department), the Congress, and our allies both in arms control negotiations and in military planning.[53]*

Without what were euphemistically termed 'national technical means' (NTMs) based on a combination of IMINT and SIGINT, verification of the arms control and arms limitation agreements of the later Cold War would have been impossible. The crucial importance of NTMs was explicitly recognized by the START treaty of 1989, which, as well as cutting strategic nuclear arsenals by about 30 per cent, required both the United States and the Soviet Union 'not to interfere with the national technical means of verification of the other Party' and 'not to use concealment measures that impede verification by national technical means'. A protocol laid down detailed conditions designed to ensure that each side was able to monitor unhindered the other's missile telemetry.[54]

The most successful KGB officer operating in the United States during the middle years of the Cold War was the Fulbright scholar Oleg Danilovich Kalugin. Of the first group of eighteen Soviet Fulbright scholars selected to study in the US in 1958, half were KGB or GRU officers operating under student cover; the remainder 'could be counted on to cooperate' with them. Four of the eighteen went to Columbia. Two (including Kalugin) were KGB, one was GRU, and the fourth, Alexander Yakovlev, later a Politburo member under Mikhail Gorbachev, became known as the 'godfather of glasnost'. Probably like the other three Fulbright scholars

---

* US and UK intelligence, however, largely missed the Soviet biological warfare programme. (Herman, 'Intelligence as Threats and Reassurance'.)

at Columbia, Kalugin was initially almost overcome by the experience of living in New York:

> In the first few weeks, I walked ceaselessly around Manhattan, over-whelmed by its power and beauty and bustle. The Soviet capital – which then looked more like an enormous village than a world-class city – had no building taller than the thirty-storey spire of Moscow State University. To such unsophisticated eyes as mine, the Empire State Building and Manhattan's other skyscrapers seemed like magnificent, otherworldly creations.

Kalugin also made an impression on New York. A profile of him in *The New York Times* called him 'a real personality kid'. He became the first (and possibly the last) KGB officer to serve on the Columbia University Student Council.[55]

Oleg Kalugin's years at Columbia launched him on a high-flying career in Soviet foreign intelligence. From 1965 to 1970, operating under cover as an embassy press officer, Kalugin was posted to the KGB residency in Washington, where he was head of Line PR (political intelligence) and deputy resident. In September 1965 a twenty-year-old army clerk in NSA, Robert Lipka, caused great excitement in the residency by arriving at the Soviet embassy on Sixteenth Street, a few blocks from the White House, and announcing that his job in NSA was to shred classified documents. Recruited by Kalugin as Agent DAN, Lipka was probably the youngest Soviet agent with access to high-grade US intelligence since the nineteen-year-old Ted Hall had offered his services at Los Alamos in 1944. For the next two years, until his posting at NSA ended, Lipka provided for money highly classified documents, which he had failed to shred, about once a fortnight through dead-letter boxes, brush contacts and meetings with his case officer. Kalugin spent what he claimed were 'endless hours' in his cramped residency office, sifting through the mass of material and choosing the most important documents to cable to the Centre before the rest followed by diplomatic bag.[56]

Only a few months after Lipka left NSA and his career as a KGB agent came to an end, the Washington residency recruited another walk-in with regular access to high-grade SIGINT. Late in 1967 Chief Warrant Officer John Anthony Walker, a communications watch officer on the staff of the Commander of US Submarine Forces in the Atlantic (COMSUBLANT), entered the Soviet embassy and announced: 'I'm a naval officer. I'd like to make some money and I'll give you some genuine stuff in return.' Despite his junior rank, Walker had access to very high-level intelligence – including the key settings of US naval ciphers. The sample batch of material which he brought to the embassy was examined with incredulity by Kalugin and the Washington resident, Boris Aleksandrovich Solomatin. According to

Kalugin, Solomatin's 'eyes widened as he leafed through the Walker papers. "I want this!" he cried.' Walker, they later agreed, was the kind of spy who turns up 'once in a lifetime'. Enabling Soviet codebreakers to crack US naval ciphers, Kalugin believed, gave the Soviet Union 'an enormous intelligence advantage' by allowing it to monitor American fleet movements. During his eighteen years as a spy, Walker formed his own spy ring, recruiting his son, elder brother and a navy friend, Jerry Whitworth. For Kalugin the greatest surprise of the Lipka and Walker cases was to discover 'how incredibly lax security still was at some of the United States' top secret installations'. The reflected glory of the two cases was to win Solomatin the Order of the Red Banner and, later, promotion to deputy head of KGB foreign intelligence. Kalugin's career also benefited. In 1974 he became the Soviet Union's youngest foreign-intelligence general.[57]

The Lipka and Walker cases also highlighted the change in motivation of Soviet agents in America since the beginning of the Cold War. Before and during the Second World War, the most valuable agents had been ideological spies. But the ideological appeal of Stalin and his successors to American radicals had waned rapidly after the Second World War. There was no new generation of Western agents like the Cambridge Five and the atom spies, inspired by belief in the ability of the Soviet Union to create a new civilization. Like Walker, most Cold War spies in the United

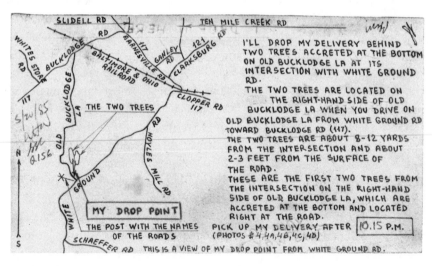

Map by US navy Chief Warrant Officer and KGB agent John Walker, showing location of 'drop point' for one of many consignments of top-secret documents.

States wanted to 'make some money'. The KGB's most valuable recruit in the CIA, Aldrich Ames, a walk-in like Lipka and Walker, made a record amount of money. In the nine years after his recruitment in April 1985, the KGB and its post-Soviet successor agency paid him at least 2.5 million dollars (probably more than any other agent in Russian history) and promised him another two million.[58]

By the mid-1970s the KGB and CIA had sharply contrasting public images. The KGB remained immune from domestic criticism. The statue of its founder, Felix Dzerzhinsky, outside its headquarters near Red Square, was the tallest in Moscow and a prominent landmark. The ambitious KGB Chairman, Yuri Andropov, steadily increased his political power after his election to the Politburo in 1973. On the death of Leonid Brezhnev in 1982, he became the first intelligence chief to become Soviet leader. The CIA, by contrast, in the wake of the Vietnam War and Watergate, faced unprecedented public criticism. The sensational disclosures during 1975, the 'Year of Intelligence', of CIA 'dirty tricks' – among them assassination plots against foreign statesmen (notably Fidel Castro) and illegal spying on US citizens during Operation CHAOS – caused widespread public revulsion. The DCI, William Colby, claimed, probably correctly, that in the aftermath of the revelations 'The CIA came under the closest and harshest public scrutiny that any such service has ever experienced not only in this country but anywhere in the world.' Senator Frank Church, chairman of the Senate Select Committee set up to investigate the abuses, declared: 'The Agency may have been behaving like a rogue elephant on the rampage.' A later Congressional report concluded more accurately that the CIA, 'far from being out of control', had been 'utterly responsive to the instructions of the President and the Assistant to the President for National Security Affairs'. Blame for officially authorized dirty tricks, however, was deflected from the White House to the Agency.[59]

Alongside accurate revelations of US covert action, there emerged during the 1970s other ill-founded allegations of CIA dirty tricks which, by dint of frequent repetition, became conventional wisdom and still appear in otherwise reliable Cold War histories. President Nixon infamously told the CIA in 1970 to try to prevent the election of Chile's Marxist President, Salvador Allende, and to make the Chilean economy 'scream'. But, as Dr Kristian Gustafson has demonstrated, the regularly repeated claims that the CIA orchestrated Allende's overthrow (and even his death) in 1973 and the rise of his successor, General Augusto Pinochet, are mistaken:

> ... The Chilean military junta was desperate not to be associated with the
> U.S ... A post-coup CIA intelligence bulletin reported Pinochet's private
> comment that 'he and his colleagues, as a matter of policy, had not given

any hints to the U.S. as to their developing resolve to act.' . . . The Chilean military's *amour propre* would have been offended by the notion that they needed the U.S. to run the coup for them. It was best and simplest, from the Chilean point of view, to keep the CIA on a string with the occasional piece of intelligence, but otherwise to keep them shut out.[60]

Though the revelations of the 'Year of Intelligence' exposed undoubted serious abuses, they also gave rise to best-selling conspiracy theories – chief among them the unfounded claim, which a majority of Americans believed and the KGB did its best to encourage, that the CIA was responsible for the assassination of John F. Kennedy.[61]* If the CIA had been involved in killing its own President, it was reasonable to conclude that there were no limits to which the Agency would not go to subvert foreign regimes and assassinate other statesmen who had incurred its displeasure. KGB 'active measures' (influence operations) successfully promoted the belief that the methods which the CIA had used to attempt to kill Castro and destabilize his regime were being employed against 'progressive' governments around the world. One Soviet active-measure operation in the Middle East in 1975 named forty-five leading statesmen who had, allegedly, been the victims of successful or unsuccessful Agency assassination attempts over the past decade. Indira Gandhi was one of a number of Third World leaders pre-occupied by supposed CIA plots against them.[62] In November 1973 she told Fidel Castro: 'What they [the CIA] have done to Allende they want to do to me also. There are people here, connected with the same foreign forces that acted in Chile, who would like to eliminate me.' The belief that Allende had been murdered in cold blood and that the Agency had marked her out for the same fate became something of an obsession. Dismissing accurate American claims that Allende had turned his gun on himself during the storming of his palace, Mrs Gandhi declared: 'When I am murdered, they will say I arranged it myself.'[63] Tragically, Mrs Gandhi paid more attention to the imaginary menace of a CIA assassination plot than to the real threat from her own bodyguards, who murdered her in 1984.

No account of American Cold War policy in the Third World omits the role of the CIA. By contrast, covert action by the KGB passes almost

---

* According to opinion polls in 1993 on the thirtieth anniversary of Kennedy's assassination, three quarters of Americans believed the CIA had murdered the President (Moynihan, *Secrecy*, pp. 219–20). Oliver Stone's film version of the conspiracy theory, *JFK*, was enormously influential. One enthusiastic US historian claimed that *JFK* probably 'had a greater impact on public opinion than any other work of art in American history' save *Uncle Tom's Cabin* (Toplin (ed.), *Oliver Stone's USA*, p. 174).

unmentioned in most histories both of Soviet foreign policy and of developing countries. The result has been a curiously lopsided account of the secret Cold War in the Third World – the intelligence equivalent of the sound of one hand clapping. The admirable history of the Cold War by John Lewis Gaddis, for example, refers to CIA covert action in Chile, Cuba and Iran, but makes no reference to the extensive KGB operations in the same countries.[64] In reality, from at least the early 1960s onwards, the KGB played an even more active global role than the CIA. The belief that the Cold War could be won in the Third World transformed the agenda of Soviet intelligence. In 1961 the youthful and dynamic Chairman of the KGB, Aleksandr Shelepin, won Khrushchev's support for the use of national liberation movements and other anti-imperialist forces in an aggressive new grand strategy against the 'Main Adversary' (the United States) in the Third World.[65] Though Khrushchev was soon to replace Shelepin with the more compliant and less ambitious Vladimir Semichastny, the KGB's grand strategy survived. The future head of KGB intelligence assessment, Nikolai Leonov, then a young foreign-intelligence officer in the First Chief (Foreign Intelligence) Directorate's (FCD) Second (Latin American) Department, was later to recall: 'Basically, of course, we were guided by the idea that the destiny of world confrontation between the United States and the Soviet Union, between Capitalism and Socialism, would be resolved in the Third World. This was the basic premise.'[66] After Khrushchev was forced to step down in 1964 and succeeded by Leonid Brezhnev, the belief that the Cold War could be won in the Third World was held with greater conviction in the Centre than in the Kremlin or the Foreign Ministry. It was enthusiastically embraced by Yuri Andropov from the moment he succeeded Semichastny as KGB Chairman in 1967.[67] By contrast, the long-serving Soviet Foreign Minister, Andrei Gromyko, was remembered by his almost equally long-serving ambassador in Washington, Anatoli Dobrynin, as a man with little interest in the Third World.[68] According to Leonov, much of the Foreign Ministry as well as Gromyko were 'openly scornful' about it.[69]

Though Andropov was careful not to appear to be treading on Gromyko's toes,[70] at most of the main moments of Soviet penetration of the Third World, from the alliance with the first Communist 'bridgehead' in the western hemisphere (to quote the KGB's codename for Castro's Cuba) in the early 1960s to the final, disastrous defence of the Communist regime in Afghanistan in the 1980s, the KGB, usually supported by the International Department of the Central Committee of the Communist Party of the Soviet Union (CPSU), had greater influence than the Foreign Ministry. Castro preferred the company of KGB officers to that of Soviet diplomats, telling the first KGB resident in Havana, Aleksandr Alekseev, that their meetings were a way of 'bypassing the Ministry of Foreign Affairs and every rule of protocol'. In 1962, largely at Castro's insistence, Alekseev replaced the unpopular Soviet ambassador. Other prominent Latin American leaders who, like Castro, preferred KGB officers to Soviet diplomats included Salvador Allende in Chile, Juan José Torres in Bolivia, Omar Torrijos (not to be confused with his son) in Panama and José Figueres Ferrer in Costa Rica. The first Soviet contact with Juan and Isabel Perón before their return to Argentina from exile in 1973 was also made by the KGB rather than by a diplomat. KGB support for the Sandinistas began almost two decades before they took power in Nicaragua in 1979.[71]

In Asia, Africa and the Middle East, as in Latin America, the main initiatives in Soviet policy during the 1960s and 1970s were more frequently taken by the KGB than by the Foreign Ministry. India, the world's largest democracy, was described by Oleg Kalugin as 'a model of KGB infiltration of a Third World government'. As in India, most of the KGB's Third World operations led to transitory successes rather than enduring influence. That, however, was not how it seemed in the 1970s. Vladimir Kryuchkov, head of the KGB First Chief (Foreign Intelligence) Directorate from 1974 to 1988, described the Non-Aligned Movement (NAM) as 'our natural allies'. In 1979 the NAM elected the unmistakably aligned Fidel Castro as its chairman – prompting a complaint from the KGB Havana residency that, 'F. Castro's vanity is becoming more and more noticeable.' Only a decade before the Soviet Union fell apart, the KGB leadership remained rashly optimistic about the success of its Third World operations. Andropov boasted to a Vietnamese minister in 1980:

> The Soviet Union is not merely talking about world revolution but is actually assisting it . . . Why did the USA and other Western countries agree on détente in the 1970s and then change their policies? Because the imperialists realized that a reduction of international tension worked to the advantage of the socialist system. During this period Angola, Mozambique, Ethiopia and Afghanistan were liberated.[72]

A decade later all four 'liberated' states had left the Soviet orbit.

Just as the KGB's enthusiasm for Castro a generation earlier had helped to launch the Soviet forward policy in the Third World, so the disastrous military intervention in Afghanistan, for which the KGB leadership bore much of the responsibility, was to bring it to an end.[73] CIA covert action, in particular its supply of shoulder-launched Stinger missiles to the *mujahideen* beginning in the summer of 1986, probably hastened the Soviet withdrawal from Afghanistan. During 1986 the CIA station in Islamabad coordinated the provision of over 60,000 tons of arms and other supplies to the *mujahideen* along over 300 infiltration routes by trucks and mules. The station chief, Milt Bearden, complained that the Agency 'needed more mules than the world seemed prepared to breed'.[74]

American covert action against the Sandinista regime in Nicaragua, first authorized by President Ronald Reagan in December 1981, was far less successful than against the Russians in Afghanistan. Secret CIA support for the inept Contra guerrilla campaign against the Sandinistas was revealed by the US media and banned by Congress. Robert Gates, then the CIA's Deputy Director of Intelligence (head of analysis), reported to the DCI, Bill Casey, in December 1984 that covert support for the Contras was counterproductive and would 'result in further strengthening of the regime and a Communist Nicaragua'. The only way to overthrow the Sandinistas would be overt military support for the Contras combined with US airstrikes. Neither Casey nor Reagan was willing to face up to this uncomfortable truth. The attempt to circumvent the Congressional ban led the White House into the black comedy of 'Iran–Contra' – an illegal attempt to divert to the Contras the proceeds of secret arms sales to Iran. The revelation of the Iran–Contra scandal in November 1986 provoked the most serious crisis of the Reagan presidency. Vice-President George Bush dictated for his diary a sequence of staccato phrases which summed up the despondency in the White House: 'The administration is in disarray – foreign policy in disarray – cover-up – Who knew what when?' A Congressional enquiry concluded that 'ultimate responsibility' for Iran–Contra lay with Reagan: 'If the President did not know what his National Security Advisors were doing, he should have.'[75]

The greatest success of Soviet Bloc intelligence operations in the West during the Cold War was probably in the field of scientific and technological intelligence. S&T provides further evidence of the asymmetry of the secret Cold War. The West had little to learn from Soviet technology. The Soviet Union had an enormous amount to learn from the West and from the US defence industry in particular.* The plans of the first US atomic bomb, obtained for Moscow by British and American agents at the end of the Second World War and used to construct the first Soviet atomic bomb in 1949, were perhaps the most important scientific secret ever obtained by any intelligence service. The early development of Soviet radar, rocketry and jet propulsion was also heavily dependent on the covert acquisition of technology from the West. The enormous flow of Western (especially American) S&T throughout the Cold War helps to explain one

---

* Though lacking in advanced micro-electronics, however, Soviet engineers found ways of using analogue processes instead in systems such as air defence missiles.

of the central paradoxes of a Soviet state which was once famously described by West German Chancellor Helmut Schmidt as 'Upper Volta with missiles',[76] a military superpower whose infant mortality and other indices of social deprivation were at Third World levels. The fact that the gap between Soviet weapons systems and those of the West was far smaller than in any other area of industrial production was due not merely to their priority within the Soviet system but also to the success of S&T collection. For most of the Cold War Soviet intelligence found the American defence industry much easier to penetrate than the US federal government.[77]

By 1975 Directorate T of the FCD, which ran KGB S&T operations, had seventy-seven agents and forty-two 'confidential contacts' working against American targets inside and outside the United States. SIGINT was also a major source. The SIGINT stations within the Washington, New York and San Francisco KGB residencies succeeded in intercepting the telephone and fax communications of the Brookhaven National Laboratory and a series of major US companies. The United States was a more important – and productive – S&T target than the rest of the world combined.[78] In 1980 61.5 per cent of the S&T received by the Soviet Military-Industrial Commission (VPK), which was mainly responsible for tasking in the military field, came from American sources (some outside the USA), 10.5 per cent from West Germany, 8 per cent from France, 7.5 per cent from Britain, and 3 per cent from Japan. In 1980 the VPK gave instructions for 3,617 'acquisition tasks', of which 1,085 were completed within a year, allegedly benefiting 3,396 Soviet research and development projects. Directorate T was its chief collection agency.[79] During the 1980s there were increasing attempts to use S&T in the Soviet civilian economy. Kryuchkov told a meeting of senior FCD staff in 1984 that 'In the last two years the quantity of material and samples handed over to civilian branches of industry has increased by half as much again', and had been used 'to real economic effect', particularly in energy and food production.[80] Kryuchkov failed to mention, however, that the sclerotic nature of Soviet industrial management made it far harder to exploit S&T in the civilian economy than in military production.* The Soviet armed forces, by contrast, became dependent on S&T. According to a KGB report in 1979, over half the development projects of the Soviet defence industry were based on S&T from the West. The Pentagon estimated in the early 1980s that probably 70 per cent of all current Warsaw

---

* The East German civilian economy found similar difficulty in making full use of Western S&T. (Macrakis, 'Does Effective Espionage Lead to Success in Science and Technology? Lessons from the East German Ministry of State Security'.)

Pact weapons systems were based in varying degree on Western – mainly US – technology.[81] *Both* sides in the Cold War – the Warsaw Pact as well as NATO – thus depended on American know-how. Intelligence is central to an understanding of the military as well as the political history of the Cold War.

So far as political-intelligence collection was concerned, the Soviet Bloc had an inbuilt advantage over the West. The authoritarian and secretive political systems of one-party states are, by their very nature, harder targets than those of democracies. Equally, however, the Soviet Bloc had an inbuilt disadvantage in intelligence assessment. In all one-party states, political-intelligence analysis (unlike most S&T) is necessarily distorted by the insistent demands of political correctness. It thus acts as a mechanism for reinforcing rather than correcting the regimes' misconceptions of the outside world. Autocrats, by and large, are told what they want to hear. One British SIS Chief defined his main role as, on the contrary, to 'tell the Prime Minister what the Prime Minister does not want to know'.[82] Western intelligence agencies, of course, have sometimes fallen far short of this exalted calling. Though the politicization of intelligence sometimes degrades assessment even within democratic systems, however, it is built into the structure of all authoritarian regimes.

The lowly status of Soviet intelligence analysis is reflected in the sparse references to it in the lengthy classified KGB Lexicon.[83] Soviet intelligence reports throughout, and for some years after, the Stalin era usually consisted only of selective compilations of relevant information on particular topics with little attempt at interpretation, for fear that they might contradict the views of the political leadership. Though intelligence analysis improved under Andropov, it remained seriously undeveloped by Western standards. Nikolai Leonov, who was dismayed to be appointed in 1971 as deputy head of the FCD assessment department, Service 1, estimates that it had only 10 per cent of the importance of the CIA's Directorate of Intelligence [Analysis]. Its prestige was correspondingly low. To be transferred there from an operational section, as happened to Leonov, was 'equivalent to moving from a guards regiment in the capital to the garrison in a provincial backwater'.[84] Vadim Kirpichenko, who later rose to become first deputy head of the FCD, recalls that pessimistic intelligence reports were kept from Brezhnev on the grounds that they 'would upset Leonid Ilyich'.[85] According to Leonov, 'All the filtration stages . . . were concerned with making sure that alarming, critical information did not come to the attention of the bosses. [Such information] was provided in a sweetened, smoothed form, with all the thorns removed in advance.'[86]

When Soviet policy suffered setbacks which could not be concealed, analysts knew they were on safe ground if they blamed them on imperialist machinations, particularly those of the United States, rather than failures of the Soviet system. As one FCD officer admitted at the end of the Cold War: 'In order to please our superiors, we sent in falsified and biased information, acting on the principle "Blame everything on the Americans, and everything will be OK".'[87] Within the Centre it was possible during the Andropov era to express much franker opinions about Third World problems – for example, about Soviet prospects in Egypt after the death of Nasser or the threat of economic collapse in Allende's Chile – than were communicated to the political leadership. From the moment that the KGB leadership had taken up a position, however, FCD dissidents kept their heads down.

The damaging effects of Soviet political correctness were made worse by the KGB's recurrent tendency to conspiracy theory, which in times of crisis escalated into a paranoid tendency. Looking back on the Cold War, Sir Percy Cradock, former chairman of the British Joint Intelligence Committee and Margaret Thatcher's Foreign Policy Adviser, was right to identify 'the main source of weakness' in the Soviet intelligence system as 'the attempt to force an excellent supply of information from the multifaceted West into an oversimplified framework of hostility and conspiracy theory'.[88] In both the early 1960s and the early 1980s, the KGB reported to the Politburo – with horrendous inaccuracy – that the United States was planning a nuclear first strike against the Soviet Union.

For most of the Cold War, one of the main weaknesses of Western intelligence analysts was their failure to grasp the degree to which political correctness and conspiracy theory degraded Soviet intelligence assessment – a weakness which ultimately derived from a lack of long-term perspective on the mishandling of information by autocratic systems. Had Western analysts in the early 1980s been aware of KGB and GRU assessments of twenty years earlier, they would doubtless have been quicker to recognize the extent of Soviet fears of the Reagan administration. On 29 June 1960 Shelepin, the KGB Chairman, personally delivered to Khrushchev an alarmist assessment of American policy, which may have derived from reports of wild talk by General Curtis LeMay, head of Strategic Air Command:

> In the CIA it is known that the leadership of the Pentagon is convinced of the need to initiate a war with the Soviet Union 'as soon as possible' . . . Right now the USA has the capability to wipe out Soviet missile bases and other military targets with its bomber forces. But over the next little while the

defence forces of the Soviet Union will grow . . . and the opportunity will
disappear.

Khrushchev took the warning seriously. Less than a fortnight later he issued
a public warning to the Pentagon 'not to forget that, as shown at the latest
tests, we have rockets which can land in a preset square target 13,000 kilometres away'. In March 1962 the GRU produced two dangerously misinformed reports which served to reinforce the KGB's earlier warning that
the Pentagon was planning a nuclear first strike. The GRU claimed that in
the previous June the United States had taken the decision to launch a surprise
nuclear attack on the Soviet Union in September 1961, but had been deterred
at the last moment by Soviet nuclear tests which showed that the USSR's
nuclear arsenal was more powerful than the Pentagon had realized.[89]

Soviet intelligence was in a similarly alarmist mood at the beginning of
the Ronald Reagan administration. In a secret speech to a major KGB
conference in May 1981, a visibly ailing Leonid Brezhnev denounced Reagan's policies as a serious threat to world peace. He was followed by Yuri
Andropov, who was to succeed him as General Secretary eighteen months
later. To the astonishment of most of his audience, the KGB Chairman
announced that, by decision of the Politburo, the KGB and GRU were for
the first time to collaborate in a global intelligence operation, codenamed
RYAN – a newly devised acronym for *Raketno-Yadernoye Napadenie*
('Nuclear Missile Attack'). Operation RYAN was to collect intelligence
on the presumed, but non-existent, plans of the Reagan administration
and its NATO allies to launch a nuclear first strike against the Soviet
Union.[90] 'Not since the end of the Second World War', Andropov informed
foreign residencies, 'has the international situation been as explosive as it
is now.'[91] As Brezhnev's successor in November 1982, Andropov retained
full control over the KGB; his most frequent visitors were senior KGB
officers.[92] Throughout his term as General Secretary, RYAN remained the
first priority of Soviet foreign intelligence. For several years, Moscow suc-
cumbed to what its ambassador in Washington, Anatoly Dobrynin, called
a 'paranoid interpretation' of Reagan's policy.[93]

The intelligence operations of the rest of the Soviet Bloc were distorted
by the requirement to collaborate with Operation RYAN. Markus Wolf,
the able long-serving head of the East German HVA (Hauptverwaltung
Aufklärung – Main Directorate for Reconnaissance), found KGB liaison
officers 'obsessed' by RYAN and the threat of a NATO first strike:

> The HVA was ordered to uncover any Western plans for such a surprise
> attack, and we formed a special staff and situation centre, as well as emer-
> gency command centres, to do this . . . Like most intelligence people, I found

these war games a burdensome waste of time, but these orders were no more open to discussion than other orders from above.[94]

Like Wolf, most KGB residencies in Western capitals were less alarmist than Andropov and the Centre. When Oleg Gordievsky, who had been recruited as an SIS agent within the KGB in 1974, joined the London residency in June 1982, he found all his colleagues in Line PR (political intelligence) sceptical about Operation RYAN. None, however, was willing to risk his career by challenging the Centre's assessment. Residencies were, in effect, ordered to search out alarming information. The Centre was duly alarmed by what they supplied and demanded more.[95] The Washington resident, Yuri Androsov, a protégé of Kryuchkov, was at pains to provide it.[96]

The Centre interpreted the announcement of the SDI ('Star Wars') programme in March 1983 as part of the psychological preparation of the American people for nuclear war. On 28 September 1983 the terminally ill Andropov issued from his sickbed a denunciation of US policy couched in apocalyptic language unparalleled since the depths of the Cold War. 'Outrageous military psychosis', he declared, had taken over the United States. 'The Reagan administration, in its imperial ambitions, goes so far that one begins to doubt whether Washington has any brakes at all preventing it from crossing the point at which any sober-minded person must stop.' Alarm within the Centre reached a climax during the NATO exercise 'Able Archer 83', held in November 1983 to practise nuclear-release procedures for a simulated DEFCON 1 coordinated nuclear attack. For a time both the Kremlin and the KGB leadership were haunted by the fear that the exercise might be intended as cover for a real nuclear first strike. Some KGB officers stationed in the West were by now more concerned by the alarmism in the Centre than by the threat of Western surprise attack.[97]

The first reliable intelligence on RYAN to reach the West came from Oleg Gordievsky, following his posting to the KGB London residency in June 1982. Gordievsky was able to supply not merely oral information but also RYAN directives from the Centre which he regularly smuggled out of the residency.[98] Though Gordievsky's British case officer, John Scarlett, who later rose to become Chief of SIS, was initially 'astonished and scarcely able to believe' the intelligence he provided,[99] it was quickly accepted as of vital importance by the Prime Minister, Margaret Thatcher, and her Foreign Secretary, Sir Geoffrey Howe, as well as by the British intelligence community. When the intelligence was shared with Washington, however, a major difference of view quickly emerged. On the British side, as Howe wrote later, during Able Archer 'Gordievsk[y] left us in no doubt of the extraordinary but genuine Russian fear of real-life nuclear strike.'[100]* Most CIA analysts disagreed – probably because of the difficulty they found in crediting the role of conspiracy theory in Soviet intelligence analysis. Some months later a Special National Intelligence Estimate (SNIE) concluded: 'We believe strongly that Soviet actions are not inspired by, and Soviet leaders do not perceive, a genuine danger of imminent conflict or confrontation with the United States.'[101] Later re-examination of the intelligence from Gordievsky and other sources led to a drastic revision of that conclusion. Robert Gates writes in his memoirs:

> Information about the peculiar and remarkably skewed frame of mind of Soviet leaders during those times that has emerged since the collapse of the Soviet Union makes me think there is a good chance – with all of the other events in 1983 – that they really felt a NATO attack was at least possible . . . U.S. intelligence had failed to grasp the true extent of their anxieties. A reexamination of the whole episode by the President's Foreign Intelligence Advisory Board [PFIAB] in 1990 concluded that the intelligence community's confidence that this had all been Soviet posturing for political effect was misplaced.[102]†

The 1990 PFIAB report, most of which was not declassified until 2015, concluded that:

> there was in fact a genuine belief among key members of Soviet leadership that the U.S. had embarked on a program of achieving decisive military superiority that might prompt a sudden nuclear attack on the U.S.S.R. . . . Although past Able Archer exercises were monitored by Soviet intelligence, the reaction by Warsaw Pact military forces and intelligence services to the 1983 exercise was unprecedented.[103]

Though the importance of single-source agent reporting was usually tactical, in the cases of both Penkovsky and Gordievsky it had major strategic significance.[104] The KGB directives during Operation RYAN supplied by Gordievsky to SIS highlighted, in addition to the Centre's fears of a surprise US nuclear attack, its sometimes woeful ignorance of

---

* Following Gordievsky's warnings, Harry Burke of the JIC Assessment Staff found evidence in technical intelligence reports of a Soviet military alert. As his boss, Michael Herman, later recalled, initially Burke 'had to fight to get his conclusion through a sceptical JIC'. (Phythian, 'Profiles in Intelligence: An Interview with Michael Herman'.)

† Though Operation RYAN had ceased to be the chief Soviet foreign-intelligence priority by the time Gorbachev became Soviet leader, partly as a result of bureaucratic inertia detailed bimonthly reports on signs of US and NATO preparations for a nuclear first strike continued until November 1991. See below, pp. 705–6.

Western society. Unaware that British blood donors are unpaid, the Centre instructed the London residency in 1983 to monitor the prices paid to them, in the belief that any increase might indicate preparations for war. The Centre also suspected that Church leaders and heads of major banks might have been secretly informed of plans for a nuclear first strike, and ordered the residency to investigate.[105]

There is no better evidence of the extent of Mikhail Gorbachev's 'new thinking' in foreign policy after he became General Secretary in March 1985 than his dissatisfaction with the bias of the KGB's political reporting. In December 1985 Viktor Chebrikov, KGB Chairman since 1982, summoned a meeting of the KGB leadership to discuss a stern memorandum from Gorbachev on 'the impermissibility of distortions of the factual state of affairs in messages and informational reports sent to the Central Committee of the CPSU and other ruling bodies' – a damning indictment of its previous political correctness. The meeting sycophantically agreed on the need to avoid sycophantic reporting, and declared it the duty of all Chekists both at home and abroad to fulfil 'the Leninist requirement that we need only the whole truth'.[106] According to Leonid Shebarshin, who succeeded Kryuchkov as head of foreign intelligence in 1988, the FCD 'no longer had to present its views in a falsely positive light'[107] – though it is difficult believe that all its officers instantly threw off the habits of a lifetime.

Throughout the Cold War there were major elements of both symmetry and asymmetry in the intelligence priorities of East and West. In KGB jargon, the United States was termed the 'Main Adversary' (*glavny protivnik*) – just as the CIA regarded its main adversary as the Soviet Union. Unlike Western intelligence agencies, however, the KGB had not one but two 'Main Adversaries'. The second was what the KGB called 'ideological sabotage' – anything which threatened to undermine the authority of the Communist one-party states in and beyond the Soviet Bloc.

The asymmetry between the priorities of the intelligence communities in East and West reflected their radically different roles within the states they served. The Cheka, founded six weeks after the Bolshevik Revolution, and its successors were central to the functioning of the Soviet system in ways that intelligence communities never were to the government of Western states. Their fundamental role within the one-party state was to monitor and repress dissent in all its forms, whether by violence or more sophisticated systems of social control involving huge surveillance networks. Informers in the German Democratic Republic were seven times more numerous even than in Nazi Germany. The KGB and its intelligence allies played a central role in the suppression of the Hungarian Uprising of 1956, the crushing of the Prague Spring in 1968, the invasion of Afghanistan in 1979 and the pressure on the Polish Communist regime to strangle the democratic Solidarity movement in 1981. More of the KGB's elite corps of illegals (deep-cover intelligence personnel posing as foreign nationals) were used to penetrate the dissident movements within the Soviet Bloc than were ever deployed against the United States or other Western targets during the Cold War.[108]

The war against the dissidents was a major part of KGB foreign as well as domestic operations. Indeed some of the most important of the foreign operations were jointly devised by senior officers of the First Chief and Fifth Directorates, responsible respectively for foreign intelligence and countering ideological subversion. Early in 1977, for example, no fewer than thirty-two 'active measures' designed to discredit and demoralize the leading dissident, Andrei Sakharov ('Public Enemy Number One', as Andropov described him), and his wife, Elena Bonner, were either in progress or about to commence both within the Soviet Union and abroad. Seeking to discredit every well-known dissident who managed to get to the West was a major KGB priority – irrespective of whether the dissident's profession had, in Western terms, anything whatever to do with politics. Though plans to maim Rudolf Nureyev, Natalia Makarova and other Soviet ballet dancers after their flight to the West seem never to have been implemented, great efforts were made to destroy their reputations. At the world chess championship in the Philippines in 1978, when the dissident Viktor Korchnoi (referred to by Soviet media only as the 'opponent' or the 'challenger') committed the unforgivable sin of competing for the title with the orthodox Anatoli Karpov, the KGB sent eighteen operations officers to try to ensure that Korchnoi lost.[109] It is possible, but not provable, that they had some effect. Korchnoi flew into a rage when a Soviet 'parapsychologist', Vladimir Zukhar, with (according to the *New York Times* correspondent) 'eyes supposedly like burning coals', took a seat near the front of the spectators. Karpov eventually won 6-5.[110]

Only when the vast apparatus of Soviet social control began to be dismantled under Mikhail Gorbachev did the full extent of the KGB's importance to the survival of the USSR retrospectively become clear. The manifesto of the hardline leaders of the August 1991 coup, of which the KGB Chairman, Vladimir Kryuchkov, was the chief organizer, implicitly acknowledged that the relaxation of the campaign against ideological subversion had shaken the foundations of the one-party state: 'Authority at all levels has lost the confidence of the population . . . Malicious mockery of all the institutions of state is being implanted. The country has in effect become ungovernable.'[111] What the plotters failed to grasp was that it was too late to turn back the clock. 'If the *coup d'état* had happened a year and a half or two years earlier', wrote Gorbachev afterwards, 'it might, presumably, have succeeded. But now society was completely changed.'[112] Crucial to the change of mood was declining respect for the intimidatory power of the KGB, which had hitherto been able to strangle any Moscow demonstration at birth. The most striking symbol of the collapse of the August coup was the toppling of the giant statue of the founder of the Cheka, Felix Dzerzhinsky, from its plinth in the middle of the square outside KGB headquarters. A large crowd, which a few years earlier would never have dared to assemble, encircled the Lubyanka and cheered enthusiastically as 'Iron Felix' was borne away, dangling in a noose suspended from a huge crane supplied by the Moscow City Government.[113]

At the time, the speed of the collapse of the Soviet system took almost all observers (including Western intelligence communities) by surprise. What now seems most remarkable, however, is less the sudden death of the Communist regime at the end of 1991 than its survival for almost seventy-five years. Without the KGB's immense system of surveillance and social control, the Soviet experience would have been significantly briefer. Arguably the KGB's most enduring achievement was thus to sustain the longest-lasting one-party state of the twentieth century. By postponing the disintegration of the Soviet Union, the KGB also prolonged the Cold War.

30

'Holy Terror': From the Cold War to 9/11

Western intelligence agencies at the end of the Cold War suffered, though they did not realize it, from a serious lack of theologians. During the Second World War and Cold War, they had been well versed in Nazi and Communist ideology. But the increasingly secularized late-twentieth-century West found it far more difficult to grasp the appeal of Islamic fundamentalism. Its incomprehension of the political power of religious extremism was vividly displayed during the crisis in Iran which led early in 1979 to the fall of the pro-Western Shah and the rise of the 78-year-old Shia Ayatollah Ruhollah Khomeini, who had lived in exile for the past fourteen years. The popular appeal of the call by Imam Khomeini (as he was best known in Iran) for the establishment of a religious ruler, the *velayat-e faqih*, was almost beyond the comprehension even of the devoutly Christian US President, Jimmy Carter. The White House aide on Iran, Gary Sick, later acknowledged: 'The notion of a popular revolution leading to the establishment of a theocratic state seemed so unlikely as to be absurd.' 'Whoever took religion seriously?' demanded one State Department official after Khomeini's rise to power.[1] Iran's religious revolution, however, was more popular than most of the political revolutions the West found easier to understand. Probably five times as many people took to the streets in Iran in 1979 as during the French Revolution almost two centuries earlier.[2]

The British ambassador in Tehran, Sir Anthony Parsons, reported to London that 'we are now witnessing a classic revolutionary situation', while the FCO Assistant Undersecretary of State for the Middle East predicted that 'the stage certainly looks set for a Lenin to emerge on the Iranian scene'. Both were mistakenly thinking in terms of a secular rather than a religious revolution.[3] Not until 22 November 1978, less than two months before the Shah was forced to flee, did the British embassy in Tehran at last cable one of Khomeini's numerous communiqués to London.[4] For some years the CIA's National Foreign Assessment Center (NFAC) had, similarly, shown little interest in Khomeini and the Iranian religious establishment. From the mid-1960s intelligence reporting on Khomeini and religion in Iran 'virtually ceased'. Until February 1978 the NFAC was unaware that Khomeini's son had died in the previous October, and it was another three months before it learned that Khomeini blamed the United States for his death. Only after the fall of the Shah in January 1979 did the CIA discover, from unclassified sources, that he had heavily cut state subsidies to religious groups.[5] An Agency post-mortem on its failure to anticipate the Iranian Revolution concluded defensively: 'No other intelligence service, whatever its organizational form, seems to have done much better.'[6]

A report to the DCI in 1983 by a group of senior advisers concluded that the failure to foresee the fall of the Shah and the rise of Khomeini derived, as in a number of other mistaken national intelligence estimates (NIEs), from the fact that they involved 'basic historical discontinuity': 'The basic problem in each was to recognize qualitative change and to deal with situations in which trend, continuity and precedent were of marginal, if not counterproductive, value.'[7] The report epitomizes the dangers of a short-term approach to strategic intelligence. Far more serious than the failure to recognize short-term 'discontinuity' in 1978–9 was the lack of long-term perspective in interpreting the political power of religious extremism.

A decade after being taken aback by the Shia Ayatollah Khomeini's rise to power in Iran, Western intelligence services found it equally difficult to grasp the nature and extent of the growing terrorist threat from Sunni extremists. The foundation in 1988 of what became the most dangerous Islamist terrorist group, Al Qaeda ('the base'), led by Osama bin Laden, failed at the time to attract the attention of Western intelligence. No US intelligence agency produced a study of its organization until 1999.[8] MI5 found it far easier to understand the secular IRA than it did the Islamist Al Qaeda. During the 1990s it had a leading role in defeating a series of well-planned IRA offensives in London. In December 1995, however, MI5 dismissively told the heads of police special branches: 'Suggestions in the press of a worldwide Islamic extremist network poised to launch terrorist attacks against the West are greatly exaggerated.'[9]

Before 9/11 most Western intelligence agencies failed to grasp that understanding the appeal of Al Qaeda and the terrorist threat which it posed required an understanding of the roots of its theology. Its leader, Osama bin Laden, regularly made dubious use of the fourteenth-century 'Mardin fatwa' of Ibn Taymiyya to justify his call for the overthrow of the Saudi monarchy and jihad against the United States.[10] His biggest theological debt was to the father of modern Islamic fundamentalism and the most influential advocate of Muslim holy war, Sayyid Qutb, who had been executed in 1966 on charges of attempting to overthrow the Egyptian government but remained almost unknown outside the Muslim world. Qutb insisted that there was no middle ground in the global conflict between Islam and what he called *jahiliyya*, the ignorance of divine guidance which he blamed for unbelief, barbarism and licentiousness. All Muslims had the duty to join in the struggle against *jahiliyya*; if they failed to do so, they were liable to be condemned as unbelievers.

Understanding the influence of Qutb also involved understanding the appeal of his conspiracy theories. He played a leading role in creating a distinctively Islamist brand of anti-Semitism. From the birth of Islam, he declared, the inherently evil Jews had been fanatically determined to destroy it: 'This is an enduring war which will never end.' In *Our Struggle with the Jews*, written only six years after the liberation of Auschwitz, Qutb denounced them as Islam's worst enemies: 'They mutilate the whole of history and falsify it . . . From such creatures who kill, massacre and defame prophets one can only expect the spilling of human blood and dirty means which would further their machinations and evil.' As well as quoting repeatedly from the fraudulent *Protocols of the Elders of Zion*, widely regarded as authentic in the Middle East, Qutb added other bizarre conspiracy theories such as the claim that Kemal Atatürk, founder of the secular Turkish state, was actually a Jew.[11]

In 1948–50, Qutb, then a schools inspector, was sent by the Egyptian Ministry of Education to the United States to study teaching methods. The unintentionally comic diatribes against American society which he published on his return did not encourage his few (probably very few) readers in the late-twentieth-century US intelligence community to take seriously the appeal of his theology to Islamist terrorists. Qutb spent much of his time in America in Greeley, Colorado, at Colorado State Teachers College (now the University of Northern Colorado). Though Greeley was a conservative town, where it was illegal to sell alcohol, its attractive young women made him feel under sexual threat: 'The American girl is well acquainted with her body's seductive capacity . . . She knows seductiveness lies in the round breasts, the full buttocks, and in the shapely thighs, sleek legs, and she shows all this and does not hide it.' Qutb traced back what he claimed was American sexual excess ('the law of the jungle') to the 'overwhelming lust for sensual pleasure' of the Pilgrim Fathers.[12]

What made Islamist terrorism a greater threat than any other to the United States in the years leading up to 9/11 was its emphasis on martyrdom missions. Qutb insisted that martyrdom was a necessary part of twentieth-century jihad. During the trial in Cairo in 1966 at which he was sentenced to death, he declared himself a martyr.[13] Thirty years later, Bin Laden told the Arab journalist Abdel Bari Atwan that 'his greatest ambition in life was to die a martyr's death and join those who had gone before him in paradise'.[14]* On 9/11, all nineteen Al Qaeda suicide hijackers believed their martyrdom mission would take them to paradise, and that most passengers on the planes they destroyed would burn in hell. A decade earlier, however, few if any Western intelligence analysts gave serious thought to the influence of Islamist theology on the terrorist threat. While head of the Defense Intelligence Agency (DIA) from 1991 to 1995, General James Clapper (later President Obama's Director of National Intelligence) knew of not a single senior-level discussion of the role of religion.[15]

In the early 1990s, intelligence services in both East and West were preoccupied not by the rise of Islamist terrorism but by the end of the Cold War and the disintegration of the Soviet Union. The CIA's assessments in 1991 of the likelihood of a coup against Mikhail Gorbachev were more realistic than those of Gorbachev himself, who underestimated the threat from the KGB Chairman, Vladimir Kryuchkov, and other hardliners. On 17 August the President's Daily Brief reported in detail on coup preparations. Next day Gorbachev was placed by the plotters under house arrest in his Black Sea dacha.[16] On this occasion, however, long-term perspective provided a misleading guide to the coup's prospects of success. As Robert Gates, DCI from 1991 to 1993, wrote later: 'Based on all prior experience in Russian and Soviet history, when you know at the outset you've got the KGB, the army and the Party all together in a coup attempt, the chances of it not succeeding based on past history are near zero.'[17] Following the humiliating failure of the August coup,[18] it seemed for a time as if the whole structure of the KGB might unravel. Kryuchkov wrote a grovelling letter to Gorbachev, pleading for the leading plotters to be spared jail because of their age and health, suggesting 'strict house arrest' as an alternative. 'In general', he claimed, 'I am very ashamed', and assured Gorbachev, 'as in the past', of his 'deep respect'. Gorbachev was unconvinced. Kryuchkov spent the next three years in jail.† The disintegration of the Soviet Union and the Soviet Bloc appeared to leave the United States as the only intelligence, as well as military, superpower.

Less than a month after the failed Moscow coup, Vadim V. Bakatin,

---

* Atwan was one of the few journalists to interview Bin Laden in his Afghan hideout.
† After Kryuchkov was amnestied in 1994, he began inventing stories that Gorbachev had advance knowledge of the coup against him. (Archie Brown, 'Vladimir Kryuchkov' (obituary), *Guardian*, 30 Nov. 2007.)

the reformist Interior Minister who had been made KGB Chairman for the final months of the Soviet Union, astonished officials in both Moscow and Washington by inviting Secretary of State James A. Baker to his office in the Lubyanka. 'The KGB has changed – or I'm not fit for the post', Bakatin told him optimistically. Baker replied: 'I don't think anything could symbolize the changes going on in the Soviet Union today any better than the fact that the Secretary of State of the United States of America is meeting here in KGB headquarters.'[19] Bakatin caused even greater astonishment in December, a few weeks before the end of the Soviet Union and his own tenure as KGB Chairman, when he invited the new US ambassador, Robert S. Strauss, to his office and handed him a thick file of classified documents on embassy eavesdropping and a valise full of electronic listening devices. 'Mr. Ambassador', said Bakatin, 'these are the plans that disclose how the bugging of your [new] embassy took place, and these are the instruments that were used. I want them turned over to your government, no strings attached.'[20] Most KGB officials were shocked by Bakatin's willingness to compromise a traditionally productive intelligence source.[21] His brief career as intelligence chief came to an abrupt end early in 1992 when the KGB's domestic and border security functions were transferred to a new Russian Ministry of Security. In December 1993 the Ministry of Security was reorganized as the Federal'naya Sluzhba Kontr-razvedky (FSK), the Federal Counter-Intelligence Service, which was itself replaced in April 1995 by today's Federal'naya Sluzhba Bezopasnosti (FSB), the Federal Security Service.

The most enduring legacy of Bakatin's months as the last Chairman of the KGB was in foreign rather than domestic intelligence. The former KGB First Chief (Foreign Intelligence) Directorate was reconstituted as an independent agency, the Sluzhba Vneshnei Razvedki (SVR), based, like its predecessor, at Yasenevo on the outskirts of Moscow. With the disintegration of the Soviet Union and the Soviet Bloc, Russian foreign intelligence lost most of its allies (with the notable exception of Cuba), and about 150 SIGINT stations on their territory.[22] At Bakatin's proposal, the first head of the SVR was Evgeny Primakov, former head of the Institute of Oriental Studies and the Institute of World Economy and International Relations (IMEMO), both parts of the Soviet Academy of Sciences, as well as one of Gorbachev's leading foreign-policy advisers and in 1990–91 a member of his Presidential Council.[23] President Yeltsin's visit to Yasenevo in September 1991 to mark Primakov's appointment as head of the SVR was the first ever by a Russian leader to foreign-intelligence headquarters.[24]

Chief among the Cold War intelligence operations to which Primakov called a halt as head of the SVR was RYAN, which had been introduced in 1981 to monitor the presumed, but non-existent, plans of the Reagan administration and its NATO allies to launch a nuclear first strike against the Soviet Union.[25] Though Operation RYAN had ceased to be the chief Soviet foreign-intelligence priority by the time Gorbachev became Soviet leader, Primakov discovered that, largely as a result of bureaucratic inertia, KGB residencies in Washington and other NATO capitals were still required, for example, to monitor the number of lights left on late at night in the Pentagon and other defence ministries, which had been identified a decade earlier as one possible indicator of preparations for surprise attack, and to submit detailed bimonthly reports to the Centre. RYAN, in Primakov's view, was 'a typical anachronism' left over from the Soviet era which continued to demand 'large financial and human resources'.[26]

Primakov had a better understanding of the West than Soviet foreign-intelligence chiefs. Less prone than they had been to attacks of conspiracy theory, he was at ease with his Western counterparts, exchanging visits with, among others, American DCIs. During Robert Gates's visit to Moscow in October 1992, the after-dinner atmosphere was so relaxed that the CIA's Director of Slavic and Eurasian Analysis, John McLaughlin, a member of the Magic Circle as well as a future Deputy DCI, demonstrated how the CIA was dealing with post-Cold War budget cuts by folding, then unfolding, a dollar bill. When the bank note was unfolded, it had turned into a hundred dollars.[27] Despite staff cutbacks,* the CIA was generally well informed on the politics of the Yeltsin presidency, which were far less opaque than those of its Soviet predecessors. According to McLaughlin:

- Our analysts anticipated the violent crisis in the fall of 1993, when Yeltsin dissolved the Communist-dominated Supreme Soviet to break the constitutional gridlock that paralyzed the country.
- In 1994, we warned of the first Chechen War.
- We were forward-leaning on the outcome of the presidential and parliamentary elections in 1995–1996 and 1999–2000, and we published and briefed extensively on corruption and the rise of Russian organized crime, long before it became such a prominent issue.
- In the economic sphere, we warned policy makers of the looming economic crisis two months before the August 1998 ruble crash and called the rebound in the economy long before business and academic experts did.

The CIA did not foresee the meteoric rise of Vladimir Putin at the end of the decade. But neither, probably, did Primakov or Putin himself.[28]

---

* In response to budget cuts designed to achieve the 'peace dividend' McLaughlin reduced staff in the CIA office of Slavic and Eurasian Analysis by 42 per cent in three years.

Primakov wrote later that 'during my tenure as director of the Foreign Intelligence Service I never met him or heard a thing about [Putin]'.[29]

The main intelligence challenge in Moscow posed by the end of the Cold War, the disintegration of the Soviet Union and the loss of its Warsaw Pact allies was to rebuild the intelligence community of the new Russian Federation. By contrast, leading NATO members on both sides of the Atlantic believed the end of the Cold War would produce a 'peace dividend' by enabling them to cut back their intelligence services as well as their armed forces. In the spring of 1992 President George H. W. Bush was widely expected to win a second term at the November elections and to take a personal interest in post-Cold War changes to the intelligence community.

The American intelligence community had greater confidence in Bush than in any President for the previous generation. The US triumph in the Cuban Missile Crisis and the phenomenal technological achievements of American spy satellites and SIGINT collection (known in much greater detail to the White House than to the public) had given Cold War presidents inflated expectations of what their intelligence communities could achieve. 'Of all the presidents I worked for [from 1968 to 1993]', recalls Robert Gates, 'only [George H. W.] Bush did not have exaggerated expectations of intelligence.'[30] Lacking a long-term understanding of the role of intelligence, most of Bush's predecessors had, at best, a confused understanding of the crucial distinction between intelligence 'secrets' and 'mysteries'. 'Secrets', such as the construction of Soviet missile bases in Cuba in 1962, were discoverable if appropriate intelligence methodology was available. 'Mysteries', such as the intentions of foreign policymakers, might either have to be inferred or be simply undiscoverable. Rightly impressed by the extraordinary detail which IMINT and SIGINT provided on the deployment of Warsaw Pact forces, presidents were disappointed and sometimes critical when the CIA failed to forecast political change abroad. 'What the hell do those clowns do out there in Langley?' Nixon famously complained when the Agency failed to foresee the overthrow of Prince Sihanouk in Cambodia in 1970. George H. W. Bush's experience as DCI gave him a clearer understanding than any previous Cold War President (with the possible exception of Eisenhower) of what it was reasonable to expect from intelligence analysts. 'Measuring intentions', he acknowledged, '. . . is an extraordinarily difficult task.'[31]

Bush's electoral defeat in November 1992, which had been forecast by almost no political pundit, aptly illustrated the difficulties of political prediction. Some of the columnists who failed to foresee Bush's demise castigated the CIA for failing to predict political change in the Soviet

Union with greater accuracy than they themselves had shown in forecasting the outcome of a presidential election in the United States.[32] Bill Clinton entered the Oval Office in January 1993, lacking Bush's deep personal interest in, and experience of, intelligence. He had less direct contact with his first DCI (James Woolsey Jr, February 1993–January 1995) than any President had ever had before with a DCI.*

The most important achievement of US intelligence during Clinton's first term was its assistance in limiting nuclear proliferation. The disintegration of the Soviet Union led to the creation, in addition to the Russian Federation, of three new nuclear powers – Ukraine, Kazakhstan and Belarus – on former Soviet territory. Ukraine had nearly 2,000 strategic nuclear warheads – more than the UK, France and China combined. At a meeting in Moscow in January 1994, Presidents Yeltsin, Clinton and Leonid Kravchuk of Ukraine agreed on the destruction in Russia, at American expense, of all warheads then in Ukraine. The agreement was possible only because of the confidence of the Clinton administration, like its Cold War predecessors, that it had precise and accurate intelligence on the former Soviet Ukrainian missile sites. Defense Secretary William Perry later described how, before the destruction of the warheads, Russian officers at the Ukrainian missile site of Pervomaysk showed him how they would have been used to attack the United States:

> I had often in my career participated in simulated war games, but that had not prepared me for this experience. I was overwhelmed with the absurdity of the situation – watching young Russian officers simulating the destruction of Washington, New York, Chicago, Los Angeles, and San Francisco, and knowing that American missiles were at that moment targeting the very spot on which we were standing. Indeed, never has the surrealistic horror of the Cold War been more vivid to me than at that moment.[33]

Nuclear material in Kazakhstan was less closely guarded than in Ukraine. In the summer of 1993, a US official was offered for sale enriched uranium from a factory in Ust-Kamenogorsk which manufactured fuel for nuclear reactors. The CIA reported that Iranian agents were already on the trail of the uranium, which was stored in a warehouse protected by little more than barbed wire. The Kazakh President, Nursultan Nazarbayev, gave his approval to a secret US operation, codenamed

---

* The almost thousand pages of Clinton's memoirs contain only a half-line reference to 'Jim Woolsey's brief tenure' as DCI. (Clinton, *My Life*, p. 737.)

SAPPHIRE, to transport the enriched uranium from over 1,000 containers in Ust-Kamenogorsk to the Oak Ridge National Laboratory in Tennessee. Lockheed C-5 transport aircraft, refuelled several times in flight, flew to Dover Air Force Base in Delaware, where the uranium was transferred to large, unmarked trucks for the journey to Oak Ridge. William Perry revealed the operation for the first time at a dramatic news conference on 23 November 1994: 'We have put this bomb-grade nuclear material forever out of the reach of potential black marketers, terrorists or a new nuclear regime.' The key to the success of SAPPHIRE, Perry believed, was cooperation between the Pentagon, the CIA, the State Department and the Department of Energy.[34] As 9/11 was to show, interdepartmental cooperation against *internal* threats to US security was far harder to achieve.

Despite the CIA's contribution to counter-proliferation in the former Soviet Union, 1994 was a disastrous year for its public reputation. On 21 February the FBI arrested a long-serving CIA analyst and counter-intelligence officer, Aldrich Ames, who had volunteered his services to the KGB in 1985. During his trial nine years later, Ames admitted having compromised 'virtually all Soviet agents of the CIA and other American and foreign services known to me', as well as providing a 'huge quantity of information on United States foreign, defense and security policies'. As Ames revealed to FBI interrogators, his KGB and SVR handlers were amazed at his ability to take highly classified files out of CIA offices for almost a decade without arousing suspicion. An investigation by the Senate Select Committee on Intelligence blamed an intelligence 'bureaucracy which was excessively tolerant of serious personal and professional misconduct among its employees, where security was lax and ineffective'. Ames was the best-paid spy in American history. The KGB and SVR had paid him $2.5 million by the time he was arrested by the FBI in 1994; a further $2.1 million had been earmarked for him in a Moscow bank account.[35] Ames was sentenced to life imprisonment without the possibility of parole.

The reputation of the CIA was further diminished by Clinton's lack of visible interest in it. The absence of personal contact between the President and his DCI (in striking contrast to the close relations between Bush and Gates) received satirical front-page publicity following a bizarre breach of White House security in 1994. *The New York Times* reported on 12 September:

> Shortly before 2 A.M. today, a small red-and-white plane flew low over 17th Street in the heart of the capital's downtown, banked left in a U-turn

near the Washington Monument, and headed straight toward the President's bedroom in the White House.

No one tried to stop it.

Secret Service agents in the White House grounds fled for their lives as the plane, a stolen Cessna 150, crashed through the branches of a magnolia tree planted by President Andrew Jackson and came to rest two storeys below the Clintons' then unoccupied bedroom.[36] Washington wits claimed that the Cessna had been piloted by Jim Woolsey in a desperate attempt to get, at last, a meeting with the President. Woolsey told the same joke after his resignation early in 1995.[37]*

Though well aware of Clinton's lack of contact with his first DCI, the media failed to notice that, unlike his two Republican predecessors in the White House, Ronald Reagan and George H. W. Bush, Clinton also failed to pay a single visit during either of his two terms to the headquarters of NSA at Fort Meade, the largest and most expensive foreign-intelligence agency not merely in the United States but in the whole of the Western world.† Bush would have discussed the cutbacks in the NSA personally with, among others, its director, Vice-Admiral John Michael 'Mike' McConnell.‡ Clinton did not do so. The cutbacks during the Clinton presidency were, almost certainly, more damaging than they would have been under Bush. Between 1992 and 1995 NSA lost a third of its budget and labour force. A Congressional enquiry concluded: 'One of the side effects of NSA's downsizing, outsourcing and transformation has been the loss of critical program management expertise, systems engineering and requirements definition skills.'[38] These contributed, on 24 January 2000, early in the final year of the Clinton presidency, to the biggest SIGINT crash in US history. According to General Mike Hayden, director of the NSA since the previous year: 'The sheer volume of collection had overwhelmed the capacity of our networks as they had been configured . . . For all intents and purposes, NSA was brain-dead.' For seventy-two hours the crash caused 'a genuine security crisis' which could only be resolved by beginning a massive hardware and software upgrade.[39]

---

* The pilot of the stolen Cessna, a Maryland truck driver with multiple personal problems, was killed in the crash.
† NSA passes unmentioned in Clinton's lengthy memoirs, save for a sentence which records that the CIA, NSA, FBI 'and our entire antiterrorist group' worked hard to prevent terrorist attacks in the two months before the new millennium. (Clinton, My Life. p. 891.)
‡ McConnell later served as President George W. Bush's Director of National Intelligence from 2007 to 2009.

Primakov and the SVR were far more publicly assertive than the US intelligence community – or than the foreign-intelligence arm of the KGB had ever been. In 1993 Primakov published a report attacking the expansion of NATO as a threat to Russian security – at a time when Yeltsin's Foreign Minister, Andrei Kozyrev, was taking a more conciliatory line. On the eve of Yeltsin's visit to Washington in September 1994, Primakov again upstaged the Foreign Ministry by publicly warning the West not to oppose the political and economic reintegration of Russia with other states which had formerly been part of the Soviet Union. Primakov's deputy, Vyacheslav Trubnikov (later his successor as head of the SVR), asserted the SVR's right to a public voice, even if it disagreed with the Foreign Ministry: 'We want to be heard . . . We express our point of view as we deem necessary.'* The revelation in 1994 of Aldrich Ames's nine years as a Russian spy in the CIA was a major morale boost for the SVR. 'Russian intelligence', boasted Primakov, 'turned out to be so highly professional that the FBI was unable to uncover any of Ames's secret dead drops, of which there were many.'[40]

Primakov took a longer view of intelligence history than any major Western intelligence chief. In 1996 publication began, under his editorship, of a six-volume history of Russian foreign intelligence, whose first volume covered the four centuries before the Soviet era. Though a mine of mostly reliable factual information, it presents a heroically sanitized interpretation of Soviet intelligence history. Even under Stalin, foreign intelligence is presented as the victim rather than the perpetrator of the Terror – despite the fact that in the late 1930s one of its chief tasks was to hunt down 'enemies of the people' abroad.[41] Primakov was a fervent admirer of the Cambridge Five, who, he claimed, 'perhaps have no equal in the history of world intelligence'. His overblown eulogy of Donald Maclean, whom he had known personally, inaccurately claimed that he was a multimillionaire aristocrat: 'A Scottish lord, he would never have gotten mixed up with Soviet intelligence for money. In fact he probably had enough money to maintain the USSR's foreign intelligence. Maclean began to cooperate with Soviet intelligence for purely ideological reasons.'[42] In 1995, to mark the seventy-fifth anniversary of the foundation of the Soviet foreign-intelligence service (of which the SVR sees itself as the heir), Primakov also ordered the publication of a volume celebrating the careers of

---

* The rivalry between the SVR and Foreign Ministry during Yeltsin's first five years as President ended in decisive victory for the SVR with Primakov's appointment to succeed Kozyrev as Foreign Minister in December 1996. (Andrew and Mitrokhin, *Mitrokhin Archive*, p. 731. Talbott, *Russia Hand*, p. 160.)

seventy-five leading intelligence officers which differs little from the uncritical hagiographies of the Soviet era.[43]

While planning his cosmetically enhanced history of Russian foreign intelligence, Primakov was unaware that the SVR had lost control of its own history. Three years earlier, there had been an unprecedented haemorrhage from KGB foreign-intelligence archives to the British SIS. The source was a former senior archivist in the KGB First Chief (Foreign Intelligence) Directorate (FCD), Vasili Mitrokhin, who from 1972 to 1982 supervised the transfer of the entire FCD archive from its overcrowded central Moscow offices in the Lubyanka to the new, Finnish-designed FCD headquarters at Yasenevo. In 1982 Mitrokhin was officially congratulated for the efficiency of the move by the FCD chief, Vladimir Kryuchkov, later Chairman of the KGB. Almost every day during the move and for two years afterwards before his retirement in 1984, Mitrokhin had taken notes of the files being transferred to Yasenevo, smuggled them back to his apartment and then to a dacha thirty-six kilometres from Moscow. Eventually, they filled a milk churn, a tin clothes-boiler, two tin trunks and two aluminium cases, all of which he buried beneath the dacha.

Kryuchkov and Mitrokhin's colleagues had no idea that he was a secret dissident. By the end of the 1960s, in the aftermath of the Soviet crushing of the Prague Spring, his political views were deeply influenced by Soviet dissidents' struggle for human rights, which he was able to follow in KGB files, supplemented by Western broadcasts. Though Mitrokhin never had any thought of aligning himself openly with the Soviet human-rights movement, the 'Chronicle of Current Events' and other samizdat publications helped to inspire him with the idea of producing a classified variant of the dissidents' attempt to document the iniquities of the Soviet system. The project began to form in his mind of compiling his own private record of KGB foreign intelligence. The transfer of FCD records to Yasenevo gave him the opportunity to do so.[44]

Mitrokhin risked his life to assemble his top-secret record of KGB foreign operations. Had it been discovered, he would have been tried in secret and probably executed with a single bullet to the back of the head. His only chance of revealing the contents of his archive was for him to escape with it to the West. The breakup of the Soviet Union at the end of 1991 and the relative weakness of border controls between Russia and some of the newly independent former Soviet republics gave Mitrokhin his chance. After secret meetings in the Baltic republics, SIS exfiltrated Mitrokhin, his family and his entire archive from Russia on 7 November 1992, the seventy-fifth anniversary of the Bolshevik Revolution. Though details of the operation still remain classified, it was so successful that for several years Russian intelligence failed to realize that Mitrokhin had left Russia and the SVR continued to pay his pension.*

Following the conviction of Aldrich Ames for espionage in 1994, there were calls in the US Congress for a 'credible, independent, and objective review of the Intelligence Community'. The White House agreed to a review. There followed the appointment in 1995 of the Presidential Commission on the Roles and Capabilities of the United States Intelligence Community (better known as the Aspin–Brown Commission after its successive chairmen), with members chosen by both Congress and the President. Its published report in March 1996, the first since the Church Commission on the intelligence community as a whole, provides an insight into the unconscious parochialism of the Washington world view of post-Cold War intelligence. Despite some specific criticisms, the Commission concluded confidently:

> Without question, the United States has the most capable intelligence apparatus of any country in the world. The information produced by this apparatus gives the United States a substantial advantage when it comes to understanding world events, predicting and preparing for unsettled times, fielding military forces, and making a host of other political and economic decisions.[45]

US technical collection capability, despite budget cuts, was (and still remains) in a class by itself. Five years later, however, 9/11 was to demonstrate serious limitations in US intelligence capability which had passed unnoticed by the Aspin–Brown Commission.

Despite the fact (unmentioned by the Commission report) that, only a decade earlier, some of the most valuable intelligence available to the CIA from inside the KGB had been provided by the British SIS and the French DST (Direction de la surveillance du territoire), it did not occur to the Commission that there was anything that American human-intelligence operations might learn from other (particularly Allied) intelligence services. All Commission members knew, however, or should have known, of the KGB directives and other intelligence of major importance provided by the SIS agent Oleg Gordievsky during Operation RYAN and the 'Able Archer' crisis of 1983 (some of it published in 1990–91), for which he was

---

* Mitrokhin's neighbours in his Moscow apartment seem to have assumed that he had moved to one of his two dachas, one some distance from Moscow. On the assessment by Western intelligence services of the Mitrokhin archive, see below, p. 714.

personally congratulated by President Reagan in the Oval Office.[46] They should equally have been aware that the best and most detailed intelligence on Soviet S&T operations in the United States had come from a DST agent in FCD Directorate T, Vladimir Vetrov (codenamed FAREWELL).[47] The Commission might also have noticed that the secrecy of Gordievsky's and Vetrov's operations a decade earlier had been better protected by British and French intelligence, despite budget cuts, than those of American agents in the KGB had been safeguarded by US intelligence.

Lacking adequate historical and comparative perspective, the Commission failed to understand that its complacent conviction that the United States had 'the most capable intelligence apparatus of any country in the world' derived not from a rigorous assessment of the evidence but from an uncritical assumption of national superiority similar to imperial China's 'Middle Kingdom complex', which has always been a defining characteristic of superpower, or would-be superpower, status. It was central, for example, to the imperial mindset of the *Pax Britannica* and the French *mission civilisatrice*.

The Aspin–Brown Commission was unaware that, at the very moment when it was producing its report, a select group of analysts in the US intelligence community was learning a great deal from copies supplied by SIS of the huge archive of top-secret KGB material which Vasili Mitrokhin had brought with him to London. Probably at British insistence, the material was not divulged to Commission members. But, when the US intelligence community was later allowed to comment publicly, the FBI called the Mitrokhin archive 'the most complete and extensive intelligence ever received from any source' and the CIA described it as 'the biggest counter-intelligence bonanza of the post-war period'. Though it contained more on Cold War operations against the United States (the KGB's 'main adversary') than any other target, there was important material on FCD operations around the world. The only European countries absent from the archive were the pocket states of Andorra, Monaco and Liechtenstein. (There was, however, interesting material on the pocket state of San Marino.) Mitrokhin had made extensive notes even on the FCD's most highly classified files, those of Directorate S, which ran illegals – KGB agents, most of Soviet nationality, working under deep cover abroad, posing as foreign citizens. Their training and the fabrication of their false identities ('legends') took years to complete.[48]

Because the secret of Mitrokhin's exfiltration with his archive was initially so tightly held, it was unknown to Aldrich Ames, who was thus unable to warn the SVR before his arrest in 1994. The response of the SVR to the first leak – in Germany – of the news of the exfiltration shows that it was taken by surprise. When the German magazine *Focus* reported in December 1996 that a former KGB officer had defected to Britain with 'the names of hundreds of Soviet spies', the SVR spokeswoman, Tatyana Samolis, ridiculed the story as 'absolute nonsense': 'Hundreds of people! That just doesn't happen! Any defector could get the name of one, two, perhaps three agents – but not hundreds!'[49] In reality, the Mitrokhin Archive contained details not of hundreds, but of thousands of KGB agents. The SVR investigation which followed the leak in Germany eventually uncovered Mitrokhin's disappearance and, presumably, the hiding places beneath one of his dachas where he had concealed his archive. The truth gradually dawned (though possibly not in full until publication of the first volume of *The Mitrokhin Archive* in 1999) that no Soviet spy at any period between the Cheka and the eve of the Gorbachev era could be certain that their secrets were safe. It was impossible for the Centre to be sure that the identity of any illegal whose training or 'legend' construction had begun before 1984 was secure.* The Mitrokhin archive caused some embarrassment for Primakov personally, because it contained a number of references to him as a KGB co-optee, codenamed MAKSIM, who had been sent on a series of missions to the Middle East and the United States. There were also references to the role of Primakov's deputy and successor, Vyacheslav Trubnikov, as a KGB officer in India, where he had made his reputation.[50]†

During the mid-1990s, as the SVR began to come to terms with the extent of Mitrokhin's revelations from its archives, it simultaneously achieved major penetrations of both the CIA and the FBI. Harold J. Nicholson, who began working for the SVR for mercenary motives in June 1994, only two months after Ames's conviction, was the most senior CIA officer ever to spy for a foreign power. Soon after his recruitment, he was made Branch Chief of the Counterterrorism Center at CIA headquarters.[51] The fact that Ames, despite repeated carelessness about his own security, had gone nine years without detection probably encouraged the less careless Nicholson to believe that he could avoid detection altogether. Suspicion fell on Nicholson, however, after he failed polygraph tests which, according to a later CIA director, had been 'reenergized after the Ames débâcle'.[52] He was arrested at Washington's Dulles airport in

---

* The Centre's attempt to rebuild an illegal network in the United States, untainted by Mitrokhin's revelations, during the first decade of the twenty-first century ended in disaster with the arrest by the FBI in 2010 of ten illegals, who had been under surveillance for some years in Operation GHOST STORIES.

† Significantly, though Primakov referred in his memoirs to Gordievsky and other major Western agents, usually to denigrate them, he made no mention of Mitrokhin.

November 1996, carrying classified documents which he planned to hand over to the SVR in Zurich. In June 1997 Nicholson was convicted of espionage and sentenced to twenty-three years' imprisonment, avoiding a harsher sentence by cooperating with the prosecution.*

By the time Nicholson was arrested in 1996, Robert P. Hanssen, the most senior FBI officer ever to spy for a foreign power, had been delivering top-secret material to the SVR at a series of dead-letter boxes in the Washington area for over a year.† While Hanssen's main motives, like Ames's and Nicholson's, were mercenary, he was also a part-time fantasist and sexual exhibitionist who set up a video link to enable a friend to watch him having sex with his wife. Though the FBI and CIA became aware that there was an unidentified SVR agent in Washington, their joint investigation was badly bungled. The chief investigators became convinced that the Russian spy was a wholly innocent and highly professional CIA officer named Brian J. Kelley. In an attempt to persuade him to confess, Kelley's family as well as he himself, were aggressively interrogated. On one occasion the investigators sent a bogus SVR officer to his front door to warn him that, because of the FBI's evidence against him, it was essential for him to escape: 'Meet us tomorrow night at the [Washington] Vienna Metro. A person will approach you. We have a passport for you, and we'll get you out of the country.' Kelley slammed the door and reported the incident to the FBI. He was eventually vindicated as the result of a file exfiltrated from SVR archives in 2000 in an operation which cost the FBI seven million dollars. The file contained tape of the US agent speaking to his Russian case officer. FBI and CIA investigators expected to hear the voice of Brian Kelley. Instead, they heard Robert Hanssen. When arrested on 18 February 2001, Hanssen asked the FBI agents: 'What took you so long?'[53]‡ In July he was sentenced to life imprisonment without the possibility of parole.

So far as counter-intelligence was concerned, the Ames, Nicholson and Hanssen cases, together with the incompetent handling of the Kelley investigation, collectively demolish the claim of the Aspin–Brown Commission in its 1996 report that the United States had 'without question . . . the most capable intelligence apparatus of any country in the world'. Despite its general belief in the global superiority of US

---

* In 2011 Nicholson was sentenced to a further eight years in prison for using one of his sons to collect over £47,000 from SVR officers in payment for his past espionage. The son was placed on probation for five years.

† Hanssen had been in contact with the GRU for several years after 1979; since Mitrokhin had access only to KGB files, there was no reference to this contact in his archive.

‡ Reinstated by the CIA in 2001, Kelley was later awarded the Distinguished Career Intelligence Medal; he retired in 2007.

intelligence, however, the Commission did briefly acknowledge that the relationship between intelligence agencies and policymakers in Washington worked less well than in several US allies:

> Intelligence must be closer to those it serves. Intelligence agencies need better direction from the policy level, regarding both the roles they perform and what they collect and analyze. Policymakers need to appreciate to a greater extent what intelligence can offer them and be more involved in how intelligence capabilities are used. Intelligence must also be integrated more closely with other functions of government, such as law enforcement, to achieve shared objectives.[54]

The British JIC had proved better than the NSC or any other American body at resolving turf battles, setting intelligence priorities, coordinating assessment by intelligence community, FCO, MOD and Treasury representatives, and gaining the confidence of policymakers. The Twentieth-Century Fund Task Force on the Future of US Intelligence, which had a British member (the author) and shadowed the Aspin–Brown Commission, expressed similar views more forcibly. It concluded that, outside the Department of Defense (DOD), most US government officials 'do not much value the [intelligence] analysis they receive'.[55]* Even DOD officials who did value intelligence reports had very little time to read them. The distinguished Harvard academic Joseph S. Nye Jr, who had a particular interest in intelligence, told the Aspin–Brown Commission, that, when serving as Assistant Secretary of Defense for International Security Affairs in 1994–5, he could rarely find more than five minutes a day to read intelligence reports. The reports he had time to read, said Nye, contained 'a lot of information, but not a lot of insight'.[56]

Nye's comment now seems a fair assessment of the limitations of US intelligence reports on terrorism in the mid-1990s. Although the 1995 National Intelligence Estimate had warned of the emergence of a 'new type of terrorism', the 9/11 Commission later concluded that 'many officials continued to think of terrorists as agents of states ... or as domestic criminals'.[57] Bruce Hoffman, the academic terrorism expert who most clearly identified the future threat from Holy Terror, did so largely because he took a much longer-term view than most intelligence agencies. Of the sixty-four terrorist groups active in 1980, only two, both closely associated with the Iranian Revolution, had a mainly religious motivation. Over the next fifteen years

---

* The Twentieth-Century Fund, a think tank based in New York, has since been renamed the Century Foundation.

there was a dramatic change. By 1995 almost half the active international terrorist groups were religiously based; all the most lethal attacks that year were carried out by religious terrorists. As Hoffman noted, so far from being a short-term late-twentieth-century deviation, the rise of religious terrorism marked a return to a much older tradition of Holy Terror. Until the French Revolution the only arguments used to justify terror had been religious.[58]

During the mid-1990s, however, religious fanatics continued to be underestimated as terrorist threats. In 1993, Khalid Sheikh Mohammed (KSM), the chief planner of the 9/11 attacks eight years later, made a first attempt, actively supported by Bin Laden, to help his nephew Ramzi Yousef plan and finance the destruction of one of the twin towers of the New York World Trade Center. Yousef showed remarkable technical ingenuity. A bomb in a truck left in the Trade Center garage ripped a hole through seven storeys of one of the towers. A thousand people were injured, though, remarkably, only six were killed. Instead of focusing on the growing threat posed by Al Qaeda to major US targets, both the Clinton administration and the media paid more attention to the naïveté of the truck bomber, Mohammed Salameh, who had only a subordinate role in the attack. Absurdly, Salameh, who had rented the truck used for the attack, tried repeatedly to reclaim from the rental company some of the $400 deposit he had paid by claiming that the truck had been stolen from him. At the third attempt, he succeeded in obtaining a partial refund and was then promptly arrested by the FBI.[59]

The intelligence investigation of the attacks on the World Trade Center both in 1993 and on 9/11 2001 was hampered by the inadequate co-operation between the FBI and the CIA which had been a recurrent problem during the Cold War.* The DCI, Jim Woolsey, complained after Yousef's arrest in 1995 and subsequent conviction:

> We didn't know what the investigation was turning up, because the investigation was all being done by law enforcement. Pursuant to Rule 6E of the Federal Rules of Criminal Procedure, anything that's obtained pursuant to a grand jury can't be shared outside the prosecutor's team. There are some limited circumstances in which they could share it, let's say, with a state or local prosecutor, but not with the intelligence community. So all that information was bottled up inside the law enforcement community for at least a couple years until the trials took place.[60]

* For five years at the beginning of the Cold War, J. Edgar Hoover had refused to share VENONA decrypts, the most valuable Soviet intelligence available to any US agency, with the CIA. See above, p. 673.

Though 'bottling up' was an old problem, it was exacerbated by changes in federal law. The CIA (now NSA) historian Dr Michael Warner concludes:

> America in the 1990s effectually revised its rules for the sharing of law enforcement and intelligence information to provide some of the highest protections against state power in any industrialized nation in history. The new rules, dubbed 'the Wall', kept vital clues from being shared by CIA and FBI officers who might have understood their broader significance.[61]

The need for closer cooperation between the FBI and the CIA was far from the only intelligence lesson not learned after the 1993 attack on the World Trade Center. The failure to take further precautions against car and truck bombings was all the more extraordinary in the light of the truck bomb attack ten years earlier on the US embassy in Beirut by an Iranian-backed Shia terrorist suicide bomber which killed sixty-three people. Of the seventeen Americans killed in 1983, eight worked for the CIA, among them the head of station and the head of Middle East intelligence analysis. Over the next year, there were further serious suicide car and truck bomb attacks on the US and French embassies in Kuwait, the US Marine and French paratrooper barracks in Beirut, and the new US Beirut embassy.[62]

The creation within the State Department of the Bureau of Diplomatic Security and the Diplomatic Security Service in 1995[63] failed to produce major reform. After Prudence Bushnell became US ambassador in Nairobi in 1996, she complained repeatedly about serious security weaknesses at her embassy. Despite the known presence of an Al Qaeda cell in Nairobi, there was little response to her complaints by the State Department. Nor was most intelligence on the cell shared with Bushnell: 'The information was highly compartmentalized, on a "need to know" basis and clearly Washington did not think the US ambassador needed to know. So, while I was aware of the Al Qaeda presence and various U.S. teams coming and going, I did not know, nor was I told, what they were learning.'[64] On 7 August 1998 huge bombs in trucks driven by suicide bombers almost demolished the US embassy and surrounding buildings in Nairobi, and, ten minutes later, badly damaged the embassy in Dar es Salaam. In Nairobi 213 were killed (only twelve of them American) and several thousand injured, of whom 150 were blinded by flying glass. In Dar es Salaam the toll was eleven dead and eighty-five wounded. The CIA had already obtained what the 9/11 Commission later judged to be 'unusually good intelligence' on the Al Qaeda cell in Nairobi which, after the bombing, provided proof of its responsibility.[65] The use of simultaneous suicide bomber attacks, first used against American targets in East Africa in 1998, was to be repeated on a much larger scale three years later inside the United States on 9/11.

'By all accounts', wrote President Clinton later in his memoirs, 'Bin Laden was poisoned by the conviction that he was in possession of the absolute truth and therefore free to play god by killing innocent people.'[66] The first Clinton administration, however, failed to grasp the extent of the new threat which he posed to the United States. As late as 1997, even the CIA's Counterterrorist Center continued to describe him as an 'extremist financier'. By contrast, the Bin Laden unit established in the CIA Operations Directorate in the previous year now recognized that he was far more than a financier, reporting that Al Qaeda's military committee was planning worldwide operations against US interests and actively trying to obtain nuclear material.[67] In February 1998 Bin Laden publicly declared war on the United States. Together with Ayman al-Zawahiri, whose Egyptian Islamic Jihad merged with Al Qaeda, he issued a fatwa in the name of the World Islamic Front against Jews and Crusaders which declared: 'The ruling to kill the Americans and their allies – civilian and military – is an individual duty for every Muslim who can do it in any country in which it is possible to do it.'[68]* Though Bin Laden was henceforth a major US intelligence target, it was not until after 9/11 that the US government adopted the elimination of Al Qaeda as a clear strategic objective.[69]

The most prescient assessment of the terrorist threat inside the United States in the few years before the 9/11 attacks came not from the intelligence community but in an unclassified official report in September 1999 by Rex Hudson of the Federal Research Division of the Library of Congress, entitled *The Sociology and Psychology of Terrorism: Who Becomes a Terrorist and Why?* Though Hudson had no access to classified material, he took a longer-term and more wide-ranging view of the terrorist threat than most intelligence analysts. He correctly identified as the main emerging threat of the 1990s 'new breeds of increasingly dangerous religious terrorists': 'The religiously motivated terrorists are more dangerous than the politically motivated terrorists because they are the ones most likely to develop and use weapons of mass destruction (WMD) in pursuit of their messianic or apocalyptic visions.'[70] The main immediate threat came

* Because of unfamiliarity with the jihadist passion for poetry, an earlier speech by Bin Laden in 1996 had become inaccurately known in the West as his 'Declaration of War against the United States'. In fact it was chiefly directed against Saudi Arabia, but most of the fifteen poetry excerpts which made this clear were not translated. (Miller, *Audacious Ascetic*, p. 252; Kendall, 'Jihadist Propaganda and Its Exploitation of the Arab Poetic Tradition', pp. 224–5.)

from suicide bombing. The most committed suicide bombers (female as well as male) of the early 1990s had come from the avowedly secular Sri Lankan Tamil Tigers (LTTE), the only terrorist group to assassinate two heads of government and one opposition leader: the Indian Prime Minister, Rajiv Gandhi, in 1991; the Sri Lankan President, Ranasinghe Premadasa, in 1993; and the Sri Lankan Leader of the Opposition, Gamini Dissanayake, in 1994.[71] Against Western, especially US, targets, however, Hudson identified the 'most dangerous type' of suicide bomber as 'the Islamic fundamentalist': 'Suicide bomber(s) belonging to al-Qaida's Martyrdom Battalion could crash-land an aircraft packed with high explosives (C-4 and semtex) into the Pentagon, the headquarters of the Central Intelligence Agency (CIA), or the White House.'[72] One of the four planes hijacked by Al Qaeda suicide bombers on 9/11 did indeed crash into the Pentagon (though it did not need high explosives to produce an explosion). Another of the hijacked planes was also heading towards an unknown high-profile Washington target when it was brought down by its passengers. So far as is known, no analyst in the US intelligence community identified as accurately as Hudson the threat of air attack by suicide bombers on prestige targets.

The most striking thing about Hudson's report, apart from its prescient insight, was how little attention it attracted at the time. Reliable open-source information on Al Qaeda was hard to come by and polluted by inventions of varying plausibility. Hudson was misled by the claims of Yossef Bodansky, Director of the US Congressional Task Force on Terrorism and Unconventional Warfare, that in the mid-1990s Bin Laden 'settled in the London suburb of Wembley', where 'he purchased property'. In the eyes of US intelligence analysts, this claim doubtless diminished the overall credibility of Hudson's report. Since Bin Laden was, at an estimated 6 foot 5 inches, probably the world's tallest leading terrorist, had a long beard and dressed in flowing robes, he would have found serious difficulty in concealing his presence in Wembley. Media reports of his presence there, however, continued. They included what MI5 dismissed as 'risible' claims by both the US television channel NBC and the London *Evening Standard* that Bin Laden regularly flew in and out of London by private jet.[73]

The British intelligence community at the dawn of the new millennium was better equipped than its US ally to deal with the smaller, but still serious, potential threat to British national security from Islamist terrorism. There was no 'Wall' on the American model to inhibit cooperation between different intelligence agencies and the police; indeed, for most of the 1990s MI5 and the police cooperated more effectively against the IRA than ever before.[74] In July 2000 an MI5 operation, codenamed LARGE, with strong police support, also uncovered the first Islamist bomb factory to be detected in Britain, set up by Moinul Abedin, a Bangladeshi-born British Muslim from Sparkbrook in Birmingham. Despite Abedin's improbable claim that he had been setting up a fireworks business, he was convicted and sentenced to twenty years' imprisonment. At the time of his arrest MI5 believed that he had no Al Qaeda connection. It interpreted his bomb factory as an isolated event, rather than the first step in a larger Islamist offensive.* In reality, Operation LARGE had discovered what has since proved to be the most active centre of jihadist plots in Britain. Since the end of the twentieth century, 10 per cent of convicted terrorists in Britain have come from Sparkbrook and four neighbouring council wards in Birmingham.[75]

A year before 9/11, in the course of its counter-proliferation operations, MI5 – without realizing it at the time – succeeded in disrupting an attempt by Al Qaeda to develop biological weapons (BW). In September 2000 the Pakistani microbiologist Rauf Ahmad attended a conference in Britain on dangerous pathogens, where he sought samples from other delegates as well as help in obtaining a bioreactor and cell counter. A search of his luggage on departure from the UK revealed £13,000, which he claimed was 'to buy equipment', documents detailing his contacts (including UK companies) and a copy of his CV. The CV revealed that Ahmad had a PhD from a university in Pakistan, had attended earlier conferences in Britain in 1997 and 1999, and had published scientific papers on anthrax. After being briefed by MI5, the British companies in contact with Ahmad ended their dealings with him. His visits to Britain, however, had much greater significance than was apparent at the time. Their purpose only became clear after 9/11, from documents found by US forces in Afghanistan late in 2001. Among them was correspondence between Islamists using the pseudonyms 'Abu Mohamed' and 'Abu Ibrahim' about procurement of equipment, cultures and training for BW production. 'Abu Mohamed' was quickly identified as Bin Laden's deputy, Ayman al-Zawahiri. 'Abu Ibrahim' took longer to track down. References in the correspondence to his foreign travels, attendance at conferences in the UK and attempts to procure dangerous pathogens, however, were discovered to match exactly the information on Ahmad in MI5 files. This discovery

---

* MI5 later changed its mind. It concluded, after further investigation, that Abedin's bomb factory was inspired by Al Qaeda's global jihad ideology, though Al Qaeda had not 'tasked or directed the operation'. (Andrew, *Defence of the Realm*, pp. 806–8. Omand, 'Keeping Europe Safe', p. 84.)

confirmed fears that Bin Laden continued to regard as 'a religious duty' the acquisition of weapons of mass destruction for use against the monstrous conspiracy of 'Jews and Crusaders' which he, like Qutb, convinced himself had threatened Islam for the last thousand years.[76]

On 3 January 2000 Al Qaeda suicide bombers on board a small boat in Aden Harbour attempted to attack a US warship, the USS *The Sullivans*. Though their boat was overloaded with explosives and sank before reaching the warship, Al Qaeda learned from its mistake. On 12 October 2000 suicide bombers detonated another, more stable, explosive-filled boat sufficiently close to the guided-missile destroyer USS *Cole* in Aden Harbour to rip a large hole in its side. Seventeen members of the crew were killed and forty injured. It was later discovered that Bin Laden wrote a poem celebrating the attack, which he recited at his son's wedding.[77] 'In the aftermath of the attack', recalled DCI George Tenet later, 'it was clear that known AQ operatives were involved, but neither our intelligence nor the FBI's criminal investigation could conclusively prove that UBL [Osama bin Laden] and his leadership had had authority, direction and control over the attack.'[78] The attempt to find proof was hampered once again by 'the Wall', which hamstrung even FBI field offices. One FBI analyst wrote in frustration over the problems of accessing intelligence needed to investigate Al Qaeda's role in the attack on USS *Cole*: 'Whatever has happened to this – someday someone will die – and wall or not – the public will not understand why we were not more effective and throwing every resource we had at certain "problems".'[79] The 9/11 Commission later concluded: 'It is now clear that everyone involved was confused about the rules governing the sharing and use of information gathered in intelligence channels.'[80]

During the 2000 election campaign the Republican candidate, George W. Bush, like his Democratic rival, Al Gore, was given regular high-level briefings by the CIA on the terrorist threat. Before the briefings, Bush, like most Americans, had never heard of Al Qaeda. Struck by the vagueness of the intelligence on Al Qaeda's plans to attack US targets, Bush told his briefers: 'Well, I assume I will start seeing the good stuff when I become president.' As Tenet wrote later, though Bush did not realize it, 'he was already seeing "the good stuff".'[81] Though convinced of the importance of intelligence, Bush lacked his father's understanding of it. In April 1999, two months before George W. Bush announced his candidacy, the CIA paid an extraordinary and unprecedented tribute to his father. In the presence of former President and Barbara Bush, CIA headquarters at Langley, Virginia, were formally renamed the George [H. W.] Bush Center for Intelligence.

Despite rows behind the scenes within the Clinton administration over the lack of response to the attack on USS *Cole*, the 2000 presidential election campaign was marked by what the 9/11 Commission later called 'a notable lack of serious discussion of the al Qaeda threat or terrorism'. The campaign culminated on 7 November in one of the closest elections in US history and the narrowest of victories for Bush, confirmed six weeks later by a 5 to 4 ruling by the Supreme Court.[82]

By George W. Bush's inauguration on 20 January 2001, Tenet believed that 'something was coming – something big – but to my great frustration we could not determine exactly what, where, when, or how'.[83] 'Mounting warning signs' of a coming terrorist attack in the spring and summer of 2001 failed to answer these questions.[84] British intelligence reports also pointed to a major Al Qaeda attack on US targets, but failed to identify the attack plan. A warning to senior Whitehall officials on 22 June reported specific threats to American interests in Saudi Arabia, Bahrain, Kuwait, Jordan, Turkey, Italy and Kenya. MI5 concluded on 6 July:

> the increase in volume [of reports] is sufficient to indicate that UBL and those who share his agenda are currently well advanced in operational planning for a number of major attacks on Western interests . . . The most likely location for an attack on Western interests by UBL and those who share his agenda is in the Gulf States, or the wider Middle East.[85]

Intelligence reports during the summer of 2001, however, did not point either to a major attack in the United States or to an operation based on hijacked aircraft.[86] MI5 overestimated the strength of US counter-terrorist security. It reported two years before 9/11: 'Intelligence suggests that whilst UBL is seeking to launch an attack inside the US, he is aware that the US will provide a tough operating environment for his organisation.' The level of security at the American airports used by the suicide hijackers on 9/11 scarcely justified MI5's belief that Al Qaeda was faced with 'a tough operating environment'. In the few years before 9/11 the Federal Aviation Authority reported repeated security violations at Logan Airport, Boston, from which two of the hijacked planes took off.[87] Contrary to widespread belief, neither Logan nor the two other airports from which the hijacked planes set out (Newark International and Washington Dulles) even had CCTV at the boarding gates.[88]

At least three eyewitnesses, ignored at the time, saw several of the hijackers studying the security checkpoints at Logan well before 9/11. One of the witnesses, an American Airlines official, confronted the ringleader of the hijackers, Mohamed Atta, after watching him video and inspect one of the Logan checkpoints in May 2001. Though Atta was reported by the official to airport security, he was never questioned.* On 9/11 the watch list maintained by the Federal Aviation Administration (FAA), which was responsible for air travel security, contained only twelve names. The FBI and CIA had hundreds more that should have been added to the list. The failure to produce an expanded list was due largely to bureaucratic infighting.[89]

In the few months before 9/11, more than two dozen Islamist messages intercepted by the NSA made clear that, to quote its director, General Mike Hayden, 'something was imminent'. One intercept from a junior Al Qaeda affiliate on the eve of 9/11 announced: 'The match is about to begin.' Another of the same day declared: 'Tomorrow is zero hour.' Neither message was translated until 12 September. It was later claimed that both gave forewarning of the 9/11 attacks. In reality, like other references to imminent attack intercepted by the NSA, neither did so. It was later concluded that they probably referred to the aftermath of the assassination on 9 September of the head of the Northern Alliance in Afghanistan, Ahmad Shah Massoud.[90] As Tenet later acknowledged: 'We – the CIA, the intelligence community, investigative bodies, the government at large – missed the exact "when and where" of 9/11. We didn't have enough dots to connect and we'll always have to live with that.'[91] Some of the dots were missing because of a strategic failure to prioritize the religious motivations of the martyrdom missions which reached their climax on 9/11. Bin Laden mocked the inability of Americans to understand the religious zeal of his followers who went on 'martyrdom' missions. He told a Pakistani interviewer after 9/11: 'We love death. The U.S. loves life. That is the big difference between us.'[92]

Important clues to Al Qaeda's preparations for aircraft hijacking in the United States were also missed because of poor communication not merely between the FBI and the CIA but also between FBI headquarters and its field offices. In July 2001 an agent in the FBI Phoenix field office sent a memo to both headquarters and the international terrorism squad in the New York field office, warning of the 'possibility of a coordinated effort by Usama Bin Ladin' to train terrorists at US aviation schools. There were, he reported, an 'inordinate number of individuals of investigative interest'

---

* The eyewitness accounts surfaced in a lawsuit brought by the family of Mark Bavis, who died in one of the hijacked Boston flights. Because the case was settled in 2011 for several million dollars without going to trial, the evidence was never aired in open court. However, the Bavis lawyers later deposited the transcripts in public archives. (Paul Sperry, '9/11 terrorists caught testing airport security months before attacks', *New York Post*, 5 Oct. 2014.)

attending these schools in Arizona. FBI HQ ignored a proposal in the memo from Phoenix for it to establish liaison with aviation schools and seek authority to obtain visa information on their foreign applicants. Managers of the FBI Bin Laden and Radical Fundamentalist units did not even see his memo until after 9/11; the New York field office read it but took no action.

Had FBI HQ acted on the Phoenix memo, it would have taken more seriously a warning on 15 August from its Minneapolis field office that Zacarias Moussaoui, a French 'Islamic extremist preparing for some future act in furtherance of radical fundamentalist goals', was taking lessons at the Pan-Am International Flight Academy in Eagan, Minnesota. Though Moussaoui was arrested by the INS for overstaying his visa, Minneapolis failed to persuade FBI HQ that he was a potential suicide hijacker. In one heated exchange, a supervisor in the Minneapolis field office told an agent at HQ that he was 'trying to keep someone from taking a plane and crashing into the World Trade Center'. The headquarters agent replied that this was not going to happen and that it was not clear that Moussaoui was a terrorist.[93] Neither the FBI's Acting Director nor its Assistant Director for Counterterrorism was briefed on the Moussaoui case.* Moussaoui was later found guilty of conspiring to kill US citizens in the 9/11 attacks.

Within the US intelligence community, the 9/11 Commission later concluded:

> The September 11 attacks fell into the void between foreign and domestic threats. The foreign intelligence agencies were watching overseas, alert to foreign threats to US interests there. The domestic agencies were waiting for evidence of a domestic threat from sleeper cells within the United States. No one was looking for a foreign threat to domestic targets. The threat that was coming was not from sleeper cells. It was foreign – but from foreigners who had infiltrated into the United States.[94]

On 10 September 2001 FBI officials told a Congressional briefing that the most imminent domestic terrorism threat was from animal-rights activists.[95] Next day, Al Qaeda mounted the greatest surprise attack on the United States since Pearl Harbor. Banner headlines in the *Washington Post* proclaimed: 'Terrorists Hijack 4 Airliners; 2 Destroy World Trade

---

* Tenet was briefed on the Moussaoui case on 23 August 2001 but later told the 9/11 Commission that 'no connection to al Qaeda was apparent to him at the time. Seeing it as an FBI case, he did not discuss the matter with anyone at the White House or the FBI.' (*9/11 Commission Report*, p. 275.)

Center; 1 Hits Pentagon; 4th Crashes.' Almost 3,000 people were killed. Bush's National Security Advisor, Condoleezza Rice, wrote later:

> No security issue ever looked quite the same again, and every day our over-whelming preoccupation was to avoid another attack. The States was the most powerful country in the world – militarily and economically. And yet, we had not been able to prevent a devastating attack by a stateless network of extremists, operating from the territory of one of the world's poorest countries [Afghanistan]. Our entire concept of what constituted security had been shaken.[96]

The facile optimism of the report only five years earlier of the Presidential Commission on the Roles and Capabilities of the United States Intelligence Community had been comprehensively exposed.

The US intelligence community had no idea what was coming next. 'At CIA', wrote George Tenet, 'we had good reason to believe that more attacks might be coming in the hours or days ahead and that 9/11 was just the opening salvo of a multipronged attack on the American mainland.'[97]* For several months intelligence analysts found it difficult to distinguish serious security threats from sometimes surreal false alarms. A week after 9/11, letters containing anthrax spores began to be posted to several news media and two Democratic US Senators, infecting twenty-two people, five fatally. 'Panic', recalls George W. Bush, 'spread across the country. Millions of Americans were afraid to open their mailboxes.' Though suspicion originally fell on Saddam Hussein and Al Qaeda, one of the most complex investigations in FBI history eventually concluded that the man responsible (though never charged) was a US government scientist, who committed suicide.[98]

A month after the 'anthrax letters' began, the White House believed it was under biological-warfare attack. While in Shanghai at the Asia Pacific Economic Cooperation summit, Bush and his National Security Advisor, Condoleezza Rice (later Secretary of State), were contacted via secure video monitor by Vice-President Dick Cheney, incongruously dressed in white tie and tails before giving a speech at a fund-raising dinner. As Bush later recalled: 'As soon as I saw Dick, I could tell something was wrong. His face was as white as his tie. "Mr President", he said, "one of the bio-detectors went off at the White House. They found traces of botulinum toxin. The chances are we've all been exposed."' Cheney reported that the FBI was testing on mice suspicious substances found in the White House

---

* During the two years after 9/11, the CIA reported to Bush an average of 400 specific threats each month. (Bush, *Decision Points*, p. 153.)

which it feared contained botulinum toxin. If the mice survived the next twenty-four hours, so would the President. But, if the mice died, 'we were goners'. The mice survived. It was, the Bureau told Bush, 'a false alarm'.[99]

A week later there was another serious security alarm in Washington. George Tenet reported to Bush that, according to 'a highly reliable source', there would be an attack on either 30 or 31 October which would be even bigger than that on the World Trade Center: 'This is the worst we've seen since 9/11.' This warning too, however, turned out to be a false alarm.[100] Tenet found it 'stunning how little reliable information was immediately available inside our own borders':

> There was no good data on how many foreigners had overstayed their visas and no tracking system to see if young men who came into this country to attend university had actually shown up for classes – or if they had changed their major from music to nuclear physics . . . In the early days [after 9/11], what we did not know about what was going on in the United States haunted us. We had to make judgements based on instinct.[101]

Three years later, the report of the 9/11 Commission argued persuasively that the failure to foresee the Al Qaeda attacks was due less to specific failures of the intelligence community than to a general 'failure of imagination': 'We do not believe leaders understood the gravity of the threat. The terrorist danger from Bin Laden and al Qaeda was not a major topic for policy debate among the public, the media, or in the Congress. Indeed, it barely came up during the 2000 presidential campaign.' The 9/11 Commission, despite its merits, failed to identify the degree to which the failure of imagination was due to short-termism. Gerald Haines, a former member of the CIA History Office, had publicly complained four years before 9/11:

> Most CIA officers and decision makers, although they use historical analogies every day, are basically ahistorical. They believe they have no time or need for history. Caught up in current crisis management and day-to-day intelligence producing activities, they fail to appreciate history's value not only as a preserver of the 'Agency's memory' (what did it do in the past, how did it react?), but as an important training mechanism, and as a tool in the overall policy making process.[102]

Those with the best understanding of the Islamist terrorist threat before 9/11, Bruce Hoffman chief among them, were those with a long-term historical perspective.

Those who do not learn from past mistakes, it has been said, are doomed to repeat them. Failure to learn from the greatest twentieth-century US intelligence failure at Pearl Harbor sixty years earlier contributed to the intelligence failure on 9/11. The 'complete surprise' of both Roosevelt and Churchill on 7 December 1941 showed how badly they had underestimated the enemy. It did not occur to either the President or the Prime Minister that the Japanese could launch such a sophisticated surprise attack on Pearl Harbor.[103] Bin Laden and Al Qaeda were similarly underestimated before 9/11, though for less racist reasons. Religious fanatics were not thought capable of such complex, secret operational planning.

The opening paragraph of the President's Daily Brief on 6 August 2001, the first PDB to raise the possibility of an Al Qaeda attack inside the United States, warned: 'Bin Ladin implied in US television interviews in 1997 and 1998 that his followers would follow the example of the World Trade Center bomber Ramzi Yousef and "bring the fighting to America".'[104] But, despite the fact that Yousef had a British degree in electrical engineering and had devised a bomb which blew a hole through seven floors of one of the Trade Center towers in 1993, the possibility that Al Qaeda was currently devising a larger-scale terrorist attack on the twin towers was not considered. Yousef had also devised a plot in 1994, financed by his uncle, Khalid Sheikh Mohammed, to place bombs on board twelve trans-Pacific airliners and explode them simultaneously in mid-flight. In a trial run in December 1994, a few weeks before his arrest for the attack on the Trade Center, Yousef planted a bomb on an airliner which killed a Japanese passenger, wounded others and blew a hole in the cabin floor – though the fuselage, remarkably, remained intact.[105] The possibility that Al Qaeda was considering using a number of commercial airliners in an attack on the United States in 2001 was also not seriously considered.

'On 9/11', wrote Bush later, 'it was obvious the intelligence community had missed something big. I was alarmed by the lapse . . .'[106] Though rightly critical in private of the lack of intelligence warning, Bush himself, despite many briefings, had only a limited grasp of the nature of Islamist terrorism. Five days after 9/11, the President vividly displayed his own 'failure of imagination' by publicly describing the war on terrorism as a 'crusade', apparently unaware that the crusades were widely regarded by Muslims as an act of aggression by Western imperialism and that, only a year earlier, Pope John Paul II had apologized for them.[107]*

In preparing the 9/11 attacks, the leadership of Al Qaeda showed greater imagination and more effective management skills than American counter-terrorist bureaucracy. It did not make Washington's mistake of underestimating its opponent. The 9/11 Commission later reported: 'What we can say with confidence is that none of the measures adopted by the

---

* Bush repeated the word 'crusade' in a speech to US troops in February 2002.

U.S. government from 1998 to 2001 disturbed or even delayed the progress of the al Qaeda plot. Across the government, there were failures of imagination, policy, capabilities, and management.'[108] Underlying these failures was what I have called 'Historical Attention-Span Deficit Disorder' (HASDD) – the lack of the long-term perspective without which it was impossible to understand adequately the threat from Islamist terrorism.

Conclusion: Twenty-First-Century Intelligence in Long-Term Perspective

Intelligence used to be, as David Dilks and I complained in 1984, the 'Missing Dimension' of most political and international-relations history. 'Academic historians', we wrote, 'have frequently tended either to ignore intelligence altogether, or to treat it as of little importance.'[1]* Successive British governments, both Conservative and Labour, welcomed historians' neglect, discouraging research on the 'missing dimension' by keeping secret all past records of the intelligence services and refusing to set a date for the release of even their earliest files.† The wartime intelligence officer Malcolm Muggeridge derived from his years in SIS the lesson that 'Secrecy is as essential to intelligence as vestments to a Mass, or darkness to a spiritualist séance, and must at all costs be maintained, quite irrespective of whether or not it serves any purpose.'[2] Sir Michael Howard, one of the official historians of wartime intelligence, wrote in 1985: 'So far as official government policy is concerned, the British security and intelligence services do not exist. Enemy agents are found under gooseberry bushes and intelligence is brought by the storks.'[3]

Though Britain and the United States were intelligence allies, there was an extraordinary contrast in the visibility of their intelligence communities. During the US 'Year of Intelligence' in 1975, the CIA had been subjected to what the DCI, William Colby, called 'the closest and harshest public scrutiny that any such service has ever experienced not only in this

---

* Intelligence had first been described as the 'missing dimension' by Sir Alexander Cadogan, PUS at the Foreign Office from 1938 to 1946.

† The government had, however, declassified many intelligence reports received by Whitehall ministries and commanders in the field during (but not before or after) the Second World War. My *Secret Service: The Making of the British Intelligence Community*, published in 1985, was made possible by tracking down intelligence-related documents which had slipped through the net of official censorship. A document removed from, say, a Foreign Office file in the National Archives might sometimes be found in a Treasury file (or vice-versa). A substantial number of private papers in a variety of archives also contained intelligence documents which Whitehall would never willingly have allowed out.

country but anywhere in the world'.[4] In Britain, even the existence of SIS was not officially acknowledged until 1992. The emergence in the rest of the 'Five Eyes' of more rational levels of public visibility for their intelligence agencies, combined with the establishment of varying systems of external accountability absent in Britain, helped to bring about the late-twentieth-century demise of the UK storks-and-gooseberry-bush tradition, the last major taboo in British politics.*

The main aims of *The Secret World*, set out in the Introduction, are 'to recover some of the lost history of global intelligence over the last three millennia, to show how it modifies current historiography, and to demonstrate its continuing relevance to intelligence in the twenty-first century'.[5]

The most recent of the world's most successful intelligence agencies, the Israeli Mossad and Shin Beth, founded in 1949, have very long-term perspectives. Both agencies derive their mission statements from the Hebrew Bible.[6] The current Israeli Prime Minister, Benjamin Netanyahu, insists on the need for Israeli intelligence to use 'both ancient and modern methods', and claims that 'Mossad does just that in the most outstanding way.' One of Mossad's distinguishing characteristics is its use of 'targeted killings' (assassinations), whose ideological justification is founded on the admonition in the Talmud: 'If someone comes to kill you, rise up and kill him first.' A majority of the many Israeli intelligence officers, officials and policymakers interviewed by Dr Ronen Bergman for his path-breaking history, *Rise and Kill First*, cited the Talmud as justification for targeted killings.[7] Even before the founding of the state of Israel, two paramilitary Zionist groups – Irgun Zvai Leumi, led by the future Israeli Prime Minister Menachem Begin, and the Stern Gang (also known as Lehi) – used targeted killing in an attempt to accelerate the end of the British mandate in Palestine. In 1947 the Stern Gang narrowly failed to blow up the Colonial Office in London. Plans for the assassination of the Foreign Secretary, Ernest Bevin, and other British ministers came less close to success, despite a letter bomb campaign.[8] The crucial decision to make 'targeted killing' secret state policy was taken by Israel's 'founding father' and first Prime Minister, David Ben-Gurion. Before independence in 1948, Ben-Gurion had opposed its use by paramilitary groups. Once the full extent of the Holocaust became known, however, he changed his mind. Ever since, writes Ronen Bergman, 'This instinct to take every measure, even the most

---

* The first major step in abandoning the traditional intelligence taboo was the Security Service Act of 1989, which, eighty years after MI5's foundation, at last placed it on a statutory footing. (Andrew, *Defence of the Realm*, section E, ch. 11.)

Mossad logo with its motto from Proverbs 11:14: 'Where no counsel is, the people fall, but in the multitude of counsellors there is safety.'

aggressive, to defend the Jewish people [has been] hardwired into Israel's DNA.' He estimates that Israel has carried out some 2,700 'targeted killing operations' – more than any other country in the Western world.[9]

Assassination has remained undeclared Israeli state policy ever since independence because of a series of operational successes. After the massacre of eleven Israeli athletes at the 1972 Munich Olympics, targeted killings were at least partly responsible for the decision by Yasser Arafat, leader of the Palestine Liberation Organization (PLO) to cease Black September terror operations in Europe. Before Munich, Golda Meir, the Israeli Prime Minister from 1969 to 1974, had prohibited targeted killing in Europe. After the massacre, she lifted the prohibition. In 1978 Mossad succeeded in assassinating Wadi Haddad, who was both head of foreign operations in the Popular Front for the Liberation of Palestine (PFLP) and a KGB agent codenamed NATSIONALIST, by poisoning his toothpaste. Haddad had devised a strategy of aircraft hijacking and terrorist attacks on 'Zionist' targets in Europe which made front-page news across the world.[10] More recently, targeted killing almost certainly helped to slow down the Iranian nuclear programme – a major potential threat to Israeli security. Some apparent operational successes, however, were counterproductive – among them the shooting in Tunis in 1988 of Arafat's charismatic chief lieutenant, Abu Jihad. Some Israeli officials now believe that Abu Jihad might have made a far more effective contribution than Arafat to the peace process.[11] The recent revelation of the scale of targeted killings has also confronted the Israeli public with the legal and moral dilemma of what Bergman calls 'two sets of laws: one for the ordinary citizens, all of us, in which murder is the most severe crime possible; and the other one, usually unwritten but very effective, for the intelligence community and the security establishment, that permits the use of aggressive measures in order to protect the country'.[12]

Thanks to recent official and unofficial disclosure of classified files, such as those which made possible Bergman's revelations on Israeli targeted killing, more reliable source material is now available on the unprecedentedly numerous intelligence operations of the twentieth century than on those of any previous century. Since the 1990s a growing number of declassified British intelligence files up to varying dates in the Cold War have become available in the National Archives – though on a smaller scale than in the United States.* Even the traditionally tightly guarded KGB archives have suffered a major haemorrhage.[13]

Research on these intelligence records has begun (though only begun) to revise historical understanding of twentieth-century politics and international relations in important ways. The declassification in 2010 of the post-war UKUSA agreement,[14] not mentioned in most twentieth-century histories of British–American relations, marked a turning point in the release of SIGINT records. Never before had two countries publicly revealed an agreement:

> to the exchange of the products of the following operations relating to foreign communications:
>
> • Collection of traffic
> • Acquisition of communications documents and equipment
> • Traffic analysis
> • Cryptanalysis
> • Decryption and translation
> • Acquisition of information regarding communications organizations, practices, procedures and equipment.[15]

The great majority of twentieth-century histories of peacetime international relations omitted all reference to these secret activities – despite the fact that, as previous chapters have shown, instances of bilateral collaboration

---

* There is great variation in the accessibility of the records of UK intelligence agencies and related official bodies. Though the British agencies have complete exemption from the requirements of the Freedom of Information Act (FOIA), MI5 declassifies many of its files (sometimes with redactions) after fifty years. SIS, by contrast, releases none of its files, though some SIS documents are to be found in declassified MI5 and other files. At the time of writing a majority of JIC minutes and memoranda are available until 1968.

between Western states in 'cryptanalysis, decryption and translation' go back to the sixteenth century.[16] SIGINT is no longer entirely absent from the history of international relations. The UKUSA declassification has led to growing recognition of its role at the centre of the 'Special Relationship' and the Five Eyes SIGINT alliance. The publication in 2019 of GCHQ's first officially 'authorized' history, together with its undertaking to give 'as many source documents from the history as we can to the National Archives',[17] will accelerate this process.

Recently declassified files on the two decades after the Second World War are also providing a new perspective on one of the most important turning points in British history – the end of the world's greatest overseas empire. Until recently, even the best histories of British decolonization made little or no reference to the role of intelligence,[18] despite the fact that, until the late 1960s, the Security Service (MI5) was responsible for intelligence in the Empire and Commonwealth as well as in Britain. New recruits to MI5 in the early Cold War could expect to spend a quarter to a third of their careers on overseas postings. For many of them, at a time when opportunities for foreign travel were more restricted than they are today, this was one of the attractions of joining MI5. One secretary recalls that, when offered a two-year posting in Colombo, 'I could hardly believe my luck.'[19]

MI5 files show that a number of former British colonies secretly agreed that its Security Liaison Officer (SLO) should stay on after independence. Among them was the government of Jawaharlal Nehru – a fact unknown until recently to Nehru's biographers.[20] For almost a quarter of a century, relations between MI5 and its Indian counterpart, the Delhi Intelligence Branch (IB or DIB), were closer and more confident than those between any other departments of the British and Indian governments.[21] Intelligence relations between Britain and independent Kenya remained so close that in 1967 an MI5 officer was appointed as both head of the research desk and Secretary of the newly-founded Kenyan National Security Executive, which reported directly to Kenyatta. The Nairobi SLO reported to London in 1968 that the officer had acquired an access to the Kenyan Special Branch and its files 'which is almost unique in Africa in this day and age'.[22]*

Further historical research on intelligence operations in Britain's remaining colonies and its intelligence liaisons with ex-colonies, which played a major role in the UKUSA SIGINT alliance, will require further

---

* At the end of the 1960s, SIS took over most of MI5's intelligence responsibilities in the Commonwealth and what remained of the Empire. The continued closure of all SIS files prevents archival research on British–Kenyan intelligence relations after the withdrawal of the SLOs.

declassification. The intelligence historian Calder Walton calls SIGINT 'the greatest secret of British decolonisation'.[23] Much of the secret remains intact. The vast majority of GCHQ and NSA files on their combined global Cold War operations are still classified. There is persuasive evidence, however, that their SIGINT operations in Hong Kong helped to reveal China's preparations for the explosion of its first nuclear weapon in 1964.[24]

Early in the twenty-first century, intelligence became headline news on both sides of the Atlantic. The headlines, however, derived not from historical revelations about UKUSA and the end of empire but from current intelligence controversies – in particular those generated by the 9/11 terrorist attacks in 2001[25] and the outbreak of the Iraq War two years later. Despite being almost 600 pages long, the *9/11 Commission Report*,[26] published in 2004, became one of the best-selling official reports in US history. The mistaken belief by US and British intelligence at the beginning of the Iraq War in 2003 that Saddam Hussein was constructing weapons of mass destruction (WMD) has become the most extensively studied intelligence failure since Pearl Harbor.

In February 2001, soon after George W. Bush became President, DCI George Tenet told Congress: 'Our most serious concern with Saddam Hussein must be the likelihood that he will seek a renewed WMD capability both for credibility and because every other strong power in the region either has it or is pursuing it.'[27] The British Joint Intelligence Committee (JIC) reported a year later: 'Although there is very little intelligence we continue to judge that Iraq is pursuing a nuclear weapons programme. We assess the programme to be based on gas centrifuge uranium enrichment . . . '[28] The fact that there was indeed 'very little intelligence' on Saddam's supposed nuclear-weapons programme should have rung alarm bells. But the high quality of SIS intelligence both on Gaddafi's WMD programmes and on the network run by the former head of the Pakistani nuclear project, Dr A. Q. Khan, which secretly supplied nuclear material to Iran, Libya and North Korea, seems to have given both the JIC and the Prime Minister, Tony Blair, exaggerated confidence in much weaker SIS intelligence on Iraqi WMD.* SIS had accurate, detailed intelligence

---

* The 2004 *Review of Intelligence on Weapons of Mass Destruction* (Butler Report) praised the success of SIS WMD intelligence operations against Libya and the A. Q. Khan network, concluding that 'it would be premature to reach conclusions about Iraq's prohibited weapons [WMD]. Much potential evidence may have been destroyed in the looting and disorder that followed the cessation of hostilities. Other material may be hidden in the sand, including stocks of agent or weapons. We believe that it would be a rash person who asserted at this stage that evidence of Iraqi possession of stocks of biological or chemical agents, or even of banned missiles, does not exist or will never be found' (para 474).

on the location of twenty-seven Libyan WMD sites. Following the over-throw of Saddam Hussein, Gaddafi invited a high-level SIS team to Libya to begin negotiations which led to their removal. An SIS combined opera-tion with German and Italian intelligence intercepted a German-registered ship carrying centrifuge parts from the A. Q. Khan network to Libya, thus providing incontrovertible evidence of Gaddafi's nuclear-weapons programme.[29]

By contrast, US and British pre-war intelligence on Saddam's supposed WMD proved to be disastrously mistaken. As Blair later acknowledged: 'The stated purpose of the conflict was to enforce UN resolutions on Saddam's WMD, and we found no WMD after taking control of the country. We thought there was an active WMD programme and there wasn't. The aftermath, following Saddam's removal in May 2003, was bloody, destructive and chaotic.'[30] The 2016 report of the official Inquiry on UK policy in Iraq from 2001 to 2009 (better known as the Chilcot Report), which included intelligence as a major theme, took seven years to complete and is 2.6 million words long.[31] It is probably the longest historical monograph in British history.

The Secret World differs from the Chilcot Report in its emphasis on the long term.[32] Common to the intelligence failures of both 9/11 and the Iraq War was serious neglect of past experience. As the previous chapter argued, before 9/11 there was a chronic lack of long-term perspective on the terrorist threat posed by religious extremism.[33] Sir Mark Allen, the leading Arabist in SIS, concluded after 9/11: 'We were just looking the wrong way . . . the failure to appreciate the significance of radical Islam since the Second World War was largely a consequence of our mindset that Arab nationalism was the key issue.'[34] The largely forgotten *Arab Bulletins* of 1916–19, possibly the best-written intelligence reports in Brit-ish history as well as the first to pay detailed attention to Arab nationalism, had taken a far longer view, emphasizing the importance of 'recording and so preserving all fresh historical data concerning Arabs and Arabic-speaking lands', as well as 'rescuing from oblivion any older facts which might help to explain the actual situation'.[35]

The attempt by the Chilcot Report in 2016 'to identify lessons for the future' from the Iraq War, despite its scrupulous examination of detailed evidence, was compromised by the report's lack of both comparative and long-term perspective. British and US belief in non-existent Iraqi WMD was part of a much larger, international intelligence failure which Chilcot does not consider. Even the intelligence services of the main powers opposed to the war – Germany, France, Russia and China chief among them – believed, like those of the United States and Britain, that Saddam *was* pursuing an active WMD programme.[36] The Chilcot Report lacks historical as well as comparative perspective. Though it goes into immense detail on the Blair government, it makes no attempt to compare his use of intelligence with that of any of his predecessors – a narrower approach than that adopted by the best previous studies of Blair's foreign, defence and domestic policy.[37]

The biggest gap in the biographies of many prime ministers continues to be their use of intelligence.[38] John Bew's rightly praised recent biography of Britain's most successful Labour Prime Minister, Clement Attlee, is a case in point.[39] Bew gives no hint that Attlee, at his own request, had far more private meetings with the Director-General of MI5 than any other twentieth-century Prime Minister (Blair included).[40] Few if any twentieth-century prime ministers were as well informed about their predecessor's handling of intelligence as Attlee was about Churchill's.[41] Harold Wilson, though he had been in Attlee's Cabinet, probably did not discover the wartime ULTRA secret until he became the next Labour Prime Minister in 1964. Most of his ministers had little experience of intelligence. The Lord Chancellor in Wilson's government, Lord Gardiner, was so suspicious of the Security Service that, unlike Attlee, he 'thought it more likely than not that MI5 was bugging the telephones in my office'. When he had confidential business to discuss with the Attorney General, Sir (later Lord) Elwyn Jones, Gardiner asked his chauffeur to drive them round, confident that 'she would never have allowed the car to be bugged without my knowledge'.* No subsequent Prime Minister replicated Wilson's (or Gardiner's) conspiracy theories. Relations between successive prime ministers and intelligence chiefs, however, have fluctuated greatly. The close links forged by Blair with Sir Richard Dearlove during his second term at Number 10, which were not limited to the Iraq War, were in striking contrast to Wilson's suspicions of his intelligence agencies.†

Before and during the Iraq War, little thought was given in London or Washington to the relevance of long-term intelligence experience to current policy. An SIS officer who gave evidence to the Chilcot Inquiry recalled that pre-war intelligence 'requirements were narrowly focused on the

---

* The Lord Chancellor was remarkably naïve as well as unnecessarily suspicious. Had MI5 broken the law and bugged Gardiner's car (which it did not), it is scarcely likely that the chauffeur would have seen them do it. (Andrew, *Defence of the Realm*, pp. 525–6.)
† Though the heads of the intelligence agencies have the right of access to the Prime Minister, ministerial responsibility for SIS and GCHQ is vested in the Foreign Secretary and that for MI5 in the Home Secretary.

operational needs of Government, the build-up to war, [with] heavy emphasis from early 2002 on Iraqi WMD': 'If we had ventilated views on Iraq's political geography and the impact of its history on its today, people would have told us to shut up.'*

The war was preceded, however, by an unprecedented American attempt to replicate perhaps the greatest public success of US Cold War intelligence. The most dramatic attempt on either side of the Atlantic to convince a global audience that Saddam had an active WMD programme was a presentation by the US Secretary of State, Colin Powell, at the Security Council on 5 February 2003. Powell and the George W. Bush administration were strongly influenced by the sensational precedent set by the US representative on the Security Council during the 1962 missile crisis, Adlai Stevenson, who had displayed hitherto top-secret U-2 imagery in public to prove that the Soviet Union was constructing missile sites on Cuba.[42] Just over forty years later, Powell displayed a much wider range of intelligence as proof that 'Saddam Hussein and his regime are concealing their efforts to produce more weapons of mass destruction':

> Some of the sources are technical, such as intercepted telephone conversations and photos taken by satellites. Other sources are people who have risked their lives to let the world know what Saddam Hussein is really up to.
>
> . . . One of the most worrisome things that emerges from the thick intelligence file we have on Iraq's biological weapons is the existence of mobile production facilities used to make biological agents.
>
> Let me take you inside that intelligence file and share with you what we know from eyewitness accounts. We have first-hand descriptions of biological weapons factories on wheels and on rails . . . In a matter of months, they can produce a quantity of biological poison equal to the entire amount that Iraq claimed to have produced in the years prior to the Gulf War.

Powell then displayed diagrams of (non-existent) mobile biological-weapons factories, and confidently announced that the United States also had 'more than a decade of proof that [Saddam] remains determined to acquire nuclear weapons'.[43]

* Redacted evidence of an SIS officer identified only as 'SIS4'. SIS4 accepted that 'in some ways' it was appropriate for SIS reports on Iraq not to deal with 'the impact of its history' since that was not what its customers wanted. The fact remains, however, that all reports on current Iraq made more sense in a historical context. (http://www.iraqinquiry.org.uk/media/98149/XXXX-XX-XX-Transcript-SIS4-part-2-declassified.pdf.)

At the time, the National Security Advisor, Condoleeza Rice, later to succeed Powell as Secretary of State, considered his presentation 'a tour de force'.[44] So did most of the Bush administration. As Powell ruefully recalls: 'Everyone remembers my UN presentation. It had enormous impact in this country and worldwide. It convinced many people that we were on the right course.'[45] Powell seemed to have repeated Adlai Stevenson's triumph at the Security Council during the Cuban Missile Crisis. But whereas Stevenson's intelligence was wholly correct, Powell's, like a British JIC report on 'Iraq's Weapons of Mass Destruction' published on Blair's initiative in September 2002, was woefully inaccurate.* Powell's 'first-hand' evidence of Iraqi biological-weapons factories was based largely on bogus intelligence from a German source codenamed CUR-VEBALL, who later admitted inventing it. The Chilcot Report noted the similarity between some of CURVEBALL's intelligence and *The Rock*, a 1996 Hollywood thriller starring Sean Connery and Nicolas Cage.[46]†

The intelligence failure over Iraqi WMD has generated a literature many times the size of this book, some of which makes ill-founded claims of intelligence 'politicization'.[47]‡ The most basic intelligence failure in 2002–3 was failure to challenge the assumption that Saddam *did* have WMD. A CIA (now NSA) historian, Michael Warner, wrote later that, over the previous few years, 'Few in Washington or London noticed . . . that the underlying hypothesis that Saddam possessed weapons of mass destruction had hardened into a non-falsifiable certainty.'[48] The Senate Select Committee on Intelligence reported in 2004: 'This "group think" led intelligence community analysts, collectors and managers both to interpret ambiguous evidence as conclusively indicative of a WMD programme and to ignore or minimise evidence that Iraq did not have active and expanding weapons of mass destruction programmes.'[49] In 2005 a report by the President's WMD Commission pointed to a basic failing in intelligence collection. US and British intelligence 'could have instructed

---

* When no WMD were discovered during or after the Iraq War, Powell's triumph turned into humiliation. It was almost a decade before he could bring himself to write an account of a day that still remains 'burned in my memory'. He wrote afterwards: 'I'll probably never write another.' (Powell, *It Worked for Me*, loc. 2610, 2701.)

† By contrast with CURVEBALL, the major UK/US agent before the Cuban Missile Crisis, Oleg Penkovsky, had both provided highly classified documentary intelligence and been questioned by SIS as well as CIA officers. See above, p. 683.

‡ The Senate Select Committee on Intelligence (SSCI) 'did not find any evidence that Administration officials attempted to coerce, influence or pressure analysts to change their judgments related to Iraq's Weapons of Mass destruction Capabilities'. (*Report of the Senate Select Committee on Intelligence on the U.S. Intelligence Community's Prewar Intelligence Assessments on Iraq*, 9 July 2004 (SSCI Iraq Report, 2004), p. 286.)

their agents to look for and report not only what sources were claiming they knew about WMD activities but also cases in which people who might have known about them if they were occurring in fact saw nothing.' But they did not do so: 'Failing to conclude that Saddam had ended his banned weapons programs is one thing – not even considering it as a possibility is another.'[50]

The errors in tasking agents derived, at least in part, from historical amnesia. When British intelligence received reports of new German weapons during the Second World War, it was well aware of the danger of sending messages to agents which they might interpret as a request to confirm the weapons' existence. Instead, agents were asked for reports on enemy weapons programmes which did not specify what it was thought the Germans might be developing. Sixty years later, the CIA failed to exercise similar caution when seeking agent intelligence on Iraqi WMD.[51*]

Even after Saddam's regime had been overthrown and no WMD discovered, the leaders of the US intelligence community gave little thought to what they might learn about their misjudgement by interrogating Saddam himself if he were captured. Over half a century previously, their predecessors had been far better prepared for the post-Second World War interrogation of the senior surviving Nazis – chief among them Hermann Göring, who, like Saddam, was a war criminal as well as Germany's highest-ranking political and military leader after Hitler's suicide. Three days after the German surrender in May 1945, Göring was interrogated by his air force opposite number, General Carl Spaatz, supreme commander of all US air forces in the European theatre, assisted by the air force historian Bruce Hopper, who was deeply aware of the historical significance of the interrogation and had prepared a series of questions. A few days later, a second lengthy interrogation began, conducted by the Interrogation Detachment of US military intelligence, using questions prepared by both Spaatz's intelligence staff and the British Air Ministry. Throughout the interrogations, Göring's questioners had the dual aim of compiling an important historical record, which the Foreign Office

---

* The last British operation (codenamed EPSILON) to collect intelligence on Nazi WMD followed the capture at the end of the war of ten German scientists who were believed to have been involved in an attempt to develop nuclear weapons. Conscious that, if questioned directly, the scientists (at least two of whom were Nazi Party members) might conceal what they knew for fear of admitting personal responsibility, British military intelligence interned them in the agreeable surroundings of a Cambridgeshire country house at Farm Hall, Godmanchester, and monitored their private conversations through an elaborate network of listening devices. Their surprised response to the news of Hiroshima on 6 August and other discussions made clear that there had been little progress towards making a German atomic bomb. (Bernstein, *Hitler's Uranium Club*.)

believed 'instructive for the future', as well as collecting evidence for the Nuremberg war crimes trials. On the errors of Nazi diplomacy Göring was remarkably frank. The whole war, he admitted, 'had been strewn with diplomatic failures and mistakes – Italy, Romania, Spain, everywhere'.[52]*

Preparations for the interrogation of Saddam in 2003 did not compare with those for Göring in 1945.† In 2003 there was a widespread but ill-founded assumption that, instead of hiding from US and UK forces, Saddam would either be killed in the invasion or kill himself. When a dishevelled Saddam, looking (as the *New York Daily News* put it) like a 'bearded bum', was found hiding in an underground hole near his former hometown of Tikrit in December 2003, there was not even a contingency plan for how to begin questioning him. No Arabic-speaking interrogator was available. A non-Arabic-speaking CIA analyst stationed in Iraq, John Nixon, who was put in charge of interrogating Saddam with the help of an interpreter a few days later, reported that basic mistakes had already been made: 'Almost anyone with experience in questioning prisoners will tell you that the first twenty-four to forty-eight hours are crucial. That's when the shock of capture is freshest and when the altered nature of a prisoner's surroundings and his new status as a detainee can lead him to divulge valuable information.'[53] By the time Saddam met Nixon, he no longer resembled a 'bearded bum'. His hair had been cut, his moustache trimmed and an unkempt beard shaved off. Saddam had recovered from the shock of capture and visibly regained much of his self-confidence. When asked about his WMD programme, he replied scornfully: 'You found me. Why don't you go find these weapons of mass destruction?'[54]

The interrogation quickly revealed, in Nixon's view, Washington's 'poor grasp of how Saddam looked at the world'. Despite Saddam's personal charisma and native cunning, Nixon found him poorly educated, with a confused grasp of international relations[55] and 'a primitive understanding of military affairs'.[56] In February 2004, two months after Saddam's capture, an Arab-speaking interrogator was at last found to succeed the non-Arab-speaking Nixon: FBI Special Agent George Piro.

---

* The records of these interrogations remain a more important historical source than those of Saddam. At Nuremberg Göring was convicted of war crimes and crimes against humanity but committed suicide by taking cyanide the night before he was due to be hanged.

† As far back as 1245–6, preparations for interrogation by the Dominican inquisition in the Lauragais region south-west of Toulouse were also arguably superior to those for the interrogation of Saddam in 2003. See above, p. 102.

As Nixon acknowledged, Saddam took an 'instant liking' to Piro,* who shrewdly (if misleadingly) gave the impression of reporting directly to President Bush. Like Nixon, Piro was left with a strong impression of 'just how little we knew about Saddam and how little he knew about us'.[57] Washington would have been less surprised to discover how little it understood Saddam if it had taken more account of past problems in understanding the mindsets of autocrats with strongly held beliefs which defied conventional logic. Probably no Western analyst or policymaker at the outbreak of the Second World War had understood Stalin's mindset well enough to realize that he gave higher priority to the assassination of the great heretic Leon Trotsky (who posed no realistic threat to Moscow from his Mexican refuge well over 6,000 miles away) than to intelligence on Adolf Hitler, who posed the greatest threat to Russia since the Emperor Napoleon. None could grasp either in the middle of the war that Hitler was so obsessed with achieving the Final Solution that he was prepared to divert resources which were desperately needed on the Eastern Front to the mass killing of Jews.[58]

As DCI from 1991 to 1993, Robert Gates, the first History PhD to head the CIA (later a long-serving Defense Secretary), displayed on his desk the maxim: 'As a general rule, the best way to achieve complete strategic surprise is to commit an act that makes no sense or is even self-destructive.' There will always be statesmen and generals who achieve surprise by these simple but effective methods.[59] Among them was the self-destructive Saddam Hussein. If Saddam had been willing to provide proof that he had no WMD, he would have avoided disastrous military defeat and the overthrow of his regime in 2003, followed three years later by his own execution for crimes against humanity. But Saddam effectively admitted to Nixon early in the interrogation that, before the US-led invasion, he 'could not comprehend the immensity of the approaching storm'. He had convinced himself that the Americans would 'possibly get bogged down or be persuaded to stop by the international community that wished to see the violence and killing stopped . . . Or the United Nations would step in and enforce a cease-fire.'[60]

During Piro's interrogation of Saddam, he collaborated with the 'Iraqi Perspectives Project', begun by the U.S. Joint Forces Command (USJF-COM) in April 2003 after the fall of Baghdad in an attempt to discover

---

* The CIA lawyer who informed Nixon that Piro was to replace him as Saddam's interrogator explained that 'the FBI . . . would try to build a criminal case against Saddam based on his alleged links to international terrorism and to crimes committed against the United States'. (Nixon, *Debriefing the President*, pp. 69, 156.)

the inner workings of the Iraqi regime. Over the next two years the Project interviewed dozens of captured senior Iraqi officers and political leaders, as well as examining hundreds of thousands of official documents from all levels of the regime. The declassified version of its report, published in 2006, was appropriately entitled 'Saddam's Delusions'.[61] On 6 April 2003, only twenty-four hours before US forces entered Baghdad, the Iraqi Defence Ministry told its troops: 'We are doing great!', and reminded staff officers to 'avoid exaggerating the enemy's abilities'. Saddam's spokesman and Information Minister, Muhammad Said Al-Sahaf (nicknamed 'Comical Ali'* in Britain and 'Baghdad Bob' in the US), became a figure of fun in Western media. During his last press conference, on 8 April, with American tanks only a few hundred metres away, he announced that US forces were about to surrender. The 'Iraqi Perspectives Project' concluded, however, that 'the evidence now clearly shows that Saddam and those around him believed virtually every word issued by their own propaganda machine'.[62] Saddam's inability to face up to the inevitability of defeat was due both to his own extraordinary capacity for self-delusion and to the fear which prevented less delusional subordinates 'telling truth to power' – both common to many previous autocrats who, like Saddam, had surrounded themselves with sycophants.

After four months' questioning, Saddam Hussein at last gave Piro a credible explanation of why he had been so reluctant to provide proof to UN weapon inspectors that he had no WMD programme. Western governments and their intelligence agencies had failed to realize that he was more fearful of attack by Iran than by the United States:

> Hussein stated he was more concerned about Iran discovering Iraq's weaknesses and vulnerabilities than the repercussions of the United States for his refusal to allow UN inspectors back into Iraq. In his opinion the UN inspectors would have directly identified to the Iranians where to inflict maximum damage on Iraq.[63]

Nixon had already found Saddam unable to 'hide his hatred of the Iranians. Sometimes he became unhinged just talking about them.'[64]† Washington's previous inability to grasp that Saddam might see Iran as a greater threat than the United States was striking evidence of its sometimes parochial world view.

---

* A variant of the nickname 'Chemical Ali' given to Saddam's cousin Ali Hassan al-Majid, after his earlier use of chemical weapons against Kurdish civilians in 1987.
† Saddam feared that Tehran would seek revenge for the eight-year Iraqi–Iranian war, for which he was responsible in the 1980s.

Most analysts at the outbreak of the Iraq War had seen their main problem as one of intelligence collection – the search for the elusive evidence of Saddam's WMD programme, which they were sure was to be discovered somewhere in Iraq. Long-term perspective would have suggested a different priority. A major study by Dick Heuer Jr of the CIA Center for the Study of Intelligence, *Psychology of Intelligence Analysis*, concluded: 'Major intelligence failures are usually caused by failures of analysis, not failures of collection. Relevant information is discounted, misinterpreted, ignored, rejected, or overlooked because it fails to fit a prevailing mental model or mind-set.'[65] The mind-set which did most to distort analysis before the Iraq War was 'mirror-imaging' – the belief that Saddam would act in what Washington believed to be in his best interest. Heuer argued controversially that, as in its assessment of Saddam, 'The US perspective on what is in another country's national interest is usually irrelevant in intelligence analysis.'[66] In 2008 the CIA made his *Psychology of Intelligence Analysis* publicly available. Heuer was one of the most outstanding analysts of the CIA's first seventy years.[*]

That intelligence continues to generate headline news has been due not merely to the prolonged official enquiries into 9/11 and the Iraq War but also to unprecedented amounts of classified material leaked by 'whistleblowers'. In 2010 the WikiLeaks website, founded by Julian Assange, began publishing online documents downloaded from State Department and military databases by US Army Private Bradley (now Chelsea) Manning.[†] The 251,287 confidential documents passed by Manning to WikiLeaks were by far the largest number ever leaked by a whistleblower.[67] When Mike Pompeo became the CIA's director early in 2017, he denounced WikiLeaks as 'a non-state hostile intelligence service'.[68]

Like much other reporting on twenty-first-century intelligence, the enormous global publicity given to WikiLeaks has been mostly devoid of historical perspective. Publication of sensitive American diplomatic documents began, on a far more modest scale, almost one and a half centuries

---

[*] The introduction to *Psychology of Intelligence Analysis* by Jack Davis (a veteran of the Directorate of Intelligence, the National Intelligence Council and the CIA Office of Training) rates Heuer as one of the four, along with Sherman Kent, Robert Gates and Douglas MacEachin, leading 'contributors to the quality of analysis' in the CIA: 'Dick Heuer was – and is – much less well known within the CIA than Kent, Gates and MacEachin. He has not received the wide acclaim that Kent enjoyed as the father of professional analysis, and he has lacked the bureaucratic powers that Gates and MacEachin could wield as DDIs. But his impact on the quality of Agency analysis arguably has been at least as important as theirs.'
[†] In 2013 Manning was sentenced to thirty-five years' imprisonment but released in 2017 after her sentence was commuted by President Obama.

before WikiLeaks – not by the press but by the US government. In the later nineteenth century some American ambassadors became reluctant to send despatches to Washington which criticized their host governments for fear that the State Department would make them public.[69] Some of the diplomatic despatches published by WikiLeaks were quite similar to those released by the State Department over a century earlier. One of the best-publicized documents during Tunisia's 'Jasmine Revolution', which overthrew the corrupt authoritarian regime of President Ben Ali at the beginning of the Arab Spring in January 2012, was a report to Washington by the US ambassador to Tunisia, Robert Godec, in July 2009, published by WikiLeaks:

> Whether it's cash, services, land, property, or yes, even your yacht, President Ben Ali's family is rumored to covet it and reportedly gets what it wants . . . Often referred to as a quasi-mafia, an oblique mention of 'the Family' is enough to indicate which family you mean. Seemingly half of the Tunisian business community can claim a Ben Ali connection through marriage . . .[70]

The publication of such reports arguably raised the reputation of the US foreign service. A limited number of ambassadors were, however, forced to leave or change their posts.

Manning's achievements as a whistleblower were far outdone by Edward Snowden, an NSA contractor who claimed that its electronic eavesdropping had spiralled out of control. In 2013 Snowden downloaded 1.5 million highly classified intelligence documents onto thumbnail drives – the largest ever breach of Western SIGINT security. Even Julian Assange was taken aback. Andrew O'Hagan, who was commissioned to ghostwrite Assange's autobiography (which was never completed), found him 'like an ageing movie star, . . . a little put out by the global superstardom of Snowden'.[71] As Snowden began to release documents for publication by global media, he took refuge in, successively, Hong Kong and Moscow. The resulting uproar fuelled international controversy on the proper limits of official surveillance in the internet age. The *Guardian* and the *Washington Post* were awarded the highest accolade in US journalism, the Pulitzer Prize for Public Service, for their articles on NSA surveillance based on Snowden's revelations. By contrast, General Mike Hayden, a former director of both the NSA and the CIA, declared himself 'viscerally angry with [Snowden] and what he had done'. So, he claimed, was 'almost everyone else in the American intelligence community'.[72]

In Britain, the customary lack of long-term intelligence perspective has led to skewed assessment of the extent of Snowden's impact. Almost none of either Snowden's supporters or opponents realized that his highly classified revelations of UKUSA SIGINT operations in 2013 had a far smaller impact on British government policy and public opinion than the mid-nineteenth-century revelation of the official interception of Mazzini's correspondence.* The Prime Minister, David Cameron, was right to claim in 2014 that in Britain, unlike the United States and Germany, Snowden had not had 'an enormous public impact': 'I think that the public reaction, as I judge it, has not been one of shock-horror; it has been much more along the lines of "The intelligence services carry out intelligence work. Good."'[73] In 1844, by contrast, the parliamentary and public reaction of Victorian Britain to the opening of Mazzini's letters, denounced by Thomas Carlyle as 'a practice near of kin to picking men's pockets', was 'one of shock-horror' which provoked furious protests in the House of Commons and the suspension of all British SIGINT operations (save on the North-West Frontier) for the next seventy years. As a result, Britain was to enter the First World War, unlike its main allies, France and Russia, without a SIGINT agency.†

The editor-in-chief of the *Guardian*, Alan Rusbridger, wrote of Snowden's achievements: 'Until the present generation of computer nerds came along, no one realised it was possible to make off with the electronic equivalent of whole libraries full of triple-locked filing cabinets and safes ...'[74]‡ Despite the novel contribution of the nerds, however, Snowden's role as the best-known whistleblower of the early twenty-first century can only be adequately understood within the long and complex history of leaks of classified material in the United States. 'Across the ideological spectrum', writes Malcolm Gladwell, 'many Americans believe both that leaking "is a problem of major proportions" and that "our particular form of government wouldn't work without it." Episodically, leaks generate political frenzy.'[75]

Though US government officials are legally prohibited from disclosing state secrets, between 1949 and 1969 an estimated 2.3 per cent of *New York Times* and *Washington Post* front-page articles were based on official leaks. Over the last century, however, there have been only about a dozen

---

* Sir David Omand, the Intelligence and Security Coordinator (and former GCHQ Director), was a rare exception. He said in evidence to the Iraq Inquiry: 'there is a long history of ministers inadvertently compromising intelligence sources from 1844 and the Mazzini affair ...' (http://www.iraqinquiry.org.uk/media/95182/2010-01-20-Transcript-Omand-S2.pdf).

† See above, pp. 383, 490–91. As a result of remarkable wartime improvisation, however, Britain's First World War SIGINT agencies became world leaders.

‡ Rusbridger, however, was wrong to claim that 'Never before has anyone scooped up en masse the top-secret files of the world's most powerful intelligence organisations, in order to make them public.' Vasili Mitrokhin had done just that in the KGB archives some years earlier in a much longer and more difficult operation. See above, pp. 712, 714–15.

federal prosecutions of official leakers.[76]* The political journalist Bob
Woodward, author of more number one non-fiction best-sellers than any
other contemporary US author, owes much of his extraordinary success
to what the former CIA director Robert Gates calls 'his ability to get
people to talk about stuff they shouldn't be talking about'.[77] For over thirty
years Woodward identified only by the codename 'Deep Throat' the first
and probably most important of his major secret sources, who provided
the crucial leads in his investigation with Carl Bernstein of the Watergate
Affair in the early 1970s. In 2005 'Deep Throat' finally identified himself
as the former Associate Director (number two) of the FBI, Mark Felt, the
most senior whistleblower in the history of the US intelligence community.[78]† A memorial plaque above an underground garage in Rosslyn,
Virginia, marks the location where Felt briefed Woodward.‡

Apart from Felt, the most celebrated American whistleblower of the
Cold War era was Daniel Ellsberg, a strategic analyst at the RAND Corporation who had also worked at the Pentagon and White House. In 1971
Ellsberg secretly gave *The New York Times* a copy of a top-secret 7,000-
page study of US decision-making in Vietnam from 1945 to 1968 which
became known as the 'Pentagon Papers'. Unlike Mark Felt, Ellsberg's
identity quickly became public knowledge. Charged on twelve felony
counts which carried a total maximum sentence of 115 years, he was found
not guilty at a trial in 1973 on the grounds of governmental misconduct
and illegal evidence gathering against him.§ Ellsberg later became a supporter of WikiLeaks, Chelsea Manning and Edward Snowden.

Ellsberg's example inspired NSA's first whistleblower, Perry Fellwock,
a 25-year-old former analyst opposed to the Vietnam War, to give an interview in 1972 to the radical *Ramparts* magazine. So little had been made
public about NSA that Fellwock was the first insider to reveal that it had a
budget larger than the CIA's and to give some details of the global UKUSA
network, but damaged his credibility by claiming total success in SIGINT
operations against the Soviet Union: 'The fact is that we're able to break
every code they've got, understand every type of communications

* A complicating factor has been the recurrent habit of branches of the federal government
to leak classified information which they believe reflects well on them.
† Woodward did not introduce Felt to Carl Bernstein, his partner in the *Washington Post*
investigation of Watergate, until 2008. (Tim Weiner, 'W. Mark Felt, Watergate Deep Throat,
Dies at 95', *The New York Times*, 19 Dec. 2008.)
‡ The garage itself, however, is scheduled for demolition.
§ President Nixon's obsession with the Pentagon Papers posed a greater threat to the national
interest than their publication. When attempts to pursue Ellsberg in the courts failed, Nixon
turned to covert action. (Andrew, *For the President's Eyes Only*, pp. 377–80. Gladwell,
'Daniel Ellsberg, Edward Snowden, and the Modern Whistle-Blower'.)

equipment and enciphering device they've got.'* *The New York Times* reported that its own 'intelligence sources both in and out of the Government had corroborated much of Mr. Fellwock's story', but 'strongly denied, however, that the United States had broken the sophisticated codes of the Soviet Union or other major powers'.[79] Before publishing the interview with Fellwock, *Ramparts* had been told by Ellsberg's lawyer that 'the government wouldn't risk exposing more secrets by publicly going after them for the article'. He was proved right. Prosecution would have been further complicated by the *New York Times* report. Its 'intelligence sources' who contradicted Fellwock's claims about the success of NSA SIGINT operations against the Soviet Union had also broken federal law but were no doubt confident that, like most who leaked state secrets to the *Times*, they would never be prosecuted. Fellwock himself gave no further interviews about NSA. After a few years of political activism he disappeared from public view, briefly re-emerging in 2013 to praise Snowden as 'a patriot'.[80]

As Snowden's success in downloading an enormous number of its files demonstrated, NSA's precautions to protect itself against whistleblowers before 2013 were seriously inadequate. In the twentieth century most major breaches of Western SIGINT security had derived not from whistleblowers but from indiscretions by Western politicians and Soviet intelligence operations. In 1911 the French Foreign Minister, Justin de Selves, had personally compromised France's most important pre-First World War intelligence source by revealing the ability of the Quai d'Orsay's *cabinet noir* to decrypt some German diplomatic traffic.[81] Repeated revelations of the contents of Soviet decrypts by post-war British ministers led Stalin in 1927 to adopt the virtually unbreakable 'one-time pad' for intelligence and high-grade diplomatic traffic. By the 1930s Soviet intelligence had considerable success in recruiting cipher and other personnel in Moscow embassies and foreign ministries abroad, which continued after the Second World War.[82] The most important UKUSA intelligence source of the early Cold War, the VENONA decrypts of Soviet intelligence telegrams, was compromised by Kim Philby and the US cipher clerk, William Weisband, who had also been recruited as a Soviet agent.[83] In 1960 two KGB agents in NSA who had defected to Moscow, Bernon F. Mitchell and William H. Martin, gave hugely embarrassing details at a press conference of US success in decrypting the communications of its friends and allies.[84] Intermittent SIGINT indiscretions by Western

* Fellwock also wrongly claimed that NSA had heard a Soviet cosmonaut, whose spacecraft malfunctioned, telling ground control before he was incinerated: 'I don't want to die, you've got to do something.' (Winslow Peck [Perry Fellwock], 'U.S. Electronic Espionage: A Memoir'.)

statesmen continued until the end of the Cold War. At the beginning of the Falklands War in 1982, the former Labour minister Ted Rowlands told the Commons: 'We have been reading [Argentina's] telegrams for many years.'[85] In a televised address from the Oval Office in April 1986 President Reagan alarmed British as well as American cryptanalysts by quoting the contents of Libyan intercepts decrypted by GCHQ and NSA in order to prove the complicity of the Gaddafi regime in the bombing of a West Berlin discothèque frequented by US troops.[86]

Since Snowden's revelations in 2013, there has been a new emphasis in the US intelligence community on the threat posed by whistleblowers. The CIA's director, Mike Pompeo, claimed in June 2017 that leaking of official secrets has 'accelerated', thanks in large part to 'the worship of Edward Snowden'.[87] Like other senior US intelligence officers, Pompeo also claims that the Snowden revelations have done serious damage to US SIGINT operations: 'In fact, a colleague of ours at NSA recently explained [in spring 2017] that more than a thousand foreign targets – people, groups, organizations – more than a thousand of them changed or tried to change how they communicated as a result of the Snowden disclosures. That number is staggering.'[88] A terrorist group which, to take a hypothetical example, discovers from the Snowden material that its phones and emails can be intercepted, but not Skype, inevitably switches to Skype when planning its next operation.[89]

Intelligence whistle-blowing is still frequently seen in too narrow and short-term a perspective. It has contributed most to understanding the roles of intelligence communities not in the West but in authoritarian regimes. Whistleblowers have greatly enhanced, arguably transformed, our knowledge of, notably, KGB operations in the Cold War, the prison camps run by North Korean state security, and the Tiananmen Square massacre of Chinese pro-democracy campaigners.

The leading whistleblower in the KGB was the senior archivist and secret dissident Vasili Mitrokhin, who for more than a decade smuggled out of its foreign intelligence headquarters an extraordinary archive of top-secret material, which was exfiltrated to Britain by SIS in 1992.[90] For some years after he arrived in London, Mitrokhin spent several days a week working on his archive, checking English translations and responding to queries about KGB operations from intelligence agencies on five continents. It was agreed from the outset that the next step would be to publish one or more books on KGB history based chiefly on his archive. In 1996, in collaboration with him, I began writing *The Mitrokhin Archive: The KGB in Europe and the West*, published three years later.[91] His (and my) ultimate aim, after we had written two books together, was always to make his entire archive publicly available – which it has been since July 2014 at Churchill College Archives Centre, Cambridge, where it attracts researchers from around the world.* Though the material in the archive which attracts most attention concerns KGB operations in the West, it also sheds new light on the secret Soviet war against dissidents. Thanks to Mitrokhin, we now know that by the middle years of the Cold War more illegals were used to search out and compromise dissidents in the Soviet Bloc than against Western targets. During the 1968 Prague Spring, for example, the KGB calculated – probably correctly – that the best strategy for penetrating the Czechoslovak reform movement was to send illegals posing as sympathetic Western journalists, business people, students and tourists. The first wave of twenty illegals sent to Czecho-slovakia to undermine the Prague Spring (Operation PROGRESS) outnumbered those used in any KGB operation in the West.[92]

Today's most important intelligence whistleblowers, though they attract only a fraction of the publicity given to Assange and Snowden, are North Korean defectors and refugees who have revealed far more about current Ministry of State Security (MSS) concentration camps than was known in the West about the Soviet Gulag run by Stalin's NKVD at the height of the Great Terror in 1936–8. The extent of Stalin's Terror was so little understood that, when Robert Conquest revealed its scale and horror thirty years later, his now celebrated book provided widespread surprise and significant scepticism.[93] By contrast, in July 2017 an NGO based in Seoul, the Transitional Justice Working Group (TJWG), published a report on Kim Jong-un's even more horrific Gulag entitled *Mapping Crimes against Humanity in North Korea*, based on interviews with 375 escapees (most of whom were not identified in order to protect their relatives). With the help of Google Earth imagery (not, of course, available in the Stalin era), the defectors and refugees were able to identify 333 killing sites as well as to give details of some of the horrors perpetrated in them. A smaller number of escapees were among those who gave evidence in 2014 to a UN commission of enquiry which reported 'systematic, widespread and gross human rights violations'. Sadistic torture, often as a means of execution, starvation, rape and forced abortion are standard practice. The enquiry chairman, Michael Kirby, a former Australian judge, compared the horrors in North Korea to those of Nazi Germany: 'The gravity, scale, duration and nature of the unspeakable atrocities committed in the country reveal a totalitarian state that does not have any

* Churchill College Archives Centre also houses the papers of, among others, Winston Churchill, Margaret Thatcher and a number of intelligence officers.

parallel in the contemporary world.'[94] Amnesty International, which has also studied satellite imagery of two of the main prison camps and interviewed escapees, accuses the Kim Jong-un regime of 'crimes against humanity'.[95]

Though much research remains to be done, intelligence is no longer a 'missing dimension' of the history of the northern hemisphere. In China, by contrast, most intelligence history is still taboo. Soon after the establishment of the People's Republic of China (PRC) in 1949, a Central Committee 'Resolution on Intelligence Work', approved by the Chinese Communist Party (CCP) Politburo, praised its major role in victory over the nationalist Kuomintang (KMT). Most of what that role was, however, remained as secret as ULTRA in post-war Britain. Among the most sensitive topics was Mao's responsibility for the purges of loyal Chinese Communists over the previous decade.[96]

Kang Sheng, the brutal security chief in Mao's Yan'an base from 1938 to 1946, had spent the previous few years in Moscow, learning from the example of the NKVD during its most paranoid phase. Kang proved an apt pupil. In Stalin's Great Terror he had purged émigré CCP members with exemplary zeal for mostly imaginary crimes, and he continued the witch-hunt in Yan'an.[97] During the screening of party cadres and hunt for enemy agents which began in 1943, almost all who operated underground in KMT or Japanese-held territory fell under suspicion; even some schoolchildren confessed to spying for the enemy. Mao was later forced to apologize in secret before his peers for the execution of many loyal Party cadres. Though Kang Sheng is now publicly vilified, most intelligence files which would damage Mao's reputation remain closed. As in Stalin's show trials, virtually every senior official overthrown during Mao's Cultural Revolution (1966–76) was denounced as an enemy agent past or present.[98]*

On its foundation in 1983, today's main Chinese intelligence agency, the Ministry of State Security (MSS), founded a department now known as the Intelligence History Research Division to stimulate the writing of both classified and unclassified intelligence histories. Probably the most important sources for published histories have been documents on the rehabilitation of former alleged intelligence traitors, such as Pan Hannian, the once reviled leader of the (non-existent) 'Pan Hannian Counter-Revolutionary Clique'. Found guilty of treason in 1963 and barbarically treated in prison and labour camp, Pan emerged from rehabilitation as one of the heroes of

---

* Among the 'traitors' exposed in 1967 was the head of China's civilian-intelligence service, Zou Dapeng. He and his wife, also a senior intelligence officer, both committed suicide.

the underground intelligence war of the Chinese Revolution. By the centenary of his birth in 2006, Han's exploits had been celebrated in almost twenty books, numerous articles and a TV drama serial.[99]

Intelligence history sells well in China, which has a flourishing 'noodle stall' market for spy stories of varying reliability. Weekly TV schedules usually include at least one espionage drama or 'documentary'.[100] Intelligence intrigues many Chinese university students. When I lectured in 2001 at Peking University (the oldest university in Beijing) on ways in which Sun Tzu and *The Art of War* had anticipated some twentieth-century Western intelligence and deception operations,[101] a forest of hands went up in the audience as soon as I finished speaking. Most of the questions which I had time to answer were put in good or excellent English.* The students' knowledge of Sun Tzu (nowadays a national hero) gave them a long-term perspective which many in Western universities lack. But the reliable information available to them on modern Chinese intelligence operations was a small fraction of that in the West. The published intelligence material on 9/11 and the war in Iraq[102] has proved too voluminous for all but the most committed Western readers. In China, by contrast, the massacre of pro-democracy protesters in Tiananmen Square in central Beijing on 4 June 1989 is still wholly taboo. The National Museum of China in Tiananmen Square, which reopened in 2011 after extensive renovation, has no exhibit which makes any mention of the protest (or of similar protests in provincial cities).

Leaked official documents which have become known as the 'Tiananmen Papers', smuggled to the West by whistleblowers sympathetic to the protesters, show that Vice-President Wang Zhen, the Prime Minister, Li Peng, and others in the ruling circle believed that the Communist regime was threatened with overthrow.[103] The documents also include some alarmist MSS reports to the Party leadership which claimed that US intelligence had penetrated the student pro-democracy movement in the hope of using it to overthrow the Communist regime. Intelligence reports on the massacre of pro-democracy demonstrators were, however, less seriously distorted than those of the army. The 38th Army Group, which was responsible for most of the bloodshed, hailed the bravery of its troops against 'rioters with clubs and steel reinforcing bars' but made no mention of the killing of demonstrators. By contrast, the MSS, while not siding with the demonstrators, frankly acknowledged that some of the troops were out of control: 'Some soldiers who were hit by rocks lost their

---

* I was informed that my lecture was the first on intelligence by an Anglophone academic at Peking University.

self-control and began firing wildly at anyone who shouted "Fascists!" or threw rocks and bricks. At least a hundred citizens and students fell to the ground in pools of blood; most were rushed to nearby Fuxing hospital by other students and citizens.'[104] Since the Tiananmen Square massacre and killings of pro-democracy demonstrators in other cities, the MSS, together with a vast army of online censors, has helped turn China into what one writer calls the 'People's Republic of Amnesia', committed to destroying popular memory of the 1989 democracy movement. As well as removing all search terms related to Tiananmen Square, official censorship even seeks to prevent any online reference to the massacre of 4 June by blocking all combinations of the numbers 4, 6 and 1989.[105]

The fact that, despite official censorship, China has the world's biggest online community makes it easy for the MSS to recruit record numbers of hackers (another taboo topic in the Chinese media) against both foreign and domestic targets. In 2015 the US Office of Personnel Management (OPM) announced that hackers (in the PRC, though it did not identify them) had stolen 'sensitive information' from its files on probably everyone subject to a US government background check during the previous fifteen years – a total of 19.7 million people and a further 1.8 million of their families, friends and other contacts. The FBI's director, James B. Comey, told reporters: 'It is a very big deal from a national security perspective and from a counter-intelligence perspective. It's a treasure trove of information about everybody who has worked for, tried to work for, or works for the United States government.' Comey believed the hackers had stolen his own SF 86 (Standard Form 86), which all applicants for security clearances had to complete: 'If you have my SF 86, you know every place I've lived since I was 18, contact people at those addresses, neighbors at those addresses, all of my family, every place I've traveled outside the United States. Just imagine if you were a foreign intelligence service and you had that data.'[106]*

Though all references to Chinese espionage are censored in Beijing, the MSS gives great prominence to the threat from foreign spies in China. In April 2016 the government inaugurated an annual 'National Security Education Day' to increase public awareness of 'foreign spy agencies and others who are fiercely carrying out infiltration, subversion, division, destruction and theft'. The quality of MSS and other official counter-espionage and

* The OPM announcement in July 2015 caused some embarrassment in Beijing since President Xi Jinping was due to make a state visit to Washington two months later. In an unconvincing attempt at damage limitation, the Chinese government blamed the theft of OPM on a handful of private Chinese hackers, whom it claimed to have arrested.

counter-subversion propaganda caused some hilarity among foreign observers. It included a sixteen-panel cartoon poster entitled 'Dangerous Love', displayed on the walls of Beijing and on the bulletin boards of national and local government offices. 'Dangerous Love' tells the story of an attractive young Chinese civil servant nicknamed Xiao Li (or Little Li), who is seduced by David, a red-haired Western visiting scholar who repeatedly tells her how beautiful she is, buys her bouquets of roses, invites her to expensive dinners and takes her on romantic walks. David is really a foreign spy more interested in state secrets than in Little Li. After she gives him classified documents from her job at a government office, they are both arrested. Little Li is handcuffed and told by the police that she has a 'shallow understanding of secrecy for a state employee'.[107] Seen in long-term perspective, the cautionary cartoon tale of Little Li was another variant of the traditional deep suspicion by the security services in autocratic regimes of the subversive potential of visiting scholars and other foreign professionals. The MSS reported to Party leaders that, ever since the founding of the PRC, the West and in particular the United States had 'done a great deal of mischief aimed at overthrowing the Communist Party and sabotaging the socialist system', trying to 'stimulate and organise political opposition using catchphrases like "democracy", "liberty", or "human rights".'[108]

On China's second National Security Education Day in April 2017 the government sought to encourage popular support for counter-espionage in Beijing by announcing cash rewards for information on foreign spies, ranging from a modest 10,000 yuan up to 500,000 yuan (over 70,000 US dollars) for really important tip-offs. In order to emphasize the importance of the counter-espionage campaign, the authorities tried to put it in long-term historical perspective by comparing it improbably with the Great Wall of China, whose construction had begun over two and a half millennia before to protect Chinese civilization from barbarian invasion. Beijing city officials in 2017 called on citizens to help 'construct an iron Great Wall to combat evil and guard against spies'.[109]

The long-term intelligence priority which today's PRC comes closest to sharing with other major powers is counter-terrorism. Liu Jieyi, China's permanent representative to the United Nations, told the Security Council early in 2017: 'Terrorism is the common enemy of mankind. Whenever and wherever and in whatever forms it occurs, it must be countered resolutely.'[110] China, however, continues to see terrorism primarily in a domestic context.[111] Its intelligence-led 'counter-terrorist' operations are chiefly directed against the Muslim ethnic Uighur population in the sparsely populated Xinjiang Uighur Autonomous Region (XUAR) in north-west China, which still has bitter memories (rarely mentioned in the 'People's Republic of Amnesia') of the closure of mosques and burning of copies of the Quran during the Cultural Revolution. Some Uighur families were forced to rear pigs.*

For most major powers, except China, the most predictable global intelligence priority over the next generation will be the continuing threat from international (primarily Islamist) terrorism. Countering that threat successfully will require a longer historical perspective than was evident in responding to the first wave of Islamist terrorism before 9/11.

The first Islamist attack to cause mass casualties in Britain was on 7 July 2005 when suicide bombers on three Tube trains and a London bus killed fifty-two people as well as themselves. I spent most of that day working on MI5's centenary history at its Thames House headquarters on Millbank, almost opposite Lambeth Palace.[112] That morning I had arrived from Cambridge at King's Cross station only to find the Tube closed because of what was mistakenly believed to be a power surge. By the time I'd walked to Thames House, it was clear there had been a terrorist attack. The impact of 7/7, as it came to be known, on the Security Service was further increased by failed (but again unanticipated) terrorist attacks a fortnight later. A senior MI5 officer later told me that even other British intelligence agencies 'did not understand just how deeply the Service felt about the July attacks, the shock, anxiety, and deep need to ensure it didn't happen again'.

In the immediate aftermath of 7/7 and 21/7, Jonathan Evans, the next Director-General of the Security Service, asked himself: 'Have they got wave after wave to throw at us?' No one could have anticipated in July 2005 that over the next decade terrorist attacks would cause only one British fatality (Lee Rigby of the Royal Regiment of Fusiliers in 2013) and, remarkably, become the rarest cause of death in mainland Britain. The success of security services' operations is best judged by things that do not happen – terrorist attacks currently chief among them.

From the later months of 2005 until the spring of 2017 major jihadist terrorist plots in Britain were detected in time to stop them. One of the main reasons for their detection was the traditional surveillance of suspects which has long been at the heart of any credible counter-terrorist (or counter-espionage) strategy, though the technology of surveillance necessarily evolves over time. But for successful surveillance during MI5's

---

* In Operation ALGA in 1970, the Kazakhstan KGB, in collaboration with 'special actions' officers from the Centre in Moscow, had set out to create a sabotage base in the XUAR with caches to conceal arms and explosives. (Andrew and Mitrokhin, *Mitrokhin Archive II*, pp. 277–83.)

Operation LARGE in 2000, an Islamist terrorist attack would probably have taken place in the UK before the 9/11 attacks in the United States.[113]

The largest surveillance operation in the history of both MI5 and the police, codenamed OVERT, was crucial to the discovery in 2006 of what MI5 judged the most dangerous terrorist conspiracy in British history – a plot to use suicide bombers to bring down in mid-air seven transatlantic aircraft bound from Heathrow to North American cities over a three-hour period. Listening devices and a hidden camera installed in a two-bedroom flat at 386a Forest Road, Walthamstow, gave the Security Service a ringside seat during the flat's conversion into an Islamist bomb factory. On 3 August the camera showed the chief plotter, Abdullah Ahmed Ali, an engineering graduate of London City University, and an assistant, Tanvir Hussain, drilling a hole in the bottom of a soft-drink bottle in order to replace its contents with liquid explosive without breaking the seal on the cap. It also revealed that the detonators for the explosive bottles which Ali, Hussain and their fellow suicide bombers planned to take on board transatlantic flights were apparently harmless AA batteries whose contents had been replaced with HMTD (hexamethylene triperoxide diamine). Though the plotters were arrested before any of their bombs were ready, in a later BBC *Panorama* programme one of the explosive devices they had intended to construct, assembled by the weapons expert Dr Sidney Alford, blew a hole in an aircraft fuselage.[114]

Ever since Walsingham's successful defeat of assassination plots against Elizabeth I,[115] message interception has also played a crucial role in counter-terrorism. While MI5 was monitoring Islamist bomb construction in a Walthamstow flat in the summer of 2006, an intercepted email sent by Ali, the chief plotter, to Pakistan appeared to give a coded indication that the terrorist attack plan was imminent: 'I've set up my mobile shop now. Now I only need to sort out an opening time.' MI5 was able to watch the plotters record 'martyrdom videos' to be made public after their deaths and (they believed) entry into paradise.[116] The legacy of Operation OVERT is the continuing ban on liquids and gels in hand luggage which since 2006 has changed the nature of air travel.

A decade without major terrorist attacks in mainland Britain came to an end with a series of attacks in 2017. The most serious was the attack on 22 May by an Islamist suicide bomber, Salman Abedi, at the end of a concert in the Manchester Arena. Twenty-three (including Abedi) were killed and 250 injured. A series of other attacks were prevented. Both the successful and unsuccessful attacks underlined once again the importance of surveillance of terrorist suspects combined with message interception.

Successful surveillance will be even more essential as terrorism moves into the age of WMD.

It is only a matter of time before we face an even more dangerous Islamist attack than that planned in Ali's Walthamstow bomb factory. As far back as 1998 Bin Laden told his followers that acquiring WMD is a 'religious duty'. A year before 9/11, without realizing it at the time, Security Service counter-proliferation operations disrupted a first attempt by Al Qaeda to obtain material in Britain to develop biological weapons.[117]

The first British Islamist to try to follow Bin Laden's instructions to obtain WMD was Dhiren Barot, a British Hindu convert to Islam who was arrested in 2004 after surveillance during Operation RHYME but not brought to trial for another two years. Barot was considered such a key figure by Al Qaeda that he was personally selected and his training supervised by Khalid Sheikh Mohammed, the chief planner of the 9/11 attacks in the United States. He wrote gleefully about a plan to explode a bomb on a tube train travelling in a tunnel beneath the Thames: 'Imagine the chaos that would be caused if a powerful explosion were to rip through here and actually rupture the river itself. This would cause pandemonium, what with the explosions, flooding, drowning, etc that would occur/ result.' Barot's ultimate ambition was to explode the first radioactive 'dirty bomb', probably in the heart of London, though he complained that 'for the time being' he had failed to acquire 'the necessary contacts'.*

He would have found it much easier today. In 2015 Chatham House produced a report entitled 'Growing Threat as Organized Crime Funnels Radioactive Materials to Terrorists'. Criminal groups in Moldova are believed to have already smuggled radioactive materials to ISIS, the so-called Islamic State in Iraq and Syria. 'Making a radiological weapon', the Chatham House report concluded, 'requires little technical and scientific expertise, and radioactive materials can be used with conventional weaponry (such as dynamite) to make a successful dirty bomb.'[118] Looming on the UK horizon, perhaps as early as the next decade, is for the first time the terrorism of the nuclear age and of chemical and biological warfare. ISIS has already used chemical weapons in Iraq. Given the opportunity, it would not hesitate to do so in Europe, probably with the help of returning jihadis.[119]

---

* More than 600 sets of keys were discovered during Operation RHYME. Police spent fourteen months visiting over 6,000 garages and lock-ups, trying to match them up; seventy-seven matches were found. The hunt continued for so long for fear that one of the premises might contain explosives or even radioactive material. (Andrew, *Defence of the Realm*, pp. 819–21.)

At the 2016 Nuclear Security Summit in Washington, attended by over fifty world leaders, the British Prime Minister, David Cameron, warned that the even greater danger of ISIS obtaining nuclear material is now 'only too real'. 'The danger of a terrorist group obtaining and using a nuclear weapon', said President Obama, is one of the greatest threats to global security . . . There is no doubt that if these madmen ever got their hands on a nuclear bomb or nuclear material, they would certainly use it to kill as many people as possible.'[120] If Bin Laden had possessed a 'dirty' radiological bomb on 9/11, he would almost certainly have used it then.

'The further backwards you look', wrote Winston Churchill, 'the further forward you can see.' His maxim is one of the keys to understanding twenty-first-century counter-terrorism. A very long-term perspective gives greater insight into the coming terrorist use of WMD than the short-term experience of low-tech terrorist attacks since 9/11. One of the great constants of the last few thousand years has been the global proliferation (once slow, now rapid) of all human inventions. WMD will not be the first exception to this iron law of history. The question now is not *whether* some future group of (probably Islamist) terrorists will use WMD but *when* they will do so.

Foreign intelligence has shown itself to be most essential during wartime and major international crises, when open sources reveal much less than usual. Intelligence both shortened the Second World War and helped to prevent the Cuban Missile Crisis ending in a Third World War. After the missile crisis, the intelligence available to both East and West on the extent and deployment of their opponents' nuclear strike force became an essential element in stabilizing the Cold War.[121] The importance of this intelligence has often been taken for granted. If US and UK intelligence had been as well informed about Saddam's WMD as they had been about those of the Soviet Union, there might have been no Iraq war in 2003. As Eisenhower realized, intelligence on what the enemy *'did not* have' was often as important as information on what they did.[122]

Though good intelligence diminishes surprise, it cannot prevent it. Even the best strategic intelligence sometimes allows us to foresee the future only as St Paul glimpsed heaven – 'through a glass, darkly'.[123] Past experience shows that intelligence analysts will be regularly surprised by the course of international relations in the twenty-first century, just as their predecessors were in the twentieth. No one in August 1914 could have predicted that in the course of the war Russia would be transformed from Europe's most authoritarian monarchy into the world's most revolutionary regime. The interwar triumph of Nazism was as unpredictable as the wartime victory of Bolshevism. When a former British ambassador to the

German Weimar Republic, Lord D'Abernon, published his two-volume memoirs in 1929, his only reference to Hitler was a footnote which mentioned that he had spent six months in prison in 1924, 'thereafter fading into oblivion'.[124] In Britain, however, it was an intelligence officer with long historical perspectives, Jack Curry of MI5, strongly influenced by an agent in the German embassy, who in 1936 was the first to argue in Whitehall that *Mein Kampf* was a better guide to Hitler's territorial ambitions than his much more moderate current rhetoric: 'It is emphatically not a case of irresponsible utterances which have been discarded by a statesman on taking power.' Curry's arguments persuaded Sir Vernon Kell, the head of MI5, but not successive British governments.[125]* His exceptional insight into Nazi Germany, however, helps to explain why, at the end of the Second World War, Kell's successor, Sir David Petrie, commissioned Curry to write a classified history of MI5 'for future guidance'.[126]

The history of intelligence is full of examples of able, well-intentioned policymakers and intelligence officers who, unlike Curry, have been seriously handicapped by their failure to comprehend the importance of past experience. At the outbreak of the First World War, Woodrow Wilson was probably the best-educated president in US history. The British Prime Minister, Herbert Asquith, had won first-class honours and a prize fellowship at Oxford University. Their failures in their use of intelligence derived not from any lack of ability but from ignorance of the historical role of intelligence. At a time when Britain was becoming world leader in SIGINT, Asquith, unlike Pitt the Elder and Pitt the Younger in the eighteenth century, showed virtually no interest in it. It almost certainly did not even occur to President Wilson that Britain's SIGINT successes included decrypting some of his own top-secret telegrams.[127]

It is not difficult to think of current world leaders with little or no discernible historical interests.[128] In academia, however, there are overdue signs of progress. Half a century ago, despite the global popularity of James Bond, intelligence history and more contemporary intelligence studies barely existed. Nowadays, they are taught in a growing minority of universities on both sides of the Atlantic. The more that is discovered about the long-term history of intelligence, the more difficult it will be for both policymakers and practitioners to ignore past experience.

---

* MI5's repeated intelligence reports showing that the policy of Appeasement encouraged, rather than diminished, Hitler's territorial ambitions had no effect on pre-war British governments.

Bibliography

9/11 Commission Report: Final Report of the National Commission on Terrorist Attacks upon the United States (New York: W. W. Norton & Co., 2004)

Abdale, Jason R., *Four Days in September: The Battle of Teutoburg* (Barnsley: Pen & Sword, 2016)

Aboul-Enein, Youssef, 'Amr ibn al-A'as, a Realistic Examination of an Early Islamic Military Strategic Planner', *Small Wars Journal*, 2012

Abram, Simon (ed.), *Islamic Hadith* (Kindle edn, 2011)

Abulafia, David, *The Great Sea: A Human History of the Mediterranean* (London: Allen Lane, 2011)

Ackroyd, Peter, *Venice* (London: Vintage Books, 2010)

Adams, Jefferson, *Historical Dictionary of German Intelligence* (Lanham, Md: Scarecrow Press, 2009)

Adams, Robyn, ' "The Service I am Here for": William Herle in the Marshalsea Prison, 1571', *Huntington Library Quarterly*, vol. 72 (2009), no. 2

Adamson, Peter, 'Before Essence and Existence: Al-Kindi's Conception of Being', *Journal of the History of Philosophy*, vol. 40 (2002), no. 3

—, *Al-Kindī* (New York: Oxford University Press, 2007)

Addison, Joseph, *Essays and Tales* (London: Cassell & Co., 1904)

Adelman, Howard Tzvi, 'A Rabbi Reads the Qur'an in the Venetian Ghetto', *Jewish History*, vol. 26 (2012)

Adkin, Mark, *The Charge: The Real Reason Why the Light Brigade was Lost* (London: Leo Cooper, 1996)

Ágoston, G., 'Information, Ideology, and Limits of Imperial Policy: Ottoman Grand Strategy in the Context of Ottoman–Habsburg Rivalry', in *The Early Modern Ottomans: Remapping the Empire* (Cambridge: Cambridge University Press, 2007), pp. 75–103

Agulhon, Maurice, *1848 ou l'apprentissage de la République 1848–1852* (Paris: Éditions du Seuil, 1973)

Aid, Matthew M., *The Secret Sentry: The Untold History of the National Security Agency* (New York: Bloomsbury, 2009)

— and Cees Wiebes (eds.), *Secrets of Signals Intelligence during the Cold War and Beyond* (London: Routledge, 2001)

Akram, A. I., *The Sword of Allah: Khalid bin al-Waleed: His Life and Campaigns* (Delhi: Adam, 2007)

Akrigg, G. P. V. (ed.), *Letters of King James VI & I* (Berkeley: University of California Press, 1984)

Al-Asmari, Abdulaziz Abdullah, 'Arab/Islamic Concept of Intelligence in the Case of Fatah Paramilitary', PhD thesis (Brunel University, 2009)

Al-Kadi, Ibrahim A., 'Origins of Cryptology: The Arab Contributions', *Cryptologia*, vol. 16 (1992), no. 2

Al-Khalili, Jim, *The House of Wisdom: How Arabic Science Saved Ancient Knowledge and Gave Us the Renaissance* (London: Penguin Books, 2011)

Al Mubarakpuri, Safiur Rahman, *The Sealed Nectar: Biography of the Noble Prophet* (Riyadh: Darussalam Publishers, 2002)

Al-Tabari, Muhammad ibn-Jarir, *The History of al-Ṭabarī*, vol. 7: *The Foundation of the Community* (New York: SUNY Press, 1987)

Alberti, Leon Battista, *De Componendis Cyfris*, ed. Augusto Buonafalce (Turin: Galimberti, 1998)

Aldhouse-Green, Miranda, *Caesar's Druids: Story of an Ancient Priesthood* (New Haven, Conn./London: Yale University Press, 2010)

Aldrich, Richard J., *The Hidden Hand: Britain, America and Cold War Secret Intelligence* (London: John Murray, 2001)

—, *GCHQ: The Uncensored Story of Britain's Most Secret Intelligence Agency* (London: HarperPress, 2010)

— and Rory Cormac, *The Black Door: Spies, Secret Intelligence and British Prime Ministers* (London: William Collins, 2016)

Alford, Stephen, *The Watchers: A Secret History of the Reign of Elizabeth I* (London: Allen Lane, 2012)

Allmand, Christopher, 'Intelligence in the Hundred Years War', in Keith Neilson and B. J. C. McKercher (eds.), *Go Spy the Land: Military Intelligence in History* (Westport, Conn.: Praeger, 1992)

Alsop, Susan Mary, *Yankees at the Court: The First Americans in Paris* (New York: Doubleday & Co., 1982)

Amann, Peter, 'The Huber Enigma: Revolutionary or Police-Spy?', *International Review of Social History*, vol. 12 (1967), no. 2

Ames, Christine Caldwell, 'Does Inquisition Belong to Religious History?', *American Historical Review*, 2005, no. 1

—, *Righteous Persecution: Inquisition, Dominicans and Christianity in the Middle Ages* (Philadelphia: University of Pennsylvania Press, 2009)

Ames, Roger T., *Sun Tzu: The Art of Warfare* (New York: Ballantine, 1993)

Andreau, Jean, and Raymond Descat, *Esclave en Grèce et à Rome* (Paris: Hachette, 2006)

Andrew, Christopher, *Théophile Delcassé and the Making of the Entente Cordiale* (London: Macmillan, 1968)

—, *The First World War: Causes and Consequences*, vol. 19 of *The Hamlyn History of the World in Colour* (London: Paul Hamlyn, 1970)

—, 'Codebreakers and Foreign Offices: The French, British and American Experience', in Christopher Andrew and David Dilks (eds.), *The Missing Dimension:*

Governments and Intelligence Communities in the Twentieth Century (London: Palgrave, 1984)

—, 'France and the German Menace', in Ernest R. May, *Knowing One's Enemies: Intelligence Assessment before the Two World Wars* (Princeton, NJ: Princeton University Press, 1984)

—, 'Churchill and Intelligence', *Intelligence and National Security*, vol. 3 (1988), no. 3

—, *Secret Service: The Making of the British Intelligence Community*, 3rd edn (London: Sceptre, 1991)

—, *For the President's Eyes Only: Secret Intelligence and the American Presidency from Washington to Bush* (London: HarperCollins, 1995)

—, 'Déchiffrement et diplomatie: Le Cabinet noir du Quai d'Orsay sous la Troisième République', *Relations Internationales*, 1976, no. 5, pp. 37–64

—, 'Secret Intelligence and British Foreign Policy 1900–1939', in Christopher Andrew and Jeremy Noakes (eds.), *Intelligence and International Relations 1900–1945* (Exeter: Exeter University Press, 1987)

—, 'The Growth of the Australian Intelligence Community and the Anglo-American Connection', *Intelligence and National Security*, vol. 4 (1989), no. 2

—, 'The British View of Security and Intelligence', in A. Stuart Farson, David Stafford and Wesley K. Wark (eds.), *Security and Intelligence in a Changing World: New Perspectives for the 1990s* (London/Portland, Oreg.: Frank Cass, 1991)

—, 'The Making of the Anglo-American SIGINT Alliance, 1940–1948', in James E. Dillard and Walter T. Hitchcock (eds.), *The Intelligence Revolution and Modern Warfare* (Chicago: Imprint Publications, 1996)

—, 'Conclusion: An Agenda for Future Research', in Rhodri Jeffreys-Jones and Christopher Andrew (eds.), *Eternal Vigilance? 50 Years of the CIA* (London: Frank Cass, 1997)

—, 'The VENONA Secret', in K. G. Robertson (ed.), *War, Resistance and Intelligence: Essays in Honour of M. R. D. Foot* (Barnsley: Pen & Sword, 1999)

—, 'Casement and British Intelligence', in Mary E. Daly (ed.), *Roger Casement in Irish and World History* (Dublin: Royal Irish Academy, 2005)

—, *The Defence of the Realm: The Authorized History of MI5*, rev. paperback edn (London: Penguin Books, 2010)

—, 'Intelligence in the Cold War', in M. P. Leffler and O. A. Westad (eds.), *The Cambridge History of the Cold War*, vol. 2: *Crises and Détente* (Cambridge: Cambridge University Press, 2010)

—, 'British Official Perceptions of Muammar Gaddafi, 1969–2011: Open Sources and Secret Intelligence', in Lawrence Freedman and Jeffrey H. Michaels (eds.), *Scripting Middle East Leaders: The Impact of Leadership Perceptions on US and UK Foreign Policy* (New York: Bloomsbury, 2013)

—, 'The Modern History of Interrogation', in Christopher Andrew and Simona Tobia (eds.), *Interrogation in War and Conflict: A Comparative and Interdisciplinary Analysis* (London: Routledge, 2014)

—, 'Intelligence and Conspiracy Theory: The Case of James Angleton in Long-Term Perspective', in Bruce Hoffman and Christian Ostermann (eds.), *Moles. Defectors and Deceptions: James Angleton and His Influence on US Counter-intelligence* (Washington, DC: Wilson Center, 2014)

— (ed.), *Codebreaking and Signals Intelligence* (London: Frank Cass, 1986)

— and David Dilks (eds.), *The Missing Dimension: Governments and Intelligence Communities in the Twentieth Century* (London: Macmillan, 1984)

— and Julie Elkner, 'Stalin and Foreign Intelligence', in Harold Shukman (ed.), *Redefining Stalinism* (London: Frank Cass, 2003)

— and Oleg Gordievsky, *KGB: The Inside Story of Its Foreign Operations from Lenin to Gorbachev* (London: Sceptre, 1991)

— and Oleg Gordievsky, *Le KGB dans le monde* (Paris: Fayard, 1990)

— and Oleg Gordievsky (eds.), *Instructions from the Centre: Top Secret Files on KGB Foreign Operations, 1975–1985* (London: Hodder and Stoughton, 1991); slightly revised US edition published as *Comrade Kryuchkov's Instructions: Top Secret Files on KGB Foreign Operations, 1975–1985* (Stanford, Calif.: Stanford University Press, 1993)

— and Gordievsky, Oleg (eds.), *More Instructions from the Centre: Top Secret Files on KGB Global Operations, 1975–1985* (London: Frank Cass, 1991)

— and A. S. Kanya-Forstner, *France Overseas: The Great War and the Climax of French Imperial Expansion* (London: Thames & Hudson, 1981)

— and Vasili Mitrokhin, *The Mitrokhin Archive: The KGB in Europe and the West* (London: Allen Lane, 1999)

——, *The Mitrokhin Archive II: The KGB and the World* (London: Allen Lane, 2005)

— and Keith Neilson, 'Tsarist Codebreakers and British Codes', in Christopher Andrew (ed.), *Codebreaking and Signals Intelligence* (London: Frank Cass, 1986)

— and Paul Vallet, 'The German Threat', in Richard Mayne, Douglas Johnson and Robert Tombs (eds.), *Cross Channel Currents: 100 Years of the Entente Cordiale* (London: Psychology Press, 2004)

— and Calder Walton, 'The Gouzenko Case and British Secret Intelligence', in J. L. Black and Martin Rudner (eds.), *The Gouzenko Affair: Canada and the Beginnings of Cold War Counter-Espionage* (Manotick, Ont.: Penumbra Press, 2006)

Antill, Peter D., *Crete 1941: Germany's Lightning Airborne Assault* (Oxford: Osprey, 2005)

Antonucci, Michael, 'War by Other Means: The Legacy of Byzantium', *History Today*, vol. 43 (1993), no. 2

Arboit, Gérald, 'Napoléon et le renseignement', Centre Français de Recherche sur le Renseignement, Note Historique no. 27 (2009)

Armstrong, Karen, *Muhammad: Prophet for Our Time* (London: Harper Perennial, 2007)

Arnold, John H., *Inquisition and Power: Catharism and the Confessing Subject in Medieval Languedoc* (Philadelphia: University of Philadelphia Press, 2001)

Aston, Sir George, *Secret Service* (London: Faber and Faber, 1930)

Aubrey, Philip, *Mr Secretary Thurloe: Cromwell's Secretary of State* (London: Athlone Press, 1990)

Auer-Véran, Francine, *Archives de l'Aéronautique Militaire de la Première Guerre Mondiale Répertoire numérique détaillé de la série A (1914–1919) et guide des sources* (Vincennes: Service Historique de la Défense, 2008)

Austin, N. J. E, and N. B. Rankov, *Exploratio: Military and Political Intelligence in the Roman World from the Second Punic War to the Battle of Adrianople* (London: Routledge, 1995)

Baden-Powell, Sir Robert (later Baron), *My Adventures as a Spy* (London: C. Arthur Pearson, 1925)

Badian, Ernst, *Collected Papers on Alexander the Great* (London: Routledge, 2012)

Baigent, Michael, and Richard Leigh, *The Inquisition* (London/New York: Viking, 1999)

Bakeless, John, *Turncoats, Traitors and Heroes: Espionage in the American Revolution*, reprint of 1959 edn (New York: Da Capo Press, 1998)

Ballantyne, Tony, 'Colonial Knowledge', in Sarah Stockwell (ed.), *The British Empire: Themes and Perspectives* (Oxford: Oxford University Press, 2008)

Bamford, James, *The Puzzle Palace: Inside the National Security Agency* (New York: Penguin Books, 1983)

—, *The Shadow Factory: The Ultra-Secret NSA from 9/11 to Eavesdropping on America* (New York: Doubleday, 2008)

—, 'Every Move You Make', *Foreign Policy*, 7 Sept. 2016

Bar-Joseph, Uri, 'Forecasting a Hurricane: Israeli and American Estimations of the Khomeini Revolution', *Journal of Strategic Studies*, vol. 36 (2013), no. 5

Barberiato, Federico, *The Inquisitor in the Hat Shop: Inquisition, Forbidden Books and Unbelief in Early Modern Venice* (Farnham: Ashgate, 2012)

Barclay, David E., *Frederick William IV and the Prussian Monarchy, 1840–1861* (Oxford: Clarendon Press, 1995)

Barker, Elton, 'Paging the Oracle: Interpretation, Identity and Performance in Herodotus' History', *Greece & Rome*, vol. 53 (2006), no. 1

Barnes, Jonathan (ed.), *The Cambridge Companion to Aristotle* (Cambridge: Cambridge University Press, 1995)

Barnett, Corelli, *The Desert Generals*, rev. edn (London: Allen & Unwin, 1983)

Barrass, Gordon S., *The Great Cold War: A Journey through the Hall of Mirrors* (Stanford, Calif.: Stanford University Press, 2009)

Barry, Jonathan, and Owen Davies (eds.), *Palgrave Advances in Witchcraft Historiography* (Basingstoke: Palgrave Macmillan, 2007)

Barry, Jonathan, Marianne Hester and Gareth Roberts, *Witchcraft in Early Modern Europe: Studies in Culture and Belief* (Cambridge: Cambridge University Press, 1996)

Bass, Streeter, 'Nathan Hale's Mission' (Langley, Va: CIA Center for the Study of Intelligence, 1996)

Batvinnis, Raymond J., *The Origins of FBI Counterintelligence* (Lawrence: University Press of Kansas, 2007)

Bayly, C. A., *Empire and Information: Intelligence Gathering and Social Communication in India, 1780–1870* (Cambridge: Cambridge University Press, 1997)

— and Tim Harper, *Forgotten Wars: The End of Britain's Asian Empire* (London: Allen Lane, 2007)

Bazeries, Étienne, and E. Burgaud, *Le Masque de fer: Révélations de la correspondance chiffrée de Louis XIV* (Paris: Firmin, Didot, 1893)

Beach, Jim, *Haig's Intelligence: GHQ and the German Army, 1916–1918* (Cambridge: Cambridge University Press, 2013)

Beard, Mary, *SPQR: A History of Ancient Rome* (London: Profile Books, 2016)

—, John North and Simon Price, *Religions of Rome*, 2 vols. (Cambridge: Cambridge University Press, 1998)

Bearden, Milt, and James Risen, *The Main Enemy: The Inside Story of the CIA's Final Showdown with the KGB* (New York: Random House, 2004)

Beauchamp, Ken, *History of Telegraphy* (London: Institution of Electrical Engineers, 2001)

Beaver, William, *Under Every Leaf: How Britain Played the Greater Game from Afghanistan to Africa* (London: Biteback, 2012)

Beeley, Philip, and Christoph J. Scriba (eds.), *The Correspondence of John Wallis (1616–1703)*, 6 vols. (Oxford: Oxford University Press, 2003–)

Beesly, Patrick, *Room 40: British Naval Intelligence 1914–18* (London: Hamish Hamilton, 1982)

Beevor, Antony, *The Second World War* (London: Weidenfeld & Nicolson, 2012)

Behrendt, Hans-Otto, *Rommel's Intelligence in the Desert Campaign, 1941–1943* (London: William Kimber, 1985)

Belchem, J. C., 'The Spy-System in 1848: Chartists and Informers. An Australian Connection', *Labour History*, 1980, no. 39

Bély, Lucien, *Espions et ambassadeurs au temps de Louis XIV* (Paris: Fayard, 1990)

—, *Les Secrets de Louis XIV: Mystères d'État et pouvoir absolu* (Paris: Tallandier, 2013)

Bennett, Gill, *'A Most Extraordinary and Mysterious Business': The Zinoviev Letter of 1924*, FCO History Note no. 14 (London: FCO, 1999)

—, *Churchill's Man of Mystery: Desmond Morton and the World of Intelligence* (London: Routledge, 2007)

Benson, Roger Louis, and Michael W. Warner (eds.), *VENONA: Soviet Espionage and the American Response, 1939–1957* (Washington, DC: National Security Agency/Central Intelligence Agency, 1996)

Berend, Ivan T., *History Derailed: Central and Eastern Europe in the Long Nineteenth Century* (Berkeley/Los Angeles: University of California Press, 2003)

Bergeron, David M., *King James and Letters of Homoerotic Desire* (Iowa City: University of Iowa Press, 1999)

Bergman, Ronen, *Rise and Kill First: The Secret History of Israel's Targeted Assassinations* (New York: Random House, 2018)

Berlière, Jean-Marc, 'A Republican Political Police? Political Policing under the French Third Republic 1875–1940', in Mark Mazower (ed.), *The Policing of Politics in the Twentieth Century* (Providence, RI, and Oxford: Berghahn Books, 1997)

Bernstein, Jeremy, *Hitler's Uranium Club: The Secret Recordings at Farm Hall*, 2nd edn (New York: Springer Verlag, 2001)

Bernstein, William, *A Splendid Exchange: How Trade Shaped the World* (London: Atlantic Books, 2008)

Berry, Lloyd E., and Robert O. Crummey (eds.), *Rude and Barbarous Kingdom: Russia in the Accounts of Sixteenth-Century English Voyagers* (Madison: University of Wisconsin Press, 1968)

Berthoud, Joël, 'L'Attentat contre Carnot. Spontanéité individuelle et action organisée dans le terrorisme anarchiste des années 1890', *Les Cahiers de l'histoire*, vol. XVI (1971), no. 1

Bethencourt, Francisco, 'L'inquisition au Portugal', in Agostino Borromeo (ed.), *L'Inquisizione: Atti del Simposio internazionale, Città del Vaticano, 29–31 ottobre 1998* (Vatican City: Biblioteca Apostolica Vaticana, 2003)

Bew, John, *Castlereagh: A Life* (Oxford: Oxford University Press, 2012)

—, *Citizen Clem: A Biography of Attlee* (London: Riverrun, 2016)

—, 'What Lessons from History Keep being Forgotten?', *World Policy Journal*, vol. 33 (2016), no. 3

Bezotosny, V. M., *Razvedka i plany storon v 1812 godu* (Moscow: Rosspen, 2005)

Biget, Jean-Louis, 'L'Inquisition en Languedoc, 1229–1329', in Agostino Borromeo (ed.), *L'Inquisizione: Atti del simposio internazionale, Città del Vaticano, 29–31 ottobre 1998* (Vatican City: Biblioteca Apostolica Vaticana, 2003)

Billington, James H., *Fire in the Minds of Men: Origins of the Revolutionary Faith* (New Brunswick, NJ: Transaction, 1999)

Bingham, Sandra, *The Praetorian Guard: A History of Rome's Elite Special Forces* (London: I. B. Tauris, 2012)

Black, Christopher F., *The Italian Inquisition* (New Haven, Conn.: Yale University Press, 2009)

Black, Jeremy, *Pitt the Elder: The Great Commoner* (Cambridge: Cambridge University Press, 1992)

—, *British Diplomats and Diplomacy, 1688–1800* (Exeter: University of Exeter Press, 2001)

—, 'Intelligence and the Emergence of the Information Society in Eighteenth-Century Britain', in Karl de Leeuw and Jan Bergstra (eds.), *The History of Information Security: A Comprehensive Handbook* (Amsterdam: Elsevier, 2007)

—, *George III: America's Last King* (New Haven, Conn.: Yale University Press, 2008)

Blair, Ann, 'Reading Strategies for Coping with Information Overload, ca. 1550–1700', *Journal of the History of Ideas*, vol. 64 (2003), no. 1

—, *Too Much to Know: Managing Scholarly Information before the Modern Age* (New Haven, Conn.: Yale University Press, 2010)

Blair, Tony, *A Journey* (London: Hutchinson, 2010)

Blaisdell, Lowell L., 'Aloysius Huber and May 15, 1848: New Insights into an Old Mystery', *International Review of Social History*, vol. 29 (April 1984), no. 1

Blanning, Tim, *The Pursuit of Glory: Europe 1648–1815* (London: Penguin Books, 2008)

—, *Frederick the Great: King of Prussia* (London: Allen Lane, 2015)

Blanqui, Louis-Auguste, 'Réponse du citoyen Auguste Blanqui' (Paris: Imprimerie Blondeau, 1848)

Blount, Thomas, *Boscobel; or, The history of the most miraculous preservation of King Charles II after the battle of Worcester, September the third, 1651. To which is added the King's own account of his adventures, dictated to Mr. Samuel Pepys.* Edited by Charles G. Thomas (London: Tylston and Edwards, 1894)

Blunt, Alison, 'Embodying War: British Women and Domestic Defilement in the Indian "Mutiny", 1857–8', *Journal of Historical Geography*, vol. 26 (2000), no. 3

Blunt, Wilfrid Scawen, *My Diaries: Being a Personal Narrative of Events, 1888–1914* (London: Martin Secker, 1932)

Bobbitt, Philip, *Terror and Consent: The Wars for the Twenty-First Century* (London: Allen Lane, 2008)

—, 'A Response to Professor Rascoff's *Presidential Intelligence*', *Harvard Law Review*, vol. 129 (2016), no. 3

Bock, F., 'Die Geheimschrift in der Kanzlei Johanns XXII', *Römische Quartalschrift*, vol. XLII (1934)

Bodansky, Yosef, *Bin Laden: The Man Who Declared War on America* (Rocklin, Ga: Prima, 1999)

Bogatyrev, Sergei, 'Ivan IV (1533–1584)', in Maureen Perrie (ed.), *The Cambridge History of Russia*, vol. 1: *From Early Rus' to 1689* (Cambridge: Cambridge University Press, 2006)

Boghardt, Thomas, *Spies of the Kaiser: German Covert Operations in Britain during the First World War Era* (Basingstoke: Palgrave Macmillan, 2004)

—, *The Zimmermann Telegram: Intelligence, Diplomacy and America's Entry into World War I* (Annapolis, Md: Naval Institute Press, 2012)

Bohlen, Charles E., *Witness to History, 1929–1969* (London: Weidenfeld & Nicolson, 1973)

Boissonade, Prosper, *Colbert: Le Triomphe de l'étatisme. La fondation de la suprématie industrielle de la France* (Paris: Marcel Rivière, 1931)

Bond, Helen K., *Caiaphas: Friend of Rome and Judge of Jesus?* (Louisville, Ky: Westminster John Knox Press, 2004)

—, *The Historical Jesus: A Guide to the Perplexed* (London: Bloomsbury, 2012)

Bonilla, Diego Navarro, ' "Secret Intelligences" in European Military, Political and Diplomatic Theory: An Essential Factor in the Defense of the Modern State (Sixteenth and Seventeenth Centuries)', *Intelligence and National Security*, vol. 27 (2012), no. 2

Bonsall, Sir Arthur, 'Bletchley Park and the RAF Y Service: Some Recollections', *Intelligence and National Security*, vol. 23 (2008), no. 6

—, *An Uphill Struggle* (Bletchley Park: Bletchley Park Trust, 2011)

Borromeo, Agostino (ed.), *L'Inquisizione: Atti del Simposio internazionale, Città del Vaticano, 29–31 ottobre 1998* (Vatican City: Biblioteca Apostolica Vaticana, 2003)

Bos, A. P., *Cosmic and Meta-Cosmic Theology in Aristotle's Lost Dialogues* (Leiden: Brill, 1989)

Bossy, John, *Under the Molehill: An Elizabethan Spy Story* (New Haven, Conn.: Yale University Press, 2001)

—, *Giordano Bruno and the Embassy Affair* (New Haven, Conn.: Yale Nota Bene, 2002)

Bosworth, A. B. and E. J. Baynham (eds.), *Alexander the Great in Fact and Fiction* (Oxford: Oxford University Press, 2000)

Bouhey, Vivien, *Les Anarchistes contre la République, 1880 à 1914: Contribution à l'histoire des réseaux sous la Troisième République* (Rennes: Presses Universitaires de Rennes, 2008)

Böwering, Gerhard, Patricia Crone, Wadad Kadi, Devin J. Stewart, Muhammad Qasim Zamam and Mahan Mirza (eds.), *The Princeton Encyclopedia of Islamic Political Thought* (Princeton, NJ: Princeton University Press, 2013)

Braddick, Michael, *God's Fury, England's Fire: A New History of the English Civil Wars* (London: Allen Lane, 2008)

Bradley, Mark Philip, 'Decolonization, the Global South, and the Cold War, 1919–1962', in M. P. Leffler and O. A. Westad (eds.), *The Cambridge History of the Cold War*, vol. 1: *Origins* (Cambridge: Cambridge University Press, 2010)

Braithwaite, Sir Rodric, *Across the Moscow River: The World Turned Upside Down* (New Haven, Conn., Yale University Press, 2002)

—, *Afgantsy: The Russians in Afghanistan 1979–89* (Oxford: Oxford University Press, 2011)

Brands, H. W., *Traitor to His Class* (New York: Doubleday, 2008)

Bréban, Alix, 'Germain Louis Chauvelin (1685–1762), ministre de Louis XV', thesis (École des Chartes, Paris, 2004)

Brendon, Piers, *Eminent Edwardians* (London: André Deutsch, 1979)

Briggs, Robin, *Witches and Neighbours: The Social and Cultural Context of European Witchcraft*, 2nd edn (Oxford: Blackwell, 2002)

Brock, Michael, and Eleanor Brock (eds.), *H. H. Asquith: Letters to Venetia Stanley*, rev. edn (Oxford: Oxford University Press, 1985)

Brodeur, Jean-Paul, 'High and Low Policing in post-9/11 Times', *Policing*, vol. 1 (2007), no. 1

—, 'High and Low Policing', in Jean-Paul Brodeur, *The Policing Web* (Oxford: Oxford University Press, 2010), ch. 7

Brooks, John, 'Preparing for Armageddon: Gunnery Practices and Exercises in the Grand Fleet prior to Jutland', *Journal of Strategic Studies*, vol. 38 (2015), no. 7

Brotton, Jerry, *This Orient Isle: Elizabethan England and the Islamic World* (London: Allen Lane, 2016)

Brown, J. M., *Modern India: The Origins of an Asian Democracy* (Oxford: Oxford University Press, 1985)

— and W. R. Louis (eds.), *The Oxford History of the British Empire*, vol. IV: *The Twentieth Century* (Oxford: Oxford University Press, 2001)

Brown, Malcolm (ed.), *T. E. Lawrence in War and Peace: An Anthology of the Military Writings of Lawrence of Arabia* (Barnsley: Frontline Books, 2015)

Brown, Peter, *Through the Eye of a Needle: Wealth, the Fall of Rome and the Making of Christianity in the West 350–550 AD* (Princeton, NJ: Princeton University Press, 2012)

Browning, Oscar (ed.), *The Despatches of Earl Gower, English Ambassador at Paris from June 1790 to August 1792* (Cambridge: Cambridge University Press, 1885)

Bruce, John (ed.), *Correspondence of King James VI of Scotland with Sir Robert Cecil and others in England, during the reign of Queen Elizabeth; with an appendix containing papers illustrative of transactions between King James and Robert Earl of Essex* (London: Camden Society, 1861)

Brugioni, Dino A., 'Arlington and Fairfax Counties: Land of Many Reconnaissance Firsts', *Northern Virginia Heritage*, February 1985

Bruneau, Thomas C., *Patriots for Profit: Contractors and the Military in US National Security* (Stanford, Calif.: Stanford University Press, 2011)

—, 'Contracting Out Security', *Journal of Strategic Studies*, vol. 36 (2013), no. 5

Brusilov, Alexei A., *A Soldier's Note-Book, 1914–1918* (Westport, Conn.: Greenwood Press, 1971)

Bryce, Trevor, *Letters of the Great Kings of the Ancient Near East: The Royal Correspondence of the Late Bronze Age* (London: Routledge, 2003)

Bulla, David W., 'Abraham Lincoln and Press Suppression Reconsidered', *American Journalism*, vol. 26 (2009), no. 4

— and Gregory A. Borchard, *Journalism in the Civil War Era* (Oxford: Peter Lang, 2010)

Buonafalce, Augusto, 'Cicco Simonetta's Cipher-Breaking Rules', *Cryptologia*, vol. 32 (2008), no. 1

Burds, Jeffrey, 'The Soviet War against "Fifth Columnists": The Case of Chechnya, 1942–4', *Journal of Contemporary History*, vol. 42 (2007), no. 2

Burger, Pierre, 'Spymaster to Louis XIV: A Study of the Papers of the Abbé Eusèbe Renaudot', in Eveline Cruikshanks (ed.), *Ideology and Conspiracy: Aspects of Jacobitism, 1689–1759* (Edinburgh: John Donald, 1982)

Burke, Aaron A., 'Canaan Under Siege: The History and Archaeology of Egypt's War in Canaan during the Early Eighteenth Dynasty', in Jordi Vidal (ed.), *Studies on War in the Ancient Near East: Collected Essays on Military History* (Münster: Ugarit-Verlag, 2010)

Burke, Peter, 'Early Modern Venice as a Center of Information and Communication', in John Martin and Dennis Romano (eds.), *Venice Reconsidered: The History and Civilization of an Italian City-State, 1297–1797* (Baltimore: Johns Hopkins University Press, 2000)

Burrows, Simon, Jonathan Conlin, Russell Goulbourne and Valerie Mainz (eds.), *The Chevalier d'Eon and His Worlds: Gender, Espionage and Politics in the 18th Century* (London: Continuum, 2010)

Bush, George W., *Decision Points* (London: Virgin, 2011)

Butcher, Tim, *The Trigger: Hunting the Assassin Who Brought the World to War*, Kindle edn (London: Chatto & Windus, 2014)

Cairncross, John, *The Enigma Spy: An Autobiography* (London: Century, 2007)

Carboni, Stefano, Trinita Kennedy and Elizabeth Marwell, 'Commercial Exchange, Diplomacy, and Religious Difference between Venice and the Islamic World', in *Heilbrunn Timeline of Art History* (New York: The Metropolitan Museum of Art, 2000–)

Carden, R. M., *German Policy toward Neutral Spain, 1914–1918* (New York: Garland, 1987)

Cardwell, John M., 'A Bible Lesson on Spying', *Studies in Intelligence*, Winter 1978

Carlyle, Thomas (ed.), *Oliver Cromwell's Letters and Speeches*, 4 vols. (Leipzig: Bernhard Tauchnitz, 1861)

Carnicer Garcia, Carlos, and Javier Marcos Rivas, *Espías de Felipe II: Los servicios secretos del Imperio español* (Madrid: La Esfera de los Libros, 2005)

Carrasco, Davíd, *Quetzalcoatl and the Irony of Empire: Myths and Prophecies in the Aztec Tradition* (Chicago: University of Chicago Press, 1982)

Cartledge, Paul, *Alexander the Great: The Hunt for a New Past*, Kindle edn (London: Pan Books, 2005)

Cattaneo, A., *Fra Mauro's Mappa Mundi and Fifteenth-Century Venice* (Turnhout: Brepols, 2011)

Catto, Jeremy, 'Currents of Religious Thought and Expression', in Michael Jones (ed.), *The New Cambridge Medieval History*, vol. 6 (Cambridge: Cambridge University Press, 2000)

Cavendish, Richard, 'Richard Cromwell Resigns as Lord Protector', *History Today*, vol. 59 (2009), no. 5

—, 'Tsar Nicholas II and Family Visit the Isle of Wight', *History Today*, vol. 59 (2009), no. 3

Cecil, Lamar, *The German Diplomatic Service, 1871–1914* (Princeton, NJ: Princeton University Press, 2015)

Central Intelligence Agency, *Intelligence in the Civil War* (Washington, DC: Central Intelligence Agency, 2007)

Chakraborty, Gayatri, *Espionage in Ancient India (from the Earliest Time to 12th Century A.D.)* (Calcutta: Minerva Associates, 1990)

Chambers, David, and Brian S. Pullan, with Jennifer Fletcher (eds.), *Venice: A Documentary History, 1450–1630* (Oxford: Blackwell, 1991)

Chambers, David Ian, 'The Past and Present State of Chinese Intelligence Historiography', *Studies in Intelligence*, vol. 56 (2012), no. 3

Chance, J. F., 'The "Swedish Plot" of 1716–17', *English Historical Review*, vol. 18 (1903)

Chandler, David, *The Campaigns of Napoleon* (London: Weidenfeld & Nicolson, 1966)

Chant, Chistopher, *Warfare and the Third Reich: The Rise and Fall of Hitler's Armed Forces* (London: Salamander, 1996)

Chapman, J. W. M, 'No Final Solution: A Survey of the Cryptanalytical Capabilities of German Military Agencies', in Christopher Andrew (ed.), *Codebreaking and Signals Intelligence* (London: Frank Cass, 1986)

[Charles I], *The Private Correspondence between King Charles I and [others]* in William Bray (ed.), *Memoirs of John Evelyn, Esq F.R.S.*, vol. 5 (London: Henry Colburn, 1827)

Charmley, John, ' "Unravelling Silk": Princess Lieven, Metternich and Castlereagh', in Lothar Höbelt and Thomas G. Otte (eds.), *A Living Anachronism?: European Diplomacy and the Habsburg Monarchy. Festschrift für Francis Roy Bridge zum 70. Geburtstag* (Vienna: Böhlau Verlag, 2010)

Chase, Philander D. (ed.), *The Papers of George Washington: Revolutionary War Series* (Charlottesville: University Press of Virginia, 1985)

Chiharu, Inaba, 'Franco-Russian Intelligence Collaboration against Japan during the Russo-Japanese War, 1904–05', *Japanese Slavic and East European Studies*, vol. 19 (1998)

Choisel, Francis, 'Charlemagne de Maupas', in B. Yvert, *Le Dictionnaire des ministres, 1789–1989* (Paris: Perrin, 1990)

Church, Clive H., *Revolution and Red Tape: The French Ministerial Bureaucracy 1770–1850* (Oxford: Clarendon Press, 1981)

Churchill, W. S., *The World Crisis*, 5 vols., vol. I: *1911–1914*; vol. II: *1915* (London: Thornton Butterworth, 1923)

—, *My Early Life* (London: Eland, 2000 [first publ. 1930])

—, *The Second World War*, 6 vols., vol. 2: *Their Finest Hour*; vol. 5: *Closing the Ring* (London: Penguin Books, 2005 [first publ. 1949; 1951])

Clarendon, Edward Hyde, Earl of, *The History of the Rebellion and Civil Wars in England*, 2 vols. (Oxford: Oxford University Press, 1843 [first publ. 1702–4])

—, *The History of the Rebellion: A New Selection*, ed. Paul Seaward (Oxford: Oxford University Press, 2009)

Clark, Christopher, *Iron Kingdom: The Rise and Downfall of Prussia, 1600–1947* (London: Allen Lane, 2006)

—, *The Sleepwalkers: How Europe Went to War in 1914* (London: Allen Lane, 2012)

Clark, Gillian, *Christianity and Roman Society* (Cambridge: Cambridge University Press, 2004)

Clarke, Jonathan, 'Restoration to Reform, 1660–1832', in Jonathan Clarke (ed.), *A World by Itself: A History of the British Isles* (London: William Heinemann, 2010)

— (ed.), *A World by Itself: A History of the British Isles* (London: William Heinemann, 2010)

Clausewitz, Carl von, *On War*, eds. Michael Howard and Peter Paret (Princeton, NJ: Princeton University Press, 1976)

Claydon, Tony, *William III and the Godly Revolution* (Cambridge: Cambridge University Press, 2004)

Clinton, Bill, *My Life* (London: Arrow Books, 2005)

Clutterbuck, Lindsay, 'The Progenitors of Terrorism: Russian Revolutionaries or Extreme Irish Republicans?', *Terrorism and Political Violence*, vol. 16 (2004), no. 1

Cobb, Richard, 'Our Man in Berne', in Richard Cobb, *A Second Identity: Essays on France and French History* (London: Oxford University Press, 1969)

—, *The Police and the People: French Popular Protest 1789–1820* (Oxford: Oxford University Press, 1970)

Cobban, Alfred, *A History of Modern France*, 2 vols. (Harmondsworth: Penguin Books, 1961)

Cohen, Raymond, 'Intelligence in the Amarna Letters', in Raymond Cohen and Raymond Westbrook (eds.), *Amarna Diplomacy: The Beginnings of International Relations* (Baltimore: Johns Hopkins University Press, 2000)

— and Raymond Westbrook (eds.), *Amarna Diplomacy: The Beginnings of International Relations* (Baltimore: Johns Hopkins University Press, 2000)

Cohn, Norman, *Warrant for Genocide: The Myth of the Jewish World Conspiracy and the Protocols of the Elders of Zion* (New York: Harper & Row, 1966)

Cole, Juan, *Napoleon's Egypt: Invading the Middle East* (London: Palgrave Macmillan, 2007)

'Conférence de M. Georges Jean Painvin', *Bulletin de l'A.R.C.*, nouvelle série, vol. VIII (May 1961)

Conley, Scott E., 'British Intelligence Operations as They Relate to Britain's Defeat at Yorktown, 1781', Master's thesis (Morgantown: West Virginia University, 1990)

Conlin, Jonathan, 'Wilkes, the Chevalier d'Eon and "the dregs of liberty": An Anglo-French Perspective on Ministerial Despotism', *English Historical Review*, vol. 120 (2005)

—, 'The Strange Case of the Chevalier d'Eon', *History Today*, vol. 60 (2010), no. 4

Conquest, Robert, *The Great Terror: A Reassessment*, rev. edn (London: Pimlico, 2008)

Conrad, Geoffrey W., and Arthur A. Demarest, *Religion and Empire: The Dynamics of Aztec and Inca Expansionism* (Cambridge: Cambridge University Press, 1984)

Cook, David, *Martyrdom in Islam* (Cambridge: Cambridge University Press, 2007)

Cooper, J. P. D., *The Queen's Agent: Francis Walsingham at the Court of Elizabeth I* (London: Faber, 2012)

Cooper, Randolf G. S., *The Anglo-Maratha Campaigns and the Contest for India: The Struggle for Control of the South Asian Military Economy* (Cambridge: Cambridge University Press, 2004)

Corera, Gordon, *The Art of Betrayal: Life and Death in the British Secret Service* (London: Weidenfeld & Nicolson, 2011)

Corvisier, André, *Louvois* (Paris: Fayard, 1983)

Cosmo, Nicola di (ed.), *Military Culture in Imperial China* (Cambridge, Mass.: Harvard University Press, 2011)

Cozzens, Peter, 'Our Ministers do not express their real opinions', Office of the Historian, US Department of State, 2011; https://history.state.gov/historical documents/frus-history/research/real-opinions

Cradock, Sir Percy, *Know Your Enemy: How the Joint Intelligence Committee Saw the World* (London: John Murray, 2002)

Creasy, Sir Edward, *Fifteen Decisive Battles of the World: From Marathon to Waterloo* (London: Oxford University Press, 1915)

Cressy, David, *Dangerous Talk: Scandalous, Seditious and Treasonable Speech in pre-Modern England* (Oxford: Oxford University Press, 2010)

Crone, Patricia, *Pre-Industrial Societies* (Oxford: Basil Blackwell, 1989)

Cronin, Audrey Kurth, 'Behind the Curve: Globalization and International Terrorism', *International Security*, XXVII (Winter 2003), no. 3

Crossan, John Dominic, and Jonathan L. Reed, *Excavating Jesus: Beneath the Stones, behind the Texts* (London: SPCK, 2001)

Cruikshanks Eveline (ed.), *Ideology and Conspiracy: Aspects of Jacobitism, 1689–1759* (Edinburgh: John Donald, 1982)

— and Howard Erskine-Hill, *The Atterbury Plot* (Basingstoke: Palgrave Macmillan, 2004)

Crumpton, Henry A., *The Art of Intelligence: Lessons from a Life in the CIA's Clandestine Service* (New York: Penguin Press, 2012)

Cubitt, Geoffrey, 'Denouncing Conspiracy in the French Revolution', *Renaissance and Modern Studies*, vol. 33 (1989)

—, 'Robespierre and Conspiracy Theories', in C. Haydon and W. Doyle (eds.), *Robespierre* (Cambridge: Cambridge University Press, 1999)

Cunliffe, Sir Barry W., *The Ancient Celts* (Oxford: Oxford University Press, 1997)

—, *Facing the Ocean: The Atlantic and Its Peoples* (Oxford: Oxford University Press, 2001)

[Curry, J. C.], *The Security Service 1908–1945*, with an introduction by Christopher Andrew (Kew: Public Record Office, 1999)

Custine, marquis Astolphe de, *Journey for Our Time: The Journals of the Marquis de Custine. Russia – 1839*, trans. and ed. Phyllis Penn Kohler (London: George Prior, 1980)

Cypess, Sandra Messinger, *La Malinche in Mexican Literature from History to Myth* (Austin: University of Texas Press, 1991)

Danan, Liora, and Alice Hunt, *Mixed Blessings: U.S. Government Engagement with Religion in Conflict-Prone Settings* (Washington, DC: CSIS Press, 2007)

Dando-Collins, Stephen, *The Ides: Caesar's Murder and the War for Rome* (Hoboken, NJ: John Wiley & Sons, 2010)

Darnton, Robert, 'The News in Paris: An Early Information Society', in Robert Darnton, *George Washington's False Teeth: An Unconventional Guide to the Eighteenth Century* (New York: W. W. Norton, 2003)

—, 'The Skeletons in the Closet: How Historians Play God', in Robert Darnton, *George Washington's False Teeth: An Unconventional Guide to the Eighteenth Century* (New York: W. W. Norton, 2003)

Darwin, John, *The Empire Project: The Rise and Fall of the British World System, 1830–1970* (Cambridge: Cambridge University Press, 2009)

Dash, Mike, 'Pass It On: The Secret That Preceded the Indian Rebellion of 1857', 2012; http://www.smithsonianmag.com/history/pass-it-on-the-secret-that-preceded-the-indian-rebellion-of-1857-105066360/?no-ist.

Daudet, Ernest, *Police politique: Chronique des temps de la restauration, d'après les rapports d'agents secrets et les papiers du cabinet noir, 1815–20* (Paris: Plon-Nourrit, 1912)

Davidsson, Elias, *Hijacking America's Mind on 9/11: Counterfeiting Evidence* (New York: Algora Publishing, 2013)

Davies, Huw, 'Integration of Strategic and Operational Intelligence during the Peninsular War', *Intelligence and National Security*, vol. 21 (2006), no. 2

—, 'Wellington's Use of Deception Tactics in the Peninsular War', *Journal of Strategic Studies*, vol. 29 (2006), no. 4.

—, 'The Influence of Intelligence on Wellington's Art of Command', *Intelligence and National Security*, vol. 22 (2007), no. 5

Davies, John G., *The Early Christian Church* (New York: Anchor Books, 1965)

Davies, Norman, *Vanished Kingdoms: The History of Half-Forgotten Europe* (London: Allen Lane, 2011)

Davies, Philip H. J., and Kristian J. Gustafson (eds.), *Intelligence Elsewhere: Spies and Espionage outside the Anglosphere* (Washington, DC: Georgetown University Press, 2013)

Davies, R. W., Oleg V. Khlevnyuk, E. A. Rees et al., *The Stalin–Kaganovich Correspondence, 1931–36* (New Haven, Conn.: Yale University Press, 2003)

Davies, Sarah, and James Harris, *Stalin's World: Dictating the Soviet Order* (New Haven, Conn.: Yale University Press, 2014)

De La Hodde [Delahodde], Lucien, *The Cradle of Rebellions: A History of the Secret Societies of France*, facsimile edn (Charleston, SC: Nabu Press, 2012)

De Vivo, Filippo, *Information and Communication in Venice: Rethinking Early Modern Politics* (Oxford: Oxford University Press, 2007)

Dear, I. C. B., and M. R. D. Foot (eds.), *The Oxford Companion to the Second World War* (Oxford: Oxford University Press, 1995)

Decock, P., 'La Dame Blanche', unpublished dissertation (Université Libre de Bruxelles, 1981)

Dedieu, Jean Pierre, 'L'Inquisition et le people en Espagne', in Agostino Borromeo (ed.), *L'Inquisizione: Atti del Simposio internazionale, Città del Vaticano, 29–31 ottobre 1998* (Vatican City: Biblioteca Apostolica Vaticana, 2003)

Deflem, Mathieu, 'International Policing in Nineteenth-Century Europe: The Police Union of German States, 1851–1866', *International Criminal Justice Review*, vol. 6 (1996)

Degtyarev, Klim, and Aleksandr Kolpakidi, *Vneshnyaya razvedka SSSR* (Moscow: Eksmo, 2009)

Delamarre, X., *Dictionnaire de la langue gauloise*, 2nd edn (Paris: Éditions Errance, 2003)

Dennis, George T. (trans. and ed.), *Maurice's Strategikon: Handbook of Byzantine Military Strategy* (Philadelphia: University of Pennsylvania Press, 1984)

— (ed.), *The Taktika of Leo VI : Text, Translation and Commentary*, rev. edn (Cambridge, Mass.: Harvard University Press, 2010)

Denniston, A. G., 'The Government Code and Cypher School between the Wars', in Christopher Andrew (ed.), *Codebreaking and Signals Intelligence* (London: Frank Cass, 1986)

Denson, Bryan, *The Spy's Son: The True Story of the Highest-Ranking CIA Officer Ever Convicted of Espionage and the Son He Trained to Spy for Russia* (New York: Atlantic Monthly Press, 2015)

Dessert, Daniel, *Argent, pouvoir et société au Grand Siècle* (Paris: Fayard, 1984)

Díaz del Castillo, Bernal, *History of the Conquest of New Spain*, trans. J. Cohen (London: Penguin Books, 1963)

Dickie, M. W., *Magic and Magicians in the Greco-Roman World* (London: Routledge, 2001)

Dictionnaire de biographie française, sous la direction de J. Balteau, A. Rastoul et M. Prévost, avec le concours de nombreux collaborateurs (Paris: Letouzey et Ané, 1929–)

Dillard, James E., and Walter T. Hitchcock (eds.), *The Intelligence Revolution and Modern Warfare* (Chicago: Imprint Publications, 1996)

Dillon, Matthew, *Omens and Oracles: Divination in Ancient Greece* (London: Routledge, 2017)

A discouerie of the treasons practised and attempted against the Queenes Maiestie and the realme, [by] Francis Throckemorton, who was for the same arraigned and condemned in Guyld Hall, in the citie of London, the one and twentie day of May last past (London: printed by Christopher Barker, 1584)

Dmitrieva, Olga, and Natalya Abramova (eds.), *Britannia and Muscovy* (New Haven, Conn.: Yale Center for British Art, 2006)

Dobrynin, Anatoly, *In Confidence* (New York: Times Books, 1995)

Doerries, Reinhard R., *Imperial Challenge: Ambassador Count Bernstorff and German–American Relations, 1908–1917* (Chapel Hill: University of North Carolina Press, 1989)

Don, Patricia Lopes, *Bonfires of Culture: Franciscans, Indigenous Leaders and the Inquisition in Early Mexico, 1524–1540* (Norman: University of Oklahoma Press, 2010)

Dorwart, Jeffery M., *The Office of Naval Intelligence: The Birth of America's First Intelligence Agency* (Annapolis, Md: Naval Institute Press, 1979)

—, 'The Roosevelt–Astor Espionage Ring', *New York History*, vol. LXII (July 1981), no. 3

Douglas, Hugh, *Jacobite Spy Wars: Moles, Rogues and Treachery* (Stroud: Sutton, 1999)

Dowling, Timothy C., *The Brusilov Offensive* (Bloomington: Indiana University Press, 2009

Duchesne. Ricardo, *The Uniqueness of Western Civilization* (Leiden: Brill, 2011)

Duffy, Christopher, *Frederick the Great: A Military Life* (London: Routledge & Kegan Paul, 1985)

Duffy, Eamon, 'The Repression of Heresy in England', in Agostino Borromeo (ed.), *L'Inquisizione: Atti del Simposio internazionale, Città del Vaticano, 29–31 ottobre 1998* (Vatican City: Biblioteca Apostolica Vaticana, 2003)

Dugdale, Blanche E. C., *Balfour: A Life of Arthur James Balfour*, 2 vols. (London: Hutchinson, 1936–7)

Duke, Alastair, 'The "Inquisition" and the Repression of Religious Dissent in the Habsburg Netherlands (1521–1566)', in Agostino Borromeo (ed.), *L'Inquisizione: Atti del Simposio internazionale, Città del Vaticano, 29–31 ottobre 1998* (Vatican City: Biblioteca Apostolica Vaticana, 2003)

Dulles, Allen W., *The Craft of Intelligence* (London: Weidenfeld & Nicolson, 1963)

Dumas, Alexandre, *Histoire de la vie politique et privée de Louis-Philippe* (Paris: Dufour et Mulat, 1852)

Dunlop, Richard, *Donovan: America's Master Spy* (New York: Skyhorse, 2014)

Dunn, Dennis J., *Caught between Roosevelt and Stalin: America's Ambassadors to Moscow* (Lexington: University Press of Kentucky, 1998)

Durey, Michael, 'Lord Grenville and the "Smoking Gun": The Plot to Assassinate the French Directory in 1798–1799 Reconsidered', *The Historical Journal*, vol. 45 (2002)

—, 'William Wickham, the Christ Church Connection and the Rise and Fall of the Security Service in Britain, 1793–1801', *English Historical Review*, vol. 121 (2006), no. 492

—, *William Wickham, Master Spy: The Secret War against the French Revolution* (London: Pickering & Chatto, 2009)

Dursteler, Eric R., 'The Bailo in Constantinople: Crisis and Career in Venice's Early Modern Diplomatic Corps', *Mediterranean Historical Review*, vol. 16 (2001), no. 2

—, 'Power and Information: The Venetian Postal System in the Mediterranean, 1573–1645', in *From Florence to the Mediterranean: Studies in Honor of Anthony Molho* (Florence: Olschki, 2009)

Dutton, Roy, *Forgotten Heroes: The Charge of the Light Brigade* (Wallasley: Infodial, 2007)

Duvernoy, Jean (ed.), *Le Registre d'Inquisition de Jacques Fournier*, 3 vols. (Paris: Mouton, 1978)

Economist, 'Sun Tzu and the Art of Soft Power', 17 December 2011

Edney, Matthew, *Mapping an Empire* (Chicago: University of Chicago Press, 1997)

Eisenhower, Dwight D., *Crusade in Europe* (New York: Doubleday, 1948)

Ekberg, Carl J., 'From Dutch to European War: Louis XIV and Louvois are Tested', *French Historical Studies*, vol. 8 (1974), no. 3

Elkner, Julie, 'Constructing the Chekist: The Cult of State Security in Soviet and Post-Soviet Russia', PhD thesis (Cambridge University, 2009)

—, *Russia and the Cult of State Security: The Chekist Tradition, from Lenin to Putin* (London: Routledge, 2011)

Elliott, J. H., *Richelieu and Olivares* (Cambridge: Cambridge University Press, 1984)

Ellis, Kenneth, *The Post Office in the Eighteenth Century: A Study in Administrative History* (London: Oxford University Press, 1958)

Emsley, Clive, 'The Home Office and Its Sources of Information and Investigation 1791–1801', *English Historical Review*, vol. 94 (1979)

Engels, Donald W., *Alexander the Great and the Logistics of the Macedonian Army* (Los Angeles: University of California Press, 1980)

Epkenhans, Michael (ed.), *Das ereignisreiche Leben eines 'Wilhelminers': Tagebücher, Briefe, Aufzeichnungen 1901 bis 1920* (Munich: Oldenbourg Wissenschaftsverlag, 2004)

Erskine, Ralph, 'The 1944 Naval BRUSA Agreement and Its Aftermath', *Cryptologia*, vol. 30 (2006), no. 1

—, 'William Friedman's Bletchley Park Diary: A Different View', *Intelligence and National Security*, vol. 22 (2007), no. 3

— and Michael Smith, *The Bletchley Park Codebreakers* (London: Biteback, 2011)

Esenwein, George Richard, *Anarchist Ideology and the Working-Class Movement in Spain, 1868–1898* (Berkeley/Los Angeles: University of California Press, 1989)

Etzioni, Amitai, 'Talking to the Muslim World: How, and with Whom?', *International Affairs*.vol. 92 (2016), no. 6

Evans, Richard, *Rereading German History: From Unification to Reunification 1800–1996* (London: Routledge, 2002)

Everth, Erich, *Die Öffentlichkeit in der Aussenpolitik von Karl V bis Napoleon* (Jena: Verlag von Gustav Fischer, 1931)

Falkenhayn, General Erich von, *The German General Staff and Its Decisions, 1914–1916* (New York: Dodd, Mead & Co., 1920)

Faught, C. Brad, *Clive: Founder of British India* (Washington, DC: Potomac Books, 2013)

Favier, Jean, 'Traits généraux et traits spécifiques de l'administration pontificale', in *Le Fonctionnement administratif de la Papauté d'Avignon* (Rome: École Française de Rome, 1990)

Ferguson, John, *Greek and Roman Religion: A Source Book* (Park Ridge, NJ: Noyes Press, 1980)

Ferguson, Kathy E., *Emma Goldman: Political Thinking in the Street* (Lanham, Md: Rowman & Littlefield Publishers, 2011)

Ferguson, Niall, *The Square and the Tower: Networks, Hierarchies and the Struggle for Global Power* (London: Allen Lane, 2017)

Ferling, John E., *The First of Men* (Knoxville: University of Tennessee Press, 1988)

Ferrill, Arther, 'Roman Military Intelligence', in Keith Neilson and B. J. C. McKercher (eds.), *Go Spy the Land: Military Intelligence in History* (Westport, Conn.: Praeger, 1992)

Ferris, John, 'Before "Room 40": The British Empire and Signals Intelligence 1898–1914', *Journal of Strategic Studies*, vol. 12 (1989), no. 4

—, 'From Broadway House to Bletchley Park: The Diary of Captain Malcolm Kennedy, 1935–1946', *Intelligence and National Security*, vol. 4 (1989), no. 3

— (ed.), *British Army and Signals Intelligence during the First World War* (Stroud: Alan Sutton, 1992)

—, 'Connaissances, influence et pouvoir: Les Services de renseignements britanniques et la Première Guerre mondiale', in Frédéric Guelton and Abdil Bicer (eds.), *Naissance et évolution du renseignement dans l'espace européen (1870–1940)* (Paris: Service Historique de la Défense, 2006)

—, 'Lord Salisbury, Secret Intelligence and British Policy toward Russia and Central Asia, 1874–1878', in John Ferris, *Intelligence and Strategy: Selected Essays* (London: Routledge, 2007)

—, 'British Intelligence and the Old World Order, 1715 to 1956', in Greg Kennedy (ed.), *Imperial Defence: The Old World Order, 1856–1956* (London: Routledge, 2008)

—, 'Signals Intelligence in War and Power Politics, 1914–2010', in Loch K. Johnson (ed.), *The Oxford Handbook of National Security Intelligence* (New York: Oxford University Press, 2010)

—, 'Towards the Second Century of Sigint', keynote address to Oriel Colloquium on Universities, Security and Intelligence Studies, 22 September 2017

Figes, Orlando, *A People's Tragedy: The Russian Revolution 1891–1924* (London: Jonathan Cape, 1996)

—, *Crimea: The Last Crusade*, Kindle edn (London: Penguin Books, 2011)

Fijnaut, Cyrille, and Gary T. Marx (eds.), *Undercover Police Surveillance in Comparative Perspective* (The Hague: Kluwer Law International, 1995)

Filby, P. William, 'Bletchley Park and Berkeley Street', *Intelligence and National Security*, vol. 3 (1988), no. 2

Filjushkin, Alexander, *Ivan the Terrible: A Military History* (London: Frontline Books, 2008)

Finkelstein, Israel, and Neil Asher Silberman, *The Bible Unearthed: Archaeology's New Vision of Ancient Israel and the Origin of Its Sacred Texts* (New York: Touchstone, 2002)

Finnegan, Terrence J., *Shooting the Front: Allied Aerial Reconnaissance in the First World War* (Stroud: The History Press, 2011)

Firth, C. H. (ed.), 'Thomas Scot's Account of His Actions as an Intelligencer during the Commonwealth', *English Historical Review*, vol. XII (1897)

Fishel, Edwin C., *The Secret War for the Union: The Untold Story of Military Intelligence in the Civil War* (New York: Houghton Mifflin, 1996)

Fishman, Ethan M., William D. Pederson and Mark J. Rozell (eds.), *George Washington: Foundation of Presidential Leadership and Character* (Westport, Conn.: Praeger, 2001)

Fishwick, Duncan, 'An Early Christian Cryptogram?', *CCHA Report*, 26 (1959)

Fitzgerald, Penelope, *The Knox Brothers* (London: Macmillan, 1977)

Fitzpatrick, John C. (ed.), *The Writings of George Washington* (Washington, DC: U.S. Government Printing Office, 1931–44)

Fleet, Kate, 'Turks, Italians and Intelligence in the Fourteenth and Fifteenth Centuries', in Çiğdem Balim-Harding and Colin Imber (eds.), *The Balance of Truth: Essays in Honour of Professor Geoffrey Lewis* (Istanbul: Isis Press, 2000)

Fleming, Thomas, 'George Washington, General', in Robert Cowley (ed.), *Experience of War* (New York: W. W. Norton, 1992)

Fletcher, Catherine, *The Divorce of Henry VIII: The Untold Story* (London: Virago, 2013)

Fletcher, Giles, *Of the Russe Commonwealth* (Cambridge, Mass.: Harvard University Press, 1966 [first publ. 1591])

Flexner, James T., *George Washington: The Forge of Experience (1732–1775)* (London: Leo Cooper, 1973)

Flower, Michael Attyah, *The Seer in Ancient Greece* (Berkeley/Los Angeles: University of California Press, 2008)

Fontenrose, Joseph, *The Delphic Oracle, Its Responses and Operations, with a Catalogue of Responses* (Berkeley/Los Angeles: University of California Press, 1981)

Forcade, Olivier, *La République secrète: Histoire des services spéciaux français de 1918 à 1939* (Paris: Nouveau Monde, 2008)

Foreign and Commonwealth Office, Historical Branch, *'My Purdah Lady': The Foreign Office and the Secret Vote 1782–1909*, History Notes No. 7 (September 1994)

Foreign Relations of the United States (Washington, DC: State Department, 1861–)

Forrest, Ian, *The Detection of Heresy in Late Medieval England* (Oxford: Oxford University Press, 2005)

Förster, Stig, and Jorg Nagler, *On the Road to Total War: The American Civil War and the German Wars of Unification, 1861–1871* (Cambridge: Cambridge University Press, 2002)

Fowler, Robert (ed.), *The Cambridge Companion to Homer* (Cambridge: Cambridge University Press, 2004)

Fowler, W. B., *British–American Relations, 1917–1918* (Princeton, NJ: Princeton University Press, 1969)

France, Jean, *Trente ans à la rue des Saussaies. Ligues et complots* (Paris: Gallimard, 1931)

Frank, Katherine, *Indira: The Life of Indira Nehru Gandhi* (London: HarperCollins, 2001)

Fraser, Antonia, *The Gunpowder Plot: Terror and Faith in 1605* (London: Weidenfeld & Nicolson, 1996)

Fraser, George MacDonald, *Flashman in the Great Game* (London: HarperCollins, 1973)

Fraser, Peter, *The Intelligence of the Secretaries of State and Their Monopoly of Licensed News, 1660–1688* (Cambridge: Cambridge University Press, 1956)

Fraser, Sarah, *The Last Highlander: Scotland's Most Notorious Clan Chief, Rebel and Double Agent* (London: HarperPress, 2012)

Freedman, Lawrence, 'Defence', in Anthony Seldon (ed.), *The Blair Effect: The Blair Government 1997–2001* (London: Little, Brown, 2001)

Freeman, Peter, 'MI1(b) and the Origins of British Diplomatic Cryptanalysis', *Intelligence and National Security*, vol. 22 (2007), no. 2

Freidel, F. B., *Franklin D. Roosevelt* (Boston: Little, Brown, 1952–73), vol. 2: *The Ordeal* (1954); vol. 3: *The Triumph* (1956)

Freitag, Sabine, Markus Mösslang and Peter Wende (eds.), *British Envoys to Germany, 1816–1866*, 2 vols. (Cambridge: Cambridge University Press, 2000–2002)

Friedlander, Alan, *The Hammer of the Inquisition: Brother Bernard Délicieux and the Struggle against the Inquisition in Fourteenth-Century France* (Leiden: Brill, 2000)

Friedman, William F., *Bletchley Park Diary*, ed. Colin MacKinnon; http://www.colin mackinnon.com/files/The_Bletchley_Park_Diary_of_William_F._Friedman_E.pdf.

Frigo, Daniela, 'Introduction', in Daniela Frigo (ed.), *Politics and Diplomacy in Early Modern Italy* (Cambridge: Cambridge University Press, 2000)

Fromkin, David, 'The Great Game in Asia', *Foreign Affairs*, Spring 1980

Fubini, Riccardo, 'Diplomacy and Government in the Italian City-States of the Fifteenth Century (Florence and Venice)', in Daniela Frigo (ed.), *Politics and Diplomacy in Early Modern Italy* (Cambridge: Cambridge University Press, 2000)

Fuhrmann, Christopher J., *Policing the Roman Empire: Soldiers, Administration and Public Order*, Kindle edn (Oxford: Oxford University Press, 2011)

Fuller, William C., Jr, 'The Russian Empire', in Ernest R. May, *Knowing One's Enemies: Intelligence Assessment before the Two World Wars* (Princeton, NJ: Princeton University Press, 1984)

—, *The Foe Within: Fantasies of Treason and the End of Imperial Russia* (Ithaca, NY: Cornell University Press, 2006)

Fursenko, Alexander, and Timothy Naftali, *'One Hell of a Gamble': Khrushchev, Kennedy, Castro and the Cuban Missile Crisis, 1958–1964* (London: John Murray, 1997)

——, *Khrushchev's Cold War: The Inside Story of an American Adversary* (New York: W. W. Norton, 2006)

Gabriel, Mary, *Love and Capital: Karl and Jenny Marx and the Birth of a Revolution* (London: Hachette, 2011)

Gabriel, Richard A., *Scipio Africanus: Rome's Greatest General* (Washington, DC: Potomac Books, 2008)

—, *Muhammad: Islam's First Great General* (Norman: University of Oklahoma Press, 2011)

Gaddis, John Lewis, *The Cold War* (London: Allen Lane, 2006)

Gaddis, Michael, *There is No Crime for Those Who Have Christ: Religious Violence in the Christian Roman Empire* (Berkeley: University of California Press, 2005)

Gannon, Paul, *Inside Room 40: The Codebreakers of World War 1* (Hersham: Ian Allan, 2010)

Garrett, Jane, *The Triumphs of Providence: The Assassination Plot, 1696* (Cambridge: Cambridge University Press, 1980)

Garthoff, Raymond L., 'The KGB Reports to Gorbachev', *Intelligence and National Security*, vol. 11 (1996), no. 2

Gasnault, Pierre, 'L'Élaboration des lettres secrètes des papes d'Avignon: Chambre et Chancellerie, in *Le Fonctionnement administratif de la Papauté d'Avignon* (Rome: École Française de Rome, 1990)

Gates, Robert, *From the Shadows* (New York: Touchstone, 1997)

Gaunt, Admiral Sir Guy, *The Yield of the Years* (London: Hutchinson, 1940)

Geifman, Anna, *Thou Shalt Kill: Revolutionary Terrorism in Russia* (Princeton, NJ: Princeton University Press, 1995)

—, *Entangled in Terror: The Azef Affair and the Russian Revolution* (Lanham, Md: Rowman and Littlefield, 2000)

Genêt, Stéphane, *Les Espions des lumières: Actions secrètes et espionnage militaire au temps de Louis XV* (Paris: Ministère de la Défense, 2013)

Gerolymatos, André, *Espionage and Treason: A Study of the Proxenia in Political and Military Intelligence Gathering in Classical Greece* (Amsterdam: J. C. Gieben, 1986)

Getty, J. Arch, and Oleg V. Naumov (eds.), *The Road to Terror: Stalin and the Self-Destruction of the Bolsheviks, 1932–1939* (New Haven, Conn.: Yale University Press, 2002)

Gevorkyan, Nataliya, Natalya Timakova and Andrei Kolesnikov, *First Person: An Astonishingly Frank Self-Portrait by Russia's President Vladimir Putin* (London: Hutchinson, 2000)

Gilbert, Martin, *Winston S. Churchill*, 8 vols. (London: Heinemann, 1966–88); vol. 3: *The Challenge of War, 1914–1916* (1971); vol. 6: *Finest Hour, 1939–1941* (1983)

—, 'Final Solution', in I. C. B. Dear and M. R. D. Foot (eds.), *The Oxford Companion to the Second World War* (Oxford: Oxford University Press, 1995)

—, *Auschwitz and the Allies* (London: Pimlico, 2001)

Gioe, David, 'The Anglo-American Special Intelligence Relationship: Wartime Causes and Cold War Consequences, 1940–63', PhD thesis (University of Cambridge, 2014)

—, Len Scott and Christopher Andrew (eds.), *An International History of the Cuban Missile Crisis: A 50-Year Retrospective* (London: Routledge, 2014)

Girard, Louis, *Napoléon III* (Paris: Hachette, 1993)

Giustiniani, Sebastiano, *Four Years at the Court of Henry VIII: Selection of Despatches Written by the Venetian Ambassador . . . January 12th, 1515, to July 26th, 1519*, ed. and trans. Rawdon Lubbock Brown, 2 vols. (Cambridge: Cambridge University Press, 2013 [first publ. 1854])

Given, James B., 'A Medieval Inquisitor at Work: Bernard Gui, 3 March 1308 to 19 June 1323', in Samuel K. Cohn, Jr, and Steven A. Epstein (eds.), *Portraits of Medieval and Renaissance Living: Essays in Memory of David Herlihy* (Ann Arbor: University of Michigan Press, 1996)

—, *Inquisition and Medieval Society: Power, Discipline and Resistance in Languedoc* (Ithaca, NY: Cornell University Press, 1997)

— (ed. and trans.), *The Fragmentary History of Priscus: Attila, the Huns and the Roman Empire, AD 430–476* (Merchantville, NJ: Evolution Publishing, 2014)

Given-Wilson, Chris, *Henry IV* (New Haven, Conn.: Yale University Press, 2016)

Gladwell, Malcolm, 'Daniel Ellsberg, Edward Snowden, and the Modern Whistle-Blower', *New Yorker*, 19 and 26 Dec. 2016

Gleichen, Edward, *A Guardsman's Memories: A Book of Recollections* (London: W. Blackwood & Son, 1932)

Glover, Michael, 'When the Congress wasn't Dancing', *History Today*, vol. 28 (1978), no. 2

Godman, Peter, *The Saint as Censor: Robert Bellarmine between Inquisition and Index* (Leiden: Brill, 2000)

—, *Silent Masters: Latin Literature and Its Censors in the High Middle Ages* (Princeton, NJ: Princeton University Press, 2000)

—, *Paradoxes of Conscience in the High Middle Ages: Abelard, Heloise and the Archpoet* (Cambridge: Cambridge University Press, 2009)

Goffman, Daniel, 'Negotiating with the Renaissance State: The Ottoman Empire and the New Diplomacy', in Virginia Aksan and Daniel Goffman (eds.), *The Early Modern Ottomans: Remapping the Empire* (Cambridge: Cambridge University Press, 2007)

Goldsworthy, Adrian Keith, *Caesar: The Life of a Colossus* (London: Weidenfeld & Nicolson, 2006)

—, *Pax Romana: War, Peace and Conquest in the Roman World* (London: Weidenfeld & Nicolson, 2016)

Goodman, Allen E., *In from the Cold: The Report of the Twentieth Century Fund Task Force on the Future of U.S. Intelligence* (Washington, DC: Brookings Institution Press, 1996)

Goodman, Michael S., 'Avoiding Surprise: The Nicoll Report and Intelligence Analysis', in Michael S. Goodman and Robert S. Dover (eds.), *Learning from the Secret Past: Cases in British Intelligence History* (Washington, D.C.: Georgetown University Press, 2011)

—, *The Official History of the Joint Intelligence Committee*, 2 vols. (London: Routledge, 2014–17)

Gorbachev, Mikhail, *The August Coup: The Truth and the Lessons* (London: HarperCollins, 1991)

Gorbunov, Evgenii, *Vostochnyiĭ rubezh: OKDVA protiviaponskoiĭ armii* (Moscow: Veche, 2010)

Gordievsky, Oleg, *Next Stop Execution* (London: Macmillan, 1995)

Gordon, Andrew, *The Rules of the Game: Jutland and British Naval Command* (London: John Murray, 1996)

Goren, Haim, Eran Dolev and Yigal Sheffy (eds.), *Palestine and World War I: Grand Strategy, Military Tactics and Culture in War* (London: I. B. Tauris, 2014)

Gorodetsky, Gabriel (ed.), *The Maisky Diaries: Red Ambassador to the Court of St James's 1932–1943* (New Haven, Conn.: Yale University Press, 2015)

Gotteri, Nicole, *La Police secrète du Premier Empire: Bulletins quotidiens adressés par Savary à l'Empereur*, 7 vols. (Paris: Champion, 1997–2004)

Grainger, John D., *The Battle of Yorktown, 1781: A Reassessment* (Woodbridge: Boydell Press, 2005)

Grant, Michael, *The Routledge Atlas of Classical History*, 5th edn (London: Routledge, 1994)

Green, Peter, 'He Found the Real Alexander', *New York Review of Books*, 22 November 2012

—, 'Questions of Class', *London Review of Books*, 25 April 2013

Green, Toby, *Inquisition: The Reign of Fear* (London: Pan Books, 2008)

Gregg, Edward, 'The Jacobite Career of John, Earl of Mar', in Eveline Cruikshanks (ed.), *Ideology and Conspiracy: Aspects of Jacobitism, 1689–1759* (Edinburgh: John Donald, 1982)

Griffin, Eric, 'The Specter of Spain in John Smith's Colonial Writing', in Robert Appelbaum and John Wood Sweet (eds.), *Envisioning an English Empire: Jamestown and the Making of the North Atlantic World* (Philadelphia: University of Pennsylvania Press, 2005)

Griffith, Samuel B. (ed. and trans.), *Sun Tzu: The Art of War*, rev. edn (Oxford: Oxford University Press, 1971)

— (ed. and trans.), *The Illustrated Art of War* (Oxford: Oxford University Press, 2005)

Grillon, Pierre (ed.), *Les Papiers de Richelieu. Section politique intérieure, correspondance et papiers d'Etat*, 6 vols. (Paris: A. Pedone, 1975–85)

Große Politik der europäischen Kabinette 1871–1914, Die. Sammlung der diplomatischen Akten des Auswärtigen Amtes, eds. Johannes Lepsius, Albrecht Mendelssohn Bartholdy and Friedrich Thimme, Reihen 1–5, 40 vols. (Berlin: Deutsche Verlagsgesellschaft für Politik und Geschichte, 1922–7)

Guelton, Frédéric, and Abdil Bicer (eds.), *Naissance et évolution du renseignement dans l'espace européen (1870–1940)* (Paris: Service Historique de la Défense, 2006)

Guillaume, A. (ed. and trans.), *The Life of Muhammad: A Translation of Isḥāq's 'Sīrat Rasūl Allāh* (Oxford: Oxford University Press, 1955)

Guillemin, Henri, 'L'Affaire Dreyfus. Le Télégramme du 2 novembre', *Mercure de France*, vol. CCCXXXIX (1960)

Guillois, Antoine, *Les Bibliothèques particulières de l'Empereur Napoléon* (Paris: Librairie Henri Leclerc, 1900)

Gürkan, Emrah Safa, 'The Efficacy of Ottoman Counter-Intelligence in the 16th Century', *Acta Orientalia Academiae Scientiarum Hungaricae*, vol. 65 (2012), no. 1

—, 'Espionage in the 16th Century Mediterranean: Secret Diplomacy, Mediterranean Go-Betweens and the Ottoman–Habsburg Rivalry', Ph.D. dissertation (Washington, DC: Georgetown University, 2012)

Gurwood, John (ed.), *The Dispatches of Field Marshal the Duke of Wellington during His Various Campaigns . . . from 1799 to 1818*, 3 vols. (London: J. Murray, 1837)

Gustafson, Kristian, 'The CIA and Chile, 1964–1974', PhD dissertation (University of Cambridge, 2005)

—, *Hostile Intent: US Covert Operations in Chile, 1964–1974* (Washington, DC: Potomac Books, 2007)

Guy, John, *Queen of Scots: The True Life of Mary Stuart* (New York: Mariner Books, 2005)

Hagen, Louis (ed.), *The Schellenberg Memoirs* (London: André Deutsch, 1956)

Hagenloh, Paul, *Stalin's Police: Public Order and Mass Repression in the USSR, 1926–1941* (Baltimore: Johns Hopkins Press, 2009)

Hague, William, *William Pitt the Younger: A Biography*, Kindle edn (London: HarperCollins, 2004)

Haigh, Christopher, *Elizabeth I*, 2nd edn (London: Longman, 1998)

Haines, Gerald, 'The CIA's Own Effort to Understand and Document Its Past: A Brief History of the CIA History Program, 1950–1955', in Rhodri Jeffreys-Jones and Christopher Andrew (eds.), *Eternal Vigilance? 50 Years of the CIA* (London: Frank Cass, 1997)

Haldon, John, *A Critical Commentary on The Taktika of Leo VI* (Cambridge, Mass.: Harvard University Press, 2014)

Hall, Henry Foljambe, *Napoleon's Notes on English History Made on the Eve of the French Revolution*, facsimile edn (Whitefish, Mont.: Kessinger Publishing, 2007)

Halperin, Charles J., 'Did Ivan IV's *Oprichniki* Carry Dogs' Heads on Their Horses?', *Canadian–American Slavic Studies*, 46 (2012)

Hamel, Debra, *The Mutilation of the Herms: Unpacking an Ancient Mystery* (North Haven, Conn.: Debra Hamel, 2012)

Hamilton, Richard F., 'War Planning: Obvious Needs, Not So Obvious Solutions', in Richard F. Hamilton and Holger H. Herwig (eds.), *War Planning 1914* (Cambridge: Cambridge University Press, 2010)

— and Holger H. Herwig (eds.), *The Origins of World War I* (Cambridge: Cambridge University Press, 2003)

—— (eds.), *War Planning 1914* (Cambridge: Cambridge University Press, 2010)

Hampson, Norman, *A Social History of the French Revolution* (London: Routledge and Kegan Paul, 1963)

Hanson, Philip, *Soviet Industrial Espionage: Some New Information* (London: RIIA, 1987)

Harari, Yuval Noah, *Sapiens: A Brief History of Humankind* (London: Vintage, 2015)

—, *Homo Deus: A Brief History of Tomorrow* (London: Vintage, 2017)

Harcave, Sidney, *Count Sergei Witte and the Twilight of Imperial Russia: A Biography* (London: Routledge, 2015)

Harding, Luke, *The Snowden Files: The Inside Story of the World's Most Wanted Man* (London: Guardian Faber, 2014)

Harding, Richard, *The Emergence of Britain's Global Naval Supremacy: The War of 1739–1748* (Woodbridge: Boydell Press, 2010)

Harris, Stephen M., *British Military Intelligence in the Crimean War, 1854–1856* (London: Frank Cass, 1999)

Harris, Tim, *Revolution: The Great Crisis of the British Monarchy, 1685–1720* (London: Penguin Books, 2007)

—, *Rebellion: Britain's First Stuart Kings* (Oxford: Oxford University Press, 2013)

Hart, Peter, *Fire and Movement: The British Expeditionary Force and the Campaign of 1914* (Oxford: Oxford University Press, 2015)

Haslam, Jonathan, *Near and Distant Neighbours: A New History of Soviet Intelligence* (Oxford: Oxford University Press, 2015)

Hassig, Ross, *Mexico and the Spanish Conquest* (Norman: University of Oklahoma Press, 2006)

Hastings, Max, *Catastrophe: Europe Goes to War 1914*, Kindle edn (London: William Collins, 2012)

—, *The Secret War: Spies, Codes and Guerrillas 1939–1945* (London: William Collins, 2015)

Hauterive, Ernest d', *La Police secrète du Premier Empire. Bulletins quotidiens adressés par Fouché à l'Empereur*, 5 vols. (Paris: Perrin et Clavreuil, 1908–64)

Hayden, Michael V., *Playing to the Edge: American Intelligence in the Age of Terror* (New York: Penguin Books, 2016)

Haynes, John Earl, and Harvey Klehr, *VENONA: Decoding Soviet Espionage in America* (New Haven, Conn.: Yale University Press, 1999)

——, *In Denial: Historians, Communism and Espionage* (San Francisco: Encounter, 2003)

—— and Alexander Vassiliev, *Spies: The Rise and Fall of the KGB in America* (New Haven, Conn.: Yale University Press, 2009)

Hearn, Karen, *Dynasties* (London: Tate Gallery, 1995)

Heather, Peter, *The Fall of the Roman Empire* (London: Macmillan, 2005)

—, *The Restoration of Rome: Barbarian Popes and Imperial Pretenders* (London: Macmillan, 2013)

Hebbert, F. J., and G. A. Rothrock, *Soldier of France: Sébastien Le Prestre de Vauban, 1633–1707* (New York: Peter Lang, 1989)

Hegghammer, Thomas, 'The Rise of Muslim Foreign Fighters: Islam and the Globalization of Jihad', *International Security*, vol. 35 (2010/11), no. 3

Heinemann, Arnim, John L. Meloy, Tarif Khalidi and Manfred Kropp (eds.), *Al-Jāḥiẓ: A Muslim Humanist for Our Time* (Würzburg: Ergon Verlag in Kommission, 2009)

Heirman, Ann, Paolo De Troia and Jan Parmentier, 'Francesco Sambiasi, a Missing Link in European Map Making in China?', *Imago Mundi*, vol. 61 (2009), no. 1

Hénin, Pierre-Yves, *Le Plan Schlieffen: Un mois de guerre, deux siècles de controverses* (Paris: Economica, 2012)

Herman, Michael, *Intelligence Power in Peace and War* (Cambridge: Cambridge University Press, 1996)

—, 'Intelligence as Threats and Reassurance', in Michael Herman and Gwilym Hughes (eds.), *Intelligence in the Cold War: What Difference Did It Make?* (London: Routledge, 2012)

Hernán, E. G., 'The Price of Spying at the Battle of Lepanto', *Eurasian Studies*, vol. II (2003), no. 2

Hertsgaard, Mark, *Bravehearts: Whistle Blowing in the Age of Snowden* (New York: Hot Books, 2016)

Herwig, Holger, 'Imperial Germany', in Ernest R. May, *Knowing One's Enemies: Intelligence Assessment before the Two World Wars* (Princeton, NJ: Princeton University Press, 1984)

—, *The First World War: Germany and Austria–Hungary 1914–1918* (London: A&C Black, 2014)

Hesk, Jon, *Deception and Democracy in Classical Athens* (Cambridge: Cambridge University Press, 2000)

Heuer, Richards J., Jr, *Psychology of Intelligence Analysis* (Washington, DC: CIA Center for the Study of Intelligence, 2007); https://www.cia.gov/library/center-for-the-study-of-intelligence/csi-publications/books-and-monographs/psychology-of-intelligence-analysis

Hewitson, Mark, *Nationalism in Germany, 1848–1866: Revolutionary Nation* (London: Palgrave Macmillan, 2010)

Hewitt, James (ed.), *Eyewitnesses to Nelson's Battles* (London: Osprey, 1972)

Hiley, Nicholas, 'The Failure of British Espionage against Germany, 1907–14', *Historical Journal*, vol. 26 (1983), no. 4

Hill, G. A., *Go Spy the Land* (London: Cassell, 1932)

Hilton, Boyd, *A Mad, Bad and Dangerous People? England 1783–1846* (Oxford: Oxford University Press, 2006)

Hingley, Richard, and Christina Unwin, *Boudica: Iron Age Warrior Queen* (London: Hambledon Continuum, 2006)

Hinsley, Sir F. H., *British Intelligence in the Second World War*, abridged edn (London: HMSO, 1993)

— and Alan Stripp (eds.), *Codebreakers: The Inside Story of Bletchley Park* (Oxford: Oxford University Press, 1993)

— et al., *British Intelligence in the Second World War: Its Influence on Strategy and Operations*, vols. 1, 2, 3i, 3ii, 4 (London: HMSO, 1979–90): vol. 2 (1981)

Hitchens, Christopher, 'Believe Me, It's Torture', *Vanity Fair*, August 2008

Hitler's Table Talk, 1941–44: His Private Conversations, eds. Norman Cameron and R. H. Stevens; introduction and preface by H. R. Trevor-Roper (London: Phoenix, 2000)

Hoare, Sir Samuel, *The Fourth Seal: The End of a Russian Chapter* (London: W. Heinemann, 1930)

Hoetzsch, Otto, *Die internationalen Beziehungen im Zeitalter des Imperialismus*, 4 vols. (Berlin: Reimar Hobbing, 1933–42)

Hoffman, Bruce, ' "Holy Terror": The Implications of Terrorism Motivated by a Religious Imperative', *Studies in Conflict and Terrorism*, vol. 18 (1995), no. 4

—, *Inside Terrorism*, 2nd edn (New York: Columbia University Press, 2006)

Hoffman, David E., *The Dead Hand: The Untold Story of the Cold War Arms Race and Its Dangerous Legacy* (New York: Doubleday, 2009)

Hoffmann, General Max, *The War of Lost Opportunities* (London: Kegan Paul, Trench, Trubner, 1924)

—, *War Diaries and Other Papers*, 2 vols., trans. Eric Sutton (London: Martin Secker, 1929)

Höhne, Heinz, *Der Krieg im Dunkeln: Die Geschichte der deutsch-russischen Spionage* (Bindlach: Gondrom 1993)

Holland, Max, 'The Lie That Linked CIA to the Kennedy Assassination', *Studies in Intelligence*, no. 11 (Fall/Winter 2001–2)

Holland, Tom, *Rubicon: The Triumph and Tragedy of the Roman Republic* (London: Little, Brown, 2003)

—, *In the Shadow of the Sword: The Battle for Global Empire and the End of the Ancient World* (London: Little, Brown, 2012)

Holmes, Richard, *Marlborough: England's Fragile Genius* (London: HarperPress, 2008)

Holst, Sanford, *Phoenician Secrets: Exploring the Ancient Mediterranean* (Los Angeles: Santorini, 2011)

Holt, Thaddeus, *The Deceivers: Allied Military Deception in the Second World War* (London: Weidenfeld & Nicolson, 2004)

Homer, *The Iliad*, trans. E. V. Rieu, ed. and rev. trans. Peter Jones (London: Penguin Books, 2014)

Honan, Park, *Christopher Marlowe: Poet and Spy* (Oxford: Oxford University Press, 2005)

Hopkins, Keith, '*Christian* Number and Its Implications', *Journal of Early Christian Studies*, vol. 6 (1998), no. 2

— and Mary Beard, *The Colosseum* (Cambridge, Mass.: Harvard University Press, 2005)

Hopkins, Lisa, *A Christopher Marlowe Chronology* (Basingstoke: Palgrave Macmillan, 2005)

Hopkins, Paul, 'Sham Plots and Real Plots in the 1690s', in Eveline Cruikshanks (ed.), *Ideology and Conspiracy: Aspects of Jacobitism, 1689–1759* (Edinburgh: John Donald, 1982)

Hopkirk, Peter, *Trespassers on the Roof of the World: The Race for Lhasa* (Oxford: Oxford University Press, 1983)

—, *The Great Game: On Secret Service in High Asia*, 2nd edn (London: John Murray, 2006)

Horn, James, 'Imperfect Understandings: Rumor, Knowledge, and Uncertainty in Early Virginia', in Peter C. Mancall (ed.), *The Atlantic World and Virginia, 1550–1624* (Chapel Hill: University of North Carolina Press, 2007)

Hornblower, Simon, and Antony Spawforth (eds.), *The Oxford Companion to Classical Civilization* (Oxford: Oxford University Press, 1998)

Hosking, Geoffrey, *Russia: People and Empire 1552–1917* (London: HarperCollins, 1997)

—, *Russia and the Russians: A History* (Cambridge, Mass.: Belknap Press, 2001)

Hossain, Kimberly Lynn, 'Was Adam the First Heretic? Diego de Simancas, Luis de Páramo, and the Origins of Inquisitorial Practice', *Archiv für Reformationsgeschichte*, vol. 97 (2006)

Howard, Michael, *British Intelligence in the Second World War*, vol. 5: *Strategic Deception* (London: HMSO, 1990)

Howe, Sir Geoffrey, *Conflict of Loyalty* (London: Macmillan, 1994)

Hoyos, Dexter (ed.), *A Companion to the Punic Wars* (Chichester: Wiley Blackwell, 2015)

Huckaby, Jessica M., and Mark E. Stout, 'Al Qaida's Views of Authoritarian Intelligence Services', *Intelligence and National Security*, vol. 25 (2010), no. 3

Hudson, Rex, *The Sociology and Psychology of Terrorism: Who Becomes a Terrorist and Why?* (Washington, DC: Federal Research Division of the Library of Congress, September 1999)

Huertner, Johannes (ed.), *Paul von Hintze: Marineoffizier, Diplomat, Staatssekretär. Dokumente einer Karriere zwischen Militär und Politik, 1903–1918* (Munich: Harald Boldt Verlag, 1998)

Hughes, Charles (ed.), 'Nicholas Faunt's Discourse Touching the Office of Principal Secretary of Estate &c. 1592', *English Historical Review*, vol. 20 (1905), no. 79

Hughes, Matthew, 'Field Marshal Viscount Allenby: One of the Great Captains of History?', in Haim Goren, Eran Dolev and Yigal Sheffy (eds.), *Palestine and World War I: Grand Strategy, Military Tactics and Culture in War* (London: I. B. Tauris, 2014)

Hugon, Alain, 'L'Affaire L'Hoste ou la tentation espagnole (1604)', *Revue d'histoire moderne et contemporaine*, vol. 42 (1995), no. 3

—, 'Les Rendez-vous manqués de Gérard de Raffis. Espionnage et retournement idéologique sous le règne de Henri IV', *Revue historique*, vol. 296 (1996), no. 1

—, *Au service du roi catholique, 'honorables ambassadeurs' et 'divins espions': Représentation diplomatique et service secret dans les relations hispano-françaises de 1598 à 1635* (Madrid: Casa de Velázquez, 2004)

Hunt, Lynn, *Culture and Class in the French Revolution* (London: Methuen, 1986)

Huskisson, William, *The Speeches of the Right Honourable William Huskisson, with a Biographical Memoir*, 3 vols. (London: John Murray, 1931)

Hutchinson, Robert, *Elizabeth's Spy Master: Francis Walsingham and the Secret War That Saved England* (Weidenfeld & Nicolson, 2006)

—, *The Spanish Armada* (London: Weidenfeld & Nicolson, 2013)

Hutton, Patrick H., *The Cult of the Revolutionary Tradition: The Blanquists in French Politics, 1864–1893* (Berkeley: University of California Press, 1981)

Hutton, Ronald, *The Restoration: A Political and Religious History of England and Wales, 1658–1667* (Oxford: Oxford University Press, 1993)

Hyam, Ronald, *Britain's Declining Empire: The Road to Decolonisation* (Cambridge: Cambridge University Press, 2008)

I Documenti Diplomatici Italiani (1908–1914) (Rome: Libreria dello Stato, 1951–)

Ianin, V. L., 'Medieval Novgorod', in Maureen Perrie (ed.), *The Cambridge History of Russia*, vol. 1: *From Early Rus' to 1689* (Cambridge: Cambridge University Press, 2006)

Ignatiev, A. A., *Piatdesiat let v stroiu*, vol. 3 (Moscow: Sovetskii Pisatel, 1952)

Iordanou, Ioanna, 'What News on the Rialto? The Trade of Information and Early Modern Venice's Centralized Intelligence Organization', *Intelligence and National Security*, vol. 31 (2016), no. 3

Isaacson, Walter, *Benjamin Franklin: An American Life* (New York: Simon & Schuster, 2003)

İsom-Verhaaren, C., 'An Ottoman Report about Martin Luther and the Emperor: New Evidence of the Ottoman Interest in the Protestant Challenge to the Power of Charles V', *Turcica*, vol. 28 (1996)

Israel, Jonathan I. (ed.), *The Anglo-Dutch Moment: Essays on the Glorious Revo-
lution and Its World Impact* (Cambridge: Cambridge University Press, 1991)
— and Geoffrey Parker, 'Of Providence and Protestant Winds: The Spanish
Armada of 1588 and the Dutch Armada of 1688', in Jonathan I. Israel (ed.), *The
Anglo-Dutch Moment: Essays on the Glorious Revolution and Its World
Impact* (Cambridge: Cambridge University Press, 1991)
Ivan IV Sochineniya (St Petersburg: Azbuka Klassiki, 2000)
Izmozik, V. S, *'Chernye kabinety': Istoria rossiiskoi perliustratsii, XVIII–nachalo
XX veka* (Moscow: Novoe literaturnoe obozrenie, 2015)
Jablonsky, David, *Churchill, the Great Game and Total War* (London: Routledge,
1991)
Jackson, David (ed.), *The Diaries of George Washington* (Charlottesville: Univer-
sity Press of Virginia, 1976)
James, W. M., *The Eyes of the Navy: A Biographical Study of Admiral Sir Regi-
nald Hall* (London: Methuen, 1955)
Jansen, Marc, and Nikita Petrov, *Stalin's Loyal Executioner: People's Commissar
Nikolai Ezhov, 1895–1940* (Stanford, Calif.: Hoover Institution Press, 2002)
Jardine, Lisa, *The Awful End of Prince William the Silent: The First Assassina-
tion of a Head of State with a Hand-Gun* (London: HarperCollins 2005)
— and William Sherman, 'Pragmatic Readers: Knowledge Transactions and
Scholarly Services in Late Elizabethan England', in Anthony Fletcher and Peter
Roberts (eds.), *Religion, Culture and Society in Early Modern Britain: Essays
in Honour of Patrick Collinson* (Cambridge: Cambridge University Press, 1994)
Jeffery, Keith, *MI6: The History of the Secret Intelligence Service, 1909–1949*
(London: Bloomsbury, 2010)
— *1916: A Global History* (London: Bloomsbury, 2015)
Jeffreys-Jones, Rhodri, 'Why was the CIA Founded in 1947?', in Rhodri Jeffreys-
Jones and Christopher Andrew (eds.), *Eternal Vigilance? 50 Years of the CIA*
(London: Frank Cass, 1997)
— and Christopher Andrew (eds.), *Eternal Vigilance? 50 Years of the CIA* (Lon-
don: Frank Cass, 1997)
Jenner, C. J., 'Turning the Hinge of Fate: Good Source and the UK–U.S. Intelli-
gence Alliance, 1940–1942', *Diplomatic History*, vol. 32 (2008), no. 2
Jensen, Richard Bach, *The Battle against Anarchist Terrorism: An International
History, 1878–1934* (Cambridge: Cambridge University Press, 2014)
Jervis, Robert, 'Reports, Politics, and Intelligence Failures: The Case of Iraq',
Journal of Strategic Studies, vol. 29 (2006)
—, *Why Intelligence Fails: Lessons from the Iranian Revolution and the Iraq War*
(Ithaca, NY: Cornell University Press, 2010)
Joffre, Field Marshal Joseph S. C., *Mémoires du Maréchal Joffre (1910–1917)*,
2 vols. (Paris: Petit-fils de Plone et Nourrit, 1932)
Johnson, James, *Venice Incognito: Masks in the Serene Republic* (Berkeley:
University of California Press, 2011)
Johnson, Loch K., 'The Aspin–Brown Intelligence Inquiry: Behind the Closed
Doors of a Blue Ribbon Commission', *Studies in Intelligence*, vol. 48 (2004), no. 3

— (ed.), *The Oxford Handbook of National Security Intelligence* (New York: Oxford University Press, 2010)

Johnston, Kenneth R., *Unusual Suspects: Pitt's Reign of Alarm and the Lost Generation of the 1790s* (Oxford: Oxford University Press, 2013)

Joint Committee on the Investigation of the Pearl Harbor Attack, *Pearl Harbor Attack: Hearings*, 79 Cong., 1 and 2 Sess. (Washington, DC: US Government Printing Office, 1946)

Jones, Clyve, 'Robert Harley and the Myth of the Golden Thread: Family Piety, Journalism and the History of the Assassination Attempt of 8 March 1711', *British Library Journal*, 2010

Jones, Frank L., 'Engaging the World: Anthony Lake and American Grand Strategy, 1993–1997', *Historical Journal*, vol. 59 (2016), no. 3

Jones, H. A., *The War in the Air: Being the Story of the Part Played in the Great War by the Royal Air Force*, vols. 2–6 (Oxford: Oxford University Press, 1922–37)

Jones, Peter, 'Antoine de Guiscard, "Abbé de la Bourlie", "Marquis de Guiscard"', *British Library Journal*, vol.8 (1982), no. 1

Jones, Peter, and Keith Sidwell (eds.), *The World of Rome: An Introduction to Roman Culture* (Cambridge: Cambridge University Press, 1997)

Jones, Seth G., and Martin C. Libicki, *How Terrorist Groups End: Lessons for Countering al Qa'ida,* (Santa Monica, Calif.: RAND Corporation, 2008)

Jordan, Don, and Michael Walsh, *The King's Revenge: Charles II and the Greatest Manhunt in British History* (London: Little, Brown, 2012)

Josephus, Flavius, *Antiquitates Judaicae*; http://www.documentacatholicaomnia. eu/04z/z_0037-0103__Flavius_Josephus__Antiquitates_Judaicae__GR.pdf.html

Jourquin, Jacques, 'Bibliothèques particulières de Napoléon', in Jean Tulard (ed.), *Dictionnaire Napoléon* (Paris: Fayard, 1989)

Jukes, Geoff, 'The Soviets and "Ultra"', *Intelligence and National Security*, vol. 3 (1988), no. 2

Juurvee, Ivo, 'Birth of Russian SIGINT during WWI on the Baltic Sea', *Intelligence and National Security*, vol. 32 (2017), no. 3

Kahn, David, *The Codebreakers: The Story of Secret Writing* (New York: Macmillan, 1967)

—, *Hitler's Spies: German Military Intelligence in World War II* (London: Hodder & Stoughton, 1978)

—, 'Codebreaking in World Wars I and II: The Major Successes and Failures, Their Causes and Their Effects', in Christopher Andrew and David Dilks (eds.), *The Missing Dimension: Governments and Intelligence Communities in the Twentieth Century* (London: Macmillan, 1984)

—, 'Pearl Harbor and the Inadequacy of Cryptanalysis', *Cryptologia*, vol. 15 (1991)

—, 'The Intelligence Failure at Pearl Harbor', *Foreign Affairs*, Winter 1991–92

—, 'Roosevelt, MAGIC and ULTRA', *Cryptologia*, vol. 14 (1992)

—, *The Reader of Gentlemen's Mail: Herbert O. Yardley and American Intelligence* (New Haven, Conn.: Yale University Press, 2004)

—, 'The Future of the Past – Questions in Cryptologic History', *Cryptologia*, vol. 32 (2008), no. 1

—, 'Intelligence Lessons in *Macbeth*', *Intelligence and National Security*, vol. 24 (2009), no. 2

—, 'The Black Code', in David Kahn, *How I Discovered World War II's Greatest Spy and Other Stories of Intelligence and Code* (Boca Raton, Fla: CTC Press, 2014)

—, 'How Garbles Tickled History', in David Kahn, *How I Discovered World War II's Greatest Spy and Other Stories of Intelligence and Code* (Boca Raton, Fla: CTC Press, 2014)

—, *How I Discovered World War II's Greatest Spy and Other Stories of Intelligence and Code* (Boca Raton, Fla: CTC Press, 2014)

Kalugin, Oleg, *Spymaster: My 32 years in Intelligence and Espionage against the West* (London: Smyth Gryphon, 1994)

Kamen, Henry, *The Spanish Inquisition: A Historical Revision* (London: Weidenfeld & Nicolson, 1997)

Kaminsky, Howard, 'The Great Schism', in Michael Jones (ed.), *The New Cambridge Medieval History*, vol. 6 (Cambridge: Cambridge University Press, 2000)

Kampmann, Christoph, 'The English Crisis, Emperor Leopold, and the Origins of the Dutch Intervention in 1688', *The Historical Journal*, vol. 55 (2012), no. 2

Karatchkova, Elena, 'The "Russian Factor" in the Indian Mutiny', in Marina Carter and Crispin Bates (eds.), *Mutiny at the Margins: New Perspectives on the Indian Uprising of 1857*, vol. 3 (New Delhi: Sage Publications India, 2013)

Karila-Cohen, Pierre, 'Les Fonds secrets ou la méfiance légitime', *Revue Historique*, 205/4, no. 636

Katzenstein, Peter J., *Disjointed Partners: Austria and Germany since 1815* (Berkeley: University of California Press, 1976)

Kautilya, *The Arthashastra*, ed. and trans. L. J. Rangarajan (New Delhi/London: Penguin Books, 1992)

Keblusek, Marika, 'Artists as Cultural and Political Agents', in Maruka Keblusek and Badeloch Noldus (eds.), *Double Agents: Cultural and Political Brokerage in Early Modern Europe* (Leiden: Brill, 2011)

Keegan, John, *Intelligence in War: Knowledge of the Enemy from Napoleon to Al-Qaeda* (London: Hutchinson, 2003)

Keene, Donald, *Emperor of Japan: Meiji and His World, 1852–1912* (New York: Columbia University Press, 2005)

Keene, Raymond, *Karpov–Korchnoi 1978: Parapsychology, Gurus and the KGB* (Edinburgh: Hardinge Simpole Publishing, 2004)

Keiger, John, *France and the Origins of the First World War* (London: Macmillan, 1983)

Kelly, Christopher, *The Roman Empire: A Very Short History* (Oxford: Oxford University Press, 2006)

—, *Attila the Hun: Barbarian Terror and the Fall of the Roman Empire* (London: Vintage, 2009)

Kelly, Ian, *Casanova* (London: Hodder & Stoughton, 2009)

Kelly, Thomas, 'The Myth of the Skytale', *Cryptologia*, vol. 22 (1998), no. 2

Kendall, Elisabeth, 'Yemen's Al-Qa'ida and Poetry as a Weapon of Jihad', in Elisabeth Kendall and Ewan Stein (eds.), *Twenty-First Century Jihad: Law, Society and Military Action* (London: I. B. Tauris, 2015)

—, 'Jihadist Propaganda and Its Exploitation of the Arab Poetic Tradition', in Elisabeth Kendall and Ahmad Khan (eds.), *Reclaiming Islamic Tradition: Modern Interpretations of the Classical Heritage* (Edinburgh: Edinburgh University Press, 2016)

Kenna, Shane, *War in the Shadows: The Irish-Americans Who Bombed Victorian Britain* (Dublin: Irish Academic Press, 2013)

Kennan, George F. *Soviet–Americam Relations, 1917–1920*, vol. 1: *Russia Leaves the War* (London: Faber and Faber, 1956)

Kennedy, Hugh, *The Great Arab Conquests: How the Spread of Islam Changed the World We Live In* (London: Weidenfeld & Nicolson, 2007)

Kennedy School of Government, Case Program, 'CIA and the Fall of the Soviet Empire: The Politics of "Getting It Right"', C16-94-12510

Kent, Sherman, 'The Need for an Intelligence Literature', in Donald P. Steury (ed.), *Sherman Kent and the Board of National Estimates: Collected Essays* (Washington, DC: CIA Center for the Study of Intelligence, 1994)

Kenyon, John Philipps, *Robert Spencer, Earl of Sunderland, 1641–1702* (London: Longmans, 1958)

Kerautret, Michel, 'Frédéric II et Napoléon (1800–1870)', *Revue de l'Institut Napoléon*, no. 181 (2000)

Kerner, Alex, 'Espionage and Field Intelligence in the Conquest of Mexico, 1519–1521', *Journal of Military History*, vol. 78 (2014), no. 2

Kessler, Pamela, *Undercover Washington* (McLean, Va: EPM Publications, 1992)

Ketchum, Robert, *Victory at Georgetown: The Campaign That Won the Revolution* (Georgetown, Washington, DC: Georgetown University Press, 1990)

Khuri, Nick, 'New Light on Able Archer '83: The Dynamics of Misperception, Escalation, and De-Escalation', MPhil thesis (University of Cambridge, 2016)

Kieckhefer, Richard, 'The Office of Inquisition and Medieval Heresy: The Transition from Personal to Institutional Jurisdiction', *Journal of Ecclesiastical History*, vol. 46 (1995)

Kiesling, Eugenia C., 'France', in Richard F. Hamilton and Holger H. Herwig (eds.), *The Origins of World War I* (Cambridge: Cambridge University Press, 2003)

Kilmeade, Brian, and Don Yaeger, *George Washington's Secret Six: The Spy Ring That Saved the American Revolution* (New York: Sentinel, 2013)

Kishlansky, Mark, *A Monarchy Transformed: Britain 1630–1714* (London: Penguin Books, 1997)

Kissinger, Henry, *Diplomacy* (New York: Simon & Schuster, 1994)

—, *On China*, Kindle edn (London: Allen Lane, 2011)

Kissling, Hans J., 'Venezia come Centro di Informazioni sui Turchi', in Hans Georg Beck et al. (eds.), *Venezia Centro di Mediazione tra Oriente e Occidente, secoli XV–XVI: Aspetti e problemi*, vol. 1 (Florence: L. S. Olschki, 1977)

Knight, Roger, *Britain Against Napoleon: The Organization of Victory 1793–1815* (London: Allen Lane, 2013)

Knott, Stephen F., *Secret and Sanctioned: Covert Operations and the American Presidency* (Oxford: Oxford University Press, 1996)

Kostin, Sergei, and Eric Raynaud, *Adieu Farewell* (Paris: Éditions Robert Laffont, 2009)

Kotani, Ken, *Japanese Intelligence in World War II* (Botley: Osprey, 2009)

Kronenbitter, Günther, *'Krieg im Frieden': Die Führung der k.u.k. Armee und die Großmachtpolitik Österreich-Ungarns 1906–1914* (Munich: Oldenbourg, 2003)

—, 'Austria–Hungary', in Richard F. Hamilton and Holger H. Herwig (eds.), *War Planning 1914* (Cambridge: Cambridge University Press, 2010)

Kronenbitter, Rita T., 'Paris Okhrana 1885–1905', *Studies in Intelligence*, vol. 10 (1966), no. 3; https://www.cia.gov/library/center-for-the-study-of-intelligence/kent-csi/vol10no3/html/v10i3a06p_0001.htm

Kruh, Louis, 'British–American Cryptanalytic Cooperation and an Unprecedented Admission by Winston Churchill', *Cryptologia*, vol. 13 (Apr. 1989), no. 2

Kruse, Elbert, and Johan Taube, 'Poslanie Ioganna Taube i Elberta Kruze', trans. Mikhail G. Rojinskiy, *Russkiy Istoricheskiy Zhurnal*, 1 July 1922

Kuhns, Woodrow J., 'Intelligence Failures: Forecasting and the Lessons of Epistemology', in Richard K. Betts and Thomas G. Mahnken (eds.), *Paradoxes of Strategic Intelligence: Essays in Honour of Michael I. Handel* (London: Frank Cass, 2003)

Kulikowski, Michael, *Rome's Gothic Wars: From the Third Century to Alaric* (Cambridge: Cambridge University Press, 2007)

Kuromiya, Hiroaki, and Andrzej Pepłoński, 'Kōzō Izumi and the Soviet Breach of Imperial Japanese Diplomatic Codes', *Intelligence and National Security*, vol. 28 (2013), no. 6

Kurzman, Charles, *The Unthinkable Revolution in Iran* (Cambridge, Mass.: Harvard University Press, 2004)

Labalme, Patricia H., and Laura Sanguineti White (eds.), *Venice: Città Excelentissima: Selections from the Renaissance Diaries of Marin Sanudo*, trans. Linda L. Carroll, (Baltimore: Johns Hopkins University Press, 2008)

Lambert, Nicholas A., *Planning Armageddon: British Economic Warfare and the First World War* (Cambridge, Mass.: Harvard University Press, 2012)

Lamont, Peter, *The Rise of the Indian Rope Trick: How a Spectacular Hoax Became History* (London: Abacus, 2004)

Lamont-Brown, Raymond, *Edward VII's Last Loves: Alice Keppel and Agnes Keyser* (London: The History Press, 2011)

Lamster, Mark, *Master of Shadows: The Secret Diplomatic Career of the Painter Peter Paul Rubens* (New York: Doubleday, 2009)

Lane, Anthony N. S., *Bernard of Clairvaux: Theologian of the Cross* (Collegeville, Minn.: Liturgical Press, 2013)

Lane Fox, Robin, *Pagans and Christians* (London: Penguin Books, 1988)

—, *Alexander the Great*, rev. edn (London: Penguin Books, 2004)

Lang, Andrew, *Pickle the Spy: Or the Incognito of Prince Charles* (London: Longmans, Green, 1897)

Langford, William, *Somme Intelligence: Fourth Army HQ 1916* (Barnsley: Pen & Sword Books, 2013)

Laqueur, Walter (ed.), *The Terrorism Reader: A Historical Anthology* (New York: New American Library, 1978)

Larner, Christina, *Enemies of God: The Witch-Hunt in Scotland* (Oxford: Blackwell, 1981)

Larsen, Daniel, 'British Intelligence and American Neutrality during the First World War', PhD thesis (University of Cambridge, 2013)

—, 'The First Intelligence Prime Minister: David Lloyd George (1916–1922)'; https://www.gov.uk/government/uploads/system/uploads/attachment_data/file/80179/Lloyd-George-as-PM.pdf.

Latham, Robert (ed.), *Samuel Pepys and the Second Dutch War: Pepys's Navy White Book and Brooke House Papers* (Aldershot: Scolar Press, 1995)

Lathrop, Charles E., *The Literary Spy: The Ultimate Source for Quotations on Espionage and Intelligence* (New Haven, Conn.: Yale University Press, 2004)

Laurent, Sébastien, 'Aux origines de la "guerre des polices": militaires et policiers du renseignement dans la République (1870–1914)', in Frédéric Guelton and Abdil Bicer (eds.), *Naissance et évolution du renseignement dans l'espace européen (1870–1940)* (Paris: Service Historique de la Défense, 2006)

Lawday, David, *Napoleon's Master: A Life of Prince Talleyrand* (London: Jonathan Cape, 2006)

—, *Danton: The Gentle Giant of Terror* (London: Jonathan Cape, 2009)

Lawrence T. E., *Seven Pillars of Wisdom* (London: Random House, 2008 [first publ. 1922])

Lazenby, J. F., *Hannibal's War: A Military History of the Second Punic War* (Warminster: Aris and Phillips, 1978)

Le Naour, Jean-Yves, *L'Affaire Malvy: Le Dreyfus de la Grande Guerre* (Paris: Hachette, 2007)

Le Roy Ladurie, Emmanuel, *Montaillou: Cathars and Catholics in a French Village 1294–1324* (London: Penguin Books, 1980)

Leeuw, Karl de, 'The Black Chamber in the Dutch Republic during the War of the Spanish Succession and Its Aftermath, 1707–1715', *The Historical Journal*, Vol. 42 (1999), no. 1

—, *Cryptology and Statecraft in the Dutch Republic* (Amsterdam: University of Amsterdam, 2000)

—, 'Cryptology in the Dutch Republic: A Case-Study', in Karl de Leeuw and Jan Bergstra (eds.), *The History of Information Security: A Comprehensive Handbook* (Amsterdam: Elsevier, 2007)

— and Jan Bergstra (eds.), *The History of Information Security: A Comprehensive Handbook* (Amsterdam: Elsevier, 2007)

Lefauconnier, Camille, 'François Sublet de Noyers (1589–1645): *Ad majorem regis et Dei gloriam*', MA thesis (École des Chartes, Paris, 2008)

Leggett, George, *The Cheka: Lenin's Political Police* (London: Clarendon Press, 1981)

Leggiere, Michael V., *Blücher: Scourge of Napoléon* (Norman: University of Oklahoma Press, 2014)

Leidinger, Hannes, 'The Case of Alfred Redl and the Situation of Austro-Hungarian Military Intelligence on the Eve of World War I', *Contemporary Austrian Studies*, vol. 23 (2014)

Leimon, M., and G. Parker, 'Treason and Plot in Elizabethan Diplomacy: The "Fame of Sir Edward Stafford" Reconsidered', *English Historical Review*, vol. 111 (1996)

Lenoe, Matthew, *The Kirov Murder and Soviet History* (New Haven, Conn.: Yale University Press, 2010)

Leonov, N. S., *Likholet'e* (Moscow: Mezhdunarodnye otnosheniia, 1995)

—, Eugenia Fediakova and Joaquín Fermandois et al., 'El general Nikolai Leonov en el CEP', *Estudios Públicos*, no. 73 (1999)

Letters which Passed between Count Gyllenborg, the Barons Gortz, Sparre, and Others: Relating to the Design of Raising a Rebellion in His Majesty's Dominions, to be Supported by a Force from Sweden (Dublin: Tho. Hume, 1717)

Levack, Brian P., 'Crime and the Law', in Jonathan Barry and Owen Davies (eds.), *Palgrave Advances in Witchcraft Historiography* (Basingstoke: Palgrave Macmillan, 2007)

Levi, Anthony, *Cardinal Richelieu and the Making of France* (London: Constable, 2000)

Levy, David, *Stalin's Man in Canada: Fred Rose and Soviet Espionage* (New York: Enigma Books, 2011)

Lewin, Ronald, *The Other Ultra* (London: Hutchinson, 1982)

Lewis, Bernard, 'The Kemalist Republic'; http://www.turkishculturalfoundation. org/education/files/TheKemalistRepublicBernardLewis.pdf

Lewis, Mark Edward, *The Early Chinese Empires: Qin and Han*, Kindle edn (Cambridge, Mass.: Harvard University Press, 2007)

Lewis, Thomas, *For King and Country* (New York: HarperCollins, 1992)

Liang, Hsi-huey, *The Rise of Modern Police and the European State System from Metternich to the Second World War* (Cambridge: Cambridge University Press, 1992)

Lieven, Dominic, *Russia Against Napoleon: The Battle for Europe, 1807 to 1814*, Kindle edn (London: Allen Lane, 2009)

—, *Towards the Flame: Empire, War and the End of Tsarist Russia* (London: Allen Lane, 2015)

Lim, Louisa, The People's Republic of Amnesia: Tiananmen Revisited (New York: Oxford University Press, 2014)

Lindberg, Carter, *The European Reformations* (Oxford: Blackwell, 1996)

Linderski, J., 'Cicero and Roman Divination', *Past & Present*, vol. 36 (1982)

Link, Arthur S. (ed.), *The Papers of Woodrow Wilson* (Princeton, NJ: Princeton University Press, 1966–92)

Livy, *The Early History of Rome: Books 1–5* trans. R. M. Ogilvie (London: Penguin Books, 2005)

Lockhart, Robert Bruce, *Memoirs of a British Agent*, 2nd edn (London/New York: Putnam, 1934)

Loewe, Michael, *Divination, Mythology and Monarchy in Han China* (Cambridge: Cambridge University Press, 1994)

Lokhova, Svetlana, 'The Evolution of the Cheka, 1917–1926', MPhil dissertation (University of Cambridge, 2002)

—, 'Stalin, the NKVD and the Investigation of the Kremlin Case: Prelude to the Great Terror', in Christopher Andrew and Simona Tobia (eds.), *Interrogation in War and Conflict: A Comparative and Interdisciplinary Analysis* (London: Routledge, 2014)

Lonchay, Henri, and Joseph Cuvelier (eds.), *Correspondance de la cour d'Espagne sur les affaires des Pays-Bas au XVII siècle*, 6 vols. (Brussels: Kiesling, 1923–37)

Louis, Georges, *Les Carnets de Georges Louis*, 2 vols. (Paris: F. Rieder, 1926)

Lowenthal, Mark M., 'Searching for National Intelligence: U.S. Intelligence and Policy before the Second World War', *Intelligence and National Security*, vol. 6 (1991), no. 4

Lowry, Bullitt, *Armistice 1918* (Kent, Ohio/London: Kent State University Press, 1996)

Lowry, Carolyn S., 'At What Cost? Spanish Neutrality in the First World War' (University of South Florida, 2009), MA thesis; http://scholarcommons.usf.edu/etd/2072

Luttwak, Edward N., *The Grand Strategy of the Byzantine Empire* (Cambridge, Mass.: Harvard University Press, 2009)

Luvaas, Jay, *Frederick the Great on the Art of War* (New York: Free Press, 1966)

—, 'Lee at Gettysburg: A General without Intelligence', *Intelligence and National Security*, vol. 5 (1990), no. 2

—, 'The Role of Intelligence in the Chancellorsville Campaign, April–May, 1863', *Intelligence and National Security*, vol. 5 (1990), no. 2

Lycett, Andrew, *Ian Fleming* (London: Weidenfeld & Nicolson, 1995)

Lynn, John A., *Wars of Louis XIV, 1664–1714* (London: Longman, 1999)

Lyons, Jonathan, *The House of Wisdom: How the Arabs Transformed Western Civilization* (London: Bloomsbury, 2009)

MacInnes, A. I., *Clanship, Commerce, and the House of Stuart* (East Linton: Tuckwell Press, 1996)

Macintyre, Ben, *Double Cross: The True Story of the D-Day Spies* (London: Bloomsbury, 2012)

Mackenzie, Compton, *Greek Memories*, 2nd edn (London: Chatto & Windus, 1939)

MacKenzie, David, *Apis: The Congenial Conspirator. The Life of Colonel Dragutin T. Dimitrijević* (Boulder, Colo.: East European Monographs, 1989)

—, *The 'Black Hand' on Trial: Salonika, 1917* (Boulder, Colo.: East European Monographs, 1995)

Mackinnon, Colin, 'William Friedman's Bletchley Park Diary: A New Source for the History of Anglo-American Intelligence Cooperation', *Intelligence and National Security*, vol. 20 (2005), no. 4

Macrakis, Kristie, 'Does Effective Espionage Lead to Success in Science and Technology? Lessons from the East German Ministry of State Security', *Intelligence and National Security*, vol. 24 (2004), no. 1

—, *Prisoners, Lovers & Spies: The Story of Invisible Ink from Herodotus to Al-Qaeda* (New Haven, Conn.: Yale University Press, 2014)

Madariaga, Isabel de, *Ivan the Terrible: First Tsar of Russia* (New Haven, Conn.: Yale University Press, 2008)

Madeira, Victor, *Britannia and the Bear: The Anglo-Russian Intelligence Wars 1917–1929* (Woodbridge: Boydell Press, 2014)

Malcolm, Noel, *Agents of Empire: Knights, Corsairs, Jesuits and Spies in the Sixteenth-Century Mediterranean World* (London: Allen Lane, 2015)

Mann, J. C., 'The Organization of Frumentarii', *Zeitschrift für Papyrologie und Epigraphik* 74 (1988)

Mansergh, Nicholas (ed.), *Constitutional Relations between Britain and India: The Transfer of Power in India*, 12 vols. (London: HMSO, 1970–83)

Marder, Arthur Jacob, *From the Dreadnought to Scapa Flow: The Royal Navy in the Fisher Era, 1904–1919* (London: Oxford University Press, 1961–70), vol. II: *The War Years: To the Eve of Jutland 1914–1916* (1961); vol. III: *Jutland and After, May 1916–December 1916* (1966); vol. IV: *1917: Year of Crisis* (1969); vol. V: *Victory and Aftermath, January 1918–June 1919* (1970)

Marquis, Hugues, *Les Agents de l'ennemi. Les Espions à la solde de l'Angleterre dans une France en révolution* (Paris: Vendémiaire, 2014)

Marriott, J. A. R., *The Life and Times of Lucius Cary, Viscount Falkland* (London: Methuen, 1907)

Marshall, Alan, *Intelligence and Espionage in the Reign of Charles II, 1660–1685* (Cambridge: Cambridge University Press, 1994)

—, 'Sir Samuel Morland and Stuart Espionage', King Charles Lecture at Bath Spa University; http://www.academia.edu/1557372/Sir_Samuel_Morland_and_Stuart_espionage, accessed 2 April 2014

Marshall, Alex, 'Russian Intelligence during the Russo-Japanese War, 1904–05', *Intelligence and National Security*, vol. 22 (2007), no. 5

Martini, Admiral Fulvio, *Nome in codice: ULISSE* (Milan: Rizzoli, 1999)

Marx, Karl, and Friedrich Engels, *Collected Works* (London: Lawrence & Wishart, 1975–2004)

Massie, Alan, *Catherine the Great: Portrait of a Woman* (London: Head of Zeus, 2012)

Massie, Robert K., *Nicholas and Alexandra* (New York: Atheneum, 1967)

Masterman, J. C., *The Double-Cross System* (London: Sphere, 1973)

—, *On the Chariot Wheel* (London: Oxford University Press, 1975)

Maugham, W. Somerset, 'Looking Back', *Sunday Express*; part 1: 30 Sept. 1962; part 2: 7 Oct. 1962

—, *Collected Short Stories* (London: Pan Books, 1976)

Maxwell-Stuart, Peter, 'The Contemporary Historical Debate, 1400–1750', in Jonathan Barry and Owen Davies (eds.), *Palgrave Advances in Witchcraft Historiography* (Basingstoke: Palgrave Macmillan, 2007)

May, Ernest R., *Knowing One's Enemies: Intelligence Assessment before the Two World Wars* (Princeton, NJ: Princeton University Press, 1984)

Mayer, Jane, 'A Deadly Interrogation', *New Yorker*, 14 November 2005

Mayr, Josef Karl, *Metternichs geheimer Briefdienst: Postlogen und Postkurse* (Vienna: Adolf Holzhausens Nachfolge, 1935)

Mazumder, Rajit K., *The Indian Army and the Making of Punjab* (New Delhi: Orient Blackswan, 2003)

McAuliffe, Mary S. (ed.), *CIA Documents on the Cuban Missile Crisis 1962* (Washington, DC: CIA, 1992)

McGuigan, Dorothy Gies, *Metternich and the Duchess* (New York: Doubleday, 1975)

McIntosh, Gregory C., *The Piri Reis Map of 1513* (Athens, Ga: University of Georgia Press, 2000)

McKee, Claire Theresa, 'British Perceptions of Tsar Nicholas II and Empress Alexandra Fedorovna 1894–1918', PhD thesis (University College London, 2014)

McLaughlin, John, 'The Changing Nature of CIA Analysis in the Post-Soviet World', 9 March 2001; https://www.cia.gov/news-information/speeches-testimony/2001/ddci_speech_03092001.html

McLellan, David (ed.), *Karl Marx, Interviews and Reflections* (Totowa, NJ: Barnes & Noble, 1981)

McLynn, Frank, *Bonnie Prince Charlie: Charles Edward Stuart* (London: Pimlico, 2003)

McNeilly, Mark, *Sun Tzu and the Art of Modern Warfare* (Oxford: Oxford University Press, 2001)

Mehta, Usha, and Usha Thakkar, *Kautilya and His Arthashastra* (New Delhi: S. Chand, 1980)

Melgounov, Sergey Petrovich, *The Red Terror in Russia* (London: J. M. Dent, 1925)

Ménage, V. L., 'The Mission of an Ottoman Secret Agent in France in 1486', *JRAS*, vol. 97 (1965), 33, no. 2

Menning, Bruce W., 'Miscalculating One's Enemies: Russian Military Intelligence before the Russo-Japanese War', *War in History*, vol. 13 (2006), no. 2

—, 'Russian Military Intelligence, July 1914: What St. Petersburg Perceived and Why It Mattered', *The Historian*, vol. 77 (2015), no. 2

Menocal, María Rosa, *The Ornament of the World* (Boston: Little, Brown, 2002)

Merlo, Grado Giovanni, 'Le origini dell'inquisizione medievale', in Agostino Borromeo (ed.), *L'Inquisizione: Atti del Simposio internazionale, Città del Vaticano, 29–31 ottobre 1998* (Vatican City: Biblioteca Apostolica Vaticana, 2003)

Merridale, Catherine, *Red Fortress: The Secret Heart of Russia's History* (London: Allen Lane, 2013)

—, *Lenin on the Train* (London: Allen Lane, 2017)

Merriman, John, *Police Stories: Building the French State* (New York: Oxford University Press, 2006)

—, *The Dynamite Club: How a Bombing in Fin-de-Siècle Paris Ignited the Age of Modern Terror* (New York: Houghton Mifflin Harcourt, 2009)

Meyer, Karl E., and Shareen Blair Brysac, *Tournament of Shadows: The Great Game and the Race for Empire in Central Asia* (London: Little, Brown, 2001)

Meyers, Eric M. (ed.), *Galilee through the Centuries: Confluence of Cultures* (Winona Lake, Ind.: Eisenbrauns, 1999)

Miller, David B., 'The Orthodox Church', in Maureen Perrie (ed.), *The Cambridge History of Russia*, vol. 1: *From Early Rus' to 1689* (Cambridge: Cambridge University Press, 2006)

Miller, Flagg, *The Audacious Ascetic: What the Bin Laden Tapes Reveal about al-Qā'ida* (London: Hurst, 2015)

Miller, Martin, 'Entangled Terrorisms in Late Imperial Russia', in Randall D. Law (ed.), *The Routledge History of Terrorism* (London: Routledge, 2015)

Miller, Stuart Creighton, *'Benevolent Assimilation': The American Conquest of the Philippines, 1899–1903* (New Haven, Conn.: Yale University Press, 1982)

Milner-Barry, P. S., ' "Action This Day": The Letter from Bletchley Park Cryptanalysts to the Prime Minister, 21 October 1941', *Intelligence and National Security*, vol. 1 (1986), no. 2

Mindich, David T. Z., 'Lincoln's Surveillance State', *The New York Times*, 5 July 2013

Mitchell, Harvey, *The Underground War against Revolutionary France: The Missions of William Wickham 1794–1800* (Oxford: Oxford University Press, 1965)

Mitrokhin, Vasili (ed.), *KGB Lexicon: The Soviet Intelligence Officer's Handbook* (London: Frank Cass, 2002)

Mohs, Polly A., *Military Intelligence and the Arab Revolt: The First Modern Intelligence War* (London: Routledge, 2008)

Mombauer, Annika, 'German War Plans', in Richard F. Hamilton and Holger H. Herwig (eds.), *War Planning 1914* (Cambridge: Cambridge University Press, 2010)

Momigliano, Arnaldo, 'Christianity and the Decline of the Roman Empire', in Arnaldo Momigliano (ed.), *The Conflict between Paganism and Christianity in the Fourth Century* (Oxford: Clarendon Press, 1963)

Monter, William, 'The Roman Inquisition and Protestant Heresy Executions in 16th-Century Europe', in Agostino Borromeo (ed.), *L'Inquisizione: Atti del Simposio internazionale, Città del Vaticano, 29–31 ottobre 1998* (Vatican City: Biblioteca Apostolica Vaticana, 2003)

Montholon, General Charles-Tristan, *Récits de la captivité de l'empereur Napoléon à Sainte-Hélène*, vol. 1 (Paris: Paulin, 1846)

Moore, R. I., *The Formation of a Persecuting Society: Power and Deviance in Western Europe, 950–1250* (Oxford: Blackwell, 1990)

—, *The War on Heresy: Faith and Power in Medieval Europe* (London: Profile Books, 2012)

Morales, A. Katherine, 'Cruelty of Ivan IV', 2005; plaza.ufl.edu/akathy/Papers

Moran, Christopher R., *Company Confessions: Revealing CIA Secrets* (London: Biteback, 2015)

Moran, Richard, *Knowing Right from Wrong: The Insanity Defense of Daniel McNaughtan* (New York: Simon and Schuster, 2000)

Moran, W. L. (ed. and trans.), *The Amarna Letters* (Baltimore: Johns Hopkins University Press, 1992)

Morgan, Ted, *FDR: A Biography* (London: Grafton, 1985)

Morris, Benny, 'Sayyid Qutb and the Jews', *The National Interest*, 20 Oct. 2010

Morris, Christopher, 'ULTRA's Poor Relations', in Christopher Andrew (ed.), *Codebreaking and Signals Intelligence* (London: Frank Cass, 1986)

Morris, Peter, 'Intelligence and Its Interpretation: Mesopotamia, 1914–1916', in Christopher Andrew and Jeremy Noakes (eds.), *Intelligence and International Relations 1900–1945* (Exeter: Exeter University Press, 1987)

Mousnier, Roland, *The Assassination of Henry IV: The Tyrannicide Problem and the Consolidation of the French Absolute Monarchy in the Early Seventeenth Century* (New York: Scribner, 1973)

Moynihan, Daniel Patrick, *Secrecy: The American Experience* (New Haven, Conn.: Yale University Press, 1998)

Muddiman, J. G. (ed.), *Notable British Trials: Trial of Charles I* (London: W. Hodge, 1928)

Mueller, Hans-Friedrich, *Roman Religion in Valerius Maximus* (London: Routledge, 2002)

Muggeridge, Malcolm, *Chronicles of Wasted Time*, vol. II: *The Infernal Grove* (London: Fontana, 1973)

Mulford, Carla, 'Benjamin Franklin's Savage Eloquence: Hoaxes from the Press at Passy, 1782', *Proceedings of the American Philosophical Society*, vol. 152 (2008), no. 4

Mulligan, Timothy P., 'Spies, Ciphers and "Zitadelle": Intelligence and the Battle of Kursk, 1943', *Journal of Contemporary History*, vol. 12 (1987), no. 2

Munch-Petersen, Thomas, *Defying Napoleon: How Britain Bombarded Copenhagen and Seized the Danish Fleet in 1807* (Stroud: Sutton Publishing, 2007)

—, 'The Secret Intelligence from Tilsit in 1807', *Napoleonica. La Revue*, vol. 3 (2013), no. 18

Murphy, Cullen, *God's Jury: The Inquisition and the Making of the Modern World* (London: Allen Lane, 2012)

Murthy, B. M. N., 'R. Shamashastry – the Scholar Who Discovered Arthashastra', *Bhavan's Journal*, 31 December 2009

Musco, Stefano, 'Intelligence Gathering and the Relationship between Rulers and Spies: Some Lessons from Eminent and Lesser-Known Classics', *Intelligence and National Security*, vol. 31 (2016), no. 7

Na'aman, Nadav, 'The Egyptian–Canaanite Correspondence', in Raymond Cohen and Raymond Westbrook (eds.), *Amarna Diplomacy: The Beginnings of International Relations* (Baltimore: Johns Hopkins University Press, 2000)

Naftali, Timothy J., 'Intrepid's Last Deception: Documenting the Career of Sir William Stephenson', *Intelligence and National Security*, vol. 8 (1993), no. 3

Nagy, John A., *George Washington's Secret Spy War: The Making of America's First Spymaster* (New York: St. Martin's Press, 2016)

Najemy, John M. (ed.). *Italy in the Age of the Renaissance: 1300–1550* (Oxford: Oxford University Press, 2004)

Nathan, Andrew, Perry Link and Liang Zhang, *The Tiananmen Papers: The Chinese Leadership's Decision to Use Force against Their Own People* (London: Abacus, 2002)

Neel, Jasper P., *Aristotle's Voice: Rhetoric, Theory, and Writing in America* (Carbondale: Southern Illinois University Press, 1994)

Neilson, Keith, 'Joy Rides'? British Intelligence and Propaganda in Russia, 1914–1917', *The Historical Journal*, vol. 24 (1981), no. 4

— and B. J. C. McKercher (eds.), *Go Spy the Land: Military Intelligence in History* (Westport, Conn.: Praeger, 1992)

Netanyahu, Iddo, *Entebbe: A Defining Moment in the War on Terrorism – the Jonathan Netanyahu Story* (New York: Balfour Books, 2003)

Nicholl, Charles, *The Reckoning: The Murder of Christopher* Marlowe, 2nd edn (London: Vintage, 2002)

Nicholson, H. B., *Topiltzin Quetzalcoatl: The Once and Future Lord of the Toltecs* (Boulder: University Press of Colorado, 2001)

Nickles, David Paull, *Under the Wire: How the Telegraph Changed Diplomacy* (Cambridge, Mass.: Harvard University Press, 2003)

Nicolai, Walter, *The German Secret Service*, trans. George Renwick (London: S. Paul, 1924)

Nieuwazny, Andrzej, 'Rien de bien certain? Le Système de renseignements français avant la campagne de Russie', *Revue Historique des armées*, 2012, no. 267

Nirenberg, David, *Communities of Violence: Persecution of Minorities in the Middle Ages* (Princeton, NJ: Princeton University Press, 2015)

Nixon, John, *Debriefing the President: The Interrogation of Saddam Hussein* (New York: Blue Rider Press, 2016)

Nordmann, Claude, 'Choiseul and the Last Jacobite Attempt of 1759', in Eveline Cruikshanks (ed.), *Ideology and Conspiracy: Aspects of Jacobitism, 1689–1759* (Edinburgh: John Donald, 1982)

Nuovo, Angela, 'A Lost Arabic Koran Rediscovered', *The Library*, 6th series, vol. 12 (1990), no. 4

Nye, Joseph S., *Bound to Lead: The Changing Nature of American Power* (New York: Basic Books, 1990)

—, *Soft Power: The Means to Success in World Politics* (New York: Public Affairs, 2004)

—, *The Powers to Lead* (Oxford: Oxford University Press, 2008)

O'Connor, John J., and Edmund F. Robertson, 'Christian Goldbach', MacTutor History of Mathematics Archive, University of St Andrews

O'Hagan, Andrew, *The Secret Life* (London: Faber & Faber, 2017)

Omand, Sir David, 'Learning from the Secret Past': unpublished address to RUSI conference, 23 October 2009

—, *Securing the State* (New York: Oxford University Press, 2010)

—, 'Keeping Europe Safe: Counterterrorism for the Continent', *Foreign Affairs*, vol. 95 (2016), no. 5

Onley, James, 'The Raj Reconsidered: British India's Informal Empire and Spheres of Influence in Asia and Africa', *Asian Affairs*, vol. XL (2009), no. 1

Ostrovsky, Victor, and Claire Hoy, *By Way of Deception* (London: Bloomsbury, 1990)

Ostryakov, Sergei Zakharovich, *Voyennye Chekisti* (Moscow: Voyenizdat, 1979)

O'Toole, G. J. A., *Honorable Treachery* (New York: Atlantic Monthly Press, 1991)

Otte, T. G., *July Crisis: The World's Descent into War, Summer 1914* (Cambridge: Cambridge University Press, 2014)

Overy, Richard, ' "Instructive for the Future": The Interrogation of the Major War Criminals in Germany', in Christopher Andrew and Simona Tobia (eds.), *Interrogation in War and Conflict: A Comparative and Interdisciplinary Analysis* (London: Routledge, 2014)

Pagden, A. R. (ed. and trans.), *Hernán Cortés: Letters From Mexico*, with an Introduction by J. H. Elliott (New York: Grossman, 1971)

Paine, Lincoln, *The Sea and Civilization: A Maritime History of the World* (London: Atlantic, 2014)

Paléologue, Maurice, *Un Grand Tournant de la politique mondiale* (Paris: Plon, 1934)

—, *Journal de L'Affaire Dreyfus, 1894–1899* (Paris: Plon, 1955)

Pantucci, Raffaello, *'We Love Death as You Love Life': Britain's Suburban Mujahedeen* (London: Hurst, 2013)

Páramo, Luis de, *De origine et progressu officii sanctae Inquisitionis eiusque dignitate et utilitate, de Romani pontificis potestate et deligata inquisitorum; edicto fidei, et ordine iudiciario sancti officij, quaestiones decem*, Libri tres (Madrid: Matriti, 1598) Cambridge University Library: Acton.b.1.230

Paret, Peter, Gordon A.Craig and Felix Gilbert (eds.), *Makers of Modern Strategy from Machiavelli to the Nuclear Age* (Oxford: Clarendon Press, 1986)

Parker, Frederick D., 'The Unsolved Messages of Pearl Harbor', *Cryptologia*, vol. 15 (1991), no. 4

Parker, Geoffrey, 'The Worst-Kept Secret in Europe? The European Intelligence Community and the Armada of 1588', in Keith Neilson and B. J. C. McKercher (eds.), *Go Spy the Land: Military Intelligence in History* (Westport Conn.: Praeger, 1992)

Passi, Sonya, 'Britain and the Iranian Revolution', MPhil dissertation (University of Cambridge, 2010)

Patel, Kiran Klaus, *The New Deal: A Global History* (Princeton, NJ: Princeton University Press)

Pavlov, Andrei, 'Fedor Ivanovich and Boris Godunov (1584–1605)', in Maureen Perrie (ed.), *The Cambridge History of Russia*, vol. 1: *From early Rus' to 1689* (Cambridge: Cambridge University Press, 2006)

— and Maureen Perrie, *Ivan the Terrible* (London: Pearson/Longman, 2003)

Pearce, Edward, *The Great Man: Sir Robert Walpole – Scoundrel, Genius and Britain's First Prime Minister* (London: Jonathan Cape, 2007)

Peck, Winslow [Perry Fellwock], 'U.S. Electronic Espionage: A Memoir', *Ramparts*, vol. 11 (1972), no. 2

Pedroncini, G., *Les Mutineries de 1917* (Paris: Presses Universitaires de France, 1999)

Peek, P. M., 'Introduction: The Study of Divination, Present and Past', in P. M. Peek (ed.), *African Divination Systems: Ways of Knowing* (Bloomington: Indiana University Press, 1991)

Pegg, Mark Gregory, *The Corruption of Angels: The Great Inquisition of 1245–1246* (Princeton, NJ: Princeton University Press, 2001)

Pelhisson, Guillaume, *Chronique (1229–1244). Suivie du Récit des Troubles d'Albi (1234)*, ed. Jean Duvernoy (Paris: Centre National de la Recherche Scientifique, 1994)

Perez, Béatrice (ed.), *Ambassadeurs, apprentis espions et maîtres comploteurs: les systèmes de renseignement en Espagne à l'époque moderne* (Paris: Presses de l'Université Paris–Sorbonne, 2010)

Perrault, Charles, *Les Hommes illustres qui ont paru en France pendant ce siècle avec leurs portraits au naturel* (Paris: Antoine Dezallier, 1696)

Perrie, Maureen, *The Cult of Ivan the Terrible in Stalin's Russia* (Basingstoke: Palgrave, 2001)

— (ed.), *The Cambridge History of Russia*, vol. 1: *From Early Rus' to 1689* (Cambridge: Cambridge University Press, 2006)

—, 'The Time of Troubles (1603–1613)', in Maureen Perrie (ed.), *The Cambridge History of Russia*, vol. 1: *From Early Rus' to 1689* (Cambridge: Cambridge University Press, 2006)

Perry, William J., *My Journey at the Nuclear Brink* (Stanford, Calif.: Stanford University Press, 2016)

Pesic, Peter, 'François Viète, Father of Modern Cryptanalysis – Two New Manuscripts', *Cryptologia*, vol. 21 (1997), no. 1

Petitfils, Jean-Christian, *Le Véritable d'Artagnan* (Paris: Tallandier, 1981)

—, *Louis XIII* (Paris: Perrin, 2008)

Philby, Kim, *My Silent War* (St Albans: Granada, 1969)

Phythian, Mark, 'Profiles in Intelligence: An Interview with Michael Herman', *Intelligence and National Security*, vol. 31 (2016), no. 2

—, 'Profiles in Intelligence: An Interview with Professor Christopher Andrew', *Intelligence and National Security*, vol. 32 (2017), no. 4

Pierre, Benoist, *Le Père Joseph: L'Éminence grise de Richelieu* (Paris: Éditions Perrin, 2007)

Piette, Diane Carraway, and Jesselyn Radack, 'Piercing the "Historical Mists": The People and Events behind the Passage of FISA and the Creation of the "Wall"', *Stanford Law and Policy Review*, vol. 17 (2006), no. 2

Pincus, Steve, *1688: The First Modern Revolution* (New Haven, Conn.: Yale University Press, 2009)

Pipes, Richard, *Russia under the Old Regime* (Harmondsworth: Penguin Books, 1974)

—, *The Unknown Lenin: From the Secret Archive*, rev. edn (New Haven, Conn.: Yale University Press, 1998)

Platonov, Sergey, *Ivan the Terrible* (Gulf Breeze, Fla: Academic International Press, 1974)

Plumb, J. H., *The Italian Renaissance* (New York: Harper Torchbooks, 1961)

Poncier, Anthony, *Les Procureurs généraux du Second Empire*, doctoral thesis, *Revue d'histoire du XIXᵉ siècle*, 2002, no. 25

Pontaut, Jean-Marie, and Jérôme Dupuis, *Les Oreilles du Président – suivi de la liste des 2000 personnes 'écoutées' par François Mitterrand* (Paris: Fayard, 1996)

Popplewell, Richard J., *Intelligence and Imperial Defence: British Intelligence and the Defence of the Indian Empire* (London: Frank Cass, 1995)

Pormann, Peter E., and Peter Adamson (eds.), *The Philosophical Works of al-Kindī* (Pakistan: Oxford University Press, 2012)

Porter, Bernard, 'The Origins of Britain's Political Police', *Warwick Working Papers in Social History*, no. 3

—, *The Refugee Question in mid-Victorian Politics* (Cambridge: Cambridge University Press, 1979)

Pottle, Mark (ed.), *Champion Redoubtable: The Diaries and Letters of Violet Bonham Carter, 1914–1945* (London: Weidenfeld & Nicolson, 1998)

Powell, Colin, *It Worked for Me: In Life and Leadership* (New York: Harper, 2012)

Pozen, David E., 'The Leaky Leviathan: Why the Government Condemns and Condones Unlawful Disclosures of Information', *Harvard Law Review*, vol. 127 (2013)

Pradel, Charles (ed.), 'Mémoires de Jean Olès sur la dernière guerre du duc de Rohan, 1627–1628', *Revue historique, scientifique et littéraire du département du Tarn*, vol. XXIV (1907)

Prange, Gordon W., *At Dawn We Slept* (New York: Penguin Books, 1982)

Preston, Andrew, 'US National Security Has Become So Expansive as to be Virtually Limitless', *Cam*, no. 81 (2017)

Preto, Paolo, *I servizi segreti di Venezia* (Milan: Il Saggiatore, 1994)

Price, Munro, *The Fall of the French Monarchy: Louis XVI, Marie-Antoinette and the Baron de Breteuil* (London: Pan Books, 2003)

—, *Napoleon: The End of Glory*, Kindle edn (Oxford: Oxford University Press, 2014)

Price, Roger, *The French Second Empire: An Anatomy of Political Power* (Cambridge: Cambridge University Press, 2001)

Primakov, Evgeny, et al., *Ocherki istorii rossiyskoi vneshnei razvedki*, 6 vols. (Moscow: Mezhdunar Otnosheniya, 1996–2007)

Primakov, Yevgeny, *Russian Crossroads: Toward the New Millennium*, trans. Felix Rosenthal (New Haven, Conn.: Yale University Press, 2004)

Prior, Robin, and Trevor Wilson, *The Somme*, rev. edn (New Haven, Conn.: Yale University Press, 2016)

Pryor, Felix, *Elizabeth I: Her Life in Letters* (London: British Library, 2004)

Public Papers of the Presidents (Washington, DC: US Government Printing Office, 1957–)

Putlitz, Wolfgang zu, *The Putlitz Dossier* (London: Allen Wingate, 1957)

Quinault, Roland, 'The French Invasion of Pembrokeshire in 1797: A Bicentennial Assessment', *Welsh History Review*, vol. 19 (1999)

Qutb, Sayyid, 'The America I Have Seen' (first publ. in Arabic 1951), in Kamal Abdel-Malek (ed.), *America in an Arab Mirror: Images of America in Arabic Travel Literature. An Anthology* (Basingstoke: Palgrave Macmillan, 2011)

Radek, Karl, 'Through Germany in a Sealed Coach' (first publ. in German 1924); https://www.marxists.org/archive/radek/1924/xx/train.htm

Radzinowicz, Leon, *A History of English Criminal Law and Its Administration from 1750*, vol. 2 (London: Macmillan, 1956)

Rakove, Jack, *Revolutionaries: Inventing the American Nation* (London: William Heinemann, 2010)

Raleigh, Sir Walter, *The War in the Air: Being the Story of the Part Played in the Great War by the Royal Air Force*, vol. 1 (Barnsley: Pen & Sword Military, 2014)

Ramm, Agatha (ed.), *The Political Correspondence of Mr Gladstone and Lord Granville, 1876–1886*, vol. 2 (Oxford: Oxford University Press, 1962)

Rancour-Laferriere, Daniel, *The Slave Soul of Russia: Moral Masochism and the Cult of Suffering* (New York: New York University Press, 1996)

Rand, Peter, *Conspiracy of One: Tyler Kent's Secret Plot against FDR, Churchill, and the Allied War Effort* (London: Lyons Press, 2013)

Randall, Willard Sterne, *Benedict Arnold: Patriot and Traitor* (London: Bodley Head, 1991)

Rangarajan, L. N. (ed), *The Arthashastra* (New Delhi: Penguin Books, 1992)

Ransom, Harry Howe, 'Secret Intelligence in the United States, 1947–1982: The CIA's Search for Legitimacy', in Christopher Andrew and David Dilks (eds.), *The Missing Dimension: Governments and Intelligence Communities in the Twentieth Century* (London: Macmillan, 1984)

Raphals, Lisa, *Divination and Prediction in Early China and Ancient Greece* (Cambridge: Cambridge University Press, 2013)

Rappaport, Helen, *Conspirator: Lenin in Exile* (New York: Basic Books, 2010)

Rapport, Mike, *1848: Year of Revolution* (London: Hachette, 2010)

Rawlings, Helen, *The Spanish Inquisition* (Oxford: Blackwell, 2006)

Rayfield, Donald, *Stalin and His Hangmen: An Authoritative Portrait of a Tyrant and Those Who Served Him* (London: Viking, 2004)

Read, Conyers, *Mr Secretary Walsingham and the Policy of Queen Elizabeth*, 3 vols. (Oxford: Clarendon Press, 1925)

Read, Piers Paul, *The Dreyfus Affair* (London: Bloomsbury, 2012)

Redworth, Glyn, *The Prince and the Infanta: The Cultural Politics of the Spanish Match* (New Haven, Conn.: Yale University Press, 2003)

Rejaji, Darius, *Torture and Democracy* (Princeton, NJ: Princeton University Press, 2009)

Report of the Iraq Inquiry [Chilcot Report], 12 vols. (London: HMSO, 2016)

Review of Intelligence on Weapons of Mass Destruction: Report of a Committee of Privy Counsellors [Butler Report], HC 898 (London: Stationery Office, 14 July 2004)

Rex, Richard, 'The Religion of Henry VIII', *The Historical Journal*, vol. 57 (2014), no. 1

Reynolds, David, 'Churchill and the British "Decision" to Fight On in 1940: Right Policy, Wrong Reasons', in Richard Langhorne (ed.), *Diplomacy and Intelligence in the Second World War* (Cambridge: Cambridge University Press, 1985)

Rhodes, P. J., *Alcibiades*, Kindle edn (Barnsley: Pen & Sword Books, 2011)

Rice, Condoleezza, *No Higher Honor: A Memoir of My Years in Washington* (New York: Simon & Schuster, 2011)

Rich, Ben, and Leo Janos, *Skunk Works* (Boston: Little, Brown, 1994)

Richmond, J. A., 'Spies in Ancient Greece', *Greece & Rome*, vol. 45 (Apr. 1998), no. 1

Ridley, Jane, *Bertie: A Life of Edward VII* (London: Random House, 2012)

Riggs, David, *The World of Christopher Marlowe* (London: Faber & Faber, 2004)

Riley-Smith, Jonathan, *The Crusades, Christianity and Islam* (New York: Columbia University Press, 2011)

Rintelen, Franz von, *The Dark Invader: Wartime Reminiscences of a German Naval Intelligence Officer*, 2nd edn (London: Frank Cass, 1997)

Roberts, Andrew, *Napoleon and Wellington: The Long Duel* (London: Phoenix, 2002)

—, *Napoleon the Great*, Kindle edn (London: Allen Lane, 2014)

—, *Elegy: The First Day on the Somme* (London: Head of Zeus, 2015)

Roberts, Geoffrey, *Stalin's General: The Life of Georgy Zhukov* (London: Icon Books, 2012)

Robertson, Geoffrey, *The Tyrannicide Brief* (London: Chatto & Windus, 2005)

Robertson, K. G. (ed.), *War, Resistance and Intelligence: Essays in Honour of M. R. D. Foot* (Barnsley: Pen & Sword, 1999)

Robson, Brian, *The Road to Kabul: The Second Afghan War 1878–1881* (London: Arms and Armour Press, 1986)

Rodger, N. A. M., *The Command of the Ocean: A Naval History of Britain, 1649–1815* (London: Allen Lane, 2004)

Rodgers, W., *Greek and Roman Naval Warfare* (Annapolis, Md: United States Naval Institute, 1937)

Rodriguéz-Salgado, Mia, 'Intelligence in the Spanish Monarchy in the Sixteenth and Early Seventeenth Centuries', unpublished paper to a conference at the German Historical Institute in London, 7 February 2014

Röhl, John C. G., *The Kaiser and His Court: Wilhelm II and the Government of Germany* (Cambridge: Cambridge University Press, 1994)

—, *Kaiser Wilhelm II, 1859–1941: A Concise Life* (Cambridge: Cambridge University Press, 2014)

—, *Wilhelm II: Into the Abyss of War and Exile, 1900–1941* (Cambridge: Cambridge University Press, 2014)

—, 'Goodbye to All That (Again)? The Fischer Thesis, the New Revisionism and the Meaning of the First World War', *International Affairs*, vol. 91 (2015), no. 1

Rojas, José Luis de, *Tenochtitlan: Capital of the Aztec Empire* (Gainesville: University Press of Florida, 2012)

Roosevelt, Elliott (ed.), *The Roosevelt Letters: Being the Personal Correspondence of Franklin Delano Roosevelt*, 3 vols. (London: Harrap, 1949–52); vol. 2: *1905–1928* (1950); vol. 3: *1928–1945* (1952)

Roosevelt, Kermit, *Countercoup: The Struggle for the Control of Iran* (New York: McGraw-Hill, 1979)

Rose, P. K., 'The Founding Fathers of American Intelligence' (Langley, Va: CIA Center for the Study of Intelligence, 1999)

Roseman, Mark, *The Wannsee Conference and the Final Solution: A Reconsideration*, rev. edn (London: Folio, 2012)

Roskill, S. W., *Hankey: Man of Secrets*, 3 vols. (London: Collins, 1970)

—, *Admiral of the Fleet Lord Beatty: The Last Naval Hero* (London: Collins, 1980)

Ross, Sir David, *Aristotle*, 6th edn (London: Routledge, 1995)

Roth, Cecil, *The Spanish Inquisition* (London: R. Hale, 1937)

Rothenberg, Gunther, 'Military Intelligence Gathering in the Second Half of the Eighteenth Century, 1740–1792', in Keith Neilson and B. J. C. McKercher (eds.), *Go Spy the Land: Military Intelligence in History* (Westport, Conn.: Praeger, 1992)

Royle, Edward, *Chartism* (London: Longman, 1996)

Russell, E., *Maitland of Lethington, the Minister of Mary Stuart: A Study of His Life and Times* (London: J. Nisbet, 1912)

Russell, Frank Santi, *Information Gathering in Classical Greece* (Ann Arbor: University of Michigan Press, 1999)

Rutledge, Steven H., *Imperial Inquisitions: Prosecutors and Informants from Tiberius to Domitian* (London: Routledge, 2001)

Ruud, Charles A., and Sergei A. Stepanov, *Fontanka 16: The Tsars' Secret Police* (Montreal/Kingston, Ont.: McGill–Queen's University Press, 1999)

Sadler, John, and Sylvie Fisch, *Spy of the Century: Alfred Redl and the Betrayal of Austria–Hungary* (Barnsley: Pen & Sword Books, 2016)

Samolis, T. R. (ed.), *Veterany vneshei razvedki Rossii: Kratkii biograficheskii* (Moscow: SVR Press, 1995)

Sand, Shlomo, *The Invention of the Jewish People* (London: Verso, 2010)

Sarotte, Mary Elise, *1989: The Struggle to Create post-Cold War Europe* (Princeton, NJ: Princeton University Press, 2009)

Sarris, Peter, *Empires of Faith: The Fall of Rome to the Rise of Islam, 500–700* (Oxford: Oxford University Press, 2011)

Satterfield, Susan, 'Livy and the Timing of Expiation in the Roman Year', *Histos*, vol. 6 (2012)

Savage, Gary, 'Foreign Policy and Political Culture in later Eighteenth-Century France', in Hamish Scott and Brendan Simms (eds.), *Cultures of Power in Europe during the Long Eighteenth Century* (Cambridge: Cambridge University Press, 2007)

Savage-Smith, Emilie (ed.), *Magic and Divination in Early Islam* (Farnham: Ashgate, 2004)

Saville, John, *1848: The British State and the Chartist Movement* (Cambridge: Cambridge University Press, 1990)

Sawyer, Ralph D., *The Tao of Spycraft: Intelligence Theory and Practice in Traditional China* (Boulder, Colo.: Westview Press, 1998)

—, *Tao of Deception: Unorthodox Warfare in Historic and Modern China* (New York: Basic Books, 2007)

—, 'Subversive Information: The Historical Thrust of Chinese Intelligence', in Philip H. J. Davies and Kristian C. Gustafson (eds.), *Intelligence Elsewhere: Spies and Espionage Outside the Anglosphere* (Washington, DC: Georgetown University Press, 2013)

Sayle, Edward F., 'The Historical Underpinnings of the U.S. Intelligence Community', *International Journal of Intelligence and CounterIntelligence*, vol. 1 (1986), no. 1

Schaeper, Thomas J., *Edward Bancroft: Scientist, Author, Spy* (New Haven, Conn.: Yale University Press, 2011)

Schama, Simon, *Citizens: A Chronicle of the French Revolution* (London: Penguin Books, 2004)

Schecter, Jerrold L., and Peter S. Deriabin, *The Spy Who Saved the World: How a Soviet Colonel Changed the Course of the Cold War* (New York: Charles Scribner's Sons, 1992)

Schieder, Theodor, *Friedrich der Grosse: Ein Königtum der Widersprüche. Biographie* (Berlin: Propyläen Verlag, 1980)

Schiff, Stacy, *A Great Improvisation: Franklin in France* (New York: Henry Holt, 2005)

Schimmelpenninck van der Oye, David, 'Tsarist Codebreaking: Some Background and Some Examples', *Cryptologia*, vol. 22 (1998), no. 4

—, 'Reforming Military Intelligence', in David Schimmelpenninck van der Oye and Bruce W. Menning (eds.), *Reforming the Tsar's Army: Military Innovation in Imperial Russia from Peter the Great to the Revolution* (Cambridge: Cambridge University Press, 2004)

Schindler, John R., 'Redl – Spy of the Century?', *International Journal of Intelligence and CounterIntelligence*, vol. 18 (2005), no. 3

Schlichting, Albert, 'A Brief Account of the Character and Brutal Rule of Vasil'evich, Tyrant of Muscovy', trans. and ed. Hugh F. Graham, *Canadian–American Slavic Studies*, vol. 9 (1975), no. 2

Schlitter, Hans (ed.), *Correspondance Secrète entre le Comte A. W. Kaunitz-Rietberg, ambassadeur impérial à Paris, et le Baron Ignaz de Koch, secrétaire de l'Impératrice Marie-Thérèse, 1750–1752* (Paris: E. Plon, Nourrit, 1899)

Schnath, Georg, *Geschichte Hannovers im Zeitalter der neunten Kur und der englischen Sukzession, 1674–1714*, 3 vols. (Hildesheim, 1976–82)

Schnurbein, S., 'Augustus in Germania and His New "Town" at Waldgirmes East of the Rhine', *Journal of Roman Archaeology*, vol. 16 (2003)

Schroeder, Paul W., *Metternich's Diplomacy at Its Zenith, 1820–1823: Austria and the Congresses of Troppau, Laibach, and Verona* (New York: Greenwood Press, 1962)

Scott, H. M., *The Birth of a Great Power System, 1740–1815* (Harlow: Longman, 2005)

Scott, Michael, *Delphi: A History of the Center of the Ancient World* (Princeton, NJ: Princeton University Press, 2014)

Scriba, Christoph J. (ed.), 'The Autobiography of John Wallis, F.R.S.', *Notes and Records of the Royal Society*, vol. 25 (1970)

Sebag Montefiore, Simon, *Prince of Princes: The Life of Potemkin* (London: Weidenfeld & Nicolson, 2000)

—, *The Court of the Red Tsar* (London: Weidenfeld & Nicolson, 2003)

—, *Young Stalin* (London: Weidenfeld & Nicolson, 2007)

Seldon, Anthony (ed.), *The Blair Effect: The Blair Government 1997–2001* (London: Little, Brown, 2001)

Seligmann, Matthew S., *Spies in Uniform: British Military & Naval Intelligence on the Eve of the First World War* (Oxford: Oxford University Press, 2006)

—, 'Naval History by Conspiracy Theory: The British Admiralty before the First World War and the Methodology of Conspiracy Theory', in Matthew S. Seligmann and David Morgan-Owen (eds.), *New Interpretations of the Royal Navy in the 'Fisher Era', Journal of Strategic Studies*, vol. 38 (2015), no. 7 (special issue)

— and David Morgan-Owen (eds.), *New Interpretations of the Royal Navy in the 'Fisher Era', Journal of Strategic Studies*, vol. 38 (2015), no. 7 (special issue)

Sengoopta, Chandak, *Imprint of the Raj: How Fingerprinting was Born in Colonial India* (London: Macmillan, 2003)

Sergeev, Evgeny, *Russian Military Intelligence in the War with Japan, 1904–05: Secret Operations on Land and at Sea* (London: Routledge, 2007)

Service, Robert, *Stalin: A Biography* (London: Macmillan, 2004)

—, *Spies and Commissars: Russia and the West in the Russian Revolution* (London: Macmillan, 2011)

Set, Shounak, 'Ancient Wisdom for the Modern World: Revisiting Kautilya and His *Arthashastra* in the Third Millennium, *Strategic Analysis*, vol. 39 (2015), no. 6

Sever, Aleksandr Kolpakidi, *Spetssluzhby Rossiyskoy Imperii. Unikal'naya entsiklopediya* (Moscow: Litres, 2010)

Sheffield, G. D., *The Somme* (London: Cassell, 2003)

Sheffy, Yigal, *British Military Intelligence in the Palestine Campaign, 1914–1918* (London: Frank Cass, 1998)

Sheldon, Rose Mary, *Intelligence Activities in Ancient Rome: Trust in the Gods But Verify* (London/New York: Frank Cass, 2005)

—, *Spies of the Bible: Espionage in Israel from the Exodus to the Bar Kokhba Revolt* (London: Greenhill, 2007)

Sherwood, Robert E., *Roosevelt and Hopkins: An Intimate History* (New York: Harper, 1948)

Shlikhting, Albert, *Novoie izvestie o Rossii vremeni Ivana Groznogo* (Leningrad, 1934)

Showalter, Dennis, *Frederick the Great: A Military History* (Barnsley: Frontline Books, 2012)

Shvets, Yuri, *Washington Station: My Life as a KGB Spy in America* (New York: Simon & Schuster, 1994)

Siebert, Benno von (ed.), *The Diplomatic Correspondence of Count Benckendorff*, 3 vols. (Berlin: Walter de Gruyter, 1928)

Siemann, Wolfram, *'Deutschlands Ruhe, Sicherheit und Ordnung.' Die Anfänge der politischen Polizei 1806–1866* (Tübingen: Max Niemeyer, 1985)

Silverstein, Adam J., *Postal Systems in the pre-Modern Islamic World* (Cambridge: Cambridge University Press, 2007)

Simms, Brendan, *Europe: The Struggle for Supremacy, 1453 to the Present* (London: Allen Lane, 2013)

Sims, John Cary, 'The BRUSA Agreement of May 17, 1943', *Cryptologia*, vol. 21 (1997), no. 1

Singh, Simon, *The Code Book: The Secret History of Codes and Codebreaking*, Epub edn (London: Fourth Estate, 2011)

Singh, Upinder, *A History of Ancient and Medieval India: From the Stone Age to the 12th Century* (Delhi: Pearson/Longman, 2008)

Sinningen, W. G., 'The Roman Secret Service', *Classical Journal*, 57 (1961)

Sisman, Adam, *Hugh Trevor-Roper: The Biography* (London: Weidenfeld & Nicolson, 2010)

Sixsmith, Martin, *Russia: A 1000-Year Chronicle of the Wild East* (London: BBC Books, 2011)

Skinner, Quentin, 'Visions of Civil Liberty', in Peter Martland (ed.), *The Future of the Past: Big Questions in History* (London: Pimlico, 2002)

Skinner, Thomas, *The Life of General Monck, late duke of Albemarle …* (Dublin: printed for Patrick Dugan, 1724)

Smith, Bradley F., *The Ultra-Magic Deals* (Novato, Calif.: Presidio, 1993)

Smith, Colin, and John Bierman, *Alamein: War Without Hate* (London: Penguin Books, 2012)

Smith, D. E., 'John Wallis as a Cryptographer', *Bulletin of the American Mathematical Society*, vol. 24 (1917)

Smith, Geoffrey, *The Cavaliers in Exile, 1640–1660* (Basingstoke: Palgrave Macmillan, 2003)

—, *Royalist Agents, Conspirators and Spies: Their Role in the British Civil Wars, 1640–1660* (Farnham: Ashgate, 2011)

Smith, Michael E., *The Aztecs* (Oxford: Blackwell, 1996)

Smoot, Betsy Rohaly, 'Impermanent Alliances: Cryptologic Cooperation between the United States, Britain, and France on the Western Front, 1917–1918', *Intelligence and National Security*, vol. 32 (2017), no. 3

Snyder, Jack, *The Ideology of the Offensive: Military Decision Making and the Disasters of 1914* (New York: Cornell University Press, 2013)

Soboleva, Tatiana, *Tainopis v Istorii Rossii: Istoriia Kriptograficheskoi Sluzhby Rossii 'XVIII' – nachala 'XX' v.* (Moscow: Mezhdunar Otnosheniia, 1994)

—, *Istoriia Shifrovalnogo Dela v Rossii* (Moscow: Olma, 2002)

Soll, Jacob, *The Information Master: Jean-Baptiste Colbert's Secret State Intelligence System* (Ann Arbor: University of Michigan Press, 2009)

—, *The Reckoning: Financial Accountability and the Making and Breaking of Nations*, Kindle edn (London: Allen Lane, 2014)

Somerset, Anne, *Queen Anne: The Politics of Passion* (London: HarperPress, 2012)

Sommerlechner, Andrea, Othmar Hageneder, Christoph Egger, Rainer Murauer and Herwig Weigl (eds.), *Die Register Innocenz' III*, vol. II, *11. Pontifikatsjahr, 1208/1209* (Vienna: Verlag der Österreichischen Akademie der Wissenschaften, 2010)

'Souvenirs du général Cartier', *Revue des Transmissions*, 1959, nos. 85, 87

Sparrow, Elizabeth, 'The Alien Office, 1792–1806', *The Historical Journal*, vol. 33 (1990), no. 2

—, *Secret Service: British Agents in France, 1792–1815* (Woodbridge: Boydell Press, 1999)

Spence, Richard B., *Wall Street and the Russian Revolution, 1905–1925* (Waterville, Ore.: Trine Day, 2017)

Sperber, Jonathan, *Karl Marx: A Nineteenth-Century Life* (New York/London: W. W. Norton, 2013)

Speyer, Dr, 'The Legal Aspects of the Sipido Case', *Journal of the Society of Comparative Legislation*, 1900

Staff, Frank, *The Penny Post 1680–1918* (Cambridge: Lutterworth Press, 1993)

Stamm-Kuhlmann, Thomas, *König in Preussens grosser Zeit. Friedrich Wilhelm III., der Melancholiker auf dem Thron* (Berlin: Siedler, 1992).

Standage, Tom, *The Victorian Internet: The Remarkable Story of the Telegraph and the Nineteenth Century's Online Pioneers* (London: Phoenix, 1999)

Standen, Heinrich von, *The Land and Government of Muscovy*, trans. and ed. Thomas Esper (Stanford, Calif.: Stanford University Press, 1967)

Steinhauer, Gustav, *Steinhauer: The Kaiser's Masterspy as Told by Himself*, ed. Sidney Felstead (London: The Bodley Head, 1930)

Stern, Virginia F., *Sir Stephen Powle of Court and Country: Memorabilia of a Government Agent for Queen Elizabeth I, Chancery Official, and English Country Gentleman* (Selinsgrove, Pa: Susquehanna University Press, 1992)

Stevenson, David, *With Our Backs to the Wall* (London: Penguin Books, 2012)

Stieber, Wilhelm J. C. E., *The Chancellor's Spy: Memoirs of the Founder of Modern Espionage*, trans. Jan Van Heurch (New York: Grove Press, 1979)

Stobo, Robert, *Memoirs of Major Robert Stobo of the Virginia Regiment* (Pittsburgh: John S. Davidson, 1854)

Stone, Norman, 'Austria–Hungary', in Ernest R. May, *Knowing One's Enemies: Intelligence Assessment before the Two World Wars* (Princeton, NJ: Princeton University Press, 1984)

Stoneman, Richard, *The Ancient Oracles: Making the Gods Speak* (New Haven, Conn./London: Yale University Press, 2011)

Storrs, Christopher, 'Intelligence and the Formulation of Policy and Strategy in Early Modern Europe: The Spanish Monarchy in the Reign of Charles II (1665–1700)', *Intelligence and National Security*, vol. 21 (2006), no. 4

Stout, Felicity, *Exploring Russia in the Elizabethan Commonwealth: The Muscovy Company and Giles Fletcher, the Elder (1546–1611)* (Manchester: Manchester University Press, 2014)

Stout, Mark, 'American Intelligence Assessment of the Jihadists, 1989–2011', in Paul Maddrell (ed.), *The Image of the Enemy: Intelligence Analysis of Adversaries since 1945* (Washington, DC: Georgetown University Press, 2015)

Strasser, G.F., 'The rise of cryptography in the European Renaissance', in Karl de Leeuw and Jan Bergstra (eds.), *The History of Information Security: A Comprehensive Handbook* (Amsterdam: Elsevier, 2007)

Strauss, Barry, *The Battle of Salamis: The Naval Encounter That Saved Greece – and Western Civilization* (New York: Simon & Schuster, 2004)

Stuart, Hannah, *Islamist Terrorism: Analysis of Offences and Attacks in the UK (1998–2015)* (London: Henry Jackson Society, 2017)

Stubbs, John, *Reprobates: The Cavaliers of the English Civil War* (London: Viking, 2011)

Sullivan, Brian R., ' "A Highly Commendable Action": William J. Donovan's Intelligence Mission for Mussolini and Roosevelt, December 1935–February 1936', *Intelligence and National Security*, vol. 6 (1991), no. 2

Sumption, Jonathan, *The Hundred Years War*, 4 vols. (London/New York: Faber and Faber, 1990–2009); vol. 1: *Trial by Battle* (1990); vol. 2: *Trial by Fire* (2001); vol. 3: *Divided Houses* (2009); vol. 4: *Cursed Kings* (2016)

—, *The Albigensian Crusade* (London/New York: Faber and Faber, 1999)

—, *Edward III: A Heroic Failure* (London: Allen Lane, 2016)

Sun Tzu, *The Art of War: Bilingual Chinese and English Text*, trans. Lionel Giles with an Introduction by John Minford (Hong Kong: Tuttle Publishing, 2016)

Sutcliffe, Marcella Pellegrino, *Victorian Radicals and Risorgimento Democrats: A Long Connection* (Woodbridge: Boydell and Brewer, 2014)

Swords, Liam, *The Green Cockade: The Irish in the French Revolution 1789–1815* (Sandycove: Glendale Publishing, 1989)

Szabo, Frank H. J., *Kaunitz and Enlightened Absolutism, 1753–1780* (Cambridge: Cambridge University Press, 1994)

Szamuely, Helen, 'Russia's First Embassies', *History Today*, vol. 63 (2013), no. 5.

Szechi, D., *Jacobitism and Tory Politics 1710–14* (Edinburgh: John Donald, 2012)

Talbott, Strobe, *The Russia Hand: A Memoir of Presidential Diplomacy* (New York: Random House, 2003)

Tanenbaum, Jan Karl, 'French Estimates of Germany's Operational War Plans', in Ernest R. May, *Knowing One's Enemies: Intelligence Assessment before the Two World Wars* (Princeton, NJ: Princeton University Press, 1984)

Tanner, Murray Scott, and James Bellacqua, *China's Response to Terrorism*, report sponsored by the US–China Economic and Security Review Commission, June 2016

Taylor, A. J. P., *The Struggle for Mastery in Europe, 1848–1918* (Oxford: Clarendon Press, 1954)

Temperley, Harold, 'Pitt's Retirement from Office, 5 Oct. 1761', *English Historical Review*, vol. XXI (1906)

Tenet, George, *At the Center of the Storm: My Years at the CIA* (New York: HarperCollins, 2007)

Thale, Mary (ed.), *Selections from the Papers of the London Corresponding Society 1792–1799* (Cambridge: Cambridge University Press, 1983)

Thomas, Marcel, *L'Affaire sans Dreyfus* (Paris: A. Fayard, 1961)

Thompson, E. P., *The Making of the English Working Class* (London: Penguin Books, 2013)

Thomson, James Westfall, and Saul K. Padover, *Secret Diplomacy, Espionage and Cryptography 1500–1815* (New York: Frederick Ungar, 1965)

Thurloe, John, *A Collection of the State Papers of John Thurloe* (London: Printed for the executor of F. Gyles, 1742)

Thwaites, N. G., *Velvet and Vinegar* (London: Grayson & Grayson, 1932)

Tibi, Bassam, 'From Sayyid Qutb to Hamas: The Middle East Conflict and the Islamization of Antisemitism', Working Paper #5, Yale Initiative for the Interdisciplinary Study of Antisemitism.

—, *Islamism and Islam* (New Haven, Conn.: Yale University Press, 2012)

Todd, Janet, *The Secret Life of Aphra Behn* (London: Pandora, 2000)

Tombs, Robert, *The English and Their History* (London: Allen Lane, 2014)

—, 'How Bloody was *la Semaine Sanglante*? A Revision', *H-France Salon*, vol. 3, no. 1; http://www.h-france.net/Salon/Salonvol3no1.pdf.

Tombs, Robert, and Isabelle Tombs, *That Sweet Enemy: The French and the British from the Sun King to the Present* (London: William Heinemann, 2006)

Topbaş, Osman Nuri, *The Prophet of Mercy Muhammad: Scenes from His Life*, translated by Abdullah Penman, 4th edn (Istanbul: Erkam Publications, 2009)

Toplin, Robert Brent (ed.), *Oliver Stone's USA: Film, History, and Controversy* (Lawrence, KN: University Press of Kansas, 2000)

Toye, Francis, *For What We Have Received* (London: Heinemann, 1950)

Treverton, Gregory F., *Covert Action* (New York: Basic Books, 1987)

— and Wilhelm Agrell (eds.), *National Intelligence Systems: Current Research and Future Prospects* (Cambridge: Cambridge University Press, 2009)

Trevor-Roper, H. R. (ed.), *Hitler's Table Talk 1941–1944* (London: Weidenfeld & Nicolson, 2000)

Troy, Thomas F., 'The Coordinator of Information and British Intelligence: An Essay on Origins', *Studies in Intelligence*, vol. 18 (Spring 1974)

—, *Donovan and the CIA: A History of the Establishment of the Central Intelligence Agency* (Frederick, Md: University Publications of America, 1981)

Tsvigun, S. K. et al. (eds.), *V. I. Lenin I VChK: Sbornik documentov (1917–1922 gg)* (Moscow: Izdatel'stvo Politicheskoi Literatury, 1975)

Tucker, Robert C., and Stephen F. Cohen (eds.), *The Great Purge Trial* (New York: Grosset and Dunlap, 1965)

Tulard, Jean, *Joseph Fiévée: Conseiller secret de Napoléon* (Paris: Arthème Fayard, 1985)

—, *Joseph Fouché* (Paris: Arthème Fayard, 1998)

Twitchett, Denis C., and Frederick W. Mote, *The Cambridge History of China*, vol. 8 (Cambridge: Cambridge University Press, 1998)

Tyerman, Christopher, *God's War: A New History of the Crusades* (London: Allen Lane, 2006)

Tzouliadis, Tim, *The Forsaken: From the Great Depression to the Gulags. Hope and Betrayal in Stalin's Russia* (London: Little, Brown, 2008)

Uehling, Greta Lynn, *Beyond Memory: The Crimean Tatars' Deportation and Return* (London: Palgrave Macmillan, 2004)

Ulfeld, Jacob, *Puteshestvie v Rossii* (Moscow: Yazyki slavianskoi kultury, 2002)

Ullrichová, Maria (ed.), *Clemens Metternich–Wilhelmine von Sagan. Ein Briefwechsel 1813–1815* (Graz/Cologne: Hermann Böhlaus Nachf., 1966)

Underdown, David, *Royalist Conspiracy in England 1649–60* (New Haven, Conn.: Yale University Press, 1960)

Urban, Mark, *The Man Who Broke Napoleon's Codes: The Story of George Scovell* (London: Faber & Faber, 2002)

Vaillé, Eugène, *Le Cabinet noir* (Paris: Presses Universitaires de France, 1950)

Vaïsse, Maurice, et al., *L'Entente Cordiale de Fachoda à la Grande Guerre* (Paris: Éditions Complexe, 2004)

Van Creveld, Martin, *Command in War* (Cambridge, MA: Harvard University Press, 1985)

Villatoux, Marie-Catherine, 'Le renseignement photographique dans la manoeuvre. L'exemple de la Grande Guerre', *Revue Historique des Armées*, 2010, no. 261

Vincent, Bernard, 'L'inquisition et l'Islam', in Agostino Borromeo (ed.), *L'Inquisizione: Atti del Simposio internazionale, Città del Vaticano, 29–31 ottobre 1998* (Vatican City: Biblioteca Apostolica Vaticana, 2003)

Vincent, David, *The Culture of Secrecy. Britain 1832–1998* (Oxford: Oxford University Press, 1998).

—, 'Surveillance, Privacy and History', 2013, http://www.historyandpolicy.org/policy-papers/papers/surveillance-privacy-and-history.

Vincent, Nicholas, 'Devil's Advocates' [review of Moore, R I, *The War on Heresy: Faith and Power in Medieval Europe* (London: Profile Books, 2012)], *Literary Review*, May 2012.

Volkogonov, Dmitri, *The Rise and Fall of the Soviet Empire: Political Leaders from Lenin to Gorbachev* (London: HarperCollins, 1998)

Volodarsky, Boris, *Stalin's Agent: The Life and Death of Alexander Orlov* (Oxford: Oxford University Press, 2015)

Volodikhin, Dmitri Mikhailovich, *Maliuta Skuratov* (Moscow: Molodaya gvardiya, 2012)

Wagner, Kim A., *The Great Fear of 1857: Rumours, Conspiracies and the Making of the Indian Uprising* (Oxford: Peter Lang, 2010)

Walker, Jonathan, *Pistols! Treason! Murder! : The rise and fall of a master spy* (Carlton, Victoria: Melbourne University Press, 2007)

Walpole, Horace, *Letters from the Hon. Horace Walpole to George Montagu, Esq. from the Year 1736 to the Year 1770* (London: Rodwell and Martin, 1818)

Walsh, Michael, 'George Koval: Atomic Spy Unmasked', *Smithsonian Magazine*, May 2009

Walsh, Patrick F., and Seumas Miller, 'Rethinking "Five Eyes" Security Intelligence Collection Policies and Practice Post Snowden', *Intelligence and National Security*, vol. 31 (2016), no. 3

Walton, Calder, *Empire of Secrets: British Intelligence, the Cold War and the Twilight of Empire* (London: HarperPress, 2013)

Walton, Charles, *Policing Public Opinion in the French Revolution: The Culture of Calumny and the Problem of Free Speech* (New York: Oxford University Press, 2009)

Walton, Timothy, *Challenges in Intelligence Analysis: Lessons from 1300 BCE to the Present* (Cambridge: Cambridge University Press, 2010)

Warner, Michael, 'The Divine Skein: Sun Tzu on Intelligence', *Intelligence and National Security*, vol. 21 (2006), no. 4

—, 'Building a Theory of Intelligence Systems', in Gregory Treverton and Wilhelm Agrell (eds.), *National Intelligence Systems: Current Research and Future Prospects* (Cambridge: Cambridge University Press, 2009)

—, *The Rise and Fall of Intelligence: An International Security History* (Washington, DC: Georgetown University Press, 2014)

Watson, Alexander, *Ring of Steel: Germany and Austria–Hungary at War, 1914–1918* (London: Penguin Books, 2014)

Watson, Derek, *Molotov: A Biography* (Basingstoke: Palgrave Macmillan, 2005)

Wawro, Geoffrey, *The Franco-Prussian War: The German Conquest of France in 1870–1871* (Cambridge: Cambridge University Press, 2005)

Weber, Ralph E., 'State Department Cryptographic Security: Herbert O. Yardley and President Woodrow Wilson's Secret Code', in *In the Name of Intelligence: Essays in Honour of Waltes Pforzheimer*, eds. Hayden B. Peake and Samuel Halpern (Washington, DC: NIBC Press, 1994), pp. 555–70

—, *Masked Dispatches: Cryptograms and Cryptology in American History, 1775–1900*, 3rd edition (NSA Center for Cryptologic History, 2013)

Wedgwood, C. V., 'Rubens and King Charles I', *History Today*, vol. 10 (1960), no. 12

Weil, M.-H. (ed.), *Les Dessous du Congrès de Vienne, d'après les documents originaux des archives du Ministère Impérial et Royal de l'Intérieur à Vienne*, 2 vols. (Paris: Librairie Payot, 1917)

Weil, Rachel, *A Plague of Informers: Conspiracy and Political Trust in William III's England* (New Haven, Conn.: Yale University Press, 2014)

Weller, Jac, *Wellington at Waterloo* (Barnsley: Frontline Books, 2010)

West, Kieran, 'Intelligence and the Development of British Grand Strategy in the First World War', PhD thesis, University of Cambridge (2010)

West, Nigel, *Historical Dictionary of World War II Intelligence* (Lanham, Md: Scarecrow Press, 2007)

—, *Historical Dictionary of World War I Intelligence* (Lanham, Md: Scarecrow Press, 2013)

Westad, Odd Arne, *The Global Cold War: Third World Interventions and the Making of Our Times* (Cambridge: Cambridge University Press, 2007)

Westrate, Bruce, *The Arab Bureau: British Policy in the Middle East, 1916–1920* (University Park: University of Pennsylvania Press, 1992)

Wheen, Francis, *Karl Marx* (London: Fourth Estate, 2000)

Whymant, Robert, *Stalin's Spy: Richard Sorge and the Tokyo Espionage Ring* (London: I. B. Tauris, 2006)

Wilcox, Jennifer, 'Revolutionary Secrets: The Secret Communications of the American Revolution'; http://www.nsa.gov/about/_files/cryptologic_heritage/publications/prewii/revolutionary_secrets.pdf

Wilhelm, Crown Prince (Friedrich Wilhelm Hohenzollern), *Memoirs of the Crown Prince of Germany* (Uckfield: Naval & Military Press, 2006)

Wilkes, Sue, *Regency Spies: Secret History of Britain's Rebels and Revolutionaries* (Barnsley: Pen & Sword, 2015)

Williams, Patrick, 'El reinado de Felipe III', in José Andrés-Gallego (ed.), *La crisis de la hegemonía española (siglo XVII)* (Madrid: Rialp, 1986)

Williams, Valentine, *The World of Action* (London: Hamish Hamilton, 1938)

Williamson, Samuel R., Jr, 'The Origins of World War I', *Journal of Interdisciplinary History*, vol. XVII (1988), no. 4

—, 'The Origins of the War', in Sir Hew Strachan (ed.), *The Illustrated Oxford History of the First World War*, rev. edn (Oxford: Oxford University Press, 2014)

— and Ernest R. May, 'An Identity of Opinion: Historians and July 1914', *Journal of Modern History*, vol. 79 (2007), no. 2

Wills, Garry, *Bomb Power: The Modern Presidency and the National Security State* (New York: Penguin, 2010)

Wilson, Frances, 'The Lost Art of Table Talk', *Literary Review*, February 2014

Wise, David, *Spy: The Inside Story of How the FBI's Robert Hanssen Betrayed America* (New York: Random House, 2003)

Witte, S., *The Memoirs of Count Witte* (New York: Doubleday, 1921)

Wolf, Markus (with Anne McElvoy), *Man without a Face: The Autobiography of Communism's Greatest Spymaster* (London: Jonathan Cape, 1997)

Wood, Michael, *Conquistadors* (London: BBC Books, 2000)

Woodham-Smith, Cecil, *The Reason Why: Story of the Fatal Charge of the Light Brigade* (London: Constable, 1953)

Woods, Kevin, James Lacey and Williamson Murray, 'Saddam's Delusions: The View from the Inside', *Foreign Affairs*, vol. 85 (2006), no. 3

Woodward, David, *The American Army and the First World War* (Cambridge: Cambridge University Press, 2014)

Worcester, Edward Somerset, Marquess of, *Three letters intercepted by Sir Tho: Fairfax in Cornwal.* (London : Printed for Edward Husband, printer to the Honorable House of Commons, 1646)

Wormald, Jenny, 'Reformations, Unions and Civil Wars, 1485–1660', in Jonathan Clarke (ed.), *A World by Itself: A History of the British Isles* (London: William Heinemann, 2010)

Wright, Lawrence, *The Looming Tower: Al Qaeda's Road to 9/11* (London: Allen Lane, 2006)

Yapp, Malcolm, 'The Legend of the Great Game', *Proceedings of the British Academy*, vol. 111 (2001)

Yardley, Herbert O., *The American Black Chamber* (Boston: Houghton Mifflin, 1931)

Yoji Koda, Vice-Admiral, 'The Russo-Japanese War: Primary Causes of Japanese Success', *[US] Naval War College Review*, vol. 58 (2005), no. 2

Zamoyski, Adam, *Rites of Peace: The Fall of Napoleon and the Congress of Vienna* (London: HarperPress, 2007)

—, *Phantom Terror: The Threat of Revolution and the Repression of Liberty, 1789–1848* (London: William Collins, 2014)

Zannini, Andrea, 'Economic and Social Aspects of the Crisis of Venetian Diplomacy in the Seventeenth and Eighteenth Centuries', in Daniela Frigo (ed.), *Politics and Diplomacy in Early Modern Italy* (Cambridge: Cambridge University Press, 2000)

Zernova, A. S., *Knigi, kirillovskoi pechati, izdannye v Moskye v XVI–XVII vekakh* (Moscow: Gosudarstvennaia biblioteka SSSR, 1958)

Zolkowski, Theodore, *German Romanticism and Its Institutions* (Princeton: Princeton University Press, 1992)

Zuckerman, Fredric S., *The Tsarist Secret Police Abroad: Policing Europe in a Modernising World* (Basingstoke: Palgrave Macmillan, 2003)

Zutshi, Patrick, 'The Political and Administrative Correspondence of the Avignon Popes, 1305–1378: A Contribution to Papal Diplomatic', in *Le Fonctionnement administratif de la Papauté d'Avignon* (Rome: École Française de Rome, 1990)

—, 'The Avignon Papacy', in Michael Jones (ed.), *The New Cambridge Medieval History*, vol. 6 (Cambridge: Cambridge University Press, 2000)

Zvonarev, K. K., *Agenturnaia razvedka*, vol. 1: *Russkaia agenturnaia razvedka do i vo vremia voiny 1914–1918* (Moscow: Izdatelskaia gruppa, 2003)

Abbreviations Used in the Notes and References

AN	Archives Nationales, Paris
BL	British Library
BN	Bibliothèque Nationale, Paris
BUL	Birmingham University Library
CAB	Cabinet Office
CCAC	Churchill College Archive Centre, Cambridge
CHAR	Chartwell papers
CO	Colonial Office
CUL	Cambridge University Library
DO	Dominions Office
FCO	Foreign and Commonwealth Office
FDRL	Franklin D. Roosevelt Library, Hyde Park, New York
FO	Foreign Office
HC Deb	House of Commons Debates
HLRO	House of Lords Records Office
HO	Home Office
HW	Government Communications Headquarters (GCHQ) files, TNA
IOLR	India Office Library and Records
IWM	Imperial War Museum
KV	MI5 (Security Service) files, TNA
LHC	Liddell Hart Centre for Military Archives, King's College London
MAE	Ministère des Affaires Étrangèrs
MECW	Marx and Engels, *Collected Works* (Lawrence & Wishart edition)
MEPO	Papers of the Metropolitan Police
NAW	National Archives, Washington, DC
NMM	National Maritime Museum
ODNB	*Oxford Dictionary of National Biography*

Parl. Deb	*Parliamentary Debates*
PHA	Joint committee on the investigation of the Pearl Harbor Attack, *Pearl Harbor Attack, Hearings*
PP	*Public Papers of the Presidents*
RG	Record Group (NAW)
RGASPI	Rossiiskii gosudarstvennyi arkhiv sotsial'no-politicheskoi istorii (Russian State Archive of Socio-Political History)
SLYU	Sterling Library, Yale University
T	Treasury
TNA	The National Archives, Kew
WC	War Cabinet
WO	War Office
WWC	Woodrow Wilson Center, Washington, DC

Notes

Introduction

1. Kent, 'Need for an Intelligence Literature'. 2. See below, pp. 15ff. 3. Interview with DCI George Tenet, *Studies in Intelligence*, vol. 42 (1998), no. 1. 4. Ransom, 'Secret Intelligence in the United States', p. 205. 5. See below, pp. 28–9. 6. Thucydides, *History of the Peloponnesian War*, book 1, 1.23. 7. See below, ch. 4. 8. Al Mubarakpuri, *Sealed Nectar*, loc. 8545; this book won first prize in a competition held by the World Muslim League in 1976 for the best biography of the Prophet Muhammad. 9. See below, ch. 6. 10. See below, ch. 7. 11. Machiavelli's often-quoted maxim appears as the first sentence of Ministry of Defence, *Understanding and Intelligence Support to Joint Operations*, Joint Doctrine Publication 2-00, Aug. 2011. 12. See below, pp. 98–9, 127–8. 13. See below, pp. 121, 158ff. 14. See below, chs. 10, 12. 15. See below, chs. 11, 14. 16. See below, ch. 15. 17. See below, pp. 421–4, 490–91, 510–11, 518, 540. 18. See below, chs. 23, 24. 19. See below, pp. 611–12. 20. See below, chs. 25–8. 21. See below, pp. 166–70. 22. See below, pp. 616–17, 657–61, 671. 23. See below, pp. 569–75. 24. Gaddis, *Cold War*. 25. Andrew, *For the President's Eyes Only*, pp. 440–41. 26. See below, pp. 701–4, 717–18. 27. Bew, 'What Lessons from History Keep being Forgotten?' 28. Skinner, 'Visions of Civil Liberty'. 29. See below, pp. 736–9, 745–53.

1 In the Beginning

1. Numbers 13:1–20. Biblical quotations are from the Authorized (King James) Version, until recently the best-known English translation. 2. Aston, *Secret Service*, pp. 32–3. The papers of Sir George Aston (1861–1938) are in the Liddell Hart Centre for Military Archives at King's College London. 3. Genesis 37–50. 4. Quran 12. 5. Andrew, *Defence of the Realm*, pp. 53–5, 222–4. 6. Clausewitz, *On War*, p. 117. 7. Numbers 13:21–33. 8. Quran 5:22–3. 9. Numbers 14:1–10. 10. Quran 5:24. 11. Numbers 14:11–39. 12. Deuteronomy 34:1–7. 13. Joshua 2:1. 14. Joshua 2:1–6. 15. Joshua 2:9–14, 24. 16. Joshua 2–6. 17. Hebrews 11:31; James 2:25. 18. Matthew 1:5. 19. Declassified articles in *Studies in Intelligence* are available on the website of the CIA Center for the Study of Intelligence. 20. Cardwell, 'A Bible Lesson on Spying'. 21. Conversation with Efraim

Halevy, 11 March 2013.   **22.** The former Mossad officer Victor Ostrovsky entitles his controversial memoirs *By Way of Deception*.   **23.** www.jns.org/news briefs/2012/12/14 (accessed 15 April 2013).   **24.** Exodus 3: 18–21; 7:16.   **25.** Finkelstein and Silberman, *Bible Unearthed*, ch. 3.   **26.** See the map of the Ancient Near East *c.*1350 BC in Cohen and Westbrook (eds.), *Amarna Diplomacy*, p. xii.   **27.** Moran (ed. and trans.), *Amarna Letters*.   **28.** Cohen, 'Intelligence in the Amarna Letters', p. 97.   **29.** Ibid., pp. 86–8.   **30.** Ibid., p. 90.   **31.** Na'aman, 'Egyptian–Canaanite Correspondence', p. 125.   **32.** Cohen, 'Intelligence in the Amarna Letters', pp. 89–90.   **33.** Ibid., p. 94.   **34.** The letter is quoted in a cuneiform biography of King Suppliuliuma I written by his son Mursili. Bryce, *Letters of the Great Kings*, pp. 187–8.   **35.** The wording of the fragment of the letter in the Amarna collection agrees closely with that quoted in Mursili's biography of his father. Ibid., pp. 193–4. The existence of the Amarna copy shows that the letter had been intercepted.   **36.** Finkelstein and Silberman, *Bible Unearthed*, ch. 3.   **37.** Abulafia, *Great Sea*, ch. 2, part V.   **38.** Finkelstein and Silberman, *Bible Unearthed*, ch. 3, Epilogue. Sheldon, *Spies of the Bible*, part I.   **39.** Mark 11:1–3.   **40.** Mark 11: 7–18.   **41.** Luke 20:19–26.   **42.** Mark 14:12–18.   **43.** Matthew 26:14–16. Mark and Luke say that Judas had been possessed by the Devil (an explanation which is not included in the FBI MICE list of possible motives).   **44.** Rutledge, *Imperial Inquisitions*, p. 3. See below, pp. 72–5.   **45.** Mark 14:44–6.   **46.** Philo, *Legatio ad Gaium*, 299–305. Bond, *The Historical Jesus*, p. 159.   **47.** Josephus, *Antiquitates Judaicae*, 18:89.   **48.** Ibid., 18:95, 123. Bond, *Caiaphas*, pp. 18ff.

2 Intelligence Operations in Ancient Greece

1. *Odyssey*, XIII, 296–9. Fowler (ed.), *Cambridge Companion to Homer*, pp. 32–3.   **2.** *Iliad*, X. Homer, *The Illiad*, trans. and ed. Rieu and Jones.   **3.** See, for example, Abulafia, *Great Sea*, p. 136.   **4.** Herodotus 7.   **5.** Herodotus 8.   **6.** Rodgers, *Greek and Roman Naval Warfare*, pp. 80–95. Strauss, *Battle of Salamis*.   **7.** Flower, *Seer in Ancient Greece*, p. 31.   **8.** Dillon, *Omens and Oracles*, pp. 33–9.   **9.** Herodotus 9.36–45. Flower, *Seer in Ancient Greece*, p. 169.   **10.** Flower, *Seer in Ancient Greece*, p. 119.   **11.** Peek, 'Study of Divination', p. 3.   **12.** Flower, *Seer in Ancient Greece*, ch. 1.   **13.** Ibid., p. 23.   **14.** Last visited by Christopher Andrew on 13 Sept. 2015.   **15.** Pindar, *Pythian* 3.29. Flower, *Seer in Ancient Greece*, p. 211.   **16.** Herodotus 9.81.   **17.** Scott, *Delphi*, p. 27.   **18.** Hesk, *Deception and Democracy*, p. 10.   **19.** Thucydides, *Peloponnesian War*, 2.34–46. https://sourcebooks.fordham. edu/ancient/pericles-funeralspeech.asp.   **20.** Thucydides, *Peloponnesian War*, 6.   **21.** Ibid., 19.   **22.** Ibid., 18.   **23.** For the evidence (not mentioned by Thucydides) that numerous Herms had their phalluses chopped off, see Hamel, *Mutilation of the Herms*, ch. 2.   **24.** Thucydides, *Peloponnesian War*, 6.27.3. Hamel, *Mutilation of the Herms*, p. 33.   **25.** Hamel, *Mutilation of the Herms*, p. 7.   **26.** Thucydides, *Peloponnesian War*, 6.18.   **27.** Hamel, *Mutilation of the Herms*, p. 37. Green, 'Questions of Class'.   **28.** Rhodes, *Alcibiades*, loc. 138.   **29.** Plutarch, *Nicias*. http:// penelope.uchicago.edu/Thayer/E/Roman/Texts/Plutarch/Lives/Nicias*.html.   **30.** Thucydides, *Peloponnesian War*, 8.45. i–ii.   **31.** Ibid., 8.48. iv–49.   **32.** Ibid., 8.81–2.

Rhodes, *Alcibiades*, loc. 1413.   **33.** The most persuasive interpretation of Alcibiades' extraordinary career is Rhodes, *Alcibiades*.   **34.** Xenophon, *Hipparchikòs*, 4.7–8. Russell, *Information Gathering in Classical Greece*, p. 104. Even Xenophon, however, had no concept of using agents-in-place to obtain strategic intelligence.   **35.** Xenophon attributed the most sophisticated use of bogus deserters not to any Greek commander but to Cyrus the Great, King of Persia over a century earlier (559–530 BC). Xenophon, *Cyropaedia*, VI, section 1. Russell, *Information Gathering in Classical Greece*, pp. 122–6.   **36.** Xenophon, *Hipparchikòs*, 9.8–9. Flower, *Seer in Ancient Greece*, p. 173.   **37.** Bos, *Cosmic and Meta-Cosmic Theology*, pp. 160–62.   **38.** Aristotle, *On Divination by Way of Dreams*. Only about 25 per cent of Aristotle's enormously varied writing survives, much of it apparently in the form of lecture notes.   **39.** Aristotle, *Politics*, 1308b20–22. Russell, *Information Gathering in Classical Greece*, p. 113.   **40.** Aristotle, *Politics*, 1313b11–16. Russell, *Information Gathering in Classical Greece*, p. 107. Aristotle implies that respectable women were not invited to these parties.   **41.** Barnes (ed.), *Cambridge Companion to Aristotle*, p. 5.   **42.** Cartledge, *Alexander the Great*, loc. 767, 1229. Ross, *Aristotle*, pp. 3–4.   **43.** Bosworth, 'Introduction' to Bosworth and Baynham, *Alexander the Great in Fact and Fiction*, p. 18.   **44.** When Ernst Badian first argued the case for Alexander's involvement in the assassination of his father in an article published in 1963, he aroused significant scholarly controversy. Over the last half-century, however, the probability of Alexander's involvement has become widely accepted by other scholars. Badian's most recent study of the assassination of Philip II, first published in 2007, places more emphasis than previously on the role of Pausanias. Badian, 'Once More the Death of Philip II', in Badian, *Collected Papers on Alexander the Great*, ch. 27. On the importance of his contribution to the understanding of Alexander the Great, see Green, 'He Found the Real Alexander'.   **45.** Badian, 'Conspiracies', in Badian, *Collected Papers on Alexander the Great*, ch. 24.   **46.** Plutarch, *Life of Alexander*, 48.5–49.2. Plutarch, *Moralia*, 339d–f. Russell, *Information Gathering in Classical Greece*, p. 114.   **47.** It is also possible that the chief plotter was Alexander himself, who had come to see Philotas as a potential threat to his authority. Cartledge, *Alexander the Great*, loc. 1010.   **48.** Cartledge, *Alexander the Great*, loc. 1824. Badian, 'Conspiracies'.   **49.** None of the more than twenty books on Alexander written by contemporaries has survived save in extracts quoted by later authors. Only one extract from a letter of Alexander is genuine beyond dispute. Lane Fox, *Alexander the Great*, ch. 1.   **50.** Because of the unheroic nature of reconnaissance for food and water, it is scarcely mentioned in any of the ancient sources. The only reference by Arrian to Alexander's logistic planning is his dismissal of Arimmas, viceroy of Syria, because he had failed to collect sufficient supplies. Arrian, *Anabasis Alexandri*, 3.6.8. Engels, *Alexander the Great and the Logistics of the Macedonian Army*, p. 66.   **51.** Engels, *Alexander the Great and Logistics*, pp. 71–2.   **52.** Arrian, *Anabasis Alexandri*, 4.4.3. Flower, *Seer in Ancient Greece*, pp. 178–81.   **53.** Arrian, *Anabasis Alexandri*, 1.25.6–8.   **54.** Ibid., 1.11.1–2; Plutarch, *Life of Alexander*, 14.5; *Itinerarium Alexandri*, 17; Pseudo-Callisthenes, 1.42. Flower, *Seer in Ancient Greece*, loc. 2340.   **55.** Cartledge, *Alexander the Great*, loc. 332.   **56.** Plutarch, *Life of Alexander*, 75. Flower, *Seer in Ancient Greece*, p. 129.

3 Intelligence and Divination in the Roman Republic

1. Livy, *History of Rome*, 6.41. https://en.wikipedia.org/wiki/Augur.   2. Cicero, *De Divinatione*, 1.1. Loeb translation: http://penelope.uchicago.edu/Thayer/E/Roman/Texts/Cicero/de_Divinatione/1*.html. Ferguson, *Greek and Roman Religion*, p. 125.   3. Cicero, *De Divinatione*, 1.82–4 (see n. 2). The case for divination is put by Cicero's Stoic brother in vol. 1 of Cicero's two-volume philosophical treatise, written in 44 BC. Cicero himself puts the case against, mostly in vol. 2.   4. Suetonius, *Lives of the Twelve Caesars: Tiberius Nero Caesar*, 2.290–91. Loeb translation: http://penelope. uchicago.edu/Thayer/E/Roman/Texts/Suetonius/12Caesars/Tiberius*/html.   5. Sheldon, *Intelligence Activities in Ancient Rome*, pp. 27–9.   6. Research into Carthage's intelligence activities is seriously impeded by the fact that virtually no Carthaginian written records survive. The habit of secrecy, inherited by Carthage from its Phoenician founders, helps to explain the lack of records (Holst, *Phoenician Secrets*, Introduction). The main reason, however, was the Roman destruction of Carthage after the Third Punic War. The principal sources on Carthage's conflict with Rome are the works of the Greek historian Polybius (*c*.204–122 BC), who was a friend and adviser to an adopted son of Scipio Africanus, and Livy (59 BC–AD 17), who incorporated in his histories the work of earlier writers which does not survive.   7. Holst, *Phoenician Secrets*, Introduction.   8. Bernstein, *Splendid Exchange*, pp. 34–5.   9. Sheldon, *Intelligence Activities in Ancient Rome*, p. 41.   10. Polybius, *Histories*, books 9, 11.   11. Valerius, *Facta et Dicta Memorabilia*, 3.7 ext. 6. Cicero, *De Divinatione*, 2.52. Loeb translation: http://penelope.uchicago.edu/Thayer/E/Roman/Texts/Cicero/de_Divinatione/2*.html. Mueller, *Roman Religion in Valerius Maximus*, p. 119.   12. Livy, *History of Rome*, 22.33.1.   13. Lazenby, *Hannibal's War* (p. 50) concludes: 'The Romans seem to have had no inkling of [Hannibal's] plan.'   14. Sheldon, *Intelligence Activities in Ancient Rome*, pp. 48–53.   15. Livy, *History of Rome*, 22.5.   16. Sheldon, *Intelligence Activities in Ancient Rome*, p. 49.   17. Plutarch, *Parallel Lives: The Life of Fabius Maximus*, 4. Loeb translation: http://penelope.uchicago.edu/Thayer/E/Roman/Texts/Plutarch/Lives/Fabius_Maximus*.html   18. Livy, *History of Rome*, 22.28.1.   19. Ibid., 23.12.1.   20. Eisenhower, *Crusade in Europe*, p. 325.   21. Plutarch, *Parallel Lives: Fabius Maximus*, 18.   22. Livy, *History of Rome*, 22.9.7. Satterfield, 'Livy and the Timing of Expiation', p. 82.   23. Holland, *Rubicon*, ch. 1. Beard, *SPQR*, p. 180. For reasons which remain obscure, two Gauls and two Greeks were also buried alive in 228 and 113 BC. Beard, North and Price, *Religions of Rome*, vol. 2, p. 158.   24. Livy, *History of Rome*, 27.   25. Ibid., 29.11.6, 14.5–14. Beard, North and Price, *Religions of Rome*, vol. 2, pp. 43–4, 158.   26. Sheldon, *Intelligence Activities in Ancient Rome*, p. 57.   27. Andreau and Descat, *Esclave en Grèce et à Rome*.   28. Sheldon, *Intelligence Activities in Ancient Rome*, pp. 57–8.   29. Livy, *History of Rome*, 30.4–6. Polybius, *Histories*, 14.1.13. Lazenby, *Hannibal's War*, pp. 206–7.   30. Polybius, *Histories*, 15.5. 7–9. Livy, *History of Rome*, 30.29.1–41. Hoyos (ed.), *Companion to the Punic Wars*, pp. 335–6.   31. Beard, *SPQR*, p. 201.   32. Plutarch, *Parallel Lives. Life of Julius Caesar*, 2.   33. Suetonius, *Lives of the Twelve Caesars: Gaius Julius Caesar*, 56.   34. Singh, *Code Book*, ch. 1.   35. Suetonius, *Lives of the Twelve Caesars: Gaius Julius Caesar*, 56.   36. Caesar, *De Bello Gallico*, 5.48. Loeb translation: http://penelope.

uchicago.edu/Thayer/E/Roman/Texts/Caesar/Gallic_War/5B*.html.   **37.** See below, p. 99.   **38.** Austin and Rankov, *Exploratio*, pp. 9–10.   **39.** Suetonius, *De Vita Caesarum: Gaius Julius Caesar*, 58.   **40.** Caesar, *De Bello Gallico*, 1.50. Loeb translation: http://penelope.uchicago.edu/Thayer/E/Roman/Texts/Caesar/Gallic_War/1B*.html. Goldsworthy, *Caesar*, pp. 230–32.   **41.** Goldsworthy, *Caesar*, pp. 230–32.   **42.** Caesar, *De Bello Gallico*, 2.19. Goldsworthy, *Caesar*, pp. 246–8.   **43.** Caesar, *De Bello Gallico*, 2.25. Loeb translation: http://penelope.uchicago.edu/Thayer/E/Roman/Texts/Caesar/Gallic_War/2*.html.   **44.** Goldsworthy, *Caesar*, pp. 248–52.   **45.** Kelly, *Roman Empire*, ch. 1.   **46.** Caesar, *De Bello Gallico*, 4.5. Loeb translation: http://penelope.uchicago.edu/Thayer/E/Roman/Texts/Caesar/Gallic_War/4*.html. **47.** Ibid., 6.17. Loeb translation: http://penelope.uchicago.edu/Thayer/E/Roman/Texts/Caesar/Gallic_War/6B*.html.   **48.** Aldhouse-Green, *Caesar's Druids*, p. 61.   **49.** Caesar, *De Bello Gallico*, 6.16 (see n. 47).   **50.** Aldhouse-Green, *Caesar's Druids*, pp. 66–7.   **51.** Ibid., p. xv.   **52.** Caesar, *De Bello Gallico*, 1.41 (see n. 40).   **53.** Ibid., 4.20 (see n. 46). **54.** Cunliffe, *Facing the Ocean*, p. 369.   **55.** Goldsworthy, *Caesar*, p. 285.   **56.** Caesar, *De Bello Gallico*, 5.14. Loeb translation: http://penelope.uchicago.edu/Thayer/E/Roman/Texts/Caesar/Gallic_War/5A*.html.   **57.** Van Creveld, *Command in War*, p. 281, n. 23.   **58.** Suetonius, *Lives of the Twelve Caesars: Gaius Julius Caesar*, 1.59. Loeb translation: http://penelope.uchicago.edu/Thayer/E/Roman/Texts/Suetonius/12Caesars/Julius*html. Plutarch's opinion of 'Salvito' (a demeaning nickname derived from his resemblance to a mime artist) concurs with that of Suetonius; Plutarch, *Parallel Lives: Life of Caesar*, 52.5.   **59.** Suetonius, *Lives of the Twelve Caesars: Gaius Julius Caesar*, 1.13.   **60.** William Shakespeare, *Julius Caesar*, Act 1, scene 2, 15–18.   **61.** Cassius Dio, *Roman History*, book 44; http://penelope.uchicago.edu/Thayer/E/Roman/Texts/Cassius_Dio/44*.html. Suetonius, *Lives of the Twelve Caesars: Gaius Julius Caesar*, 81. Dando-Collins, *The Ides*, pp. 77–8.   **62.** Goldsworthy, *Caesar*, ch. 23.   **63.** Suetonius, *Lives of the Twelve Caesars: Gaius Julius Caesar*, 82.   **64.** Kelly, *Roman Empire*, ch. 1.

4 *The Art of War* and the *Arthashastra*

1. Ames, *Sun Tzu*, pp. 22–4. The name Sun Tzu ('Master Sun') is so well established in English that I use it rather than the current Chinese pinyin transliteration Sūn Zǐ. For the first twelve chapters of *The Art of War*, I have used the 1910 translation by Lionel Giles, reprinted alongside the original Chinese text in Sun Tzu, *The Art of War: Bilingual Chinese and English Text*. For the final chapter 13 I have preferred the English translation in Griffith (ed. and trans.), *Sun Tzu: The Art of War*.   **2.** Sir Basil Liddell Hart, Foreword to Griffith (ed. and trans.), *Sun Tzu: The Art of War*.   **3.** Sun Tzu, *The Art of War* (bilingual edition), 11:26.   **4.** Griffith (ed. and trans.), *Sun Tzu: The Art of War*, ch. 13.   **5.** Ibid.   **6.** Sun Tzu, *The Art of War* (bilingual edition), 1:17, 18.   **7.** See above, pp. 29–30.   **8.** Griffith (ed. and trans.), *Sun Tzu: The Art of War*, p. ix.   **9.** Sawyer, *Tao of Spycraft*, p. 530.   **10.** Lewis, *Early Chinese Empires*, ch. 4.   **11.** Ibid., loc. 1250.   **12.** Loewe, *Divination, Mythology and Monarchy*, p. 186.   **13.** Griffith (ed. and trans.), *Sun Tzu: The Art of War*, p. 137.

14. Ibid., pp. 113, 141.   **15.** Ibid., p. ix.   **16.** Kissinger, *On China*, loc. 269.   **17.** Sawyer, *Tao of Spycraft*, pp. 250–52.   **18.** Sawyer, 'Subversive Information', pp. 37–8.   **19.** Twitchett and Mote, *Cambridge History of China*, vol. 8, p. 53.   **20.** Andrew, *First World War*, pp. 92–3.   **21.** Kissinger, *On China*, loc. 437.   **22.** On dating and authorship, see, inter alia, Mehta and Thakkar, *Kautilya and His Artha-shastra*, ch. 1.   **23.** *Mahabharata*, book 12, section LXIX.   **24.** *Arthashatra*, 1.11.   **25.** *Arthashastra*, 1.19.16, 9–24.   **26.** Rangarajan (ed.), *Arthashastra*, p. 157.   **27.** *Arthashastra*, 1.10.17–20.   **28.** Report by Megasthenes, the ambassador to the court of Chandragupta Maurya of Seleucus, the Greek ruler of Persia and Babylon; a similar account was later given by the Greek historian Strabo (*c.*64 BC–AD 19). Chakraborty, *Espionage in Ancient India*, p. 20.   **29.** *Arthashastra*, 1.12.2.   **30.** *Arthashastra*, 9.6.54, 55   **31.** See below, pp. 623–4.   **32.** See below, pp. 681–2.   **33.** Andrew, *For the President's Eyes Only*, pp. 252–3.   **34.** *Arthashastra*, 1.15.60.   **35.** *Arthashastra*, 1.12.20–23. Rangarajan (ed.), *Arthashastra*, p. 506.   **36.** *Art of War*, 13.22. Griffith (ed. and trans.), *Sun Tzu: The Art of War*, p. 149.   **37.** *Arthashastra*, 13.1.21.   **38.** Andrew and Mitrokhin, *Mitrokhin Archive II*, pp. 266–7, 324, 326.   **39.** Murthy, 'R. Shamashastry'.   **40.** Speech by Shivshankar Menon to the Indian Institute for Defence Studies and Analyses (IDSA), 18 Oct. 2012. Menon was Foreign Secretary from 2006 to 2009 and National Security Adviser from 2011 to 2014.   **41.** There had been five previous English translations, all inadequate. The very first foreign translation, into French by the Jesuit Father J. J. M. Amiot, may have been read by the young Napoleon. Griffith (ed. and trans.), *Sun Tzu: The Art of War*, p. 2.   **42.** Andrew, *Defence of the Realm*, ch. 1. Sun Tzu was mentioned in interwar MI5 lectures.   **43.** Griffith (ed. and trans.), *Illustrated Art of War*, pp. 17, 141–3. *Economist*, 'Sun Tzu and the Art of Soft Power'.   **44.** Dulles, *Craft of Intelligence*, p. 14.   **45.** Kissinger, *On China*, loc. 540.   **46.** Ibid., loc. 2364.   **47.** Ibid., loc. 543.   **48.** Defense Security Service, Security Research Center, *Recent Espionage Cases 1975–1999*, Sept. 1999. 'Huge Data Loss from China is Seen from Espionage', *The New York Times*, 30 Nov. 1985. 'Chin Believed Planted in US as Spy', *Washington Post*, 6 Dec. 1985. 'CIA Aide Called a "Living Lie" for 30 Years', *Los Angeles Times*, 28 Nov. 1985. 'Money wasn't Main Motive for Spying for China, Chin Testifies', *Los Angeles Times*, 7 Feb. 1986.   **49.** Warner, 'Divine Skein'. Warner, 'Building a Theory of Intelligence Systems'.   **50.** An activist from the Falun Gong movement (banned in China) also succeeded in infiltrating a press conference and heckling Hu. 'In Hu's Visit to the U.S., Small Gaffes May Overshadow Small Gains', *The New York Times*, 22 April 2006.   **51.** Nye, *Bound to Lead*. Nye, *Soft Power*.   **52.** Sun Tzu, *The Art of War* (bilingual edition), 3.3.   **53.** Nye, *Soft Power*, p. x.   **54.** *Economist*, 'Sun Tzu and the Art of Soft Power'.

5 The Roman Empire and the *Untermenschen*

1. See above, pp. 52–3.   **2.** Sheldon, *Intelligence Activities in Ancient Rome*, ch. 11.   **3.** Tacitus, *Annals*, 1.55. Loeb translation: http://penelope.uchicago.edu/Thayer/E/Roman/Texts/Tacitus/Annals/1D*.html.   **4.** Velleius Paterculus, *The*

Roman History, II. 118. Loeb translation: http://penelope.uchicago.edu/Thayer/ Roman/E/Texts/Velleius_Paterculus/home.html.   5. Cassius Dio, *Roman History*, 56.20.5.   6. Sheldon, *Intelligence Activities in Ancient Rome*, ch. 11.   7. Lucius Annaeus Florus, *Epitome of Roman History*, 2.30.36–7. Loeb translation: http://penelope.uchicago.edu/Thayer/E/Roman/Texts/Florus/Epitome/2H*.html.   8. Tacitus, *Annals*, 1.61.   9. Suetonius, *Lives of the Twelve Caesars: D. Octavius Caesar Augustus*, 23. Loeb translation: http://penelope.uchicago.edu/Thayer/E/ Roman/Texts/Suetonius/12Caesars/augustus*.html.   10. Ibid., 35.1.   11. Rut-ledge, *Imperial Inquisitions*, Introduction.   12. Suetonius, *De Vita Caesarum: Augustus*, 69 (see n. 9).   13. Ibid., 67.   14. Rutledge, *Imperial Inquisitions*, Introduc-tion.   15. Tacitus, *Annals*, 1.74.1–3. Loeb translation: http://penelope.uchicago. edu/Thayer/E/Roman/Texts/Tacitus/Annals/1E*.html. Rutledge, *Imperial Inquisi-tions*, p. 11.   16. Seneca, *On Benefits*, 3.26.1. Sheldon, *Intelligence Activities in Ancient Rome*, p. 152.   17. Suetonius, *Lives of the Twelve Caesars: Caius Caesar Caligula*, 15.   Loeb translation: http://penelope.uchicago.edu/Thayer/E/Roman/ Texts/Suetonius/12Caesars/Caligula*.html. 18. Suetonius, *Lives of the Twelve Cae-sars: Nero Claudius Caesar*, X.   19. Tacitus, *Annals*, 15.60–64.   20. Suetonius, *Lives of the Twelve Caesars: Caius Caesar Caligula*, 56–7.   21. Tacitus, *Annals*, 12.64. Loeb translation: http://penelope.uchicago.edu/Thayer/E/Roman/Texts/ Tacitus/Annals/12B*.html.   22. Suetonius, *Lives of the Twelve Caesars: Nero*, 34, 40. Loeb translation: http://penelope.uchicago.edu/Thayer/E/Roman/Texts/ Suetonius/12Caesars/Nero*.html.   23. Cassius Dio, *Roman History*, 62. Loeb translation: http://penelope.uchicago.edu/Thayer/E/Roman/Texts/Cassius_ Dio/62*.html.   24. Tacitus, *Annals*, 14.32. Loeb translation: http://penelope. uchicago.edu/Thayer/E/Roman/Texts/Tacitus/Annals/14B*.html.   25. Cassius Dio, *Roman History*, 62 (see n. 23).   26. https://en.wikipedia.org/wiki/Temple_ of_Claudius,_Colchester. 27. Hingley and Unwin, *Boudica*.   28. Sheldon, *Intelligence Activities in Ancient Rome*, p. 274, n. 62.   29. Bingham, *Praetorian Guard*, ch. 2.   30. Fuhrmann, *Policing the Roman Empire*, loc. 1499.   31. *Historia Augusta: Hadrian*, 11.4–6. Loeb translation: http://penelope.uchicago.edu/Thayer/E/ Roman/Texts/Historia_Augusta/Hadrian/1*.html.   32. *Historia Augusta: Didius Julianus*, 5.8. Loeb translation: http://penelope.uchicago.edu/Thayer/E/Roman/ Texts/Historia_Augusta/Didius_Julianus*.html. Fuhrmann, *Policing the Roman Empire*, loc. 1512.   33. Eusebius, *Ecclesiastical History*, VI. 40.   34. Ferrill, 'Roman Military Intelligence', p. 18.   35. Aurelius Victor, *De Caesaribus*, 39–45. Fuhrmann, *Policing the Roman Empire*, loc. 1523.   36. Sinningen, 'Roman Secret Service', p. 69.   37. Sheldon, *Intelligence Activities in Ancient Rome*, ch. 13.   38. On MI5 membership statistics, see Andrew, *Defence of the Realm*, appendix 2.   39. Beard, *SPQR*, p. 487.   40. Goldsworthy, *Pax Romana*, loc. 6627, 6678.   41. Lane Fox, *Pagans and Christians*, pp. 626, 666.   42. Stoneman, *The Ancient Oracles*, ch. 13.   43. Kelly, *Attila the Hun*, ch. 1.   44. Luttwak, *Grand Strategy of the Byzantine Empire*, loc. 5809. The quotation is from the eleventh-century *Strategikon* by Kekaumenos (sections 32–3), but sums up the conclusions of earlier military manuals going back to the *Strategikon* of the Emperor Maurikios (582–602).   45. Ammianus Marcellinus, *Res Gestae a fine Corneli Taciti*, 31.2.1–11.

Loeb translation: http://penelope.uchicago.edu./Thayer/E/Roman/Texts/
Ammian/31*.html.   **46.** Kelly, *Attila the Hun*, ch. 2.   **47.** Ibid., pp. 25–7.   **48.**
Kulikowski, *Rome's Gothic Wars*, p. 93.   **49.** Sarris, *Empires of Faith*, p. 9.   **50.**
Kelly, *Attila the Hun*, ch. 1. Heather, *The Fall of the Roman Empire*, loc. 3198ff.
Ammianus Marcellinus, *Res Gestae a fine Corneli Taciti*, 31.13 (see n. 45).   **51.**
See above, pp. 45–9.   **52.** Ammianus Marcellinus, *Res Gestae a fine Corneli Taciti*,
book 31.1.1,3 (see n. 45).   **53.** Kelly, *Attila the Hun*, ch. 24.   **54.** Ibid., pp. 47,
69–75.   **55.** Ibid., pp. 107–9. Given (ed. and trans.), *Fragmentary History of
Priscus*, fragments 5, 6.   **56.** Given (ed. and trans.), *Fragmentary History of
Priscus*, fragment 7. Kelly, *Attila the Hun*, pp. 120–25.   **57.** Kelly, *Attila the Hun*,
chs. 13–16.   **58.** Given (ed. and trans.), *Fragmentary History of Priscus*, fragments
8, 8.1.   **59.** Ibid., fragment 11.   **60.** Kelly, *Attila the Hun*, p. 162. Edekon, Bigilas
and Maximinos (in Given's translation) are referred to by Professor Kelly as Edeco,
Vigilas and Maximinus.   **61.** Kelly, *Attila the Hun*, Prologue.   **62.** Heather, *The Fall
of the Roman Empire*, ch. 8. Kelly, *Attila the Hun*, ch. 24.   **63.** See above, p. 62.   **64.**
See below, pp. 169–70.   **65.** See below, pp. 681–2.   **66.** See below, pp. 687–8.

6 Muhammad and the Rise of Islamic Intelligence

1. Topbaş, *Prophet of Mercy Muhammad*, p. 621.   **2.** Quran 43:80.   **3.** Al-Asmari,
'Arab/Islamic Concept of Intelligence', p. 118.   **4.** Armstrong, *Muhammad*, loc.
1244.   **5.** Al Qaeda training manual, lesson 11, espionage (Uk/Bm-76 Translation);
www.fas.org/irp/world/para/manualpart1_3.pdf.   **6.** Al-Asmari, 'Arab/Islamic
Concept of Intelligence', p. 56.   **7.** On the Hadiths (*ahadith*), see Bowering et al.
(eds.), *Princeton Encyclopedia of Islamic Political Thought*, pp. 211–14. The two
most revered canonical collections of Hadiths are those of al-Bukhari, completed
in the mid-ninth century, and his student Ibn Muslim.   **8.** Abram, *Islamic Hadith*,
2.723.   **9.** Al Qaeda training manual, lesson 11, espionage (Uk/Bm-76 Translation); www.fas.org/irp/world/para/manualpart1_3.pdf.   **10.** Sahih Muslim: book
019, Hadith no. 4394. http://hadithcollection.com/sahihmuslim/147-Sahih%20
Muslim%20Book%2019.%20Jihad%20and%20Expedition/12752-sahih-muslim-
book-019-hadith-number-4394.html.   **11.** Quran 3.123–5, 8:9–18. Hadiths provide
further detail.   **12.** Abram, *Islamic Hadith*, 5.327   **13.** Islamic sources identify over
forty individuals whose killing was ordered or approved by Muhammad: http://
www.wikiislam.net/wiki/List_of_Killings_Ordered_or_Supported_by_Muhammad.
14. Abram, *Islamic Hadith*, 5.369.   **15.** Ibid., 5.371. Al-Bukhari, *Hadith*, 5.59:
370–72. Al-Tabari, *History of al-Ṭabari*, vol. 7, p. 100.   **16.** Guillaume (ed. and
trans.), *Life of Muhammad*, pp. 675–6.   **17.** Abram, *Islamic Hadith*, 5.325.   **18.**
Ibid., 5.319.   **19.** http://www.hadithcollection.com/sahihbukhari/85-/3499-sahih-
bukhari-volume-004-book-052-hadith-number-268.html.   **20.** Al-Asmari, 'Arab/
Islamic Concept of Intelligence', pp. 112–13.   **21.** Quran 17:81.   **22.** Quran
9:25.   **23.** Luttwak, *Grand Strategy of the Byzantine Empire*, loc. 3871.   **24.**
Dennis (trans. and ed.), *Maurice's Strategikon*, book XI.   **25.** Luttwak, *Grand
Strategy of the Byzantine Empire*, loc. 889.   **26.** Ibid., loc. 2708.   **27.** Sarris,

Empires of Faith, loc. 6011.   28. Akram, *Sword of Allah*, ch. 35.   29. Ibid., ch. 30.   30. Ibid., ch. 34.   31. Kennedy, *Great Arab Conquests*, p. 121.   32. Al Qaeda training manual, lesson 11, espionage (Uk/Bm-76 Translation); www.fas.org/irp/world/para/manualpart1_3.pdf.   33. http://www.defence.pk/forums/military-history-strategy/127922-quotes-khalid-bin-al-walid.html#ixzz2XaVp2kRc, accessed 29 June 2013.   34. Pantucci, *'We Love Death as You Love Life'*.   35. Richard Stengel, 'Osama bin Laden and the Idea of Progress', *Time*, 21 Dec. 2001.   36. Kennedy, *Great Arab Conquests*, p. 78.   37. This account was set down by the ninth-century Egyptian chronicler Ibn Abd al-Hakam. The incomplete source material on Amr's career is discussed in Aboul-Enein, 'Amr ibn al-A'as'.   38. Kennedy, *Great Arab Conquests*, p. 83.   39. Akram, *Sword of Allah*, ch. 34.   40. Meyers (ed.), *Galilee through the Centuries*, pp. 380ff. Kennedy, *Great Arab Conquests*. The source of the story of the Arabs' entry into Caesarea through the secret water channel, Ahmad Ibn Yahya al-Baladhuri, is generally regarded as a reliable source for the early history of Muslim expansion.   41. Haldon, *Critical Commentary on The Taktika of Leo VI*.   42. Dennis (trans. and ed.), *Taktika of Leo VI*, p. 487.   43. Ibid., p. 477.   44. Ibid., p. 487.   45. Ibid. I am grateful for this reference to Dr Kristian Gustafson.   46. Quran 49.12.   47. Quran 24:27.   48. Silverstein, *Postal Systems in the Pre-Modern Islamic World*, chs. 1, 2.   49. Ibid., pp. 86–7.   50. Ibid., p. 187.   51. Holland, *In the Shadow of the Sword*, pp. 427–8.   52. Silverstein, *Postal Systems in the Pre-Modern Islamic World*, pp. 87, 187. Crone, *Pre-Industrial Societies*, p. 41.   53. Silverstein, *Postal Systems in the Pre-Modern Islamic World*, pp. 79–80.   54. Heinemann et al. (eds.), *Al-Jahiz*.   55. Al-Asmari, 'Arab/Islamic Concept of Intelligence', p. 120.   56. Ibid.   57. The agents were called *uyun* (literally 'eyes'). Ibid., p. 32.   58. Lyons, *House of Wisdom*. Al-Khalili, *House of Wisdom*.   59. Al-Khalili, *House of Wisdom*.   60. Adamson, *Al-Kindī*, ch. 1.   61. Pormann and Adamson (eds.), *Philosophical Works of al-Kindī*. Adamson, 'Before Essence and Existence'.   62. Adamson, *Al-Kindī*, p. 6.   63. Ibid., ch. 1.   64. Al-Kadi, 'Origins of Cryptology'. On Caesar's ciphers, see above, pp. 46–7.   65. Ibid. Singh, *Code Book*, loc. 392–426.

7 Inquisitions and Counter-Subversion

1. Andrew and Mitrokhin, *Mitrokhin Archive*, chs. 19, 20.   2. Pegg, *Corruption of Angels*, p. 4. Sumption, *Albigensian Crusade*, ch. 1.   3. Innocent III to papal legates, 3 Feb. 1209; Sommerlechner et al. (eds.), *Die Register Innocenz' III*, vol. II, 11, no. 226, p. 379.   4. Lane, *Bernard of Clairvaux*, pp. 166–8. One of the papal legates to whom Innocent III wrote was Abbot Arnald of Clairvaux.   5. Pegg, *Corruption of Angels*, p. 4.   6. Ibid., ch. 2. Sumption, *Albigensian Crusade*, ch. 6.   7. Pegg, *Corruption of Angels*, ch. 2.   8. Ames, *Righteous Persecution*, p. 42.   9. Pegg, *Corruption of Angels*.   10. Andrew, 'Modern History of Interrogation'.   11. Biget, 'L'Inquisition en Languedoc, 1229–1329', p. 66.   12. Baigent and Leigh, *Inquisition*, p. 33.   13. Murphy, *God's Jury*, ch. 2.   14. Duvernoy (ed.), *Registre d'Inquisition de Jacques Fournier*, vol. 1, pp. 49–54.   15. Pegg,

Corruption of Angels, p. 48.   16. Pelhisson, *Chronique*, pp. 60–65. Cf. Ames, *Righteous Persecution*, pp. 29–32.   17. The most influential exposition of this interpretation is Moore, *War on Heresy*.   18. See below, pp. 599–601.   19. Moore, *War on Heresy*, ch. 17.   20. Biget, 'L'Inquisition en Languedoc, 1229–1329' pp. 44–5, 80–83. Ames, *Righteous Persecution*, pp. 28–9.   21. Andrew and Mitrokhin, *Mitrokhin Archive*, pp. 450–51.   22. Le Roy Ladurie, *Montaillou*.   23. Duvernoy (ed.), *Registre d'Inquisition de Jacques Fournier*, vol. 2, pp. 633–43.   24. Moore, *Formation of a Persecuting Society*, pp. 64–5.   25. Duvernoy (ed.), *Registre d'Inquisition de Jacques Fournier*, vol. 1, p. 222.   26. Nirenberg, *Communities of Violence*, pp. 63–7.   27. Sumption, *Hundred Years War*, vol. 1, pp. 379–80.   28. Politburo decision, 2 Oct. 1937; Getty and Naumov (eds.), *Road to Terror*, document 164. See below, p. 598.   29. Kieckhefer, 'Office of Inquisition and Medieval Heresy'.   30. Andrew and Gordievsky, *KGB*, p. 149. See below, p. 620.   31. Baigent and Leigh, *Inquisition*, pp. 36–7. For an example of the invitations to regional notables, see 'The Expenditures made for the Sermon or the Indulgence of the Lord Inquisitor in the City of Carcassonne on Sunday, April 24 [1323]'; AN, Doat Ms 34, 24 April 1323.   32. See, for example: 'For the expenditures made to burn Raimon Maistre of Villemoustaussou, Bernard de Bosco of Béziers, Peire Julian of Narbonne and Johan Conils, inhabitant of Béziers . . .', AN, Doat Ms 34, 24 April 1323.   33. 'For the expenditures made by order of the Lord Inquisitor', AN, Doat Ms 34, 24 April 1323.   34. Duffy, 'Repression of Heresy in England', p. 446.   35. Murphy, *God's Jury*, p. 4.   36. I am grateful for this information to Professor Peter Godman.   37. Godman, *Saint as Censor*.   38. Ibid.   39. Ibid., pp. 45–8.   40. Andrew and Mitrokhin, *Mitrokhin Archive*, p. 3.   41. Menocal, *Ornament of the World*, p. 47.   42. Kamen, *Spanish Inquisition*, ch. 3.   43. Roth, *Spanish Inquisition*, pp. 41–6. Kamen, *Spanish Inquisition*, p. 47.   44. Kamen, *Spanish Inquisition*, p. 207.   45. Ibid., pp. 59–60. Rawlings, *Spanish Inquisition*, pp. 14–16.   46. Kamen, *Spanish Inquisition*, pp. 61–5.   47. Ibid., ch. 2.   48. Ibid., pp. 94–5.   49. Duke, 'The "Inquisition" and the Repression of Religious Dissent'. The Netherlands had, writes Duke, 'a mongrel imperial-papal inquisition'.   50. Duffy, 'Repression of Heresy in England', pp. 451–6. Professor Duffy comments: 'Most English dioceses mounted no sustained campaign against heresy, and the reluctance of the bishops and their officers was certainly a factor in this inactivity.'   51. Ibid., pp. 467–8.   52. Kamen, *Spanish Inquisition*, pp. 95–101.   53. See below, pp. 698–70.   54. Hossain, 'Was Adam the First Heretic?'   55. Páramo, *De origine et progressu officii sanctae Inquisitionis*, book 1. Book 2 continues the history of inquisitions up to the 1590s; book 3 is an inquisitorial manual.   56. On the two other forms of torture most frequently employed by the Spanish Inquisition, the rack and the strapado, see Kamen, *Spanish Inquisition*, pp. 187–9; Murphy, *God's Jury*, ch. 3.   57. Rejali, *Torture and Democracy*, p. 280.   58. Bush, *Decision Points*, ch. 6.   59. Hitchens, 'Believe Me, It's Torture'.

8 Renaissance Venice and the Rise of Western Intelligence

1. Ackroyd, *Venice*, p. 102. De Vivo, *Information and Communication in Venice*, p. 51.   2. Ackroyd, *Venice*, p. 101.   3. Decree of Council of Ten, 12 July 1481;

Chambers and Pullan (eds.), *Venice*, p. 16.   **4.** Ibid., pp. 92–3.   **5.** Iordanou, 'What News on the Rialto?', p. 314.   **6.** Kissling, 'Venezia come Centro di Informazioni sui Turchi'.   **7.** Plumb, *Italian Renaissance*, p. 102.   **8.** Cattaneo, *Fra Mauro's Mappa Mundi*.   **9.** Quoted by Plumb, *Italian Renaissance*, p. 144.   **10.** Harari, *Sapiens*, pp. 319–25, 330–31.   **11.** Heirman, De Troia and Parmentier, 'Francesco Sambiasi, a Missing Link in European Map Making in China?'   **12.** Burke, 'Early Modern Venice as a Center of Information and Communication', p. 392. De Vivo, *Information and Communication in Venice*, p. 91.   **13.** On the diplomatic system and balance of power among Italian city-states in long-term perspective, see Kissinger, *Diplomacy*, pp. 20–24.   **14.** Frigo, 'Introduction', p. 10.   **15.** Jardine and Sherman, 'Pragmatic Readers'. De Vivo, *Information and Communication in Venice*, p. 75.   **16.** Preto, *I servizi segreti*, pp. 198–209.   **17.** Ibid., pp. 217–25.   **18.** Ibid., p. 219.   **19.** Malcolm, *Agents of Empire*, p. 223.   **20.** Goffman, 'Negotiating with the Renaissance State', p. 71.   **21.** Gürkan, 'The Efficacy of Ottoman Counter-Intelligence', p. 23.   **22.** Gürkan, 'Espionage in the 16th Century Mediterranean', pp. 396–7.   **23.** Nuovo, 'A Lost Arabic Koran Rediscovered'.   **24.** Adelman, 'A Rabbi Reads the Qur'an'.   **25.** Speech by Mustafa Kemal, 25 Nov. 1925; Lewis, 'Kemalist Republic', p. 22.   **26.** İsom-Verhaaren, 'An Ottoman Report'.   **27.** Malcolm, *Agents of Empire*, pp. 224–8.   **28.** Gürkan, 'Espionage in the 16th Century Mediterranean', p. 97.   **29.** Ibid.   **30.** Preto, *I servizi segreti*, pp. 76–8.   **31.** Giustiniani, *Four Years at the Court of Henry VIII*, vol. 1, p. 90.   **32.** Rex, 'The Religion of Henry VIII', p. 29.   **33.** Giustiniani; report to Senate after his return to Venice, 10 Oct. 1519; Giustiniani, *Four Years at the Court of Henry VIII*, vol. 2, p. 314. His estimate of Wolsey's age was probably correct.   **34.** Labalme and Sanguineti White (eds.), *Venice: Città Excelentissima*, pp. 202–3.   **35.** De Vivo, *Information and Communication in Venice*.   **36.** Zutshi, 'Political and Administrative Correspondence', pp. 380–81. Bock, 'Die Geheimschrift in der Kanzlei Johanns XXII'.   **37.** Alberti, *De Cyfris*, ed. Buonafalce; also entitled in some editions *De Componendis Cyfris*.   **38.** See above, p. 99.   **39.** Kahn, *Codebreakers*, pp. 127–30.   **40.** Labalme and Sanguineti White (eds.), *Venice: Città Excelentissima*, pp. 218–19.   **41.** See above, pp. 98–9.   **42.** Gürkan, 'Efficacy of Ottoman Counter-Intelligence', pp. 22–3.   **43.** Labalme and Sanguineti White (eds.), *Venice: Città Excelentissima*, p. 34.   **44.** Sanudo diary: ibid., p. 219. On the functioning of the Collegio, see de Vivo, *Information and Communication in Venice*, p. 37.   **45.** Sanudo diary: Labalme and Sanguineti White (eds.), *Venice: Città Excelentissima*, p. 219.   **46.** Decree of Council of Ten, 20 Sept. 1539; Chambers and Pullan (eds.), *Venice*, p. 17.   **47.** Preto, *I servizi segreti*, pp. 55–74.   **48.** De Vivo, *Information and Communication in Venice*, pp. 41–2.   **49.** Ibid.   **50.** Ibid.   **51.** Murphy, *God's Jury*, loc. 1455.   **52.** The leading study of the Venetian use of masks from the thirteenth to the eighteenth century is Johnson, *Venice Incognito*.   **53.** Addison, *Essays* (c.1703).   **54.** Johnson, *Venice Incognito*, p. 53.   **55.** Ibid., pp. 105–7.   **56.** news.nationalgeographic.com/news/2007/08/070829-venice-plague.html, accessed 31 July 2013.   **57.** Mark Twain, *The Innocents Abroad, or, The New Pilgrim's Progress* (Hartford, Conn.: American Pub. Co., 1871), ch. 22.   **58.** A rare exception to the lack of research on the role of intelligence in the establishment of New Spain is Kerner, 'Espionage and Field Intelligence'.   **59.** Conrad and Demarest, *Religion and Empire*, pp. 49–50. Kerner, 'Espionage and Field Intelligence', p. 479.   **60.** Smith, *Aztecs*, p. 277.   **61.** Díaz, *History of the Conquest of New Spain*, pp. 82–7.   **62.** Ibid., pp. 98–114.   **63.** Ibid., pp. 140–66.   **64.** Ibid., pp. 195–203.   **65.** Carrasco, *Quetzalcoatl and the Irony of Empire*, ch. 4. Díaz, *History of the Conquest of New Spain*, pp. 114–15.   **66.** Díaz, *History of the Conquest of New Spain*, pp. 152, 214–83, 353–413. Kerner, 'Espionage and Field Intelligence', pp. 487–99. Harari, *Sapiens*, pp. 328–30. Harari, *Homo Deus*, pp. 9–10. Rojas, *Tenochtitlan*, pp. 36–9.   **67.** Harari, *Sapiens*, p. 330.   **68.** Wood, *Conquistadors*, chs. 3, 4.   **69.** See above, p. 114.   **70.** See below, pp. 138–40.   **71.** Pesic, 'François Viète', pp. 3–4.   **72.** Ibid., pp. 4–6.   **73.** Kahn, *Codebreakers*, pp. 118, 995.   **74.** Pesic, 'François Viète', pp. 5–6.   **75.** Kahn, *Codebreakers*, pp. 117–18.   **76.** A translation of Viète's memoir to Sully, written before his death in February 1603, appears in Pesic, 'François Viète' pp. 22–7.   **77.** De Leeuw, 'Cryptology in the Dutch Republic', p. 334.   **78.** S. Tomokiyo, 'Spanish Ciphers during the Reign of Philip II'; http://www.h4.dion.ne.jp/~room4me/america/code/spanish3.htm, accessed 27 Aug. 2013.   **79.** De Leeuw, 'Cryptology in the Dutch Republic', p. 334.   **80.** See below, ch. 10.

9 Ivan the Terrible and the Origins of Russian State Security

1. Perrie, *Cult of Ivan the Terrible*, p. 1.   **2.** Bogatyrev, 'Ivan IV', pp. 257–8.   **3.** Ibid. Pavlov and Perrie, *Ivan the Terrible*, p. 118.   **4.** The use of dogs' heads is attested by four independent contemporary sources. Halperin, 'Did Ivan IV's *Oprichniki* Carry Dogs' Heads?'   **5.** Ibid.   **6.** Jansen and Petrov, *Stalin's Loyal Executioner.*   **7.** Volodikhin, *Maliuta Skuratov*, ch. 7.   **8.** On Ivan's wars, see Filjushkin, *Ivan the Terrible.*   **9.** de Madariaga, *Ivan the Terrible*, p. 231. Merridale, *Red Fortress*, p. 93.   **10.** Schlichting, 'Brief Account of the Character and Brutal Rule of Vasil'evich, Tyrant of Muscovy', pp. 207, 223–4.   **11.** Standen, *Land and Government of Muscovy*, p. 21.   **12.** Merridale, *Red Fortress*, p. 93.   **13.** Ianin, 'Medieval Novgorod', p. 210.   **14.** Standen, *Land and Government of Muscovy*, pp. 26–7. In addition to Standen's first-hand account, there are other contemporary descriptions in Kruse and Taube, 'Poslanie Ioganna Taube i Elberta Kruze', and Schlichting, 'Brief Account of the Character and Brutal Rule of Vasil'evich'.   **15.** Halperin, 'Did Ivan IV's *Oprichniki* Carry Dogs' Heads?', pp. 51–2.   **16.** Pavlov and Perrie, *Ivan the Terrible*, p. 30. Merridale, *Red Fortress*, p. 72.   **17.** Primakov et al., *Ocherki istorii rossiyskoi vneshnei razvedki*, vol. 1, p. 31.   **18.** Ibid., p. 27.   **19.** See below, pp. 619–27.   **20.** On the Ottomans' lack of permanent embassies and printing presses, see above, pp. 122–3.   **21.** Zernova, *Knigi, kirillovskoi pechati, izdannye v Moskye*, pp. 11–25. Miller, 'The Orthodox Church', p. 357.   **22.** Primakov et al., *Ocherki istorii rossiyskoi vneshnei razvedki*, vol. 1. The SVR account is based chiefly on Chancellor's own account but adds some details from the Dvina Chronicle, an eighteenth-century compilation which drew on earlier records.   **23.** Chancellor, 'The First Voyage to Russia', in Berry and Crummey (eds.), *Rude and*

Barbarous Kingdom, pp. 18–27.   **24.** See, for example, Ivan IV to Elizabeth, 24 Oct. 1570, TNA SP 102/49; Russian text and English translation at http://eng.history.ru/content/view/131/87/.   **25.** Bogatyrev, 'Ivan IV', p. 257.   **26.** Primakov et al., *Ocherki istorii rossiyskoi vneshnei razvedki*, vol. 1, p. 26. The SVR account of Nepeya's reception in Lunsky (London) derives from Russian sources.   **27.** Ivan IV to Elizabeth, 24 Oct. 1570, TNA SP 102/49; Russian text and English translation at http://eng.history.ru/content/view/131/87/.   **28.** Primakov et al., *Ocherki istorii rossiyskoi vneshnei razvedki*, vol. 1.   **29.** Ivan IV to Elizabeth, 24 Oct. 1570, TNA SP 102/49; Russian text and English translation at http://eng.history.ru/content/view/131/87/.   **30.** Brotton, *This Orient Isle*, pp. 40, 59.   **31.** 'The first voyage made by Master Anthony Jenkinson, from the City of London, toward the land of Russia, begun the twelfth day of May, in the year 1557', in Berry and Crummey (eds.), *Rude and Barbarous Kingdom*, pp. 46–58.   **32.** Following his return to England in 1554, Chancellor's detailed description of Muscovy was written down by the author and teacher Clement Adams, who is believed to have been a former Fellow of King's College, Cambridge; Chancellor also wrote his own 'book of the great and mighty Emperor of Russia, etc'. *ODNB* Richard Chancellor.   **33.** Chancellor, 'Of Moscow, the chief city of the kingdom, and of the emperor thereof', in Berry and Crummey (eds.), *Rude and Barbarous Kingdom*, pp. 23–7.   **34.** Chancellor, 'Of their religion', in Berry and Crummey (eds.), *Rude and Barbarous Kingdom*, pp. 35–8.   **35.** Chancellor, 'Of the discipline of war amongst the Russes', in Berry and Crummey (eds.), *Rude and Barbarous Kingdom*, pp. 27–30.   **36.** *ODNB* Anthony Jenkinson.   **37.** Ibid.   **38.** Pavlov and Perrie, *Ivan the Terrible*, p. 137.   **39.** *ODNB* Anthony Jenkinson.   **40.** There is no mention of Randolph in Alford, *Watchers* or in Cooper, *Queen's Agent*.   **41.** Berry and Crummey (eds.), *Rude and Barbarous Kingdom*, p. 62.   **42.** Turberville, 'To Dancie', in Berry and Crummey (eds.), *Rude and Barbarous Kingdom*, p. 75.   **43.** Sir Thomas Randolph, 'A Mission to Muscovy', in Berry and Crummey (eds.), *Rude and Barbarous Kingdom*, pp. 65–70.   **44.** *ODNB* Thomas Randolph.   **45.** Berry and Crummey (eds.), *Rude and Barbarous Kingdom*, p. 70.   **46.** Pavlov and Perrie, *Ivan the Terrible*, pp. 153–4.   **47.** There is a first-hand account in Schlichting, 'Brief Account of the Character and Brutal Rule of Vasil'evich', pp. 259–61. Other contemporary accounts are in Standen, *Land and Government of Muscovy*, p. 28; Kruse and Taube, 'Poslanie Ioganna Taube i Elberta Kruze' p. 51; de Madariaga, *Ivan the Terrible*, p. 258.   **48.** Translation prepared for the Queen of Ivan IV to Elizabeth, 24 Oct. 1570, TNA SP 102/49; published by Pryor, *Elizabeth I*.   **49.** *ODNB* Anthony Jenkinson.   **50.** *ODNB* Jerome Horsey.   **51.** See above, pp. 121–2, 124.   **52.** Sir Jerome Horsey, 'Travels'; in Berry and Crummey (eds.), *Rude and Barbarous Kingdom*, pp. 294–5.   **53.** Primakov et al., *Ocherki istorii rossiyskoi vneshnei razvedki*, vol. 1, p. 33.   **54.** Sir Jerome Horsey, 'Travels', in Berry and Crummey (eds.), *Rude and Barbarous Kingdom*, p. 260.   **55.** Ibid., p. 233.   **56.** Ibid., p. 362.   **57.** Pavlov, 'Fedor Ivanovich and Boris Godunov', p. 267.   **58.** Merridale, *Red Fortress*, p. 104.   **59.** Pavlov, 'Fedor Ivanovich and Boris Godunov', p. 285.   **60.** Ibid., p. 266–7.   **61.** *ODNB* Giles Fletcher.   **62.** Fletcher, *Of the Russe Commonwealth*, ch. 7; in Berry and Crummey (eds.), *Rude and Barbarous Kingdom*, pp. 132–5.   **63.**

Berry and Crummey (eds.), *Rude and Barbarous Kingdom*, p. 107.   64. Merridale, *Red Fortress*, pp. 114–15, 122. Perrie, 'The Time of Troubles', pp. 412–13.

10 Elizabeth I, Walsingham and the Rise of English Intelligence

1. Quoted by Sir Keith Thomas in his review of Alford, *Watchers*, in the *Guardian*, 17 Aug. 2012.   2. *ODNB* Francis Walsingham.   3. Ibid.   4. Sumption, *Edward III*, ch. 1.   5. Sumption, *Hundred Years War*, vol. 1, p. 447.   6. Given-Wilson, *Henry IV*, p. 411.   7. Ibid., p. 411, n. 19.   8. Sumption, *Hundred Years War*, vol. 4: *Cursed Kings*, p. 209.   9. *ODNB* Francis Walsingham.   10. Haigh, *Elizabeth I*, p. 72.   11. A statement attributed to Sir Maurice Oldfield.   12. Lindberg, *European Reformations*, p. 295.   13. On the identification of 'Pompeo Pellegrini' as Anthony Standen, see Read, *Mr Secretary Walsingham*, vol. 3, pp. 288–92.   14. See below, pp. 173–4.   15. See below, pp. 183–4.   16. Guy, *Queen of Scots*, chs. 1–7.   17. Duke of Norfolk and his Council to Cecil, 21 April 1560, *CSP Foreign Elizabeth*, vol. 2. Cecil to William Petre, 21 June 1560, *CSP Foreign Elizabeth*, vol. 3.   18. Throckmorton to Cecil, 3 May 1560, *CSP Foreign Elizabeth*, vol. 3.   19. Throckmorton to Cecil, 3 May 1560, *CSP Foreign Elizabeth*, vol. 3. No record appears to survive of any further dealings with Beaumont.   20. Throckmorton to Privy Council, 19 July 1560, *CSP Foreign Elizabeth*, vol. 3.   21. Guy, *Queen of Scots*, pp. 491–2.   22. James Hamilton of Bothwellhaugh to Raulet, 18 Aug, 1970, *Calendar of the Cecil Papers in Hatfield House*, vol. 1.   23. *ODNB* Charles Bailly. Cooper, *Queen's Agent*, p. 194. Alford, *Watchers*, pp. 49–50.   24. Cooper, *Queen's Agent*, pp. 57–8.   25. Hutchinson, *Elizabeth's Spy Master*, p. 58.   26. Guy, *Queen of Scots*, p. 450.   27. The painting also included Mary's husband, Philip II. The identity of the painter is uncertain. Hearn, *Dynasties*, p. 81.   28. Killigrew (Edinburgh) to Burghley, 17 March 1573; Killigrew (Edinburgh) to Burghley and Leicester, 4 and 7 April 1573; *CSP Foreign Elizabeth*, vol. 3. S. Tomokiyo, 'Ciphers during the Reign of Queen Elizabeth I', http://www.h4.dion. ne.jp/~room4me/america/code/elizabeth.htm, accessed 6 Sept. 2013.   29. Russell, *Maitland of Lethington*, pp. 501–2.   30. Cooper, *Queen's Agent*, pp. 130–32.   31. See above, pp. 139–40.   32. Thomas Wilson to Earl of Leicester, 22 March 1577, *CSP Foreign Elizabeth*, vol. 21.   33. The despatch had been intercepted by a Huguenot (French Protestant) general and decrypted by Aldegonde. Cooper, *Queen's Agent*, pp. 267–8.   34. TNA SP 106/1, no. 58. Kahn, *Codebreakers*, p. 120. http:// cryptiana.web.fc2.com/code/spanish3.htm.   35. Thomas Wilson to Walsingham, 30 June 1577, *CSP Foreign Elizabeth*, vol. 13.   36. *ODNB* Thomas Phelippes.   37. Walsingham to William Davison, 20 March 1578, *CSP Foreign Elizabeth*, vol. 12.   38. William Davison to Walsingham and other Secretaries, 5 April 1578, *CSP Foreign Elizabeth*, vol. 12. The decrypt sent with this despatch does not survive.   39. Maurice of Nassau to Walsingham, 14/24 March 1585; English translation of decrypted letter from Mendoza to the Prince of Parma, 17/24 Feb. 1585. *CSP Foreign Elizabeth*, vol. 19.   40. For Henry IV, see below, p. 198.   41. Jardine, *Awful End of Prince William the Silent*, Introduction.   42. Ibid., p. 101.   43. See

above, pp. 83–4.   **44.** Alford, *Watchers*, p. 103.   **45.** *ODNB* Robert Persons.   **46.** *ODNB* Edmund Campion.   **47.** Alford, *Watchers*, p. 67.   **48.** *ODNB* Robert Persons.   **49.** *ODNB* Edmund Campion.   **50.** Riggs, *World of Christopher Marlowe*, p. 140.   **51.** Ibid., p. 130.   **52.** Honan, *Christopher Marlowe*, pp. 144–5. Nicholl, *The Reckoning*, p. 448.   **53.** *ODNB* Nicholas Faunt.   **54.** Buttery Book, Corpus Christi College, Cambridge, Archives.   **55.** Hopkins, *Christopher Marlowe Chronology*, p. 85.   **56.** See below, pp. 186–7.   **57.** Alford, *Watchers*, p. 160.   **58.** *CSP Scotland, 1581–3*, no. 432.   **59.** Text in French with English translation in Bossy, *Giordano Bruno and the Embassy Affair*, Appendix 4, pp. 197–200.   **60.** In the first edition of *Giordano Bruno and the Embassy Affair*, Bossy identified the secretary as de Courcelles. In 2002, after discovering persuasive new evidence, he identified him instead as Laurent Feron. Ibid., pp. 46–55.   **61.** *ODNB* Lord Henry Howard.   **62.** Alford, *Watchers*, chs. 10, 11. *ODNB* Francis Throckmorton.   **63.** Cooper, *Queen's Agent*, p. 208.   **64.** *A discouerie of the treasons practised and attempted . . .*   **65.** Throckmorton to Elizabeth I, undated [June or early July 1584], TNA SP 12/171 folio 2.   **66.** Cooper, *Queen's Agent*, p. 208.   **67.** Bossy, *Under the Molehill*.   **68.** *ODNB* Gilbert Gifford.   **69.** Guy, *Queen of Scots*, p. 466.   **70.** See below, pp. 187–8.   **71.** Babington to Mary, 6 July 1586, TNA SP 12/193/54.   **72.** Mary to Babington, 17 July 1586, TNA SP 12/193/55.   **73.** Mary to Babington (with fraudulent insertion by Phelippes), ibid.   **74.** Alford, *Watchers*, pp. 219–35.   **75.** Cooper, *Queen's Agent*, p. 293.   **76.** Guy, *Queen of Scots*, ch. 29. Alford, *Watchers*, pp. 236–9.   **77.** Guy, *Queen of Scots*, pp. 479–82. Alford, *Watchers*, pp. 239–40.   **78.** *ODNB* Thomas Phelippes.   **79.** Cooper, *Queen's Agent*, pp. 396–7.   **80.** Pompeo Pellegrini to Jacopo Manucci (one of Walsingham's servants), 7 May 1587, TNA SP 94/2 part 2, f82.   **81.** Walsingham to Standen, [April or early May 1587], TNA SP 98/1, pt 1, f18.   **82.** http://www.nationalarchives.gov.uk/spies/spies/standen/st1.htm.   **83.** See below, pp. 682–3.   **84.** Cooper, *Queen's Agent*, pp. 396–7.   **85.** *ODNB* Sir Stephen Powle. Stern, *Sir Stephen Powle*.   **86.** Stephen Powle to Walsingham, 3/13 Feb. 1588, *CSP Foreign Elizabeth*, vol. 21, part 1.   **87.** Ibid., 10/20 Feb. 1588.   **88.** Alford, *Watchers*, p. 253. On Santa Cruz, see above, p. 180.   **89.** Salisbury MSS, 7.96–7; cited by *ODNB* Thomas Phelippes.   **90.** *ODNB* Edward Stafford. Leimon and Parker, 'Treason and Plot in Elizabethan Diplomacy'.   **91.** Hutchinson, *Spanish Armada*.   **92.** Cooper, *Queen's Agent*, p. 421.   **93.** Alford, *Watchers*, p. 263.   **94.** Cooper, *Queen's Agent*, pp. 428–30.   **95.** Alford, *Watchers*, pp. 264–6.   **96.** *ODNB* Thomas Phelippes.   **97.** *ODNB* Anthony Standen. *ODNB* Anthony Bacon.   **98.** Hughes (ed.), 'Nicholas Faunt's Discourse'.   **99.** See above, pp. 171–2.   **100.** See above, pp. 172–3.   **101.** *ODNB* Christopher Marlowe.   **102.** Nicholl, *The Reckoning*, ch. 25.   **103.** On the interaction between drama and intelligence, see Christopher Andrew and Julius Green, *Stars and Spies* (forthcoming).   **104.** British Library, Harley MS 6848, fols. 185–6; MS 6853, fols. 307–8; cited by *ODNB* Christopher Marlowe.   **105.** Nicholl, *The Reckoning*, ch. 29.   **106.** Ibid., ch. 36.   **107.** *ODNB* Christopher Marlowe.   **108.** Nicholl, *The Reckoning*, pp. 31–3. On Poley's role in the Babington Plot, see above, p. 176.   **109.** *ODNB* Robert Devereux, 2nd Earl of Essex.   **110.** *ODNB* Roderigo Lopez.   **111.** Cooper,

Queen's Agent, pp. 266–7.   **112.** Alford, *Watchers*, p. 305.   **113.** Lisa Jardine, 'A Tale for Our Times'; http://news.bbc.co.uk/1/hi/magazine/5159022.stm.   **114.** Alford, *Watchers*, p. 305.   **115.** *ODNB* Roderigo Lopez.   **116.** *ODNB* Thomas Phelippes.   **117.** Alford, *Watchers*, p. 310.   **118.** Ibid., pp. 310–14.   **119.** http://www.andrewgrahamdixon.com/archive/readArticle/245.

11 The Decline of Early Stuart and Spanish Intelligence

1. *ODNB* Lord Henry Howard.   **2.** Bruce (ed.), *Correspondence of King James VI. of Scotland*, p. xxxiv.   **3.** See above, pp. 173–4.   **4.** *ODNB* Robert Cecil.   **5.** Ibid.   **6.** Apology by Thomas Phelippes, ?May 1603, TNA SP 14/1/119.   **7.** See above, pp. 177–8.   **8.** Phelippes to Cranborne [Cecil], 29 and 31 Jan. 1605; *CSP Domestic James I*, vol. 12, nos. 42, 44.   **9.** *Daemonologie*, published in 1597.   **10.** *ODNB* Robert Cecil. On Stafford, see above, pp. 183–4.   **11.** Fraser, *Gunpowder Plot*, p. 123.   **12.** Ibid., p. 124.   **13.** *ODNB* Robert Catesby.   **14.** Fraser, *Gunpowder Plot*, p. 164.   **15.** *ODNB* Gunpowder Plot; *ODNB* Guy Fawkes.   **16.** *ODNB* Guy Fawkes.   **17.** Fraser, *Gunpowder Plot*, pp. 191–2.   **18.** Mousnier, *Assassination of Henry IV*.   **19.** See below, pp. 206–7.   **20.** See above, p. 192.   **21.** See below, pp. 196–7.   **22.** Hugon, *Au service du roi catholique*, p. 41.   **23.** See above, pp. 133–6.   **24.** Philip III to 7th Duke of Medina Sidonia, 29 July 1608, John D. Rockefeller Library (Special Collections), Williamsburg, VA.   **25.** Ibid., 11 June 1609.   **26.** Horn, 'Imperfect Understandings', pp. 534–6.   **27.** Ibid., p. 540. Griffin, 'The Specter of Spain', p. 122.   **28.** Harari, *Sapiens*, p. 331.   **29.** Hugon, *Au service du roi catholique*.   **30.** Rodriguéz-Salgado, 'Intelligence in the Spanish Monarchy'.   **31.** Hugon, *Au service du roi catholique*, p. 52.   **32.** Ibid., p. 410.   **33.** A translation of Viète's memoir to Sully, written before his death in February 1603, appears in Pesic, 'François Viète', pp. 22–7.   **34.** Hugon, *Au service du roi catholique*, pp. 260–61.   **35.** Hugon, 'Les Rendez-vous manqués de Gérard de Raffis'.   **36.** Hugon, 'L'Affaire L'Hoste'. Hugon, *Au service du roi catholique*, pp. 175, 613–14.   **37.** Ibid., p. 175.   **38.** Ibid., pp. 391, 433–4.   **39.** Ibid., p. 127.   **40.** Ibid., pp. 410–11.   **41.** The original of the letter from Jean de Quercy to Philip III, dated 10 Dec. 1613, is in the Simancas archives; the text is published in Hugon, *Au service du roi catholique*, appendix 3.   **42.** Hugon, *Au service du roi catholique*, p. 430.   **43.** Ibid., pp. 421, 430, 581.   **44.** Petitfils, *Louis XIII*, pp. 187–90.   **45.** Ibid., p. 288.   **46.** Ibid., p. 219.   **47.** Ibid., chs. 6, 7.   **48.** See below, pp. 206, 211–12.   **49.** Hugon, *Au service du roi catholique*, p. 21.   **50.** Ibid., p. 191.   **51.** Petitfils, *Louis XIII*, pp. 288–9. The main source for the intimate detail of Louis's sexual relationship with Queen Anne is the journal of his doctor, Jean Héroard.   **52.** Hugon, *Au service du roi catholique*, pp. 421, 430, 581.   **53.** Ibid., pp. 431–2.   **54.** See above, pp. 170–71.   **55.** *ODNB* Robert Persons.   **56.** Harris, *Rebellion*, p. 2.   **57.** Hugon, *Au service du roi catholique*, p. 412. Spanish archives, cited by Hugon, add to the information on Creswell in the *ODNB* entries on Robert Persons and Joseph Creswell.   **58.** Ibid., p. 615.   **59.** Ibid., p. 595.   **60.** Bergeron, *King James and Letters of Homoerotic Desire*.   **61.** Stubbs, *Reprobates*,

p. 53.   62. Kishlansky, *Monarchy Transformed*, p. 104.   63. Ibid. Redworth, *The Prince and the Infanta*.   64. Petitfils, *Louis XIII*, pp. 369–73.   65. *CSP Venice, 1621–3*, p. 289.   66. Ibid., *1623–5*, p. 601.   67. *ODNB* Thomas Phelippes.   68. On Viète, see above, pp. 137–9.   69. Pradel (ed.), 'Mémoires de Jean Olès', pp. 155–7. Kahn, *Codebreakers*, p. 157.   70. Richelieu to Louis XIII, 22 Aug. 1628 (referring to incidents during the siege over the previous few months); Grillon (ed.), *Papiers de Richelieu*, vol. 3, pp. 450–51.   71. Condé (Toulouse) to Richelieu, 8 Aug. 1628: Grillon (ed.), *Papiers de Richelieu*, vol. 3, pp. 421–2.   72. Perrault, *Hommes illustres*, p. 57.   73. Grillon (ed.), *Papiers de Richelieu*, vol. 3, p. 421n.   74. Perrault, *Hommes illustres*, p. 57. http://www.juvisy.fr/wp-content/uploads/chronologie-de-Juvisy.pdf, accessed 10 Jan. 2014.   75. 'Mémoire pour convier les Rochelois à se rendre', 20 Aug. 1628; Grillon (ed.), *Papiers de Richelieu*, vol. 3, pp. 445–7.   76. M. de La Ville-aux-Clercs to Richelieu, 21 Sept. 1628; ibid., pp. 496–7.   77. Petitfils, *Louis XIII*, p. 367.   78. Hugon, *Au service du roi catholique*, p. 208.   79. Preto, *I servizi segreti*, p. 219.   80. Lamster, *Master of Shadows*, pp. 149–50.   81. Ibid., p. 144.   82. Ibid., pp. 191–2.   83. Ibid., pp. 196–7.   84. Ibid., pp. 209–10.   85. Wedgwood, 'Rubens and King Charles I'.   86. Ibid. Lamster, *Master of Shadows*, ch. 7.   87. See below, pp. 218–19.   88. Pierre, *Le Père Joseph*.   89. Petitfils, *Louis XIII*, p. 496.   90. The most persuasive interpretation of the some-times conflicting evidence on the *journée des dupes* is Petitfils, *Louis XIII*, ch. 15.   91. Hugon, *Au service du roi catholique*, p. 595.   92. Blanning, *Pursuit of Glory*, loc. 5017.   93. There is, for example, no reference to Rossignol (though a number to Père Joseph) in the classic study by J. H. Elliott, *Richelieu and Olivares*, or in the most recent British biography of Richelieu, by Anthony Levi. Petitfils, *Louis XIII*, contains numerous references to Père Joseph but mentions Rossignol only in passing as one of those whose company Richelieu enjoyed and esteemed (pp. 590, 605).   94. Vaillé, *Cabinet noir*, p. 53.   95. Ibid., pp. 53–4.   96. Hugon, *Au service du roi catholique*, p. 24, n. 19.   97. Levi, *Cardinal Richelieu*, p. 288, n. 12.   98. Vaillé, *Cabinet noir*, pp. 54–5.   99. Elliott, *Richelieu and Olivares*, pp. 112, 144–5, 154.   100. Ibid., p. 137.   101. Ibid., p. 164.   102. Perrault, *Hommes illustres*, pp. 57–8.   103. Vaillé, *Cabinet noir*, p. 57.   104. Mazarin to Hiérosme de Nouveau, *Surintendant des Postes*, 18 Jan.1660; Vaillé, *Cabinet noir*, pp. 63–4.   105. Perrault, *Hommes illustres*, pp. 57–8.   106. The present-day Académie Française's brief biography of Perrault describes him as Colbert's 'spokesman in the Académie'. http://www.academie-francaise.fr/les-immortels/charles-perrault, accessed 10 Jan. 2014. There is, surprisingly, no mention of Rossignol in Soll, *Information Master*. On Colbert and the *cabinet noir*, see Vaillé, *Cabinet noir*, pp. 59–66.

12 Intelligence and Regime Change in Britain

1. Review by Keith Thomas of Braddick, *God's Fury*; *Guardian*, 8 March 2008.   2. Marriott, *Life and Times of Lucius Cary*, p. 5.   3. *ODNB* Lucius Cary, 2nd Viscount Falkland.   4. *ODNB* Richard Royston. Additional material on Wright's allegation in 1897 edition of *Dictionary of National Biography*.   5. Stubbs,

Reprobates, p. 331.   **6.** Braddick, *God's Fury*, pp. 143–4.   **7.** *ODNB*. Richard Chaloner.   **8.** http://www.historyofparliamentonline.org/volume/1604-1629/member/tomkins-nathaniel-1584-1643.   **9.** Smith, *Royalist Agents, Conspirators and Spies*, p. 55.   **10.** *ODNB* John Wallis.   **11.** Scriba (ed.), 'Autobiography of John Wallis', p. 38.   **12.** http://books.google.co.uk/books/about/The_king_s_Cabinet_opened.html?id=-kk-AAAAcAAJ&redir_esc=y, accessed 18 March 2014.   **13.** Charles to the Queen, 5 March 1645; *King's Cabinet opened*, p. 8.   **14.** Ibid., pp. 43–4.   **15.** [Charles I], *Private Correspondence*, pp. 139–40.   **16.** *King's Cabinet opened*, p. 48.   **17.** *ODNB* Thomas Savile. http://www.historyofparliamenton line.org/volume/1604-1629/member/savile-sir-thomas-1590-16579.   **18.** [Charles I], *Private Correspondence*, pp. 139–40.   **19.** See above, pp. 176–9.   **20.** Kishlansky, *Monarchy Transformed*, pp. 158–9.   **21.** Robertson, *Tyrannicide Brief*, pp. 190–92.   **22.** Jordan and Walsh, *King's Revenge*, p. 2.   **23.** Ibid., pp. 76–8.   **24.** Firth (ed.), 'Thomas Scot's Account of His Actions', p. 118.   **25.** *ODNB* Thomas Scott.   **26.** Firth (ed.), 'Thomas Scot's Account of His Actions', p. 126.   **27.** *ODNB* Thomas Scott.   **28.** Ibid.; http://bcw-project.org/biography/thomas-scot, accessed 12 March 2014.   **29.** Firth (ed.), 'Thomas Scot's Account of His Actions', p. 119. For details of Werden's role in the Civil War and later use of his services by the Duke of York, who in 1685 succeeded his brother as James II, see *ODNB* Robert Werden.   **30.** *ODNB* Robert Werden.   **31.** Firth (ed.), 'Thomas Scot's Account of His Actions', p. 118.   **32.** Ibid., p. 121.   **33.** *ODNB* John Wallis.   **34.** Firth (ed.), 'Thomas Scot's Account of His Actions', p. 121.   **35.** See below, p. 251.   **36.** Jordan and Walsh, *King's Revenge*, pp. 81–2.   **37.** *ODNB* Robert Werden.   **38.** Stubbs, *Reprobates*, p. 406.   **39.** Clarendon, *History of the Rebellion*, p. 350.   **40.** Ibid., p. 351.   **41.** Ibid., p. 352.   **42.** See below, p. 236.   **43.** 'The King's own account of his adventures, dictated to Mr. Samuel Pepys', in Blount, *Boscobel*, pp. 140–41.   **44.** Clarendon, *History of the Rebellion*, vol. 2, p. 781.   **45.** *ODNB* Edward Hyde.   **46.** Thurloe to Sir Harbottle Grimston, ?May 1660; Thurloe, *State Papers*, 7.914. http://www.british-history.ac.uk/thurloe-papers/vol7/pp912-915.   **47.** Cromwell to Thurloe, 28 July 1655; in Carlyle (ed.), *Oliver Cromwell's Letters and Speeches*, vol. 3, pp. 139–40.   **48.** *ODNB* Sealed Knot.   **49.** Westbury [Edward Villiers] (London) to Mons[ieur] Barsiere [Sir Edward Hyde], au cheval noir, rue St Honore, Paris, 2 February 1653 [1654]; Thurloe, *State Papers*, 2.64.   **50.** *ODNB* Sealed Knot.   **51.** http://bcw-project.org/military/royalist-conspiracies/penruddocks-uprising, accessed 22 March 2014.   **52.** Aubrey, *Mr Secretary Thurloe*, p. 101. Smith, *Royalist Agents, Conspirators and Spies*, pp. 204–6.   **53.** Details of the cipher given by Thurloe to Manning at http://www.h4.dion.ne.jp/~room4me/america/code/thurloe.htm, accessed 23 March 2014.   **54.** *CSP 1655*, pp. 192–3, 235.   **55.** Aubrey, *Mr Secretary Thurloe*, pp. 102ff.   **56.** Thurloe, *State Papers*, 5.534; www.british-history.ac.uk/thurloe-papers/vol5.   **57.** Marshall, 'Sir Samuel Morland and Stuart Espionage'. *ODNB* Sir Samuel Morland.   **58.** Marshall, *Intelligence and Espionage*, p. 24.   **59.** http://www.h4.dion.ne.jp/~room4me/america/code/thurloe.htm, accessed 10 April 2014.   **60.** *ODNB* John Thurloe.   **61.** *ODNB* George Downing. On Downing Street, see https://www.gov.uk/government/history/10-downing-street, accessed

14 April 2014. 62. *ODNB* George Downing. 63. *CSP Venice, 1655–6*, p. 188. 64. Aubrey, *Mr Secretary Thurloe*, p. 94. 65. *ODNB* John Thurloe. 66. Ibid. Aubrey, *Mr Secretary Thurloe*. 67. *ODNB* George Booth. 68. *ODNB* Thomas Scot. 69. Skinner, *Life of General Monck*, p. 199. 70. Ibid., pp. 193–4. 71. Ibid., p. 197. 72. Ibid., p. 201. 73. Ibid., p. 211. 74. Ibid., pp. 208–9. 75. Ibid., p. 233. 76. *ODNB* Thomas Scot. 77. *ODNB* John Thurloe. 78. Thurloe, *State Papers*, 7.837–8. *ODNB* George Downing. 79. Hutton, *Restoration*, pp. 17–19. *ODNB* John Grenville. 80. *ODNB* George Downing. 81. *ODNB* John Thurloe. 82. Firth (ed.), 'Thomas Scot's Account of His Actions', p. 116. 83. Jordan and Walsh, *King's Revenge*, p. 195. 84. Firth (ed.), 'Thomas Scot's Account of His Actions', p. 117. 85. Ibid., p. 123. 86. Jordan and Walsh, *King's Revenge*, p. 241. 87. Ibid., pp. 270–71. 88. *ODNB* William Blencowe. 89. Jordan and Walsh, *King's Revenge*, pp. 271–8. 90. Marshall, *Intelligence and Espionage*, pp. 345–6. 91. *ODNB* John Okey. 92. *ODNB* George Downing. 93. Jordan and Walsh, *King's Revenge*, pp. 298–9. 94. Marshall, *Intelligence and Espionage*, pp. 292–3. *ODNB* Joseph Williamson. 95. Marshall, *Intelligence and Espionage*, pp. 295–6. 96. Ibid., pp. 296–8. Jordan and Walsh, *King's Revenge*, pp. 302–4. *ODNB* John Lisle. 97. *ODNB* Thomas Goffe. CSP col., 5.54, 345. 98. Jordan and Walsh, *King's Revenge*, pp. 315–16. *ODNB* Aphra Behn. Todd, *Secret Life of Aphra Behn*, chs. 7, 8, 9. 99. Fraser, *Intelligence of the Secretaries of State*, ch. 4. *ODNB* Samuel Pepys. 100. Herman, *Intelligence Power*, p. 223. 101. Pepys, diary, 22 June 1667; http://www.pepys.info/1667/1667jun.html#19. 102. Kishlansky, *Monarchy Transformed*, p. 245. *ODNB* Charles II. 103. Fraser, *Intelligence of the Secretaries of State*, ch. 5. 104. *ODNB* John Wallis. 105. John Ellis to Wallis, 7 Oct. 1669; Beeley and Scriba (eds.), *Correspondence of John Wallis*, vol. 3, p. 252. 106. Wallis to Harbord, 15 Aug. 1691, 'Letter Book of Dr John Wallis, 1651–1701', BL Add. MS 32499; transcript in Smith, 'John Wallis as a Cryptographer', pp. 90–93. 107. Marshall, *Intelligence and Espionage*, chs. 4, 5. Cressy, *Dangerous Talk*, ch. 9. 108. Cressy, *Dangerous Talk*, pp. 210–11. 109. *ODNB* Sir Edmund Berry Godfrey. 110. *ODNB* Titus Oates. 111. *ODNB* Edward Colman. 112. *ODNB* Robert Spencer. 113. Cressy, *Dangerous Talk*, p. 259. 114. *ODNB* Titus Oates.

13 Intelligence in the Era of the Sun King

1. Blanning, *Pursuit of Glory*, loc. 8473. 2. Bély, *Secrets de Louis XIV*, pp. 17–18. 3. Ibid. See above, p. 206. 4. Vaillé, *Cabinet noir*, pp. 83–4. 5. Ibid., p. 76. 6. Soll, *Information Master*, pp. 3–4. 7. Dessert, *Argent, pouvoir et société*, pp. 293–4. 8. Soll, *Reckoning*, loc. 1761. 9. Ibid., loc. 1784. 10. Petitfils, *Véritable d'Artagnan*. 11. Bély, *Secrets de Louis XIV*, p. 198. Soll, *Reckoning*, loc. 1790. 12. Soll, *Information Master*, pp. 84–93, 144. 13. Ibid., ch. 1. Soll subtitles his book *Jean-Baptiste Colbert's Secret State Intelligence System*. 14. Vaillé, *Cabinet noir*, p. 88. 15. Ibid., p. 69. 16. Hebbert and Rothrock, *Soldier of France*. 17. Lynn, *Wars of Louis XIV*, p. 22. 18. Ibid., ch. 4. 19. Bély, *Secrets de Louis XIV*,

pp. 306–7.   20. Ekberg, 'From Dutch to European War', p. 396.   21. See above, p. 213.   22. Soll, *Reckoning*, ch. 6.   23. Vaillé, *Cabinet noir*, pp. 69–70.   24. Bély, *Secrets de Louis XIV*, pp. 390–96.   25. Ibid., pp. 236–7.   26. See above, pp. 236–7.   27. Kenyon, *Robert Spencer*, pp. 35–41.   28. Pincus, *1688*, pp. 317–19.   29. *ODNB* Nassau van Zuylestein.   30. Kampmann, 'English Crisis'.   31. Kishlansky, *Monarchy Transformed*, pp. 278–9.   32. Israel and Parker, 'Of Providence and Protestant Winds', pp. 338–41.   33. Marshall, *Intelligence and Espionage*, p. 301.   34. Pincus, *1688*, ch. 8. Harris, *Rebellion*, pp. 296–7, 303–5.   35. *ODNB* John Wallis.   36. Leeuw, 'Black Chamber in the Dutch Republic', p. 138.   37. Ibid., p. 138.   38. Claydon, *William III and the Godly Revolution*, p. 93.   39. Wallis to Nottingham, 1 Aug. 1689, *CSP Domestic 1689*.   40. French decrypt enclosed with Wallis to Nottingham, 10 Aug. 1689, *CSP Domestic 1689*.   41. Wallis to Nottingham, 13 Aug. 1698, 'Letter Book of Dr John Wallis, 1651–1701', BL Add. MS 32499; transcript in Smith, 'John Wallis as a Cryptographer', p. 86.   42. Wallis to Nottingham, 10 Aug. 1689, *CSP Domestic 1689*.   43. Wallis to [Richard] Hampden, 3 Aug. 1698, 'Letter Book of Dr John Wallis, 1651–1701', BL Add. MS 32499; transcript in Smith, 'John Wallis as a Cryptographer', p. 87.   44. Wallis to Harbord, 15 Aug. 1691, 'Letter Book of Dr John Wallis, 1651–1701', BL Add. MS 32499; transcript in Smith, 'John Wallis as a Cryptographer', p. 91.   45. Ibid., p. 90.   46. Wallis to James Johnston (ambassador in Berlin), 9 June 1692, 'Letter Book of Dr John Wallis, 1651–1701', BL Add. MS 32499; transcript in Smith, 'John Wallis as a Cryptographer', p. 94.   47. Portrait by Sir Godfrey Kneller of John Wallis, 1701; Examination Schools, University of Oxford.   48. Wallis to Earl of Shrewsbury, 5 Nov. 1689, *CSP Domestic 1689*. Wallis to Earl of Nottingham, 22 Dec. 1689, *CSP Domestic 1689*.   49. Wallis to Earl of Nottingham, 22 Dec. 1689, *CSP Domestic 1689*.   50. Wallis to Earl of Shrewsbury, 5 Nov. 1689, *CSP Domestic 1689*. Wallis to Earl of Nottingham, 22 Dec. 1689, *CSP Domestic 1689*. Earl of Nottingham to Wallis, 31 Dec. 1689, *CSP Domestic 1689*.   51. Smith, 'John Wallis as a Cryptographer' pp. 82–96. Kahn, *Codebreakers*, p. 169. See below, p. 263.   52. Wallis to Nottingham, 12 Nov. 1689, 'Letter Book of Dr John Wallis, 1651–1701', BL Add. MS 32499; transcript in Smith, 'John Wallis as a Cryptographer', pp. 88–9.   53. Wallis to Harbord, 15 Aug. 1691, 'Letter Book of Dr John Wallis, 1651–1701', BL Add. MS 32499; transcript in Smith, 'John Wallis as a Cryptographer', pp. 92–3.   54. Holmes, *Marlborough*, p. 130f.   55. Schnath, *Geschichte Hannovers*, vol. 2, pp. 354–8. Leeuw, 'Black Chamber in the Dutch Republic', pp. 139–41.   56. Wallis to Tilson, 20 March 1701, 'Letter Book of Dr John Wallis, 1651–1701', BL Add. MS 32499; transcript in Smith, 'John Wallis as a Cryptographer', p. 84. On the British–Hanoverian codebreaking alliance established after the Hanoverian succession, see above, p. 270.   57. Ibid., pp. 83–4. Kahn, *Codebreakers*, p. 169.   58. Bély, *Secrets de Louis XIV*, pp. 454, 457.   59. *ODNB* John Drummond.   60. Bély, *Secrets de Louis XIV*, p. 457.   61. Cressy, *Dangerous Talk*, p. 228.   62. Weil, *A Plague of Informers*, pp. 104–6.   63. Pincus, *1688*, p. 444.   64. *ODNB* John Churchill.   65. See below, p. 267.   66. See above, pp. 224–5.   67. Weil, *Plague of Informers*, pp. 104–6.   68. Ibid., pp. 108–13. *ODNB* William Fuller.   69. Nottingham to Jephson, 2 July

1690, *CSP Domestic 1690*.   70. See above, pp. 238–41.   71. Weil, *Plague of Informers*, pp. 108–13. *ODNB* William Fuller.   72. Pincus, *1688*, p. 439.   73. *ODNB* Sir George Barclay. *ODNB* Thomas Prendergast (also known as Prendergrass); Weil, *Plague of Informers*, ch. 7.   74. *ODNB* James Fitzjames, Duke of Berwick.   75. *ODNB* John Drummond.   76. Kishlansky, *Monarchy Transformed*, ch. 13.   77. Somerset, *Queen Anne*. Kishlansky, *Monarchy Transformed*, p. 316.   78. Holmes, *Marlborough*, p. 479.   79. *ODNB* William Cadogan.   80. Holmes, *Marlborough*, pp. 216–17.   81. Ibid., pp. 176–7, 215–16.   82. *ODNB* Jean de Robethon.   83. Holmes, *Marlborough*, p. 261.   84. Ibid., pp. 8–9.   85. Ibid., p. 297.   86. Leeuw, 'Black Chamber in the Dutch Republic', pp. 142–4.   87. Blencowe, 'French Ministers Letterbook 1702–1712', BL Add. MSS 32,306; cited by Leeuw, 'Black Chamber in the Dutch Republic'.   88. *ODNB* William Blencowe.   89. Leeuw, 'Black Chamber in the Dutch Republic', p. 146.   90. Ibid., pp. 144–6.   91. Schnath, *Geschichte Hannovers*, vol. 2, p. 358.   92. Leeuw, 'Black Chamber in the Dutch Republic', pp. 147–52.   93. Holmes, *Marlborough*, pp. 215–16. Leeuw, 'Black Chamber in the Dutch Republic', p. 146.   94. Kishlansky, *Monarchy Transformed*, p. 332.   95. Holmes, *Marlborough*, p. 411.   96. Lynn, *Wars of Louis XIV*, loc. 1093.   97. Kishlansky, *A Monarchy Transformed*, p. 47.   98. *ODNB* Daniel Defoe.   99. John Kerrigan, 'The Secret Agent', *Guardian*, 8 March 2008.   100. *ODNB* Robert Harley. Others have argued that the £20,000 paid to Scottish politicians was the overdue payment of salaries and pensions.   101. Jones, 'Antoine de Guiscard'.   102. The best account of the assassination attempt is Jones, 'Robert Harley and the Myth of the Golden Thread'. See also Jones, 'Antoine de Guiscard' and *ODNB* Robert Harley (both of which repeat the 'golden thread' story).   103. *ODNB* Matthew Prior.   104. *ODNB* John Churchill.

14 Codebreakers and Spies in Ancien Régime Europe

1. Szechi, *Jacobitism and Tory Politics*, ch. 1.   2. Ibid., ch. 1 and Conclusion.   3. *ODNB* John Erskine, Earl of Mar.   4. MacInnes, *Clanship, Commerce, and the House of Stuart*, p. 200.   5. Foreign and Commonwealth Office, Historical Branch, 'My Purdah Lady', p. 3. Ellis, *Post Office in the Eighteenth Century*, p. 74. On George I's previous experience of codebreaking, see above, pp. 255–6, 264.   6. See above, p. 263.   7. Ellis, *Post Office in the Eighteenth Century*, p. 73.   8. Ibid.   9. Chance, 'The "Swedish Plot" of 1716–17'. *Letters which Passed between Count Gyllenborg, the Barons Gortz, Sparre, and Others*. On the publication of Charles I's correspondence, see above, pp. 216–18.   10. Pearce, *Great Man*, p. 152.   11. Ellis, *Post Office in the Eighteenth Century*, p. 73.   12. See above, p. 254.   13. *ODNB* Edward Willes.   14. Ellis, *Post Office in the Eighteenth Century*, p. 129.   15. Ibid. *ODNB* Edward Willes. Codebreakers, Corbiere among them, are underrepresented in the otherwise admirably comprehensive *ODNB*.   16. On Kelly, see *ODNB* George Kelly.   17. *ODNB* James Butler, 2nd Duke of Ormond.   18. Pearce, *Great Man*, p. 163.   19. *ODNB* Francis Atterbury.   20. Pearce, *Great Man*, p. 159.   21. *ODNB* Christopher Layer.   22. Deposition of William Squire

concerning the arrest of Christopher Layer, 29 Sept. 1722, CUL MS Ch(H)69/2/28.   23. *ODNB* Christopher Layer.   24. *ODNB* John Erskine, Earl of Mar.   25. 'T. Illington' (Francis Atterbury) to 'Mr Musgrave' (Earl of Mar), decrypted 'true Copy' of 'the Original Letter', CUL MS Ch(H)69/4/11. It was later claimed during Atterbury's trial that the correspondence was forged.   26. *ODNB* Francis Atterbury. *ODNB* John Erskine, Earl of Mar. Pearce, *Great Man*, p. 151.   27. *Declaration of James the Third King of England, Scotland and Ireland, &c . . . , with a cover addressed [from Lucca] to M. Lunelle at Slaughter's Coffee House*, 10 Sept. 1722, CUL MS Ch(H)69/5/23.   28. *ODNB* Robert Walpole. *ODNB* Francis Atterbury. Pearce, *Great Man*, pp. 169–70.   29. Anxious to avoid implicating either himself or Atterbury in Jacobite conspiracy, Kelly claimed that Harlequin was in fact a present from himself to Mrs Barnes, his former landlady. Mrs Barnes was duly called before the investigating committee and confirmed that the 'little dog' had indeed been meant for Mrs Atterbury. Examination of Jane Barnes before a Committee of the Council (signed by Mrs Barnes), London, 23 May 1722, CUL MS Ch(H)69/5/4.   30. Cruickshanks and Erskine-Hill, *Atterbury Plot*, pp. 208–9.   31. Ibid., p. 209.   32. Ibid., pp. 209–10.   33. See above, p. 179.   34. Jonathan Swift, *Gulliver's Travels*, part III.   35. Ellis, *Post Office in the Eighteenth Century*, pp. 128–30. *ODNB* Edward Willes.   36. BL Add. MSS 32270; cited, with other references, by Ellis, *Post Office in the Eighteenth Century*, p. 73. There has so far been no detailed research on the Austrian decrypts.   37. Ellis, *Post Office in the Eighteenth Century*, p. 73.   38. There is no mention of codebreaking in Genêt, *Espions des lumières*.   39. Soboleva, *Istoriia Shifroval-nogo Dela v Rossii*, pp. 117–19. Izmozik, 'Chernye kabinety', pp. 609–10. O'Connor and Robertson, 'Christian Goldbach'.   40. Soboleva, *Istoriia Shifrov-alnogo Dela v Rossii*, pp. 119–29. Izmozik, 'Chernye kabinety', pp. 77–83. Kahn, *Codebreakers*, p. 617. Massie, *Catherine the Great*, ch. 8. La Chétardie's intercepted despatches are at http://elcocheingles.com/Memories/Texts/Shetardie/Shetardie.htm.   41. Kahn, *Codebreakers*, pp. 163–5.   42. Schlitter (ed.), *Correspondance Secrète*, p. 124.   43. Ibid., pp. 124–5.   44. Ibid., p. 117.   45. Ibid., p. 124.   46. Szabo, *Kaunitz and Enlightened Absolutism*, p. 20.   47. Kahn, *Codebreakers*, pp. 163–5.   48. Genêt, *Espions des lumières*, pp. 7–9.   49. Thomson and Padover, *Secret Diplomacy*, p. 165.   50. Savage, 'Foreign Policy and Political Culture', pp. 307–8. Conlin, 'The Strange Case of the Chevalier d'Eon'.   51. Darnton, 'The News in Paris', pp. 56–7.   52. Genêt, *Espions des lumières*, p. 455.   53. BL Add. MSS 32686–32992. Foreign and Commonwealth Office, Historical Branch, 'My Purdah Lady'.   54. Andrew, *Secret Service*, p. 3.   55. On Chauvelin, see Bréban, 'Germain Louis Chauvelin'.   56. *ODNB* James Waldegrave.   57. Ibid.   58. *Dictionnaire de biographie française*, vol. 14, p. 30.   59. Ibid., vol. 7, p. 722. There is no mention in the *Dictionnaire* of Bussy's recruitment as a British agent.   60. Harding, *Emergence of Britain's Global Naval Supremacy*, pp. 33ff.   61. *Dictionnaire de biographie française*, vol. 7, p. 722.   62. *ODNB* James Waldegrave. *Dictionnaire de biographie française*, vol. 7, p. 722.   63. Douglas, *Jacobite Spy Wars*, pp. 50–51. Genêt, *Espions des lumières*, pp. 203–5.   64. *ODNB* Dudley Bradstreet. Douglas, *Jacobite Spy Wars*, chs. 7, 8.   65. See above, p. 272.   66. Douglas, *Jacobite*

Spy Wars, chs. 10, 11. *ODNB* Flora Macdonald. 67. McLynn, *Bonnie Prince Charlie*, p. 384. 68. *ODNB* Charles Edward Stuart. 69. Douglas, *Jacobite Spy Wars*, p. 55. 70. Lang, *Pickle the Spy*. 71. Douglas, *Jacobite Spy Wars*, p. 224. 72. Ibid., pp. 226–8. 73. Frederick's *Principes généraux* of 1748, cited in Luvaas, *Frederick the Great on the Art of War*, p. 114. 74. Frederick's interest in spies tends to be underestimated. There is no mention, for example, in the excellent studies by Clark, *Iron Kingdom*, and Showalter, *Frederick the Great: A Military History*. 75. Frederick II ('the Great'), 'Military Instructions' to his generals, article XII; http://www.au.af.mil/au/awc/awcgate/readings/fred_instructions.htm. 76. Genêt, *Espions des lumières*, pp. 98–9. 77. Frederick II ('the Great'), 'Military Instructions' to his generals, article XII; http://www.au.af.mil/au/awc/awcgate/readings/fred_instructions.htm. 78. Ibid. 79. Everth, *Öffentlichkeit in der Aussenpolitik*, pp. 355–60. Simms, *Europe: The Struggle for Supremacy*, p. 112. 80. Schieder, *Friedrich der Grosse*, p. 178. Blanning, *Frederick the Great*, p. 202. 81. The surviving records of the Deciphering Branch contain no French decrypts for the period 1756–62; Ellis, *Post Office in the Eighteenth Century*, p. 73. However, other sources show that the British cabinet discussed the text of at least one important French decrypt in August 1761; see below, p. 289. 82. Horace Walpole to George Montagu, 21 Oct. 1759; *Letters from the Hon. Horace Walpole to George Montagu, Esq.*, pp. 179–80. 83. Blanning, *Frederick the Great*, pp. 221–3. Duffy, *Frederick the Great*, pp. 146–54. 84. Black, *British Diplomats and Diplomacy*, p. 143. 85. *Dictionnaire de biographie française*, vol. 7, pp. 722–3. 86. Bussy to Choiseul, 30 Aug. 1761; cited by Black, *Pitt the Elder*, p. 215. 87. *Dictionnaire de biographie française*, vol. 7, pp. 722–3. 88. Black, *Pitt the Elder*, p. 217. 89. *ODNB* John Stuart, 3rd Earl of Bute. 90. Black, *Pitt the Elder*, p. 220. 91. Kahn, *Codebreakers*, pp. 172–3. Temperley, 'Pitt's Retirement from Office, 5 Oct. 1761'. 92. 'Secret Service' [A History of the Secret Vote up to 1914], p. 4, TNA T1/11689/25138. 93. Massie, *Catherine the Great*, ch. 41. 94. Ellis, *Post Office in the Eighteenth Century*, p. 73. 95. Massie, *Catherine the Great*, ch. 42. 96. Sebag Montefiore, *Prince of Princes*, pp. 48–52.

15 Intelligence and American Independence

1. Tombs and Tombs, *That Sweet Enemy*, p. 155. 2. Alsop, *Yankees at the Court*, p. 25. 3. Tombs and Tombs, *That Sweet Enemy*, p. 158. 4. Conlin, 'Strange Case of the Chevalier d'Eon'. Conlin, 'Wilkes, the Chevalier d'Eon and "the dregs of liberty"' 5. Ibid. 6. Lucy Peltz, curator of eighteenth-century portraits at the National Portrait Gallery, quoted in 'Portrait mistaken for 18th-century lady is early painting of transvestite', *Guardian*, 6 June 2012. 7. Conlin, 'Strange Case of the Chevalier d'Eon'. On the complex issues raised by d'Éon's unprecedented career, see Burrows et al. (eds.), *Chevalier d'Eon and His Worlds*. 8. www.beaumontsociety.org.uk/downloads/Biography.pdf. 9. Tombs and Tombs, *That Sweet Enemy*, p. 163. 10. Schaeper, *Edward Bancroft*, pp. 195–8. 11. *ODNB* Benjamin Franklin. 12. Isaacson, *Benjamin Franklin*, ch. 13. 13. Ibid. 14. 'Engagement of Dr Edwards [Bancroft] to correspond with P. Wentworth and Lord

Stormont, and the means of conducting that correspondence', 13 Dec. 1776, BL Add. MSS 34, 413.   **15.** Isaacson, *Benjamin Franklin*, ch. 13; Schaeper, *Edward Bancroft*, pp. 125–32.   **16.** Schaeper, *Edward Bancroft*, pp. 179–80, 188–9. Tombs and Tombs, *That Sweet Enemy*, p. 172.   **17.** Isaacson, *Benjamin Franklin*, ch. 13.   **18.** Schaeper, *Edward Bancroft*, p. 147.   **19.** Rakove, *Revolutionaries*, p. 250. Schaeper, *Edward Bancroft*, ch. 7.   **20.** Ibid., p. 90.   **21.** Isaacson, *Benjamin Franklin*, p. 342.   **22.** Schaeper, *Edward Bancroft*, p. 99.   **23.** Isaacson, *Benjamin Franklin*, p. 357.   **24.** Rose, 'Founding Fathers of American Intelligence'. Isaacson, *Benjamin Franklin*, ch. 13.   **25.** Schaeper, *Edward Bancroft*, p. 115.   **26.** Ibid., p. 93.   **27.** Ibid., p. 94.   **28.** Ibid., p. 96.   **29.** Andrew and Mitrokhin, *Mitrokhin Archive*, pp. 137–41.   **30.** Isaacson, *Benjamin Franklin*, ch. 13. Schaeper, *Edward Bancroft*, p. 139.   **31.** Rose, 'Founding Fathers of American Intelligence'.   **32.** Ellis, *Post Office in the Eighteenth Century*, p. 73. See above, pp. 287–91.   **33.** Schaeper, *Edward Bancroft*, p. 159.   **34.** Ibid., pp. 142, 160.   **35.** See below, pp. 306–7.   **36.** Schaeper, *Edward Bancroft*, p. 161.   **37.** Kahn, *Codebreakers*, p. 187.   **38.** Washington to Colonel Elias Dayton, 26 July 1777. The original is in the Walter L. Pforzheimer Collection on Intelligence Service (in Washington when consulted by the author, now at Yale).   **39.** Andrew, *For the President's Eyes Only*, p. 6. Nagy, *George Washington's Secret Spy War*.   **40.** Jackson (ed.), *Diaries of George Washington*, vol. 1, pp. 144–5. Washington's less frank published account of his mission made him a celebrity on both sides of the Atlantic. http://www.mountvernon.org/education/primary-sources-2/article/the-journal-of-major-george-washinton/.   **41.** Flexner, *George Washington*, chs. 5, 6. Ferling, *First of Men*, ch. 2. Lewis, *For King and Country*, chs. 9, 10.   **42.** Washington to Robert Hunter Morris, 5 Jan. 1766; Fitzpatrick (ed.), *Writings of George Washington*, vol. 1, p. 268.   **43.** Washington to John Hancock, 21 July 1775; Chase (ed.), *Papers of George Washington: Revolutionary War Series*, vol. 1, p. 138.   **44.** Fitzpatrick (ed.), *Writings of George Washington*, vol. 3, p. 407n.   **45.** Chase (ed.), *Papers of George Washington: Revolutionary War Series*, vol. 1, p. 38. Cf. pp. 57, 79, 91, 138, 306, 332–3, 399, 410, 421, 437, 458, 459.   **46.** Ibid., vol. 3, pp. 528–9.   **47.** Bass, 'Nathan Hale's Mission'. Kilmeade and Yaeger, *George Washington's Secret Six*, pp. 20–26.   **48.** Andrew, *For the President's Eyes Only*, p. 8.   **49.** Kessler, *Undercover Washington*, p. 123.   **50.** O'Toole, *Honorable Treachery*, p. 42. Fleming, 'George Washington, General'. Andrew, *For the President's Eyes Only*, pp. 9–10.   **51.** Kilmeade and Yaeger, *George Washington's Secret Six*, p. 58.   **52.** Ibid., pp. 35–6.   **53.** Rose, 'Founding Fathers of American Intelligence'.   **54.** See above, pp. 228–30.   **55.** Randall, *Benedict Arnold*, chs. 18, 19. *ODNB* Benedict Arnold.   **56.** Bakeless, *Turncoats, Traitors and Heroes*, p. 335.   **57.** Grainger, *Battle of Yorktown*, ch. 3.   **58.** 'Aristarchus' to George III, report no. 83, 15 Jan. 1781, Royal Archives. *George III – The Genius of the Mad King*, BBC2, 30 Jan. 2017. Valentine Low, 'The ageing spy who saved George III', *The Times*, 28 Jan. 2017.   **59.** Conley, 'British Intelligence Operations', chs. 4, 5.   **60.** The latest study of the Yorktown campaign is Ketchum, *Victory at Yorktown*.   **61.** Fitzpatrick (ed.), *Writings of George Washington*, vol. 23, pp. 189–90. Cf. pp. 210, 308n.   **62.** Mulford, 'Benjamin Franklin's Savage Eloquence'.   **63.** Fitzpatrick (ed.), *Writings of George Washington*, vol. 24,

p. 98. 64. Soll, *Reckoning*, ch. 10. Fishman, Pederson and Rozell (eds.), *George Washington*, p. 175. 65. Sayle, 'Historical Underpinnings of the U.S. Intelligence Community', p. 9. 66. Andrew, *For the President's Eyes Only*, pp. 11–12. On the publishing history of *The Spy*, see the introduction by J. E. Morpurgo to the Oxford University Press edition, first published in 1988. 67. See below, pp. 422–4, 458, 527–8.

16 The French Revolution and the Revolutionary Wars

1. Tombs and Tombs, *That Sweet Enemy*, p. 193. 2. *ODNB* John Frederick Sackville. 3. Browning (ed.), *The Despatches of Earl Gower*, p. xvii. 4. *ODNB* George Granville Leveson Gower. 5. Marquis, *Agents de l'ennemi*, p. 35. 6. *ODNB* William Augustus Miles. 7. *ODNB* Hugh Elliot. 8. Browning (ed.), *Despatches of Earl Gower*, pp. 38–9. 9. Hague, *William Pitt the Younger*, loc. 5185. 10. Browning (ed.), *Despatches of Earl Gower*, p. 22. 11. Cobban, *History of Modern France*, vol. 1, pp. 164–5. 12. Price, *Fall of the French Monarchy*, ch. 7. 13. Ibid., ch. 8. 14. Browning (ed.), *Despatches of Earl Gower*, p. 98. 15. Price, *Fall of the French Monarchy*, ch. 8. 16. Marquis, *Agents de l'ennemi*, pp. 91–111. 17. *ODNB* William Pitt the Younger. 18. Tombs and Tombs, *That Sweet Enemy*, p. 207. 19. Monro's main reports from Paris were published in 1885 as a supplement (which has since been little noticed) to Browning (ed.), *Despatches of Earl Gower*. 20. On Monro's previous experience in penetrating English groups suspected of support for French republicanism, see Monro to Grenville, 10 Jan. 1793, in Browning (ed.), *Despatches of Earl Gower*, p. 277. 21. Monro to Grenville, 4 and 6 Sept. 1792, in ibid., pp. 225–9, 232–5. 22. Cobban, *History of Modern France*, vol. 1, pp. 196–8. Schama, *Citizens*, pp. 624–5, 635. 23. Monro to Grenville, 4 Sept. 1792, in Browning (ed.), *Despatches of Earl Gower*, p. 229. 24. Monro to Grenville, 17 Dec. 1792, in ibid., pp. 260–61. *ODNB* Thomas Paine. *ODNB* Robert Merry. 25. Monro to Grenville, 31 Dec. 1792, in Browning (ed.), *Despatches of Earl Gower*, pp. 268–9. 26. Monro to Grenville, 7 Jan. 1793, in ibid., pp. 272–3. 27. Monro to Grenville, 21 Jan. 1793, in ibid., p. 279. 28. Price, *Fall of the French Monarchy*, ch. 8. 29. Monro to Grenville, 10 Jan. 1793, in Browning (ed.), *Despatches of Earl Gower*, pp. 276–7. 30. Swords, *Green Cockade*, p. 116. 31. Marquis, *Agents de l'ennemi*, pp. 39–41. 32. Walton, *Policing Public Opinion*, Introduction. Cobban, *History of Modern France*, vol. 1, p. 210. 33. In *Reflections on the Revolution in France*. 34. Walton, *Policing Public Opinion*, Introduction. 35. Church, *Revolution and Red Tape*, pp. 86–8. 36. Robespierre, speech of 8 Thermidor, Year II: http://www.youscribe.com/catalogue/ressources-pedagogiques/savoirs/sciences-humaines-et-sociales/discours-de-robespierre-303751. 37. Marquis, *Agents de l'ennemi*, pp. 47–52. 38. Cobb, *Police and the People*, pp. 6–13. 39. Lawday, *Danton*, ch. 19. 40. Cobb, *Police and the People*, pp. 6–13. 41. Ibid., p. 17. 42. Schama, *Citizens*, loc. 14662. 43. Hunt, *Culture and Class in the French Revolution*, p. 41. 44. Cubitt, 'Robespierre and Conspiracy Theories'. 45. Robespierre, speech of 8 Thermidor, Year II: http://www.youscribe.com/catalogue/ressources-pedagogiques/savoirs/sciences-humaines-et-sociales/discours-de-robespierre-303751. 46. Tombs, *The English and Their History*, pp.

184–5.   47. Sparrow, 'Alien Office'. *ODNB* Evan Nepean.   48. Durey, *William Wickham, Master Spy*, chs. 1, 2. *ODNB* William Wickham.   49. Ibid.   50. Thale (ed.), *Selections from the Papers of the London Corresponding Society*, p. 27.   51. Cressy, *Dangerous Talk*, pp. 245–6.   52. Thale (ed.), *Selections from the Papers of the London Corresponding Society*, p. 113. Durey, *William Wickham, Master Spy*, loc. 1015.   53. Durey, *William Wickham, Master Spy*, loc. 1015, 1039.   54. *ODNB* William Wickham.   55. Thompson, *Making of the English Working Class*, ch. 1.   56. Emsley, 'Home Office and Its Sources', p. 559.   57. Tombs, *The English and Their History*, p. 591.   58. Grenville to Wickham, 9 Dec. 1794; http://www.napoleon-series.org/research/government/british/Espionage/c_espionageChapter1.html#_ftn5.   59. The late, great Richard Cobb saw Wickham as a somewhat comic figure; Cobb, 'Our Man in Berne'. More recent research takes him much more seriously. Roger Knight concludes that Wickham 'deserves his recently bestowed title of "Master Spy"' Knight, *Britain Against Napoleon*, p. 123. Durey, *William Wickham, Master Spy*, ch. 3.   60. Marquis, *Agents de l'ennemi*, p. 177.   61. Ibid., pp. 180–81.   62. Mitchell, *Underground War against Revolutionary France*, pp. 256–60.   63. Durey, *William Wickham, Master Spy*, ch. 3.   64. Hilton, *A Mad, Bad and Dangerous People?*, p. 84.   65. Durey, *William Wickham, Master Spy*, ch. 4.   66. Cobban, *History of Modern France*, vol. 1, p. 245.   67. Durey, *William Wickham, Master Spy*, loc. 2217.   68. Marquis, *Agents de l'ennemi*, p. 194.   69. Durey, *William Wickham, Master Spy*, loc. 2316.   70. Ibid., ch. 4.   71. Marquis, *Agents de l'ennemi*, p. 199.   72. Wickham to Talbot, 27 Nov. 1797; Sparrow, *Secret Service*, p. 3. For evidence of the penetration of Wickham's Swiss office, see Marquis, *Agents de l'ennemi*, pp. 150–51.   73. Tombs and Tombs, *That Sweet Enemy*, p. 223. Quinault, 'French Invasion of Pembrokeshire'.   74. Johnston, *Unusual Suspects*, ch. 12. Wilkes, *Regency Spies*, pp. 33–8. Walsh's reports are in TNA HO 42/41.   75. On Thelwall, see above, p. 329.   76. Wilson, 'Lost Art of Table Talk', p. 1.   77. Johnston, *Unusual Suspects*, ch. 12.   78. Roberts, *Napoleon the Great*, loc. 3306.   79. Harari, *Sapiens*, pp. 317–18.   80. Knight, *Britain Against Napoleon*, p. 144.   81. Ibid., p. 146.   82. Rodger, *Command of the Ocean*, p. 458. Knight, *Britain Against Napoleon*, p. 145.   83. Cole, *Napoleon's Egypt*, ch. 1.   84. Rodger, *Command of the Ocean*, pp. 458–9.   85. Ibid., p. 459.   86. Knight, *Britain Against Napoleon*, p. 147.   87. Ibid., p. 92.   88. Ibid., p. 148.   89. Durey, 'Lord Grenville and the "Smoking Gun"' Durey, *William Wickham, Master Spy*, p. 101.   90. Tombs and Tombs, *That Sweet Enemy*, loc. 5553.   91. Hague, *William Pitt the Younger*, loc. 7882.   92. Marquis, *Agents de l'ennemi*, pp. 248–51.   93. Knight, *Britain Against Napoleon*, p. 91.   94. Durey, *William Wickham, Master Spy*, loc. 2511.   95. Durey, *william wickham, Master spy* loc. 3803.   96. Knight, *Britain Against Napoleon*, p. 151.   97. Ibid.   98. Durey, *William Wickham, Master Spy*, ch. 7. *ODNB* William Wickham.   99. Durey, *William Wickham, Master Spy*, loc. 3226.   100. *ODNB* Edward Willes. Black, *British Diplomats and Diplomacy*, p. 134.   101. See above, p. 239.   102. On Napoleon's invasion plans and the British response, see Knight, *Britain Against Napoleon*, ch. 9.   103. Roberts, *Napoleon the Great*, loc. 6577ff. https://www.theguardian.com/world/2014/sep/27/plot-kill-napoleon-linked-to-cabinet-minister-castlereagh.

17 The Napoleonic Wars

1. Van Creveld, *Command in War*, p. 66. 2. Ibid., p. 68. 3. Roberts, *Napoleon and Wellington*, loc. 2264, 2299. 4. Arboit, 'Napoléon et le renseignement'. 5. Kerautret, 'Frédéric II et Napoléon (1800–1870)'. 6. Hall, *Napoleon's Notes on English History*, p. 184. 7. Guillois, *Bibliothèques particulières de l'Empereur Napoléon*, p. 9. 8. Jourquin, 'Bibliothèques particulières de Napoléon'. Arboit, 'Napoléon et le renseignement'. 9. Vaillé, *Cabinet noir*, p. 315. 10. See below, pp. 353–4. 11. Vaillé, *Cabinet noir*, pp. 322–3. 12. Montholon, *Récits de la captivité de l'empereur Napoléon*, vol. 1, pp. 211–12. 13. Roberts, *Napoleon the Great*, loc. 4354. 14. Walton, *Policing Public Opinion*, pp. 219–25. 15. Tulard, *Joseph Fouché*, loc. 2214, ch. 13. For the daily reports sent by Fouché to Napoleon, see Hauterive, *Police secrète du Premier Empire: Bulletins quotidiens adressés par Fouché à l'Empereur*. 16. Tulard, *Joseph Fouché*, ch. 14. 17. *ODNB* Sir George Rumbold. Tulard, *Joseph Fouché*, loc. 2459, ch. 15. 18. Roberts, *Napoleon the Great*, loc. 2173. 19. Montholon, *Récits de la captivité de l'empereur Napoléon*, vol. 1, p. 212. 20. Tulard, *Joseph Fouché*, loc. 2265. 21. Ibid., ch. 14. 22. Roberts, *Napoleon the Great*, loc. 10526. For the daily reports sent by Savary to Napoleon, see Gotteri, *Police secrète du Premier Empire: Bulletins quotidiens adressés par Savary à l'Empereur*. 23. Tombs and Tombs, *That Sweet Enemy*, p. 240. 24. Andrew, *Secret Service*, p. 5. 25. Knight, *Britain Against Napoleon*, pp. 285, 460. 26. *Parl. Deb.*, 1808, 10, p. 55. 27. Ibid., p. 63; cited by Munch-Petersen, 'Secret Intelligence from Tilsit'. 28. Andrew, *Secret Service*, p. 4. 29. Roberts, *Napoleon and Wellington*, loc. 2511. 30. Tombs and Tombs, *That Sweet Enemy*, p. 281. 31. Roberts, *Napoleon and Wellington*, loc. 11093f. 32. Ibid., loc. 1295. 33. Cooper, *Anglo-Maratha Campaigns*, pp. 307–10. 34. Ibid., pp. 82–120. 35. Ibid., pp. 98–9. 36. Gurwood (ed.), *Dispatches of Field Marshal the Duke of Wellington*, vol. 2, p. 540. 37. Davies, 'Influence of Intelligence', pp. 629–30. 38. Popplewell, *Intelligence and Imperial Defence*, pp. 9–11. 39. Davies, 'Integration of Strategic and Operational Intelligence', pp. 202–3. 40. Urban, *Man Who Broke Napoleon's Codes*, chs. 11–14. 41. http://www.nationalarchives.gov.uk/spies/ciphers/scovell/sc1.htm. 42. Urban, *Man Who Broke Napoleon's Codes*, pp. 249–50. 43. See above, pp. 216–18. 44. See above, pp. 271–2. 45. Ellis, *Post Office in the Eighteenth Century*, p. 131. On the Willes dynasty of cryptanalysts, see above, pp. 276, 348, 383. 46. Urban, *Man Who Broke Napoleon's Codes*, p. 262. 47. Ibid., pp. 261–2. 48. Ibid., pp. 272–5. 49. Nieuwazny, 'Rien de bien certain?' 50. Bezotosny, *Razvedka i plany storon v 1812 godu*. 51. Soboleva, *Istoriia Shifrovalnogo Dela v Rossii*, ch. 8. 52. Kahn, *Codebreakers*, p. 617. 53. See below, pp. 353–4, 359. 54. Clark, *Iron Kingdom*, pp. 303–4. Stamm-Kuhlmann, *König in Preussens grosser Zeit*, pp. 299–31. 55. Bezotosny, *Razvedka i plany storon v 1812 godu*. 56. Ibid. Lieven, *Russia Against Napoleon*, loc. 1777ff. 57. Bezotosny, *Razvedka i plany storon v 1812 godu*. 58. Lieven, *Russia Against Napoleon*, loc. 1738. 59. Lawday, *Napoleon's Master*, pp. 226–7. 60. Vaillé, *Cabinet noir*, p. 316. 61. Lawday, *Napoleon's Master*, pp. 215–16. 62. Kahn, *Codebreakers*, pp. 617–18. 63. Lieven, *Russia Against Napoleon*, loc. 1694. 64. Roberts, *Napoleon the Great*, loc. 11256. 65.

See above, p. 44. **66.** Roberts, *Napoleon the Great*, loc. 11634. **67.** Lieven, *Russia Against Napoleon*, loc. 4943. **68.** Roberts, *Napoleon the Great*, loc. 11659, ch. 25. **69.** Ibid., loc. 11780, ch. 25. **70.** *ODNB* Robert Wilson. **71.** Lieven, *Russia Against Napoleon*, loc. 5103. **72.** Chandler, *Campaigns of Napoleon*, p. 834. **73.** *ODNB* Robert Wilson. **74.** Lieven, *Russia Against Napoleon*, loc. 9772. Roberts, *Napoleon the Great*, loc. 13414. **75.** Lieven, *Russia Against Napoleon*, loc. 9776. **76.** Ibid., loc. 9790. **77.** Ibid., loc. 9798. **78.** Kahn, *Codebreakers*, pp. 617–18. Soboleva, *Istoriia Shifrovalnogo Dela v Rossii*, ch. 8. The excellent study by Dominic Lieven, *Russia Against Napoleon*, makes no mention of Russian breaking of French ciphers. **79.** Roberts, *Napoleon the Great*, loc. 13854. **80.** Price, *Napoleon: The End of Glory*, loc. 5382. **81.** Blanning, *Pursuit of Glory*, loc. 13079. **82.** *ODNB* Colquhoun Grant. **83.** Roberts, *Napoleon the Great*, loc. 14415. **84.** Ibid., loc. 14408. **85.** Weller, *Wellington at Waterloo*, pp. 139–40. Clark, *Iron Kingdom*, loc. 7101. **86.** Roberts, *Napoleon the Great*, loc. 14553.

18 Intelligence and Counter-Revolution. Part I

1. Glover, 'When the Congress wasn't Dancing'. **2.** Weil (ed.), *Dessous du Congrès de Vienne*, vol. 1, *Avant-propos*. **3.** Ibid., pp. x–xi. **4.** See above, pp. 278–9. **5.** Zamoyski, *Phantom Terror*, p. 433. **6.** Weil (ed.), *Dessous du Congrès de Vienne*, vol. 1, p. xi. **7.** Zamoyski, *Phantom Terror*, p. 497. **8.** Zamoyski, *Rites of Peace*, loc. 1398. **9.** Hager to Silber, 1 July 1814; Weil (ed.), *Dessous du Congrès de Vienne*, vol. 1, p. 10. **10.** Zamoyski, *Rites of Peace*, loc. 4060. **11.** Ibid., loc. 4052. **12.** There are numerous examples of such *chiffons* in Weil (ed.), *Dessous du Congrès de Vienne*, vols. 1, 2. **13.** Hager to La Roze, 1 July 1814; ibid., vol. 1, p. 11. **14.** Schmidt to Hager, 7 Oct. 1814; ibid., vol. 1, pp. 239–40. **15.** Note by Hager, 28 Sept. 1814; ibid., vol. 1, p. 138. **16.** Zamoyski, *Rites of Peace*, loc. 4498. **17.** Schmidt to Hager, 17 Oct. 1814; Weil (ed.), *Dessous du Congrès de Vienne*, vol. 1, p. 326. **18.** Report to Hager, 3 Nov. 1814; Hager to Emperor, 5 Nov. 1814; ibid., vol. 1, pp. 460–61, 466. **19.** Silber to Hager, 27 Sept. 1814; ibid., vol. 1, p. 127. **20.** Report to Hager, 4 Oct. 1814; ibid., vol. 1, p. 211. **21.** Report to Hager, 14 Oct. 1814; Hager to Emperor, 15 Oct. 1814; ibid., vol. 1, p. 280. **22.** Zamoyski, *Rites of Peace*, loc. 2245. **23.** Bernstorff to Copenhagen (intercepted), 13 July 1814; Weil (ed.), *Dessous du Congrès de Vienne*, vol. 1, p. 22. **24.** Report to Hager, 13 August 1814; ibid., vol. 1, p. 52. **25.** Agent 'Freddi' to Hager, 22 Sept. 1814; ibid., vol. 1, p. 65. **26.** Agent report to Hager, 28 Oct. 1814; ibid., vol. 1, pp. 422–3. **27.** Silber to Hager, 3 Oct. 1814; ibid., vol. 1, pp. 200–201. **28.** Report to Hager, 3 Oct. 1814; ibid., vol. 1, p. 205. **29.** Report to Hager, 2 Oct. 1814; ibid., vol. 1, pp. 191–3. **30.** Ullrichová (ed.), *Clemens Metternich–Wilhelmine von Sagan*. **31.** Agent report to Hager, 14 Oct. 1814; Weil (ed.), *Dessous du Congrès de Vienne*, vol. 1, p. 316. **32.** Report to Hager, 1 Oct. 1814; ibid., vol. 1, p. 193. **33.** Zamoyski, *Rites of Peace*, loc. 3863. McGuigan, *Metternich and the Duchess*, pp. 318–19. On Lamb's numerous affairs, see *ODNB* Frederick Lamb. **34.** Ullrichová (ed.), *Clemens Metternich–Wilhelmine von Sagan*. **35.** See, for example, agent reports to Hager of 28 May, 2, 4, 5, 6 and

11 June 1815; Weil (ed.), *Dessous du Congrès de Vienne*, vol. 2, pp. 598, 613–15, 620, 642.   **36.** Intercepted letter from a Swiss doctor, 7 June 1815; ibid., vol. 2, p. 623.   **37.** Zamoyski, *Rites of Peace*, loc. 7889. *ODNB* Charles Stewart, 3rd Marquess of Londonderry.   **38.** Zamoyski, *Rites of Peace*, loc. 4498.   **39.** Goehausen to Hager, 9 Nov. 1814; Weil (ed.), *Dessous du Congrès de Vienne*, vol. 1, p. 498.   **40.** Zamoyski, *Rites of Peace*, loc. 5032.   **41.** Report to Hager, 12 Oct. 1814; Weil (ed.), *Dessous du Congrès de Vienne*, vol. 1, p. 272.   **42.** Zamoyski, *Rites of Peace*, loc. 5009.   **43.** Ibid., loc. 4381. Price, *Napoleon: The End of Glory*, loc. 2514.   **44.** Price, *Napoleon: The End of Glory*, loc. 2595. Price was the first to carry out research in the Clam-Martinic papers.   **45.** Zamoyski, *Rites of Peace*, loc. 7308.   **46.** Price, *Napoleon: The End of Glory*, loc. 297.   **47.** Ibid., loc. 5390.   **48.** Report to Hager, 6 June 1815; Weil (ed.), *Dessous du Congrès de Vienne*, vol. 2, p. 616.   **49.** Zamoyski, *Rites of Peace*, loc. 8630.   **50.** Schroeder, *Metternich's Diplomacy at Its Zenith*, ch. 1.   **51.** Berend, *History Derailed*, p. 212.   **52.** Mayr, *Metternichs geheimer Briefdienst*, p. 215.   **53.** Ibid.   **54.** Charmley, '"Unravelling Silk"'   **55.** Zamoyski, *Phantom Terror*, p. 434.   **56.** Charmley, '"Unravelling Silk"'   **57.** Bew, *Castlereagh*, p. 546.   **58.** Zamoyski, *Phantom Terror*, p. 206.   **59.** George H. Rose (Berlin) to Castlereagh, no. 69, 29 Oct. 1817; Freitag, Mösslang and Wende (eds.), *British Envoys to Germany*, vol. 1, pp. 76–7.   **60.** Schroeder, *Metternich's Diplomacy at Its Zenith*, ch. 1.   **61.** George H. Rose (Berlin) to Castlereagh, no. 100, 30 Sept. 1819; Freitag, Mösslang and Wende (eds.), *British Envoys to Germany*, vol. 1, p. 113.   **62.** *Karlsbader Beschlüsse – Universitätsgesetz vom 20. September 1819*; http://www.heinrich-heine-denkmal.de/dokumente/karlsbad1.shtml.   **63.** Katzenstein, *Disjointed Partners*, p. 57.   **64.** Hosking, *Russia: People and Empire*, pp. 144–57.   **65.** Zamoyski, *Phantom Terror*, p. 338. On Kamptz, see Zolkowski, *German Romanticism and Its Institutions*, pp. 132–4.   **66.** Zamoyski, *Phantom Terror*, p. 343.   **67.** Zamoyski, *Phantom Terror*, p. 344.   **68.** Ruud and Stepanov, *Fontanka 16*, p. 21.   **69.** Zamoyski, *Phantom Terror*, pp. 344–5.   **70.** Ibid., ch. 23, loc. 5602.   **71.** Ibid., loc. 5608.   **72.** Karila-Cohen, 'Fonds secrets ou la méfiance légitime'.   **73.** Zamoyski, *Phantom Terror*, pp. 359–60.   **74.** Ibid., p. 361.   **75.** Ibid., p. 377.   **76.** Ibid., p. 350.   **77.** Ibid., ch. 22.   **78.** Custine, *Journey for Our Time*, pp. 50–51.   **79.** Ibid., p. 95.   **80.** Ibid., p. 169.   **81.** Ibid., pp. 12–13.   **82.** Rancour-Laferriere, *Slave Soul of Russia*, p. 256, n. 82.   **83.** Karila-Cohen, 'Fonds secrets ou la méfiance légitime'.   **84.** 'Aux armes, citoyens!', 12 May 1839; https://www.marxists.org/francais/blanqui/1839/appel.htm.   **85.** The most detailed, if sometimes confused, account of the insurrection is in the four volumes of trial records (though Blanqui and Barbès refused to give evidence): Cour des Pairs, *Attentat des 12 et 13 mai 1839*.   **86.** Hilton, *A Mad, Bad and Dangerous People?*, p. 617. Royle, *Chartism*, p. 75.   **87.** Moran, *Knowing Right from Wrong*, p. 58.   **88.** See above, pp. 326–9.   **89.** Andrew, *Secret Service*, p. 15.   **90.** Belchem, 'The Spy-System in 1848'. Cf. Radzinowicz, *History of English Criminal Law*, vol. 2, chs. 2–6.   **91.** Zamoyski, *Phantom Terror*, p. 403.   **92.** Vincent, 'Surveillance, Privacy and History'.   **93.** 'Post-office espionage: the English Fouché', *Northern Star*, 22 June 1844. Sutcliffe, *Victorian Radicals and Risorgimento Democrats*, p. 45.   **94.** HC Deb, vol. 75, 14 June 1844.   **95.** Ibid., 24 June 1844.   **96.** Ibid.   **97.** Ibid., 24 June 1844.   **98.** Vincent, 'Surveillance, Privacy and History'.   **99.** Ellis, *Post Office in the*

Eighteenth Century, Appendix 4.   100. Ibid., p. 131.   101. See below, pp. 509–11.
102. Agulhon, *1848*, pp. 22–3.   103. De La Hodde [Delahodde], *Cradle of Rebellions*,
title page, Preface (by publisher), p. iii.   104. Blanqui, 'Réponse du citoyen Auguste
Blanqui'.   105. Hutton, *Cult of the Revolutionary Tradition*, p. 21.   106. Amann,
'The Huber Enigma'. Agulhon, *1848*, pp. 23, 63–4. Blaisdell, 'Aloysius Huber and
May 15, 1848'.   107. De La Hodde [Delahodde], *Cradle of Rebellions*, p. 27.   108.
Tombs and Tombs, *That Sweet Enemy*, p. 345.   109. Ibid., p. 346.   110. Clark, *Iron
Kingdom*, p. 469.   111. Zamoyski, *Phantom Terror*, ch. 30. http://www.habsburger.
net/de/kapitel/ja-duerfens-denn-des-die-revolution-1848?language=de.

19 Intelligence and Counter-Revolution. Part II

1. Wheen, *Karl Marx*, pp. 102–3.   2. Ibid., p. 125.   3. Marx, *The Eighteenth
Brumaire of Louis Bonaparte*.   4. Wheen, *Karl Marx*, pp. 130–34.   5. McLellan
(ed.), *Karl Marx, Interviews and Reflections*, pp. 15–16.   6. Clark, *Iron Kingdom*,
p. 483.   7. Ibid., p. 493.   8. Ibid., p. 484.   9. Ibid., p. 485.   10. https://www.
marxists.org/archive/marx/works/1849/05/19c.htm.   11. Porter, *Refugee Question*, pp. 150–51.   12. Ibid., pp. 27–8.   13. Letter from Marx, Engels and Willich,
The Spectator, 15 June 1850. *MECW*, vol. 10, p. 381.   14. Ibid.   15. Wheen, *Karl
Marx*, p. 163.   16. Ibid., pp. 162–3.   17. Ibid., pp. 163–4.   18. *ODNB* Political
Refugees in Britain, 1826–1905.   19. Porter, *Refugee Question*, p. 58.   20. Ibid.,
p. 150.   21. Ibid., p. 152.   22. Deflem, 'International Policing'.   23. Extracts from
Wilhelm Hirsch's account of his work as a Prussian police spy in London appear
in Marx, *Herr Vogt*, Appendix 4. They were first published by August Willich in
the *New-Yorker Criminal-Zeitung* in April 1853 under the title 'Die Opfer der
Moucharderie, Rechtfertigungsschrift von Wilhelm Hirsch'.   24. Tombs, *The English and Their History*, p. 467.   25. Extracts from Wilhelm Hirsch's account of his
work as a Prussian police spy in London appear in Marx, *Herr Vogt*, Appendix
4.   26. Gabriel, *Love and Capital*, pp. 163–5. Sperber, *Karl Marx*, pp. 275–6.   27.
See below, pp. 440–41.   28. Gabriel, *Love and Capital*, p. 169.   29. Report by
unidentified Prussian agent, autumn 1852; McLellan (ed.), *Karl Marx, Interviews
and Reflections*, pp. 32–4.   30. Sperber, *Karl Marx*, pp. 281–5.   31. Wheen, *Karl
Marx*, pp. 271–2.   32. Vaillé, *Cabinet noir*, pp. 392–5.   33. Girard, *Napoléon
III*.   34. Choisel, 'Charlemagne de Maupas'.   35. Price, *French Second Empire*,
p. 84.   36. Choisel, 'Charlemagne de Maupas'.   37. Poncier, *Procureurs généraux
du Second Empire*.   38. Porter, *Refugee Question*, ch. 6.   39. Ibid., p. 171.   40.
Ibid., pp. 192–4.   41. Ibid., p. 151.   42. Marx, 'Portents of the Day', 11 March
1858 *MECW*, vol. 15.   43. Wheen, *Karl Marx*, pp. 238–43.   44. Marx, *Herr
Vogt*, *MECW*, vol. 17.   45. Jenny Marx to Mrs Weydemeyer, March 1861; McLellan (ed.), *Karl Marx, Interviews and Reflections*, p. 39.   46. Sperber, *Karl Marx*,
p. 333.   47. Marx summarizes his conspiracy theories about Palmerston in note
16 to Marx, *Herr Vogt*; *MECW*, vol. 17. The conspiracy theories appear frequently
in both his newspaper articles and his correspondence.   48. Wheen, *Karl Marx*,
p. 286.   49. Deflem, 'International Policing'. Dr Deflem's pioneering study fails to

make the connection between the Austro-Prussian War and the demise of the Police Union.   50. Sperber, *Karl Marx*, p. 379.   51. Marx, *Civil War in France*, *MECW*, vol. 22.   52. Sperber, *Karl Marx*, p. 380.   53. On the controversial issue of the death toll during the suppression of the Commune, see Tombs, 'How Bloody was *la Semaine Sanglante*? A Revision'.   54. Wheen, *Karl Marx*, p. 342.   55. Sperber, *Karl Marx*, ch. 13. Wheen, *Karl Marx*, pp. 344–7.   56. Andrew, *Secret Service*, p. 17. Wheen, *Karl Marx*, pp. 165–6.   57. Metropolitan Police reports of 24 May, 15 June 1872; TNA HO45/9303/11335. Porter, 'Origins of Britain's Political Police'.   58. Scotland Yard report to Home Office, 'Carl Marx – Naturalisation', 17 Aug. 1874, TNA HO45/9366/36228; Wheen, *Karl Marx*, pp. 356–7.   59. Wheen, *Karl Marx*, pp. 381–2.   60. Ibid., p. 299.   61. Porter, *Refugee Question*, p. 210.   62. Memo by Superintendent Adolphus Williamson, 22 Oct. 1880, TNA MEPO 2/134. Porter, 'Origins of Britain's Political Police'.

20 The Telegraph, Mid-Century Wars and the 'Great Game'

1. Standage, *Victorian Internet*, p. 2.   2. Figes, *Crimea*, loc. 5681.   3. Harris, *British Military Intelligence in the Crimean War*, p. 76.   4. *ODNB* Raglan.   5. Ibid.   6. Andrew, *Secret Service*, pp. 8–9.   7. Beaver, *Under Every Leaf*, pp. 12–14. Andrew, *Secret Service*, p. 9.   8. *ODNB* Charles Cattley.   9. Figes, *Crimea*, loc. 4193.   10. Woodham-Smith, *The Reason Why*. Dutton, *Forgotten Heroes*. Adkin, *The Charge*. Figes, *Crimea*, loc. 4642. *ODNB* James Thomas Brudenell, 7th Earl of Cardigan.   11. *ODNB* Charles Cattley. Harris, *British Military Intelligence in the Crimean War*, was the first to reveal the importance of Cattley's intelligence role in the Crimea.   12. Figes, *Crimea*, ch. 6.   13. *ODNB* Charles Cattley. Harris, *British Military Intelligence in the Crimean War*.   14. Standage, *Victorian Internet*, p. 146.   15. *ODNB* George Hamilton Gordon, 4th Earl of Aberdeen. *ODNB* William Howard Russell.   16. Primakov et al., *Ocherki istorii rossiyskoi vneshnei razvedki*, vol. 1, ch. 21.   17. See above, pp. 353–5.   18. Karatchkova, ' "Russian Factor" in the Indian Mutiny'. Hopkirk, *Great Game*, pp. 295–6. Fraser, *Flashman in the Great Game*. On the complex origins of the phrase 'Great Game', see Yapp, 'Legend of the Great Game'.   19. Harari, *Sapiens*, pp. 332–3. Edney, *Mapping an Empire*.   20. Wagner, *Great Fear of 1857*. Dash, 'Pass It On: The Secret That Preceded the Indian Rebellion of 1857'.   21. Beauchamp, *History of Telegraphy*, pp. 108–10.   22. *ODNB* Robert Montgomery. Aditi Vatsa, 'When telegraph saved the empire', *Indian Express*, 18 Nov. 2012; http://archive.indian express.com/news/when-telegraph-saved-the-empire/1032618/0.   23. Hopkirk, *Great Game*, p. 289.   24. Wagner, *Great Fear of 1857*, p. 226.   25. *The Times*, 6 Aug. 1857. Blunt, 'Embodying War'.   26. Wagner, *Great Fear of 1857*, p. 226. *ODNB* Alexander Duff.   27. Sengoopta, *Imprint of the Raj*, p. 48.   28. Bayly, *Empire and Information*, p. 327. *ODNB* William Stephen Raikes Hodson.   29. Bayly, *Empire and Information*, p. 328   30. See above, pp. 227ff.   31. *ODNB* William Stephen Raikes Hodson.   32. Ibid. Meyer and Brysac, *Tournament of Shadows*, pp. 146–7.   33. Bayly, *Empire and Information*, p. 319.   34. Ibid., p.

322.   35. Brown, *Modern India*, p. 152.   36. Bayly, *Empire and Information*, pp. 332–4.   37. Wagner, *Great Fear of 1857*, pp. 12–14.   38. Andrew, *For the President's Eyes Only*, pp. 19–20.   39. Central Intelligence Agency, *Intelligence in the Civil War*, p. 33.   40. Andrew, *For the President's Eyes Only*, p. 20. Brugioni, 'Arlington and Fairfax Counties: Land of Many Reconnaissance Firsts'.   41. Luvaas, 'Lee at Gettysburg'.   42. Luvaas, 'Role of Intelligence in the Chancellorsville Campaign'.   43. Luvaas, 'Lee at Gettysburg'.   44. Fishel, *Secret War for the Union*, pp. 551–3. Central Intelligence Agency, *Intelligence in the Civil War*, p. 20. Andrew, *For the President's Eyes Only*, p. 22.   45. See above, p. 403.   46. Andrew, *Secret Service*, pp. 9–10. Beaver, *Under Every Leaf*, ch. 1.   47. Jean-Claude Bologne, 'Il ne manque pas un bouton de guêtre'; http://www.canalacademie.com/ida4894-Il-ne-manque-pas-un-bouton-de-guetre.html.   48. Wawro, *Franco-Prussian War*, p. 94.   49. Ibid., p. 97.   50. Andrew, *Secret Service*, p. 12.   51. Braithwaite, *Afgantsy*, p. 23. On the role of Russian intelligence, see the forthcoming study by David Schimmelpenninck van der Oye, *Russia's Great Game: The Struggle for Mastery in Central Asia*.   52. On the survey, see above, pp. 406–7.   53. Meyer and Brysac, *Tournament of Shadows*, pp. 208–10. Hopkirk, *Great* Game, pp. 330–32. *ODNB* Thomas George Montgomerie.   54. Meyer and Brysac, *Tournament of Shadows*, p. 211.   55. *ODNB* Thomas George Montgomerie. Meyer and Brysac, *Tournament of Shadows*, p. 221.   56. Meyer and Brysac, *Tournament of Shadows*, p. 221.   57. Ferris, 'Lord Salisbury, Secret Intelligence and British Policy toward Russia and Central Asia'.   58. Ferris, 'Before "Room 40" ' p. 433.   59. Ferris, 'Lord Salisbury, Secret Intelligence, and British Policy toward Russia and Central Asia'.   60. Popplewell, *Intelligence and Imperial Defence*, p. 21.   61. Ferris, 'Lord Salisbury, Secret Intelligence, and British Policy toward Russia and Central Asia', p. 20.   62. Robson, *Road to Kabul*, ch. 5.   63. Ibid., ch. 6.   64. Ferris, 'Before "Room 40"', p. 433.   65. Robson, *Road to Kabul*, p. 118.   66. Ibid., p. 192. *ODNB* Sir Pierre Louis Napoleon Cavagnari.   67. Robson, *Road to Kabul*, chs. 8, 9.   68. Braithwaite, *Afgantsy*, pp. 15, 25–6.   69. Meyer and Brysac, *Tournament of Shadows*, p. 200.   70. Nickles, *Under the Wire*, p. 98.   71. See above, p. 383.   72. See below, pp. 454–70.   73. Ramm (ed.), *Political Correspondence of Mr Gladstone and Lord Granville,* vol. 2, pp. 32–5.   74. Monson to Lansdowne, 21 Feb. 1902; TNA Lansdowne papers, FO 800/124.   75. Nickles, *Under the Wire*, pp. 169–70.   76. Larsen, 'British Intelligence and American Neutrality', ch. 1.   77. Cozzens, 'Our Ministers Do Not Express Their Real Opinions'.   78. Ibid.   79. Larsen, 'British Intelligence and American Neutrality', ch. 1. Weber, 'State Department Cryptographic Security', pp. 562–3. *Foreign Relations of the United States, 1898*, pp. 692–769.

21 'The Golden Age of Assassination'

1. Clutterbuck, 'The Progenitors of Terrorism', pp. 154ff.   2. Jensen, *Battle against Anarchist Terrorism*, p. 25. Miller, 'Entangled Terrorisms in Late Imperial Russia', pp. 445–6.   3. See above, p. 374.   4. Ruud and Stepanov, *Fontanka 16*, ch. 2.   5. 'La Police russe en France', 29 June 1914, AN F⁷14, 605.   6. Andrew and

Gordievsky, *KGB*, pp. 42–3.   7. 'La Police russe en France', 29 June 1914, AN F⁷14, 605.   8. Andrew and Gordievsky, *KGB*, pp. 42–3.   9. Brodeur, 'High and Low Policing'.   10. Andrew, *Secret Service*, pp. 16–19. Kenna, *War in the Shadows*, chs. 7–8.   11. Andrew, *Secret Service*, p. 19.   12. Zuckerman, *Tsarist Secret Police Abroad*, pp. 133–5.   13. Miller, 'Entangled Terrorisms in Late Imperial Russia', p. 103. Zuckerman, *Tsarist Secret Police Abroad*, pp. 136–7.   14. Bouhey, *Anarchistes contre la République*, pp. 220–25, 280–84. Merriman, *Dynamite Club*, pp. 68–74.   15. Merriman, *Dynamite Club*, ch. 5.   16. Ibid., pp. 145–56. Bouhey, *Anarchistes contre la République*, pp. 276–7.   17. Merriman, *Dynamite Club*, p. 150.   18. Jensen, *Battle against Anarchist Terrorism*, p. 187.   19. Berlière, 'A Republican Political Police?'   20. Berthoud, 'L'Attentat contre Carnot'.   21. 'Caserio at the Guillotine', *The New York Times*, 16 Aug. 1894.   22. Esenwein, *Anarchist Ideology and the Working-Class Movement in Spain*, pp. 197–8. Jensen, *Battle against Anarchist Terrorism*, pp. 38, 133–8.   23. Andrew, *Secret Service*, p. 20.   24. Jensen, *Battle against Anarchist Terrorism*, p. 141.   25. Ibid., ch. 5.   26. Bouhey, *Anarchistes contre la République*, pp. 303–4.   27. France, *Trente ans à la rue des Saussaies*, pp. 100, 176–7.   28. 'Polices étrangères en France', 19 June 1914, AN F⁷14, 605.   29. Jensen, *Battle against Anarchist Terrorism*, ch. 5.   30. Ridley, *Bertie*, pp. 339–40.   31. Lamont-Brown, *Edward VII's Last Loves*, pp. 81–2.   32. Speyer, 'Legal Aspects of the Sipido Case', pp. 434–9.   33. Jensen, *Battle against Anarchist Terrorism*, pp. 187–203.   34. Tombs and Tombs, *That Sweet Enemy*, pp. 400ff.   35. Andrew, *Defence of the Realm*, pp. 5–7. On Lenin's time in London, see Rappaport, *Conspirator*, pp. 91–7, 157–69, 184–7.   36. Röhl, *Wilhelm II: Into the Abyss*, pp. 133–4.   37. Jensen, *Battle against Anarchist Terrorism*, pp. 204–5.   38. Andrew, *Defence of the Realm*, p. 5. See below, p. 481.   39. Report of the President's Commission on the Assassination of President Kennedy (the Warren Commission), Appendix 7.   40. Jensen, *Battle against Anarchist Terrorism*, pp. 248–50.   41. Ibid., p. 252.   42. Pipes, *Russia under the Old Regime*, ch. 11.   43. Cohn, *Warrant for Genocide*.   44. Geifman, *Thou Shalt Kill*, ch. 2.   45. Geifman, *Entangled in Terror*. Ruud and Stepanov, *Fontanka 16*, ch. 7.   46. Massie, *Nicholas and Alexandra*, pp. 59–60, 99.   47. Miller, 'Entangled Terrorisms in Late Imperial Russia', pp. 105–6.   48. Ruud and Stepanov, *Fontanka 16*, ch. 7.   49. Ibid., ch. 9.   50. Rappaport, *Conspirator*, pp. 164, 186.   51. Andrew and Gordievsky, *KGB*, p. 54.   52. Billington, *Fire in the Minds of Men*, pp. 476–7.   53. Lenin, 'Chto Delat'?', quoted in Hosking, *Russia and the Russians*, p. 359.   54. Andrew and Gordievsky, *KGB*, pp. 52–4. Sebag Montefiore, *Young Stalin*, p. 242.   55. These examples of the large amount of important material found by Svetlana Lokhova in Stalin's Okhrana file have been among those included in her presentations to the Cambridge Intelligence Seminar and will subsequently feature in her published work.   56. Clark, *Sleepwalkers*, ch. 1.   57. MacKenzie, *Apis*, chs. 10–12. Clark, *Sleepwalkers*, ch. 1.   58. Clark, *Sleepwalkers*, p. 42. Hastings, *Catastrophe*, loc. 470.   59. Clark, *Sleepwalkers*, pp. 48, 58–9. Butcher, *Trigger*, ch. 10.   60. Butcher, *Trigger*, ch. 11.   61. Hastings, *Catastrophe*, Prologue.   62. Butcher, *Trigger*, loc. 3764.   63. Mackenzie, *'Black Hand' on Trial*, p. 259.   64. Ibid., part II.

22 The Great Powers and Foreign Intelligence

1. Andrew, *Secret Service*, pp. 22–4. 2. Brendon, *Eminent Edwardians*, pp. 216–19. Baden-Powell, *My Adventures as a Spy*, pp. 11–12, 88, 159. 3. Andrew, *Secret Service*, p. 25. 4. Churchill, *My Early Life*. 5. Andrew, *Secret Service*, pp. 28–30. 6. Edmonds, Unpublished Memoirs, ah.19, LHC Edmonds MSS III/4. Edmonds misremembered the date of his appointment to the 'Special Section'. 7. Gleichen, *Guardsman's Memories*, pp. 314–16. 8. Andrew, *Secret Service*, p. 50. 9. Herwig, 'Imperial Germany', pp. 64–5. 10. See below, pp. 460–62. 11. Cecil, *German Diplomatic Service*, p. 142. 12. Herwig, 'Imperial Germany' pp. 65–8. 13. Fuller, *The Foe Within*, pp. 151–2. 14. See above, p. 434. 15. Andrew, *Defence of the Realm*, p. 12. 16. Huertner (ed.), *Paul von Hintze*, pp. 121ff. Röhl, *Wilhelm II: Into the Abyss*, ch. 11. 17. Röhl, *Wilhelm II: Into the Abyss*, p. 264. 18. Ibid., ch. 11. Epkenhans (ed.), *Das ereignisreiche Leben eines 'Wilhelminers'*. 19. Röhl, *Kaiser and His Court*, pp. 203–4. 20. Lieven, *Towards the Flame*, loc. 1744. 21. Menning, 'Russian Military Intelligence', p. 218. 22. I am grateful for this information to Svetlana Lokhova. 23. Soboleva, *Istoriia Shifrovalnogo Dela v Rossii*, pp. 269–71. Izmozik, 'Chernye kabinety', pp. 297–300. 24. Harcave, *Count Sergei Witte*, p. 80. 25. Soboleva, *Istoriia Shifrovalnogo Dela v Rossii*, pp. 271–2. 26. Andrew, *Théophile Delcassé*, pp. 74, 233. 27. Lamsdorf to Osten Sacken, 10 Jan. 1902, quoting extracts from German decrypts; MAE Nelidov MSS. 28. Correspondence in TNA FO371/123; Andrew and Neilson, 'Tsarist Codebreakers and British Codes'. 29. Andrew, *Secret Service*, pp. 403, 442. 30. Madeira, *Britannia and the Bear*, pp. 43–8. 31. See above, pp. 455–6. 32. Cavendish, 'Tsar Nicholas II and Family'. 33. Erskine and Smith, *Bletchley Park Codebreakers*. 34. Röhl, *Kaiser Wilhelm II, 1859–1941*, pp. 95–7. Vaïsse et al., *L'Entente Cordiale*, pp. 106–9. 35. Nickles, *Under the Wire*, pp. 170–71. 36. See below, pp. 592–3, 662. 37. See above, pp. 428, 434. 38. See above, pp. 426ff. 39. Andrew, *Théophile Delcassé*, pp. 130–31, 239, 241. 40. Andrew, 'Déchiffrement et diplomatie', p. 43. 41. Thomas, *L'Affaire sans Dreyfus*, p. 76. Read, *Dreyfus Affair*, p. 59. 42. Paléologue, *Journal de L'Affaire Dreyfus*, pp. 13–14. Though Paléologue is known to have made changes to the text of his journal before publication, what he says about the *cabinet noir* and intelligence, with which he was personally involved as *sous-directeur chargé des affaires réservées*, appears accurate and can sometimes be corroborated from other sources. 43. Thomas, *L'Affaire sans Dreyfus*, p. 76. Read, *The Dreyfus Affair*, p. 59. 44. Reports of Commissariat Spécial de Marseille of 29 Aug., 8 Sept., 10 Sept., 10 Oct., I Dec. 1896; MAE to Sûreté, acknowledging receipt, 8 Dec. 1896. AN F⁷12, 829. 45. Andrew, 'Déchiffrement et diplomatie', p. 44. 46. R. de Billy, 'Souvenirs', pp. 15–16, de Billy MSS, MAE. 47. Bazeries and Burgaud, *Le masque de fer*. 48. Andrew, 'Déchiffrement et diplomatie', pp. 44–50. 49. Read, *The Dreyfus Affair*, p. 191. 50. Guillemin, 'L'Affaire Dreyfus'. Andrew, 'Déchiffrement et diplomatie', p. 48. 51. *Dossier personnel* of Étienne Bazeries, Archives de la Guerre, SHD Vincennes. 52. Guillemin, 'L'Affaire Dreyfus'. Andrew, 'Déchiffrement et diplomatie', p. 48. 53. Robert Harris, 'The Whistle-Blower Who Freed Dreyfus', *New*

York Times, 17 Jan. 2014. **54.** Andrew, 'France and the German Menace', p. 133. **55.** There are incomplete series of Balasy's intelligence reports in the Hanotaux and Delcassé MSS (MAE). **56.** Andrew, *Théophile Delcassé*, pp. 98–100. **57.** Tombs and Tombs, *That Sweet Enemy*, p. 429. **58.** Andrew, *Théophile Delcassé*, pp. 98–100. The most recent account of the role of SIGINT during the Fashoda crisis, by a historian in the US State Department, follows this interpretation; Nickles, *Under the Wire*, pp. 165–6. **59.** Paléologue, 'Éventualité d'un accord franco-italien au sujet de la Méditerranée', 30 septembre 1913, MAE, Italie N.S. 12. Paléologue refers to 'un télégramme déchiffré hier'; the verb 'décrypter' did not yet exist. 'Déchiffrer' could mean either 'decipher' or 'decrypt'; in this instance the meaning is clearly 'decrypt'. **60.** *Documents diplomatiques français*, 3ème série, tôme VIII, no. 223. **61.** Andrew, *Théophile Delcassé*, pp. 195–6. **62.** Hénin, *Plan Schlieffen*, ch. 5. Paléologue, *Grand Tournant*, pp. 63–5. **63.** A study by Senator Maxime Lecomte in 1914 listed 300 published works and fifty magazine articles which had discussed the possibility of a German attack on France through Belgium; Hénin, *Plan Schlieffen*, p. 258. **64.** Andrew, *Defence of the Realm*, pp. 148–9. **65.** Röhl, *Kaiser Wilhelm II*, p. 87. **66.** See below, pp. 494–5. **67.** Menning, 'Miscalculating One's Enemies'. **68.** Sergeev, *Russian Military Intelligence in the War with Japan*, p. 57. **69.** Yoji Koda, 'Russo-Japanese War', p. 37. **70.** Menning, 'Miscalculating One's Enemies'. **71.** Yoji Koda, 'Russo-Japanese War', p. 42. **72.** Ferris, 'Before "Room 40"'. Morris, 'Intelligence and Its Interpretation', pp. 80–81. **73.** Kronenbitter, 'Paris Okhrana 1885–1905'. **74.** Haverna, 'Note sur l'organisation et le fonctionnement du service cryptographique de la Sûreté Générale, 7 Sept 1917', pp. 1–2; AN F⁷14, 605. **75.** Soboleva, *Istoriia Shifrovalnogo Dela v Rossii*, p. 283. For further details on Krivosh-Nemanich, see http://konstantynowicz.info/constantinovich/konstantinovich/Russian_military_intelligence/renucci_fraucci_frauchi_frautchi_artuzov/index.html. **76.** Both the Delcassé papers (MAE) and Sûreté files (AN F⁷12, 829 and F⁷12, 830) contain Japanese diplomatic decrypts. A note on an intercept of 3 Feb. 1906 records: 'From this point onwards, a [Japanese] cipher came into use which cannot be decrypted'; F⁷12, 830. On Delcassé's attempts to mediate between Russia and Japan, see Andrew, *Théophile Delcassé*, pp. 291–9. **77.** Andrew, *Théophile Delcassé*, pp. 289–301. *Grosse Politik der europäischen Kabinette, 1871–1914*, vol. XIXii, no. 6306. **78.** See below, pp. 477–8. **79.** Lamsdorf to Nelidov, 8 June 1905, MAE Nelidov MSS. Andrew, *Théophile Delcassé*, p. 74. **80.** Haverna, 'Note sur l'organisation et le fonctionnement du service cryptographique de la Sûreté Générale, 7 Sept. 1917', pp. 1–2, AN F⁷14, 605. **81.** Zvonarev, *Agenturnaia razvedka*, vol. 1, pp. 80–81. Marshall, 'Russian Intelligence during the Russo-Japanese War', p. 690. **82.** Haverna, 'Note sur l'organisation et le fonctionnement du service cryptographique de la Sûreté Générale, 7 Sept 1917', pp. 1–2, AN F⁷14, 605. **83.** Haverna, 'Note sur l'organisation et le fonctionnement du service cryptographique de la Sûreté Générale, 7 Sept 1917'; Andrew, 'Déchiffrement et diplomatie', pp. 51–3. **84.** Lieven, *Towards the Flame*, pp. 223–4.

23 Intelligence and the Coming of the First World War

1. On current historiographical controversies about the pre-war Royal Navy, see Seligmann and Morgan-Owen (eds.), *New Interpretations of the Royal Navy in the 'Fisher Era'*. 2. Andrew, *Secret Service*, pp. 46–7. 3. Andrew, *Defence of the Realm*, pp. 9–10, 13–14. 4. Ibid., pp. 11–12. 5. Boghardt, *Spies of the Kaiser*, pp. 13–20. 6. See above, p. 454. 7. 'Report and Proceedings of a Sub-Committee of the Committee of Imperial Defence Appointed by the Prime Minister to Consider the Question of Foreign Espionage in the United Kingdom', Oct. 1909; TNA, CAB 16/8. Andrew, *Defence of the Realm*, pp. 1, 13–21. 8. Andrew, *Defence of the Realm*, p. 18. 9. Sumption, *Hundred Years War*, vol. 3: *Divided Houses*, p. 289. 10. Andrew, *Defence of the Realm*, pp. 1, 25. 11. Taylor, *Struggle for Mastery in Europe*, p. 467. 12. Clark, *Sleepwalkers*, p. 205. 13. Andrew, 'Déchiffrement et diplomatie', pp. 53–5. 14. Röhl, *Wilhelm II: Into the Abyss*, pp. 1002–3. 15. On the Russian ability to decrypt Italian telegrams, see below, pp. 491, 499. 16. Andrew, *Defence of the Realm*, pp. 29–31. 17. Churchill to Sir Edward Grey, 22 Nov. 1911, CCAC Churchill MSS, CHAR 13/1/25. 18. Andrew, *Defence of the Realm*, pp. 37–8. 19. On pre-war gunnery ranges see Brooks, 'Preparing for Armageddon'. 20. Andrew, *Defence of the Realm*, pp. 44–5. 21. 'Reduction of Estimates for Secret Services', 19 March 1920, House of Lords Record Office, Lloyd George MSS F/9/2/16. 22. Andrew, *Secret Service*, p. 79. 23. Jeffery, *MI6*, p. 34. Hiley, 'Failure of British Espionage', pp. 884–8. 24. Seligmann, *Spies in Uniform*, pp. 247–8, 261–2. 25. Jeffery, *MI6*, pp. 31–2. *ODNB* Sir Henry Hughes Wilson. 26. Jeffery, *MI6*, p. 50. 27. Interviews by Christopher Andrew with Diana Pares, 1984. 28. Mackenzie, *Greek Memories*, p. 324. 29. Williams, *World of Action*, pp. 334–5. 30. Andrew, 'Déchiffrement et diplomatie', pp. 54–5. 31. See above, pp. 477–8. 32. Andrew, 'Déchiffrement et diplomatie', p. 57. 33. Ibid., pp. 55–7. See below, pp. 491–2. 34. Soboleva, *Istoriia Shifrovalnogo Dela v Rossii*, pp. 283–4. 35. See above, p. 455. 36. Menning, 'Russian Military Intelligence'. Kronenbitter, '*Krieg im Frieden*', pp. 236–7. 37. Lieven, *Towards the Flame*, p. 313. 38. Sadler and Fisch, *Spy of the Century*. 39. Menning, 'Russian Military Intelligence'. 40. Ibid. 41. Fuller, 'Russian Empire', p. 125. 42. Ignatiev, *Piatdesiat let v stroiu*, p. 1089; cited by Fuller, 'Russian Empire', p. 124. 43. Lieven, *Towards the Flame*, p. 154. 44. Williamson, 'Origins of the War', p. 17. 45. See above, ch. 21. 46. Röhl, *Wilhelm II: Into the Abyss*, p. 1017. 47. Clark, *Sleepwalkers*, p. 397. 48. Williamson, 'Origins of the War', p. 18. 49. Clark, *Sleepwalkers*, p. 394. 50. Louis, *Carnets de Georges Louis*, vol. 2, pp. 18–19. Andrew, 'Déchiffrement et diplomatie', p. 55. 51. Poincaré, 'Notes journalières', BN, n.a.fr. 16026ff. 52. Soboleva, *Istoriia Shifrovalnogo Dela v Rossii*, pp. 283–4. See above, pp. 485–6. 53. See above, p. 278. 54. Kahn, *Codebreakers*, pp. 263–4. Nickles, *Under the Wires*, pp. 166–7. On the Kaunitz era, see above, pp. 278–9. 55. Siebert later published three volumes of the diplomatic correspondence between St Petersburg and the London embassy. Siebert (ed.), *Diplomatic Correspondence*. 56. Clark, *Sleepwalkers*, p. 422. 57. Ibid., p. 421. 58. Otte, *July Crisis*, p. 95. 59. Ibid., p. 169. 60. San

Giuliano to Italian ambassadors in Berlin, St Petersburg, Vienna and Belgrade (tels), 16 July 1914; *I Documenti Diplomatici Italiani*, vol. XII, no. 272. Williamson, 'Origins of World War I', p. 809. **61.** Lieven, *Towards the Flame*, p. 318. **62.** Clark, *Sleepwalkers*, p. 428. **63.** See above, p. 485. **64.** Poincaré, 'Notes journalières', BN, n.a.fr.16027. **65.** Clark, *Sleepwalkers*, pp. 313, 361. **66.** Poincaré wrote in his diary as they were arriving in Russia, 'How far it is from the Caillaux trial! Viviani, however, is preoccupied by it.' 'Notes journalières', 19 July 1914, BN, n.a.fr.16027. **67.** Andrew, 'Déchiffrement et diplomatie', p. 57. **68.** Poincaré, 'Notes journalières', 22 July 1914, BN, n.a.fr.16027. **69.** Andrew, 'Déchiffrement et diplomatie', p. 57. **70.** Clark, *Sleepwalkers*, p. 472. **71.** Ibid., p. 480. **72.** Crown Prince Wilhelm, *Memoirs*, p. 241. **73.** Röhl, *Kaiser Wilhelm II*, pp. 153–4. **74.** Crown Prince Wilhelm, *Memoirs*, p. 242. **75.** Röhl, *Kaiser Wilhelm II*, p. 157. **76.** Andrew and Vallet, 'German Threat'. **77.** *ODNB* John Denton Pinkstone French, 1st earl of Ypres. **78.** Hamilton and Herwig, *War Planning 1914*, p. 133. **79.** Kahn, 'How Garbles Tickled History', p. 366. **80.** Kiesling, 'France', pp. 253–5. **81.** Tanenbaum, 'French Estimates of Germany's Operational War Plans', pp. 170–71. **82.** Herwig, *First World War*. **83.** Joffre, *Mémoires*, vol. 1, p. 21. **84.** Fuller, *Foe Within*, p. 151. See above, p. 453. **85.** See below, p. 497. **86.** See above, pp. 497–81. **87.** Andrew, *Defence of the Realm*, pp. 50–51. **88.** Steinhauer, *Steinhauer*, p. 37. **89.** Crown Prince Wilhelm, *Memoirs*.

24 The First World War. Part 1

1. See above, pp. 486–7. **2.** Hoffmann, *War Diaries*, vol. I. Kahn, *Codebreakers*, pp. 622–7. **3.** Hoffmann, *War of Lost Opportunities*, p. 28. Soboleva, *Istoriia Shifrovalnogo Dela v Rossii*, ch. 13. **4.** Kahn, *Codebreakers*, pp. 629–33. On the Caesar cipher, see above, p. 46. **5.** Höhne, *Krieg im Dunkeln*, pp. 174–6. Fuller, *Foe Within*, p. 153. **6.** Nicolai, *German Secret Service*, p. 123. **7.** Hoffmann, *War of Lost Opportunities*, p. 132. **8.** See above, pp. 354–5. **9.** http://www.globalsecurity.org/military/world/sukhomlinov-effect.htm. **10.** Lieven, *Towards the Flame*, p. 148. **11.** See above, pp. 454–5, 470–71, 485–6. **12.** See above, pp. 354–6. **13.** Fuller, *Foe Within*, pp. 184–9. **14.** Asquith to his daughter Violet, 29 and 31 Aug. 1914; text in Pottle (ed.), *Champion Redoubtable: The Diaries and Letters of Violent Bonham Carter*. **15.** Soboleva, *Istoriia Shifrovalnogo Dela v Rossii*, ch. 13. **16.** See above, p. 456. **17.** Hoare, *Fourth Seal*, p. 57. **18.** Entry for Sir Samuel Hoare, *Who Was Who*. On Russian recipients of the awards, see above, p. 489, and below, p. 501. **19.** See above pp. 457–8. **20.** Sir George Buchanan to Lord Grey, 23 Aug. and 13 Oct. 1915, TNA FO 800/75. McKee, 'British Perceptions of Tsar Nicholas II and Empress Alexandra Fedorovna', p. 276. **21.** Soboleva, *Istoriia Shifrovalnogo Dela v Rossii*, ch. 13. **22.** Falkenhayn, *German General Staff and Its Decisions*, p. 142. **23.** Soboleva, *Istoriia Shifrovalnogo Dela v Rossii*, ch. 13. On Fetterlein, see above, pp. 457–8, and below, p. 576. **24.** Brusilov, *Soldier's Note-Book*, pp. 208–18. **25.** Dowling, *Brusilov Offensive*. Jeffery, *1916*, ch. 6. **26.** Sir

George Buchanan to Lord Grey, 12 and 14 June 1915, TNA FO 371/2452. Fuller, *Foe Within*, p. 182.   **27.** Fuller, *Foe Within*, pp. 1–2, 190–94, 205.   **28.** Ibid., pp. 209–10.   **29.** Ibid., ch. 8.   **30.** Ibid., pp. 233–4.   **31.** Hoare, *Fourth Seal*, p. 54.   **32.** Andrew, *Defence of the Realm*, pp. 53–5.   **33.** See above, p. 318.   **34.** See above, p. 412.   **35.** Andrew, *Secret Service*, p. 133.   **36.** Finnegan, *Shooting the Front*, p. 40.   **37.** Raleigh, *War in the Air*, vol. 1, p. 341. Hart, *Fire and Movement*, pp. 231–2.   **38.** Beach, *Haig's Intelligence*, p. 145.   **39.** Raleigh, *War in the Air*, vol. 1, p. 9. Jones, *War in the Air*, vol. 2, pp. 149–60; vol. 3, pp. 307, 314.   **40.** Villatoux, 'Le renseignement photographique dans la manoeuvre'.   **41.** Finnegan, *Shooting the Front*, pp. 66–8.   **42.** Raleigh, *War in the Air*, vol. 1, p. 9. Jones, *War in the Air*, vol. 2, pp. 149–60; vol. 3, pp. 307, 314.   **43.** Beach, *Haig's Intelligence*, p. 145.   **44.** Sheffield, *The Somme*, p. 34.   **45.** Beach, *Haig's Intelligence*, pp. 145–6. See below, pp. 562–3, 565.   **46.** Jones, *War in the Air*, vol. 5, pp. 160–245.   **47.** Mohs, *Military Intelligence and the Arab Revolt*, pp. 50–51. See below, pp. 528–30.   **48.** West, 'Intelligence and the Development of British Grand Strategy', p. 210.   **49.** Keegan, *Intelligence in War*, p. 31.   **50.** See above, pp. 415–18.   **51.** Andrew, *Secret Service*, pp. 86–7.   **52.** Jurvee, 'Birth of Russian SIGINT'.   **53.** Andrew, *Secret Service*, pp. 88–90.   **54.** Churchill, 'Exclusively Secret' memorandum, 8 Nov. 1914, TNA HW 3/4.   **55.** Asquith to Venetia Stanley, 18 Aug. 1914; Brock and Brock (eds.), *H. H. Asquith Letters to Venetia Stanley*, p. 176.   **56.** Ibid.   **57.** Asquith to Venetia Stanley, 24 Aug. 1914, enclosing copy of secret telegram from Sir John French to Lord Kitchener of 24 Aug.; ibid., pp. 190–92.   **58.** Andrew, *Secret Service*, pp. 90–91.   **59.** Ibid., p. 91.   **60.** Ibid., pp. 91–3.   **61.** Beesly, *Room 40*, ch. 5. Andrew, *Secret Service*, p. 97.   **62.** Churchill, *World Crisis*, vol. I, p. 466.   **63.** Andrew, *Secret Service*, p. 498.   **64.** Marder, *Dreadnought to Scapa Flow*, vol. II, p. 142. Naval Staff Monograph, vol. XII (1925), pp. 120–21. MOD Naval Historical Branch.   **65.** Marder, *Dreadnought to Scapa Flow*, vol. II, pp. 143–4.   **66.** Naval Staff Monograph, vol. XII (1925), p. 144. MOD Naval Historical Branch.   **67.** Churchill, *World Crisis*, vol. II, pp. 128ff.   **68.** Marder, *Dreadnought to Scapa Flow*, vol. II, pp. 140, 161, 167. Roskill, *Admiral of the Fleet Lord Beatty*, pp. 114–16. Andrew, *Secret Service*, pp. 99–100.   **69.** Gilbert, *Winston S. Churchill*, vol. 3: *Challenge of War*, p. 359.   **70.** Page to Wilson, 17 March 1918, Wilson Papers, reel 95, Library of Congress, Washington. The first to quote an extract from this letter was James, *Eyes of the Navy*, p. xvii. The full text was first tracked down by Dr Dan Larsen, 'British Intelligence and American Neutrality', p. 11.   **71.** Page to Wilson, 17 March 1918; Larsen, 'British Intelligence and American Neutrality', p. 11.   **72.** See below, pp. 519, 538.   **73.** See above, p. 56.   **74.** Andrew, *Secret Service*, p. 96.   **75.** Army Security Agency, 'Historical Background of the Signal Security Agency', vol. II, pp. 17–18; NAW, RG 457, NC3-457-77-1.   **76.** Fitzgerald, *Knox Brothers*, pp. 90–92, 137. Andrew, *Secret Service*, p. 94.   **77.** Professor E. R. Vincent, Unpublished Memoirs, p. 107; Corpus Christi College, Cambridge, Archives.   **78.** Fitzgerald, *Knox Brothers*, p. 93.   **79.** Original copy in Denniston MSS, CCAC DENN 3/3. The title page reveals that the verses are by Knox.   **80.** Andrew, *Secret Service*, pp. 452–3.   **81.** Ibid., pp. 95–7.   **82.** Ibid., pp. 107–8. Larsen, 'British Intelligence and American Neutrality', ch. 5.   **83.** Andrew, 'Déchiffrement et diplomatie', pp. 58–9.   **84.** Carden, *German*

Policy toward Neutral Spain, pp. 67–8, 78. Lowry, 'At What Cost?', pp. 30–31.　**85.** See above, p. 478.　**86.** See below, pp. 540–41.　**87.** See below, p. 544.　**88.** Adams, *Historical Dictionary of German Intelligence*, p. 1.　**89.** Kahn, *Hitler's Spies*, p. 35. Beach, *Haig's Intelligence*, p. 157. See below, p. 531.　**90.** Boghardt, *Spies of the Kaiser*, p. 121.　**91.** Ibid., p. 128.　**92.** Ibid., p. 121.　**93.** Andrew, *Defence of the Realm*, pp. 77–9. Boghardt, *Spies of the Kaiser*, p. 128.　**94.** Introduction by Arthur S. Link to Doerries, *Imperial Challenge*, p. xiv.　**95.** See above, pp. 389–90.　**96.** Andrew, *For the President's Eyes Only*, p. 31.　**97.** Boghardt, *Spies of the Kaiser*, p. 128.　**98.** Andrew, *For the President's Eyes Only*, p. 31.　**99.** On the prewar history of the US Secret Service see above, pp. 435–6.　**100.** Andrew, *For the President's Eyes Only*, pp. 31–4.　**101.** Rintelen, *Dark Invader*, pp. 80, 126. Andrew, *For the President's Eyes Only*, pp. 33–4.　**102.** Gaunt, *Yield of the Years*, p. 135.　**103.** Ibid., pp. 137–8. Boghardt, *Zimmermann Telegram*, pp. 108–9.　**104.** Boghardt, *Zimmermann Telegram*, pp. 108–13. Andrew, *For the President's Eyes Only*, pp. 34–5.　**105.** Andrew, *Secret Service*, pp. 101–2.　**106.** William Clarke, '40 O.B. and GC & CS 1914 to 1945', chs. 1, 2, CCAC Clarke MSS CLKE3.　**107.** Jeffery, *1916*, loc. 2195.　**108.** Andrew, *Secret Service*, pp. 103–5.　**109.** For an analysis of the 'many reporting failures' and other errors, in addition to 'almost criminal ineptitude' in the handling of SIGINT, which contributed to the Grand Fleet's failure to cut off Scheer's escape route, see Gordon, *Rules of the Game*, ch. 22, p. 508.　**110.** Marder, *Dreadnought to Scapa Flow*, vol. III, pp. 172–86. Roskill, *Admiral of the Fleet Lord Beatty*, pp. 179–83. Clarke, 'Jutland 31.5.16', CCAC Roskill MSS ROSKILL 3/6. Andrew, *Secret Service*, pp. 107–8.　**111.** Jeffery, *MI6*, pp. 83–5. Intelligence reports in TNA ADM223/637, cited by Jeffery, *1916*, loc. 2291.　**112.** https://www.fbi.gov/news/stories/2004/july/blacktom_073004. http://www.smithsonianmag.com/history/sabotage-in-new-york-harbor-123968672/?no-ist.　**113.** Andrew, *For the President's Eyes Only*, p. 37.　**114.** Andrew, *Secret Service*, pp. 145–7, 165–6. Jeffery, *MI6*, pp. 47–53.　**115.** Andrew, *Secret Service*, p. 166.　**116.** Beach, *Haig's Intelligence*, p. 322.　**117.** Roberts, *Elegy*, loc. 888.　**118.** Beach, *Haig's Intelligence*, p. 217.　**119.** Lawrence, *Seven Pillars of Wisdom*, Introduction, ch. 6.　**120.** Mohs, *Military Intelligence and the Arab Revolt*, pp. 36–7, 159.　**121.** Ibid., pp. 73–4.　**122.** Ibid., p. 36.　**123.** Ibid., pp. 9–10.　**124.** Hogarth's comments are reproduced in the introduction to the Cambridge Archives edition of *The Arab Bulletin*, 4 vols. (1986).　**125.** Lawrence, *Seven Pillars of Wisdom*, Introduction, ch. 6.　**126.** Brown (ed.), *T. E. Lawrence in War and Peace*, p. 293.　**127.** Westrate, *Arab Bureau*, ch. 4.　**128.** Ibid., pp. 207–8.　**129.** Beach, *Haig's Intelligence*, pp. 157–8.　**130.** Ibid., p. 204.　**131.** Ibid., p. 158.　**132.** Langford, *Somme Intelligence*, loc. 1620.　**133.** Robertson to Haig, 29 July 1916, Haig Papers, TNA WO 256/11; cited in Larsen, 'British Intelligence and American Neutrality', p. 80.　**134.** Haig Diary, 21 Oct. 1916, Haig Papers, 159, National Library of Scotland, Edinburgh; cited in ibid., p. 98.　**135.** See above, p. 158.　**136.** See above, p. 336.　**137.** Unpublished Hall memoirs (ghostwritten by Ralph Strauss), draft chapter C, CCAC HALL 3/2.　**138.** Hankey Diary, 20 Nov. 1916, CCAC; cited in Larsen, 'British Intelligence and American Neutrality', p. 133.　**139.** Larsen, 'British Intelligence and American Neutrality', pp. 80–81. Prior and Wilson, *The Somme*, pp. 196–7.　**140.** Official

History of MI1b, TNA HW 7/35. **141.** A. G. Denniston, untitled MS memoir on Room 40, n.d., CCAC Deniniston MSS DENN 1/3. **142.** Roskill, *Hankey*, vol. 1, p. 247. **143.** Fowler, *British–American Relations*, pp. 10, 13, 19. Andrew, *For the President's Eyes Only*, pp. 38–9. **144.** Thwaites, *Velvet and Vinegar*, pp. 154–5. Gaunt, *Yield of the Years*, pp. 192–4. Andrew, *For the President's Eyes Only*, pp. 39–40. **145.** Larsen, 'First Intelligence Prime Minister'. **146.** Ibid. **147.** Andrew, *For the President's Eyes Only*, pp. 41–2. **148.** Boghardt, *Zimmermann Telegram*, p. 104. **149.** Andrew, *For the President's Eyes Only*, p. 42. Boghardt, *Zimmermann Telegram*, pp. 107–9. **150.** Larsen, 'First Intelligence Prime Minister'. Larsen, 'British Intelligence and American Neutrality', ch. 8. **151.** Page to Wilson, draft, February 1917, Page Papers, 1090.5, Box 3, Journal 1917, Harvard University Houghton Library. This document, which had laid undisturbed in the Page papers for many years, was discovered by Dr Dan Larsen; Larsen, 'British Intelligence and American Neutrality', p. 197. **152.** Dugdale, *Balfour*, vol. 2, p. 138. **153.** Andrew, *For the President's Eyes Only*, pp. 44–5. **154.** Mohs, *Military Intelligence and the Arab Revolt*, pp. 125–6. **155.** *PWW*, vol. 51, pp. 519–27. Andrew, *For the President's Eyes Only*, pp. 45–6.

25 The First World War. Part 2

1. Roskill, *Hankey*, vol. I, pp. 356–7, 380–84. Marder, *Dreadnought to Scapa Flow*, vol. IV, chs. 6, 7, 10. **2.** Andrew, *Secret Service*, pp. 120–22. Marder, *Dreadnought to Scapa Flow*, vol. IV, pp. 264–8. **3.** Merridale, *Lenin on the Train*, pp. 58–69, 257–61. **4.** Ibid., ch. 6. **5.** Röhl, *Kaiser Wilhelm II*, p. 170. **6.** Andrew, *Defence of the Realm*, p. 99. **7.** Radek, 'Through Germany in a Sealed Coach'. Merridale, *Lenin on the Train*, pp. 151–2. **8.** Andrew, *Defence of the Realm*, pp. 95–6, 100. **9.** Andrew, *First World War*, pp. 42–3. **10.** Watson, *Ring of Steel*, pp. 462–3. **11.** Figes, *People's Tragedy*, pp. 416–17. **12.** Watson, *Ring of Steel*, p. 463. **13.** Andrew, *For the President's Eyes Only*, pp. 46–7. **14.** Ibid., p. 47. **15.** On Voska, see above, p. 523. **16.** Maugham, 'Looking Back'. Andrew, *For the President's Eyes Only*, pp. 47–8. **17.** Figes, *People's Tragedy*, pp. 418–19. **18.** Andrew, *Defence of the Realm*, pp. 95–6. **19.** Fuller, *Foe Within*, pp. 241–2. **20.** Tombs and Tombs, *That Sweet Enemy*, p. 490. Pedroncini, *Les Mutineries de 1917*. **21.** Andrew, *Defence of the Realm*, p. 101. **22.** Ibid. **23.** Ibid., pp. 101–2. **24.** Fowler, *British–American Relations*, pp. 113–18. Jeffery, *MI6*, p. 119. **25.** Maugham, 'His Excellency', in *Collected Short Stories*, vol. III. **26.** Andrew, *Defence of the Realm*, pp. 102–3. **27.** Ibid., p. 103. **28.** Leggett, *Cheka*, pp. 15–19. **29.** Ibid., pp. 281–2. **30.** Kennan, *Soviet–American Relations*, vol. I, pp. 401–2, 454–5. **31.** Service, *Spies and Commissars*, p. 110. **32.** Andrew and Gordievsky, *KGB*, pp. 62–3. **33.** Leggett, *Cheka*, pp. 41–51. **34.** Ibid., pp. 73, 293. **35.** Ibid., ch. 4. **36.** Andrew and Gordievsky, *KGB*, pp. 68–9. **37.** 17 RGASPI F. 76 d. 3 0. 10, p. 1. This letter was discovered by Svetlana Lokhova, who includes the text in her MPhil thesis, 'The Evolution of the Cheka', p. 12. Though there is no date on the letter, the archive catalogue states that it was written on 30 August 1918. **38.** Andrew and Mitrokhin, *Mitrokhin Archive*, p. 34. **39.**

Tsvigun et al. (eds.), *V. I. Lenin i VChK*, no. 198. **40.** Ostryakov, *Voyennye Chekisti*, ch. 1. **41.** Lockhart, *Memoirs of a British Agent*, ch. 10. Andrew, *Defence of the Realm*, p. 95. **42.** Lockhart, *Memoirs of a British Agent*, pp. 276–7, 322. Hill, *Go Spy the Land*, p. 238. Andrew and Gordievsky, *KGB*, pp, 71–80. **43.** See above, pp. 440–41. **44.** Andrew and Mitrokhin, *Mitrokhin Archive*, p. 31. **45.** Leggett, *Cheka*, p. 17. **46.** Report from the Cheka of the town and district of Morshansk in the first issue of the Cheka weekly, dated 22 Sept. 1918; Mitrokhin Archive k-9, 112, CCAC. **47.** *ODNB* Edgar Cox. Beach, *Haig's Intelligence*, pp. 301–2. **48.** Decock, 'La Dame Blanche', chs. 5–8 (quotation from p. 149). Andrew, *Secret Service*, pp. 168–9. **49.** Andrew, *Secret Service*, pp. 170–71. Beach, *Haig's Intelligence*, pp. 289–90. **50.** Andrew, *Secret Service*, pp. 171–2. Major-General S. S. Butler, 'France 1916–1918', microfilm copy, IWM. Beach, *Haig's Intelligence*, pp. 289–302. **51.** General Sir James Marshall-Cornwall, unpublished memoirs, ch. 4, p. 7, IWM. **52.** http://www.annales.org/archives/x/pain vin.html. **53.** 'Souvenirs du général Cartier', pp. 19–20. 'Conférence de M. Georges Jean Painvin', p. 50. **54.** 'Le chiffre ADFGX'; http://www.apprendre-en-ligne.net/crypto/subst/adfgvx.html. **55.** Beach, *Haig's Intelligence*, pp. 307–8. **56.** Sheffy, *British Military Intelligence in the Palestine Campaign*, pp. 222–56. Stevenson, *With Our Backs to the Wall*, pp. 148–55. Ferris (ed.), *British Army and Signals Intelligence*, pp. 297–9. **57.** Woodward, *American Army and the First World War*, chs. 16–19. **58.** Stevenson, *With Our Backs to the Wall*, p. 183. **59.** Smoot, 'Impermanent Alliances'. Omand, 'Learning from the Secret Past'. **60.** See above, p. 534. **61.** Friedman, *Bletchley Park Diary*. **62.** See above, pp. 567–8. **63.** 'Memorandum on Scope and Activities of MI1c in New York', 27 April 1917, Wiseman papers, series 1, box 6, folder 174, SLYU. **64.** Wiseman to Cumming, 6 Sept. 1918, Wiseman papers, series 1, box 6, folder 171, SLYU. **65.** Wiseman to Reading, 26 July 1918, Wiseman papers, series 1, box 3, folder 74, SLYU. **66.** Admiral John Godfrey, unpublished memoirs, vol. 5, pp. 132–7, CCAC GDFY 1/6. **67.** Wiseman to Murray, 14 Sept. 1918; Murray to Wiseman, Wiseman papers, series 1, box 2, folder 53, SLYU. Andrew, *For the President's Eyes Only*, p. 57. **68.** *PWW*, vol. 42, pp. 16–17. **69.** Andrew, *For the President's Eyes Only*, p. 63. **70.** Ibid., pp. 53–4. **71.** *PWW*, vol. 51, pp. 345–8. **72.** Ibid., pp. 527–8. **73.** See above, pp. 604–5. **74.** CX [MI1c] reports of October 1918, cited in Beach, *Haig's Intelligence*, p. 318. **75.** Röhl, *Kaiser Wilhelm II*, p. 176. **76.** Toye, *For What We Have Received*, pp, 153–5. Toye misremembered the exact date. **77.** Marder, *Dreadnought to Scapa Flow*, vol. V, pp. 172–5. **78.** The intercepts are in TNA ADM 137/964. **79.** Lowry, *Armistice 1918*, pp. 84, 126. Larsen, 'The Frist Intelligence Prime Minister'. Though, as with most MI1b intercepts, the decrypts do not survive, the cables exchanged between House and Wilson are to be found in *PWW*, vol. 51. **80.** *PWW*, vol. 51, pp. 594–5. **81.** Larsen, 'British Intelligence and American Neutrality'. **82.** Decock, 'La Dame Blanche', chs. 5–8 (quotation from p. 149). Andrew, *Secret Service*, pp. 168–9. **83.** Andrew, *Secret Service*, p. 173. **84.** Beach, *Haig's Intelligence*, pp. 314–16. **85.** Major-General S. S. Butler, 'France 1916–1918', microfilm copy, IWM. Andrew, *Secret Service*, p. 173. **86.** Stevenson, *With Our Backs to the Wall*, p. 540. **87.** Andrew, *First World War*, p. 50.

26 SIGINT and HUMINT between the Wars

1. Andrew, *For the President's Eyes Only*, p. 68.   2. Andrew, *Defence of the Realm*, pp. 186–7.   3. Jeffery, *MI6*, p. 245.   4. Andrew, *Defence of the Realm*, p. 186.   5. See above, pp. 556–9.   6. Andrew and Mitrokhin, *Mitrokhin Archive*, p. 37.   7. Report of the All-Russia Central Executive Committee and the Council of People's Commissars, 5 Dec. 1919.   8. Lokhova, 'Evolution of the Cheka', pp. 20–21. Lokhova is the first to discover the record of Dzerzhinsky's interrogation of Nikolai Aleksandrovich Pavlov (alias 'Kozul'), a twenty-year-old member of Kuznetsov's gang, on 15 February 1919. An English translation of this document is included in 'Evolution of the Cheka' as Appendix A.   9. Dzerzhinsky, 'Inquiry into the damage to Lenin's furniture', Sept. 1922; RGASPI, F. 76 op. 3 d. 268 l. 2–3. This document was cited for the first time in Lokhova, 'Evolution of the Cheka', pp. 21–2.   10. Andrew, *Defence of the Realm*, pp. 117, 122. On MI5's far more extensive, though under-resourced, operations before the Second World War, see ibid., pp. 179ff, 191ff.   11. Andrew and Mitrokhin, *Mitrokhin Archive*, pp. 43–5. On Savinkov, see ibid., pp. 43–4.   12. Ibid., pp. 45–6. Jeffery, *MI6*, pp. 182–4. On Reilly, see above, p. 560.   13. Andrew and Mitrokhin, *Mitrokhin Archive*, p. 46.   14. Andrew and Gordievsky, *KGB*, pp. 94–5.On Fetterlein's role in the Tsarist *cabinet noir*, see above, p. 458. On his role at GC&CS, see Denniston, 'Government Code and Cypher School', p. 55; Brigadier John H. Tiltman, 'Experiences 1920–1939'; https://www.nsa.gov/public_info/_files/tech_journals/experiences.pdf.   15. Filby, 'Bletchley Park and Berkeley Street', p. 280.   16. W. F. Friedman, 'Six Lectures on Cryptography', p. 18, NAW, RG457 SRH-004.   17. Filby, 'Bletchley Park and Berkeley Street', p. 280.   18. Curzon to Crewe, 2 Feb. 1923, CUL Crewe MSS 12.   19. Andrew and Kanya-Forstner, *France Overseas*, p. 232.   20. Andrew, *Secret Service*, p. 245.   21. Ibid., pp. 262–3, 296. On Fetterlein's previous career as a leading Tsarist codebreaker, see above, pp. 457–8, 489.   22. See above, pp. 535–6, 538–9.   23. Andrew, *Secret Service*, p. 268.   24. Ibid., pp. 268–9.   25. Cabinet conclusions, 15 Sept. 1920, TNA CAB 23/23.   26. Cabinet conclusions, 3 May 1923, TNA CAB 23/45. Cf. Curzon to Bonar Law, 5 May 1923, HLRO Davidson MSS.   27. Cmd. 1869 (1923).   28. Andrew, *Secret Service*, pp. 292–3.   29. Ibid., pp. 296–7.   30. Title written by Curzon on envelope containing French intercepts; IOLR Curzon MSS Eur. F 112/320.   31. Curzon to Crewe, 13 Oct., 12 Nov., 12 Dec. 1923, CUL Crewe MSS 12. Curzon to Baldwin, 9 Nov. 1923, IOLR Curzon MSS Eur. F 112/320.   32. Churchill to Austen Chamberlain, 21 Nov. 1924, BUL Chamberlain MSS AC 51/58.   33. *Parliamentary Debates (Commons)*, 5th series, vol. CCVI, 26 May 1927, cols. 2257–8.   34. Andrew, *Defence of the Realm*, pp. 148–51.   35. Bennett, *'A Most Extraordinary and Mysterious Business'*, p. 26.   36. Andrew, 'Secret Intelligence and British Foreign Policy', p. 20.   37. See above, pp. 510–11.   38. Churchill to Austen Chamberlain, 22 Nov. 1924, BUL Chamberlain MSS AC 51/61. Andrew, *Secret Service*, pp. 315–16.   39. Conversation with Fetterlein noted by William Friedman in 1943. Friedman, *Bletchley Park Diary*, p. 12.   40. Andrew, *Secret Service*, pp. 331–3.   41. Hankey to Lloyd George, 8 Oct. 1920, HLRO Davidson MSS.   42. French archives also include

Austrian, Belgian, German, Greek and Romanian decrypts; SHD 6 N 233, 249–52. **43.** Denniston, 'Government Code and Cypher School', p. 55. **44.** See above, pp. 478, 484. **45.** Unpublished memoirs of Alexandre Millerand, quoted by permission of his son, the late Jacques Millerand. **46.** Decrypted telegram from Mayer, the German ambassador in Paris, to Berlin, no. 85, 18 Jan. 1921; SHD 6 N 250. Millerand kept a number of other German decrypts in his papers (MAE). **47.** Forcade, *La République secrète*, pp. 178–80. **48.** See above, p. 569. **49.** Kahn, *Reader of Gentlemen's Mail*, chs. 7, 8. **50.** Yardley, *American Black Chamber*, p. 215. **51.** *Documents on British Foreign Policy, 1919–1939*, 1st series, vol. 14, p. 297. **52.** Yardley, *American Black Chamber*, p. 224. **53.** Unclassified review of Kahn, *Reader of Gentlemen's Mail*, by Thomas R. Johnson, *Studies in Intelligence*, vol. 48 (2004), no. 2 **54.** Andrew, *For the President's Eyes Only*, p. 71. **55.** Yardley, *American Black Chamber*, pp. 232–4. **56.** W. F. Friedman, 'A Brief History of the Signal Intelligence Service', 29 June 1942, pp. 9–10; RG 457: SRH-029, NAW. **57.** Stimson diary, 1 June 1931, SLYU. Stimson kept no diary during his early months as Secretary of State. His account of the closure of the Black Chamber comes from later comments in his diary on the publication of Yardley's memoirs. **58.** Andrew, *Defence of the Realm*, pp. 72–3, 104–6. **59.** Hannah, 'Many Lives', RLEW 5/41, CCAC; cited in Moran, *Company Confessions*, p. 31. **60.** Yardley, *American Black Chamber*. **61.** Hannah, 'Many Lives' RLEW 5/41, CCAC; Moran, *Company Confessions*, ch. 3. **62.** Andrew and Gordievsky, *KGB*, pp. 192–4. **63.** Kahn, *Reader of Gentlemen's Mail*, p. 134. **64.** Gorbunov, *Vostochnyii rubezh: OKDVA protiv iaponskoii armii*. **65.** Stalin to Kaganovich (late June or 1 July 1932); Davies et al. (eds.), *The Stalin–Kaganovich Correspondence, 1931–36*, document 42. **66.** RGASPI 558/11/185/126-32. Davies and Harris, *Stalin's World*, pp. 123–4. **67.** Patel, *New Deal*, p. 143. **68.** See above, p. 499. **69.** See above, pp. 457–8. **70.** Andrew and Mitrokhin, *Mitrokhin Archive*, pp. 47, 67–9. **71.** Primakov et al., *Ocherki istorii rossiyskoi vneshnei razvedki*, vol. 3, ch. 13. **72.** Andrew and Mitrokhin, *Mitrokhin Archive*, pp. 67–9. **73.** Bohlen, *Witness to History*, p. 20. **74.** Dunn, *Caught between Roosevelt and Stalin*, p. 75. **75.** Preface by Graham Greene to Philby, *My Silent War*. **76.** See above, p. 171. **77.** Andrew and Mitrokhin, *Mitrokhin Archive*, p. 137. **78.** See below, pp. 625–6. **79.** Andrew and Elkner, 'Stalin and Foreign Intelligence', p. 75. **80.** See above, p. 574. **81.** Yagoda, draft circular, c.20 Jan. 1935; Lenoe, *The Kirov Murder and Soviet History*, document 100. Lenoe did not, however, have access to the files on the investigation of the Kremlin plot discovered by Lokhova. **82.** Lokhova, 'Stalin, the NKVD and the Investigation of the Kremlin Case', pp. 37–42. **83.** Ibid., pp. 42–4. **84.** Ibid., pp. 49–54. **85.** Lokhova, 'Stalin, the NKVD and the Investigation of the Kremlin Case', pp. 49–50. I am grateful to Svetlana Lokhova for additional information on Alexei Sinelobov. **86.** Tzouliadis, *The Forsaken*, ch. 12. **87.** Jansen and Petrov, *Stalin's Loyal Executioner*, p. 207. **88.** Politburo decision, 2 October 1937; Getty and Naumov (eds.), *Road to Terror*, document 164. **89.** See below, pp. 623–4. **90.** 'Concerning the Terroristic Activity of the Trotskyist–Zinovievist Counter-Revolutionary Bloc', 29 July 1936; Getty and Naumov (eds.), *Road to Terror*, document 73. **91.** Andrew and Gordievsky, *KGB*, pp.

148–9. **92.** Resolution of the February–March 1937 Central Committee Plenum on 'Lessons of the wrecking, diversionary and espionage activities of the Japanese-German-Trotskyist agents'; Getty and Naumov (eds.), *Road to Terror*, document 145. **93.** Tucker and Cohen (eds.), *Great Purge Trial*. **94.** Ibid. **95.** Andrew and Gordievsky, *KGB*, p. 157. **96.** Andrew and Elkner, 'Stalin and Foreign Intelligence', pp. 71–2. **97.** Andrew and Gordievsky, *KGB*, p. 154. **98.** Andrew and Mitrokhin, *Mitrokhin Archive*, p. 95.

27 The 'Big Three' and Second World War Intelligence

1. See above, pp. 451, 480, 510, 582–3. **2.** See above, pp. 441–2, 594–8, 600–602. **3.** Dorwart, *Office of Naval Intelligence*, pp. 104–11. Andrew, *For the President's Eyes Only*, pp. 76–7. **4.** See above, p. 527. **5.** PSF Anecdotes FDRL. Andrew, *For the President's Eyes Only*, pp. 77–8. **6.** See above, pp. 567, 570. **7.** Freidel, *Franklin D. Roosevelt*, vol. 2: *The Ordeal*, pp. 18, 30–31, 77. **8.** Brands, *Traitor to His Class*, p. 134. **9.** Freidel, *Franklin D. Roosevelt*, vol. 2: *The Triumph*, p. 66. **10.** Andrew, *For the President's Eyes Only*, p. 81. **11.** Dorwart, 'The Roosevelt–Astor Espionage Ring'. **12.** Roosevelt (ed.), *Roosevelt Letters*, vol. 3, p. 100. **13.** Astor to FDR, 26 Sept. 1934, PSF 92, Astor File, FDRL. FDR to Astor, 26 Sept. 1934, Astor Papers, FDRL. **14.** Astor to FDR, n.d., PSF 92, 'Amusing Things' File, FDRL. **15.** Correspondence in PSF 92, Astor File, FDRL; cited by Andrew, *For the President's Eyes Only*, pp. 83–4. **16.** See above, p. 483. **17.** Andrew, *For the President's Eyes Only*, p. 84. **18.** Sullivan, '"A Highly Commendable Action"'. Andrew, *For the President's Eyes Only*, pp. 85–6. **19.** Andrew, *For the President's Eyes Only*, pp. 86–7. Memorandum of White House conference, 14 Nov. 1938; cited in Lowenthal, 'Searching for National Intelligence'. **20.** Preston, 'US national security'. **21.** Astor to FDR, 'Sunday night', n.d. [1939], PSF Astor File, FDRL. **22.** Correspondence in PSF 92 and PPF 40, Astor File, FDRL; cited in Andrew, *For the President's Eyes Only*, p. 93. **23.** Andrew, *For the President's Eyes Only*, pp. 93–4. Jeffery, *MI6*, pp. 439–41. **24.** Andrew, *For the President's Eyes Only*, pp. 94–6. **25.** See above, p. 563. **26.** Roosevelt (ed.), *Roosevelt Letters*, vol. 2, p. 311. **27.** Jeffery, *MI6*, pp. 438–43. Naftali, 'Intrepid's Last Deception'. **28.** Stimson, 'Notes after Cabinet Meeting', 4 April 1941; cited in Troy, 'Coordinator of Intelligence and British Intelligence', pp. 89–90. **29.** Troy, 'Coordinator of Information and British Intelligence', pp. 107–9. Troy, *Donovan and the CIA*, Appendix B. **30.** Godfrey, unpublished memoirs, vol. 5, pp. 132–7, CCAC GDFY 1/6. **31.** Andrew, *For the President's Eyes Only*, pp. 104–5. **32.** Ibid., p. 105. **33.** Ibid., p. 106. On the closure of the Black Chamber, see above, pp. 588–9. **34.** 'Historical Background of the Signal Security Agency', part 3, p. 308; NAW RG 457: SRH-001. Andrew, 'Codebreakers and Foreign Offices', pp. 52–3. **35.** See above, pp. 576, 582–3. **36.** Bennett, *Churchill's Man of Mystery*. **37.** ODNB Ralph Wigram. **38.** Putlitz, *Putlitz Dossier*, ch. 12. **39.** Andrew, *Defence of the Realm*, pp. 198–9. **40.** Ibid., pp. 200–201. **41.** Ibid., pp. 195–203. **42.** Andrew, 'Secret Intelligence and British Foreign Policy', p. 24. **43.** Andrew, *Defence of the Realm*, pp.

195–209.   44. Andrew, 'Churchill and Intelligence', pp. 181–2. Jeffery, *MI6*, pp. 347–8.   45. See above, pp. 577–84.   46. Information from Michael Herman, who helped to arrange Margaret Thatcher's visit. GC&CS had been renamed GCHQ.   47. Milner-Barry, 'Action This Day'.   48. Andrew, *Secret Service*, ch. 13. Jeffery, *MI6*, pp. 382–6.   49. Andrew, 'Churchill and Intelligence', pp. 190–91.   50. Reynolds, 'Churchill and the British "Decision" to Fight On'.   51. Andrew, *Secret Service*, p. 477.   52. Andrew, *Defence of the Realm*, p. 223. Andrew, *Secret Service*, p. 476.   53. Blunt, *My Diaries*, vol. 2, p. 288.   54. See above, p. 574. Andrew, *Secret Service*, pp. 290–91.   55. Andrew and Mitrokhin, *Mitrokhin Archive*, pp. 100–101.   56. Gorodetsky (ed.), *The Maisky Diaries*, p. 90.   57. Andrew and Mitrokhin, *Mitrokhin Archive*, pp. 105–6.   58. Primakov et al., *Ocherki istorii rossiyskoi vneshnei razvedki*, vol. 3, p. 17.   59. Andrew and Elkner, 'Stalin and Foreign Intelligence', p. 71.   60. Andrew and Mitrokhin, *Mitrokhin Archive*, pp. 108–12.   61. Andrew and Gordievsky, *KGB*, p. 181.   62. Volodarsky, *Stalin's Agent*, ch. 18. Andrew and Mitrokhin, *Mitrokhin Archive*, pp. 113–14.   63. Andrew and Mitrokhin, *Mitrokhin Archive*, p. 100.   64. Andrew and Gordievsky, *KGB*, pp. 180–81.   65. Andrew and Mitrokhin, *Mitrokhin Archive*, p. 112.   66. Ibid., pp. 114–15.   67. Centre to 'Gennady' (Ovakimian), 27 Jan. 1941, WWC Vassiliev White Notebook 1, pp. 16–18.   68. See above, p. 599.   69. Centre to 'Gennady' (Ovakimian), 27 Jan. 1941, WWC Vassiliev White Notebook 1, pp. 16–18.   70. See above, p. 593.   71. Andrew and Mitrokhin, *Mitrokhin Archive*, p. 122.   72. Andrew and Elkner, 'Stalin and Foreign Intelligence', pp. 77–8.   73. Ibid., pp. 78–9.   74. Samolis (ed.), *Veterany vneshei razvedki Rossii*, p. 154.   75. Andrew and Mitrokhin, *Mitrokhin Archive*, p. 125.   76. Whymant, *Stalin's Spy*, part 3.   77. Interview by Christopher Andrew with Yuri Rastvorov in Washington, DC, Nov. 1987. Rastvorov worked with Tolstoy in the wartime Fifth Directorate. In 1954 Rastvorov defected from the KGB Tokyo residency to the United States.   78. See above, pp. 456–8.   79. Kuromiya and Pepłoński, 'Kōzō Izumi and the Soviet Breach'. Hastings, *Secret War*, pp. 184–7.   80. Andrew and Gordievsky, *KGB*, pp. 281–3.   81. See above, p. 611.   82. Stimson diary, 2 Jan. 1941, SLYU.   83. *PHA*, part 2, p. 288; part 4, p. 1734. Kahn, 'Roosevelt, MAGIC and ULTRA', p. 292.   84. *PHA*, part 11, pp. 5278–81.   85. Ibid., p. 5475. On Watson's role in the White House, see Morgan, *FDR*, p. 444.   86. *PHA*, part 11, p. 5475.   87. *FRUS 1941*, vol. 4, pp. 299–300.   88. *PHA*, part 11, pp. 5475–6.   89. Ibid.   90. Kotani, *Japanese Intelligence in World War II*, pp. 136–8.   91. *MBPH*, vol. 4, no. 16A; vol. 4, Appendix, nos. 14, 114, 162. Andrew, *For the President's Eyes Only*, p. 111.   92. Andrew, *For the President's Eyes Only*, pp. 112–13.   93. *PHA*, part 11, p. 5284.   94. Morgan, *FDR*, pp. 613–14.   95. *PHA*, part 14, pp. 1413–15.   96. *PHA*, part 9, pp. 4002–3.   97. Details in *PHA*, part 14, pp. 1413–15.   98. *PHA*, part 10, pp. 4660–64.   99. *PHA*, part 11, pp. 5281–4.   100. Prange, *At Dawn We Slept*, p. 553.   101. *PHA*, part 9, p. 4099; part 11, pp. 5283–4.   102. Sherwood, *Roosevelt and Hopkins*, pp. 430–31.   103. Andrew, *For the President's Eyes Only*, pp. 118–19.   104. *PHA*, part 12, pp. 200–202.   105. Prange, *At Dawn We Slept*, p. 558.   106. Berle diary, 7 Dec. 1941, FDRL.   107. Lewin, *The Other Ultra*, p. 67.   108. Andrew, *For the President's Eyes Only*, p. 119.   109. Kahn, 'Intelligence Failure at Pearl Harbor'. Kahn, 'Pearl Harbor and the Inadequacy of Cryptanalysis'.   110. Parker, 'The Unsolved Messages of Pearl Harbor'.   111. See below, pp. 637–8.   112. Ferris, 'From Broadway House to Bletchley Park'.   113. Gilbert, *Winston S. Churchill*, vol. 6: *Finest Hour*, pp. 1267–8.

28 Intelligence and the Victory of the Grand Alliance

1. Kahn, 'Roosevelt, MAGIC and ULTRA', pp. 306–8.   2. Andrew, *For the President's Eyes Only*, p. 125. The Japanese reached similar conclusions; Kotani, *Japanese Intelligence in World War II*, p. 87.   3. Andrew, *For the President's Eyes Only*, p. 138.   4. Kahn, 'Black Code'.   5. Kruh, 'British–American Cryptanalytic Cooperation', p. 126.   6. Behrendt, *Rommel's Intelligence*, p. 146. Jenner, 'Turning the Hinge of Fate', p. 169.   7. Jenner, 'Turning the Hinge of Fate', pp. 170–71.   8. Ibid., pp. 175–6.   9. Ibid., p. 192.   10. Kahn, *Hitler's Spies*, p. 195.   11. Jenner, 'Turning the Hinge of Fate', pp. 169–70.   12. Ibid., p. 168.   13. Dear and Foot (eds.), *Oxford Companion to the Second World War*, pp. 326–8, 1167.   14. Jablonsky, *Churchill, the Great Game and Total War*, pp. 160–61. Aldrich and Cormac, *Black Door*, p. 116.   15. Dear and Foot (eds.), *Oxford Companion to the Second World War*, pp. 326–8, 1167.   16. Hinsley and Stripp (eds.), *Codebreakers*, p. 37. Hastings, *Secret War*, p. 409.   17. Churchill, *Second World War*, vol. 2: *Their Finest Hour*, p. 529.   18. See above, pp. 543–4.   19. The use of intelligence in the war against the U-boats is told in great detail in Hinsley et al., *British Intelligence in the Second World War*, 4 vols. For a more concise account, see the one-volume abridged edition, chs. 10, 18, 34, 37.   20. West, *Historical Dictionary of World War II Intelligence*, pp. 14–15.   21. The best up-to-date overview of British–American wartime and post-war intelligence collaboration is Gioe, 'Anglo-American Special Intelligence Relationship'.   22. Andrew, *For the President's Eyes Only*, pp. 135–7.   23. Hinsley et al., *British Intelligence in the Second World War*, vol. 2, p. 48.   24. Denniston, 'The Government Code and Cypher School', p. 56. Erskine, 'William Friedman's Bletchley Park Diary', p. 371.   25. The complete text of BRUSA remained classified until 1995; Sims, 'BRUSA Agreement of May 17, 1943'. On Strong, see above, p. 609.   26. Interviews by Christopher Andrew with Sir Harry Hinsley, March–April 1994.   27. See above, pp. 565–6.   28. Friedman, *Bletchley Park Diary*.   29. Interviews by Christopher Andrew with Sir Harry Hinsley, March–April 1994.   30. BBC interview cited in *New York Times* obituary of William F. Bundy, 7 Oct. 2000.   31. Service, *Spies and Commissars*, p. 110.   32. Herman, *Intelligence Power*, p. 283.   33. Hastings, *Secret War*, p. 447.   34. B-Dienst war diary, quoted in Kahn, 'Codebreaking in World Wars I and II', p. 145.   35. Kahn, 'Codebreaking in World Wars I and II', p. 154.   36. See above, pp. 483–5, 533, 610–11.   37. Kahn, 'Codebreaking in World Wars I and II', p. 155.   38. *Hitler's Table Talk*, 17 Feb. 1942.   39. Ibid., 22 May 1942.   40. Gilbert, 'Final Solution', provides a valuable introduction to the vast literature on the Holocaust. On Wannsee, see Roseman, *Wannsee Conference and the Final Solution*.   41. Lathrop, *Literary Spy*, p. 18.   42. Paret et al. (eds), *Makers of Modern Strategy*, p. 492.   43. See above, pp. 575–6.   44. Sebag Montefiore, *Stalin: Court of the Red Tsar*, p. 451.   45.

Hastings, *Secret War*, pp. 229–36.   46. Sebag Montefiore, *Stalin: Court of the Red Tsar*, p. 452. Service, *Stalin*, pp. 428–9.   47. SD report, 28 Jan. 1943; Chant, *Warfare and the Third Reich*.   48. Hastings, *Secret War*, p. 469.   49. Jukes, 'The Soviets and "Ultra"'. Mulligan, 'Spies, Ciphers and "Zitadelle"'. Andrew and Gordievsky, *KGB*, pp. 316–17. Haslam, *Near and Distant Neighbours*, pp. 118–19.   50. Cairncross, *Enigma Spy*, pp. 95ff.   51. Andrew and Mitrokhin, *Mitrokhin Archive*, p. 159. Andrew and Gordievsky, *KGB*, p. 314. Samolis (ed.), *Veterany Vneshei razvedki Rossii*, p. 154.   52. Hastings, *Secret War*, pp. 188–9.   53. See above, p. 621.   54. Andrew and Mitrokhin, *Mitrokhin Archive*, pp. 157–8.   55. Report on Activities of Security Service, 26 March 1943, TNA KV 4/83.   56. Andrew, *Defence of the Realm*, p. 280   57. Andrew and Mitrokhin, *Mitrokhin Archive*, pp. 157–9.   58. Andrew, *Defence of the Realm*, p. 249.   59. Masterman, *On the Chariot Wheel*, ch. 21.   60. Masterman, *Double-Cross System*, p. xii. Andrew, *Defence of the Realm*, pp. 255–6, 285.   61. Andrew, *Defence of the Realm*, p. 239.   62. Ibid., pp. 285–7.   63. Ibid., pp. 287–90.   64. Roberts, *Stalin's General*, p. 167.   65. Hastings, *Secret War*, p. 326.   66. Mulligan, 'Spies, Ciphers and "Zitadelle"', p. 250.   67. Excerpt from captured German document in US Office of Naval Intelligence, 'Espionage–Sabotage–Conspiracy. German and Russian Operations 1940 to 1945', p. 51; NAW RG 242, box 70.   68. Hastings, *Secret War*, p. 327.   69. Andrew and Mitrokhin, *Mitrokhin Archive II*, p. xxvii.   70. Rayfield, *Stalin and His Hangmen*, pp. 394–5. Uehling, *Beyond Memory*.   71. Gilbert, *Auschwitz and the Allies*.   72. Hastings, *Secret War*, p. 480.   73. Trevor-Roper, memorandum, summer 1943, TNA HW19/347; cited in Hastings, *Secret War*, p. 470.   74. Hastings, *Secret War*, p. 470.   75. Hastings, *Secret War*, pp. 460–64.   76. Churchill, *Second World War*, vol. 5: *Closing the Ring*, p. 338.   77. Howard, *British Intelligence*, vol. 5: *Strategic Deception*, pp. 105–7.   78. Holt, *Deceivers*, ch. 13. Macintyre, *Double Cross: The True Story of the D-Day Spies*.   79. Bonsall, 'Bletchley Park and the RAF Y Service'.   80. Unpublished X-2 history, Box 2, RG 226, NAW; Andrew, *For the President's Eyes Only*, pp. 139–40.   81. Andrew, *Defence of the Realm*, p. 305.   82. Ibid., pp. 305–8.   83. Ibid., p. 308.   84. Ibid., p. 309.   85. Andrew and Mitrokhin, *Mitrokhin Archive*, pp. 183–4.   86. Ibid., pp. 165–6.   87. Ibid., pp. 141–2.   88. Minute by Molotov on report from Washington embassy which he forwarded to Stalin on 23 Sept 1942; http://www.loc.gov/exhibits/archives/sovi.html#obj4.   89. Wellington A. Samouce, 'I Do Understand the Russians', pp. 52–3, Samouce papers, US Army Military History Institute, Carlisle Barracks, Pa.   90. See below, p. 675.   91. Andrew and Mitrokhin, *Mitrokhin Archive*, pp. 175–7.   92. See above, p. 638.   93. Kotani, *Japanese Intelligence in World War II*, p. 98.   94. Ibid., p. 159.   95. Ibid., p. 160.   96. Ibid., pp. 97–8.   97. Ibid., p. 142.   98. Ibid., p. 144.   99. Ibid., p. 101.   100. Ibid., p. 105.   101. Haynes, Klehr and Vassiliev, *Spies*, p. 47.   102. Walsh, 'George Koval'.   103. Haynes, Klehr and Vassiliev, *Spies*, p. 47.   104. Andrew and Mitrokhin, *Mitrokhin Archive*, pp. 169, 790–91.   105. Haynes, Klehr and Vassiliev, *Spies*, p. 37.   106. Walsh, 'George Koval'.   107. Andrew and Mitrokhin, *Mitrokhin Archive*, pp. 151–2, 167–9. Haynes, Klehr and Vassiliev, *Spies*, pp. 94–102.   108. Interviews by Christopher Andrew with Theodore Hall (who lived in Cambridge in the street next to Andrew) in 1996. Andrew and Mitrokhin, *Mitrokhin Archive*, pp. 169–70.   **109.** Ibid., p. 169.   **110.** William J. Broad, 'Putin Toasts His Spy; From Sioux City to Birobidzhan and Back', *International Herald Tribune*, 17 Nov. 2007.

29 The Cold War and the Intelligence Superpowers

1. Andrew, *For the President's Eyes Only*, pp. 149–56.   **2.** Ibid., pp. 161–2.   **3.** Truman, Memorandum for the Secretaries of State, War and the Navy, 12 Sept. 1945, Naval Aide Files, box 10, file 1, Harry S. Truman Library. Smith, *Ultra-Magic Deals*, p. 212.   **4.** Andrew, 'Making of the Anglo-American SIGINT Alliance'.   **5.** Gioe, 'Anglo-American Special Intelligence Relationship', ch. 5.   **6.** See above, pp. 255–6, 270.   **7.** Email to author from Michael Herman, 29 July 2017.   **8.** On interwar breaches of SIGINT security, see above, pp. 575–80, 583–90.   **9.** Gioe, 'Anglo-American Special Intelligence Relationship', was the first to use the declassified SIGINT agreements.   **10.** COS (45), confidential annexe, 31 July 1945, TNA CAB 76/36; Special Order by Sir Edward Travis (Director GCHQ), 7 May 1945, TNA FO 371/39171: both cited in Aldrich, *Hidden Hand*, pp. 1–3.   **11.** Andrew, 'Intelligence in the Cold War'.   **12.** Andrew, *For the President's Eyes Only*, ch. 6.   **13.** Ibid., p. 5 and ch. 13. This volume attempts an assessment, on the fragmentary evidence available, of varying presidential attitudes towards SIGINT.   **14.** Andrew, *For the President's Eyes Only*, pp. 484–5.   **15.** See above, p. 206.   **16.** On the 'one-time pad', see above, p. 584.   **17.** On the historical controversies aroused by the VENONA decrypts, far greater in the US than in the UK, see Haynes and Klehr, *In Denial*.   **18.** Andrew, 'VENONA Secret'.   **19.** Benson and Warner (eds.), *VENONA*. Haynes and Klehr, *VENONA*. Andrew, 'VENONA Secret'.   **20.** Andrew, *Defence of the Realm*, pp. 423–6.   **21.** *ODNB* Sir Arthur Bonsall; further information kindly supplied by Sir David Omand, author of the *ODNB* biography.   **22.** Selwyn Lloyd to E. M. Jones (Director, GCHQ), 30 Sept. 1956, TNA AIR 20/10621.   **23.** Garthoff, 'The KGB Reports to Gorbachev', p. 228.   **24.** Andrew and Mitrokhin, *Mitrokhin Archive*, ch. 21.   **25.** Ibid., pp. 233–5.   **26.** Martini, *Nome in codice: ULISSE*, pp. 19–20.   **27.** Andrew and Mitrokhin, *Mitrokhin Archive*, pp. 200, 361–2, 459, 601, 603, 608–9, 621, 628, 630, 718. On DARIO, see the additional information in the Italian edition, *L'Archivio Mitrokhin* (Milan: Rizzoli, 1999), pp. 693–4.   **28.** Andrew and Mitrokhin, *Mitrokhin Archive*, pp. 458–9, 625–6.   **29.** The first detailed account, with some documentary evidence, of the bugging carried out from the Elysée in the Mitterrand era was Pontaut and Dupuis, *Les Oreilles du Président*; quotation from p. 215.   **30.** Andrew, *For the President's Eyes Only*, pp. 163–5.   **31.** Ibid., pp. 168–70.   **32.** Jeffreys-Jones, 'Why was the CIA Founded in 1947?', pp. 26–7.   **33.** Andrew, *For the President's Eyes Only*, p. 171.   **34.** Ibid., pp. 171–2.   **35.** See above, p. 619.   **36.** Jeffery, *MI6*, pp. 606–7.   **37.** Aldrich and Cormac, *Black Door*, pp. 154–5.   **38.** Roosevelt, *Countercoup*, pp. 199–209. To conceal the role of SIS, the first edition of *Countercoup* claimed inaccurately that 'the original proposal' for the operation came from the Anglo-Iranian Oil Company; this was later changed to 'British Intelligence'. 'Iran 1953: The Strange Odyssey of Kermit Roosevelt's *Countercoup*',

National Security Archive Electronic Briefing Book No. 468, 12 May 2014, http://nsarchive.gwu.edu/NSAEBB/NSAEBB468/. **39.** Andrew, 'Intelligence in the Cold War'. **40.** The extensive literature on US covert action includes: *Final Report of the Select Committee to Study Governmental Operations with Respect to Intelligence Activities*, [Church Committee], 94 Cong., 2 Sess., Report no. 755 (April 26, 1976); Treverton, *Covert Action*; Andrew, *For the President's Eyes Only*. **41.** Andrew and Gordievsky, *KGB*, ch. 9. **42.** See above, pp. 599–601. **43.** Andrew and Gordievsky, *KGB*, ch. 9. **44.** Ibid., pp. 416–17. Krotov told his recollections of Rajk's trial and execution to Gordievsky. **45.** See above, pp. 623–4. **46.** Andrew and Mitrokhin, *Mitrokhin Archive*, pp. 464–6. **47.** Ibid., p. 446. **48.** Andrew, 'Intelligence in the Cold War'. **49.** On the top-secret construction and operation of the U-2, see Rich and Janos, *Skunk Works*. **50.** Andrew, *For the President's Eyes Only*, chs. 6, 7. **51.** Gioe, Scott and Andrew (eds.), *International History of the Cuban Missile Crisis*. **52.** Perry, *My Journey at the Nuclear Brink*, pp. 3–4. Edward Wilson, 'Thank you Vasili Arkhipov, the man who stopped nuclear war', *Guardian*, 27 Oct. 2012. **53.** Gates, *From the Shadows*, p. 562. **54.** START Treaty, 31 July 1989, Articles IX, X; Protocol on telemetric information (text published by US Arms Control and Disarmament Agency). **55.** Kalugin, *Spymaster*, pp. 29–32. Interviews with Oleg Kalugin by Christopher Andrew. **56.** Kalugin, *Spymaster*, pp. 82–3. Andrew and Mitrokhin, *Mitrokhin Archive*, pp. 23–4, 267–9. **57.** Kalugin, *Spymaster*, pp. 84–90. Andrew and Mitrokhin, *Mitrokhin Archive*, pp. 268–9. **58.** Andrew and Mitrokhin, *Mitrokhin Archive*, pp. 287–8. **59.** Andrew, *For the President's Eyes Only*, pp. 402–4. **60.** Gustafson, 'The CIA and Chile, 1964–1974'. Gustafson, *Hostile Intent*. **61.** Andrew and Mitrokhin, *Mitrokhin Archive*, ch. 14. Holland, 'The Lie That Linked CIA to the Kennedy Assassination'. **62.** Andrew and Mitrokhin, *Mitrokhin Archive II*, pp. 18, 326. **63.** Frank, *Indira*, pp. 368, 374–5. **64.** Gaddis, *Cold War*. **65.** Andrew and Mitrokhin, *Mitrokhin Archive*, pp. 236–7. Andrew and Mitrokhin, *Mitrokhin Archive II*, p. 40. **66.** Leonov, Fediakova and Fermandois et al., 'El general Nikolai Leonov en el CEP'. **67.** Andrew and Mitrokhin, *Mitrokhin Archive*, p. 10. **68.** Dobrynin, *In Confidence*, pp. 404–5. **69.** Leonov, *Likholet'e*, p. 141. **70.** Dobrynin, *In Confidence*, pp. 209–10, 404–5, 408. **71.** Andrew and Mitrokhin, *Mitrokhin Archive II*, chs. 2–6. **72.** Ibid., pp. 12, 115, 471. Kalugin, *Spymaster*, pp. 126–30. **73.** Andrew and Mitrokhin, *Mitrokhin Archive II*, chs. 21, 22. **74.** Bearden and Risen, *Main Enemy*; quotation from p. 312. Westad, *Global Cold War*, pp. 353–7, 375–7. **75.** Andrew, *For the President's Eyes Only*, pp. 478–93, 497. Westad, *Global Cold War*, pp. 339–48, 374. **76.** 'From "Upper Volta with Missiles" to "Nigeria with Snow"'. http://russialist.org/from-upper-volta-with-missiles-to-nigeria-with-snow/. **77.** Andrew, 'Intelligence in the Cold War'. **78.** Andrew and Mitrokhin, *Mitrokhin Archive*, pp. 167–70, 280–87. **79.** Hanson, *Soviet Industrial Espionage*. The documents and statistics supplied by the French agent in Directorate T, Vladimir Vetrov (codenamed FAREWELL), on which Hanson bases his analysis, complement the KGB files noted by Mitrokhin. On Vetrov, see also Kostin and Raynaud, *Adieu Farewell*; and Andrew and Gordievsky, *Le KGB dans le monde*, pp. 619–25. **80.** Andrew and Gordievsky (eds.), *Instructions from the Centre*, pp. 37, 49–50. **81.** Andrew and Mitrokhin,

Mitrokhin Archive, pp. 280–87, 723–5. **82.** Comment by Sir Maurice Oldfield to Christopher Andrew. **83.** Mitrokhin (ed.), *KGB Lexicon*. **84.** Leonov, *Likholet'e*, pp. 120–22. **85.** Interview with Vadim Kirpichenko, *Vremya Novostey*, 20 Dec. 2004. **86.** Leonov, *Likholet'e*, pp. 129–31. **87.** Andrew and Mitrokhin, *Mitrokhin Archive*, p. 722. *Izvestia*, 24 Sept. 1991. **88.** Cradock, *Know Your Enemy*, ch. 17. **89.** Fursenko and Naftali, *'One Hell of a Gamble'*, pp. 51–2, 155, 168. **90.** Andrew and Gordievsky (eds.), *Instructions from the Centre*, ch. 4. **91.** Kalugin, *Spymaster*, pp. 302–3. Kalugin considered the tone of Andropov's cable 'paranoid'. **92.** Volkogonov, *Rise and Fall of the Soviet Empire*, p. 351. **93.** Dobrynin, *In Confidence*, p. 523. **94.** Wolf, *Man without a Face*, p. 222. **95.** Andrew and Gordievsky, *KGB*, pp. 582–603. Andrew and Gordievsky (eds.), *Instructions from the Centre*, ch. 4. **96.** Shvets, *Washington Station*, pp. 29, 74–5. Shvets had access to Androsov's reports as a member of the FCD First (North American) Department at the Centre from 1982 to 1985, and was then posted to Washington as a Line PR officer in Androsov's residency. **97.** Andrew and Gordievsky, *KGB*, pp. 591–605. The best analysis of recently declassified documents on the crisis is Khuri, 'New Light on Able Archer '83'. **98.** Some of the KGB RYAN directives are published in Andrew and Gordievsky (eds.), *Instructions from the Centre*, ch. 4. **99.** Gordievsky, *Next Stop Execution*, p. 262. **100.** Howe, *Conflict of Loyalty*, pp. 349–50. **101.** 'Implications of Recent Soviet Military-Political Activities', SNIE 11-10-84/ JX. **102.** Gates, *From the Shadows*, p. 273. **103.** US Executive Office, President's Foreign Intelligence Advisory Board, 'The Soviet "War Scare"', 15 Feb. 1990 (declassified Oct. 2015), pp. vi, viii, 7 (cited in Khuri, 'New Light on Able Archer '83', p. 37). The PFIAB report is available online at: http://nsarchive.gwu.edu/nukevault/ebb533-The-Able-Archer-War-Scare-Declassified-PFIAB-Report-Released/ 2012-0238-MR.pdf. **104.** Omand, *Securing the State*, p. 35. **105.** Andrew and Gordievsky (eds.), *Instructions from the Centre*, pp. 70–73. **106.** Garthoff, 'The KGB Reports to Gorbachev', pp. 226–7. **107.** Interview with Leonid Shebarshin, *Daily Telegraph*, 1 Dec. 1992. **108.** Andrew and Mitrokhin, *Mitrokhin Archive*, chs. 15, 16. **109.** Ibid., pp. 423–5, 480–81, 727–8. **110.** Keene, *Karpov–Korchnoi 1978*. **111.** The text of the appeal of the 'State Committee for the State of Emergency' was published in *The Times* on 19 August 1991. **112.** Gorbachev, *August Coup*, p. 31. **113.** Andrew and Mitrokhin, *Mitrokhin Archive*, p. 730.

30 'Holy Terror': From the Cold War to 9/11

1. Andrew, *For the President's Eyes Only*, pp. 440–41. **2.** Kurzman, *Unthinkable Revolution in Iran*, p. viii. **3.** Parsons to FCO, 15 Jan. 1979; Lucas to Weir, 16 Jan. 1979, TNA FCO 8/3351; cited in Passi, 'Britain and the Iranian Revolution', Introduction. **4.** Stephen Lamport to Gorham, 22 Nov. 1978, TNA FCO 8/3208; cited in Passi, 'Britain and the Iranian Revolution', Introduction. **5.** Jervis, *Why Intelligence Fails*, pp. 85–7. **6.** Ibid., p. 119. **7.** Kuhns, 'Intelligence Failures'. Bobbitt, *Terror and Consent*, p. 292. **8.** *9/11 Commission Report*, p. 341. **9.** Andrew, *Defence of the Realm*, p. 801. **10.** On Bin Laden's misinterpretation of the Mardin fatwa, see http://www.israinternational.com/component/content/art

icle/42-rokstories/318-muslim-scholars-recast-ibn-taymiyyahs-fatwa-on-jihad.html.
11. Morris, 'Sayyid Qutb and the Jews'. Tibi, *Islamism and Islam*.   12. Qutb, 'The
America I Have Seen'.   13. Cook, *Martyrdom in Islam*, pp. 138–9.   14. Abdel
Bari Atwan, 'Osama bin Laden's death: A leader's wish fulfilled', *Guardian*, 2 May
2011.   15. Danan and Hunt, *Mixed Blessings*, p. 24. 'Religion' is conspicuously
absent from the most recent analysis of the world view of Clinton's first National
Security Advisor; Jones, 'Engaging the World'.   16. Andrew, *For the President's
Eyes Only*, pp. 538–9.   17. Kennedy School of Government, Case Program, 'CIA
and the Fall of the Soviet Empire', p. 55.   18. See above, pp. 699–700.   19. 'Baker
Visits a Much-Changed KGB', *Los Angeles Times*, 14 Sept. 1991.   20. Peter Grier,
'Cleaning the Bug House', *Air Force Magazine*, Sept. 2012. The new embassy
building was still unfinished.   21. On KGB bugging of the US embassy and the
ambassador's residence during the Soviet era, see above, pp. 592–3, 662.   22.
Andrew, *For the President's Eyes Only*, p. 540.   23. Primakov, *Russian Cross-
roads*, chs. 1–5.   24. Ibid., p. 89.   25. See above, p. 695.   26. Primakov, *Russian
Crossroads*, p. 97.   27. Information from John McLaughlin.   28. McLaughlin,
'Changing Nature of CIA Analysis'.   29. Primakov, *Russian Crossroads*, p. 3.   30.
Interview by Christopher Andrew with Robert Gates, 14 March 1994.   31. Andrew,
For the President's Eyes Only, pp. 538–9.   32. Ibid., p. 539.   33. Perry, *My Jour-
ney at the Nuclear Brink*, pp. 91–2.   34. Ibid., pp. 100–101. Hoffmann, *The Dead
Hand*, ch. 21. On Oak Ridge, see above, p. 666.   35. Senate Select Committee on
Intelligence, 'An Assessment of the Aldrich H. Ames Espionage Case and Its Implications for U.S. Intelligence' 1 Nov. 1994. https://www.cia.gov/news-information/
featured-story-archive/ames-mole-hunt-team.html.   36. Maureen Dowd, 'Crash
at the White House: The Overview; Unimpeded, Intruder Crashes Plane Into White
House', *The New York Times*, 13 Sept. 1994.   37. Warner, *Rise and Fall of Intelligence*, p. 260.   38. Aid, *Secret Sentry*, p. 198.   39. Hayden, *Playing to the Edge*,
ch. 1.   40. Primakov, *Russian Crossroads*, p. 107.   41. Primakov et al., *Ocherki
istorii rossiyskoi vneshnei razvedki*.   42. Primakov, *Russian Crossroads*, pp. 110–
11.   43. Samolis (ed.), *Veterany vneshei razvedki Rossii*.   44. Andrew and
Mitrokhin, *Mitrokhin Archive*, Introduction to paperback edn and ch. 1.   45. The
Commission report, entitled *Preparing for the 21st Century: An Appraisal of U.S.
Intelligence*, was published on 1 March 1996; https://www.gpo.gov/fdsys/pkg/
GPO-INTELLIGENCE/content-detail.html.   46. See above, pp. 695–7.   47.
Andrew and Mitrokhin, *Mitrokhin Archive*, pp. 619–20.   48. Ibid., Introduction
to paperback edn and ch. 1.   49. *Nevavisimaya Gazeta*, 10 Dec. 1996; Reuter
reports, 10 Dec. 1996.   50. Andrew and Mitrokhin, *Mitrokhin Archive*, p. 17.   51.
'C.I.A. Officer Admits Spying for Russians'; www.nytimes.com/1997/03/04/us/
cia-officer-admits-spying-for-russians.html. Denson, *Spy's Son*.   52. Hayden,
Playing to the Edge, p. 278.   53. Wise, *Spy*. Interviews by Christopher Andrew
with the late Bryan J. Kelley.   54. *Preparing for the 21st Century: An Appraisal
of U.S. Intelligence*, 1 March 1996; https://www.gpo.gov/fdsys/pkg/GPO-
INTELLIGENCE/content-detail.html.   55. Andrew, 'Conclusion: An Agenda for
Future Research', pp. 224–5.   56. Johnson, 'Aspin–Brown Intelligence
Inquiry'.   57. *9/11 Commission Report*, p. 108.   58. Hoffman, '"Holy Terror"'.

Hoffman, *Inside Terrorism*, ch. 4.   **59.** Ralph Blumenthal, 'The Twin Towers: The Investigation; Insistence on Refund for a Truck Results in an Arrest in Explosion', *The New York Times*, 5 March 1993.   **60.** http://www.pbs.org/wgbh/pages/front-line/shows/gunning/interviews/woolsey.html.   **61.** Warner, *Rise and Fall of Intelligence*, p. 284. Piette and Radack, 'Piercing the "Historical Mists"'.   **62.** Jane Mayer, 'Ronald Reagan's Benghazi', *New Yorker*, 5 May 2014.   **63.** https://www.state.gov/m/ds/rls/rpt/c47602.htm.   **64.** Interview with Ambassador Prudence Bushnell, 2005; http://adst.org/2012/08/prudence-bushnell-on-the-us-embassy-nairobi-bombings/.   **65.** *9/11 Commission Report*, pp. 115–16.   **66.** Clinton, *My Life*, p. 798.   **67.** *9/11 Commission Report*, p. 109.   **68.** Wright, *Looming Tower*, pp. 260–61.   **69.** *9/11 Commission Report*, p. 108.   **70.** Hudson, *Sociology and Psychology of Terrorism*, pp. 3–4, 62.   **71.** Ibid., pp. 135–40.   **72.** Ibid., p. 15.   **73.** Andrew, *Defence of the Realm*, pp. 802–3.   **74.** Ibid., pp. 771–3, 784–5.   **75.** Stuart, *Islamist Terrorism*.   **76.** Andrew, *Defence of the Realm*, pp. 807–8.   **77.** Kendall, 'Yemen's Al-Qa'ida and Poetry as a Weapon of Jihad', p. 247.   **78.** Tenet, *At the Center of the Storm*, loc. 2247.   **79.** *9/11 Commission Report*, p. 271. Warner, *Rise and Fall of Intelligence*, p. 284.   **80.** *9/11 Commission Report*, p. 271.   **81.** Tenet, *At the Center of the Storm*, loc. 2348.   **82.** *9/11 Commission Report*, pp. 192–8.   **83.** Tenet, *At the Center of the Storm*, loc. 2492.   **84.** Ibid., loc. 2500.   **85.** Andrew, *Defence of the Realm*, pp. 808–9.   **86.** Ibid., p. 809.   **87.** Ibid., p. 806.   **88.** Davidsson, *Hijacking America's Mind*, pp. 5off.   **89.** 'Fifteen Years after 9/11'; https://www.cybersecurityintelligence.com/blog/15-years-after-9-11-1624.html.   **90.** Hayden, *Playing to the Edge*, pp. 44–5.   **91.** Tenet, *At the Center of the Storm*, loc. 3135.   **92.** Richard Stengel, 'Osama bin Laden and the Idea of Progress', *Time*, 21 Dec. 2001.   **93.** *9/11 Commission Report*, pp. 273–5.   **94.** Ibid., p. 263.   **95.** 'Fifteen Years after 9/11'; https://www.cybersecurityin-telligence.com/blog/15-years-after-9-11-1624.html.   **96.** Rice, *No Higher Honor*, p. 79.   **97.** Tenet, *At the Center of the Storm*, loc. 330.   **98.** Bush, *Decision Points*, pp. 157–8. FBI, Amerithrax or Anthrax Investigation; https://www.fbi.gov/history/famous-cases/amerithrax-or-anthrax-investigation.   **99.** Bush, *Decision Points*, pp. 152–3.   **100.** Ibid., pp. 158–60.   **101.** Tenet, *At the Center of the Storm*, loc. 3827.   **102.** Haines, 'CIA's Own Effort', p. 201.   **103.** See above, p. 636.   **104.** *9/11 Commission Report*, p. 261.   **105.** Ibid., pp. 72–3; http://www.globalsecurity.org/security/profiles/yousef_bombs_philippines_airlines_flight_434.htm.   **106.** Bush, *Decision Points*, p. 135.   **107.** Peter Ford, 'Europe cringes at Bush "crusade" against terrorists', *Christian Science Monitor*, 19 Sept. 2001.   **108.** *9/11 Commission Report*, executive summary.

Conclusion: Twenty-First-Century Intelligence in Long-Term Perspective

1. Andrew and Dilks, *Missing Dimension*, p. 1.   **2.** Muggeridge, *Chronicles of Wasted Time*, vol. II: *The Infernal Grove*, pp. 122–3.   **3.** Andrew, *Defence of the Realm*, p. 753.   **4.** See above, p. 687.   **5.** See above, p. 11.   **6.** See above, p. 18.

7. Talmud, Sanhedrin 72a. Bergman, *Rise and Kill First*. 8. Andrew, *Defence of the Realm*, pp. 350–60. 9. Bergman, *Rise and Kill First*. 10. On Haddad's terrorist operations and role as a KGB agent, see Andrew and Mitrokhin, *Mitrokhin Archive II*, ch. 13. 11. Bergman, *Rise and Kill First*, pp. 322–3. 12. Interview with Ronen Bergman, *The Times of Israel*, 26 Jan. 2018; https://www.timesofisrael.com/how-israels-leaders-use-targeted-killings-to-try-to-stop-history/. 13. See above, pp. 712–13, 714. 14. See above, pp. 670–71, 673–4. 15. Warner, *Rise and Fall of Intelligence*, p. 143. 16. See above, pp. 166–70. 17. https://www.gchq.gov.uk/news-article/gchq-celebrate-centenary-2019. 18. Among them are Bayly and Harper, *Forgotten Wars*; Brown and Louis (eds.), *Oxford History of the British Empire*, vol. IV: *Twentieth Century*; Hyam, *Britain's Declining Empire*; Mansergh (ed.), *Constitutional Relations between Britain and India*. Bradley, 'Decolonization, the Global South, and the Cold War, 1919–1962' mentions the role of the CIA but, surprisingly, not that of British intelligence. 19. Andrew, *Defence of the Realm*, pp. 330–31. 20. Himanshi Dhawan, 'Documents reveal Nehru govt shared information on Netaji with Britain's MI5', *Times of India*, 12 April 2015. 21. Andrew, *Defence of the Realm*, pp. 442–6. 22. Ibid., pp. 463–9, 472–3, 481–2. 23. Walton, *Empire of Secrets*, pp. 151–5. By unanimous decision of the judges, this volume won the 2014 Longman History Today book prize. 24. Aldrich, *GCHQ*, ch. 8. 25. See above, pp. 727–30. 26. See above, pp. 726, 728. 27. Warner, *Rise and Fall of Intelligence*, p. 290. 28. JIC report, 15 March 2002; *Review of Intelligence on Weapons of Mass Destruction* (Butler Report), para 272. 29. Andrew, 'British Official Perceptions of Muammar Gaddafi'. 30. Blair, *A Journey*, p. 374. 31. *Report of the Iraq Inquiry* (Chilcot Report), 12 vols. 32. See below, pp. 738–45. 33. See above, ch. 30. 34. Bobbitt, *Terror and Consent*, p. 314. 35. See above, pp. 529–30. 36. This was a point made in evidence to the Chilcot Inquiry by the Intelligence and Security Coordinator, Sir David Omand; http://www.iraqinquiry.org.uk/media/95182/2010-01-20-Transcript-Omand-S2.pdf. 37. In an earlier study of Blair's defence policy, for example, Sir Lawrence Freedman, a member of the Iraq Inquiry, had taken a much longer-term view; Freedman, 'Defence', in Seldon (ed.), *Blair Effect*. 38. The great exception is the pioneering study by Aldrich and Cormac, *The Black Door: Spies, Secret Intelligence and British Prime Ministers*, which includes intelligence material omitted by many prime ministerial biographers. 39. Bew, *Citizen Clem*. 40. Andrew, *Defence of the Realm*, pp. 321–2, 350–55, 411–12. 41. Aldrich and Cormac, *Black Door*, ch. 6. 42. Andrew, *For the President's Eyes Only*, p. 298. 43. Presentation by Colin Powell to the UN Security Council, 5 Feb. 2003. 44. Rice, *No Higher Honor*, p. 200. 45. Powell, *It Worked for Me*, loc. 2676. 46. https://www.theguardian.com/uk-news/2016/jul/06/movie-plot-the-rock-inspired-mi6-sources-iraqi-weapons-claim-chilcot-report. 47. Jervis, *Why Intelligence Fails*, pp. 123–4. 48. Warner, *Rise and Fall of Intelligence*, p. 292. 49. SSCI Iraq Report, 2004, p. 18. On this colloquial use of the 'groupthink' concept, see Jervis, *Why Intelligence Fails*, pp. 129–30. 50. Commission on the Intelligence Capabilities of the United States Regarding Weapons of Mass Destruction (President's WMD Commission), *Report to the President of the United States*, 31 March 2005, p. 155. Jervis, *Why Intelligence Fails*, p. 152. 51. Jervis, *Why Intelligence Fails*, pp.

150–51.   52. Overy, "'Instructive for the Future'".   53. Nixon, *Debriefing the President*, p. 67.   54. Ibid., p. 25.   55. Ibid., pp. 6, 8, 71.   56. Ibid., p. 138.   57. https://www.cbsnews.com/news/interrogator-shares-saddams-confessions/.   58. See above, pp. 621–5, 645–6, 655–6.   59. Andrew, *For the President's Eyes Only*, p. 538.   60. Nixon, *Debriefing the President*, p. 137.   61. Woods, Lacey, and Murray, 'Saddam's Delusions: The View from the Inside'.   62. Ibid.   63. Saddam made the admission not in formal interrogation but in 'casual conversation'. SSA Piro, 'Casual Conversation [with Saddam Hussein], June 11, 2004'; http://nsarchive.gwu.edu/NSAEBB/NSAEBB279/24.pdf. Piro's 'casual conversation' with Saddam made a considerable impression on Bush; Bush, *Decision Points*, pp. 268–9.   64. Nixon, *Debriefing the President*, p. 96.   65. Heuer, *Psychology of Intelligence Analysis*. Though this study was completed in 2008, it was based on previous drafts and research over thirty years.   66. Ibid., ch. 6.   67. O'Hagan, *Secret Life*, p. 27.   68. https://www.cia.gov/news-information/speeches-testimony/2017-speeches-testimony/pompeo-delivers-remarks-at-csis.html.   69. See above, pp. 422–4.   70. http://www.businessinsider.com/tunisia-wikileaks-2011-1?IR=T.   71. O'Hagan, *Secret Life*, p. 98.   72. Hayden, *Playing to the Edge*, p. 421.   73. Aldrich and Cormac, *Black Door*, pp. 569–76.   74. Alan Rusbridger, Foreword to Harding, *Snowden Files*.   75. Gladwell, 'Daniel Ellsberg, Edward Snowden, and the Modern Whistle-Blower'.   76. Pozen, 'The Leaky Leviathan'.   77. Woodward quotes Gates's comment on his website, bobwoodward.com.   78. Bob Woodward, 'How Mark Felt Became "Deep Throat"', *Washington Post*, 20 June 2005.   79. 'Ex-Code Analyst Explains His Aim', *The New York Times*, 19 July 1972.   80. Adrian Chen, 'After 30 Years of Silence, the Original NSA Whistleblower Looks Back'; http://gawker.com/after-30-years-of-silence-the-original-nsa-whistleblow-1454865018.   81. See above, p. 478.   82. See above, pp. 583–4, 591–3, 675.   83. See above, p. 673.   84. See above, p. 675.   85. Aldrich, *GCHQ*, pp. 399–400.   86. Andrew, *For the President's Eyes Only*, pp. 483–4.   87. 'Trump CIA director blames "worship of Edward Snowden" for rise in leaks', *Guardian*, 24 June 2017.   88. https://www.cia.gov/news-information/speeches-testimony/2017-speeches-testimony/pompeo-delivers-remarks-at-csis.html.   89. Alan Judd, 'Edward Snowden, MI5, The Guardian: who are the bad guys?', *Daily Telegraph*, 9 Oct. 2013.   90. See above, pp. 712–13.   91. Andrew and Mitrokhin, *Mitrokhin Archive*, Introduction to paperback edn and ch. 1. Three other books are based on secret exfiltration of additional important material from KGB foreign-intelligence files: Andrew and Gordievsky (eds.), *Instructions from the Centre* and *More Instructions from the Centre*; Haynes, Klehr and Vassiliev, *Spies*.   92. Andrew and Mitrokhin, *Mitrokhin Archive*, ch. 15.   93. Conquest, *Great Terror*.   94. Conor Gaffey, 'North Korean Defectors are Using Google Earth to Identify Killing Sites and Mass Graves in Kim Jong Un's Totalitarian State', *Newsweek*, 21 July 2017. United Nations, Human Rights Council, *Report of the Commission of Inquiry on Human Rights in the Democratic People's Republic of Korea*. UN doc A/HRC/25/CRP. 1, 7 February 2014   Amnesty International Annual Report 2016/17; https://www.amnesty.org/en/countries/asia-and-the-pacific/north-korea/report-korea-democratic-peoples-republic-of/.   95. Amnesty International, 'North Korea prison camps very much in working order', 22 Nov. 2016; https://www.

amnesty.org/en/latest/news/2016/11/north-korea-prison-camps-very-much-in-working-order/. **96.** Chambers, 'Past and Present State', p. 32. **97.** Andrew and Mitrokhin, *Mitrokhin Archive II*, pp. 270–71. **98.** Chambers, 'Past and Present State', pp. 31–4. **99.** Ibid., pp. 37–40. **100.** Ibid., p. 40. **101.** See above, p. 66. **102.** See above, p. 736ff. **103.** Nathan, Link and Liang, *Tiananmen Papers*. **104.** MSS, 'Situation at Muxidi on the evening of the 3rd', Important Intelligence (*Yaoqin*), 2 a.m., 4 June 1989. Nathan, Link and Liang, *Tiananmen Papers*. **105.** Lim, *People's Republic of Amnesia*. **106.** Ellen Nakashima, 'Hacks of OPM databases compromised 22.1 million people, federal authorities say', *Washington Post*, 9 July 2015. Julie Hirschfeld Davis, 'Hacking of Government Computers Exposed 21.5 Million People', *The New York Times*, 9 July 2015. **107.** *Guardian*, 19 April 2016; *The New York Times*, 21 April 2016; *Daily Telegraph*, 21 April 2016. **108.** MMS report to Party Central, 'On ideological and political infiltration into our country from the United States and other international political forces', 1 June 1989; Nathan, Link and Liang, *Tiananmen Papers*, pp. 446ff. **109.** BBC News, 'Beijing offers hefty cash reward for spy tip-offs', 10 April 2017; http://www.bbc.co.uk/news/world-asia-china-39550673. **110.** http://www.chinadaily.com.cn/business/2017-02/14/content_28194717.htm. **111.** Tanner and Bellacqua, *China's Response to Terrorism*. **112.** Though others in the building worked under cover, as Official Historian I was publicly identified. **113.** See above, p. 722. **114.** Andrew, *Defence of the Realm*, pp. 828–33. **115.** See above, pp. 163–6, 170, 173–8. **116.** Andrew, *Defence of the Realm*, pp. 830–31. **117.** Ibid., pp. 807–8. **118.** Beyza Unal, 'Growing Threat as Organized Crime Funnels Radioactive Materials to Terrorists', 13 Oct. 2015; https://www.chathamhouse.org/expert/comment/growing-threat-organized-crime-funnels-radioactive-materials-terrorists. **119.** 'Isis would use chemical weapons in attack on UK, says minister', *Guardian*, 1 Jan. 2017. 'Chemical weapons found in Mosul in Isis lab, say Iraqi forces', *Guardian*, 29 Jan. 2017. 'ISIS militants launch multiple chemical weapons attacks on Iraqi troops', *Newsweek*, 17 April 2017. **120.** https://www.theguardian.com/us-news/2016/apr/01/obama-nuclear-security-summit-stop-madmen-isis-terrorism. https://www.gov.uk/government/publications/nuclear-security-summit-2016. **121.** See above, p. 684. **122.** See above, pp. 682–3. **123.** 1 Corinthians 13:12. **124.** Andrew, *Defence of the Realm*, pp. 842–3. **125.** Ibid., pp. 198–206. **126.** Petrie originally wanted only a record of MI5's recent, mainly wartime, history. Curry, however, insisted on going back to MI5's origins. Andrew, Introduction to [Curry], *The Security Service, 1908–1945*. Minute by Petrie, 29 March 1946, TNA KV 4/3. **127.** See above, pp. 510–11, 538–9. **128.** See, for example, Tom McCarthy, 'Trump voices confusion over US history: "Why was there a civil war?"', *Guardian*, 1 May 2017.

Acknowledgements

My greatest debts are to Corpus Christi College, Cambridge, where I have been a Fellow since 1967, and to the Cambridge University Faculty of History, which appointed me assistant lecturer (later Professor of Modern and Contemporary History) in the same year. Their support enabled me to become the first Cambridge academic to teach the history of intelligence at a time when the subject still provoked some scholarly scepticism.

The Cambridge Intelligence Seminar, which for the past two decades has met at Corpus Christi every Friday in term-time, has been a constant source of inspiration during the writing of *The Secret World*. Though most participants are students and academics, they have also included former intelligence officers, among them ex-heads of Russian foreign intelligence and Mossad as well as of Western agencies. Before every seminar, I and other convenors meet for tea in the Old Combination Room by a painting widely believed to be the only contemporary portrait of the College's greatest writer, Christopher Marlowe, who was recruited to the Elizabethan secret service while still a student. His portrait is a constant reminder to us of the importance of long-term perspective. At a time when Elizabeth I faced both serious assassination plots and the looming threat of Spanish invasion, intelligence from both espionage and codebreaking was as important as at almost any subsequent moment in British history.*

The three-millennia time-span and wide geographical range of *The Secret World* have made assistance from friends and academic colleagues in tracking down elusive intelligence sources essential. But for help from friends in Paris in navigating French bureaucracy while I was still a PhD student (more difficult then than now), I might never have gained access to the French SIGINT files which began my interest in intelligence history and are quoted in this book.† Some of my acknowledgements are, sadly, posthumous. Our neighbours in the Newnham area of Cambridge who had worked in Bletchley Park, as well as the retired Soviet spy in the next street, are no more, but *The Secret World* draws on interviews with them. In the final years of the Cold War, I had the great privilege of working closely (and for three years secretly) with Oleg Gordievsky, who made a daring escape from Moscow in

---

* See above, ch. 10.
† Further details in Phythian, 'Profiles in Intelligence: An Interview with Professor Christopher Andrew'.

1985 after a decade as the leading Western agent in the KGB. In 1992 came my appointment as visiting Beton Michael Kaneb Professor of National Security at Harvard and other transatlantic research opportunities which helped to shape the long-term interpretation in this book of US intelligence. In 1995 I began a collaboration with the former KGB archivist Vasili Mitrokhin (not publicly announced until the publication of our first book four years later), who had smuggled out of KGB archives what the FBI called 'the most complete and extensive intelligence ever received from any source'. This intelligence is now available to researchers at the Churchill College Archives Centre, Cambridge. The Mitrokhin Archive makes an extraordinary contrast with that of the Security Service (MI5), to which I had access as MI5's first (and so far only) Official Historian from 2003 to 2010 and which I quoted extensively in its centenary history.

There is no space, alas, to thank by name all those who assisted me while I was writing *The Secret World*. I am deeply grateful, however, to all the following for responding to queries or for commenting on segments of the text or for notably extending my grasp of intelligence by allowing me to supervise their PhD theses (in a minority of cases, for all three): Professor Richard Aldrich, Dr Christian Bak, Gill Bennett, Dr Ronen Bergman, Professor Tim Blanning, Dr David Burke, Dr Johnny Chavkin, Professor Tony Craig, Professor Julie Fedor, Professor André Gerolymatos, Dr David Gioe, Professor Peter Godman, Dr Kristian Gustafson, George Hart, Professor Lord (Peter) Hennessy, Michael Herman, Professor Bruce Hoffman, Dr Ioanna Iordanou, Professor Peter Jackson, Dr David Kahn, Dr Elisabeth Kendall, Professor Neil Kent, Professor Georg Kreis, Stuart Laing, Dr Dan Larsen, Svetlana Lokhova, Dr Victor Madeira, Dr Tom Maguire, Dr Cornelia Manegold, Keith Melton, Sir David Omand, Jeremy Paterson, Hayden Peake, Dr Kevin Quinlan, Dr John Ranelagh, Professor Richard Rex, Dr Dina Rezk, Emily Salamon-Andrew, Dr Christian Schlaepfer, Dr Adam Shelley, Dr Will Styles, Dr Isabelle Tombs, Professor Robert Tombs, Professor Maurice Vaïsse, Dr Mathilde Von Bülow, Dr Calder Walton, Dr Michael Warner, Baron Wilson of Dinton, J. D. Work and Dr Patrick Zutshi.

As with most of my previous books on intelligence, the skill and support of my editor at Penguin, Stuart Proffitt, and my literary agent, Bill Hamilton, have been indispensable. I have been very fortunate too in my copyeditor, Mark Handsley, and in the proofreading work of Stephen Ryan. Errors that remain are, of course, my responsibility. I shall be grateful to readers kind enough to point them out to me.

I've greatly valued the opportunities given me by lecturing on Swan Hellenic cruises and while presenting BBC Radio and TV programmes to explore some of the intelligence locations in *The Secret World*. During voyages on the inimitable *Minerva*, these included sites as diverse as Archangel, Mount Nebo and the intelligence rooms of the Doge's Palace in Venice. In the Yeltsin era, the BBC fulfilled my ambition of carrying out interviews in the former KGB (now FSB) headquarters, the Lubyanka. I've learned much from the BBC producers with whom I've worked, especially Ian Bell. During the decade when we worked together on annual series of Radio 4's *What If?*, Ian encouraged me to present programmes on ancient and medieval, as well as recent, history – a rare privilege for a modern historian.

The students at Cambridge University from whom I've learnt much when teaching intelligence history have a long historical lineage which goes back to Christopher Marlowe and Elizabethan England. Talking to school audiences while writing *The Secret World* has made me realize the resonance of intelligence among even younger students. In 2015 I was one of the judges of the BBC TV programme *Blue Peter*'s Operation PETRA which aimed to identify Britain's best potential spies aged between eight and fourteen. The first task of the final shortlist during a weekend in Manchester was to identify and track down a mysterious picture which turned out to be the portrait of Marlowe (a copy of the Corpus Christi original) in Manchester Art Gallery. The three winners – two ten-year-olds and one aged thirteen – were presented with their certificates (but not recruited) by the Director-General of MI5 in its London HQ, where TV cameras were allowed for the first time.

My book is dedicated to seven young family members who have been a constant inspiration during the writing of *The Secret World*.

Christopher Andrew
March 2018

Index

Abdullah (Abu Bakr's son), 87
Abdullah ibn Atik, 89–90
Abdullah ibn Jahsh, 87
Abdullah-Khan, ruler of Shirvan, 150
Abdur Rahman, Afghan Amir ('The
    Iron Amir'), 421
Abedi, Salman, 757
Abedin, Moinul, 722
Aberdare, Lord, 400
Aberdeen, Lord, 359, 365–6,
    368, 405–6
Ablis, Geoffroy d', 102–3
Abu Al-Fadl Al-Abbas, 88
Abu al-Faraj al-Isfahani, 97
Abu Bakr, 87, 93
Abu Jihad, 733
Abu Rafi, 89–90
Abu Sufyan, 92
Abu'l Abbas As-Saffah, 96–7
Abwehr (German intelligence agency),
    573, 626, 646–7, 652, 653–4,
    656, 658–61
Acheson, Dean, 670
Act of Settlement, English (1701), 264
Act of Union (1707), 265
Adam, Robert, 303†
Adams, Arthur Alexandrovich, 664–5
Adams, John, 295, 299, 309
Adcock, Frank, 518
Addington, Henry, 336, 337–8
Addison, Joseph, 131
    Cato, 303
Adrianople, Battle of (378), 81–2
aerial reconnaissance

early ballooning experiments,
    411–12
First World War: Western Front,
    505–8, 562, 563
Second World War: Middle East,
    508, 529, 565
Aéronautique Militaire, 506
Aeschylus, 31
Afghanistan
    CIA covert actions in
        (1980s), 690–91
    First Anglo-Afghan war (1839–42),
        419
    mujahideen in, 690–91
    Northern Alliance, 725
    North-West Frontier, 416, 418,
        419–21, 449–50, 451
    Second Anglo-Afghan War (1878–
        80), 419–21
    Soviet war in (1980s), 689, 690, 699
Agadir crisis (1911), 477–8, 479, 484,
    485
Agasse, Guillaume, 106
'Age of Discovery', 120–21
Ageloff, Sylvia, 624
agents provocateurs, 61–2, 220, 238,
    273, 389, 394, 575
Agis II, Spartan king, 35
Ahmad, Rauf, 722–3
aircraft, 505, 507
airport security, 724–5, 757
Aix-la-Chapelle, Congress of (autumn
    1818), 370
Akhenaten, Pharaoh, 19

Akram, A. I., 94
Alam Halfa, Battle of (August–September 1942), 640
Alaric, Visigoth leader, 82
Albam, Abram Mironovich, 620
Albania, 678–9
Albert, Dr Heinrich, 521–2
Alberti, Leon Battista, 127–8
Alcibiades, 30, 34, 35–6
Aldegonde (Philips of Marnix, Lord of Saint-Aldegonde), 139–40, 166–9
Aldrich, Winthrop W., 605
Alekseev, Aleksandr, 689–90
Alekseev, General Mikhail, 486
Alembert, Jean d', 291
Alexander I, Tsar, 340, 343*, 352–3, 354–5, 356–7, 358–9, 360, 498, 499
  at Congress of Vienna, 363, 366–7
Alexander II, Tsar, 154, 406, 425, 427, 437
Alexander III, Tsar, 154, 428, 436
Alexander the Great, 37–9, 45–6, 333
Alexander Severus, Roman emperor, 76
Alexandra, Princess (wife of Edward VII), 433
Alexandra, Tsarina (wife of Nicholas II), 500
Alexandrovich, Vyacheslav Alekseevich, 557, 558
Alexandrovskaya Sloboda (country estate of Ivan IV), 141, 142, 151–2
Alexei, Tsarevich (son of Nicholas II), 500
Alfield, Thomas, 171
Alfonso XIII, King of Spain, 429
Alford, Dr Sidney, 757
Alford, Stephen, 190
Ali, Abdullah Ahmed, 757, 758
Alien Office, London, 323, 324*, 327, 329, 332–3
  'Inner Office' of, 336, 337
Allen, Sir Mark, 737
Allen, William, 171, 172, 176

Allenby, Field Marshal Viscount Edmund, 564–5
Allende, Salvador, 687–8, 690
All-Russian Co-operative Society (ARCOS), 583, 584
Alma, Battle of the (20 September 1854), 403–4
Almereyda, Miguel, 551
Alonne, Abel Tasien d', 264
Alvensleben, Count, 469
Amalric, Arnaud, 101
Ambrose, Stephen, 672
American Revolutionary War, 5, 294–311
Ames, Aldrich, 687, 709, 713, 714
Amiens, Peace of (1802), 321, 336–7
Ammianus Marcellinus, 80, 81–2
Amnesty International, 752
Ampthill, Lord, 467
Amr ibn al-As, 94–5
Anabaptists, 110
anarchist movement, nineteenth century, 429–31, 432–3
Ancre, Concino Concini, marquis d', 201–2
André, John, 303, 303†, 306
Andreev, Nikolai, 558
Andrew, Christopher
  Defence of the Realm, 10*, 10†, 90†, 548*, 658*, 722*, 732*, 738*, 758*
  Mitrokhin Archive, The (with Vasili Mitrokhin), 750–51
  For the President's Eyes Only, 676*, 748§
  Secret Service: The Making of the British Intelligence Community, 731†
  Timewatch documentary on Cumming, 482§, 582*
Androcles (Athenian demagogue), 34
Andropov, Yuri, 105, 130†, 687, 689, 690, 693, 694, 695–6, 699
Androsov, Yuri, 696
Angiolillo, Michele, 431

Anglo-Dutch wars (seventeenth century), 226, 235–6, 237
Ankhesenamen, Queen, 21
Annas (father-in-law of Caiaphas), 25*
Anne, Queen of England, 250, 261, 266, 269
Anne of Austria, 201, 202–3, 204, 212
anti-Semitism
  in Elizabethan era, 189
  Islamist brand of, 703
  medieval conspiracy theories, 106–7
  Nazi and fascist, 437, 645–6, 655–6, 732, 743
  Protocols of the Elders of Zion (forgery), 437, 703
  and Spanish Inquisition, 113
Antraigues, comte d', 343*
Appeasement policy in 1930s, 612–13, 614–16, 760*
Arab Bulletin, The, 529–30, 737
  Arab Rising against Turkish rule (1916), 508, 530, 541
Arabian Peninsula, 3, 86–92, 93
  Arab armies' military conquest in 630s/640s, 93–5
  Arab nationalism, 508, 530, 541, 737
  Arab Poetic Tradition, 720*
  pre-Islamic, 86†
Arabic language, 98, 99, 111, 123, 334, 742
  Arabic science and mathematics, 47, 97–9
Arafat, Yasser, 733
Aragon, Catherine of, 125, 126
Archibald, James F. J., 523
Arco, Antonio de, 200–201, 202–3
Argenson, comte d', 280
Argentina, 750
Ariovistus (Germanic ruler), 47
Aristander of Telmessus, 35–6
Aristotle, 36–7
Arisue, Major-General Seizo, 664
Arlington, Earl of, Sir Henry Bennet, 234, 236, 237–8

Arlington Hall, Virginia, 643
Arminius (Cheruscan leader), 70–71
Armstrong, Karen, *Muhammad: Prophet for Our Time,* 3*
Arnold, Benedict, 305–6
Arnold, John, 258
Arrian of Nicomedia, 35
Artagnan, Charles d', 243–4
Arthashastra (Mauryan dynasty manual), 3, 54–5, 55*, 60–66
Arundel, Charles, 183–4
Al-Asbahani, 86†
Ascham, Anthony, 221
Ashkenazi, Solomon Nathan, 124
Asim ibn Thabit, 91
Asma bint Marwan, 90
Aspin–Brown Commission (1995–6), 713–14, 716–17, 727
Asquith, Herbert, 6, 458, 474, 475, 477, 494, 499, 510–11, 532, 603, 760
Assange, Julian, 745, 746
assassination
  anarchist 'propaganda of the deed', 429–31, 432–3
  in the *Arthashastra*, 62, 63, 85
  of Bogolepov in Russia (1901), 437
  of Buckingham, 195, 207
  in Chinese tradition, 59, 85
  CIA's plans for Castro, 63, 85, 677, 680, 687, 688
  of Concini in Paris (April 1617), 201–2
  failures of protective security, 429–31, 433
  of Franz Ferdinand in Sarajevo, 444–8, 487
  frumentarii in Roman world, 77
  of Grand Duke Sergei (1905), 438
  by handgun, 169–70
  of Henry IV of France, 169, 195
  of Sergei Kirov (1 December 1934), 594–5
  MGB's plans for Tito, 85, 681–2
  and Muhammad, 89–90

assassination – (cont.)
   and nineteenth-century police
      forces, 426–7
   Operation FOXLEY (SOE plan to
      kill Hitler), 338†, 646
   pre-First World War 'golden age of',
      425, 427, 428–31, 432–3, 437–9,
      442, 444–8, 487
   pursuit of Charles I's regicides, 219,
      221, 230–32, 233–5
   Roman plot against Attila, 83–4, 85
   royalist plot on Napoleon (May
      1803), 337–8
   and Rushdie fatwa, 90, 90†
   in Serbia, 442–3
   of Sir William Curzon Wyllie (1909),
      619
   and Stalin, 62–3, 85, 623–4
   Talmud injunction to 'rise and kill
      first', 732–4
   and Tamil Tigers (LTTE), 721
   of Trotsky, 62–3, 624
   of Tsar Alexander II (March 1881),
      154, 425, 427, 437
   of Tsar Peter III, 291
   as undeclared Israeli state policy,
      732–4
   of US presidents, 429, 435–6, 688
   use of poison, 63
   of William I, Prince of Orange
      (1584), 85, 169–70
   Yamamoto's plane shot down (April
      1943), 638
Assaye, Battle of (1803), 345
Aston, Sir George, 13, 452
Astor, Vincent, 605–6
Atahualpa, Inca ruler, 136
Atatürk, Mustafa Kemal, 123
Atta, Mohamed, 724–5
Atterbury, Francis, Bishop of Rochester,
   272–5, 279
Attila, Hun leader, 82–5
Attlee, Clement, 673, 678–9, 738
Atwan, Abdel Bari, 704
Augsburg, League of, 247

Augustus, Emperor, 70, 72, 75
Aurelius Victor, 77
Auschwitz II (Birkenau), 656
Australia, 670–71
Austria
   1848 disturbances in, 384–5, 388
   annexation of by Nazi Germany
      (1938), 613
   'black chamber' (Geheime Kabinets-
      Kanzlei), 277, 278, 279, 363–4,
      365, 369–70, 489
   confrontation with Serbia (summer
      1914), 487–8, 490–91, 492, 493
   and First World War, 486, 502, 523
   French decrypts in mid-eighteenth
      century, 278
   and French Revolutionary
      wars, 317
   Galician uprising (1846), 369
   intelligence during Congress of
      Vienna, 363–7
   Kaunitz's intelligence operations, 5,
      278–9, 363
   Metternich's repression of students,
      372–3
   and Napoleonic Wars, 357
   Prussian defeat of (1866), 398
   Redl as Russian agent, 486
   rule in the Balkans, 443, 444, 471
   Russian decrypts of despatches, 485,
      488, 491, 492
   and Seven Years War (1756–63),
      278, 287, 288
   SIGINT agency in Vienna (pre-First
      World War), 489, 491
Austrian Succession, War of the, 278,
   285–6
authoritarian regimes
   Aristotle on, 37
   Committee of Public Safety in
      Revolutionary France, 321, 322–3,
      325, 326
   and conspiracy theories, 106, 326,
      594, 598–602, 619–20, 625–6,
      651, 680–82, 694–8

counter-subversion campaigns, 4, 26, 100–17, 130†, 574–5, 698–700, 751

crimes against humanity in North Korea, 751–2

as harder intelligence targets than democracies, 693

intelligence analysis as distorted in, 326, 344, 372, 375, 594, 603, 693–8

and media control/censorship, 108–10, 754

mindsets of autocrats, 26, 339, 344, 693, 743, 744, 745

and monopoly of truth, 100, 108–10, 115, 693

see also 'telling truth to power'

and whistle-blowing, 750–51, 753–4

Ay (Tutankhamun's vizier), 21

Azev, Evno, 437–9

Aztec Empire, Spanish conquest of, 132–6, 137

Babington, Anthony, 175–9, 188, 192, 200

Bacon, Anthony, 185–6, 188, 189*

Baden, Prince Max of, 569

Baden-Powell, Robert, 449–50

Badoer, Angelo, 203

Badoglio, Marshal Pietro, 607

Badr, Battle of (624), 88–9, 91

Baghdad, 97, 98

'House of Wisdom', 4, 98–9, 127, 128

Bagration, Princess Catherine, 366–7

Bahadur Shah (last Mughal ruler), 409–10

Bailly, Charles, 164–5

Baines, Richard, 171–2, 173, 186, 187

Bakatin, Vadim V., 704–5

Baker, James A., 705

Al-Baladhuri (historian), 95

Balaklava, Battle of (25 October 1854), 404

Balasy-Belvata, Jules de, 462–3, 464–5

Baldwin, Stanley, 580, 582, 583

Balfour, Arthur J., 523, 539, 543*, 548

Balkans region, 442–8, 471, 487, 489

Ball, Joseph, 581

balloonists, 411–12

Balta'ah, Hatib ibn Abi, 91

Bancroft, Edward, 296–8, 299–301

Bangya, János, 392–3

Banqueting House, Whitehall Palace, 209, 219

BARBAROSSA, operation (22 June 1941), 326*, 627

Barbès, Armand, 383, 384

Barclay, Sir George, 260

Barclay de Tolly, Mikhail, 352–3, 354–5, 358, 359, 498

Barillon, Paul, marquis de Branges, 248, 249

Barkstead, John, 233

Barnes, Jonathan, 37

Barot, Dhiren, 758

Barr, Joel, 666

Barras, Admiral de, 307

Barrère, Camille, 488

Barry, Madame du, 292

Bastian, Madame Marie-Caudron ('Auguste'), 459–60

Bates, David Homer, 411

Batiushin, General N. S., 550

Bavis, Mark, 725*

Bay of Pigs landing (1961), 677, 680

Bazeries, Étienne, 460, 461, 463, 468, 470

Bazna, Elyesa, 656–7

Beach, Jim, Haig's Intelligence, 530*

Beachy Head, Battle of (July 1690), 255

Beale, Robert, 185

Beard, Mary, 77

Beardall, Captain John R., 629, 631, 632–3, 635

Bearden, Milt, 691

Beatty, Admiral Earl David, 513, 514–15, 524, 525, 526

Beauchamp, Alphonse de, 341†

Beaumarchais, Pierre-Augustin Caron de, 293, 294

Beaumont Society (transgender support group), 294

Beaverbrook, Lord, 543–4
Bedborough, George, 431–2
Bedell Smith, Walter, 377–8
Beevor, Antony, 647
Begin, Menachem, 732
Behn, Aphra, 235, 236, 237, 303†
Belarus, 708
Belasyse, John, 224
Belchem, J. C., 380
Beletsky, S. P., 440, 441
Belgium, 494–5, 562
Bell, Eddie, 516, 538
Bellarmine, Robert, 109†
Ben Ali, President of Tunisia, 746
Benavides, Cristobal de
    Benavente y, 207
Benckendorff, General Aleksandr
    Kristoforovich von, 374
Benedict XII, Pope (Jacques Fournier),
    105–6
Ben-Gurion, David, 732
Bennett, Ralph, 641
Bentivoglio, Guido, 202
Bentley, Elizabeth, 673
Berchtold, Leopold, 487–8
Beresford, General William, 347*
Bergman, Dr Ronen: Rise and Kill
    First, 732–3, 734
Beria, Lavrenti, 110, 152*, 620, 626–7,
    654, 655, 667
Berle, Adolf A., 608, 634, 662
Berlin, Isaiah, 375
Bernard, Martin, 383
Bernard, Simon, 396–7
Bernardo, Lorenzo, 124
Bernstein, Carl, 748
Bernstorff, Johann Heinrich von, 519,
    521, 535, 540, 541–2
Berthier, Marshal, 344
Bertin, Rose, 294
Berwick, Duke of, 257, 259–60, 269
Bethmann Hollweg, Theobald von,
    488, 489–90, 493
Bevan, Colonel J. H., 652, 657
Bevin, Ernest, 732

Bew, John, 10, 738
Béziers, Languedoc, 101
Bienvenu-Martin, Jean-Baptiste, 492
Bigelow, John, 422
Bignon, Louis de, 352
bin Laden, Osama, 94, 702–3, 704,
    718, 720, 721, 723, 724, 725,
    758, 759
Binder, Baron Franz von, 370
Bingham, John, 423
Birch, Frank, 518, 524
Birmingham, 722
Bismarck, Major Busso von, 498
Bissell, Richard, 63
Black, Jeremy: Pitt the Elder, 289*
Blaine, James G., 423
Blair, Tony, 736, 737, 738
'Blanchardie, Martin', 324
Bland, Sir Nevile, 618–19
Blanning, Tim, 210
Blanqui, Auguste, 378–9, 383–4
Blencowe, William, 256, 263, 264, 270
Blenheim, Battle of (1704), 261, 262
Bletchley Park, 'Station X' at, 1, 120,
    509, 517–18, 616, 617, 635, 640,
    641, 642, 671–2
  Air Section, 642, 674
  John Cairncross at, 649
  ELINT successes, 674
  extraordinary talent at, 644
  SSA fact-finding mission to
    (1943), 642–4
  state-of-the-art technology at, 648
Blücher, Gebhard Leberecht von, 361
Blunt, Anthony, 621, 649–50, 653, 661
Blyumkin, Yakov, 557–8
Bodansky, Yossef, 721
Boer War (1899–1902), 449, 450–51
Bogolepov, N. P., 437
Bogrov, Dmitri, 439
Bohlen, 'Chip', 592
Boisdeffre, General Raoul de, 462
Boleyn, Anne, 126
Bolingbroke, Viscount, 276
Bolivia, 690

Bolsheviks
    Churchill's hatred of, 575, 578–9,
        583, 626
    German aid to (First World War),
        544–7
    Lenin's 'April Theses', 545
    Revolution (October 1917), 7,
        552–3, 555, 759
    split with Mensheviks, 440, 442, 545
Bonaparte, Joseph, 344, 348, 349–52
Bonaparte, Napoleon, 1, 38, 53, 288,
    316
    coup d'état (November 1799), 336
    and 'Coup of 18 Fructidor', 331
    crowns himself emperor (1804), 339
    defeat of (1814), 359–60
    in Egypt (1798–9), 333–6
    escape from Elba (February 1815),
        360–61, 368
    ignores intelligence at Waterloo,
        361–2
    royalist plot to assassinate (May
        1803), 337–8
    Russian campaign of, 352–3, 354,
        358–9
    sacks Fouché as chief of police, 342–3
    Statistical Bureau, 339–40, 344, 345
    use of/view of intelligence, 339,
        339†, 340–41, 342, 344, 352,
        353–4, 357–8
Bonar Law, Andrew, 579
Bonch-Bruevich, Vladimir, 560
Bonham, Sir George, 443
Bonis, François, 280
Bonner, Elena, 699
Bonnet Rouge (left-wing newspaper),
    551
Bonneval, baron de, 286
Bonrepaus, Usson de, 248–9
Bonsall, Arthur 'Bill', 642, 674
Booth, Sir George, 228
Booth, John Wilkes, 435
Borghese, Pauline, 354
Borodino, Battle of (7 September
    1812), 358

Bosnia and Herzegovina, 443, 444, 471
Bossy, John: Giordano Bruno and the
    Embassy Affair, 173*
Boudicca, Queen, 74–5
Bougainville, Admiral Louis-Antoine
    de, 321
Bouillé, marquis de, 315–16
Bourdin, Martial, 431
Boyce, Ernest, 560, 575*
Boy-Ed, Captain Karl, 522, 523
Boyle, Edward, 644*
the Boyne, Battle of (1 July 1690), 255
Braddock, General Edward, 302
Bradshaw, John, 218–19
Bradstreet, Dudley, 283
Braithwaite, Sir Rodric, 416, 421
Bratton, Colonel Rufus S., 629
Bresci, Gaetano, 430, 433
Brest-Litovsk, Treaty of (March 1918),
    556, 557, 558, 561
Breteuil, marquis de, 315–16
Brezhnev, Leonid, 687, 689, 693, 695
Briand, Aristide, 585
Bridd, John, 159
Brillon, Madame de, 299
Britain
    7 July 2005 attacks in London, 756
    Act of Union (1707), 265
    Anglo-French Entente Cordiale
        (1904), 464
    and Congress of Vienna, 338, 365, 366
    decolonization, 735–6
    destruction of Steinhauer's network,
        495–6
    Duke of Newcastle and espionage,
        280–81
    embassy security issues, 456–7, 591–2
    exaggerated official secrecy, 8–9, 734
    fear of republicanism during French
        Revolution, 326–9
    General Staff introduced (1906), 452
    'German finance for pacifism' claims
        (First World War), 551–2, 553–5
    intelligence as taboo subject, 731,
        732, 734

Britain – (cont.)
  intelligence during American war,
    295, 296–8
  intelligence special relationship
    with US, 7, 8, 169, 516, 565–7,
    608, 609, 641–4, 670–71,
    673–4, 735
  during 'July Crisis' (1914), 494
  Nootka Sound crisis, 313–14
  post-First World War intelligence
    cuts, 573, 574
  pre-First World War German
    invasion/espionage scares,
    472–6, 474
  Royal Navy mutinies (1797), 332
  Russian decrypts of despatches, 456,
    457, 458
  and Seven Years War (1756–63),
    278, 287–91
  supports Cadoudal conspiracy (May
    1803), 337–8
  weak First World War ciphers, 500
  see also Victorian-era Britain
British Museum, 66
brothels, 16–17, 342, 367, 547
Browning, Lieutenant-Colonel Freddie,
  581–2
Browning, Oscar, 313
Bruce, David, 605
Brücker, Martin-Joseph, 459
Bruneau, Jacques, 199
Bruno, Giordano, 109†, 173*
Brunswick-Lüneburg, house of, 255
Brusilov, General Alexei, 498*, 502,
  549, 550
Buchanan, Sir George, 500, 502, 552–3
Buckingham, George Villiers, Duke of
  (favourite of James I), 195, 203–5,
  206–7, 208
Bukharin, Nikolai, 601
Bulgakov, Mikhail: The Master and
  Margarita, 143
Bulgaria, 501
Buller, General Sir Redvers, 450–51
Bullitt, William C., Jr, 592–3, 607

Bülow, Bernhard von, 454, 458, 469,
  470–71, 479
Bundy, William F. B, 643
Bureau of Diplomatic Security, 719
Burgess, Guy, 621, 649, 673
Burgoyne, General John, 299
Burke, Edmund, 321, 322
Burke, Frank, 521
Burke, Harry, 697*
Burtsev, Vladimir, 438
Bush, George H. W., 672, 691, 707–8,
  710, 723
Bush, George W., 67–8, 116–17, 723,
  724, 727–8, 729, 736
Bushnell, Prudence, 719
Bussche-Haddenhausen, Baron Hilmar
  von dem, 490*
Bussy, François de, 281, 282, 287, 288–9
Butcher, Tim: The Trigger, 444*
Bute, Earl of, 289, 290
Butler Report (Review of Intelligence
  on Weapons of Mass Destruction,
  2004), 736
Byrne, James F., 670
Byron, Lord, 132*
Byzantium, 80, 86, 92–3, 94, 95–6

cabinet noir (black chamber), French
  1890s–1914 period, 459–60, 461,
  463–4, 467–9, 470, 478, 479,
  483–4, 485, 488, 492, 749
  Étienne Bazeries at, 460, 461, 463,
    468, 470
  as bureau du secret under Louis XV,
    282*
  and Colbert, 245
  disrupted by the Fronde, 212
  and Gladstone, 421–2
  and Louis XIV, 242, 247–8
  and Louis Napoleon, 395
  and Metternich's correspondence,
    357, 370
  and Napoleon, 340, 341, 342, 357
  relative decline in eighteenth
    century, 277

Richelieu founds (c.1633), 5, 210–11
Rossignol as key figure, 210, 211, 212, 242
Čabrinović, Nedeljko, 444–5, 446
Cadogan, Sir Alexander, 613–14, 615, 617, 731*
Cadogan, William, 261–2, 264–5
Cadoudal, Georges, 338
Caesar, Julius, 46–53, 51*, 70, 82, 333
Caesarea, Byzantine Palestine, 95
Caiaphas (high priest), 25, 26
Caillaux, Madame Henriette, 485, 491–2
Caillaux, Joseph, 478, 479, 484–5, 491–2, 551
Cairncross, John, 621, 649
Cairo Museum of Egyptian Antiquities, 21
Calchas (mythical diviner), 40*
Caleb (biblical spy), 15, 16
Caligula, Roman emperor, 73, 75
Callen, Sylvia, 624–5
Callwell, Major-General Charles, 449
Calmette, Gaston, 484, 485, 491
Cambodia, 707
Cambridge, Field Marshal the Duke of, 415
Cambridge University, 643
   Cambridge spy ring, 183, 593, 621, 649–51, 661–2, 673, 711
   Churchill College Archives Centre, 751
   King's College, 155, 158, 517, 518
Cameron, Dr Archibald, 285
Cameron, David, 747, 759
Campion, Edmond, 171
Canaan, 2, 3, 13, 14–20, 21–2
Canada, 670–71, 672*
Canaris, Admiral, 656*
Cannae, Battle of (216 BC), 43–4, 82
Canning, George, 343–4
Cannon, James, 624–5
Cánovas del Castillo, Antonio, 429, 431
Cao Cao, Chinese warlord, 58
Capello, Carlo, 126
Carbonari, Italian, 379, 397
Carcassonne, Languedoc, 102–3, 108

Cardigan, James Brudenell, 7th Earl of, 404
Cardonnel, Adam de, 262
Cardwell, Edward, 415
Cardwell, John M., 17–18
Carlos I, King of Portugal, 428
Carlsbad Decrees (1819), 372–3
Carlyle, Thomas, 381, 747
Carmarthen, Lord, 312
Carnot, Sadi, President of France, 428–9, 430–31, 447
Caroline, Queen, 281
Carson, Sir Edward, 551
Carter, Jimmy, 701
Carter, John Franklin ('Jay Franklin'), 605
Carthaginian Empire, 41–5
Cartier, Colonel François, 564
Cartledge, Paul, 34–5
cartography
   in ancient Rome, 50, 50†
   Chinese, 121†
   Great Trigonometrical Survey of India, 407, 416–18
   Jervis's during Crimean War, 403, 414
   and Ottoman Empire, 120–21, 121*
   Salviati World Map (1525), 120
   T&S Department in Britain, 414, 415
   Venetian Mappa Mundi (c.1450), 120
Casanova, Giacomo, 131
Caserio, Sante, 430–31
Casey, Bill, 691
Casimir, Duke John, 181
Cassius Dio, 73–4
Castelnau, Michel de, 173, 175
Castelnau, Pierre de, 100–101
Castlereagh, Lord (Robert Stewart), 338, 365, 366, 370–71
Castro, Fidel, 63, 677, 680, 687, 688, 689–90
Catesby, Robert, 193, 195
Cathar heresy in Languedoc, 4, 100–102, 104, 104*, 105–6
Catherine the Great, 287, 291

Catholic Church
  'Albigensian Crusade', 100–102
  burning of heretics, 100, 101, 104,
    108, 109†, 114–15
  Capuchin order, 209
  censorship in Middle Ages, 109
  Charles II's death bed conversion,
    222, 236
  Council of Trent (1551), 123*
  English Catholics in Elizabethan/
    Stuart era, 158, 161, 173–5,
    176–7, 193, 222
  execution of Protestant 'heretics',
    110, 110*
  and Henry VIII, 125
  'inquisitions', 4, 100, 102–6, 102§,
    107–8, 109–10, 111–13, 115–16,
    742†
  'Investiture Controversy', 100
  and James II, 236, 240, 248–9
  and Napoleon, 340–41
  Nicholas II's dislike of, 456*
  Papacy and Italian Wars, 128
  Papacy's use of ciphers, 127
  papal bureaucracy, 100
  parti dévot in France, 200, 207
  and plots to overthrow Elizabeth I,
    158, 164–6, 173–9
  'Popish Plot' (late 1670s), 238,
    239–40, 241
  in revolutionary France, 317
  Roman Inquisition (Holy Office),
    107, 109–10
  Third Republic anticlericalism, 484
Cattley, Charles (alias Calvert), 404–5
Caux, Bernard de, 102
Cavagnari, Major Sir Louis, 419–20
Cave, Sir George, 553
Cavendish-Bentinck, Victor, 617
Cecil, Robert, 662
Cecil, Sir Robert (Earl of Salisbury),
  189–90, 191–2, 193, 203
Cecil, William (Lord Burghley), 150,
  156, 158, 174, 177, 532
  cutbacks in intelligence, 185

  death of (1598), 190
  fear of foreign-backed Catholic plots,
    163–4
  and 'Lopez Plot', 188–9
  and Mary, Queen of Scots, 175, 179,
    191
  Powle as agent of, 181
  and Ridolfi Plot, 165
  and Somer's decryption, 162–3, 162†
  and Treaty of Edinburgh (1560), 163
Celle, Lower Saxony, 255–6
censorship and media control
  in authoritarian states, 108–10, 754
  ecclesiastical in Middle Ages, 109–10
  French on pre-First World War
    codebreaking, 464
Central Intelligence Agency (CIA)
  accounting procedures, 310
  Ames spy trial (1994), 709, 711, 713
  and *The Art of War*, 66, 67
  Bay of Pigs fiasco (1961), 677, 680
  Castro assassination plans, 63, 85,
    677, 680, 687, 688
  Center for the Study of Intelligence,
    67, 300, 305, 309*, 745
  Bill Clinton's lack of interest in,
    709–10
  Congressional oversight, 17–18
  covert actions during Cold War, 8,
    677–8, 679–80, 690–91
  Director of Central Intelligence
    (DCI) role, 378, 676, 677, 702,
    706, 707–8, 710
  failure in Indonesia (1958), 679–80
  founding of (1947), 677
  Franklin declared a 'Founding
    Father', 295, 299
  headquarters at Langley, Virginia, 303
  on Mitrokhin archive, 714
  National Foreign Assessment Center
    (NFAC), 701–2
  need for closer cooperation with
    FBI, 718–19, 725
  'perception management', 299
  post-Cold War budget cuts, 706

public criticism in mid-1970s, 17–18, 687, 688

and *Studies in Intelligence*, 9, 17–18

SVR penetration of, 715–16

Tenet on main mission of, 2

'the Wall' (federal law over sharing information), 719, 723

use of 'waterboarding', 4, 116–17

VENONA secret kept from, 673, 718*

Central Intelligence Group (CIG), 676

Chaloner, Richard, 216

Chamberlain, Austen, 582–3, 584

Chamberlain, Joseph, 450, 464–5

Chamberlain, Neville, 612, 614, 615–16

Chambers, Whittaker, 662, 673

Chamillart, Michel de, 262

Champagny, Jean-Baptiste de Nompère de, 355–6

Chanak crisis (1922), 577

Chancellor, Richard, 147–8, 149–50, 156

Chandler, Arthur B., 411

Chapman, Eddie, 653

Charles I, King of England, 204, 204*, 207–9, 214–20, 232, 271, 348

Charles II, King of England, 219, 220, 221, 230–35, 236–7, 248, 283

Charles V, Holy Roman Emperor (Charles I of Spain), 113, 120, 123*, 129, 137

Charles VI, King of France, 159

Charles X, King of France, 375–6

Charles XII, King of Sweden, 271, 272

Charteris, Brigadier-General John, 507, 528, 531, 563, 564, 565

Chartist movement in Britain, 379–80, 385

Chasteau-Martin, Henri, 190*

Châteauneuf, Baron de, 176

Chauvelin, Germain, 281

Chebrikov, Viktor, 698

Chechnya, 655

Cheka (later GPU, OGPU, NKVD, KGB)

Administration for Special Tasks (abduction/assassination), 599, 622–4

brutality against 'class enemies', 556–7, 561

as central to one-party state, 574–5, 698–700

counter-espionage section, 557–8, 561

creation of (20 December 1917), 7, 110–11, 555–6

emblems and symbols of, 555

foreign-intelligence department (INO), 594, 620, 623

influence of LSRs, 557–8

Japanese decrypts published (1932), 589–90

and Kremlin Plot, 595–7

Lubyanka in Moscow, 558, 561, 700

MGB plans for Tito's assassination, 85, 681–2

and Mirbach's assassination (July 1918), 558

and Okhrana tradecraft, 561

post-war imaginary enemies, 680–82

and Russian Civil War, 557, 559, 573–4

Second World War THRONE operation with GRU, 646

SINDIKAT and TREST operations, 575–6, 646

tendency to conspiracy theory, 594, 598–602, 619–20, 625–6, 651, 680–82, 694–8, 706

and terror, 556–7, 558–9, 573–4, 600–602, 620–21, 751

wartime ethnic cleansing by, 654–5

see also KGB

Cheliadnin-Fedorov, Prince Ivan Petrovich, 144

Cheney, Dick, 727–8

Cherkasov, Nikolai, 143

Cherniavsky, Mikhail, 596

Chernomazov, Miron, 441

Chernyshev, Alexander, 354, 357, 498

Cheval, Joseph, 394

Chicherin, Georgi, 577
Chilcot Report (2016), 737–9
Chile, 687–8, 690
Chin, Larry Wu-tai, 67
China
  assassination tradition in, 59, 85
  Boxer Rebellion, 66
  Communist–Kuomintang civil war,
    66, 752
  'counter-terrorist' operations, 755–6
  first nuclear weapon (1964), 736
  hackers in, 754
  Han dynasty, 57–8, 57†
  intelligence history in, 752–3
  Mao's Cultural Revolution, 66, 752,
    755–6
  Middle Kingdom, 59
  Ming dynasty, 57, 198
  Ministry of State Security (MSS),
    752, 753–5
  Nixon's visit to (1972), 67
  official censorship in, 754
  public campaigns over foreign spies
    in, 754–5
  Qing dynasty, 59–60, 198
  Qin's terracotta warriors, 57
  science and technology espionage,
    67, 69
  spies in pre-Sun Tzu civil
    wars, 56*
  'Three Kingdoms' period, 58
  Tiananmen Square massacre, 750,
    753–4
  see also Sun Tzu: The Art of War
    (Sunzi bingfa)
Chisholm, John, 166
Choiseul, duc de, 288–9, 292
Cholmeley, Richard, 187
Cholula, central Mexico, 135
Christiancy, Isaac P., 423
Chrysaphius, 83, 84
Church, Senator Frank, 679, 687
Church, Major G. R. M., 467
Church, Ralph Edwin, 677
Church of England, 114, 161, 220

Churchill, John (later Duke of
  Marlborough), 250, 257, 261–5,
  267, 268
Churchill, Winston, 524
  on Battle of Jutland, 525
  becomes Prime Minister
    (May 1940), 616
  Bletchley Park codebreakers' appeal
    to, 617
  and 'Blinker' Hall, 515
  and Boer War, 450–51, 451
  on breaking of US Black Code,
    638–9
  as covert action enthusiast, 679
  and creation of GC&CS, 612
  denied access to intercepts (1924),
    582–3
  and Double-Cross System, 651–3,
    657, 659, 660
  enthusiasm for intelligence, 336, 451,
    480, 510, 511–12, 591*, 603, 612,
    619, 652
  first two years as Prime Minister, 56
  and First World War naval
    intelligence, 7, 512, 513, 514–15
  and Gallipoli expedition, 532
  Gilbert's eight-volume biography,
    477, 671
  Great Contemporaries, 575, 619
  on Haig's Somme offensive, 532–3
  hatred of Bolshevism, 575, 578–9,
    583, 626
  interest in all aspects of intelligence,
    634, 635
  on Lenin's 'sealed' train, 545
  on long-term and historical
    perspective, 759
  and operation OVERLORD (1944),
    659, 660
  papers of at Churchill College, 751*
  racist underestimation of Japanese,
    636, 728–9
  and Second World War intelligence
    coordination, 617, 618
  at 'Siege of Sidney Street' (1910), 560

SIGINT while peacetime Prime
   Minister, 671
and SOE, 619
and Stalin, 626, 650
on U-boat peril, 641
and ULTRA intelligence, 616–17,
   640–41, 671
as war correspondent, 450–51
Ciano, Count Galeazzo, 16*
Cicero, 40, 47, 49†, 52*
Cincar-Marković, Dimitrije, 442
Cistercian order, 101
Civil War, American (1861–5), 6,
   411–14
Civil War, English (1642–9),
   214–15, 221
   King's Cabinet opened, The (1645),
   217, 217–18
   Waller Plot (1643), 215–16
Civil War, Russian (1918–20), 557,
   559, 573–4, 575, 626
Civil War, Spanish (1936–9), 622, 682
Clam-Martinic, Count Karl, 368
Clapper, General James, 704
Clarendon, 4th Earl of, 396, 397
Clark, Christopher, 493*
Clarke, Sir William, 346
Clarke, William F., 524
Claudius, Roman emperor, 73, 75, 75†
Claudius Pulcher, 41
Clausewitz, Carl von, 14–15, 54
Clayton, Brigadier-General Gilbert F.,
   528–9
Clemenceau, Georges, 462, 551, 584
Cleveland, Grover, 435
Clifford, Clark, 678
Clifford, Sir Thomas, 236
Cline, Ray, 679–80
Clinton, Bill, 708, 709–10
Clinton, Sir Henry, 301, 305, 306, 307
Cobb, Richard, 324
Cobban, Alfred, 314–15, 331
codebreaking see cryptanalysis
codes and ciphers
   Abbasid use of, 98–9, 127, 128

ADFGX (later ADFGVX) (First
   World War German), 564
in ancient Egypt, 20†
Caesar's 'substitution ciphers', 46–7,
   99, 497
cipher telegrams, 421
Enigma machine, 56†, 616–17,
   640–41, 671
during First World War, 497–500,
   504, 533–4, 563–4
French advances in late-nineteenth-
   century, 460
Geheimschreiber messages, 648
Japanese, 467–8, 469, 470
Japanese naval JN25b, 634–5,
   637–8
of Mary, Queen of Scots, 166
MI-8 in USA, 569
in ninth-century Baghdad, 98–9
Ottoman failings, 128–9
Papacy's use of, 127
'polyalphabetic substitution', 127
'Red Code' (US diplomatic code,
   1876), 423–4
SHARK (U-boat version of
   Enigma), 641
Soviet 'one-time pad', 584, 672,
   673–4, 749
Spanish security as poor, 139–40
Spartan 'skytale' claims, 46†
Swedish, 272, 348
'Triplecodex' (1914), 479
and Tsar Alexander I, 360
US 'Black Code', 638–9
US naval ciphers during Cold War,
   685–6
see also cryptanalysis
coffee houses, 238, 257
Cohen, Lona, 673
Cohen, Morris, 673
Coke, Sir Edward, 189
Coke, Sir John, 204*, 208, 219
Colbert, Jean-Baptiste, 212, 213,
   243–5, 247, 267, 268
Colby, William, 731–2

Colchester (Camulodunum), 74–5

Cold War
   analysis of effects of intelligence on,
      682–3, 684
   arms control/limitation agreements,
      684
   British official secrecy, 8–9, 736
   CIA covert actions during, 8, 677–8,
      679–80, 690–91
   CIA failure in Indonesia (1958),
      679–80
   Cuban Missile Crisis, 683–4, 707,
      739, 740, 759
   early codebreaking successes
      of US, 673
   and Eisenhower's dictum, 181
   ELINT successes during, 674
   IMINT revolution during, 683,
      684, 707
   intelligence on opponents' nuclear
      strike force, 683, 684, 759
   KGB 'active measures' (influence
      operations), 8, 688, 689–91
   KGB covert actions during, 8,
      680–82, 688–91
   KGB cryptanalysis during, 674
   neglect of SIGINT in studies of,
      8, 671–3
   'peace dividend' at end of, 707
   role of HUMINT in, 676
   SIGINT secrecy during, 671, 674
   Soviet penetration of foreign
      ministries in West, 675
   and Third World states, 8, 674,
      688–91
   Truman Doctrine, 676–7
   US 'bomber gap' and 'missile gap'
      myths, 682–3
   VENONA decrypts, 672, 718*, 749

Coleman, Edward, 240
Coleridge, Samuel Taylor, 332–3
Colonna, Marco Antonio, 128
'Colossus' (world's first electronic
   computer), 648
Colt, Henry, 258

Columbia University, New York,
   684–5
Columbus, Christopher, 120
Comey, James B., 754
Commodus, Roman emperor, 75–6
Commonwealth of England, 219–30
Communist Correspondence Commit-
   tee, Brussels, 386
Communist International (Comintern),
   465, 581
Communist League, 388, 393–4
Communist Party of America, 665
Communist Party of Great Britain
   (CPGB), 578, 581
Communist Party of the Soviet Union
   689, 698
Conan Doyle, Sir Arthur, 420*
Condé, Henri II of Bourbon, prince de,
   205, 206
Condé, Louis de Bourbon, prince de,
   245, 246, 247
Conquest, Robert, 751
Conrad, Joseph, *The Secret Agent*, 431

conspiracy theories
   and authoritarian regimes, 106, 326,
      594, 598–602, 619–20, 680–82,
      694–8
   Catholic plots in Elizabethan era,
      163–4, 170–72, 175, 188–9
   and First World War pacifism, 551–2,
      553–5, 554
   and Indian Mutiny, 410–11
   Islamist brand of anti-Semitism,
      703, 723
   of Ivan the Terrible, 141–2, 144–5,
      146, 150–51, 152, 153–4
   and Jacobite cause, 258–9
   Kennedy assassination, 688
   medieval, 106–7
   and Metternich, 369, 371, 372, 375
   nineteenth-century anarchist
      movement, 432
   over Russian First World War
      disasters, 502–4
   and Paris Commune, 398–400

'Popish Plot' (late 1670s), 238,
   239–40, 241
in revolutionary France, 317–19,
   322–3, 324–6
and secret societies, 372, 373–4,
   376–7
Constant, Benjamin, 375
Constantine, Grand Duke, 373
Constantine, Roman emperor, 32‡,
   76*, 77, 78
Constantini, Francesco, 591
Constantini, Secondo, 591, 592
Constantinople, 78, 92–3, 122, 124,
   125, 132
Conti, prince de, 280
Contra guerrilla campaign,
   Nicaragua, 691
Conway, Sir Edward, 205
Coolidge, Calvin, 587
Cooper, Dr Tarnya, 160–61
Cooper, Duff, 652–3
Cooper, James Fenimore, 310–11
Copenhagen, Battle of
   (March 1801), 336
Corbet, Miles, 233
Corbiere, Anthony, 272
Cornwallis, Lord, 306, 307–8
Cortés, Hernán, 132–6, 137, 195
Costa Rica, 681–2, 690
Cotton, Joseph P., 588
counter-subversion
   in 1840s France, 383
   in authoritarian states, 4, 100–17,
      130†, 574–5, 698–700, 751
   bizarre conspiracy theories, 106–7
   bureaucracy and record-keeping, 4,
      100, 102–3, 102§
   Catholic 'inquisitions', 4, 100,
      102–6, 102§, 107–8, 109–10,
      111–13, 115–16
   in China, 754–5
   and denunciations, 103
   fear of professional revolutionaries
      (1820s–1840s), 369, 371, 372–5,
      376–81, 383–4, 552*

in France under restored Bourbons,
   375–6
German police union (1851–66),
   391, 398
KGB role in, 698–700, 751
MI5 in Britain (1917–8), 551–2,
   553–5, 554
Okhrana in Russia, 7, 425–6, 428,
   434, 436, 437–42, 574, 603
Spanish autos da fé, 111–12, 115
Spanish Inquisition as milestone, 111
Stalinist show trials, 107, 108, 600,
   601, 620, 667
Third Section in Tsarist Russia,
   374–5, 376–8, 425
Courland, Duchess of, 368
Coventry, Sir Henry, 240
covert operations
   British during Cold War, 678–9
   British intelligence on First World
      War German, 522–4
   British Operation VALUABLE in
      Communist Albania (1948),
      678–9
   Church Committee report (1976),
      679, 687
   CIA 'dirty tricks' disclosures (1975),
      687, 688
   CIA during Cold War, 8, 677–8,
      679–80, 690–91
   CIA in Third World, 8, 690–91
   defined, 677–8
   Doolittle report's endorsement of
      (1954), 679
   First World War German in USA,
      520, 521–4, 527, 528, 542, 604
   and Benjamin Franklin, 295–6,
      298–300, 308–9
   German in First World War
      revolutionary Russia, 544–7
   as intelligence method from earliest
      times, 2
   KGB 'active measures' in Third
      World, 8, 688, 689–91
   KGB during Cold War, 680–82

MI1c attempts to keep Russia in
    First World War, 547–9
and Mossad, 18–19
Okhrana in Western Europe,
    426, 428
in Old Testament, 14
overthrow of Guatemalan regime
    (1954), 679
restoration of Shah in Iran (1953), 679
Roman plot against Attila, 83–4, 85
royalist during English Civil War,
    214–16
in Sun Tzu and the *Arthashastra*,
    56, 59, 64
US in Italian 1948 elections, 678, 679
Wiseman's in First World War USA,
    535
Cox, Brigadier Edgar, 562–3, 564, 572
Cradock, Sir Percy, 694
Craig, Daniel, 27
Cranmer, Thomas, 114–15
Cresswell, Joseph, 203
Cressy, David, *Dangerous Talk*, 280†
Creveld, Professor Van, 339‡
Crimean War (1853–6), 402–6
Croesus, ruler of Lydia, 32†
Croissy, Colbert de, 253–4
Cromwell, Oliver, 5, 221, 223–4,
    227, 230
Cromwell, Richard, 227–8
Crone, Matthew, 258
Crowe, Sir Eyre, 482, 582
cryptanalysis
    and Aldegonde, 139–40, 166–9
    and American Civil War, 411
    during American Revolutionary War,
        301, 308
    Austrian during Congress of Vienna,
        363–4, 365
    Babington Plot deception/forgery,
        177, 179, 180, 192
    and Étienne Bazeries, 460, 461,
        463, 468
    black chambers in Celle and
        Hanover, 255–6, 264, 270

and William Blencowe, 256, 263,
    264, 270
breaking of FLORADORA (Nazi
    diplomatic cipher), 642
British Government of India, 410,
    419
Chiffrierabteilung (code department)
    of OKW, 639, 644
Civil War revival in England,
    216–18, 221
Deciphering Branch closure (1844),
    6, 337, 383, 747
Deciphering Branch in Britain, 6,
    276–7, 288, 289–90, 300, 301,
    337, 348–9, 357, 410, 421, 449
decline of Deciphering Branch in
    Britain, 337, 348–9, 357
and diplomatic telegrams, 421, 422,
    533–4, 535–41, 542
Dutch assistance to Elizabethan
    England, 7, 166–70
early Cold War successes of US, 673
Enigma machines captured at
    Stalingrad, 648
during First World War, 497–502,
    504, 509–19, 529–30, 532, 533–4,
    535–42, 563–4, 571, 603,
    671, 747†
Franco-Russian collaboration,
    467–8, 469–70
and Frederick the Great, 287
French (1890s–1914 period), 459,
    460, 461, 463–4, 468–9, 478, 479,
    483–5, 488, 491, 749
French interwar decrypts, 584–5
French official censorship on, 464
'frequency analysis', 4, 99, 127, 347
and George I, 270, 271, 279, 643
and Christian Goldbach, 277
'Great Paris Cipher', 347–52, 350–51
in *Gulliver's Travels*, 275–6
HYPO (later FRUPac) unit (US
    after Pearl Harbor), 637–8
interwar period, 576–80, 583–90,
    616–17

Japanese RED and PURPLE ciphers
  cracked, 610–12, 627, 628, 671†
by KGB during Cold War, 674
Al-Kindi and invention of, 4, 98–9,
  127, 497
in Louis XIV's France, 242, 245, 277
and James Lovell, 308
in mid-eighteenth-century Vienna,
  277, 278–9
and Samuel Morland, 225–6
during Napoleonic Wars, 340–41,
  347–52, 357–8, 359, 360
and Georges Painvin, 564
and Thomas Phelippes, 167, 177,
  179, 180, 183, 189, 205, 242
Philip II likens to witchcraft, 137,
  138, 139, 140
in pre-First World War Vienna,
  489, 491
publication of decrypts, 216–19,
  271–2, 348
by the Raj, 467
Renaissance agencies, 5
and Renaissance Venice, 127,
  128–9, 137
and Richelieu, 205–6, 210–11, 672
and Antoine Rossignol, 205–6, 210,
  211, 212, 213, 242, 245*,
  247, 672
and Russian Empire, 353, 357–9,
  360, 454–7, 467–8, 469–71, 478,
  485, 488, 491–2, 497, 499–502
during Russo-Japanese War, 467–8
Scovell during Peninsular War,
  347–8, 349–52, 350–51
and Seven Years War (1756–63),
  288, 289–90
SHARK (U-boat version of
  Enigma), 641
sixteenth-century pool of talent,
  137, 138
and John Somer, 162, 162†, 166, 167
and Giovanni Soro, 127, 128, 129, 137
Soviet decrypts of Japanese
  despatches, 589–90

Soviets as best by early 1930s, 590
and Spanish Armada preparations,
  183
Spanish in seventeenth-century, 211
Third World diplomatic traffic in
  Cold War, 674
Travis–Strong agreement (BRUSA,
  May 1943), 642–3
ULTRA intelligence (Second World
  War), 8, 56†, 616–17, 640–42,
  648, 649, 652, 669, 671–2
US failure to crack JN25b before
  Pearl Harbor, 634–5
by Vienna cabinet noir, 369–70
and François Viète, 137, 138–9,
  140, 198
and Francis Wallis, 301
and John Wallis, 216–17, 221,
  237–8, 242, 251–5, 256
and George Washington, 308
and Edward Willes, 271, 272, 273,
  274, 276, 337
see also Bletchley Park, 'Station X'
  at; cabinet noir (black chamber),
  French; codes and ciphers
cryptography see codes and ciphers;
  cryptanalysis
Cuba, 8, 63, 589, 689, 705
  CIA's Castro assassination plans, 63,
    85, 677, 680, 687, 688
  Cuban Missile Crisis (1962), 683–4,
    707, 739, 740, 759
anČubrilović, Vaso, 445, 447
Culloden, Battle of (16 April 1746),
  283
Cumberland, Duke of, 283
Cumming, Commander Mansfield,
  477, 481–3, 512, 528, 532, 534,
  548, 571–2, 606
Cunliffe, Sir Barry, 49–50
Currie, Lauchlin, 662
Curry, Jack, 614, 615–16, 760
Curtis Wright, David, 78†
Curzon, Lord, 576–7, 579–80
Custine, marquis de, 377–8

cyberwarfare, 10, 754
Czechoslovakia, 613, 614–15, 616,
    699, 712, 751
Czolgosz, Leon Frank, 435–6

D'Abernon, Lord, 759–60
Daily Herald, 578
Daily Mail, 472–3, 579, 581–2
Dalton, Hugh, 619
Damascus, 95, 97
Daniels, Josephus, 603–4
Dansey, Claude, 550
Danton, Georges, 314, 318, 324–5
Dar es Salaam terror attack (7 August
    1998), 719–20
Darnley, Lord, 163
Darnton, Robert, 280
Dati, Leonardo, 127
Davies, Joseph E., 593, 597
Davis, Jack, 745*
Davison, F. Trubee, 605
Davison, William, 169
Dead Sea Scrolls, 58‡
'dead-letter boxes', 269, 298, 300, 716
Deane, Silas, 296, 298
Dearlove, Sir Richard, 738
Decianus, Catus, 74–5
declassification of intelligence files, 8,
    9*, 17, 665*, 671, 672, 697, 731†,
    734, 734*, 735–6
defence industry, US, 692
Defense Intelligence Agency (DIA), 704
Defoe, Daniel, 265
Delahodde, Lucien, 383, 384
Delarue, Francis, 260
Delcassé, Théophile, 459, 462, 463,
    464, 465, 468, 469, 478, 485
Delessert, Gabriel, 383
Delhi Intelligence Branch
    (IB or DIB), 735
Delphic oracle, 32, 43, 44, 73
    role of Pythia, 32, 32*, 78
    Serpent Column, 32, 32‡
Demyanov, Alexander, 646–7
Dendy, Edward, 232

Denmark, 291, 343
Denniston, A. G. 'Alastair', 509–10,
    517, 533, 576*, 585, 642
Department of Defense (DOD), US,
    717
Deubner, Ludwig, 497
Deutsch, Arnold, 593
Deutscher, Isaac, 598
Dhingra, Madan Lal, 619
Díaz del Castillo, Bernal, 134, 135–6
Dickens, Charles, 380
Didius Julianus, Roman emperor, 76
Digby, John, 196
Dilks, David, 731
Dimitrijevic, Dragutin ('Apis'), 442,
    443–4, 445, 446, 447–8
Diocletian, Roman emperor, 77
Diodorus Siculus, 34
Diomedes, 27–8
diplomacy
    early-modern overlap with
        intelligence, 208
    embassy security issues, 456–7, 458,
        459–60, 592–3, 662, 674–5, 719
    and Ivan the Terrible, 146, 147–54
    Ottoman lack of permanent
        embassies, 122, 123
    Ottoman prohibition of printing,
        122–3
    Renaissance turning point, 4, 5, 121
    Rubens's for Philip IV, 207–9
    Russian lack of permanent
        embassies, 146, 148–9
    Russian lack of print culture, 146–7
    system of resident ambassadors,
        121–2, 149–50, 154, 155–6
    and the telegraph, 421
    of US in nineteenth century, 422–4
    US publishing of main
        correspondence, 422–3, 745–6
    Venetian ambassadors, 122,
        123–4, 125
'Diplomatic Revolution', in mid-
    eighteenth century, 278
Diplomatic Security Service, 719

Directorate of Military Operations
    (DMO), British, 452–3, 473,
    476, 482
Dissanayake, Gamini, 721
Diviciacus (or Divitiacus), 49
divination and portents
    in ancient Greece, 30–31, 35–7, 54–5
    in ancient Rome, 40–41, 42, 43, 44,
        50–52, 51*, 52*, 54–5, 73, 74, 77–8
    Chinese beliefs, 56–8, 58*
    prohibited in *The Art of War* (*Sunzi
        bingfa*), 54–5, 55*, 58
Dobrynin, Anatoli, 689, 695
Doge, Venetian, 118
Doge's Palace, Venice, 128, 128*,
    130, 130*
Dolomieu, Déodat Gratet de, 334*
Dolon (Trojan spy), 27–8
domestic intelligence and internal
    surveillance
    and the *Arthashastra*, 61–2, 63, 65–6
    in Britain during French Revolution,
        326–9, 332–3, 336
    caliphs' *Barid*, 96, 97
    Charles II's reign, 238
    and Chartist movement, 379–80
    CIA's operation CHAOS in USA, 687
    in early Stuart era, 193–5
    Elizabethan England, 171–9, 188–9
    and English Civil War, 214–18
    and English Commonwealth,
        220–21, 222, 226
    in Louis XIV's France, 242–3
    Louis XV's *Secret du Roi*, 280
    and Louis Napoleon, 395–6
    and Mazarin, 212–13
    Mitterrand's secret office in
        France, 675–6
    and Muhammad, 87–90, 91
    and Napoleon, 341–3
    on post-1848 émigrés in Britain, 388,
        389–91, 396–7
    and Queen Victoria's funeral
        (1901), 434
    and Renaissance Venice, 130, 131–2

and Richelieu, 205–6, 209–10
Shin Bet in Israel, 18
surveillance of anarchists, 432–3
twenty-first-century counter-
    terrorism, 756–8
of William III, 258
see also counter-subversion
Dominican Friars, 102, 103–4, 105,
    742†
Don Juan of Austria, 140, 167, *168*
Dönitz, Admiral Karl, 641
Donovan, William J. 'Wild Bill', 606–7,
    608–10, 634
Dori, Leonora, 201
Dorislaus, Isaac, 219
Dorislaus, Isaac (the younger), 226
Dorset, John Frederick Sackville, 3rd
    Duke of, 312–13, 312*
double-agents
    during American Revolutionary War,
        296–8, 299–300
    B1a (MI5's Second World War
        double-agent section), 650, 651,
        652–3, 659
    Alexander Demyanov in Second
        World War, 646–7
    Earl of Mar, 273
    FORTITUDE deceptions before
        D-Day landings, 657–61
    and Frederick the Great, 286
    MI5 in First World War
        Germany, 548
    Sicinnus at Salamis, 29–30
    Anthony Standen, 185–6
    Sun Tzu's category of, 55, 67
    Walsingham's, 165–6, 175–6
Douglas, Wing Commander W. S., 506–7
Dover, Treaty of (1670), 236, 248
Downing, George, 227, 230, 232–3
Draga, Queen of Serbia, 442
Drake, Sir Francis, 180–81, 184
Dreadnought battleship, 472
Drelincourt, Anne, Lady Primrose, 284
Dreyfus, Captain Alfred, 453, 459,
    460–62

Druids, 49
Drummond, Sir Eric, 548, 592
Dual Alliance, Franco-Russian, 458–9,
    491, 492
Dubois, Louis, 342
Duchâtel, Charles Marie Tanneguy, 378
Duff, Reverend Alexander, 409
Duggan, Larry, 299, 593
Dulles, Allen, 2, 63, 66, 67, 678
Dumba, Constantin, 523
Dumouriez, General Charles-
    François, 322
Duncan, Abram, 380
Duncombe, Thomas, 381
Dundas, Henry, 333, 335, 336
Dunlap, Staff Sergeant Jack E., 675*
Duroc, Géraud, 342
Duval, Émile-Joseph, 551
dynamite, 425, 429, 520–21
Dzerzhinsky, Felix Edmundovich, 555,
    557, 558, 559, 561, 574, 575, 603,
    687, 700

East India Company (EIC), 346,
    406–7, 410
Ebner, Hermann, 393
Écija, Francisco Fernández de, 196
Edekon (Hun envoy), 83–4, 85
Eden, Anthony, 618
Eden, William, 297, 298, 313
Edinburgh Castle occupation (1573),
    166
Edmonds, Brigadier-General Sir James,
    452, 474–6
Edward, Prince of Wales (future
    Edward VII), 433–4, 457–8
Edward III, King of England, 159
Egesta (city state in Sicily), 33–4
Egypt
    Alexander the Great's occupation,
        39, 333
    'Amarna letters', 19–20, 20*, 21
    city-states in Canaan, 19–20
    cryptography in, 20†
    Muslim conquest of (639–41), 95

Napoleon in (1798–9), 333–6
Qutb in, 703–4
Eisenhower, Dwight D., 43, 181, 640,
    661, 671–2, 682, 683, 759
    as covert-action enthusiast,
        679–80
Eisenstein, Sergei: Ivan the Terrible,
    141, 143
Eitingon, Leonid, 624
El Alamein, Battle of (October–
    November 1942), 640–41
Elbeuf, Duke and Duchess of, 202
Elibank, Alexander Murray of, 285
ELINT (low-level communications/
    electronic signals), 674
Eliot, George, 170, 171
Elizabeth, Empress of Austria, 428,
    431, 432
Elizabeth (Elizaveta), Empress of
    Russia, 277, 290
Elizabeth I, Queen of England
    Babington Plot against (1586), 173,
        175–9, 183, 192, 200
    death of (March 1603), 192
    excommunicated (1570), 109*,
        137, 164
    and 'Lopez Plot', 188–9
    'the Rainbow portrait', 190
    'Ridolfi Plot' against (1571),
        164–6, 200
    size and multiplicity of courts, 170
    succession plans for, 191–2
    Throckmorton Plot against (1583),
        173, 191
Elizabethan England
    Church of England, 114,
        161, 220
    cryptanalysis, 162–3
    diplomatic ties with Ivan the
        Terrible, 147–54
    fear of foreign-backed Catholic plots,
        163–4, 170–72, 175
    foreign intelligence, 137, 140, 160,
        161, 162–3, 164–9, 171–7,
        180–86, 189–90

intelligence apparatus, 4, 5, 150,
  151, 158, 160, 161, 162–3,
  164–83, 184–5
intelligence apparatus after
  Walsingham, 185–90
as period of intense insecurity, 158
SIGINT alliance with Dutch, 7,
  166–70
travel books, 147
war with Spain, 140, 175, 192, 532
Elliot, Hugh, 313–14
Elliott, John, 212
Ellis, Havelock, *Psychology of Sex*, 431–2
Ellis, John, 237
Ellsberg, Daniel, 748
Emmery, Joseph, 361
Engels, Friedrich, 386, 389, 400
England
  Act of Union (1707), 265
  'Battle of Watling Street' (AD 60 or
    61), 75
  burning of Protestants under Mary,
    114–15
  Caesar's invasions of (55/54 BC), 49–50
  'Glorious Revolution' (1688), 249–51
  Iceni threat to Roman rule, 71–2, 73–5
  intelligence decline in early
    seventeenth century, 203–5
  loss of French possessions (sixteenth
    century), 160
  pre-Tudor intelligence operations,
    159–60
  Restoration (1660), 230
  revival of intelligence in Civil
    War era, 214
  see also Elizabethan England
Enigma machines, 56†, 616–17,
  640–41, 648, 671
Enukidze, Abel, 595
Éon de Beaumont, Chevalier d', 292–4
Ephialtes of Trachis, 29
Erasmian humanism, 115*, 120
Erfurt, Congress of (1808), 356
Ernest, Prince, Duke of
  Cumberland, 363

Erskine, Ralph, 'William Friedman's
  Bletchley Park Diary', 643*
Erskine, Thomas, 328
Essex, Earl of, 188–9
Estaing, Admiral d', 297–8
Esterhazy, Ferdinand, 461, 462
Eugénie, Empress, 395
Evans, Jonathan, 10†, 756
Evans, Sir Richard, 390
Evelyn, John, 231, 233
Ewart, Lieutenant-General Sir John
  Spencer, 473, 476, 482
Ewing, Sir Alfred, 509, 512,
  516–17, 518

Fabius Maximus, Quintus, 43,
  44, 358
'Fagot, Henri' (agent of Walsingham),
  161, 173–4
Falkenhayn, Erich von, 493–4,
  501, 520
Falkland, Lucius Cary,
  2nd Viscount, 214
Falklands War (1982), 750
Fashoda crisis (1898), 463–4
Faunt, Nicholas, 172, 186
Fawkes, Guido ('Guy'), 194–5
Federal Aviation Administration
  (FAA), 724, 725
Federal Bureau of Investigation (FBI)
  Bureau of Investigation as forerunner
    of, 435, 521, 527–8, 568
  interrogation of Saddam (2004),
    742–4
  on Mitrokhin archive, 714
  need for closer cooperation with
    CIA, 718–19, 725
  pre-9/11 intelligence on US aviation
    schools, 725–6
  Second World War cooperation with
    SIS, 608
  SVR penetration of, 716
  'the Wall' (federal law over sharing
    information), 719, 723
  and VENONA secret, 673, 718*

Federal Research Division, Library of
    Congress, 720
Federov, Ivan, 147
Federovich, Pavel, 595
Fedor I, Tsar, 154–6
Fedor II, Tsar (Fedor Borisovich
    Godunov), 156–7
Fejérváry–Mayer Codex, 133*
Fellers, Colonel Bonner, 639, 640
Fellwock, Perry, 748–9
Felt, Mark, 748
Felton, John, 164*
Ferdinand I, Emperor of Austria, 384–5
Ferdinand II, Habsburg emperor, 209
Ferdinand II, King of Aragon, 111,
    112–13
Ferdinand III, King of Castile, 111
Ferner, Robert O., 611
Feron, Laurent, 174
Ferrand, W. B., 380
Ferris, John, 'Signals Intelligence in
    War and Power Politics', 672*
Ferry, Abel, 492
Fersen, Count Hans Axel von, 315–16
Fetterlein, Ernst, 457, 458, 501–2, 576,
    577, 584
Fiévée, Joseph, 342
Figaro (French newspaper), 468, 484,
    485, 491–2
Figl, Andreas, 489, 491
Figliazzi, Giovanni, 180
Figueres Ferrer, José, 690
First World War
    air power during, 505–8
    Allied Meuse–Argonne offensive
        (autumn 1918), 565
    Arab Bureau in Cairo, 528–30
    Arab Rising against Turkish rule
        (1916), 508, 530
    Armistice Day (11 November 1918),
        572
    armistice negotiations, 569–70, 571
    Austrian ultimatum to Serbia,
        490–91, 492, 493
    Battle of the Atlantic, 515, 519, 544

bombarding of Hartlepool, 513
British Expeditionary Force (BEF),
    494, 496, 506
British naval operations, 6–7,
    512–16, 525–6, 543–4, 543*
British victory at Amiens (8 August
    1918), 564
Brusilov's June offensive (1916),
    498*, 502
Brusilov's June offensive (1917), 549,
    550
build-up to (summer 1914), 487–94
cryptanalysis during, 497–502, 504,
    509–19, 529–30, 532, 533–4,
    535–42, 563–4, 571, 603, 671,
    747†
cutting of German transatlantic
    cables, 509, 518
Dardanelles campaign, 515, 532
French Plan XVII, 494–5
French troop mutinies (1917),
    550–51
German diplomatic telegrams
    decrypted, 516–17, 519
German espionage in neutral USA,
    520–24, 527, 528, 542, 604
'German finance for pacifism' claims,
    551–2, 553–5
German invasion of France, 494, 495
German POWs, 531, 564, 572
German sabotage department,
    520–21, 522
German spring offensive (1918),
    561–4
German Verdun offensive (1916),
    501, 507
German victory on Eastern
    Front, 544
as intelligence turning point, 6, 7
interdepartmental SIGINT rivalries
    in Britain, 644
'July Crisis' (1914), 485, 488,
    489–94
in Middle East, 508, 528–30,
    541, 564–5

and military intelligence, 7, 311,
497–502, 506–8, 511–12, 519–20,
528–33, 536–42, 568–9, 571, 671

naval intelligence during, 7, 495,
508–11, 512–19, 524–6, 533,
536, 543*

outbreak of (1914), 453–4, 494

poor British telephone security, 520,
530, 531

pre-war military intelligence, 453–5,
494–5

psychological warfare on Eastern
Front, 547

Russian disasters on Eastern Front,
498, 499, 502–4

Russian mobilization, 486, 492, 495

Russian troop mutinies (1917),
549, 550

'Schlieffen Plan', 465–6, 494–5

SIGINT on Eastern Front, 497–502

spy mania during, 502–5

trench warfare on Western Front,
506, 519–20, 530–31, 533,
563, 564

U-boat warfare, 515, 519,
536–7, 543–4

US declaration of war
(April 1917), 542

US peace proposals (1916), 534, 536

Fish, Hamilton, 423

Fisher, Admiral Sir John, 510, 513,
514, 515

Fisher, Sir Warren, 615

Fitin, Pavel, 625, 627

Fitzgerald, Lord Robert, 313*

Flaminius, Gaius, 42–3

Flashman novels, 406

Fleming, Ian, 610

Fletcher, Giles, 155–6

Fleury, Cardinal, 281–2

Flint, Charles, 337

Florus, Lucius Annaeus, 71

Flotow, Hans von, 490–91

Flynn, Michael, 380

Foch, Marshal Ferdinand, 563, 572

Fogolino, Marcello, 207

Fondère, Hyacinthe, 478

Fontenoy, Battle of (1745), 279

foreign intelligence
agent recruitment, 64, 69

amateur espionage by foreign army
officers, 449–50

American Revolutionary War, 5,
294–8, 299–301, 302–8, 309–11

in the Arthashastra , 63–4

black chambers in Celle and
Hanover, 255–6, 264, 270

British during First World War,
516–19, 533–42

British during French Revolution,
313–14, 314*, 317–21, 323–4,
329–31, 333–5, 336, 337

British in Napoleonic France,
342, 343

Byzantine, 92–3

Charles II's reign, 236, 237–8

during Congress of Vienna, 363–7

and Hernán Cortés, 132–6, 137, 195

documents purloined from
embassies/consulates, 456–7, 458,
459–60

in early Stuart era, 192, 203–5

early-modern overlap with
diplomacy, 208

Elizabethan England, 137, 140, 160,
161, 162–3, 164–9, 171–7,
180–86, 189–90

and English Commonwealth, 220,
224–7

of future Charles II, 221–2

and the 'Glorious Revolution',
249–50

history of Russian intelligence
(edited by Primakov), 711–12

Hundred Years War, 107*, 159,
159*, 160, 476

Incas' lack of, 136

Intelligence Department (ID) in
Britain, 449, 450–51

and Ivan the Terrible, 146

foreign intelligence – (*cont.*)
  in Louis XIV's France, 242, 244–5, 248, 268
  Louis XV's *Secret du Roi*, 279–80
  in Louis XVI's France, 292–4
  as low priority in 1870–1914 period, 449
  as most essential in wartime and crises, 759
  Okhrana Foreign Agency, 426, 428, 434, 437, 457, 458–9, 468, 470
  in one-party states, 594, 693
  Ottoman weaknesses in, 122–4
  on post-1848 émigrés in Britain, 389–91, 392–4, 400–401
  pre-Tudor England, 159–60
  pursuit of Charles I's regicides, 219, 221, 230–35
  and Renaissance Venice, 119–20, 121, 122, 124, 125–31, 207
  and Richelieu, 206–7, 210–12, 268
  Room 40 (Admiralty Old Building), 516–19, 533–41, 542
  Franklin Roosevelt's interest in, 605–7
  Rouillé on French, 280
  Russian in Napoleonic Wars, 354–60
  Soviet hunt for 'enemies of the people' (late 1930s), 621–4, 680, 711
  Soviet operations on Trotsky/Sedov, 598–600, 622–5
  Soviet penetration of foreign embassies, 591–3, 594, 627–8, 749
  Spain in seventeenth century, 195, 196–201, 202–3, 207–9, 210, 211–12
  Spain's inferiority under Philip II, 137
  and Walsingham, 151, 154, 154†, 160, 161
  and George Washington, 301, 301–5, 308, 309–11
  and William III, 255–8, 259–60, 268
  see also cryptanalysis; double-agents; military intelligence; signals intelligence (SIGINT)
Forrestal, James, 670

Fort Duquesne (now Pittsburgh), 302
Fort Meade, Maryland, 672, 675*, 710
Fouché, Joseph, 341–2, 360, 426–7
  sacked as chief of police, 342–3
Fouquet, Nicolas, 243–4
Fouquier-Tinville, Antoine, 324, 325
Fournier, Jacques, Bishop of Pamiers, 105–6
France
  anarchist terror attacks of 1890s, 429–31, 432
  Anglo-French Entente Cordiale (1904), 464
  British interwar decrypts, 576–7, 580, 584–5
  decrypts by Austria (mid-eighteenth century), 278
  defeats by Marlborough (1704–8), 261, 262
  Dreyfus Affair, 453, 459, 460–62
  DST, 713, 714
  'Dual Alliance' with Russia, 458–9
  Edict of Nantes, 200
  February Revolution (1848), 384, 386
  Franco-Prussian War (1870–71), 398
  the *Fronde* (revolts, 1648–53), 212
  Huguenot Protestants in, 200, 205–6
  Hundred Days of Napoleon, 361–2
  Hundred Years War, 107, 159–60, 159*, 476
  interwar decrypts, 584–5
  Jacobite exile community in, 256–7
  and James II in Ireland (1689–90), 251–2, 255
  July Days (1830), 376
  July Monarchy of Louis-Philippe, 378, 384, 395
  Louis XIII's marriage to Anne of Austria, 201, 202–3
  Louis Napoleon's coup (2 December 1851), 387
  Mitterrand's secret office in Elysée Palace, 675–6
  Okhrana Foreign Agency in Paris, 426, 428, 458–9, 468, 470

Paris as spy centre during American
  war, 295–8
parliamentary scrutiny of intelligence
  budget (from 1818), 375, 378
post-First World War intelligence
  cuts, 585
pre-First World War mishandling of
  SIGINT, 483–5
republican rising in Paris (1839),
  378–9, 383
restored Bourbon monarchy
  (1815–30), 375–6
revival of intelligence under
  Richelieu, 205, 209, 268
Rouillé on French foreign
  intelligence, 280
Second Empire (1852–70), 387,
  395–6, 398
Second Republic, 386–7
Section du Chiffre at War Ministry,
  519, 533, 564, 585
security of foreign embassies in aris,
  459–60
and Seven Years War (1756–63),
  278, 286, 288–9, 290
seventeenth-century Spanish agents
  in, 198–201, 202–3, 207
Soviet agents in Cold War Quai
  d'Orsay, 675
St Bartholomew's Day massacre
  (1572), 161
'Statistical' (espionage) Section, 459,
  460–61, 462
support for American rebels, 5, 294,
  297–9, 307–8
Third Republic, 398, 432, 483–5
troop mutinies (1917), 550–51
and Turkish War of Independence
  (1919–23), 576–7
Vauban's fortifications, 246
war with Spain (from 1635),
  211–12
see also Bonaparte, Napoleon;
  cabinet noir (black chamber),
  French; French Revolution

Francis (Franz) I, Emperor of Austria,
  363, 364, 365, 369
Francis II, King of France, 161–2, 163
Franco-Dutch War (1672), 246
Franco-Prussian War (1870–71), 398,
  414–15
Franklin, Benjamin, 295–6, 298, 299,
  300, 308–9
Franz Ferdinand, Archduke, 444–8, 487
Franz Joseph, Emperor of Austria, 384
Fraser, Lionel, 524
Frederick I, Duke (later King) of
  Prussia, 253
Frederick II, King of Denmark, 146
Frederick II ('the Great'), King of
  Prussia, 279, 285–7, 288, 290,
  291, 340
Frederick William III, King of Prussia,
  353–4, 360, 363
Frederick William IV, King of Prussia,
  388, 389, 394
French, Field Marshal Sir John, 494,
  511, 528
'French and Indian Wars', 302
French Revolution
  Agence Royale (royalist intelligence
    service), 330, 331
  British intelligence during, 313–14,
    314*, 317–21, 323–4, 329–31,
    336, 337
  British republican expatriates in
    Paris, 319–20
  Civil Constitution of the Clergy
    (1790), 317
  Comité de défense générale, 321
  Committee of Public Safety, 321,
    322–3, 325, 326
  'Coup of 18 Fructidor' (1797), 331
  Directory (1795–9), 330–35
  failed French royalist plot (1799), 335
  French landing at Fishguard (1797),
    331–2
  initial enthusiasm for, 314–15
  Louis XVI's 'flight to Varennes'
    (June 1791), 315–17

French Revolution – (cont.)
  Napoleon's coup d'état (November
    1799), 336
  outbreak of (1789), 312–13
  'partial elections' (spring 1797), 331
  royalist émigré spy networks, 323–4
  'September massacres' (1792),
    318–19, 505
  the Terror (1793–4), 318, 321–6
  trial and execution of king (January
    1793), 320–21
French Revolutionary wars
  British intelligence failure over
    Egypt, 333–5, 336
  fall of Verdun (1792), 318
  France's citizen army, 322
  French declaration of war on Britain
    (1793), 321
  naval intelligence, 508–9
  Nelson's victory at Aboukir Bay
    (1798), 335
  spy mania in Paris during, 505
  start of (1792), 317
  Wickham as unofficial intelligence
    chief, 336, 532
French Wars of Religion (from 1562),
  137–8
  St Bartholomew's Day massacre
    (1572), 161
Friedman, William F., 565–6, 576, 588,
  610–11, 643
Fritigern, Visigoth leader, 81, 82
Frizer, Ingram, 187–8
Frost, John, 328
Fuchs, Klaus, 667, 668, 673
Fugger family of Augsburg, 244
Fulbright scholars, 684–5
Fuller, Thomas, 155–6
Fuller, William, 258–9
Fuller, Professor William C., 504

Gabriel, Richard, Scipio Africanus, 45*
Gaddafi regime in Libya, 672†, 736–7,
  750
Gaddis, John Lewis, 8, 689

Gama, Vasco da, 121
Gandhi, Indira, 64, 688
Gandhi, Mahatma, 65
Gandhi, Rajiv, 721
Gardiner, Lord, 738
Gardiner, S. R., 216
Garfield, James A., 435
Gasperi, Alcide de, 678
Gates, Robert, 684, 691, 697, 704, 706,
  707, 743, 745*, 748
Gaultier, Abbé François, 267
Gaunt, Admiral Sir Guy, 522–3, 537
GCHQ (Government Communication
  Headquarters), 10*, 644, 671,
  674, 735, 736, 738†
Geddes, Sir Auckland, 586
Gehlen, Major-General Reinhard, 647
gelignite, 425, 429
Genêt, Stéphane: Les Espions des
  lumières, 282*
Geneva, 327, 329–30, 428, 431
George I, King of Great Britain (George
  Louis I of Hanover), 255–6, 262,
  264, 269, 270, 271, 279, 643, 671
George I, King of Greece, 428
George II, King of Great Britain, 281
George III, King of United Kingdom,
  289, 300–301, 303, 306–7, 308
George IV, King of United Kingdom, 370
George William of Celle, 255
Gérard, Balthasar, 170
Gerasimov, A. V., 438
Gerlach, Leopold von, 394
German Confederation (Deutscher
  Bund), 368–9, 371–3, 384–5,
  387–8, 391, 398
German Democratic Republic, 692*,
  695–6, 698
Germania (Roman province), 70–71, 74
Germanicus (nephew of Tiberius), 71
Germany
  'blank cheque' to Vienna
    (July 1914), 488
  British intelligence on German WW1
    operations, 522–4

British military/naval attachés in
(pre-First World War), 482
during 'July Crisis' (1914), 492–4
First World War aid to Bolsheviks in
Russia, 544–7
First World War military intelligence,
519–20, 530, 531
loss of First World War military
records, 488–9
military collapse at end of First
World War, 572
naval mutinies (November 1918), 571
pre-First World War military
intelligence, 453–5
pre-First World War naval expansion,
472, 477
Russian decrypts of despatches,
454–6, 470–71, 478, 485–6
sabotage operations in neutral USA
(First World War), 520, 521, 522,
527, 528, 542, 604
'Schlieffen Plan', 465–6, 494–5
SIGINT agency established (First
World War), 497–8, 502
unrestricted U-boat warfare in First
World War, 537, 543–4
Versailles Treaty restrictions on, 573
Versailles war reparations, 585
Weimar Republic, 573, 759–60
see also Nazi Germany
Gerolymatos, André, 30–31*
Gershuni, Grigory, 437
Giancana, Salvatore 'Sam', 63
Giavarina, Francesco, 227
Gifford, Gilbert, 161, 176
Gilbert, Sir Martin, 671
Giles, Dr Lionel, 66
Gisevius, Hans-Bernd, 656*
Giustiniani, Sebastiano, 125–6
Given-Watson, Chris, 159*
Gladstone, William Ewart, 421–2, 427
Gladwell, Malcolm, 747
Gleichen, Lord Edward, 449, 452
'Glorious Revolution', English (1688),
249–51

Godfrey, Admiral John, 610
Godfrey, Sir Edmund Berry, 239
Godunov, Boris, 154–7
Godunov, Semen Nikitich, 156, 157
Goebbels, Joseph, 648
Goffe, Thomas, 235
Goldbach, Christian, 277
Goldheim, Friedrich, 394
Golovin, Petr, 155‡
Goltz, Baron Bernhard von der, 291
Gonse, General Charles-Arthur, 462
Google Earth imagery, 751
Gorbachev, Mikhail, 684, 697†, 698,
699–700, 704, 706
Gorchakov, Prince Mikhail, 456
Gordian I, Roman emperor, 72
Gordievsky, Oleg, 696–7, 713–14
Gore, Al, 723
Göring, Hermann, 741–2
Gorsky, Anatoly Veniaminovich, 621,
650, 663
Görtz, Georg Heinrich von, 271
Goths, 79–80, 81
Gough, General Sir Hubert, 563
Gournay-sur-Aronde (Oise), 49*
Government Code and Cypher School
(GC&CS), 576, 577–80, 583,
584–5, 612, 644
Baldwin government indiscretion
(1927), 583–4, 616–17
Enigma machine ciphers cracked
(1940–42), 616–17
Japanese decrypts by in 1920s/30s,
585, 590
Gower, Earl, 313, 314, 316, 324*
Grabež, Trifko, 444–5, 447
Graham, Sir James, 381, 382
Grand Duke Nikolai Nikolyaevich, 575
Grant, Colquhoun, 361
Grant, Ulysses S., 413–14, 423
Granville, Earl, 421–2
Grasse, Admiral de, 307
Gratian, Western emperor, 81
Great Exhibition (London, 1851),
391–2

Greece, ancient, 2, 27–9
  Alexander the Great, 37–9,
    45–6, 333
  and military intelligence, 30–31, 33–6
  oracles, 30, 31–2, 32†, 43, 44, 73, 78
  Peloponnesian War, 3, 29, 32–5
  Persian Wars, 2, 29–31
  seers and diviners, 30–31,
    35–7, 54–5
Greene, Graham, 593
Greene, Mary, 238
Greenglass, David, 668
Gregory IX, Pope, 102, 105
Gregory XIII, Pope, 161
Gregory XIV, Pope, 138*
Greif, Police Lieutenant, 392
Grenville, Lord, 317, 327, 330, 333, 335
Grenville, Sir John, 230
Grew, Joseph C., 629
Grey, Sir Edward, 458, 480, 490, 494
Grey, Nigel de, 518, 536, 542
Grigulevich, Iosif, 63, 622, 623–4,
    681, 682
Gromyko, Andrei, 689
Guadalcanal, Solomon Islands, 638
Guaras, Antonio de, 167
Guardian newspaper, 535–6, 746, 747
Guatemala, 679
Guerchy, comte de, 293
Guiscard, Antoine de, 265–7
Guise, Duke of, 174, 175, 183
Gulag, Soviet, 26, 378, 602, 751
  use of term 'Gulag', 561*
Gunpowder Plot (1605), 193–5
Gustafson, Dr Kristian, 687–8
Gustavus Adolphus, King of
    Sweden, 209
Gwyn, Nell, 237
Gwynne, H. A., 580
Gyllenborg, Count Karl, 271

Haddad, Wadi, 733
Hadrian, Roman emperor, 76
Hager, Baron Franz von, 363, 364–5,
    366, 367

Haig, Field Marshal Earl Douglas, 507,
    528, 530–31, 532–3, 562–3, 564,
    565, 572
Haines, Gerald, 728
Haldane, R. B., 450, 475, 476, 505
Hale, Nathan, 303
Halevy, Efraim, 18
Halifax, Lord, 614, 615, 616
Hall, Theodore 'Ted', 667–8, 685
Hall, Admiral Sir William Reginald
    'Blinker', 512, 515–16, 518,
    522, 523, 532, 533–4, 536–40,
    541–2, 581–2
  gains control of both Room 40
    sections, 543
  and Franklin D. Roosevelt, 567,
    604–5, 609
  and Woodrow Wilson, 569, 570
Hamilton, James, 164
Han Fei (Chinese philosopher), 55†
Hanbury Williams, General
    Sir John, 500
Handel, Michael, 9
Hankey, Maurice, 532, 534, 543*,
    544, 584
Hannibal (Carthaginian general),
    42–5, 44*
Hanotaux, Gabriel, 462
Hanover, 255–6, 264, 270, 271, 671
Hanssen, Robert P., 716
Harari, Yuval, 198
Harcourt, Lewis, 511*
Harcourt, Sir William Vernon, 427
Hardenberg, Prince Karl
    August von, 368
Hardinge, Sir Charles, 456, 457, 538,
    539, 577
Hardy, Thomas (secretary of LCS),
    328–9
Harington, Sir 'Tim', 577
Harley, Robert, 265–7, 269–70
Harnack, Arvid, 593, 594, 625
Harriman, Averell, 636
Harris, Sir James, 281
Harris, Tomás, 658, 659, 660

Harvey, George, 407

Hastings, Sir Max, 647

Hatfield House, 190†

Haverna, Jacques-Paul-Marie, 468, 470, 483–4

Hawazin, Bedouin tribe, 92

Hayden, General Mike, 710, 746

Hayes, Rutherford B., 414

Heath, Admiral Sir Herbert, 482

Heather, Peter, 81†

Heinsius, Anthonie, 251, 263, 264

Helen of Troy, 28

Helphand, Alexander, 544

Henderson, Sir Edmund, 401

Henrietta Maria, Queen, 204, 217–18

Henry, Major Hubert-Joseph, 459, 460–61

Henry II, King of France, 161–2

Henry III, King of France, 169, 176

Henry IV, King of France, 137–8, 139, 140, 169, 195

Henry VIII, King of England, 125–6, 159

Herbette, Maurice, 484

Herle, William, 170

Herman, Michael, 671, 697*

Herodotus, 29, 30–31, 32†

Herschell, Lord, 518

Herzen, Aleksandr, 378

Hesiod, 31

Hessian mercenaries, 295–6

Heuer, Dick: *Psychology of Intelligence Analysis*, 745

Heydrich, SS General Reinhard, 645

Hill, Richard, 266

Hilton, Boyd, 331

Hilton, Paris, 68

Himmat Bahadur Gosavi, 345

Himmler, Heinrich, 645, 646, 648, 656

Hindenburg, Paul von, 544

Hinsley, Harry, 642, 643

Hintze, Paul von, 454

Hipper, Admiral Franz von, 512–13, 514–15, 525

Hirohito, Emperor, 632, 670

Hiroshima atomic bomb (6 August 1945), 669

Hirota (Foreign Minister in Tokyo), 590–91

Hirsch, Wilhelm, 391, 392

Hiskey, Clarence, 665

Hiss, Alger, 299, 593, 662, 663

historical and long-term perspective, 476, 552, 694, 737–9, 739*, 741, 745, 760

and appeal of Islamic fundamentalism, 9–10, 701–4

Churchill's maxim on, 759

Jack Curry's warnings over Hitler, 760

and declassification of intelligence files, 8, 9*, 17, 665*, 671, 672, 697, 731†, 734, 734*, 735–6

on future terrorist threat, 756, 759

on Islamist terrorism, 1, 10, 701–4, 728–9, 730, 737, 756, 759

of Israeli intelligence agencies, 732

in modern China, 753, 755

need for in intelligence analysis, 1, 9–10, 11, 707, 730, 745

post-war interrogation of senior Nazis, 741–2

and pre-Iraq War intelligence, 738–9, 745

Snowden's classified revelations, 746–7

and whistle-blowing, 750–51

Hitler, Adolf

abolishes Abwehr (February 1944), 656

Appeasement policy towards, 612–13, 614–16, 760*

and British naval ciphers, 644

operation FOXLEY (SOE plan to kill), 338†, 646

prestige damaged by Stalingrad, 648

racist underestimation of Slavs, 70, 71, 627, 646

strategic incompetence of, 646

style of government, 644

triumph of as unpredictable, 759–60

on US 'Black Code', 640

views on spies, 645

Hittite Empire, 20, 21
Ho Chi Minh, 66–7
Hoare, Sir Samuel, 500, 504, 548
Hobart-Hampden, Ernest, 585
Hodson, Major W. S. R., 409–10
Hoffman, Bruce, 10, 717, 718, 728
Hoffmann, Colonel Max, 497, 498
Hogarth, D. G., 529–30
Hojeda, Alonso de, 111
Holford, George, 338
Hollis, Lord, 242
Holmes, Captain Jasper, 638
Holmes, Richard (military
    historian), 261
Holmes, Sherlock, 420*
Holocaust, 645–6, 655–6, 732, 743
Holt-Wilson, Eric, 553
Holy Roman Empire, 100, 113,
    249–50, 250*, 251, 264
  abolished by Napoleon (1806), 369
  War of the League of Cambrai, 128
Holyoake, George, 396
Homberg, Octave, 463–4
Homer
  Iliad, 2, 27–8
  Odyssey, 27, 28
Honeyman, John, 304*
Hong Kong, 736
Hooker, General 'Fightin' Joe', 412–13
Hoover, Herbert, 588
Hoover, J. Edgar, 608, 673, 718*
Hope, Admiral W. W., 512
Hopkins, Harry, 632, 633
Hopman, Albert, 455
Hopper, Bruce, 741
Hopton, John, 114
Horsey, Sir Jerome, 150*, 154–5,
    154†, 155*
Hötzendorf, Kurt Conrad von, 486, 487
House, 'Colonel' Edward M., 522, 523,
    528, 534–5, 547, 548, 566, 567,
    568, 570, 571
Howe, Admiral Lord, 508
Howard, Sir Michael, 731
Howe, Sir Geoffrey, 696–7

Howe, Sir William, 303
Hu Jintao, President of China, 67–8
Huber, Aloysius, 384
Huddlestone, Father, 222
Hudson, Rex, 720, 721
Hughes, Charles Evans, 586
Hugo, Victor, 395
human sacrifice, 44, 49, 136
Humanité, L' (French newspaper), 485
Humbert, General, 336
Humbert of Romans, 102
Hume, David, 293
Hunayn, Battle of (630), 92
Hundred Years War, 107, 159–60,
    159*, 476
Hungary, 681, 699
Huns, 79–81, 79‡, 82–5
Huntel, Police Commissioner, 391
Huskisson, William, 323, 324*, 327
Hussain, Tanvir, 757
Hussein, Saddam, 736, 737, 738,
    739–40, 741
  interrogation of (2003–4), 741,
    742–4
Hyde, Anne, 249
Hyde, Edward (later Lord Clarendon),
    222, 223, 224, 225, 230, 237, 238

Ibn al-Haytham, 98
Ignatiev, A. A., 487
Ignatiev, Nikolai, 406
Ilić, Danilo, 445, 446–7
Illuminati, the (secret society), 376
imagery intelligence (IMINT), 411,
    412, 508, 683, 684, 707
Inca Empire, 136–7
India
  British colonial Government, 6*,
    345, 410, 418–19, 467
  British Indian army, 410, 416,
    419, 467
  'chupatty movement' (1857), 407
  codebreaking by the Raj, 467
East India Company (EIC), 346,
    406–7, 410

First Anglo-Afghan war
  (1839–42), 419
Government of India Acts (1858), 410
Great Trigonometrical Survey of,
  407, 416–18
KGB operations in, 64, 690
Maratha Empire, 345
Maratha wars, 345
Mauryan dynasty, 3, 54, 60–62,
  63–4, 85, 425*
Mughal, 198
pandit missions during 'Great Game',
  416–18
post-independence intelligence
  relationship with UK, 735
Punjab border expedition (1877–8),
  419
Second Anglo-Afghan War (1878–
  80), 419–21
Wellington's campaigns in, 345–6
see also Arthashastra (Mauryan
  dynasty manual)
Indian Mutiny (1857–8), 406–7, 408–11
  cartridge cases as immediate cause,
  407–8
Indonesia, 679–80
informers
  and Catholic 'inquisitions', 107–8, 112
  in Chartist movement, 379–80
  and classical Greece, 34, 37
  at Congress of Vienna, 363, 364–6
  delatores in Rome, 24–5, 72–3, 75
  and denunciations, 73, 103, 131–2
  frumentarii in Roman world, 76–7
  in German Democratic Republic, 698
  Boris Godunov's, 155, 156
  of Jacobite sympathizers, 257
  KGB, 107–8, 698–9
  to Louis XV's Secret du Roi, 280
  and Ming emperors, 59
  in Napoleonic France, 342
  on post-1848 émigrés in Britain, 388,
  389–91
  in Prussian political system, 394
  in Renaissance Venice, 119, 131–2

and secret societies, 383–4
stool pigeons during French Terror,
  324–5
Ingenohl, Admiral Friedrich von,
  512, 513
Ingushetia, 655
Innocent III, Pope, 101
intelligence analysis
  academic research and journals,
  9, 745
  during American Civil War, 412–14
  distorted by racist stereotypes, 409,
  420, 466–7, 636, 728–9
  as distorted in authoritarian regimes,
  326, 344, 372, 375, 594, 603,
  693–8
  and downfall of Umayyad dynasty,
  96–7
  and Duke of Marlborough, 261–5
  Kent as founding father in US, 1, 9
  lack of long-term historical
  perspective, 9–10, 11, 707, 745
  Nazi failure over OVERLORD,
  656–7
  Twentieth-Century Fund report on
  (1996), 717
  as underdeveloped in USSR, 693–8
  Western failure to grasp Soviet
  weaknesses, 694, 697
Intelligence and National Security
  (academic journal), 9
International Working Men's Association (IWMA, First International),
  398, 399–400
interrogation
  by Abwehr of Russian partisans, 654
  of Dmitri Bogrov, 439
  brutality during, 88–9, 106, 130,
  164, 174, 559
  by Caesar during Gallic Wars, 47,
  48, 49
  by Cheka, 559, 595–6, 600, 654, 681
  and clerical inquisitions, 4, 102–3,
  105–6, 116, 742†
  of the Decembrists, 373

interrogation – (*cont.*)
  and denunciations, 103
  by FBI, 709, 716, 742–3
  of Guido ('Guy') Fawkes, 194–5
  'file and dossier approach', 103
  of First World War German POWs,
    531, 572
  Kremlin Plot, 595–6
  of LCS leaders, 328–9
  post-war of senior Nazis, 741–2
  of Saddam (2003–4), 741, 742–4
  of Sarajevo assassins (June 1914),
    446–7
  of Thomas Scot, 231
  and Spanish Inquisition, 116, 117
  at Walsingham's house, 165
  'waterboarding', 4, 116–17
Iran
  CIA/SIS operation to restore Shah
    (1953), 679
  fatwa on Rushdie, 90, 90†
  Ministry of Intelligence and Security
    (MOIS), 90†
  nuclear programme, 733
  revolution (1979), 9–10, 701–2
  Saddam's fear/hatred of, 744
  US secret arms sales to, 691
Iraq
  Colin Powell's UN presentation (5
    February 2003), 739–40
  bogus CURVEBALL source on
    WMD, 740
  Iraq War (2003), 11, 736–7,
    738–9, 759
  'Iraqi Perspectives Project' (by
    USJFCOM), 743–4
  Muslim conquest of, 94
  President's WMD Commission
    report (2005), 740–41
  Senate Select Committee on
    Intelligence report (2004), 740
  WMD intelligence, 736–8, 739–41,
    745, 759
Irarraga, Diego de, 199–200
Ireland

Fenian bombing campaigns in
  London, 427–8
  IRA offensives in London (1990s),
    702
  and Napoleon, 335–6
  Wickham as Chief Secretary in, 337
Irgun Zvai Leumi (paramilitary Zionist
  group), 732
Isaacson, Walter, 297*
Isabella, Archduchess, ruler of Spanish
  Netherlands, 204*, 207, 208
Isabella I of Castile, 111, 112–13
Ibn Ishaq (biographer of
  Muhammad), 90*
ISIS (Islamic State in Iraq
  and Syria), 758–9
Islam
  Abbasid dynasty, 96–9, 127, 128
  Barid (Caliphate messenger service),
    96, 97
  Caliphate established, 3, 93
  Crimean Tatars, 405
  dominance in Arabian Peninsula, 3,
    86–92, 93
  early history of, 87–8
  fundamentalism, 9–10, 701–4
  golden age of science and
    mathematics, 97–9
  Hadiths, 3, 88, 90*, 91, 99
  Kaaba in Mecca, 92
  'Mardin fatwa' of Ibn Taymiyya, 702
  military conquest in 630s/640s, 93–5
  Moorish kingdoms in Spain, 111
  Muslim tribes of the Caucasus,
    405, 415
  and Quraish tribe, 87–9, 91–2
  Uighur population in north-west
    China, 755–6
  Umayyad dynasty, 95, 96–7
  see also Muhammad
Islamist terrorism
  1993 World Trade Center attack,
    718–19, 729
  7 July 2005 attacks in London, 756
  and age of WMD, 10, 722–3, 758–9

and Arab Poetic Tradition, 720*
in Britain, 721–2, 756–7
British intelligence, 721–2, 756–7
car and truck bombings, 719
emphasis on martyrdom missions,
  703–4, 721, 725
eulogizing of Muhammad's agent
  network, 88
growth of movements/groups
  (1980s/90s), 717–18
historical and long-term perspective
  on, 1, 10, 701–4, 728–9, 730, 737,
  756, 759
Rex Hudson on, 720, 721
Manchester Arena attack (22 May
  2017), 757
need for closer FBI–CIA
  cooperation, 718–19, 725
religious motivations for, 702–4, 725
report of the 9/11 Commission, 717,
  719, 723, 724, 726, 728,
  729–30, 736
and Sunni extremists, 702–4
theological roots of, 10, 701–4
underestimated in West (1990s), 718,
  728–9, 737
US embassy attack in Beirut
  (1983), 719
and US embassy security, 719
US intelligence reports on
  (mid-1990s), 717
see also Al Qaeda
Israel, state of, 18–19, 732–4
Istanbul, 32‡, 99
Italian Wars (1494–1559), 128, 129
Italy
  anarchist terrorists in 1890s, 430,
    431, 432, 433
  British embassy in Rome, 591–2
  Carbonari (secret societies), 379
  conquest of Ethiopia, 606–7
  cryptanalysis during Second World
    War, 644
  embassies in Soviet Bloc, 675
  Fascist, 606–7, 644

and 'July Crisis' (1914), 493
George P. Marsh in 1870s Rome,
  422–3
nineteenth-century nationalists,
  380–82, 396–7, 747
poor cipher and embassy
  security, 489
Renaissance, 4, 121–2
and 'Triplecodex' (1914), 479
US covert action in 1948 elections,
  678, 679
see also Venice, Renaissance
Ivan III, 'the Great', 146
Ivan IV, 'the Terrible'
  constant fear of conspiracies, 141–2,
    144–5, 146, 150–51, 152, 153–4
  diplomatic ties with England,
    147–54
  and dog's head symbol, 142–3, 145
  Giles Fletcher on, 156
  fragmentary sources on, 141
  kills his son Ivan, 154
  Novgorod massacre (1570), 145
  oprichniki (security service) of,
    142–5, 150, 151, 152, 153–4, 155
  and print culture, 147
  reign of terror, 144–6, 150, 151, 152,
    153
  Stalin as admirer of, 141, 145
Ivanov, General Nikolai, 502
Izumi, Kozo, 627–8

Jackson, George, 366
Jackson, Admiral Thomas, 524,
  525, 543*
Jacobite cause
  1715 Rebellion, 270
  agent network, 269
  and Atterbury, 272–5
  'Elibank Plot' (1752), 285
  and European powers, 270,
    271–2, 281
  French invasion of Britain cancelled
    (1744), 282
  Fuller's conspiracy theories, 258–9

Jacobite cause (*cont.*)
  intelligence network, 269, 270,
    283, 284
  in Ireland (1689–90), 251–2, 254–5
  James II's court in exile, 256
  plots against William III, 256–7,
    259–60
  Rising (1745–6), 283–4
  Swedish negotiations, 271–2, 279, 348
  and William III's government/armed
    forces, 257–8
Jagow, Gottlieb von, 490–91
Al-Jahiz, 97
James, Edwin, 396–7
James, Commander William
  'Bubbles', 543
James I, King of England (James VI of
  Scotland), 163, 164, 193
  accession to English throne, 192
  Buckingham as favourite of, 195,
    203–4
  declares war on Spain (1624),
    204, 207
  intelligence and foreign policy of,
    192, 203–5
  secret correspondence with Cecil,
    191–2
James II, King of England, 220, 236,
  240, 241, 248, 249, 250–51
  campaign in Ireland (1689–90),
    251–2, 254–5
  death of (1701), 260–61
  exile court at Saint-Germain-en-
    Laye, 256–7, 259, 260–1
James V, King of Scotland, 161
Jamestown, Virginia, 195–8
Japan
  atomic bombs dropped on (August
    1945), 669–70
  and BARBAROSSA, 627
  cryptanalysis during Second World
    War, 644
  decrypts by UK and US in
    1920s/30s, 585–7, 588, 589, 590,
    610–11

German embassy in Tokyo, 593–4
  intelligence during Second World
    War, 663–4
  intelligence preparations for Pearl
    Harbor, 630
  Kwantung Army, 627
  main ciphers cracked by USA,
    610–12
  naval code JN25b, 634–5, 637–8
  Nicholas II's hatred of, 466–7
  Pacific islands of, 606
  Pearl Harbor attack (1941), 7,
    633–6, 677
  RED and PURPLE ciphers cracked,
    610–12, 627, 628, 671†
  Russo-Japanese War (1904–5), 455,
    466–8, 469, 478–9
  'southern solution' (war with Britain
    and US), 627, 628
  surrender in Second World War
    (August 1945), 670
  USSR publishes decrypts, 589–90
  'Winds Messages' to foreign
    embassies (November 1941), 631
Jaupain, François, 262–3
Jay, John, 303*
Jeffery, Professor Keith, 525, 553*, 614
Jellicoe, Admiral Earl John, 481,
  512–13, 525–6, 543
Jena, Battle of (October 1806),
  339‡, 354
Jenkins, Roy, 644*
Jenkins' Ear, War of (1739), 282
Jenkinson, Anthony ('Anton Iankin'),
  148, 149, 150–51, 153–4
Jericho, Israelite conquest story,
  16–18, 22
Jervis, Major Thomas Best, 403, 414
Jesuit missions, 121, 170–73, 176, 203
Jesus of Nazareth, 22–6, 22*, 24*, 86
Jews
  in Constantinople, 124
  expulsion from Spain (1492), 113
  ICOR (Soviet rival to Zionist
    movement), 665

and medieval conspiracy theories,
106–7
in medieval Spain, 111–13
Nazi genocide, 645–6, 655–6, 732,
743
in nineteenth-century Vienna, 364
persecution of in Russian Empire,
436–7
Protocols of the Elders of Zion
(anti-Semitic forgery), 437, 703
and Spanish Inquisition, 111–13, 115
Talmud injunction to 'rise and kill
first', 732–4
JFK (Oliver Stone film), 688*
Jie Xuan, 59
Jodl, General Alfred, 646
Joffre, Marshal Joseph, 494–5, 506
John XXII, Pope, 106–7, 127
John the Baptist, 22
John Paul II, Pope, 729
Johnson, Thomas R., 587
Joint Intelligence Committee (JIC), 10,
617–18, 626, 634, 697*, 717,
734*, 736
'Iraq's Weapons of Mass Destruction'
(2002 report), 740
Jones, Lord Elwyn, 738
Jones, John Paul, 300
Joseph (Old Testament), 2, 13
Joseph I, Emperor, 264
Joseph de Paris, Père (François Le Clerc
du Tremblay), 209, 210*, 211
Joshua (Old Testament), 3, 13, 14,
16–18
Joubert, Charles, 325
Joynson-Hicks, William ('Jix'), 583, 584
Judas Iscariot, 2, 24–5
Julian the Apostate, Roman emperor, 78
Jutland, Battle of (1916), 525–6,
533, 543*
Juvenal, 50*

Kab ibn Al-Ashraf, 89
Kahn, David: *The Codebreakers*, 20†,
46†, 271*

Kalmyks (Buddhist Mongol herdsmen),
655
Kalugin, Oleg, 64, 684–6, 690
Kamen, Henry, 115
Kamenev, Lev, 441, 600
Kamptz, Karl Albert von, 374
Kang Sheng, 752
Kaplan, Fanya (Dora), 559
Kapnist, Pyotr, 456
Karachai (Turkic shepherds), 654–5
Karpov, Anatoli, 699
Kasahara, Lieutenant-Colonel
Yukio, 590
Kashmir, Maharajah of, 419
Kaunitz, Prince Wenzel Anton, 5,
278–9, 363
Kautilya (or Chanakya), 60
Kawabe, Torashiro, 590
Kaye, Sir John, 408
Kazakhstan, 708–9
Keill, John, 270–71
Keith, Robert, 290–91
Kell, Vernon, 66, 477, 479–80, 481,
483, 495, 532, 552, 553–5, 614,
615, 760
Kelley, Brian J., 716
Kelly, Christopher, 81†
Kelly, George, 272, 273, 274
Kelly, Thomas: 'The Myth of the
Skytale', 46†
Kendall, Elizabeth: 'Jihadist
Propaganda and Its Exploitation
of the Arab Poetic Tradition', 720*
Kennan, George, 556, 592
Kennedy, President John F., 295, 435,
680, 688
Kennedy, Captain Malcolm, 635–6
Kent, Sherman, 1, 9, 10, 745*
Kent, Tyler, 592
Kenya, 719–20, 735
Keppel, Alice, 433
Kerensky, Alexander, 504, 549, 552–3
Kernochan, Frederic, 605
Kerrigan, John, 265
Keynes, John Maynard, 517

KGB
'active measures' in Third World, 8,
688, 689–91
agents in Cold War USA, 684–7,
709, 711
Bakatin as last chairman of, 704–5
Cheka as forerunner, 7, 110–11
Cold War penetration of embassies
in Moscow, 674–5
covert actions during Cold War, 8,
680–82, 688, 689–91
covert activity as 'active measures', 2
cryptanalysis during Cold War, 674
First Chief (Foreign Intelligence)
Directorate (FCD), 689, 692,
693–4, 698, 712–13, 714
Gordievsky as agent of SIS, 696,
713–14
and 'ideological subversion', 4, 100,
105, 107–8, 130†, 698–700, 751
ignorance of Western society, 697–8
illegals, 593–4, 622, 626, 665, 666,
673, 681–2, 699, 714–15, 751
as immune from domestic criticism
in 1970s, 687
informers, 107–8, 698–9
and Kennedy assassination
conspiracy theories, 688
and Mitrokhin (FCD) archive,
712–13, 714–15, 747‡, 750–51
network of informers, 107–8
officers as more influential than
diplomats, 689–90
subversion in India, 64, 690
Khadijah bint Khuwaylid, 87, 88
Khalid ibn al-Walid, 93–4, 95
Khalid Sheikh Mohammed, 718,
729, 758
Khan, Dr A. Q., 736
Al-Khatmi, Umayr-ibn Adiy, 90
Khnumhotep II, Egyptian nobleman, 20†
Khomeini, Ayatollah Ruhollah, 9–10,
90, 701–2
Khrushchev, Nikita, 601, 683, 689,
694–5

Kibalchich, Nikolai, 425
Kicke, Abraham, 232–3
Kiderlen-Wächter, Alfred von, 477–8
Killigrew, Henry, 166
Kim Jong-un, 751–2
Kimmel, Admiral Husband, 634
Al-Kindi, Yaqub ibn Ishaq, 4, 98–9,
127, 347, 497
King, John, 327
Kipling, Rudyard, *Kim*, 416
Kirby, Michael, 752
Kirov, Sergei, 594–5
Kirpichenko, Vadim, 693
Kishlansky, Mark, 261
Kissinger, Henry, 58, 59, 66–7
Kitchener, General Sir Herbert, 451,
463, 511*
Klement, Rudolf, 622–3
Klotz, Louis-Lucien, 484
Klyuchevsky, Vasily, 277*
Knatchbull-Hugessen, Sir Hughe, 656
Kneller, Sir Godfrey, 253
Knollys, Charlotte, 433
Knowlton, Thomas, 303
Knox, Alfred Dillwyn, 517–18, 524
Knox, Frank, 631, 633
Knyvett, Sir Thomas, 194
Koch, Baron Ignaz von, 278, 279
Koda, Vice-Admiral Yoji, 466, 467
Kolychev, Filipp, 143–4
Komissarov, M. S., 437
Konovalets, Yevhen, 623
Konoye, Prince, 627
Korchnoi, Viktor, 699
Kordt, Theodor, 614
Korean War (1950–53), 679
Korotkov, Aleksandr, 625
Kotzebue, August von, 372
Koval, Zhorzh ('George') Abramovich,
664–7, 668
Kozyrev, Andrei, 711
Kramer, Lieutenant-Commander
Alwin D., 629, 632, 633
Krasin, Leonid, 577, 578
Kravchuk, Leonid, 708

Krivosh-Nemanich, Vladimir, 468
Kropotkin, Pyotr, 429
Kropotkin, Sasha, 549
Krötenschield, Boris, 662
Krotov, Valeri, 681
Krüger, Karl, 526–7
Kryuchkov, Vladimir, 690, 692, 696,
    699, 704, 712
Kubesch, Herr, 391
Kullback, Dr Solomon, 645
Kuomintang (KMT), 66, 752
Kuropatkin, General Alexei, 467
Kutepov, General Aleksandr, 575
Kutuzov, Prince Mikhail, 358, 359
Kuznetsov, Iakov, 574
Kyd, Thomas, 187

La Chétardie, marquis de, 277
La Fayette, marquis de, 297, 301
La Rochelle, siege of (1628), 205–7
Lac, Jean-André de, 334*
Laflotte, Alexandre de, 324–5
Lake Trasimene, Battle of (217 BC), 42–3
Lamartine, Alphonse de, 384
Lamb, Frederick, 367
Lamb, George, 204*, 208
Lamballe, princesse de, 318–19
Lambe, Dr John, 206–7
Lambeth Palace, 220
Lamsdorf, Count, 454, 455–6, 469
Lancken, Oskar von der, 478
Landau, Captain Henry, 562
Landezen, Abram, 428
Lando, Antonio di, 119
Lando, Girolamo, 205
Lang, Andrew, 284
Lansdowne, Lord, 422
Lansing, Robert, 522, 527–8, 540, 541,
    548, 568, 570
Larsen, Daniel, 'British Intelligence and
    American Neutrality', 533*, 538
Las Cases, Mémorial de Sainte-Hélène
    (1823), 375
Lassen, Lieutenant-Commander
    Alfred, 520

Latimer, Hugh, 114
Latsis, Martyn Yanovich, 556–7
Latzarus, Louis, 491
Lauragais region (near Toulouse), 102,
    742†
Laurent, General Charles, 495
Lavaur, Languedoc, 101
Lawrence, T. E. ('Lawrence of Arabia'),
    508, 528–9, 530
Layer, Christopher, 273
Le Clerc de Noisy, 337
Le Peletier, Claude, 247
Le Queux, William, 472–3, 474, 476
Le Roy Ladurie, Emmanuel, 106
Le Tellier, Michel, 245†
League of Nations, 568
Leahy, Admiral, 676
leaks, official, 747–8
Leboeuf, Marshal, 414–15
Lee, Arthur, 294–5, 299–300
Lee, Duncan, 593
Lee, Henry, 301
Lee, General Robert E., 411, 412–13
Legare, Alexander Brown, 604
Legitimation League, 431–2
Leibniz, Gottfried Wilhelm von,
    256, 270*
Leicester, Earl of, 166, 170
Leipzig, Battle of (October 1813), 359
LeMay, General Curtis, 683, 694–5
Lenin
    arrival at the Finland Station (April
        1917), 545
    and Bolshevik–Menshevik split,
        440, 442
    and Brest-Litovsk, 556, 561
    creation of Cheka, 555–6
    deceived by police spies (early
        1917), 393
    execution of brother Alexander
        (1887), 436
    and German 'sealed' train, 545, 546
    as 'German spy', 549–50, 551
    Kaplan's assassination attempt
        on, 559

Lenin – (cont.)
  on Lloyd George, 577
  and Okhrana penetration of RSDLP,
    440–41
  Okhrana surveillance of, 440, 441
  and Solovetsky Island concentration
    camp, 561
  stays in London, 434, 441, 545
  support for terror, 557, 574
  as victim of carjack, 574, 595
Lenoe, Matthew, *The Kirov Murder
  and Soviet History*, 595*
Leo VI 'The Wise', Eastern emperor,
  95–6
Leonidas, King of Sparta, 29
Leonov, Nikolai, 689, 693
Leopold I, Habsburg emperor, 246,
  247, 249–50
Leopold II, King of the Belgians, 465–6
Leotychidas (son of Agis), 35*
lepers, 106
Lerma, Duke of, 195*
Leuthen, Battle of (December 1757), 288
Lhasa, Tibet, 417–18
L'Hoste, Nicolas, 199
Li Peng, 753
Liddell Hart, Sir Basil, 54, 612*
Lieven, Dorothea, 370–71
Lincoln, Abraham, 311, 411–12,
  422, 435
Link, Arthur S., 520, 540–41
Lionne, Hugues de, 213
Lipka, Robert, 685
Lippomano, Girolamo, 125
Lisle, Sir John, 234
Litvinov, Maxim, 560, 578
Liu Jieyi, 755
Livy, 40, 42–3, 44, 44*, 45
Lloyd, Selwyn, 674
Lloyd George, David, 531, 532, 534,
  535–6, 538–9, 579
  Anglo-Soviet trade negotiations
    (1920–21), 577–8
  and convoy system, 543–4
Lockhart, John Bruce, 534

Lockhart, Robert Bruce, 559–60
Lockheed, 683
Logan Airport, Boston, 724–5
Lokhova, Svetlana, 441–2, 591*,
  595, 597
London
  7 July 2005 attacks in, 756
  Boudicca's burning of, 75
  Fenian bombing campaigns in, 427–8
  interception of Mazzini's letters,
    380–83, 747
  IRA offensives in (1990s), 702
  Lenin in, 434, 441, 545
  Marx as refugee in, 388–91
London Corresponding Society
  (LCS), 327–9
London Virginia Company, 195–6
Londonderry (Derry),
  siege of (1689), 251
Lopez, Alfonso, 211
Lopez, Dr Roderigo, 188–9
Loredan, Leonardo, 118
Los Alamos laboratories, New Mexico,
  667, 668, 673
Loubet, Émile, 459
Louis IX, King of France, 102
Louis XIII, King of France, 201, 205
  and Concini assassination, 201–2
  consummation of marriage to Anne
    of Austria, 201, 202–3
  and cryptanalysis, 206, 211,
    212, 672
  and *journées des dupes*, 209–10
Louis XIV, King of France, 206, 212,
  242–7, 249–50, 460, 672
  death of (1715), 267–8
  and James II, 248–9, 250, 254–5,
    256, 260–61
  and Madame de Maintenon, 247–8
  and Nine Years War (1688–97), 251,
    268
  and Poland, 252–3, 255
  secret diplomacy with Charles II,
    237, 248
  and state finance, 244†, 247, 267

Louis XV, King of France, 279, 281,
  282, 287, 292
  and Benjamin Franklin,, 295
  invasion of Britain cancelled
    (1744), 282
  Secret du Roi, 279–80, 292–3
Louis XVI, King of France, 279, 307,
  313, 314
  arrest and imprisonment (1792),
    317, 319
  attempted escape from Paris (June
    1791), 315–17
  and *Secret du Roi*, 293–4
  trial and execution of (January
    1793), 320–21
Louis XVII, death in prison of (1795),
  330, 360
Louis XVIII, King of France, 316, 330,
  331, 341§, 360, 361, 375
Louis of Battenberg, Prince, 510
Louis Napoleon (Napoleon III), 387,
  395–7, 415
Louis Philippe, King of France, 376,
  378, 384
Louvois, marquis de, 245–7, 248, 460
Lovell, James, 308, 309
Lowe, Thaddeus S. C., 411–12
Lucan, 49†, 50*
Lucan, George Bingham,
  3rd Earl of, 404
Lucheni, Luigi, 431
Lucius Vitellius, 25–6
Ludendorff, General Erich, 497–8, 544,
  550, 561–2, 564
Ludlow, Edmund, 233–4, 235*
Lusitania, sinking of (1915), 521
Luther, Martin, ninety-five theses
  (1517), 109
Luttwak, Edward, 93
Luvaas, Jay, 412, 413
Luxembourg, duc de, 246
Lvovna, Frida, 620
Lynam, George, 327, 329
Lytton, Edward Bulwer-Lytton, 1st
  Earl, 418–19, 420, 459

MacArthur, General Douglas, 636
Macaulay, Thomas Babington, 381–2,
  392, 409
Macdonald, Flora, 283–4
MacDonald, J. Ramsay, 580, 581, 582
Macdonald, Marshal Jacques, 360
Macdonogh, General Sir George,
  506, 507
MacDougall, Major-General Sir
  Patrick, 415
MacEachin, Douglas, 745*
Macedonia, 443
Machiavelli, Nicolo, 4
Mackenzie, Compton, 483, 512
Mackey, John Ross, 290
Maclean, Donald, 621, 649, 650,
  673, 711
Maclean, Sir Fitzroy, 601
Mafia, 63
Mahabharata, 60–61, 64
Al-Mahdi, Caliph, 97
Maintenon, Madame de, 247–8
Maitland of Lethington,
  Sir William, 166
Makarios of Chios, 123
Makarova, Natalia, 699
Malato, Charles, 429
Malcolm, Noel, 122
Malinche (ex-slave woman), 133–4,
  135, 136, 195
Malinovsky, Roman, 440–41, 561
Maliuta Skuratov (Grigory Luky-
  anovich Skuratov-Belski), 143–4,
  145, 152, 155
Malobabić, Rade, 444
Malplaquet, Battle of (1709), 265
Malta, 334
Malvy, Louis, 551
Al-Mamum, Caliph, 97
Manasco, Carter, 677
Manasevich-Manuilov, Ivan, 468, 470
MANHATTAN Project, 664–8, 669,
  673, 691
Manning, Bradley (now Chelsea), 745,
  746, 748

Manning, Henry, 224–5
Al-Mansur, Caliph, 97
Manteuffel, Otto von, 394
Mao Zedong, 66, 67, 752
Mar, John Erskine, Earl of, 270, 273, 274
Marchand, Major Jean-Baptiste, 463
Marco Polo, 119
Mardonius (Persian commander), 31
Maret, Hugues-Bernard, 352
María, Sister (adviser to Philip IV), 210
Maria Anna, Infanta (sister of Philip IV), 204
Maria Theresa, Habsburg empress, 278–9, 287
Marie-Antoinette, 297, 307, 315–16, 317, 319
Marie-Thérèse (daughter of Marie-Antoinette), 316
Marillac, Michel de, 209–10
Mark Antony, 72
Marlowe, Christopher, 172–3, 186–7
  killing of, 176†, 187–8
Marmont, Marshal Auguste, 348
the Marne, Battle of (1915), 506
Marquis, Hugues: Agents de l'ennemi, 324*
Marris, Sir William, 78*
Marsh, George P., 422–3
Marshall, General Sir James, 507
Marshall Islands, 606
Marshall-Cornwall, General Sir James, 528, 563
Martin, William H., 675, 749
Martini, Admiral Fulvio, 675
Martov, Yuli, 441
Marvell, Andrew, 236
Marwan II, Caliph, 96
Marwand, Battle of (July 1880), 420*
Marx, Jenny, 386, 388–9, 393, 397
Marx, Karl
  Civil War in France, The (pamphlet), 399, 400
  Cologne congress (August 1848), 387, 388, 393
  and Cologne show trial (1852), 393–4
  Communist Correspondence Committee, 386
  Communist Manifesto, The (with Engels), 397
  complaints against 'spy system', 389–90, 520
  death of (14 March 1883), 400
  deceived by Bangya, 392–3
  editor of Neue Rheinische Zeitung, 387, 388
  and First International, 398, 399–400
  and French Second Empire, 397
  on French Second Republic, 386–7
  on Indian Mutiny, 408*
  and Paris Commune, 398–9
  as refugee in London, 388–91
  writing of Das Kapital, 394, 398, 400
Mary, Queen of Scots, 5, 151*, 161–2, 163–4, 165, 166–7, 192
  and plots to overthrow Elizabeth I, 173–9
  secret correspondence with English supporters, 173–5, 176–9, 191, 192
  trial and execution of (February 1587), 179–80
Mary I, Queen of England, 114–15, 137
Mary II, Queen of England, 249, 250, 251, 258
Mary of Guise, Scottish Queen Regent, 161, 162–3
Mary of Modena, 248, 249
Massachusetts Institute of Technology (MIT), 596
Massoud, Ahmad Shah, 725
Masterman, J. C., 651
Matha, Louis, 429
Matsuoka, Yosuke, 664
Mauborgne, Major-General Joseph, 611
Maubourg, General Latour, 347*

Maugham, W. Somerset, 549, 552–3

Maupas, Charlemagne de, 395

Maurice, Eastern emperor, 93

Maurya, King Chandragupta, 60, 62

Maximilian I, Emperor, 128

Maximinos, 83

Mayenne, Charles de Guise,
     Duke of, 138

Mayne, Sir Richard, 388

Mazarin, Cardinal Jules, 212–13, 242,
     243, 244

Mazzini, Giuseppe, 380–82, 747

McAdoo, William G., 522

McCarthy, Senator Joseph, 672–3

McConnell, Vice-Admiral John
     Michael 'Mike', 710

McCormack, Alfred, 637

McCrea, Captain John, 637

McIntire, Rear Admiral Ross T., 633

McKinley, President William, 429,
     435–6

McLaughlin, John, 706

McLynn, Frank, 284

McNutt, Russell 'Russ', 666

Meade, General George G., 413

Méchin, Alexandre-Edme, 375–6

Medici, Marie de', Queen Regent of
     France, 201–2, 209–10

medieval warfare, role of
     intelligence, 78†

Medina Sidonia, Duke of, 183, 184, 196

Megiddo offensive (September
     1918), 565

Mehmedbašić, Muhamed, 445–6

Meir, Golda, 733

Melfort, Lord, 252, 256, 260–61

Melville, Superintendent William,
     433–5, 475, 481

Mendoza, Antonio de, 133*

Mendoza, Bernardino de, 138, 167,
     169, 174, 175, 177, 183–4

Menon, Shivshankar, 65–6

Menzies, Stewart, 336, 608, 616, 617, 652

Mérargues, Louis de Lagonia de, 199

Mercader, Ramón, 63, 624

Mercurius Aulicus (Civil War news-
     sheet), 215

Merridale, Catherine, 155

Merry, Robert, 319

Mesnager, Nicolas, 267

message interception
     during Allied final offensive (1814),
          359–60
     and 'Amarna letters', 20–21, 20*
     and American Civil War, 411
     during American Revolutionary
          War, 301
     Atterbury's correspondence, 273,
          274–5
     Britain and Louis XIV's
          correspondence, 252–3, 255
     British as naïve about, 421–2
     British debate on (1844), 381–3
     British Government of India, 410
     of cipher telegrams, 421
     during Congress of Vienna, 363, 365–6
     correspondence of Moray's assassin
          Hamilton, 164
     and counter-terrorism, 757
     and Edinburgh Castle occupation
          (1573), 166
     English embassy in Paris
          (1570s/1580s), 167
     First World War German naval
          messages, 7, 509, 510–11, 512–19,
          524–6
     by France in pre-First World War
          period, 488
     French Revolutionary Wars, 337
     during the Fronde (1648–53), 212
     during German spring offensive
          (1918), 563–4
     by Germany during First World War,
          497–8, 502, 504, 519
     Home Office Warrants (HOWs)
          system, 480, 495
     interwar period, 576–80, 582–4,
          616–17
     King's correspondence captured at
          Naseby, 216–18, 219

message interception – (*cont.*)
  letter-opening by Third Section in
    Russia, 374
  and Louis Napoleon, 395
  in Louis XIV's France, 242–3,
    245, 248
  by Marlborough, 263, 264
  Marlborough's to James II, 257
  Mary of Guise's letters to French
    court, 162–3
  Mary's Babington Plot
    correspondence, 176–9
  and Mazarin, 212–13
  Mazzini's letters in London,
    380–83, 747
  in months before 9/11 attacks, 725
  'Moritz' apparatus (First World
    War), 520
  and Muhammad, 91
  and Napoleon, 341
  by the Okhrana, 425–6
  by the Papacy, 127
  during Peninsular War, 347–52, 403
  of Philip II's correspondence, 138,
    139–40, 166–7, 180
  poor British telephone security (First
    World War), 520, 530, 531
  pre-First World War German naval
    intelligence, 479–80
  Richelieu's interception of Huguenot
    letters, 205–6
  and Richelieu's *cabinet noir*,
    210–11
  during Seven Years War (1756–63),
    288, 289
  and Soro's decryptions, 128, 129
  Swedish negotiations with Jacobites,
    271–2, 279, 348
  by John Thurloe, 224, 225, 226
  of Trotsky's and Sedov's
    correspondence, 599
  by Vienna *cabinet noir*, 363–4, 365
Messersmith, George S., 608
Metropolitan Police Force in London,
  380, 388, 396, 400–401

Criminal Investigation Department
  (CID), 401
Special Branch, 428, 431–2, 433–5,
  504, 552, 553, 578
Special Irish Branch (est. 1883), 427–8
Metternich, Prince Klemens von
  and Carlsbad Decrees (1819), 372–3
  on Charles X's royal coup (1830), 376
  and Congress of Vienna, 363–4, 366,
    367, 369
  correspondence opened by the
    French, 357, 370
  and death of Castlereagh, 371
  fear of Italian nationalists, 380–81
  flees to London (March 1848), 385
  intelligence network of, 369–70
  obsession with surveillance, 365
  obsessive fear of conspiracy/
    revolution, 369, 371, 372, 375
  purpose of intelligence for, 372
  sexual liaisons, 366, 367, 370
Mexico, 536–8, 540, 598, 623–4
MI1b (War Office SIGINT agency)
  First World War US and German
    SIGINT, 533–42
  merged with Room 40 as GC&CS,
    576
  Room 40 as rival, 533
MI5 (Security Service)
  7 July 2005 attacks in London, 756
  attitude to Appeasement, 612–13,
    614, 615–16, 760*
  attitude to declassification of files,
    9*, 734*
  B1a (Second World War double-agent
    section), 650, 651, 652–3, 659
  belief that Lenin a German spy, 515
  Defence of the Realm (official
    history of by Andrew), 10*, 10†,
    90†, 548*, 658*, 722*, 732*,
    738*, 758*
  dismisses Islamic extremist threat
    (1995), 702
  double-agents in First World War
    Germany, 548

and Empire/Commonwealth, 735
and First World War 'British
    Bolshevism', 551–2, 553–5, 554
and First World War spy mania, 505
in-house history (1921), 480
intelligence reports on Al Qaeda
    (summer 2001), 724
and IRA offensives in London
    (1990s), 702
and Islamist terrorism in UK, 721–2,
    756–7
and media claims on Bin Laden, 721
Melville as 'chief detective', 435
ministerial responsibility for, 738†
and neutral US during Second World
    War, 609
operation LARGE (July 2000), 722,
    756–7
OVERT surveillance operation
    (2006), 757–8
post-First World War intelligence
    cuts, 574
Rimington as first female head of, 9
and Rushdie fatwa, 90†
Secret Service Bureau as forerunner
    of, 66, 477, 479–80, 495,
    532, 603
Security Service 1908–1945, The
    (classified history of by
    Curry), 760
size of in early Cold War, 77
sources in German embassy (late
    1930s), 612–13, 614, 615
and Zinoviev letter (October
    1924), 581
MI6/SIS (Secret Intelligence Service;
    MI1c)
    attempts to keep Russia in First
        World War, 547–9
    attitude to Appeasement, 614–15,
        617–18
    attitude to declassification of files,
        734*, 735*
    Chief of ('C'), 223*, 483
    Cold War covert actions, 678–9

and Empire/Commonwealth,
    735*
existence officially acknowledged
    (1992), 9, 483, 677, 732
and First World War, 512, 526–7,
    528, 534–5
Gordievsky as agent of, 696, 697,
    713–14
Hoare in St Petersburg/Petrograd,
    500, 504, 548
intelligence special relationship with
    US, 566–7, 608, 609
and Iraqi WMD intelligence,
    736–7, 739
La Dame Blanche network, 562,
    571–2
and Ramsay MacDonald,
    580–81, 582
ministerial responsibility for, 738†
Moscow head of station, 560
and neutral US during Second World
    War, 608–9
official history of, 10*, 614*
operations on Libya and A. Q. Khan
    network, 736–7
post-First World War intelligence
    cuts, 573
receives Mitrokhin (FCD) archive
    (1992), 712–13, 714–15,
    747‡, 750
Secret Service Bureau as forerunner
    of, 477, 481, 532, 603
Section IX on Soviet activity, 662
Venlo humiliation (November
    1939), 618
MI-8 (first specialized US SIGINT
    agency), 569
    Cipher Bureau (Black Chamber),
        586–9
    Japanese decrypts by in 1920s,
        586–7, 588, 589
Miasoiedov, Sergei, 502–3
Middleton, Charles, 250
Mieselbach, Colonel J. F., 345
Miles, William, 313–14

military intelligence
  Alexander II's reforms in
    Russia, 406
  and American Civil War,
    411, 412–14
  and Amr ibn al-As, 95
  and ancient Greece, 30–31, 33–6
  Arab Bureau in Cairo (First World
    War), 528–30
  and Augustus, 70–71
  Austrian during Napoleonic
    Wars, 357
  British Intelligence Branch (IB), 415
  British military attachés, 414
  Byzantine, 93, 95–6
  and Julius Caesar, 47–51, 53, 82
  Richard Chancellor in Ivan IV's
    Russia, 150
  Clausewitz on, 14–15
  collapse of Russian system
    (1917), 550
  and Hernán Cortés, 132–6, 137, 195
  during Crimean War, 403,
    404–5, 406
  Directorate of Military Operations
    (DMO), British, 452–3, 473,
    476, 482
  Dreyfus Affair, 453, 459, 460–62
  and Duke of Marlborough,
    261–5, 268
  Encyclopédie (1751–72) on, 279
  failures over Dutch Medway attack
    (1667), 236
  Field Intelligence Department (Boer
    War), 452
  and First World War, 7, 311,
    497–502, 506–8, 511–12, 519–20,
    528–33, 536–42, 568–9, 571, 671
  Franco-Prussian War (1870–71),
    414–15
  and Frederick the Great, 285–7
  French (1890s–1914 period), 453,
    459, 460–66, 494–5
  French Deuxième Bureau, 459, 462,
    465, 495, 585

  French pre-First World War
    deficiencies, 494–5
  German military attachés, 453, 454,
    460, 461
  German sabotage department (First
    World War), 520–21, 522
  and Indian Mutiny, 409
  Japanese, 466, 467
  in Kaiser's Germany, 453
  and Khalid ibn al-Walid, 94
  in Louis XIV's France, 246–7, 268
  MO5 (War Office counter-espionage
    department), 452, 474–6
  and Muhammad, 3, 86, 87–9, 91, 92,
    94, 96, 97
  Napoleon's view of, 339, 339†, 340,
    344, 352
  and Pearl Harbor attack, 7, 630–63,
    634, 677
  Peninsular War, 346–52, 403
  pre-First World War, 453–5, 494–5
  pre-First World War German
    espionage network in Britain, 477
  Revolutionary/Napoleonic Wars,
    333–5
  Roman neglect of, 70, 71–2, 74, 77,
    79, 81–2
  Russian agents in Napoleonic Paris,
    354–6
  and Russian campaign of Napoleon,
    352–3, 354
  Russian military attachés, 487
  Scipio's grasp of, 45, 82
  Sektion IIIb of German General
    Staff, 453, 475, 495
  Signal Security Agency (SSA),
    642, 643–4
  Soviet Fourth Department (later
    GRU), 406, 590, 593–4, 596, 620,
    625, 626, 627, 646, 664–5
  Soviet penetration of
    MANHATTAN Project, 664–8,
    669, 673, 691
  Statistical Bureau of Napoleon,
    339–40, 344, 345

Sun Tzu's 'Divine Skein', 55–6
US Military Intelligence Division (MID), 569, 573
US Signal Intelligence Service (SIS), 610–12, 627, 628–30, 631–3, 634, 637, 645
and George Washington, 302–6
and Wellington, 345–52
and William III's landing in England, 249–50
Millais, Sir John, 543
Miller, Flagg, *The Audacious Ascetic*, 720*
Millerand, Alexandre, 585
Milner-Barry, Stuart, 617
Mirabeau, comte de, 313–14
Mirbach, Count Robert, 558
Mirbach, Count Wilhelm, 557, 558
Mirebeau (Côte d'Or), 49*
Miremont, Raymond du Falga de, 104
Mitchell, Bernon F., 675, 749
Mitrokhin, Vasili, 654, 712–13, 714–15, 747‡, 750–51
Mitterrand, François, 675–6
Mocenigo, Giovanni, 138–9
Moldova, 758
Molotov, Vyacheslav, 597*, 662
Moltke, Helmuth von, 455, 488–9
Momigliano, Arnaldo: 'Christianity and the Decline of the Roman Empire', 79*
Monck, General George, 228–9, 230, 305–6
Mongol Empire, 78†
Monmouth, Earl of, 258
Monro, Captain George, 317–21
Monson, Sir Edmund, 422, 463
Montagu, Ralph, 242
Montaigne, Michel de, 109–10
Montaillou, Pyrenean village, 105–6
Montalivet, comte de, 378
Monteagle, Lord, 193, 194, 194, 195
Montebello, marquis de, 459
Monteleón, Duke of, 198
Montgomerie, Captain Thomas, 416–18

Montgomery, Field Marshal Sir Bernard, 640, 641, 661
Montgomery, Robert, 408, 409
Montholon, Charles-Tristan de, 341*
Montoya, Pedro López de, 116
Moore, R. I., 105*, 106
Moran, W. L., 19
Moray, James Stewart, 1st Earl of, 163–4
Mordvinov, A. A., 374*
Morenheim, Baron, 428
Moreo, Comendador, 138
Morgan, Thomas, 176, 200
Morice, Sir William, 236
Morland, Samuel, 225–6, 228
Morning Post, 579, 580
Moroccan Crisis
First (1905), 468–9, 478, 485
Second (1911), 477–8, 479, 484, 485
Morton, Desmond, 612
Moses (Musa), 1–2, 3, 13, 14–16, 19, 86*
Mossad (Israeli foreign-intelligence agency), 18–19, 732, 733, 733
Mossadeq, Mohammed, 679
Motecuhzoma II ('Montezuma'), 133, 134, 135–6
Mott, Sir Nevill, 667
Mountbatten, Vice-Admiral Lord Louis, 652
Moussaoui, Zacarias, 726
Mozhaysk, Treaty of (1562), 146
Muawiyah ibn Abu Sufyan, 95
Al Mubarakpuri, Safiur Rahman, 3
Muggeridge, Malcolm, 731
Muhammad
    agent network inside Mecca, 87–8
    assassinations ordered by, 89–90
    biographical information on, 90*
    condemns brutality during interrogation, 88–9
    conquest of Mecca (630), 91–2
    death of (632), 92, 93
    divine revelations, 86–7, 99
    doctrine of Holy War (militant *jihad*), 93

Muhammad – (*cont.*)
flight to Medina (the *Hijrah*), 87
and force of arms, 3, 86, 88
and intelligence collection, 3, 86,
87–9, 91, 92, 94, 96, 97
killed spies as martyrs, 91
mentions of in Quran, 2*
Muhammad ibn Maslama, 89
Munich Crisis (1938), 607, 614, 615,
617–18
Munich Olympics massacre (1972), 733
Murano, island of, 120
Muravyov, Count Mikhail, 459
Murray, Sir Archibald, 508, 541
Murray, Arthur C., 568
Muscovy (later Russia) Company,
London, 148, 149, 150, 152, 153,
154†, 155, 156
Mussolini, Benito, 606–7, 640
Mysore Oriental Library (now Oriental
Research Institute), 65

Nadolny, Rudolf, 520
Nagasaki atomic bomb (9 August
1945), 670
Nain Singh ('Chief Pandit'), 417–18
Nairobi terror attack (7 August 1998),
719–20
Nakajima, Minato, 630
Napoleonic Wars
Battle of Jena (October 1806),
339‡, 354
Battle of Trafalgar (1805), 338*
British capture of Danish fleet
(1807), 343
French invasion of Portugal
(1807), 344
intelligence during, 340–41, 342–4,
346–58
Napoleon's defeat (1814), 359–60
and Napoleon's study of history, 340
naval intelligence, 508–9
Peninsular War, 344, 346–52, 403
Russian campaign of Napoleon,
352–3, 354, 358–9

Treaties of Tilsit (July 1807), 343*,
354
Narodna Odbrana (Serb nationalist
organization), 444
Naseby, Battle of (June 1645), 216
Nassau, Maurice of, 169
National Intelligence Authority (NIA),
676
National Portrait Gallery, London,
160–61, 161*
National Security Agency (NSA), 8,
206‡, 634, 635, 644, 736
cutbacks under Clinton, 710
Perry Fellwock as whistleblower, 748–9
founding of (1952), 672
Islamist messages intercepted
(summer 2001), 725
network crash at (January 2000), 710
poor Cold War security at, 675
Edward Snowden as whistleblower,
746–7, 749, 750
National Security Council (NSC), 677,
678, 717
naval intelligence
Admiralty's First World War failures,
524–5, 526, 533, 543*
and 'Blinker' Hall, 515–16, 518
breaking of First World War U-boat
ciphers, 519
British in First World War, 508–9,
512–19, 524–5
British Naval Intelligence Division,
481–2, 509, 512–19, 524–6, 543,
544, 578
Enemy Submarines Section (E1), 544
First World War German naval codes
captured, 510, 519
and French Revolutionary/
Napoleonic wars, 508–9
German in First World War, 495, 519
German Nachrichten-Abteilung
('N'), 454, 475, 477, 479, 480–81,
495–6
German sabotage department (First
World War), 520–21, 522

ID 25 (section 25), 570–71
Office of Naval Intelligence (US),
    569, 604, 605, 630
and Pacific War, 637–8, 663–4
and Pearl Harbor attack,
    634–5
pre-First World War British targets in
    Germany, 481–2
Room 40 (Admiralty Old Building),
    511, 512–15, 516–19, 524–6, 532,
    533, 536–42, 544
Room 40 becomes section 25 (ID 25)
    of US Naval Intelligence Division,
    524, 543, 544
Room 40 merged with MI 1(b) as
    GC&CS, 576
'Swedish roundabout' (First World
    War), 518–19, 536
US naval ciphers during Cold War,
    685–6
US navy Code and Signal Section
    (later OP-20-G), 610, 611–12,
    628–30, 631–3, 634, 637, 643
US after Pearl Harbor, 637–8
naval operations
Anglo-German rivalry, 472, 477
Anglo-Russian naval talks (June
    1914), 490
Battle of Leyte Gulf (October
    1944), 664
Battle of Midway (June 1942), 638
Battle of the Coral Sea (May 1942),
    638
British during American War,
    297–8, 307
convoy system in First World War,
    543–4
First World War British, 6–7,
    512–16, 525–6, 543–4, 543*
First World War U-boat warfare,
    515, 519, 536–7, 543–4
German High Seas Fleet, 472,
    512–16, 525–6, 570–71
Japanese victory at Tsushima (1905),
    466, 469

Revolutionary/Napoleonic Wars,
    333–5, 336, 343
Salamis (480 BC), 2, 29–30, 56
Second World War U-boat warfare,
    641–2
Triple Alliance secret agreement
    (1913), 479
Washington Naval Conference
    (1921–2), 586–7, 589
see also Royal Navy
Nazarbayev, Nursultan, 708–9
Nazi Germany
annexation of Austria (1938), 613
anti-Semitism, 437, 645–6, 655–6,
    732, 743
Chiffrierabteilung (code department)
    of OKW, 639, 644
and Czechoslovakia, 613, 614–15,
    616
death camps, 645–6, 656
decrypts of US 'Black Code', 639
the Final Solution, 645–6, 655–6,
    732, 743
Göring's Forschungsamt, 644
as motivation for Soviet Agent
    recruitment, 593
Pers Z at Foreign Ministry, 644
Salon Kitty, Berlin brothel, 16*
Soviet agents in, 593–4, 625
triumph of as unpredictable,
    759–60
Nazi–Soviet Pact (August 1939), 621,
    622, 623
Nebel, Colonel Fritz, 564
Nehru, Jawaharlal, 735
    Discovery of India, The, 65
Nelson, Admiral Horatio, 334–5,
    336
Nepean, Evan, 327
Nepeya, Osip, 148–9
Nephro, Jerome, 237*
Nero, Roman emperor, 73, 75
Nesselrode, Count Carl von, 355–6,
    357, 366
Netanyahu, Benjamin, 18–19, 732

Netherlands
  Anglo-Dutch wars (seventeenth
    century), 226, 235–6, 237
  burning of heretics in, 114
  capture of Spanish treasure fleet
    (1610), 203
  Dutch black chamber, 264
  Dutch Republic, 226–7, 235–6
  Dutch United Provinces, 249
  enters war against Britain (1780), 300
  Habsburg, 113–14, 137, 139–40,
    167, 204*
  Marlborough's intelligence on, 264
  Revolt against Spain, 114, 137,
    139–40, 166–70
  United Provinces, 300
Neubourg, Ludwig, 264
Neue Rheinische Zeitung (newspaper),
  387, 388
New England, 235
New Oxford Shakespeare, 187
New Spain (Nueva España)
  conquest of Aztec Empire,
    132–6, 137
  conquest of Inca Empire, 136–7
  and English settlement, 192, 195
  falling revenues from, 203
New Testament, 2, 17, 22–6
  John's Gospel, 25*
  Luke's Gospel, 23
  Mark's Gospel, 23*
  surveillance of Jesus by authorities,
    23, 24
New World
  Asian empires' lack of interest in, 198
  early English settlement of, 195–8
  Spanish intelligence collection in,
    132–6, 137, 195, 196–8
New York Times, The, 523, 685, 699,
  709–10, 747, 748, 749
New York World Fair (1939), 667
New Zealand, 670–71
Newcastle, Henry Pelham-Clinton, 5th
  Duke of (Secretary of War, 1850s),
  402, 403, 405–6

Newcastle, Thomas Pelham-Holles, 1st
  Duke of, 278, 280–81, 282, 284,
  287–8, 290
Nicholas I, Tsar, 156, 373–4, 376–8, 405
Nicholas II, Tsar, 6, 436, 454–6, 488, 576
  at Cowes Regatta (1909), 457–8
  despising of the Japanese, 466–7
  as First World War commander-in-
    chief, 500–501
  and German decrypts, 470–71, 485–6
  state visit to France (1901), 459
Nicholson, Arthur, 487
Nicholson, Harold J., 715–16
Nicolai, Colonel Walter, 498
Niebuhr, Marcus, 394
Nienburg, 255, 270
Nikolaev, Leonid, 594–5
Nimitz, Admiral Chester W., 638
Nin, Andreu, 622
Nine Years War (1688–97), 251, 268
Nivelle, General Robert, 550
Nixon, John, 742–3
Nixon, Richard, 67, 687, 707, 748§
Nobel, Alfred, 425
Noble, Sir Andrew, 591
Nolan, Captain Louis, 404
Non-Aligned Movement (NAM), 690
Norfolk, Duke of (executed 1572),
  164, 165, 166
North, Lord, 297, 299, 308
North Korea, 750, 751–2
Northampton, Henry Howard, Earl of,
  173, 174, 191, 192
Northbrook, Earl of, 418
Northcliffe, Lord, 473
Northern Star (Chartist newspaper),
  379–80, 381
Norway, 672*
Nottingham, Earl of, 238*, 251, 252–3,
  254
Nouveau, Hiérosme de, 212–13
Noyers, François Sublet de, 210
nuclear weapons
  A. Q. Khan network, 736
  and China, 736

Cuban Missile Crisis, 683–4, 707, 739, 740, 759
and disintegration of USSR, 708–9
EPSILON (British operation on Nazi capability), 741*
first Soviet bomb (1949), 691
Iranian nuclear programme, 733
and Islamist terrorism, 759
MANHATTAN Project, 664–8, 669, 673, 691
NATO exercise 'Able Archer 83' (1983), 696, 713–14
PFIAB report (1990), 697
role of intelligence on in Cold War, 682, 683, 684
SDI ('Star Wars') programme (1983), 696
Soviet fears in early 1960s and 1980s, 694–8, 705–6, 713–14
Soviet operation RYAN (early 1980s), 695–8, 705–6, 713–14
START treaty (1989), 684
US secret operation SAPPHIRE (1994), 708–9
Numidia, kingdom of, 45
Nuovo, Angela, 123
Nureyev, Rudolf, 699
Nye, Lieutenant-General Sir Archibald, 652
Nye, Joseph S., Jr, 68, 717

Oak Ridge facility, Tennessee, 666–7, 668, 709
Oates, Titus, 238–40, 241, 258, 259
Obama, Barack, 672‡, 759
Obrenovic, Alexander, King of Serbia, 442
Odysseus, 27–9
Office of Strategic Services (OSS), 605, 658, 673, 676
O'Hagan, Andrew, 746
Okamoto, Major-General Kiyotomi, 664
Okey, Colonel John, 233
Old Testament/Tanakh, 1–2, 3, 13–18
Adam and Eve, 116

Israelites' conquest of Promised Land, 16–18, 21–2
Israelites' escape from Egypt, 13, 15, 16–17, 19
Moses' agents in Canaan, 1–2, 3, 13, 14–16, 17–18, 19
and the Phoenicians, 41
prophecy of Zechariah, 22
Olivares, Count-Duke, Don Gaspar de Guzmán, 204, 208, 209, 210, 211–12
Oliver, Admiral of the Fleet Sir Henry 'Dummy', 509, 512, 513, 514, 524, 543*
Oliver, Isaac, 190
Oliver, James Harrison, 604
Omand, Sir David, 674*, 747*
open-source information, 19, 122, 147, 340, 453, 529, 721
Oppenheim, E. Phillips, 473*
oracles
and abolition of Paganism in Rome, 77–8
at Antium, 73
of Didyma and Zeus Philios, 77*
in Greece, 30–33, 32†, 43, 44, 73, 78
of Zeus Ammon at Siwah oasis, 39
Orléans, Louis, duc d', 159
Orléans, Philippe, duc d', 273
Orlov, Alexander, 621, 622, 682
Orlov, Boris, 500*
Orlov, Grigory, 291
Ormond, Duke of, 267, 272
Orsini, Felice, 396, 397
Ostrogoths, 79
Ott, Colonel Eugen, 594
Ottoman Empire
Arab Rising against (1916), 508, 530, 541
and the Balkans, 443
and cartography, 120–21, 121*
cryptanalysis failings, 4, 128–9
diplomatic and political intelligence failings, 122, 123–4

Ottoman Empir – (*cont.*)
  First World War defeats in Middle
    East (1917–18), 564–5
  Hejaz Expeditionary Force (HEF), 541
  military superiority to Venice, 122, 132
  no interest in European New World
    activities, 198
  prohibition of printing, 122, 123
Oudenarde, Battle of (1708), 261
Oudinot, Marshal Nicolas, 357
Ovakimian, Gayk, 624
Ozaki, Hotsumi, 627

Pacific War (Second World War),
    637–8, 663–4
Page, Dr Walter Hines, 516, 538–40
Paget, Sir James, 608
Paine, Thomas, 319, 320
Painvin, Georges, 564
Palatine, Princess, 248
Paléologue, Maurice, 465
Palestine Liberation Organization
    (PLO), 733
Palmer, Alexander Mitchell, 605
Palmer, Captain G. S., 467
Palmerston, Lord, 391, 396, 397–8, 406
Pamplona, siege of (1813), 403
Pan Hannian, 752–3
Panama, 690
Panin, Nikita Petrovich, 353
Panizzardi, Alessandro, 461, 464
Papen, Franz von, 522, 523–4
Páramo, Luis de, 115–16
Pares, Diana, 482§
Paris, Treaty of
    1762, 290
  May 1814, 369
  20 November 1815, 369
  March 1856, 406
Paris Commune (1871), 398–9, 400
Paris Peace Conference (1919), 584
Parker, Frederick D., 635
Parker, Geoffrey, 246*
Parker, John F., 435
Parker, Matthew, 172, 219

Parlett, Sir Harold, 585†
Parma, Alessandro Farnese, Duke of,
    137, 169, 170, 184
Parrott, George, 481
Parry, Sir Thomas, 193
Parsons, Sir Anthony, 701
Pašić, Nikola, 443–4, 445, 447–8
Pasov, Zelman, 620
Paterculus, Velleius, 71
Patrick, Marsena Rudolph, 412–13
Patton, General George S., 657
Paul III, Pope, 109
Paulus, General Friedrich, 647
Pavlović, Milovan, 442
Pavlovich, Yuri, 500
Pearl Harbor attack (1941), 7, 633–6,
    677, 728–9
Peek, Philip, 31
Peel, Sir Robert, 380–81
Peking University, 753
Pelham, Henry, 282, 284, 285, 287
Pelhisson, Guillaume, 104
Pelloux, General Luigi, 432
Pendézec, General Jean-Marie, 465, 466
Penkovsky, Oleg, 683, 697, 740†
Penruddock, Colonel John, 224
Penruddock Uprising (1655), 224
'Pentagon Papers', 748
People's Will (*Narodnaya Volya*), 425,
    426, 428
Pepys, Samuel, 226, 229, 236, 253
Perceval, Spencer, 343
Percy, Thomas, 194–5
Pergamum, kingdom of, 44
Pericles, 30, 33
Périgord, Dorothée de, 368
Perkins, Frances, 633
Perl, William, 666
Perón, Juana nd Isabel, 690
Perrault, Charles, 206, 213
Perry, William, 708, 709
Pershing, General John J. 'Black Jack', 565
Persian Empire, 2, 29–31, 35–6, 93,
    94, 198
Persons, Robert, 170–71, 203

Pertinax, Roman emperor, 76
Peru, 423
Pesaro, Zuane, 205
Peter I, King of Serbia, 443
Peter III, Tsar of Russia, 290–91
Peter of Verona (Peter the Martyr), 105
Peters, Yakov Khristoforovich, 557, 560
Petitfils, Jean-Christian, 201
Petrie, Sir David, 652, 653, 760
Phelippes, Thomas, 167, 177, 183, 185,
    189, 242
    Babington Plot deception/forgery,
        177, 179, 180, 192
    tests Venetian cipher, 205
Philby, Kim, 593, 621, 649–50, 661–2,
    673, 749
Philip II, King of Macedon, 34, 37–8
Philip II, King of Spain, 1, 5, 85, 113,
    114, 115, 116, 161
    and assassination of William the
        Silent (1584), 170
    interception of correspondence of,
        138, 139–40, 166–7, 180
    likens cryptanalysis to witchcraft,
        137, 138, 139, 140
    marriage to Mary Tudor, 137
    new Armada (1596), 190
    opposes Henry IV's accession in
        France, 138
    and Robert Persons, 203
    and plots to overthrow Elizabeth I,
        163, 164
    Spanish Armada (1588), 1, 161,
        180–83, 184
Philip III, King of Spain, 195, 196–8, 203
Philip IV, King of Spain, 198, 203, 204,
    207–9, 210
Philip V ('the Tall'), King of France, 106
Philip VI, King of France, 106–7
Philo of Alexandria, 25–6
Philotas (Macedonian commander), 34
Phoenicians, 41–5
photography
    First World War aerial
        reconnaissance, 506–7, 508

from high-altitude spy-planes, 683
    Thornton-Pickard camera, 507
Phythian, Mark: 'Profiles in
    Intelligence', 697*
Pichon, Stephen, 484
Picquart, Colonel Georges, 461–2
Piłsudski, Jósef, 486
Pindar, 31–2
Pinochet, General Augusto, 687–8
Piri, Ahmed Muhiddin (Piri Reis), 121*
Piro, George, 742–4
Pitt, William ('the Elder'), 287–90
Pitt, William ('the Younger'), 312, 313,
    314, 323, 343
    attempts to avoid war (1789–92), 317
    expands 'secret service', 326–7
    fears French invasion of Ireland
        (1798), 336
    and LCS interrogations, 328–9
    Wickham as unofficial intelligence
        chief, 336, 532
Pius V, Pope (Antonio Ghislieri), 109,
    109*, 110, 110*, 164
Pius VII, Pope, 340–41
Pizarro, Francisco, 136–7
Plataea, Battle of (479 BC), 30–31, 32
Platonov, Sergey, 145*
Plehve, V. K., 438
Pliny the Elder, 49†
'Plug Plot' in Britain (1842), 379
Plumb, Sir J. H. ('Jack'), 1*, 120
Plutarch, 35, 37, 38
Pohl, Hugo von, 479
Poincaré, Raymond, 464, 484, 485,
    488, 491, 492, 577, 580, 585
Poland, 152, 252–3, 255, 280, 376,
    486, 699
Poley, Robert, 176, 187–8
Polignac, Jules de, 376
Polk, Frank L., 527, 548, 568
Polybius, 45
Pompadour, Madame de, 280, 292
Pompeo, Mike, 745, 750
Pompey, 51*
Ponsonby, Arthur, 573, 580–81

Pontius Pilate, 22, 23, 23†, 25–6
'Popish Plot' (late 1670s), 238,
    239–40, 241
Popović, Cvetko, 445
Popular Front for the Liberation of
    Palestine (PFLP), 733
Port Moresby, New Guinea, 638
Portland, William Bentinck, 1st Duke
    of, 259–60
Portland, William Cavendish-Bentinck,
    3rd Duke of, 328, 343
Portugal, 211, 344
Potiorek, General Oskar, 444, 445
Potsdam conference (July 1945), 669
Pourtalès, Friedrich von, 470
Powell, Colin, 739–40
Powhatan Indians, 196
Powle, Stephen, 181–3
Premadasa, Ranasinghe, 721
Prendergast, Thomas, 260
press
    British during Napoleonic Wars,
        340, 344
    expansion of in Britain during
        1830s, 379
    in Napoleonic France, 340, 342
    the telegraph and war reporting,
        402–3, 405–6
Prestonpans, Battle of (1745), 283
Primakov, Evgeny, 705–7, 711–12, 715*
Princip, Gavrilo, 444–5, 446–7
printing presses, 109, 120, 122–3, 147
Prior, Matthew, 267
Priscus of Panium, 83, 84
Priuli, Girolamo, 121
proxenoi, 30–31*
Prussia
    1848 disturbances in, 384, 387–8
    assassination attempt against king
        (1850), 389
    and Carlsbad Decrees (1819), 372–3
    and Congress of Vienna, 363, 367–8
    defeat of Austria (1866), 398
    Franco-Prussian War (1870–71),
        398, 414–15

Frederick the Great's rule in, 279,
    285–7, 288, 290, 291, 340
and French ciphers before Jena, 353–4
informers in political system, 394
and Napoleonic Wars, 339‡, 340–41,
    342, 353–4
notoriety of police, 390–91
and Seven Years War (1756–63),
    278, 286, 287, 288, 290–91
surveillance of émigrés in Britain,
    389–91, 392–4
victory at Waterloo (18 June 1815),
    361–2
psychological warfare
    in The Art of War and the
        Arthashastra, 64
    Franklin's against British, 295–6, 308–9
    German on First World War Eastern
        Front, 547
Puertocarrera, Alonso Hernández, 134*
Puibaraud (or Puybaraud), Louis, 430
Pujol, Juan (GARBO), 657–61, 658
Punch magazine, 381
Putin, Vladimir, 668, 706–7
Putlitz, Wolfgang zu, 612–13, 615

Qadisiyya, Battle of (640), 94
Al Qaeda, 4, 10, 88, 116–17, 702–3, 718
    9/11 attacks, 10, 11, 704, 720, 721,
        726–7, 729–30, 736
    attacks on US ships in Aden (2000),
        723, 724
    attempts to develop biological
        weapons, 722–3, 758
    East African embassy attacks, 719–20
    intelligence reports on (summer
        2001), 724
    Khalid as a role model, 94
    NSA message intercepts (summer
        2001), 725
    pre-9/11 intelligence on US aviation
        schools, 725–6
    report of the 9/11 Commission, 717,
        719, 723, 724, 726, 728,
        729–30, 736

underestimation of in West, 718, 729
Quadruple Alliance (20 November
    1815), 369
Quercy, Jean de, 200
Quetzalcoatl (Aztec god), 135
Quraish tribe in Arabia, 87–9, 91–2
Quran, 2*, 89, 90*, 92, 99, 123
    espionage references in, 86, 96
    Musa (Moses) story, 2, 14, 15, 86*
Qutb, Sayyid, 703–4

Rabinovich, Dr Grigory, 599
Rachkovsky, Pyotr, 426, 428, 434,
    437, 458–9
Radó, Alexander, 649
Radolin, Prince Hugo von, 455, 462
Raffis, Gérard de, 199
Raglan, Lord, 402–3, 404, 405, 406
Rahab (biblical harlot), 16–17
Raimon VI, Count of Toulouse, 101
Raimon VII, Count of Toulouse, 102
Rajk, László, 681
Ramillies, Battle of (1706), 261, 262
Ramparts magazine, 748–9
Randolph, Sir Thomas, 151–2
Raskolnikov, Fedor, 580
Rasputin, Grigory, 500, 503
Rathom, John R., 523
Ratibor, Prince Max von, 519
Ravachol, François-Claudius, 429
Ravaillac, François, 195
Ravenna, 82
Rawlings, Helen, 115*
Rawlinson, General Henry, 530
Reading, Lord, 567
Reagan, Ronald, 206‡, 672, 691, 694,
    695, 696, 713–14, 750
Réalmont, siege of (1628), 205
reconnaissance
    and Alexander the Great, 38
    and ancient Rome, 41
    Boer War, 451, 452
    Caesar's differentiating of roles, 47
    and Condé, 246
    eighteenth-century battlefield, 279
    failure at Brandywine Creek, 304
    and Ivan the Terrible, 145
    and Napoleon, 339†
    and Second World War Russian
        partisans, 654
    in the Taktika, 95–6
    and Xenophon of Athens, 36
    see also aerial reconnaissance
Redl, Colonel Alfred, 486
Reformation, Protestant
    Catholic persecution of Protestants,
        110, 110*
    failure to root in Spain, 115, 115*
    and Holy Roman Empire, 113
    and the Low Countries, 113–14
    and printing presses, 109
    and Queen Mary in England, 114–15
Reille, General Charles, 349
Reilly, Sidney ('ace of spies'), 560, 575
Renaissance, European, 4–5, 121–2
    humanism, 115*, 120, 124
    world lead in intelligence, 120, 121
    see also Venice, Renaissance
Renaudot, Abbé, 256
Repin, Ilya, 154
Retz, Cardinal de, 326
Revolutions of 1848 in Europe, 384–5,
    386, 387–8
Rey, Antoine-Claude, 323–4
Rheims seminary, 171–3, 186, 187
Rhesus, Thracian king, 28
Ribbentrop, Joachim von, 612–13,
    627, 633
Ribemont-sur-Ancre (Somme), 49*
Rice, Condoleezza, 727, 740
Richelieu, Cardinal, 5, 205–2067,
    209–12, 268
Riddell, Lord, 494
Ridley, Thomas, 114
Riezler, Kurt, 490
Rigby, Lee, 756
Rimington, Stella, 9
Rinaldi, Nicolò, 124–5
Rintelen von Kleist, Franz, 522, 523
Riordane, Germaine (or John), 234

Robert II, King of France, 100*

Roberts, Field Marshal Lord, 421, 452

Robertson, Thomas 'Tar', 651, 659

Robertson, Field Marshal Sir William,
    531-2, 541

Robespierre, Maximilien, 314, 323, 325-6

Robethon, Jean de, 262, 264

Rock, The (1996 Hollywood
    thriller), 740

Roessler, Rudolf, 649

Rogers, Daniel, 167

Rogers, Samuel, 332

Röhl, Professor John, 479*, 493*

Romania, 501

Rome, ancient
    adoption of Christianity (AD 312), 77-8
    Alaric's sack of Rome (410), 82
    Antonine Constitution (212), 78-9
    assassination of emperors, 75, 76, 425*
    barbarian invasions in West, 79-81,
        79*, 82
    civil wars, 51, 51*, 52, 70
    Colosseum, 79, 79†
    defeat at Adrianople (378), 81-2
    defeat at Cannae (216 BC), 43-4, 82
    defeat in Teutoburg forest (AD 9),
        70-71, 74
    delatores (informers) in, 24-5, 72-3, 75
    divination and portents, 40-41, 42,
        43, 44, 50-52, 51*, 52*, 54-5, 73,
        74, 77-8
    East–West division formalised (395), 78
    Empire in the East *see* Byzantium
    end of Western Empire, 82
    Etruscan augurs, 40*
    frumentarii, 76-7
    Gallic Wars, 46-51, 82
    'general agents' (*agentes in rebus*), 77
    Hun threat to Eastern Empire, 82-5
    and the Iceni in Britain, 71-2, 73-5
    Julio-Claudian dynasty, 70-75
    Mater Magna ('Great Mother'), 44
    mid-third-century crisis, 76, 77
    Praetorian Guard, 75-6
    Punic Wars, 41-5, 82

Scipio's use of spies, 45

Sibylline Books (*Libri Sibyllini*), 43-4

strategic intelligence as neglected, 70,
    71-2, 74, 77, 79, 81-2

underestimation of barbarians, 70,
    71-2, 74, 79, 80, 81-2

Rommel, Field-Marshal Irwin, 639-41

Romulus Augustulus, Western
    emperor, 82

Roosevelt, Franklin, 7, 299, 311
    Assistant Secretary of the Navy
        (1913-20), 522, 567, 603-5, 609
    death of (12 April 1945), 668
    gentlemen spies of (The Room/Club),
        605-6, 607-8
    Hundred Days (1933), 605
    lack of interest in SIGINT, 628,
        634-5, 639
    and MAGIC (Japanese) decrypts,
        628-30, 631-3, 634, 635, 637
    meeting with 'Blinker' Hall (1918),
        567, 604-5, 609
    racist underestimation of Japanese,
        636, 728-9
    and US Second World War neutrality,
        607, 608-9

Roosevelt, Kermit, 605, 679

Roosevelt, Theodore, 469, 522

Root, Elihu, 587

Rose, George, 371-2

Rose, P. K., 'The Founding Fathers of
    American Intelligence', 295*,
    303*, 309*

Rosenberg, Ethel, 8, 668

Rosenberg, Julius, 8, 666

Rosmer, Alfred, 623

Ross, Bishop of (John Leslie), 164

Rosselli,, Johnny, 63

Rossignol, Antoine, 205-6, 210, 211,
    212, 213, 242, 245*, 247, 672

Rosso, Andrea, 129

Rotter, Charles, 482

Rouillé, Antoine Louis, 280

Rouvier, Maurice, 469, 478, 485

Rowlands, Ted, 750

Rowlett, Frank B., 610–11
Royal Air Force (RAF), 642
Royal Australian Navy, 510
Royal Flying Corps (RFC), 505–8, 565
Royal Geographical Society, 416, 418
Royal Navy, 235–6, 297, 298, 301,
    307, 335, 338, 454, 457–8, 508
  and Anglo-Russian naval talks (June
    1914), 490
  First World War, 512–16, 525–6, 543*
  launch of *Dreadnought* class
    (1906), 472
  mutinies (spring 1797), 332
  opposes First World War convoy
    system, 543–4
  Parrott's spying for 'N', 481
  pre-First World War German
    espionage network, 477
Royston, Richard, 214
Ruadh, Alasdair ('Pickle'), 284–5
Rubens, Peter Paul, 207–9
Ruffey, General Pierre, 495
Rumbold, Sir George, 342
Rundstedt, Field Marshal Gerd von, 661
Rusbridger, Alan, 747
Rushdie, Salman: *Satanic Verses*, 90
Russell, Lord John, 382
Russell, William Howard, 402–3, 405–6
Russian Empire
  1905 Revolution, 438, 545
  abolition of serfdom (1861), 406
  agents in Napoleonic Paris, 354–7
  assassination of Tsar Peter III, 291
  cabinet noir, 353, 357, 455–8,
    467–8, 470, 478, 485, 488, 491,
    492, 497, 499–501, 576
  and Congress of Vienna, 363, 366–7
  conspiracy theories over First World
    War disasters, 502–4
  Cossack regiments, 358, 359–60, 437
  and cryptanalysis, 353, 357–9, 360,
    454–7, 467–8, 469–71, 478, 485,
    488, 491–2, 497, 499–502
  Decembrist Revolt (December 1825),
    373–4

'Dual Alliance' with France, 458–9
educational system, 374–5
expansion in Central Asia (1860s–80s),
    415–16
February Revolution (1917), 503, 504
Fedor I's regency council, 154–6
and First World War, 6
First World War use of 'Caesar
    cipher', 497
Goldbach's codebreaking, 277
'Great Game' with Britain on
    North-West Frontier, 406, 416–21
intelligence in Napoleonic Wars,
    354–60, 406
invasion of East Prussia (1914),
    453–4, 495
lack of permanent embassies, 146,
    148–9, 154
lack of print culture, 146–7
Lukovsky case (1834), 376–7
military intelligence in First World
    War, 497, 498–502
and Napoleonic Wars, 343*, 352–3,
    354–60, 406
Okhrana, 7, 425–6, 428, 434,
    436–42, 457, 458–9, 468, 470,
    500, 574, 603
oprichniki (Ivan IV's security
    service), 142–5, 150, 151, 152,
    153–4, 155
origins of diplomacy and foreign
    intelligence, 146
poor diplomatic–military intelligence
    coordination, 486–7, 497, 498–9
and Seven Years War (1756–63),
    278, 287, 290–91
state-sponsored anti-Semitism, 436–7
Sukhomlinov treason trial (1917),
    503–4
surveillance of émigrés in Britain,
    400–401
Tatar raid on Moscow (1571), 153–4
'Time of Troubles', 141, 157
uprising in Russian Poland
    (1830), 376

Russian Federation
  FSB (Federal Security Service), 705
  SVR–Foreign Ministry rivalry, 711
  see also SVR (Russian Federation
    foreign-intelligence service)
Russian Provisional Government, 504,
  544, 545, 547, 549–50, 552–3
Russian Social Democratic Labour
  Party (RSDLP), 439–41, 442
  Bolshevik–Menshevik split, 440,
    442, 545
  German aid to Bolsheviks (First
    World War), 544–7
Russo-Japanese War (1904–5), 455,
  466–8, 469, 478–9
Rybkina, Zoya, 650*
Rykov, Alexei, 440*, 601

Sabatier, Pierre, 103
sabotage
  sinking of the *Lusitania*, 521
  First World War German, 520–21,
    522, 527, 528, 542, 604
Sadighi, Mehdi Seyed, 90†
Sagan, Wilhelmine, Duchess of, 366, 367
Al-Sahaf, Muhammad Said ('Comical
  Ali'/'Baghdad Bob'), 744
Saint-Aulaire, Comte de, 580
Sainte-Beuve, Charles Augustin, 368
Saint-Just, Louis-Antoine de, 322,
  325, 326
Saint-Mihiel, Battle of (September
  1918), 565
Saint-Pierre, Jean de, 102
Saint-Simon, duc de, 245‡
Sakharov, Andrei, 699
Salamanca, Battle of (22 July 1812),
  348, 349
Salameh, Mohammed, 718
Salamis, Battle of (480 BC), 2, 29–30, 56
Salisbury, Lord, 418
Sallust, 50*
Salon Kitty, Berlin brothel, 16*
the Sambre, Battle of (57 BC), 47–8
Samolis, Tatyana, 715

San Giuliano, Antonio di, 491
Sand, Karl, 372
Sanders, Detective-Constable John,
  396, 397
Sanders, John Hitchens, 388
Sandherr, Colonel Jean, 460–62
Sandinistas in Nicaragua, 690, 691
Santa Cruz, Marquis of, 180, 183
Sanudo, Marin, 118–19, 130
Sanzo, Tsuda, 466–7
Sarant, Alfred, 666
Saratoga, Battle of (October 1777),
  298–9, 306
Sargent, Aaron A., 423
Savarkar, V. D., 410–11
Savary, René, 342, 343, 355
Savile, Thomas, Earl of Sussex, 218
Savinkov, Boris, 438, 575, 619
Savoy, Prince Eugène of, 262
Saxe, Maurice de, 279
Saxony, 287
Sazonov, Sergei, 487, 488, 491, 492, 493
Scarlett, Sir John, 223*, 696
Schaedel, Dr Herbert, 639
Scheer, Admiral Reinhard, 525, 526,
  570, 571
Scheurer-Kestner, Auguste, 462
Schlichting, Albert, 144
Schmidt, Helmut, 692
Schoen, Wilhelm von, 494
Schulz, Lieutenant Lester R., 632
Schulze-Boysen, Harro, 593, 594, 625–6
Schurz, Carl, 387, 388
Schuyler, Eugene, 423
Schwartzkoppen, Colonel Maximilian
  von, 460, 461
Schweppenburg, General Baron Geyr
  von, 613, 614, 615
science and technology espionage
  Chinese, 67, 69
  and civilian economy in Soviet bloc, 692
  Soviet, 596–7, 714
  Soviet during Cold War, 691–3
  Soviet penetration of MANHATTAN
    Project, 664–8, 669, 673, 691

Scipio Africanus, 44–6, 82

Scot, Thomas, 216*, 220–21, 222, 223, 228–9, 231, 232

Scot, William, 235, 237

Scotland
  1715 Jacobite Rebellion, 270
  Act of Union (1707), 265
  Edinburgh Castle occupation (1573), 166
  Elizabethan era, 161–4
  future Charles II invades England from, 221–2
  Jacobite Rising (1745–6), 283–4
  'Lords of the Congregation', 162, 163
  Treaty of Edinburgh (6 July 1560), 163

Scott, Charles, 304

Scott, H. M.: The Birth of a Great Power System, 292*

Scovell, George, 347–8, 349–52, 350–51

Sealed Knot plot (1654), 224

Second World War
  Allied intelligence collaboration, 7, 8, 169, 566–7, 608, 609, 641–4
  'Battle of the Atlantic', 641–2
  Battle for Crete (20 May–1 June 1941), 56†
  Battle of Kursk (June 1943), 649, 653, 656
  Berlin–Rome–Tokyo Axis, 611
  British Security Coordination (BSC) in New York, 609
  fall of Tobruk (June 1942), 640
  'fifth column' scares, 618–19
  German Blitzkriegs in Low Countries and France, 618–19
  German SIGINT during, 644
  as an intelligence war, 603
  North Africa campaign, 639–41
  operation OVERLORD (1944), 657–61
  outbreak of (1939), 607–8
  Pacific War, 637–8, 663–4
  Red Army advance to Berlin, 653–4
  Russian partisans behind German lines, 653–4

Soviet penetration of Roosevelt administration, 662–3, 669, 673

Stalingrad (1942–3), 646, 647–8, 656, 664

U-boat warfare, 641–2

ULTRA intelligence, 8, 56†, 616–17, 640–42, 648, 649, 652, 669, 671–2

Secret Service Bureau, British
  destruction of Steinhauer's network, 495–6
  Foreign Department, 481–3, 532
  founding of (1909), 66, 476–7, 532, 603
  minimal resources, 479–80
  pre-war offices at 2 Whitehall Court, 483, 483*
  see also MI5 (Security Service); MI6/SIS (Secret Intelligence Service; MI1c)

secret societies
  Carbonari in Italy, 379, 397
  conspiracy theories, 372, 373–4, 376–7
  decline in Bourbon restoration France, 375
  Delahodde's book about, 383
  the Illuminati, 376
  Société des Saisons, 378–9, 383
  and students, 372

security, personal
  Cheka failures over Lenin, 574, 595
  of Elizabeth I, 170
  and Emperor Augustus, 72
  failures of protective security, 429–31, 433, 435–6, 445–6, 447
  of Franz Ferdinand in Sarajevo, 445–6, 447
  and Julius Caesar, 52–3
  of Kaiser Wilhelm II, 434
  Praetorian Guard in Rome, 75–6
  at Queen Victoria's funeral (1901), 434
  and Stalin, 594–5
  of US presidents, 435–6

Security Service Act (1985), 732*

Sedan, Battle of (September 1870), 415

Sedov, Lev, 598–9, 600

Sefeloge, Maximilian Joseph, 389

Segestes (Germanic barbarian), 70–71
Segur, Philippe, 341
Selves, Justin de, 478, 749
Semichastny, Vladimir, 689
Seneca, 73
Septimius Severus, Roman emperor, 76
Serbia, 442–3, 447–8, 489
    Austria confrontation with (summer
        1914), 487–8, 490–91, 492, 493
    Black Hand in, 443–8
Serebryansky, Yakov, 599, 622, 623
Serocold, Claude, 518
Serov, Ivan, 654, 655
Seso, Carlos de, 115
Seven Years War (1756–63), 278,
    286, 287–91
Sévigné, Madame de, 242–3
Seward, William, 422
Seymour, Lord Henry, 184
Shakespeare, William, 51, 126, 147, 186–7
Shamashastry, Dr Rudrapatnam, 65
Sharpe, Colonel George G., 412, 413
Shaw, Byam, 553, 554
Shebarshin, Leonid, 698
Sheffy, Yigal, 565
Shelepin, Aleksandr, 689, 694
Sher Ali, Afghan Amir, 418, 419
Shin Bet (Israeli domestic security
    service), 18, 732
Short, General Walter, 634
Shpigelglass, Sergei, 620
Shrewsbury, Earl (later Duke) of, 258
Shuisky, Prince Andrei Mikhailovich, 146
Sibylline Books (Libri Sibyllini), 43–4, 44†
Sicinnus (Greek double-agent), 29–30
Sick, Gary, 701
Siebert, Benno von, 489–90
'Siege of Sidney Street' (1910), 560
signals intelligence (SIGINT)
    Baldwin government tightens
        security procedures, 582–3
    British–American SIGINT accords
        (1946/48), 670–71, 673–4, 734–5
    Chiffrierabteilung (code department)
        of OKW, 639, 644

and colonial Government of India, 6*
European innovation in sixteenth
    century, 127
FDR's Second World War neglect of,
    610
and First World War, 6–7
in First World War Middle East, 564–5
French pre-First World War
    mishandling of, 483–5
German establishment of agency
    (First World War), 497–8, 502
Göring's Forschungsamt, 644
Lincoln's interest in, 411–12
MI-8 (first specialized US agency), 569
neglect of in studies of Cold War, 8,
    671–3
Pers Z at Foreign Ministry, 644
public recognition by heads of state,
    206, 206‡
Richelieu founds cabinet noir, 5,
    210–11
Russia as pre-First World War world
    leaders, 470, 485, 497
and SD (intelligence arm of Nazi
    SS), 644
and Second World War, 7–8, 169
Signal Security Agency (SSA), 642,
    643–4
and Soviet S&T espionage, 692
UK/US Second World War alliance,
    7, 8, 169, 566–7, 608, 609, 641–4
US navy Code and Signal Section
    (later OP-20-G), 610, 611–12,
    628–30, 631–3, 634, 637, 643
US reorganization after Pearl
    Harbor, 637
US Signal Intelligence Service (SIS),
    610–12, 627, 628–30, 631–3, 634,
    637, 645
    see also cryptanalysis; message
        interception
Sihanouk, Prince, 707
Silber (Vienna police chief), 364, 365
Simonetta, Francesco (Cicco), 127*
Simonides of Ceos, 29

Simpson, Sir James, 405, 406
Sims, Admiral (US navy), 543
Sinan Pasha, Grand Admiral, 123
Sinclair, Admiral Sir Hugh 'Quex',
    575*, 578, 614
Sinelobov, Alexei, 597
Sipiagin, S. N., 437
Sipido, Jean-Baptiste, 433
Siqueiros, David Alfaro, 623–4
Sixtus IV, Pope, 111
Sixtus V, Pope, 138
Skeres, Nicholas, 187–8
Skinner, Dr Thomas, 228–9
Skinner, Quentin, 10
Skyfall (Bond film), 27
Skype, 750
Slutsky, Abram, 601, 620
Small, Albert W., 611
Smith, F. E., 532–3
Smith, Captain John, 196
Smolensk, Battle of (16 August
    1812), 359
'Snettisham Treasure', 74*
Snowden, Edward, 746–7, 748, 749, 750
Socialist Workers Party (SWP) in USA,
    599, 624–5
Socialist-Revolutionary (SR) Party in
    Russia, 437–9
Société des Saisons (Blanqui's secret
    society), 378–9, 383
Sokollu Pasha, Mehmed, 123–4, 129
Solomatin, Boris Aleksandrovich, 685–6
Somer, John, 162–3, 162†, 166, 167
Somers, Abbé Michael, 321, 323
the Somme, Battle of (1916), 508, 520,
    528, 530–31, 532–3
Sophia of Hanover, 264
Sorensen, Theodore, 680
Sorge, Richard, 593–4, 626, 627
Soro, Giovanni, 127, 128, 129, 137
Souers, Admiral Sidney W., 676
Soult, Marshal Nicolas, 403
'South Sea Bubble' (1720), 272
Southwick, George, 193
Soviet Bloc in Europe

covert action as central to
    establishment of, 680
disintegration of, 705
dissident movements within, 699,
    712, 751
Hungarian Uprising (1956), 699
and operation RYAN, 695–6
Prague Spring (1968), 699, 712, 751
repressive role of intelligence, 698–9
security services of, 680–81
Solidarity movement in Poland, 699
Soviet Union
    August 1991 coup, 699–700, 704
    Bedell Smith's Custine comparisons,
        377–8
    breaks Japanese PURPLE code,
        627, 628
    British interwar decrypts, 577–80,
        583–4, 616–17
    Cambridge spy ring, 183, 593, 621,
        649–51, 661–2, 673, 711
    censorship and media control, 110
    Cheka founded, 7, 110–11
    Council of People's Commissars
        (Sovnarkom), 556, 557
    'Curzon ultimatum' to, 579–80
    diplomatic relations with USA
        (1933), 586
    disintegration of, 700, 704–7, 708–9
    dissidents' struggle for human
        rights, 712
    early Cold War 'Zionist
        conspirators', 680–81
    'envoys' plot (1918), 559–60, 561
    Fifth Directorate, 627–8
    foreign embassies in Moscow,
        674–5, 749
    German invasion of
        (BARBAROSSA, 22 June 1941),
        326*, 627
    Germany embassy (from April 1918),
        557–8
    Great Patriotic War, 628
    Left Socialist Revolutionaries
        (LSRs), 557–8

Soviet Union – (*cont.*)
  loss of intelligence operatives to
    purges, 621, 623
  military technology gained through
    S&T, 691–3
  Moscow as new capital city, 556
  operation RYAN (early 1980s),
    695–8, 705–6, 713–14
  penetration of Roosevelt
    administration, 662–3, 669, 673
  purges of intelligence operatives, 620
  Red Terror, 556–7, 558–9, 573–4
  Stalinist show trials, 107, 108, 600,
    601, 620, 667
  Stalin's Great Terror (1936–8), 104,
    105, 107–8, 141, 143, 318, 326*,
    594–602, 620–21, 711, 751, 752
  UK breaks off diplomatic relations
    (1927), 583–4, 616–17
  ULTRA intelligence given to by
    Cairncross, 649
  US embassy in Moscow, 592–3,
    662, 674–5
  wartime ethnic cleansing by
    intelligence agencies, 654–5
  see also Cheka (later GPU, OGPU,
    NKVD, KGB); KGB; Lenin;
    Stalin, Joseph
Sovin, Alexander Grigoryevich, 152
Spaatz, General Carl, 741
Spain
  Anglo-Spanish peace treaty (1604),
    192, 195
  cipher security as poor, 139–40
  Council of State, 195, 196, 202
  Drake attacks Cádiz harbour (April
    1587), 180–81, 184
  Dutch Revolt, 114, 137, 139–40,
    166–70
  English agents working for, 183–4,
    200, 203
  failure of Protestantism in, 115, 115*
  Ferdinand and Isabella as joint
    rulers, 111, 112–13
  First World War neutrality, 519
  and French Wars of Religion, 137, 138
  inferiority in foreign intelligence
    under Philip II, 137
  intelligence in seventeenth century, 195,
    196–201, 202–3, 207–9, 210, 211–12
  James I declares war on (1624),
    204, 207
  Jewish population in Middle Ages,
    111–13
  Joseph Bonaparte as king, 344, 348,
    349–52
  loss of Portugal (1640), 211
  Moorish (Muslim) kingdoms, 111
  Nootka Sound crisis, 313–14
  war with France (from 1635), 211–12
Spanish–American War (1898), 116, 423–4
Spanish Armada (1588), 1, 161,
    180–83, 184
Spanish Inquisition, 4, 111–13, 115,
    116, 130
Spanish Succession, War of the
    (1702–14), 261–7, 268
Special Operations Executive (SOE),
    338†, 609, 646
  creation of (1940), 619
  SIS takes over, 678
Spencer, Earl (First Lord of the
    Admiralty), 333
Speransky, Mikhail, 355
spice trade, 119, 121
spies and agents
  Alexander I's in Paris, 354–5, 357
  American Revolutionary War, 294–8,
    299–301, 302–8, 309–11
  in ancient China, 56*
  in ancient Indian culture, 60–62, 63–4
  anti-Nazi 'Lucy Ring' in Switzerland,
    649
  in Aztec Empire, 133, 135
  Aphra Behn, 235, 236, 237, 303†
  Boudicca's, 74–5
  British guaranteed indefinite
    anonymity, 343–4
  British in Jacobite ranks (1740s/50s),
    283, 284–5

British in Napoleonic France, 342
British in revolutionary France,
    313–14, 314*, 317–21, 323–4
British–American in Cold War GRU/
    KGB, 683, 696–8
buried in Westminster Abbey, 237,
    237‡, 303, 303†
Byzantine, 93, 95–6
Cadogan's network in France, 262
caliphs' use of, 96, 97
Cambridge spy ring, 183, 593, 621,
    649–51, 661–2, 673, 711
Carthaginian, 42
of Sir Robert Cecil, 190, 193
against Charles I's regicides,
    219, 221
Chinese view of, 58, 59, 60
Cold War motivation as money not
    ideology, 686–7
at Congress of Vienna, 363, 364–6
Culper spy ring (set up 1778), 305
of early Caliphate armies, 94, 95
English agents working for Spain,
    183–4, 200, 203
of English Commonwealth, 220–21
escapes of Soviet agents due to
    Philby, 673, 749
FDR's gentlemen spies (The Room/
    Club), 605–6, 607–8
in First World War German
    shipyards, 526–7
Fouché's agent network, 342
Frederick the Great's categories of,
    286–7
of French Committee of Public
    Safety, 322, 323
French word espionnage, 279
frumentarii in Roman world, 76–7
Gaunt's Czech-American ring, 523
German naval in Britain, 454
Boris Godunov's, 155, 156
history of spy scares before wars,
    107, 476
and Hundred Years War, 107*, 159,
    159*, 160, 476

illegals, 593–4, 622, 626, 665, 666,
    673, 681–2, 699, 714–15, 751
Jacobite network, 269, 270, 283, 284
Japanese at Port Arthur, 466, 467
Judas Iscariot, 2, 24–5
KGB in Cold War USA, 684–7,
    709, 711
La Dame Blanche in First World War
    Belgium, 562, 571–2
in London Corresponding Society
    (LCS), 327–9
and Karl Marx, 389–91, 392–3, 397–9
MI5's in German embassy (late
    1930s), 612–13, 614, 615
Moses' in Canaan, 1–2, 3, 13, 14–16,
    17–18, 19
Muhammad's, 87–8, 89–90, 91, 92
of the Okhrana, 425–6, 437–41, 457
Ottoman, 120, 120†, 123
parliamentary in Civil War, 216–18
pre-Tudor England, 159–60
royalist in Civil War, 214–15
royalist émigrés during French
    Revolution, 323–4
Russian in Austria, 486
selling to highest bidder, 124–5
during Seven Years War (1756–63),
    288–9
of seventeenth-century Spain,
    198–200, 207
Soviet, 299, 593–4, 625
Soviet in foreign embassies, 591–2,
    627–8, 749
Soviet in Nazi Germany, 593–4, 625
Soviet penetration of
    MANHATTAN Project, 664–8,
    669, 673, 691
Stafford as Spanish agent (1580s), 183–4
Steinhauer's German agents in Britain,
    475, 477, 479, 480–81, 495–6
Sun Tzu's five types of, 55
surveillance of émigré revolutionaries,
    388, 389–91, 392–4
and system of resident ambassadors,
    121–2, 149–50, 154, 155–6

spies and agents – (cont.)
   Thurloe's in The Hague, 227
   Van Lew's network in Richmond,
     Virginia, 413–14
   Venetian, 119–20, 121, 122, 124,
     125–6, 207
   Waldegrave's in France, 281, 282
   of Walsingham, 151, 154, 154†, 160,
     161, 165–6, 171–4, 175–6,
     180–86
   Wellington's use of, 345–7
   William III's at Saint-Germain-en-
     Laye, 256–7, 259
Spina, Carlos, 203
Spinola, Andrea, 121
Spiridonova, Maria, 557
Spring Rice, Cecil, 456–7, 522, 534,
   548, 567
Spurinna (Caesar's haruspex), 51–2, 52*
spy fiction, 431
   James Bond, 2, 27, 483
   James Fenimore Cooper: The Spy,
     310–11
   Edwardian spy novelists, 472–3,
     474, 476
spy satellites, 683, 707
Sri Lanka, 721
SS (Nazi Schutzstaffel), 142, 644, 645,
   646, 648, 656
St Albans, 75
St Bernard of Clairvaux, 101
St Cyprian, 108
St Dominic Guzman, 103–4
St John, Henry, 266
Stadion, Johann von, 357
Stafford, Sir Edward, 183–4
Stalin, Joseph
   as admirer of Ivan the Terrible, 141, 145
   as admirer of Skuratov, 143
   and assassination of enemies, 62–3
   and Churchill, 626, 650
   constant fear of conspiracies, 146,
     152, 594, 598–602, 619–20,
     625–6, 680–82
   death of (5 March 1953), 682

   deceived by police spies (early
     1917), 393
   enthusiasm for intelligence, 7, 591, 603
   fears Japanese attack, 589–90, 591, 627
   Great Terror (1936–8), 104, 105,
     107–8, 141, 143, 318, 326*,
     594–602, 620–21, 711, 751, 752
   ignores BARBAROSSA intelligence,
     625–7
   Kremlin Plot to kill, 595–7
   marshal's uniform of, 648
   move to paranoia in mid-1930s,
     594–5, 596, 597, 598–602,
     619–20, 680–82
   obsession with Trotsky, 598–600,
     621–5, 680, 743
   Okhrana surveillance of, 7, 441–2, 603
   as own intelligence analyst, 594
   personal archive, 441, 445
   and personal security, 594–5
   plans for Tito's assassination, 681–2
   post-war imaginary enemies, 680–82
Stalingrad, 646, 647–8, 656, 664
Standen, Anthony (alias Pompeo Pellegrini),
   161, 180–81, 182, 185–6, 188*
Standen, Baron von, 144, 145
Stanley, Venetia, 511
Stanton, Edwin M., 411*
Stark, Admiral Harold R. 'Betty', 633–4
START treaty (1989), 684
Stayley, William, 240–41
Steenkerque, Battle of (1692), 286
Steinhauer, Gustav, 434, 454, 475, 480,
   481, 495–6
Stephenson, William, 608, 609
Stern Gang (Lehi) (paramilitary Zionist
   group), 732
Stettinius, Edward, 522
Steuart Davis,, 604
Stevenson, Adlai, 739, 740
Stewart, Sir Charles, 365, 367
Stewart, William Rhinelander, 605
Stieber, Wilhelm, 390–91, 393–4, 520
Stimson, Henry L., 588–9, 611, 628,
   633–4, 637, 670

Stobo, Major Robert, 302*
Stolypin, Pyotr, 429, 438, 439
Stoneman, Dr Richard, 32*
Stormont, Lord, 296, 298
Strabo, 49
Strang, Sir William, 679
strategic deception
  in *The Art of War*, 56, 66
  B1a (MI5's Second World War
    double-agent section), 650, 651,
    652–3, 659
  and 'Blinker' Hall, 516
  Cheka SINDIKAT and TREST
    operations, 575–6, 646
  Double-Cross System (Second World
    War), 8, 29, 575–6, 651–3, 656,
    657–61
  German before BARBAROSSA,
    626
  London Controlling Section (LCS),
    651, 652, 657
  and Mossad, 18–19
  and Muhammad, 89–90, 91–2
  NKVD and GRU THRONE
    operation, 646
  operation MINCEMEAT (1943),
    652, 656
  and operation OVERLORD
    (1944), 657
  and Russian Brusilov offensive
    (1916), 502
  and Salamis (480 BC), 2, 29–30, 56
  sanctioned by Pope Innocent III, 101
  Soviet Operation MARS (November
    1942), 647
  the Trojan Horse, 2, 28–9
  Washington during Revolutionary
    War, 304, 305, 306
Strategikon (Byzantine warfare
    manual), 93
Strauss, Robert S., 705
Strong, Brigadier-General George V.,
    609, 642
Stuart, Charles (British minister to
    Portugal), 347

Stuart, Charles Edward ('Young
    Pretender'), 282, 283–5
Stuart, James Francis Edward (son of
    James II, The Old Pretender), 249,
    250, 269, 270, 274, 281
  and Atterbury, 272–5
Studies in Intelligence (journal), 9, 10,
    17–18
submarines
  and Cuban Missile Crisis, 683–4
  First World War U-boat warfare,
    515, 519, 536–7, 543–4
  pre-First World War German
    construction of, 482
  Second World War U-boat warfare,
    641–2
Suchet, Marshal Louis-Gabriel, 352
Sudoplatov, Pavel Anatolievich, 623
Suetonius, 41, 46, 47, 49†, 51, 52*, 53,
    72, 73
Suez Crisis (1956), 674
Suffolk, Lord Thomas Howard, Earl of,
    192, 193–4
Sukarno, Achmed, 679–80
Sukhomlinov, Ekaterina, 503
Sukhomlinov, Vladimir, 487, 498–9, 502–4
Sully, duc de, 139
Sumption, Jonathan, 78†, 107, 159*, 476
Sun Tzu: *The Art of War* (*Sunzi
    bingfa*), 753
  authorship of, 54
  and concept of 'soft power', 68, 69
  as far ahead of its time, 56–7
  five types of agents, 55–6
  and intelligence-based warfare, 4,
    55–6, 66–7, 68
  international reputation of, 3, 54, 66–9
  and kingdom of Cao Wei, 58
  'know the enemy and know
    yourself', 56, 63
  and Mao Zedong, 66, 67
  prohibition of omens, 54–5, 55*, 58
  purpose of book, 54*
  revered in Communist China, 3, 66, 67
  and subversion, 64

Sunderland, Robert Spencer, 2nd Earl of, 240
Sunderland, Charles Spencer, 3rd Earl of, 262
Suppiluliuma I, Hittite king, 21
Svechin, Colonel Mikhail, 486
SVR (Russian Federation foreign-intelligence service), 621, 705, 709, 711, 715–16, 715*
  Mitrokhin archive, 712–13, 714–15, 747‡, 750–51
  official history of Russian foreign intelligence, 145–6, 147, 148, 154, 406, 620, 711–12
  Primakov as first head of, 705–7, 711–12, 715
Sweden, 209, 271–2, 279, 348, 518–19, 536, 541–2
Sweeney, Inspector John, 431–2
Swift, Jonathan: Gulliver's Travels, 275–6
Switzerland, 327, 329–30, 331, 335, 498
Sykes, R. A., 625
Szapáry, Frigyes (Friedrich), 491, 492
Szymańska, Halina, 656*

Tabula Peutingeriana (Roman map), 50†
Tacitus, 49†, 72, 73–5
Taft, William Howard, 116
Talbot, James, 330, 331, 335, 337
Tallard, Marshal Camille de, 262
Talleyrand-Périgord, Charles Maurice de, 356–7, 360
  at Congress of Vienna, 365, 368
  and second Treaty of Paris (November 1815), 369
Tallmadge, Benjamin, 304–5
Tamil Tigers (LTTE), 721
Tannenberg, Battle of (August 1914), 497, 502, 504
Tarquinius Superbus, 43
Taschereau, Jules, 383–4
Tassis, Juan Bautista de, 198–9, 207
Tatars, Crimean, 655
Tate, William, 331
Taylor, A. J. P., 478

Techen, Carl, 394
Tehran conference (November 1943), 656
telegraph, 6, 402–3, 405–6
  and American Civil War, 411
  First World War cutting of German cables, 509, 518
  and Indian Mutiny, 408
  and practice of diplomacy, 421
'telling truth to power'
  and Bancroft during American War, 300–301
  and El Dorado myth, 137
  and First World War Arab Bureau, 530
  Hager's reports to Metternich, 366
  and Louis Napoleon, 395
  and Louis XIV, 246–7
  and Napoleon, 344, 358
  and Robespierre, 326
  and Saddam, 744
  and Soviet intelligence analysis, 693, 698
  and Walsingham, 160
  and Wellington, 345–6
Tenet, George, 2, 723, 724, 725, 727, 728, 736
Tennyson, Alfred, 'Charge of the Light Brigade', 404
Tenochtitlan (Aztec capital), 135–6
terrorism
  Black September, 733
  bombs fitted with timing devices, 427
  'Combat Organization' of SRs in Russia, 437–9
  Fenian bombing campaigns in London, 427–8
  'International Conference for the Defence of Society against the Anarchists' (1898), 432–3
  IRA offensives in London (1990s), 702, 721–2
  Munich Olympics massacre (1972), 733
  and nineteenth-century police forces, 426–8
  Okhrana attack in Geneva (1886), 428
  People's Will in Russia, 425, 426, 428

pre-First World War 'golden age of assassinations', 425, 427, 428–31, 432–3, 437–9, 444–8, 487
   Serbian against Austrian rule, 444–8
   Stern Gang in London (1947), 732
   suicide bombing, 720–21
   US intelligence reports on (mid-1990s), 717
   see also Islamist terrorism
Thatcher, Margaret, 160, 694, 696, 751*
Thelwall, John, 329, 332–3
Themistocles, 29–30
Theobalds, estate in Royston, 190, 192
Theodorovic, Belimir, 442–3
Theodosius, Roman emperor, 77–8
Theodosius II, Eastern emperor, 83–4
Thermopylae, Battle of, 29
Thiers, Adolphe, 395, 398
Third World
   Cold War covert actions in, 8, 688–91
   Cold War diplomatic traffic of, 674
   intelligence analysis in Andropov era, 694
Thirty Years War (1618–48), 203–4, 209
Thomson, Basil, 504, 552, 553, 578
Thornley, R. H., 646
Thornton, John, 295
Thou, Jacques-Auguste de, 138
Throckmorton, Francis, 173–4, 191
Throckmorton, Sir Nicholas, 162–3
Thucydides, 3, 30, 33, 34, 35–6
Thurloe, John, 223–8, 229–30
Thurstan, Edward, 537
Thwaites, Norman, 535, 566
Thwaites, Major-General Sir William, 473, 577
Tiberius, Roman emperor, 24–5, 72–3
Tibet, 417–18
Tikhomirov, Lev, 428
Times, The, 381, 399, 408, 427, 435, 578, 621
   Crimean War coverage, 402–3, 405–6
Tinkler, Charles A., 411
Tinsley, Richard, 526
Tintoretto, Domenico, 130

Tirpitz, Alfred von, 513
Tisamenus of Elis, 31, 32
Tissaphernes (Persian satrap), 35–6
Tisza, István, 488
Tito, Marshal, 62, 63, 85, 680–82
Tittoni, Tommaso, 484
Tlaxcala confederacy, 134–5
TNT, 520–21
Tocqueville, Alexis de, 386
Todd, Janet, 235†
Togo, Shigenori, 630, 670
Tojo, General Hideki, 630
Tolstoy, Sergei, 627
Tombs, Robert, 329
Tomkins, Nathaniel, 216
Tonge, Dr Israel, 239
Topbas, Osman Nuri: The Prophet of Mercy Muhammad, 3*
Topographical and Statistical Department (T&S), British, 414, 415
Torcy, M de, 248, 264, 266, 267
Torquemada, Tomás de, 111
Torres, Juan Jose, 690
Torrijos, Omar, 690
torture, 4, 106, 116–17, 130, 137, 164, 174, 189
Totonac people, 134
Toulouse, 101, 102, 104, 742†
Tourzel, marquise de, 316
Townsend, Robert, 305*
Toye, Francis, 570–71
trade and commerce
   Anglo-Soviet trade negotiations (1920–21), 577–8
   commercial intelligence and Renaissance Venice, 119, 121‡
   and Phoenician Empire, 41
   spice trade, 119, 121
   trade routes in Old Testament times, 19–20, 41
   transatlantic trade with New World, 121
Trafalgar, Battle of (1805), 338*
Transitional Justice Working Group (TJWG), 751

Travis, Commander Edward, 642
Tresham, Francis, 193
Trevor-Roper, Hugh, 656
Triple Alliance, 479, 479†, 493
Triple Entente (1907), 470–71, 472
Trojan War, 2, 27–9
Trotsky, Leon, 556, 598–600, 621–3, 680, 743
    assassination of (20 August 1940), 62–3, 624
    first attack on (24 May 1940), 623–4, 681
    Fourth International, 600, 622, 623
Troubetzkoi, Prince Vasili, 343*
Trubnikov, Vyacheslav, 711, 715
Truman, Harry S., 8, 668, 671
    disavowal of covert action, 677–8
    dislike of peacetime HUMINT, 670, 676
    Truman Doctrine, 676–7
    VENONA secret kept from, 673
Trumbull, Sir William, 248, 257
Tschirsky, Heinrich von, 488
Tsushima, Battle of (1905), 466, 469
Tunisia, 746
Turberville, George, 151
Turenne, vicomte de, 246, 247
Turing, Alan, 518
Turkish War of Independence (1919–23), 576–7
Tutankhamun, Pharaoh, 20–21
Twain, Mark, 132
Twentieth-Century Fund (think tank), 717
Tyrconnell, Earl of, 252

U-2 (first high-altitude spy-plane), 683
Udney, John, 334
Ukraine, 708
Ulbricht, Walter, 680
Ulyanov, Alexander, 436
Umar ibn al-Khattab, 93, 95
Umberto I, King of Italy, 428, 430, 433, 447
Umm Al-Fadl, 88
United States

2000 presidential election campaign, 723, 724, 728
arrival of troops in Europe (1917–18), 561, 563, 565
Aspin–Brown Commission (1995–6), 713–14, 716–17, 727
assumption of national superiority, 713–14
Black Tom attack (July 1916), 527, 528, 604
Bureau of Investigation, 435, 521, 527–8, 568
challenges Europe's lead in intelligence, 5–6
Coordinator of Information (COI) post, 609–10
Department of Homeland Security, 435
diplomatic relations with USSR (1933), 586
Director of Central Intelligence (DCI) role, 378, 676, 677, 702, 706, 707–8, 710
embassy security in Russia, 458, 592–3, 662, 674–5
expectation of surprise Japanese attack (late 1941), 630–31
and First World War, 515, 516, 519, 520, 527–8, 533–42
German sabotage in (First World War), 520, 521, 522, 527, 528, 542, 604
growth of intelligence agencies during First World War, 568–9
intelligence coordination problem, 568, 609–10, 611–12, 628–30, 631–3, 634, 637
intelligence special relationship with UK, 7, 8, 169, 516, 565–7, 608, 609, 641–4, 670–71, 673–4, 735
Iran–Contra scandal (1986), 691
MAGIC (Japanese) decrypts, 611–12, 628–30, 631–3, 634, 635, 637, 669–70
MI1b decrypts of diplomatic telegrams, 533–4, 535–6, 538–9, 566, 571, 760

National Security Act (26 July
  1947), 677
policy in the Third World, 8
poor airport security in pre-9/11
  years, 724–5
post-9/11 scares and false alarms, 727–8
post-First World War intelligence
  cuts, 573, 587, 588–9
publishing of diplomatic
  correspondence, 422–3
Second World War intelligence
  failures, 7
Secret Service, 435–6, 521–2,
  527–8, 568
Secret Service Fund, 310
Soviet penetration of Roosevelt
  administration, 662–3, 669, 673
Truman Doctrine, 676–7
'Year of Intelligence' (1975), 687–8,
  731–2
see also Central Intelligence Agency
  (CIA); Federal Bureau of
  Investigation (FBI)
Urban VII, Pope, 138*
Uritsky, Moisei Solomonovich, 559
US Army Air Force (USAAF), 642
Ustinov, Jona 'Klop', 612, 613, 614
Utrecht, Treaty of (1713), 267, 269

Vaillant, Auguste, 429–30
Valens, Eastern emperor, 81, 82
Valentian, Roman emperor, 78
Valerius Probus, 46
Valley Forge, Pennsylvania, 304
Van Lew, Elizabeth, 413–14
Vansittart, Sir Robert, 612, 615
Varro, 50*
Varus, Publius Quinctilius, 70–71
Vauban, Sébastien Le Prestre de, 243, 246
Vedic religion, 60
Velázquez, Diego, 208
Venanges (now Fort Franklin), 302
'Vengeur, Le' (pre-First World War
  'French agent'), 465, 466
Venice, Renaissance

Archivio Centrale, 119, 120
Bridge of Sighs, 132*
and commercial intelligence, 119, 121‡
Council of Ten, 118, 122, 124, 125,
  126, 127, 128, 129–30, 131, 138–9
and cryptanalysis, 127, 128–9
end of mercantile supremacy, 121
informers in, 119, 131–2
and Italian Wars (1494–1559), 128, 129
lion's mouth (bocca di leone)
  letterboxes, 131–2, 131†
and masks, 130–31
military inferiority to Ottomans,
  122, 132
obsession with secrets and secrecy,
  118–19, 126, 129–30
Phelippes tests ciphers of, 205
political-intelligence collection, 119–20,
  121, 122, 124, 125–31, 207
as printing capital, 122–3
state inquisitors, 130, 131
trading empire, 119–20, 132
Vergennes, comte de, 293, 294, 296,
  298, 299, 301
Versailles, Palace of, 242
Versailles, Treaty of (1919), 573, 585
Vetrov, Vladimir, 714
Victoria, Queen, 391, 427, 434
Victoria, Queen of Spain, 429
Victorian-era Britain
  Chartist movement, 379–80, 385
  debate on letter-opening (1844), 381–3
  Deciphering Branch closure (1844),
    6, 337, 383, 410, 421, 449, 747
  Fenian 'Dynamite War' (1881–5), 427
  Great Exhibition (London, 1851), 391–2
  'Great Game' with Russia on
    North-West Frontier, 406, 416–21
  intelligence decline, 6, 414
  Intelligence Department (ID) in War
    Office, 449, 450–51
  lack of 'political police', 380
  as safe haven for continental
    revolutionaries, 380, 388–9, 396,
    400–401

Vienna, Congress of (1814–15), 363–6
  Final Act (9 June 1815), 368–9
  and Napoleon's escape from Elba, 368
  sexual liaisons/pillow talk at, 366–8
Viète, François, 137, 138–9, 140, 198
Vietnam War, 66, 687, 748
Viguié, Léopold, 432
Villars, Marshal Claude Louis
    Hector de, 265
Villiers, Edward, 224
Vincent, Professor E. R., 643
Virgil, *Aeneid*, 2, 28
Visigoths, 79–80, 81–2
Viskovaty, Ivan Mikhailovich, 146,
    147, 149, 151, 152, 154
Vitoria, Battle of (June 1813), 349
Vivian, Valentine, 592
Viviani, René, 485, 491, 492
Vladimir of Staritsa, 144
Vo Nguyen Giap, 66–7
Vock, Maksim Yakovlevich von, 374–5
Vogt, Karl, 397
Volkonsky, Prince, 367
Voroshilov, Kliment, 590
Voska, Emanuel, 523, 549
Vyshinsky, Andrei, 601, 667

Wadleigh, Julian, 593
Wagner, Kim, 407
Wakley, Thomas, 382
Waldegrave, first Earl, 281, 282
Wales, 331–2
Walker, Colonel James, 418
Walker, John Anthony, 685–6, 686
Wallace, Robert, 381
Waller, Edmund, 215–16
Wallis, John, 216–17, 221, 237–8, 242,
    251–5, 256, 257, 263
Walpole, Horace, 288, 293
Walpole, Sir Robert, 273, 274, 281, 282
Walsh, James, 332–3
Walsingham, Sir Francis, 5, 532, 757
  Babington Plot deception/forgery,
      177, 179, 180
  'Book of Secret Intelligences', 160

  death of (6 April 1590), 185
  Dutch alliance with, 166, 167–70
  early life and career, 158–9
  Elizabeth presents painting to, 166
  fear of foreign-backed Catholic plots,
      163–4, 175
  as Foreign Secretary and intelligence
      chief, 4, 158
  and Jerome Horsey, 154, 154†, 155*
  ill-health of, 160
  intelligence operations run from
      home, 160, 165
  and Mary, Queen of Scots, 175, 179
  personal management of intelligence,
      184–5
  portrait of, 160–61
  as Protestant ideologue, 161
  and Thomas Randolph, 151
  and Ridolfi Plot, 165
  and Spanish Armada, 180–83, 184
  spies and agents of, 151, 154, 154†,
      160, 161, 165–6, 171–4, 175–6,
      180–86
  and Throckmorton Plot (1583), 173–5
Walsingham, Thomas, 188
Walton, Calder, 736
Wang Ch'ung, 58*
Wang Mang, 57†
Wang Zhen, 753
Wannsee conference (January 1942), 645
War of the League of Cambrai
    (1508–16), 128
Warner, Michael, 67, 719, 740
Warrender, Vice-Admiral Sir George, 513
Wartburg festival (18 October 1817),
    371–2
Washington, George, 5–6, 301–11
Washington Naval Conference
    (1921–2), 586–7, 589
Washington Post, 746, 747, 748
Waterbury, Lawrence, 604
Watergate, 687, 748
Waterloo, Battle of (18 June 1815),
    338†, 361–2, 369
Watson, General Edwin 'Pa', 628–9

Weisband, William, 673, 749
Welles, Captain Roger, 604
Wellesley, Henry, 347
Wellesley, Richard, 342, 345
Wellington, Arthur Wellesley, Duke of,
    338†, 340
  campaigns in India, 345–6
  Napoleon's underestimation of, 345
  Peninsular War, 344, 346–52, 403
  use of intelligence, 344, 345–52
  victory at Waterloo (18 June 1815),
    361–2
Wemyss, Admiral Sir Rosslyn, 529
Wentworth, Paul, 297, 298, 299, 300
Werden, Robert, 220, 222
Westphalen, Ferdinand von, 388–9,
    390–91, 393
Whalley, Edward, 234–5
whistleblowers, 11, 462, 745, 746–7,
    748–9, 750
  and authoritarian regimes, 750–51,
    753–4
White, Dick, 653
White, Harry Dexter, 593, 662
Whitehall Palace, 170
Whitford, Walter, 219
Whitworth, Jerry, 686
Whytock, Roslyn, 548*
wicker men, 49
Wickham, William, 327, 328, 329–31,
    336, 337, 532
Wigram, Ralph, 612
WikiLeaks website, 745–6, 748
Wilhelm, Crown Prince
    ('Little Willy'), 496
Wilhelm II, Kaiser, 434–5, 453, 454–5,
    465–6, 475, 478–9, 496
  abdication of, 570
  during 'July Crisis', 492–4
Willes, Edward, 271, 272, 273, 274,
    276, 337, 383
Willes, Edward (junior), 276, 348
Willes, Francis, 276, 301
Willes, Francis (last of the cryptanalyst
    dynasty), 383

Willes, Revd William, 276
William I, Prince of Orange ('William
    the Silent'), 85, 166, 167
  assassination of (1584), 169–70
William III, King of England
  declared joint ruler with Mary
    (1689), 251
  and domestic intelligence, 258
  and foreign intelligence, 255–8,
    259–60, 268
  invasion of England (1688), 249–50
  and Nine Years War (1688–97), 251
  personality of, 251
  threat of Jacobite cause, 257–8, 259–60
  use of double agents, 286
  and Wallis' decryptions, 251–5
Williams, Walter, 174
Williamson, Adolphus 'Dolly', 401
Williamson, Sir Joseph, 234, 235, 236,
    237, 238, 240
Willich, August, 389, 390
Willys (Willis), Sir Richard, 224, 228
Wilson, Admiral Sir Arthur, 514
Wilson, Major-General Sir Charles, 414
Wilson, Harold, 400, 738
Wilson, Field Marshal Sir Henry, 482
Wilson, Sir Henry, 578
Wilson, Sir Horace, 614
Wilson, Sir Robert, 359
Wilson, Thomas, 167
Wilson, Woodrow, 6, 311, 424, 522,
    534–6, 605, 760
  and armistice negotiations,
    569–70, 571
  British decryption of
    communications of, 534, 535–6,
    539, 566, 571, 760
  ends diplomatic relations with
    Germany (1917), 537
  and First World War German
    operations in US, 521–2
  ignorance of MI1c operations on US
    soil, 566–7
  and influence operation in Petrograd,
    548–9

Wilson, Woodrow – (*cont.*)
  the Inquiry (peace conference
    preparation), 567
  lack of interest in US intelligence
    agencies, 527–8, 568, 569
  speech to Congress (2 April 1917), 542
  vision of post-war world, 542, 568
  and Wiseman, 534–5, 567–8
  and Zimmermann telegram, 540–41
Winant, John, 636
Wingate, Sir Reginald, 541
Wiseman, Sir William, 534–5, 547–9,
  566, 571
  and Woodrow Wilson, 534–5, 567–8
Wissembourg, Battle of (August
  1870), 415
Witte, Sergei, 456
Wolf, Markus, 695–6
Wolsey, Cardinal Thomas, 125–6
Woodhull, Abraham, 305*
Woodward, Bob, 748
Woollcombe, Major Malcolm 'Woolly',
  582, 614–15
Woolsey, James, Jr, 708, 710, 718
Worcester, Battle of (3 September
  1651), 222
Wordsworth, Dorothy, 332
Wordsworth, William, 315, 332–3
World Trade Center, New York
  1993 attack on, 718–19, 729
  9/11 attacks, 10, 11, 704, 720, 721,
    726–7, 729–30, 736
Wotton, Sir Henry, 191
Wright, John, 214
Wu-pei Chih (Ming military compen-
  dium), 57
Württemberg, Duke of, 286
Wyllie, Sir William Curzon, 619

Xenophon of Athens, 36
Xerxes, King of Persia, 30
Xi Jinping, 754*

Yagoda, Genrikh, 110, 152*, 595, 597,
  601, 602
Yakovlev, Alexander, 684
Yakub Khan, Afghan Amir, 419
Yakushev, Aleksandr, 575
Yalta conference (February 1945),
  655, 663
Yamamoto, Admiral Isoroku, 637–8
Yao Li (Chinese assassin), 59
Yardley, Herbert, 569, 586–9
Yarmouk, Battle of (636), 94
Yeltsin, Boris, 673, 705, 708, 711
Yevseev, Dmitri Gavrilovich, 561
Yezhov, Nikolai, 110, 143, 152*,
  597–8, 601, 620–21
Yitzhaki, Rabbi Shlomo (Rashi), 19
Yoshikawa, Takeo, 630
Younger, Alex, 483
Yousef, Ramzi, 718, 729
Yugoslavia, 680, 681

Zalkind, Ivan, 556
Zama, Battle of (202 BC), 45
al-Zawahiri, Ayman, 720, 722
Zborowski, Mark, 599, 623
Žerajić, Bogdan, 444
Zhdanov, A. A., 141*
Zheng He, Chinese admiral, 121†
Zhitomirsky, Dr Yacov, 440
Zhou Enlai, 67
Zhukov, Marshal Georgi, 648, 653
Zieten, General von, 362
Zimmermann telegram (1917), 519,
  536–41, 538, 540, 542, 543, 671
Zinoviev, Grigory, 441, 546, 581, 600
Zinoviev letter (October 1924), 581–2
Zionist movement, 665, 732
Zola, Émile, 'J'Accuse . . .!', 462
Zou Dapeng, 752*
Zukhar, Vladimir, 699
Zúñiga, Baltasar de, 199
Zuylestein, William Nassau van, 249